A BREAKTHROUGH IN THE CONCEPT OF A THESAURUS

Now, for the first time, there is a thesaurus which provides a concise definition at every main entry and a brief verbal illustration of the word used in context to help take the guesswork and error out of word selection. Words are clearly distinguished, and the relationship between the main entry and its synonyms is clarified to facilitate proper word choice. Furthermore, because exact synonyms are not always desirable, listings include related words, idiomatic phrases, and antonyms.

THE MERRIAM-WEBSTER THESAURUS represents a whole new concept, one which will delight the general user with its simplicity and the scholar with its completeness. As a guide to more precise and effective use of the language, it is unmatched.

"It is so ample and easy to use that for many it will largely supersede Roget."
—*The Wall Street Journal*

(More....)

RESOUNDING PRAISE FOR A MAJOR PUBLISHING EVENT

"This new Merriam-Webster volume represents a genuinely fresh approach to the thesaurus concept evolved by Peter Mark Roget more than a century ago. Because the language itself has vastly grown since Roget's time, this new thesaurus is based on contemporary American-English. Secondly, every entry is not only provided with its synonyms and antonyms but also with idiomatic equivalents, related words and contrasting words, a structure which offers the reader an infinitely broader choice than the original based on a 19th-century English vocabulary....A distinct advance in analysis of language, in accessibility, in contemporaneity, and in convenience."

— *John Barkham Reviews*

"Every home, office, school or library should own a copy....It's so good, it should have been thought of before."

— *The Hartford Courant*

The
Merriam-Webster
Thesaurus

A Merriam-Webster®

PUBLISHED BY POCKET BOOKS NEW YORK

POCKET BOOKS, a Simon & Schuster division of
GULF & WESTERN CORPORATION
1230 Avenue of the Americas, New York, N.Y. 10020

This is the **POCKET BOOKS** concise edition of
WEBSTER'S COLLEGIATE THESAURUS

Copyright © 1978 by G. & C. Merriam Co.
Philippines copyright © 1978 by G. & C. Merriam Co.

Published by arrangement with G. & C. Merriam Co.
Library of Congress Catalog Card Number: 75-45167

ISBN: 0-671-42694-X

First Pocket Books printing August, 1978

15   14   13   12   11   10   9   8   7

POCKET and colophon are trademarks of Simon & Schuster.

Printed in the U.S.A.

Preface

WEBSTER'S POCKET THESAURUS is based on the recently published Webster's Collegiate Thesaurus and is designed especially to meet the day-to-day needs of those who want a compact and handy thesaurus. In this book we have been able to eliminate much of the bulk and weight of the larger volume while retaining the basic features that have caused Webster's Collegiate Thesaurus to be so well received.

The basic premise behind both books is that the user of a thesaurus is seeking a more appropriate term than the one he has in mind. This very broad concept is scarcely consonant with the typical thesaurus presentation of "synonyms" and sometimes "antonyms". In point of fact, the user may be seeking a synonym, a word stronger or weaker in force, one of slightly different meaning, a more starchy or more folksy word, an idiomatic phrase that conveys the same idea, or a word that to a greater or less degree contrasts with his starting point. Patently, all these possible uses cannot be subsumed reasonably under the rather unitary notions of "synonym" and "antonym". Perhaps the longevity of Roget's *Thesaurus* rests on the simple fact that in spite of its complexity and lack of guidance, it does spread before the user a greater body of material to browse through than any comparable book heretofore available. Webster's Pocket Thesaurus is designed to present a similar range of material but in a readily available and highly structured form that minimizes the consultant's need to grope and guess.

In earlier Merriam-Webster publications the pattern of supplementing synonym lists with lists of related and contrasted words, words that were relevant to the group under study yet not quite synonyms or antonyms respectively, was extensively tested. This favorably received feature not only allowed more precise delineation of synonyms and antonyms but provided the user with much additional significant and pertinent assistance. The same plan of supplementing synonyms and antonyms with genuinely germane collateral material has been made a feature of this new thesaurus.

Additional features of Webster's Pocket Thesaurus designed to facilitate its use are the provision at each main entry of a concise statement of the segment of denotation in which a group of words can be construed as synonyms, a strictly alphabetical organization, and the entry at its own alphabetical place of each word that appears as a synonym at a main entry. The absence or inadequate handling of the first of these features is a major flaw in most existent thesauruses. Though many justifications have been offered for avoiding the second, they all boil down to the implausible notion that the members of a group of words are synonymous but some are more synonymous than others! Perhaps unfairly, one can't help feeling that the only valid explanation for non-alphabetical listing of properly chosen synonyms appears in one specialized dictionary of synonyms whose author comments. "Apologies are in order, however, for my inability to maintain alphabetical order within the categories, the plea being of course lack of time." Finally, since no one can anticipate where the user's search may start, it seems only logical to enter each synonym in such a way that it can serve as a convenient starting point in his searching.

Though Webster's Pocket Thesaurus is based on Webster's Collegiate Thesaurus, its ultimate authority lies in Webster's Third New International Dictionary and the Merriam-Webster research file of nearly 13,000,000 instances of words in actual use by a wide range of writers and speakers. In preparing the Pocket Thesaurus the chief organizational change was the replacement of the synonym list at each secondary entry with a cross-reference to the appropriate main entry. In addition a few specialized or abstruse entries were eliminated and a few synonyms not likely to be of general interest were dropped.

Webster's Pocket Thesaurus was prepared by Kathleen M. Doherty, assistant editor, under the immediate supervision of E. Ward Gilman, senior editor.

Explanatory Notes

How to Use Webster's Pocket Thesaurus

Every thesaurus user should read these Explanatory Notes because a thorough understanding of the scope, content, and structure of the book is essential to its effective employment. The key lines at the bottom of the text pages direct the user to these Explanatory Notes.

Since the English lexicon contains an incalculable number of fixed combinations, senses, subsenses, and nuances of meaning (for example, Webster's Third New International Dictionary records some 251 distinguishable meanings for the verb *set* and its fixed combinations), *it is essential that the thesaurus be used in conjunction with an adequate dictionary.*

Scope of Webster's Pocket Thesaurus

This book is concerned with the general vocabulary of the English language. Since the user may actually be hindered rather than helped by a vocabulary diluted with obsolete, archaic, or extremely rare terms or with specialized or technical jargon, such words have been omitted.

Structure and Content

Entry Order The body of the book consists of main and secondary entries introduced by alphabetically ordered boldface headwords, as

> **raid** *vb* **1** to make a raid on < Indians *raided* the
> settlers frequently >
> *syn* foray, harass, harry, maraud
> *rel* despoil, devastate, ravage, sack, spoliate,
> waste; loot, plunder, rifle, rob
> **2** *syn* see INVADE 1

> **raider** *n syn* see MARAUDER

> **rail** *n syn* see RAILING

where *raid, raider,* and *rail* are the headwords introducing either a main entry (as **raid** *vb* 1), or a secondary entry (as **raid** *vb* 2, **raider** *n,* or **rail** *n*).

Homograph headwords are entered in historical order: the one first used in English is entered first, as

till *prep*
till *conj*
till *vb*

Verbs used predominantly with one or two prepositions or adverbs may be headwords introducing main or secondary entries; in this case, they are entered with the verb segment in boldface type followed by the parenthetical element or elements in lightface type. Such verb + particle combinations immediately follow their base verb in alphabetical order:

put *vb* ———————— base-verb homograph
put (back) *vb*
put (on) *vb* ————— verb + particle combinations
put (on *or* **upon)** *vb*
put *n* ——————————— noun homograph

Fixed verb + adverb collocations commonly entered in dictionaries as two-word verbs have boldface entry at their appropriate alphabetical positions in this book. However, they follow any verb + particle combinations occurring in the same alphabetical sequence:

take *vb* ———————— base verb
take (from) *vb* ———— verb + particle combinations
take (to) *vb*
take away *vb* ————— two-word verb collocations
take back *vb*
take down *vb*
take in *vb*
take off *vb*

Headwords ordinarily conform to normal dictionary practices: for instance, they are styled as singular nouns or infinitive verbs. Special situations (as plural usage or variant spellings) are signaled by the use of boldface subheads, as

crossroad *n, usu* **crossroads** *pl but sing or pl in constr* **syn** see JUNCTURE 2

woe *n* ... 3 *usu* **woes** *pl* **syn** see DISASTER

catercorner (*or* **catty-corner** *or* **kitty-corner**) *adv* **syn** see DIAGONALLY

where **crossroads** and **woes** are subheads indicating plural usage, and **catty-corner** and **kitty-corner** are subheads showing variant spellings of the headwords.

The Main Entry and Its Basic Elements Each main entry consists of a headword followed by a part-of-speech label, a sense number when needed, a meaning core with a brief verbal illustration, and a list of synonyms. Lists of related words, idiomatic equivalents, contrasted words, and antonyms follow the synonym list if they are called for.

A typical main entry is

calm *adj* **1** free from storm or rough activity < the
wind died and the sea became *calm*>
syn halcyon, hushed, placid, quiet, still, stilly,
untroubled
rel inactive, quiescent, reposing, resting; pacific,
smooth, tranquil, unruffled
idiom calm as a millpond, still as death
con agitated, disturbed, perturbed, restless,
turbulent, uneasy
ant stormy

where the italic part-of-speech label *adj* indicates that the headword is an
adjective. Other such labels used in the book are: *adv* (adverb), *conj* (conjunction), *interj* (interjection), *n* (noun), *prep* (preposition), *pron* (pronoun),
and *vb* (verb).

Individual senses of multisense entries (as **calm** *adj*) are introduced by a
boldface sense number (as **1**).

The meaning core, as at **calm 1**

free from storm or rough activity

indicates the area of meaning in which a group of words (in this case *calm,
halcyon, hushed, placid, quiet, still, stilly,* and *untroubled*) are considered to
be synonymous.

In other words, the meaning core pinpoints the exact relationship between the main-entry headword and its synonyms.

A meaning core may be supplemented by a usage note introduced by a
lightface dash when additional information or comments on syntax or usage are required:

yet *adv* **1** beyond this — used as an intensive to
stress the comparative degree

Some interjections express feelings but otherwise are untranslatable into
substitutable meaning; in such cases, the meaning core itself may be replaced by a usage note:

good-bye *interj* — used as a conventional expression
of good wishes at parting

Each meaning core is followed by a verbal illustration enclosed by angle
brackets, as

< the wind died and the sea became *calm*>

that exemplifies a typical use of the headword (here, **calm**) in its pertinent
sense (**1**). The verbal illustration also offers the thesaurus user a frame for
testing the suitability of the synonyms and/or related words with regard to
his particular needs. Two verbal illustrations may appear after a meaning
core that is broad enough to subsume alternatives (as both a literal and an
extended use):

see *vb* **1** to take cognizance of by physical
or mental vision < *saw* that the boat was being
driven ashore > < the only one who *saw* the truth >

Such double illustrations have been chosen with discretion and are used sparingly in this book.

The boldface italic abbreviation *syn* introduces a synonym list that appears at each main entry on a line below the meaning core and the verbal illustration. This list may consist of only one synonym (as *here* at **hitherto** *adv* 2) or of many (as *halcyon, hushed, placid, quiet, still, stilly,* and *untroubled* at **calm** *adj* 1). Each synonym in a main-entry list has a boldface entry at its own alphabetical place.

A compare cross-reference may appear at the end of a main-entry *syn* list. This cross-reference introduced by the italic word *compare* is used (1) when two or more groups of synonyms are very closely related and it is felt that the user examining one list should be aware of the existence of the other list or lists:

> **assassin** *n* a person hired or hirable to
> commit murder <found out who paid the *assassin*>
> *syn* bravo, cutthroat, gun, gunman, ‖gunsel, gunslinger,
> hatchet man, hit man, torpedo, triggerman; *compare* MURDERER

> **murderer** *n* one who kills a human being
> <a *murderer* who wouldn't hesitate to kill in cold blood>
> *syn* homicide, killer, manslayer, slayer; *compare* ASSASSIN

and (2) when the user should be warned that certain words have evolved derivative senses that tend to blur precise sense boundaries and consequently cause an overlapping of senses or of meaning, thus making those words somewhat less desirable choices for the user in terms of preciseness than other words in their lists. A comparison of the main entries

> **ration** *n* an amount allotted or made available
> especially from a limited supply <saved up their gasoline
> *ration* for a vacation trip>
> *syn* allotment, allowance, apportionment, measure,
> meed, part, portion, quantum, quota, share; *compare* SHARE 1

> **share** *n* **1** something belonging to, assumed by, or falling to
> one (as in division or apportionment) <wanted his *share* of
> the prize money>
> *syn* allotment, allowance, bite, cut, lot,
> part, partage, portion, quota, slice; *compare* RATION

reveals the usage overlap of the synonyms *allotment, allowance, part, portion, quota,* and *share* which are indeed valid synonyms at both entries.

The Secondary Entry and Its Basic Elements A secondary entry consists of a boldface headword followed by a part-of-speech label, a boldface sense number when needed, and a *syn* see cross-reference in small capitals directing the user to the appropriate main entry in whose *syn* list the secondary entry appears (followed when needed by a lightface sense number of the main entry). Lists of related words, idiomatic equivalents, contrasted words, or antonyms that are specifically applicable to the secondary-entry headword in the relationship indicated by the *syn* see cross-reference may be included as well. A typical secondary entry is

> **placid** *adj* 1 *syn* see CALM 1
> *rel* irenic, peaceful, serene, unagitated, unstirring
> *ant* roiled

where **placid** is the headword, *adj* is the part-of-speech label, **1** is the sense number of the secondary entry, and *syn* see CALM 1 is the *syn* cross-reference directing the user to the main entry **calm 1** where *placid* is a synonym.

Main and Secondary Entries: Elements Common to Both All, some, or none of the following lists may appear at both main and secondary entries in this order: related words, idiomatic equivalents, contrasted words, and antonyms.

The boldface abbreviation *rel* introduces a list of related words. The related words — words that are almost but not quite synonymous with the headword — are included at an entry next after the synonym list. For example, at the main entry

> **splendid** *adj*...
> 2 extraordinarily or transcendently impressive...
> *syn* glorious, gorgeous, magnificent, proud,
> resplendent, splendiferous, splendorous, sublime,
> superb
> *rel* eminent, illustrious; grand, impressive, lavish,
> luxurious, royal, sumptuous; divine, exquisite,
> lovely; incomparable, matchless, peerless,
> superlative, supreme, unparalleled, unsurpassed;
> surpassing, transcendent

the *rel* list is composed of twenty terms separated into five subgroups that each share a common likeness or relation with the headword and its synonyms. On the other hand, at the secondary entry

> **splendiferous** *adj syn* see SPLENDID 2
> *rel* dazzling, marvelous; smashing, walloping;
> rattling, ripping, screaming, terrific

three subgroups of eight terms were selected as being distinctively related to *splendiferous* rather than to the whole synonym group in the context indicated by the *syn* see cross-reference to **splendid 2.** Related words appearing at a main entry are not ordinarily repeated at the secondary entries. The user should therefore check the main entry when seeking the most complete groupings of related words. Related words as such are not entered in boldface at their own alphabetical places. They may, of course, be synonyms in other lists or head their own main entries.

The boldface italic abbreviation *idiom* introduces a list of idiomatic equivalents that are essentially the same in meaning as the members of a synonym group. An *idiom* list at a main entry includes phrases that are generally pertinent to the entire *syn* list and the headword, as the ones at

> **speak** *vb* **1** to articulate words in order to express
> thoughts...
> *syn* talk, utter, verbalize, vocalize, voice
> *rel*...
> *idiom* break silence, give voice (*or* tongue *or* utterance) to,
> let fall, make public (*or* known), open
> one's mouth (*or* lips), put in (*or* into) words, say one's say,
> speak one's piece

while a secondary-entry list, as the one at

> **retaliate** *vb syn* see RECIPROCATE
> *rel*...
> *idiom* even the score, get back at, get

even with, give in kind, give one a
dose of his own medicine, give one tit for
tat, pay one in his own coin, settle (*or*
square) accounts, turn the tables on

features idioms that are particularly appropriate equivalents of its headword in the context indicated by the *syn* see cross-reference. Idiomatic
equivalents, including those fixed verb + preposition combinations that
function as idioms rather than as literal meanings of the verb are not entered in boldface at their own alphabetical places in this book.

The boldface italic abbreviation *con* introduces a list of contrasted words
— words that are strongly contrastable but not quite antonymous with the
headword — that may appear at an entry:

> **watchful** *adj* paying close attention usually
> with a view to anticipating approaching
> danger or opportunity . . .
> *syn* . . .
> *rel* . . .
> *idiom* . . .
> *con* careless, heedless, thoughtless; in-
> advertent; absentminded, abstracted,
> faraway

> **alert** *adj* **1** *syn* see WATCHFUL
> *rel* . . .
> *idiom* . . .
> *con* inattentive, unmindful; aloof,
> detached, indifferent, unconcerned

At the main entry **watchful** *adj* the *con* list is composed of seven words
separated into three subgroups that each share at least one aspect of contrast to the headword and its *syn* list, while the *con* list at the secondary
entry **alert 1** comprises six words separated into two such subgroups. Contrasted words appearing at a main entry are not ordinarily repeated at the
secondary entries. The thesaurus user should therefore check the main entry when seeking the most complete groupings of contrasted words. Contrasted words as such are not entered in boldface at their own alphabetical
places. They may, of course, be synonyms in other lists or head their own
main entries.

The boldface italic abbreviation *ant* introduces the last possible element
of a main or secondary entry: an antonym or list of antonyms, as at the
entry

> **perfect** *adj* . . . **2** . . .
> *ant* imperfect

or at the entry

> **quiet** *adj* . . . **4** not showy or obtrusive . . .
> *ant* gaudy, loud

When antonyms are drawn from different classes of opposites, members of
the two groups are separated by a semicolon, as at the entry

> **assistance** *n syn* see HELP 1
> *rel* . . .
> *con* . . .
> *ant* impediment, impeding;
> obstructing, obstruction

antonyms that are opposites
with intermediates

antonyms that are reverse
opposites

Like related and contrasted words, antonyms as such are not entered in boldface at their own alphabetical places. They may, of course, be synonyms in other lists or head their own main entries.

Main and Secondary Entries: The One Arbitrary Rule Ideally, a book such as this should be free of all arbitrary restraints and curtailments. In practice, however, its editors found that one rule was essential: *No word may appear in more than one list at a main or secondary entry.* For example, *nice* is a synonym at **pleasant** *adj* **1**. The applicable sense of *nice* is found in Webster's Third New International Dictionary at the entry ¹**nice** ... *adj* ... **7** (binding substitute) **+7b**, where the definitions are

> : pleasant and satisfying: as ... **b** : ENJOYABLE,
> PLEASING, DELIGHTFUL <a *nice* time at
> the party> <*nice* and warm by the fire> <we have
> four *nice* bedrooms upstairs to make them
> comfortable —Willa Cather>

However, one might reasonably construe senses **7e** (: MILD, CLEMENT, PLEASING <the *nice* weather of late spring> <the *nice* old days of the past>) and **7g** (: FITTING, APPROPRIATE, SUITABLE <the *nice* clothes she wears> <not a *nice* word for use in church>) as a basis for entering *nice* as a related word as well as a synonym at **pleasant 1**, while sense **8** in Webster's Third New International Dictionary

> : most inappropriate : UNPLEASANT, UNATTRACTIVE,
> TREACHEROUS — used ironically <a chronic alcoholic
> is certainly a *nice* one to talk about
> temperance> <a *nice* friend, who would have
> me ... cover myself with eternal infamy —J.A.
> Froude> <got himself in a *nice* fix>

could be construed as evidence for entering *nice* as both a contrasted word and an antonym at **pleasant 1**. Obviously, the thesaurus user would not be helped by an entry showing any word in such an involved relationship with itself.

Labels, Punctuation, and Symbols

Labels Words that are labeled *cap* or *usu* [ally] *cap* in Webster's Third New International Dictionary are capitalized in this book. Thus, the synonyms *Gehenna, Pandemonium, Sheol,* and *Tophet* are so styled at the main entry **hell** *n* as are the related words *Styx* and *Tartarus.* A term that is capitalized in a main-entry *syn* list is also capitalized when it appears as a boldface secondary entry at its own alphabetical position:

Gehenna *n syn* see HELL

If only one entered sense of a word is capitalized, an italic *cap* label followed by a boldface capitalized subhead is attached to the affected sense:

pandemonium *n* **1** *cap* **Pandemonium** *syn* see HELL
  2 *syn* see SINK 1
  3 *syn* see DIN

In addition to the part-of-speech label, an italic plural label may be added when a word or a sense of a word is sometimes, often, usually, or always used in the plural. Typical examples of these labels are found at

years *n pl syn* see OLD AGE

where *pl* indicates that the headword **years** is always plural in form and construction in this particular application, and at

road *n* **1** *often* **roads** *pl syn* see HARBOR 3
  2 *syn* see WAY 1
  3 *syn* see WAY 2

where sense **1** (and only that sense) of the headword **road** is often but not always used in the plural, and at

minutia *n, usu* **minutiae** *pl* **1** *syn* see
  INS AND OUTS
  2 *syn* see TRIVIA

where the label preceding both senses indicates that the headword **minutia** is usually used in the plural in both of these applications, and at the main entry

trivia *n pl but sometimes sing in constr*

where the label is qualified to show that this plural noun may sometimes be used with a singular verb, and at

common *n* **1** **commons** *pl but sing or pl in*
  constr syn see COMMONALTY

which indicates that **common** occurs as a plural noun in sense **1** but may occur with either singular or plural verbs, and at

outdoors *n pl but sing in constr* the space where
  air is unconfined <every night he let the dog
  run in the *outdoors*>

whose label indicates that while the word *outdoors* is a plural noun, it consistently takes a singular verb. Use of these labels conforms to the treatment of plurals in Webster's Third New International Dictionary.

An italic subject guide phrase pointing to something with which the headword is associated may precede a meaning core in a very few instances, as at

set *vb*... **11** *of a fowl* to incubate eggs
  by crouching upon them...

Punctuation A comma links items (as synonyms, idiomatic equivalents, members of a single group or subgroup of related or contrasted words or of antonyms) that are alike in their relation to the headword, as at

conservative *adj*... **2**...
  syn controlled, discreet, moderate, reasonable,
  restrained, temperate, unexcessive, unextreme
  rel cautious, chary, wary; circumspect, politic, proper,
  prudent
  con expansive, unconstrained; excessive, freewheeling,
  uncontrolled, unrestrained

A semicolon signals a break in continuity and is used in *rel* and *con* lists (as between the two subgroups in the *rel* and *con* lists at **conservative 2** above) to separate subgroups of words which differ in their relation to the headword. A semicolon is also used to separate antonyms that belong to different classes of opposites, as

> **arise** *vb* **1** *syn* see RISE 4
> **ant** recline; slump

where the two antonyms are so separated. A semicolon may also appear at the end of a main-entry *syn* list to introduce a compare cross-reference, as shown at **honorable** *adj* **1**:

> *syn* estimable, high-principled, noble,
> sterling, worthy; *compare* VENERABLE 1

Parentheses enclose variant spellings, as at the main entry **cake** *vb* **1** where

> encrust (*or* incrust)

is a synonym, and at the secondary entries, where that particular synonym is styled

> **encrust** (*or* **incrust**) *vb* *syn* see CAKE 1

Parentheses also enclose a particle or particles usually associated with a base word, as

> **adore** *vb*... **3** to love, admire, or enjoy
> excessively...
> *syn* dote (on *or* upon), idolize, worship

> **dote** (on *or* upon) *vb* *syn* see ADORE 3

Similarly, parentheses may indicate usage alternatives in idiomatic expressions, as at **slavery** *n* **2** where

> *idiom* the yoke (*or* chains) of slavery

alerts the user that he may choose one of two noun elements when employing this particular idiom. Parentheses are also used in main-entry *syn* lists to enclose plural suffixes of words that are sometimes, often, or usually but not always used in the plural:

> **scad** *n*, *usu* **scads** *pl* a great number or abundance...
> *syn* gob(s), heap, jillion, load(s), million,
> oodles, quantities, ...

Parentheses enclose material indicating a typical, or occasionally, a sole object of reference, as in the meaning core of **express** *vb* **2**

> to give expression to (as a thought, an opinion,
> or an emotion)

where they enclose an adjunct, or at entries such as **abrogate** *vb* **2**

> **ant** establish, fix (*as a right, a quality, or
> a custom*)

where an antonym or a group of antonyms are associated with a particular object or objects of reference — a restriction or limitation to which the thesaurus user should be alerted.

Symbols   A warning symbol is used in this book in the form of the double bars ‖.

The double bars prefixing some terms warn the user that the employment of such a term may involve a problem of diction too complex for presentation in a thesaurus, or a restriction in usage. Consequently, the thesaurus user should consult a dictionary if he is in doubt about the stylistic level or appropriateness of the word or if he is unfamiliar with its meaning. For example, ‖**fat cat** (a synonym of **notable** *n* 1), ‖**chuff** (a synonym of **sullen** *adj*), and ‖**puxy** (a synonym of **swamp** *n*) are all double-barred in this book because they carry stigmatizing or regional labels in Webster's Third New International Dictionary.

The
Merriam-Webster
Thesaurus

A

aback *adv syn* see UNAWARES

abaft *adv* toward or at the stern (of a vessel) <headed *abaft* for a smoke>
syn aft, astern
rel after, back, behind
ant forward

abaft *prep* to the rear of <huddled in a nook *abaft* the chimney>
syn back of, behind

abalienate *vb syn* see TRANSFER 4

abandon *vb* 1 to give up without intent to return or re-claim <*abandoned* his family>
syn chuck, desert, forsake, quit, renounce, throw over
rel cast (off), discard, disuse, drop, junk, scrap; reject, repudiate
idiom have done with, leave flat, quit cold, run out on, turn one's back on (*or* upon), walk out on
con hold, keep, possess, retain; redeem, rescue, save; acquire, gain, get, procure, win; cherish, foster
ant re-claim
2 *syn* see RELINQUISH
ant retain

abandon *n* 1 *syn* see UNCONSTRAINT
2 carefree disregard for consequences <behave with *abandon*>
syn impulsiveness, uninhibitedness, unrestraint; *compare* UNCONSTRAINT
rel freedom, liberty, license; exuberance, heedlessness, laxity, laxness, looseness, unruliness, wildness; incontinence, licentiousness, wantonness; fun, games, play, sport
con constraint, inhibitedness, inhibition, restraint; repression, suppression
ant self-restraint

abandoned *adj* 1 *syn* see DERELICT 1
2 free from moral restraint <led a thoroughly *abandoned* life>
syn dissolute, licentious, profligate, reprobate, self-abandoned, unprincipled
rel debased, debauched, depraved, perverted, riotous; incorrigible; lascivious, lecherous, lewd, wanton; corrupt, degenerate
idiom dead to honor, gone to the bad, lost to shame, rotten (to *or* at) the core

con ethical, high-principled, moral, reputable, virtuous; correct, decent, decorous, proper, seemly
ant scrupulous, upright

abase *vb syn* see HUMBLE
rel demote, diminish, downgrade, reduce; fawn, grovel, toady; cower, cringe, truckle
con elevate, lift, raise
ant exalt; extol

abash *vb syn* see EMBARRASS 1
rel abase, demean, humble, humiliate
idiom make one eat humble pie
ant embolden, reassure

abashment *n syn* see EMBARRASSMENT

abate *vb* 1 *syn* see ABOLISH 1
2 *syn* see ANNIHILATE 2
3 *syn* see DECREASE
4 to lessen in force or intensity <the storm *abated* slowly>
syn ‖bate, die (down *or* away), ease off, ebb, fall, let up, lull, moderate, relent, slacken, subside, wane
rel decrease, diminish, dwindle, lessen, weaken
idiom run its course
con augment, expand, extend, increase; mount, rage, soar, surge
ant revive; rise

abatement *n syn* see DEDUCTION 1
con enlargement, increase
ant addition

abbreviate *vb syn* see SHORTEN
rel attenuate, extenuate
con enlarge, increase; amplify, dilate, expand
ant lengthen; extend

ABC *n* 1 *usu* ABC's *pl syn* see ALPHABET 1
2 *often* ABC's *pl syn* see ALPHABET 2

abdicate *vb* 1 to part formally or definitely with a position of honor or power <the king *abdicated* the throne in order to marry a commoner>
syn demit, renounce, resign; *compare* RELINQUISH
rel abandon, leave, relinquish, surrender; drop; withdraw
con appropriate, arrogate, confiscate; grab, seize, take over, wrest

ant assume, usurp
2 *syn* see DISCARD
con keep, retain, treasure

abdomen *n* the part of the body between the chest and the pelvis <intense pain in the lower *abdomen*>
syn belly, ||gut, paunch, stomach, tummy, venter
rel bay window, ||breadbasket, corporation, pod, pot, potbelly; middle, midriff, midsection

abduct *vb syn* see KIDNAP
rel grab, seize

abecedarian *n syn* see AMATEUR 2

aberrant *adj* 1 *syn* see ABNORMAL 1
rel different, disparate, divergent; eccentric, odd, peculiar, strange; exceptional, unusual
con natural, normal, regular, typical; customary, usual, wonted
ant true (*to a type*)
2 *syn* see ERRANT 2

aberration *n* 1 *syn* see DEVIATION 1
rel abnormality; mistake, slip; curiosity, oddity, prodigy, rarity
con average, mean, norm; normality
ant conformity; regularity
2 *syn* see INSANITY 1
ant soundness (*of mind*)

abet *vb* 1 *syn* see INCITE
rel egg, exhort, goad, prod, spur, urge; advocate, countenance, encourage, endorse
con forbid, prevent, prohibit; debar, deter, discourage
2 *syn* see HELP 1

abettor *n syn* see CONFEDERATE

abeyance *n* a state of temporary inactivity <the warm dry weather kept his asthma in *abeyance*>
syn abeyancy, cold storage, doldrums, dormancy, intermission, interruption, latency, quiescence, quiescency, suspension
rel break, interval, pause, respite
con activeness, activity, stir
ant continuance

abeyancy *n syn* see ABEYANCE
ant continuancy

abeyant *adj syn* see LATENT
rel deferred, intermitted, postponed, stayed, suppressed; repressed
con refreshed, renewed, restored
ant active, operative; revived

abhor *vb* 1 *syn* see HATE
2 *syn* see DESPISE
con dote (on *or* upon), like, love
ant admire

abhorrence *n syn* see ABOMINATION 2
rel distaste, repellency; dismay, horror
con affection, attachment, love
ant admiration; enjoyment

abhorrent *adj* 1 *syn* see HATEFUL 2
ant admirable
2 *syn* see REPUGNANT 1
rel antipathetic; uncongenial, unsympathetic
con alluring, attractive, captivating; enticing, seductive, tempting
ant congenial

---

syn synonym(s)   *rel* related word(s)
ant antonym(s)   *con* contrasted word(s)
idiom idiomatic equivalent(s)
|| use limited; if in doubt, see a dictionary

abide *vb* 1 *syn* see STAY 2
rel adhere, cleave, cling, stick; dwell, live, reside
con go, leave, quit; move, remove, shift
ant depart
2 *syn* see CONTINUE 1
rel linger; exist, subsist
con avoid, elude, escape, evade
ant pass
3 *syn* see BEAR 10
rel accept, receive; accede, consent
idiom put up with
4 *syn* see RESIDE 1

abiding *adj syn* see SURE 2
rel durable, lasting, perdurable, persistent
con ephemeral, impermanent, short-lived, transient, transitory

ability *n* 1 physical, mental, or legal power to perform <he has the *ability* to accomplish whatever he sets his mind to>
syn adequacy, capability, capacity, competence, might, qualification, qualifiedness
rel address, adroitness, cleverness, dexterity; aptitude, aptness, facility, knack
idiom what it takes
con impotence, inadequacy, incapability, incompetence
ant inability
2 natural or acquired proficiency especially in a particular activity <he has unusual *ability* in planning and designing>
syn command, expertise, expertism, expertness, knack, know-how, mastership, mastery, skill
rel adroitness, deftness, efficiency, handiness, proficiency; ingenuity, resourcefulness; talent
con inadequacy, incompetence, ineffectualness, unfitness; fatuity, futility, inanity

abject *adj syn* see DOWNTRODDEN

abjure *vb* to give up (something formerly adhered to) irrevocably and usually solemnly or formally <an immigrant solemnly *abjuring* allegiance to his former country>
syn forswear, palinode, recall, recant, retract, take back, unsay, withdraw
rel disavow, disown, renounce, repudiate; abandon, desert, forsake; cede, relinquish, surrender
idiom eat one's words

ablaze *adj* 1 *syn* see BURNING 1
2 *syn* see ALIGHT 2

able *adj* possessed of or marked by a high level of efficiency and ability <an *able* student always near the head of his class>
syn au fait, capable, competent, good, proper, qualified, wicked
rel effective, effectual, efficient; expert, proficient, skilled, skillful; alert, clever, keen, sharp; brainy, brilliant, intelligent, smart; enterprising, go-ahead, up-and-coming
con ineffective, ineffectual, inefficient; incapable, incompetent, unqualified; fair, indifferent, mediocre; lackluster, maladroit
ant inept; unable

abnegation *n syn* see RENUNCIATION

abnormal *adj* 1 departing significantly from the normal or a norm <the *abnormal* rains caused flooding>

syn aberrant, anomalous, atypical, deviant, deviative, heteroclite, preternatural, unrepresentative, untypical

rel divergent, offtype; irregular, unnatural; uncustomary, unusual, unwonted; heteromorphic; paratypic

con common, familiar, natural, ordinary, regular, typical; customary, usual, wonted

ant normal

2 **syn** see IRREGULAR 1

abode *n syn* see HABITATION 2

abolish *vb* 1 to bring to an end often by formal or concerted action < *abolish* a tax >

syn abate, abrogate, annihilate, annul, circumduct, invalidate, negate, nullify, quash, undo, vitiate

rel cancel, disallow, disannul, repeal, rescind, revoke, vacate

idiom bring to naught, make void, set aside

con conserve, preserve, save; keep, retain

2 **syn** see ANNIHILATE 2

con found, institute

ant establish

abominable *adj syn* see HATEFUL 2

rel accursed, cursed; loathsome, offensive, repugnant, revolting

con applaudable, commendable

ant laudable (*as practices, customs*); delightful, enjoyable

abominate *vb syn* see HATE

rel curse, damn, objurgate

idiom hold in abomination, take an aversion to

con admire, regard

ant enjoy; esteem

abomination *n* 1 one that is a source of utter disgust or intense dislike < found the new tax form an *abomination* of confused complexity >

syn anathema, bête noire, black beast, bugbear, detestation, hate

rel annoyance, pest, plague, trial; bogey, bugaboo, incubus

con delectation, delight, joy, pleasure; treasure

2 a feeling of extreme disgust and dislike < they hold every indulgence in *abomination* >

syn abhorrence, aversion, detestation, hate, hatred, horror, loathing, repugnance, repugnancy, repulsion, revulsion

rel contempt, despite, disdain, scorn; disfavor, dislike, disrelish, distaste

con admiration, regard, respect; fondness, liking, relish, taste; approbation, approval, countenance, favor; acceptance, tolerance

ant esteem; enjoyment

aboriginal *adj syn* see NATIVE 2

rel primeval, primitive, primordial, pristine; barbarian, barbaric, barbarous, savage

con advanced, progressive; civilized, cultured; sequent, successive

abortion *n syn* see FREAK 2

abortive *adj syn* see FUTILE

rel unformed; immature, unmatured, unripe

con accomplished, completed, concluded, finished

ant consummated

abound *vb syn* see TEEM

abounding *adj syn* see ALIVE 5

rel full, jammed, packed, stuffed

about *adv* 1 in every direction < looked carefully *about* >

syn around, round, round about

2 in a circuitous way or course < took the long way *about* >

syn circuitously, round about

3 **syn** see NEARLY

4 here or there without plan or order < left his tools lying *about* >

syn anyhow, any which way, anywise, around, at random, haphazard, haphazardly, helter-skelter, random, randomly

rel back and forth, hither and thither, to and fro; aimlessly, carelessly, casually

5 in the vicinity < talked to the people standing *about* >

syn near, near-at-hand, nearby

idiom close by

6 in the opposite direction < he turned *about* and saw her >

syn again, around, back, backward, in reverse, round, round about

idiom in one's course

about *prep* 1 in the vicinity of < *about* five miles to go >

syn around, circa, close on, near, nearby, nigh

idiom hard by, not far from

2 **syn** see APROPOS

idiom in point of, with regard to

3 **syn** see OVER 3

4 here and there upon or within < traveled *about* the country >

syn round, through, throughout

idiom all over

about–face *n syn* see REVERSAL 1

above *adv* 1 *syn* see OVER 4

ant below

2 higher on the same page or on a preceding page < earlier examples appear *above* >

syn supra

ant below, infra

above *prep* 1 *syn* see OVER 1

ant below

2 **syn** see BEYOND 2

aboveboard *adj syn* see STRAIGHTFORWARD 2

rel open, scrupulous; artless, ingenuous, unsophisticated

con clandestine, covert, furtive, secret, surreptitious; deceitful; crooked, devious, oblique

ant underhand, underhanded

abracadabra *n syn* see GIBBERISH 3

rel mystification; argot, cant, jargon

abrade *vb* 1 to injure or flaw by frictional action < wind-driven sand *abraded* the glass >

syn chafe, corrade, erode, gall, graze, rub, ruffle, wear

rel corrode, eat away, fret; grate, rasp, scrape

2 **syn** see CHAFE 3

rel burn

3 **syn** see ANNOY 1

rel disorganize, disturb, flurry, rattle; confuse, distract, perturb

con calm, relieve, soothe

Abraham's bosom *n syn* see HEAVEN 2

abreast *adj* 1 *syn* see UP-TO-DATE

2 *syn* see FAMILIAR 3

abridge *vb* 1 to make less by in some manner restricting <laws that *abridge* freedom of speech>
syn curtail, diminish, lessen, minify
rel limit, narrow, reduce, restrict; minimize
con augment, broaden, enlarge, extend
ant amplify
2 *syn* see SHORTEN
con amplify, augment, enlarge, increase
ant expand, extend

abridgment *n* a shortened version of a larger work or treatment produced by condensing and omitting without basic alteration of intent and language <an *abridgment* of a dictionary>
syn abstract, boildown, breviary, breviate, brief, condensation, conspectus, epitome, synopsis
rel aperçu, compendium, digest, outline, précis, sketch, syllabus; capsule, summary; sum, summation, summing-up
con elaboration; paraphrase
ant expansion

abroad *adv syn* see OVERSEAS

abrogate *vb* 1 *syn* see ANNUL 4
rel abate, extinguish
con establish, found; confirm, ratify
ant institute (*as by enacting or decreeing*)
2 *syn* see ABOLISH 1
rel extinguish; blot out, cancel, obliterate; ruin, wreck
con support, uphold
ant establish, fix (*as a right, a quality, or a custom*)

abrupt *adj* 1 *syn* see PRECIPITATE 1
rel hastened; casual, informal, unceremonious; quick, speedy
con dilatory, laggard; easy, relaxed
ant deliberate, leisurely
2 *syn* see BLUFF
rel brisk, crisp, sharp; impetuous, quick, ready
con calm, easy, relaxed
3 *syn* see STEEP 1
rel perpendicular, plumb, vertical
con inclined, slanting; flat, level, plane, smooth
ant sloping

abruptly *adv syn* see SHORT 1

abscess *n* a localized swollen area of infection containing pus <had an *abscess* on his leg>
syn boil, carbuncle, furuncle, pimple, pustule
rel lesion, sore, trauma; botch, ulcer

abscond *vb syn* see ESCAPE 1
rel go, leave, quit, withdraw
idiom do the disappearing act, skip out, take French leave
con render, surrender, yield
ant give (oneself) up

absence *n* the state of being absent or missing <the *absence* of news was disturbing>
syn dearth, default, defect, lack, ‖miss, privation, want; *compare* FAILURE 3

rel deficiency, drought, inadequacy, insufficiency; exigency, necessity, need; vacuum, void; nonappearance, nonattendance
con abundance, copiousness, plenty
ant presence

absent *adj* 1 not now present <all missed their *absent* friend>
syn away, gone, lacking, missing, omitted, wanting
ant present
2 *syn* see ABSTRACTED
rel absorbed; forgetful, heedless
con attending, hearkening, listening; considerate, thoughtful
ant attentive

absentminded *adj syn* see ABSTRACTED
rel unnoticing, unobserving, unperceiving, unseeing; heedless, inattentive
idiom lost in thought
con alert; aware
ant wide-awake

absolute *adj* 1 *syn* see PERFECT 2
rel pure, sheer, simple
con circumscribed, limited, partial, restricted
2 *syn* see PURE 2
rel abstract, ideal; real, true
con imperfect, incomplete
ant mixed, qualified
3 *syn* see UTTER
4 exercising power or authority without external restraint <an *absolute* monarch>
syn arbitrary, autarchic, autocratic, despotic, monocratic, tyrannical, tyrannous; *compare* TOTALITARIAN 1
rel dictatorial, magisterial; authoritarian, totalitarian; domineering, imperious, masterful; plenipotential, plenipotentiary, unlimited
con circumscribed, limited, restrained, restricted; constitutional, lawful
5 *syn* see ACTUAL 2
6 *syn* see ULTIMATE 3
rel ideal, transcendent, transcendental; autonomous, free, independent, sovereign; boundless, eternal, infinite
con circumscribed, limited, restricted; conditional, contingent, dependent

absolutely *adv syn* see EASILY 2

absolution *n syn* see PARDON
rel condonation
con censure, reprehension, reprobation
ant condemnation

absolve *vb* 1 *syn* see EXEMPT
2 *syn* see EXCULPATE
rel discharge, free, release
con condemn, doom, sentence; chasten, discipline, punish
ant charge (with), hold (to)

absorb *vb* 1 to take in and make a part of one's being <*absorb* knowledge from reading>
syn assimilate, imbibe, incorporate, inhaust, insorb
rel embody, imbue, impregnate, infuse, permeate
con disgorge, eject, expel, vomit; discharge, eliminate, emit, give off, pass
ant exude, give out
2 *syn* see MONOPOLIZE
rel concern, engage, immerse, involve, preoccupy
con diffuse, disperse, scatter

---

ant dissipate (*as time, attention*)

absorbed *adj syn* see INTENT
  rel involved
  idiom caught up in, up to the elbows (*or* ears) in
  con apathetic, disinterested, indifferent, unconcerned; uninterested; absent, abstracted
  ant distracted

absorbing *adj syn* see ENGROSSING
  ant irksome

abstain *vb* 1 *syn* see DENY 3
  rel abnegate, eschew, forgo; decline, refuse, reject, spurn
  idiom dispense with, do without, let alone
  con pamper; gratify, regale; sate, satiate, surfeit
  ant indulge
  2 *syn* see REFRAIN 1

abstemious *adj* marked by restraint in satisfying desires (as for food, drink, or pleasure) < an *abstemious* man, little given to self-indulgence >
  syn abstentious, abstinent, continent, self-restraining, sober, temperate; *compare* SOBER 3
  rel self-abnegating, self-denying; ascetic, austere; sparing
  con greedy, rapacious, voracious; epicurean, sybaritic, voluptuous
  ant gluttonous

abstentious *adj syn* see ABSTEMIOUS
  ant gluttonous

abstinence *n syn* see TEMPERANCE 2
  rel renunciation
  con gorging, sating, surfeiting; immoderateness, overdoing, unrestraint; crapulence, excess, extravagance
  ant self-indulgence

abstinent *adj syn* see ABSTEMIOUS
  ant gluttonous

abstract *adj* 1 having conceptual rather than concrete existence < the *abstract* perfect society >
  syn hypothetical, ideal, theoretical, transcendent, transcendental
  rel academic, impractical, utopian, visionary; speculative, undemonstrable; conceptual, notional; inconcrete
  con corporeal, material, objective, phenomenal, physical; actual, factual, real
  ant concrete
  2 *syn* see NEUTRAL

abstract *n syn* see ABRIDGMENT
  con enlargement, expansion
  ant amplification

abstract *vb* 1 *syn* see DETACH
  rel divide, part, separate
  con insinuate, interpolate, interpose
  ant insert, introduce
  2 *syn* see STEAL 1

abstracted *adj* withdrawn in mind and inattentive to external matters < seemed *abstracted* and remote >
  syn absent, absentminded, bemused, distrait, faraway, inconscient, lost, preoccupied
  rel engrossed, intent, rapt; oblivious, unmindful, unminding; heedless, inattentive
  idiom in a brown study, lost in thought, lost to the world
  con attentive, vigilant, watchful, wide-awake; noticing, noting, observant, seeing
  ant alert

abstruse *adj syn* see RECONDITE
  rel complex, complicated, intricate, knotty; abstract, hypothetical, ideal
  con clear, evident, manifest, palpable; clear, lucid, perspicuous; easy, facile, simple
  ant obvious, plain

absurd *adj syn* see FOOLISH 2
  rel comic, droll, funny; asinine, fatuous, simple; irrational, unreasonable
  con logical, ratiocinative, subtle
  ant rational, sensible

absurdity *n syn* see FOOLISHNESS

abundance *n syn* see PROSPERITY 2
  rel adequacy, competence, enough, plenty, sufficiency; lavishness, prodigality
  idiom enough and to spare
  con deficiency, inadequacy, insufficiency, lack, paucity

abundant *adj syn* see PLENTIFUL
  rel lavish, lush, luxuriant, profuse; crammed, crowded, thick; common
  idiom in good supply
  con infrequent, rare, uncommon; inadequate, scanty
  ant scarce

abuse *vb* 1 *syn* see DECRY 2
  ant praise
  2 to put to a bad or improper use < *abuse* the prerogatives of office >
  syn misapply, misemploy, mishandle, misimprove, misuse, pervert, prostitute
  rel mar, spoil; corrupt, debase, desecrate, profane
  idiom make ill use of
  con esteem, honor, respect
  3 *syn* see EXPLOIT 2
  4 to treat without compassion and usually in a hurtful manner < parents who *abuse* children >
  syn ill-treat, ill-use, maltreat, mistreat, misuse, outrage
  rel damage, harm, hurt, impair, injure; oppress, persecute, wrong; manhandle, mess (up)
  idiom do one dirt, do violence to
  con cherish, prize, treasure; esteem, revere, reverence, venerate
  ant honor, respect

abuse *n* vehemently and usually coarsely expressed condemnation or disapproval < had an unequaled vocabulary of *abuse* >
  syn billingsgate, contumely, invective, obloquy, scurrility, vituperation
  rel calumny, defamation, malignment, mud; vilification; cursing, profanity, swearing; berating, railing, rating, reviling
  con acclaim, laudation, praise; applause, commendation, compliment
  ant adulation

abusive *adj* coarse, insulting, and contemptuous in character or utterance < an *abusive* denunciation >
  syn contumelious, invective, opprobrious, scurrile, scurrilous, truculent, vituperative, vituperatory, vituperous
  rel affronting, insulting, offending, outraging; dirty, odious, offensive; aspersing, maligning, vilifying
  con acclaiming, extolling, lauding, praising; eulogistic, panegyrical; flattering

ant complimentary; respectful
abut *vb syn* see ADJOIN
abutting *adj syn* see ADJACENT 3
   rel connecting, joining; impinging
   con detached, disengaged; disassociated, disconnected, disjoined, parted, separated
abysm *n syn* see GULF 2
abysmal *adj* 1 *syn* see BOTTOMLESS 2
   2 *syn* see DEEP 1
   rel illimitable, infinite
abyss *n* 1 *syn* see HELL
   2 *syn* see GULF 2
   3 *syn* see DEPTH 2
academic *adj* 1 *syn* see PEDANTIC
   con ignorant, illiterate, unlettered; down=
   to-earth, everyday, practical, realistic,
   straightforward
   2 *syn* see THEORETICAL 1
   rel impractical, utopian, visionary; chimerical, imaginary
accede *vb syn* see ASSENT
   rel concur, cooperate; allow, let, permit
   con decline; balk, shy, stick; expostulate,
   kick, object, protest; fight, oppose, resist,
   withstand
   ant demur
accelerate *vb syn* see SPEED 3
   rel drive, impel
   idiom get going, make up for lost time
   con clog, hamper; delay, detain, slow
   ant decelerate; retard
accent *n* 1 *syn* see INFLECTION
   2 *syn* see EMPHASIS
   rel cadence, meter, rhythm; beat, pulsation, pulse, throb
accentuation *n syn* see EMPHASIS
   con evenness, sameness, steadiness, uniformity
   ant inaccentuation
accept *vb* 1 *syn* see APPROVE 1
   rel fancy, like, relish; admire, esteem
   con discountenance, disesteem, dislike,
   disrelish
   ant reject
   2 to take or sustain without protest or
   repining <a losing candidate must *accept*
   the decision of the electorate>
   syn bear (with), endure, pocket, swallow,
   tolerate, tough (out); *compare* BEAR 10
   rel acquiesce (in), agree (to *or* with),
   assent (to), subscribe (to); respect; bow,
   capitulate, yield
   idiom put up with
   con disavow, disown; brush (aside), deny,
   reject, repudiate
   3 *syn* see BELIEVE 1
   4 *syn* see APPREHEND 1
acceptable *adj syn* see DECENT 4
   rel average, commonplace, ordinary; bearable, endurable, supportable
   con insupportable, intolerable, unbearable, unendurable
   ant unacceptable
acceptably *adv syn* see WELL 4
acceptant *adj syn* see RECEPTIVE 1
acceptation *n syn* see MEANING 1
accepted *adj* 1 *syn* see USUAL 1
   rel conventional, established, recognized;
   correct, orthodox, proper, right

---

syn synonym(s)   *rel* related word(s)
ant antonym(s)   *con* contrasted word(s)
idiom idiomatic equivalent(s)
‖ use limited; if in doubt, see a dictionary

idiom according to custom (*or* use)
   con irregular, questionable, unacceptable,
   unconventional; incongruent, unconformable, unorthodox
   2 *syn* see ORTHODOX 1
acceptive *adj syn* see RECEPTIVE 1
access *n* 1 *syn* see ATTACK 3
   rel onset; taking; pang, stitch, twinge
   2 *syn* see OUTBURST 1
   3 *syn* see DOOR 2
   rel passage, route
   con departure, retreat, withdrawal
   ant egress; outlet
accessible *adj* 1 *syn* see OPEN 4
   rel approachable
   con limited, restricted; remote
   2 *syn* see OPEN 5
   ant inaccessible
accession *n syn* see ADDITION
   ant discard
accessory *n* 1 *syn* see APPENDAGE
   rel accompaniment, concomitant; accretion, addition, increment
   2 *syn* see CONFEDERATE
   ant principal
accessory *adj syn* see AUXILIARY
   rel secondary, subordinate, tributary;
   coincident, concomitant, concurrent; adventitious, incidental
   con constitutional, ingrained, inherent,
   intrinsic; cardinal, fundamental, vital;
   essential, indispensable, necessary
   ant constituent, integral
accident *n* 1 absence of positive plan or
   intent <we stopped there by *accident*>
   syn chance, fortuity, hap, luck
   rel fluke, fortune, hazard
   con design, premeditation
   ant intent
   2 a chance event bringing injury, loss, or
   distress <the school was closed by an
   accident to the heating system>
   syn casualty, misadventure, mischance,
   mishap
   rel calamity, catastrophe, disaster, tragedy; misfortune; chance, destiny, fate,
   kismet
   con foreordination, predestination
accidental *adj* resulting from chance
   <an *accidental* meeting>
   syn casual, chance, contingent, fluky,
   fortuitous, incidental, odd; *compare* RAN-
   DOM, UNINTENTIONAL
   rel conditional, dependent; coincident,
   coincidental; inadvertent, undesigned,
   unintended, unintentional, unmeant, unplanned, unpurposed, unwitting
   con designed, intended, purposed; constitutional, inherent, intrinsic; innate
   ant planned; essential
accidentally *adv syn* see INCIDENTALLY
   1
acclaim *vb syn* see COMMEND 2
   rel cheer, root (for); exalt, magnify; glorify, honor
   con berate, rate, revile; damn, execrate,
   objurgate; censure, denounce
   ant vituperate
acclaim *n syn* see APPLAUSE
   rel homage, honor, reverence; éclat, glory
   con abuse, invective, obloquy; censure,
   condemnation, denunciation, reprobation
   ant vituperation

acclamation n syn see APPLAUSE

acclimate vb syn see HARDEN 2

acclimatize vb syn see HARDEN 2

accolade n syn see HONOR 2

accommodate vb 1 syn see ADAPT
    rel bow, defer, submit, yield; alter,
    change, modify, vary
    con alienate, estrange
    ant constrain
    2 syn see HARMONIZE 3
    3 syn see OBLIGE 2
    rel cater (to), humor, indulge
    con annoy, harass, harry; irk, vex, worry
    ant incommode
    4 syn see CONTAIN 2
    rel encase, enclose
    5 syn see HARBOR 2

accommodations n pl shelter, food, and
    services (as at a hotel) <searched for
    accommodations as night drew near>
    syn lodging, lodgment, room and board
    rel bed; room; keep; housing, shelter
    idiom bed and breakfast

accompaniment n 1 something added to a
    principal thing usually to increase its
    impact or effectiveness <her song had a
    soft orchestral accompaniment>
    syn augmentation, complement, enhance-
    ment, enrichment
    rel accessory, addition, supplement; aid,
    assistance, help
    2 an accompanying individual, situation,
    or occurrence <smog is an inevitable
    accompaniment of excessive numbers of
    automobiles>
    syn associate, companion, concomitant,
    consort, fellow, mate
    rel attendant, colleague, comrade, part-
    ner; corollary, equivalent

accompany vb to go or be together with
    <accompanied his wife to the theater>
    syn attend, bear, ‖bring, ‖carry, chaperon,
    companion, company, conduct, consort
    (with), convoy, escort
    rel associate, combine, join, link; defend,
    guard, protect, safeguard, shield; guide,
    lead, pilot, steer
    idiom bear one company, go along with,
    go hand in hand with
    con leave, quit, withdraw; abandon, for-
    sake

accompanying adj syn see CON-
    COMITANT

accomplice n syn see CONFEDERATE
    rel aider, assistant, helper; flunky, stooge

accomplish vb syn see GAIN 1

accomplished adj syn see CONSUMMATE
    1
    rel adept, expert, masterly, proficient; all-
    around, many-sided, versatile

accomplishment n 1 syn see ACQUIRE-
    MENT
    rel art, craft, skill; adeptness, expertise,
    expertness, proficiency
    2 syn see ACTION 1

accord vb 1 syn see AGREE 4
    rel coincide, concur; blend, coalesce, fuse,
    merge
    con differ, disagree; compare, contrast
    ant conflict
    2 syn see GRANT 1
    rel allot
    con deny, gainsay; refuse; detain, hold,
    reserve

    ant withhold
    3 syn see GIVE 2

accord n 1 syn see HARMONY 2
    rel affinity, attraction, empathy, sympa-
    thy; solidarity, union
    idiom community of interest(s)
    con conflict, contention, difference; ani-
    mosity, antipathy, hostility
    ant dissension, strife; antagonism
    2 syn see AGREEMENT 2
    3 syn see HARMONY 1

accordant adj syn see HARMONIOUS 2

accordingly adv syn see THEREFORE
    idiom by reason of that (or this), for that
    (or this) reason

according to prep syn see BY 5

accost vb 1 syn see ADDRESS 7
    rel buttonhole
    con ignore, overlook, slight; avoid, elude,
    evade, shun
    2 to approach boldly or in a challenging
    or sometimes a defensive manner <ac-
    costed by a beggar who demanded mon-
    ey>
    syn confront, face, front
    rel affront, insult, offend, outrage; annoy,
    bother; challenge, dare, outface
    idiom come face to face with, meet face
    to face
    3 syn see ADDRESS 4
    rel call (to), hail, halloo; buttonhole; dog,
    hound, pester, worry

accouchement n syn see CONFINEMENT
    2

account n 1 syn see BILL 1
    2 syn see USE 3
    con immateriality, inconsequence, insignif-
    icance, unimportance; bootlessness, fruit-
    lessness, futility
    3 syn see WORTH 1
    4 syn see REGARD 4
    rel consequence, dignity, distinction, note;
    reputation, repute
    5 syn see EXPLANATION 2
    6 syn see SCORE 4
    7 a statement of real or purported events,
    occurrences, or conditions <wrote an
    account of his travels>
    syn chronicle, history, narrative, report,
    story, version; compare STORY 2

account vb 1 syn see CONSIDER 3
    rel appraise, assess, estimate, evaluate,
    rate; esteem
    con underestimate, underrate, undervalue
    2 syn see EXPLAIN 3
    rel answer, elucidate, expound, interpret

accountable adj syn see RESPONSIBLE
    con absolute, arbitrary, autocratic; imperi-
    ous, magisterial, masterful
    ant unaccountable

accouter vb syn see FURNISH 1
    rel attire, dress; adorn, deck, decorate,
    embellish; fix (up), prepare, ready

accouterment n, usu accouterments pl syn
    see EQUIPMENT
    rel appointment(s); furnishing(s); bravery,
    regalia, trappings

accredit vb 1 syn see APPROVE 2
    rel commend, recommend; attest, certify,
    vouch (for)
    con belittle, deprecate, depreciate, disap-
    prove; reject, repudiate
    2 syn see ASCRIBE

3 *syn* see AUTHORIZE 1
   rel introduce, present

accretion *n syn* see ADDITION
   rel enlargement; attachment, joining, uniting; adjunct, appendage

accroach *vb* **1** *syn* see ARROGATE 1
   2 *syn* see APPROPRIATE 1

accumulate *vb* to bring together and form a store of < *accumulate* knowledge>
   syn amass, cumulate, garner, hive, lay up, roll up, stockpile, store (up), uplay; *compare* HOARD
   rel assemble, collect, gather, lay by, lay down, lay in; heap, mass, pile, stock; fund, hoard, treasure
   idiom squirrel away
   con decrease, diminish, lessen; deal, dispense, distribute, dole (out); dispel, disperse, scatter; consume, expend, spend, use, use up
   ant dissipate

accumulation *n* a mass, quantity, or number that has accumulated < an *accumulation* of rubbish>
   syn agglomeration, aggregation, amassment, collection, colluvies, conglomeration, cumulation, hoard, trove
   rel bank, heap, mass, pile; cumulus, reserve, stock, store
   con dispersal, dispersion, scattering

accumulative *adj syn* see CUMULATIVE
   rel aggregative, conglomerative; augmentative, multiplicative
   con contractile, contractive, reducing, reductive; dispelling, dispersing, dispersive, dissipative, scattering

accuracy *n syn* see PRECISION

accurate *adj* **1** *syn* see CORRECT 2
   con slipshod, slovenly; careless, heedless, lax
   ant inaccurate
   2 *syn* see CERTAIN 3

accurately *adv syn* see JUST 1

accursed *adj syn* see EXECRABLE 1
   rel abhorrent, abominable, detestable, hateful, odious; offensive, repugnant, revolting
   con admirable, estimable; honorable; divine, holy, sacred
   ant blessed

accuse *vb* to declare one guilty of a fault or offense < *accused* her daughter of neglecting her children>
   syn arraign, charge, criminate, impeach, incriminate, inculpate, indict, tax
   rel blame, censure, criticize, denounce, reprobate; complain
   idiom bring charges (against), point the finger at, prefer charges (against)
   con absolve, acquit, exonerate, vindicate; accept, approve, endorse, sanction
   ant exculpate

accustom *vb* to make something familiar or acceptable through use or experience < *accustom* oneself to city life>
   syn familiarize, habituate, inure, use, wont
   rel accommodate, adapt, adjust; acclimatize, harden, season

con alienate, estrange, wean; abjure, reject, repudiate; rebuff, repel, repulse, scorn
   ant disaccustom

accustomed *adj* **1** *syn* see HABITUAL 2
   2 *syn* see USUAL 1
   rel commonplace, everyday; conventional, regulation, standard
   con infrequent, occasional, uncommon; erratic, odd, peculiar, queer, singular
   ant unaccustomed

ace *n* **1** *syn* see HAIR
   2 *syn* see PARTICLE

acedia *n syn* see SLOTH 2

acerb *adj* **1** *syn* see SOUR 1
   2 *syn* see SARCASTIC

acerbate *vb syn* see EXACERBATE

acerbic *adj* **1** *syn* see SOUR 1
   2 *syn* see SARCASTIC

acerbity *n* **1** *syn* see ACRIMONY
   rel acidity, sourness, tartness; crabbedness, dourness, saturninity, surliness; acridity, bitterness; harshness, roughness
   con blandness, gentleness, mildness, smoothness; amiability, complaisance, good nature
   ant mellowness
   2 *syn* see SARCASM

acetose *adj syn* see SOUR 1

ache *vb* **1** *syn* see HURT 4
   2 *syn* see COMPASSIONATE
   rel deplore; sorrow (over); comfort, console, solace
   3 *syn* see LONG

ache *n syn* see PAIN 1
   rel injury; rack
   con alleviation, assuagement, mitigation; relief; comfort, ease

acheronian *adj syn* see GLOOMY 3

acherontic *adj syn* see GLOOMY 3

achieve *vb* **1** *syn* see PERFORM 2
   rel complete, conclude, finish; conquer, overcome, surmount
   idiom bring to a happy issue, bring to pass
   con begin, commence, start
   ant fail (in *or* to do)
   2 *syn* see GAIN 1
   rel acquire, get, obtain, secure; actualize; arrive, come
   idiom gain one's end
   con depart, deviate, swerve; avoid, elude, escape, shun
   ant miss

achievement *n* **1** *syn* see FEAT 2
   con omission, slighting
   ant failure
   2 *syn* see ACQUIREMENT

Achilles' heel *n syn* see SOFT SPOT 2

aching *adj syn* see PAINFUL 1
   rel achy

acicular *adj syn* see POINTED 1

aciculate *adj syn* see POINTED 1

acid *adj syn* see SOUR 1
   con bland, mild, neutral
   ant sweet; alkaline, basic

acidulous *adj syn* see SOUR 1
   rel biting, cutting, sharp; piquant, pungent
   con bland, mild, neutral; mellow, smooth, suave
   ant saccharine

acknowledge *vb* **1** to show often grudgingly by word or deed that one knows of

---

syn synonym(s)   *rel* related word(s)
ant antonym(s)   *con* contrasted word(s)
idiom idiomatic equivalent(s)
‖ use limited; if in doubt, see a dictionary

and agrees to or with something < *acknowledge* the justice of a complaint >
syn admit, allow, avow, concede, confess, fess (up), grant, let on, own, own up
rel disclose, divulge, reveal, tell; announce, declare, proclaim, publish
con disallow, disavow, disown, ||nix, reject; contradict, gainsay, impugn, negate, negative
ant deny
2 to take notice of and accept as being as stated < he is generally *acknowledged* to be the leader in his profession >
syn admit, agree, recognize
rel accept, receive; concede, consider, deem, hold, view
con disregard, neglect, slight; reject, repudiate, spurn
ant ignore

acknowledgment *n syn* see CREDIT 4

acme *n syn* see APEX 2

acoustic *adj syn* see AUDITORY

acquaint *vb* 1 *syn* see INTRODUCE 4
idiom make acquainted
2 *syn* see INFORM 2
rel disclose, divulge, reveal; accustom, habituate
con hold, hold back, reserve, withhold; conceal, hide

acquaintance *n* 1 knowledge of something based on personal exposure < had a considerable *acquaintance* with modern poetry >
syn experience, familiarity, intimacy, inwardness
rel apprehension, grasp, ken; appreciation, awareness, consciousness
con inexperience, unfamiliarity; greenness, verdancy
2 *syn* see FRIEND
rel associate, companion, comrade, crony
con outsider, stranger

acquainted *adj syn* see FAMILIAR 3

acquiesce *vb syn* see ASSENT
rel accommodate, adapt, adjust, reconcile; bow, coincide, concur
con balk, demur, shy (away); kick, protest, remonstrate; differ, dissent
ant object

acquiescence *n* weak or passive agreement to what is asked or demanded < his childish *acquiescence* to all claims on his time >
syn compliance, conformity, resignation
rel complaisance; submissiveness; deference
con contumaciousness, insubordination; independence, self-assurance
ant rebellion, rebelliousness

acquiescent *adj syn* see PASSIVE 2

acquire *vb* 1 *syn* see GET 1
rel achieve, reach; add
con alienate, convey, transfer; abandon, relinquish, surrender, yield
ant forfeit
2 *syn* see EARN 1
rel accumulate, amass, collect, cumulate, garner
3 *syn* see DEVELOP 4

acquirement *n* a power or skill that results from persistent endeavor and cultivation < proud of his scholastic *acquirements* >

syn accomplishment, achievement, acquisition, attainment, finish
rel accretion, addition; advance, advancement; education, erudition, knowledge
con dearth, defect, lack, privation, want

acquisition *n syn* see ACQUIREMENT
rel accession, increment; assets, belongings, means, possessions

acquisitive *adj syn* see COVETOUS
rel demanding, exacting, exigent
con eschewing, forbearing, forgoing; sacrificing
ant abnegating, self-denying

acquit *vb* 1 *syn* see EXCULPATE
rel discharge, free, liberate, release; justify
con condemn, damn, doom, proscribe, sentence
ant convict
2 *syn* see BEHAVE 1

acres *n pl syn* see ESTATE 3

acrid *adj* having or being a noticeable, persistent, and usually unpleasant flavor or sometimes odor < the tonic had an *acrid* aftertaste >
syn amaroidal, astringent, austere, bitter, harsh, sharp
rel biting, caustic, cutting; piquant, pungent; cloying, oversweet, saccharine
con palatable, sapid, tasty, toothsome; delectable, delicious, luscious
ant savory

acrimonious *adj syn* see ANGRY
rel cranky, cross, irascible, splenetic, testy; belligerent, contentious, quarrelsome
con benign, benignant, kind, kindly
ant irenic, peaceable

acrimony *n* sharpness or rancor manifested in words, manner, or disposition < the dispute was renewed with increasing *acrimony* >
syn acerbity, asperity, mordancy
rel bitterness, ill will, malevolence, malice, malignity, spite, spleen; animosity, animus, antipathy, rancor
con civility, courtesy, graciousness, politeness; diplomacy, urbanity
ant suavity

acroamatic *adj syn* see RECONDITE

across *adv* 1 so as to intersect the length of something < cut the board *across* >
syn athwart, crossways, crosswise
2 *syn* see OVER 1

across *prep* from one side to the other < drew the curtain *across* the window >
syn athwart, cross, over

act *vb* 1 to present a role or performance on or as if on the stage < *acted* the part of Hamlet's father >
syn discourse, do, enact, impersonate, perform, personate, play, playact
rel characterize, portray, represent; masquerade; counterfeit, feign, sham, simulate
2 *syn* see ASSUME 4
idiom act a part, put on an act (of)
3 *syn* see BEHAVE 1
rel perform
4 to perform the duties or function of < he *acted* as president for over a year >
syn function, officiate, serve
idiom do duty (as), discharge the office (of), serve in the office (*or* capacity) of
5 to perform especially in an indicated way < the laxative *acted* quickly >

syn behave, function, operate, perform, react, take, work
idiom take effect
6 *syn* see FUNCTION 3
act *n syn* see ACTION 1
rel exploit, feat
actify *vb syn* see VITALIZE
acting *adj syn* see TEMPORARY
action *n* **1** something done or effected < a kindly *action* >
syn accomplishment, act, deed, doing, thing
rel discharge, effectuation, execution, fulfillment, performance; activity, behavior, operation, reaction, work; procedure, proceeding, process
2 *syn* see BATTLE
rel affray, combat, conflict, fray
3 *syn* see SERVICE 1
4 *syn* see SUIT 1
activate *vb syn* see VITALIZE
rel arouse, awaken, rally, rouse, stir, wake, waken
ant arrest
active *adj* **1** being at work or in effective operation < marginal mines that are *active* only when prices are high >
syn alive, dynamic, functioning, live, operative, running, working
rel assiduous, busy, diligent, industrious; energetic, strenuous, vigorous; alert, wide‑awake; rushing
con dormant, latent, quiescent; idle, inert, passive, supine; dead, dull, slow
ant inactive; abeyant
2 *syn* see AGILE
rel animated, spirited, vivacious; flexible, graceful, supple
con inert, lumpish, torpid
ant inactive
3 *syn* see ENERGETIC 2
rel expeditious, prompt, ready
con disinterested, indifferent, unconcerned
actively *adv syn* see SERIOUSLY 1
activity *n syn* see EXERCISE 2
activize *vb syn* see VITALIZE
actor *n* **1** one who takes part in an exhibition simulating happenings in real life < had been an *actor* on the stage and in television >
syn impersonator, mime, mimic, mummer, performer, playactor, player, thespian, trouper
2 *syn* see PARTICIPANT
rel mainstay, supporter, sustainer, upholder
con abettor, backer, patron, promoter
actual *adj* **1** existing in act < our *actual* intentions >
syn existent, extant
ant possible, potential
2 existing in or based on fact < problems of *actual* life >
syn absolute, factual, genuine, hard, positive, sure-enough
rel commonplace, everyday, ordinary, routine, usual; concrete, real, tangible
con conjectural, hypothetical, theoretical; putative, reputed, supposititious

ant apparent, nominal
3 *syn* see REAL 3
rel material, objective, phenomenal, physical; authentic, bona fide, legitimate
con abstract, transcendent, transcendental; academic, speculative, theoretical; fabulous, fictitious, mythical
ant ideal; imaginary
actuality *n* **1** *syn* see EXISTENCE 1
rel actualization, externalization, incarnation, materialization; achievement, attainment
con abstraction, ideality, transcendence
ant possibility, potentiality
2 something that has existence < the *actualities* of daily life >
syn materiality, reality
rel basis, essence, substance; embodiment, incarnation
3 *syn* see FACT 1
actually *adv syn* see VERY 2
actuate *vb* **1** *syn* see MOVE 5
2 *syn* see MOBILIZE 1
rel excite, galvanize, provoke; arouse, rouse, stir; vitalize
act up *vb syn* see CUT UP 2
acumen *n syn* see WIT 3
rel acuteness, sharpness
con denseness, density, slowness
ant obtuseness, obtusity
acuminate *adj syn* see POINTED 1
acuminous *adj syn* see POINTED 1
acute *adj* **1** *syn* see POINTED 1
rel barbed, prickly, spiky, spined, spiny
ant blunt
2 *syn* see SHARP 4
rel cutting, incisive, trenchant; piercing
con crass, dense, dull, slow, stupid
ant obtuse
3 perceiving clearly and sensitively < an *acute* ear >
syn keen, perceptive, sensitive, sharp
rel observant, penetrating, probing; accurate, meticulous, precise
con imperceptive, insensitive; imprecise, inaccurate; inexact, uncritical
ant dull
4 elevated in pitch < an *acute* note >
syn argute, high, piercing, piping, sharp, shrill, thin, treble
rel penetrating; reedy, screechy, shrieky, shrilly, squeaky; tinny
con bass, deep, low
ant grave
5 *syn* see SHARP 8
6 serious to the point of approaching a crisis < an *acute* housing shortage >
syn climacteric, critical, crucial, desperate, dire
rel afflictive, grave, serious; aggravated, intensified; dangerous, hazardous, menacing, perilous, precarious, threatening; exigent, urgent
adage *n syn* see SAYING
adamant *adj syn* see INFLEXIBLE 2
rel immobile, immovable; unsubmitting
con placable, relenting, submitting; complaisant, obliging; subdued, submissive
ant yielding
adamantine *adj syn* see INFLEXIBLE 2
rel immobile, immovable; unsubmitting
con placable, relenting, submitting; complaisant, obliging; subdued, submissive

---

syn synonym(s)   *rel* related word(s)
ant antonym(s)   *con* contrasted word(s)
idiom idiomatic equivalent(s)
‖ use limited; if in doubt, see a dictionary

ant yielding

adapt *vb* to bring into correspondence or make suitable < *adapted* himself easily to the company he found himself with >
syn accommodate, adjust, conform, fit, quadrate, reconcile, square, suit, tailor, tailor-make
rel qualify, temper; acclimate, acclimatize
ant unfit

adaptable *adj* 1 *syn* see VERSATILE
2 *syn* see PLASTIC
con intractable, irreconcilable, nonconforming, refractory, unaccommodating
ant inadaptable, unadaptable

adapted *adj syn* see ASSORTED 2

add *vb* 1 to bring in or join on something more so as to form a larger or more inclusive whole < *added* music to his accomplishments >
syn annex, append, subjoin, superadd, take on
rel affix, attach, fasten, superimpose, tack (on); augment, enlarge, increase; burden, clutter, cumber, encumber, saddle
con abstract, detach; curtail, decrease, diminish, lessen, reduce
ant deduct, subtract
2 to combine numbers or quantities into one sum < *add* up a column of figures >
syn cast, figure, foot, sum, summate, tot, total, totalize, tote
rel calculate, compute, estimate, reckon; score, tally

added *adj syn* see ADDITIONAL

addendum *n*, *sometimes* **addenda** *pl but sing or pl in constr syn* see APPENDIX 1

addict *vb syn* see HABITUATE 2
rel bias, dispose, incline, predispose; address, apply, direct
con alienate, estrange; detach, disengage, disincline, indispose
ant wean

addict *n* a person who by habit or strong inclination indulges in something < a science fiction *addict* >
syn aficionado, buff, devotee, fan, habitué, hound, lover, votary
rel enthusiast, fanatic, zealot; hobbyist, putterer, tinkerer

addition *n* something else that tends to increase something else (as in size, number, or content) < there are several new *additions* to our staff >
syn accession, accretion, augmentation, increase, increment, raise, rise
rel accessory, adjunct, appanage, appurtenance, supplement; continuation, extension, rider; accrual, accruement, accumulation
con deduction, lessening, reduction

additional *adj* being or coming by way of addition < gave *additional* reasons to justify his position >
syn added, another, else, farther, fresh, further, more, new, other
rel accessory, adscititious, collateral, extra, supplemental, supplementary

additionally *adv* 1 *syn* see ALSO 2
2 *syn* see AGAIN 4

additive *adj syn* see CUMULATIVE
rel component, constituent, elemental

additory *adj syn* see CUMULATIVE

addle *vb syn* see CONFUSE 2

rel confound, dumbfound, nonplus; amaze, astound, flabbergast
idiom addle one's wits
con animate, enliven, quicken, vivify
ant refresh (*mentally*)

address *vb* 1 *syn* see DIRECT 2
2 *syn* see SEND 1
3 to occupy (oneself or one's attention or efforts) with something < *addressed* himself to the job and soon finished it >
syn apply, bend, buckle (down), devote, direct, give, throw, turn
rel associate, connect, couple, link, relate; aim, level, point
idiom bring (oneself) into relation with something, tax (one's energies) with something
con disregard, ignore, overlook
4 to communicate directly to or with < *addressed* the governor with his petition >
syn accost, apply (to), approach, bespeak, memorialize
rel speak (to), talk (with); appeal (to); apostrophize; petition
con ignore, overlook, pass up, slight; avoid, cut, disregard
5 *syn* see TALK 7
6 to affix directions for delivery < *address* a letter >
syn direct, superscribe
7 to seek the attention of usually orally and in order to gain recognition < *address* a stranger to ask directions >
syn accost, call (to), greet, hail, salute
rel converse, speak, talk
idiom attract one's attention
8 to direct one's attention to in the role of a suitor < ready to marry the first man that *addressed* her >
syn court, make up (to), pursue, spark, sue, sweetheart, woo
rel attend, escort, squire; neck, pet, romance, rush, smooch, spoon
idiom make a play for, pay (one's) addresses to, run after

address *n* 1 the quality or state of being ready or skillful < to bring off such a coup requires *address* >
syn adroitness, deftness, dexterity, dexterousness, prowess, readiness, skill, sleight; *compare* TACT
rel competence, efficiency, expertise, know-how, proficiency; craft, finesse; ingeniousness, ingenuity, resourcefulness
con inadequacy, ineptitude, ineptness, unskillfulness; awkwardness, clumsiness, gawkiness, lubberliness, stupidity
2 *syn* see TACT
rel dexterity, ease, facility; cleverness, readiness; affability, graciousness
con awkwardness, clumsiness, gaucheness; boorishness, churlishness
ant maladroitness
3 *syn* see BEARING 1
4 *syn* see SPEECH 2

adduce *vb* to bring forward for consideration < *adduce* evidence in support of a hypothesis >
syn advance, allege, cite, lay, offer, present
rel animadvert, comment, commentate, remark; document, exemplify, illustrate;

prefer, proffer, propose, submit, suggest, tender

add up *vb syn* see AMOUNT 1

add up (to) *vb syn* see MEAN 2

adept *n syn* see EXPERT
ant bungler, incompetent

adept *adj syn* see PROFICIENT
rel clever; adroit, deft, dexterous
con amateurish, dabbling, dilettantish; awkward, clumsy, maladroit
ant bungling, inapt, inept

adequacy *n* 1 *syn* see ABILITY 1
rel equality, satisfactoriness, sufficiency
idiom enough on the ball
ant inadequacy, inadequateness
2 *syn* see ENOUGH

adequate *adj* 1 *syn* see SUFFICIENT 1
con meager, scanty, sparse
ant inadequate, unadequate
2 *syn* see DECENT 4

adequately *adv* 1 *syn* see ENOUGH 1
2 *syn* see WELL 4

adequation *n syn* see EQUIVALENCE

adhere *vb syn* see STICK 2
rel combine, join, link, unite
con disjoin, disunite

adherence *n* 1 a physical adhering < the close *adherence* of scales to a plant bud >
syn adhesion, bond, cling, clinging, coherence, cohesion, stickage, sticking
rel agglutination, cementation, concretion, conglutination; congelation, set, setting, solidification
con detachment, disjunction, parting, separation
2 *syn* see ATTACHMENT 1
con fickleness, inconstancy

adherent *n syn* see FOLLOWER
rel backer, champion, upholder
con apostate, recreant; deserter, forsaker; adversary, antagonist, opponent
ant renegade

adhesion *n* 1 *syn* see ADHERENCE 1
ant nonadhesion
2 *syn* see ATTACHMENT 1
con fickleness, inconstancy

adhesive *adj syn* see STICKY 1

adieu *interj syn* see GOOD-BYE

adieu *n syn* see PARTING

ad interim *adj syn* see TEMPORARY
ant permanent

adipose *adj syn* see FATTY 1

adiposity *n syn* see OBESITY

adit *n syn* see DOOR 2

adjacent *adj* 1 *syn* see NEIGHBORING
ant remote
2 *syn* see CONVENIENT 2
3 having a common border < the brothers built on *adjacent* lots >
syn abutting, adjoining, approximal, bordering, conterminous, contiguous, juxtaposed, touching
rel closest, nearest, next; consecutive, successive; attached, connected, joined, linked
con distant, far, remote, removed; parted, separated
ant nonadjacent

---

adjoin *vb* to be contiguous or adjacent to < the new suburb *adjoins* farmland >
syn abut, border, butt (on *or* against), communicate, join, line, march, neighbor, touch, verge
rel meet, run (into); end

adjoining *adj syn* see ADJACENT 3
ant detached

adjourn *vb* 1 *syn* see DEFER
rel curb, hold back, restrain
con advance, expedite, further, promote
2 to bring to a formal close < *adjourn* the legislature >
syn dissolve, prorogate, prorogue, recess, rise, terminate
rel break up, close, disband, discontinue, disperse; stay, suspend
con open; mobilize, muster, rally
ant convene, convoke

adjudge *vb syn* see JUDGE 1
rel accord, allot, assign, award, grant

adjudicate *vb syn* see JUDGE 1

adjunct *n syn* see APPENDAGE
rel accretion, addition; appanage; affix, attachment, fixture

adjust *vb* 1 *syn* see ADAPT
rel accord, correspond; attune, harmonize
2 to alter so as to make efficient or more efficient < *adjust* a carburetor >
syn fix, regulate, tune (up)
rel correct, rectify, right; balance, stabilize, steady, trim, true; arrange, order, rig
idiom make right, put (*or* set) in order, put right (*or* to rights), set right (*or* to rights)
con disarrange, disorder, disturb, upset
ant derange
3 *syn* see HABITUATE 2

adjuvant *adj syn* see AUXILIARY
rel synergistic
con antagonistic, negating, negativing, neutralizing; hindering, impeding, obstructing
ant counteractive

ad–lib *vb syn* see IMPROVISE

admeasure *vb syn* see ALLOT

admeasurement *n syn* see SIZE 1

adminicular *adj syn* see CORROBORATIVE

administer *vb* 1 to supervise the affairs or the provision, use, or conduct of especially in the capacity of an agent or steward < *administer* justice >
syn administrate, carry out, execute, govern, render
rel conduct, direct, manage, run, supervise
2 to provide in appropriate amount < *administer* a laxative >
syn apportion, deal (out), dispense, dole (out), mete (out), portion (out), share out
rel distribute, give, give out, issue; allot, assign, consign; allocate, ration
3 *syn* see GIVE 10

administrate *vb syn* see ADMINISTER 1

administrator *n syn* see EXECUTIVE

admirable *adj syn* see WORTHY 1

admiration *n* 1 *syn* see WONDER 2
rel surprise; ecstasy, rapture, transport
con aloofness, indifference, unconcern
2 *syn* see REGARD 4
rel appreciation; adoration, reverence, veneration, worship
con detestation, hate, hatred, loathing; dislike, disrelish, distaste

---

syn synonym(s)	*rel* related word(s)
ant antonym(s)	*con* contrasted word(s)
idiom idiomatic equivalent(s)	
‖ use limited; if in doubt, see a dictionary	

ant abhorrence

admire *vb* **1** to view with an elevated feeling of pleasure < *admired* the scene that spread out before them >
syn appreciate, cherish, delight (in), relish; *compare* APPRECIATE 1
rel adore, revere, reverence, venerate, worship
idiom go into raptures over, take delight in
con disesteem, disfavor, dislike, disrelish, mislike
ant disdain
2 to hold in high esteem < *admired* his ability to get things done >
syn consider, esteem, regard, respect
rel appreciate, cherish, prize, treasure, value
idiom have (*or* hold) a high opinion of, rate highly, set (great) store by, think much (*or* highly) of
con abominate, detest, hate, loathe; contemn, despise, disdain, scorn
ant abhor

admirer *n syn see* AMATEUR 1
admissible *adj syn see* PERMISSIBLE
admission *n syn see* DOOR 2
admit *vb* **1** *syn see* TAKE 10
rel allow, permit, suffer; entertain, harbor, house, lodge, shelter
con debar, exclude, shut out; bar, block, hinder, obstruct
ant eject, expel
2 *syn see* ACKNOWLEDGE 1
rel acquiesce, agree, assent, subscribe
ant gainsay
3 *syn see* ENTER 2
rel induct, initiate, install; insert, interject, interpose
con debar, shut out; eject, expel, oust
ant exclude
4 *syn see* ACKNOWLEDGE 2

admittance *n syn see* DOOR 2
admix *vb syn see* MIX 1
admixture *n* **1** an added ingredient that alters the character of something < her love had a marring *admixture* of selfishness >
syn adulterant, alloy, denaturant
rel doctor, fortification, taint; accretion, addition; bit, dash, shade, smack, spice, tinge
2 *syn see* MIXTURE

admonish *vb syn see* REPROVE
rel caution, forewarn, warn
idiom have a word with
con applaud, approve, compliment
ant commend

admonishing *adj syn see* MONITORY
admonishment *n syn see* REBUKE
admonition *n* **1** *syn see* REBUKE
2 *syn see* WARNING
admonitory *adj syn see* MONITORY
ado *n syn see* STIR 1
rel effort, exertion, pains, trouble; confusion, hurly-burly, turmoil, uproar
con calm, peace, serenity, tranquillity; quiet, silence, stillness

adolescence *n syn see* YOUTH 1
ant senescence
adopt *vb* to make one's own what in some fashion one owes to another < *adopt* a new style >

syn embrace, espouse, take on, take up
rel affect, assume; appropriate, arrogate, take, usurp; domesticate, naturalize
idiom adapt to one's own ends, go in for
con reject, spurn; abjure, forswear, renounce
ant discard; repudiate

adoption *n syn see* ESPOUSAL 4
adorable *adj* **1** *syn see* LOVABLE
2 *syn see* DELIGHTFUL
adoration *n* deep, ardent, and often excessive attachment or love < the *adoration* given popular heroes >
syn idolatry, idolization, worship
rel affection, attachment, devotion, love; crush, infatuation, passion, weakness
con antipathy, aversion; disfavor, dislike, distaste
ant detestation

adore *vb* **1** *syn see* REVERE
rel extol, laud, praise
con curse, execrate
2 *syn see* LOVE 2
3 to love, admire, or enjoy excessively < she *adores* and spoils her grandchildren >
syn dote (on *or* upon), idolize, worship
rel admire, esteem, love; coddle, indulge, pamper, spoil
idiom be silly over
con abhor, abominate, hate, loathe; contemn, despise, disdain, scorn
ant detest
4 *syn see* LOVE 1

adorn *vb* to add something nonessential to enhance the appearance or beauty of < a hat *adorned* with feathers >
syn beautify, bedeck, deck, decorate, dress (up), embellish, garnish, ornament, prank, trim
rel enrich, furbish, smarten, spruce (up); bedizen, dandify, fancy up; enhance, heighten, intensify
con clear, divest, expose, strip, uncover; deface, mar, scar, spoil
ant disfigure

ad rem *adj syn see* RELEVANT
adroit *adj* **1** *syn see* DEXTEROUS 1
ant maladroit
2 *syn see* SKILLFUL 2
3 *syn see* CLEVER 4
rel astute, perspicacious, shrewd; intelligent, quick-witted, smart; artful, subtle
con dense, dull, stupid; apathetic, heavy, impassive, phlegmatic, stodgy
ant stolid

adroitness *n* **1** *syn see* ADDRESS 1
2 *syn see* ART 1
adscititious *adj syn see* ADVENTITIOUS
adulation *n syn see* FLATTERY
rel acclaim, applause
ant abuse
adult *adj syn see* MATURE 1
rel aged
con adolescent, pubescent
ant juvenile, puerile
adulterant *n syn see* ADMIXTURE 1
adulterate *vb* to alter fraudulently usually for profit < sausage *adulterated* with cereal products >
syn debase, doctor, dope (up), load, sophisticate, weight

rel cut, dilute; denaturalize, denature, manipulate, tamper (with); defile, impurify, pollute, taint; deacon
con better, improve; augment, fortify, supplement
ant refine

adumbrate *vb* **1** to give a hint or indication of something to come < social unrest that *adumbrated* the revolt >
syn foreshadow, hint, prefigurate, prefigure, shadow (forth); *compare* SUGGEST 5
rel augur, bode, forebode, foretell, portend, presage; lower, menace, threaten; symbolize, typify
idiom cast its shadow before
2 *syn* see FORETELL
rel argue, bespeak, betoken, indicate
3 *syn* see SKETCH
4 *syn* see SUGGEST 5
rel denote, mean, signify
5 *syn* see OBSCURE

adumbration *n syn* see SHADE 1
rel hint, intimation, suggestion; sign, symptom, token; emblem, symbol, type
con disclosure, discovery, divulgence
ant revelation

advance *vb* **1** to cause to proceed or progress toward a goal < warm rains *advanced* the crops >
syn encourage, forward, foster, further, promote, serve
rel aid, assist, help; accelerate, quicken, speed
con hinder, impede; delay, slow; curb, restrain
ant retard; check
2 to raise in rank or position < was *advanced* to the presidency >
syn elevate, prefer, promote, upgrade
rel aggrandize, exalt, raise, uplift; glorify, immortalize, magnify
ant hold back; reduce (*in rank*)
3 *syn* see LEND
4 *syn* see ADDUCE
rel air, broach, expose
5 to go forward in space or time or toward an objective < prices *advanced* sharply >
syn get along, get on, march, move, proceed, progress
rel heighten, increase, intensify; develop, mature
idiom forge ahead, gain ground, get ahead, make headway (*or* progress), make one's way, make rapid strides
con retire, retreat, retrograde, withdraw
ant recede

advance *n* **1** *syn* see PROGRESS 2
2 forward movement especially on a course of action or development < the recent *advance* of technology >
syn advancement, anabasis, headway, march, ongoing, proficiency, progress
rel betterment, furtherance, improvement; development, evolution; breakthrough
con retreat, retrogression; ebbing, retiring, withdrawal
ant recession

3 *syn* see OVERTURE 1
rel offer, proffer

advanced *adj* **1** *syn* see PRECOCIOUS
con retrograde, retrogressive
ant backward
2 *syn* see LIBERAL 3
rel adventurous, daring, venturesome
ant conservative

advancement *n* **1** the act of raising or the status of being raised in grade, rank, or dignity < his *advancement* in his profession was rapid >
syn elevation, preference, preferment, prelation, promotion, upgrading
rel aggrandizement, dignification, magnification, raising, uplifting
con demotion, downgrading, reduction
ant degradation
2 *syn* see ADVANCE 2

advantage *n* **1** *syn* see BETTER 2
2 *syn* see WELFARE
3 something giving one person or side a position of superiority (as in a contest) < he had the *advantage* of greater height >
syn allowance, bulge, ‖deadwood, draw, edge, handicap, head start, odds, ‖overhand, start, vantage; *compare* BETTER 2
rel drop, jump, lead, running start; ascendancy, domination, leadership; mastery, superiority, upper hand, whip hand
idiom ace in the hole, inside track
con embarrassment, hamper, hindrance, impediment, inconvenience
ant disadvantage
4 *syn* see USE 3
rel betterment, improvement; enhancement; heightening
con damage, harm, hurt, injury
ant detriment
5 *syn* see GOOD 1

advantage *vb syn* see BENEFIT

advantageous *adj* **1** yielding a profit < sold on very *advantageous* terms >
syn gainful, good, lucrative, moneymaking, paying, profitable, remunerative, well≈paying, worthwhile
rel acceptable, agreeable, desirable, pleasing, satisfactory, satisfying
idiom in the black, paying its (own) way
con disadvantageous, unfavorable, unprofitable; damaging, hurtful
2 *syn* see GOOD 1
rel remedial, salutary; conducive, contributory, implemental, instrumental; advisable, expedient
con unfavorable; inconvenient; deleterious, detrimental
ant disadvantageous

advenient *adj syn* see ADVENTITIOUS

advent *n syn* see ARRIVAL 1
rel approach, nearing
ant exit

advential *adj syn* see ADVENTITIOUS

adventitious *adj* coming from without and not participating in the fundamental nature of something < *adventitious* notions that have corrupted the primitive doctrine >
syn adscititious, advenient, advential, supervenient
rel accidental, casual, contingent, fortuitous, incidental

---

syn synonym(s)   *rel* related word(s)
ant antonym(s)   *con* contrasted word(s)
idiom idiomatic equivalent(s)
‖ use limited; if in doubt, see a dictionary

con constitutional, essential, intrinsic; inborn, inbred, innate
ant inherent

adventure *n* an undertaking or experience that involves hazard and requires boldness < recounted the *adventures* of his solitary voyage >
syn emprise, enterprise, exploit, feat, gest, venture
rel hazard, peril, risk; quest; achievement

adventure *vb syn* see VENTURE 1

adventuresome *adj syn* see ADVENTUR-OUS
ant unadventurous; cautious

adventurous *adj* courting danger or exposing oneself to danger beyond the call of duty or courage < *adventurous* boys scrambled over the cliff face >
syn adventuresome, audacious, daredevil, daring, foolhardy, rash, reckless, temerarious, venturesome, venturous
rel bold, doughty, intrepid; brash, harebrained, hotheaded, impetuous, imprudent, madcap, overconfident
con shrinking, timid, timorous; afraid, alarmed, fearful, scared; apprehensive, uneasy
ant unadventurous; cautious

adversary *n syn* see OPPONENT
rel assaulter, attacker
con backer, supporter, upholder
ant ally

adverse *adj* 1 acting against or in a contrary direction < hindered by *adverse* forces >
syn antagonistic, anti, antipathetic, opposed, opposing, oppugnant
rel contrary, counter, counteractive; hindering, impeding, obstructive; hostile, unfriendly
con coactive, collaborative, cooperative; adjuvant, synergistic; favorable, propitious
2 being opposed to one's interests < an *adverse* balance of trade >
syn detrimental, negative, unfavorable
rel deleterious, harmful, hurtful, injurious; disadvantageous, prejudicial, unpropitious, unsatisfactory
con advantageous, favorable, positive, propitious, satisfactory

adversity *n syn* see MISFORTUNE
rel distress, misery, suffering; deprivation, destitution, indigence, poverty
con bliss, felicity, happiness; comfort, ease
ant prosperity

advert *vb syn* see REFER 3
rel animadvert, note, notice, observe, remark
con disregard, ignore, neglect, overlook

advertent *adj syn* see ATTENTIVE 1

advertise *vb* 1 *syn* see DECLARE 1
rel recount, relate, report; communicate, impart; ballyhoo, promote, propagandize, publicize
con conceal, repress, suppress; bury, hide, obscure
2 *syn* see PUBLICIZE
3 *syn* see PROMOTE 3

advertisement *n syn* see DECLARATION
rel ballyhoo, promotion, propaganda, publicity

advertising *n syn* see PUBLICITY

advice *n* 1 recommendation regarding a decision or course of conduct < benefited from his *advice* on study habits >
syn advisement, counsel
rel direction, guidance, instruction, teaching; admonition; caution, cautioning, forewarning, warning
2 *syn* see NEWS

advisable *adj syn* see EXPEDIENT
rel commendable, desirable; becoming, seemly, suitable; sensible
ant inadvisable

advise *vb* 1 *syn* see COUNSEL
rel caution, forewarn, warn; coax, induce, persuade, win (over)
con bedazzle, misadvise, mislead
2 *syn* see CONFER 2
rel deliberate
3 *syn* see INFORM 2
rel disclose, let out, reveal; communicate, impart

advised *adj syn* see DELIBERATE 1
rel intended, intentional, meant; knowing, purposeful, willful

advisement *n syn* see ADVICE 1

advocate *n syn* see EXPONENT

advocate *vb* 1 *syn* see ENCOURAGE 2
2 *syn* see SUPPORT 2
rel justify, vindicate; advance, forward, promote
idiom hold a brief for
con assail, attack; combat, fight, oppose
ant impugn

aegis *n* 1 *syn* see DEFENSE 1
2 *syn* see BACKING

aeneous *adj syn* see BRAZEN 4

aeon *n syn* see AGE 2

aerial *adj* 1 *syn* see AIRY 1
2 *syn* see LOFTY 6
3 *syn* see AIRY 3
rel immaterial, incorporeal; impalpable, imperceptible, imponderable

aesthete *n syn* see CONNOISSEUR
rel perfectionist, stickler; fussbudget, old maid
con barbarian; clod, lout, oaf

affable *adj* 1 *syn* see GRACIOUS 1
rel courteous, polite; suave, urbane; loquacious, talkative
con crabbed, glum, surly; reticent, withdrawn; silent, taciturn, uncommunicative
ant reserved
2 *syn* see GENTLE 2

affair *n* 1 something done or dealt with < trying to get at the truth of the *affair* >
syn business, concern, matter, shooting match, thing
rel care, lookout, responsibility; pie, proceeding
idiom cup of tea
2 *syn* see BUSINESS 8
3 *syn* see LOVE AFFAIR
4 *syn* see AMOUR 2

affect *vb* 1 *syn* see ASSUME 4
2 *syn* see FREQUENT

affect *vb* to produce a usually mental or emotional effect on one capable of reaction < much *affected* by the touching scene >
syn carry, get, impress, influence, inspire, move, strike, sway, touch
rel actuate, draw, drive, impel; penetrate, pierce

idiom work on

affectation *n syn* see POSE 2
  rel ostentation, pretentiousness
  con ingenuousness, naiveté, naturalness, simplicity, unsophistication
  ant artlessness

affected *adj* 1 *syn* see INTERESTED
  2 *syn* see SELF-CONSCIOUS
  3 *syn* see GENTEEL 3
  4 *syn* see PRECIOUS 4
  5 *syn* see ARTIFICIAL 3

affecting *adj syn* see MOVING 2
  rel piteous, pitiable, pitiful; distressful, distressing, disturbing, troubling

affection *n* 1 *syn* see FEELING 3
  rel leaning, penchant, propensity; bias, predilection; bent, faculty, turn
  con aversion, hate, hatred; dislike, distaste
  ant antipathy
  2 *syn* see LOVE 1
  rel sympathy, tenderness, warmth; attention, concern, interest; doting, enjoying
  con coolness, frigidity
  ant coldness

affection *vb syn* see LOVE 2

affection *n* 1 *syn* see DISEASE 1
  rel access, attack, paroxysm, spell; derangement, disordering, disturbance
  2 *syn* see QUALITY 1

affectionate *adj syn* see LOVING
  rel sympathetic, tender, warm
  con apathetic, impassive, stolid; remote, uninterested, withdrawn
  ant cold; undemonstrative

affective *adj syn* see EMOTIONAL 2

affectivity *n syn* see FEELING 3

affianced *adj syn* see ENGAGED 2

affianced *n syn* see BETROTHED

affiche *n syn* see POSTER

affiliated *adj syn* see RELATED
  con autonomous, free, independent
  ant unaffiliated

affiliation *n syn* see ASSOCIATION 1

affinity *n* 1 *syn* see ATTRACTION 2
  con antipathy, aversion; dislike, distaste; repugnance, repellency, repulsion
  2 *syn* see LIKENESS
  rel accord

affirm *vb syn* see ASSERT 1
  rel attest, certify, guarantee, vouch, witness; say, state
  con debate

affirmative *adj syn* see POSITIVE 6

affix *vb syn* see FASTEN 1
  rel add, annex, append, subjoin
  con disengage, disjoin
  ant detach

afflation *n syn* see INSPIRATION

afflatus *n syn* see INSPIRATION

afflict *vb* to inflict upon one something hard to endure <he was *afflicted* with boils>
  syn agonize, crucify, excruciate, harrow, martyr, martyrize, rack, smite, strike, torment, torture, try, wring
  rel annoy, harass, harry, pester, plague, press, worry; bother, irk, vex; lacerate, wound

---

syn synonym(s)   *rel* related word(s)
ant antonym(s)   *con* contrasted word(s)
idiom idiomatic equivalent(s)
‖ use limited; if in doubt, see a dictionary

---

  con console, delight, gladden, please, rejoice; ease, relieve, solace
  ant comfort

afflicted *adj syn* see WOEFUL 1

affliction *n* 1 *syn* see TRIAL 1
  rel mischance, mishap
  con alleviation, assuagement, easement, relief
  ant consolation, solace
  2 *syn* see SORROW
  3 *syn* see SICKNESS 1

afflictive *adj* 1 *syn* see PAINFUL 1
  2 *syn* see DEPLORABLE
  3 *syn* see BITTER 2

affluent *adj syn* see RICH 1
  rel acquisitive, grasping
  con poor; bankrupt, impoverished
  ant impecunious; straitened

affranchise *vb syn* see ENFRANCHISE

affray *n* 1 *syn* see BRAWL 2
  2 *syn* see CLASH 2

affright *vb syn* see FRIGHTEN
  rel bewilder, confound
  con animate, fire, inspire
  ant embolden, nerve

affront *vb* 1 *syn* see OFFEND 3
  rel criticize, dispraise
  con compliment; laud, praise; dignify, honor
  2 *syn* see CONFRONT 1

affront *n* a speech or an action designed to impugn the honor or worth of someone or something <her costume was an *affront* to the solemnity of the occasion>
  syn contumely, despite, indignity, insult, slap
  rel dishonor, flouting, offense, outrage, slight; aspersion, barb, defamation, dig
  idiom slap in the face
  con deference, homage, honor; adulation, compliment, flattery

aficionado *n syn* see ADDICT

afield *adj syn* see AMISS 2

afire *adj* 1 *syn* see BURNING 1
  2 *syn* see ALIGHT 2

aflame *adj* 1 *syn* see BURNING 1
  2 *syn* see ALIGHT 2

aflicker *adj syn* see ALIGHT 2, ablaze, afire, aflame, aglow

à fond *adv syn* see WELL 3

aforementioned *adj syn* see SUCH 1

aforesaid *adj syn* see SUCH 1

aforethought *adj syn* see DELIBERATE 1

afraid *adj* 1 suffering the effects of apprehension, fear, or terror <too *afraid* to even cry for help>
  syn aghast, anxious, ‖ascared, fearful, frightened, scared, scary, terrified; *compare* FEARFUL 2
  rel shrinking, shy, timid, timorous; cautious, chary, wary; jumpy, skittish
  idiom frightened out of one's wits, in a (blue) funk, scared to death, terror stricken
  con confident, dauntless, fearless; assured, collected, poised, self-possessed
  ant unafraid
  2 *syn* see FEARFUL 2
  idiom all of a twitter (*or* flutter)
  ant unafraid; sanguine
  3 *syn* see DISINCLINED

afresh *adv* 1 *syn* see OVER 7
  2 *syn* see NEW

‖**African dominoes** *n pl syn* see DICE
aft *adv syn* see ABAFT
 rel hind, posterior
 con ahead, before, forward
 ant fore
after *adv* so as to follow in time or space
 <*after*, we turned toward home>
 syn afterward, afterwhile, behind, by and
 by, infra, later, latterly, next, subsequently
 rel abaft, aft, astern
 idiom after a time (*or* while), in the wake
 of
 con ahead, forward
 ant before
after *prep* **1** so as to resemble or follow in
 some respect <named *after* his father>
 syn for, from
 2 later in time or lower in place or rank
 <*after* our discussion>
 syn behind, below, following, next, since,
 subsequent to
 con ante, ere, in advance of, preceding,
 prior to
 ant before
 3 *syn* see BEYOND 1
after *adj* **1** *syn* see SUBSEQUENT 1
 2 *syn* see POSTERIOR 2
 con antecedent, preceding, prior
after all *adv syn* see HOWEVER
aftereffect *n syn* see EFFECT 1
 rel remainder, residual, residuum
afterlife *n* **1** *syn* see ETERNITY 2
 2 *syn* see HEREAFTER 2
afterlight *n syn* see REVIEW 5
aftermath *n syn* see EFFECT 1
 rel remainder, residual, residuum
aftertime *n syn* see FUTURE
afterward *adv syn* see AFTER
afterward *n syn* see FUTURE
afterwhile *adv syn* see AFTER
afterword *n syn* see EPILOGUE 1
afterworld *n syn* see HEREAFTER 2
again *adv* **1** *syn* see ABOUT 6
 2 *syn* see OVER 7
 3 *syn* see THEN 1
 4 as another point, fact, or instance
 <*again*, consider taxes>
 syn additionally, also, besides, further, in
 addition, then; *compare* ALSO 2
 idiom by the same token, into the bargain, on top of that
 5 as an alternative and especially a converse <he may win and *again* he may
 not>
 syn contra, contrariwise, contrary, contrawise, conversely, oppositely, vice versa;
 compare HOWEVER
 idiom at the same time, be that as it may,
 just the same, on the other hand
again and again *adv syn* see OFTEN
against *prep* **1** directly opposite <stood
 against the crowd and shouted for order>
 syn contra, facing, fronting, over against,
 toward, vis-à-vis
 idiom counter to, face to face with
 2 so as to touch <vines trained *against*
 the wall>
 syn to, touching
 idiom in contact with, next to
 3 *syn* see VERSUS 1
 4 without being prevented or obstructed
 by <succeeded *against* grave handicaps>
 syn despite, in spite of, notwithstanding,
 regardless of

idiom in the face of
 5 *syn* see FROM 2
 6 *syn* see APROPOS
agape *adj syn* see AGHAST 2
age *n* **1** *syn* see OLD AGE
 ant youth
 2 *often* **ages** *pl* a long or seemingly long
 period of time <haven't seen her for
 ages>
 syn aeon, blue moon, coon's age, dog's
 age, donkey's years, eternity, long
 idiom month of Sundays, ‖right smart
 spell
 con flash, instant, minute, moment, second, split second, trice
 3 *syn* see PERIOD 2
age *vb syn* see MATURE
aged *adj* **1** being in the declining phase of
 life <*aged* pensioners>
 syn ancient, elderly, old, olden
 rel pensioned (off), retired, superannuated; senior; hoary, patriarchal, venerable;
 doddering, senescent, senile, tottery
 idiom along in years, getting on, getting
 on (*or* along) in years, gray with age, on
 one's last legs, stricken with years
 con juvenile, puerile
 ant youthful
 2 *syn* see ANCIENT 1
 3 *syn* see RIPE 3
ageless *adj syn* see ETERNAL 4
agency *n syn* see MEAN 2
 rel antecedent, cause, determinant; gear
agenda *n syn* see PROGRAM 1
agent *n* **1** *syn* see MEAN 2
 rel doer, executive, executor, performer;
 actor, worker; activator, energizer
 2 one who acts for another <diplomatic
 agents serving abroad>
 syn assignee, attorney, deputy, factor,
 proxy; *compare* DELEGATE
 rel go-between, middleman; instrument,
 minister, tool; commissioner, institor,
 proctor, procurator, representative, steward; buyer, commissionaire
 ant principal
 3 *syn* see SPY
age-old *adj syn* see ANCIENT 1
agglomerate *n syn* see AGGREGATE 1
 rel heap, mass, pile
agglomeration *n* **1** *syn* see ACCUMULA-
 TION
 rel association, combination
 2 *syn* see AGGREGATE 2
aggrandize *vb* **1** *syn* see INCREASE 1
 rel amplify, build up
 2 *syn* see EXALT 1
 ant belittle
aggrandizement *n syn* see APOTHEOSIS 2
aggravate *vb* **1** *syn* see INTENSIFY
 rel augment, enlarge, increase, multiply;
 aggrandize
 con extenuate, palliate
 ant alleviate
 2 *syn* see IRRITATE
 rel disturb, perturb, upset; annoy, bedevil
 con calm, tranquilize
 ant appease
aggravation *n syn* see ANNOYANCE 2
aggregate *n syn* see AMOUNT 1
aggregate *n* **1** a mass or body formed of
 particles or parts that retain their individuality <an *aggregate* of ill-planned ar-
 guments>

syn agglomerate, agglomeration, aggregation, conglomerate, conglomeration; *compare* ACCUMULATION
ant constituent, element
2 *syn* see BODY 5
ant individual, unit; particular
3 *syn* see WHOLE 1

aggregation *n* 1 *syn* see AGGREGATE 1
ant constituent, element
2 *syn* see ACCUMULATION
rel backlog, reserve, stockpile
3 *syn* see GATHERING 2

aggress *vb syn* see ATTACK 1

aggression *n* 1 *syn* see ATTACK 1
2 *syn* see ATTACK 2
rel incursion, inroad, invasion, raid; irruption
ant resistance

aggressive *adj* marked by bold determination and readiness for conflict <an *aggressive* fighter>
syn assertive, assertory, militant, pushful, pushing, pushy, self-assertive
rel belligerent, combative, contentious, scrappy; domineering, imperious, masterful, tough; energetic, hard-hitting, strenuous, vigorous
con passive, unassertive; meek, submissive, yielding

aggressiveness *n syn* see ATTACK 2

aggrieve *vb* 1 *syn* see DISTRESS 2
rel abuse, misuse, outrage; pain
con delight, gladden, please
2 *syn* see WRONG
rel afflict, torment, try; annoy, harass, harry, plague, worry
con benefit, profit

aghast *adj* 1 *syn* see AFRAID 1
rel appalled, horrified, horror-struck; undone, unmanned
idiom scared stiff (*or* white)
2 struck by an intense emotional reaction (as surprise, disgust, or bewilderment) <*aghast* at the lack of discipline>
syn agape, confounded, dismayed, dumbfounded, overwhelmed, shocked, thunderstruck
rel agog, amazed, startled; awed, awestricken; astonished, flabbergasted, surprised
idiom struck all of a heap, taken aback, unable to believe one's eyes (*or* senses)
con acceptant, acquiescent, tolerant

agile *adj* acting or moving with easy alacrity <an *agile* mind>
syn active, brisk, brisky, catty, lively, nimble, sprightly, spry, volant, yare, zippy
rel adroit, deft, dexterous; fleet, quick, speedy; limber, lissome, lithe, supple; light-footed, tripping
con inactive, inert, passive; heavy, lethargic, logy; dull, slow, sluggish
ant torpid

agitable *adj syn* see EXCITABLE

agitate *vb* 1 *syn* see SHAKE 4
rel bounce, joggle, jounce; actuate, drive, impel, move
con lull, quiet, still

2 *syn* see DISCOMPOSE 1
rel exasperate, irritate, peeve, provoke, rile, ruffle
ant calm, tranquilize
3 *syn* see DISCUSS 1
rel air, broach, ventilate; consider; assail, attack

agitation *n syn* see COMMOTION 2
rel ado, bustle, disturbance, stir
ant tranquillity

agitator *n syn* see INSTIGATOR

aglow *adj syn* see ALIGHT 2
rel gleaming, glowing, shining; lucent, luminous, radiant

agnate *adj* 1 *syn* see RELATED
2 *syn* see LIKE

agog *adj syn* see EAGER
rel aroused, roused, stirred; excited, galvanized, stimulated; restive; zestful
ant aloof

agonize *vb* 1 *syn* see AFFLICT
rel distress, trouble; chafe, fret, gall
2 *syn* see WRITHE 1
rel bear, endure, suffer

agonizing *adj syn* see EXCRUCIATING
rel exquisite, fierce, intense, vehement, violent

agony *n syn* see DISTRESS
con repose, rest

agrarian *adj syn* see WILD 1

agree *vb* 1 *syn* see ACKNOWLEDGE 2
rel allow, concede, grant, own
con except, exclude
ant deny
2 *syn* see ASSENT
rel allow, concede, grant; receive; acknowledge, admit
con expostulate, kick, object, remonstrate; balk, demur, jib; oppose, resist, withstand
ant protest (against); differ (with)
3 to achieve harmony (as of opinion, feeling, or purpose) <they *agreed* finally on all major issues>
syn coincide, concert, concord, concur, harmonize
rel coact, cooperate, unite
idiom fall in with, hit it off with
con bicker, quarrel, squabble, wrangle; argue, debate, dispute, hassle
ant differ; disagree
4 to exist or go together without conflict or incongruity <his conclusion *agrees* with the evidence>
syn accord, check, check out, cohere, comport, conform, consist, consort, correspond, dovetail, fit (in), ||gee, go, harmonize, jibe, march, quadrate, rhyme, square, suit, tally
rel approach, equal, match, rival, touch; complete, fulfill, round out, supplement
idiom go hand in hand
con negate, negative, nullify; clash, conflict, jar
ant differ (from)

agree (with) *vb syn* see SUIT 4

agreeability *n syn* see AMENITY 1

agreeable *adj* 1 *syn* see PLEASANT 1
rel delectable, delightful
ant disagreeable
2 *syn* see CONSONANT 1
con conflicting, inharmonious, jarring, uncongenial

agreeableness *n syn* see AMENITY 1

---

syn synonym(s)   *rel* related word(s)
ant antonym(s)   *con* contrasted word(s)
idiom idiomatic equivalent(s)
‖ use limited; if in doubt, see a dictionary

agreed *adv syn* see YES 1

agreement *n* **1** *syn* see HARMONY 2
ant disagreement
2 a settlement reached by parties to a
dispute or negotiation < the company has
reached an *agreement* with the striking
workers >
syn accord, deal, understanding; *compare*
CONTRACT
rel cartel, concordat, convention, entente,
pact; compact, contract, covenant, treaty;
engagement
3 *syn* see TREATY
4 *syn* see CONTRACT

agrestal *adj syn* see WILD 1

agrestic *adj syn* see RURAL

agriculture *n* the science or business of
raising useful plants and animals < opening the country for *agriculture* >
syn farming, husbandry

aground *adj* being or becoming forced
onto the ground or shore < the boat is
aground and breaking up >
syn beached, grounded, stranded
idiom high and dry, on the rocks
ant afloat

ahead *adv* **1** *syn* see BEFORE 1
con after
ant behind
2 further on in the direction in question
< the road stretched *ahead* toward the
west >
syn alee, forth, forward, onward

ahead of *prep syn* see BEFORE 1

aid *vb syn* see HELP 1
rel alleviate, lighten, mitigate, relieve
ant impede

aid *n* **1** *syn* see HELP 1
2 *syn* see HELP 2
rel alleviation, assuagement, mitigation;
backing, support
idiom a leg up
con check, curb, restraint; bar, obstacle,
obstruction
ant impediment
3 *syn* see HELPER
4 *syn* see ASSISTANT 2
rel aider, befriender, benefactor, minis-
trant, succorer; striker

aidant *adj syn* see HELPFUL 1

aide *n syn* see ASSISTANT 2

aide-de-camp *n syn* see ASSISTANT 2

aiding *adj syn* see HELPFUL 1

ail *vb syn* see TROUBLE 1
rel afflict, try
idiom be the matter (with), give one trouble
con alleviate, ease, relieve; comfort, console, solace

ailing *adj syn* see UNWELL
rel debilitated, enfeebled, gone, strengthless, weak; droopy, limp, sapless, spiritless
con hale, lusty, robust, rugged, vigorous

ailment *n* **1** *syn* see DISEASE
2 *syn* see UNREST

aim *vb* **1** *syn* see DIRECT 2
rel concentrate, fix, focus
idiom draw a bead on, take aim
2 to have as a controlling desire something that transcends one's present capacity for attainment < from a boy he had
aimed at high office >
syn aspire, pant

rel attempt, endeavor, essay, strive, try;
design, intend, propose, purpose; covet,
crave, yearn (for)
idiom have an eye to, reach for the stars,
set one's eyes upon
3 *syn* see INTEND 2
rel choose, desire, want, wish; expect
idiom have (*or* keep) in view, promise
oneself (to)
4 *syn* see SLANT 2

aim *n syn* see AMBITION 2
rel desideratum, desire, idol, urge
idiom end in view

aimless *adj syn* see RANDOM

air *n* **1** *syn* see BEARING 1
rel manner, style
2 *usu* **airs** *pl syn* see POSE 2
rel loftiness, ostentation, pretentiousness,
show; complacency, self-importance, vainglory, vanity
3 a pervading influence that colors outward appearance or apparent character
< the village had an *air* of decay >
syn atmosphere, aura, feel, feeling, mood,
semblance
rel character, property, quality
con basis, essence, reality
4 *syn* see MELODY

air *vb syn* see EXPRESS 2
rel discover, divulge, reveal; broadcast,
declare, proclaim, publish
idiom make public, noise (*or* sound)
abroad, spread far and wide

airless *adj syn* see STUFFY 1

airman *n syn* see PILOT 2

airy *adj* **1** of or relating to air < clouds
drifting on *airy* currents >
syn aerial, atmospheric, pneumatic
rel gaseous, vaporous
2 *syn* see LOFTY 6
rel exposed, windswept; supernal
3 resembling or suggesting air especially
in lightness or lack of substance < *airy*
persiflage >
syn aerial, ethereal, vaporous, vapory
rel frivolous, light, volatile; rare, rarefied,
tenuous, thin; dainty, delicate, diaphanous, exquisite, spirituel
con corporeal, material, physical; bulky,
massive, massy
ant substantial
4 *syn* see ELASTIC 2
rel animated, high-spirited, spirited
5 *syn* see WINDY 1

akin *adj* **1** *syn* see RELATED
2 *syn* see LIKE
rel kindred; according, agreeing, conforming, harmonizing
con extraneous, foreign
ant alien

alacrity *n* promptness in responding or
acting < accepted the invitation with *alacrity* >
syn dispatch, expedition, goodwill,
promptitude, readiness
rel briskness, eagerness; enthusiasm, fervor, heartiness, zeal; promptness, quickness
con hesitation, procrastination, temporiza-
tion, vacillation; apathy, indifference, lethargy, phlegm, sluggishness
ant dilatoriness

a la mode *adj syn* see STYLISH

alarm *n* **1** a signal that warns or calls to action < the door's squeak gave the *alarm* >
  syn alert, SOS, tocsin
  rel caution, forewarning, prenotice, warning
  2 *syn* see FEAR 1
  rel upset; strain, stress, tension
  con calm, calmness, serenity, tranquillity; equanimity, sangfroid
  ant assurance; composure

alarm *vb syn* see FRIGHTEN
  rel amaze, astonish, surprise
  idiom give one a turn
  con comfort, console, solace
  ant assure, relieve

alarmable *adj syn* see EXCITABLE

albeit *conj syn* see THOUGH

album *n syn* see ANTHOLOGY

alcohol *n syn* see LIQUOR 2

alcoholic *adj syn* see SPIRITUOUS

alcoholized *adj syn* see INTOXICATED 1

alcove *n syn* see SUMMERHOUSE

alee *adv syn* see AHEAD 2

alehouse *n* an establishment serving primarily beer and ale < warm country *alehouses* >
  syn beer garden, beer hall, ‖beerhouse, bierstube, mughouse, stube; *compare* BAR 4
  rel barrelhouse, bistro, bottle club, brasserie, cabaret, café, honky-tonk, nightclub, rathskeller, roadhouse, wineshop

alembicated *adj syn* see PRECIOUS 4

alert *adj* **1** *syn* see WATCHFUL
  rel attentive, heedful, mindful; careful
  idiom all eyes and ears, on (one's) guard, on the alert
  con inattentive, unmindful; aloof, detached, indifferent, unconcerned
  2 *syn* see INTELLIGENT 2
  rel apt, prompt, quick, ready
  con lackadaisical, languid, listless
  3 *syn* see LIVELY 1
  rel frisky; mercurial
  idiom full of life
  con inactive, indolent
  ant inert

alert *n syn* see ALARM 1

alfresco *adj syn* see OUTDOOR

algetic *adj syn* see PAINFUL 1

alias *n syn* see PSEUDONYM

alibi *n syn* see EXCUSE 1

alien *adj syn* see EXTRINSIC
  rel exotic, outlandish, strange; incompatible, incongruous, inconsonant
  con cognate, kindred, related; compatible, congenial, congruous, consonant; germane, material, pertinent, relevant
  ant akin; assimilable

alien *n syn* see STRANGER
  con national, subject
  ant citizen

alien *vb* **1** *syn* see ESTRANGE
  rel alter, change, convert
  con accommodate, adjust, conform, reconcile
  ant unite; reunite

  2 *syn* see TRANSFER 4
  rel give up, hand over, relinquish

alienate *vb* **1** *syn* see TRANSFER 4
  rel give up, hand over, relinquish
  2 *syn* see ESTRANGE
  rel alter, change, convert
  con accommodate, adjust, conform, reconcile
  ant unite; reunite

alienation *n* **1** *syn* see ESTRANGEMENT
  2 *syn* see INSANITY 1

alight *vb* to come to rest after or as if after a flight, a descent, or a fall < snowflakes *alighting* on the bare trees >
  syn land, light, perch, roost, set down, settle, sit down, touch down
  rel drop, fall, tumble
  con arise, ascend, rise, soar

alight *adj* **1** *syn* see BURNING 1
  2 made bright by or as if by fire < her face *alight* with joy >
  syn ablaze, afire, aflame, aflicker, aglow
  rel bright, effulgent, fulgent, refulgent; blazing, flaming, flaring, glowing
  con dark, dusky, gloomy, heavy, lowery, shadowed, shadowy

align *vb syn* see LINE 1
  rel adjust, fix, regulate
  con unsettle

alike *adj syn* see LIKE
  con separate
  ant unlike; different

alikeness *n syn* see LIKENESS

aliment *n syn* see FOOD 2

alimentary *adj syn* see NUTRITIVE 1

alimentation *n syn* see LIVING

alimentative *adj syn* see NUTRITIVE 1

alimony *n syn* see LIVING

alive *adj* **1** *syn* see LIVING 1
  con inactive, inert
  ant dead, defunct
  2 *syn* see EXTANT 1
  3 *syn* see ACTIVE 1
  rel fresh, green, verdant
  con dormant, inactive, quiescent
  ant dead, extinct
  4 *syn* see AWARE
  rel vigilant, watchful, wide-awake; intelligent, quick, quick-witted
  con heedless, inattentive, oblivious, unmindful; careless, neglectful, negligent
  ant blind (to)
  5 full of vigorous life, animation, or activity < the streets were *alive* with shoppers >
  syn abounding, overflowing, replete, rife, swarming, teeming, thronged
  rel crowded, populous, thick; filled, flush, full
  con barren, empty, vacant, void; unoccupied, unpopulated, untenanted

all *adj* **1** *syn* see WHOLE 4
  rel full, plenary
  2 each member or individual of < *all* my friends came with me >
  syn each, every
  ant no

all *adv* **1** without exception < the money was *all* spent >
  syn all in all, altogether, exactly, in toto, just, purely, quite, stick, totally, utterly, wholly
  idiom in its entirety

---

syn synonym(s)   *rel* related word(s)
ant antonym(s)   *con* contrasted word(s)
idiom idiomatic equivalent(s)
‖ use limited; if in doubt, see a dictionary

2 *syn* see APIECE

all *pron* 1 *syn* see EVERYTHING
2 *syn* see EVERYBODY

all *n syn* see WHOLE 1

all–around *adj* 1 *syn* see VERSATILE
rel complete, consummate
2 not narrowly particularized < taking an *all-around* view of the problem >
syn comprehensive, general, global, inclusive, overall, sweeping
rel broad, extensive, panoramic, wide; all= inclusive, unexcluding, unexclusive, wide= ranging; synoptic
con express, particular, specific; narrow, precise, restricted; individual, singular

allay *vb* 1 *syn* see RELIEVE 1
con arouse, rouse, stir; excite, provoke, stimulate; aggravate, enhance
ant intensify
2 *syn* see CALM
rel ease, soften, subdue; deaden, dull, temper; disburden, disembarrass, disencumber; deliver, free, release
con aggravate, enhance, heighten, magnify, worsen
ant intensify

all but *adv* 1 *syn* see NEARLY
2 *syn* see ALMOST 2

allege *vb syn* see ADDUCE
rel affirm, assert, avouch, avow, declare, profess; recite, recount, rehearse, state
con contradict, deny, gainsay, impugn, negate, negative; controvert, disprove, rebut, refute
ant contravene

alleged *adj* of questionable truth or genuineness < had doubts of the *alleged* miracle >
syn ostensible, pretended, professed, purported, so-called, supposed; *compare* SUP=POSED 1
rel credible, plausible, specious; doubtful, dubious, questionable; self-styled, soi= disant, would-be
idiom in name only
con authentic, bona fide, genuine, veritable; actual, real, true; delusory, erroneous, fallacious, false, illusory, imaginary, unreal

allegiance *n syn* see FIDELITY 1
rel firmness; consecration, dedication; deference, homage, honor
con alienation, disaffection; disloyalty, treason

allegiant *adj syn* see FAITHFUL 1

allegory *n* 1 a method of indirect representation (as in literature or art) of ideas or truths < by *allegory* such abstractions as love and fear can be depicted >
syn figuration, symbolism, symbolization, typification
2 a literary form that tells a story to present a truth or enforce a moral < Orwell's *Animal Farm* is a well-known English *allegory* >
syn apologue, fable, myth, parable; *compare* MYTH 1

allergy *n syn* see ANTIPATHY 2
rel rejection, repulsion, revulsion
con affinity, attraction, sympathy

alleviate *vb syn* see RELIEVE 1
rel cure, remedy
idiom temper the wind to the shorn lamb
con augment, heighten, intensify

ant aggravate

alleviation *n syn* see EASE 3

all–fired *adj syn* see UTTER

alliance *n* 1 *syn* see ASSOCIATION 1
2 an association (as of nations) for a common object < a world *alliance* in support of peace >
syn anschluss, coalition, confederacy, confederation, federation, league, union; *compare* UNIFICATION
rel association, club, order, society

allied *adj syn* see RELATED
rel linked, united; parallel, similar
con alien, extraneous, foreign; discrete, separate, several
ant unallied

all in *adj syn* see EFFETE 2
idiom at last gasp

all in all *adv* 1 *syn* see ALL 1
2 *syn* see ALTOGETHER 3

allineate *vb syn* see LINE 1

allness *n syn* see ENTIRETY 1

allocate *vb* 1 *syn* see ALLOT
con reserve, sequester, stockpile
2 *syn* see DESIGNATE 3

allocution *n syn* see SPEECH 2

allot *vb* to give as one's share, portion, role, or place < *allotted* himself a daily hour for exercise >
syn admeasure, allocate, allow, apportion, assign, give, lot, mete (out)
rel deal (out), dispense, distribute, dole (out); equip, fit out, furnish; accord, grant, vouchsafe; appoint, ordain, prescribe
con detain, hold, hold back, keep, retain, withhold; appropriate, arrogate, confiscate

allotment *n* 1 *syn* see SHARE 1
2 *syn* see RATION

all–out *adj syn* see TOTAL 5

all over *adv syn* see EVERYWHERE 1

allover *adj syn* see OMNIPRESENT

‖**all–overs** *n pl syn* see JITTERS

allow *vb* 1 *syn* see ALLOT
rel bestow, confer
con refuse
2 *syn* see ACKNOWLEDGE 1
rel accede, acquiesce, assent
con confute, refute, reject
ant disallow
3 *syn* see LET 2
rel brook, endure, stand, tolerate; defer, submit, yield
con avert, prevent, ward (off)
ant inhibit

allowable *adj syn* see PERMISSIBLE

allowance *n* 1 *syn* see RATION
rel assignment; appropriation, grant, subsidy
2 *syn* see SHARE 1
3 *syn* see ADVANTAGE 3
rel aid, assistance, help; bounty, grant, subsidy
4 *syn* see PERMISSION
rel countenance, favor; indulgence, toleration
con refusal, rejection; contradiction, contravention, negation
5 a taking into account of extenuating circumstances or of contingencies < we must make *allowance* for the inexperience of youth >
syn concession
rel accommodation, adaptation, adjustment; extenuation, mitigation, palliation

alloy *n* **1** *syn* see ADMIXTURE 1
2 *syn* see MIXTURE
all–powerful *adj syn* see OMNIPOTENT
all right *adv syn* see YES 1
all right *adj syn* see DECENT 4
all round (*or* **all around**) *adv syn* see EV-
ERYWHERE 1
all there *adj syn* see SANE 2
all told *adv syn* see ALTOGETHER 3
allude *vb syn* see REFER 3
  rel hint, imply, intimate, suggest
allure *vb* **1** *syn* see ATTRACT 1
  rel delude; woo
  con avoid, elude, eschew, shun; alienate,
  disaffect, estrange, wean
2 *syn* see LURE
allure *n syn* see CHARM 3
allurement *n* **1** *syn* see ATTRACTION 1
2 *syn* see LURE 2
alluring *adj syn* see ATTRACTIVE 1
  rel appetizing; beguiling, delusive
  con repellent; disagreeable, displeasing,
  uninviting, unlikable, unpleasant
  ant repulsive
almighty *adj syn* see OMNIPOTENT
almost *adv* **1** *syn* see NEARLY
2 not actually but in effect < he paid
  almost nothing for it >
  syn all but, as good as, as much as, essentially, practically, well-nigh; *compare*
  VIRTUALLY
  idiom for all practical purposes, in effect,
  just about, to all intents and purposes
alms *n pl syn* see DONATION
aloft *adv syn* see OVER 4
  rel high; skyward, upward
  idiom in the clouds
alone *adj* **1** separated from others < the
  house was *alone* on a windy ridge >
  syn apart, detached, isolate, isolated,
  removed, unaccompanied
  rel out-of-the-way, private, remote, retired, secluded, withdrawn
  idiom off the beaten track
  con adjacent, close-by, near-at-hand,
  nearly, neighboring, nigh
2 *syn* see LONE 1
3 having no equal or rival and being single in kind or excellence < a drug *alone* in
  its curative powers >
  syn matchless, only, peerless, unequaled,
  unique, unmatched, unparalleled, unrivaled; *compare* SUPREME
  rel inimitable; incomparable, unexcelled,
  unsurpassed; excellent, good, superior
  idiom second to none
  con common, commonplace, everyday,
  ordinary, usual; accustomed, conventional,
  customary, regular
4 *syn* see ONLY 2
alone *adv syn* see ONLY 1
aloneness *n syn* see SOLITUDE
along *adv* **1** so as to make forward
  progress < hurrying *along* toward town >
  syn forth, forward, on, onward; *compare*
  AHEAD 1
2 *syn* see ALSO 2
alongside *prep syn* see BESIDE 1

aloof *adj* **1** *syn* see INDIFFERENT 2
  rel arrogant, disdainful, haughty, proud;
  chilly, cold, cool, frigid; constrained, reserved, restrained, reticent, standoffish
  con affable, companionable, gregarious,
  sociable, social; friendly, neighborly
  ant familiar; outgoing
2 *syn* see UNSOCIABLE
alp *n syn* see MOUNTAIN 1
alpha *n syn* see BEGINNING
  ant omega
alphabet *n* **1** a set of characters in which a
  language can be written < the Greek *alphabet* >
  syn ABC(s), christcross-row, letters
2 the simplest fundamental part or level
  < learning the *alphabet* of science >
  syn ABC's, elements, fundamentals,
  grammar, principles, rudiments
  rel beginning, commencement, start; outset
  idiom first steps
  con entirety, total, whole; details, minutiae, trivia
already *adv* **1** *syn* see BEFORE 2
2 *syn* see EVEN 2
also *adv* **1** in the same manner < those *also*
  serve who support the workers >
  syn correspondingly, likewise, similarly,
  so
  idiom in like manner
2 in addition to that < he was stern but
  also just >
  syn additionally, along, as well, besides,
  futhermore, item, likewise, more, moreover, still, too, withal, yea, yet
  idiom into the bargain, on top of that, to
  boot
3 *syn* see AGAIN 4
alter *vb* **1** *syn* see CHANGE 1
  rel accommodate, adapt, adjust, moderate, modulate, temper; doctor
  idiom work a change (in)
  con conserve, keep, preserve, retain
  ant fix
2 *syn* see STERILIZE
alteration *n* **1** *syn* see CHANGE 1
  rel accommodation, adaptation, adjustment; conversion, metamorphosis, transformation; fluctuation, shilly-shally, vacillation, wavering
  con perdurability, permanence, stability;
  continuance, endurance, persistence
  ant fixation, fixity
2 *syn* see TRANSITION
3 *syn* see CONVERSION 2
altercate *vb syn* see QUARREL
  rel agitate, argue, debate, dispute
  con accord, get along; accommodate,
  adapt, adjust, conform
  ant concur
altercation *n syn* see QUARREL
  rel argument; combat, contest
  con agreement, concord, consonance,
  harmony; empathy, like-mindedness, sympathy, understanding
  ant accord; concurrence
alterity *n syn* see DISSIMILARITY
alternate *adj* **1** *syn* see INTERMITTENT
  rel alternant, alternating, rotating; complementary, corresponding, reciprocal
  con sequent, successive
  ant consecutive

---

syn synonym(s)   *rel* related word(s)
ant antonym(s)   *con* contrasted word(s)
idiom idiomatic equivalent(s)
‖ use limited; if in doubt, see a dictionary

2 *syn* see SUBSTITUTE 1
rel equivalent, proxy, replacing; exchangeable, interchangeable; makeshift, provisional, tentative

alternate *vb syn* see ROTATE 2
rel fluctuate, oscillate, sway, waver; recur, return, revert
con follow, succeed

alternate *n syn* see SUBSTITUTE

alternately *adv syn* see INSTEAD

alternation *n syn* see SUCCESSION 2
rel recurrence, return, reversion; reappearance, repetition

alternative *adj syn* see SUBSTITUTE 1
rel equivalent, proxy, replacing; exchangeable, interchangeable; makeshift, provisional, tentative

alternative *n syn* see CHOICE 1
rel attainable, contingency, possibility

alternatively *adv syn* see INSTEAD

although *conj syn* see THOUGH

altitude *n syn* see HEIGHT
rel apex, eminence, peak, summit
con depth

altitudinous *adj syn* see HIGH 1

altogether *adv* 1 *syn* see WELL 3
2 *syn* see ALL 1
3 as a total < *altogether* it cost over a thousand dollars>
syn all told, in all, quite
idiom taken together
4 with minor exceptions or flaws < *altogether* the party was a success>
syn all in all, by and large, en masse, generally, on the whole
idiom all things considered, as a whole, for the most part, generally speaking, in the main

altruistic *adj syn* see CHARITABLE 1
rel considerate, kind, unselfish; bounteous, bountiful, generous, liberal, openhanded; bighearted, magnanimous, nobleminded
con egotistic, self-centered, selfish, selfseeking; illiberal, mean, niggardly, stingy, ungenerous
ant egoistic

always *adv* 1 on every relevant occasion < *always* made the same mistake>
syn constantly, continuously, ever, invariably, perpetually
rel frequently, often, regularly, usually
idiom in every case (*or* instance), without exception
con rarely, seldom
ant never
2 *syn* see EVER 2

‖**amah** *n syn* see NURSEMAID

amalgam *n syn* see MIXTURE

amalgamate *vb syn* see MIX 1
rel compact, consolidate, unify
con crumble, decompose, disintegrate; disperse, dissipate, scatter

amalgamation *n* 1 *syn* see MIXTURE
2 *syn* see CONSOLIDATION 2

amaranthine *adj syn* see EVERLASTING 1

amaroidal *adj syn* see ACRID

amass *vb syn* see ACCUMULATE
ant distribute

amassment *n syn* see ACCUMULATION

amateur *n* 1 one having a marked and usually informed taste or liking for something < an *amateur* of fine fabrics>

syn admirer, devotee, fan, fancier, votary
rel crank, enthusiast, faddist, infatuate, ‖nut, zealot; aesthete, cognoscente, connoisseur, dilettante; illuminato, illuminist
con abecedarian, dabbler, tyro; adept, expert
2 one who follows a pursuit without attaining mastery or professional status < a nation handicapped by *amateurs* in high office>
syn abecedarian, dabbler, dilettante, nonprofessional, smatterer, tyro, uninitiate
rel beginner, greenhorn, neophyte; apprentice, novice, probationer; potterer, putterer, tinker
con adept, virtuoso, wizard
ant expert, master; professional

amateurish *adj* lacking or marked by lack of expert skill or finish < an *amateurish* actor>
syn dabbling, dilettante, dilettantish, dilettantist, jackleg, unaccomplished, unfinished, ungifted, unskilled
rel clumsy, crude, green, raw, untutored; defective, deficient, faulty, flawed
con accomplished, expert, gifted, skilled
ant professional

amative *adj syn* see EROTIC

amatory *adj syn* see EROTIC
rel admiring, attracted, yearning

amaze *vb syn* see SURPRISE 2
rel affect, impress, move, strike, touch

amaze *n syn* see WONDER 2
rel confoundment; surprise

amazement *n syn* see WONDER 2
rel confoundment; surprise

amazing *adj syn* see MARVELOUS 1

amazon *n syn* see VIRAGO

ambidextrous *adj* 1 *syn* see TWO-HANDED 2
2 *syn* see VERSATILE
3 *syn* see INSINCERE

ambience *n syn* see ENVIRONMENT

ambient *n syn* see ENVIRONMENT

ambiguity *n* expression or an expression obscure because subject to more than one interpretation < a speech full of *ambiguities*>
syn amphibology, double entendre, double meaning, equivocality, equivocation, equivoque, tergiversation
rel dodge, evasion, hedge, quibble, shift, subterfuge; cavil, haggling, hair-splitting, quibbling; obscurity, uncertainty, vagueness
con definiteness, expressness, specificity; clearness, exactness, precision
ant explicitness; lucidity

ambiguous *adj* 1 *syn* see OBSCURE 3
rel doubtful, dubious, questionable
con clear, lucid, perspicuous; categorical, express, specific
ant explicit
2 *syn* see DOUBTFUL 1

ambit *n* 1 *syn* see CIRCUMFERENCE
2 *syn* see RANGE 2

ambition *n* 1 strong desire for advancement < a life ruled by *ambition*>
syn ambitiousness, aspiration, pretension
rel drive, go-ahead, push; anxiety, avidity, eagerness, keenness; energy, enterprise, spirit; goad, incentive, motive, spur
con contentment, satisfaction; faineance, indolence, lethargy, sloth

2 an object of desire or intent < his *ambition* was to have enough to live on without working >
syn aim, goal, mark, objective, quaesitum, target; *compare* INTENTION
rel design, intent, purpose; desire, fancy, hope, wish; dream, ideal, nirvana
3 *syn* see ENTERPRISE 4

ambitious *adj* **1** marked by intense desire for advancement (as in power, fame, or wealth) < a ruthlessly *ambitious* politician >
syn aspiring, emulous, vaulting
rel aggressive, enterprising, go-ahead, pushing, up-and-doing; energetic, hard-working, indefatigable; anxious, avid, eager, keen
con apathetic, phlegmatic, stolid; faineant, indolent, lazy, slothful
2 of a kind to try or exceed one's powers of performance < an *ambitious* scheme to recover gold from seawater >
syn grandiose, lofty, pretentious, utopian, visionary
rel audacious, bold, daring; chimerical, extravagant, high-flown, impractical, unrealistic
con easy, plain, straightforward; feasible, practicable, realistic; unpretentious
ant modest

ambitiousness *n syn* see AMBITION 1
ambivalent *adj syn* see EQUIVOCAL 2
amble *vb syn* see SAUNTER
rel dally, dawdle, dillydally, loiter
ambrosial *adj* **1** *syn* see DELIGHTFUL
2 *syn* see SWEET 2
ambulant *adj syn* see ITINERANT
ant bedfast, bedridden
ambulate *vb syn* see WALK 1
ambulatory *adj syn* see ITINERANT
ambuscade *n syn* see AMBUSH
ambush *vb syn* see SURPRISE 1
rel assail, assault, attack; ensnare, entrap, snare, trap
ambush *n* a device to entrap an enemy by lying in hiding until a surprise attack is feasible < planned an *ambush* on the cliff above the trail >
syn ambuscade, ambushment
rel lure, snare, trap; blind, cover, hideout, retreat
ambushment *n syn* see AMBUSH
ameliorate *vb* **1** *syn* see IMPROVE 1
rel alleviate, lighten, mitigate, relieve
con damage, harm, hurt, impair, injure, mar, spoil; aggravate, intensify
ant worsen; deteriorate
2 *syn* see IMPROVE 3
amenable *adj* **1** *syn* see RESPONSIBLE
rel open, subject; dependent, subordinate
con autarchic, free
ant independent (of); autonomous
2 *syn* see OBEDIENT
rel subdued, tame; receptive, responsive, willing; adaptable, impressionable, malleable, plastic, pliable, pliant
con fierce, mulish, obstinate, stubborn, truculent

ant recalcitrant, refractory
amend *vb* **1** *syn* see CORRECT 1
rel repair; elevate, lift, raise
con corrupt, debauch, deprave, pervert, vitiate
ant debase
2 *syn* see IMPROVE 1
rel advance, forward, promote
ant worsen; impair
amends *n pl syn* see REPARATION
amenity *n* **1** the quality of being pleasant or agreeable < a discussion conducted in perfect *amenity* > < the *amenity* of the climate >
syn agreeability, agreeableness, amiability, cordiality, enjoyableness, geniality, gratefulness, pleasance, pleasantness, sweetness and light
rel attractiveness, charm, delightfulness; fascination, pleasingness
con disagreeableness, distastefulness, unattractiveness, unpleasantness
2 a feature that makes for pleasantness or ease < among the *amenities* of the house is central air-conditioning >
syn comfort, convenience, facility
rel betterment, enhancement, enrichment, improvement; excellence, merit, quality, virtue
con difficulty, hardship, trial, vicissitude
3 *pl* amenities *syn* see MANNER 5
4 *syn* see LUXURY
5 *syn* see COURTESY 1
rel civility, courteousness, politeness; affability, cordiality, geniality, graciousness, sociability
con discourtesy, impoliteness, incivility; affront, indignity, insult; acrimony
ant rudeness
ament *n syn* see FOOL 4
amerce *vb syn* see PENALIZE
amercement *n syn* see FINE
amiability *n syn* see AMENITY 1
amiable *adj* **1** of a generally agreeable nature especially in social interaction < the meeting ended on an *amiable* note >
syn complaisant, easy, good-humored, good-natured, good-tempered, lenient, mild, obliging
rel affable, cordial, genial, gracious; courteous, mannerly; benign, benignant, kind, kindly; responsive, warm, warmhearted
idiom easy to get along with
con discourteous, ill-mannered, ill-natured, impolite, rude; crabbed, dour, unsociable
ant unamiable; surly
2 *syn* see GENTLE 2
amicable *adj* **1** characterized by peaceableness and goodwill < the negotiators joined in *amicable* discussion >
syn friendly, neighborly
rel empathic, like-minded, sympathetic, understanding; accordant, agreeing, concordant, frictionless, harmonious; pacific, peaceable, peaceful
con bellicose, belligerent, combative, contentious, pugnacious, quarrelsome; antipathetic, hostile, suspicious, uncooperative
2 *syn* see HARMONIOUS 3
amical *adj syn* see HARMONIOUS 3
amid *prep* **1** in or into the central part of < the bomb burst *amid* the crowd >

syn among, mid, midst
  idiom in (*or* into) the middle of, in (*or* into) the midst of, in (*or* into) the thick of
2 *syn* see AMONG 1
3 *syn* see DURING
amigo *n syn* see FRIEND
amiss *adv* 1 in a mistaken, inappropriate, or reprehensible way < I feel you judge him *amiss* >
  syn faultily, incorrectly, wrongly
  rel inaccurately; indiscreetly, unwisely
  con accurately, correctly, properly, rightly; cleverly, wisely
  ant right
2 out of the proper course < our planning had gone *amiss* >
  syn afield, astray, awry, badly, unfavorably, wrong; *compare* HARD 5
  idiom beside (*or* off) the mark
  con auspiciously, famously, favorably, promisingly, propitiously, well
  ant aright
amiss *adj* 1 *syn* see BAD 1
2 *syn* see FAULTY
3 *syn* see BLAMEWORTHY
amity *n syn* see GOODWILL 1
  rel accord, agreement, concord, harmony; amicableness, neighborliness
  con animosity, antagonism, antipathy, hostility; conflict, contention, discord, dissension, strife
  ant enmity
amnesty *n syn* see PARDON
among *prep* 1 surrounded by < the valley nestled *among* high mountains >
  syn amid, mid, midst
2 *syn* see AMID 1
3 *syn* see BETWEEN
amorist *n syn* see GALLANT 2
amorous *adj syn* see EROTIC
  rel enamored, infatuated; lustful
  con aloof, detached, indifferent; cold, cool; apathetic, impassive, unconcerned
  ant frigid
amorousness *n syn* see LOVE 2
amorphous *adj syn* see FORMLESS
amount *vb* 1 to make up as a total < their expenses *amounted* to just a hundred dollars >
  syn add up, aggregate, come, number, run (to *or* into), sum (to *or* into), total
  rel comprehend, comprise, embody, include, incorporate, reach, subsume
2 to be essentially equivalent < that utter terror that *amounts* to madness >
  syn approach, correspond (to), equal, match, partake (of), rival, touch
  rel hint, imply, intimate, smack (of), suggest
  idiom be near to, come to the same thing as, have all the earmarks (*or* features) of
amount *n* 1 *syn* see BODY 5
2 *syn* see SUBSTANCE 2
amour *n* 1 *syn* see LOVE AFFAIR
2 an illicit or informal sexual relation < memoirs devoted to accounts of his *amours* >
  syn affair, intrigue, liaison
  rel entanglement, intimacy, relationship; love affair, romance
3 *syn* see LOVE 2
amour propre *n* 1 *syn* see PRIDE 2
2 *syn* see CONCEIT 2

rel complacency, self-complacency, self-satisfaction, smugness; pride
amphibological *adj syn* see OBSCURE 3
amphibology *n syn* see AMBIGUITY
ample *adj* 1 *syn* see SPACIOUS
  rel distended, expanded, inflated, swollen
  con scant, skimpy, spare; cramped, exiguous, narrow, strait
  ant meager; circumscribed
2 *syn* see PLENTIFUL
  rel lavish, prodigal, profuse; handsome
  idiom enough and to spare
  con scrimpy, spare, sparse; beggarly, miserable, niggardly
  ant meager, scant
amplify *vb* 1 *syn* see EXPAND 4
  rel augment, extend, increase; unfold
  con abbreviate, shorten
  ant abridge, condense
2 *syn* see EXPAND 3
amplitude *n* 1 *syn* see SIZE 2
2 *syn* see BREADTH 2
  con closeness, limitation, restriction, straitness
  ant narrowness
3 *syn* see EXPANSE
  rel bigness, greatness, largeness; capaciousness, commodiousness, roominess, spaciousness
  con circumscription, restriction
  ant straitness; limitation
amply *adv syn* see WELL 4
amulet *n syn* see CHARM 2
  rel lucky piece, rabbit-foot
amuse *vb* to pass or cause to pass time in pleasant or agreeable activity < simple toys to *amuse* children on long trips >
  syn divert, entertain, recreate
  rel absorb, distract, engross; animate, enliven, fleet, quicken; beguile, charm, delight, enchant, fascinate, wile; while
  con fatigue, irk, jade, pall (on), tire, wear (on), weary; bore, ennui
amusement *n syn* see ENTERTAINMENT
ana *n syn* see ANTHOLOGY
anabasis *n syn* see ADVANCE 2
anachronism *n* 1 a chronological error < *anachronisms* of several centuries mar some earlier chronicles >
  syn misdate, misdating, mistiming, parachronism
  rel antedate, anticipation, prochronism, prolepsis; metachronism, postdate
2 one that is inappropriately situated especially in time < born centuries too late, he was an *anachronism* in modern urban society >
  syn solecism
  rel bevue, faux pas, gaffe; defect, flaw, mistake, slip
anadem *n syn* see WREATH
anagogic *adj syn* see MYSTICAL 1
  rel esoteric, occult, recondite; allegorical, symbolical
analects *n pl syn* see ANTHOLOGY
analgesic *n syn* see ANODYNE 1
  ant irritant
analogous *adj syn* see LIKE
  rel convertible, corresponding, interchangeable; kindred
analogue *n syn* see PARALLEL
  rel cognate, congener
analogy *n* 1 *syn* see LIKENESS

2 expression or an expression involving explicit or implied comparison of things basically unlike but with some striking similarities < God can be described only by *analogy* >
  syn metaphor, simile, similitude
  rel ambiguity, equivocation, equivoque, tergiversation
  con demonstration, description, formulation

analphabet *n syn see* ILLITERATE

analysis *n* 1 separation of a whole into its fundamental elements or constituent parts < *analysis* of a problem >
  syn breakdown, breakup, dissection, resolution
  rel division, separation; decomposition, disintegration
  con combination, union; concatenation, integration, unification
  ant synthesis
  2 *syn see* EXAMINATION

analytic *adj syn see* LOGICAL 2
  rel deep, profound; acute, keen, sharp; penetrating, piercing
  con constructive, creative, inventive

analytical *adj syn see* LOGICAL 2

analyze *vb* to divide a complex whole into its constituent parts or elements < *analyze* the plot of a novel >
  syn anatomize, break down, decompose, decompound, dissect, resolve
  rel divide, part, separate; assort, classify, pigeonhole; examine, inspect, investigate, scrutinize
  con articulate, concatenate, integrate
  ant compose, compound; construct

anamnesis *n syn see* MEMORY 2

Ananias *n syn see* LIAR

anarch *n syn see* REBEL

anarchism *n* 1 a political theory opposed to all forms of government and advocating voluntary cooperation and interaction of individuals and groups in satisfying their common needs < the doubtful premises of *anarchism* about human nature >
  syn anarchy
  rel utopianism; communism, Marxism, syndicalism
  con absolutism, authoritarianism, dictatorship; elitism
  2 *syn see* DISORDER 2

anarchist *n syn see* REBEL

anarchy *n* 1 absence of effective government or the resulting social disorder < complete *anarchy* followed the breakdown of communications >
  syn chaos, lawlessness, mobocracy, ochlocracy
  rel confusion, disorder, disorganization
  idiom mob rule (*or* law), reign of terror
  2 *syn see* ANARCHISM
  3 *syn see* DISORDER 2

anastomose *vb syn see* INTERJOIN

anathema *n* 1 *syn see* CURSE 1
  rel censure, condemnation, denunciation, reprehension, reprobation, reproof
  con eulogy, laudation, praise

2 *syn see* ABOMINATION 1
  rel leper, pariah, outcast, untouchable

anathematize *vb syn see* EXECRATE 1
  rel impugn, reproach
  con approbate, approve, countenance, endorse, favor

anatomize *vb syn see* ANALYZE

ancestor *n* 1 a person from whom one is descended < proud of his pioneer *ancestors* >
  syn antecedent (used in pl.), ascendant, forebear, forefather, primogenitor, progenitor
  ant descendant
  2 *syn see* FORERUNNER 2

ancestry *n* one's progenitors or their character or quality as a whole < a man of noble *ancestry* >
  syn blood, descent, extraction, lineage, origin, pedigree
  rel family, kindred, line, race, stock; derivation, source; breed, breeding
  ant descendants; posterity

anchor *vb syn see* FASTEN 2
  rel imbed, plant
  idiom make fast (*or* secure)

anchorage *n syn see* HARBOR 3

ancient *adj* 1 persisting from the distant past < an *ancient* monument >
  syn aged, age-old, antediluvian, antique, hoary, Noachian, old, timeworn, venerable; *compare* OBSOLETE
  rel primal, primeval, primordial, pristine; forgotten, immemorial, remote, traditional; ageless, dateless
  idiom old as time, older than God (*or* the hills), out of the dim past
  con current, fresh, new, novel, prevailing, up-to-date
  ant modern
  2 *syn see* AGED 1
  rel doddering, doting, fading, sinking, waning, wasting
  idiom old as Methuselah (*or* the hills)

ancient *n syn see* OLDSTER

ancilla *n syn see* HELPER

ancillary *adj* 1 *syn see* AUXILIARY
  2 *syn see* CONCOMITANT

androgynous *adj syn see* BISEXUAL

android *n syn see* ROBOT 1

anecdote *n syn see* STORY 2
  rel recital, relation; episode, event, incident

anemic *adj syn see* PALE 2

anent *prep syn see* APROPOS

anesthetic *adj syn see* INSENSIBLE 5
  rel impenetrable, impermeable, impervious; obtuse
  con responsive, sensitive

anesthetic *n syn see* ANODYNE 1
  ant stimulant

anesthetized *adj syn see* NUMB 1

anew *adv* 1 *syn see* OVER 7
  2 *syn see* NEW

anfractuous *adj syn see* WINDING

angel *n syn see* SPONSOR
  rel ‖butter-and-egg man

angelic *adj syn see* SAINTLY

anger *n* emotional excitement induced by intense displeasure < a man easily aroused to *anger* >
  syn fury, indignation, ire, mad, rage, wrath

---

syn synonym(s)   *rel* related word(s)
ant antonym(s)   *con* contrasted word(s)
idiom idiomatic equivalent(s)
‖ use limited; if in doubt, see a dictionary

rel ‖dander, dudgeon, ‖Dutch, huff, ‖monkey, pet, pique, temper; annoyance, exasperation, infuriation, irritation
ant forbearance

anger *vb* **1** to make angry <their constant heedless interruptions *angered* her>
syn enrage, incense, infuriate, ire, mad, madden, steam up, umbrage
rel annoy, irk, vex; aggravate, exasperate, irritate, nettle, provoke, rile; affront, offend, outrage
idiom burn one up, make one hot under the collar, put (*or* get) one's dander up, set one by the ears
con appease, conciliate, mollify, placate, propitiate, soothe
ant gratify; pacify

2 to be or become angry <he *angers* easily>
syn blow up, boil, boil over, bristle, burn, flare (up), fume, rage, seethe
rel chafe, fret, stew; rant, rave, storm
idiom breathe fire, fly into a rage, get hot under the collar, get one's blood (*or* dander) up, hit the ceiling, lose one's temper, see red
ant calm (down)

angle *vb syn* see HINT 4

angle *n* **1** *syn* see VIEWPOINT 2
2 *syn* see PHASE
rel detail, item, particular
3 *syn* see TURN 4

angle *vb* **1** *syn* see SLANT 2
2 *syn* see SLANT 3

angry *adj* feeling or showing strong displeasure or bad temper <*angry* at the children's lack of consideration>
syn acrimonious, choleric, heated, indignant, irate, ireful, mad, ‖pissed, ‖pissed off, shirty, waxy, wrathful, wrathy, wroth, wrothful, wrothy
rel aggravated, exasperated, perturbed, put out, riley, upset, uptight, worked up, wrought (up); angered, enraged, incensed, infuriate, infuriated, maddened, sore, vexed; orey-eyed, red-faced, wild-eyed
idiom foaming at the mouth, hot under the collar, in a taking, in a temper (*or* rage), mad as a hornet (*or* wet hen)
con calm, placid, tolerant; content, pleased, satisfied

anguish *n syn* see SORROW
rel anxiety, worry; ache, pain, pang, throe; torment, torture
con comfort, consolation, solace; alleviation, assuagement, mitigation
ant relief

angular *adj* **1** *syn* see RUDE 1
2 *syn* see LEAN
rel lathy, ribby, weedy
con chubby, chuffy
ant rotund

anima *n syn* see SOUL 1

animadversion *n* a remark or statement that constitutes an adverse and usually uncharitable criticism <her spiteful *animadversions* on her neighbors' children>
syn aspersion, obloquy, reflection, slam, slur, stricture
rel censure, criticism, reprehension; accusation, imputation, insinuation; captiousness, carping, caviling, faultfinding
con acclaim, extolling, laudation, praise; approbation, approval

ant commendation

animadvert *vb syn* see REMARK 2
rel declare, say, state, tell, utter; descant, dilate, expatiate, perorate; adduce, offer, present
con disregard, ignore, overlook

animal *n syn* see BEAST

animal *adj* **1** *syn* see BRUTISH
2 *syn* see CARNAL 2
rel bestial, brutal, brutish
con intellectual, mental, psychic; reasoning, thinking; nonphysical, spiritual
ant rational

animalism *n syn* see ANIMALITY
rel lasciviousness, lecherousness, lechery, licentiousness, lustfulness, unchastity; sensualism, sensuality, voluptuousness

animality *n* the animal aspect or quality of human beings or human nature <his violent reaction was sheer *animality*>
syn animalism, carnality, fleshliness
rel maleness, masculinity, virility; sensuality; brutishness, coarseness, grossness
ant spirituality

animalize *vb syn* see DEBASE 1

animate *adj* **1** *syn* see LIVING 1
rel breathing, viable
ant inanimate
2 *syn* see LIVELY 1
rel active, dynamic, live; activated, energized, vitalized
con dead, inanimate, lifeless; passive
ant inert

animate *vb* **1** *syn* see ENCOURAGE 1
rel invigorate, refresh, renew; fortify, reinforce, strengthen
idiom give a lift (to), put on (*or* upon) one's mettle, raise the spirits of
2 *syn* see QUICKEN 1
3 *syn* see FIRE 2
rel activate, actuate, motivate; drive, impel, move
con check, curb, restrain; frustrate, thwart
ant inhibit

animated *adj* **1** *syn* see LIVING 1
rel activated, energized, vitalized
con passive
ant inert
2 *syn* see LIVELY 1
rel exuberant, high-spirited, zestful
con enervated, spiritless; comatose
ant dejected, depressed

animating *adj syn* see INVIGORATING

animation *n syn* see SPIRIT 5

animosity *n syn* see ENMITY
con amity; esteem
ant goodwill

animus *n* **1** *syn* see INTENTION
2 *syn* see SOUL 1
3 *syn* see ENMITY
rel grudge; bias, discrimination, prejudice
con partiality, predilection; sympathy
ant favor

annals *n pl syn* see HISTORY 2

annex *vb* **1** *syn* see ADD 1
rel associate, connect, join, link, unite
con disengage; divorce, part, separate
2 *syn* see GET 1
3 *syn* see APPROPRIATE 1
4 *syn* see STEAL 1

annex *n* a subsidiary structure associated with a main building <built an *annex* to the museum to hold a new collection>

syn arm, block, ell, extension, wing
rel addition, continuation

annihilate *vb* **1** *syn* see ABOLISH 1
2 to destroy utterly < matter cannot be *annihilated* >
syn abate, abolish, blot out, eradicate, exterminate, extinguish, extirpate, murder, root out, uncreate, uproot, wipe (out)
rel cancel, efface, erase, expunge, obliterate
con renew, restore; create, discover, invent; fashion, forge, form, make, shape
3 *syn* see DESTROY 1
4 *syn* see SLAUGHTER 3
rel rout
5 *syn* see CRUSH 5

annihilative *adj* *syn* see DESTRUCTIVE

annotate *vb* to add or append comment < *annotate* a volume of poems >
syn gloss
rel construe, elucidate, explain, expound; comment, commentate, remark

announce *vb* **1** *syn* see DECLARE 1
rel communicate, impart
con hush (up), smother, stifle, suppress
2 to point to as a future occurrence or development < the shortening days *announce* the coming of winter >
syn forerun, foreshow, harbinger, herald, preindicate, presage
rel augur, forebode, forecast, foretell, predict
3 *syn* see INDICATE 2
rel present, set forth, show (forth)

announcement *n* *syn* see DECLARATION
rel affirmation, assertion, averment, statement

annoy *vb* **1** to disturb and upset nervously < her persistent prying soon *annoyed* her hostess >
syn abrade, bother, ‖bug, chafe, exercise, fret, gall, irk, provoke, ruffle, vex; *compare* IRRITATE
rel agitate, disturb, perturb, upset
idiom get in one's hair
con comfort, console, solace; content, gratify, please, satisfy
ant soothe
2 *syn* see WORRY 1
rel badger, bait, chivy, heckle, hector; chafe, distress, gall, rub
idiom get (*or* grate) on one's nerves, rub one the wrong way
con disregard, ignore, overlook; appease, calm, dulcify, mollify; cool, lull, subdue

annoyance *n* **1** the act of annoying < devoted himself to the *annoyance* of his patient wife >
syn bothering, harassment, irking, provocation, provoking, vexation, vexing
rel pestering, teasing
2 the state or feeling of being annoyed < her *annoyance* increased as he continued to pester her >
syn aggravation, bother, botheration, exasperation, pother
rel anger, indignation, ire, wrath; aversion, repugnance, repulsion, revulsion; disgust, dislike, distaste

con appreciation, enjoyment, liking, pleasure
3 something that causes an annoyed state or feeling < his constant baiting was an *annoyance* to her >
syn besetment, bother, botheration, botherment, exasperation, irritant, nuisance, pest, pester, ‖pesterment, plague
rel affliction, aggravation, distress, provocation, trial; riding

annual *n* *syn* see YEARBOOK

annuary *n* *syn* see YEARBOOK

annul *vb* **1** *syn* see ERASE
rel abstract, dispose (of), eliminate, remove
2 *syn* see NEUTRALIZE
rel outweigh, overbalance
3 *syn* see ABOLISH 1
rel counteract, negative, neutralize; blot out, cancel, efface, obliterate; extinguish
idiom make void, set aside
con enact, ordain, pass
4 to deprive of legal validity, force, or authority < *annul* a marriage >
syn abrogate, discharge, dissolve, quash, vacate, void
rel abolish, cancel, countermand, invalidate, nullify, undo
idiom make void

annunciate *vb* *syn* see DECLARE 1
rel affirm, assert, asseverate, aver; profess, protest; pronounce, state

anodyne *n* **1** something used to relieve or prevent pain < opium and its derivatives are still our most potent *anodynes* >
syn analgesic, anesthetic, pain-killer
rel calmative, depressant, sedative, tranquilizer; hypnotic, somnifacient, soporific, stupefacient
2 something that soothes or, often, dulls or deadens the senses or sensibilities < the kind of religion that is no more than an *anodyne* >
syn narcotic, nepenthe, opiate
ant energizer, stimulant; irritant

anomalous *adj* **1** *syn* see IRREGULAR 1
rel monstrous, prodigious
2 *syn* see ABNORMAL 1
rel foreign, peculiar, singular, strange; monstrous, prodigious
con accustomed, customary, usual, wonted

anon *adv* **1** *syn* see PRESENTLY 1
2 *syn* see THEN 1

anonym *n* *syn* see PSEUDONYM

anonymous *adj* not identified by name < saved by an *anonymous* hero >
syn innominate, nameless, undesignated, unnamed
rel incognito, unidentified, unknown, unrecognized, unspecified
ant named, onymous

another *adj* **1** *syn* see THAT 1
2 *syn* see ADDITIONAL
rel second

anschauung *n* *syn* see INTUITION

anschluss *n* *syn* see ALLIANCE 2

answer *n* **1** something spoken or written by way of return to a question or demand < a sullen *answer* >
syn antiphon, rejoinder, reply, respond, response, retort, return

---

syn synonym(s)   *rel* related word(s)
ant antonym(s)   *con* contrasted word(s)
idiom idiomatic equivalent(s)
‖ use limited; if in doubt, see a dictionary

rel comment, observation, remark; defense, justification; rebuttal, refutation; replication

con inquiry, interrogation, query, question, quiz

2 something attained by mental effort and especially by computation < got the *answer* by trial-and-error methods >
syn result, solution

answer *vb* **1** to say, write, or do something in response (as to a question) < *answered* his critics with documented facts >
syn come in, rejoin, reply, respond, retort, return
rel acknowledge, recognize; disprove, rebut, refute; countercharge, recriminate
idiom come back (at), make reply (to)
con ask, inquire, interrogate, query, question, quiz
2 *syn* see SATISFY 5

answerable *adj syn* see RESPONSIBLE
rel bound, compelled, constrained, duty-bound, obligated, obliged

Antaean *adj syn* see HUGE

antagonism *n* **1** *syn* see ENMITY
rel opposition, oppugnancy, resistance, withstanding; conflict, difference, disagreement, discord, friction
con concord, consonance, harmony; agreement, understanding
ant accord; comity

2 an opposing state, action, or position < the natural *antagonism* of predators and prey >
syn antithesis, con, contradistinction, contraposition, contrariety, opposition, opposure
rel disagreement, discrepancy, disparity, incongruity; annulling, negation, nullification; counteraction
con agreement, congruity; alliance, association, rapport; empathy, sympathy

antagonist *n syn* see OPPONENT
con adherent, henchman, partisan
ant supporter

antagonistic *adj* **1** *syn* see BITTER 3
2 *syn* see ADVERSE 1
rel discordant, incompatible, inconsonant; averse, disinclined, indisposed, unwilling; conflicting, hostile
con advantageous, beneficial; auspicious, benign, propitious
ant favorable

3 *syn* see ANTIPATHETIC 1
rel adverse, counter, counteractive, reactive; discordant; antonymous, opposing, oppugnant

ante *adv syn* see BEFORE 1
ante *prep syn* see BEFORE 1
ante *n syn* see BET
antecede *vb syn* see PRECEDE 2
antecedence *n syn* see PRIORITY
antecedent *n* **1** *syn* see CAUSE 1
rel forebear, forerunner, precursor; agency, instrumentality, means
con sequel; upshot
ant consequence

2 *syn* see FORERUNNER 2
3 — used in pl. *syn* see ANCESTOR 1
antecedent *adj syn* see PRECEDING
ant consequent; subsequent

antecedently *adv syn* see BEFORE 1
antecessor *n syn* see FORERUNNER 2

antedate *vb syn* see PRECEDE 2
antediluvian *adj syn* see ANCIENT 1
antediluvian *n syn* see FOGY
anterior *adj syn* see PRECEDING
con after, back, hind, hinder, rear
ant posterior

anthology *n* a collection of selected artistic and especially literary pieces or passages < an *anthology* of sacred music >
syn album, ana, analects, florilegium, garland, miscellany, omnibus, posy
rel collection, compilation; delectus, treasure-house, treasury

anthropoid *adj* resembling man < *anthropoid* apes >
syn anthropomorphic, anthropomorphous, humanoid, manlike

anthropomorphic *adj syn* see ANTHROPOID
anthropomorphous *adj syn* see ANTHROPOID
anti *n syn* see OPPONENT
anti *adj syn* see ADVERSE 1
ant pro

antic *n syn* see PRANK
rel artifice, wile; romp

antic *adj* **1** *syn* see FANTASTIC 2
rel foolish; comic, comical, farcical, laughable, ludicrous
con prudent, sensible, wise; conventional, formal; grave, sedate, serious, solemn, somber

2 characterized by a light gay quality < a briskly *antic* and delightful tale >
syn frolicsome, playful, rollicking, sprightly
rel gay, lively, spirited; light, whimsical; casual, easy, suave
con constrained, controlled, curbed, guarded, inhibited, restrained

3 *syn* see PLAYFUL 1

anticipant *adj syn* see EXPECTANT 1
anticipate *vb* **1** *syn* see PREVENT 1
rel forecast, foretell, presage
idiom be one step ahead of
con disregard, ignore, neglect, overlook, slight

2 *syn* see FORESEE
rel await, contemplate, expect; foretaste
idiom be on the lookout (*or* watch) for, look forward to, look (*or* watch) out for

anticipation *n syn* see EXPECTANCY 1
anticipative *adj syn* see EXPECTANT 1
anticipatory *adj syn* see EXPECTANT 1
antidote *n syn* see REMEDY 2
rel negator, neutralizer, nullifier, offset; backfire

antipasto *n syn* see APPETIZER
antipathetic *adj* **1** having a natural or inherent opposition < national needs *antipathetic* to peace >
syn antagonistic, clashing, conflicting, contrariant, contrary, discordant
rel antipodal, antithetical, antonymous, contradictory, opposite
idiom at cross purposes, at daggers drawn, at war with one another
con agreeing, consonant, correspondent, harmonious; coactive, collaborative, cooperative
ant concordant

2 arousing marked aversion or dislike < found his sister's husband in every way *antipathetic* >

syn aversive, kindless, repellent, repugnant, uncongenial, ungenial, unsympathetic

rel abhorrent, obnoxious; disgustful, disgusting, distasteful, loathsome, repulsive

con compatible, consonant, sympathetic; alluring, attractive, charming; agreeable, pleasant, pleasing, satisfying, soothing

ant congenial

3 *syn* see ADVERSE 1

antipathy *n* 1 *syn* see ENMITY

rel disrelish, distaste, repellency, repugnance; avoidance, escape, eschewal, evasion

con liking, partiality, predilection, prepossession; attachment, love; attraction, taste (for)

ant affection (for)

2 the state of mind induced by what is antipathetic <a strong *antipathy* to modern art>

syn allergy, aversion, dyspathy

rel abhorrence, dislike, disrelish, distaste, repellency, repugnance; avoidance, escape, eschewal, evasion

con liking, partiality, predilection, prepossession; affection, attachment, love; attraction

ant taste (for)

antiphon *n* *syn* see ANSWER 1

antipodal *adj* *syn* see OPPOSITE

antipode *n* *syn* see OPPOSITE

antipodean *adj* *syn* see OPPOSITE

antipole *n* *syn* see OPPOSITE

antiquate *vb* *syn* see OUTDATE

antiquated *adj* *syn* see OLD-FASHIONED

con modern, new, novel

ant modernistic

antique *adj* 1 *syn* see ANCIENT 1

rel ancestral, dateless, immemorial, legendary, time-honored, traditional

con advanced, current, recent

2 *syn* see OLD-FASHIONED

antisocial *adj* averse to the society of others <a pure scholar, remote and *antisocial*>

syn eremitic, misanthropic, reclusive, reserved, solitary, standoffish

rel ascetic, austere, cold, remote; cynical, introverted, withdrawn

con affable, friendly, gregarious; communicative, outgoing, sociable

ant social

antithesis *n* 1 *syn* see ANTAGONISM 2

2 *syn* see OPPOSITE

antithetical *adj* *syn* see OPPOSITE

anxiety *n* *syn* see CARE 2

rel doubt, mistrust, uncertainty; distress, misery, suffering; dread; panic

con composure, equanimity, sangfroid; aplomb, confidence, self-possession; certainty, certitude, faith, trust

ant security

anxious *adj* 1 *syn* see AFRAID 1

rel agitated, apprehensive, jittery, perturbed, upset, worried; alarmed, bothered, disquieted, troubled, uneasy

idiom ill at ease

---

syn synonym(s)   *rel* related word(s)
ant antonym(s)   *con* contrasted word(s)
idiom idiomatic equivalent(s)
‖ use limited; if in doubt, see a dictionary

con calm, collected, cool, easy, imperturbable, unruffled; assured, confident, sanguine, sure

2 *syn* see EAGER

rel importunate, pressing, urgent

idiom all agog, bursting to

con averse, disinclined, hesitant, indisposed, reluctant

ant loath

anyhow *adv* *syn* see ABOUT 4

anytime *adv* *syn* see EVER 4

anyway *adv* *syn* see EVER 5

any which way *adv* *syn* see ABOUT 4

anywise *adv* 1 *syn* see ABOUT 4

2 *syn* see EVER 5

A1 *adj* *syn* see EXCELLENT

apace *adv* *syn* see FAST 2

apart *adv* 1 as a discrete item <taken *apart*, his view seemed sound enough>

syn independently, individually, one by one, separately, severally, singly

idiom one at a time

2 excluded from consideration <these slips *apart*, he had done very well>

syn aside

idiom to one side

3 in or into parts <tore the sheets *apart*>

syn asunder, sky-high

idiom all to pieces, to bits (*or* flinders)

apart *adj* *syn* see ALONE 1

apart from *prep* *syn* see EXCEPT

apartheid *n* *syn* see SEGREGATION

apartment *n* 1 a set of rooms (as in a private house or a block) rented or leased for use as a dwelling place <had a tiny top-floor *apartment*>

syn ‖chambers, flat, lodging(s), rental, rooms, suite, tenement

2 *syn* see ROOM 1

apathetic *adj* *syn* see IMPASSIVE 1

rel dull, inert, languid, sluggish, torpid; anesthetic, impassible, insensible, insensitive; callous, unmoved, untouched; limp, spiritless

con aroused, awake, aware, conscious, impressionable, perceptive, receptive; vigilant, watchful, wide-awake

ant alert

apathy *n* 1 lack of emotional responsiveness <hid her sorrow behind a dull brooding *apathy*>

syn impassivity, insensibility, phlegm, stoicism, stolidity, unresponsiveness

rel inertness, passivity, supineness; aloofness, detachment, indifference, unconcern; lethargy, torpidity, torpor; listlessness, numbness, stupefaction, stupor

con ardor, fervor, passion, responsiveness, warmth; alertness, awareness, concern, solicitude

ant zeal; enthusiasm

2 lack of interest or concern <public *apathy* toward the school crisis>

syn disinterest, disregard, heedlessness, indifference, insouciance, lassitude, lethargy, listlessness, unconcern, unmindfulness

rel callousness, hardness, insensitivity, obduracy, unawareness; coldness, halfheartedness, lukewarmness; calmness, dispassion, dispassionateness

con attentiveness, concern, heedfulness, interest; awareness, mindfulness, sensitivity, solicitude; ardency, fervency, passion, warmth, zeal

ape *vb syn* see MIMIC
  rel caricature; emulate, rival
  idiom make like

aperçu *n syn* see COMPENDIUM 1

aperitive *adj syn* see PALATABLE

aperture *n* a discontinuity allowing passage <the mouse squeezed through a narrow *aperture* in the wall>
  syn hole, opening, orifice, outlet, vent
  rel discontinuity, gap, hiatus, interstice; bore, perforation, pinhole, prick, puncture; chasm, cleft, cut, gash, slash, slit; breach, break, rupture

apery *n syn* see MIMICRY

apex *n* 1 *syn* see TOP 1
  rel extremity, limit, spire
  ant nadir
  2 the culminating point <the *apex* of his career>
  syn acme, apogee, capsheaf, capstone, climax, comble, crescendo, crest, crown, culmen, culmination, meridian, ne plus ultra, noon, noontide, peak, pinnacle, sublimity, summit, zenith
  rel last word, prime, quintescence, ultimate; achievement, attainment, consummation, realization
  ant nadir
  3 *syn* see POINT 9
  rel cap, crest, peak, prominence, spire

aphorism *n syn* see MAXIM

aphrodisia *n syn* see LUST 2

aphrodisiac *adj syn* see EROTIC
  ant anaphrodisiac

apiarist *n syn* see BEEKEEPER

apical *adj syn* see TOP 1

apiculturist *n syn* see BEEKEEPER

apiece *adv* by, for, or to each one <gave the boys a dollar *apiece* >
  syn all, aside, each, ‖per, per capita, per caput
  rel individually, one by one, respectively, severally, singly, successively

apish *adj syn* see SLAVISH 3

aplomb *n syn* see CONFIDENCE 2
  rel poise, savoir faire; coolness, imperturbability, levelheadedness, nonchalance; composure, ease, easiness, equanimity, sangfroid
  idiom presence of mind
  con bewilderment, distraction, perplexity; befuddlement, confusion, fluster, fuddlement; discomfiture, embarrassment, perturbation
  ant shyness

apocalypse *n syn* see REVELATION
  rel envisioning, foresight, precognition, prevision

apocalyptic *adj* 1 *syn* see PROPHETIC
  2 *syn* see OMINOUS

apocryphal *adj syn* see SPURIOUS 3
  rel false, erroneous, inaccurate, incorrect, untrue, wrong; doubtful, dubious, questionable
  idiom open to question
  con accurate, correct, established, factual, true, truthful, veracious; authentic

apogee *n syn* see APEX 2

Apollyon *n syn* see DEVIL 1

apologetic *adj syn* see REMORSEFUL

apologetic *n syn* see APOLOGY 1

apologia *n syn* see APOLOGY 1
  rel clarification, elucidation, explanation, interpretation

apologue *n syn* see ALLEGORY 2

apology *n* 1 a presentation intended to justify or defend something <the white paper is essentially an *apology* for recent foreign policy>
  syn apologetic, apologia, defense, justification; *compare* EXCUSE 1
  rel excuse, extenuation, mitigation, palliation; advocating, advocation, championing, espousal, espousing, support
  idiom pleading one's cause, putting in a good word for, speaking up for
  con blame, censure, condemnation, decrial, reprehension, reprobation
  2 an acknowledgment expressing regret for a wrong, improper, or discommoding act <murmured a brief *apology* for her lateness>
  syn excuse, regrets; *compare* EXCUSE 1
  rel amends, atonement; acknowledgment, admission, concession, confession, mea culpa; reparation, redress, satisfaction
  3 *syn* see EXCUSE 3

aporetic *adj syn* see INCREDULOUS

apostasy *n syn* see DEFECTION
  rel perfidy, treacherousness

apostate *n syn* see RENEGADE
  rel bolter; dissenter, nonconformist, recusant
  con adherent, follower, partisan; convert, proselyte

apostatize *vb syn* see DEFECT

a posteriori *adj syn* see INDUCTIVE

apostle *n syn* see MISSIONARY

apothecary *n syn* see DRUGGIST

apothegm *n syn* see MAXIM

apotheosis *n* 1 the consummate form, example, or instance (as of a quality) <the *apotheosis* of vulgarity>
  syn epitome, last word, quintessence, ultimate; *compare* EMBODIMENT
  rel acme, culmination, height, peak, summit
  idiom ‖the living end
  2 a raising to a state of eminent triumph or glory <the *apotheosis* of a folk hero>
  syn aggrandizement, deification, dignification, exaltation, glorification
  rel elevation, ennoblement, enshrinement, idolization, immortalization, lionization
  con debasement, defamation, degradation, denigration, sullying

appall *vb syn* see DISMAY 1
  rel awe, faze, overawe
  con brace (up), buck up, cheer (up); assure, hearten, inspire, inspirit
  ant embolden, nerve

appalling *adj syn* see FEARFUL 3
  rel daunting, dismaying, horrifying; bewildering, confounding, dumbfounding
  con assuring, heartening, inspiriting
  ant reassuring

appanage *n syn* see RIGHT 2

apparatus *n syn* see EQUIPMENT
  rel implement, instrument, tool, utensil; furnishings, provisions, supplies

apparel *vb syn* see CLOTHE
  rel appoint
  con bare, denude
  ant divest

apparel *n syn* see CLOTHES
apparent *adj* 1 *syn* see CLEAR 5
rel ponderable; noticeable, prominent; discernible, observable, perceivable
idiom plain as day, plain to be seen
con ambiguous, hidden, obscure
ant inapparent
2 being other than seems to be the case < her *apparent* goodwill masked an inner loathing >
syn Barmecidal, illusive, illusory, ostensible, seeming, semblant
rel deceptive, delusive, delusory, misleading; credible, plausible, specious; factitious, fake, false, pseudo, sham, supposititious, suppositious
con genuine, true, valid; basic, essential, fundamental, inherent, intrinsic
ant actual, real
apparently *adv syn* see OSTENSIBLY
apparition *n* a visible appearance of something not present and especially of a dead person < illusions that the superstitious see as *apparitions* >
syn bogey, eidolon, ghost, ‖haunt, phantasm, phantom, revenant, shade, shadow, specter, spectrum, spirit, ‖spook, umbra, wraith
rel delusion, hallucination, illusion; corposant, foxfire, ignis fatuus, jack-o'-lantern, marshfire, Saint Elmo's fire, will-o'-the-wisp
appeal *n* 1 *syn* see PRAYER
rel asking, requesting, solicitation
con claim, demand, exaction; kick, objection, protest
2 *syn* see ATTRACTION 1
3 *syn* see CHARM 3
rel draw; pleasantness
con disagreeableness, unpleasantness
appeal *vb* 1 *syn* see BEG
2 *syn* see PETITION
3 *syn* see INTEREST
appealing *adj syn* see ATTRACTIVE 1
appear *vb* 1 to become visible < the sun *appeared* from behind a cloud >
syn emerge, loom, show
rel arrive, come; arise, emanate, issue, materialize, outcrop, rise, spring
idiom come in sight, come into view, meet (*or* strike) the eye, show one's face
con go, leave; depart, retire, withdraw
ant disappear, vanish
2 *syn* see SEEM
idiom give an appearance of, strike one as
appearance *n* 1 the state or form in which one appears < his disheveled *appearance* surprised his guests >
syn aspect, look, mien, seeming
rel air, bearing, countenance, demeanor, manner
2 *usu* **appearances** *pl* outward and often deceptive indication or look < to all *appearances* he was guilty >
syn face, guise, seeming, semblance, show, showing, simulacrum; *compare* MASK

appease *vb* 1 *syn* see PACIFY
rel calm (down), ease, soothe; extenuate, gloss (over), palliate, whitewash
con annoy, bother, irk, vex; anger, enrage, incense, infuriate; discompose, disturb, perturb, upset
ant exasperate
2 *syn* see SATISFY 3
rel ease, relieve; cater (to), coddle, pamper, spoil
ant aggravate
appellation *n syn* see NAME 1
appellative *n syn* see NAME 1
append *vb syn* see ADD 1
appendage *n* something accompanying or attached to another thing to which it is usually subordinate or nonessential < people to whom culture is a mere *appendage* to life >
syn accessory, adjunct, appendix, appurtenance
rel auxiliary, incidental, subsidiary, supplement; collateral, extra, nonessential
appendix *n* 1 additional material subjoined to a writing and especially a book < a dictionary with an *appendix* of new words >
syn addendum, codicil, rider, supplement
2 *rel* APPENDAGE, accessory, adjunct, appurtenance
apperception *n syn* see RECOGNITION 1
rel apprehension, grasp, perception; comprehension, understanding
appertain *vb* 1 *syn* see BELONG 2
2 *syn* see BEAR (on *or* upon)
appetence *n syn* see APPETITE 1
appetent *adj syn* see EAGER
rel craving, desirous, lusting, yearning
idiom consumed with desire
appetite *n* 1 a natural enjoyment of food < all fell to with a hearty *appetite* >
syn appetence, stomach, taste
rel gluttony, greed, hunger, voracity; epicurism, gourmandise
2 *syn* see DESIRE 1
rel cupidity, greed, urgency
con abnegation, asceticism, renunciation, self-denial; distaste, revulsion
3 an attraction toward something < had a great *appetite* for gossip >
syn fondness, inclination, liking, soft spot, taste, weakness
rel bent, bias, flair, leaning, penchant, proclivity, propensity
con disinclination, dislike, distaste; disinterest, unconcern
appetition *n syn* see DESIRE 1
appetizer *n* food or drink served before a meal to stimulate appetite < *appetizers* such as cocktails and canapés >
syn antipasto, hors d'oeuvre, whet, zakuska
rel dainty, delicacy, goody, tidbit; savory
appetizing *adj syn* see PALATABLE
ant disgusting, nauseating
applaud *vb* 1 *syn* see COMMEND 2
rel boost, plug
ant censure; admonish

---

syn synonym(s)   *rel* related word(s)
ant antonym(s)   *con* contrasted word(s)
idiom idiomatic equivalent(s)
‖ use limited; if in doubt, see a dictionary

2 to express enthusiastic approval < *applauded* wildly when his team won a point >
syn cheer, rise (to), root
rel acclaim, extol, laud, praise; eulogize, glorify, magnify, panegyrize
con deride, mock, ridicule, taunt; contemn, disdain, scorn, scout
ant boo; hiss

applause *n* public expression of approbation < her appearance was greeted with *applause* >
syn acclaim, acclamation, plaudit(s)
rel cheers, hand, ovation, round; cheering, clapping, rooting
con derision, mockery, ridicule, taunting; Bronx cheer, raspberry
ant booing, hissing

‖**apple knocker** *n syn* see RUSTIC
apple–polish *vb syn* see FAWN
apple–polisher *n syn* see SYCOPHANT
‖**applesauce** *n syn* see NONSENSE 2
appliance *n syn* see USE 1
applicability *n syn* see USE 3
con irrelevance, unsuitability
ant inapplicability

applicable *adj* 1 *syn* see RELEVANT
rel alliable, associable, compatible, congenial, connective
con incompatible, uncongenial; inappropriate, unfit, unsuitable
ant inapplicable
2 *syn* see FIT 1
rel correct, good, seemly
idiom as it ought to be, as it should be
con improper, incorrect

applicant *n syn* see CANDIDATE
application *n* 1 *syn* see ATTENTION 1
rel busyness, zeal; energy, indefatigability
con bemusement, wool-gathering; faineance, laziness, sloth
ant indolence
2 *syn* see USE 1
3 *syn* see EXERCISE 1
4 *syn* see PRAYER

applicative *adj syn* see RELEVANT
applicatory *adj syn* see RELEVANT
apply *vb* 1 *syn* see ADDRESS 3
rel set about, take on, undertake; drudge, grind, toil
idiom burn the midnight oil, keep one's nose to the grindstone, work like a horse (or dog or ‖nigger); concern (oneself) with something, set (one's hand) to something
con let slide, neglect, pass over, slight
2 *syn* see BEAR (on or upon)
idiom come into relation with
3 *syn* see RESORT 2
rel appeal, petition; beg, beseech, entreat, implore, supplicate; importune, press, urge
idiom make application to
4 *syn* see USE 2

apply (to) *vb syn* see ADDRESS 4
appoint *vb* 1 *syn* see DESIGNATE 2
rel accredit, authorize, commission
con cashier, discharge, dismiss; debar, exclude, reject
2 *syn* see FURNISH 1
rel embellish, enrich, furbish, garnish; dress up, set off, spruce (up)
con denude, dismantle, divest, strip
appointment *n* 1 *syn* see JOB 2
2 *syn* see ENGAGEMENT 3

apportion *vb* 1 *syn* see ALLOT
rel divide, partition, share
con assemble, collect, gather
2 to separate something into shares with care and accuracy and distribute it among a number < Christ *apportioned* the loaves and fishes >
syn divide, ‖divvy, parcel, portion, prorate, quota, ration, share, ‖shift
rel accord, award, bestow, distribute; give, grant, present; part, separate, split
3 *syn* see ADMINISTER 2
rel dish out, serve

apportionment *n syn* see RATION
apposite *adj syn* see RELEVANT
rel felicitous, happy; opportune, pat, seasonable, timely
idiom to the point (or purpose)
con awkward, inept; casual, haphazard, hit-or-miss, random
ant inapposite, inapt

appositeness *n syn* see ORDER 11
appraisal *n* 1 *syn* see ESTIMATE 1
2 *syn* see ESTIMATION 1
appraise *vb syn* see ESTIMATE 1
rel adjudge, deem, esteem, judge; audit, examine, inspect, scrutinize
idiom set (or place) a value on, take the measure of

appraisement *n* 1 *syn* see ESTIMATE 1
2 *syn* see ESTIMATION 1
appreciable *adj syn* see PERCEPTIBLE
rel noticeable; apparent, clear, evident, manifest, obvious, plain; concrete, material, real, substantial
con impalpable, imperceptible, imponderable, insensible, intangible
ant inappreciable

appreciate *vb* 1 to hold in high estimation < *appreciate* the kindness of a friend >
syn apprize, cherish, esteem, prize, treasure, value; *compare* ADMIRE 1
rel admire, regard, respect; adore, ‖eat up, enjoy, like, love, relish
idiom rate highly, set great store by, think much (or well) of
con contemn, disapprove, disdain, scorn; decry, depreciate, disparage
ant despise
2 *syn* see ADMIRE 1
rel enjoy, like, savor
con contemn, disdain, scorn
3 *syn* see KNOW 1
rel catch, seize, take in

appreciation *n syn* see TESTIMONIAL 3
apprehend *vb* 1 to recognize the existence or meaning of < as a child learns to *apprehend* the relation between naughtiness and punishment >
syn accept, catch, compass, comprehend, conceive, cotton (to or on to), ‖dig, follow, grasp, make out, see, take, take in, tumble (to), twig, understand
rel realize, recognize, sense; absorb, digest, seize; catch on, wise (up); penetrate
idiom catch (or get) the drift of, get the idea, get through one's head, make head or tail of
ant misapprehend
2 *syn* see ARREST 2
3 *syn* see FORESEE
rel dread, fear

idiom be on pins and needles, have one's heart in one's mouth, wait with bated breath

4 *syn* see KNOW 1

idiom be acquainted with, be cognizant of

apprehensible *adj syn* see UNDERSTANDABLE

apprehension *n* **1** *syn* see IDEA

2 *syn* see ARREST

3 fear that something is going or will go wrong < had the strongest *apprehension* about her sister's health >

syn apprehensiveness, foreboding, misgiving, premonition, prenotion, presage, presentiment

rel agitation, angst, anxiety, care, concern, disquiet, disquietude, solicitude, unease, uneasiness, worry; alarm, dread, fear, panic

idiom the anxious seat

con assurance, composure, equanimity, sangfroid, self-possession; faith, reliance, trust

ant confidence

apprehensive *adj* **1** *syn* see AWARE

2 *syn* see FEARFUL 2

ant confident

apprehensiveness *n syn* see APPREHENSION 3

apprentice *n syn* see NOVICE

rel starter; amateur

con adept, expert, specialist

apprenticed *adj syn* see BOUND 2

apprise *vb syn* see INFORM 2

rel announce, communicate, declare, proclaim, publish; disclose, discover, divulge, reveal, tell

idiom make known to, serve (one) notice

apprize *vb syn* see APPRECIATE 1

approach *vb* **1** to come or go near or nearer < as a boy *approaches* manhood >

syn approximate, near, nigh

rel achieve, arrive (at), attain, gain, hit, make, reach; draw on

idiom come to close quarters with

con recede, retire, retreat, withdraw; depart, go, leave

2 *syn* see ADDRESS 4

rel advise, confer, consult, counsel, negotiate, parley; beg, beseech, entreat, implore, plead, supplicate

3 *syn* see REACH 3

4 *syn* see AMOUNT 2

con depart, deviate, digress; differ, disaccord, disharmonize, vary

5 *syn* see BORDER 3

approach *n syn* see OVERTURE 1

rel attempt, endeavor, essay, try; call, invitation

ant withdrawal

approaching *adj syn* see FORTHCOMING

approbate *vb syn* see APPROVE 1

approbation *n* warmly commending acceptance or agreement < expressed *approba­tion* of their progress >

syn approval, benediction, blessing, favor, OK (*or* okay)

rel commendation, countenance, goodwill, sanction; admiration, esteem, liking, regard, respect; pleasure, satisfaction

con censure, condemnation, criticism, disapproval, disfavor, reprehension; annoyance, disgust, irritation; distress, regret, sorrow

ant disapprobation

approbative *adj syn* see FAVORABLE 1

approbatory *adj syn* see FAVORABLE 1

appropinquity *n syn* see PROXIMITY

appropriate *vb* **1** to take over as if by preeminent right < limitations on the right of the state to *appropriate* private proper­ty >

syn accroach, annex, arrogate, commandeer, confiscate, expropriate, preempt, seize, sequester, take; *compare* ARROGATE 1

rel grab, grasp, snatch; claim, exact, extort, wrench; conscript, draft, press

idiom help oneself to, lay hold of, make free with, take possession of

2 *syn* see STEAL 1

rel despoil, spoil; forage, raid

3 *syn* see ARROGATE 1

appropriate *adj* **1** *syn* see FIT 1

rel apposite, germane, pertinent, relevant; opportune, pat, seasonable, timely

con incompatible, incongruous, inconsonant

ant inappropriate

2 *syn* see GOOD 2

rel agreeable, desirable, enjoyable, pleasant; acceptable, admissible, eligible, entitled, right, worthy

con disagreeable undesirable, unpleasant; inadmissible, ineligible, unworthy, wrong

ant inappropriate

3 *syn* see JUST 3

con unfair, unjustified, unmerited, unreasonable; unsuitable

ant inappropriate

4 *syn* see TRUE 7

ant inappropriate

appropriately *adv syn* see WELL 4

appropriateness *n* **1** *syn* see USE 3

2 *syn* see ORDER 11

appropriation *n* property (as money) set apart or given by official or formal action for a predetermined use by others < an increased *appropriation* for public housing >

syn grant, subsidy, subvention

rel allotment, allowance, stipend; aid, assistance, grant-in-aid, help

approval *n syn* see APPROBATION

rel applause, commendation, compliment; acceptance, endorsement, sanction, suffrage

con depreciation, derogation, disparagement

ant disapproval

approve *vb* **1** to find acceptable < they were unable to *approve* his behavior >

syn accept, approbate, countenance, favor, go (for), hold (with)

rel back (up), stand by, support, sustain, uphold; bear, endure, put up (with), tolerate

idiom be in favor of, pat on the back, take kindly to, think well (*or* highly) of, view with approval (*or* favor)

---

syn synonym(s)   *rel* related word(s)
ant antonym(s)   *con* contrasted word(s)
idiom idiomatic equivalent(s)
‖ use limited; if in doubt, see a dictionary

con deprecate, disfavor, dislike, frown (on *or* upon); object (to), oppose
ant disapprove
2 to give an often formal expression of approval and support <the committee *approved* the plans for the new clubhouse>
syn accredit, certify, endorse, OK (*or* okay), sanction
rel applaud, compliment, commend; confirm, initial, ratify; clear
con refuse, reject, repudiate, spurn; censure, condemn, criticize, reprehend, reprobate
ant disapprove
approving *adj syn see* FAVORABLE 1
approximal *adj syn see* ADJACENT 3
approximate *adj* 1 *syn see* COMPARATIVE
2 *syn see* RUDE 3
approximate *vb* 1 *syn see* APPROACH 1
idiom be in the neighborhood of
2 *syn see* ESTIMATE 3
approximately *adv syn see* NEARLY
idiom in round numbers, right about
ant exactly, precisely
appulse *n syn see* IMPACT
appurtenance *n syn see* APPENDAGE
rel appointment (*usu* appointments *pl*), equipment, furnishings; furniture
appurtenant *adj syn see* AUXILIARY
a priori *adj syn see* DEDUCTIVE
apriorism *n syn see* ASSUMPTION 2
apropos *adj syn see* RELEVANT
rel meet, proper
con clumsy, gauche, inappropriate, inept
ant malapropos
apropos *prep* in reference to <it is impossible to reach a decision *apropos* this matter at present>
syn about, against, anent, as for, as regards, as respects, as to, concerning, in re, in respect to, re, regarding, respecting, touching, toward, with respect to
apt *adj* 1 having a tendency or inclination <it is *apt* to be cool late in the evening>
syn given, inclined, liable, likely, prone
rel disposed, minded, predisposed
con averse, disinclined, indisposed, loath; doubtful, improbable, unlikely
2 *syn see* FIT 1
rel apposite, apropos, pertinent, relevant; compelling, convincing, telling; exact, nice, precise
con awkward, clumsy, maladroit
ant inapt, inept
3 *syn see* QUICK 2
rel alert, brainy, bright; gifted, talented
con laggard
aptness *n* 1 *syn see* ORDER 11
rel helpfulness, propitiousness
2 *syn see* GIFT 2
‖**apurpose** *adv syn see* INTENTIONALLY
apyrous *adj syn see* NONCOMBUSTIBLE
aquake *adj syn see* TREMULOUS
aqua vitae *n syn see* LIQUOR 2
aqueduct *n syn see* CHANNEL 1
aquiculture *n syn see* HYDROPONICS
aquiver *adj syn see* TREMULOUS
arab *n* 1 *syn see* VAGABOND
‖2 *syn see* PEDDLER
arable *adj* suitable for tilling and for growing crops <used their *arable* land intensively>

syn cultivable, cultivatable, tillable
rel fat, fertile, fruitful, productive
con barren, sterile, unfertile, unfruitful, unproductive
arbiter *n syn see* JUDGE 1
rel moderator
arbitrary *adj* 1 characterized by or given to willful and often unwise or irrational choices and demands <a proud fitful *arbitrary* nature>
syn capricious, erratic, freakish, vagarious, wayward, whimsical, whimsied
rel undisciplined, unruly, wild, willful; arrogant, unconstrained, unreasonable; careless, heedless, impetuous, indiscreet, precipitate, rash; kooky, screwball, zany
con circumspect, discreet, heedful, judicious, politic, reflective; calculating, discriminative, judicial, prudent, well-advised
2 *syn see* ABSOLUTE 4
rel authoritarian, dictatorial, magisterial, oracular
con lawful, legal, licit, rightful
ant legitimate
arbitrate *vb syn see* JUDGE 1
rel intermediate, intervene, mediate; appease, placate, soothe
arbitrator *n* 1 *syn see* MODERATOR
2 *syn see* JUDGE 1
arbor *n* a shelter (as in a garden) formed of vines or branches or of latticework covered with climbing shrubs or vines <the children picnicked under the *arbor*>
syn bower, pergola
rel belvedere, casino, cocky, gazebo, summerhouse
arc *n syn see* CURVE
arcadia *n syn see* UTOPIA
arcane *adj syn see* MYSTERIOUS
rel eerie, uncanny, weird; anagogic, mystical
arced *adj syn see* CURVED
arch *n syn see* CURVE
arch *adj* 1 *syn see* FIRST 3
rel conspicuous, notable, noteworthy; extraordinary, extreme
2 *syn see* SAUCY 1
rel impish, mischievous, playful, roguish, waggish; bold, cheeky, cocky, flippant, fresh; derisive, mocking, twitting
con modest, quiet, respectful, submissive
3 *syn see* COY 2
archaic *adj* 1 *syn see* OLD-FASHIONED
idiom behind the times, of the old school
con fresh, modern, new, novel; fashionable
ant up-to-date
2 *syn see* PRIMITIVE 3
arched *adj syn see* CURVED
archetypal *adj syn see* TYPICAL 1
archetype *n* 1 *syn see* ORIGINAL 1
2 *syn see* MODEL 2
archfiend *n syn see* DEVIL 2
archilochian *adj syn see* SARCASTIC
archimage *n syn see* MAGICIAN 1
architect *n syn see* FATHER 2
architecture *n syn see* MAKEUP 1
archive *n, usu* **archives** *pl* 1 *syn see* LIBRARY
2 *syn see* DOCUMENT
rel papers, parchments, scrolls, writings; clippings, cuttings, excerpts, extracts, fragments, gleanings, remains

arciform *adj syn* see CURVED

arctic *adj syn* see COLD 1
rel bitter, boreal, hyperborean; numbing, rigorous; hibernal, hiemal
idiom cold as charity, cold enough to freeze a brass monkey
ant torrid

ardent *adj* 1 *syn* see IMPASSIONED
rel enthusiastic, urgent; avid, desirous, eager, keen
con calm, composed, imperturbable, nonchalant; apathetic, impassive, phlegmatic; disinterested, dispassionate, impartial, uninterested
ant cool
2 very deep or moving < had an *ardent* longing for knowledge >
syn extreme, intense
rel crying, importunate, insistent, urgent; great, mighty, powerful, strong
con feeble, minimal, slight, trivial
3 *syn* see EAGER
rel hasty, impetuous, impulsive, precipitate; fervid, fiery, hectic, hot; uncontrolled, ungoverned; earnest, intent, urgent, vehement
con dull, heavy, inert, leaden, lumpish; languid, lethargic, listless; apathetic, impassive, phlegmatic
ant easygoing
4 *syn* see FAITHFUL 1
5 *syn* see HOT 1
6 *syn* see SPIRITUOUS

ardor *n* 1 *syn* see PASSION 6
rel avidity; gusto, spirit, verve, zest; excitement, galvanization, quickening, stimulation
con aloofness, detachment, disinterest, unconcern; apathy, lackadaisy, languor, listlessness
ant coolness; indifference
2 *syn* see EAGERNESS
rel ardency, fervor, warmth
3 *syn* see FIDELITY 1
rel adoration, love, worship

arduous *adj* 1 *syn* see HARD 6
2 *syn* see STEEP 1
3 *syn* see TIGHT 4

arduously *adv syn* see HARD 8
con easily, facilely
ant effortlessly

area *n* 1 a distinguishable extent of surface and especially of the earth's surface < a large wooded *area* >
syn belt, region, territory, tract, zone
rel expanse, stretch; district, locality, place; lot, plot, section; terrain; circuit
2 *syn* see LOCALITY 1

arena *n syn* see SCENE 4

arete *n syn* see EXCELLENCE

argent *adj syn* see SILVERY

argentate *adj syn* see SILVERY

argenteous *adj syn* see SILVERY

argentine *adj syn* see SILVERY

argot *n syn* see DIALECT 2

arguable *adj syn* see MOOT

argue *vb* 1 *syn* see DISCUSS 1

rel analyze, investigate, review, sift, study, ventilate; expostulate, object, protest, remonstrate
2 to contend in words < *arguing* about who should answer the phone >
syn argufy, bicker, dispute, hassle, quibble, squabble, wrangle; *compare* QUARREL
rel differ, disaccord, disagree, dissent; balk, demur, jib; clash, conflict
idiom bandy words, have it out, join (or take) issue
con accord, agree, concur
3 *syn* see INDICATE 2
4 *syn* see MAINTAIN 2

argue (into) *vb syn* see INDUCE 1

argufy *vb syn* see ARGUE 2

argument *n* 1 *syn* see REASON 3
rel basis, foundation; position, posture, stance, standpoint
2 a vigorous often heated discussion of a moot question < their continuing *argument* over household expenses >
syn contention, controversy, dispute, hurrah, rumpus
rel argumentation, debate, disputation, polemic; disagreement, dissension, squabbling; embroilment, fuss, hassle, wrangle
3 *syn* see SUBJECT 2
rel position, proposition, statement, thesis

argumentation *n* the act or art or an exercise of one's powers of argument < noted for his skill in *argumentation* >
syn debate, dialectic, disputation, forensic, mooting
rel argument, controversy, dispute; declamation, elocution, eloquence, oratory, rhetoric

argumentative *adj syn* see CONTENTIOUS 2

argute *adj* 1 *syn* see SHREWD
2 *syn* see ACUTE 4

aria *n syn* see SONG 2

arid *adj* 1 *syn* see DRY 1
rel barren, infertile, sterile, unfruitful
con fecund, fertile, fruitful
2 lacking in interest or liveliness < some of the most *arid* prose ever written >
syn bromidic, dry, dryasdust, dull, dusty, insipid, tedious, uninteresting, wearīful, wearisome; *compare* TEPID 2, UNORIGINAL
rel drab, dreary, flat, heavy, lackluster, leaden, unanimated, unlively; academic, bookish, pedantic; boring, humdrum, monotonous, unimaginative, uninspired
con appealing, bright, lively, sparkling, stimulating, vigorous, vivid

aright *adv syn* see WELL 1

arise *vb* 1 *syn* see RISE 4
ant recline; slump
2 *syn* see ROLL OUT
3 *syn* see SPRING 1
rel ensue, follow, succeed
4 *syn* see BEGIN 2

aristarch *n syn* see CRITIC

aristo *n syn* see GENTLEMAN

aristocracy *n* the highest stratum of a society < the self-centered attitude of some *aristocracies* >
syn aristoi, blue blood, carriage trade, crème de la crème, elite, flower, gentility, gentry, haut monde, optimacy, patriciate, quality, society, upper class, upper crust, who's who

---

syn synonym(s)   *rel* related word(s)
ant antonym(s)   *con* contrasted word(s)
idiom idiomatic equivalent(s)
‖ use limited; if in doubt, see a dictionary

rel nobility, noblesse, patricians; county; beau monde, bon ton, jet set, smart set
con canaille, mob, rabble, riffraff; commoners, commons, masses, people, plebeians

aristocrat *n syn* see GENTLEMAN
ant commoner
aristoi *n syn* see ARISTOCRACY
arithmetic *n syn* see COMPUTATION
arm *n* 1 *syn* see INLET
2 *syn* see ANNEX
3 *syn* see POWER 4
arm *vb syn* see FURNISH 1
rel prepare, ready
idiom put in (*or* into) shape
ant disarm
armament *n syn* see DEFENSE 1
armamentarium *n syn* see SUPPLY
armed forces *n pl syn* see TROOP 2
armistice *n syn* see TRUCE
armor *n syn* see DEFENSE 1
rel cloak, mantle, shroud, veil; buckler, cover, screen, shelter
armory *n* a place where military arms and supplies are stored < the problem of weapon theft from *armories* >
syn arsenal, depot, dump, magazine
army *n syn* see MULTITUDE 1
rel crush, horde, mob, press, throng
aroma *n* 1 *syn* see FRAGRANCE
2 *syn* see SMELL 1
rel fetor, mephitis, reek, stench, stink
aromal *adj syn* see SWEET 2
rel penetrating, piquant, pungent
ant acrid
aromatic *adj syn* see SWEET 2
ant acrid
aromatize *vb syn* see SCENT 2
around *adv* 1 *syn* see ABOUT 1
2 *syn* see THROUGH 1
3 *syn* see ABOUT 4
4 *syn* see ABOUT 6
around *prep syn* see ABOUT 1
around *adj syn* see EXTANT 1
around–the–clock *adj syn* see CONTINUAL
arouse *vb syn* see STIR 1
rel alert, excite, work up; electrify, thrill; fire, inflame
idiom fan the fire (*or* flame), raise to fever heat, set on fire, stir one's blood (*or* feelings)
con allay, alleviate, assuage, ease, mitigate, relieve; mollify, pacify, placate
ant calm, quiet
arraign *vb syn* see ACCUSE
rel cite, summon; test, try
idiom bring to book, call to account
con absolve, acquit, exculpate, exonerate, vindicate; defend, justify
arrange *vb syn* see ORDER 1
rel assort, categorize, pigeonhole, sort
con disorder, disorganize, disturb, unsettle; confuse, jumble, muddle, tumble; disperse, scatter
ant derange, disarrange
2 *syn* see DESIGN 3
3 *syn* see PLAN 2
4 *syn* see NEGOTIATE 1
rel design, plan, project, scheme
5 *syn* see HARMONIZE 4
arrangement *n syn* see ORDER 3
rel layout, lineup, setup; method, system

ant disarrangement
arrant *adj* 1 *syn* see UTTER
rel plain, pure, regular, sheer
2 *syn* see SHAMELESS
array *vb syn* see ORDER 1
ant disarray
2 *syn* see CLOTHE
array *n* 1 *syn* see GROUP 3
2 *syn* see DISPLAY 2
rel exhibition, exposing, showing; arranging, marshaling, ordering
arrear *n, usu* arrears *pl syn* see DEBT 3
arrearage *n* 1 *syn* see DEBT 3
2 *syn* see INDEBTEDNESS 1
arrect *adj* 1 *syn* see ERECT
2 *syn* see ATTENTIVE 1
arrest *vb* 1 to bring to a halt < science cannot yet *arrest* the process of aging >
syn check, halt, interrupt, stall, stay; *compare* STOP 3
rel balk, frustrate, thwart; choke, obstruct, stop (up); delay, detain, hamper, hinder, restrain, retard; interfere, interpose, intervene; contain, stem, withstand
idiom bring to a halt (*or* stand *or* standstill), bring up short, check in full career, cut short
con advance, forward, further, promote; expedite, hasten, quicken, speed
2 to take and hold in custody under authority of the law < *arrested* for murder >
syn apprehend, ‖bust, detain, nab, pick up, pinch, pull in, run in; *compare* CATCH 1
rel immure, imprison, incarcerate, jail, lock (up), ‖slough; attach
idiom lay by the heels, lay hands on
con discharge, free, liberate, release
arrest *n* the taking and holding of a person in custody under authority of the law < unwilling to submit to *arrest* >
syn apprehension, arrestation, arrestment, detention, ‖nab, pickup, pinch
rel capture, catch, collar, seizure, taking
con discharge, freeing, liberation, release
arrestation *n syn* see ARREST
arresting *adj syn* see NOTICEABLE
rel attractive, enchanting, fascinating; affective, appealing, impressive, moving, touching
idiom enough to make one stop and take notice
con common, familiar, ordinary, run-of-the-mill; hackneyed, stereotyped, trite
arrestive *adj syn* see NOTICEABLE
arrestment *n syn* see ARREST
arride *vb syn* see PLEASE 2
rel beguile, divert, entertain, recreate
idiom tickle one's fancy
con bore, ennui, jade, weary
arrival *n* 1 the reaching of a destination < the train was late in its *arrival* >
syn advent, coming
rel appearance, emergence, entrance, issuance, manifestation
con disappearance, going, leaving, withdrawal; recession, retirement, retreat
ant departure
2 *syn* see SUCCESS
arrive *vb* 1 *syn* see COME 1
con get away, go, retire
ant depart
2 *syn* see SUCCEED 3

arriviste *n syn* see UPSTART
arrogance *n syn* see PRIDE 3
  ant humility
arrogant *adj syn* see PROUD 1
  rel domineering, imperative, peremptory; affected, artificial, highfalutin, mannered, showy
  idiom too big for one's britches
  con humble; deferential, submissive; abject, obsequious, subservient, truckling
  ant meek
  2 *syn* see POMPOUS 1
arrogate *vb* 1 to claim or take over in a high-handed manner < *arrogated* to himself the right to make all decisions >
  syn accroach, appropriate, assume, commandeer, preempt, usurp; *compare* APPROPRIATE 1
  rel annex, preempt, preoccupy, sequester; grab, seize, take, take over
  idiom help oneself to, make free with, take into one's own hands
  con cede, relinquish, resign, surrender, yield
  ant renounce
  2 *syn* see APPROPRIATE 1
arrondi *adj syn* see CURVED
arroyo *n syn* see RAVINE
*****arse** *n syn* see BUTTOCKS
arsenal *n* 1 *syn* see ARMORY
  2 *syn* see DEPOT 2
arsonist *n syn* see INCENDIARY
arsy–varsy *adj syn* see UPSIDE-DOWN 2
art *n* 1 a usually acquired proficiency in doing or performing < there's an *art* to competent public speaking >
  syn adroitness, craft, cunning, dexterity, expertise, know-how, skill
  rel capability, competence, handiness, proficiency; address, finesse, ‖savvy
  con clumsiness, maladroitness
  2 *syn* see CUNNING 2
  rel acuteness, astuteness
  con candor, frankness, sincerity; directness, straightforwardness, bluffness, bluntness
  3 *syn* see TRADE 1
artery *n syn* see WAY 1
artful *adj syn* see SLY 2
  rel diplomatic, oily, politic, smooth, suave; facile, specious, superficial; adroit, dexterous
  ant artless
artfulness *n syn* see CUNNING 2
article *n* 1 *syn* see POINT 1
  rel division, section, segment
  2 *syn* see ESSAY 2
  rel critique, manifesto, report, statement, study, survey
  3 *syn* see THING 3
  rel detail, particular
articled *adj syn* see BOUND 2
articulate *adj* 1 *syn* see VOCAL 1
  rel clear, distinct, intelligible
  ant inarticulate; dumb
  2 *syn* see VOCAL 3
  rel meaningful, significant; garrulous, prolix, talkative; uttering, venting

ant inarticulate
articulate *vb* 1 *syn* see INTEGRATE 3
  rel connect, join, relate; methodize, order, organize, systematize; adjust, coordinate, harmonize, regulate; assemble, collect, gather; unify
  con dissect, resolve; divide, part, separate
  2 to form speech sounds < regional differences in *articulating* the letter *r* >
  syn enunciate, phonate, pronounce, say
  rel sound, utter
articulation *n syn* see VOCALIZATION
artifice *n* 1 *syn* see CUNNING 2
  rel ingenuity, inventiveness, originality; adroitness, cleverness, keenness, quickness, shrewdness; adeptness, proficiency
  2 *syn* see TRICK 1
  rel chicane, chicanery, trickery; knavery, rascality, skulduggery; deceit, dissimulation, duplicity, guile
artificial *adj* 1 *syn* see SYNTHETIC
  rel fabricated, fashioned, made
  con native
  ant natural
  2 taking the place of something else and especially of something finer or more costly < *artificial* diamonds >
  syn dummy, ersatz, false, imitation, mock, sham, simulated, spurious, substitute; *compare* FICTITIOUS 2, SPURIOUS 3
  rel fake, papier-mâché, ‖pretend, unreal; hollow, painted
  con authentic, bona fide, genuine, real, sure-enough, true, veritable
  3 lacking in spontaneity and genuineness < exchanged *artificial* smiles >
  syn affected, assumed, feigned, put-on, spurious
  rel histrionic, insincere, overdone, quaint, stagy, theatrical, unnatural; cute, cutesy, goody-goody, mincing, overrefined, simpering; contrived, forced, labored
  con genuine, sincere, spontaneous, unaffected
artist *n syn* see EXPERT
  rel ace, crackerjack, first-rater, shark, topnotcher; genius, prodigy, wonder
artiste *n syn* see EXPERT
artless *adj syn* see NATURAL 5
  rel free, relaxed; aboveboard, forthright, straightforward; childlike, trusting, unsuspicious; untouched, virginal
  con cunning, insidious, sly, wily; calculating, designing, intriguing, scheming; artificial, insincere
  ant artful; affected
arty *adj syn* see PRETENTIOUS 3
arty–crafty *adj syn* see PRETENTIOUS 3
as *conj syn* see BECAUSE
as a rule *adv syn* see USUALLY 2
‖**ascared** *adj syn* see AFRAID 1
ascend *vb* 1 to move upward to or toward a summit < *ascend* a mountain >
  syn climb, escalade, escalate, mount, scale, upclimb, upgo
  rel clamber, get up, scramble, shin; crest, surmount, top
  idiom scale the heights, work one's way up
  ant descend
  2 *syn* see RISE 4
ascendancy *n syn* see SUPREMACY
ascendant *n* 1 *syn* see SUPREMACY

---

syn synonym(s)   *rel* related word(s)
ant antonym(s)   *con* contrasted word(s)
idiom idiomatic equivalent(s)
‖ use limited; if in doubt, see a dictionary

2 *syn* see ANCESTOR 1
 rel forerunner, precursor, predecessor
 ant descendant
ascendant *adj syn* see DOMINANT 1
ascension *n syn* see ASCENT
ascent *n* a moving upward or an upward movement < the slow *ascent* of the creaky old elevator>
 syn ascension, rise, rising
 rel elevation, raising, uplifting
 ant descent
ascertain *vb syn* see DISCOVER 3
 rel ask, inquire, interrogate, query, question; appraise, inspect, observe, survey, view; consider, contemplate, study, weigh
 con assume, presume; conjecture, guess, surmise
ascetic *adj syn* see SEVERE 1
 rel abstemious, abstinent, forbearing; self-abasing, self-abnegating, self-denying, self-forgetful, selfless; disciplined, restrained, schooled, trained
 con epicurean, sensual, sensuous, sybaritic; abandoned, dissolute, licentious, self-indulgent
 ant luxurious, voluptuous
ascribe *vb* to refer especially to a supposed cause, source, or author <a manuscript commonly *ascribed* to Saint Augustine>
 syn accredit, assign, attribute, charge, credit, impute, lay, refer
 rel attach (to), connect (with), fix (on or upon), pin (on), saddle (on or upon or with); affix, fasten; conjecture, guess, surmise; adduce, advance, allege, cite
aseptic *adj syn* see UNDEMONSTRATIVE
as for *prep syn* see APROPOS
as good as *adv* **1** *syn* see NEARLY
 2 *syn* see ALMOST 2
ash *n* the residue left when material is consumed by fire <cold whitened *ash* on the hearth>
 syn ashes, cinders, clinkers
 rel dross, scoria, slag; charcoal, coal(s), coke, ember(s); fumes, smoke, soot
ashake *adj syn* see TREMULOUS
ashamed *adj* humiliated or disconcerted usually by feelings of guilt, disgrace, or impropriety <*ashamed* of her brother's noisy boasting>
 syn chagrined, mortified, shamed
 rel abashed, discomfited, embarrassed; abased, humbled, humiliated; abject, hangdog, mean; contrite, penitent, repentant
 idiom unable to show one's face
 con arrogant, assured, overbearing, self-assured; vain, vainglorious
 ant proud
ashen *adj syn* see PALE 1
 rel corpselike, ghostly, macabre; blanched, bleached, decolorized, faded
ashes *n pl syn* see ASH
ashiver *adj syn* see TREMULOUS
ashy *adj syn* see PALE 1
aside *adv* **1** in a slanting or sloping direction <his head hung *aside* as if he lacked the strength to hold it up>
 syn aslant, aslope, obliquely, sideways, sidewise, slant, slantingly, slantingways, slantly, slantways, slantwise, ‖slaunchways, slopeways; *compare* SIDEWAYS 1
 rel askance, askant, askew, awry; downgrade, downhill

 con erectly, uprightly, vertically
 2 *syn* see APART 2
 3 *syn* see APIECE
‖**aside** *prep syn* see NEAR 2
aside *n syn* see DIGRESSION
aside from *prep syn* see EXCEPT
asinine *adj syn* see SIMPLE 3
 rel puerile; absurd, irrational, unreasonable
 con prudent, sage, sane, sapient, wise; clever, intelligent, knowing, smart; rational, reasonable
 ant judicious, sensible
ask *vb* **1** to call upon for an answer or information <*asked* him to explain his behavior>
 syn catechize, examine, inquire, interrogate, query, question, quiz
 rel argue, canvass, debate, deliberate, discuss, review, talk (over)
 con answer, rejoin, reply, respond, retort
 2 to seek to obtain by making one's needs or desires known <*asked* for time to consider the problem>
 syn bespeak, desire, request, solicit
 rel claim, demand, exact, require; beg, beseech, entreat, implore, importune
 idiom put in for
 3 *syn* see DEMAND 2
 4 *syn* see INVITE
 rel canvass, request, seek
askance *adv* **1** *syn* see AWRY 1
 ant directly
 2 with absence of approval or trust <a proceeding one must view more than a little *askance*>
 syn distrustfully, doubtfully, mistrustfully, skeptically, suspiciously
 rel captiously, critically, cynically, doubtingly; deprecatingly, depreciatively, disparagingly
 con approvingly, favorably
askant *adv syn* see AWRY 1
 ant directly
asker *n syn* see SUPPLIANT
askew *adv syn* see AWRY 1
 ant straight
aslant *adv syn* see ASIDE 1
asleep *adj* **1** *syn* see DEAD 1
 2 *syn* see NUMB 1
 3 *syn* see INACTIVE
as long as *conj syn* see BECAUSE
aslope *adv syn* see ASIDE 1
as much as *adv syn* see ALMOST 2
asomatous *adj syn* see IMMATERIAL 1
aspect *n* **1** *syn* see APPEARANCE 1
 rel countenance, face, visage; air, bearing, port, presence
 2 *syn* see PHASE
 rel point of view, slant, standpoint
asperity *n* **1** *syn* see DIFFICULTY 1
 rel austerity, bitterness, grimness, harshness, inclemency, severity, stringency
 con blandness, gentleness, mildness, softness
 2 *syn* see INEQUALITY 1
 3 *syn* see ACRIMONY
 rel harshness, keenness, roughness, sharpness; irritability, snappishness, tartness, waspishness
 con blandness, smoothness, suavity, urbanity; courtesy, gallantry
 ant amenity

asperous *adj syn* see ROUGH 1
asperse *vb* 1 *syn* see MALIGN
  rel deride, mock, taunt; affront, insult, offend
  con applaud, commend, compliment
  2 *syn* see BAPTIZE
aspersion *n syn* see ANIMADVERSION
  rel abuse, invective, muck, vituperation; backbiting, calumny, detraction, scandal, slander; lampoon, libel, pasquinade, skit, squib
  con eulogy, extolling, laudation, praise; acclaim, acclamation, applause, plaudits; commendation, compliment
asphyxiate *vb syn* see SUFFOCATE
aspirant *n syn* see CANDIDATE
aspiration *n syn* see AMBITION 1
  rel aim, direction, goal, objective; desire, lust, passion, urge
aspire *vb* 1 *syn* see AIM 2
  rel hunger, long, pine, thirst; bid (for), strain (for *or* after), struggle (for), try (for)
  idiom cry for the moon, have at heart, have one's heart set on, reach for (*or* keep one's eyes on) the stars
  con condescend, deign, look down (on); grovel, stoop, wallow
  2 *syn* see RISE 4
aspiring *adj syn* see AMBITIOUS 1
  rel desirous, impassioned, urgent; wanting, wishful, yearning
as regards *prep syn* see APROPOS
as respects *prep syn* see APROPOS
ass *n* 1 *syn* see DONKEY 1
  2 *syn* see FOOL 1
*ass *n syn* see BUTTOCKS
assail *vb syn* see ATTACK 1
  rel beat, belabor, buffet, pound, pummel
  idiom round on
assailment *n syn* see ATTACK 1
assassin *n* a person hired or hirable to commit murder <found out who paid the *assassin*>
  syn bravo, cutthroat, gun, gunman, ‖gunsel, gunslinger, hatchet man, hit man, torpedo, triggerman; *compare* MURDERER
  rel apache, desperado, goon, ‖gorilla, highbinder, strong arm, thug
assassinate *vb syn* see MURDER 1
assault *n syn* see ATTACK 1
  rel brush, clash, invasion, melee, skirmish; brawl, contest, fracas, set-to
assault *vb syn* see ATTACK 1
  rel battle, fight, war; clash, collide, encounter, engage; skirmish
assay *vb* 1 *syn* see TRY 5
  rel venture
  idiom make an effort to
  2 *syn* see ESTIMATE 1
  rel demonstrate, prove, test, try; analyze, resolve; calculate, compute, reckon
assemblage *n syn* see GATHERING 1
assemble *vb* 1 *syn* see CONVOKE
  2 *syn* see GATHER 6
  rel associate, combine, unite; convene, convoke
  con dispel, dissipate, scatter; leave, part, quit, separate

---

  ant disperse
  3 *syn* see GROUP 1
  rel accumulate, aggregate, amass, garner; bunch, clump; bank, heap, mound, pile, stack
  con dispel, dissipate, scatter; leave, part, quit, separate; break up, disband
  ant disperse
  4 *syn* see MAKE 3
assembly *n* 1 *syn* see GATHERING 2
  rel association, band, conclave, party, troupe
  2 *syn* see GROUP 1
  rel crowd, push; faction, interest, sect, wing; brotherhood, fellowship, fraternity
  con masses, multitude; canaille, rabble, riffraff, ruck, trash
assent *vb* to give or express one's consent or concurrence <*assented* grudgingly to her plans for the evening>
  syn accede, acquiesce, agree, consent, subscribe, yes
  rel adopt, embrace, espouse; accept; abide, bear (with), endure, stand, suffer, tolerate; down, stomach, swallow, take; defer, relent, submit, yield
  idiom be at one with, cast one's vote for, give the nod of approval, go along with, see eye to eye with
  con rebuff, refuse, reject, scorn, scout, spurn; deny, gainsay
  ant dissent
assert *vb* 1 to state firmly, positively, or assuredly <he continued to *assert* his innocence>
  syn affirm, aver, avouch, avow, constate, declare, depose, predicate, profess, protest
  rel adduce, advance, allege, cite, claim, pretend; announce, broadcast, disseminate, proclaim, promulgate, publish, spread
  idiom have it
  con contradict, contravene, dispute, gainsay, negate, negative, traverse; confute, disprove, rebut, refute
  ant deny; controvert
  2 *syn* see MAINTAIN 2
  rel declare, express, utter, voice; advance, state, stipulate, submit
assertive *adj* 1 *syn* see EMPHATIC
  2 *syn* see AGGRESSIVE
  rel affirmative; arbitrary, dogmatic, peremptory, positive; assured, certain, cocksure, opinionated, opinionative, self-assured, sure; confident, presumptuous, sanguine, self-confident
  con bashful, diffident, modest, shy; amenable, biddable, docile, submissive
  ant retiring; acquiescent
assertory *adj syn* see AGGRESSIVE
assess *vb* 1 *syn* see LEVY
  2 *syn* see ESTIMATE 1
  rel calculate, compute; account, consider, deem, reckon, weigh
assessment *n* 1 *syn* see ESTIMATION 1
  2 *syn* see ESTIMATE 1
  3 *syn* see TAX 1
asset *n* 1 assets *pl syn* see MEAN 3
  rel bankroll, money; equity; principal
  ant liabilities
  2 *syn* see CREDIT 3
  rel distinction, glory, honor, ornament
  con detriment, disadvantage, discredit, liability

---

ant handicap

asshead *n syn* see FOOL 1

assiduous *adj* marked by careful attention or persistent application < learned to speak French fluently by *assiduous* practice >
syn diligent, industrious, operose, sedulous; *compare* BUSY 1
rel hardworking, laborious, moiling; indefatigable, tireless, untiring, unwearied, zealous
idiom hard at it
con casual, haphazard, happy-go-lucky, hit-or-miss, intermittent, random; careless, lax, remiss, slack, sloppy, slovenly; indolent, lazy, slothful
ant desultory

assiduously *adv syn* see HARD 3

assign *vb* 1 *syn* see TRANSFER 4
2 *syn* see ALLOT
rel establish, fix, set, settle
3 *syn* see ASCRIBE
rel associate, link, relate; classify, pigeonhole
4 *syn* see PRESCRIBE 2
rel decide, determine; commit, consign, entrust, relegate

assignation *n syn* see ENGAGEMENT 3
rel agreement, arrangement, understanding; get-together

assignee *n syn* see AGENT 2

assignment *n syn* see TASK 1
rel incumbency, liability, obligation, responsibility

assimilate *vb* 1 *syn* see ABSORB 1
rel imbue, infuse, ingrain, inoculate, leaven, suffuse; adopt, embrace, espouse; corner, engross, monopolize
2 *syn* see EQUATE 2

assimilation *n syn* see RECOGNITION 1
rel awareness, consciousness, mindfulness

assist *vb syn* see HELP 1
rel accompany, attend, escort; concur, cooperate
con clog, fetter, trammel; forestall, prevent; burden, encumber, handicap, tax, weigh down
ant hamper; impede

assist *n syn* see HELP 1

assistance *n syn* see HELP 1
rel backing, supporting, upholding; advantage, avail, profit, use; appropriation, grant, subsidy, subvention
con checking, hampering, hindering, hindrance; balking, foiling, frustration, thwarting
ant impediment, impeding; obstructing, obstruction

assistant *n* 1 *syn* see HELPER
2 a person who takes over part of the duties of a superior < started as *assistant* to the secretary >
syn aid, aide, aide-de-camp, coadjutant, coadjutor, lieutenant
rel acolyte, attendant, second; flunky, henchman, minion, stooge; girl Friday, right-hand man; agent, attorney, deputy, factor, proxy; fall guy, patsy; co-worker, workfellow, yokemate

assistive *adj syn* see HELPFUL 1

assize *n* 1 *syn* see LAW 1
2 *syn* see STANDARD 4

associate *vb syn* see JOIN 1

rel amalgamate, blend, coalesce, merge, mingle, mix; ally, confederate, federate, league
con alienate, estrange; divide, divorce, part

associate *n* 1 *syn* see PARTNER
rel affiliate, ally, confederate, leaguer; abettor, accomplice, collaborator
2 *syn* see COLLEAGUE
3 a person regularly frequenting the company of another < a man is judged by the *associates* he keeps >
syn buddy, chum, comate, companion, comrade, crony, ‖cully, pal, running mate; *compare* FRIEND
rel acquaintance, friend, sympathizer; confidant, familiar, intimate; brother-in-arms, comrade-in-arms
4 *syn* see ACCOMPANIMENT 2
rel complement, correlate, correlative, counterpart, match; correspondent
con competitor, rival; adversary, antagonist, opponent

association *n* 1 the quality or state of being associated < worked in close *association* with the courts >
syn affiliation, alliance, cahoots, combination, conjointment, conjunction, connection, hookup, partnership, tie-up, togetherness
rel coaction, collaboration, concert, cooperation, teamwork; conviviality, gaiety, joviality, sociability
con aloofness, apartness, disjunction, disunion, isolation, separation
ant disassociation, dissociation
2 an organization of persons sharing a common interest or purpose < a buyers' *association* >
syn brotherhood, club, congress, fellowship, fraternity, guild, league, order, society, sodality, union
rel alliance, axis, bloc, coalition, federation, organization; faction, interest, sect, wing; combine, gang, machine, ring
3 *syn* see LEAGUE 4
4 something (as a feeling or recollection) associated in the mind with a particular person or thing < the thought of her childhood home always carried an *association* of loving warmth >
syn connotation, hint, implication, overtone, suggestion, undertone
rel image, picture, vision; appearance, fantasy, illusion, mirage

assort *vb* to arrange systematically < *assort* yarn by color >
syn categorize, class, classify, group, pigeonhole
rel arrange, methodize, order, systematize; distribute, divide, separate; screen, sift; stratify
con derange, disarrange, disorder, disorganize; commingle, jumble, mingle, mix, scramble

assorted *adj* 1 *syn* see MISCELLANEOUS
con chosen, picked, preferred, selected
2 corresponding in such manner or degree as to be appropriately associated < they made a well-*assorted* pair >
syn adapted, conformable, fitted, matched, suited
rel chosen, picked, preferred, selected; associated, bracketed, coupled, linked

con confused, disordered, fouled-up, haywire, jumbled, muddled, scrambled
assortment *n* 1 *syn* see VARIETY 2
2 *syn* see MISCELLANY 1
assuage *vb* 1 *syn* see RELIEVE 1
rel placate
con augment, increase, recruit, reinforce; enhance, exaggerate, heighten, intensify, magnify, strengthen
ant exacerbate
2 *syn* see PACIFY
rel calm, ease, relax, slack, slacken, soothe
con annoy, inflame, nettle, provoke, ruffle, vex
as such *adv* *syn* see PER SE
assumably *adv* *syn* see PRESUMABLY
assume *vb* 1 *syn* see DON 2
2 *syn* see DON 1
3 *syn* see ARROGATE 1
rel grab, seize, snatch, take
idiom take over the helm, take possession (*or* command)
4 to take on or present a false or deceptive appearance < their gaiety was *assumed* >
syn act, affect, bluff, counterfeit, fake, feign, pretend, put on, sham, simulate
rel camouflage, cloak, conceal, disguise, dissemble, hide, mask
idiom make believe
5 *syn* see PRESUPPOSE
rel affirm, assert, aver, predicate, profess; allow, concede, grant
6 *syn* see UNDERSTAND 3
assumed *adj* *syn* see ARTIFICIAL 3
rel factitious, synthetic; deceptive, delusory, illusory, insubstantial, unreal
con authentic, bona fide, genuine, veritable; real, true
assumption *n* 1 *syn* see PRESUPPOSITION
2 something that is taken for granted or advanced as fact < decisions based on *assumptions* about the nature of society >
syn apriorism, posit, postulate, postulation, premise, presumption, presupposition, supposition, thesis
rel conjecture, guess, surmise; hypothesis, theory; axiom, fundamental, law, principle, theorem
asssurance *n* 1 *syn* see WORD 8
rel parole, promise; troth; plight; agreement, compact, covenant, pact, understanding
2 *syn* see CERTAINTY
rel credit; dependence, reliance, trust
con suspicion, uncertainty; disbelief, incredulity, unbelief
ant mistrust; dubiousness
3 *syn* see SAFETY
4 *syn* see CONFIDENCE 2
rel composure, equanimity, sangfroid
con agitation, disquiet, jumpiness, nervousness, shakiness, skittishness; anxiety, doubt, foreboding, funk, perturbation, trepidation
ant alarm
5 *syn* see TEMERITY

rel brazenness, cockiness, presumption; conceit, self-conceit, self-importance, vanity
con diffidence, modesty, shyness, timidity; self-depreciation, self-effacement, unassumingness, unpretentiousness
assure *vb* 1 *syn* see ENSURE
con abash, discomfit, embarrass; buffalo, bulldoze, cow, daunt, intimidate, shake; demoralize, disquiet, unman, unnerve
ant alarm
2 to make one sure or certain of something < pinched his arm to *assure* himself he was awake >
syn convince, persuade, satisfy
idiom bring (*or* drive) home to, lead one to believe, sell one on something
assured *adj* 1 *syn* see CONFIDENT 1
rel collected, composed, cool, imperturbable, unflappable, unruffled; game, plucky, resolute, spunky
con abashed, discomfited, disconcerted, embarrassed, rattled; hesitant, insecure, reluctant, uncertain; apprehensive, timorous
2 *syn* see DECIDED 1
rel certain, fixed, set
con ambiguous, uncertain; enigmatic, mysterious, obscure
assuredness *n* *syn* see CERTAINTY
astern *adv* *syn* see ABAFT
rel rear
con ahead, before, forward
as to *prep* 1 *syn* see APROPOS
2 *syn* see BY 5
astonish *vb* *syn* see SURPRISE 2
rel overwhelm; affright, alarm, terrify
astonishing *adj* *syn* see MARVELOUS 1
astound *vb* *syn* see SURPRISE 2
astounding *adj* *syn* see MARVELOUS 1
astral *adj* 1 *syn* see STELLAR 1
2 *syn* see DREAMY 1
3 *syn* see EXALTED 1
astray *adv* *syn* see AMISS 2
astricted *adj* *syn* see CONSTIPATED
astringent *adj* 1 *syn* see ACRID
rel puckery
con bland, mellow, mild
2 *syn* see SEVERE 1
rel biting, cutting, incisive, penetrating, piercing, stabbing; brisk, caustic, keen, sharp
con lax, loose, relaxed, slack, weak; unexacting
3 *syn* see TONIC 1
astucious *adj* *syn* see SHREWD
rel discreet, foresighted, prudent; cunning, sly, wily
con ingenuous, naive, simple, unsophisticated; dull, heavy, obtuse, slow; arid, barren, staid, stuffy, uninspired
ant gullible
astucity *n* *syn* see WIT 3
astute *adj* 1 *syn* see SHREWD
rel discreet, foresighted, prudent; cunning, sly, wily
con ingenuous, naive, simple, unsophisticated; dull, heavy, obtuse, slow; arid, barren, staid, stuffy, uninspired
ant gullible
2 *syn* see SLY 2
rel subtile, subtle; keen, knowing, sharp
idiom slippery as an eel, too clever by half

---

syn synonym(s)   *rel* related word(s)
ant antonym(s)   *con* contrasted word(s)
idiom idiomatic equivalent(s)
‖ use limited; if in doubt, see a dictionary

con aboveboard, forthright, straightforward; ingenuous, naive, simple, unsophisticated

astuteness *n syn* see WIT 3

asudden *adv syn* see SHORT 1

asunder *adv syn* see APART 3
idiom all to pieces, one part from the other, to shreds

as usual *adv syn* see USUALLY 1

asweat *adj syn* see SWEATY

as well *adv* 1 *syn* see ALSO 2
idiom over and above
2 *syn* see EVEN 1

as well as *prep syn* see BESIDES 1

as yet *adv syn* see HITHERTO 1

asylum *n* 1 *syn* see SHELTER 1
2 *syn* see REFUGE 1
rel inviolability; security
3 an institution for the care of the insane < demand for improved *asylums* >
syn booby hatch, ||bughouse, crazy house, loony bin, madhouse, ||nuthouse
rel farm, home, institution, sanatorium
idiom ||funny farm, insane (*or* lunatic) asylum, mental hospital (*or* institution), state hospital

asymmetric *adj syn* see LOPSIDED

at all *adv* 1 *syn* see EVER 5
2 *syn* see EVER 4

ataraxy *n syn* see EQUANIMITY

atavism *n syn* see REVERSION 1

ataxia *n syn* see CONFUSION 3

at close hand *adv syn* see CLOSE

atelier *n syn* see STUDIO

athenaeum *n syn* see LIBRARY

athirst *adj* 1 *syn* see THIRSTY 1
rel dehydrated, desiccated, dried up
2 *syn* see EAGER
con lackadaisical, languid, listless; autistic, withdrawn

athletic *adj syn* see MUSCULAR 2
rel active, energetic, strenuous, vigorous
con delicate; decadent, effete, flabby, soft

athletics *n pl* physical activities engaged in for exercise or pleasure < went in heavily for *athletics* >
syn games, sports
rel calisthenics, exercise, gymnastics; drill, practice, workout; amusement, diversion, entertainment, pastime, recreation

athwart *adv* 1 *syn* see ACROSS 1
2 *syn* see OVER 1

athwart *prep syn* see ACROSS

atiptoe *adj syn* see EXPECTANT 1

atmosphere *n* 1 *syn* see AIR 3
rel character, flavor, property, quality; characteristic, individuality, peculiarity; impression, suggestion
2 *syn* see ENVIRONMENT

atmospheric *adj syn* see AIRY 1

atom *n syn* see PARTICLE
rel dash, touch, trace; shade, smack, spice, soupçon, suggestion, suspicion, tincture, tinge

atomize *vb syn* see DESTROY 1

at once *adv* 1 *syn* see TOGETHER 1
2 *syn* see AWAY 3

atone *vb syn* see EXPIATE
rel compensate, pay, recompense, satisfy; appease, conciliate, propitiate
idiom set one's house in order

atone (for) *vb syn* see COMPENSATE 1

atramentous *adj syn* see BLACK 1

at random *adv syn* see ABOUT 4

atrocious *adj* 1 *syn* see OUTRAGEOUS 2
rel flagitious, infamous, iniquitous, vicious; barbarous, savage; glaring, rank; abominable, contemptible, despicable, execrable, odious, vile
con fine, righteous, upright, virtuous; benign, righteous, kindly
ant humane
2 *syn* see OFFENSIVE
rel displeasing, distasteful
con alluring, magnetic

atrociousness *n syn* see ENORMITY 1

atrocity *n syn* see ENORMITY 1

atrophy *n syn* see DETERIORATION 1

attach *vb syn* see FASTEN 1
rel associate; add, annex, append; bind, tie
con disassociate, dissociate; disembarrass, disencumber, disengage, disentangle
ant detach

attachment *n* 1 the state of being firmly attached to someone or something (as by affection, sympathy, or self-interest) < his *attachment* to an outworn code >
syn adherence, adhesion, constancy, faithfulness, fidelity, loyalty
rel firmness, staunchness, steadfastness; allegiance, devotion, fealty
con disloyalty, faithlessness, infidelity, unfaithfulness; aloofness, distance, remoteness; disinterest, disregard, unconcern, unmindfulness
ant detachment
2 *syn* see LOVE 1
rel piety; devotedness
con antipathy, disinclination, dislike; alienation, disaffection, estrangement
ant aversion

attack *vb* 1 to act in violent opposition < cavalry *attacked* the Indian camp >
syn aggress, assail, assault, beset, fall (on *or* upon), storm, strike
rel invade, irrupt; charge, raid, rush; besiege, blockade, encompass, invest; beleaguer, beset, harass, harry, press; turn (on)
idiom gang up on, light into, sail into, set upon, take the offensive
con defend, guard, protect, shield; combat, oppose, resist, withstand
2 to begin to work vigorously (as at a task) < *attack* a problem >
syn bang away (at), tackle
rel buckle (to *or* down *or* down to), fall to, pitch in, wade (in *or* into)
idiom address (*or* apply *or* devote) oneself to, give oneself up to
con dawdle, lag, poke, putter

attack *n* 1 an act of attacking especially in the form of an attempt to injure, destroy, or defame < insecticides that are essential for successful *attack* on insect pests >
syn aggression, assailment, assault, offense, offensive, onfall, onset, onslaught
rel charge, descent, drive, foray, push, raid, sally, sortie; blitz, incursion, inroad, surprise; action, battle
con championing, justification, protection, support, vindication; opposition, resistance; defending, guarding, protecting, sheltering
ant defense

2 action or an attitude in a struggle that calls for or is opposed by defense < his policy had always been one of *attack* >
syn aggression, aggressiveness, belligerence, combativeness, fight, pugnacity
rel bellicosity, chauvinism, jingoism, warmongering; activation, militarization, mobilization, muster
con submissiveness, yielding
3 an episode of bodily or mental disorder < a sudden *attack* of dizziness >
syn access, fit, seizure, spell, throe, turn; *compare* SIEGE
rel outbreak, paroxysm, spasm; affection, ailment, complaint, disease, disorder
attain vb syn see GAIN 1
idiom gain one's end, make good
attainable adj syn see AVAILABLE 1
attainment n syn see ACQUIREMENT
attempt vb syn see TRY 5
rel begin, commence, inaugurate, initiate, start; venture
idiom give (something) a try, take a crack (or whack) at
con accomplish, achieve, effect, execute, fulfill, perform; attain, compass, gain, reach
ant succeed
attempt n an effort made to do or accomplish something < made a determined *attempt* to improve her writing >
syn endeavor, essay, hassle, striving, struggle, trial, try, undertaking
rel care, effort, pains, trouble; beginning, commencement, initiation, offer, shy, start
con accomplishment, achievement, attainment, finish, fulfillment
attend vb 1 syn see LISTEN
idiom be attentive (to), give heed (to)
2 syn see TEND 2
rel govern, oversee, supervise; direct, handle, manage, regulate, run; aid, assist, help
3 syn see ACCOMPANY
rel associate, fraternize, join, mingle, mix
attendant adj syn see CONCOMITANT
attendant n syn see HELPER
attending adj syn see CONCOMITANT
attention n 1 a focusing of the mind on something < gave the problem careful *attention* >
syn application, concentration, consideration, debate, deliberation, heed, study
rel assiduity, diligence, industry, sedulity, sedulousness; notice, observation, regard, remark; absorption, engrossment, immersion, intentness
con absence, absentmindedness, abstraction, detachment, remoteness, withdrawal; disinterest, indifference, unconcern, unmindfulness
ant inattention
2 syn see NOTICE 1
rel awareness, consciousness, mindfulness, sensibility
con disregard, heedlessness, insensibility, unawareness, unconsciousness
3 syn see COURTESY 1

rel deference, homage, honor, reverence; benignity; considerateness, consideration, kindliness, solicitude
con neglect, negligence; aloofness, indifference, unconcern; discourtesy
attentive adj 1 concentrating one's attention on something < listeners *attentive* to the speaker's appeal >
syn advertent, arrect, heedful, intentive, observant, regardful
rel alert, aware, mindful; agog, eager, interested, keen; concentrating, earnest, intent; open-eared, open-eyed
idiom all ears (or eyes), on the ball, paying attention
con absorbed, abstracted, bemused, preoccupied; absentminded, daydreaming, faraway, oblivious, wandering, woolgathering
ant absent; inattentive
2 syn see THOUGHTFUL 3
con aloof, indifferent
ant inattentive; neglectful
attenuate vb 1 syn see THIN 1
rel lessen; sap; dissipate; constrict, contract, deflate, shrink
con amplify, dilate, distend, expand, inflate, swell; augment, enlarge, increase; enrich
2 syn see WEAKEN 1
3 syn see THIN 2
attenuate adj 1 syn see THIN 1
2 syn see THIN 2
attenuated adj syn see THIN 2
attest vb 1 syn see CERTIFY 1
rel confirm, corroborate, substantiate, verify; support, sustain, uphold, warrant; affirm, asseverate, depone, swear, testify
con confute, controvert, disprove, refute; contradict, deny, gainsay
2 syn see INDICATE 2
rel authenticate, confirm, substantiate
con falsify, misrepresent; distort, garble, pervert, twist, warp
ant belie
3 syn see TESTIFY 1
attestation n syn see TESTIMONY
at times adv syn see SOMETIMES
attire vb syn see CLOTHE
rel accouter, appoint, arm, equip, outfit
con bare, denude, dismantle, strip
ant divest
attire n syn see CLOTHES
attirement n syn see CLOTHES
attitude n 1 syn see POSTURE 1
rel air, demeanor, port, presence
2 syn see POSITION 1
rel point of view; bias, predilection, prejudice, prepossession
attitudinize vb syn see POSE 4
attorney n 1 syn see AGENT 2
rel alternate, locum tenens, stand-in, substitute, supply
2 syn see LAWYER
attorney-at-law n syn see LAWYER
attract vb 1 to exert an irresistible or compelling influence on < her beauty *attracted* all eyes >
syn allure, bewitch, captivate, charm, draw, enchant, fascinate, magnetize, take, wile
rel entice, lure, seduce, tempt; beguile, draw (in), intrigue, inveigle, suck (in); enrapture, entrance; court, invite, solicit

---

syn synonym(s)   **rel** related word(s)
ant antonym(s)   **con** contrasted word(s)
idiom idiomatic equivalent(s)
‖ use limited; if in doubt, see a dictionary

con fend (off), hold (off *or* away), rebuff, repulse; disgust, offend, revolt
ant repel
2 *syn* see INTEREST

attracting *adj syn* see ATTRACTIVE 1

attraction *n* 1 a quality that elicits admiration or pleased responsiveness < yielding to the *attraction* of the balmy afternoon >
syn allurement, appeal, attractiveness, call, draw, drawing power, lure, pull, seduction
rel charm, glamour, interest; delight, pleasure; bait, hook, snare
con offensiveness, repulsiveness, ugliness
2 a relationship characteristic of individuals that are drawn together naturally or involuntarily and exert a degree of influence on one another < the *attraction* between iron and the magnet >
syn affinity, sympathy
rel accord, concord, harmony
idiom drawing together
con conflict, discord, friction, tension

attractive *adj* 1 having the power to attract < an area *attractive* to wildlife >
syn alluring, appealing, attracting, bewitching, captivating, charming, drawing, enchanting, engaging, fascinating, glamorous, magnetic, mesmeric, prepossessing, seductive, siren
rel beautiful, bonny, comely, fair, lovely, pretty; Circean, enticing, fetching, luring, tempting; interesting, taking, winning; beckoning, come-hither, inviting, provocative, tantalizing, teasing; likable, simpatico
con abhorrent, distasteful, obnoxious, repugnant; loathsome, offensive, repulsive, revolting; antipathetic, unsympathetic
ant repellent, repelling; forbidding
2 *syn* see BEAUTIFUL
rel agreeable, goodly, ||likely, pleasing, sightly
con homely, ill-favored, plain, uncomely, unprepossessing
ant unattractive

attractiveness *n syn* see ATTRACTION 1

attribute *n* 1 *syn* see QUALITY 1
rel particularity, singularity, specialty; brand, earmark, impress, stamp
2 *syn* see SYMBOL 1

attribute *vb syn* see ASCRIBE
rel calendar, chronologize, date, place

attrition *n syn* see PENITENCE

attritional *adj syn* see REMORSEFUL

attune *vb syn* see HARMONIZE 3
rel balance, compensate, counterbalance; accord, agree; fix, rectify, regulate
idiom put in tune, set to rights (*or* in order)
con divide, separate, wean

||**atween** *prep syn* see BETWEEN 2

||**atwixt** *prep syn* see BETWEEN 2

atypical *adj syn* see ABNORMAL 1
rel irregular, unnatural; different, divergent; exceptional, odd, peculiar, queer, strange
con customary, usual
ant typical; representative

auberge *n syn* see HOTEL

au courant *adj* 1 *syn* see AWARE
2 *syn* see UP-TO-DATE
3 *syn* see FAMILIAR 3

audacious *adj* 1 *syn* see BRAVE 1

rel adventurous, daredevil, daring, foolhardy, rash, reckless, venturesome; brash, brazen, shameless
con calculating, cautious, chary, wary; judicious, prudent, sane, wise; careful, circumspect, discreet
2 *syn* see ADVENTUROUS
rel fearless, valiant, valorous
con careful, circumspect, discreet; calculating, cautious, chary, wary
3 *syn* see INSOLENT 2
4 free from constraint and formality < found life an *audacious* ever-changing adventure >
syn uncurbed, ungoverned, unhampered, uninhibited, unrestrained, untrammeled
rel emancipated, free, independent; easy, relaxed; careless, heedless, thoughtless; self-absorbed, self-centered, selfish
con checked, curbed, governed, hampered, inhibited, restrained, trammeled; careful, cautious, heedful, mindful, thoughtful; considerate, generous, self-abnegating, self-effacing; drab, dull, pedestrian

audacity *n syn* see TEMERITY
rel cheek, effrontery, face, gall; brass, brazenness, cockiness; forwardness, impudence, resolution; courage, mettle, spirit
con calculation, caution, wariness; shyness, timidity, timorousness; agitation, disquiet, nervousness, perturbation, trepidation
ant circumspection

audible *adj syn* see AURAL 1
ant inaudible

audience *n* 1 *syn* see HEARING 2
rel attention, consideration, ear
2 *syn* see FOLLOWING 2
rel admirers, devotees, fanciers, fans, votaries

audile *adj syn* see AUDITORY

audit *n syn* see EXAMINATION
rel investigation, probe; check, control, corrective

audition *n syn* see HEARING 2

auditory *adj* of, relating to, or experienced through the sense of hearing < *auditory* disorders >
syn acoustic, audile, aural; *compare* AURAL 1

au fait *adj* 1 *syn* see ABLE
2 *syn* see FAMILIAR 3
3 *syn* see DECOROUS 1

au fond *adv syn* see ESSENTIALLY 1

Augean stable *n syn* see SINK 1

aught (*or* ought) *n syn* see ZERO 1

augment *vb* 1 *syn* see INCREASE 1
2 *syn* see INCREASE 2

augment *n syn* see INCREASE 1
rel exalt, hike, raise
con attenuate, decrease, dwindle; abridge; alleviate, assuage, relieve
ant abate

augmentation *n* 1 *syn* see ACCOMPANIMENT 1
rel adjunct, annex, attachment, fixture, reinforcement; bonus, boot, extra, plus
2 *syn* see ADDITION
con subtraction

augur *n syn* see PROPHET

augur *vb* 1 *syn* see FORETELL
rel argue, bespeak, indicate

2 to indicate or suggest a future probability <their enthusiasm *augurs* well for the success of the enterprise>
syn betoken, bode, forebode, foreshadow, foreshow, foretoken, omen, portend, presage, promise
rel hint, imply, intimate, suggest; prefigure, shadow (forth)
idiom bid fair to, give promise (*or* fair promise) of, hold out hope of, lead one to believe (*or* expect)

augury *n syn* see FORETOKEN
rel anticipation, premonition, presentiment
con accomplishment, effecting, effectuation, fulfillment; actualization, materialization, realization; appearance, emergence, forthcoming, issuance

august *adj syn* see GRAND 1
rel splendid, sublime, superb; impressive, moving, striking; awe-inspiring, awful, fearful, overwhelming

au naturel *adj syn* see NUDE 2

aura *n syn* see AIR 3
rel appearance, aspect, suggestion; aureole, radiance

aural *adj* **1** heard or perceived with the ear <responded to *aural* stimuli>
syn audible, auricular; *compare* AUDITORY
2 *syn* see AUDITORY

aureate *adj syn* see RHETORICAL
rel baroque, rococo
con moderate, quiet, restrained, sober, temperate
ant austere

auricular *n syn* see AURAL 1

aurora *n syn* see DAWN 1

auslander *n syn* see STRANGER

auspex *n syn* see PROPHET

auspices *n pl syn* see BACKING

auspicious *adj* **1** *syn* see FAVORABLE 5
rel hopeful; golden, halcyon, roseate, rosy
con ominous, portentous, unpropitious; adverse, antagonistic
ant inauspicious; ill-omened
2 *syn* see TIMELY 1

austere *adj* **1** *syn* see SEVERE 1
rel bald, bare, simple, unadorned, undecorated, unembellished, unornamented; earnest, grave, serious, sober, somber
con complicated, elaborate, fancy, flamboyant, fussy, ornate; frivolous, light, light-minded, shallow, superficial
2 *syn* see ACRID
rel biting, keen, rough
con bland, mellow, smooth, soft
3 *syn* see GRIM 2

autarchic *adj* **1** *syn* see ABSOLUTE 4
rel commanding, dogmatic, imperious; nonconstitutional, undemocratic
2 *syn* see FREE 1
rel self-dependent, self-reliant, self-sufficient

autarkic *adj syn* see FREE 1
rel self-dependent, self-reliant, self-sufficient

authentic *adj* **1** worthy of acceptance because of accuracy <an *authentic* portrayal of ancient customs>
syn convincing, credible, faithful, trustworthy, trusty
rel accurate, dependable, factual, reliable, sure; solid, sound, straight, valid; authoritative, cathedral, official, standard
idiom all wool and a yard wide; to be depended (*or* relied) on
con incredible, unconvincing, untrustworthy; equivocal, obscure, uncertain, vague; hypothetical, purported, putative, supposed, supposititious; debatable, doubtful, questionable; nonstandard
ant inauthentic
2 being exactly as appears or is claimed <an *authentic* masterpiece>
syn blown-in-the-bottle, bona fide, genuine, indubitable, pukka, questionless, real, right, simon-pure, sure-enough, true, undoubted, undubitable, unquestionable, veritable, very
rel cognizable, identifiable, knowable, recognizable; honest, pure, unadulterated, unalloyed
con deceptive, delusive, delusory, false, misleading, wrong; unidentifiable, unrecognizable
ant spurious
3 *syn* see CERTAIN 3

authenticate *vb* **1** *syn* see CONFIRM 2
rel accredit, approve, endorse; demonstrate, prove, test, try; avouch, vouch (for)
con reject, repudiate, spurn; contradict, deny, negate
ant impugn

author *n syn* see FATHER 2
rel origin, source; ancestor, parent, procreator

authoritarian *adj* **1** *syn* see DICTATORIAL
rel heavy-handed, high-handed, oppressive, strict, stringent
ant libertarian; anarchistic
2 *syn* see TOTALITARIAN 1
rel fascistic, nazi; patriarchal
ant democratic

authoritative *adj* **1** *syn* see OFFICIAL
2 *syn* see TRUE 9
rel attested, authenticated, circumstantiated, confirmed, proven, validated, verified; convincing, indisputable, irrefutable, sure, unrefutable; cathedral, cathedratic
con contestable, controversial, debatable, disputable, refutable; dubious, questionable, suspect, unreliable
3 *syn* see DICTATORIAL
4 *syn* see ORTHODOX 1

authority *n* **1** *syn* see EXPERT
2 *syn* see POWER 7
rel governance, government, rule
3 *syn* see INFLUENCE 1
rel example, exemplar, ideal, model, pattern, standard; force, power, pressure

authorization *n syn* see PERMISSION

authorize *vb* **1** to invest with power or the right to act <I did not *authorize* him to speak for me>
syn accredit, commission, empower, enable, license
rel approve, countenance, endorse; aid, assist, help, support, subserve; advance, facilitate, forward, further, promote

---

syn synonym(s)   *rel* related word(s)
ant antonym(s)   *con* contrasted word(s)
idiom idiomatic equivalent(s)
‖ use limited; if in doubt, see a dictionary

con bar, disallow, enjoin, forbid, interdict, prohibit
2 *syn* see ENTITLE 2
rel allow, let, permit; approve, countenance, endorse
idiom give one the right to
3 *syn* see INVEST 2

auto *n syn* see CAR
auto *vb* 1 *syn* see DRIVE 5
2 *syn* see RIDE 1
autobiographer *n syn* see BIOGRAPHER
autobiographist *n syn* see BIOGRAPHER
autobiography *n syn* see BIOGRAPHY
rel diary, journal, letters
autocar *n syn* see CAR
autochthonous *adj syn* see NATIVE 2
con alien, extraneous, extrinsic, foreign; imported, introduced
ant naturalized
autocracy *n syn* see TYRANNY
autocratic *adj syn* see ABSOLUTE 4
rel arrogant, haughty, overbearing, overweening
con deferential, submissive, yielding; forbearing, indulgent, lenient, tolerant
autodidactic *adj syn* see SELF-TAUGHT
autograph *vb syn* see SIGN 1
autognosis *n syn* see SELF-KNOWLEDGE
autoist *n syn* see MOTORIST
automatic *adj* 1 *syn* see SPONTANEOUS
rel prompt, quick, ready; accustomed, confirmed, habitual, habituated
2 *syn* see PERFUNCTORY
automaton *n* 1 *syn* see ROBOT 1
2 *syn* see ROBOT 2
automobile *n syn* see CAR
automobilist *n syn* see MOTORIST
autonomous *adj syn* see FREE 1
rel self-governed; unconstrained, uncontrolled, unsubordinated
con controlled, subordinated; governed, ruled; affiliated, allied
autopsy *n* examination of the body after death usually to determine the cause of death < the *autopsy* of a murder victim>
syn necropsy, ‖post, postmortem, postmortem examination
autoschediasm *n syn* see IMPROVISATION
autoschediastic *adj syn* see EXTEMPORANEOUS
auxiliary *adj* capable of supplying or intended to supply aid or support < an *auxiliary* police unit>
syn accessory, adjuvant, ancillary, appurtenant, collateral, contributory, subservient, subsidiary
rel complementary, supplementary; peripheral, secondary, subordinate, tributary; backing, supporting, upholding; aiding, assisting, helping
con chief, leading, main, principal; sole, solitary, unique
avail *vb syn* see BENEFIT
rel answer, fill, fulfill, meet, satisfy
con damage, harm, hurt, injure
avail *n syn* see USE 3
rel interest; appositeness, suitability
con inappropriateness, unsuitableness
available *adj* 1 that is accessible or may be obtained < the best pen *available* at the present time>
syn attainable, disponible, gettable, obtainable, procurable, securable

rel accessible, convenient, handy
idiom to be had
con unattainable, unobtainable; absent, deficient, lacking, missing
ant unavailable
2 *syn* see PURCHASABLE 1
avarice *n syn* see CUPIDITY
rel frugality, parsimony, thrift; miserliness, niggardliness, parsimoniousness, stinginess; acquisitiveness, covetousness, graspingness, piggishness
con extravagance; bountifulness, bounty, generosity, liberality, munificence, openhandedness
ant prodigality
avariciousness *n syn* see CUPIDITY
avenge *vb* to inflict punishment by way of repayment for < *avenge* an insult>
syn redress, revenge, venge, vindicate
rel compensate, pay (back), pay out, recompense, repay, requite, retaliate, retribute; chasten, chastise, punish; correct, right
idiom get an eye for an eye, get even with, settle accounts, wreak one's vengeance
con condone, disregard, ignore, overlook; absolve, amnesty, forgive, pardon, remit; bear, endure, stand, suffer, tolerate
avengement *n syn* see RETALIATION
avenging *n syn* see RETALIATION
avenue *n* 1 *syn* see WAY 1
‖2 *syn* see DRIVEWAY
aver *vb syn* see ASSERT 1
rel defend, hold, justify, maintain
con deny
average *n* something (as a number, quantity, or condition) that represents a middle point between extremes < somewhat sweeter than *average*>
syn mean, median, norm, par
ant maximum; minimum
average *adj syn* see MEDIUM
rel common, familiar, ordinary; customary, usual
idiom common or garden variety
con choice, excellent, exceptional, prime, superior; conspicuous, noticeable, outstanding, prominent; bad, inferior, low-grade, poor, punk
averagely *adv syn* see ENOUGH 2
avernal *adj syn* see INFERNAL 2
averse *adj syn* see DISINCLINED
rel balky, contrary, perverse; flinching, quailing, recoiling, resistant, shrinking; uncongenial, unsympathetic
ant avid (of *or* for)
aversion *n* 1 *syn* see DISLIKE
rel antagonism, antipathy, hostility; dread, fear, horror
con bias, partiality; leaning, propensity, taste
ant predilection
2 *syn* see ANTIPATHY 2
rel abhorrence, distaste, repellency, repugnance, repulsion, revulsion; disgust, dread, loathing
con bias, partiality, penchant; flair, inclination, leaning, taste
ant attachment; predilection
3 *syn* see ABOMINATION 2
ant delight
aversive *adj syn* see ANTIPATHETIC 2

avert *vb* **1** *syn* see TURN 6
rel remove, transfer
2 *syn* see PREVENT 2
rel anticipate; balk, foil, frustrate, thwart;
check, halt, stay, stop
con advance, further, promote

aviary *n* a house, enclosure, or large cage
for confining live birds < the zoo's *aviary* >
syn birdhouse
rel dovecote, dovehouse; columbary, pigeon house

aviator *n* *syn* see PILOT 2

avid *adj* *syn* see EAGER
rel covetous, craving, desirous, wanting,
wishful; importunate, insistent, pressing,
urgent; gluttonous, omnivorous
con aloof, disinterested, uninterested;
disinclined, indisposed, loath
ant indifferent; averse

avidity *n* *syn* see CUPIDITY

avoid *vb* *syn* see ESCAPE 2
rel avert, deflect, divert, obviate, prevent,
ward (off); debar, exclude, preclude; forbid, prohibit
idiom give a miss (*or* a wide berth), have
no truck with, set one's face against, steer
clear of, turn one's back on
con court, invite, solicit
ant face; meet

avoidance *n* *syn* see ESCAPE 2

avouch *vb* *syn* see ASSERT 1
rel confirm, corroborate; acknowledge,
admit, confess, own
con deny, impugn

avow *vb* **1** *syn* see ASSERT 1
rel defend, maintain, vindicate; asseverate,
swear, testify
2 *syn* see ACKNOWLEDGE 1
con repudiate, withdraw

avowry *n* *syn* see PATRON SAINT

await *vb* *syn* see EXPECT 1
rel abide, stay, wait
idiom bide one's time, sweat (*or* tough) it
out

awake *vb* **1** *syn* see WAKE 1

awake *adj* *syn* see AWARE
rel vigilant, watchful; aroused, awakened,
roused, stirred up; excited
con drowsy, sleepy, slumberous, somnolent; inactive, inert, supine

awaken *vb* **1** *syn* see WAKE 1
2 *syn* see STIR 1
rel fire, inflame; alert
idiom stir the feelings (*or* blood) of
con arrest, check, retard, subdue; calm,
compose, restrain

awanting *prep* *syn* see WITHOUT 2

award *vb* **1** *syn* see GRANT 1
rel allocate, allot, apportion, assign;
dower, endow, endue
2 *syn* see GIVE 2

award *n* *syn* see HONOR 2

aware *adj* marked by realization, perception, or knowledge often of something not
generally realized, perceived, or known
< *aware* of her own inner weakness >
syn alive, apprehensive, au courant,
awake, cognizant, conscious, conversant,

knowing, mindful, sensible, sentient, ware,
witting
rel acquainted, apprised, informed; alert,
heedful; impressionable, perceptive, receptive
con anesthetic, impassible, insensible,
insensitive; ignorant, unknowing
ant unaware

awash *adj* *syn* see FULL 1

away *adv* **1** from this or that place
< come *away* at once >
syn hence, thence
rel forth, out, therefrom
2 at some distance from a place expressed
or implied < he lived several blocks
away >
syn off, over
rel afar, far; apart, aside
3 without hesitation or delay < fire *away*
when you see the target >
syn at once, directly, first off, forthwith,
immediately, instanter, instantly, now,
PDQ, right, right away, right off, straight,
straight away, straight off, straightway
rel momentarily, promptly, ‖pronto,
punctually; expeditiously, quickly, speedily, swiftly

away *adj* *syn* see ABSENT 1

awe *n* *syn* see REVERENCE 2
rel esteem, regard, respect, veneration,
worship; admiration, amazement, wonder,
wonderment
con despite, scorn; arrogance, insolence,
superciliousness

awe *vb* *syn* see FRIGHTEN

aweless *adj* *syn* see BRAVE 1

awful *adj* *syn* see FEARFUL 3
rel impressive, moving; august, imposing,
majestic; splendid, superb; grave, serious,
solemn; ominous, portentous

‖awful *adv* *syn* see VERY 1

awfully *adv* *syn* see VERY 1

awkward *adj* **1** *syn* see CLUMSY 1
rel blundering, bumbling, bungling;
clownish, lubberly, oafish; cumbrous,
hulking, ponderous
idiom all thumbs
2 marked by a lack of grace, ease, skill, or
fitness (as in action or speech) < his *awkward* approach to the problem >
syn bumbling, clumsy, gauche, halting,
ham-handed, heavy-handed, inept, lumbering, maladroit, unhandy, unhappy,
wooden; *compare* CLUMSY 1
rel rigid, stiff; discomfited, disconcerted,
embarrassed; bunglesome, bungling, inefficient, inexpert, unskillful
con adept, adroit, dexterous, expert, finished, polished, proficient, skilled, skillful,
smooth; easy, effortless, facile, simple
ant deft; graceful
3 *syn* see INCONVENIENT
4 *syn* see INFELICITOUS

awry *adv* (*or adj*) **1** deviating from a
straight line or direction < the coverlet
was pulled *awry* >
syn askance, askant, askew, ‖cam, cock=
a-hoop, cockeyed, crookedly
rel aside, aslant, obliquely, slantways
con even, straight, true; directly, undeviatingly
2 *syn* see AMISS 2
rel erroneously, faultily, untruly; aside

ax *vb syn* see DISMISS 3
axiom *n* 1 *syn* see PRINCIPLE 1
2 *syn* see MAXIM

‖**ayah** *n syn* see NURSEMAID
aye *adv syn* see YES 1

B

Babbitt *n syn* see PHILISTINE
babblative *adj syn* see TALKATIVE
babble *vb* 1 *syn* see GIBBER
2 to talk nonsensically <silly people *babbling* on about trivia>
syn blabber, blather, drivel, drool, gabble, prate, prattle, twaddle, ‖waffle
rel clack, jaw, rattle, run on, yak, yammer, yap
idiom run off at the mouth
3 *syn* see CHAT 1
babble *n* 1 *syn* see CHATTER
2 *syn* see GIBBERISH 1
babe *n syn* see BABY 1
babel *n syn* see DIN
con hush, noiselessness; peace, quiet, silence
babushka *n syn* see KERCHIEF 1
baby *n* 1 a very young child esp. in the first year of life <the love of a mother for her *baby*>
syn babe, bantling, infant, neonate, newborn
rel bambino, little one, toddler, tot; nursling, suckling, weanling; bratling
idiom babe in arms
2 *syn* see WEAKLING
‖3 *syn* see GIRL FRIEND 2
baby *vb* to treat with special, excessive, or fond care <*baby* a sick husband>
syn cater (to), cocker, coddle, cosset, cotton, humor, indulge, mollycoddle, pamper, spoil
rel dry-nurse, wet-nurse; dote (on *or* upon), favor; gratify, please, satisfy
con control, discipline, restrain; abuse, ill-treat, ill-use, mistreat, oppress; neglect, overlook, slight
baby buggy *n syn* see BABY CARRIAGE
baby carriage *n* a four-wheeled push carriage with a folding top for a baby <used the *baby carriage* to wheel home firewood>
syn baby buggy, bassinet, ‖perambulator, ‖pram
babyhood *n syn* see INFANCY 1
babyish *adj syn* see CHILDISH
bacchanal *n syn* see ORGY 2
bacchanalia *n syn* see ORGY 2
back *n* 1 the surface or part most remote from the front <the *back* of his neck>
syn posterior, rear, rearward
rel extremity, tail; reverse
con anterior
ant front
2 *syn* see SPINE

back *adv syn* see ABOUT 6
back *adj* 1 distant from settled areas <*back* regions in the hill country>
syn frontier, outlandish, remote, unsettled
rel uncultivated, uninhabited, unoccupied, unpopulated, wild

con built-up, settled, urban
2 *syn* see POSTERIOR 2
ant front
back *vb* 1 *syn* see SUPPORT 2
rel aid, assist, help; abet
2 *syn* see CAPITALIZE
3 *syn* see MOUNT 5
4 *syn* see RECEDE 1
con advance, progress
back answer *n syn* see RETORT 2
backbiting *n syn* see DETRACTION
rel animadversion, reflection, stricture; abuse, invective, obloquy, vituperation
con accolade, commendation, encomium, eulogy, laudation, paean, panegyric, praise, tribute; adulation, blarney, compliment, flattery, soft soap
backbiting *adj syn* see LIBELOUS
backbone *n* 1 *syn* see SPINE
2 *syn* see FORTITUDE
rel hardihood; heart
con irresoluteness, irresolution
ant backbonelessness, spinelessness
3 *syn* see MAINSTAY
backchat *n syn* see BANTER
backcountry *n syn* see FRONTIER 2
‖**backdoor trots** *n pl but sing or pl in constr syn* see DIARRHEA
back down *vb* to withdraw from a previous agreement or stand <a politician *backing down* on an earlier promise>
syn back off, back out, backpedal, backwater, crawfish (out), cry off, declare off, renege, resile, welsh
rel disavow, recall, recant, retract, take back, withdraw; backtrack; beg off, weasel (out); balk, demur, hold back, stickle
idiom get out of, go back on
backer *n syn* see SPONSOR
rel ally, protagonist; bankroller, ‖grubstaker, ‖meal ticket, promoter
backer–up *n syn* see SPONSOR
backfire *vb* to have the reverse of the desired effect <the new policy *backfired* disastrously>
syn backlash, boomerang, bounce (back), kick back
rel fall (through), fizzle, miscarry, miss, ricochet
idiom come to grief, go on the rocks, ‖lay an egg
con come off, succeed, work out
backhouse *n syn* see PRIVY 1
backing *n* aid or support given to an undertaking <the project had the *backing* of the city fathers>
syn aegis, auspices, patronage, sponsorship
rel championship, cooperation, fosterage; guidance, tutelage; encouragement; assistance, help, support
backland *n syn* see FRONTIER 2

backlash *vb syn* SEE BACKFIRE
backlog *n syn* SEE RESERVE
back of *prep syn* SEE ABAFT
back off *vb syn* SEE BACK DOWN
back out *vb syn* SEE BACK DOWN
backpack *n* a carrying case (as of canvas or nylon) held on the back by shoulder straps < carried his supplies in a *backpack* >
syn haversack, knapsack, pack, packsack, rucksack
backpedal *vb syn* SEE BACK DOWN
rel dodge, duck, elude, evade, get around, shirk, sidestep
backset *n syn* SEE SETBACK
backside *n syn* SEE BUTTOCKS
backslide *vb syn* SEE LAPSE
rel regress, retrovert, return, revert; defect, desert, tergiversate, turn
idiom fall away, fall (*or* sink *or* slide *or* slip) back into, give in to
backsliding *n syn* SEE LAPSE 2
backstabbing *n syn* SEE DETRACTION
backstage *adj or adv* off or away from the part of the stage visible to the audience < *backstage* sounds that gave the impression of a storm >
syn offstage
idiom behind the scenes
ant onstage
backstop *vb syn* SEE SUPPORT 2
back talk *n* impudent and insolent talk < do as you're told and no *back talk* >
syn guff, ||jaw, ||lip, mouth, sass, sauce
rel cheek, impudence, insolence
||**backveld** *n syn* SEE FRONTIER 2
backward *adv syn* SEE ABOUT 6
backward *adj* 1 directed, turned, or executed backward < the *backward* swimming of the crayfish >
syn retral, retrograde
rel inverted, reversed
ant advance, forward
2 *syn* SEE DISINCLINED
rel bashful, diffident
3 *syn* SEE SHY 1
4 *syn* SEE RETARDED
5 holding to outworn or traditional views, ideas, or principles < had a *backward* attitude toward social inferiors >
syn benighted, ignorant, unenlightened, unprogressive
rel conservative, reactionary; obtuse, stupid, thickheaded; bigoted, hidebound, narrow; blind; unenlightened, uninformed
con advanced, aware, enlightened, forward-looking, progressive, unbenighted
6 not developing or progressing especially in economic and social areas < *backward* nations using primitive farming methods >
syn behindhand, underdeveloped, undeveloped, unprogressive
rel poor, struggling; medieval; benighted, retarded, uncultivated, uncultured
idiom behind the times
con forward-looking, progressive; civilized, cultivated, cultured; modern
ant advanced

backwash *n syn* SEE FRONTIER 2
backwater *n syn* SEE FRONTIER 2
backwater *vb syn* SEE BACK DOWN
rel dodge, duck, elude, evade, get around, shirk, sidestep
backwoods *n pl but sing or pl in constr*
syn SEE FRONTIER 2
||**backwoodser** *n syn* SEE RUSTIC
backwoodsman *n syn* SEE RUSTIC
bad *adj* 1 falling short of a standard of what is satisfactory < a *bad* repair job >
syn amiss, ||bum, ||crappy, dissatisfactory, poor, ||punk, rotten, unsatisfactory, up, wrong
rel deficient, inadequate, inferior; careless, slipshod; defective, disordered, off, unsound; execrable, ||lousy, miserable, ||pisspoor, wretched; inadmissible, objectionable, unacceptable; insufferable, intolerable
idiom below par, not up to snuff (*or* scratch)
con excellent, fine, meritorious; acceptable, adequate, sound
2 *syn* SEE WRONG 1
rel arrant, peccant; graceless, improper, indecorous, untoward; disorderly, misbehaving, naughty, rowdy, ruffianly, unruly; froward, perverse
ant good
3 *syn* SEE EVIL 5
4 *syn* SEE EVIL 6
5 having undergone decay < one *bad* apple can spoil the barrel >
syn decayed, putrid, rotten, spoiled
rel fusty, stale; mildewed, moldered, moldy, moth-eaten, musty, rancid, worm-eaten, decomposed, putrefied, putrifacted; tainted, turned
con crisp, dewy, fresh, sweet, unspoiled; choice, picked, prime
ant good
6 *syn* SEE NAUGHTY 1
7 *syn* SEE TOUGH 8
8 arousing discomfort or distaste < a *bad* smell >
syn ||chiselly, disagreeable, displeasing, rotten, sour, unhappy, unpleasant
rel disgusting, foul, nauseating, noisome, noxious, offensive, repulsive, sickening; abhorrent, hateful, loathsome, obnoxious; uneasy; thankless, ungrateful; distasteful, distressing, sticky; ungracious, unhandsome
con agreeable, pleasant, pleasing, refreshing, soothing; unoffensive
9 *syn* SEE HARMFUL
10 *syn* SEE DOWNCAST
11 *syn* SEE NULL
bad actor *n syn* SEE TROUBLEMAKER
bad books *n pl syn* SEE DISLIKE
badge *n* 1 *syn* SEE INSIGNIA
2 *syn* SEE HONOR 2
badger *vb syn* SEE BAIT 2
rel plague, tease, worry
badinage *n syn* SEE BANTER
rel chaffing, guying, japery, joshing, kidding, sport
badland *n syn* SEE WASTE 1
||**bad lot** *n syn* SEE WASTREL 1
badly *adv* 1 *syn* SEE HARD 5
2 *syn* SEE AMISS 2
ant well

---

syn synonym(s)	*rel* related word(s)
ant antonym(s)	*con* contrasted word(s)
idiom idiomatic equivalent(s)
|| use limited; if in doubt, see a dictionary

badman *n syn* see OUTLAW
   rel criminal; villain; hood, hoodlum, hooligan, thug; blackguard, devil, knave, rascal, rapscallion, rascallion, rogue, scoundrel

bad–tempered *adj syn* see ILL-TEMPERED
   rel cantankerous, cranky, crusty, temperamental, touchy
   con forbearing, long-suffering, patient
   ant good-tempered

Baedeker *n syn* see HANDBOOK

baffle *vb syn* see FRUSTRATE 1
   rel confound, dumbfound, flummox, mystify, nonplus, puzzle; addle, ball up, befuddle, confuse, fog, mix up, muddle; discomfit, disconcert, embarrass, faze, rattle
   con enlighten, illuminate

bag *n* 1 a container made of a flexible material and open or opening at the top <a grocery *bag*>
   syn ‖poke, pouch, sack
   ‖2 *syn* see HAG 2

bag *vb syn* see CATCH 1
   rel clench, ‖cop, ‖glom, hook, land, nab, net, sack, scoop
   idiom lay by the heels

baggage *n syn* see WANTON

‖bagged *adj syn* see INTOXICATED 1

bagnio *n syn* see BROTHEL

bail *n syn* see GUARANTEE 1

bail *vb syn* see DIP 2

bailiwick *n syn* see FIELD
   rel district, jurisdiction, neighborhood, place, quarter, realm; beat, circuit, round, walk

bait *vb* 1 *syn* see MOLEST
   2 to persist in tormenting or harassing another < *baiting* him with gibes about his humble origin>
   syn badger, bullyrag, chivy, heckle, hector, hound, ride
   rel annoy, bother, bedevil, devil, rag, worry; harass, harry, haze, vex; ‖bug, nag, pester, push around
   3 *syn* see LURE

bait *n* 1 *syn* see LURE 2
   ‖2 *syn* see SNACK

bake *vb* 1 *syn* see BURN 3
   2 *syn* see FIRE 6

baking *adj syn* see HOT 1

balance *n* 1 the stability resulting from the equalization of opposing forces <keeping his emotional *balance* when under stress>
   syn counterpoise, equilibrium, equipoise, equiponderation, poise, stasis
   rel collectedness, composure, cool, coolness, coolth, equanimity, repose, sangfroid; aplomb, assurance, self-assurance, self-possession; control, self-control, stability, steadiness; stagnancy, stagnation
   con imbalance, unbalance; instability, nervousness, shakiness, uncontrol, unsteadiness
   2 *syn* see SYMMETRY
   rel congruity, consistency, correspondence, sameness
   con disbalance, disharmony, disproportion, incongruity, inconsistency, irregularity, overbalance, unbalance
   ant imbalance
   3 *syn* see REMAINDER

balance *vb syn* see COMPENSATE 1

   rel adjust, attune, harmonize, tune; accord, agree, correspond; even, level, square
   idiom strike a balance

bald *adj* 1 *syn* see HAIRLESS
   rel bobbed, clipped, cropped, polled, shaven, sheared
   con bushy, hairy, hirsute, shaggy; unshaven, unshorn; fleecy, furry, woolly; downy, fuzzy, pilose, pubescent
   2 *syn* see BARE 1
   rel austere, severe; plain, unadorned, undecorated, unembellished, ungarnished, unornamented; colorless, lackluster, lifeless, lusterless, uncolored

balderdash *n syn* see NONSENSE 2

baldhead *n* one who has a bald head
   syn baldpate, ‖baldy, ‖skinhead

baldpate *n syn* see BALDHEAD

‖baldy *n syn* see BALDHEAD

balefire *n syn* see BEACON 1

baleful *adj syn* see SINISTER
   rel deadly, evil, harmful, pernicious; bodeful, foreboding; unfavorable, unpromising
   con auspicious, benign, favorable, promising, propitious; advantageous, beneficial
   ant beneficent
   2 *syn* see OMINOUS

balk *n syn* see TIMBER 2

balk *vb* 1 *syn* see FRUSTRATE 1
   idiom stand in the way of
   con back, support, uphold; aid, assist, help
   ant forward
   2 *syn* see DEMUR
   rel decline, refuse, turn down; flinch, hang back, quail, recoil, shrink
   con capitulate, give in

balky *adj syn* see CONTRARY 3
   rel immovable, inflexible, unbending, unmanageable; averse, disinclined, hesitant, indisposed, loath, reluctant
   con subdued, submissive, tame

ball *n* a more or less spherical body or mass <a *ball* of string>
   syn globe, orb, rondure, round, sphere
   rel egg, oval, ovoid

ball *vb* to form into a more or less spherical body or mass < *balled* the cookie dough with her hands>
   syn conglobate, conglobe, ensphere, round, sphere
   rel bead, pill; clot, wad

balladmonger *n syn* see POETASTER

ball and chain *n* 1 *syn* see RESTRICTION 1
   ‖2 *syn* see WIFE

ballast *vb syn* see STABILIZE

ballerina *n syn* see DANCER

ballet girl *n syn* see DANCER

ballot *n* 1 a piece of paper used to cast a vote in an election <deliberately spoiled his *ballot*>
   syn ticket, vote
   rel Australian ballot, Indiana ballot, Massachusetts ballot, office-block ballot, office-group ballot, party-column ballot, secret ballot
   2 *syn* see SUFFRAGE

ballot *vb syn* see ELECT 2

‖ballup *n syn* see CONFUSION 3

ball up *vb syn* see CONFUSE 2

ballyhoo *vb syn* see TOUT
balm *n* 1 *syn* see OINTMENT
   2 *syn* see FRAGRANCE
balm *vb syn* see CALM
balmy *adj* 1 *syn* see SWEET 2
   rel musky; refreshing, rejuvenating, re-storative; pleasant, pleasing
   2 *syn* see GENTLE 1
   rel agreeable, delightful, gratifying, pleasant, pleasing; allaying, assuaging, balsamic, easing, lightening, relieving, soothing
   con annoying, bothering, bothersome, irking, irksome, vexing
   ‖3 *syn* see FOOLISH 2
‖**baloney** *n syn* see NONSENSE 2
balustrade *n syn* see RAILING
bamboozle *vb syn* see DUPE
   rel bilk, diddle, swindle
ban *vb syn* see FORBID
   rel illegalize, outlaw
   con approve, authorize; suffer, tolerate
ban *n syn* see TABOO
banal *adj syn* see INSIPID 3
   rel hackneyed, pedestrian, trite, warmed-over; bromidic, commonplace, corny, platitudinous, stock; bewhiskered, hoary, old; asinine, fatuous, silly, simple
   con fresh, new, novel; different, uncommon, unusual; stimulating, zesty; choice, rare, recherché
   ant original
banality *n syn* see COMMONPLACE
banausic *adj* 1 *syn* see DULL 9
   2 *syn* see MATERIALISTIC
band *n syn* see STRIP 1
   rel belt, border, edge, line; tape; fascia, taenia; streak, vein
band *vb* 1 *syn* see BELT 1
   2 *syn* see UNITE 2
   rel amalgamate, unionize; consociate; club, team (up)
   con disintegrate, disperse, dissolve, separate
   ant break up, disband
band *n* 1 *syn* see COMPANY 4
   rel assembly, bevy, body, bunch, covey, group; detachment, detail
   2 *syn* see GROUP 1
   3 *syn* see ORCHESTRA
bandage *vb* to cover with a bandage
   < *bandage* wounds >
   syn bind, dress
bandanna *n syn* see KERCHIEF 1
bandar–log *n syn* see CHATTERBOX
bandbox *adj syn* see DAPPER
bandeau *n syn* see STRIP 1
banderole *n syn* see FLAG
‖**bandido** *n syn* see OUTLAW
   rel brigand, footpad, highwayman, holdup man; bravo, cutthroat, gunman, villain; gangster, mobster, racketeer
banding *n syn* see STRIP 1
bandit 1 *n syn* see OUTLAW
   rel brigand, footpad, highwayman, holdup man; bravo, cutthroat, villain; gangster, mobster, racketeer; jayhawker
   2 *syn* see MARAUDER

syn synonym(s)   *rel* related word(s)
ant antonym(s)   *con* contrasted word(s)
idiom idiomatic equivalent(s)
‖ use limited; if in doubt, see a dictionary

bandwagon *n syn* see FASHION 3
bandy *vb syn* see EXCHANGE 3
   rel chuck, flip, pitch, throw, toss; banter; answer, repay, retort
   idiom bat (*or* beat) back and forth
bandy *adj syn* see BOWLEGGED
bandy–legged *adj syn* see BOWLEGGED
bane *n* 1 *syn* see POISON
   2 *syn* see DOWNFALL 2
baneful *adj* 1 *syn* see PERNICIOUS
   rel injurious; insalubrious, noisome, unhealthy, unwholesome
   con benign, favorable, propitious; advantageous, helpful, profitable; healthful, salubrious, salutary, wholesome
   ant beneficial
   2 *syn* see OMINOUS
‖**bang** *vb syn* see SURPASS 1
bang *n* 1 *syn* see BLOW 1
   2 a loud percussive or explosive noise
   < slammed the book shut with a *bang* >
   syn blast, boom, burst, clap, crack, crash, slam, smash, wham
   rel noise, report, sound; discharge, explosion, pop, shot; howl, roar, roll, rumble, thunder
   3 *syn* see THRILL
   4 *syn* see SMASH 6
   5 *syn* see VIGOR 2
bang *adv syn* see JUST 1
bang away (at) *vb syn* see ATTACK 2
bang–up *adj syn* see EXCELLENT
banish *vb* to eject by force or authority from a country, state, or sovereignty
   < *banish* an enemy of the king >
   syn cast out, deport, displace, exile, expatriate, expel, expulse, ‖lag, ostracize, oust, relegate, run out, transport; *compare* EJECT 1
   rel disfellowship, excommunicate, rusticate; debar, exclude, shut out; drive out, eject, evict, turn out; bump, can, cashier, discharge, dismiss, fire, put out, sack; blackball, blacklist, boycott
banishment *n syn* see EXILE 1
banister *n syn* see RAILING
bank *n* 1 *syn* see PILE 1
   rel snowbank; snowdrift; cloudage, fogbank
   2 *syn* see SHORE
   rel bankside, levee, riverfront, streamside; lakefront, lakeshore, lakeside, margin; oceanfront, seabank, seabeach, seaboard, seafront, sea frontage, sea line, sea sands, shingle
   idiom water's edge
bank *vb syn* see HEAP 1
   rel compact, concentrate
bank *vb* to place money in a bank < *banks* half his paycheck every week >
   syn deposit
   rel invest, lay aside, lay away, salt away, salt down, save, set aside, sock away; cache, coffer, hoard, squirrel (away), stash
   con draw out, take out, withdraw; disburse, expend, fork (over *or* out), lay out, pay (out), spend
bank (on *or* upon) *vb syn* see RELY (on *or* upon)
   rel intend, plan; bet (on), gamble (on), stake, venture, wager
   idiom bank the rent on, bet one's bottom dollar on, go bail on, lay money on

bankroll *vb syn* see CAPITALIZE

bankrupt *vb* **1** *syn* see DEPLETE
  rel break, impair, incapacitate
  con rebuild, repair, restore, revive; augment, bolster, fortify, strengthen
  2 *syn* see STRIP 2
  3 *syn* see RUIN 3
  4 *syn* see RUIN 2

banned *adj* **1** *syn* see FORBIDDEN
  2 *syn* see CONTRABAND

banner *n syn* see FLAG
  rel banneret

banner *adj syn* see EXCELLENT

bannerol *n syn* see FLAG

banquet *n syn* see DINNER
  rel bridale, feed, ||gaudy, harvest home, repast, ||tuck, ||tuck-in, ||tuck-out

bantam *adj* **1** *syn* see SMALL 1
  2 *syn* see SAUCY 1

banter *vb* **1** to make fun of good-naturedly < the students resented their teacher's *bantering* them about mistakes >
  syn chaff, fool, fun, jest, ||jive, joke, jolly, josh, kid, rag, razz, rib
  rel deride, guy, mock, quiz, rally, ridicule, satirize, taunt, tease, twit
  idiom make fun of, make merry with, poke fun at
  2 *syn* see FACE 3
  3 *syn* see COAX

banter *n* animated back-and-forth exchange of remarks < entertained the group with their jolly *banter*>
  syn backchat, badinage, ||cross talk, persiflage, repartee, snip-snap
  rel chitchat, gossip, gossipry, small talk; rallying, teasing; exchange, give-and-take
  con debate, deliberation, discussion

bantling *n syn* see BABY 1

baptismal name *n syn* see GIVEN NAME

baptize *vb* **1** to administer the rite of baptism < a child *baptized* in the Catholic Church>
  syn asperse, christen, immerse, sprinkle
  rel cleanse, purify, regenerate
  2 *syn* see NAME 1

bar *n* **1** a solid piece of material usually rectangular and considerably longer than it is wide < a *bar* of gold >
  syn billet, ingot, rod, slab, stick, strip
  2 something that stands in the way of some objective < his religion was a *bar* to membership in that exclusive club >
  syn barricade, barrier, blank wall, block, blockade, fence, roadblock, stop, wall
  rel clog, encumbrance, hamper, hindrance, impediment; hurdle, obstacle, obstruction, stumbling block; check, checkrein, control, curb; bamboo curtain, iron curtain; difficulty, hardship, vicissitude
  3 *syn* see OBSTACLE
  rel check, checkrein, control, curb
  con accommodation, convenience, facility, service
  ant advantage
  4 *syn* see COURT 2
  5 a room or public establishment where alcoholic beverages are served < nightly discussions in the *bar* >
  syn barroom, ||boozer, ||bucket shop, buvette, cantina, cocktail lounge, drinkery, drunkery, ||gin mill, ||groggery, ||grogshop, lounge, pothouse, pub, ||public house,

||rum-hole, rummery, ||rum-mill, rumshop, saloon, tap, taproom, tavern, watering hole, watering place; *compare* ALEHOUSE
  rel barrelhouse, bistro, bottle club, cabaret, café, dive, honky-tonk, nightclub, rathskeller, roadhouse, wineshop

bar *vb* **1** *syn* see LIMIT 2
  2 *syn* see EXCLUDE
  rel block, hinder; leave out, omit, pass over; banish, deport, exile, ostracize
  con accept, receive, welcome; allow, let, permit
  ant admit, include
  3 *syn* see HINDER
  rel halt, stop
  con back, support, uphold

bar *prep syn* see EXCEPT

barathrum *n syn* see HELL

barb *n syn* see SHAFT 2

barbarian *adj* **1** of, relating to, or characteristic of people that are not fully civilized < the *barbarian* tribes that sacked Rome>
  syn barbaric, barbarous, Gothic, Hunnic, Hunnish, rude, savage, uncivil, uncivilized, uncultivated, wild
  rel heathenish, vandal, vandalic; backward, coarse, crude, ill-mannered, primitive, rough; untamed; uncouth, uncultured; beastish, bloodthirsty, brutal, cruel, ferocious, inhuman
  con gentle, peaceful, subdued, submissive, tame; cultured, enlightened, humane, sophisticated; genteel, refined, well-bred, well-mannered
  ant civilized
  2 *syn* see BARBARIC 1

barbaric *adj* **1** marked by a lack of restraint, cultivated taste, and refinement < the *barbaric* use of color and ornament>
  syn barbarian, barbarous, graceless, outlandish, tasteless, vulgar, wild
  rel coarse, crude, rough, rude, uncouth; flamboyant, florid, ornate, ostentatious, showy; blatant, flashy, garish, gaudy, loud, tawdry; cacophonous, harsh, raucous; aggressive
  con quiet, restrained, soft, subdued; concinnous, cultivated, elegant, polished, refined; smooth, sophisticated, urbane
  2 *syn* see BARBARIAN 1

barbarism *n* a word or expression which in form or use offends against contemporary standards of correctness or purity in a language < many writers consider *irregardless* a *barbarism* >
  syn corruption, impropriety, slangism, solecism, vernacularism, vernacularity, vulgarism
  rel neologism; colloquialism, foreignism; shibboleth; Goldwynism, Irish bull, malaprop, malapropism, spoonerism; caconym; error, lapse, misuse, slip

barbarous *adj* **1** *syn* see BARBARIAN 1
  2 *syn* see OUTRAGEOUS 1
  3 *syn* see BARBARIC 1
  rel backward, benighted, cretinous, ignorant, illiterate, lowbrow, philistine, uneducated, unlettered, unread, unschooled, untaught, untutored
  con aware, informed, sophisticated, with-it; finished, polished, rounded; well-bred,

well-mannered; educated, intelligent, learned, schooled; erudite, well-read
4 *syn* see FIERCE 1
rel heartless, uncompassionate, unmerciful; atrocious, monstrous, outrageous; bloody, butcherly, sanguinary; fiendish, sadistic
con forbearing, lenient, merciful, tolerant; compassionate, sympathetic, tender; benevolent, humane, humanitarian
ant clement

barbate *adj syn* see BEARDED

barber *n* one whose occupation is primarily cutting hair
syn haircutter
rel coiffeur, coiffeuse, friseur, hairdresser, hair stylist; beautician, cosmetologist; clipper, cropper, shaver

bard *n* **1** a poet-singer who sang or recited verse to the accompaniment of a stringed instrument (as a harp) < *bards* were the theater of olden times>
syn jongleur, minstrel, troubadour
rel meistersinger, minnesinger, rhapsodist; gleeman; skald; conteur
2 *syn* see POET

bardlet *n syn* see POETASTER

bardling *n syn* see POETASTER

bare *adj* **1** lacking a natural or usual cover or finish <the room looked *bare* without curtains and pictures>
syn bald, naked, nude
rel denuded, dismantled, divested, peeled, stripped, uncovered; baldish, depilated, hairless; unattired, unclad, unclothed, undressed, unrobed; arid, bleak, desert, desolate
con attired, clad, clothed, dressed, garbed; furry, hairy; green, leafy, luxuriant, verdant; complete, consummate, finished, perfect
ant covered
2 *syn* see OPEN 2
3 *syn* see EMPTY 1
rel barren, depleted, destitute, dried-up, emptied, exhausted; unfilled, unstocked, unsupplied
con bountiful, bursting, chock-full, complete, crammed, laden, overflowing, overfull, replete, stuffed; full, stocked, supplied
4 *syn* see VERY 4

bare *vb syn* see STRIP 2
rel disclose, exhibit, expose, reveal, show, unveil
con camouflage, cloak, disguise, dissemble, mask; apparel, attire, dress, garb, invest, robe
ant cover

barefaced *adj syn* see SHAMELESS
rel blunt, candid, frank, open, plain, temerarious; indecent, indecorous, unseemly
con covert, secret, secretive, stealthy; cautious, circumspect, discreet, tactful
ant furtive

barefisted *adj or adv syn* see BARE‑HANDED

barefoot *adj* **1** wearing no shoes or stockings <always went *barefoot* in the summer>
syn shoeless, unsandaled, unshod
con socked, stockinged; sockless; booted, sandaled, shod
2 *syn* see DISCALCED

bare-handed *adj or adv* without covering on the hands <box *bare-handed*>
syn barefisted, bareknuckle
ant gloved

bareknuckle *adj or adv syn* see BARE‑HANDED

barely *adv syn* see JUST 2
con amply; adequately, enough, sufficiently

barf *vb syn* see VOMIT

bargain *n* **1** an advantageous purchase <at that price the car is a *bargain*>
syn buy, closeout, pennyworth, steal
rel deal; giveaway
con cheat, flimflam, gouge, sticking, sting
2 *syn* see CONTRACT

bargain *vb* **1** *syn* see HAGGLE 2
rel arrange, confer, negotiate; compromise
2 *syn* see TRADE 1

barge *vb syn* see LUMBER

bark *vb syn* see SNAP 1

barkeeper *n* **1** *syn* see SALOONKEEPER
2 *syn* see BARTENDER

‖**barmaid** *n syn* see BARTENDER

barman *n syn* see BARTENDER

Barmecidal *adj syn* see APPARENT 2

barnacle *n syn* see PARASITE

‖**barney** *n syn* see QUARREL

barnyard *adj syn* see OBSCENE 2

baron *n syn* see MAGNATE

baronial *adj syn* see GRAND 1

baroque *adj syn* see ORNATE
rel embellished, gilt, ornamented, scrolled
con austere, gray

barrage *n* a vigorous expulsion or projection of many things at once <the announcement was met with a *barrage* of protests>
syn bombardment, broadside, burst, cannonade, drumfire, fusillade, hail, salvo, shower, storm, volley
rel burst, eruption, flare, outburst, stream, surge, tornado

barrel *n* **1** *syn* see CASK
2 *syn* see MUCH

barrel *vb syn* see HURRY 2

barrelhouse *n syn* see DIVE

barrelhouse *vb syn* see HURRY 2

barren *adj* **1** *syn* see STERILE 1
rel childless, fallow, heirless, issueless
con pregnant; fertile
ant fecund
2 deficient in production of vegetation and especially crops <*barren* deserts and wastelands>
syn hardscrabble, infertile, unbearing, unfertile, unproductive
rel fallow; irreclaimable, uncultivable, unhusbanded, untillable, wild; bleak, depleted, improverished, poor, worn-out; vegetationless, verdureless; arid, desert, dry, parched
con arable, fruitful, productive; fat, rich; lush, luxuriant; green, verdant, verdurous
ant fertile

barren *n syn* see WASTE 1

---

barricade *n syn* see BAR 2
barrier *n syn* see BAR 2
barring *prep syn* see EXCEPT
barroom *n syn* see BAR 5
bar sinister *n syn* see STIGMA
bartender *n* one who serves alcoholic beverages at a bar < worked for some years as a *bartender* >
  syn barkeeper, ||barmaid, barman, mixologist, tapster; *compare* SALOONKEEPER
barter *vb syn* see TRADE 1
basal *adj* 1 *syn* see FUNDAMENTAL 1
  rel pedimental; bottommost, lowermost, lowest, nethermost, undermost
  con highest, uppermost
  2 *syn* see ELEMENTARY 1
base *n* 1 something on which another thing is reared or built or by which it is supported or fixed in place < the *base* of a lamp >
  syn basement, basis, bed, bedrock, bottom, footing, foundation, ground, groundwork, hardpan, infrastructure, rest, seat, seating, substratum, substruction, substructure, underpinning, understructure; *compare* BASIS 1
  rel bolster, buttress, framework, prop, stand, stay, support; foot
  2 *syn* see BASIS 1
  3 *syn* see BOTTOM 3
base *vb* to supply or to serve as a basis < *based* his accusation on sound evidence >
  syn bottom, establish, found, ground, predicate, rest, stay
  rel build, construct, fix, plant, seat, set up
base *adj* 1 *syn* see IGNOBLE 1
  2 *syn* see CHEAP 2
  3 contemptible because beneath minimal standards of human decency < a *base* lying cheat >
  syn despicable, ignoble, low, low-down, servile, sordid, squalid, ugly, vile, wretched; *compare* CONTEMPTIBLE
  rel beggarly, lousy, sorry; abominable, disgraceful, loathsome; bad, evil, wicked; base-minded, low-minded, meanspirited; caitiff, cowardly, dastardly, recreant; unworthy; dirty, filthy; degrading, humiliating, ignominious
  con honest, honorable, upright; virtuous; ethical, moral, righteous; fair, forbearing, open-minded, patient, reasonable, tolerant, understanding
  ant noble
baseborn *adj* 1 *syn* see IGNOBLE 1
  2 *syn* see ILLEGITIMATE 1
baseless *adj* being without cause or occasion < anxious old ladies with their *baseless* fears >
  syn bottomless, foundationless, gratuitous, groundless, uncalled-for, unfounded, ungrounded, unwarranted
  rel false, wrong; indefensible, reasonless, unjustifiable, unsolid, unsupported, unsustained, untenable; empty, idle, vain; needless, pointless, senseless, unnecessary, unneeded
  con actual, real, reasonable, true; authentic, bona fide, genuine, valid
basement *n syn* see BASE 1
bash *n* 1 *syn* see BLOW 1

  2 *syn* see SHINDIG 1
bashful *adj syn* see SHY 1
  rel timorous; recoiling, shrinking; mousy; abashed, embarrassed; blushful
  con assured, bold, intrepid; arrogant, barefaced, brazen, impudent, shameless; loquacious, talkative
  ant brash, forward
basic *adj* 1 *syn* see FUNDAMENTAL 1
  rel capital, chief, main, principal
  2 *syn* see ELEMENTAL 1
basic *n syn* see ESSENTIAL 1
basically *adv syn* see ESSENTIALLY 1
basin *n syn* see DEPRESSION 2
basis *n* 1 something that supports or sustains anything immaterial < his argument rested on a *basis* of conjecture >
  syn base, bedrock, footing, foundation, ground, groundwork, infrastructure, root, substratum, underpinning; *compare* BASE 1
  rel axiom, fundamental, law, principle, theorem; assumption, postulate, premise, presumption, presupposition; essence, heart
  2 *syn* see BASE 1
  3 something serving as a reason or justification for an action or opinion < resented such a challenge without *basis* or reason >
  syn foundation, warrant
  rel call, justification, right; ground(s), reason
bask *vb* 1 *syn* see SUN
  2 *syn* see WALLOW 3
bassinet *n syn* see BABY CARRIAGE
bastard *n* 1 one born out of wedlock < bore a *bastard* before she was fifteen >
  syn by-blow, catch colt, chance child, come-by-chance, filius nullius, filius populi, illegitimate, love child, natural child, whoreson, woods colt
  2 *syn* see HYBRID
bastard *adj* 1 *syn* see ILLEGITIMATE 1
  2 *syn* see SPURIOUS 3
bastardize *vb syn* see DEBASE 1
bastardy *n syn* see ILLEGITIMACY 1
baste *vb* 1 *syn* see BEAT 1
  rel clobber, ||larrup, mill, whip
  2 *syn* see SCOLD 1
bastille *n syn* see JAIL
bastille *vb syn* see IMPRISON
bastinado *n syn* see BLOW 1
bastion *n syn* see BULWARK
bat *n* 1 *syn* see BLOW 1
  2 *syn* see CUDGEL
  ||3 *syn* see SPEED 2
  4 *syn* see BINGE 1
||**bat** *n syn* see HAG 2
bat *vb syn* see WANDER 1
bat *vb syn* see WINK
batch *n syn* see GROUP 3
bate *vb* ||1 *syn* see ABATE 4
  ||2 *syn* see DECREASE
  3 *syn* see EXCLUDE
bath *n, usu* **baths** *pl syn* see SPA 1
||**bath** *vb syn* see BATHE 1
bathe *vb* 1 to clean oneself with a bath < *bathed* only on Saturday nights >
  syn ||bath, shower, tub, wash
  rel soap; douse, soak
  2 to flow or splash against < waves *bathed* the rocky shore >
  syn lap, lave, lip, wash
  rel drench, soak, sop, souse; flush

bathetic adj 1 syn see TRITE
 2 syn see SENTIMENTAL
bathtub gin n syn see MOONSHINE 2
bating prep syn see EXCEPT
baton n syn see CUDGEL
batter vb 1 to affect (as by repeated blows)
 so severely as to disfigure or damage <so
 battered in the fight he couldn't even
 crawl away> <a boat battered to pieces
 by stormy seas>
  syn ||bung up, mangle, maul
  rel disable, disfigure; maim, mutilate;
  cripple, lame; bruise, contuse, lacerate;
  baste, clobber, pummel; shatter, wreck
  idiom beat black and blue, beat to pieces
  (or shreds), beat within an inch of one's
  life
 2 syn see BEAT 1
battery n syn see GROUP 3
battle n a hostile meeting between opposing military forces <the battle continued
 until nightfall>
  syn action, engagement
  rel brush, clash, encounter, pitched battle, scrimmage, skirmish; assault, attack,
  onset, onslaught, sortie; combat, conflict,
  contest, fight; hostilities
battle vb syn see CONTEND 1
  rel clash, scrimmage; assail, assault, attack, bombard
battle cry n a word or phrase used as a
 slogan by a faction <"death to the invader" was the battle cry>
  syn cry, motto, rallying cry, war cry;
  compare CATCHWORD
battlesome adj syn see QUARRELSOME 2
||batty adj syn see INSANE 1
bauble n syn see KNICKKNACK
bavardage n syn see SMALL TALK
bawd n syn see PROSTITUTE
bawdy house n syn see BROTHEL
bawl vb 1 syn see ROAR
  rel holler, scream, screech, shout, shriek,
  squall, yammer, yell
 2 to cry and weep loudly or lustily especially from distress <the baby bawled and
 kicked when its bottle was taken away>
  syn howl, squall, wail, yowl; compare
  CRY 2, ROAR
  rel blubber, boohoo, cry, sob, weep
bawl out vb syn see SCOLD 1
  rel condemn, denounce
  idiom read a lecture (or lesson)
bay n, usu **bays** pl syn see HONOR 2
bay vb syn see HOWL 1
bay n syn see INLET
baygall n syn see SWAMP
bayou n syn see INLET
bay window n syn see POTBELLY
bazoo n ||1 syn see MOUTH 1
 2 syn see RASPBERRY
be vb to have actuality or reality <I think,
 therefore I am>
  syn breathe, exist, live, move, subsist
  rel hold, obtain, stand; abide, continue,
  endure, go on, persist, prevail, remain;
  come
beach n syn see SHORE

  rel oceanfront; lakeshore, lakeside
beach vb syn see SHIPWRECK 1
beached adj syn see AGROUND
beacon n 1 a signal fire usually on an
 elevated place <a beacon on the hill to
 warn of danger>
  syn balefire, watchfire
  rel flare; bonfire
 2 syn see LIGHTHOUSE
beak n 1 syn see BILL 1
 2 syn see NOSE 1
 3 syn see PROMONTORY
 ||4 syn see JUDGE 2
beak vb syn see PECK 1
be-all and end-all n 1 syn see ESSENCE
 2
 2 syn see WHOLE 1
beam n 1 syn see TIMBER 2
 2 syn see RAY 1
 3 syn see BUTTOCKS
beam vb 1 syn see SHINE 1
 2 syn see SMILE
beaming adj syn see BRIGHT 1
||bean n syn see HEAD 1
beanery n syn see EATING HOUSE
beany adj syn see SPIRITED 2
bear vb 1 syn see CARRY 1
  rel shoulder
 2 syn see BEHAVE 1
 3 to have attached to one <the bottle
 bears the label "poisonous">
  syn carry, have, possess
  rel display, exhibit, show
  con lack, need, want
 4 syn see ACCOMPANY
 5 to give birth to offspring <she has
 borne several children>
  syn ||birth, ||born, bring forth, deliver
  idiom bring abed, bring to bed, bring to
  birth, give birth to, have a baby
  con abort, miscarry
 6 syn see PRESS 8
 7 syn see PRESS 1
 8 syn see PROCREATE 1
 9 to bring forth a product <the apple
 trees bear every year>
  syn produce, turn out, yield
  rel breed, engender, generate, propagate,
  reproduce; fructify, fruit; fabricate, fashion, form, make, shape; create, invent
 10 to put up with something trying or
 difficult <can't bear the tension of the
 work>
  syn abide, brook, digest, endure, go,
  lump, stand, ||stick, stick out, stomach,
  suffer, support, sustain, swallow, sweat
  out, take, tolerate; compare ACCEPT 2
  rel afflict, torment, torture, try; allow,
  condone, countenance, permit; acquiesce,
  bow, defer, submit, yield
  idiom make do, put up with, take lying
  down
  con decline, refuse, reject, spurn; avoid,
  bypass, elude, evade, shun
 11 syn see HEAD 3
bear (on or upon) vb to have a connection
 especially logically <this situation bears
 directly upon the question under discus-
 sion>
  syn appertain, apply, pertain, relate
  rel refer; affect, concern, involve, touch;
  correspond, parallel
  idiom have to do with, tie in with

---

syn synonym(s)   rel related word(s)
ant antonym(s)   con contrasted word(s)
idiom idiomatic equivalent(s)
|| use limited; if in doubt, see a dictionary

bear (with) *vb syn* see ACCEPT 2
bearable *adj* capable of being borne < his outrageous behavior is hardly *bearable*>
syn endurable, livable, sufferable, supportable, sustainable, tolerable
rel acceptable, admissible, allowable, satisfactory
con insufferable, insupportable, intolerable, unendurable, unsupportable
ant unbearable
beard *n* the natural growth of hair on a man's face < some men look better with *beards*>
syn beaver, whiskers; *compare* SIDE-WHISKERS
rel charley, galways, goatee, imperial, spade beard, Vandyke; fuzz
beard *vb syn* see FACE 3
idiom beard the lion in his den
bearded *adj* having a beard < an old *bearded* philosopher>
syn barbate, bewhiskered, whiskered
rel beardy; goateed; hairy; stubbed, stubbly, unshaven
con barefaced, clean-faced, clean-shaven, shaven, smooth-faced, whiskerless
ant beardless
bear down *vb syn* see CONQUER 1
bearer *n* 1 *syn* see MESSENGER
2 a man who carries baggage and supplies for travelers < native *bearers* serving the safari>
syn carrier, drogher, porter
rel boy, cargador, coolie; redcap, skycap
bearing *n* 1 the way in which or the quality by which a person outwardly manifests his personality < a dowager with a regal *bearing*>
syn address, air, comportment, demeanor, deportment, mien, port, presence, set
rel aspect, brow, visage; attitude, carriage, pose, posture, stand; poise; display, front; behavior, conduct
2 *syn* see BIRTH 1
bearish *adj syn* see CANTANKEROUS
bear out *vb syn* see CONFIRM 1
bear up *vb syn* see SUPPORT 4
beast *n* a lower animal as distinguished from man < *beasts* of the field>
syn animal, brute, creature, ‖critter
rel beastie, varmint; quadruped
beastly *adj syn* see BRUTISH
beat *vb* 1 to strike repeatedly < robbed and *beaten* by thugs>
syn baste, batter, belabor, buffet, drub, ‖dump, hammer, lam, lambaste, paste, pelt, pound, pummel, thrash, tromp, wallop, whop
rel bastinado, baton, bludgeon, cudgel, fustigate, pistol-whip; flog, lace, lash, tan, whip; lay on, maul, muss up, rough (up)
idiom give one beans, rain blows on
2 *syn* see WHIP 2
3 *syn* see SCOUR 2
4 *syn* see WHIP 3
5 *syn* see WAG
6 *syn* see HAMMER 1
7 *syn* see SURPASS 1
idiom beat (all) hollow
8 *syn* see NONPLUS 1
9 *syn* see CHEAT
10 *syn* see FRUSTRATE 1
11 *syn* see SCOOP 3

12 *syn* see PULSATE
13 *syn* see WIN 1
beat *n* 1 *syn* see RHYTHM
2 *syn* see SCOOP
beat down *vb syn* see CONQUER 1
beating *n syn* see DEFEAT 1
rel lump(s)
beatitude *n syn* see HAPPINESS
rel ecstasy, rapture, transport
con affliction, trial, tribulation; anguish, grief, sorrow, woe; agony, suffering
ant despair, dolor
beau *n* 1 *syn* see BOYFRIEND 1
2 *syn* see BOYFRIEND 2
Beau Brummel *n syn* see FOP
beau ideal *n syn* see MODEL 2
idiom shining example
‖**beaut** *n syn* see BEAUTY
beauteous *adj syn* see BEAUTIFUL
beautiful *adj* very pleasing or delightful to look at < the most *beautiful* woman in the world>
syn attractive, beauteous, ‖bonny, comely, fair, good-looking, handsome, lovely, pretty, pulchritudinous, stunning, well-favored
rel choice, elegant, exquisite; glorious, resplendent, splendid, sublime, superb; eye-appealing, eye-filling, ‖proper; personable, pleasing
con offensive, repugnant, repulsive, revolting; homely, plain, ordinary, unattractive, unbeauteous, uncomely, unhandsome, unlovely, unpretty
ant ugly, unbeautiful
beautiful people *n pl syn* see SMART SET
beautify *vb syn* see ADORN
rel glamorize, prettify
con deface, disfigure; damage, mar, spoil
ant uglify
beauty *n* a physically attractive woman < a charming woman and a *beauty* to boot>
syn ‖beaut, eyeful, knockout, looker, lovely, stunner
rel charmer, dazzler, dream, eye-opener, good-looker, peach; belle, toast
idiom raving beauty
con dog, gorgon, hag, slattern, witch
beaver *n syn* see BEARD
becalm *vb syn* see CALM
because *conj* for the reason that < I left *because* I was bored>
syn as, as long as, ‖being, 'cause, considering, for, inasmuch as, now, seeing, since, whereas
idiom in view of the fact
because of *prep syn* see OVER 6
becloud *vb* 1 *syn* see OBSCURE
rel befuddle, confuse, perplex, puzzle
con illuminate
2 *syn* see CONFUSE 4
become *vb* 1 to commence to be < *became* sick yesterday>
syn come, ‖come over, get, go, grow, run, turn, wax
rel arise, mount, rise, soar
idiom get to be, turn out to be
2 *syn* see SUIT 4
3 *syn* see FLATTER
becoming *adj syn* see DECOROUS 1
rel attractive, flattering; tasteful

con unattractive, unflattering; distasteful; inappropriate, unfitting, unrespectable, unsuitable
ant unbecoming

becomingly *adv syn see* WELL 4
becrush *vb syn see* CRUSH 2
bed *n syn see* BASE 1
bed *vb* 1 to put to bed < getting the children *bedded* >
syn tuck (in)
rel cradle
2 *syn see* RETIRE 4
bedamn *vb syn see* SWEAR 3
bedaub *vb syn see* SMEAR 1
bedaze *vb syn see* DAZE 2
bedazzle *vb syn see* DAZE 1
bedcover *n syn see* BEDSPREAD
bedeck *vb syn see* ADORN
rel bedaub, bedizen
bedevil *vb syn see* WORRY 1
bedfast *adj syn see* BEDRIDDEN
bedim *vb syn see* OBSCURE
con highlight, illuminate
bedlamite *n syn see* LUNATIC 1
bedlamite *adj syn see* INSANE 1
bedog *vb syn see* TAIL
bedraggled *adj syn see* SHABBY 1
bedridden *adj* confined to one's bed by illness or injury < a *bedridden* invalid >
syn bedfast
rel confined, incapacitated, laid up; feeble, infirm, sickly, weak
idiom flat on one's back
con healed, well; hale, healthy, whole
ant ambulant, ambulatory
bedrock *n* 1 *syn see* BASE 1
2 *syn see* BASIS 1
bedspread *n* an often ornamental outer covering for a bed < an appliquéd *bedspread* >
syn bedcover, counterpane, coverlet, ‖coverlid, spread
bee *n syn see* CAPRICE
rel idea; impulse
beef *n* 1 *syn see* MUSCLE 1
2 *syn see* POWER 4
3 *syn see* QUARREL
‖**beef** *vb syn see* GRIPE
beef (up) *vb syn see* INCREASE 1
beefheaded *adj syn see* STUPID 1
beef–witted *adj syn see* STUPID 1
beefy *adj syn see* HUSKY 1
beekeeper *n* one who engages in the production of and caring for bees and honey < special masks and gloves for *beekeepers* >
syn apiarist, apiculturist, beeman, beemaster
beeline *vb syn see* HURRY 2
Beelzebub *n syn see* DEVIL 1
beeman *n syn see* BEEKEEPER
beemaster *n syn see* BEEKEEPER
beer garden *n syn see* ALEHOUSE
beer hall *n syn see* ALEHOUSE
‖**beerhouse** *n syn see* ALEHOUSE
beetle *vb* 1 *syn see* HANG 4
2 *syn see* BULGE
beetlehead *n syn see* DUNCE

beetleheaded *adj syn see* STUPID 1
‖**beezer** *n syn see* NOSE 1
befall *vb syn see* HAPPEN 1
befit *vb syn see* SUIT 4
befitting *adj* 1 *syn see* FIT 1
ant unbefitting
2 *syn see* DECOROUS 1
befittingly *adv syn see* WELL 1
befog *vb* 1 *syn see* OBSCURE
2 *syn see* CONFUSE 4
3 *syn see* PUZZLE
befool *vb syn see* DUPE
before *adv* 1 so as to precede something in order or time < racing on *before* to give warning >
syn ahead, ante, antecedently, beforehand, fore, forward, in advance, precedently, previous
con behind; abaft, aft, astern
ant after
2 in time past < had heard that joke *before* >
syn already, earlier, erstwhile, formerly, heretofore, once, previously; *compare* THEN 1
ant after
3 until now or then < you'll get it tomorrow and not *before* >
syn beforehand, earlier, sooner
before *prep* 1 coming before in space or time < be home *before* dark >
syn ahead of, ante, ere, in advance of, preceding, prior to, to; *compare* UNTIL
con since, subsequent to
ant after
2 in the presence of < stood *before* the court >
syn confronting, facing
idiom face to face with
3 *syn see* UNTIL
beforehand *adv* 1 *syn see* BEFORE 1
2 *syn see* BEFORE 3
befoul *vb* 1 *syn see* CONTAMINATE 2
2 *syn see* MALIGN
befuddle *vb syn see* CONFUSE 2
rel daze
befuddlement *n syn see* HAZE 2
rel confusion, mix-up
con clearheadedness, lucidness
beg *vb* to ask for or ask one for something urgently < *beg* one's life from an attacker > < *beg* a stranger for help >
syn appeal, beseech, brace, conjure, crave, entreat, implore, importune, invoke, plead, pray, supplicate
rel ask, call (on), request, solicit; petition, sue; besiege, demand, press; nag, worry
idiom throw oneself at the feet of (*or* on the mercy of)
con hint, intimate, suggest
‖**begats** *n pl* 1 *syn see* GENEALOGY
2 *syn see* OFFSPRING
begem *vb syn see* BEJEWEL
beget *vb* 1 *syn see* FATHER
2 *syn see* PROCREATE 1
beggar *n* 1 one who begs especially habitually or as a livelihood < *beggars* crying out to tourists >
syn bummer, cadger, moocher, panhandler, ‖schnorrer
rel deadbeat, freeloader, sponge, sponger; ‖bindle stiff, hobo, tramp
2 *syn see* SUPPLIANT

---

syn synonym(s)   *rel* related word(s)
ant antonym(s)   *con* contrasted word(s)
idiom idiomatic equivalent(s)
‖ use limited; if in doubt, see a dictionary

3 *syn* see PAUPER

beggared *adj syn* see POOR 1

beggarly *adj syn* see CONTEMPTIBLE
rel wretched; ‖cheesy, trashy; measly, paltry

beggary *n* 1 *syn* see POVERTY 1
2 *syn* see MENDICANCY

begin *vb* 1 to carry out the first act or step of an action or operation < *began* his lecture with a joke>
syn commence, embark (on *or* upon), enter, get off, inaugurate, initiate, jump (off), kick off, launch, lead off, open, set to, start, take up, tee off
rel establish, found, institute; introduce, usher in; broach; attack, tackle; prepare; break in; dig in
idiom get the show on the road, get to work, get underway
con cease, desist, discontinue, quit, stop; close, complete, conclude, finish, terminate; abandon, forsake, leave, quit; back out, renege, withdraw
ant end
2 to come into existence < not since civilization *began* has there been such distress >
syn arise, commence, originate, start; *compare* SPRING 1
rel spring; open
idiom raise its head
con end, finish, terminate

beginner *n syn* see NOVICE

beginning *n* the first part or stage of a process or development < the first few chapters at the *beginning* of the novel >
syn alpha, birth, commencement, dawn, dawning, day spring, genesis, onset, opening, opening gun, outset, outstart, setout, start
rel creation, inception, origin, origination, root, source, spring; anlage, rudiment, sprout; prologue; appearance, emergence, rise; incipiency, infancy
idiom the word go
con consummation, termination; closing, completion, conclusion; omega
ant end, ending

beginning *adj* 1 *syn* see INITIAL 1
2 *syn* see ELEMENTARY 1

begird *vb* 1 *syn* see BELT 1
2 *syn* see SURROUND 1

begirdle *vb* *syn* see BELT 1

begone *vb* *syn* see GET OUT 1

begrime *vb* *syn* see SOIL 2

begrudge *vb* *syn* see ENVY

beguile *vb* 1 *syn* see MANIPULATE 2
2 *syn* see DECEIVE
rel entice, lure, seduce
3 *syn* see WHILE

beguiling *adj* *syn* see MISLEADING

béguin *n* *syn* see INFATUATION

behave *vb* 1 to act in a specified way < *behave* as people of good breeding should >
syn acquit, act, bear, carry, comport, conduct, demean, deport, disport, do, go on, move, quit
rel control, direct, manage
idiom make as if (*or* as though); be on one's best behavior, mind one's p's and q's
ant misbehave, misconduct
2 *syn* see ACT 5

behavior *n* one's actions in general or on a particular occasion < his flustered *behavior* before women >
syn comportment, conduct, deportment, tenue
rel bearing, demeanor, mien; action, manner, way
con misbehavior, misconduct

behead *vb* to sever the head < nobles *beheaded* for treason >
syn decapitate, decollate, guillotine, head, neck
idiom bring to the block

behemoth *n syn* see GIANT

behemothic *adj syn* see HUGE

behest *n syn* see COMMAND 1
rel demand; prompting, request, solicitation

behind *adv syn* see AFTER

behind *prep* 1 *syn* see ABAFT
2 *syn* see AFTER 2

behind *n syn* see BUTTOCKS

behindhand *adj* 1 *syn* see NEGLIGENT
2 *syn* see BACKWARD 6
3 *syn* see TARDY
ant beforehand

behold *vb syn* see SEE 1

beholden *adj syn* see INDEBTED

beholder *n syn* see SPECTATOR

being *n* 1 *syn* see EXISTENCE 1
rel character, individuality, personality
ant nonbeing
2 *syn* see THING 4
3 *syn* see ENTITY 1
4 *syn* see ESSENCE 1
5 *syn* see HUMAN

‖**being** *conj syn* see BECAUSE

bejewel *vb* to ornament with or as if with jewels < a *bejeweled* headdress > < cobwebs all *bejeweled* with glittering morning dew >
syn begem, beset, enjewel, gem, jewel
rel bespangle, spangle; diamond; encrust

belabor *vb syn* see BEAT 1

belated *adj* 1 *syn* see TARDY
2 *syn* see OLD-FASHIONED

belch *vb* 1 to expel gas suddenly from the stomach through the mouth < ate and ate until he *belched* >
syn burp, eruct, eructate
2 *syn* see ERUPT 1

beldam *n* 1 a woman of advanced years < a crotchety *beldam* hunched over the fire >
syn dame, gammer, grandam; *compare* GAFFER, OLDSTER
rel grandmother, granny; grand dame; matron; matriarch
idiom old girl
con damsel, lass, maid, miss
2 *syn* see HAG 2

beleaguer *vb* 1 *syn* see BESIEGE
rel siege, storm
idiom set upon from all sides
2 *syn* see WORRY 1

belfry *n* 1 *syn* see BELL TOWER
‖2 *syn* see HEAD 1

belie *vb syn* see MISREPRESENT
rel contradict, contravene, negative; controvert, disprove; conceal, disguise, hide
con bespeak, betoken, indicate; disclose, discover, reveal
ant attest

belief *n* **1** the act of assenting intellectually to something proposed as true or the state of mind of one who so assents < offered ready *belief* to anyone he trusted >
syn credence, credit, faith
rel assurance, certainty, certitude, conviction, sureness; acquiescence, assent; trust; credibility, trustworthiness
con distrust, doubt, mistrust, uncertainty; incredulity; question
ant disbelief, unbelief
2 *syn* see OPINION
rel doctrine, dogma, fundamental, law, precept, principle; concept, idea

believable *adj* worthy of belief < the author's bizarre characterizations are hardly *believable* >
syn colorable, credible, creditable, plausible
rel likely, possible, probable, tenable; conceivable, rational, reasonable; presumable, supposable; unquestionable; convincing, impressive, persuasive, satisfying; meaningful, solid, substantial
con improbable, unlikely; doubtable, doubtful, dubious, fishy, questionable; specious; implausible, incredible; inconceivable, untenable; fabulous, mythological
ant unbelievable

believe *vb* **1** to have a firm conviction in the reality of something < *believes* in ghosts >
syn accept, ‖buy, swallow
rel accredit, credit, trust; admit
idiom have no doubts about, hold the belief that, take (*or* accept) as gospel, take at one's word, take one's word for
con discredit, distrust, doubt, mistrust, question, suspect; challenge, dispute, reject, turn down
ant disbelieve, misbelieve
2 *syn* see FEEL 3
3 *syn* see UNDERSTAND 3

belittle *vb syn* see DECRY 2
rel criticize, discredit; underestimate, underrate, undervalue
con intensify; boast, crow
ant aggrandize; magnify

belittlement *n syn* see DETRACTION

bell *vb syn* see RING

‖**bell cow** *n syn* see LEADER 1

bellicose *adj syn* see BELLIGERENT
rel aggressive, assertive; factious, fighting, rebellious
idiom full of fight
con gentle, moderate, temperate
ant amicable; pacific

belligerence *n syn* see ATTACK 2

belligerent *adj* having or taking an aggressive or fighting attitude < a *belligerent* reply to a diplomatic note >
syn bellicose, combative, contentious, gladiatorial, militant, pugnacious, quarrelsome, ‖ructious, scrappy, truculent, warlike; *compare* QUARRELSOME 2
rel battling, fighting, warring; attacking, invading; aggressive, antagonistic, fierce, hostile; ardent, hot, hot-tempered

con neutral; pacific, pacifist, peaceable, peaceful; conciliatory; amicable
ant friendly

‖**belling** *n syn* see SHIVAREE

bellow *vb syn* see ROAR
rel bark, bay, yelp; cry, wail; low, moo

bell ringer *n syn* see SMASH 6

bell tower *n* a tower that supports or shelters a bell or group of bells < a *bell tower* stood free from the church >
syn belfry, campanile, carillon

bellwether *n syn* see LEADER 1

belly *n syn* see ABDOMEN

bellyache *n syn* see STOMACHACHE

‖**bellyache** *vb syn* see GRIPE

‖**bellyacher** *n syn* see GROUCH

belong *vb* **1** to be suitable, appropriate, or advantageous or to be in a proper or fitting place or situation < the boxes *belong* in the attic >
syn fit, go, set
rel become, befit, suit; accord, agree, chime, harmonize; correspond, match, tally
idiom have one's place
2 to be the property of (a person or thing) < the books *belong* to the library >
syn appertain, pertain, vest
3 to be an attribute, part, adjunct, or function (of a person or thing) < good humor and wit *belong* to his personality >
syn indwell, inhere
idiom run in one's blood (*or* family)

belongings *n pl syn* see POSSESSION 2

beloved *adj syn* see FAVORITE 1

beloved *n* **1** *syn* see SWEETHEART 1
2 *syn* see GIRL FRIEND 2
3 *syn* see BOYFRIEND 2

below *adv* **1** in or at a lower position than something expressed or implied < several business establishments were situated *below* >
syn beneath, under, underneath
ant above
2 lower on the same page or on a following page < for additional examples see *below* >
syn infra
ant above, supra

below *prep* **1** in a lower position relative to some other object or place < lives just *below* me >
syn beneath, under, underneath
con over
ant above
2 *syn* see AFTER 2

belt *n* **1** a strip of flexible material worn around the waist < a leather *belt* >
syn ceinture, cincture, girdle, sash, waistband
rel baldric, cummerbund; band
2 *syn* see AREA 1
rel stretch, strip

belt *vb* **1** to bind about or around with or as if with a belt < gold lamé *belting* the gown >
syn band, begird, begirdle, cincture, encincture, engird, engirdle, gird, girdle
rel tie (up); loop; sash; circle, encircle, ring
2 *syn* see SLAM 1

belt *n syn* see BLOW 1

belvedere *n syn* see SUMMERHOUSE

---

syn synonym(s)   *rel* related word(s)
ant antonym(s)   *con* contrasted word(s)
idiom idiomatic equivalent(s)
‖ use limited; if in doubt, see a dictionary

bemean *vb syn see* HUMBLE
bemedaled *adj* having or wearing decorations especially as awarded by the military < the general's *bemedaled* uniform >
syn beribboned, decorated
bemired *adj syn see* MUDDY 1
bemoan *vb syn see* DEPLORE 1
rel regret; complain
con applaud, cheer, huzzah; delight, jubilate, rejoice
ant exult
bemuse *vb syn see* DAZE 2
rel addle; perplex, puzzle
con enlighten, illuminate
bemused *adj syn see* ABSTRACTED
benchmark *n syn see* STANDARD 3
bend *vb* 1 *syn see* CURVE
rel arch, curl, double, hook
ant straighten
2 *syn see* GIVE 12
3 *syn see* INCLINE 3
4 *syn see* ADDRESS 3
bend (over) *vb syn see* HANG 4
bend *n* 1 *syn see* TURN 2
2 *syn see* TURN 4
3 *syn see* CURVE
bender *n syn see* BINGE 1
bending *adj syn see* CROOKED 1
beneath *adv syn see* BELOW 1
beneath *prep syn see* BELOW 1
ant above, over
benediction *n* 1 *syn see* BLESSING 1
2 *syn see* GRACE 1
3 *syn see* APPROBATION
4 *syn see* GOOD 1
benefact *vb syn see* HELP 1
benefaction *n syn see* DONATION
benefic *adj syn see* GOOD 1
rel desirable, pleasing, satisfying
con damaging, harmful, injurious
ant malefic
beneficence *n syn see* DONATION
beneficial *adj syn see* GOOD 1
rel salutary, wholesome
con baneful, deleterious, noxious, pernicious
ant detrimental, harmful
benefit *n* 1 *syn see* GOOD 1
2 *syn see* WELFARE
rel account, behalf, sake; gain, profit
con catastrophe, disaster, misfortune; detriment
ant harm, ill
benefit *vb* to be useful or profitable to < medicines that *benefit* mankind >
syn advantage, avail, profit, serve, work (for)
rel advance, ameliorate, better, contribute (to), favor, improve; relieve, succor; build, further, promote; aid, assist, help
idiom do a world of good
con hinder, impede; damage, impair, injure; distress, upset; afflict, anguish; oppose
ant harm, hurt
benet *vb syn see* CATCH 3
benevolence *n* 1 *syn see* GOODWILL 1
con animosity, bitterness, ill will; antagonism, hostility; inimicality, unkindliness; stinginess
2 *syn see* GIFT 1
benevolent *adj* 1 *syn see* GENEROUS 1
rel beneficent; charitable; humane; compassionate, tenderhearted

con cruel, inhuman, malicious, spiteful
ant malevolent
2 *syn see* CHARITABLE 1
rel bighearted, freehearted, generous, greathearted, largehearted, liberal, openhanded; public-spirited; do-good
con niggardly, stingy; callous, indifferent, insensitive, unconcerned, unfeeling
benighted *adj* 1 *syn see* IGNORANT 1
rel backward, unenlightened; uninformed
idiom in the dark
con informed, intelligent
2 *syn see* BACKWARD 5
benightedness *n syn see* IGNORANCE 1
benign *adj* 1 *syn see* KIND
rel gracious
con malevolent, malicious, malignant, spiteful; acrid, caustic, mordant
ant malign
2 *syn see* FAVORABLE 5
rel gentle, mild; benevolent, charitable, humane; clement, forbearing, merciful
con menacing, threatening
ant malign
benignant *adj syn see* KIND
rel mild; gracious
con malevolent, malicious, spiteful; relentless
ant malignant
benison *n syn see* BLESSING 1
bent *n* 1 *syn see* LEANING 2
2 *syn see* GIFT 2
con antipathy, aversion; inability, incapacity
bent *adj* 1 *syn see* CURVED
2 *syn see* DECIDED 2
benumb *vb* 1 *syn see* DEADEN 1
2 *syn see* DAZE 2
benumbed *adj syn see* NUMB 1
bequeath *vb* 1 *syn see* WILL
con disinherit, exheridate
2 *syn see* HAND DOWN
bequest *n syn see* LEGACY 1
berate *vb syn see* SCOLD 1
con acclaim, praise; applaud; commend, compliment
berceuse *n syn see* LULLABY
bereave *vb syn see* DEPRIVE 2
bereaved *adj* suffering the death of a loved one < the *bereaved* family >
syn bereft
rel distressed, sorrowing
bereft *adj syn see* BEREAVED
beribboned *adj syn see* BEMEDALED
berth *n* 1 *syn see* WHARF
2 *syn see* JOB 2
beseech *vb syn see* BEG
beset *vb* 1 *syn see* BEJEWEL
2 *syn see* ATTACK 1
3 *syn see* BESIEGE
4 *syn see* INFEST 1
5 *syn see* SURROUND 1
idiom come at from all directions (*or* sides)
besetment *n syn see* ANNOYANCE 3
beside *prep* 1 at or by the side of < left the car *beside* the road >
syn alongside, by, ‖fornent, next to
rel near, opposite
2 *syn see* NEAR 2
3 *syn see* BESIDES 1
4 *syn see* EXCEPT
besides *adv* 1 *syn see* ALSO 2

idiom at that
2 *syn* see AGAIN 4
besides *prep* **1** in addition to < *besides* being tall, he's thin >
syn as well as, beside, beyond, over and above
idiom along with, together with
2 *syn* see EXCEPT
besides *adj syn* see ADDITIONAL
besiege *vb* to surround an enemy in a fortified or strong position so as to prevent ingress and egress < Troy was *besieged* by Greeks for ten years >
syn beleaguer, beset, blockade, invest
rel encircle, encompass, hem (in), surround; trap; assail, assault, attack
besmear *vb* 1 *syn* see SMEAR 1
2 *syn* see TAINT 1
besmirch *vb syn* see TAINT 1
besoil *vb syn* see SOIL 2
besotted *adj syn* see INFATUATED
bespangle *vb syn* see SPANGLE 1
bespatter *vb* 1 *syn* see SPOT 1
2 *syn* see MALIGN
bespeak *vb* 1 *syn* see RESERVE 2
2 *syn* see ADDRESS 4
3 *syn* see ASK 2
idiom put in for
4 *syn* see INDICATE 2
bespeckle *vb syn* see SPECKLE 1
bespectacled *adj* having or wearing glasses < *bespectacled* thesaurists >
syn spectacled
bespot *vb syn* see SPOT 1
besprinkle *vb syn* see SPRINKLE 1
best *adj* much more than half < passed the *best* part of a month at the shore >
syn better, ‖bettermost, greater, largest, most
best *vb* 1 *syn* see CONQUER 2
2 *syn* see SURPASS 1
3 *syn* see DEFEAT 2
best *n* the choicest one or part < always gave the *best* that she had >
syn choice, cream, elite, fat, flower, pick, pride, prime, primrose, prize, top
rel gem; nonesuch, nonpareil; exemplar, model, paragon, pattern
idiom cock of the walk, flower of the flock, one in a thousand (*or* million)
ant worst
bestain *vb syn* see STAIN 1
‖**best bib and tucker** *n syn* see FINERY
best girl *n syn* see GIRL FRIEND 1
bestial *adj syn* see BRUTISH
bestialize *vb syn* see DEBASE 1
bestir *vb syn* see STIR 1
bestow *vb* 1 *syn* see USE 2
2 *syn* see STOW
3 *syn* see HARBOR 2
4 *syn* see GIVE 1
bestower *n syn* see DONOR
bestrew *vb syn* see STREW 1
bestride *vb* 1 *syn* see MOUNT 5
2 to sit with one leg on each side < boys *bestriding* a fallen log >
syn straddle, ‖striddle, stride
bet *n* something of value (as money) staked on a winner-take-all basis on the outcome

of an uncertainty < laid a *bet* at three to one on the champion >
syn ante, pot, stake, wager
bet *vb syn* see GAMBLE 1
bête noire *n syn* see ABOMINATION 1
bethink *vb syn* see REMEMBER
betide *vb syn* see HAPPEN 1
betimes *adv* 1 *syn* see EARLY 1
2 *syn* see EARLY 2
‖3 *syn* see SOMETIMES
betoken *vb* 1 *syn* see INDICATE 2
2 *syn* see AUGUR 2
betray *vb* 1 *syn* see DECEIVE
rel ensnare, entrap, snare, trap
2 to prove faithless or treacherous < *betrayed* his own people by going over to the enemy >
syn cross, double-cross, sell, sell out, ‖split
rel desert, renegade; give away, inform, turn in; collaborate; apostatize
idiom act (*or* play) the traitor, break faith, round on, sell down the river
3 *syn* see REVEAL 1
rel demonstrate, evidence, evince, manifest, show; betoken, indicate
con defend, guard, protect, safeguard, shield
betrayer *n syn* see INFORMER
betrothal *n syn* see ENGAGEMENT 2
betrothed *n* either member of a couple engaged to be married
syn affianced, intended
rel fiancé, husband-to-be; bride-to-be, fiancée, wife-to-be
betrothed *adj syn* see ENGAGED 2
betrothing *n syn* see ENGAGEMENT 2
betrothment *n syn* see ENGAGEMENT 2
better *adj* 1 *syn* see BEST
2 more worthy or pleasing than an alternative < it is *better* to lose gracefully than to win arrogantly >
syn ‖bettermost, preferable, superior; *compare* GOOD
rel exceeding, exceptional, surpassing; choice, desirable, excellent
idiom more than a match for
ant worst
better *adv syn* see MORE 2
ant worse
better *n* 1 *syn* see SUPERIOR
2 a superior or winning position < had the *better* of the argument >
syn advantage, superiority, upper hand, victory, whip hand; *compare* ADVANTAGE 3
rel success, triumph, win
con collapse, defeat, disadvantage, loss; beating, drubbing, licking
ant worse
better *vb* 1 *syn* see IMPROVE 1
ant worsen
2 *syn* see SURPASS 1
‖**bettermost** *adj* 1 *syn* see BETTER 2
2 *syn* see BEST
between *prep* **1** in common to (as in position, in a distribution, or in participation) < a treaty *between* three powers >
syn among
2 in the time, space, or interval that separates < *between* the ages 12 and 20 >
syn ‖atween, ‖atwixt, ‖betwixt, in between, tween, twixt

---

syn synonym(s)   *rel* related word(s)
ant antonym(s)   *con* contrasted word(s)
idiom idiomatic equivalent(s)
‖ use limited; if in doubt, see a dictionary

‖**betwixt** *prep syn* see BETWEEN 2
bevel *adj syn* see DIAGONAL
beveled *adj syn* see DIAGONAL
‖**bever** *n syn* see SNACK
beverage *n syn* see DRINK 1
bevy *n syn* see GROUP 1
bewail *vb syn* see DEPLORE 1
  ant rejoice
beware *vb* to be cautious < *beware* of the dog>
  syn look out, mind, watch out
  rel attend, heed, notice, watch
  idiom be on one's guard, be on the lookout (*or* watch), keep at a safe distance, take care (*or* heed)
  con disregard, ignore, neglect
bewhiskered *adj syn* see BEARDED
bewilder *vb* 1 *syn* see PUZZLE
  rel baffle, fuddle, muddle
  2 *syn* see CONFUSE 2
bewitch *vb* 1 to practice witchcraft on < *medicine* men who *bewitch* ignorant tribesmen>
  syn charm, enchant, ensorcell, hex, spell, voodoo, witch
  rel bedevil, demonize, overlook, possess, sorcerize; beglamour, dazzle, trick
  idiom cast a spell on (*or* over), give (*or* cast) the evil eye, put a curse on
  2 *syn* see ATTRACT 1
  rel beglamour, ‖snow
bewitched *adj syn* see ENAMORED 3
bewitching *adj syn* see ATTRACTIVE 1
  con forbidding, grim
bewitchment *n syn* see MAGIC 1
beyond *adv* 1 on or to the farther side < a house with mountains *beyond* >
  syn farther, further, ‖yon, yonder
  2 *syn* see OVER 1
beyond *prep* 1 on or to the farther side of < the store is just *beyond* the next house>
  syn after, outside, past, without
  2 out of the reach, sphere, or comprehension of < it's *beyond* me how he did it>
  syn above, past
  idiom beyond one's depth (*or* power), over (*or* above) one's head, too deep (*or* much) for
  3 *syn* see BESIDES 1
beyond *adj syn* see ADDITIONAL
beyond *n syn* see HEREAFTER 2
‖**b'hoy** *n syn* see TOUGH
bias *n* 1 *syn* see LEANING 2
  2 *syn* see PREJUDICE 1
  rel inclination, predisposition; slant, standpoint, viewpoint
  con dispassionateness; fairness, justness
bias *adj syn* see DIAGONAL
bias *vb* 1 *syn* see SLANT 3
  2 *syn* see INCLINE 3
  3 *syn* see PREJUDICE 2
biased *adj* 1 *syn* see DIAGONAL
  2 exhibiting or characterized by a highly personal and unreasoned distortion of judgment < a *biased* estimate of the book's worth>
  syn colored, jaundiced, one-sided, partial, partisan, prejudiced, prepossessed, tendentious, unindifferent, unneutral, warped
  rel bent, disposed, inclined, predisposed; influenced, interested, swayed; opinionated
  con detached, dispassionate, impartial, neutral, open-minded; fair, honest, just

  ant unbiased
bibber *n syn* see DRUNKARD
bibble-babble *n syn* see CHATTER
bibelot *n syn* see KNICKKNACK
Bible *n* the sacred volume of Christians < students of the *Bible* >
  syn Book, Holy Writ, Sacred Writ, Scripture
  idiom Book of Books, Good Book, Word of God
bibliopole *n syn* see BOOKDEALER
bicker *vb* 1 *syn* see ARGUE 2
  rel battle, contend, fight, war
  2 *syn* see QUARREL
  3 *syn* see RATTLE 1
bickering *n syn* see QUARREL
bicycle *n* a pedal-propelled vehicle with two wheels tandem, a steering handle, and a saddle seat < ten-speed *bicycles* >
  syn bike, cycle, two-wheeler, velocipede
bid *vb* 1 *syn* see COMMAND
  rel summon
  con interdict, prohibit
  ant forbid
  2 *syn* see INVITE
  rel request
biddable *adj syn* see OBEDIENT
  rel amiable, good-natured, obliging
  con mulish, obstinate, stiff-necked, stubborn
  ant recalcitrant
bidding *n syn* see COMMAND 1
  rel call, summoning
biddy *n* 1 *syn* see MAID 2
  2 *syn* see HAG 2
bide *vb* 1 *syn* see STAY 2
  rel continue
  2 *syn* see RESIDE 1
bierstube *n syn* see ALEHOUSE
biff *n syn* see BLOW 1
‖**biff** *vb syn* see STRIKE 2
‖**biffy** *n syn* see PRIVY 1
bifold *adj syn* see TWOFOLD 1
big *adj* 1 of significant size or scope < a *big* expanse of mud > < *big* plans>
  syn considerable, extensive, hefty, large, large-scale, major, sizable
  rel bumper, hulking, whacking, whopping; clumsy, unwieldy; ample, biggish, capacious, commodious, comprehensive, copious, roomy, spacious, voluminous, distended, inflated, swollen
  con paltry, piddling, trivial; slight, small; insignificant; minute, tiny, wee
  ant little
  2 *syn* see LARGE 1
  3 *syn* see PREGNANT 1
  4 *syn* see FULL 1
  rel flushed, overflowing; cloyed, glutted, sated, satiated, satisfied
  idiom full to bursting (*or* overflowing), full to the ears, stuffed to the gills
  con empty
  5 *syn* see IMPORTANT 1
  6 *syn* see PRETENTIOUS 3
  7 *syn* see GENEROUS 1
‖**big** *adv syn* see VERY 1
big *n syn* see NOTABLE 1
big boy *n syn* see NOTABLE 1
‖**big bug** *n syn* see NOTABLE 1
‖**big cheese** *n syn* see NOTABLE 1
‖**big chief** *n syn* see NOTABLE 1
‖**biggety** *adj syn* see WISE 5

‖**biggie** *n syn* see NOTABLE 1

big gun *n syn* see NOTABLE 1

‖**big house** *n syn* see JAIL

bight *n syn* see INLET

big name *n syn* see CELEBRITY 2

bigness *n syn* see SIZE 2

‖**big noise** *n syn* see NOTABLE 1

bigot *n syn* see ENTHUSIAST

   rel approver, liker, relisher; mumpsimus, racist, segregationist

   con depreciator, disparager, knocker; disliker, disrelisher, hater, loather, misliker

bigoted *adj syn* see ILLIBERAL

   rel lily-white; conservative

big shot *n syn* see NOTABLE 1

big-timer *n syn* see NOTABLE 1

‖**big wheel** *n syn* see NOTABLE 1

bigwig *n syn* see NOTABLE 1

bike *n syn* see BICYCLE

bilge *n syn* see NONSENSE 2

bilk *vb* 1 *syn* see FRUSTRATE 1

   con fulfill

   2 *syn* see CHEAT

   3 *syn* see ESCAPE 2

   rel dodge, shake

bill *n* 1 the jaws of a bird with their projecting horny covering < the huge *bill* of the toucan >

   syn beak, neb, nib, pecker

   2 *syn* see PROMONTORY

   3 *syn* see VISOR 1

bill *n* 1 a statement of the amount due a creditor < *bills* from the grocer and doctor >

   syn account, invoice, reckoning, score, statement, tab

   rel charges, damage

   idiom statement of account

   2 *syn* see CHECK 2

   3 *syn* see POSTER

   4 *syn* see DOLLAR

billet *n syn* see JOB 2

billet *vb* 1 to assign quarters to soldiers < the troops were *billeted* in private homes >

   syn canton, quarter

   rel bed, house, lodge, put up; bestow

   2 *syn* see HARBOR 2

billet *n syn* see BAR 1

billet-doux *n syn* see LOVE LETTER

billingsgate *n syn* see ABUSE

billy *n syn* see CUDGEL

billy club *n syn* see CUDGEL

‖**bim** *n syn* see WANTON

bimanal *adj syn* see TWO-HANDED 2

bimanual *adj syn* see TWO-HANDED 1

‖**bimbo** *n syn* see WANTON

binary *adj syn* see TWOFOLD 1

bind *vb* 1 *syn* see TIE 1

   con release

   ant unloose

   2 *syn* see BANDAGE

‖**bindle stiff** *n syn* see VAGABOND

‖**bing** *n syn* see PILE 1

binge *n* 1 a drunken revel < hung over after a weekend *binge* >

   syn bat, bender, blowoff, booze, brannigan, bum; bust, carousal, carouse, compotation, drunk, jag, orgy, ran-tan, rowdy-

dow, soak, souse, spree, tear, ‖time, toot, wassail

   rel bacchanal, bacchanalia, debauch; blast, ‖blowout; ‖bun

   2 *syn* see SPREE 1

bio *n syn* see BIOGRAPHY

biocide *n syn* see PESTICIDE

biographer *n* one who writes a biography < irresponsible *biographers* whose work is more fiction than fact >

   syn autobiographer, autobiographist, Boswell, memoirist

biography *n* a more or less detailed account of the events and circumstances of a person's life < wrote a *biography* of his grandfather >

   syn autobiography, bio, confessions, life, memoir

   rel diary, journal, letters; adventures, history, story; profile; obit, obituary

biologic *n syn* see DRUG 1

bird *n syn* see RASPBERRY

birdbrain *n syn* see SCATTERBRAIN

birdhouse *n syn* see AVIARY

birdman *n syn* see PILOT 2

bird-witted *adj syn* see GIDDY 1

birr *n syn* see ENERGY 2

birth *n* 1 the act or process of bringing forth young from the womb < had a very hard *birth* after a prolonged labor >

   syn bearing, ‖birthing, childbearing, childbirth, delivery, parturition

   rel abortion, miscarriage, slip

   2 *syn* see BEGINNING

birth *vb* ‖1 *syn* see BEAR 5

   2 *syn* see SPRING 1

birth control *n* control of the number of children born especially by preventing or lessening the frequency of conception < cultural and religious aspects of *birth control* >

   syn contraception

   rel rhythm method; planned parenthood; vasectomy; (the) pill

‖**birthing** *n syn* see BIRTH 1

birthmark *n* 1 a congenital pigmented area on the skin < *birthmarks* often appear on the neck >

   syn mole, nevus

   2 *syn* see CHARACTERISTIC 1

birth pang *n, usu* **birth pangs** *pl syn* see LABOR 2

birthright *n* 1 *syn* see RIGHT 2

   2 *syn* see HERITAGE 1

bisexual *adj* being structurally and functionally both male and female < many lower animals are *bisexual* >

   syn androgynous, hermaphrodite, hermaphroditic

bistered *adj syn* see DARK 3

bistro *n syn* see NIGHTCLUB

bit *n* 1 *syn* see MORSEL 1

   2 *syn* see PARTICLE

   3 *syn* see END 4

   4 *syn* see WHILE 1

bit *vb syn* see RESTRAIN 1

bit by bit *adv syn* see GRADUALLY

‖**bitch** *vb* 1 *syn* see GRIPE

   2 *syn* see DECEIVE

bitch (up) *vb syn* see BOTCH

bitchy *adj syn* see MALICIOUS

bite *vb* 1 to seize with the teeth so that they enter < *bite* into a pear >

---

syn synonym(s)   *rel* related word(s)
ant antonym(s)   *con* contrasted word(s)
idiom idiomatic equivalent(s)
‖ use limited; if in doubt, see a dictionary

syn champ, chomp

rel gnaw, nibble, tooth; ‖chaw, chew, crunch, masticate, munch; ‖scrunch; eat

idiom sink one's teeth into

2 syn see EAT 3

3 syn see SMART

bite n 1 syn see MORSEL 1

2 syn see SNACK

3 syn see SHARE 1

biting adj syn see INCISIVE

‖bitsy adj syn see TINY

bitter adj 1 syn see ACRID

rel acerb, acid, bitterish

con delicious; bland, flat, insipid

2 difficult to accept mentally < the bitter truth>

syn afflictive, distasteful, galling, grievous, painful, unpalatable

rel annoying, distressing, disturbing, woeful; bad, disagreeable, displeasing, offensive, unpleasant; galling, provoking, vexatious

con agreeable, gratifying, satisfying

3 marked by intense animosity < bitter contempt>

syn antagonistic, hostile, rancorous, virulent, vitriolic

rel alienated, divided, estranged; irreconcilable

4 syn see SEVERE 3

con mild, springlike, summery

bitter–ender n syn see DIEHARD 1

bitterly adv syn see HARD 6

bivouac vb syn see CAMP

‖bivvy vb syn see CAMP

bizarre adj 1 syn see STRANGE 4

2 syn see FANTASTIC 2

con normal, ordinary, regular

blab n syn see CHATTER

blab vb syn see GOSSIP

blab (out) vb syn see REVEAL 1

blabber vb syn see BABBLE 2

blabber n syn see CHATTER

blabber n syn see CHATTERBOX

blabbermouth n syn see CHATTERBOX

blabmouth n syn see CHATTERBOX

black adj 1 having the color of soot or coal < a black hearse>

syn atramentous, ebon, ebony, inky, jet, jetty, onyx, pitch-black, pitch-dark, pitchy, raven, sable

rel blackish; charcoal, slate; piceous; dusky, swart, swarthy; brunet

idiom black as a crow (or a shoe or the ace of spades), black as hell (or night)

ant white

2 syn see DIRTY 1

3 syn see GLOOMY 3

4 syn see UTTER

black vb syn see BRUISE 1

black (out) vb syn see ERASE

black and white n syn see PRINT 2

black–a–vised adj syn see DARK 3

black beast n syn see ABOMINATION 1

‖blackcoat n syn see CLERGYMAN

black dog n syn see SADNESS

blacken vb syn see MALIGN

idiom blacken one's good name, give one a black eye, throw mud at

black eye n 1 a bruise about the eye < got a black eye in a fight>

syn mouse, shiner

rel contusion

2 syn see STIGMA

blackguard n syn see VILLAIN 1

black out vb syn see FAINT

blackout n syn see FAINT

blague n syn see NONSENSE 2

blah n syn see NONSENSE 2

blah adj syn see DULL 9

blamable adj syn see BLAMEWORTHY

blame vb syn see CRITICIZE

rel accuse, charge; impute

idiom lay at one's door (or doorstep), lay (or put) the blame on

con exculpate, vindicate; praise

blame n responsibility for misdeed or delinquency < accepted the blame for his foolish act>

syn culpability, fault, guilt, onus

rel accountability, answerability, liability; accusation, charge, imputation; censure, condemnation, denunciation, reprehension

idiom burden of guilt

con commendation, compliment; acclaim, applause, praise

blamed adj 1 syn see DAMNED 2

2 syn see UTTER

blameful adj syn see BLAMEWORTHY

blameless adj 1 syn see INNOCENT 2

2 syn see GOOD 11

rel unimpeachable

ant blameworthy

blameworthy adj deserving reproach and punishment < though not criminal, his behavior was certainly blameworthy>

syn amiss, blamable, blameful, censurable, culpable, demeritorious, guilty, reprehensible, sinful, unholy

rel illaudable, uncommendable, unpraiseworthy, unpretty; delinquent, faultful; punishable; foolish, irresponsible, reckless

idiom at fault, to blame

con faultless, flawless, impeccable, irreproachable, unimpeachable; guiltless, innocent, sinless; creditable, high-principled, upright

ant blameless; unblamable

blanch vb syn see WHITEN 1

blanch (over) vb syn see PALLIATE

blanch vb syn see RECOIL

blanched adj syn see PALE 1

bland adj 1 syn see SUAVE

rel good-natured, ingratiating

con bluff, crusty, gruff

ant brusque

2 syn see GENTLE 1

3 syn see INSIPID 3

con pungent, savory, spicy, zestful

blandish vb syn see COAX

rel flatter; beguile, charm

con threaten

blandishment n syn see FLATTERY

blank adj 1 syn see EXPRESSIONLESS

2 syn see UTTER

blank n syn see OMISSION

blank check n syn see CARTE BLANCHE

blanket vb syn see COVER 3

blankety–blank adj 1 syn see DAMNED 2

2 syn see UTTER

blankness n syn see VACUITY 2

blank wall n syn see BAR 2

blare vb 1 syn see BLAZE

2 syn see SCREAM 4

blaring adj syn see LOUD 1

blarney *vb syn* see COAX
blarney *n syn* see FLATTERY
blasé *adj syn* see SOPHISTICATED 2
  con awed, wide-eyed; artless, naive, natural, unsophisticated
blasphemous *adj syn* SEE SACRILEGIOUS
blasphemy *n* 1 impious or irreverent language < cursing God is *blasphemy* >
  syn cursing, cussing, execration, imprecation, profanity, swearing
  rel affront, indignity, insult; abuse, billingsgate, scurrility, vituperation
  con reverence, veneration, worship
  ant adoration
  2 *syn* see PROFANATION
  rel abuse, befouling, shaming
blast *n syn* see BANG 2
blast *vb* 1 to ruin or to injure severely, suddenly, or surprisingly < we'll have no peaches; frost *blasted* the blossoms this year >
  syn blight, dash, nip
  rel destroy, ruin, wreck; damage, injure, spoil; shrivel, stunt, wither
  2 *syn* see SLAM 1
  3 *syn* see WHIP 2
blasted *adj* 1 *syn* see DAMNED 2
  2 *syn* see UTTER
blat *vb syn* see EXCLAIM
blatant *adj* 1 *syn* see VOCIFEROUS
  rel screaming; obtrusive
  con modest, soft-spoken
  2 *syn* see GAUDY
  3 *syn* see SHAMELESS
blather *vb syn* see BABBLE 2
blather *n syn* see NONSENSE 2
blatherskite *n syn* see NONSENSE 2
‖**blatter** *n syn* see CHATTER
blaze *vb* to burn or appear to burn brightly < the hot sun *blazed* down >
  syn blare, flame, flare, glare, glow
  rel illuminate, illumine, light; radiate, shine; coruscate, fulgurate, scintillate, sparkle; incandesce
blaze (abroad) *vb syn* see DECLARE 1
blazes *n pl syn* see HELL
blazing *adj* 1 *syn* see BURNING 1
  2 *syn* see IMPASSIONED
blazon *vb syn* see DECLARE 1
bleach *vb syn* see WHITEN 1
bleak *adj* 1 *syn* see GRIM 2
  2 *syn* see GLOOMY 3
blear *vb syn* see DULL 4
blear *adj syn* see FAINT 2
blear-eyed *adj syn* see STUPID 1
blear-witted *adj syn* see STUPID 1
bleary *adj* 1 *syn* see FAINT 2
  2 *syn* see EFFETE 2
bleat *vb syn* see GRIPE
bleed *vb* 1 *syn* see EXUDE
  2 *syn* see FLEECE 1
bleeding *adj* 1 *syn* see DAMNED 2
  2 *syn* see UTTER
blemish *vb syn* see INJURE 1
blemish *n* an imperfection (as a spot or crack) < a *blemish* on the face >
  syn defect, flaw, vice
  rel fault, scar; blister, blotch; disfigurement, pockmark, wart; catch, snag, tear

---

blench *vb syn* see RECOIL
blench *vb syn* see WHITEN 1
blend *vb* 1 *syn* see MIX 1
  rel combine, integrate
  con resolve, separate
  2 *syn* see HARMONIZE 4
blend *n syn* see MIXTURE
blending *adj syn* see HARMONIOUS 1
bless *vb* 1 to make holy by religious rite or word < the priest *blessed* the water and wine >
  syn consecrate, hallow, sanctify
  rel dedicate
  con defile, desecrate, profane
  2 *syn* see PRAISE 2
blessed *adj* 1 *syn* see HOLY 1
  2 *syn* see DAMNED 2
  3 *syn* see UTTER
blessedness *n syn* see HAPPINESS
  con agony, suffering
  ant misery
blessing *n* 1 an expression or utterance of good wishes < on departing, he received his father's *blessing* >
  syn benediction, benison
  rel Godspeed, valediction
  2 *syn* see APPROBATION
  3 *syn* see GOOD 1
  4 *syn* see GRACE 1
‖**bless out** *vb syn* see SCOLD 1
blight *vb syn* see BLAST 1
blighted *adj* 1 *syn* see DAMNED 2
  2 *syn* see UTTER
‖**blighter** *n syn* see WRETCH 1
blimp *n* 1 *syn* see FATTY
  2 *syn* see REACTIONARY
  3 *cap syn* see STUFFED SHIRT
blind *adj* 1 lacking the power to see < kittens are *blind* at birth >
  syn ‖dark, eyeless, sightless, stone-blind, visionless
  rel dim-sighted, purblind, short-sighted; blindish; blindfolded; unseeing
  idiom blind as a bat
  con seeing, sighted; keen, sharp
  2 *syn* see INTOXICATED 1
  3 *syn* see DULL 7
blind *vb syn* see DAZE 1
blind *n* 1 *syn* see FRONT 3
  2 *syn* see DECOY 2
blind alley *n syn* see DEAD END
blinding *adj* 1 *syn* see DAMNED 2
  2 *syn* see UTTER
blink *vb* 1 *syn* see WINK
  2 to shine intermittently < we'll signal by *blinking* the headlights >
  syn flash, flicker, twinkle
  rel glimmer, scintillate, shimmer
blink (at) *vb syn* see CONNIVE 1
blink (at *or* away) *vb syn* see NEGLECT
‖**blinking** *adj* 1 *syn* see DAMNED 2
  2 *syn* see UTTER
blip *vb* 1 *syn* see SLAP 1
  2 *syn* see CENSOR
bliss *n* 1 *syn* see HAPPINESS
  con dolor, misery, woe
  ant anguish
  2 *syn* see HEAVEN 2
blissfulness *n syn* see HAPPINESS
  rel ecstasy, euphoria, exaltation; heaven, paradise
blister *vb syn* see LAMBASTE 3
blistering *adj* 1 *syn* see HOT 1

---

syn synonym(s)   *rel* related word(s)
ant antonym(s)   *con* contrasted word(s)
idiom idiomatic equivalent(s)
‖ use limited; if in doubt, see a dictionary

‖2 *syn* see DAMNED 2
blithe *adj* 1 *syn* see CHEERFUL 1
  2 *syn* see MERRY
  ant atrabilious, morose
blithering *adj syn* see UTTER
blithesome *adj syn* see MERRY
blitz *vb syn* see BOMBARD
‖**bloat** *n syn* see DRUNKARD
bloated *adj syn* see POMPOUS 1
bloc *n syn* see COMBINATION 2
block *n* 1 *syn* see BAR 2
  2 *syn* see ANNEX
block *vb* 1 *syn* see HINDER
  2 *syn* see INTERCEPT
  3 *syn* see FILL 1
block (out) *vb syn* see SKETCH
blockade *n* 1 *syn* see BAR 2
‖2 *syn* see MOONSHINE 2
blockade *vb syn* see BESIEGE
block and block *adj syn* see FULL 1
blockhead *n syn* see DUNCE
blockheaded *adj syn* see STUPID 1
blockish *adj syn* see STUPID 1
block out *vb syn* see SCREEN 3
‖**bloke** *n syn* see MAN 3
blond *adj* 1 of a pale soft yellow color
  < *blond* hair >
  syn flaxen, golden, straw
  rel blondish; platinum; champagne, tow-
  headed
  con dark; brunet
  2 *syn* see FAIR 3
blood *n* 1 the fluid that circulates in the
  heart, arteries, capillaries, and veins of a
  vertebrate animal < *blood* covered the
  battlefield >
  syn ‖claret, gore
  rel ichor; humor
  2 *syn* see ANCESTRY
  3 *syn* see MURDER
  4 *syn* see FOP
blood-and-guts *adj syn* see INTENSIVE
bloodbath *n syn* see MASSACRE
bloodless *adj* 1 *syn* see PALE 2
  rel colorless; lifeless
  con alive; vigorous; florid
  ant plethoric; sanguine
  2 *syn* see INSENSIBLE 5
bloodshed *n syn* see MASSACRE
bloodstained *adj syn* see BLOODY 1
bloodsucker *n syn* see PARASITE
bloodthirsty *adj syn* see MURDEROUS
bloody *adj* 1 affected by or involving the
  shedding of blood < a *bloody* knife >
  < when will this long and *bloody* conflict
  cease? >
  syn bloodstained, ensanguined, gory,
  imbrued, sanguinary, sanguine, sanguineous
  rel bloodthirsty, grim, murderous, slaugh-
  terous; cutthroat, red-handed
  2 *syn* see MURDEROUS
bloom *n* 1 *syn* see FLOWER 1
  2 a state or time of beauty, freshness, and
  vigor < the *bloom* of youth >
  syn blossom, flush
  rel glow
  3 a rosy appearance of the cheeks < recovered all her health and *bloom* >
  syn blossom, blush, flush, glow
bloom *vb syn* see BLOSSOM
‖**blooming** *adj* 1 *syn* see DAMNED 2
  2 *syn* see UTTER

blooper *n* 1 *syn* see ERROR 2
  2 *syn* see FAUX PAS
blossom *n* 1 *syn* see FLOWER 1
  rel capitulum, corymb, cyme, inflores-
  cence, panicle, raceme, spike, umbel
  2 *syn* see BLOOM 2
  3 *syn* see BLOOM 3
blossom *vb* to produce flowers or be in
  flower < lilacs *blossom* in the spring >
  syn bloom, blow, burgeon, effloresce,
  flower, outbloom
  rel bud; leaf; shoot; open, unfold
  idiom burst into bloom, come into flower,
  put forth blossoms (*or* flowers *or* bloom)
  con fade, fall, wither
blot *n syn* see STIGMA
  rel blemish, flaw, defect
blot *vb syn* see STAIN 1
blotch *vb syn* see SPLOTCH
blot out *vb* 1 *syn* see ERASE
  2 *syn* see ANNIHILATE 2
‖**blotter** *n syn* see DRUNKARD
‖**blotto** *adj syn* see INTOXICATED 1
bloviate *vb syn* see ORATE
blow *vb* 1 to produce a current of air on
  < let the wind *blow* your hair dry >
  syn fan, ruffle, wind, winnow
  2 *syn* see BOAST
  3 *syn* see PANT 1
  4 *syn* see WASTE 2
  5 *syn* see TREAT 3
  ‖6 *syn* see BOTCH
  7 *syn* see GO 2
blow *n syn* see BREAK 4
blow *vb syn* see BLOSSOM
blow *n* 1 a forceful sharp stroke (as with
  the fist or an instrument) < struck him a
  sudden *blow* >
  syn bang, bash, bastinado, bat, belt, biff,
  bop, crack, ‖ding, ‖douse, pound, slam,
  slosh, smack, smash, sock, ‖swap, thwack,
  wallop, ‖welt, whack, whop; *compare*
  CUFF, HIT 1
  rel recumbentibus, slug, ‖souse; clip, pelt,
  plug, punch, swat
  2 *syn* see IMPACT
blow-by-blow *adj syn* see CIRCUMSTAN-
  TIAL
blowen *n syn* see HARLOT 1
blower *n syn* see BRAGGART
blowhard *n syn* see BRAGGART
‖**blow in** *vb syn* see COME 1
blown-in-the-bottle *adj syn* see AU-
  THENTIC 2
‖**blow off** *vb syn* see GRIPE
‖**blowoff** *n syn* see BINGE 1
‖**blowout** *n syn* see SHINDIG 1
blowsy *adj syn* see SLATTERNLY
  ant spruce
blow up *vb* 1 *syn* see EXPLODE 1
  2 *syn* see DISCREDIT 2
  3 *syn* see ANGER 2
blowy *adj syn* see WINDY 1
blub *vb syn* see CRY 2
blubber *vb syn* see CRY 2
bludgeon *n syn* see CUDGEL
bludgeon *vb syn* see INTIMIDATE
blue *adj* 1 *syn* see DOWNCAST
  2 *syn* see RISQUÉ
  3 *syn* see UTTER
blue *n syn* see OCEAN
blue blood *n* 1 *syn* see GENTLEMAN
  2 *syn* see ARISTOCRACY

‖**bluebottle** *n syn* see POLICEMAN
bluecoat *n syn* see POLICEMAN
blue–eyed *adj syn* see FAVORITE 1
blue moon *n syn* see AGE 2
bluenose *n syn* see PRUDE
bluenosed *adj syn* see PRIM 1
blueprint *n syn* see PLAN 1
   rel outline, sketch
blueprint *vb syn* see PLAN 2
blue–ribbon *adj syn* see EXCELLENT
blues *n pl but sometimes sing in constr syn*
   see SADNESS
bluff *adj* direct and unceremonious in
speech or manner < *bluff* aggressive questions >
   syn abrupt, blunt, breviloquent, brief,
brusque, crusty, curt, gruff, rough, short,
short-spoken, snippety, snippy
   rel hearty, honest, sincere; barefaced,
candid, direct, forthright, frank, no-nonsense, outspoken, plainspoken, straightforward; bearish, rude, tactless; sharp, tart;
laconic, terse
   idiom to the point
   con civil, courteous, courtly, gallant,
polite; diplomatic, urbane
   ant smooth, suave
bluff *vb* 1 *syn* see DECEIVE
   rel fool, joke, trick
   2 *syn* see ASSUME 4
blunder *vb* 1 *syn* see STUMBLE 3
   2 *syn* see WALLOW 2
   3 *syn* see BOTCH
blunder (away) *vb syn* see WASTE 2
blunder *n syn* see ERROR 2
blunderbuss *n syn* see STUMBLEBUM
blunderer *n syn* see STUMBLEBUM
blunt *adj* 1 *syn* see DULL 6
   rel unpointed, unsharp; insensitive
   con acuminate, acute
   ant keen, sharp
   2 *syn* see BLUFF
   con politic, smooth, suave
   ant subtle; tactful
blunt *vb* 1 *syn* see DULL 3
   2 *syn* see DEADEN 1
   3 *syn* see DULL 5
   4 *syn* see WEAKEN 1
‖**blunt** *n syn* see MONEY
blur *n syn* see STIGMA
blur *vb* 1 *syn* see TAINT 1
   2 *syn* see CONFUSE 4
   3 *syn* see DULL 4
blurb *n syn* see PUFF 3
blurt (out) *vb syn* see EXCLAIM
blush *vb* to turn or glow red in the face
< *blushed* from embarrassment >
   syn color, crimson, flush, glow, mantle,
pink, pinken, redden, rose, rouge
blush *n syn* see BLOOM 3
bluster *vb* 1 *syn* see ROAR
   rel blast, storm, rage
   2 *syn* see INTIMIDATE
blustering *adj syn* see WILD 6
blustery *adj syn* see WILD 6
board *vb* 1 to get aboard of < *boarded* the
wrong bus >
   syn embark

rel embus, emplane, entrain
   idiom get on
   con debus, deplane, detrain; land
   ant debark, disembark, get off
   2 *syn* see HARBOR 2
   rel care (for), cherish, nurture, tend
board *n* 1 **boards** *pl syn* see DRAMA
   2 *syn* see TABLE 1
boast *vb* to express pride in oneself or
one's accomplishments < *boasting* about
all the girl friends he had >
   syn blow, brag, cock-a-doodle-doo, crow,
gasconade, mouth, prate, puff, rodomontade, vaunt
   rel pique, plume, preen, pride, quack;
gush, vapor; aggrandize, exalt, glory, triumph; bluster, ‖bounce, bully, ruffle,
swash, swashbuckle, swagger; flaunt, parade, show off
   idiom blow one's horn, congratulate oneself, hug oneself, pat oneself on the back
   con belittle, decry, degrade, disparage,
knock, minimize, run down
   ant depreciate
boaster *n syn* see BRAGGART
boastful *adj* given to or characterized by
boasting < a *boastful* old windbag >
   syn braggadocian, braggart, braggy, rodomontade, self-glorifying, vaunting
   rel arrogant, pretentious; cock-a-hoop,
exultant; big-headed, conceited, swelled-
headed; self-aggrandizing, self-applauding,
self-flattering, vainglorious
   idiom having a high opinion of oneself,
seeing oneself larger than life
   con self-depreciating, self-effacing, unassuming; bashful, demure, sheepish, shy,
timid; quiet, reserved, restrained, retiring
   ant modest
bob *vb syn* see TAP 1
bobbery *n syn* see BRAWL 2
bobble *vb syn* see BOTCH
‖**bobby** *n syn* see POLICEMAN
‖**bodacious** *adj syn* see NOTEWORTHY
bode *vb syn* see AUGUR 2
bodement *n syn* see FORETOKEN
bodiless *adj syn* see IMMATERIAL 1
bodily *adj* of or relating to the human
body < *bodily* pain >
   syn carnal, corporal, corporeal, fleshly,
physical, somatic
   rel animal, sensual
   con intellectual, mental, psychic, psychological; spiritual, unworldly
boding *n syn* see FORETOKEN
body *n* 1 *syn* see HUMAN
   2 *syn* see CORPSE
   3 the main, central, or essential part < the
body of the discussion dealt with ways to
ensure equal opportunities for all >
   syn bulk, core, corpus, mass, staple, substance; *compare* ESSENCE 2, SUBSTANCE 2,
TENOR 1
   rel majority; sum, total, whole; basis,
crux, fundamental, gravamen; gist, pith
   con angle, aspect, facet, feature, side;
accessory, extension, offshoot, side issue
   4 a discrete portion of matter < unknown *bodies* in space >
   syn bulk, mass, object, volume
   5 a determinable or measurable whole
< collected a large *body* of evidence >
   syn aggregate, amount, budget, bulk,
quantity, quantum, total

---

syn synonym(s)   *rel* related word(s)
ant antonym(s)   *con* contrasted word(s)
idiom idiomatic equivalent(s)
‖ use limited; if in doubt, see a dictionary

rel extent, range; number, stock, sum, whole

6 *syn* see GROUP 3

7 *syn* see SUBSTANCE 2

body (forth) *vb syn* see REPRESENT 2

boeotian *n syn* see PHILISTINE

bog *n syn* see SWAMP

bog (down) *vb syn* see DELAY 1

bogey *n syn* see APPARITION

boggle *vb* **1** *syn* see DEMUR

2 *syn* see BOTCH

3 *syn* see STAGGER 5

bogus *adj syn* see COUNTERFEIT

rel forged; imitation

con bona fide, good

ant authentic, genuine, real

Bohemian *n* a person (as an artist) who has an unconventional life-style that often reflects protest against or indifference to convention <a gathering place for radicals and *Bohemians*>

syn maverick, nonconformist

rel beat, beatnik, dropout, hippie; iconoclast; eccentric, original; recusant

con conformer, conventionalist, formalist, pedant

bohunk *n syn* see OAF 2

boil *n syn* see ABSCESS

boil *vb* **1** *syn* see SEETHE 4

2 to prepare (as food) in a liquid heated to the point that it begins to give off steam < *boil* eggs>

syn parboil, seethe, simmer, stew

rel coddle, poach; decoct; steam

3 *syn* see ANGER 2

4 *syn* see RUSH 1

boil down *vb syn* see SIMPLIFY

boildown *n syn* see ABRIDGMENT

‖**boiled** *adj syn* see INTOXICATED 1

boiling *adj syn* see HOT 1

boil over *vb syn* see ANGER 2

boisterous *adj* **1** *syn* see TURBULENT 1

2 *syn* see VOCIFEROUS

rel brawling, noisy, riotous, rollicking, rowdy

con sedate, sober, staid; noiseless

boko *n syn* see NOSE 1

bold *adj* **1** *syn* see BRAVE 1

con pusillanimous, shrinking, timid, timorous

ant cowardly

2 *syn* see WISE 5

rel audacious; bluff

con mousy, quiet, shy

3 *syn* see INSOLENT 2

‖**boldacious** *adj syn* see INSOLENT 2

bold–faced *adj syn* see WISE 5

boldhearted *adj syn* see BRAVE 1

boldness *n syn* see INSOLENCE

bollix *vb syn* see BOTCH

Bolshevik *n syn* see COMMUNIST

‖**Bolshie** *n syn* see COMMUNIST

bolster *vb* **1** *syn* see SUPPORT 4

rel reinforce, strengthen

2 *syn* see SUPPORT 5

bolt *n syn* see THUNDERBOLT

bolt *vb* **1** *syn* see START 1

2 *syn* see RUSH 1

3 *syn* see RUN 2

4 *syn* see EXCLAIM

5 *syn* see GULP

bomb *n* **1** *syn* see FAILURE 5

‖**2** *syn* see FORTUNE 4

bomb *vb syn* see BOMBARD

bombard *vb* to assault with bombs or shells <cities *bombarded* by planes and artillery>

syn blitz, bomb, cannonade, shell

rel barrage, strafe, strike

idiom open up on, pour a broadside into

bombardment *n syn* see BARRAGE

bombast *n* pretentious inflated speech or writing <adolescent *bombast* about Youth and Destiny>

syn fustian, highfalutin, lexiphanicism, rant, rhapsody, rhetoric, rodomontade

rel grandiloquence, magniloquence; flatulence, orotundity, tumidity, turgidity; heroics, pyrotechnics, sesquipedality; Johnsonese; spread-eagleism; nonsense

idiom purple prose

bombastic *adj syn* see RHETORICAL

rel flatulent

con unimpassioned; unaffected

‖**bombed** *adj syn* see INTOXICATED 1

bombinate *vb syn* see HUM

bona fide *adj syn* see AUTHENTIC 2

bona fides *n syn* see GOOD FAITH

bonanza *n* a place of great abundance or a source of great wealth or opportunity <the town proved to be a *bonanza* for entrepreneurs>

syn eldorado, Golconda, gold mine, mine, treasure-house, treasure trove, treasury

bond *n* **1** *usu bonds pl syn* see SHACKLE

2 *syn* see CONTRACT

3 a uniting or binding element or force <the *bonds* of friendship>

syn knot, ligament, ligature, link, nexus, tie, vinculum, yoke

rel bridge, connection, connective, liaison; interrelationship, relationship

4 *syn* see ADHERENCE 1

5 *syn* see GUARANTEE 1

bondage *n* the state of subjection to an owner or master <prisoners sold into *bondage*>

syn enslavement, helotry, peonage, serfage, serfdom, servility, servitude, slavery, thrall, thralldom, villenage, yoke

rel subjection, subjugation

con freedom, independence, liberty

bondman *n syn* see SLAVE 1

bondslave *n syn* see SLAVE 1

bondsman *n syn* see SLAVE 1

bone *n* **1** *bones pl syn* see DICE

‖**2** *syn* see DOLLAR

bone (up) *vb syn* see CRAM 4

bone–dry *adj* **1** *syn* see DRY 1

2 *syn* see DRY 3

bonehead *n syn* see DUNCE

boneless *adj syn* see WEAK 4

boner *n* **1** *syn* see ERROR 2

2 *syn* see FAUX PAS

‖**boneyard** *n syn* see CEMETERY

bong *vb syn* see RING

boniface *n syn* see SALOONKEEPER

‖**bonkers** *adj syn* see INSANE 1

bonne bouche *n syn* see DELICACY

bonnet *n syn* see DECOY 2

‖**bonny** *adj syn* see BEAUTIFUL

bon vivant *n syn* see EPICURE

rel bon viveur, boulevardier, high liver, man-about-town, sport

bony *adj syn* see LEAN

boo *n syn* see RASPBERRY

boo *n syn* see MARIJUANA
boob *n* 1 *syn* see DUNCE
  2 *syn* see PHILISTINE
‖**boo–boo** *n syn* see FAUX PAS
booby *n syn* see DUNCE
booby hatch *n syn* see ASYLUM 3
booby trap *n syn* see PITFALL
boodle *n* 1 *syn* see FORTUNE 4
  2 *syn* see SPOIL
boodle *vb syn* see CHEAT
boohoo *vb syn* see CRY 2
book *n* 1 a collection of folded, cut, bound, and usually printed sheets <a *book* of poems>
  syn tome, volume
  rel publication, work, writing; scroll; booklet, brochure, folder, leaflet, magazine, pamphlet; compendium, handbook, manual, monograph, textbook, tract, treatise; codex; novel
  2 *cap* Book *syn* see BIBLE
book *vb* 1 *syn* see LIST 3
  2 *syn* see TIME 1
  3 *syn* see RESERVE 2
bookdealer *n* one who deals in books <sold his library to a *bookdealer*>
  syn bibliopole, bookman, bookseller
  rel bouquiniste
bookie *n syn* see BOOKMAKER
bookish *adj syn* see PEDANTIC
  rel booksy, highbrow
book–learned *adj syn* see PEDANTIC
bookmaker *n* one who determines odds and receives and pays off bets <*bookmakers* who welsh on paying off winners>
  syn bookie, layer
  rel pricemaker; runner
bookman *n syn* see BOOKDEALER
bookseller *n syn* see BOOKDEALER
booky *adj syn* see PEDANTIC
boom *n* 1 *syn* see BANG 2
  2 *syn* see PROSPERITY 4
boomerang *vb syn* see BACKFIRE
booming *adj syn* see FLOURISHING
boon *n* 1 *syn* see GIFT 1
  2 *syn* see GOOD 1
boon *adj syn* see MERRY
‖**boondocks** *n pl syn* see FRONTIER 2
‖**boonies** *n pl syn* see FRONTIER 2
boor *n* an uncouth ungainly fellow <an ill-mannered *boor*>
  syn ‖boothoon, chuff, churl, clodhopper, clown, grobian, mucker
  rel barbarian, vulgarian; looby, lubber; farmer, loon, rustic, swain; ‖carl; bohunk; boob, buffoon, oaf
  con slicker, smoothy; gentleman; cosmopolitan, cosmopolite, sophisticate
boorish *adj* uncouth in manner or appearance <a *boorish* fellow lacking all grace>
  syn churlish, cloddish, clodhopping, clownish, ill-bred, loutish, lowbred, lubberly, lumpish, robustious, rugged, swainish, uncivilized, uncultured, unpolished, unrefined; *compare* COARSE 3
  rel barbarian, barbaric, outlandish, tasteless, vulgar; bucolic, countrified, inurbane, provincial, rustic, yokelish; ill-mannered,

impolite, rude, uncivil, ungracious; graceless, unpoised
  con cultivated, cultured, refined; suave, urbane; courteous, courtly, genteel, polite, well-bred; graceful, gracious, poised
boost *vb* 1 *syn* see RAISE 9
  2 *syn* see INCREASE 1
  3 *syn* see PROMOTE 3
  ‖4 *syn* see SHOPLIFT
boost *n syn* see RISE 3
‖**booster** *n syn* see DECOY 2
boot *n* 1 *syn* see THRILL
  2 *syn* see NOVICE
boot (out) *vb* 1 *syn* see EJECT 1
  2 *syn* see DISMISS 3
‖**boot hill** *n syn* see CEMETERY
bootleg *n syn* see MOONSHINE 2
bootleg *vb syn* see SMUGGLE
bootless *adj syn* see FUTILE
  rel frustrating; profitless, worthless
bootlick *vb syn* see FAWN
bootlick *n syn* see SYCOPHANT
bootlicker *n syn* see SYCOPHANT
bootlicking *adj syn* see FAWNING
booty *n syn* see SPOIL
booze *vb syn* see DRINK 3
booze *n* 1 *syn* see LIQUOR 2
  2 *syn* see BINGE 1
‖**boozed** *adj syn* see INTOXICATED 1
‖**boozehound** *n syn* see DRUNKARD
boozer *n* 1 *syn* see DRUNKARD
  ‖2 *syn* see BAR 5
‖**boozy** *adj syn* see INTOXICATED 1
‖**bop** *n syn* see BLOW 1
borasca *n syn* see POVERTY 1
bordello *n syn* see BROTHEL
border *n* 1 a line or relatively narrow space that marks the outermost bound of something <the *border* of the rug>
  syn brim, brink, edge, fringe, hem, margin, perimeter, periphery, rim, selvage, skirt, verge; *compare* CIRCUMFERENCE
  rel butts and bounds, lines, metes and bounds; bound, circumference, confine, end, extremity, limit, termination; boundary, frontier, march, pale; beginning, door, entrance, threshold; sideline; lip
  con inside, interior; recesses; center; body, bulk, mass, whole
  2 *syn* see FRONTIER 1
border *vb* 1 to form a border to <hedges *border* the park>
  syn bound, define, edge, fringe, hem, margin, outline, rim, skirt, surround, verge
  rel circumscribe, encircle, enclose, frame; contour, delineate, mark (off), outline, set off; flank, line, side; trim
  2 *syn* see ADJOIN
  3 to come to be closely similiar to a specified thing <ideas that *border* on the absurd>
  syn approach, trench, verge
  rel approximate, compare, near
  idiom come close (*or* near) to
bordering *adj syn* see ADJACENT 3
borderland *n syn* see FRONTIER 1
borderline *adj syn* see DOUBTFUL 1
bore *vb* 1 *syn* see PERFORATE
  2 *syn* see GAZE 1
bore *vb* to induce a state of boredom in <*bored* to death by his endless sermon>
  syn ennui, pall, tire, weary
  rel jade; fatigue, wear; annoy, irk, irritate; afflict, bother, discomfort

---

syn synonym(s)   *rel* related word(s)
ant antonym(s)   *con* contrasted word(s)
idiom idiomatic equivalent(s)
‖ use limited; if in doubt, see a dictionary

idiom put one to sleep

con amuse, entertain; excite, fascinate, intrigue; absorb, beguile, engross, enthrall, grip; enliven, freshen, invigorate, quicken, stimulate

ant interest

boreal *adj syn see* COLD 1

boredom *n syn see* TEDIUM

rel fatigue, weariness; disgust, distaste

con amusement, diversion, entertainment; excitement, fascination; engrossment, enthrallment

boresome *adj syn see* IRKSOME

rel deadly, dreary, dull, humdrum, monotonous

con amusing, entertaining; exciting, fascinating, intriguing; absorbing, engrossing, enthralling, gripping, stimulating

ant interesting

boring *adj syn see* IRKSOME

born *adj syn see* INHERENT

‖**born** *vb syn see* BEAR 5

borné *adj syn see* LITTLE 2

bosh *n syn see* NONSENSE 2

bosom *n syn see* HEART 1

bosomy *adj syn see* BUXOM

boss *n syn see* LEADER 2

‖**boss** *adj syn see* EXCELLENT

boss *vb syn see* SUPERVISE

bossy *adj syn see* MASTERFUL 1

‖**bosthoon** *n syn see* BOOR

Boswell *n syn see* BIOGRAPHER

botch *vb* to do or proceed ineffectively or badly through clumsiness, stupidity, or lack of ability < a complete incompetent —*botches* everything he puts his hand to >

syn bitch (up), ‖blow, blunder, bobble, boggle, bollix, bugger up, bumble, bungle, cobble, dub, flub, fluff, foozle, fumble, goof (up), gum (up), louse up, mess, ‖muck, mucker, muff, ‖screw (up)

rel butcher, mangle, murder, mutilate; mar, ruin, spoil; destroy, wreck; hash; tinker; misconduct, mishandle, mismanage; confuse, disorder

idiom play (*or* wreak) havoc with, play hell with

botch *n syn see* MESS 3

botchery *n syn see* MESS 3

botchy *adj syn see* SLIPSHOD 3

bother *vb* 1 *syn see* DISCOMPOSE 1

2 *syn see* ANNOY 1

bother *n* 1 *syn see* ANNOYANCE 2

2 *syn see* ANNOYANCE 3

3 *syn see* INCONVENIENCE

botheration *n* 1 *syn see* ANNOYANCE 2

2 *syn see* ANNOYANCE 3

bothering *n syn see* ANNOYANCE 1

botherment *n syn see* ANNOYANCE 3

bothersomeness *n syn see* INCONVENIENCE

bottega *n syn see* STUDIO

bottle (up) *vb* 1 *syn see* RESTRAIN

2 *syn see* CORNER

bottom *n* 1 the under surface as opposed to the top surface < gum was stuck to the *bottom* of her shoe >

syn sole, underneath, underside, undersurface

rel belly, underbelly, underbody; base, floor, foot, ground

con acme, apex, cap, crest, crown, tip, upper

ant top

2 *syn see* BUTTOCKS

3 the lower or lowest point < the *bottom* of the page >

syn base, foot, nadir

rel basement, floor, ground; end; low

con acme, apex, pinnacle, zenith

ant top

4 *syn see* BASE 1

5 *syn see* ESSENCE 2

bottom *vb syn see* BASE

bottom *adj* 1 *syn see* BOTTOMMOST

2 *syn see* FUNDAMENTAL 1

bottom dog *n syn see* VICTIM 2

bottomless *adj* 1 *syn see* BASELESS

rel reasonless, unjustifiable, unsupportable

2 extremely deep < the *bottomless* sea >

syn abysmal, fathomless, plumbless, plummetless, soundless, unfathomable; *compare* DEEP 1

rel endless, infinite

bottommost *adj* that is at the very bottom < the ladder's *bottommost* rung >

syn bottom, lowermost, lowest, nethermost, rock-bottom, undermost

con top, upper, uppermost

ant topmost

bough *n syn see* LIMB

bought *adj syn see* READY-MADE

‖**boughten** *adj syn see* READY-MADE

boulevard *n syn see* WAY 1

bounce *vb* 1 *syn see* JUMP 1

2 *syn see* DISMISS 2

‖3 *syn see* INTIMIDATE

bounce (back) *vb* 1 *syn see* RECOVER 3

2 *syn see* BACKFIRE

bouncer *n* ‖1 *syn see* LIE

rel exaggeration, hyperbole, overstatement

idiom tall tale

2 a person employed to restrain or eject disorderly persons (as at a bar) < tossed out by the *bouncer* >

syn chucker, ‖chucker-out, houseman

rel goon, muscleman, strong arm

bouncy *adj syn see* ELASTIC 2

bound *n* 1 *usu* bounds *pl syn see* ENVIRONS 1

2 *syn see* LIMIT 1

bound *vb* 1 *syn see* DEMARCATE 1

2 *syn see* BORDER 1

bound *adj* 1 *syn see* FINITE

2 obliged to serve a master or in a clearly defined capacity for a certain length of time by the terms of a contract or mutual agreement < brought to the American colonies as a *bound* servant >

syn apprenticed, articled, indentured

rel contracted; enslaved

con free, freed

3 *syn see* CONSTIPATED

bound *vb syn see* JUMP 1

boundary *n syn see* ENVIRONS 1

bounded *adj syn see* FINITE

ant unbounded

bounder *n syn see* CAD

boundless *adj syn see* LIMITLESS

bounteous *adj* 1 *syn see* LIBERAL 1

con cheap, illiberal, scant

ant niggardly

2 *syn see* PLENTIFUL

con insufficient, scant, sparse

bountiful *adj* 1 *syn see* LIBERAL 1

2 *syn* see PLENTIFUL

bouquet *n* 1 cut flowers arranged for wear or display <a *bouquet* of spring flowers>
syn nosegay, posy
rel arrangement; boutonniere, corsage; spray; wreath; garland, festoon; lei
2 *syn* see COMPLIMENT 1
3 *syn* see FRAGRANCE

Bourbon *n syn* see REACTIONARY

bout *n* 1 *syn* see SPELL 1
2 *syn* see SIEGE

boutade *n syn* see CAPRICE

bow *vb syn* see YIELD 2

bow *n* 1 *syn* see CURVE
2 *syn* see TURN 4

bow *vb syn* see CURVE

bowdlerize *vb syn* see CENSOR

bowed *adj* 1 *syn* see CURVED
2 *syn* see BOWLEGGED

bowel *vb syn* see EVISCERATE

bower *n syn* see ARBOR

bowery *n syn* see SKID ROW

bowl *n syn* see STADIUM

‖**bowl** (down *or* out) *vb syn* see WHIP 2

bowl (down *or* over) *vb syn* see FELL 1

bowlegged *adj* having legs bent outward <a *bowlegged* cowboy>
syn bandy, bandy-legged, bowed
rel bent, crooked, curved, misshapen

bowwow *n syn* see DOG 1

‖**box** *n* 1 *syn* see HUT
2 *syn* see PREDICAMENT

box *n syn* see CUFF

box *vb syn* see SLAP 1

boxing *n* the art of attack and defense with the fists practiced as a sport <he liked *boxing*—at least as a spectator sport>
syn fisticuffs, prizefighting, pugilism, ring

boy *n* 1 a male person not fully matured <a *boy* of nine>
syn lad, laddie, shaveling, son, stripling, tad
rel gamin, ragamuffin, street arab, urchin; hobbledehoy, whippersnapper; schoolboy
idiom little shaver, small fry
2 *syn* see MAN 3

boyfriend *n* 1 a man who is a woman's usual or preferred escort or companion <went to the movies with her *boyfriend*>
syn beau, gentleman friend, swain, young man
rel admirer
2 a man who shares with a woman a strong and usually sexually oriented mutual attraction <moved in with her *boyfriend*>
syn beau, beloved, flame, inamorato, lover, steady, sweetheart, truelove
rel crush, heartthrob; fiancé
3 *syn* see LOVER 1

brabble *vb syn* see QUARREL

brabble *n* 1 *syn* see QUARREL
2 *syn* see CHATTER

brace *n* 1 *syn* see COUPLE
2 *syn* see SUPPORT 3
3 **braces** *pl syn* see SUSPENDERS

brace *vb* 1 *syn* see GIRD 3

2 *syn* see SUPPORT 4
3 *syn* see BEG

bracing *adj syn* see INVIGORATING

bracket *vb* 1 *syn* see JOIN 1
2 *syn* see COMPARE 2

brag *vb syn* see BOAST
con apologize, deprecate

braggadocian *adj syn* see BOASTFUL

braggadocio *n syn* see BRAGGART

braggart *n* one who boasts <too much of a *braggart* about his strength>
syn blower, blowhard, boaster, braggadocio, bragger, ‖gasbag, puckfist, rodomont, rodomontade, vaunter
rel bluffer, blusterer, loudmouth, miles gloriosus, ranter, raver, windbag
con Milquetoast

braggart *adj syn* see BOASTFUL

bragger *n syn* see BRAGGART

braggy *adj syn* see BOASTFUL

Brahmin *n syn* see INTELLECTUAL 2

brain *n* 1 *syn* see MIND 1
2 *syn* see INTELLECT 2
3 *often* **brains** *pl syn* see INTELLIGENCE 1

brainchild *n syn* see INVENTION

brainless *adj syn* see SIMPLE 3

brainpower *n syn* see INTELLIGENCE 1

brainsick *adj syn* see INSANE 1

brainwork *n syn* see THOUGHT 1

brainy *adj syn* see INTELLIGENT 2

brake *vb syn* see HINDER
rel slow, stop

branch *n* 1 *syn* see LIMB
rel branchlet
2 *syn* see CREEK 2

brand *n* 1 *syn* see MARK 7
2 *syn* see STIGMA

brandish *vb syn* see SHOW 4

brand–new *adj* conspicuously new and unused <a *brand-new* car right out of the showroom>
syn fire-new, mint, spang-new, spanking-new, span-new, spick-and-span
rel untouched, unused; clean, fresh, pristine
con hand-me-down, secondhand, used; outworn, shabby, worn, worn-out
ant old

brannigan *n* 1 *syn* see BINGE 1
2 *syn* see QUARREL

brash *adj* 1 *syn* see RASH 1
2 *syn* see EXUBERANT 1
3 *syn* see TACTLESS
4 *syn* see PRESUMPTUOUS
rel bold, brazen; rash, reckless; headlong, impetuous; cocksure

brashness *n* 1 *syn* see TEMERITY
2 *syn* see EFFRONTERY

brass *n* ‖1 *syn* see MONEY
2 *syn* see EFFRONTERY

brassbound *adj* 1 *syn* see ILLIBERAL
2 *syn* see INFLEXIBLE 2
3 *syn* see PRESUMPTUOUS

brass hat *n syn* see SUPERIOR

brassy *adj* 1 *syn* see SHAMELESS
2 *syn* see BRAZEN 4

brave *adj* 1 having or showing no fear when faced with something dangerous, difficult, or unknown <made a *brave* attempt to save the burning house>
syn audacious, aweless, bold, boldhearted, bravehearted, chin-up, courageous, dauntless, doughty, fearless, gallant, game, greathearted, ‖gutsy, heroic, intrepid, lion-

---

syn synonym(s)   *rel* related word(s)
ant antonym(s)   *con* contrasted word(s)
idiom idiomatic equivalent(s)
‖ use limited; if in doubt, see a dictionary

hearted, manful, manly, ‖plucked, plucky, soldierly, spunky, stalwart, stout, stout-hearted, unafraid, unblenched, unblenching, undauntable, undaunted, unfearful, unfearing, valiant, valorous

rel daring, defiant, gritty, hardy, mettle-some, resolute, spirited, steadfast, unapprehensive, undismayed, unflinching, unfrightened, unquailing, unshrinking, unswerving, unwincing, unyielding, venturesome; chivalrous, noble, preux; confident

con cringing, flinching, frightened, pusillanimous, scared, shrinking, timid; chickenhearted, fainthearted, lily-livered, nerveless, soft, spineless, unmanly, weakhearted, weak-kneed, yellow

ant cowardly, craven

2 *syn* see COLORFUL

3 *syn* see GOOD 1

brave *vb syn* see FACE 3
con avoid

bravehearted *adj syn* see BRAVE 1

bravery *n syn* see FINERY

bravo *n syn* see ASSASSIN

brawl *vb syn* see QUARREL

brawl *n* 1 *syn* see QUARREL

2 a rough, noisy, and often prolonged hand-to-hand fight usually involving several people < windows and furniture were broken in the barroom *brawl* >

syn affray, bobbery, broil, dogfight, donnybrook, fight, fracas, fray, free-for-all, knock-down-and-drag-out, maul, melee, mellay, ‖muss, rough-and-tumble, row, rowdydow, ruction, scrap, scrimmage, scuffle, set-to; *compare* QUARREL

rel fistfight, fisticuffs, slugfest; struggle, tussle; conflict, contention, contest, riot; altercation, embroilment, imbroglio, quarrel, wrangle; commotion, disturbance, eruption, hubbub, pandemonium, ruckus, rumpus, turn-to, ‖turnup, upheaval, uproar; incident, ‖rumble

idiom a coming to blows, exchange of blows

brawling *adj syn* see QUARRELSOME 2

brawlsome *adj syn* see QUARRELSOME 2

brawly *adj syn* see QUARRELSOME 2

brawn *n syn* see MUSCLE 1

brawny *adj syn* see MUSCULAR 2

rel lusty, red-blooded, vigorous, vital; tough

con lanky, lean, rawboned, skinny, thin

ant scrawny

bray *vb syn* see PULVERIZE 1

brazen *adj* 1 *syn* see INSOLENT 2

2 *syn* see SHAMELESS

3 *syn* see GAUDY

4 of the color of polished brass < a *brazen* sky at sunset >

syn aeneous, brassy

rel bronze

brazenfaced *adj syn* see SHAMELESS

breach *n* 1 the act or offense of failing to keep the law or to do what law, duty, or obligation requires < sued for *breach* of contract > < his behavior was a gross *breach* of good manners >

syn contravention, infraction, infringement, transgression, trespass, violation

rel disregard, nonobservance; delinquency, dereliction, neglect

con conformance, conformity, observance

ant observance

2 *syn* see GAP 1

3 an interruption of accustomed friendly relations < a trivial misunderstanding caused a *breach* between the brothers >

syn break, fissure, fracture, rent, rift, rupture, schism, split; *compare* SCHISM 3

rel division, separation, severance; alienation, estrangement; difference, discord, disharmony, dissension, disunity, strife, variance; secession, withdrawal; falling-out, quarrel

idiom parting of ways

con integrity, solidarity, union, unity; communion, community; accord, concord, harmony

4 *syn* see GAP 2

breach *vb* 1 *syn* see OPEN 3

rel bore, penetrate

2 *syn* see VIOLATE 1

bread *n* 1 *syn* see FOOD 1

2 *syn* see LIVING

‖3 *syn* see MONEY

bread and butter *n syn* see LIVING

breadth *n* 1 *syn* see EXPANSE

2 spaciousness of extent < the *breadth* of his knowledge on the subject is awesome >

syn amplitude, comprehensiveness, fullness, scope, wideness

rel compass, gamut, orbit, range, reach, sweep; expanse, spread, stretch

con limitation, restriction

ant narrowness

breadthen *vb syn* see BROADEN

break *vb* 1 *syn* see GIVE 12

2 *syn* see PLOW

3 *syn* see VIOLATE 1

ant observe

4 *syn* see ESCAPE 1

5 *syn* see FAIL 5

idiom go broke

6 *syn* see RUIN 3

7 *syn* see DEGRADE 1

8 *syn* see DISPROVE 1

9 *syn* see COMMUNICATE 1

10 *syn* see SOLVE 2

11 *syn* see DECODE

12 *syn* see HAPPEN 1

13 *syn* see GET OUT 2

‖14 *syn* see CLEAR 9

break *n* 1 *syn* see GAP 1

2 *syn* see GAP 3

3 *syn* see INTERLUDE

4 a usually short rest period < took a *break* for coffee >

syn blow, breath, breather, breathing space (*or* spell), respite, ten; *compare* PAUSE

5 *syn* see BREACH 3

6 *syn* see FAUX PAS

7 *syn* see OPPORTUNITY

breakable *adj syn* see FRAGILE 1

break down *vb* 1 *syn* see ANALYZE

2 *syn* see DECAY

3 *syn* see COLLAPSE 2

breakdown *n* 1 *syn* see NERVOUS BREAKDOWN

2 *syn* see COLLAPSE 2

3 *syn* see ANALYSIS 1

break in *vb* 1 *syn* see HOUSEBREAK

idiom break and enter

2 *syn* see INTERRUPT 2

breakneck *adj syn* see FAST 3
break out *vb syn* see ERUPT 2
breakout *n syn* see ESCAPE 1
breakthrough *n syn* see RISE 3
break up *vb* 1 *syn* see SEPARATE 1
  2 *syn* see DISBAND
breakup *n syn* see ANALYSIS 1
breast *n syn* see HEART 1
breast-feed *vb syn* see NURSE 1
breastwork *n syn* see BULWARK
breath *n* 1 *syn* see HINT 2
  2 *syn* see BREAK 4
breathe *vb* 1 *syn* see BE
  2 *syn* see REST 3
  3 to draw (as air) into and expel from the lungs < *breathe* clean air >
  syn respire
  rel exhale, inhale
  4 *syn* see CONFIDE 1
breathe (in) *vb syn* see INHALE
breathe (out) *vb syn* see EXHALE
breather *n syn* see BREAK 4
breathing *n syn* see INSTANT 1
breathing space (*or* spell) *n syn* see BREAK 4
breathless *adj* 1 *syn* see EAGER
  2 *syn* see STUFFY 1
bred-in-the-bone *adj syn* see INVETERATE 1
breech *n syn* see BUTTOCKS
breed *vb* 1 *syn* see PROCREATE 1
  2 *syn* see FATHER 1
  3 *syn* see GENERATE 3
  4 *syn* see GROW 1
breed *n syn* see TYPE
breeding *n syn* see CULTURE
  rel civility, courtesy, gentility, grace
  con barbarism; boorishness; coarseness, grossness; discourtesy, rudeness
  ant vulgarity
breeding ground *n* a place or environment which favors growth < the slum was a *breeding ground* for crime >
  syn forcing bed, forcing house, hotbed, hothouse
breeze *n syn* see SNAP 1
breeze *vb* to proceed quickly and easily < *breezed* through customs >
  syn waltz, zip
  rel skim, slide, slip
  con drag, falter, flag, lag, trail
breezy *adj* 1 *syn* see WINDY 1
  2 *syn* see EASYGOING 3
breviary *n syn* see ABRIDGMENT
breviate *n syn* see ABRIDGMENT
breviloquent *adj* 1 *syn* see CONCISE
  2 *syn* see BLUFF
brew *vb syn* see LOOM 2
brew *n syn* see MISCELLANY 1
bribable *adj syn* see VENAL 1
bribe *vb* to give or promise money or favor to a person in a position of trust to influence his judgment or conduct < *bribed* a building inspector >
  syn buy, buy off, fix, have, ‖lubricate, sop, square, tamper (with)
  rel approach; corrupt, instigate, suborn; soften (up), sweeten

idiom grease the palm (*or* hand), oil the palm (*or* hand), tickle the palm
bridal *n syn* see WEDDING
bridewell *n syn* see JAIL
bridle *vb syn* see RESTRAIN 1
  rel repress; suppress; control, manage; govern, rule
  con air, express, utter, ventilate, voice
  ant vent
brief *adj* 1 *syn* see SHORT 1
  rel fleeting, momentary, passing, transient
  ant long
  2 *syn* see CONCISE
  3 *syn* see BLUFF
brief *n syn* see ABRIDGMENT
briefly *adv* in a few words < he answered *briefly* and to the point >
  syn concisely, in brief, in short, laconically, shortly, succinctly, tersely
  rel accurately, crisply, exactly, precisely
  idiom in a capsule, in a nutshell, in a word, to make a long story short
  con diffusely, long-windedly, profusely, prolixly, protractedly, verbosely, wordily; at length, comprehensively, fully
‖**brig** *n syn* see JAIL
brigand *n syn* see MARAUDER
bright *adj* 1 shining or glowing with light < the *bright* sun >
  syn beaming, brilliant, effulgent, fulgent, incandescent, lambent, lucent, lucid, luminous, lustrous, radiant, refulgent
  rel clear, light, undimmed; illuminated, lighted; coruscating, flashing, gleaming, glistening, glittering, scintillating, shimmering, sparkling; blazing, flaming, glowing; burnished, polished, shiny; sunshiny
  con dark, dusky, gloomy, murky, tenebrous; colorless, drab, dreary, lackluster, leaden; somber; cloudy, gray, overcast, shadowy; moonless, starless, sunless; faint, pale, weak
  ant dim; dull
  2 *syn* see COLORFUL
  3 *syn* see GLAD 2
  4 *syn* see FAVORABLE 5
  5 *syn* see INTELLIGENT 2
  rel advanced, precocious
  con retarded
  ant dense, dull
  6 *syn* see LIVELY 1
brilliant *adj* 1 *syn* see BRIGHT 1
  ant subdued
  2 *syn* see INTELLIGENT 2
  rel erudite, learned; sage, wise
brim *n syn* see BORDER 1
brimful *adj* 1 *syn* see FULL 1
  2 *syn* see BIG 3
brimming *adj* 1 *syn* see FULL 1
  2 *syn* see BIG 3
brine *n syn* see OCEAN
bring *vb* 1 *syn* see CONVERT 1
  ‖2 *syn* see ACCOMPANY
  3 *syn* see SELL 4
bring about *vb syn* see EFFECT 1
bring around *vb syn* see INDUCE 1
bring down *vb syn* see FELL 1
bring forth *vb syn* see BEAR 5
bring in *vb* 1 *syn* see YIELD 5
  2 *syn* see SELL 4
  3 *syn* see EARN 1
bring off *vb syn* see EFFECT 2
bring out *vb syn* see SAY 1

---

syn synonym(s)   *rel* related word(s)
ant antonym(s)   *con* contrasted word(s)
idiom idiomatic equivalent(s)
‖ use limited; if in doubt, see a dictionary

bring up *vb* **1** to give a child a parent's fostering care <the orphan was *brought up* by his aunt>
syn ‖fetch up, raise, rear
rel breed, cultivate, foster, nurture; feed, nourish, provide (for); discipline, educate, train
con abuse, ill-use, maltreat; neglect
2 *syn* see STOP 4
3 *syn* see REFER 3
4 *syn* see BROACH
5 *syn* see VOMIT
brink *n* **1** *syn* see BORDER 1
2 *syn* see VERGE 2
‖**briny** *n syn* see OCEAN
brio *n syn* see SPIRIT 5
brisk *adj syn* see AGILE
rel adroit; quick
con inactive, torpid
ant sluggish
brisky *adj syn* see AGILE
bristle *vb syn* see ANGER 2
brittle *adj syn* see SHORT 6
broach *n syn* see BROOCH
broach *vb* to open up (a subject) for discussion <would be awkward to *broach* the matter now>
syn bring up, introduce, moot, ventilate
rel interject, interpose; mention, speak (about); propose, suggest
con hush (up), quash, stifle, suppress; black out, censor
broad *adj* **1** *syn* see LIBERAL 3
2 *syn* see EXTENSIVE 1
3 *syn* see RISQUÉ
broadcast *n syn* see DECLARATION
broadcast *vb* **1** *syn* see STREW 1
2 *syn* see DECLARE 1
rel communicate, radio, televise, transmit
idiom spread a report, spread far and wide
broaden *vb* to grow or become broad or broader <the street *broadens* into an avenue>
syn breadthen, widen
rel expand; spread (out); open
con contract, shrink; slim, thin
ant narrow
broad–minded *adj syn* see LIBERAL 3
broadside *n syn* see BARRAGE
Brobdingnagian *adj syn* see HUGE
brocard *n syn* see MAXIM
‖**brogue** *vb syn* see IDLE
broil *vb syn* see BURN 3
broil *n syn* see BRAWL 2
broiling *adj syn* see HOT 1
broke *adj syn* see POOR 1
broken–down *adj syn* see SHABBY 1
broker *n syn* see GO-BETWEEN 2
bromide *n syn* see COMMONPLACE
bromidic *adj syn* see ARID 2
‖**Bronx cheer** *n syn* see RASPBERRY
brooch *n* an ornament with a pin or clasp now worn usually by women <a diamond *brooch*>
syn broach, clip, pin
brood *n syn* see OFFSPRING
brood *vb* **1** *syn* see SET 11
2 *syn* see MOPE 1
brook *vb syn* see BEAR 10
brook *n syn* see CREEK 2
brothel *n* an establishment where prostitutes ply their trade <madam of the local *brothel*>
syn bagnio, bawdy house, bordello, call house, cathouse, crib, disorderly house, fancy house, ‖hookshop, ‖joyhouse, lupanar, parlor house, seraglio, sporting house, stew, whorehouse
idiom house of ill fame (*or* repute), house of prostitution
brotherhood *n syn* see ASSOCIATION 2
brouhaha *n* **1** *syn* see DIN
2 *syn* see COMMOTION 3
brow *n syn* see FOREHEAD
browbeat *vb syn* see INTIMIDATE
browbeater *n syn* see BULLY 1
brownie *n syn* see FAIRY
‖**brownnose** *vb syn* see FAWN
‖**brownnose** *n syn* see SYCOPHANT
‖**brownnoser** *n syn* see SYCOPHANT
brown study *n syn* see REVERIE
browse *vb* to read through, study, or examine cursorily <*browsed* through the book looking for illustrations>
syn dip (into), flip (through), glance (at *or* over), leaf (through), riff (through), riffle (through), run (through *or* over), scan, skim (through), thumb (through)
rel go (through *or* over), look (over), peruse, skip (through)
idiom give the once over, run the eye over
con examine, study; delve (into), dig (into)
ant pore (over)
bruise *n* an injury involving rupture of small blood vessels and discoloration without break in the overlying skin <got an ugly *bruise* when he fell>
syn contusion; *compare* BLACK EYE
rel ‖boo-boo; abrasion, scrape, scratch
idiom black-and-blue spot (*or* mark)
bruise *vb* **1** to inflict a bruise on <fell down and *bruised* his hip>
syn black, contuse
rel batter, ‖bung up
2 *syn* see CRUSH 2
bruit (about) *vb syn* see DECLARE 1
rel hint, intimate, rumor, suggest
bruja *n syn* see WITCH 1
brume *n syn* see HAZE 1
brummagem *adj syn* see COUNTERFEIT
brunet *adj syn* see DARK 3
brush *vb* to touch or strike lightly (as in passing) <they *brushed* fenders but no real damage was done>
syn glance, graze, kiss, shave, skim
rel bump, clash, collide, sideswipe; clip, contact, scrape, touch
brush *n* **1** *syn* see ENCOUNTER
rel clash, engagement
2 *syn* see CLASH 2
brush up *vb syn* see TOUCH UP
brusque *adj syn* see BLUFF
brutal *adj* **1** *syn* see BRUTISH
2 *syn* see SEVERE 3
brutalize *vb syn* see DEBASE 1
brute *adj syn* see BRUTISH
brute *n syn* see BEAST
brutish *adj* marked by animal traits and by a lack of man's dignity or refinement <a graceless *brutish* hulk of a man>
syn animal, beastly, bestial, brutal, brute, feral, ferine, swinish
rel animalistic; coarse, crude; base, low, mean, scurvy, vile

bubble *vb* 1 *syn* see SLOSH 1
　2 *syn* see SEETHE 4
bubble *n syn* see PIPE DREAM
buccaneer *n syn* see PIRATE
buck *n* 1 *syn* see MAN 3
　2 *syn* see FOP
　‖3 *syn* see DOLLAR
　4 *syn* see SAWHORSE
buck *vb* 1 *syn* see RESIST
　2 *syn* see CARRY 1
　3 *syn* see PASS 9
buck (off) *vb syn* see THROW 2
buck *vb syn* see PULVERIZE 1
bucket *n syn* see JAIL
bucket *vb syn* see HURRY 2
‖**bucket shop** *n syn* see BAR 5
buckle (down) *vb* 1 *syn* see ADDRESS 3
　2 *syn* see PITCH IN 1
buckle (under) *vb syn* see YIELD 2
buckram *adj syn* see STIFF 4
buck up *vb syn* see COMFORT
bucolic *adj syn* see RURAL
　ant urbane
bucolic *n syn* see RUSTIC
bud *n* 1 *syn* see CHILD 1
　2 *syn* see SEED 2
buddy *n syn* see ASSOCIATE 3
‖**buddy–buddy** *adj syn* see INTIMATE 4
‖**budge** *n syn* see LIQUOR 2
budget *n syn* see BODY 5
budtime *n syn* see SPRING 5
buff *n syn* see ADDICT
buff *vb syn* see POLISH 1
buffalo *vb* 1 *syn* see FRUSTRATE 1
　2 *syn* see NONPLUS 1
buff–bare *adj syn* see NUDE 2
buffet *n syn* see CUFF
buffet *vb* 1 *syn* see SLAP 1
　2 *syn* see BEAT 1
‖**buffet** *n syn* see EATING HOUSE
‖**bufflehead** *n syn* see DUNCE
‖**buffle–headed** *adj syn* see SIMPLE 3
buffoon *n syn* see CLOWN 3
‖**buffy** *adj syn* see INTOXICATED 1
bug *n syn* see ENTHUSIAST
‖**bug** *vb syn* see ANNOY 2
bugbear *n syn* see ABOMINATION 1
‖**bugger** *n syn* see SNOT
‖**bugger** *vb syn* see EXHAUST 4
bugger up *vb syn* see BOTCH
‖**buggy** *adj* 1 *syn* see ENTHUSIASTIC
　2 *syn* see INSANE 1
‖**buggy** *n syn* see CAR
‖**bughouse** *n syn* see ASYLUM 3
‖**bughouse** *adj syn* see INSANE 1
‖**bugs** *adj* 1 *syn* see INSANE 1
　2 *syn* see ENTHUSIASTIC
build *vb* 1 to form or fashion a structure
< will *build* either a garage or carport >
syn construct, erect, put up, raise, rear,
uprear; *compare* ERECT 3, MAKE 3
rel fabricate, fashion, frame, manufacture;
run up, throw up; prefabricate
con demolish, destroy, dismantle, level,
pull down, raze, take down, tear down,
wreck
　2 *syn* see MAKE 3
　3 *syn* see INCREASE 1

---

syn synonym(s)　*rel* related word(s)
ant antonym(s)　*con* contrasted word(s)
idiom idiomatic equivalent(s)
‖ use limited; if in doubt, see a dictionary

---

　4 *syn* see INCREASE 2
build (on) *vb syn* see RELY (on *or* upon)
build *n syn* see PHYSIQUE
　rel conformation
building *n* a usually roofed and walled
structure built for permanent use < a
building with four apartments >
syn fabric, structure; *compare* EDIFICE,
HUT
build up *vb* 1 *syn* see ERECT 5
　2 *syn* see PUBLICIZE
buildup *n syn* see PUBLICITY
‖**built** *adj syn* see CURVACEOUS
built–in *adj syn* see INHERENT
bulge *vb* to extend outward beyond the
usual or normal line < the box was so full
that the sides *bulged* >
syn beetle, jut, overhang, poke, pouch,
pout, project, protrude, protuberate, stand
out, stick out
rel bag, belly, dilate, distend, expand,
swell
bulge *n* 1 *syn* see PROJECTION 1
　rel bump, lump, swelling
　con depression, hollow, pit
　2 *syn* see ADVANTAGE 3
bulk *n* 1 a body of usually material substance that constitutes a thing or unit
< his industry was proven by the *bulk* of
his accomplishment > < a great dark *bulk*
blocked the alley >
syn mass, volume
rel bigness, greatness, largeness, magnitude, quantity, totality
　2 *syn* see BODY 4
　3 *syn* see BODY 5
　4 *syn* see BODY 3
bulk *vb syn* see LOOM 3
bull *n* 1 *syn* see ERROR 2
　‖2 *syn* see NONSENSE 2
　‖3 *syn* see POLICEMAN
bull *adj syn* see LARGE 1
‖**bull band** *n syn* see SHIVAREE
bulldoze *vb* 1 *syn* see INTIMIDATE
　rel menace, threaten; harass, harry
　2 *syn* see PUSH 3
bulldozer *n syn* see BULLY 1
bullet *vb syn* see HURRY 2
bullfighter *n* one who fights bulls
< moved with the grace of an experienced
bullfighter >
syn matador, toreador, torero
rel banderillero; cuadrillero, picador;
cuadrilla
bullheaded *adj syn* see OBSTINATE
bullwork *n syn* see WORK 2
bully *n* 1 an insolent, overbearing person
who persists in tormenting another < a
big *bully* who picked on little kids >
syn browbeater, bulldozer, harasser, harrier, hector, intimidator; *compare* TOUGH
rel annoyer, antagonizer, heckler, persecu-
tor, pest, tease, tormenter
　2 *syn* see PIMP 1
bully *adj syn* see EXCELLENT
bully *vb syn* see INTIMIDATE
　rel torment, torture; menace, threaten
　ant coax
bullyboy *n syn* see TOUGH
bullyrag *vb* 1 *syn* see INTIMIDATE
　2 *syn* see BAIT 2
bulwark *n* an aboveground defensive structure that forms part of a fortification

<the *bulwarks* were woefully under-manned>
syn bastion, breastwork, parapet, rampart
rel citadel, fort, fortress, stronghold
con bunker, dugout
bulwark *vb syn* see DEFEND 1

‖**bum** *vb syn* see HUM

bum *vb syn* see IDLE

bum *n* 1 *syn* see VAGABOND
2 *syn* see SLUGGARD

‖**bum** *adj syn* see BAD 1

bum ‖*n syn* see BINGE 1

bumble *vb syn* see HUM

bumble *vb* 1 *syn* see BOTCH
2 *syn* see STUMBLE 3

bumbling *adj syn* see AWKWARD 2

‖**bumfuzzle** *vb syn* see CONFUSE 2

bummel *vb syn* see SAUNTER

bummer *n* 1 *syn* see BEGGAR 1
2 *syn* see MARAUDER

bumming *n syn* see MENDICANCY

bump *vb* 1 to meet with or come up against forcibly <the two cars *bumped* with a great crumpling of fenders>
syn clash, collide, ‖prang
rel bang, carom, crash, hit, knock, slam, strike; impinge; jar, jolt
idiom whang together
2 *syn* see HAPPEN 2
3 *syn* see DEGRADE 1

bump *n* 1 *syn* see IMPACT
2 a swelling of tissue usually resulting from a blow <fell and got a *bump* on his head>
syn bunch, knot, lump, ‖pumpknot
rel protuberance, swelling
3 a marked unevenness in a road surface likely to jolt a passing vehicle
syn ‖cahot, thank-you-ma'am
rel chuckhole, mudhole, pothole, rut
4 *syn* see GIFT 2

bumpkin *n syn* see RUSTIC

bump off *vb syn* see MURDER 1

‖**bump-off** *n syn* see MURDER

bunch *n* 1 *syn* see BUMP 2
2 *syn* see GROUP 3
3 *syn* see SET 5
4 *syn* see GROUP 1

bunco steerer *n syn* see SWINDLER

bundle *n* 1 *syn* see GROUP 3
2 *syn* see FORTUNE 4

bundle up *vb* to dress warmly <*bundle up*, it's cold outside>
syn ‖hap, muffle, wrap (up)
rel envelop, mummify, swaddle, swathe

bung *vb syn* see THROW 1

bung-full *adj syn* see FULL 1

bungle *vb syn* see BOTCH

bungle *n syn* see ERROR 2

bungler *n syn* see STUMBLEBUM

bung up *vb syn* see BATTER 1

bunk *vb syn* see HARBOR 1

bunk *vb* 1 *syn* see ESCAPE 1

bunk *n syn* see NONSENSE 2

bunk *vb syn* see DECEIVE

bunkum *n syn* see NONSENSE 2

‖**bunkum** *adj* 1 *syn* see EXCELLENT
2 *syn* see HEALTHY 1

Bunyanesque *adj syn* see HUGE

buoy (up) *vb syn* see SUPPORT 5

buoyancy *n syn* see EBULLIENCE

buoyant *adj syn* see ELASTIC 2

burble *vb* 1 *syn* see SLOSH 1

2 *syn* see CHAT 1

burden *n* 1 *syn* see LOAD 1
2 *syn* see LOAD 3

burden *vb* to lay a heavy load on or to lie like a heavy load on a person or thing <*burdened* his men with needless heavy work> <I won't *burden* you with this lengthy story>
syn charge, clog, cumber, encumber, lade, load, lumber, saddle, task, tax, weigh, weight
rel overburden, overload, overweigh; handicap; afflict, oppress
idiom bear down on (*or* upon)
con alleviate, ease, lighten, relieve, unload; disburden, disencumber
ant unburden

burden *n syn* see SUBSTANCE 2

burdensome *adj syn* see ONEROUS

burdensomely *adv syn* see HARD 8

bureaucrat *n* a member of a bureaucracy <*bureaucrats* were blamed for the error>
syn mandarin
rel civil servant, functionary, official

burg *n* a small, insignificant, remote town <the *burg* had only two stores and one gas station>
syn hick town, jerkwater town, mudhole, one-horse town, Podunk, tank town, whistle-stop
rel cowtown; crossroads; jumping-off place; hamlet, village
con city, metropolis

burgee *n syn* see FLAG

burgeon *vb* 1 *syn* see INCREASE 2
2 *syn* see BLOSSOM

burghal *adj syn* see URBAN

burgher *n syn* see TOWNSMAN

burglarize *vb* to commit an act of breaking open and entering with a felonious purpose the dwelling house of another by night <that night several homes were *burglarized*>
syn burgle; *compare* HOUSEBREAK, ROB 1
rel knock over, rob; ransack, rifle; screw

burgle *vb syn* see BURGLARIZE

burial *n* 1 *syn* see GRAVE
2 the act or ceremony of burying <his *burial* took place yesterday>
syn entombment, inhumation, interment, sepulture
rel burying, exequies, funeral, obsequies; deposition; deep six
con disinterment, exhumation

burial ground *n syn* see CEMETERY

buried *adj syn* see ULTERIOR

burke *vb* 1 *syn* see SUPPRESS 3
2 *syn* see SKIRT 3

burlesque *n* 1 *syn* see MOCKERY 2
2 *syn* see CARICATURE 2

burlesque *vb syn* see MIMIC

burly *adj syn* see HUSKY 1

‖**burn** *n syn* see CREEK 2

burn *vb* 1 *syn* see SHINE 1
2 to undergo combustion <the wood is too green to *burn*>
syn combust
rel fire, flame, ignite, kindle, light; consume, use; smolder, sputter
3 to be hot as if on fire <sand *burning* in the blazing sun>
syn bake, broil, cook, melt, roast, scorch, swelter

rel parch, toast, warm; char
con chill, cool, freeze
4 *syn* see ANGER 2
5 *syn* see SMART
6 *syn* see FIRE 6
‖7 *syn* see CHEAT
burn (up) *vb syn* see IRRITATE
burnable *adj syn* see COMBUSTIBLE 1
burning *adj* 1 on fire < the *burning* house >
syn ablaze, afire, aflame, alight, blazing, conflagrant, fiery, flaming, flaring, ignited, lighted
rel aglow, glowing, incandescent
idiom in flames
con burned-out, cold
2 *syn* see HOT 1
ant icy
3 *syn* see FEVERISH 2
4 *syn* see IMPASSIONED
5 *syn* see PRESSING
burnish *vb syn* see POLISH 1
burnished *adj syn* see LUSTROUS 1
burn off *vb syn* see CLEAR 9
burnsides *n pl syn* see SIDE-WHISKERS
burp *vb syn* see BELCH 1
burro *n syn* see DONKEY 1
burrow *n* 1 *syn* see LAIR 1
2 *syn* see HOVEL
burrow *vb syn* see SNUGGLE
burst *vb* 1 *syn* see EXPLODE 1
2 *syn* see SHATTER 1
3 *syn* see PLUNGE 2
burst (forth) *vb syn* see ERUPT 2
burst *n* 1 *syn* see OUTBREAK 1
2 *syn* see OUTBURST 1
3 *syn* see BANG 2
4 *syn* see BARRAGE
bury *vb* 1 to deposit (a corpse) in or as if in the earth < the pharaohs were *buried* in pyramids > < *buried* at sea >
syn entomb, inhume, inter, lay away, plant, put away, sepulcher, sepulture, tomb; *compare* ENTOMB 1
rel inurn; coffin
idiom consign to the grave, lay to rest, put six feet under
con dig (up), disentomb, disinter, exhume, untomb; burn, cremate
2 *syn* see HIDE
burying ground *n syn* see CEMETERY
‖**bus** *n syn* see CAR
bush *n syn* see FRONTIER 2
‖**bush up** *vb syn* see HIDE
bushwa *n syn* see NONSENSE 2
business *n* 1 *syn* see FUNCTION 1
2 *syn* see PATRONAGE 2
3 *syn* see WORK 1
4 activity concerned with the supplying and distribution of commodities < the lumber *business* depends heavily on the housing *business* >
syn commerce, industry, trade, traffic
5 *syn* see ENTERPRISE 3
6 *syn* see AFFAIR 1
7 *syn* see DOODAD
8 something personal to oneself < that is none of your *business* >

syn affair, concern, lookout, occasions, palaver
businessman *n syn* see MERCHANT
buss *vb syn* see KISS 1
bust *vb* 1 *syn* see RUIN 3
2 *syn* see DEGRADE 1
ant promote
3 *syn* see FAIL 5
‖4 *syn* see ARREST 2
bust *n* ‖1 *syn* see CUFF
2 *syn* see FAILURE 5
3 *syn* see BINGE 1
4 *syn* see RAID 2
‖**busthead** *n syn* see MOONSHINE 2
bustle *vb syn* see HURRY 2
bustle *n* 1 *syn* see STIR 1
2 *syn* see COMMOTION 4
bustling *adj* full of activity < a *bustling* frontier town >
syn busy, fussy, hopping, humming, hustling, lively, popping
rel active, brisk, energetic
idiom on its way, on the go (*or* move), up and doing
busty *adj syn* see BUXOM
busy *adj* 1 engaged in activity < I can't stop to talk. I'm *busy* >
syn employed, engaged, occupied, working; *compare* ASSIDUOUS
idiom at work, on the fly
con idle, inactive
ant free
2 *syn* see BUSTLING
3 *syn* see IMPERTINENT 2
busy *vb syn* see ENGAGE 4
busybody *n* one who concerns himself with affairs not his own < a meddlesome *busybody* who saw all and tattled all she saw >
syn butt-in, ‖buttinsky, intermeddler, kibitzer, meddler, Meddlesome Mattie, nose, nosey Parker, Paul Pry, polypragmatist, pragmatic, pragmatist, prier (*or* pryer), quidnunc, rubber, rubberneck, snoop, ‖sticky-beak; *compare* GOSSIP 1, INFORMER
rel gossip, gossipmonger, newsmonger, rumormonger, scandalmonger, tabby, talebearer, telltale
idiom curiosity shop, question box
busybody *vb syn* see SNOOP
2 *syn* see MEDDLE
but *conj* 1 *syn* see ONLY
2 *syn* see EXCEPT 1
but *prep syn* see EXCEPT
but *adv* 1 *syn* see ONLY 1
2 *syn* see JUST 3
butcher *vb syn* see SLAUGHTER 1
2 *syn* see SLAUGHTER 2
butchery *n syn* see MASSACRE
butt *n* 1 *syn* see TARGET 1
2 *syn* see LAUGHINGSTOCK
3 *syn* see FOOL 3
butt (on *or* **against)** *vb syn* see ADJOIN
‖**butt** *n* 1 *syn* see BUTTOCKS
2 *syn* see CIGARETTE
butt *n syn* see CASK
butterball *n syn* see FATTY
butt in *vb* 1 *syn* see INTRUDE 1
con abstain, forbear, restrain
2 *syn* see MEDDLE
butt-in *n syn* see BUSYBODY
‖**buttinsky** *n syn* see BUSYBODY

---

buttocks *n pl* the part of the back on which a person sits < gave the boy a whack across the *buttocks* >
syn backside, beam, behind, bottom, breech, ||butt, ||can, cheeks, derriere, ||duff, fanny, fundament, hams, haunches, heinie (*or* hiney), hind end, ||hinder, hunkers, ||keister, nates, podex, posterior, rear, rear end, rump, seat, ||stern, tail, tail end, ||tokus, ||twat
idiom seat of one's pants

button–down *adj syn* see CONVENTIONAL 1

buttress *n syn* see SUPPORT 3

buttress *vb syn* see SUPPORT 4

buvette *n syn* see BAR 4

buxom *adj* having an amply developed bosom < a *buxom* young woman >
syn bosomy, busty, chesty, full-bosomed; *compare* CURVACEOUS
rel ||stacked; full-figured, Junoesque, shapely, well-developed, well-proportioned

buy *vb* 1 to acquire something for money or the equivalent < *bought* a new car >
syn purchase, take
rel acquire, get, obtain, procure
ant sell
2 *syn* see RANSOM
3 *syn* see BRIBE
||4 *syn* see BELIEVE 1

buy *n syn* see BARGAIN 1

buyable *adj syn* see VENAL 1

buyer *n syn* see PURCHASER

buy off *vb syn* see BRIBE

buzz *vb* 1 *syn* see HUM
2 *syn* see HISS
||3 *syn* see TELEPHONE

buzz *n syn* see REPORT 1

||**buzzed** *adj syn* see INTOXICATED 1

by *prep* 1 *syn* see BESIDE 1
2 *syn* see NEAR 2
3 *syn* see VIA 1
4 *syn* see VIA 2

5 with reference to < sorted *by* color >
syn according to, as to

by *adv syn* see OVER 5

by *interj syn* see GOOD-BYE

by all odds *adv syn* see FAR AND AWAY

by a long shot *adv syn* see FAR AND AWAY

by and by *adv* 1 *syn* see AFTER
2 *syn* see PRESENTLY 1

by–and–by *n syn* see FUTURE

by and large *adv syn* see ALTOGETHER 3

by–blow *n syn* see BASTARD 1

by dint of *prep syn* see VIA 2

bye–bye *interj syn* see GOOD-BYE

by far *adv syn* see FAR AND AWAY

bygone *adj* 1 *syn* see FORMER 2
2 *syn* see OLD-FASHIONED
3 *syn* see EXTINCT 2

by long odds *adv syn* see FAR AND AWAY

by means of *prep syn* see VIA 2

byname *n syn* see NICKNAME

by odds *adv syn* see FAR AND AWAY

by ordinary *adv syn* see USUALLY 2

bypass *vb* 1 *syn* see SKIRT 1
2 *syn* see SKIRT 3

byplace *n syn* see NOOK

by–product *n syn* see OUTGROWTH 2

by–sitter *n syn* see SPECTATOR

bystander *n syn* see SPECTATOR

by stealth *adv syn* see SECRETLY

by–talk *n syn* see SMALL TALK

by the bye *adv syn* see INCIDENTALLY 2

by the way *adv syn* see INCIDENTALLY 2

by–the–way *adj syn* see INDIFFERENT 2

by virtue of *prep syn* see VIA 2

by way of *prep* 1 *syn* see VIA 1
2 *syn* see VIA 2

byword *n* 1 *syn* see SAYING
2 *syn* see CATCHWORD
3 *syn* see NICKNAME

Byzantine *adj syn* see COMPLEX 2

C

cab *n syn* see TAXICAB

||**cab** *n syn* see CRUD

cabal *n* 1 *syn* see CLIQUE
2 *syn* see PLOT 2

cabalistic *adj syn* see MYSTERIOUS

cabaret *n syn* see NIGHTCLUB

||**cabbage** *n syn* see MONEY

cabbage *vb syn* see STEAL 1

cabbagehead *n syn* see DUNCE

cabin *n syn* see HUT

||**caboose** *n syn* see HUT

||**caboose** *n syn* see JAIL

||**ca' canny** *n syn* see SLOWDOWN 2

cache *vb syn* see HIDE
con discover, unearth

cachet *n syn* see STATUS 2

||**cack** *vb syn* see VOMIT

cackle *vb syn* see CHAT 1

cackle *n syn* see CHATTER

cacophonic *adj syn* see DISSONANT 1

cacophonous *adj syn* see DISSONANT 1

cad *n* a person without gentlemanly instincts < gloated over his rival's distress like the *cad* that he was >
syn bounder, cur, rotter, yellow dog
rel boor, churl, clown, lout; guttersnipe, mucker, vulgarian; ||creep; bastard, heel, louse, rat, stinker
idiom Jack Nasty
ant gentleman

cadaver *n syn* see CORPSE

cadaverous *adj* 1 *syn* see GHASTLY 2
2 *syn* see EMACIATED
rel careworn, haggard, pinched, worn

cadence *n syn* see RHYTHM
rel accent, accentuation, emphasis, stress; pulsation, pulse, throb

cadency *n syn* see RHYTHM

cadet *n syn* see PIMP 1

cadger *n syn* see BEGGAR 1

cadging *n syn* see MENDICANCY

caducity *n syn* see OLD AGE
rel childishness, dotardy, dotingness

café *n* **1** *syn* see EATING HOUSE
  2 *syn* see NIGHTCLUB
cage *vb syn* see ENCLOSE 1
  rel imprison, incarcerate, jail
cagey *adj syn* see SHREWD
cageyness *n syn* see CUNNING 2
cahoots *n pl syn* see ASSOCIATION 1
‖**cahot** *n syn* see BUMP 3
cajole *vb syn* see COAX
  rel beguile, deceive, delude; tantalize;
  crowd, push
cake *vb* **1** to cover with a surface layer
  <the floor was *caked* with filth>
  syn crust, encrust (*or* incrust), incrustate,
  rime
  rel besmear, coat, smear, spread; cover,
  daub
  2 *syn* see HARDEN 1
  rel compress, condense, contract, shrink
cakewalk *n syn* see RUNAWAY
calaboose *n syn* see JAIL
calamitous *adj* **1** *syn* see FATAL 2
  2 *syn* see DEPLORABLE
calamity *n syn* see DISASTER
  rel collapse, ruin, wreck; affliction, cross,
  trial, tribulation, visitation
  con fortune, luck; benefaction; favor, gift
  ant boon
calamity howler *n syn* see PESSIMIST
calculate *vb* to determine or approximate a
  mathematical value (as speed, cost, or
  quantity) <*calculate* the cost of a new
  car>
  syn cipher, compute, estimate, figure,
  reckon
  rel consider, study, weigh; ascertain, determine, discover; appraise, evaluate, price,
  value; assess, prize, rate
  con conjecture, guess, surmise
calculate (on *or* upon) *vb syn* see RELY
  (on *or* upon)
calculating *adj syn* see CAUTIOUS
  rel artful, crafty, cunning, guileful, sly,
  wily
  con improvident, imprudent, indiscreet
  ant rash, reckless
calculation *n syn* see COMPUTATION
calembour *n syn* see PUN
calendar *n syn* see PROGRAM 1
calenture *n syn* see PASSION 6
caliber *n* **1** *syn* see QUALITY 2
  rel ability, capability, capacity; force,
  power
  2 *syn* see QUALITY 3
caliginous *adj syn* see DARK 1
call *vb* **1** to speak or utter in a loud distinct carrying voice <*call* for help>
  syn cry, hallo, holler, hollo, shout, vociferate, yell; *compare* SHOUT 1
  rel bawl, bellow, hoot, howl, roar,
  scream, screech, shriek, shrill, whoop,
  yowl
  con murmur, whisper
  2 *syn* see DEMAND 1
  3 *syn* see SUMMON 2
  rel assemble, collect, gather, round up;
  bid, invite
  4 *syn* see CONVOKE

5 *syn* see TELEPHONE
6 *syn* see NAME 1
7 *syn* see PREDICT 2
8 *syn* see ESTIMATE 3
9 *syn* see FORETELL
10 *syn* see VISIT 2
call (for) *vb syn* see DEMAND 2
call (to) *vb syn* see ADDRESS 7
call *n* **1** the natural vocal sound of an animal and especially a bird <the clear *call*
  of a bellbird>
  syn cry, note, song
  rel cheep, chirp, peep, twitter, warble
  2 *syn* see ATTRACTION 1
  3 *syn* see OCCASION 3
  4 *syn* see VISIT 1
call down *vb syn* see REPROVE
caller *n syn* see VISITOR 1
‖**callet** *n syn* see PROSTITUTE
call girl *n syn* see PROSTITUTE
call house *n syn* see BROTHEL
calligraphy *n syn* see HANDWRITING
call in *vb syn* see SUMMON 2
calling *n* **1** *syn* see MISSION
  2 *syn* see TRADE 1
  3 *syn* see WORK 1
‖**callithump** *n syn* see SHIVAREE
call off *vb syn* see CANCEL 2
callous *adj syn* see UNFEELING 2
  rel indurated, set
callow *adj* **1** *syn* see YOUNG 1
  2 *syn* see INEXPERIENCED
callowness *n syn* see INEXPERIENCE
call up *vb* to summon for active military
  duty <*called up* the army reserves>
  syn order up; *compare* DRAFT 1
  rel mobilize
  idiom call to the colors
  ant discharge, muster out
calm *n syn* see QUIET 1
calm *adj* **1** free from storm or rough activity <the wind died and the sea became
  calm>
  syn halcyon, hushed, placid, quiet, still,
  stilly, untroubled
  rel inactive, quiescent, reposing, resting;
  pacific, smooth, tranquil, unruffled
  idiom calm as a millpond, still as death
  con agitated, disturbed, perturbed, restless, turbulent, uneasy
  ant stormy
  2 free from mental or emotional distress
  or agitation <a man who remained *calm*
  under stress>
  syn collected, composed, easy, easygoing,
  placid, poised, possessed, self-composed,
  self-possessed, serene, tranquil
  rel cool, imperturbable, nonchalant, unflappable, unruffled; even-tempered, impassive, phlegmatic, steady; firm, stable,
  staunch
  con discomposed, disturbed, perturbed,
  upset; anxious, bothered, confused, nervous; fidgety, jittery, jumpy, shaky, tense
  ant agitated
calm *vb* to relieve from or bring to an end
  whatever distresses, agitates, or disturbs
  <that inner faith that *calms* the troubled
  spirit>
  syn allay, balm, becalm, compose, lull,
  quiet, ‖quieten, settle, soothe, ‖soother,
  still, tranquilize

---

syn synonym(s)   *rel* related word(s)
ant antonym(s)   *con* contrasted word(s)
idiom idiomatic equivalent(s)
‖ use limited; if in doubt, see a dictionary

rel alleviate, assuage, mitigate, relieve; appease, mollify, pacify, placate; relax, steady
con bother, discompose, disquiet, disturb, flurry, perturb, stir up, upset
ant agitate; arouse

calmant *n syn* see SEDATIVE
calmative *n syn* see SEDATIVE
calmness *n syn* see EQUANIMITY
calumniate *vb syn* see MALIGN
ant eulogize; vindicate
calumnious *adj syn* see LIBELOUS
calumny *n syn* see DETRACTION
rel animadversion, reflection, stricture
con encomium, panegyric, tribute; adulation, compliment, flattery
ant eulogy; vindication
calvary *n syn* see TRIAL 1
‖**cam** *adv syn* see AWRY 1
camaraderie *n* a spirit of friendly goodwill typical of comrades < the easy *camaraderie* of a cozy neighborhood bar >
syn comradery, good-fellowship
rel affability, friendliness, gregariousness, sociability; cheer, conviviality, jollity
con aloofness, coldness, frigidity, inaccessibility, reclusiveness, remoteness, self-containment; exclusiveness, self-sufficiency, unsociability
camarilla *n syn* see CLIQUE
cameraman *n syn* see PHOTOGRAPHER
camerist *n syn* see PHOTOGRAPHER
camouflage *vb syn* see DISGUISE
rel becloud, befog, dim
camp *n* 1 a place where a number of people (as vacationers or soldiers) live temporarily together in usually more or less casual housing < planned to summer at a fishing *camp* in Maine >
syn campground, encampment
2 *syn* see CLIQUE
3 *syn* see HUT
camp *vb* to live temporarily in a camp or the outdoors < *camped* under the trees for the night >
syn bivouac, ‖bivvy, encamp, ‖laager, ‖maroon, tent
idiom rough it
con decamp
campanile *n syn* see BELL TOWER
campestral *adj syn* see RURAL
camp follower *n syn* see PROSTITUTE
campground *n syn* see CAMP 1
‖**cample** *vb syn* see SCOLD 1
‖**can** *n* 1 *syn* see JAIL
2 *syn* see TOILET
3 *syn* see BUTTOCKS
‖**can** *vb syn* see DISMISS 3
Canaan *n syn* see HEAVEN 2
canaille *n syn* see RABBLE 2
canal *n syn* see CHANNEL 1
canard *n syn* see LIE
rel hoax, humbug, mare's-nest, sell, spoof; artifice, dodge, trick
‖**canary** *n syn* see INFORMER
cancel *vb* 1 *syn* see ERASE
2 to give up something previously arranged or agreed on < decided to *cancel* his appointment with the dentist >
syn call off, drop, scrub
rel end, terminate; annul, invalidate, rescind, revoke; give up, relinquish, surrender

cancel (out) *vb syn* see NEUTRALIZE
candid *adj* 1 *syn* see FAIR 4
rel aboveboard, forthright, straightforward; honest, scrupulous, upright
2 *syn* see FRANK
ant evasive
candidate *n* one who seeks an office, honor, position, or award < examining *candidates* for editorial positions >
syn applicant, aspirant, hopeful, seeker
rel nominee; dark horse; also-ran, has-been; campaigner, electioneerer, stumper, whistle-stopper
candy *vb syn* see SUGARCOAT 1
canine *n syn* see DOG 1
canker *vb syn* see DEBASE 1
cankered *adj syn* see CANTANKEROUS
cannabis *n syn* see MARIJUANA
canned *adj* 1 *syn* see CONDENSED
2 *syn* see INTOXICATED 1
cannibalic *adj syn* see FIERCE 1
canniness *n* 1 *syn* see PRUDENCE 1
2 *syn* see CUNNING 2
‖**cannon** *n syn* see PICKPOCKET
cannonade *n syn* see BARRAGE
cannonade *vb syn* see BOMBARD
canny *adj* 1 *syn* see CLEVER 4
2 *syn* see SPARING
3 *syn* see WISE 4
canon *n* 1 *syn* see LAW 1
2 *syn* see DOCTRINE
canonical *adj syn* see ORTHODOX 1
‖**cant** *adj syn* see LIVELY 1
cant *vb syn* see SLANT 1
cant *n* 1 *syn* see DIALECT 2
rel diction, language, phraseology, vocabulary; idiom, speech
2 *syn* see TERMINOLOGY
3 *syn* see HYPOCRISY
cantankerous *adj* habitually ill-humored, irritable, and disagreeable < one of our more *cantankerous* fellow workers >
syn bearish, cankered, cranky, cross-grained, crotchety, ornery, rantankerous, vinegarish, vinegary, waspish, waspy; *compare* IRASCIBLE, IRRITABLE
rel dour, morose, sour; crabbed, cross, crusty, huffy, petulant, prickly, snappish; dyspeptic, ill-conditioned, ill-natured; liverish
idiom like a bear with a sore paw
con benign, kindly, mellow, mild; amiable, congenial, friendly, pleasant, well-disposed; benevolent, gracious, kind
canter *n syn* see VAGABOND
cantina *n syn* see BAR 5
canting *adj syn* see HYPOCRITICAL
canton *vb syn* see BILLET 1
‖**canty** *adj syn* see LIVELY 1
canvass *vb* 1 *syn* see SCRUTINIZE 1
2 *syn* see DISCUSS 1
3 *syn* see SOLICIT 1
cap *vb* 1 *syn* see SURMOUNT 3
2 *syn* see PUZZLE
3 *syn* see COVER 3
4 *syn* see SURPASS 1
5 *syn* see CLIMAX
capability *n* 1 *syn* see ABILITY 1
rel art, craft, cunning, skill
con inability, disability
ant incapability, incompetence
2 *syn* see EFFICACY 1
capable *adj syn* see ABLE

ant incapable

capacious *adj syn see* SPACIOUS
   rel dilatable, distensible, expandable, expansive, extensile; abundant, copious, plentiful
   ant exiguous

capacity *n* 1 *syn see* ABILITY 1
   rel bent, faculty, gift, knack, talent; twin; caliber, stature
   con impotence, ineffectiveness, powerlessness
   ant incapacity
   2 *syn see* STATUS 1

cape *n syn see* PROMONTORY

caper *vb syn see* GAMBOL
   idiom cut capers

caper *n* 1 *syn see* ESCAPADE
   2 *syn see* PRANK
   rel devilment, impishness, mischief, roguery, waggishness

‖capernoited *adj syn see* INTOXICATED 1

capital *adj* 1 *syn see* EGREGIOUS
   2 *syn see* CHIEF 2
   rel cardinal, essential, vital; basic, fundamental, underlying
   3 *syn see* EXCELLENT

capital *n syn see* MEAN 3

capitalize *vb* to supply capital for or to
   < agreed to *capitalize* the venture >
   syn back, bankroll, finance, grubstake, stake
   rel aid, assist, help, subsidize, support; fund; promote, sponsor

capitulate *vb syn see* YIELD 2

capitulation *n syn see* SURRENDER

capper *n syn see* DECOY 2

caprice *vb* an arbitrary, impulsive, and often illogical notion or change of mind < given to sudden *caprices* and random fancies >
   syn bee, boutade, conceit, crank, crotchet, fancy, freak, humor, maggot, megrim, notion, vagary, whigmaleerie, whim, whimsy
   rel mood, temper, vein; contrariety, inconsistency, perversity; characteristic, foible, habit, mannerism, peculiarity, trait, trick

capricious *adj* 1 *syn see* ARBITRARY 1
   2 *syn see* INCONSTANT 1
   rel humorsome, moody; effervescent
   con constant, steady
   ant steadfast
   3 *syn see* UNCERTAIN 1

capsheaf *n syn see* APEX 2

capstone *n syn see* APEX 2

capsule *adj syn see* CONDENSED

caption *n* an explanatory or identifying comment accompanying a pictorial illustration < the *captions* were under the wrong figures >
   syn legend, underline

captious *adj syn see* CRITICAL 1
   rel demanding, exacting, finicky; contrary, perverse; irritable, peevish, petulant, snappish, snappy, testy
   con judicious, sensible, wise; rational, reasonable; knowing, knowledgeable

---

ant appreciative

captivate *vb syn see* ATTRACT 1
   rel delight, gratify, please; entterall, grip, hold, mesmerize, spellbind
   ant repulse

captivated *adj syn see* ENAMORED 3

captivating *adj syn see* ATTRACTIVE 1

capture *vb syn see* CATCH 1

Capuan *adj syn see* LUXURIOUS 3

car *n* a usually private passenger-carrying automotive vehicle < drove a shabby old *car* >
   syn auto, autocar, automobile, buggy, ‖bus, machine, motor, motorcar
   rel coach, convertible, coupe, hardtop, limousine, phaeton, roadster, runabout, sedan, station wagon, touring car; ‖crate, ‖clunker, ‖heap, ‖jalopy, junker, ‖wreck

caravansary *n syn see* HOTEL

carbon *n syn see* REPRODUCTION

carbon copy *n syn see* REPRODUCTION

carbuncle *n syn see* ABSCESS

carcass *n syn see* CORPSE

‖carcel *n syn see* JAIL

card *n* 1 *syn see* WAG 1
   2 *syn see* PROGRAM 1
   3 *syn see* MENU

card *vb syn see* SCHEDULE 1

cardboard *adj syn see* STIFF 4
   rel unlifelike, unreal, unrealistic

cardinal *adj* 1 *syn see* ESSENTIAL 2
   2 *syn see* CENTRAL 1

care *n* 1 *syn see* SORROW
   rel strain, stress, tension
   2 a burdened or disquieted state of mind < a mind full of *care* and sadness >
   syn anxiety, concern, concernment, disquiet, solicitude, unease, uneasiness, worry
   rel apprehension, foreboding, misgiving, suspense; agitation, disturbance, perturbation; alarm, consternation, dismay, fear
   con calm, ease, peace, quietude; assurance, comfort, easiness
   3 *syn see* TRIAL 2
   4 serious and heedful attentiveness < attended his words with *care* >
   syn carefulness, concern, consciousness, heed, heedfulness, regard; *compare* ATTENTION 1
   rel curiosity; enthusiasm, interest; consideration, solicitude, thoughtfulness; effort, exertion, pains, trouble; alertness, vigilance, watchfulness
   con carelessness, disregard, heedlessness, unconcern; boredom, disinterest, ennui
   5 *syn see* OVERSIGHT 1
   6 *syn see* CUSTODY

care (for) *vb* 1 *syn see* TEND 2
   2 *syn see* MINISTER (to)
   idiom take care of

careen *vb syn see* LURCH 2

career *vb syn see* COURSE

carefree *adj* 1 *syn see* HAPPY-GO-LUCKY
   2 *syn see* IRRESPONSIBLE

careful *adj* 1 *syn see* CAUTIOUS
   rel attentive, heedful, observant
   2 closely attentive to details or showing such attention < *careful* workmanship >
   syn conscientious, conscionable, exact, fussy, heedful, meticulous, painstaking, punctilious, punctual, scrupulous
   rel accurate, nice, precise; deliberate, studied; foresighted, provident, prudent;

---

syn synonym(s)   *rel* related word(s)
ant antonym(s)   *con* contrasted word(s)
idiom idiomatic equivalent(s)
‖ use limited; if in doubt, see a dictionary

critical, discriminating, finical, finicky; observant, particular, religious; duteous, dutiful, intent
con disorderly, lax, negligent, slack, slipshod, slovenly; heedless, neglectful, remiss
ant careless
carefulness *n syn* see CARE 4
careless *adj* 1 lacking in or showing lack of care and attention < *careless* of the harm his neglect might do to others > < unwilling to accept such *careless* shoddy work >
syn feckless, heedless, inadvertent, irreflective, thoughtless, uncaring, unheeding, unrecking, unreflective, unthinking; *compare* INCAUTIOUS, RASH 1
rel forgetful, inattentive, oblivious, unmindful; lax, neglectful, negligent, slack, unconcerned, uninterested; inadequate, incapable, unfit, unqualified
con careful, heedful, thoughtful; concerned, considerate, punctilious, scrupulous
ant careful
2 *syn* see IRRESPONSIBLE
3 *syn* see NEGLIGENT
4 *syn* see SLIPSHOD 3
5 *syn* see SLOVENLY 1
caress *vb* to express interest, affection, or love by touching or handling < *caress* a frightened child >
syn cosset, cuddle, dandle, fondle, love, pet
rel cocker, coddle, indulge, pamper; coquet, dally, flirt, toy, trifle; nuzzle, pat, stroke
careworn *adj syn* see HAGGARD
rel distressed, troubled; exhausted, fagged, jaded, tuckered
ant carefree
cargo *n syn* see LOAD 1
caricature *n* 1 *syn* see MOCKERY 2
2 a grotesque or bizarre imitation < a doting attentiveness that was a sickly *caricature* of motherhood >
syn burlesque, parody, takeoff, travesty
rel lampoon, libel, pasquinade; laughingstock, mockery; cheat, fake, imitation, phony, sham; bosh, bunk, gammon, hokum, moonshine; clinquant, pinchbeck, shoddy, tinsel
carillon *n syn* see BELL TOWER
caritas *n syn* see MERCY
cark *vb* 1 *syn* see TROUBLE 1
2 *syn* see WORRY 3
carnage *n syn* see MASSACRE
carnal *adj* 1 *syn* see BODILY
rel material, substantial; earthly, earthy
2 characterized by physical rather than intellectual or spiritual orientation < giving too much heed to the *carnal* aspects of day-to-day life >
syn animal, fleshly, sensual; *compare* SENSUOUS
rel bodily, corporal, corporeal, physical; coarse, gross, obscene, vulgar; earthly, earthy, mundane, temporal, worldly; lascivious, lewd, lustful, wanton; Pandemic, sensuous
con ethical, moral, noble, righteous, virtuous; aerial, ethereal, otherworldly, supernal; chaste, decent, modest, pure
ant spiritual; intellectual

carnality *n syn* see ANIMALITY
carom *vb syn* see GLANCE 1
carousal *n syn* see BINGE 1
carouse *n syn* see BINGE 1
carouse *vb syn* see REVEL 1
carp (at) *vb syn* see NAG
carper *n syn* see CRITIC
‖**carpet** *vb syn* see SCOLD 1
idiom call on the carpet, take to task
carpet knight *n syn* see HEDONIST
carping *adj syn* see CRITICAL 1
rel blaming, criticizing, reprehending, reprobating; jawing, railing, upbraiding; blameful, condemnatory, damnatory, objurgatory, reproachful, reprobatory
con applauding, commendatory, complimentary; approving, endorsing; extolling, laudatory, praiseful
ant fulsome
carriage *n* 1 *syn* see TRANSPORTATION 1
2 *syn* see POSTURE 1
carriageable *adj syn* see PORTABLE
carriage trade *n syn* see ARISTOCRACY
carrier *n* 1 *syn* see BEARER 2
2 *syn* see MESSENGER
3 *syn* see VECTOR
carrot *n syn* see REWARD
carry *vb* 1 to be the agent or means by which someone or something is shifted from one place to another < *carried* the child on his shoulder >
syn bear, buck, convey, ferry, ‖hump, ‖jag, lug, pack, tote, transport
rel bring, fetch, take; move, remove, shift, transfer; send, transmit
‖2 *syn* see ACCOMPANY
3 *syn* see AFFECT
4 *syn* see BEAR 3
5 *syn* see CONDUCT 4
6 *syn* see BEHAVE 1
7 *syn* see SUPPORT 4
8 *syn* see STOCK
carrying *n syn* see TRANSPORTATION 1
carry off *vb syn* see KILL 1
carry on *vb* 1 *syn* see CONDUCT 3
2 *syn* see CUT UP 2
3 *syn* see PERSEVERE
carry out *vb* 1 *syn* see ADMINISTER 1
rel complete, finalize; discharge, effect, effectuate, fulfill; prosecute, transact
idiom put in force (*or* into effect); sign, seal, and deliver
2 *syn* see EFFECT 2
carrytale *n syn* see GOSSIP 1
carry through *vb* 1 *syn* see EFFECT 2
2 *syn* see CONTINUE 1
carte blanche *n* full discretionary power < was given *carte blanche* to build, landscape, and furnish the house >
syn blank check, free hand
rel license, prerogative, right; authority, power; say, say-so
idiom power of attorney
carte d'entrée *n syn* see TICKET 2
carte du jour *n syn* see MENU
cartel *n* 1 *syn* see DEFIANCE 1
rel gage, gauntlet, glove; blow, slap
2 *syn* see SYNDICATE
rel corporation; multinational; consortium, merger
carve *vb* 1 *syn* see CUT 5
2 *syn* see SCULPTURE
Casanova *n* 1 *syn* see GALLANT 2

2 *syn* see WOLF

cascade *n syn* see WATERFALL

||**cascade** *vb syn* see VOMIT

case *n* 1 *syn* see EVENT 4

2 *syn* see ORDER 9

3 *syn* see SUIT 1

4 *syn* see INSTANCE

rel circumstance, episode, event, incident, occurrence; condition, situation, state

5 *syn* see ECCENTRIC

case *n syn* see HULL

||**case** *vb syn* see SCRUTINIZE 1

case history *n syn* see INSTANCE

cash *n syn* see MONEY

cashier *vb* 1 *syn* see DISMISS 3

rel eject, expel, oust; bar, eliminate, exclude; pass over, shelve

con appoint, designate, elect, name; employ, engage, hire

2 *syn* see DISCARD

cash in *vb syn* see DIE 1

cask *n* a vessel made of staves, headings, and hoops <a *cask* of cider>

syn barrel, butt, hogshead, keg, pipe, tun

Cassandra *n syn* see PESSIMIST

cassock *n syn* see CLERGYMAN

cast *vb* 1 *syn* see THROW 1

rel broadcast, disperse, distribute, scatter

2 *syn* see DIRECT 2

3 *syn* see DISCARD

rel abandon, leave, relinquish, surrender, yield; dismiss, drop

|4 *syn* see VOMIT

5 *syn* see ADD 2

6 *syn* see PLAN 2

cast *n* 1 *syn* see LOOK 2

2 *syn* see PREDICTION

3 *syn* see COLOR 1

4 *syn* see HINT 2

5 *syn* see TYPE

6 *syn* see FORM 1

cast about *vb syn* see SEEK 1

cast away *vb* 1 *syn* see WASTE 2

2 *syn* see SHIPWRECK 1

castaway *n syn* see OUTCAST

cast down *vb syn* see HUMBLE

cast down *adj syn* see DOWNCAST

castigate *vb* 1 *syn* see PUNISH 1

rel baste, beat, belabor, drub, pummel, thrash; berate, rail, rate, tongue-lash, upbraid, wig; penalize

2 *syn* see LAMBASTE 3

castigation *n syn* see PUNISHMENT

castigatory *adj syn* see PUNITIVE

castle *n syn* see MANSION

castle-builder *n syn* see DREAMER

cast out *vb* 1 *syn* see BANISH

||2 *syn* see QUARREL

castrate *vb* 1 *syn* see STERILIZE

2 *syn* see UNNERVE

rel bleed, drain, empty, exhaust

casual *adj* 1 *syn* see ACCIDENTAL

rel unplanned, unpremeditated; extemporaneous, extempore, impromptu, improvised, offhand; impulsive, spontaneous

con advised, considered, deliberate, intentional, planned, premeditated, studied

ant deliberate

2 *syn* see INDIFFERENT 2

3 *syn* see EASYGOING 3

con ceremonial, conventional, formal

4 *syn* see LITTLE 3

casually *adv syn* see INCIDENTALLY 1

casualty *n* 1 *syn* see ACCIDENT 2

2 *syn* see FATALITY 2

3 *syn* see VICTIM 2

casuistry *n syn* see FALLACY 2

|**cat** *n syn* see MAN 3

|**cat** *vb syn* see VOMIT

cataclysm *n* 1 *syn* see FLOOD 2

2 *syn* see DISASTER

cataclysmic *adj syn* see FATAL 2

catacomb *n syn* see CRYPT

catalog *n syn* see LIST

rel program, prospectus, syllabus

catalog *vb* 1 *syn* see INVENTORY

2 *syn* see LIST 3

rel admit, enter, introduce; count, enumerate, number

catalyst *n syn* see STIMULUS

cataplasm *n syn* see POULTICE

cataract *n* 1 *syn* see WATERFALL

2 *syn* see FLOOD 2

catastrophe *n syn* see DISASTER

catastrophic *adj syn* see FATAL 2

catcall *n syn* see RASPBERRY

catch *vb* 1 to obtain physical mastery and possession of <the cat *caught* a mouse>

syn bag, capture, collar, ||cotch, get, nail, prehend, secure, take; *compare* ARREST 2, SEIZE 2

rel clutch, grab, snatch; clasp, grasp, grip; ensnare, entangle, entrap, snare, tangle, trap

con free, release

ant miss

2 *syn* see SEIZE 2

3 to put at a disadvantage or bring under control by or as if by enmeshing in a net <*caught* in the fallacy of his own argument>

syn benet, catch up, ensnare, entangle, entrap, snare, tangle, trap; *compare* ENTANGLE 3

rel baffle, confound, nonplus, perplex, stick, stump; abash, disturb, embarrass, put out; confuse, flurry, fluster, rattle

4 *syn* see DUPE

5 *syn* see FIND 1

6 *syn* see MARRY 1

7 to come up with often unexpectedly <the storm *caught* them unawares>

syn ||cotch, overhaul, overtake, take

rel reach

idiom come upon

8 *syn* see SEIZE 3

9 *syn* see INTERCEPT

10 *syn* see CONTRACT 1

idiom fall ill (of *or* with), fall victim to

11 *syn* see FASTEN 2

12 *syn* see STRIKE 2

13 *syn* see APPREHEND 1

catch colt *n syn* see BASTARD

catching *adj syn* see INFECTIOUS 2

2 *syn* see INFECTIOUS 1

catch on *vb syn* see DISCOVER 3

catchphrase *n syn* see CATCHWORD

catchpole *n syn* see DELEGATE

catch up *vb* 1 *syn* see CATCH 3

2 *syn* see ENTHRALL 2

catchword *n* a word or phrase that catches the eye or ear and is repeated so

often that it becomes representative of a
political party, school of thought, or point
of view <"new deal" became the *catchword* of supporters and critics of Franklin
Roosevelt>
  syn byword, catchphrase, phrase, shibboleth, slogan, watchword; *compare* BATTLE
CRY
  rel household word; maxim, motto
catchy *adj syn* see FITFUL
catechize *vb syn* see ASK 1
categorical *adj* 1 *syn* see ULTIMATE 3
  con conjectural, hypothetical, suppositious; conditional, contingent, dependent,
relative
  2 *syn* see EXPLICIT
  rel certain, positive, sure; direct, downright, forthright
  con ambiguous; doubtful, dubious, problematic, questionable
  3 *syn* see POSITIVE 1
categorically *adv syn* see EXPRESSLY 1
categorize *vb syn* see ASSORT
  rel identify, nail down, peg, put down
category *n syn* see CLASS 1
cater (to) *vb* 1 *syn* see BABY
  idiom make much of
  2 *syn* see INDULGE 1
cateran *n syn* see MARAUDER
catercorner (*or* **catty-corner** *or* **kitty-
corner**) *adv syn* see DIAGONALLY
cater–cousin *n syn* see FRIEND
caterwaul *vb syn* see QUARREL
catharsis *n syn* see PURIFICATION
catholic *adj* 1 *syn* see UNIVERSAL 2
  rel comprehensive, inclusive; general,
generic, indeterminate; extensive, large-
scale
  ant parochial; provincial
  2 *syn* see ECLECTIC 2
catholicon *n syn* see PANACEA
cathouse *n syn* see BROTHEL
catlike *adj syn* see STEALTHY 2
catnap *n syn* see NAP
catnap *vb syn* see NAP
‖**catouse** *n syn* see COMMOTION 3
cat's–paw *n syn* see TOOL 2
catty *adj* 1 *syn* see STEALTHY 2
  2 *syn* see AGILE
  3 *syn* see MALICIOUS
‖**caulk** (off) *vb syn* see NAP
‖**caulker** *n syn* see DRAM
causatum *n syn* see EFFECT 1
cause *n* 1 that (as a person, fact, or condition) which is responsible for an effect
<the storm was the *cause* of all our dif-
ficulties>
  syn antecedent, determinant, occasion,
reason
  rel goad, impulse, incentive, inducement,
motive, spring; origin, prime mover, root,
source; author, creator, generator, originator
  con consequence, effect, issue, outcome,
result
  2 *syn* see MOTIVE 1
  3 *syn* see OCCASION 3
  4 *syn* see SUIT 1
cause *vb* 1 *syn* see GENERATE 3
  2 *syn* see EFFECT 1
  rel elicit, evoke, provoke
  idiom be at the root of, give origin to, set
on foot

'cause *conj syn* see BECAUSE
causerie *n syn* see CHAT 2
caustic *adj* 1 marked by sharp and often
witty incisiveness <a *caustic* critic>
  syn mordacious, mordant, salty, scathing,
trenchant; *compare* SARCASTIC
  rel biting, cutting, incisive; acrid, bitter,
pungent, tart; acute, keen, sharp; ironic,
sarcastic, satiric, stinging; harsh, rough,
severe, stringent; crisp, pithy, succinct,
terse
  con gentle, mild; cordial, gracious; bland,
diplomatic, suave, urbane
  ant genial
  2 *syn* see SARCASTIC
causticity *n syn* see SARCASM
caution *n* 1 *syn* see WARNING
  2 *syn* see PRUDENCE 1
caution *vb syn* see WARN 1
cautionary *adj syn* see MONITORY
cautioning *adj syn* see MONITORY
cautious *adj* marked by careful prudence
especially in reducing or avoiding risk or
danger <a *cautious* approach to mar-
riage>
  syn calculating, careful, chary, circumspect, considerate, discreet, gingerly,
guarded, safe, wary
  rel alert, vigilant, watchful; cagey, canny,
cozy, foresighted, precautious, shrewd;
forethoughtful, prethoughtful, provident,
prudent; calculating, scheming, shrewd;
expedient, judicious, politic
  idiom on one's guard, on the safe side,
playing it safe
  con daring, rash, reckless, venturesome;
headlong, impetuous, precipitate
  ant adventurous, temerarious
cavalier *adj syn* see PROUD 1
cave *n* a usually natural underground
chamber <the limestone *caves* of Ken-
tucky>
  syn cavern, grotto, subterrane, subterranean
cave *vb* 1 *syn* see GIVE 12
  2 *syn* see YIELD 2
cave (in) *vb syn* see COLLAPSE 2
caveat *n syn* see WARNING
cavern *n syn* see CAVE
cavernous *adj* 1 suggestive of a cave <a
cavernous fireplace that gulped in wood>
  syn chasmal, gaping, yawning
  rel commodious, vast
  2 *syn* see HOLLOW 1
cavil *vb syn* see QUIBBLE 1
caviler *n syn* see CRITIC
caviling *adj syn* see CRITICAL 1
  rel contrary, perverse; demanding, exacting; finicky, fussy, picky; mean, petty,
small; hairsplitting, niggling, nitpicking
  con amiable, complaisant, good-natured,
tolerant; accommodating, easy, obliging
cavillous *adj syn* see CRITICAL 1
cavity *n syn* see HOLE 3
cavort *vb syn* see GAMBOL
  rel carry on, cut up, horse (around),
horseplay, roughhouse
caw *vb syn* see SQUALL 1
cease *vb syn* see STOP 3
  rel close, conclude, end, finish, terminate;
intermit
  con continue, persist; extend, prolong,
protract; arise, originate, rise, spring

cease *n syn* see END 2
cease-fire *n syn* see TRUCE
ceaseless *adj* 1 *syn* see CONTINUAL
  2 *syn* see EVERLASTING 1
cede *vb* 1 *syn* see RELINQUISH
  rel accord, concede, grant, vouchsafe
  con hold, hold back, keep back, retain, withhold
  2 *syn* see TRANSFER 4
ceinture *n syn* see BELT 1
‖**celeb** *n syn* see CELEBRITY 2
celebrate *vb* 1 *syn* see KEEP 2
  2 *syn* see PRAISE 2
celebrated *adj syn* see FAMOUS 2
celebrious *adj syn* see FAMOUS 2
celebrity *n* 1 *syn* see FAME 2
  ant obscurity
  2 a widely known and popularly esteemed person < youngsters making a great to-do over sports *celebrities* >
  syn big name, ‖celeb, luminary, name, notability, notable, somebody
  rel hero, immortal, mahatma, star, superstar; lion; personage, worthy; cynosure
  idiom center of attraction, person of note (*or* mark)
  con back number; nobody
celerity *n* 1 *syn* see HASTE 1
  rel alacrity, briskness, legerity
  2 *syn* see SPEED 2
celestial *adj* of, relating to, or befitting heaven or the heavens < *celestial* music from an angelic choir >
  syn empyreal, empyrean, heavenly
  rel ethereal, supernal, transcendental; otherworldly, unearthly, transmundane; beatific, blessed, elysian, Olympian
  con earthly, earthy, mundane, sublunary, worldly; chthonian, hellish, infernal
  ant terrestrial, uncelestial
cemetery *n* a piece of land used for burying the dead < the quiet peace of a country *cemetery* >
  syn ‖boneyard, ‖boot hill, burial ground, burying ground, God's acre, graveyard, memorial park, necropolis, polyandrium, potter's field
  rel churchyard; catacomb
  idiom city of the dead
censor *vb* to remove matter considered objectionable by expurgation or alteration < *censor* a movie >
  syn blip, bowdlerize, expurgate, screen
  rel cut out, excise, exscind; blue-pencil, delete, edit, red-pencil; bleach, clean (up), purge, purify; narrow, restrain, restrict
censorious *adj syn* see CRITICAL 1
  rel chiding, reproachful, reproaching; condemnatory, condemning, denouncing, denunciatory, reprehending; accusatory, culpatory
  con acclaiming, acclamatory, extolling, laudatory, lauding, praising; adulatory, complimentary, flattering
  ant eulogistic
censurable *adj syn* see BLAMEWORTHY
  rel improper, incorrect, objectionable, wrong, wrongful; discreditable, doubtful, questionable; inadmissible, unacceptable

---

  con correct, proper, right; acceptable, admissible; creditable
  ant uncensurable
censure *vb syn* see CRITICIZE
  rel rebuke, reprimand, reproach, reprove; contemn, disdain, scorn, scout, strafe; disallow, disapprove, oppose, reject, stigmatize
  con applaud, compliment, recommend; allow, approve, support
  ant commend
center *n* 1 a point or part in a surface or solid more or less equidistant from the periphery < the *center* of the earth >
  syn core, middle, midpoint, midst
  rel inside, interior
  con circumference, compass, perimeter, periphery; bounds, confines, limits
  2 one eminent in or central to a particular activity, condition, or interest < a *center* of international trade >
  syn focal point, focus, heart, hub, nerve center, polestar, seat; compare ESSENCE 2
  3 a source or point of origin (as of an influence, pressure, or effect) < the group proved a *center* of discontent >
  syn core, heart, pith, quick, root
  rel activator, dynamo, energizer, stimulant
center *adj syn* see MIDDLE 1
  2 *syn* see MIDDLE 2
centermost *adj syn* see MIDDLE 1
central *adj* 1 occupying a dominant or supremely important position < the *central* theme of American foreign policy >
  syn cardinal, overriding, overruling, pivotal, ruling
  rel dominant, paramount, predominant, preponderant; important, significant; outstanding, salient, signal; chief, essential, foremost, leading, main; all-absorbing, controlling, master; focal, key; basic, fundamental, primary, radical
  con insignificant, minor, trivial, unimportant; borderline, marginal
  ant peripheral
  2 *syn* see MIDDLE 2
centralizing *adj syn* see INTEGRATIVE
centripetal *adj syn* see INTEGRATIVE
‖**cep** *prep syn* see EXCEPT
cerate *n syn* see OINTMENT
cerberus *n syn* see CUSTODIAN
cerebral *adj* 1 *syn* see MENTAL 1
  2 *syn* see INTELLECTUAL 2
cerebrate *vb syn* see THINK 5
cerebration *n syn* see THOUGHT 1
ceremonial *adj* stressing or concerned with careful attention to form and detail < his *ceremonial* approach to everyday life >
  syn ceremonious, conventional, formal, solemn, stately
  rel mannered, studied, stylized; liturgical, ritual, ritualistic; august, courtly, imposing, lofty; fixed, rigid, set, starchy, stiff
  con casual, easy, informal, relaxed; artless, ingenuous, open, sincere
ceremonial *n* 1 *syn* see FORM 2
  2 *syn* see RITE 2
ceremonious *adj syn* see CEREMONIAL
  rel decorous, proper, seemly; impressive, moving, striking; grandiose, imposing, majestic
  ant unceremonious

---

syn synonym(s)   *rel* related word(s)
ant antonym(s)   *con* contrasted word(s)
idiom idiomatic equivalent(s)
‖ use limited; if in doubt, see a dictionary

ceremony *n* **1** *syn* see FORM 2
2 *syn* see RITE 2
certain *adj* **1** *syn* see FIRM 4
  rel assured, certified, guaranteed, warranted; ensured, insured, sure
  2 constituting an indeterminate and otherwise unidentified part of a group or whole < *certain* students dispute this finding >
  syn some, various
  rel a, an, one; many, numerous; divers, several, sundry
  con no; all
  3 being such beyond a doubt < no *certain* likeness of this saint survives >
  syn accurate, authentic, dependable, reliable
  rel credible, plausible, well-grounded
  con counterfeit, false, spurious; controversial, doubtful, dubious, questionable
  ant uncertain
  4 *syn* see INFALLIBLE 2
  5 *syn* see POSITIVE 3
  rel confirmable, demonstrable, establishable, provable, verifiable; doubtless, trustworthy, unerring
  con controversial, iffy
  ant uncertain
  6 *syn* see INEVITABLE
  rel indefeasible, irrevocable, unalterable, written; fated, predestinated, predetermined
  ant uncertain
  7 *syn* see SURE 5
  rel assured, confident, sanguine
  con hesitant, indecisive, vague, wavering; doubtful, dubious, questionable
  ant uncertain
certainty *n* a state of mind in which one is free from doubt < answered with complete *certainty* >
  syn assurance, assuredness, certitude, confidence, conviction, sureness, surety
  rel belief, credence, faith; absoluteness, definiteness, dogmatism, positiveness, positivism; firmness, staunchness, steadiness
  con doubt, mistrust, skepticism, unsureness; fluctuation, irresolution, shifting, trimming, vacillation, wavering; obscurity, vagueness
  ant uncertainty
certify *vb* **1** to testify usually formally and in writing to the truth or genuineness of something < *certify* a student's college transcript >
  syn attest, vouch, witness
  rel assert, aver, avouch, avow, profess
  2 *syn* see WARRANT 2
  3 *syn* see APPROVE 2
  rel authorize, commission, license
  con antagonize, counter, oppose
certitude *n* *syn* see CERTAINTY
  rel cocksureness
  con uncertainty
  ant doubt
‖**cess** *n* *syn* see TAX 1
cessation *n* *syn* see END 2
cesspit *n* *syn* see SINK 1
cesspool *n* *syn* see SINK 1
‖**chack** *n* *syn* see SNACK
chafe *vb* **1** *syn* see ANNOY 1
  2 *syn* see ABRADE 1
  3 to make sore or raw through friction < the high stiff collar *chafed* his neck >

  syn abrade, excoriate, fret, gall, rub
  rel damage, hurt, impair, injure; flay, peel, skin; inflame, irritate; graze, scrape, scratch
  con ease, relieve, soothe
chaff *vb* *syn* see BANTER 1
  idiom make merry over
chaffer *vb* *syn* see HAGGLE 2
  rel beg, coax, plead
chafing *adj* *syn* see IMPATIENT 1
chagrined *adj* *syn* see ASHAMED
  rel crushed, disconcerted; discomposed, perturbed, upset
  idiom put out of countenance
chain *n* **1 chains** *pl syn* see SHACKLE
  2 *syn* see SUCCESSION 2
  3 *syn* see SYNDICATE
chain *adj* **1** *syn* see CUMULATIVE
  2 *syn* see TRITE
chair *vb* *syn* see PRESIDE
chair car *n* *syn* see PARLOR CAR
chalk (out) *vb* *syn* see SKETCH
chalk up *vb* *syn* see GET 1
challenge *vb* **1** *syn* see DEMAND 1
  2 *syn* see QUESTION 2
  3 *syn* see FACE 3
  rel question; dispute; strive, struggle, try
  idiom throw down the (*or* one's) gage
  con by-pass, evade
  4 *syn* see STIR 1
challenge *n* **1** *syn* see DEMUR 2
  2 *syn* see DEFIANCE 1
  rel calling, claiming, demanding, exacting; importuning, insistence
chamber *n* **1** *syn* see ROOM 1
  ‖**2 chambers** *pl syn* see APARTMENT 1
chamber *vb* *syn* see HARBOR 1
champ *vb* **1** *syn* see CHEW 1
  rel crush, macerate, mash, smash
  2 *syn* see BITE 1
  rel nibble, nip; gum, mouth, mumble; peck, pick
champaign *n* *syn* see FIELD
champion *n* *syn* see EXPONENT
champion *vb* *syn* see SUPPORT 2
  rel battle, contend, fight (for)
  idiom put in a good word for, stand behind (*or* back of), stand up for
  con resist, withstand; denounce, condemn
  ant combat
champion *adj* **1** *syn* see EXCELLENT
  rel distinguished, illustrious, outstanding, splendid
  2 *syn* see FIRST 3
chance *n* **1** *syn* see ACCIDENT 1
  con certainty, inevitability, necessity; destiny, fate, foreordination, predestination
  ant law
  2 an unpurposed, unpredictable, and uncontrollable master force < the folly of depending on *chance* for success in life >
  syn fortune, hazard, luck
  rel advantage, break, fluke; fate, lot; contingency
  3 *syn* see OPPORTUNITY
  rel likelihood, possibility, probability; outlook, prospect
chance *vb* **1** *syn* see HAPPEN 1
  2 *syn* see HAPPEN 2
  3 *syn* see GAMBLE 2
  4 *syn* see VENTURE 1
  idiom put at (*or* in) hazard

con cherish, protect, safeguard, secure

chance *adj syn* see ACCIDENTAL
rel careless, heedless, offhand

chance child *n syn* see BASTARD 1

chancy *adj* 1 *syn* see UNCERTAIN 1
rel hazardous, risky, speculative, unsound; precarious, ticklish, touchy, tricky
idiom hanging by a thread, on thin ice (*or* slippery ground)
con safe, secure, sound, stable
2 *syn* see DANGEROUS 1

change *vb* 1 to make or become different < *changed* her will again and again > < our needs *change* as we grow older >
syn alter, modify, mutate, refashion, turn, vary; *compare* TRANSFORM
rel convert, metamorphose, transform, transmute; diversify, variegate; exchange, interchange
idiom go (*or* pass through) a change
con establish, fix, set
2 *syn* see TRANSFORM
3 *syn* see REVERSE 1
4 *syn* see STERILIZE
5 to make substitution for or among < it's time to *change* the subject >
syn replace, shift
rel exchange, swap, trade; substitute
6 *syn* see EXCHANGE 2

change *n* 1 a making different < saw a gradual *change* of attitude in the community >
syn alteration, modification, mutation, turn, variation
rel aberration, deviation, divergence; diversification; shift; innovation
ant uniformity
2 a result of such change < amazed at the *changes* in the town >
syn innovation, mutation, novelty, permutation, sport, vicissitude
rel conversion, metamorphosis, transformation, transmutation; shift, substitute, surrogate; avatar

changeable *adj* 1 alterable or changing under slight provocation < *changeable* April weather >
syn changeful, fluid, mobile, mutable, protean, unsettled, unstable, unsteady, variable, weathery; *compare* INCONSTANT 1, MUTABLE 2
rel adaptable, impressionable, plastic, pliant; ever-changing, kaleidoscopic; restless, unfixed; inconstant, uncertain, vicissitudinous
con constant, invariable, permanent; certain, fixed, immutable, unalterable, unmodifiable; abiding, enduring, persistent
ant unchangeable; unchanging
2 *syn* see MUTABLE 2
3 *syn* see INCONSTANT 1

changeabout *n syn* see REVERSAL 1

changeful *adj syn* see CHANGEABLE 1
rel active, dynamic, live; lively, vigorous
con durable, lasting, perdurable, stable; steady, uniform
ant changeless, unchanging

changeover *n syn* see CONVERSION 2

---

channel *n* 1 passage through which a fluid (as water) flows or is led < the river cut a new *channel* to the sea >
syn aqueduct, canal, conduit, course, duct, watercourse
rel pass, passage, way
2 *syn* see MEAN 2
3 *syn* see PIPELINE

channel *vb syn* see CONDUCT 4

chant *vb syn* see SING 1

chaos *n* 1 *syn* see CONFUSION 3
2 *syn* see ANARCHY 1
rel misrule, unruliness

chap *n syn* see MAN 3

chaperon *vb* 1 *syn* see ACCOMPANY
rel guide, overlook, oversee, supervise
2 *syn* see SUPERVISE

chapfallen *adj syn* see DOWNCAST

chaplet *n syn* see WREATH

character *n* 1 an arbitrary or conventional device used in writing or printing < an inscription in runic *characters* >
syn mark, sign, symbol
rel cipher, device, monogram; letter
2 *syn* see CHARACTERISTIC 1
3 *syn* see QUALITY 1
rel distinction, uniqueness, uniquity
4 *syn* see TYPE
5 *syn* see DISPOSITION 3
rel soul, spirit; courage, mettle, resolution; intellect, intelligence, mind
6 *syn* see ROLE 1
7 *syn* see STATUS 1
8 *syn* see CREDENTIALS
9 *syn* see NOTABLE 1
10 *syn* see ECCENTRIC
‖11 *syn* see HUMAN
12 *syn* see REPUTATION 2

character assassination *n syn* see DETRACTION

characteristic *adj* being or revealing a quality specific or identifying to an individual or group < her *characteristic* down-to-earth approach to a problem >
syn diacritic, diagnostic, distinctive, idiosyncratic, individual, peculiar, proper
rel especial, particular, special, specific; natural, normal, regular, typical
con general, generic, universal
ant uncharacteristic

characteristic *n* 1 something that marks or sets apart < *characteristics* that distinguish man from lower primates >
syn birthmark, character, feature, point, trait; *compare* QUALITY 1
rel badge, mark, sign, token; flavor, odor, savor, smack, tang; differentia; singularity
2 *syn* see QUALITY 1

characterize *vb* 1 *syn* see SKETCH
2 to be a peculiar or significant quality or feature of something < a man *characterized* by quiet dignity >
syn distinguish, individualize, individuate, mark, qualify, signalize, singularize
rel define, describe, differentiate, identify; peculiarize, personalize
idiom be a feature of

characterless *adj* lacking in character or solid qualities < a drab *characterless* little man that no one ever seemed to notice >
syn namby-pamby, pantywaist, wishy-washy
rel childish, infantile; sissified, sissy, unmanly; futile, weak; impotent, powerless

---

syn synonym(s)   *rel* related word(s)
ant antonym(s)   *con* contrasted word(s)
idiom idiomatic equivalent(s)
‖ use limited; if in doubt, see a dictionary

con manly, strong, vigorous, virile

charade *n syn* see PRETENSE 2

chare *n syn* see TASK 1

charge *vb* 1 *syn* see BURDEN
2 *syn* see LOAD 3
3 *syn* see PERMEATE
4 *syn* see ENTRUST 1
5 *syn* see COMMAND
rel ask, request, solicit; adjure
6 *syn* see ACCUSE
rel impugn, reprehend, reproach
idiom bring (*or* prefer) charges
con excuse, forgive, pardon, remit; acquit
ant absolve
7 *syn* see ASCRIBE
8 *syn* see RUSH 1

charge *n* 1 *syn* see LOAD 3
rel business, devoir, place
2 *syn* see OBLIGATION 2
3 *syn* see OVERSIGHT 1
4 *syn* see COMMAND 1
5 *syn* see PRICE 1

chargeless *adj syn* see FREE 5

charger *n syn* see COURSER

charioteer *vb syn* see DRIVE 5

charisma *n syn* see CHARM 3

charitable *adj* 1 having or showing interest in or concern for the welfare of others <spent generously for *charitable* aid to the needy>
syn altruistic, benevolent, eleemosynary, good, humane, humanitarian, philanthropic
rel accommodating, helpful, obliging; benign, kindhearted, kindly, sympathetic
2 *syn* see FORBEARING
rel benevolent, considerate, kindly, thoughtful
con cold, harsh, heartless, unfeeling
ant uncharitable

charity *n* 1 *syn* see MERCY
rel affection, attachment, love; altruism, benevolence, humaneness; kindliness; amity, friendliness, goodwill
con malevolence, malignancy, malignity, spite, spleen
ant ill will, malice
2 *syn* see DONATION

charivari *n syn* see SHIVAREE

charlatan *n* one who pretends unscrupulously to knowledge or skill <the professions overrun with *charlatans* and rogues>
syn mountebank, quack, quacksalver, quackster, saltimbanque; *compare* IMPOSTER
rel bluff, four-flusher, sham

Charlie McCarthy *n syn* see STOOGE 1

charm *n* 1 *syn* see SPELL
2 an object worn or cherished to ward off evil or attract good fortune <the Indian medicine bag is essentially a *charm*>
syn amulet, fetish, juju, luck, mascot, periapt, phylactery, talisman, zemi
3 a quality or combination of qualities that is wholly attractive and irresistible <the *charm* of her smile>
syn allure, appeal, charisma, fascination, glamour, magnetism, witchcraft, witchery
rel allurement, attraction, attractiveness, lure; agreeableness, delightfulness, gratefulness

con hatefulness, obnoxiousness, odiousness, repulsiveness; distastefulness, unpleasantness

charm *vb* 1 *syn* see ATTRACT 1
2 *syn* see BEWITCH 1

charmed *adj syn* see ENAMORED 3

charmer *n syn* see MAGICIAN 1

charming *adj syn* see ATTRACTIVE 1
ant charmless

chart *n* 1 a stylized or symbolic depiction of something incapable of direct verbal or pictorial representation (as because of complexity or abstractness) <a *chart* of anticipated economic progress>
syn graph, map
rel plan, plat, plot, scheme
2 *syn* see TABLE 2

chart *vb syn* see PLAN 2

charter *n syn* see DEED 3

charter *vb syn* see HIRE 1

chary *adj* 1 *syn* see CAUTIOUS
rel disinclined, hesitant, loath, reluctant; economical, frugal, sparing, thrifty; constrained, inhibited, restrained
2 *syn* see SPARING

chase *vb* 1 *syn* see FOLLOW 2
con flee, fly
2 *syn* see HUNT 1
3 *syn* see EJECT 1
4 *syn* see RUSH 1
5 *syn* see COURSE

chase *n syn* see HUNTING
2 *syn* see GAME 3

chaser *n syn* see WOLF

chasm *n* 1 *syn* see GULF 2
2 *syn* see RAVINE
3 *syn* see OMISSION
4 *syn* see SCHISM 3

chasmal *adj syn* see CAVERNOUS 1

chaste *adj* free from every trace of the lewd or salacious <was as *chaste* in language as in conduct>
syn clean, decent, immaculate, modest, pure, spotless, stainless, unblemished, undefiled, unsullied
rel ethical, moral, righteous, virtuous; maidenly, virgin, virginal; becoming, decorous, proper, seemly; abstinent, continent
con coarse, gross, obscene, ribald, vulgar; lascivious, lecherous, licentious, lustful; gluttonous, incontinent, self-indulgent
ant unchaste

chasten *vb syn* see PUNISH 1
rel abase, humble, humiliate; afflict, try
con baby, humor, indulge, spoil
ant pamper

chastise *vb syn* see PUNISH 1
rel baste, beat, belabor, pummel, thrash

chastisement *n syn* see PUNISHMENT

chat *vb* 1 to emit a ready flow of inconsequential talk <*chats* on the phone for hours>
syn babble, burble, cackle, chatter, chin≈ chin, clack, clatter, ‖dish, dither, gab, gabble, ‖gas, jaw, ‖natter, patter, prate, prattle, rattle, run on, smatter, talk, tinkle, twaddle, twiddle, twitter, yak, yakety≈ yak, yammer, yatter; *compare* CONVERSE
rel yap; blab, gossip; gush, lallygag; confabulate
idiom beat one's gums, ‖chew the fat (*or* rag), ‖shoot (*or* bat) the breeze, ‖shoot (*or* sling) the bull

con discourse, expound; declaim, harangue, hold forth, orate, preach
2 *syn* see CONVERSE

chat *n* 1 *syn* see CHATTER
2 an informal conversation < had a satisfactory little *chat* with the new assistant >
syn causerie, chin, prose, rap, talk, yarn; *compare* CONVERSATION 2
rel gossip, tête-à-tête
idiom bull session, rap session
con debate, deliberation, discussion
3 *syn* see CONVERSATION 1

chateau *n syn* see MANSION

chattel *n* 1 **chattels** *pl syn* see POSSESSION 2
2 *syn* see SLAVE 1

chatter *vb* 1 *syn* see GIBBER
2 *syn* see CHAT 1

chatter *n* idle and often loud and incessant talk < schoolgirl *chatter* >
syn babble, bibble-babble, blab, blabber, ‖blatter, brabble, cackle, chat, chin-chin, ‖chin music, chitchat, chitter-chatter, clack, gab, gabble, gibble-gabble, jabber, palaver, prate, prattle, stultiloquence, talkee-talkee, tittle-tattle, yak, yakety-yak, yak-yak, yatter
rel ‖bull, gossip, small talk
idiom tongue wagging

chatterbox *n* one who engages in chatter < that old *chatterbox* will talk your arm off >
syn bandar-log, blabber, blabbermouth, blabmouth, chatterer, chewet, gabber, jabberer, magpie, prater, prattler
rel busybody, gossip, newsmonger, quidnunc, scandalmonger, tabby, tattletale

chatterer *n syn* see CHATTERBOX

chatty *adj syn* see TALKATIVE

‖**chaw** *vb* 1 *syn* see CHEW 1
2 *syn* see PONDER 2

chawbacon *n syn* see RUSTIC

cheap *adj* 1 costing little < produce is usually *cheaper* in summer >
syn inexpensive, low, low-cost, low-priced, popular, reasonable, uncostly, undear
rel bargain-basement, bargain-counter, cut-rate, reduced; dirt-cheap
con dear, high, high-priced
ant costly, expensive
2 of inferior quality < *cheap* furniture is never a bargain >
syn base, cheesy, common, mean, ‖ornery, paltry, poor, rubbishing, rubbishly, rubbishy, shoddy, sleazy, tatty, trashy, trumpery; *compare* INFERIOR 2
rel cheap-jack, valueless, worthless; flashy, garish, meretricious, tawdry; brummagem, fake, phony, sham; bad, rotten, terrible
con capital, excellent, fine, good; first-class, first-rate, high-class, high-grade, superior, tip-top, top-notch
ant precious
3 *syn* see CONTEMPTIBLE
rel wrong; base, low, vile; measly, paltry, petty, trifling

ant noble

cheapen *vb syn* see DEPRECIATE 1

cheap-jack (*or* **cheap-john**) *n syn* see PEDDLER

cheapskate *n syn* see MISER

cheat *n* 1 *syn* see DECEPTION 1
2 *syn* see IMPOSTURE
rel bamboozlement, cozening, hoaxing; chicane, chicanery, trickery
3 *syn* see SWINDLER

cheat *vb* to obtain something (as money) from or an advantage over by dishonesty and trickery < *cheated* out of his inheritance by a grasping lawyer >
syn beat, bilk, boodle, ‖burn, chisel, chouse, cozen, ‖crook, defraud, diddle, do, ‖doodle, ‖dry-shave, ‖duff, flimflam, gyp, ‖mace, ‖mump, overreach, ream, ‖screw, sucker, swindle, take; *compare* EXTORT 1, FLEECE 1
rel befool, dupe, fool, gull, slick; bunco, con, fudge, short; beguile, deceive, delude, double-cross, mislead

cheater *n syn* see SWINDLER

check *vb* 1 *syn* see ARREST 1
rel cease, desist, discontinue, stop; repress, suppress; circumvent, foil, frustrate, thwart
ant expedite
2 *syn* see RESTRAIN 1
rel baffle, balk; obviate, preclude, prevent
ant accelerate (*of speed*); advance (*as of hopes, plans*); release (*of feelings, energies*)
3 *syn* see TRY 1
4 *syn* see AGREE 4

check *n* 1 *syn* see SETBACK
2 a statement of charges for food and drink consumed (as at a restaurant) < shocked at the size of the *check* >
syn bill, tab
rel damage, score

check out *vb* ‖1 *syn* see DIE 1
2 *syn* see AGREE 4

check over *vb syn* see SCRUTINIZE 1

check-over *n syn* see EXAMINATION

check up *vb syn* see SCRUTINIZE 1

checkup *n syn* see EXAMINATION

cheek *n* 1 **cheeks** *pl syn* see BUTTOCKS
2 *syn* see EFFRONTERY

cheeky *adj syn* see WISE 5

cheep *vb syn* see CHIRP

cheer *vb* 1 *syn* see COMFORT
2 *syn* see ENCOURAGE 1
3 *syn* see APPLAUD 2

cheerful *adj* 1 marked by or suggestive of lighthearted ease of mind and spirit < a *cheerful* smile >
syn blithe, cheery, ‖chirk, chirpy, chirrupy, lightsome, sunbeamy, sunny; *compare* LIVELY 1
rel airy, carefree, debonair, jaunty; animated, gay, lighthearted, lively, vivacious; buoyant, corky
idiom in good (*or* high) spirits, of good cheer
con blue, dejected, depressed, melancholy; dispirited, heavyhearted; joyless, mournful, sorrowful, woeful; dour, morose, saturnine, sullen; doleful, lugubrious; austere, forbidding, grim, stern
ant gloomy, glum
2 *syn* see GLAD 2
ant cheerless

‖cheerio *interj syn* see GOOD-BYE
cheerless *adj syn* see GLOOMY 3
  rel dejecting
  ant cheerful
cheery *adj* 1 *syn* see GLAD 2
  2 *syn* see CHEERFUL 1
cheeseparer *n syn* see MISER
cheeseparing *adj syn* see STINGY
  rel cheap, grudging, mean, shabby; illiberal
cheesy *adj syn* see CHEAP 2
chef d'oeuvre *n* 1 *syn* see MASTERPIECE
  1
  2 *syn* see SHOWPIECE
‖chemist *n syn* see DRUGGIST
cherish *vb* 1 *syn* see NURSE 2
  rel conserve, preserve, save; entertain, harbor, keep, shelter; defend, guard, safeguard, shield
  con reject, repudiate, scorn
  ant abandon
  2 *syn* see APPRECIATE 1
  rel revere, reverence, venerate
  idiom hold in high esteem
  con disregard, forget, ignore, overlook, slight
  ant neglect
  3 *syn* see ADMIRE 1
‖cherry *n syn* see VIRGINITY
chest *n syn* see TREASURY 2
chesty *adj syn* see BUXOM
chew *vb* 1 to crush or grind with the teeth
  < *chew* your food well >
  syn champ, ‖chaw, chomp, ‖chonk, chumble, chump, crunch, masticate, munch, ruminate, scrunch
  rel bite; gnaw, nibble; consume, devour, eat; gum, mumble
  ‖2 *syn* see SCOLD 1
chewet *n syn* see CHATTERBOX
‖chew out *vb syn* see SCOLD 1
chiaus *n syn* see SWINDLER
chic *n syn* see FASHION 3
chic *adj syn* see STYLISH
chicane *vb* 1 *syn* see QUIBBLE 1
  2 *syn* see DUPE
chicane *n syn* see DECEPTION 1
  rel artifice, feint, gambit, maneuver, ploy, ruse, stratagem, trick, wile; furtiveness, surreptitiousness, underhandedness
  con forthrightness, straightforwardness
chicanery *n syn* see DECEPTION 1
  rel intrigue, machination, plot; furtiveness, surreptitiousness, underhandedness
  con forthrightness, straightforwardness; honesty, honor, integrity, probity
chichi *adj* 1 *syn* see SHOWY
  2 *syn* see PRECIOUS 4
chick *n* 1 *syn* see CHILD 1
  ‖2 *syn* see GIRL FRIEND 1
chickabiddy *n syn* see CHILD 1
chicken *n syn* see COWARD
‖chicken *adj syn* see COWARDLY
chide *vb syn* see REPROVE
  rel berate, rate, scold, upbraid
  con applaud, compliment; approve, endorse, sanction
  ant commend
chiding *n syn* see REBUKE
chief *n* 1 *syn* see LEADER 2
  rel dictator, duce, führer
  2 *syn* see NOTABLE 1
chief *adj* 1 *syn* see FIRST 3

2 standing apart by reason of superior importance, significance, or influence < his *chief* claim to consideration is his unquestionable uprightness >
  syn capital, ‖cock, dominant, main, major, number one, outstanding, predominant, preeminent, principal, star, stellar
  rel primal, primary, prime; important, prominent, significant; consequential, momentous, weighty; effective, potent, telling; controlling, master, ruling
  con inconsequential, minor, trivial, unimportant; collateral, contingent, secondary
chiefly *adv syn* see GENERALLY 1
chieftain *n syn* see LEADER 2
chiffer *n syn* see NUMBER
child *n* 1 a young person < a movie for both *children* and adults >
  syn bud, chick, chickabiddy, chit, juvenile, kid, moppet, ‖nipper, puss, youngling, young one, youngster, youth
  rel minor; adolescent, teenager, teener, teenybopper; brat, bratling, dickens, runabout; cherub, innocent, lamb, sweetling
  idiom a slip of a boy (*or* girl), small fry, young hopeful
  ant adult, grown-up
  2 children *pl syn* see OFFSPRING
childbearing *n* 1 *syn* see BIRTH 1
  2 *syn* see LABOR 2
childbed *n syn* see CONFINEMENT 2
childbirth *n* 1 *syn* see BIRTH 1
  2 *syn* see LABOR 2
childing *adj* 1 *syn* see PREGNANT 1
  2 *syn* see FERTILE
childish *adj* significantly deficient in maturity < a *childish* and spiteful attitude >
  syn babyish, immature, infantile, infantine, prekindergarten, puerile
  rel asinine, fatuous, foolish, silly, simple; naive, unsophisticated; arrested, backward, moronic, retarded, slow, ‖wanting
  ant adult
child's play *n syn* see SNAP 1
chill *vb syn* see DISCOURAGE 1
chill *adj* 1 *syn* see COLD 1
  2 *syn* see COLD 2
  rel distant, formal, reserved, solitary, standoffish, uncompanionable, withdrawn; abstracted, disinterested, uninterested
  con easy, gregarious, informal; sociable
chiller *n syn* see THRILLER
chillsome *adj syn* see COLD 1
chilly *adj syn* see COLD 1
chime *n syn* see HARMONY 2
chime *vb syn* see RING
chime in *vb* 1 *syn* see INTERRUPT 2
  2 *syn* see SAY 1
chimera *n syn* see PIPE DREAM
chimerical *adj syn* see FICTITIOUS 1
  rel ambitious, pretentious, utopian; deceptive, delusive, delusory; fabulous, mythical; absurd, preposterous
  con believable, plausible, rational, reasonable; possible, practicable
  ant feasible
chiming *adj syn* see HARMONIOUS 1
chin *n syn* see CHAT 2
chin *vb syn* see CONVERSE
chin–chin *vb syn* see CHAT 1
chin–chin *n syn* see CHATTER
‖chinchy *adj syn* see STINGY
chine *n syn* see RIDGE 1

Chinese puzzle *n syn* see MYSTERY
Chinese wall *n syn* see OBSTACLE
chink *n syn* see CRACK 3
  rel interruption
chink *vb syn* see JINGLE
‖**chink** *n syn* see MONEY
chinkle *vb syn* see JINGLE
‖**chin music** *n syn* see CHATTER
chintzy *adj syn* see GAUDY
chin–up *adj syn* see BRAVE 1
chip *vb syn* see CHIRP
chip in *vb* 1 *syn* see CONTRIBUTE 1
  2 *syn* see INTERRUPT 2
chipper *vb syn* see CHIRP
chipper *adj* 1 *syn* see LIVELY 1
  2 *syn* see NEAT 2
‖**chippy** *n syn* see DOXY 1
‖**chips** *n pl syn* see MONEY
chirk *adj* 1 *syn* see LIVELY 1
  2 *syn* see CHEERFUL 1
chirk (up) *vb syn* see ENCOURAGE 1
‖**chirm** *n syn* see DIN
‖**chirm** *vb syn* see CHIRP
chirography *n syn* see HANDWRITING
chirp *vb* to make a short, sharp, and usually repetitive sound < sparrows *chirping* on the lawn >
  syn cheep, chip, chipper, ‖chirm, chirrup, clutter, peep, tweedle, tweet, twitter
chirpy *adj syn* see CHEERFUL
chirrup *vb syn* see CHIRP
chirrupy *adj syn* see CHEERFUL 1
chisel *vb* 1 *syn* see SCULPTURE
  2 *syn* see CHEAT
chisel (in) *vb* 1 *syn* see INTRUDE 1
‖**chiselly** *adj syn* see BAD 8
chit *n syn* see CHILD 1
chit *n syn* see NOTE 2
chitchat *n* 1 *syn* see CHATTER
  2 *syn* see SMALL TALK
chitter *vb syn* see CHIRP
chitter–chatter *n* 1 *syn* see CHATTER
  2 *syn* see SMALL TALK
chivalrous *adj syn* see GENEROUS 1
  rel knightly, manly, noble
  con churlish common, low
chivy *vb* 1 *syn* see FOLLOW 2
  2 *syn* see BAIT 2
  rel afflict, torment, try; chase, pursue, trail
choate *adj syn* see WHOLE 3
chockablock *adj syn* see FULL 1
chock–full *adj syn* see FULL 1
choice *n* 1 the act, right, opportunity, or faculty of choosing or deciding < the *choice* lies with the electorate >
  syn alternative, ‖druthers, election, option, preference, selection
  rel decision, determination, finding, judgment, verdict; appraisal, evaluation, rating
  2 *syn* see BEST
choice *adj* having qualities that appeal to a fine or highly refined taste < a few *choice* spirits gathered nightly to discuss the day's events >
  syn dainty, delicate, elegant, exquisite, rare, recherché, select, superior
  rel incomparable, peerless, preeminent, prime, superlative, supreme, surpassing,

transcendent, unsurpassed; chosen, culled, picked, selected
  con common, ordinary; average, fair, mediocre, medium, middling, run-of-the-mill, second-rate; drab, dull, lackluster, lusterless
  ant indifferent
‖**choicy** *adj syn* see NICE 1
choke *vb* 1 to check normal breathing especially by compressing or obstructing the windpipe < *choked* by a bone in the throat >
  syn strangle, throttle; *compare* SUFFOCATE
  2 *syn* see SUFFOCATE
  3 *syn* see FILL 1
  4 *syn* see LOAD 3
choke (off) *vb syn* see SILENCE
‖**chokey** *n syn* see JAIL
choking *n syn* see REPRESSION 1
choleric *adj* 1 *syn* see IRASCIBLE
  rel acrimonious, angry, fiery, indignant, irate, mad, spunky, wrathful, wroth; captious, carping, faultfinding
  con calm, serene, tranquil; composed, cool, nonchalant
  ant ‖placid
  2 *syn* see ANGRY
chomp *vb* 1 *syn* see CHEW 1
  2 *syn* see BITE 1
‖**chonk** *vb syn* see CHEW 1
choose *vb* 1 to fix upon one among alternatives as the one to be taken, accepted, or adopted < *chose* the largest apple but found it sour >
  syn cull, elect, mark, opt (for), optate, pick, pick out, prefer, select, single (out), take
  rel adopt, embrace, espouse; crave, desire, love, want, wish
  con decline, refuse, repudiate, spurn; abnegate, forbear, forgo
  ant reject; eschew
  2 *syn* see WILL
  rel favor, prefer
  ‖3 *syn* see DESIRE 1
choosy *adj syn* see NICE 1
chop *vb* 1 *syn* see FELL 2
  2 to cut into fragments by repeated strokes < *chop* meat and onions for hash >
  syn hash, mince
  rel cut up, dice, fragment
  idiom cut to bits, make mincemeat of
chop *n syn* see CUFF
chop–chop *adv syn* see FAST 2
chore *n* 1 *syn* see TASK 1
  2 *syn* see TASK 2
  rel trial, tribulation
chortle *vb syn* see LAUGH
chorus *n syn* see HARMONY 1
chosen *adj syn* see SELECT 1
chouse *n syn* see TRICK 1
chouse *vb syn* see CHEAT
‖**chow** *n* 1 *syn* see FOOD 1
  2 *syn* see MEAL
chowchow *adj syn* see MISCELLANEOUS
chowchow *n syn* see MISCELLANY 1
chowderhead *n syn* see DUNCE
chrism *n syn* see OINTMENT
christcross–row *n syn* see ALPHABET 1
christen *vb* 1 *syn* see BAPTIZE
  2 *syn* see NAME 1

---

syn synonym(s)   *rel* related word(s)
ant antonym(s)   *con* contrasted word(s)
idiom idiomatic equivalent(s)
‖ use limited; if in doubt, see a dictionary

Christian *adj syn* see DECOROUS 1
Christian name *n syn* see GIVEN NAME
Christmas *n* a festival or holiday commemorating the birth of Christ < gave presents on *Christmas*>
syn Nativity, noel, Xmas, yule, yuletide
chronic *adj* 1 *syn* see HABITUAL 2
2 *syn* see USUAL 1
chronicle *n* 1 *syn* see HISTORY 2
2 *syn* see ACCOUNT 7
rel narration, recital, recountal
chthonian *adj syn* see INFERNAL 1
chthonic *adj syn* see INFERNAL 1
chubby *adj syn* see ROTUND 2
ant slim
chuck *vb* 1 *syn* see DISCARD
2 *syn* see EJECT 1
3 *syn* see ABANDON 1
||**chuck** *n syn* see HARBOR 3
chucker *n syn* see BOUNCER 2
||**chucker–out** *n syn* see BOUNCER 2
chuckhole *n syn* see POTHOLE
chuckle *vb syn* see LAUGH
chucklehead *n syn* see DUNCE
chuckleheaded *adj syn* see STUPID 1
chuff *n* 1 *syn* see BOOR
2 *syn* see MISER
||**chuff** *adj syn* see SULLEN
||**chuffy** *adj syn* see STOCKY
||**chuffy** *adj syn* see SULLEN
chum *n syn* see ASSOCIATE 3
chumble *vb syn* see CHEW 1
chummy *adj* 1 *syn* see FAMILIAR 1
2 *syn* see INTIMATE 4
chump *n* ||1 *syn* see HEAD 1
2 *syn* see DUNCE
3 *syn* see FOOL 3
chump *vb syn* see CHEW 1
||**chumpy** *adj syn* see STOCKY
chunk *n syn* see LUMP 1
chunky *adj syn* see STOCKY
rel chubby, rotund
||**chunter** *vb syn* see MUMBLE
church *n* 1 *syn* see HOUSE OF WORSHIP
2 *syn* see RELIGION 2
church *adj syn* see ECCLESIASTICAL
churchly *adj syn* see ECCLESIASTICAL
churchman *n syn* see CLERGYMAN
churchmanly *adj syn* see ECCLESIASTICAL
churl *n syn* see BOOR
ant aristocrat, gentleman
churlish *adj syn* see BOORISH
rel crude, discourteous; blunt, brusque, crusty, curt, gruff; dour, surly; naive, unschooled
con bland, politic, smooth; polished, sophisticated
ant courtly
churn *vb syn* see SEETHE 4
chute *n syn* see WATERFALL
cicatrix *n syn* see SCAR
cicatrize *vb syn* see SCAR
||**cig** *n syn* see CIGARETTE
cigarette *n* a paper-wrapped tube of finely cut smoking tobacco < dependence on *cigarettes* >
syn ||butt, ||cig, ||coffin nail, fag, ||gasper, ||pill, ||skag, smoke
cimmerian *adj syn* see INFERNAL 2
cinch *n syn* see SNAP 1
cinch *vb syn* see ENSURE
cincture *n syn* see BELT 1

cincture *vb syn* see BELT 1
cinders *n pl syn* see ASH
cine *n syn* see MOVIE
||**cinema** *n syn* see MOVIE
cipher *n* 1 *syn* see ZERO 1
2 *syn* see NUMBER
3 *syn* see MONOGRAM
4 *syn* see NONENTITY
cipher *vb* 1 *syn* see CALCULATE
||2 *syn* see SOLVE 2
ciphering *n syn* see COMPUTATION
circa *prep syn* see ABOUT 1
Circean *adj syn* see ENTICING
circle *n* 1 *syn* see RANGE 2
2 *syn* see CYCLE 1
3 *syn* see SET 5
rel acquaintance; cronies, friends, intimates; associates, companions, comrades
4 *syn* see CLIQUE
circle *vb* 1 *syn* see SURROUND 1
2 *syn* see TURN 1
circuit *n* 1 *syn* see CIRCUMFERENCE
rel course, route, way; journey, tour, travels, trip
2 *syn* see REVOLUTION 1
3 *syn* see TOUR 2
4 *syn* see LEAGUE 4
circuitous *adj syn* see INDIRECT 1
ant straight
circuitously *adv syn* see ABOUT 2
circular *adj* 1 *syn* see ROUND 1
2 *syn* see INDIRECT 1
circulate *vb* 1 *syn* see SPREAD 1
rel exchange, interchange; flow; revolve, rotate
2 *syn* see MOBILIZE 1
circulation *n syn* see REVOLUTION 1
circulator *n syn* see GOSSIP 1
circumambages *n pl syn* see VERBIAGE 1
circumambulate *vb syn* see WANDER 1
circumbendibus *n syn* see VERBIAGE 1
circumduct *vb* 1 *syn* see TURN 1
2 *syn* see ABOLISH 1
circumference *n* a continuous line or course about an area < strolled along the *circumference* of the reservoir >
syn ambit, circuit, compass, perimeter, periphery; *compare* BORDER 1
rel boundary, bounds, confines, limits; border, margin, rim
circumlocution *n syn* see VERBIAGE 1
con conciseness, concision, pithiness, succinctness, terseness; compactness
circumnavigate *vb syn* see SKIRT 2
circumscribe *vb syn* see LIMIT 2
rel fetter, hamper, trammel
con amplify, distend, inflate, swell; enlarge
ant dilate, expand
circumscribed *adj syn* see DEFINITE 1
rel bound, bounded, finite; confined, cramped, strait
circumscription *n* 1 *syn* see RESTRICTION 1
2 *syn* see RESTRICTION 2
circumspect *adj syn* see CAUTIOUS
rel meticulous, punctilious, scrupulous
con adventurous, daredevil, foolhardy; careless, heedless; bold
ant audacious
circumstance *n* 1 *syn* see OCCURRENCE
rel detail, item, particular; component, constituent, element, factor

2 *syn* see FATE

circumstantial *adj* marked by careful attention to relevant details <gave a *circumstantial* account of his adventure>
syn blow-by-blow, clocklike, detailed, full, itemized, minute, particular, particularized, thorough
rel accurate, exact, nice, precise; complete, replete; close, strict
con compendious, concise, laconic, pithy, short, succinct, terse; abbreviated, curtailed, cut, pruned, shortened, trimmed
ant abridged; summary

circumvent *vb* 1 *syn* see FRUSTRATE 1
rel befool, dupe, hoodwink, trick; avoid, elude, escape, evade
ant conform (*to laws, orders*); cooperate (*with persons*)

2 *syn* see SKIRT 2

3 *syn* see SKIRT 3

circumvolution *n syn* see REVOLUTION 1

cit *n syn* see TOWNSMAN

citadel *n syn* see FORT

citation *n syn* see ENCOMIUM
rel award, guerdon, reward

cite *vb* 1 *syn* see REMEMBER

2 *syn* see MENTION

3 *syn* see ADDUCE
rel count, enumerate, number, tell

citizen *n* 1 *syn* see TOWNSMAN

2 a person regarded as a member of a sovereign state, entitled to its protection, and subject to its laws <the subtle bond between the *citizen* and the nation>
syn national, subject
con foreigner, stranger
ant alien

city *adj syn* see URBAN

civic *adj syn* see PUBLIC 1

civil *adj* 1 *syn* see PUBLIC 1

2 adequate in courtesy <made a *civil* inquiry about their health>
syn courteous, genteel, mannerly, polite, well-mannered; *compare* COURTLY
rel cultivated, refined, well-bred; accommodating, affable, cordial, obliging; bland, diplomatic, gracious, politic, suave, urbane
con boorish, churlish, loutish, uncouth; discourteous, ill-mannered, impolite, ungracious
ant uncivil; rude

civilities *n pl syn* see MANNER 5

civilized *adj* 1 *syn* see DECOROUS 1

2 *syn* see SUAVE

Civitas Dei *n syn* see HEAVEN 2

||**clabber** *vb syn* see CURDLE

clack *vb* 1 *syn* see CHAT 1

2 *syn* see RATTLE 1

clack *n* 1 *syn* see CHATTER

2 *syn* see GOSSIP 1

clad *vb* 1 *syn* see CLOTHE

2 *syn* see SHEATHE

||**claggy** *adj* 1 *syn* see STICKY 1

2 *syn* see MUDDY 1

claim *vb* 1 *syn* see DEMAND 1
rel adduce, advance, allege; assert, defend, justify, maintain, vindicate
con abnegate, forgo; refuse, reject, repudiate; disavow, disown

ant disclaim; renounce

2 *syn* see MAINTAIN 2

claim *n* 1 a real or assumed right to demand something as one's own or one's due <his genial wit was his greatest *claim* to fame>
syn ||dibs, pretense, pretension, title
rel birthright, prerogative, privilege, right; affirmation, assertion, declaration, protestation

2 *syn* see INTEREST 1

clamant *adj syn* see PRESSING

clamber *vb syn* see SCRAMBLE 1

clamor *n* 1 *syn* see COMMOTION 4

2 *syn* see DIN

3 *syn* see COMMOTION 1

clamor *vb syn* see ROAR
rel claim, demand; agitate, debate, dispute
idiom make the welkin ring, raise the roof

clamorous *adj* 1 *syn* see VOCIFEROUS
rel articulate, eloquent, vocal, voluble; adjuring, begging, imploring, importunate
ant taciturn

2 *syn* see PRESSING

clamp *n syn* see HOLD

clampdown *n syn* see REPRESSION 2

clan *n* 1 *syn* see FAMILY 1

2 *syn* see CLIQUE

clandestine *adj syn* see SECRET 1
rel illegitimate, illicit; artful, foxy, sly
con aboveboard, forthright, straightforward
ant open

clandestinely *adv syn* see SECRETLY

clangorous *adj syn* see NOISY

clap *n syn* see BANG 2

claptrap *n syn* see NONSENSE 2

||**claret** *n syn* see BLOOD 1

clarify *vb* 1 *syn* see PURIFY 1

2 to make clear and understandable <felt a need to *clarify* his position on the question>
syn clear, clear up, elucidate, explain, illuminate, illustrate; *compare* EXPLAIN 1
rel settle, straighten out; define, delineate, formulate; analyze, break down, simplify
idiom make plain
con befog, cloud, obfuscate, obscure; confuse, foul up, muddle, ||snafu

clarion *adj syn* see FAIR 2

clarity *n* notable precision of thought or expression <*clarity* of expression depends on use of exactly the right words in precisely the right way>
syn clearness, limpidity, lucidity, perspicuity, plainness
rel articulateness, articulation; care, exactitude, fussiness, meticulousness, nicety, precision; accuracy, correctitude, propriety
con haziness, imprecision, indefiniteness, unclearness, vagueness; inexactness, laxity, looseness, sloppiness, slovenliness
ant obscurity

||**clarty** *adj* 1 *syn* see MUDDY 1

2 *syn* see STICKY 1

clash *vb* 1 *syn* see BUMP 1

2 to be markedly out of harmony <garish colors that *clashed* almost painfully>
syn conflict, disaccord, discord, disharmonize, jangle, jar, mismatch
rel fret, gall, grate, try
idiom swear at one another

---

con accord, blend, conform, correspond; fit, meet, suit

ant harmonize

clash *n* **1** *syn* see IMPACT

2 a sharp and usually brief conflict especially between military units < recurrent border *clashes* >

syn affray, brush, fray, melee, mellay, scrimmage, skirmish

rel brawl, broil, fracas, riot, row, rumpus, scrap, set-to; action, battle, conflict, engagement; embroilment, encounter

idiom clash of arms, passage at (*or* of) arms

clashing *adj syn* see ANTIPATHETIC 1

clasp *n syn* see HOLD

clasp *vb* **1** *syn* see EMBRACE 1

2 *syn* see TAKE 4

class *n* **1** a unit or a subunit of a larger whole made up of members sharing one or more characteristics < miniaturization of circuitry made possible a whole new *class* of small computers and calculators >

syn category, grade, group, grouping, league, pigeonhole, tier

rel brand, color, description, feather, genre, grain, ilk, kidney, kind, nature, order, sort, stamp, style, type; bracket, branch, denomination, division, head, section; genus, species

2 *syn* see QUALITY 3

3 *syn* see TYPE

class *vb* **1** *syn* see ASSORT

2 to put into an appropriate class < he is generally *classed* among our leading theoretical physicists >

syn classify, evaluate, grade, rank, rate

rel appraise, gauge, judge; divide, part, separate; allot, assign; account, assess, consider, hold, reckon, regard; mark, score

classic *adj* **1** *syn* see EXCELLENT

2 *syn* see VINTAGE 1

3 *syn* see TYPICAL 1

classic *n syn* see MASTERPIECE 1

classical *adj* **1** *syn* see EXCELLENT

2 *syn* see VINTAGE 1

3 *syn* see TYPICAL 1

classify *vb* **1** *syn* see ASSORT

2 *syn* see CLASS 2

‖**classy** *adj syn* see STYLISH

clatter *vb* **1** *syn* see RATTLE 1

2 *syn* see CHAT 1

clatter *n syn* see COMMOTION 4

clattery *adj syn* see NOISY

claviger *n syn* see CUSTODIAN

‖**clawback** *n syn* see SYCOPHANT

clean *adj* **1** free from dirt < kept a *clean* house in a dirty neighborhood >

syn cleanly, immaculate, spotless, taintless, unsoiled, unsullied

rel bright, shining, sparkling; fresh, pure, untainted, wholesome

idiom clean as a whistle (*or* new penny)

con dingy, grimy, grubby, messy, mussy, slovenly; filthy, foul, noisome

ant dirty, unclean

2 *syn* see INNOCENT 2

3 *syn* see CHASTE

ant unclean

4 *syn* see FAIR 5

clean *vb* **1** *syn* see PURIFY 1

2 to make clean < *cleaned* his car every week >

syn cleanse, clean up

rel do, neaten, order, police, spruce, straighten (up), tidy, trim; brighten, freshen, furbish, recondition; renew, renovate

idiom make spick-and-span

con begrime, daub, dirty, sully; besmirch, defile, foul, pollute

ant soil

3 *syn* see DRESS 3

clean–cut *adj syn* see EXPLICIT

clean–limbed *adj syn* see SHAPELY

cleanly *adj syn* see CLEAN 1

rel neat, orderly, spick-and-span, tidy, trim; dainty, fastidious, fussy, nice

con disheveled, disorderly, slipshod, sloppy, slovenly, unkempt

ant uncleanly

cleanse *vb* **1** *syn* see CLEAN 2

rel disinfect, sanitize, sterilize

2 *syn* see PURIFY 1

3 *syn* see PURIFY 2

cleansing *n syn* see PURIFICATION

clean up *vb* **1** *syn* see CLEAR 6

2 *syn* see CLEAN 2

3 *syn* see SETTLE 7

‖**clean up** (on) *vb syn* see WHIP 2

clear *adj* **1** *syn* see FAIR 2

2 *syn* see TRANSPARENT 1

3 *syn* see TRANSLUCENT 3

rel milky, opalescent

4 free from obscurity or ambiguity < his account of the accident was perfectly *clear* >

syn clear-cut, crystal, lucent, lucid, luculent, luminous, pellucid, perspicuous, translucent, transparent, transpicuous, unambiguous, unblurred; *compare* UNDERSTANDABLE

rel apprehensible, comprehensible, graspable, knowable, understandable; plain, simple, straightforward, uncomplicated, unperplexed; defined, definite

idiom clear as day (*or* crystal), plain as the nose on one's face

con clouded, dark, mysterious, unclear; hazy, ill-defined, vague

ant obscure

5 readily perceived or apprehended < a *clear* case of embezzlement >

syn apparent, conspicuous, distinct, evident, manifest, obvious, open-and-shut, openhanded, palpable, patent, plain, straightforward, unambiguous, unequivocal, univocal, unmistakable; *compare* SELF-EXPLANATORY, UNDERSTANDABLE

rel appreciable, perceptible, recognizable, sensible, tangible; overt, public, published, unhidden, unobscured; exact, precise

con dim, dusky, gloomy, murky; cryptic, dark, enigmatic, equivocal, indistinct, vague; arcane, esoteric, mysterious, occult

ant obscure

6 *syn* see EMPTY 1

clear *adv syn* see WELL 3

clear *vb* **1** *syn* see EXCULPATE

2 *syn* see CLARIFY 2

3 *syn* see VACATE 2

4 *syn* see RID

rel eliminate, rule out; clean, cleanse

5 to make right by presenting what is due < *clear* one's accounts >

syn clear off, discharge, liquidate, pay, pay up, quit, satisfy, settle, square

rel close, pay off, repay, sink, solve
6 to obtain as a profit or return <he *cleared* several thousand on the deal>
syn clean up, gain, make, net
rel acquire, get, obtain, secure; earn, win; accumulate, gather, glean, pick up
7 *syn* see EXTRICATE 2
8 to pass over or by < *cleared* the hurdle with perfect form>
syn hurdle, leap, negotiate, over, overleap, surmount, vault
9 to become fair <the weather *cleared* later in the day>
syn ‖break, burn off
rel ameliorate, better, improve, meliorate; settle, stabilize
10 *syn* see VANISH
clear away *vb* **1** *syn* see REMOVE 4
2 *syn* see EXTRICATE 2
clear-cut *adj* **1** *syn* see CLEAR 4
2 *syn* see EXPLICIT
3 *syn* see INCISIVE
rel clear, distinct, manifest, plain; definite, explicit, express; exact, nice, precise
con fogged, hazy, misty; confused, muddled; obscured, overcast
4 *syn* see DECIDED 1
rel indubitable, undisputed, undoubted, unquestioned
idiom beyond a shade (or shadow) of doubt, past dispute
clearness *n* *syn* see CLARITY
clear off *vb* *syn* see CLEAR 5
clear out *vb* *syn* see GET OUT 1
clear-sightedness *n* *syn* see WIT 3
clear up *vb* **1** *syn* see CLARIFY 2
2 *syn* see SOLVE 2
cleavage *n* *syn* see SCHISM 3
cleave *vb* *syn* see STICK 2
rel associate, combine, conjoin, join, link, unite
con alienate, disaffect, disunite, estrange, separate
cleave *vb* **1** *syn* see CUT 5
2 *syn* see TEAR 1
rel divide, divorce, separate; chop, hew
con join, link, unite; attach, fasten
cleft *n* **1** *syn* see CRACK 3
2 *syn* see RAVINE
3 *syn* see SCHISM 3
clemency *n* **1** *syn* see MERCY
rel gentleness, mildness; equitableness, fairness, justness
con austerity, severity, sternness; rigidity, rigorousness, strictness; inexorableness, inflexibility, obduracy
ant harshness
2 *syn* see FORBEARANCE 2
rel endurance, sufferance
con firmness, hardness, inflexibility, obdurateness, relentlessness, rigidity
ant harshness
clement *adj* *syn* see FORBEARING
rel compassionate, sympathetic, tender; benign, benignant, kind, kindly; benevolent, charitable, humane
con austere, severe, stern; rigid, rigorous, strict, stringent

ant harsh; barbarous
clench *n* *syn* see HOLD
clergyman *n* one duly ordained to the service of God in the Christian church <the responsibility of the *clergyman* to the whole community>
syn ‖blackcoat, cassock, churchman, cleric, clerical, clerk, ‖devil-dodger, divine, ‖dominie, ecclesiast, ecclesiastic, ‖Holy Joe, minister, parson, preacher, pulpitarian, pulpiteer, pulpiter, reverend, sermonizer, sky pilot
rel evangelist, missionary; chaplain, curate, pastor, vicar; father, priest, shepherd; predicant
idiom man of God, man of the cloth
cleric *n* *syn* see CLERGYMAN
clerical *n* *syn* see CLERGYMAN
clerisy *n* *syn* see INTELLIGENTSIA
clerk *n* *syn* see CLERGYMAN
clerkish *adj* *syn* see NICE 1
clever *adj* **1** *syn* see SKILLFUL 2
2 *syn* see DEXTEROUS 1
3 *syn* see INTELLIGENT 2
rel apt, prompt, quick, ready; able, capable, competent; all-around, many-sided, versatile
idiom quick as a flash, sharp (or smart) as a whip
con asinine, fatuous, foolish, simple
ant dull
4 highly skilled in devising or contriving <very *clever* about getting her own way>
syn adroit, canny, cunning, dexterous, ingenious, ‖sleighty, slim, sly; *compare* SKILLFUL 2
rel able, adept, expert, handy, masterly, proficient, skilled, skillful; capable, competent, qualified; crafty, deceitful, slick, tricky
con awkward, clumsy, gauche, inept, maladroit; dilatory, laggard, slow, sluggish; incapable, incompetent, inept, unqualified
5 pleasing because of aptness, sparkle, and usually wit <delighted her audience with a series of *clever* comparisons>
syn good, scintillating, smart, sprightly
rel bright, brilliant, coruscating, dazzling, sparkling; piquant, racy, salty; fanciful, whimsical; amusing, entertaining, pleasing; facetious, funny, humorous, witty; laughable, risible
con drab, dull, humdrum, monotonous, stodgy; barren, empty, inane; fatuous, pointless; absurd, foolish, nonsensical, ridiculous
ant stupid
‖**cleverly** *adv* *syn* see WELL 3
cliché *n* *syn* see COMMONPLACE
cliché *adj* *syn* see TRITE
clichéd *adj* *syn* see TRITE
click *vb* *syn* see SUCCEED 2
client *n* *syn* see CUSTOMER
clientage *n* *syn* see FOLLOWING 2
clientele *n* *syn* see FOLLOWING 2
climacteric *adj* *syn* see ACUTE 6
climate *n* *syn* see ENVIRONMENT
climatize *vb* *syn* see HARDEN 2
climax *n* *syn* see APEX 2
climax *vb* to bring to or come to a satisfying termination <the feast was *climaxed* by a glorious plum pudding>

---

syn synonym(s)   *rel* related word(s)
ant antonym(s)   *con* contrasted word(s)
idiom idiomatic equivalent(s)
‖ use limited; if in doubt, see a dictionary

syn cap, crown, culminate, finish off, round off, top off

rel content, please, satisfy; conclude, end, finish, terminate

climb *vb syn* see ASCEND 1

∥**clinch** *vb syn* see EMBRACE 1

clinch *n syn* see HOLD

clincher *n syn* see TRUMP CARD

cling *vb syn* see STICK 2

cling *n syn* see ADHERENCE 1

clinging *n syn* see ADHERENCE 1

clink *vb syn* see JINGLE

∥**clink** *n syn* see JAIL

clinkers *n pl syn* see ASH

∥**clip** *vb syn* see EMBRACE 1

clip *n syn* see BROOCH

clip *vb* 1 *syn* see CUT 6

2 *syn* see MOW

3 *syn* see REDUCE 2

4 *syn* see OVERCHARGE 1

clique *n* a narrowly exclusive group of people usually held together by a common often selfish interest or purpose < there was a politically minded *clique* on the campus >

syn cabal, camarilla, camp, circle, clan, coterie, in-group, mob, ring; *compare* SET 5

clitter *vb syn* see RATTLE 1

cloak *n syn* see MASK 2

cloak *vb syn* see DISGUISE

rel blanket, curtain, screen, shroud, veil

ant uncloak

clobber *vb* ∥1 *syn* see WHIP 2

2 *syn* see SLAM 1

clochard *n syn* see VAGABOND

clock *vb syn* see TIME 2

∥**clock** *n syn* see SET 11

clocklike *adj syn* see CIRCUMSTANTIAL

clockwise *adj syn* see RIGHT-HANDED

clod *n* 1 *syn* see LUMP 1

2 *syn* see DUNCE

cloddish *adj syn* see BOORISH

clodhopper *n* 1 *syn* see RUSTIC

2 *syn* see BOOR

clodhopping *adj syn* see BOORISH

clodpate *n syn* see DUNCE

clodpoll *n syn* see DUNCE

clog *n syn* see ENCUMBRANCE

clog *vb* 1 *syn* see BURDEN

2 *syn* see HAMPER

3 *syn* see FILL 1

cloggy *adj syn* see STICKY 1

cloister *vb syn* see SECLUDE

cloistered *adj syn* see SECLUDED

clonk *vb syn* see THUD

∥**Cloot** *n, usu* **Cloots** *pl syn* see DEVIL 1

∥**Clootie** *n syn* see DEVIL 1

close *vb* 1 to fill an opening with an appropriate closure < be sure to *close* the gate >

syn ∥put to, shut

rel bang, clap, slam; block, choke, clog, obstruct, occlude, stop; debar, exclude

ant open

2 *syn* see SCREEN 3

3 to bring or come to a limit or to a natural or appropriate stopping point < *closed* the meeting as soon as the discussion was over >

syn complete, conclude, consummate, determine, do, end, finish, halt, terminate, ultimate, wind up, wrap up

rel cease, desist, quit, stop; finalize, write off

idiom call it a day, set a period to

con begin, commence, enter (on *or* upon), inaugurate, initiate, start

4 *syn* see FILL 1

5 *syn* see DECREASE

6 *syn* see MEET 6

close *n* 1 *syn* see END 2

2 *syn* see FINALE

ant opening

∥**close** *n syn* see COURT 1

close *adj* 1 *syn* see SILENT 3

idiom close as a clam

con candid, frank, plain

ant open

2 *syn* see STUFFY 1

rel humid, muggy, sticky

3 *syn* see STINGY

ant liberal

4 having the constituent parts massed closely together < a paper of fine *close* texture >

syn compact, crowded, dense, thick, tight

rel compacted, compressed, condensed, consolidated, constricted, contracted; firm, solid, substantial; impenetrable, impermeable; close-grained

con lax, loose, slack; unconsolidated

5 *syn* see TIGHT 3

6 not far removed (as in space, time, or relationship) from something stipulated or understood < true and veritable are *close* synonyms > < the park is very *close* to the river > < it is *close* to closing time >

syn immediate, near, near-at-hand, nearly, nigh, proximate; *compare* NEIGHBORING

rel abutting, adjacent, adjoining, contiguous; convenient, handy; nearest, nearmost, next

idiom at hand, at one's fingers' ends (*or* fingertips), under one's nose

con distant, far, faraway, far-off, removed

ant remote

7 *syn* see FAMILIAR 1

con cool, remote, withdrawn

ant aloof

close *adv* into proximity with respect to space, time, or approach < hoping to come *closer* to the truth of the matter >

syn at close hand, hard, near, nearby, nigh

rel almost, nearabout, nearly

idiom as near as no matter (*or* never mind), in hailing (*or* spitting) distance, within an inch (*or* an ace) of, within a stone's throw

con afar, distantly, far

ant remotely

close-at-hand *adj* 1 *syn* see NEIGHBORING

2 *syn* see CONVENIENT 2

close-by *adj* 1 *syn* see NEIGHBORING

2 *syn* see CONVENIENT 2

closed *adj syn* see SELF-SUFFICIENT

closed book *n syn* see MYSTERY

closed-minded *adj syn* see OBSTINATE

closefisted *adj syn* see STINGY

rel clinging, clutching, grasping, keeping, tenacious

close in *vb syn* see ENCLOSE 1

close-lipped *adj syn* see SILENT 3

closely *adv syn* see HARD 4

rel carefully, heedfully, mindfully, thoughtfully; meticulously, minutely, punctiliously, scrupulously *con* carelessly, heedlessly, thoughtlessly

closemouthed *adj syn* see SILENT 3

close off *vb syn* see ISOLATE

close on *prep syn* see ABOUT 1

close out *vb syn* see SELL OUT 1

closeout *n syn* see BARGAIN 1

‖**closet** *n syn* see PRIVY 1

closet *adj* 1 *syn* see PRIVATE 2
  2 *syn* see THEORETICAL 1

close-tongued *adj syn* see SILENT 3

closing *n syn* see END 2

closing *adj syn* see LAST

closure *n syn* see END 2

clot *n syn* see GROUP 3

clot *vb syn* see COAGULATE

clothe *vb* to cover with or as if with garments <forests *clothe* the rocky slopes>
  syn apparel, array, attire, clad, dress, enclothe, garb, garment, raiment
  rel costume, do up, dress up, tog (up *or* out); cloak, mantle, robe; accouter, equip, outfit, rig (out); bedrape, drape, swathe; endue, invest
  con dismantle, divest, strip
  ant unclothe

clothes *n pl* a person's garments as a whole <dressed in new *clothes* from the skin out>
  syn apparel, attire, attirement, clothing, dress, duds, habiliment(s), rags, raiment, rigging, things, togs
  rel array, garb, toggery, vestments, vesture; costume, getup, outfit, rig

clothing *n* 1 *syn* see CLOTHES
  2 *syn* see ROLE 1

cloud *n syn* see MULTITUDE 1

cloud *vb* 1 *syn* see OBSCURE
  rel addle, befuddle, confuse, muddle; distract, perplex, puzzle
  2 *syn* see CONFUSE 4
  3 *syn* see TAINT 1

clouded *adj syn* see DOUBTFUL 1

cloudless *adj syn* see FAIR 2

cloudy *adj* 1 *syn* see OVERCAST
  2 *syn* see HAZY
  3 *syn* see MURKY 3

clough *n syn* see RAVINE

clout *n* 1 *syn* see CUFF
  2 *syn* see PULL 1

clout *vb* 1 *syn* see STRIKE 2
‖ 2 *syn* see STEAL 1

clove *n syn* see RAVINE

clown *n* 1 *syn* see RUSTIC
  2 *syn* see BOOR
  3 a performer (as in a circus) who entertains by grotesque appearance and actions <children delighted by the antics of the *clowns*>
  syn buffoon, harlequin, merry-andrew, zany
  rel comedian; fool, jester, mountebank; mime, mummer
  4 *syn* see ZANY 1

clownish *adj syn* see BOORISH
  rel awkward, clumsy, gauche; green, raw, rough, rude, uncouth
  ant urbane

cloy *vb syn* see SATIATE

con excite, pique, provoke, stimulate
  ant whet

club *n* 1 *syn* see CUDGEL
  2 *syn* see ASSOCIATION 2

club car *n syn* see PARLOR CAR

‖**cluck** *n syn* see DUNCE

clue *n syn* see HINT 1

clue (*or* **clew**) *vb syn* see INFORM 2

clump *n* 1 *syn* see GROUP 3
  rel clutter, hodgepodge, jumble, omnium-gatherum
  2 *syn* see LUMP 1

clump *vb syn* see LUMBER

clumsy *adj* 1 lacking in physical ease and grace usually because of coarse cumbersome build or poor coordination <a *clumsy* boy constantly stumbling over his own feet> <the *clumsy* gait of a young puppy>
  syn awkward, gawky, lumbering, lumpish, splathering, splay, ungainly; *compare* AWKWARD 2
  rel butterfingered, heavy-handed, left-handed, unhandy; graceless, inelegant, uncouth; bulky, hulking, unwieldy
  idiom all thumbs, fingers all thumbs
  con comely, shapely, well-formed, well-proportioned; apt, deft, handy, quick, ready
  2 *syn* see AWKWARD 2

clunk *vb syn* see THUD

clunker *n syn* see JALOPY

cluster *n* 1 *syn* see GROUP 3
  2 *syn* see GROUP 1

cluster *vb syn* see GROUP 1
  rel accumulate, aggregate, associate, cumulate; bundle, package, parcel

clutch *vb syn* see SEIZE 2
  rel clench, clinch, gripe; cherish, harbor, hold, keep

clutch *n syn* see HOLD

clutch *n syn* see GROUP 3

clutter *n* 1 *syn* see CONFUSION 3
  2 a disordered nondescript mass or group <a *clutter* of ornaments on the mantel>
  syn hash, hugger-mugger, jumble, jungle, litter, mash, mishmash, muddle, rummage, scramble, shuffle, tumble
  rel hodgepodge, macédoine, medley, mélange; disarray, mess, muss, ruck
  con arrangement, array, order; grouping, ordering, pigeonholing, ranking, sorting

‖**cly** *vb syn* see STEAL 1

coact *vb syn* see INTERACT

coacting *adj syn* see COOPERATIVE

coactive *adj syn* see COOPERATIVE

coadjutant *n syn* see ASSISTANT 2

coadjute *vb syn* see UNITE 2

coadjutor *n syn* see ASSISTANT 2

coadunate *vb syn* see JOIN 1

coadunation *n syn* see UNIFICATION

coagment *vb syn* see JOIN 1

coagulate *vb* to alter by chemical reaction from a liquid to a more or less firm jelly <the blood *coagulated* and closed the wound>
  syn clot, congeal, gel, gelate, gelatinize, jell, jellify, jelly, set
  rel concrete, harden, solidify; curdle, inspissate; compact, concentrate, consolidate; coalesce; freeze; dehydrate, dry; condense, thicken
  con deliquesce, fluidify, liquefy, liquesce; flux, fuse, melt, run

---

syn synonym(s)   *rel* related word(s)
ant antonym(s)   *con* contrasted word(s)
idiom idiomatic equivalent(s)
‖ use limited; if in doubt, see a dictionary

coalesce vb syn see JOIN 1
  rel adhere, cleave, cling, stick; blend, fuse, merge, mingle, mix
coalition n 1 syn see UNIFICATION
  2 syn see COMBINATION 2
  3 syn see ALLIANCE 2
coarct vb syn see RESTRAIN 1
coarse adj **1** made up of relatively large particles < *coarse* sand >
  syn grainy, granular
  rel caked, cakey, lumpy, particulate
  2 syn see CRUDE 5
  3 deficient in refinement of manner and delicacy of feeling < a *coarse* practical man lacking all social graces >
  syn crass, crude, gross, incult, inelegant, low, raw, rough, rude, uncouth, uncultivated, uncultured, unrefined, vulgar; *compare* BOORISH
  rel raffish, roughneck, rowdy, vulgarian; common, tacky
  con considerate, courtly, gracious; cultivated, polished, refined
  4 syn see OBSCENE 2
  ‖**5** syn see WILD 6
coast n syn see SHORE
coast vb syn see SLIDE 6
coax vb to influence or persuade by artful ingratiation < *coaxed* her friend to help her with her work >
  syn ‖barter, blandish, blarney, cajole, con, soft-soap, sweet-talk, wheedle
  rel pester, plague, tease; importune, press, urge; get, induce, persuade, prevail; entice, inveigle, lure, tempt; butter (up)
  con coerce, compel, constrain, force, oblige; browbeat, bulldoze, cow, intimidate
  ant bully
cob vb syn see SURPASS 1
cobble vb syn see BOTCH
  rel confuse, foul up, snafu, snarl (up)
cobweb n syn see WEB 2
cock n **1** syn see FAUCET
  2 syn see LEADER 2
  ‖**3** syn see NONSENSE 2
‖**cock** adj syn see CHIEF 2
cock vb syn see LORD
cock n syn see PILE 1
cock vb syn see HEAP 1
cock-a-doodle-doo vb syn see BOAST
cock-a-hoop adj **1** syn see EXULTANT
  2 syn see AWRY 1
Cockaigne n syn see UTOPIA
cock-and-bull story n syn see LIE
cock-a-whoop adj syn see EXULTANT
cockcrow n syn see DAWN 1
cockcrowing n syn see DAWN 1
cocker vb syn see BABY
‖**cocket** adj syn see SAUCY
cockeyed adj **1** syn see AWRY 1
  2 syn see INTOXICATED 1
cockle vb syn see RIPPLE
cocksure adj syn see SURE 5
cocktail lounge n syn see BAR 5
‖**coco** n syn see HEAD 1
coconspirator n syn see CONFEDERATE
‖**coconut** n syn see HEAD 1
cocotte n syn see PROSTITUTE
coddle vb syn see BABY
codicil n syn see APPENDIX 1
coefficient adj syn see COOPERATIVE
coerce vb syn see FORCE 2

  rel beset, push, urge; browbeat, bulldoze, bully, cow, intimidate; menace, terrorize, threaten
coercion n syn see FORCE 4
  rel menace, menacing, threat, threatening
coetaneous adj syn see CONTEMPORARY 1
coeval adj syn see CONTEMPORARY 1
coexistent adj syn see CONTEMPORARY 1
coexisting adj syn see CONTEMPORARY 1
coffee shop n syn see EATING HOUSE
coffer n syn see TREASURY 2
‖**coffin nail** n syn see CIGARETTE
cogency n syn see POINT 3
  rel pertinence, relevance; bearing, concern, connection
cogent adj **1** syn see VALID
  rel compelling, constraining, forceful, forcible, potent, powerful, puissant; inducing, persuasive, justified; well-founded, well-grounded
  con ineffective, ineffectual, inefficacious; feeble, forceless, impotent, powerless, weak
  2 syn see WELL-FOUNDED
  rel consequential, influential, momentous, weighty; meaningful, significant
cogitable adj syn see THINKABLE 1
cogitate vb **1** syn see THINK 5
  rel conceive, envisage, envision, imagine
  2 syn see PLOT
cogitation n syn see THOUGHT 1
cogitative adj syn see THOUGHTFUL 1
cognate adj syn see RELATED
  rel common, general, generic, universal
  con different, disparate, divergent, diverse, various
cognizance n syn see NOTICE 1
cognizant adj syn see AWARE
  con forgetful, oblivious, unmindful; heedless, ignoring, neglectful, slighting, unmindful
  ant ignorant
cognize vb syn see KNOW 1
cognomen n syn see NAME 1
cognoscente n syn see CONNOISSEUR
  rel ‖dab, proficient, specialist; authority, critic, judge
cohere vb **1** syn see STICK 2
  rel blend, coalesce, fuse, merge; associate, combine, connect, join, unite
  con disembarrass, disentangle, untangle
  2 syn see AGREE 4
coherence n **1** syn see ADHERENCE 1
  rel integrity, solidarity, union, unity
  ant incoherence
  2 syn see CONSISTENCY
cohesion n **1** syn see ADHERENCE 1
  ant incohesion
  2 syn see SOLIDARITY
cohort n **1** syn see PARTNER
  2 syn see FOLLOWER
coil n syn see COMMOTION 3
coil vb syn see WIND 2
  rel revolve, rotate, turn
‖**coin** n syn see MONEY
  idiom coin of the realm
coinage n syn see INVENTION
coincide vb syn see AGREE 3
  rel accord, correspond, jibe, tally; equal, match
  con deviate, divagate, divaricate, diverge; bias, skew, twist, warp

ant differ

coincident *adj syn* see CONCOMITANT

coincidentally *adv syn* see TOGETHER 1

coincidently *adv syn* see TOGETHER 1

coinstantaneously *adv syn* see TOGETHER 1

cojones *n pl syn* see COURAGE

cold *adj* 1 marked by a deficiency of warmth <a *cold* day>
syn arctic, chill, chillsome, chilly, cool, freezing, frigid, frore, frosty, gelid, glacial, icy, nippy, shivery
rel biting, bleak, chilling, cutting, nipping, polar, raw, sharp; frozen, iced, wintry; bracing, brisk, crisp, snappy
con calid, genial, mild
ant warm
2 lacking cordiality or emotional warmth <a *cold* greeting>
syn chill, emotionless, frigid, glacial, icy, indifferent, unemotional
rel unenthusiastic, unresponsive, unsympathetic
con cordial, friendly, genial, hearty, warm; empathic, sympathetic
3 *syn* see MATTER-OF-FACT 3
4 *syn* see FRIGID 3
ant hot
5 *syn* see GLOOMY 3
6 *syn* see DEAD 1
7 *syn* see INSENSIBLE 2

cold–blooded *adj* 1 *syn* see UNFEELING 2
2 *syn* see MATTER-OF-FACT 3

cold feet *n syn* see FEAR 1

coldhearted *adj syn* see UNFEELING 2
ant warmhearted

‖**cold meat** *n syn* see CORPSE

cold–shoulder *vb syn* see CUT 7

cold storage *n syn* see ABEYANCE

colic *n syn* see STOMACHACHE

coliseum *n syn* see STADIUM

‖**coll** *vb syn* see EMBRACE 1

collapse *vb* 1 *syn* see GIVE 12
rel break up, disintegrate, shatter
idiom fall to pieces
2 to lose energy, stamina, or control under stress <exhausted to the point of *collapsing* helplessly on the bed>
syn break down, cave (in), drop, ‖flake out, give out, peg out, succumb, wilt
rel droop, fail, languish, weaken; exhaust, fag, flag, play out, tire, weary
con enliven, invigorate, stimulate

collapse *n* 1 *syn* see NERVOUS BREAKDOWN
2 a sudden and grave failure <the *collapse* of an overextended market>
syn breakdown, crack-up, crash, debacle, smash, smashup, wreck
rel breakup, disorganization, disruption, undoing; cataclysm, catastrophe; destruction, ruination, ruining; failure

collar *vb* 1 *syn* see CORNER
2 *syn* see CATCH 1
3 *syn* see STEAL 1

collate *vb syn* see COMPARE 2

collateral *adj* 1 *syn* see CONCOMITANT
2 *syn* see INDIRECT 2

3 *syn* see CORROBORATIVE
4 *syn* see SUBORDINATE
rel allied, cognate, kindred, related; complementary, corresponding, reciprocal
con major, prominent
5 *syn* see AUXILIARY
‖**collateral** *n syn* see REFUSE

colleague *n* one affiliated with another usually through a common office or profession <he claims to speak for his *colleagues* in the Senate>
syn associate, compatriot, compeer, confrere
rel consociate, copartner, fellow, partner; co-worker, workfellow; buddy, chum, companion, crony, pal; aide, assistant, helper

collect *vb* 1 *syn* see GATHER 6
con assort, sort; sever, sunder; deal, dispense, divide, dole
ant disperse; distribute
2 *syn* see INFER
3 *syn* see COMPOSE 4
4 *syn* see GROUP 1
rel align, array, dispose, marshal, order, rank
con broadcast, disperse, distribute, scatter

collected *adj* 1 *syn* see CALM 2
rel peaceful, quiet, still
ant distraught
2 *syn* see COOL 2
rel assured, confident, sanguine, sure; complacent, self-satisfied, smug
con disordered, troubled

collection *n* 1 *syn* see GATHERING 2
rel band, crew, outfit, party
2 *syn* see ACCUMULATION
rel assortment, medley, miscellany, variety; bunch, clump, cluster, group; armamentarium; boiling, caboodle, kit, lot

‖**college** *n syn* see JAIL

collide *vb syn* see BUMP 1
rel atomize, fragment, pulverize, shatter, smash, splinter; break up, crunch, scrap

collimate *vb syn* see PARALLEL 2

collision *n syn* see IMPACT
rel dilapidation, ruin, wreck; demolishment, destruction

collocate *vb syn* see PARALLEL 2

collogue *vb* ‖1 *syn* see PLOT
2 *syn* see CONFER 2

colloque *vb syn* see CONVERSE

colloquial *adj syn* see VERNACULAR

colloquial *n syn* see VERNACULAR 3

colloquium *n syn* see CONFERENCE 2

colloquy *n* 1 *syn* see CONVERSATION 1
2 *syn* see CONVERSATION 2
3 *syn* see CONFERENCE 2

collude *vb syn* see PLOT

collusion *n syn* see COMPLICITY

colluvies *n* 1 *syn* see ACCUMULATION
2 *syn* see MISCELLANY

collywobbles *n pl but sing or pl in constr*
syn see STOMACHACHE

Colonel Blimp *n syn* see STUFFED SHIRT

color *n* 1 a property of a visible thing recognizable only when rays of light fall upon it and serving to distinguish things otherwise visually identical (as in size, shape, or texture) <the green *color* of foliage turns rainbow-hued in autumn>
syn cast, hue, shade, tinge, tint, tone
2 *syn* see MASK 2

---

3 *syn* see VERISIMILITUDE

4 *syn* see POSITION 1

5 *syn* see FLAG

6 something used to impart visible color to something <dyed her curtains with one of the new easy-to-use *colors*>
syn colorant, dye, dyestuff, pigment, stain, tincture

color *vb* 1 *syn* see EMBROIDER
rel disguise, distort, fake, misrepresent
con constrain, minimize, reduce, soften, temper; blue-pencil, censor, edit

2 *syn* see MISREPRESENT

3 *syn* see BLUSH

colorable *adj syn* see BELIEVABLE
rel cogent, compelling, convincing, sound, telling, valid

colorant *n syn* see COLOR 6

colored *adj syn* see BIASED 2

colorful *adj* making a fine display of usually showy color <a *colorful* bed of asters>
syn brave, bright, colory, gay, vivid
rel blatant, florid, garish, gaudy, loud; flashy, showy, splashy
con blanched, bleached, pallid, wan; dim, dull, faint, pale, weak
ant colorless

coloring *n* 1 *syn* see MASK 2

2 *syn* see EXAGGERATION

colorless *adj* 1 *syn* see PALE 1

2 lacking in sparkle and vitality <an accurate but *colorless* recital of facts>
syn drab, dull, flat, lackluster, lifeless, lusterless, prosaic, prosy
rel blurry, hazy, obscure, vague; feeble, insipid, milk-and-water, namby-pamby, weak, wishy-washy; unimaginative, uninspired
con clear, concise, exact, precise; exciting, provocative, rousing, stimulating, stirring
ant colorful

3 *syn* see NEUTRAL
rel aloof, remote, withdrawn

colory *adj syn* see COLORFUL

colossal *adj syn* see HUGE

colporteur *n syn* see MISSIONARY

colt *n syn* see NOVICE

coltish *adj syn* see PLAYFUL 1

columbary *n syn* see DOVECOTE

column *n* 1 *syn* see PILLAR 1

2 *syn* see SUPPORT 3

coma *n* 1 *syn* see FAINT

2 *syn* see LETHARGY 1

comate *n syn* see ASSOCIATE 3

comatose *adj* 1 *syn* see INSENSIBLE 2

2 *syn* see LETHARGIC
rel anesthetic, impassible, insensitive
ant awake

comb *vb* 1 *syn* see SORT 2

2 *syn* see SCOUR 2
rel examine, inspect, scrutinize; investigate, probe, sift

combat *vb syn* see RESIST
rel battle, contend, war

combat *n syn* see SERVICE 1

combative *adj syn* see BELLIGERENT
rel energetic, strenuous, vigorous; manful, manly, virile
ant pacifistic

combativeness *n syn* see ATTACK 2

‖**combe** *n syn* see VALLEY

combination *n* 1 *syn* see UNIFICATION

2 individuals or organized interests banded together to further a common end <a *combination* of citizens devoted to holding down taxes>
syn bloc, coalition, combine, faction, party, ring
rel cartel, pool, syndicate, trust; cabal, circle, clique, coterie, set

3 *syn* see ASSOCIATION 1

combine *vb* 1 *syn* see JOIN 1
rel amalgamate, blend, commingle, fuse, mingle, mix; consolidate, unify
con divide, divorce, part
ant separate

2 *syn* see EMBODY 2

3 *syn* see UNITE 2
rel agree, coincide; merge, pool

combine *n* 1 *syn* see COMBINATION 2

2 *syn* see SYNDICATE

comble *n syn* see APEX 2

combust *vb syn* see BURN 2

combustible *adj* 1 capable of catching or being set on fire <*combustible* materials should be stored away from open fire>
syn burnable, flammable, ignitable, inflammable
rel comburent, combustive; burning, firing, igniting, kindling
con fireproof; flameproof, nonflammable; fire-resistant, fire-resistive, fire-retardant
ant incombustible, noncombustible

2 *syn* see EXCITABLE

come *vb* 1 to attain to a destination <when will they *come*>
syn arrive, in, get, get in, reach, show, show up, turn up
rel approach, near, nigh
con depart, leave, quit, retreat, withdraw
ant go

2 *syn* see AMOUNT 1

3 *syn* see HAPPEN 1

4 *syn* see BECOME 1

come (from) *vb* 1 *syn* see SPRING

2 *syn* see ORIGINATE 5

come (in) *vb* 1 *syn* see ENTER 1

comeback *n syn* see RETORT 2

come by *vb syn* see VISIT 2

come-by-chance *n syn* see BASTARD 1

comedian *n* 1 *syn* see HUMORIST 2

2 *syn* see WAG 1

come down (with) *vb syn* see CONTRACT 1

comedown *n* a loss of status <bitter over their *comedown* in the world>
syn descent, discomfiture, down; *compare* SETBACK
rel collapse, crash, downfall, fall, ruin, smash, undoing, wreck
con advance, headway, progress
ant rise

comedy *n syn* see HUMOR 4

come in *vb syn* see ANSWER 1

comely *adj* 1 *syn* see BEAUTIFUL
ant homely

2 *syn* see DECOROUS 1

come off *vb* 1 *syn* see SUCCEED 2

2 *syn* see HAPPEN 1

come-off *n syn* see ESCAPE 2

come-on *n* 1 *syn* see LURE 2

‖2 *syn* see FOOL 3

3 *syn* see SWINDLER

come out *vb* 1 *syn* see GET OUT 2

2 *syn* see DEBUT

come out (with) *vb syn* see SAY 1
come over *vb* 1 *syn* see VISIT 2
  2 *syn* see BECOME 1
come round *vb syn* see RECOVER 2
comestible *adj syn* see EDIBLE
comestibles *n pl syn* see FOOD 1
come through *vb* 1 *syn* see SURVIVE 2
  2 *syn* see CONTRIBUTE 1
comeuppance *n syn* see DUE 1
comfort *n* 1 *syn* see HELP 1
  2 *syn* see AMENITY 2
comfort *vb* to make or try to make
brighter a person overcome by grief or
misery < *comforting* her widowed sister
with words of hope >
  syn buck up, cheer, console, solace, upraise
  rel brighten, gladden, lighten; allay, alleviate, assuage, mitigate, relieve; refresh,
renew, restore; reassure; commiserate,
condole, sympathize
  idiom give a lift to
  con torment, torture, try; distress, trouble, worry; annoy, irk, vex
  ant afflict; bother
comfortable *adj* 1 *syn* see SUFFICIENT 1
  2 enjoying or providing conditions that
make for comfort and security < lived in
a *comfortable* home on a quiet street >
  syn comfy, cozy, cushy, easeful, easy,
snug, soft
  rel agreeable, grateful, gratifying, welcome; pleasant, pleasing; restful; comforting, consoling, solacing; content, pleased,
satisfied
  con distressing, perturbing, troubling;
annoying, bothering, irking, vexing; inferior, miserable, poor, substandard,
wretched
  ant uncomfortable
  3 *syn* see PROSPEROUS 3
  idiom in comfortable circumstances
‖**comfortable** *n syn* see QUILT
comforter *n syn* see QUILT
comfortless *adj syn* see UNCOMFORT-
ABLE
comfy *adj syn* see COMFORTABLE 2
comic *adj syn* see LAUGHABLE
  rel antic, fantastic, grotesque; mocking,
ridiculing
  ant tragic
comic *n syn* see HUMORIST 2
comical *adj syn* see LAUGHABLE
  rel absurd, foolish, silly; impish, roguish,
sportive, waggish
  con doleful, dolorous, lugubrious, melancholy
  ant pathetic
comicality *n syn* see HUMOR 4
comicalness *n syn* see HUMOR 4
coming *n syn* see ARRIVAL 1
coming *adj* 1 *syn* see FORTHCOMING
  2 *syn* see NEXT
coming in *n*, *usu* **comings in** *pl syn* see
REVENUE
comingle *vb syn* see MIX 1
comity *n syn* see GOODWILL 1

  rel accord, concord, harmony; camaraderie, companionship, comradeship, good‡
fellowship
comma *n syn* see PAUSE
command *vb* to issue orders or an order to
< the general *commanded* the troops to
advance >
  syn bid, charge, direct, enjoin, instruct,
order, tell, warn
  rel demand, exact, require; coerce, compel, constrain, force, oblige; conduct, control, manage; ask, call (on), request, say
  ant comply, obey
command *n* 1 a direction that must or
should be obeyed < failure to obey a direct *command* subjects the soldier to
grave penalties >
  syn behest, bidding, charge, dictate, injunction, mandate, order, word
  rel direction, directive, instruction; canon,
law, ordinance, precept, rule, statute;
devoir, duty, obligation, responsibility
  2 *syn* see POWER 1
  rel rule
  3 *syn* see ABILITY 2
  rel aplomb, assurance, confidence, poise
  con incertitude, insecurity, uncertainty,
unsureness; indecisiveness, vagueness
commandeer *vb* 1 *syn* see APPROPRIATE
1
  2 *syn* see ARROGATE 1
comme il faut *adj syn* see DECOROUS 1
commemorate *vb* 1 *syn* see KEEP 2
  2 *syn* see MEMORIALIZE 2
commemorative *adj syn* see MEMORIAL
commemoratory *adj syn* see MEMORIAL
commence *vb* 1 *syn* see BEGIN 1
  2 *syn* see BEGIN 2
  idiom come into being (*or* existence)
commencement *n syn* see BEGINNING
commend *vb* 1 *syn* see COMMIT 1
  rel resign, yield; proffer, tender
  2 to indicate one's warm approval < the
teacher *commended* her pupils' studious
attitude >
  syn acclaim, applaud, compliment, hail,
kudize, praise, recommend, ‖roose
  rel eulogize, extol; approve, countenance,
endorse, support
  con blame, criticize, reprehend, reprobate;
chide, rebuke, reprimand, reproach, reprove
  ant censure; admonish
commendable *adj syn* see WORTHY 1
commensurable *adj syn* see PROPOR-
TIONAL
commensurate *adj syn* see PROPOR-
TIONAL
comment *n* 1 *syn* see REMARK 2
  2 *syn* see CRITICISM 1
comment *vb syn* see REMARK 2
  rel construe, elucidate, explain, explicate,
expound; annotate, gloss
commentary *n syn* see REMARK 2
commentate *vb syn* see REMARK 2
commerce *n* 1 *syn* see CONTACT 2
  2 a situation characterized by mutual
exchange (as of ideas) < those who feel
that art should have no *commerce* with
morality >
  syn communion, dealings, intercourse,
traffic, truck

---

syn synonym(s)   *rel* related word(s)
ant antonym(s)   *con* contrasted word(s)
idiom idiomatic equivalent(s)
‖ use limited; if in doubt, see a dictionary

rel communication, congress, contact, exchange, interchange, intercommunication; basis, common ground, takeoff

3 *syn* see BUSINESS 4

commie *n syn* see COMMUNIST

commination *n syn* see CURSE 1

commingle *vb syn* see MIX 1
rel integrate, unify

comminute *vb syn* see PULVERIZE 1

commiserable *adj syn* see PITIFUL 1

commiserate *vb syn* see COMPASSIONATE

commiseration *n syn* see PITY

commission *vb* **1** *syn* see AUTHORIZE 1
rel appoint, designate, name, nominate; bid, charge, command, enjoin, instruct, order

2 *syn* see DELEGATE

commit *vb* **1** to assign (as to a person) especially for use or safekeeping <it is unwise to *commit* all power and authority to one man> <sainted beings who *commit* their spirits to God>
syn commend, confide, consign, entrust, hand over, relegate, turn over
rel allocate, allot, assign, destine, ordain; move, remove, shift, transfer; deliver, give, offer, submit; delegate, deputize
idiom give into the charge (*or* hands) of

2 to be responsible for or guilty of (an offense or wrongdoing) <*commit* a crime>
syn perpetuate, pull
rel accomplish, achieve, do, effectuate, execute, perform, pull off; contravene, transgress, trespass, violate; offend, scandalize, sin

commitment *n syn* see OBLIGATION 2

committal *n syn* see OBLIGATION 2

commix *vb syn* see MIX 1

commixture *n syn* see MIXTURE

commodious *adj syn* see SPACIOUS
con cramped, narrow, strait
ant incommodious

commodities *n pl syn* see MERCHANDISE
rel articles, items, things

common *adj* **1** generally shared in or participated in by members of a community <our *common* civic responsibilities>
syn communal, conjoint, conjunct, intermutual, joint, mutual, public, shared
rel general, generic, universal; like, reciprocal, similar; corporate
con personal, private, restricted
ant individual

2 *syn* see GENERAL 2
rel popular, public

3 *syn* see IMPURE 3

4 taking place often <a *common* occurrence>
syn customary, everyday, familiar, frequent
rel repetitious, routine, usual
con infrequent, occasional, unfrequent; casual, chance, incidental
ant rare, uncommon

5 *syn* see GENERAL

6 conforming to a type without noteworthy excellences or faults <just a *common* everyday sort trying to get by in life>
syn commonplace, ordinary, prosaic, uneventful, unexceptional, unnoteworthy

rel down-to-earth, matter-of-fact, prosy, unexciting; dull, flat, trite, stale, uninteresting
con exceptional, noteworthy, remarkable; excellent, marvelous, prodigious, wonderful; aberrant, divergent, eccentric
ant extraordinary

7 *syn* see DECENT 4

8 *syn* see CHEAP 2

9 *syn* see INFERIOR 2

‖**10** *syn* see EASYGOING 3

common *n* **1** **commons** *pl but sing or pl in constr syn* see COMMONALTY

2 an often improved and ornamentally planted open space for public use in a built-up area <in summer a band played on the village *common*>
syn green, plaza, square
rel garden, park, pleasance, pleasure ground

commonage *n syn* see COMMONALTY

commonalty *n* persons without rank or authority or the political estate made up of these <laws that both the gentles and the *commonalty* recognized as just>
syn commonage, commoners, common men, commune, people, plebeians, plebes, plebs, populace, rank and file, third estate
rel masses, mob, multitude, proletariat, public
con aristocracy, elite, gentility, nobility; classes, gentry, nobs

commoners *n pl syn* see COMMONALTY

commonition *n syn* see WARNING

commonly *adv syn* see USUALLY 2
idiom more often than not

common men *n pl syn* see COMMONALTY

commonplace *n* an idea or expression deficient in originality or freshness <lazily exchanging *commonplaces* over their beer>
syn banality, bromide, cliché, platitude, prosaicism, prosaism, rubber stamp, shibboleth, tag, truism
rel chestnut, corn, prose, stereotype; inanity, shallowness, wishy-washiness; threadbareness, triteness
ant profundity

commonplace *adj* **1** *syn* see COMMON 6

2 *syn* see GENERAL 1

3 *syn* see PROSAIC 3

4 *syn* see TRITE
idiom a dime a dozen, as everyday as breakfast

common sense *n syn* see SENSE 6

commorancy *n syn* see HABITATION 2

commotion *n* **1** a state of often disorderly civic unrest <the whole city was in *commotion* over the new restrictions>
syn clamor, convulsion, ferment, outcry, tumult, upheaval, upturn
rel insurgence, insurrection, mutiny, rebellion, revolt, riot, uprising

2 a state of usually mental or emotional excitement <this challenge threw him into great *commotion* of mind>
syn agitation, confusion, dither, flap, lather, pother, stew, tumult, turbulence, turmoil
rel discomposure, disquiet, flurry, fluster, perturbation, upset; annoyance, bother, irritation, vexation; strain, tension
con calm, placidity, quietude, relaxation, serenity

3 a noisy and often unruly disturbance
< the children created a *commotion* over
missing the circus >

syn brouhaha, ‖catouse, coil, foofaraw,
furore, fuss, hurrah, ruckus, rumpus, shindig, shindy, to-do, uproar

rel din, hubbub, hullabaloo, pandemonium, racket; fracas, ruction, row

4 a state of noisy confusion < never saw
such *commotion* as the time the old sow
got out and knocked the preacher into the
midden >

syn bustle, clamor, clatter, hassle, hubbub, hurly-burly, lather, moil, pother,
rowdydow, ruction, storm, to-do, tow=
row, tumult, turmoil, uproar, whirl,
whoopla; *compare* DIN, STIR 1

con calmness, order, peace, quiet

commove *vb syn* see ELATE
communal *adj syn* see COMMON 1
commune *n syn* see COMMONALTY
communicable *adj* 1 *syn* see INFECTIOUS
2

2 *syn* see COMMUNICATIVE
communicate *vb* 1 to make known < *communicated* the whole story under a pledge
of secrecy >

syn break, convey, impart, pass on, transmit

rel betray, disclose, discover, divulge, ‖let
out, reveal, tell; hint, imply, let on, suggest; broadcast, disseminate, publicize

con conceal, hide, obscure, screen, veil;
dissemble; distort, garble, twist, warp;
camouflage, disguise

2 *syn* see ADJOIN
communication *n* 1 *syn* see MESSAGE 1

2 *syn* see CONTACT 2

3 interchange of thoughts or opinions
through shared symbols < the difficulties
of *communication* between people of different cultural backgrounds >

syn communion, converse, intercommunication, intercourse

rel exchange, interchange; conversing,
discussing, talking; conversation, discussion, talk; advice, intelligence, news, tidings

communicative *adj* inclined to talk freely
and sometimes indiscreetly < too *communicative* to be trusted with a secret >

syn communicable, expansive; *compare*
FRANK

rel garrulous, loquacious, talkative, voluble; conversational; demonstrative, effusive, gushing

con constrained, guarded, inhibited, restrained; bridled, controlled, curbed

communion *n* 1 *syn* see COMMERCE 2

2 *syn* see COMMUNICATION 3

3 *syn* see CONTACT 2

4 *syn* see RELIGION 2

Communist *n* a member of the Russian
Communist party < restructuring of Rus-
sia by the *Communists* >

syn Bolshevik, ‖Bolshie, commie, comrade, Red

rel fellow traveler, pink, pinko; Leninist,
Marxist, Stalinist, Trotskyist; apparatchik

---

community *n syn* see SOCIETY 3
commutable *adj syn* see INTERCHANGE-
ABLE
commute *vb syn* see TRANSFORM
compact *adj* 1 *syn* see PITHY

2 *syn* see CLOSE 4

rel hard; appressed, bunched, packed

con loose, slack, unconstrained; rare,
tenuous, thin

compact *vb syn* see UNIFY 1

rel compress, condense, contract; combine, unite; set, solidify

con disperse, dissipate; fluff, loosen

compact *n syn* see CONTRACT
compacting *adj syn* see INTEGRATIVE
companion *n* 1 *syn* see ASSOCIATE 3

rel colleague, fellow, partner; chaperon,
escort

2 *syn* see MATE 5

3 *syn* see ACCOMPANIMENT 2

companion *vb syn* see ACCOMPANY
companionable *adj syn* see SOCIAL 1

rel amiable, complacent, good-natured

con uncongenial, unsympathetic; reserved,
taciturn, uncommunicative

companionship *n syn* see COMPANY 1
company *n* 1 association between individuals especially on pleasant or intimate
terms < we always enjoyed his *company* >

syn companionship, fellowship, society

rel camaraderie, comradeship, consociation

2 persons visiting especially in one's house
< invited *company* for dinner >

syn guests, visitors; *compare* VISITOR 1

3 *syn* see GATHERING 2

4 a group of persons associated in a joint
effort or for a common purpose < a *company* of thieves lay in wait by the highway >

syn band, corps, outfit, party, troop,
troupe

rel crew, gang, pack, team; circle, clique,
coterie, set; association, club, order, society; crowd, horde, mob, throng; group

5 *syn* see ENTERPRISE 3

company *vb syn* see ACCOMPANY
comparable *adj syn* see LIKE

ant disparate

comparative *adj* being such in comparison
with an expressed or implied standard or
absolute < living in *comparative* poverty >

syn approximate, near, relative

rel equivalent, like, similar

con genuine, real, true

ant absolute

compare *vb* 1 *syn* see EQUATE 2

2 to examine side by side or point by
point in order to establish likenesses and
differences < *compare* the effects of two
diets on weight loss >

syn bracket, collate, contrast

rel approach, equal, match, rival, touch;
examine, inspect, observe, scan, scrutinize,
size (up); consider, contemplate, ponder,
study, weigh

comparison *n syn* see LIKENESS
compass *vb* 1 *syn* see SURROUND 1

2 *syn* see GET 1

3 *syn* see APPREHEND 1

compass *n* 1 *syn* see CIRCUMFERENCE

rel domain, field, sphere; enclosure

2 *syn* see ENVIRONS 1
3 *syn* see RANGE 2
rel bounds, limits; circumscription, limitation, restriction

compassion *n* 1 *syn* see SYMPATHY 2
rel charity, clemency, grace, lenity, mercy; benevolence, humaneness, humanity
con aloofness, indifference, unconcern; cruelty, harshness, mercilessness; implacability, relentlessness
2 *syn* see PITY

compassionate *adj syn* see TENDER
rel clement, forbearing; piteous, pitiful
con grim, implacable, merciless, relentless, unrelenting; adamant, inexorable, inflexible, obdurate

compassionate *vb* to feel or express compassion for < a kindly man who *compassionated* all human misery >
syn ache, commiserate, feel (for), pity, sympathize (with)
rel grieve (over), regret, repine; lament, mourn, sorrow (for *or* over); deplore
con accept, endure, tolerate; disregard, ignore, overlook, pass over

compassionless *adj syn* see UNFEELING 2
compatible *syn* see CONSONANT 1
rel appropriate, fit, fitting, meet, proper, suitable
ant incompatible

compatriot *n syn* see COLLEAGUE
compeer *n syn* see COLLEAGUE
compel *vb syn* see FORCE 2
compellation *n syn* see NAME 1
compendiary *adj syn* see CONCISE
compendious *adj syn* see CONCISE
rel close, compact
con amplified, elaborated, expanded, inflated; complete, full

compendium *n* 1 a condensed treatment of a subject < prepared a *compendium* of the state laws dealing with education >
syn aperçu, digest, pandect, précis, sketch, survey, syllabus, sylloge
rel abridgment, abstract, brief, conspectus, epitome; overview
con elaboration, expansion
2 *syn* see HANDBOOK

compenetrate *vb syn* see PERMEATE
compensate *vb* 1 to make good the defects of < her kind heart *compensated* for her nosy ways >
syn atone (for), balance, counterbalance, counterpoise, countervail, make up, offset, outweigh, redeem, set off
rel abrogate, annul, invalidate, negate, nullify; counteract, negative, neutralize; better, fix (up), improve, repair; redress
idiom make amends (*or* reparations), make matters right
2 *syn* see PAY 1
3 to make proper payment to (as for injury, loss, *or* damage) < *compensated* a worker injured on the job >
syn indemnify, pay, recompense, reimburse, remunerate, repay, requite
rel recoup, refund
idiom make restitution (*or* reparation)

compensation *n syn* see REPARATION
compete *vb* 1 to strive to gain mastery or obtain a prize < students *competing* for a scholarship >

syn contend, contest, rival, vie
rel dispute; battle, fight, strive, struggle; attempt, essay, try
2 *syn* see RIVAL 2
rel approach, equal, match, touch

competence *n* 1 *syn* see ENOUGH
2 *syn* see ABILITY 1
rel appropriateness, fitness, suitability
ant incompetence

competent *adj* 1 *syn* see ABLE
rel adept, finished, masterly, polished
ant incompetent
2 *syn* see SUFFICIENT 1

competition *n* 1 *syn* see CONTEST 1
2 *syn* see CONTEST 2
3 *syn* see RIVAL

competitor *n syn* see RIVAL
complacence *n syn* see CONCEIT 2
complacency *n syn* see CONCEIT 2
complacent *adj* feeling or showing an often excessive or unjustified satisfaction and pleasure in one's status, possessions, or attainments < had the *complacent* air of superiority that often mars an ignorant self-made man >
syn priggish, self-complacent, self-contented, self-pleased, self-satisfied, smug
rel assured, confident, self-assured, self≠ confident, self-possessed; conceited, egoistic, egotistic
con humble, modest; diffident, shy

complain *vb* to express discontent, resentment, or regret usually peaceably and as if seeking sympathy < a nice girl but given to *complaining* over trifles >
syn fuss, kick, murmur, repine, wail, whine; *compare* GRIPE 2, GRUMBLE 1
rel fret, worry; nag, pester
idiom air a grievance, find fault, register a complaint, sing (*or* cry) the blues
con accept, condone, countenance, tolerate

complainer *n syn* see GROUCH
complaint *n syn* see DISEASE 1
complaisant *adj syn* see AMIABLE 1
rel accommodating, agreeable, generous, indulgent; submissive
con harsh, rigorous, stern; determined, firm, masterful

complement *n* 1 something that makes up a deficiency in another thing < bought the farm with its *complement* of equipment and livestock >
syn supplement
rel correlate, counterpart; makeweight
2 *syn* see ACCOMPANIMENT 1
3 *syn* see COUNTERPART 1

complete *adj* 1 *syn* see WHOLE 3
2 *syn* see UNABRIDGED
3 *syn* see WHOLE 4
4 brought to completion < each *complete* revolution of the earth >
syn completed, concluded, done, down, ended, finished, terminated, through
rel accomplished, achieved, effected, executed, realized; attained, compassed
idiom all over, done with, set at rest
ant incomplete
5 *syn* see EXHAUSTIVE
ant incomplete
6 *syn* see UTTER

complete *vb* 1 *syn* see CLOSE 3
rel accomplish, achieve, discharge, effect, execute, fulfill, perform

idiom carry through, go through with
2 *syn* see FULFILL 1

completed *adj syn* see COMPLETE 4

completely *adv* 1 *syn* see DOWN 2
idiom down to the ground
2 *syn* see THOROUGHLY 2
3 *syn* see WELL 3

completeness *n* 1 *syn* see ENTIRETY 1
2 *syn* see INTEGRITY 2

complex *adj* 1 made up of two or more
separable or identifiable elements < the
complex vascular system of higher
plants >
syn composite, compound
rel blended, compounded, mingled,
mixed; heterogeneous, varied; elaborate,
intricate, involved; complicated, confused,
mixed-up
con homogeneous, uniform
ant simple
2 difficult to comprehend because of a
multiplicity of interrelated elements < a
complex plot to undermine the government by discrediting its leaders >
syn Byzantine, complicated, daedal, elaborate, gordian, intricate, involved, knotty,
labyrinthine, sophisticated
rel bewildering, confusing, distracting,
disturbing; baffling, confounding, mysterious, mystifying, perplexing, puzzling,
equivocal, obscure, vague; involute, invo-
luted, reticular
con clear, defined, definite, distinct, plain,
recognizable, uncomplicated, uninvolved;
comprehensible, explicable, intelligible,
knowable
ant simple

complex *n syn* see SYSTEM 1
con constituent, element, factor; member,
part, piece, portion; detail, item, particular
ant component

complexion *n syn* see DISPOSITION 3
rel kind, sort, style, type

complexion *vb syn* see TINT

complexionless *adj syn* see PALE 1

compliance *n syn* see ACQUIESCENCE
rel amenability, docility, obedience, trac-
tability; deference, submission, submissiveness
con contumacy, obstinacy, stubbornness
ant frowardness

complicate *vb* to make complex, involved,
or difficult < a disagreement *complicated*
by intense personal animosities >
syn entangle, ‖muck, muddle, perplex,
ravel, snarl, tangle
rel jumble, ‖snafu; derange, disarrange,
disorder, mix up, upset
con arrange, order; disentangle, straighten
(out), untangle
ant simplify

complicated *adj* 1 *syn* see ELABORATE 2
2 *syn* see COMPLEX 2
rel arduous, difficult, hard; abstruse,
recondite
con easy, facile, light; clear-cut, precise,
straightforward
ant simple

---

syn synonym(s)   *rel* related word(s)
ant antonym(s)   *con* contrasted word(s)
idiom idiomatic equivalent(s)
‖ use limited; if in doubt, see a dictionary

complicity *n* association with an improper
or unlawful activity < failed to prove his
complicity in the cover-up >
syn collusion, connivance
rel implication, involvement; engineering,
machination, manipulation, wire-pulling

compliment *n* 1 an expression of regard or
praise < a man meriting the *compliments*
and homage of his fellows >
syn bouquet, kudo, orchid(s)
rel trade-last; laud, laudation, praise;
accolade, commendation, honor; bless-
ing(s), congratulation(s), felicitation(s);
encomium, eulogy, tribute
con dig, gibe, jeer, slam
ant taunt
‖2 *syn* see GIFT 1

compliment *vb syn* see COMMEND 2
idiom take off one's hat to
con belittle, decry, denigrate, depreciate,
disparage, run down

complimentary *adj syn* see FREE 5

comply *vb syn* see OBEY

component *n syn* see ELEMENT 2
con admixture, amalgam, blend, compound, mixture
ant composite; complex

comport *vb* 1 *syn* see AGREE 4
2 *syn* see BEHAVE 1

comportment *n* 1 *syn* see BEARING 1
2 *syn* see BEHAVIOR

compose *vb* 1 *syn* see CONSTITUTE 1
rel consist (of)
2 to bring into being by mental and especially artistic effort < *compose* a ballad or
a history of England >
syn create
rel devise, invent, make up, originate;
dream up
3 *syn* see CALM
rel ease, lessen, soften; comfort, console,
solace
con agitate, embroil, trouble, unsettle
ant discompose
4 to bring oneself or one's emotions under
control < *composed* himself and turned to
face the new attack >
syn collect, contain, control, cool, recollect, rein, repress, restrain, simmer
down, smother, suppress
rel down, mitigate, moderate, modulate,
pocket, temper, tune down; bottle (up),
check, hold in; ease (off *or* up), let up,
relax, slacken
idiom calm down, control one's feelings
(*or* emotions), get hold of oneself, master
one's feelings, pull oneself together

composed *adj* 1 *syn* see CALM 2
2 *syn* see COOL 2
rel quiet, still; sedate, serious, staid; repressed, suppressed
con concerned, worried
ant discomposed, ruffled

composite *adj syn* see COMPLEX 1

composite *n syn* see MIXTURE
rel combination, union

composition *n* 1 *syn* see MAKEUP 1
2 *syn* see COMPROMISE
3 *syn* see ESSAY 2

compos mentis *adj syn* see SANE 2

compost *n syn* see MIXTURE

composure *n syn* see EQUANIMITY
ant discomposure, perturbation

compotation *n syn* see BINGE 1

compound *vb* 1 *syn* see JOIN 1
2 *syn* see MIX 1
3 *syn* see INCREASE 1

compound *adj syn* see COMPLEX 1

compound *n syn* see MIXTURE

comprehend *vb* 1 *syn* see APPREHEND 1
2 *syn* see KNOW 1
rel envisage, envision, see
3 *syn* see INCLUDE

comprehendible *adj syn* see UNDER-STANDABLE
ant incomprehensible

comprehensible *adj syn* see UNDER-STANDABLE
ant incomprehensible

comprehensive *adj* 1 *syn* see ENCYCLO-PEDIC
2 *syn* see ALL-AROUND 2
idiom in depth

comprehensiveness *n syn* see BREADTH 2

compress *vb* 1 *syn* see CONTRACT 3
rel compact, consolidate; cram, crowd, press, squeeze
con disperse, dissipate, scatter
ant stretch; spread
2 *syn* see PRESS 1

comprise *vb syn* see CONSTITUTE 1

compromise *n* a settlement reached by mutual concession < the company and the union agreed to a *compromise* on fringe benefits >
syn composition
rel golden mean, mean, middle ground, middle way; agreement, compact, contract, pact; arrangement, bargain, understanding
idiom happy medium

compromise *vb syn* see ENDANGER
rel blast, blight, mar, queer, ruin, spoil
idiom cook one's goose; play havoc (*or* hob) with, settle one's hash

compulsatory *adj syn* see MANDATORY

compulsion *n syn* see FORCE 4
rel driving, impelling, pressing; exigency, necessity, need; pressure, stress
con coaxing, inducing, persuasion; choice, election, option, preference

compulsory *adj syn* see MANDATORY

compunction *n* 1 *syn* see PENITENCE
rel conscience, conscientiousness, punctiliousness, scrupulosity, scrupulousness
con brazenness, callousness, hardness, insensitivity; disinterest, indifference, unconcern; obduracy, recalcitrance
2 *syn* see QUALM
rel disinclination; hesitancy, hesitation

compunctious *adj syn* see REMORSEFUL

computation *n* the act or action of calculating mathematically < by his *computation* they could not possibly afford a new car >
syn arithmetic, calculation, ciphering, estimation, figuring, reckoning

compute *vb syn* see CALCULATE

comrade *n* 1 *syn* see ASSOCIATE 3
rel consort, fellow, mate; adjunct, ally, auxiliary
2 *syn* see COMMUNIST

comradery *n syn* see CAMARADERIE

comstock *n syn* see PRUDE

con *vb* 1 *syn* see SCRUTINIZE 1

2 *syn* see MEMORIZE

con *n* 1 *syn* see OPPONENT
ant pro
2 *syn* see ANTAGONISM 2

con *vb* 1 *syn* see DUPE
2 *syn* see COAX

‖con *n syn* see CONVICT

concatenate *vb syn* see INTEGRATE 3

concavity *n syn* see DEPRESSION 2

conceal *vb syn* see HIDE
rel camouflage, disguise, dissemble
idiom keep (something) dark
con betray, divulge; evidence, evince, manifest
ant reveal

concealed *adj syn* see ULTERIOR

concede *vb* 1 *syn* see ACKNOWLEDGE 1
rel cede, relinquish, waive
con agitate, argue, debate, discuss; answer, confute, refute; controvert
ant dispute
2 *syn* see GRANT 1
con refuse, reject
ant deny

conceit *n* 1 *syn* see IDEA
2 an attitude of regarding oneself with favor < his constant boasting was an indication of *conceit* >
syn amour propre, complacence, complacency, conceitedness, consequence, egoism, egotism, narcissism, outrecuidance, pride, self-admiration, self-complacency, self-conceit, self-consequence, self-esteem, self-exaltation, self-glory, self-importance, self-love, self-opinion, self-pride, swelled head, swellheadedness, vainglory, vainness, vanity
rel assurance, pomposity, self-partiality, smugness, stuffiness
con humbleness, humility, self-depreciation, unpretentiousness
ant modesty
3 *syn* see CAPRICE

‖conceit *vb syn* see UNDERSTAND 3

conceited *adj syn* see VAIN 3

conceitedness *n syn* see CONCEIT 2

‖conceity *adj syn* see VAIN 3

conceivable *adj* 1 *syn* see THINKABLE 2
2 *syn* see PROBABLE

conceive *vb* 1 *syn* see THINK 1
rel excogitate; cogitate, speculate; meditate, ponder, ruminate
2 *syn* see APPREHEND 1
rel heed, mark, note, notice, observe, remark
3 *syn* see UNDERSTAND 3
rel judge; deem, feel

concenter *vb* 1 *syn* see FASTEN 3
2 *syn* see CONVERGE

concentrate *vb* 1 *syn* see FASTEN 3
rel establish, set, settle
2 *syn* see UNIFY 1
rel assemble, collect, gather; heap, mass, pile
con dispel, disperse; attenuate, dilute, extenuate, rarefy, thin; dispense, distribute
ant dissipate
3 *syn* see CONTRACT 3
4 *syn* see CONVERGE

concentrated *adj* 1 *syn* see STRONG 3
2 *syn* see WHOLE 5
rel complete, entire, total
3 *syn* see INTENSE 1

concentrating *adj syn* see INTEGRATIVE
concentration *n syn* see ATTENTION 1
  rel enthrallment, raptness
  ant distraction
concept *n syn* see IDEA
  con percept, sensation, sense-datum, sensum
conception *n syn* see IDEA
conceptual *adj* existing or dealing with what exists only in the mind < *conceptual* analysis of a problem>
  syn ideal, ideational, notional
  rel abstract, transcendent, transcendental; absolute, categorical, ultimate; obscure, remote; fanciful, imaginary, visionary
  con practical, pragmatic, realistic; concrete, material, substantial, tangible
concern *n* 1 *syn* see INTEREST 3
  2 *syn* see AFFAIR 1
  3 *syn* see BUSINESS 8
  4 *syn* see CARE 4
  5 *syn* see CONSIDERATION 3
  6 *syn* see UNCERTAINTY
  rel faltering, irresolution; apprehension, misgiving; inquietude, suspense
  7 *syn* see CARE 2
  rel attention, consideration, thoughtfulness
  con aloofness, incuriousness, indifference
  ant unconcern
  8 *syn* see ENTERPRISE 3
  9 *syn* see GADGET 1
concerned *adj syn* see INTERESTED
concerning *prep syn* see APROPOS
concernment *n syn* see CARE 2
concert *vb* 1 *syn* see NEGOTIATE 1
  rel argue, debate, discuss; concur, cooperate, unite
  2 *syn* see AGREE 3
concert *n syn* see HARMONY 1
concession *n syn* see ALLOWANCE 5
conciliate *vb syn* see PACIFY
  rel intervene, mediate; persuade, prevail; calm, quiet, soothe, tranquilize
  con alienate, disaffect, estrange; foment, incite; excite, pique, provoke, stimulate
  ant antagonize
concise *adj* presented with or given to brevity of expression < a *concise* statement of the problem> < a very *concise* thinker>
  syn breviloquent, brief, compendiary, compendious, curt, laconic, short, short and sweet, succinct, summary, terse; *compare* PITHY
  rel abridged, compressed, condensed; marrowy, meaty, pithy; lean
  con diffuse, long-winded, prolix, rambling, voluble, wordy
  ant redundant; verbose
concisely *adv syn* see BRIEFLY
conclude *vb* 1 *syn* see DECIDE
  2 *syn* see CLOSE 3
  idiom ring down the curtain
  ant open
  3 *syn* see INFER
concluded *adj syn* see COMPLETE 4
concluding *adj syn* see LAST

ant opening
conclusion *n* 1 *syn* see INFERENCE 2
  2 *syn* see FINALE
  3 *syn* see END 2
  4 *syn* see DECISION 1
conclusive *adj* putting an end to debate or question usually by reason of irrefutability < the evidence was *conclusive* and no defense was possible>
  syn definitive
  rel cogent, compelling, convincing, telling; incontrovertible, irrefragable, irrefrangible, irrefutable, unanswerable; deciding, decisive, determinant, determinate, determinative; clear, precise, unambiguous
  con doubtful, dubious, problematic, questionable; credible, plausible, specious; ambiguous, cryptic, enigmatic, obscure
  ant inconclusive
concoct *vb syn* see CONTRIVE 2
  rel conceive, envisage, envision; create, discover, originate
concomitant *adj* occurring in company with < good manners are likely to be *concomitant* with good behavior>
  syn accompanying, ancillary, attendant, attending, coincident, collateral, incident, satellite
  rel accessory, adjuvant, supplementary; correlative, corresponding
concomitant *n syn* see ACCOMPANIMENT 2
concord *n* 1 *syn* see HARMONY 2
  rel amity, comity, friendship, goodwill; calmness, peace, placidity, serenity, tranquillity
  con conflict, contention, difference, dissension, strife, variance
  ant discord
  2 *syn* see HARMONY 3
  3 *syn* see HARMONY 1
  4 *syn* see TREATY
concord *vb syn* see AGREE 3
concordance *n syn* see HARMONY 2
concordant *adj syn* see HARMONIOUS 1
concours *n syn* see CONTEST 2
concourse *n* a coming, flocking, or flowing together < they doubt the universe originated in a chance *concourse* of atoms>
  syn concursion, confluence, gathering, junction, meeting
  rel association, joining, linkage
  con disassociation, parting, separation
concrete *vb* 1 *syn* see HARDEN 1
  2 *syn* see JOIN 1
concupiscence *n syn* see LUST 2
concupiscent *adj syn* see LUSTFUL 2
concur *vb* 1 *syn* see UNITE 2
  rel accord, agree, harmonize, jibe
  2 *syn* see AGREE 3
  rel accede, acquiesce, assent, consent
  ant contend; altercate
concurrent *adj syn* see CONTEMPORARY 1
concurrently *adv syn* see TOGETHER 1
concursion *n syn* see CONCOURSE
concuss *vb* 1 *syn* see SHAKE 4
  2 *syn* see FORCE 2
concussion *n syn* see IMPACT
  rel beating, buffeting, jarring, jolting, pounding, shaking; blow, clip, clout
condemn *vb* 1 *syn* see CRITICIZE
  rel belittle, decry, depreciate, disparage; deprecate, disapprove

---

syn synonym(s)   *rel* related word(s)
ant antonym(s)   *con* contrasted word(s)
idiom idiomatic equivalent(s)
‖ use limited; if in doubt, see a dictionary

idiom damn with faint praise, find fault with
con applaud, commend, compliment; acclaim, eulogize, extol, laud, praise; condone, excuse, forgive, pardon
2 *syn* see SENTENCE
con deliver, redeem, rescue, save

condemned *adj syn* see DAMNED 1
rel fallen, fated

condensation *n syn* see ABRIDGMENT

condense *vb* 1 *syn* see CONTRACT 3
rel compact, consolidate; curtail, minimize
con amplify
2 *syn* see EPITOMIZE 1
con broaden, expand, extend, widen
ant amplify

condensed *adj* made shorter and typically simpler < a *condensed* biography >
syn canned, capsule, epitomized, pocket, potted
rel abbreviated, abridged, bobbed, bobtail, bobtailed, curtailed, shortened
con elaborated, polished, refined; amplified, enlarged, expanded

condescend *vb syn* see STOOP 1

condign *adj syn* see JUST 3
rel grim, rigorous, stern, strict, stringent; atrocious, awful, dreadful, horrible

condition *n* 1 something that limits or qualifies an agreement or offer < included the *condition* that any heir contesting the will would be automatically disinherited >
syn provision, proviso, reservation, stipulation, strings, terms
rel prerequisite, requirement, requisite; exception, exemption, limitation, modification, qualification, restriction, saving clause
2 *syn* see ESSENTIAL 2
3 *syn* see STATE 1
4 *syn* see ORDER 9
5 *syn* see ORDER 10
6 *syn* see DISEASE 1

conditional *adj* 1 containing or dependent on a condition < our agreement is *conditional* on your raising the needed funds >
syn provisional, provisionary, provisory, tentative
rel iffy, obscure, uncertain; limited, modified, qualified, restricted
con fixed, set, sure
ant unconditional
2 *syn* see DEPENDENT 1
rel provisional, tentative; problematic, questionable; fortuitous, incidental
ant unconditional

condonable *adj syn* see JUSTIFIABLE
rel acceptable, tolerable

condone *vb syn* see EXCUSE 1
rel disregard, forget, ignore, overlook
con deplore, deprecate, disapprove; impugn, reproach

conduce *vb syn* see CONTRIBUTE 2

conduct *n* 1 *syn* see OVERSIGHT 1
2 *syn* see BEHAVIOR
rel bearing, demeanor, mien, posture, stance

conduct *vb* 1 *syn* see GUIDE
2 *syn* see ACCOMPANY
rel convey, transmit
3 to have the direction of and responsibility for < he had *conducted* a small market for many years >

syn carry on, direct, keep, manage, operate, ordain, run
rel administer, handle, head, oversee, supervise; arrange, control, keep up, order, regulate, rule; engineer, lead, pilot, steer
4 to act as a conduit for < shady transactions that *conducted* profits away from the stockholders >
syn carry, channel, convey, funnel, pipe, siphon, traject, transmit
rel remove, separate, take away, withdraw
5 *syn* see BEHAVE 1

conduit *n* 1 *syn* see CHANNEL 1
2 *syn* see PIPELINE

confab *vb syn* see CONFER 2

confabulate *vb syn* see CONFER 2

confabulation *n* 1 *syn* see CONVERSATION 1
2 *syn* see CONVERSATION 2
3 *syn* see CONFERENCE 1

confederacy *n syn* see ALLIANCE 2

confederate *n* one associated with another or others in a wrong or unlawful act < conspiring with his *confederates* to overthrow the government >
syn abettor, accessory, accomplice, coconspirator, conspirator
rel collaborator, fellow traveler; associate, colleague, fellow, partner

confederation *n syn* see ALLIANCE 2

confer *vb* 1 *syn* see GIVE 2
rel allot, provide; vouchsafe
2 to carry on a conversation or discussion usually directed toward reaching a decision or settlement < the President *conferred* with his cabinet about the scandal >
syn advise, collogue, confab, confabulate, consult, huddle, parley, powwow, treat
rel bargain, chaffer, deal, negotiate; argue, debate, discuss; converse, speak, talk
idiom put one's head together with

conference *n* 1 an interchanging of views < took several hours of *conference* to find a solution to the problem >
syn confabulation, deliberation, discussion, rap, ventilation
2 a meeting for the purpose of serious discussion and interchange of views < the association held a *conference* on the problems of aging >
syn colloquium, colloquy, palaver, rap session, seminar
rel round robin, round table
3 *syn* see TALK 4
4 *syn* see LEAGUE 4

conferrer *n syn* see DONOR

confess *vb syn* see ACKNOWLEDGE 1
idiom make a clean breast, open one's heart

confessions *n pl syn* see BIOGRAPHY

confidant *n syn* see FRIEND

confide *vb* 1 to tell confidentially < shyly *confided* her secret >
syn breathe, whisper
rel hint, insinuate, intimate, suggest
con advertise, broadcast, proclaim, publish
2 *syn* see COMMIT 1
rel bestow, present

confidence *n* 1 *syn* see TRUST 1
con distrust, mistrust; despair, hopelessness

ant doubt; apprehension

2 a feeling or showing of adequacy and reliance on oneself and one's powers < had serene *confidence* in his own ability to win through >

syn aplomb, assurance, self-assurance, self-assuredness, self-confidence, self-trust; *compare* EQUANIMITY

rel courage, mettle, resolution, spirit, tenacity; brashness, impudence, presumption

con apprehension, incertitude, misgiving, self-depreciation, self-doubt, uncertitude

ant diffidence

3 *syn* see CERTAINTY

4 *syn* see EFFRONTERY

confidence man *n syn* see SWINDLER

confident *adj* **1** marked by a strong, fearless, and bold belief in oneself and one's capacities < faced his accusers with a *confident* air >

syn assured, sanguine, secure, self-assured, self-confident, undoubtful

rel certain, cocksure, cocky, perky, positive, sure; self-possessed, self-reliant; bold, brave, courageous, dauntless, fearless, intrepid, unafraid, undaunted, valiant

con jittery, nervous, uneasy; afraid, daunted, fearful; doubtful, dubious

ant apprehensive

2 *syn* see SURE 5

3 *syn* see PRESUMPTUOUS

confidential *adj* **1** *syn* see PRIVATE 2

2 *syn* see FAMILIAR 1

rel secret; tried, trustworthy, trusty

configuration *n syn* see FORM 1

confine *vb* **1** *syn* see LIMIT 2

2 *syn* see IMPRISON

confine *n, usu* **confines** *pl* **1** *syn* see ENVIRONS 1

2 *syn* see LIMIT 1

rel circumference, compass, periphery

3 *syn* see RANGE 2

confined *adj syn* see CRAMPED

confinement *n* **1** *syn* see RESTRICTION 2

2 the state attending and consequent to childbirth < had a long difficult *confinement* >

syn accouchement, childbed, lying-in

rel parturition; labor, travail

confirm *vb* **1** *syn* see RATIFY

rel accede, acquiesce, assent, consent, subscribe; validate

idiom make good

con decline, refuse, reject

2 to attest to the truth, genuineness, accuracy, or validity of something < a surprise witness *confirmed* his account of the incident >

syn authenticate, bear out, corroborate, justify, substantiate, validate, verify

rel attest, certify, vouch, witness; back, support, underpin, uphold, warrant; check, check out

con confute, controvert, disprove, refute; contravene, gainsay, impugn, negative, traverse

ant deny; contradict

confirm (in) *vb syn* see HABITUATE 2

confirmation *n syn* see TESTIMONY

confirmative *adj*   *syn*   see   CORROBORATIVE

confirmatory *adj*   *syn*   see   CORROBORATIVE

confirmed *adj* **1** *syn* see HABITUAL 2

2 *syn* see INVETERATE 1

confiscate *vb syn* see APPROPRIATE 1

confiture *n syn* see JAM

conflagrant *adj syn* see BURNING 1

conflagration *n syn* see FIRE 1

conflict *n* **1** *syn* see CONTEST 1

rel argument, controversy, dispute

2 *syn* see CONTEST 2

3 *syn* see DISCORD

conflict *vb syn* see CLASH 2

rel differ, disagree, vary; disturb, interfere

idiom run against the tide

conflicting *adj* **1** *syn* see ANTIPATHETIC 1

2 *syn* see INCONSONANT 1

confluence *n syn* see CONCOURSE

conform *vb* **1** *syn* see ADAPT

rel attune, harmonize, tune

2 *syn* see AGREE 4

con conflict, differ, disagree

ant diverge

3 *syn* see HARMONIZE 3

4 *syn* see OBEY

idiom toe the line

conformable *adj syn* see ASSORTED 2

rel appropriate, fitting, suitable; applicable, usable

conformation *n syn* see FORM 1

conforming *adj syn* see DECOROUS 1

conformity *n* **1** *syn* see CONSISTENCY

2 *syn* see ACQUIESCENCE

confound *vb* **1** *syn* see PUZZLE

idiom take aback

2 *syn* see MISTAKE 1

ant discriminate, distinguish

3 *syn* see EMBARRASS

4 *syn* see DISPROVE 1

confounded *adj* **1** *syn* see AGHAST 2

2 *syn* see DAMNED 2

3 *syn* see UTTER

confoundedly *adv syn* see EVER 6

confrere *n* **1** *syn* see COLLEAGUE

2 *syn* see PARTNER

confront *vb* **1** to stand over against in the role of an adversary or enemy < he *confronted* his accusers with perfect aplomb >

syn affront, encounter, face, meet; *compare* MEET 6

rel beard, brave, challenge, defy; flout, scorn, scout; oppose, resist, withstand

idiom come to close quarters with, come up against

con avoid, elude, evade

2 *syn* see ACCOST 2

confronting *prep syn* see BEFORE 2

confuse *vb* **1** *syn* see EMBARRASS

2 to make unclear in mind or purpose < found the city hustle and noise very *confusing* >

syn addle, ball up, befuddle, bewilder, ‖bumfuzzle, discombobulate, distract, dizzy, fluster, fuddle, mix up, ‖mizzle, ‖momble, muddle, mull, throw off, throw out

rel misguide, mislead; agitate, bother, discompose, disquiet, flurry, perturb, upset

---

syn synonym(s)   *rel* related word(s)
ant antonym(s)   *con* contrasted word(s)
idiom idiomatic equivalent(s)
‖ use limited; if in doubt, see a dictionary

3 *syn* see PUZZLE
4 to make indistinct the elements or true character of (as a discussion) < *confuse* an issue in a debate >
syn becloud, befog, blur, cloud, fog, muddy
rel complicate, confound, involve, mix up
idiom lose in a fog
con clarify, elucidate; simplify
5 to throw into disorder < surging waves *confused* the waters > < her accounts were totally *confused* >
syn foul up, jumble, mix up, muddle, ‖snafu, snarl up, tumble; *compare* DISORDER 1
rel derange, disarrange, disorder, disorganize, disturb, mess (up), unsettle
idiom put in a flutter, throw into confusion
6 *syn* see MISREPRESENT
7 *syn* see MISTAKE 1
ant differentiate

confusion *n* **1** *syn* see RUIN 3
2 *syn* see EMBARRASSMENT
3 a condition in which things are out of their normal or proper places or relationships < the room was in complete *confusion* >
syn ataxia, ‖ballup, chaos, clutter, disarray, disorder, huddle, misorder, muddle, ‖mullock, pell-mell, snarl, topsy-turviness
rel derangement, disarrangement, disturbance; foul-up, mess, mix-up, muck, ‖mux, ‖snafu; babel, din, hullabaloo, pandemonium
con methodization, ordering, organization, systematization; method, order, system
4 *syn* see COMMOTION 2
rel disorder, disorganization, disturbance; discomfiture, embarrassment

confute *vb* *syn* see DISPROVE 1
congé *n* *syn* see PARTING
congeal *vb* **1** *syn* see HARDEN 1
rel chill, cool, freeze
2 *syn* see COAGULATE
congenial *adj* *syn* see HARMONIOUS 3
ant uncongenial
2 *syn* see CONSONANT 1
rel companionable, cooperative, social; affable, cordial, genial, gracious, sociable; pleasant, pleasing
ant uncongenial; antipathetic (*of persons*); abhorrent (*of tasks, responsibilities*)
3 *syn* see PLEASANT 1
4 *syn* see GRACIOUS 1
congenital *adj* **1** *syn* see INNATE 1
2 *syn* see INHERENT
congeries *n* *syn* see GATHERING 2
congest *vb* *syn* see FILL 1
conglobate *vb* *syn* see BALL
conglobe *vb* *syn* see BALL
conglomerate *adj* *syn* see MISCELLANEOUS
conglomerate *n* **1** *syn* see AGGREGATE 1
2 *syn* see SYNDICATE
conglomeration *n* **1** *syn* see ACCUMULATION
2 *syn* see AGGREGATE 1
congratulate *vb* to express to another one's pleasure in his good fortune or success < *congratulate* a friend when he wins a race >

syn felicitate
rel applaud, laud, praise; bless, compliment
idiom pat one on the back, tender (*or* offer) congratulation, wish one joy, wish one well
con belittle, depreciate, disparage, knock, run down, slur
congregate *vb* *syn* see GATHER 6
rel swarm, teem
ant disperse
congregation *n* *syn* see GATHERING 2
rel audience, disciples, following, public
congress *n* *syn* see ASSOCIATION 2
congress *vb* *syn* see GATHER 6
congruity *n* *syn* see CONSISTENCY
congruous *adj* **1** *syn* see CONSONANT 1
rel appropriate, fit, fitting, meet; proper, seemly
ant incongruous
2 *syn* see HARMONIOUS 2
conjectural *adj* *syn* see SUPPOSED 1
con demonstrated; unquestionable
conjecture *n* *syn* see THEORY 2
ant fact
conjecture *vb* to draw an inference from slight or inadequate evidence < when he failed to arrive on time she *conjectured* that he was drinking again >
syn guess, presume, pretend, suppose, surmise, think; *compare* INFER, UNDERSTAND 3
rel assume, expect, suspect; believe, deem, feel; conceive, fancy, imagine; conclude, estimate, gather, glean, infer, judge
idiom hazard a conjecture, take for granted
con demonstrate, prove, test, try; ascertain, determine, discover, learn
conjoin *vb* **1** *syn* see JOIN 1
2 *syn* see UNITE 2
conjoint *adj* **1** *syn* see COMMON 1
2 *syn* see COOPERATIVE
conjointly *adv* *syn* see TOGETHER 3
conjointment *n* *syn* see ASSOCIATION 1
conjugal *adj* *syn* see MATRIMONIAL
conjugality *n* *syn* see MARRIAGE 1
conjugate *vb* *syn* see JOIN 1
conjunct *adj* *syn* see COMMON 1
conjunction *n* *syn* see ASSOCIATION 1
conjuration *n* *syn* see SPELL
conjure *vb* *syn* see BEG
conjurer *n* **1** *syn* see MAGICIAN 1
2 *syn* see MAGICIAN 2
conjuring *n* **1** *syn* see MAGIC 1
2 *syn* see MAGIC 2
conjury *n* *syn* see MAGIC 1
‖**conk** *n* **1** *syn* see NOSE 1
2 *syn* see HEAD 1
‖**conk** *n* *syn* see HIT 1
conk *vb* *syn* see DIE 1
con man *n* *syn* see SWINDLER
rel shill
con mark, sucker, victim; greenhorn
connate *adj* **1** *syn* see INNATE 1
2 *syn* see INHERENT
3 *syn* see RELATED
connatural *adj* **1** *syn* see INNATE 1
2 *syn* see RELATED
connect *vb* *syn* see JOIN 1
ant disconnect
connection *n* **1** *syn* see ASSOCIATION 1
2 *syn* see JOINT 1

3 *syn* see JOB 2

4 *syn* see RELIGION 2

connivance *n syn* see COMPLICITY

connive *vb* **1** to secretly favor or sympathize with something improper or illicit < *connive* at treason >
syn blink (at), wink (at)
rel condone, disregard, ignore, overlook, tolerate
idiom close (*or* shut) one's eyes to, let go by (*or* get by) one's eye, regard with indulgence
con disapprove, disfavor, frown (at *or* upon); disallow, reject, repudiate; disdain, scorn, scout, spurn

2 *syn* see PLOT

connoisseur *n* a person who enjoys with discrimination and appreciation of subtleties and details especially in matters of culture or art < a *connoisseur* of fine wines >
syn aesthete, cognoscente, dilettante
rel bon vivant, epicure, gourmet; adept, authority, critic, expert
con abecedarian, amateur, dabbler, tyro

connotation *n syn* see ASSOCIATION 4

connote *vb* **1** *syn* see MEAN 2

2 *syn* see SUGGEST 1

connubial *adj syn* see MATRIMONIAL

connubiality *n syn* see MARRIAGE 1

conquer *vb* **1** to overcome or gain dominion over by force of arms < leaders who have tried and failed to *conquer* the world >
syn bear down, beat down, crush, defeat, overpower, reduce, subdue, subjugate, vanquish; *compare* DEFEAT 2, OVERTHROW 2, WHIP 2, WIN 1
rel baffle, balk, circumvent, foil, frustrate, outwit, override, thwart; bend, control, master, overmaster, subject, worst
idiom bring one to one's knees, trample in the dust, trample underfoot
con bow, cave, give up, succumb, yield; capitulate, surrender

2 to gain mastery over something by getting the better of obstacles and difficulties < trials faced by the men who *conquered* Mount Everest >
syn best, master, overcome, prevail, triumph; *compare* OVERCOME 1

3 *syn* see OVERCOME 1

conqueror *n syn* see VICTOR 1

conquest *n syn* see VICTORY 1
rel defeating, overthrow, rout, routing, subdual

consanguine *adj syn* see RELATED

‖consarned *adj* **1** *syn* see DAMNED 2

2 *syn* see UTTER

conscience *n syn* see QUALM

conscienceless *adj syn* see UNSCRUPULOUS
rel devious, shifty, tricky, unfair
ant conscientious

conscientious *adj* **1** *syn* see UPRIGHT 2
ant conscienceless

2 *syn* see CAREFUL 2

conscionable *adj syn* see CAREFUL 2

conscious *adj* **1** *syn* see AWARE
rel noticing, noting, observing, perceiving, remarking; vigilant, watchful
con forgetful, oblivious, unmindful; disregarding, ignoring, overlooking
ant unconscious

2 *syn* see SELF-CONSCIOUS

consciousness *n syn* see CARE 4

conscribe *vb syn* see DRAFT 1

conscript *vb syn* see DRAFT 1

consecrate *vb* **1** *syn* see DEVOTE 1
con desecrate, profane; defile, pollute

2 *syn* see BLESS 1

consecrated *adj syn* see HOLY 1

consecution *n* **1** *syn* see ORDER 5

2 *syn* see SUCCESSION 2

consecutive *adj* following one after another in orderly fashion < it rained for five *consecutive* days >
syn sequent, sequential, serial, subsequent, subsequential, succedent, succeeding, successional, successive; *compare* NEXT
rel after, ensuing, following, later; enlarging, increasing, progressive
con antecedent, preceding, prior

consecutively *adv syn* see TOGETHER 2

consent *vb syn* see ASSENT
rel allow, let, permit; approve, sanction; concur
con decline; balk, demur, stick, stickle

consent *n* **1** *syn* see PERMISSION

2 *syn* see AGREEMENT 2

consentaneous *adj syn* see UNANIMOUS

consentient *adj syn* see UNANIMOUS

consequence *n* **1** *syn* see EFFECT 1
con origin, root, source
ant antecedent

2 *syn* see IMPORTANCE
rel exigency, need; fame, honor, renown, reputation, repute

3 *syn* see STATUS 2

4 *syn* see CONCEIT 2

consequent *adj syn* see RATIONAL

consequential *adj syn* see IMPORTANT 1

consequently *adv syn* see THEREFORE

conservancy *n syn* see CONSERVATION 1

conservation *n* **1** a deliberate planned guarding and protecting of something felt as precious < *conservation* of our natural resources >
syn conservancy, husbanding, preserval, preservation, salvation, saving
rel attention, care, cherishing, protection; control, directing, governing, management, managing, supervising, supervision
con neglect, squandering, waste

2 *syn* see PRESERVATION 1

conservative *adj* **1** tending to resist or oppose change < took a very *conservative* stance politically >
syn die-hard, fogyish, old-line, orthodox, reactionary, right, tory, traditionalistic
con modern, progressive, radical
ant advanced

2 kept or keeping within bounds < equally *conservative* in speech and action >
syn controlled, discreet, moderate, reasonable, restrained, temperate, unexcessive, unextreme
rel cautious, chary, wary; circumspect, politic, proper, prudent

---

syn synonym(s)   *rel* related word(s)
ant antonym(s)   *con* contrasted word(s)
idiom idiomatic equivalent(s)
‖ use limited; if in doubt, see a dictionary

con expansive, unconstrained; excessive, freewheeling, uncontrolled, unrestrained

conservative n syn see DIEHARD 1

conservatory n syn see GREENHOUSE

conserve vb syn see SAVE 3
rel keep up, maintain, support, sustain
con dissipate, fritter, squander, waste

conserve n syn see JAM

consider vb 1 to give serious thought to < *consider* the risk you would be taking>
syn contemplate, excogitate, mind, perpend, ponder, study, think (out or over), weigh
rel meditate, muse, ruminate; cogitate, reason, reflect, speculate, think; examine, inspect, look (at), scan, scrutinize, see
idiom bestow thought to, chew the cud over, revolve (or turn over) in one's mind
con disregard, ignore, neglect, overlook, slight
2 syn see EYE 1
rel envisage, envision
3 to come to view, judge, or classify < he *considered* thrift essential to success>
syn account, deem, reckon, regard, view; compare FEEL 3
rel conceive, fancy, imagine, think; conclude, gather, infer, judge, rule
4 syn see ADMIRE 1
5 syn see FEEL 3

considerable adj 1 syn see IMPORTANT 1
2 tending more to the large than the small < buckled down with his ax and made a *considerable* impression on the woodpile>
syn good, respectable, ||right smart, sensible, sizable, ||smart
rel able, capable, competent; active, effective, efficacious; important, notable, significant; goodly, pretty, substantial, tidy
con insignificant, meager, slight, trivial; big, grand, great, huge
3 syn see BIG 1

considerably adv syn see WELL 8

considerate adj 1 syn see CAUTIOUS
2 syn see THOUGHTFUL 3
rel kind, kindly; compassionate, sympathetic, tender, warmhearted; amiable, complaisant, obliging
ant inconsiderate
3 syn see GENEROUS 1

considerately adv syn see WELL 2
rel solicitously, tenderly; altruistically, benevolently, charitably
con austerely, harshly, severely, strictly

considerateness n syn see CONSIDERATION 3

consideration n 1 syn see ATTENTION 1
2 syn see MOTIVE 1
3 thoughtful and sympathetic attention < showed great *consideration* to the needs of others>
syn concern, considerateness, regard, solicitude
rel awareness, heed, heedfulness, mindfulness; forbearance, mercy, quarter
con disregard, heedlessness, unconcern, unmindfulness; inconsiderateness; contempt, despite, disdain, disinterest, scorn
4 syn see REGARD 4

considered adj syn see DELIBERATE 1
rel intentional, voluntary, willful
con impulsive, instinctive, spontaneous; headlong, impetuous, precipitate

ant unconsidered

considering conj syn see BECAUSE

consign vb 1 syn see COMMIT 1
rel resign, surrender, yield
2 syn see SEND 1

consist vb 1 to have existence or a place < our national strength *consists* not solely in military readiness>
syn dwell, exist, inhere, lie, reside
rel be, subsist; abide, repose, rest
idiom have one's (or a) place
2 syn see AGREE 4

consistency n agreement or harmony of parts, traits, or features < his adversary had to admit the *consistency* of his position>
syn coherence, conformity, congruity, correspondence; compare HARMONY 2
rel agreement, concord, consonance; likeness, similarity; apposition, aptness, felicity, fitness, suitability
con incoherence, incongruity; impropriety, inappropriateness, unsuitability
ant inconsistency

consistent adj 1 syn see SAME 3
2 syn see CONSONANT 1

consistently adv syn see USUALLY 1

consociate n syn see PARTNER

console vb syn see COMFORT
rel calm, relieve, tranquilize; animate, hearten, inspirit
idiom lift the spirits of
con agitate, discompose, disquiet, disturb, perturb, upset

consolidate vb syn see UNIFY 1
rel amalgamate, blend, fuse, merge; set, solidify
con part, sever, sunder; liquefy, melt

consolidating adj syn see INTEGRATIVE

consolidation n 1 syn see UNIFICATION
2 a union of two or more businesses < *consolidation* is often accompanied by a new corporate name>
syn amalgamation, merger
ant dissolution

consonance n 1 syn see HARMONY 2
con discrepancy, incompatibility, incongruousness
ant discord
2 syn see HARMONY 1
ant dissonance

consonant adj 1 conforming (as to a pattern, a standard, or a relationship) without discord or difficulty < his performance was seldom *consonant* with his very real abilities>
syn agreeable, compatible, congenial, congruous, consistent, sympathetic; compare HARMONIOUS 2
rel accordant, conformable, harmonious; coincident, concurrent; en rapport
con discordant, discrepant; incompatible, incongruous, inconsistent
ant inconsonant
2 syn see HARMONIOUS 1
ant dissonant
3 syn see LIKE
4 syn see RESONANT

consort n 1 syn see ACCOMPANIMENT 2
2 syn see SPOUSE

consort vb syn see AGREE 4

consort (with) vb syn see ACCOMPANY 1

consortium n syn see ASSOCIATION 2

conspectus *n syn* see ABRIDGMENT
conspicuous *adj* **1** *syn* see CLEAR 5
　2 *syn* see NOTICEABLE
　rel celebrated, eminent, illustrious; showy
　con common, everyday, ordinary; covert,
　secret; concealed, hidden
　ant inconspicuous
conspiracy *n syn* see PLOT 2
　rel sedition, treason; disloyalty, faithless-
　ness, falsity, perfidiousness, perfidy,
　treacherousness, treachery
　con faith, faithfulness, fealty, loyalty
conspirator *n syn* see CONFEDERATE
conspire *vb syn* see PLOT
‖**constable** *n syn* see POLICEMAN
constancy *n syn* see ATTACHMENT 1
constant *adj* **1** *syn* see FAITHFUL 1
　rel abiding, clinging, enduring, lasting,
　persistent, persisting
　con capricious, mercurial
　ant fickle, inconstant
　2 *syn* see INFLEXIBLE 3
　con fluctuant, fluctuating, fluctuational,
　unstable
　ant inconstant, variable
　3 *syn* see SAME 3
　4 *syn* see STEADY 2
　5 *syn* see CONTINUAL
　rel chronic, confirmed, inveterate; dogged,
　obstinate, pertinacious; persevering
　con alternate, intermittent, recurrent;
　infrequent, occasional, sporadic
　ant fitful
constantly *adv syn* see ALWAYS 1
　idiom day after day, day in, day out
　ant occasionally
constate *vb syn* see ASSERT 1
consternate *vb syn* see DISMAY 1
consternation *n syn* see FEAR 1
　rel confusion, muddle, muddlement; be-
　wilderment, distraction, perplexity
　con composure, equanimity, phlegm,
　sangfroid; aplomb, poise, self-command,
　self-possession
constipate *vb syn* see STULTIFY
constipated *adj* being unable to defecate
　regularly and without difficulty < com-
　plained that she was constantly *con-
　stipated* >
　syn astricted, bound, costive, obstipated
constituent *n syn* see ELEMENT 2
　rel division, fraction, part, portion
　con complex, economy, organism; system;
　amalgam, blend, composite, compound
　ant aggregate, whole
constitute *vb* **1** to be all or a fundamental
　part of the substance of < water *consti-
　tutes* the greater part of the human
　body >
　syn compose, comprise, form, make,
　make up
　rel embody, incorporate, integrate; com-
　plement, complete, fill out, flesh (out)
　2 *syn* see ENACT 1
　3 *syn* see FOUND 2
constitution *n* **1** *syn* see PHYSIQUE
　2 *syn* see MAKEUP 2
constitutional *adj syn* see INHERENT

　con anomalous, irregular, unnatural
　ant advenient
constitutional *n syn* see WALK 1
　rel ambulation, footwork, legwork, per-
　ambulation
constitutive *adj syn* see ESSENTIAL 2
constrain *vb* **1** *syn* see FORCE 2
　2 *syn* see RESTRAIN 1
　3 *syn* see DENY 3
　rel abridge, curtail, deprive; ban, bar,
　disallow, enjoin
　4 *syn* see IMPRISON
　5 *syn* see PRESS 1
　6 *syn* see DISTRESS 2
constrained *adj syn* see RESERVED 1
constrainment *n syn* see RESTRICTION 2
constraint *n* **1** *syn* see FORCE 4
　rel repression, suppression; driving, im-
　pelling, impulsion; goad, motive, spring,
　spur
　2 *syn* see RESTRICTION 2
constrict *vb* **1** *syn* see CONTRACT 3
　rel curb, restrain; circumscribe, confine,
　limit, restrict
　con enlarge, expand, increase, maximize
　2 to make narrow or narrower < the mus-
　cles that *constrict* the sphincter >
　syn constringe, narrow
　rel gather, plait, pucker; compress, con-
　strain, squeeze; astringe
　con broaden, dilate, distend, widen
　ant expand
constringe *vb syn* see CONSTRICT 2
construal *n syn* see EXPLANATION 1
construct *vb* **1** *syn* see MAKE 3
　2 *syn* see BUILD 1
　3 *syn* see ERECT 5
construction *n* **1** *syn* see MAKEUP 1
　2 *syn* see EXPLANATION 1
constructive *adj syn* see IMPLICIT 2
　rel inferential, ratiocinative; construable,
　interpretable, renderable
　con clear, evident, obvious, patent
　ant manifest
construe *vb syn* see EXPLAIN 1
consuetude *n syn* see HABIT 1
consult *vb syn* see CONFER 2
　rel cogitate, counsel, deliberate; consider,
　examine, review
consume *vb* **1** to bring to an end by or as
　if by the action of a destroying force
　< the village was *consumed* by fire >
　syn devour, eat, eat up, exhaust, use up
　rel destroy, raze, ruin, wreck; annihilate,
　extinguish; crush, overwhelm, suppress
　con bolster, brace, buttress, hold up,
　prop, stay, support, sustain; build, con-
　struct, create, make, produce; renew, re-
　store
　2 *syn* see WASTE 2
　3 *syn* see GO 4
　4 *syn* see EAT 1
　5 to eat or drink usually gluttonously or
　without measure < *consumed* dozens of
　burgers and a case of beer >
　syn polish off, punish, put away, put
　down, shift, swill; *compare* EAT 1
　rel absorb, ingest; devour, gobble (up),
　gorge, wolf; down, gulp, guzzle, inhale,
　swallow
　idiom dispose of
　6 *syn* see MONOPOLIZE
consumedly *adv syn* see EVER 6

---

syn synonym(s)　　*rel* related word(s)
ant antonym(s)　　*con* contrasted word(s)
idiom idiomatic equivalent(s)
‖ use limited; if in doubt, see a dictionary

consuming adj syn see ENGROSSING

consummate adj 1 brought to the highest possible point of perfection < the difficult allegro passages displayed her *consummate* skill >
  syn accomplished, finished, perfected, ripe, virtuosic; *compare* PERFECT 2
  rel faultless, flawless, impeccable, perfect; practiced, skilled, trained; able, gifted, talented; inimitable, peerless, superb, superlative, supreme, transcendent, unsurpassable
  con callow, crude, green, raw, rough, uncouth; defective, deficient, inadequate
  2 *syn* see UTTER

consummate vb syn see CLOSE 3

consumption n syn see TUBERCULOSIS

contact n 1 the state of being in or coming into close association or connection < shuddered at the *contact* of his icy hand >
  syn contingence, touch
  rel closeness, contiguity, nearness, propinquity, proximity; impingement, taction, touching; association, connection, relation; oneness, union, unity
  con breach, break, rift, rupture, split; insularity, isolation, seclusion, segregation, separation; distance, farness, remoteness
  2 a situation permitting exchange of ideas and opinions < tried for several days to get in *contact* with her brother >
  syn commerce, communication, communion, intercommunication, intercourse
  rel association, companionship, fellowship; oneness, union, unity; accord, concord, harmony, rapport; empathy, sympathy, understanding

contact vb syn see REACH 4

contagion n syn see POISON
  rel contamination, corruption, pollution, taint; miasma

contagious adj 1 syn see INFECTIOUS 2
  2 syn see INFECTIOUS 3

contain vb 1 syn see COMPOSE 4
  2 to have or be capable of having within < the box *contained* family papers > < a mug that will *contain* a quart of ale >
  syn accommodate, hold
  rel harbor, house, lodge, shelter; admit, receive, take, take in
  3 syn see INCLUDE

contaminate vb 1 to debase by making impure or unclean < feared her child's morals would be *contaminated* by others >
  syn defile, pollute, soil, taint; *compare* TAINT 1
  rel corrupt, debase, debauch, deprave, pervert, vitiate; harm, injure, spoil
  con better, elevate, improve
  ant purify
  2 to render unfit for use by the introduction of unwholesome or undesirable elements < water *contaminated* by sewage >
  syn befoul, foul, pollute
  rel infect; poison; dirty, soil
  ant purify

contemn vb syn see DESPISE

contemplate vb 1 syn see EYE 1
  rel ponder, reflect, study; examine, inspect, scan, scrutinize
  2 syn see CONSIDER 1

  rel drift, roam
  3 syn see INTEND 2
  idiom have in view

contemplative adj syn see THOUGHTFUL 1
  rel musing, weighing; reasoning
  idiom in a brown study

contemporaneous adj syn see CONTEMPORARY 1

contemporary adj 1 existing or occurring at the same time < the story has come down from several *contemporary* sources >
  syn coetaneous, coeval, coexistent, coexisting, concurrent, contemporaneous, simultaneous, synchronal, synchronic, synchronous
  rel accompanying, attendant, attending, coincident, concomitant; current, existing, present; associated, connected, linked, related
  con antecedent, foregoing, preceding, previous, prior; ensuing, following, succeeding
  2 *syn* see PRESENT
  3 *syn* see UP-TO-DATE

contempt n 1 syn see DESPITE 1
  rel antipathy, aversion; distaste, repugnance
  con awe, fear, reverence
  ant regard
  2 *syn* see DISGRACE
  3 *syn* see DEFIANCE 2

contemptible adj arousing or meriting scorn or disdain < a *contemptible* attempt to blame his wife for his failure >
  syn beggarly, cheap, despicable, despisable, mean, pitiable, pitiful, scummy, scurvy, shabby, sorry; *compare* BASE 3
  rel abhorrent, abominable, detestable, hateful, odious; abject, ignoble, sordid; bad, inferior, poor, sad; disgusting, scrimy, shameful; outcast
  con creditable, estimable, honorable, noble; high-minded, high-principled, principled, true, upright; honest, square, straight
  ant admirable

contend vb 1 to strive in opposition to someone or something < *contending* against the temptation to look behind him >
  syn battle, fight, oppugn, tug, war
  rel combat, oppose, resist, withstand; contest, cope (with), vie
  2 *syn* see MAINTAIN 2
  rel report, say, tell; charge, enjoin, urge; dictate, prescribe
  3 *syn* see COMPETE 1
  rel combat, oppose, resist, withstand; confront, encounter, face, meet, stand

content vb syn see SATISFY 3
  rel delight, thrill, tickle; bewitch, captivate, charm, enrapture
  con disappoint, dishearten, displease
  ant discontent

contention n 1 syn see DISCORD
  rel altercation, quarrel, squabble, wrangle; argument, controversy, dispute
  con agreement, coincidence, concurrence
  2 *syn* see ARGUMENT 2
  3 *syn* see THESIS 1

contentious adj 1 syn see BELLIGERENT
  rel contrary, froward, perverse; captious, carping, caviling, faultfinding

con calm, serene, tranquil; amiable, complaisant, good-natured, obliging
ant peaceable

2 prone to wordy contention < a *contentious* old chap, always ready for an argument >
syn argumentative, controversial, disputatious, litigious, polemical
rel fiery, hasty, hotheaded, impetuous, peppery; belligerent, bellicose, scrappy
con amiable, complaisant, good-natured, obliging; agreeable, cooperative, understanding

conterminous *adj syn* see ADJACENT 3
contest *vb* **1** *syn* see COMPETE 1
rel endeavor
2 *syn* see RESIST

contest *n* **1** earnest struggle for superiority or victory < the rival factions continued in *contest* for several years >
syn competition, conflict, emulation, rivalry, strife, striving, tug-of-war, warfare
rel brush, encounter, skirmish; action, battle, engagement

2 a competitive encounter between groups or individuals < there were *contests* of skill and of wit >
syn competition, concours, conflict, meet, meeting, rencontre
rel proving, testing, trial, trying

contestation *n syn* see THESIS 1
contiguity *n syn* see PROXIMITY
contiguous *adj* **1** *syn* see ADJACENT 3
rel close, near, nearby, nigh
con apart, separate; distant, remote
2 *syn* see NEIGHBORING

contiguously *adv syn* see IMMEDIATELY 1
contiguousness *n syn* see PROXIMITY
continence *n syn* see TEMPERANCE 2
rel self-restraint; moderation, temperateness; chasteness, chastity, purity
con self-indulgence; excessiveness, inordinateness; lasciviousness, lecherousness, lewdness, licentiousness, wantonness
ant incontinence

continent *adj syn* see ABSTEMIOUS
rel bridled, curbed, inhibited, restrained; chaste, pure
con self-indulgent, spoiled
ant incontinent

contingence *n syn* see CONTACT 1
contingency *n syn* see JUNCTURE 2
rel break, chance, occasion, opportunity
contingent *adj* **1** *syn* see ACCIDENTAL
rel unanticipated, unforeseeable, unforeseen; likely, possible, probable
con certain, inevitable, necessary
2 *syn* see DEPENDENT 1

continual *adj* continuing without intermission and seemingly without end < they were tired of her *continual* nagging >
syn around-the-clock, ceaseless, constant, continuous, endless, everlasting, incessant, interminable, minutely, perpetual, timeless, unceasing, unending, unintermitted, unintermittent, uninterrupted, unremitting
rel abiding, enduring, persistent, persisting, staying; unvarying, unchanging, un-

failing, unflagging, unwaning; relentless, running, steady
con ephemeral, evanescent, impermanent, short-lived, temporary, transient, transitory

continually *adv syn* see TOGETHER 2
continuance *n syn* see RUN 2
rel constancy, longevity, permanence; survival

continuation *n* **1** uninterrupted existence or succession < the *continuation* of political disorder in Northern Ireland >
syn continuity, duration, endurance, persistence
rel extension, prolongation, protraction
ant termination
2 *syn* see RUN 2
ant cessation

continue *vb* **1** to remain indefinitely in existence or in a particular state or course < many traditional beliefs still *continue* > < do you expect to *continue* in school for the rest of your life? >
syn abide, carry through, endure, last, perdure, persist
rel carry on, carry over, ride, run on; outlast, outlive, survive; remain, stay
con cease, desist, discontinue, quit; arrest, check, interrupt; defer, intermit, postpone, stay, suspend
ant discontinue
2 *syn* see RESUME 2

continuing *adj syn* see OLD 2
continuity *n syn* see CONTINUATION 1
continuous *adj syn* see CONTINUAL
ant discontinuous
continuously *adv* **1** *syn* see TOGETHER 2
2 *syn* see ALWAYS 1
contort *vb syn* see DEFORM
rel bend, curve, twist
contour *n syn* see OUTLINE
contra *prep syn* see AGAINST 1
contra *adv syn* see AGAIN 5
contra *n syn* see OPPOSITE

contraband *adj* prohibited or excluded by law or treaty < fur or feathers from endangered species are *contraband* in advanced nations >
syn banned, hot
rel disapproved, proscribed, taboo; forbidden, prohibited; excluded, shut out
contraband *vb syn* see SMUGGLE
contraception *n syn* see BIRTH CONTROL
contract *n* a usually legally enforceable arrangement between two or more parties < a *contract* for a new roof >
syn agreement, bargain, bond, compact, convention, covenant, pact, transaction; *compare* AGREEMENT 2, TREATY
contract *vb* **1** to become affected by a disease or disorder < *contracted* a severe cold that later turned into pneumonia >
syn catch, come down (with), get, sicken (with *or* of), take
rel acquire, obtain; decline, fail, sink, weaken; afflict, derange, disorder, indispose, upset; bring on, cause, induce; succumb (to)
idiom be laid by the heels by, fall (a) victim to
2 *syn* see INCUR
3 to make or become smaller in bulk or volume < *contract* a muscle >

---

syn synonym(s)   *rel* related word(s)
ant antonym(s)   *con* contrasted word(s)
idiom idiomatic equivalent(s)
‖ use limited; if in doubt, see a dictionary

syn compress, concentrate, condense, constrict, shrink
rel decrease, diminish, dwindle, lessen, reduce
con dilate, distend, inflate, swell
ant expand

contracted *adj syn* see ENGAGED 2

contradict *vb syn* see DENY 4
rel dispute; belie, falsify, garble
con authenticate, substantiate, verify
ant corroborate; confirm

contradiction *n syn* see DENIAL 2

contradictory *n syn* see OPPOSITE

contradictory *adj syn* see OPPOSITE
rel negating, nullifying; adverse, antagonistic, counteractive
con agreeing, jibing, squaring, tallying
ant corroboratory; confirmatory

contradistinction *n syn* see ANTAGONISM 2

contraposition *n syn* see ANTAGONISM 2

contraption *n syn* see DEVICE 2

contrariant *n syn* see ANTIPATHETIC 1

contrariety *n syn* see ANTAGONISM 2

contrariwise *adv syn* see AGAIN 5
idiom on (*or* to) the contrary

contrary *n syn* see OPPOSITE

contrary *adj* 1 *syn* see OPPOSITE
2 *syn* see ANTIPATHETIC 1
3 obstinately self-willed in refusing to concur, conform, or submit < why be *contrary* about something that you cannot change >
syn balky, cross-grained, froward, ornery, perverse, restive, wayward, wrongheaded
rel headstrong, intractable, recalcitrant, refractory, unruly; contumacious, insubordinate, rebellious; dissentient, dissident, nonconforming, nonconformist, recusant; obstinate, stubborn
con amenable, biddable, docile, obedient, tractable; amiable, obliging; acquiescent, compliant; forbearing, long-suffering, tolerant
ant complaisant

contrary *adv syn* see AGAIN 5

contrast *vb syn* see COMPARE 2

contravene *vb* 1 *syn* see VIOLATE 1
rel encroach, intrude, overstep, trespass
2 *syn* see DENY 4
rel combat, fight, oppose, resist; abjure, disclaim, disown, exclude, reject, repudiate, spurn
con accept, agree, subscribe (to); admit, allow, own
ant uphold (*as a principle*); allege (*as a right or claim*)

contravention *n syn* see BREACH 1
rel crime, offense, sin, vice

contrawise *adv syn* see AGAIN 5

contretemps *n syn* see MISFORTUNE

contribute *vb* 1 to give in common with others < *contribute* to a fund for handicapped children >
syn chip in, come through, kick in, pitch in, subscribe; *compare* GIVE 1
idiom put something in the pot, sweeten the kitty
2 to have a share in something (as an act or effect) < careful planning *contributed* greatly to the success of the project >
syn conduce, redound, tend

rel aid, help, assist; add (to), augment, supplement; fortify, recruit, reinforce, strengthen
idiom do one's bit, have a hand in
con detract, minus, subtract, take away

contribution *n syn* see DONATION

contributory *adj syn* see AUXILIARY

contrite *adj syn* see REMORSEFUL

contriteness *n syn* see PENITENCE

contrition *n syn* see PENITENCE

contriturate *vb syn* see PULVERIZE 1

contrivance *n* 1 *syn* see DEVICE 2
2 *syn* see INVENTION

contrive *vb* 1 *syn* see PLOT
rel develop, elaborate, work out
2 to use ingenuity in making or doing or achieving an end < *contrived* a useful camp stove from a few bricks and a piece of screen >
syn concoct, cook (up), devise, dream up, formulate, frame, hatch (up), invent, make up, vamp (up)
rel plan, plot, project, scheme; fabricate, fashion, make, manufacture; handle, manipulate, move; rig

control *vb* 1 *syn* see COMPOSE 4
rel adjust, regulate; curb, master, quell, subdue
2 *syn* see GOVERN 3
rel regulate, supervise; discipline
idiom put through the mill (*or* a course of sprouts), take in hand

control *n syn* see POWER 1

controlled *adj syn* see CONSERVATIVE 2

controversial *adj syn* see CONTENTIOUS 2

controversy *n* 1 *syn* see ARGUMENT 2
2 *syn* see QUARREL

controvert *vb syn* see DISPROVE 1
rel challenge, oppugn, question

contumacious *adj syn* see INSUBORDINATE
rel contrary, froward, perverse; alienated, disaffected, estranged, irreconcilable
con acquiescent, compliant, resigned
ant obedient

contumacy *n syn* see DEFIANCE 2

contumelious *adj* 1 *syn* see ABUSIVE
2 *syn* see INSOLENT 2
ant obsequious

contumely *n* 1 *syn* see ABUSE
rel animadversion, aspersion, reflection, stricture
idiom hard (*or* bitter) words
2 *syn* see AFFRONT

contuse *vb syn* see BRUISE 1

contusion *n syn* see BRUISE

conundrum *n syn* see MYSTERY

convalesce *vb syn* see IMPROVE 3

convenance *n syn* see FORM 3

convene *vb* 1 to begin a session (as of a legislature or conference) < the council *convened* at 10 o'clock >
syn meet, open, sit
idiom hold a meeting (*or* session)
2 *syn* see SUMMON 2
rel convoke, muster
3 *syn* see CONVOKE

convenience *n* 1 *syn* see AMENITY 2
2 *syn* see TOILET

convenience *vb syn* see OBLIGE 2

convenient *adj* 1 *syn* see GOOD 2
2 situated within easy reach < left his glasses *convenient* to his book >

syn adjacent, close-at-hand, close-by, handy, near-at-hand, nearby

rel close, near, nigh; immediate, next

idiom at one's beck and call, at one's fingertips, in one's immediate neighborhood, under one's nose

ant inconvenient

convention *n* 1 *syn* see TREATY

2 *syn* see CONTRACT

rel accord, understanding

3 *syn* see FORM 3

rel canon, law, precept, rule; custom, practice

conventional *adj* 1 according with or based on generally accepted and well-established usage < took a very *conventional* view of his duty >

syn button-down, orthodox, square, straight; *compare* TRADITIONAL 1

rel moderate, sober, temperate; constrained, restrained; dependable, reliable, responsible; conscientious, fastidious, nice, punctilious, scrupulous; conservative, traditionalistic

ant unconventional

2 *syn* see TRADITIONAL 1

3 *syn* see CEREMONIAL

rel decent, decorous, proper, seemly; correct, precise, right

con lax, negligent, remiss, slack; artless, ingenuous, naive, natural, simple, unsophisticated

ant unconventional

converge *vb* to come to or trend toward a common point < the main streets *converge* on a central square >

syn concenter, concentrate, focus, meet

idiom come to a center, come (*or* run) together

conversant *adj* 1 *syn* see AWARE

ant ignorant

2 *syn* see FAMILIAR 3

rel sensible; up-to-date; apprehending, comprehending, perceptive, percipient

con unfamiliar; nescient

ant unconversant

conversation *n* 1 oral exchange of information or ideas < leaned against the fence in casual *conversation* >

syn chat, colloquy, confabulation, converse, dialogue, parley

rel discussion; discourse, speech, talk

2 an instance of conversational exchange < had a long *conversation* about family problems >

syn colloquy, confabulation, dialogue, talk; *compare* CHAT 2

rel debate, deliberation, discussion, ventilation; comment, observation, remark; cross talk, repartee

conversation piece *n* *syn* see CURIOSITY 2

converse *vb* to engage in conversation < they *conversed* quietly while waiting for their friend >

syn chat, chin, colloque, talk, visit, yarn; *compare* CHAT 2

converse (in) *vb* *syn* see SPEAK 3

---

syn synonym(s)   *rel* related word(s)

ant antonym(s)   *con* contrasted word(s)

idiom idiomatic equivalent(s)

‖ use limited; if in doubt, see a dictionary

---

converse *n* 1 *syn* see CONVERSATION 1

2 *syn* see COMMUNICATION 3

converse *adj* *syn* see OPPOSITE

converse *n* *syn* see OPPOSITE

conversely *adv* *syn* see AGAIN 5

conversion *n* 1 fundamental alteration in one's system of beliefs < Judaism does not encourage *conversion* of gentiles >

syn metanoia, rebirth

rel about-face, reversal, turning; reclamation, regeneration

idiom change of heart

2 change of one thing to another usually by substitution < *conversion* of locomotives from steam to diesel power >

syn alteration, changeover, shift, transformation

rel change, modification, qualification; metamorphosis, mutation, permutation, transmutation; innovation, novelty

convert *vb* 1 to induce (another or others) to accept the validity of something (as a belief, course of action, or point of view) < Chinese missionaries *converted* many Japanese to Buddhism >

syn bring, lead, move, persuade

rel redeem, reform, save; bend, bias, incline, sway; actuate, budge, impel; proselyte, proselytize

2 *syn* see TRANSFORM

rel fabricate, forge, make, manufacture; apply, employ, use, utilize

convey *vb* 1 *syn* see CARRY 1

2 *syn* see COMMUNICATE 1

rel project, put across

3 *syn* see TRANSFER 4

rel commit, consign, relegate

4 *syn* see CONDUCT 4

conveyance *n* 1 *syn* see TRANSPORTATION 1

2 *syn* see DEED 3

3 *syn* see VEHICLE 3

convict *n* a person serving time in prison after conviction as a criminal < mixing hardened *convicts* with juvenile offenders >

syn ‖con, jailbird, ‖lag, loser, prison bird

rel long-termer, longtimer; ‖stir bug; recidivist, repeater

conviction *n* 1 *syn* see CERTAINTY

con dubiety, dubiosity, uncertainty; disbelief, incredulity, unbelief

2 *syn* see OPINION

rel doctrine, dogma, tenet

convince *vb* 1 *syn* see ASSURE 2

2 *syn* see INDUCE 1

convincing *adj* 1 *syn* see AUTHENTIC 1

2 *syn* see VALID

convivial *adj* *syn* see SOCIAL 1

rel lively, vivacious; jocund, jolly, merry

con grave, sedate, serious, sober, solemn, somber; reserved, reticent, silent

ant taciturn; stolid

convoke *vb* to bring together by or as if by summons < the ruler *convoked* his council >

syn assemble, call, convene, summon; *compare* SUMMON 2

rel collect, congregate, gather; ask, bid, invite, request; meet, sit

con adjourn, close, dissolve, prorogue, recess, suspend; disperse, scatter

convoluted *adj* *syn* see WINDING

convoy *vb syn* see ACCOMPANY
  rel defend, guard, protect, safeguard,
shield
convulse *vb syn* see SHAKE 4
convulsion *n syn* see COMMOTION 1
  rel cataclysm, disaster; quaking, rocking,
shaking, tottering, trembling
cook *vb* 1 to make ready or fit for eating
by the use of heat < liked everything well=
cooked >
  syn do
  2 *syn* see BURN 3
cook (up) *vb syn* see CONTRIVE 2
cookshop *n syn* see EATING HOUSE
cool *adj* 1 *syn* see COLD 1
  ant warm
  2 freed or giving the impression of freedom from all agitation or excitement
< they looked *cool* and very formidable >
  syn collected, composed, disimpassioned,
imperturbable, nonchalant, unflappable,
unruffled; *compare* HAPPY-GO-LUCKY
  rel calm, placid, serene, tranquil; aloof,
detached, indifferent; impassive, phlegmatic, stolid; assured, confident, self-
possessed
  con fervent, fervid, impassioned, passionate, perfervid; discomposed, disturbed,
flurried, flustered, perturbed, upset
  ant ardent; agitated
  3 *syn* see UNSOCIABLE
  ‖4 *syn* see MARVELOUS 2
cool *vb* 1 *syn* see COMPOSE 4
  2 *syn* see MURDER 1
cooler *n syn* see JAIL
coolness *n syn* see EQUANIMITY
‖**coon** *vb syn* see STEAL 1
coon's age *n syn* see AGE 2
‖**coony** *adj syn* see CLEVER 4
coop *n syn* see JAIL
coop *vb syn* see ENCLOSE 1
  rel bar, block, hinder, impede, obstruct
cooperate *vb syn* see UNITE 2
  rel agree, coincide
  con annul, negate, nullify; negative, neutralize
  ant counteract
cooperative *adj* involving joint action in
producing a result < the need of *cooperative* efforts to effect lasting social change >
  syn coacting, coactive, coefficient, conjoint, synergetic, synergic
  rel collaborative, concerted; noncompeti-
tive, uncompetitive
  con competitive, emulous, rivaling, vying;
antagonistic, conflicting, oppugnant
  ant counteractive
coordinate *vb syn* see HARMONIZE 3
coordinate *n* 1 *syn* see OPPOSITE NUM-
BER
  2 *syn* see MATE 5
‖**cop** *vb syn* see STEAL 1
cop *n syn* see POLICEMAN
copartner *n syn* see PARTNER
copious *adj syn* see PLENTIFUL
  rel exuberant, lush, luxuriant
  con exiguous, scant, scanty, scrimpy,
spare, sparse; slender, slight, slim, tenuous, thin
  ant meager
‖**cop out** *vb syn* see DIE 1
‖**copper** *n syn* see POLICEMAN
copy *n* 1 *syn* see IMITATION

2 *syn* see REPRODUCTION
  rel counterpart, parallel; impress, impression, imprint, print; effigy, image, likeness
  ant original
copy *vb* to make a copy of < had her more
valuable jewelry *copied* >
  syn duplicate, imitate, reduplicate, replicate, reproduce
  rel ditto, repeat; counterfeit, fake, sham,
simulate; ape, burlesque, mock, parody,
take off, travesty
  ant originate
coquet *vb syn* see TRIFLE 1
coquette *n syn* see FLIRT
coquettish *adj syn* see COY 2
cordial *adj syn* see GRACIOUS 1
  rel responsive, sympathetic, tender, warm,
warmhearted; heartfelt, hearty, sincere,
wholehearted
  con cold, cool, frigid, frosty; aloof, detached, disinterested, indifferent; reserved,
silent, taciturn
cordiality *n syn* see AMENITY 1
  rel responsiveness, sympathy, understanding, warmth; mutuality, reciprocity; approbation, approval, favor
  con cross-purposes, difference, disagreement, misunderstanding, odds, variance;
disapprobation, disapproval, disfavor
core *n* 1 *syn* see CENTER 1
  2 *syn* see BODY 3
  3 *syn* see SUBSTANCE 2
  rel consequence, import, importance,
significance
  4 *syn* see CENTER 3
  rel base, basis, foundation; beginning,
commencement, origin, start
‖**corker** *n syn* ‖DILLY, crackerjack, ‖daisy,
dandy, humdinger, jim-dandy, knockout,
‖lalapalooza, ‖lulu, nifty
corkscrew *vb syn* see WIND 2
corner *n* 1 *syn* see PREDICAMENT
  2 *syn* see MONOPOLY
corner *vb* to get into one's control or a
position from which escape is difficult
< *cornered* him at a party and tried to
borrow a hundred dollars >
  syn bottle (up), collar, tree
  rel bother, disturb, put out, trouble; capture, catch, nab, seize, trap
  idiom chase up a tree, drive (*or* run) into
a corner, get (*or* have) on the ropes
cornerwise *adv syn* see DIAGONALLY
corny *adj syn* see TRITE
corollary *n syn* see EFFECT 1
coronal *n syn* see WREATH
coronet *n syn* see WREATH
corporal *adj syn* see BODILY
corporation *n syn* see POTBELLY
corporeal *adj* 1 *syn* see BODILY
  2 *syn* see MATERIAL 1
corps *n syn* see COMPANY 4
corpse *n* a dead body especially of a human being < concealed the *corpse* under
some rubbish >
  syn body, cadaver, carcass, ‖cold meat,
‖deader, mort, remains, stiff
  rel carrion; bones
corpselike *adj* 1 *syn* see DEATHLY 1
  2 *syn* see GHASTLY 1
corpsy *adj syn* see DEATHLY 1
corpulence *n syn* see OBESITY
corpulent *adj syn* see FAT 2

corpus *n* **1** *syn* see BODY 3
  2 *syn* see OEUVRE
corrade *vb syn* see ABRADE 1
corral *vb syn* see ENCLOSE 1
correct *vb* **1** to set right something that is
  wrong < *correct* a misstatement >
  syn amend, emend, mend, rectify, right
  rel ameliorate, better, improve; redress,
  remedy, revise; make over, reform; adjust,
  fix, regulate
  con damage, harm, hurt, impair, injure,
  mar, spoil
  2 *syn* see PUNISH 1
  con baby, coddle, cosset, humor, indulge,
  pamper, spoil
correct *adj* **1** *syn* see DECOROUS 1
  rel careful, meticulous, punctilious, scrupulous
  2 conforming to or agreeing with fact
  < the *correct* solution to the problem >
  syn accurate, exact, nice, precise, proper,
  right, rigorous
  rel faithful, true, undistorted, veracious,
  veridical; faultless, flawless, impeccable,
  perfect
  con fallacious, false, wrong; defective,
  faulty, flawed, imperfect
  ant incorrect
correction *n syn* see PUNISHMENT
correctitude *n syn* see ORDER 7
corrective *n syn* see REMEDY 2
correctly *adv syn* see WELL 1
correctness *n* **1** *syn* see ORDER 7
  2 *syn* see PRECISION
correlate *vb* **1** *syn* see COUNTERPART 1
  2 *syn* see PARALLEL
correspond *vb syn* see AGREE 4
correspond (to) *vb syn* see AMOUNT 2
correspondence *n syn* see CONSISTENCY
  ant divergence
correspondent *n syn* see PARALLEL
corresponding *adj syn* see LIKE
correspondingly *adv syn* see ALSO 1
corridor *n syn* see PASSAGE 4
corrival *n syn* see RIVAL
corroborate *vb syn* see CONFIRM 2
  con invalidate, negate, nullify
  ant contradict
corroborative *adj* serving or tending to
  corroborate < *corroborative* evidence >
  syn adminicular, collateral, confirmative,
  confirmatory, corroboratory, verificatory
  rel ancillary, auxiliary, supplementary,
  supportive; assisting, helping
  con confutative, refutative, refutatory;
  contradictory, negatory
corroboratory *adj   syn*   see   COR-
  ROBORATIVE
corrode *vb syn* see EAT 3
corrosive *adj syn* see SARCASTIC
corrosiveness *n syn* see SARCASM
corrugation *n syn* see WRINKLE
corrupt *vb* **1** *syn* see DEBASE 1
  rel abase, degrade; ruin, wreck
  con amend, correct, reform
  2 *syn* see DECAY
  rel befoul, defile, foul; smirch, tarnish
corrupt *adj* **1** *syn* see VICIOUS 2

  rel crooked, devious, oblique; baneful,
  deleterious, detrimental, noxious, pernicious; abased, degraded, low
  2 seeking sordid advantage with little
  regard to moral or legal bars < a *corrupt*
  politician >
  syn mercenary, praetorian, unethical,
  unprincipled, unscrupulous, venal; *compare* CROOKED 2, VENAL 1
  rel undependable, unreliable, untrustworthy; faithless, inconstant, unfaithful;
  double-dealing, perfidious, treacherous,
  two-faced; bribable, corruptible; black-
  guardly, knavish, reprobate
  con ethical, principled, scrupulous, upright; dependable, reliable, trustworthy,
  trusty
  3 *syn* see CROOKED 2
corrupted *adj syn* see DEBASED
corruptible *adj syn* see VENAL 1
corruption *n* **1** *syn* see VICE 1
  2 *syn* see BARBARISM
corsair *n syn* see PIRATE
coruscate *vb syn* see FLASH 1
coruscation *n syn* see FLASH 1
corybantic *adj syn* see FURIOUS 2
coryphée *n syn* see DANCER
cosmic *adj syn* see UNIVERSAL 2
cosmopolitan *adj* **1** exhibiting or characterized by a sophistication and savoir faire
  arising from cultured urban life and wide
  travel < had a thoroughly *cosmopolitan*
  outlook on life >
  syn metropolitan, urbane; *compare* SO-
  PHISTICATED 2
  rel civilized, polished, smooth; sophisticated, worldly-wise; cultivated, cultured
  con boorish, cloddish, rude, rustic; insular, parochial, provincial
  2 *syn* see UNIVERSAL 2
cosmos (*or* **kosmos**) *n syn* see UNIVERSE
cosset *vb* **1** *syn* see CARESS
  2 *syn* see BABY
cost *n* **1** *syn* see PRICE 1
  2 *syn* see EXPENSE 1
  3 *syn* see EXPENSE 2
costive *adj* **1** *syn* see CONSTIPATED
  2 *syn* see STINGY
costless *adj syn* see FREE 5
costly *adj* **1** commanding or being a large
  price < the scarcer an item becomes the
  more *costly* it is >
  syn dear, expensive, high; *compare* PRE-
  CIOUS 1
  rel excessive, exorbitant, extravagant,
  inordinate, steep, stiff; fancy, premium,
  top
  con inexpensive, low, low-priced, reasonable
  ant cheap
  2 *syn* see PRECIOUS 1
costume *n* style of clothing and adornment
  < her *costume* was always suitable to the
  occasion >
  syn dress, getup, guise, outfit, rig, setout,
  turnout
  rel fashion, mode, style
cot *n syn* see HUT
||**cotch** *vb* **1** *syn* see SEIZE 2
  2 *syn* see CATCH 1
  3 *syn* see CATCH 7
coterie *n syn* see CLIQUE
cottage *n syn* see HUT

---

syn synonym(s)   *rel* related word(s)
ant antonym(s)   *con* contrasted word(s)
idiom idiomatic equivalent(s)
|| use limited; if in doubt, see a dictionary

cotton vb 1 syn see BABY
2 syn see FAWN

cotton (to or on to) vb syn see APPREHEND 1

cottony adj syn see SOFT 3

couch vb 1 syn see WORD
2 syn see LOWER 3

couch n syn see LAIR 1

couleur de rose adj syn see HOPEFUL 2

couloir n syn see PASSAGE 4

counsel n syn see ADVICE 1

counsel vb to give advice to or about < counseled him to wait for a more propitious occasion>
syn advise, recommend
rel admonish, reprehend, warn; direct, order, prescribe; charge, enjoin, prompt, urge; advocate, suggest

count vb 1 to ascertain the total of units in a collection by noting one after another < counted the sheep in the pasture>
syn enumerate, number, numerate, tale, tally, tell
rel add, cast, figure, foot, sum, tot, total; calculate, compute, estimate, reckon; tell off
2 syn see MATTER
3 syn see WEIGH 3

count (on) vb syn see RELY (on or upon)

count (on or upon) vb syn see EXPECT 1

countenance n 1 syn see LOOK 2
idiom (the) cut of one's jib
2 syn see FACE 1

countenance vb 1 syn see ENCOURAGE 2
rel applaud, commend; back, champion, support, uphold
con deride, ridicule; criticize, reprehend, reprobate; reproach, reprove
ant discountenance
2 syn see APPROVE 1

counter vb syn see OPPOSE 1

counter n syn see OPPOSITE

counter adj syn see OPPOSITE
rel hostile, inimical; adverse, antagonistic, anti, oppugnant; hindering, impeding, obstructive

counteract vb syn see NEUTRALIZE
rel correct, fix, rectify, right
con cooperate, coordinate, synergize; back, reinforce, support

counteractant n syn see REMEDY 2

counteractive n syn see REMEDY 2

counteragent n syn see REMEDY 2

counterbalance vb syn see COMPENSATE 1
rel amend, correct, rectify
con overbalance, unbalance

counterblow n syn see RETALIATION

countercheck vb syn see NEUTRALIZE

counterfactual adj syn see FALSE 1

counterfeit vb syn see ASSUME 4
rel ape, copy, imitate, mimic

counterfeit adj being an imitation intended to mislead or deceive < counterfeit money> < counterfeit sympathy>
syn bogus, brummagem, fake, false, phony, pinchbeck, pseudo, sham, snide, spurious; compare SPURIOUS 3
rel feigned, pretended, simulated; deceptive, delusive, delusory, misleading; fraudulent
con authentic, veritable; actual, real, true; unquestionable, valid

ant bona fide, genuine

counterfeit n syn see IMPOSTURE
rel copy, facsimile, reproduction; dummy, simulacrum

countermeasure n syn see REMEDY 2

counterpane n syn see BEDSPREAD

counterpart n 1 something that completes or complements < export controls as a counterpart of domestic distribution controls>
syn complement, correlate, pendant; compare PARALLEL
rel analogue, correlate, correspondent; equal, equivalent, like, match
con counterpoint, opposite
2 syn see PARALLEL
3 syn see EQUAL
4 syn see OPPOSITE NUMBER

counterpoise n syn see BALANCE 1

counterpoise vb syn see COMPENSATE 1
rel ballast, poise, stabilize, steady, trim
con capsize, overturn, upset

counterpole n syn see OPPOSITE

countersign n syn see PASSWORD 1

counterstep n syn see REMEDY 2

countertype n syn see PARALLEL

countervail vb syn see COMPENSATE 1
rel amend, correct, rectify; foil, frustrate, thwart; overcome, surmount

countless adj syn see INNUMERABLE

count out vb syn see EXCLUDE

countrified adj syn see RURAL

country n the nation-state to which one belongs or from which one originated < returned to his own country after years of exile>
syn fatherland, home, homeland, land, mother country, motherland, soil

country adj syn see RURAL

country jake n syn see RUSTIC

countryman n syn see RUSTIC

couple vb 1 syn see JOIN 1
2 syn see HITCH 2
rel hook up, ‖inspan

couple n two individuals of the same or a similar kind that occur, function, or are considered together < a couple of ideas for improving the book> < the happiest couple I know>
syn brace, doublet, duo, dyad, pair, twosome
rel span, team, yoke

coupling n syn see JOINT 1

courage n a quality of mind or temperament that enables one to stand fast in the face of opposition, hardship, or danger < had the kind of courage that could appreciate a danger yet steadfastly face it>
syn cojones, dauntlessness, guts, heart, mettle, ‖moxie, pluck, resolution, spirit, spunk; compare FORTITUDE
rel audacity, boldness, bravery, doughtiness, fearlessness, intrepidity; gallantry, heroism, valor; backbone, fortitude, grit, sand; assurance, determination, firmness, persistence, tenacity
con chickenheartedness, faintheartedness, unmanliness, yellowness; baseness, cravenness, poltroonery, pusillanimity; timidity, timorousness
ant cowardice

courageous adj syn see BRAVE 1

rel fiery, high-spirited; strong, tenacious
con afraid, apprehensive, fearful
ant pusillanimous

courier *n syn* see MESSENGER

course *n* 1 *syn* see WAY 2
rel circuit, orbit, range, scope
2 *syn* see CHANNEL 1
3 way of acting or proceeding <hard to decide on the best *course* to follow>
syn line, policy, polity, procedure, program
rel design, pattern, plan, platform, scheme; manner, system, way
idiom course of action
4 *syn* see PROGRESS 2
5 *syn* see SUCCESSION 2

course *vb* to proceed with great celerity (as in pursuing or competing) <the fox *coursed* after the hare>
syn career, chase, race, rush, speed, tear; *compare* RUSH 1
rel hasten, hurry, hustle; dart, dash, scamper, scoot, scurry; run, sprint
idiom step on the gas, stir one's stumps

courser *n* a strong vigorous horse formerly used in mounted combat <heroes mounted on great fiery *coursers*>
syn charger, war-horse

court *n* 1 an open space wholly or partly enclosed (as by buildings or walls) <the window looked on the *court*>
syn ‖close, courtyard, curtilage, enclosure, quad, quadrangle, yard
2 a place or the persons assembled for the administration of justice <the *court* was called to order>
syn bar, lawcourt, tribunal
3 *syn* see JUDGE 1

court *vb syn* see ADDRESS 8
rel allure, attract, captivate, charm

courteous *adj syn* see CIVIL 2
rel attentive, considerate, thoughtful
con blunt, brusque, curt, gruff; insolent, overbearing, supercilious
ant discourteous

courtesan *n syn* see HARLOT 1

courtesy *n* 1 courteous behavior or a courteous act <noted for her *courtesy* and graciousness> <such little *courtesies* take little time but often brighten lonely lives>
syn amenity, attention, gallantry
rel affability, cordiality, geniality, graciousness; comity, complaisance; chivalry, civility, courteousness, courtliness; attentiveness, considerateness, consideration, thoughtfulness
con boorishness, churlishness; impoliteness, incivility, rudeness, ungraciousness
ant discourtesy
2 *syn* see FAVOR 4

courtly *adj* marked by elaborate and often ceremonious courtesy <this was indeed a *courtly* gentleman of the old school>
syn gallant, gracious, preux, stately; *compare* CIVIL 2
rel august, dignified, imposing, lofty; prim, starchy, stiff, stilted, studied; ceremonious, conventional, formal; civilized

con discourteous, ill-mannered, impolite, rude, uncivil, ungracious; boorish, coarse, gross, loutish, uncouth, vulgar
ant churlish

courtyard *n syn* see COURT 1

cousinage *n syn* see KIN 2

cousinhood *n syn* see KIN 2

cove *n syn* see INLET

covenant *n syn* see CONTRACT

covenant *vb syn* see VOW
rel agree, concur

cover *vb* 1 *syn* see DEFEND 1
2 *syn* see HIDE
3 to spread over or put something over <a smile *covered* her face> <*cover* the garden with manure>
syn blanket, cap, crown, overcast, overlay, overspread
rel conceal, hide, screen; defend, protect, shield; enclose, enfold, envelop, shroud, wrap; overspread, superimpose, superpose
con display, exhibit, expose
ant bare, uncover
4 *syn* see TRAVEL 2
5 *syn* see SET 11

cover *n* 1 *syn* see SHELTER 1
rel concealment, hiding, screen; safety, security
ant exposure
2 *syn* see MASK 2

coverlet *n syn* see BEDSPREAD

‖**coverlid** *n syn* see BEDSPREAD

covert *adj* 1 *syn* see SECRET 1
rel camouflaged, cloaked, disguised, dissembled, masked
con candid, frank, open
ant overt
2 *syn* see ULTERIOR
con direct, forthright; honest, square, straight

covert *n syn* see SHELTER 1

covertly *adv syn* see SECRETLY

covet *vb syn* see DESIRE 1
con abjure, forswear
ant renounce

covetous *adj* having or marked by an urgent and often unscrupulous desire for possessions <the *covetous* eye of an avid collector>
syn acquisitive, desirous, grabby, grasping, greedy, itchy, prehensile
rel esurient, gluttonous, rapacious, ravenous, voracious; hoggish, lickerish, piggish, swinish; avid, eager, keen; envious, jealous; grudging, selfish
con generous, liberal, munificent; ungrudging, unselfish; abstemious, abstinent, ascetic, austere; moderate, restrained, temperate

covey *n syn* see GROUP 1

covin *n syn* see PLOT 2

cow *vb syn* see INTIMIDATE
rel appall, daunt, dismay; abash, discomfit, disconcert, embarrass, faze, rattle
con cower, cringe, fawn, toady, truckle

coward *n* one who shows or yields to ignoble fear <a treacherous *coward* who betrayed his friends to save his own skin>
syn chicken, craven, dastard, funk, funker, poltroon, quitter, yellowbelly
rel baby, fraidycat, invertebrate, jellyfish, milksop, scaredy-cat; caitiff, recreant
con gallant, hero, palladin, stalwart; ideal, model, pattern, standard

---

syn synonym(s)   *rel* related word(s)
ant antonym(s)   *con* contrasted word(s)
idiom idiomatic equivalent(s)
‖ use limited; if in doubt, see a dictionary

coward *adj syn* see COWARDLY

cowardly *adj* marked by or arising from a base lack of courage < a *cowardly* desertion >
syn ‖chicken, coward, cowhearted, craven, gutless, lily-livered, milk-livered, poltroon, poltroonish, poor-spirited, pusillanimous, spunkless, unmanly, white-livered, yellow
rel afraid, chickenhearted, fainthearted, fearful, timid, timorous; funky, panicky; caitiff, dastardly, recreant, vile, worthless
con courageous, fearless, intrepid, valiant; daring, reckless, temerarious
ant brave

cower *vb syn* see FAWN
rel blench, flinch, quail, recoil, shrink, wince
con browbeat, bulldoze, bully, cow, intimidate; bristle, strut, swagger

cowering *adj syn* see FAWNING

cowhearted *adj syn* see COWARDLY

coxcomb *n syn* see FOP

coy *adj* 1 *syn* see SHY 1
rel decent, decorous, nice, proper, seemly
con brash, brazen, impudent
2 marked by a light playful artlessness < glanced up with a *coy* twinkle in her eye >
syn arch, coquettish, roguish
rel capricious, kittenish, lively, mischievous, playful, skittish
con serious, sober, thoughtful

cozen *vb* 1 *syn* see CHEAT
2 *syn* see DECEIVE

cozy *adj* 1 *syn* see COMFORTABLE 2
rel safe, secure
2 *syn* see INTIMATE 4

crab *vb syn* see GRIPE
idiom fret and fume

crab *n syn* see GROUCH

crabbed *adj syn* see SULLEN
rel blunt, brusque, crusty, gruff; choleric, cranky, splenetic, testy; huffy, irascible, irritable, snappish
con amiable, complaisant, good-natured, obliging; benign, benignant, kind, kindly; agreeable, pleasing; affable, genial, gracious

crabber *n syn* see GROUCH

crabby *adj syn* see SULLEN

crabwise *adv syn* see SIDEWAYS 1

crack *vb syn* see DECODE
rel puzzle out

crack *n* 1 *syn* see BANG 2
rel splintering, splitting; percussion
2 *syn* see JOKE 1
rel dig, fling, potshot
idiom flash of wit
3 a usually narrow opening, break, or discontinuity made by splitting and rupture < a *crack* in the ice >
syn chink, cleft, fissure, rift, rima, rimation, rime, split
rel rent; discontinuity, interstice, interval; cranny, niche; crevasse, crevice
4 *syn* see INSTANT 1
idiom flash of lightning
5 *syn* see BLOW 1
6 *syn* see FLING 1

crack *adj syn* see PROFICIENT
rel excellent, superior

crackbrain *n syn* see CRACKPOT
idiom cracked wit

crackbrained *adj syn* see INSANE 1

crackdown *n syn* see REPRESSION 2
rel quashing
idiom lowering the boom

cracked *adj syn* see INSANE 1
idiom ‖off in the upper story

crackerjack *n* *syn* ‖DILLY, ‖corker, ‖daisy, dandy, humdinger, jim-dandy, knockout, ‖lalapalooza, ‖lulu, nifty

crackerjack *adj syn* see PROFICIENT

‖crackers *adj syn* see INSANE 1

cracking *adj syn* see MONSTROUS 1

crackpot *n* one given to extremely eccentric or lunatic ideas or actions < a *crackpot* who wrote threatening letters to public figures >
syn crackbrain, crank, cuckoo, ding-a-ling, harebrain, kook, lunatic, nut, screwball
rel case, character, ‖dingbat, eccentric, oddball, oddity, ‖wack; loon, loony, madman, maniac

crack-up *n* 1 *syn* see NERVOUS BREAKDOWN
2 *syn* see CRASH 3
3 *syn* see COLLAPSE 2
rel decline, deterioration

‖cracky *adj syn* see INSANE 1

cradlesong *n syn* see LULLABY

craft *n* 1 *syn* see ART 1
2 *syn* see TRADE 1
rel job
3 *syn* see CUNNING 2

craftiness *n syn* see CUNNING 2

crafty *adj syn* see SLY 2
rel adroit, clever, tidy; acute, keen, sharp; deceitful, fawning, ‖sleekit, ‖sleeky

cragged *adj syn* see ROUGH 1

craggy *adj syn* see ROUGH 1

cram *vb* 1 to fill (a limited space) forcibly with more than is practicable or fitting < *crammed* the suitcase chock-full and had to sit on it to close it >
syn jam, jam-pack, ‖pang, ram, stuff, tamp; *compare* LOAD 3, PRESS 7
rel pack, stive; fill, heap; chock, choke; press, shove, thrust; drive, force; squeeze, wedge
2 *syn* see PRESS 7
3 *syn* see GULP
rel overeat
idiom pack it in
4 to study intensively or under pressure < had to *cram* all night before the exam >
syn bone (up), ‖mug (up)
rel study; review
idiom burn the midnight oil

cram-full *adj syn* see FULL 1

crammed *adj syn* see FULL 1
idiom crammed full, crammed to the bursting point, fit (*or* ready) to burst
ant emptied

cramp *n* 1 *syn* see RESTRICTION 1
rel shackle
2 *syn* see RESTRICTION 2
rel constipation, stultification

cramp *adj syn* see CRAMPED

cramped *adj* having insufficient size or capacity < a *cramped* cubbyhole of an office >
syn confined, cramp, incommodious, squeezy, ‖tucked up
rel close, narrow, tight, two-by-four; little, minute, small, tiny

con commodious, unconfined
ant spacious
crank *n* 1 *syn* see CAPRICE
2 *syn* see CRACKPOT
rel freak
3 *syn* see GROUCH
cranky *adj* 1 *syn* see INSANE 1
2 *syn* see CANTANKEROUS
rel contrary, difficult, froward, perverse
3 *syn* see IRASCIBLE
rel bad-humored, ill-humored; disagreeable; ugly
idiom out of sorts
cranny *n* *syn* see NOOK
‖**crap** *n* *syn* see NONSENSE 2
‖**crap out** *vb* *syn* see FAINT
‖**crappy** *adj* *syn* see BAD 1
crash *vb* *syn* see FAIL 5
ant skyrocket
crash *n* 1 *syn* see BANG 2
2 *syn* see IMPACT
3 a wrecking or smashing especially of a vehicle < an air *crash* >
syn crack-up, pileup, ‖prang, smash, smashup, ‖stramash, wreck
rel accident; collision
4 *syn* see COLLAPSE 2
crashing *adj* *syn* see UTTER
crass *adj* *syn* see COARSE 3
rel churlish, loutish
ant refined
crate *n* *syn* see JALOPY
crave *vb* 1 *syn* see BEG
2 *syn* see DESIRE 1
con contemn, despise, disdain, scorn
ant spurn
3 *syn* see LONG
idiom have a craving for
4 *syn* see DEMAND 2
craven *adj* *syn* see COWARDLY
craven *n* *syn* see COWARD
craving *n* *syn* see DESIRE 1
crawfish (out) *vb* *syn* see BACK DOWN
crawl *vb* 1 *syn* see CREEP 1
rel grovel; worm
2 *syn* see TEEM
‖3 *syn* see LAMBASTE 3
craze *vb* *syn* see MADDEN 1
craze *n* *syn* see FASHION 3
rel enthusiasm, fever
crazed *adj* *syn* see INSANE 1
craziness *n* *syn* see FOOLISHNESS
crazy *adj* 1 *syn* see INSANE 1
rel doting, gaga, moonstruck; beeheaded, silly; erratic, possessed
idiom as crazy as a loon, having a screw loose, having bats in one's belfry, not having all one's marbles (*or* buttons)
ant sane
2 *syn* see FOOLISH 2
rel goofy, senseless
idiom beyond the realm of reason, out of all reason
con practical, reasonable, reasoned, sensible
ant sane
‖**crazy** *adv* *syn* see VERY 1
crazy house *n* *syn* see ASYLUM 3

cream *n* 1 *syn* see OINTMENT
2 *syn* see BEST
idiom (the) top cream
‖**cream** *vb* *syn* see WHIP 2
crease *n* *syn* see WRINKLE
create *vb* 1 *syn* see GENERATE 1
idiom call into being
2 *syn* see FOUND 2
3 *syn* see COMPOSE 2
rel conceive, formulate; imagine
creation *n* *syn* see UNIVERSE
creative *adj* *syn* see INVENTIVE
rel causal, institutive, occasional; Promethean
ant uncreative
creator *n* *syn* see FATHER 2
rel brain(s), brainpower, mastermind
creature *n* 1 *syn* see BEAST
2 *syn* see HUMAN
3 *syn* see SYCOPHANT
credence *n* *syn* see BELIEF 1
rel acceptance, accepting, admission, admitting; confidence, reliance, trust
con skepticism; distrust, mistrust; disbelief, incredulity, unbelief
credentials *n pl* something presented or held by one as proof that he is what or who he claims to be < her academic *credentials* were excellent >
syn character, recommendation, reference, testimonial
rel document(s), documentation, paper(s), voucher; accreditation, certification, endorsement, sanction
credible *adj* 1 *syn* see BELIEVABLE
rel satisfying, satisfactory; solid, sound, straight, valid
idiom to be believed
con unsatisfactory; preposterous, ridiculous
ant incredible
2 *syn* see AUTHENTIC 1
rel likely, probable; rational, reasonable; conclusive, determinative
ant incredible
credit *n* 1 *syn* see BELIEF 1
rel confidence, reliance, trust
2 *syn* see INFLUENCE 1
rel fame, renown, reputation, repute
con disrepute, ignominy, obloquy, opprobrium
ant discredit
3 one that enhances another < he is a *credit* to his family >
syn asset
rel honor
4 favorable notice or attention resulting from an action or achievement < took all the *credit* for the idea >
syn acknowledgment, recognition
rel attention, notice; distinction, fame, honor; glory, kudos
credit *vb* 1 *syn* see FEEL 3
con disbelieve, pooh-pooh
ant discredit
2 *syn* see ASCRIBE
creditable *adj* 1 *syn* see BELIEVABLE
ant discreditable
2 *syn* see RESPECTABLE 1
rel satisfactory; suitable
ant discreditable
credo *n* *syn* see IDEOLOGY

---

syn synonym(s)   *rel* related word(s)
ant antonym(s)   *con* contrasted word(s)
idiom idiomatic equivalent(s)
‖ use limited; if in doubt, see a dictionary

credulous *adj* ready or inclined to believe especially on slight or insufficient evidence < deceiving the *credulous* young girls >
syn unsuspecting, unsuspicious, unwary
rel believing; accepting, unquestioning; trustful, trusting; green, inexperienced; naive, simple, unsophisticated; dupable, gullible
con mistrustful, suspecting, suspicious; careful, wary; doubtful, doubting, questioning
ant incredulous, skeptical

creed *n* 1 *syn* see RELIGION 1
2 *syn* see RELIGION 2
3 *syn* see IDEOLOGY

creek *n* ‖1 *syn* see INLET
rel ria
2 a natural stream of water normally smaller than and often tributary to a river < went wading in the *creek* >
syn ‖branch, brook, ‖burn, ‖crick, gill, race, ‖rindle, ‖rithe, rivulet, ‖run, runnel, stream
rel ‖beck, brooklet, ‖rigolet, rill, rillet, runlet, streamlet; freshet; ditch, watercourse; wadi

creep *vb* 1 to move along a surface in a prone or crouching position < a cat *creeping* through the grass >
syn crawl, slide, snake
rel glide, slither; sneak, steal, tiptoe; edge, inch; sniggle, wriggle
2 *syn* see STEAL 3
3 *syn* see SNEAK

crème de la crème *n* *syn* see ARISTOCRACY

crepehanger *n* *syn* see PESSIMIST

crescendo *n* *syn* see APEX 2

crest *n* 1 *syn* see TOP 1
rel cap
2 *syn* see RIDGE 1
3 *syn* see APEX 2

crest *vb* *syn* see SURMOUNT 3

crestfallen *adj* *syn* see DOWNCAST
idiom ‖in a funk
ant elated

cretin *n* *syn* see FOOL 4
rel zombie

crew *n* *syn* see GROUP 1
rel aggregation, collection, congregation; gang, retinue, set

crib *n* 1 *syn* see BROTHEL
2 *syn* see PONY
rel plagiarism

‖**crib** *vb* *syn* see GRIPE

‖**crick** *n* *syn* see CREEK 2

crime *n* 1 a serious breach of the public law < armed robbery is a *crime* >
syn misdeed, offense
rel criminality, illegality, lawlessness; delict, delictum; breach, break, infringement, transgression, violation; wrong, wrongdoing; felony
2 *syn* see EVIL 3

crimeless *adj* *syn* see INNOCENT 2

criminal *adj* *syn* see UNLAWFUL

criminal *n* one who has committed a usually serious offense < car thieves and other *criminals* >
syn felon, lawbreaker, malefactor, offender
rel scofflaw; transgressor, trespasser, wrongdoer; crook, ‖twicer; gangster, hood,

mobster, racketeer, thug; fugitive, outlaw; convict, jailbird

criminate *vb* *syn* see ACCUSE
ant exonerate

crimp *vb* 1 *syn* see CRUMPLE 1
2 *syn* see RESTRAIN 1

crimp *n* *syn* see OBSTACLE

crimple *vb* *syn* see CRUMPLE 1

crimson *vb* *syn* see BLUSH
ant blanch

cringe *vb* *syn* see FAWN
rel blench, flinch, quail, recoil, wince; ‖croodle, crouch, shrink
idiom bow and scrape, eat dirt

cringing *adj* *syn* see FAWNING
rel obeisant, prostrate
idiom bowing and scraping, eating dirt, eating humble pie, on one's hands and knees

crinkle *vb* *syn* see CRUMPLE 1

crinkle *n* *syn* see WRINKLE
rel crimp

cripple *vb* 1 *syn* see MAIM
rel lame
2 *syn* see PARALYZE 1
3 *syn* see WEAKEN 1

crisis *n* *syn* see JUNCTURE 2

crisp *adj* 1 *syn* see SHORT 6
con flabby, flaccid, limp
2 *syn* see INCISIVE
rel piquing, provoking, stimulating

crisscross *vb* *syn* see INTERSECT

criterion *n* *syn* see STANDARD 3
rel adjudgment, judgment

critic *n* one given to harsh or captious judgment < chronic *critics* of the administration >
syn aristarch, carper, caviler, criticizer, faultfinder, knocker, momus, smellfungus, Zoilus
rel Monday morning quarterback; nitpicker, quibbler; belittler, disparager; complainer; censurer; muckraker, mudslinger
con backer, supporter; partisan; advocate, champion, protagonist

critic *adj* *syn* see CRITICAL 1

critical *adj* 1 exhibiting the spirit of one who looks for and points out faults and defects < constant *critical* comments about her attire >
syn captious, carping, caviling, cavillous, censorious, critic, faultfinding, hypercritical, overcritical
rel discerning, discriminating, penetrating; finicky, fussy, particular; belittling, demeaning, disparaging, humbling, lowering
con cursory, shallow, superficial; encouraging, flattering, praising
ant uncritical
2 *syn* see ACUTE 6
rel conclusive, decisive, determinative; consequential, important, momentous, significant, weighty

criticism *n* a discourse that evaluates or analyzes something (as a work of art or literature) < read every *criticism* of the new play >
syn comment, critique, notice, review, reviewal
rel analysis, examination, study; commentary, observation; opinion; appraisal, assessment, estimate, rating

criticize *vb* to make adverse comments about (someone or something) openly,

often publicly, and with varying severity
< *criticized* his opponent's liberal views>
syn blame, censure, condemn, cut up,
denounce, denunciate, knock, pan, rap,
reprehend, reprobate, skin; *compare* LAM-
BASTE 3, REPROVE, SCOLD 1
rel blast, castigate, fulminate (against),
fustigate, roast, scathe
idiom find fault with, pull (*or* pick *or*
tear) to pieces, take to task
con approve, countenance, endorse, OK
(*or* okay)
ant praise

criticizer *n syn* CRITIC, aristarch, carper,
caviler, faultfinder, knocker, momus,
smellfungus, Zoilus

critique *n syn see* CRITICISM

‖**critter** *n syn see* BEAST

croak *vb* 1 *syn see* GRUMBLE 1
rel complain, quarrel
‖2 *syn see* DIE 1

‖**croaker** *n syn see* PHYSICIAN

croaking *adj syn see* HOARSE 1

croaky *adj syn see* HOARSE 1

‖**crocked** *adj syn see* INTOXICATED 1

crone *n syn see* HAG 2
rel frump, slattern, sloven

crony *n syn see* ASSOCIATE 3
idiom bosom buddy

‖**crooch** *vb syn see* CROUCH

‖**croodle** *vb syn see* SNUGGLE

crook *vb* 1 *syn see* CURVE
‖2 *syn see* STEAL 1
‖3 *syn see* CHEAT

crooked *adj* 1 departing from a straight
line or course < a *crooked* road>
syn bending, curving, devious, twisting;
compare CURVED, WINDING
rel oblique; circuitous, indirect, roundabout; errant, meandering, rambling, serpentine, snaky, tortuous, winding; zigzag
con direct, undeviating
ant straight
2 deviating from rectitude < *crooked* police officers on the take>
syn corrupt, dishonest, snide; *compare*
CORRUPT 2, VENAL 1
rel devious, indirect, shifty, underhand;
double-dealing, fraudulent; deceitful, lying,
untruthful; ruthless, unscrupulous
con aboveboard, forthright, straightforward; conscientious, honorable, just,
proper, righteous, scrupulous, upright
ant honest, straight

crookedly *adv syn see* AWRY 1
ant straight

crop *n syn see* HARVEST 2

crop *vb* 1 *syn see* TOP 1
rel chop, hew, slash; detach, disengage
2 *syn see* MOW
3 *syn see* CUT 6
rel snip

cropping *n syn see* HARVEST 1

cross *n* 1 *syn see* TRIAL 1
idiom a cross to bear
2 *syn see* HYBRID

cross *vb* 1 *syn see* DENY 4
2 *syn see* BETRAY 2

idiom bite the hand that feeds one, stab
in the back
3 *syn see* TRAVERSE 4
4 to cause (an animal or plant) to breed
with one of a different kind < *crossing* a
horse with an ass results in a mule>
syn crossbreed, cross-mate, hybridize,
interbreed, intercross
rel mongrelize
5 *syn see* INTERSECT
idiom lie (*or* be) athwart

cross *adj syn see* IRASCIBLE
rel captious, carping, caviling, faultfinding
idiom cross as a bear

cross *prep syn see* ACROSS

crossbred *n syn see* HYBRID

crossbreed *vb syn see* CROSS 4

crossbreed *n syn see* HYBRID

crosscut *vb syn see* INTERSECT

cross-examination *n* a thorough, typically formal questioning for full information < *cross-examination* of a hostile wit-
ness>
syn grill, grilling, interrogation, third
degree
rel debriefing; questioning

cross-grained *adj* 1 *syn see* CANTAN-
KEROUS
2 *syn see* CONTRARY 3
rel difficult

crossing *adj syn see* TRANSVERSE

cross-mate *vb syn see* CROSS 4

crosspatch *n syn see* GROUCH

crossroad *n, usu* **crossroads** *pl but sing or
pl in constr syn see* JUNCTURE 2

‖**cross talk** *n syn see* BANTER

crossways *adv syn see* ACROSS 1
rel transversely; askew, awry, crisscross
con lengthwise
ant longways

crosswise *adv syn see* ACROSS 1
con longways
ant lengthwise

crosswise *adj syn see* TRANSVERSE
ant lengthwise

crotchet *n syn see* CAPRICE
rel eccentricity, kink, kinkiness, quirk,
twist
idiom bee in one's bonnet (*or* brain), flea
in one's nose, kink in one's horn, maggot
in one's brain

crotchety *adj syn see* CANTANKEROUS

crouch *vb* to stoop low with the limbs
close to the body < *crouched* behind a
rock and watched>
syn ‖crooch, huddle, hunch, scrooch
(down); *compare* SQUAT
rel bend, bow, dip, duck; hunker (down),
‖quat, squat, stoop, ‖swat; cower, cringe,
flinch, quail, wince; grovel

crow *vb syn see* BOAST
rel cry, exult, jubilate

crowd *vb* 1 *syn see* PRESS 1
rel ram, shove
2 *syn see* PRESS 7
rel bunch, cluster

crowd *n* 1 a usually large group of people
< a *crowd* gathered before the palace>
syn crush, drove, horde, multitude, press,
push, squash, throng; *compare* MULTI-
TUDE 1
rel army, host, legion; flock, gaggle, herd,
swarm; mob, rabble, rout

---

syn synonym(s)   *rel* related word(s)
ant antonym(s)   *con* contrasted word(s)
idiom idiomatic equivalent(s)
‖ use limited; if in doubt, see a dictionary

2 *syn* see GATHERING 2
rel huddle, parley; troop; herd; rally
3 *syn* see MULTITUDE 1
4 *syn* see SET 5
crowded *adj* 1 *syn* see FULL 1
rel overcharged, overloaded
ant uncrowded
2 *syn* see CLOSE 4
ant uncrowded
crown *n* 1 *syn* see TOP 1
2 *syn* see WREATH
rel diadem, tiara
3 *syn* see APEX 2
crown *vb* 1 *syn* see SURMOUNT 3
2 *syn* see COVER 3
3 *syn* see CLIMAX
crown (with) *vb syn* see ENDOW 1
crucial *adj syn* see ACUTE 6
rel deciding, decisive, important; necessary, vital; clamorous, compelling, crying, imperative, insistent, pressing
crucible *n syn* see TRIAL 1
crucify *vb syn* see AFFLICT
rel bedevil, bother, browbeat
idiom kill by inches, nail to the cross, put on the rack
crud *n* a deposit or incrustation of something filthy, greasy, or sticky < machinery all covered with *crud* >
syn ‖cab, goo, gook, gunk; *compare* GOO 1
rel filth, muck, slime, sludge; debris, junk, rubbish, trash
‖cruddle *vb syn* see CURDLE
crude *adj* 1 *syn* see UNREFINED 3
2 *syn* see COARSE 3
rel backward, ignorant, unenlightened; boorish, cloddish, clodhopping, ill-bred, loutish, lowbred; savage; insensible
3 *syn* see RUDE 1
rel immature, unmatured; coarse, graceless
con cultivated, cultured, refined; developed, matured, ripened
ant consummate, finished
4 *syn* see OBSCENE 2
rel blue, risqué
idiom rated X
5 rough in plan or execution < *crude* imitations, completely lacking in the original artistry >
syn coarse, inexpert, prentice; *compare* RUDE 1
rel amateurish, unproficient, unskilled, untaught, untrained; raw, rough, rude, unfinished, unpolished; inadequate, ineffective, inferior, poor
con finished, perfected, polished
ant expert
cruel *adj syn* see FIERCE 1
rel atrocious, heinous, monstrous, outrageous; bestial, bloodthirsty, brutish; heartless, implacable, relentless; impiteous, unpitying
con compassionate, sympathetic, tender; clement, forbearing, lenient, merciful; humane, kindly
‖cruise *vb syn* see GO 1
cruise *n syn* see VOYAGE
rel sail
‖cruiser *n syn* see PROSTITUTE
crumb *n syn* see PARTICLE
crumble *vb syn* see DECAY

rel mush, squash
crumbly *adj syn* see SHORT 6
rel rubbery
‖crump *adj syn* see SHORT 6
crumple *vb* 1 to press or twist into folds or wrinkles < *crumple* a piece of paper >
syn crimp, crimple, crinkle, ‖crunkle, rimple, ruck (up), ‖ruckle, rumple, screw, scrunch, wrinkle
rel crease, fold; buckle, cockle; wad
ant smooth
2 *syn* see GIVE 12
crunch *vb syn* see CHEW 1
crunchy *adj syn* see SHORT 6
‖crunkle *vb syn* see CRUMPLE 1
crusading *adj syn* see EVANGELICAL
crush *vb* 1 *syn* see PRESS 3
rel ‖scruze, squeeze
2 to reduce or be reduced to a pulpy or broken mass < *crushed* rose petals >
syn becrush, bruise, mash, ‖mush (up), pulp, squash
rel press, squeeze; contuse; batter, maim; beat, pound; dash, quash, ‖quat, smash; comminute, powder, pulverize, triturate
3 *syn* see PULVERIZE 1
4 *syn* see PRESS 1
5 to bring to an end by destroying or defeating < the police *crushed* the rebellion >
syn annihilate, extinguish, put down, quash, quell, quench, squash, suppress; *compare* SUPPRESS 2
rel ‖quelch, repress, squelch, strangle; beat down, conquer, defeat, subdue, subjugate; ruin, wreck; abolish, demolish, destroy; blot out, obliterate
idiom crush (*or* grind) under one's heel, ride down into the dust, roll (*or* trample) in the dust
6 *syn* see CONQUER 1
idiom bring one to his knees
7 *syn* see PRESS 7
crush *n* 1 *syn* see CROWD 1
2 *syn* see INFATUATION
rel calf love, puppy love
‖crust *n syn* see EFFRONTERY
crust *vb syn* see CAKE 1
crusty *adj* 1 *syn* see BLUFF
rel irritable, snappish, waspish; choleric, cranky, irascible, splenetic, testy; crabbed, dour, saturnine, surly
2 *syn* see OBSCENE 2
crux *n syn* see SUBSTANCE 2
cry *vb* 1 *syn* see CALL 1
rel bleat
2 to show distress, grief, or pain by tears and usually incoherent utterances < the little girl *cried* when she fell down >
syn blub, blubber, boohoo, ‖pipe, sob, wail, weep; *compare* BAWL 2, WHIMPER
rel sniff, snivel, whimper, whine; break down, choke up; groan, moan, sigh; bemoan, bewail, keen, lament, mourn, sorrow; bawl, howl, squall, yowl
idiom cry one's eyes (*or* heart) out, ‖pipe one's eye, shed tears
3 *syn* see SHOUT 1
4 *syn* see PUBLICIZE
cry *n* 1 *syn* see BATTLE CRY
rel slogan
2 *syn* see REPORT 1
3 *syn* see FASHION 3

4 *syn* see CALL 1
　rel screech, squawk; squeak; caw
cry down *vb syn* see DECRY 2
　ant cry up
crying *adj* 1 *syn* see PRESSING
　rel necessary, needed
　2 *syn* see OUTRAGEOUS 2
cry off *vb syn* see BACK DOWN
cry out *vb syn* see EXCLAIM
crypt *n* a subterranean chamber < a burial *crypt* >
　syn catacomb, undercroft, vault
　rel cell; chamber, compartment, room; cave, cavern, grotto
cryptanalyze *vb syn* see DECODE
cryptic *adj* being intentionally obscure and mysterious < the senator made some *cryptic* statements about intelligence operations >
　syn dark, Delphian, enigmatic, mystifying; *compare* OBSCURE 3
　rel equivocal, murky, obscure, opaque, tenebrous, unclear, uninformative, vague; incomprehensible, inexplicable, strange, unfathomable; abstruse, mysterious; evasive, secretive
crystal *adj syn* see CLEAR 4
　idiom clear as crystal, crystal clear
cry up *vb syn* see PRAISE 2
　idiom beat the drum for, praise to the skies
　ant cry down
cubby *n syn* see CUBBYHOLE
cubbyhole *n* an excessively small room or place < a cramped *cubbyhole* of an office >
　syn cubby, mousehole, pigeonhole
　rel recess; niche; cubicle
　idiom hole in the wall
‖**cubes** *n pl syn* see DICE
cuckoo *n syn* see CRACKPOT
cuckoo *adj syn* see INSANE 1
cuddle *vb* 1 *syn* see CARESS
　rel embrace, enfold, hold
　2 *syn* see SNUGGLE
cudgel *n* a short solid stick used as a weapon or an instrument of punishment < beat the prisoner with a *cudgel* >
　syn bat, baton, billy, billy club, bludgeon, club, knobkerrie, mace, nightstick, ‖shillelagh, spontoon, truncheon, war club
　rel birch, cane, ferule, hickory, paddle, rattan, rod, switch; blackjack; quarterstaff; bastinado
cue *n syn* see HINT 1
cuff *vb syn* see SLAP 1
cuff *n* a sharp blow typically delivered with the hand < gave him a good *cuff* in the face >
　syn box, buffet, ‖bust, chop, clout, haymaker, ‖paste, poke, punch, slap, smack, sock, spank, ‖spat, ‖swack; *compare* BLOW 1, HIT 1
　rel bat, blow, clip, wallop
cul-de-sac *n syn* see DEAD END
　rel stalemate
cull *vb* 1 *syn* see GLEAN
　rel accumulate, amass, collect, round up

2 *syn* see CHOOSE 1
　rel discriminate
　idiom separate the sheep from the goats, separate the wheat from the chaff
‖**cull** *n syn* see FOOL 3
‖**cully** *n syn* see ASSOCIATE 3
culmen *n syn* see APEX 2
culminate *vb syn* see CLIMAX
culmination *n syn* see APEX 2
　rel extremity, limit, maximum
culpability *n syn* see BLAME
　con blamelessness, innocence
　ant inculpability
culpable *adj syn* see BLAMEWORTHY
　rel impeachable, indictable
　ant inculpable
cult *n* 1 *syn* see RELIGION 1
　2 *syn* see RELIGION 2
cultivable *adj syn* see ARABLE
　ant uncultivable
cultivatable *adj syn* see ARABLE
　ant uncultivatable
cultivate *vb* 1 *syn* see TILL
　rel crop, farm, manage
　2 *syn* see NURSE 2
　rel raise, rear; educate, instruct, teach, train; ameliorate, better, improve
　con disregard, ignore, neglect, slight
　3 *syn* see GROW 1
　rel develop, mature, ripen
cultivated *adj syn* see GENTEEL 1
　rel courteous, polite
　ant uncultivated
cultivation *n syn* see CULTURE
culture *n* enlightenment and excellence of taste acquired by intellectual and aesthetic training < a man of *culture* is known by his reading >
　syn breeding, cultivation, polish, refinement
　rel education, enlightenment, erudition, learning; gentility, manners; discrimination, taste; savoir-faire, sophistication, urbanity; class, elegance
　con greenness, ignorance, inexperience, verdancy; crudeness, vulgarity
cultured *adj syn* see GENTEEL 1
　rel educated, enlightened, erudite, learned, literate; civilized
　ant uncultured
culverhouse *n syn* see DOVECOTE
cumber *vb syn* see BURDEN
cumbersome *adj syn* see UNWIELDY
　rel irksome, tiresome, wearisome
cumbrance *n syn* see ENCUMBRANCE
　rel burden, charge, pressure
cumbrous *adj syn* see UNWIELDY
　rel clogging, hampering, hindering, impeding
cumshaw *n syn* see GRATUITY
cumulate *vb syn* see ACCUMULATE
　rel obtain, secure
　ant dissipate
cumulation *n syn* see ACCUMULATION
　rel stockpile; snowball
cumulative *adj* increasing or produced by addition of like or similar things < the *cumulative* effect of several drugs >
　syn accumulative, additive, additory, chain, summative
　rel accumulated, amassed; augmenting, increasing, multiplying; advancing, heightening, intensifying, magnifying, snowballing

---

syn synonym(s)　　*rel* related word(s)
ant antonym(s)　　*con* contrasted word(s)
idiom idiomatic equivalent(s)
‖ use limited; if in doubt, see a dictionary

con dispersed, dissipated, scattered

cunning *adj* **1** *syn* see CLEVER 4
rel well-devised, well-laid, well-planned; crackerjack, masterful
idiom too clever by half
2 *syn* see SLY 2
rel acute, keen, sharp; knowing, smart; wary
idiom not to be caught with chaff
con artless, naive, unsophisticated

cunning *n* **1** *syn* see ART 1
rel deftness, dexterousness; adeptness, expertness; cleverness, ingeniousness, ingenuity
2 skill in devising or using indirect or subtle methods <a woman able to maneuver people with great *cunning* >
syn art, artfulness, artifice, cageyness, canniness, craft, craftiness, foxiness, slyness, wiliness
rel savvy, sharpness, shrewdness; cleverness, ingeniousness, ingenuity; agility, facility, finesse, slickness; subtlety; insidiousness, shiftiness, trickiness
3 *syn* see DECEIT 1
idiom satanic cunning, the cunning of the serpent

cupidity *n* intense desire for possessions and wealth <the sight of so much money aroused his *cupidity* >
syn avarice, avariciousness, avidity, greed, rapacity
rel acquisitiveness, greediness, possessiveness, rapaciousness; eagerness, voracity; craving, desire; lust; infatuation, passion

cur *n* **1** *syn* see SNOT 1
rel riffraff
2 *syn* see CAD

curative *adj* restoring or tending to restore to a state of normalcy or health <a *curative* drug>
syn curing, healing, remedial, remedying, restorative, sanative, sanatory, vulnerary, wholesome
rel medicable, medicative, medicinal; corrective, therapeutic; invigorating, tonic; beneficial, helpful, salutary, wholesome

curb *vb* **1** *syn* see HAMPER
2 *syn* see DENY 3
rel repress, suppress
ant goad
3 *syn* see RESTRAIN 1
rel fetter, hamper, hog-tie, manacle, shackle
idiom hold in leash, keep a tight rein on
con unbridle, unleash
ant spur

curd *vb syn* see CURDLE

curdle *vb* to cause to become coagulated or thickened and often sour <hot weather will *curdle* milk>
syn ||clabber, ||cruddle, curd, ||lopper, turn
rel clot, coagulate, condense, thicken; ferment; go off, sour, spoil

cure *n* **1** *syn* see REMEDY 1
2 *syn* see REMEDY 2

cure *vb* to rectify an unhealthy or undesirable condition <aspirin *cured* his headache>
syn heal, remedy
rel doctor, medicate; restore; ameliorate, better, improve

cure-all *n syn* see PANACEA

cureless *adj syn* see HOPELESS 2

curing *adj syn* see CURATIVE

curio *n syn* see KNICKKNACK

curiosity *n* **1** *syn* see INTEREST 3
rel inquisitiveness, questioning
ant disinterest
2 something that arouses interest especially because of uncommon or exotic characteristics <an architectural *curiosity* >
syn conversation piece, oddity
rel exception, nonesuch, rarity; marvel, prodigy, wonder; anomaly; freak, monstrosity
idiom something to write home about

curious *adj* **1** *syn* see INQUISITIVE 1
rel searching; analytical; prurient
ant incurious
2 interested in what is not one's personal or proper concern <a *curious* old woman prying into her neighbors' affairs>
syn inquisitive, inquisitorial, inquisitory, ||nibby, nosy, peery, prying, snoopy
rel interfering, intermeddling, meddling, tampering; examining, inspecting, scrutinizing; impertinent, intrusive, meddlesome
idiom consumed (*or* burning up *or* eaten up) with curiosity, curious as a cat (*or* monkey)
con aloof, detached, disinterested, indifferent, unconcerned, uninterested; apathetic, impassive, phlegmatic, stolid
ant incurious
3 *syn* see STRANGE 4

curl *vb syn* see WIND 2
rel crook; roll; ringlet; kink
con straighten, unkink, unwind
ant uncurl

currency *n syn* see MONEY

current *adj* **1** *syn* see PRESENT 1
rel topical, up-to-date
con antiquated, antique, obsolete
2 *syn* see PREVAILING
rel accustomed, customary; a la mode, fashionable, modern, popular
ant antique

current *n* **1** *syn* see FLOW
2 *syn* see TENDENCY 1

curry *vb syn* see WHIP 2

curse *n* **1** a denunciation that conveys a wish or threat of evil <the dying man's *curse* against his family>
syn anathema, commination, imprecation, malediction, malison
rel execration, objurgation; damning, denunciation; blasphemy, profanation, profanity, sacrilege
ant blessing
2 *syn* see SWEARWORD
3 *syn* see PLAGUE 1

curse *vb* **1** *syn* see EXECRATE 1
rel blaspheme; blight; doom
idiom call down curses on the head of, call down evil on
ant bless
2 *syn* see SWEAR 3
idiom ||curse up a storm

cursed *adj* **1** *syn* see DAMNED 2
rel hateful
2 *syn* see EXECRABLE 1
rel disgusting; odious
ant blessed

cursing *n syn* see BLASPHEMY 1

cursive *adj syn* see EASY 9

cursory *adj syn* see SUPERFICIAL 2
rel fast, hasty, hurried, quick, rapid, speedy, swift; brief, short; casual, desultory, haphazard, random
con careful, meticulous, scrupulous
ant painstaking

curt *adj* 1 *syn* see CONCISE
2 *syn* see BLUFF
rel imperious, peremptory
ant voluble

curtail *vb* 1 *syn* see SHORTEN
ant prolong, protract
2 *syn* see ABRIDGE 1
ant extend

curtains *n pl but sing in constr syn* see DEATH 1

curtilage *n syn* see COURT 1

curvaceous *adj* having a shapely figure marked by pronounced curves < *curvaceous* bikini-clad girls swarmed over the beach >
syn ||built, curvesome, curvilinear, curvy, Junoesque, rounded, ||stacked, well-developed; *compare* BUXOM, SHAPELY
rel shapeful, shapely, statuesque, well-proportioned; attractive, charming, pleasing
idiom ||built (*or* stacked) like a brick outhouse

curvation *n syn* see CURVE

curvature *n syn* see CURVE

curve *vb* to swerve or cause to swerve from a straight line or course < the road *curves* to the right >
syn bend, bow, crook, round; *compare* WIND 3
rel deflect, divert, turn; deviate, swerve, veer; coil, curl, spiral, twist, wind; incurve
ant straighten

curve *n* something (as a line or surface) that curves or is curved < a slight *curve* to her eyebrows >
syn arc, arch, bend, bow, curvation, curvature, round
rel incurvation, incurvature; inflection; rondure; circuit, circumference, compass

curved *adj* having or characterized by a curve or curves < a *curved* vault >
syn arced, arched, arciform, arrondi, bent, bowed, curvilinear, round, rounded; *compare* CROOKED 1
rel declinate; embowed, incurvate, incurved; excurved; bending, twisted, twisting
ant straight

curvesome *adj syn* see CURVACEOUS

curvilinear *adj* 1 *syn* see CURVED
2 *syn* see CURVACEOUS

curving *adj syn* see CROOKED 1

curvy *adj syn* see CURVACEOUS

cushy *adj syn* see COMFORTABLE 2

cusp *n syn* see POINT 9

cuspidate *adj syn* see POINTED 1

cuss *n* 1 *syn* see SWEARWORD
2 *syn* see MAN 3

cuss *vb syn* see SWEAR 1
idiom ||cuss up a blue streak

---

syn synonym(s) *rel* related word(s)
ant antonym(s) *con* contrasted word(s)
idiom idiomatic equivalent(s)
|| use limited; if in doubt, see a dictionary

---

cussed *adj syn* see DAMNED 2

cussing *adj syn* see BLASPHEMY 1

cussword *n syn* see SWEARWORD

custodian *n* one that guards, protects, or maintains (as property or records) < was the *custodian* of the manor for many years >
syn cerberus, claviger, ||custodier, custos, guardian, keeper, warden, watchdog
rel curator, steward; castellan, governor; overseer, supervisor

||custodier *n syn* see CUSTODIAN

custody *n* the act or duty of guarding and preserving < the government has *custody* of all state gifts >
syn care, guardianship, keeping, safekeeping, trust, ward
rel caretaking; charge, management, supervision; protection

custom *n* 1 *syn* see HABIT 1
rel precedent; ritual; mold; fixture, institution; prescription, rubric; canon, law, precept, rule
idiom matter of course
con departure, deviation, shift; exception; irregularity
2 *syn* see PATRONAGE 2

custom *adj syn* see CUSTOM-MADE

customarily *adv syn* see USUALLY 1
rel conventionally, traditionally; normally, ordinarily; routinely
idiom as a matter of course
con rarely; never
ant occasionally

customary *adj* 1 *syn* see USUAL 1
rel acknowledged, recognized, understood; standard; conventional, orthodox, traditional; prescriptive, regulation, stipulated
idiom being the customary (*or* usual) thing
con occasional; infrequent, inhabitual, sporadic, uncommon; irregular
ant uncustomary
2 *syn* see COMMON 4
rel household, popular; general, universal
ant uncustomary

custom–built *adj syn* see CUSTOM-MADE

customer *n* one that patronizes or uses the services of something (as a store or restaurant) < many *customers* in the shop >
syn client, patron
rel buyer, consumer, purchaser; shopper

customized *adj syn* see CUSTOM-MADE

custom–made *adj* made according to personal order and individual specifications < he always wore a *custom-made* suit >
syn custom, custom-built, customized, custom-tailored, made-to-order, tailor-made
ant mass-produced

custom–tailored *adj syn* see CUSTOM–MADE

custos *n syn* see CUSTODIAN

cut *vb* 1 to penetrate with or as if with a sharp edge < *cut* his hand on a broken bottle >
syn gash, incise, pierce, slash, slice, slit
rel cleave, dissever, sever, sunder; rend, rip, rive, tear; lacerate, wound
2 *syn* see SHORTEN
3 *syn* see REDUCE 2

4 *syn* see MOW
5 to penetrate and divide with an edged tool or instrument < *cut* the melon into slices >
syn carve, cleave, dissect, dissever, sever, slice, split, sunder
rel divide, part, separate; chop, dice, hash, mince, mow
idiom lay open
6 to reduce by severing parts < the barber *cut* his hair too short >
syn clip, crop, pare, prune, shave, shear, skive, trim
rel cut back, dock, lop, poll, pollard, shrub; amputate; curtail
7 to refuse social recognition especially by way of rebuke < his friends *cut* him after the scandal broke >
syn cold-shoulder, ostracize, snob, snub
rel disdain, ignore, rebuff, reject, slight, turn away; affront, insult, offend
idiom give the cold shoulder (to), show one his place, slam the door in one's face, slam the door on, slap one in the face, turn aside (*or* away) from, turn one's back (on *or* upon)
8 *syn* see DILUTE
9 *syn* see FELL 2
10 *syn* see OPERATE 2
cut *n* **1** *syn* see PART 1
2 *syn* see SHARE 1
3 *syn* see TRENCH
4 *syn* see TYPE
cut *adj syn* see INTOXICATED 1
cut back *vb* **1** *syn* see SHORTEN
2 *syn* see REDUCE 2
cut down *vb syn* see REDUCE 2

cut in *vb syn* see INTRUDE 1
cut off *vb* **1** *syn* see KILL 1
2 *syn* see INTERCEPT
3 *syn* see ISOLATE
4 *syn* see DISINHERIT 1
cutoff *n syn* see SHORTCUT
cut out *vb* **1** *syn* see EXCISE
2 *syn* see SUPPLANT 1
cutpurse *n syn* see PICKPOCKET
cutthroat *n syn* see ASSASSIN
cutting *adj syn* see INCISIVE
rel piercing, probing
cut up *vb* **1** *syn* see CRITICIZE
2 to behave in a boisterously comic or unruly manner < children *cutting up* in front of company >
syn act up, carry on, horse, horseplay
rel caper, cavort, romp; clown; show off; roughhouse; misbehave
idiom cut a dido (*or* shine), cut up rough, ‖kick up a shindy, raise Cain (*or* Ned), whoop it up
cutup *n syn* see ZANY 2
cycle *n* **1** a complete course of recurrent operations or events < a 24-hour *cycle* of medication >
syn circle, round, wheel; *compare* SUCCESSION 2
rel chain, sequel, sequence, series; course, run; circuit, loop, ring
2 *syn* see BICYCLE
cyclone *n syn* see TORNADO
cyclopean *adj syn* see HUGE
ant lilliputian
cynical *adj syn* see SARDONIC
cyprian *n syn* see WANTON
czar *n syn* see MAGNATE

D

dab *vb syn* see SMEAR 1
‖**dab** *n syn* see EXPERT
dabbler *n syn* see AMATEUR 2
con adept, artist, connoisseur; expert, master, professional
dabbling *adj syn* see AMATEURISH
rel sciolistic, shallow, sophomoric, superficial
con adept, capable, competent
‖**dabster** *n syn* see EXPERT
dad *n syn* see FATHER 1
dada *n syn* see FATHER 1
dad-blamed *adj* **1** *syn* see DAMNED 2
2 *syn* see UTTER
dad-blasted *adj* **1** *syn* see DAMNED 2
2 *syn* see UTTER
dad-burned *adj* **1** *syn* see DAMNED 2
2 *syn* see UTTER
daddy *n syn* see FATHER 1
daedal *adj syn* see COMPLEX 2
daffy *adj syn* see INSANE 1
daft *adj syn* see INSANE 1
daily *adj* of each or every day < *daily* prayers for the dead >
syn diurnal, quotidian
con nocturnal; alternate, intermittent,

periodic, recurrent, spasmodic; erratic, fitful, fluctuating, infrequent, irregular; occasional, sporadic
ant nightly
dainty *n syn* see DELICACY
dainty *adj* **1** *syn* see CHOICE
rel beautiful, bonny, fair, lovely, pretty; delectable, delicious, delightful; airy, diaphanous, ethereal, light
con coarse, vulgar
ant gross
2 *syn* see NICE 1
rel acute, penetrative, perceptive
con careless, neglectful, negligent, thoughtless
‖**daisy** *n syn* ‖DILLY, ‖corker, crackerjack, dandy, humdinger, jim-dandy, knockout, ‖lalapalooza, ‖lulu, nifty
dale *n syn* see VALLEY
dally *vb* **1** *syn* see TRIFLE 1
rel frolic, gambol, play, rollick, romp, sport; caress, cosset, cuddle, dandle, fondle, pet
2 *syn* see DELAY 2
con fleet, rush, scurry, skedaddle
ant hasten
dam *vb syn* see HINDER
rel repress, suppress

con air, express, utter, vent

damage *n syn* see INJURY 1
rel impairment, marring; deterioration, dilapidation, disrepair, ruining, wrecking; deleteriousness, disadvantage, drawback
con amelioration, betterment, improvement; benefit, profit; advantage, service, use
ant repair

damage *vb syn* see INJURE 1
rel demolish, destroy, raze, ruin, wreck; deteriorate, dilapidate; abuse, ill-treat, maltreat, mistreat, misuse, outrage
con ameliorate, amend, better, improve; mend
ant repair

damaged *adj* having been injured < *damaged* merchandise >
syn flawed, impaired, marred, spoiled
rel blemished, broken, imperfect, injured, unsound
con flawless, good, intact, unbroken, unhurt, unimpaired, uninjured, unmarred, whole; corrected, improved, rectified, repaired
ant undamaged

damaging *adj syn* see HARMFUL

dame *n* 1 *syn* see MATRIARCH
2 *syn* see BELDAM 1

damn *vb* 1 *syn* see SENTENCE
rel castigate, discipline, penalize, punish; banish, cast out, expel
con deliver, ransom, redeem, rescue; reward
ant save
2 *syn* see EXECRATE 1
rel abominate; vituperate
3 *syn* see SWEAR 3

damn *n syn* see PARTICLE

damnable *adj* 1 *syn* see EXECRABLE 1
rel abhorrent, abominable, detestable, hateful, odious; damned
con admirable, commendable, estimable; laudable, praiseworthy
2 *syn* see DAMNED 2
3 *syn* see UTTER

damned *adj* 1 being doomed to eternal punishment < a *damned* soul >
syn condemned, doomed, lost
rel anathematized, cursed, reprobate; done for
idiom gone to blazes, hell bound
con delivered, ransomed, redeemed
ant saved
2 deserving censure or strong disapproval —often used as a generalized expression of annoyance < this *damned* door won't open >
syn blamed, blankety-blank, blasted, bleeding, blessed, blighted, blinding, ‖blinking, ‖blistering, ‖blooming, confounded, ‖consarned, cursed, cussed, dadblamed, dad-blasted, dad-burned, damnable, dang, darn (or durn), dashed, doggone, dratted, execrable, goldarn, infernal, perishing, so-and-so
3 *syn* see UTTER

damned *adv syn* see VERY 1

---

damp *adj* slightly or relatively wet < her dress was still *damp* >
syn dampish, dank, moist, moisty, wettish
rel drenched, saturated, soaked, soaking; soggy, water-logged
con arid, dry

dampen *vb syn* see MUFFLE 2

dampish *adj syn* see DAMP

damsel *n syn* see GIRL 1

dance *vb* 1 to perform a rhythmic and patterned succession of steps usually to music < the band was good enough to *dance* to >
syn foot (it), hoof (it), prance, step, tread
rel shuffle, trip, truck
idiom ‖cut a rug, trip the light fantastic
2 *syn* see FLIT 2
rel quaver, quiver, shake, tremble, wobble

dancer *n* a professional performer of dances < *dancers* performing a ballet >
syn ballerina, ballet girl, coryphée, dancing girl, danseur, danseuse, figurant, figurante, hoofer
rel chorine, chorus boy, chorus girl, chorus man; danseur noble, premier danseur, premiere danseuse, prima ballerina

dancing girl *n syn* see DANCER

dandle *vb syn* see CARESS
rel disport, play, sport

dandy *n* 1 *syn* see FOP
con clod, lout, lump, oaf, slob, slouch
ant sloven
2 *syn* ‖DILLY, ‖corker, crackerjack, ‖daisy, humdinger, jim-dandy, ‖lalapalooza, ‖lulu, nifty, peach

‖dandy *adj* 1 *syn* see MARVELOUS 2
2 *syn* see EXCELLENT
rel grand, hunky-dory, keen, nifty, swell
idiom fine and dandy
con ‖bum, ‖crummy, grim, ‖lousy, ‖putrid, rotten
ant blah

dang *adj* 1 *syn* see DAMNED 2
2 *syn* see UTTER

danger *n* the state of being exposed to injury, pain, or loss < they are seeking a place where children can play without *danger* >
syn hazard, jeopardy, peril, risk
rel menace, precariousness, threat; emergency, exigency, pass; precipice
idiom dangerous ground, thin ice
con safety; exemption, immunity; defense, guard, protection, safeguard, shield
ant security

dangerous *adj* 1 attended by or involving the possibility of injury, pain, or loss < a *dangerous* crossing >
syn chancy, ‖dangersome, hairy, hazardous, jeopardous, parlous, perilous, risky, treacherous, unhealthy, unsound, wicked; *compare* GRAVE 3
rel insecure, precarious, uncertain, unsafe; chance, haphazard, hit-or-miss, random; critical, menacing, serious, threatening
idiom beset (or fraught) with danger, on a collision course
con certain, reliable; harmless, innocent
ant safe, secure
2 *syn* see GRAVE 3

‖dangersome *adj syn* see DANGEROUS 1

dangle *vb syn* see HANG 1

dank *adj syn* see DAMP

danseur *n syn* see DANCER
danseuse *n syn* see DANCER
dap *vb syn* see GLANCE 1
dapper *adj* trimly neat and tidy <a *dapper* dresser, always neat as a pin>
syn bandbox, doggish, doggy, natty, sassy, sparkish, spiffy, spruce, sprucy, well-groomed; *compare* NEAT 2, STYLISH
rel chichi; jaunty, rakish; showy
con dowdy, drab, unstylish; disheveled, disordered, slipshod, sloppy, slovenly, unkempt, untidy; blowsy, dowdy, frowsy, shabby, slatternly
dappled *adj syn* see VARIEGATED
con pure, smooth, spotless, unbroken, uniform
dare *vb syn* see FACE 3
rel change, hazard, risk
idiom take the bull by the horns
con avoid, evade; flee, run
dare *n syn* see DEFIANCE 1
daredevil *adj syn* see ADVENTUROUS
con timid, timorous; cautious, chary, circumspect, wary; discreet, judicious, prudent, sane, sensible
daring *adj syn* see ADVENTUROUS
dark *adj* 1 deficient in light <a *dark* room>
syn caliginous, dim, dun, dusk, dusky, gloomy, lightless, murky, obscure, somber, tenebrous, unilluminated
rel cloudy, dull, shadowy, shady; pitch-black, pitch-dark
con bright, brilliant, luminous, radiant; enlightened, illuminated, illumined, lighted
ant light
2 *syn* see CRYPTIC
rel abstruse, esoteric, hidden, occult, recondite; anagogic, cabalistic, darkling, mystic, mystical; complicated, intricate, knotty
con clear, perspicuous; easy, facile, light, simple
ant lucid
3 of dark complexion <her *dark* good looks>
syn bistered, black-a-vised, brunet, dark-skinned, dusky, swart, swarth, swarthy
con blond, fair, light; ruddy, tawny
‖4 *syn* see BLIND 1
darken *vb syn* see OBSCURE
ant illuminate
dark-skinned *adj syn* see DARK 3
darling *n syn* see SWEETHEART 1
darling *adj* 1 *syn* see FAVORITE 1
2 *syn* see DELIGHTFUL
darn (*or* **durn**) *adj syn* see DAMNED 2
2 *syn* see UTTER
dart *n syn* see SHAFT 2
dart *vb syn* see FLY 1
rel hasten, hurry, precipitate, speed; run, scamper, scoot, scurry, sprint, spurt
con dally, dawdle, delay, linger, tarry; lumber, plod, slog, trudge
dash *vb* 1 *syn* see RUSH 1
rel run, scamper, scoot, scurry, sprint
con dally, dawdle, delay, linger, tarry; lumber, plod, slog, trudge
2 *syn* see RUN 1
3 *syn* see BLAST 1
4 *syn* see FRUSTRATE 1
dash *n* 1 *syn* see SPIRIT 5
rel energy, force, might, power, strength; intensity, vehemence; impressiveness

con apathy, dullness, languor, lethargy, listlessness, sluggishness, stagnation, torpor
2 *syn* see HINT 2
rel impress, impression, stamp
dashed *adj* 1 *syn* see DAMNED 2
2 *syn* see UTTER
dashing *adj* 1 *syn* see LIVELY 1
2 *syn* see STYLISH
rel flashy, flaunting; dapper, jaunty, spiffy, spruce
idiom cutting a fine figure
con unfashionable, unstylish; modest, unostentatious, unpretentious
ant drab
dastard *n syn* see COWARD
date *vb* to go or take on a date <he *dated* her several times that winter>
syn see, take out
rel accompany, escort; court, woo
idiom go out with
date *n* 1 *syn* see ENGAGEMENT 3
2 *syn* see ESCORT 1
dated *adj syn* see OLD-FASHIONED
ant up-to-the-minute
dateless *adj syn* see ETERNAL 4
ant ephemeral
daub *vb syn* see SMEAR 1
rel spatter, speckle, spot; dapple, fleck, variegate
daunt *vb syn* see DISMAY 1
rel browbeat, bully, cow, intimidate; baffle, foil, frustrate, thwart
con arouse, awaken, rally, rouse, stir, waken; actuate, drive, impel, move; activate, energize, vitalize
ant enhearten
dauntless *adj syn* see BRAVE 1
rel indomitable, invincible, unconquerable
con hesitant, reluctant
ant poltroon
dauntlessness *n syn* see COURAGE
ant poltroonery
dawdle *vb* 1 *syn* see IDLE
2 *syn* see DELAY 2
rel amble, saunter, stroll; stay, wait; toy, trifle; fritter, waste
idiom fritter away time
con arouse, rally, rouse, stir; hasten, hurry, speed
dawdler *n syn* see LAGGARD
dawn *n* 1 the first appearance of light in the morning <birds which sing at *dawn*>
syn aurora, cockcrow, cockcrowing, dawning, daybreak, daylight, light, morn, morning, sunrise, sunup
rel prime
idiom break of day, crack of dawn, first blush (*or* flush) of day, first light, peep of day, the wee small hours
2 *syn* see BEGINNING
ant sunset
dawning *n* 1 *syn* see DAWN 1
2 *syn* see BEGINNING
ant sunset
day *n* 1 the time of light between one night and the next <waiting for *day* to dawn>
syn daylight, daytime
rel light, sunlight, sunshine
con dark, nighttime
ant night
2 *usu* **days** *pl syn* see PERIOD 2

daybreak *n syn* see DAWN 1
daydream *n syn* see FANCY 4
  rel conceiving, fancying, imagination, imagining
  con substantiality, tangibility; authenticity, truth, verity
daydreaming *adj syn* see DREAMY 1
daydreamy *adj syn* see DREAMY 1
daylight *n* 1 *syn* see DAWN 1
  syn see DAY 1
dayspring *n syn* see BEGINNING
daystar *n syn* see SUN 1
daytime *n syn* see DAY 1
daze *vb* 1 to confuse with light <the bright sunlight *dazed* him>
  syn bedazzle, blind, dazzle
  rel overcome, overpower, overwhelm; dizzy
  2 to dull or deaden the powers of the mind through some disturbing experience or influence <*dazed* by the news of the accident>
  syn bedaze, bemuse, benumb, paralyze, petrify, stun, stupefy
  rel bewilder, confound, disorder, distract, dumbfound, mystify; befuddle, confuse, fuddle, muddle; dazzle, dizzy; rock
  con enhance, expand, heighten, sharpen; alert, arouse, waken
daze *n syn* see HAZE 2
dazzle *vb syn* see DAZE 1
dead *adj* 1 devoid of life <a *dead* person>
  syn asleep, cold, deceased, defunct, departed, exanimate, extinct, inanimate, late, lifeless, spiritless, unanimated
  rel bloodless, breathless; gone, reposing; inactive, inert; belowground, buried
  idiom dead as a doornail, gone the way of all flesh, out of one's misery, pushing up daisies
  con animate, animated, living, vital; being, existing; active, live
  ant alive
  2 *syn* see DEATHLY 1
  rel insensible, insentient, numb, unfeeling, unresponsive; inanimate, unconscious
  con feeling, responsive, sensitive, sentient; animate, animated, living, spirited, vivacious
  ant alive
  3 *syn* see NUMB 1
  4 *syn* see OBSOLETE
  ant living; viable
  5 *syn* see EXTINCT 2
  6 *syn* see DULL 7
  rel bleak, dismal
  con glorious, resplendent
  7 *syn* see UTTER
dead *adv syn* see DIRECTLY 1
deaden *vb* 1 to impair in vigor, force, activity, or sensation <the news *deadened* his distress>
  syn benumb, blunt, desensitize, dull, mull, numb
  rel anesthetize, paralyze, unnerve; stun, stupefy
  con animate, vivify; energize, invigorate; activate, vitalize

---

syn synonym(s)   *rel* related word(s)
ant antonym(s)   *con* contrasted word(s)
idiom idiomatic equivalent(s)
‖ use limited; if in doubt, see a dictionary

---

  ant enliven
  2 *syn* see MUFFLE 2
dead end *n* a course which leads to nothing further <had reached a *dead end* in negotiations>
  syn blind alley, cul-de-sac, impasse, pocket
  rel corner, hole; deadlock, halt, standstill; bottleneck
deadened *adj* 1 *syn* see DEATHLY 1
  2 *syn* see NUMB 1
‖**deader** *n syn* see CORPSE
deadfall *n syn* see PITFALL
deadliness *n syn* see FATALITY 1
deadlock *n syn* see DRAW 4
  rel condition, posture, situation, state; dilemma, plight, predicament, quandary
  con decision, determination, resolution, solution
deadly *adj* 1 causing or causative of death <a *deadly* disease>
  syn deathly, fatal, lethal, mortal, mortiferous, pestilent, pestilential; *compare* PERNICIOUS
  rel destroying, destructive; killing, slaying; internecine; baneful, noxious, pernicious; poisonous, toxic, virulent
  con healthful, healthy, wholesome; advantageous, beneficial, restorative, sanative
  2 *syn* see PERNICIOUS
  con harmless, innocuous, inoffensive, unoffending
  3 *syn* see DEATHLY 1
deadpan *adj syn* see EXPRESSIONLESS
dead to rights *adv syn* see RED-HANDED
deadweight *n syn* see LOAD 3
‖**deadwood** *n syn* see ADVANTAGE 3
deaf *adj syn* see OBSTINATE
deal *vb* 1 *syn* see DISTRIBUTE 1
  rel partake, participate, share
  con receive, take; detain, hold, hold back, keep, retain, withhold; appropriate, arrogate, confiscate
  2 *syn* see GIVE 10
  rel impart, mete, render
  con annul, cancel, remove, rescind, revoke
deal (out) *vb syn* see ADMINISTER 2
  rel dish, dish out, help, serve; offer, present, proffer, tender
  con hold, hold back, keep, retain, withhold
deal (with) *vb syn* see TREAT 2
  rel control, direct; clear, rid, unburden
  con misconduct, misdirect, mishandle, mismanage; disregard, ignore, neglect; burden, cumber, encumber
deal *n* 1 *syn* see AGREEMENT 2
  2 treatment received in a transaction from another <a fair *deal*>
  syn shake
dealer *n syn* see MERCHANT
dealings *n pl syn* see COMMERCE 1
  rel affairs, business, concerns, doings, matters, things; proceedings
deambulatory *adj syn* see ITINERANT
dean *n syn* see LEADER 1
dear *adj* 1 *syn* see FAVORITE 1
  2 *syn* see LOVING
  3 *syn* see COSTLY 1
  con inexpensive, low, moderate, modest, nominal
  ant cheap
dear *n syn* see SWEETHEART 1

dearth *n syn* see ABSENCE
rel infrequency, rareness, scarcity, uncommonness; exiguousness, meagerness, scantiness, scantness; paucity, insufficiency
con superfluity, surplus; lavishness, prodigality, profusion
ant excess

death *n* **1** the end or the ending of life
< *death* of a man > < *death* of an enterprise >
syn curtains, decease, defunction, demise, dissolution, grim reaper, (the) Pale Horse, passing, quietus, silence, sleep
rel annihilation, ending, expiration, extinction, grave, termination
idiom crossing the bar
ant life
2 *syn* see FATALITY 2

deathful *adj syn* see DEATHLY 1

deathless *adj syn* see IMMORTAL 1
rel eternal; abiding, lasting, persisting

deathlike *adj* **1** *syn* see DEATHLY 1
2 *syn* see GHASTLY 2

deathly *adj* **1** suggesting death (as in inertness or appearance) < fell in a *deathly* faint >
syn corpselike, corpsy, dead, deadened, deadly, deathful, deathlike
rel cadaverous, haggard, wasted; ghastly, grisly, gruesome, macabre; appalling, dreadful, horrible
con healthy, hearty, robust; stout, sturdy; energetic, strenuous, vigorous
2 *syn* see DEADLY 1

debacle *n* **1** *syn* see DEFEAT 1
2 *syn* see COLLAPSE 2

debar *vb syn* see EXCLUDE
rel forbid, interdict; block, hinder, impede, obstruct
con accept, receive; allow, let, permit
ant admit

debark *vb syn* see DISEMBARK

debase *vb* **1** to cause to become impaired in quality or character < vulgarly outrageous movies that *debase* the taste of the people >
syn animalize, bastardize, bestialize, brutalize, canker, corrupt, debauch, demoralize, deprave, pervert, poison, rot, stain, vitiate, warp; *compare* ADULTERATE
rel damage, harm, impair, injure, mar, spoil; contaminate, defile, dishonor, pollute, taint; commercialize
con enhance, heighten; lift, raise; ameliorate, better, improve
ant elevate; amend
2 *syn* see HUMBLE
rel cripple, debilitate, disable, enfeeble, sap, undermine, weaken
con acclaim, laud, praise; refresh, rejuvenate, renew, restore
3 *syn* see ADULTERATE
rel damage, impair, worsen; corrupt, defile, spoil
idiom play the devil (*or* the mischief) with
con amend, upgrade

debased *adj* being lowered in quality or character < became *debased* in his greed for money >
syn corrupted, debauched, depraved, perverted, vitiate, vitiated
rel decadent, degenerate, degenerated, deteriorated; abandoned, dissolute, profligate, reprobate

con ameliorated, bettered, improved; elevated, lifted, raised
ant elevated

debatable *adj syn* see MOOT
ant undebatable

debate *n* **1** *syn* see ARGUMENTATION
rel controverting, rebutting, refuting
2 *syn* see ATTENTION 2

debate *vb syn* see DISCUSS 1
rel altercate, quarrel, wrangle; confute, controvert, disprove, rebut, refute; demonstrate, prove; contend, contest
con agree, coincide, concur; affirm, aver, maintain, profess

debauch *vb* **1** *syn* see DEBASE 1
rel decoy, inveigle, lure, seduce, tempt
con amend, remedy; clean, cleanse, purge, purify; preserve, reclaim, save
2 *syn* see SEDUCE 2

debauch *n syn* see ORGY 2

debauched *adj syn* see DEBASED
rel lascivious, lecherous, lewd, libertine, libidinous, licentious, wanton
con delivered, reclaimed, redeemed, rescued, saved; chaste, decent, pure; moral, virtuous; continent, temperate

debilitate *vb syn* see WEAKEN 1
rel devitalize; attenuate, extenuate; harm, hurt, mar, spoil
con energize, vitalize; fortify, reinforce, strengthen; refresh, rejuvenate, renew, restore; rally, rouse, stir
ant invigorate

debility *n syn* see INFIRMITY 1

debris *n syn* see REFUSE
rel dregs, dross, rubble

debt *n* **1** *syn* see EVIL 2
2 *syn* see INDEBTEDNESS 1
3 something (as money) that is owed
< struggling to keep ahead of his *debts* >
syn arrear(s), arrearage, due, indebtedness, liability; *compare* INDEBTEDNESS 1
rel default, deficit, delinquency, nonpayment, outstandings; debit, demurrage
con asset, credit; compensation, refund, reimbursement, remuneration

debunk *vb syn* see EXPOSE 4

debut *vb* to make one's formal entrance into society < she *debuted* on her 20th birthday >
syn come out
idiom make one's bow

decadence *n syn* see DETERIORATION 1
rel regress, regression, regressiveness, retrogradation, retrograding, retrogression, retrogressiveness; debasement, degradation
con advance, progress, progression; amelioration, bettering, betterment, improvement
ant rise; flourishing

decadent *adj syn* see EFFETE 3

decamp *vb* **1** *syn* see GET OUT 1
2 *syn* see ESCAPE 1
rel exit, go, leave, quit, retire, withdraw; avoid, elude, evade, shun
con arrive, come

decapitate *vb* **1** *syn* see BEHEAD
2 *syn* see DESTROY 1

decay *vb* to undergo or to cause to undergo destructive changes < apples *decaying* in the basket >
syn break down, corrupt, crumble, decompose, disintegrate, molder, ‖perish, putrefy, putresce, rot, spoil, taint, turn

rel deteriorate; debilitate, enfeeble, sap, undermine, weaken; contaminate, defile, pollute; dilapidate, ruin, wreck; curdle, ferment, sour, work; dry-rot

idiom go bad, go to pot, go to seed, go to wrack and ruin

con mature, ripen; refresh, renew, restore; activate, energize, vitalize; cleanse, purify; galvanize, quicken, stimulate, strengthen

decayed *adj* 1 *syn* see EFFETE 3

2 *syn* see BAD 5

decease *n syn* see DEATH 1

decease *vb syn* see DIE 1

deceased *adj syn* see DEAD 1

deceit *n* 1 the act or practice of imposing upon the credulity of others by dishonesty, fraud, or trickery < he was full of *deceit* in his business dealings >

syn cunning, dissemblance, dissimulation, duplicity, guile

rel chicane, chicanery, deception, double-dealing, fraud, trickery; artifice, craft; cheating, cozening, defrauding, entrapping, overreaching, trapping

con honesty, scrupulosity, scrupulousness, uprightness; candidness, candor, frankness, openness; forthrightness, straightforwardness

2 *syn* see IMPOSTURE

deceitful *adj syn* see DISHONEST 1

rel artful, crafty, cunning, foxy, guileful, insidious, sly, tricky, wily; clandestine, furtive, stealthy, underhand, underhanded; deceptive, delusive, delusory, misleading

con assuring, convincing, reassuring

ant trustworthy

deceive *vb* to lead astray or frustrate by underhandedness < advertising that *deceives* the public >

syn beguile, betray, ‖bitch, bluff, ‖bunk, cozen, delude, double-cross, four-flush, humbug, illude, juggle, mislead, mock, sell out, suck in, take in, two-time

rel cheat, defraud, do, overreach; circumvent, outwit; bamboozle, befool, dupe, gull, hoax, hoodwink, spoof, trick, victimize; throw off

idiom pull one's leg, pull the wool over one's eyes, put something over (or across), take for a ride, take into camp, throw off the scent (or track)

con correct, disabuse, rectify, unblind; acquaint, advise, apprise, inform

ant undeceive; enlighten

deceiving *adj syn* see MISLEADING

ant undeceiving; enlightening

decelerate *vb syn* see DELAY 1

ant accelerate

decency *n syn* see DECORUM 1

rel appropriateness, fittingness, fitness, suitability; ceremoniousness, conventionality, formality

con impropriety, indecorousness, unseemliness; inappropriateness, unfitness, unsuitability; discourteousness, impoliteness, rudeness

ant indecency

decent *adj* 1 *syn* see DECOROUS 1

con awkward, clumsy, gauche, inept, maladroit; discomfiting, disconcerting, embarrassing; crude, rough, rude, uncouth

2 *syn* see CHASTE

rel noble; good, right; rigid, strict; ascetic, austere, severe

con lewd; libertine, wanton; abandoned, dissolute, profligate, reprobate

ant indecent; obscene

3 *syn* see RESPECTABLE 5

4 better than mediocre but less than excellent < the accommodations were *decent* >

syn acceptable, adequate, all right, common, good, respectable, right, satisfactory, sufficient, tolerable, unexceptionable, unexceptional, unimpeachable, unobjectionable; *compare* RESPECTABLE 5, SUFFICIENT 1

rel average, fair, mediocre, middling

con imperfect, inadequate, unacceptable, unsatisfactory; excellent, fine, superior

5 *syn* see SUFFICIENT 1

decently *adv syn* see WELL 1

deception *n* 1 the act of deliberately deceiving < resort to falsehood and *deception* in avoiding the tax >

syn cheat, chicane, chicanery, dipsy-doodle, dirt, dishonesty, double-dealing, dupery, fourberie, fraud, hanky-panky, highbinding, indirection, sharp practice, subterfuge, ‖suck-in, trickery

rel cunning, deceit, dissimulation, duplicity, guile; cheating, cozening, defrauding, overreaching; bamboozling, befooling, duping, gulling, hoaxing, hoodwinking; manipulation; ride, ‖snow job

con candidness, frankness, openness; honesty, integrity, probity; artlessness, ingenuousness, naiveté

2 *syn* see IMPOSTURE

rel delusion, hallucination, illusion, mirage

3 *syn* see FALLACY 2

deceptive *adj syn* see MISLEADING

rel colorable, plausible, specious; apparent, illusory, ostensible, seeming

con authentic, bona fide, genuine, veritable; actual, real, true; dependable, reliable, trustworthy

deceptiveness *n syn* see FALLACY 2

decide *vb* to come or to cause to come to a conclusion < he *decided* how to solve the problem >

syn conclude, determine, figure, resolve, rule, settle

rel gather; adjudge, adjudicate, judge; conjecture, guess, surmise; establish, fix, set

idiom cast the die, make up one's mind, settle in one's mind

con falter, hesitate, vacillate, waver; fluctuate, oscillate; balk, demur, scruple, shy

decided *adj* 1 beyond any doubt or ambiguity < a *decided* advantage over her opponent >

syn assured, clear-cut, definite, pronounced

rel determined, resolved; certain, positive, sure; categorical, explicit, express, unequivocal; clear, obvious, unmistakable, runaway

con doubtful, dubious, problematic, uncertain; equivocal, obscure, vague

---

syn synonym(s)   *rel* related word(s)
ant antonym(s)   *con* contrasted word(s)
idiom idiomatic equivalent(s)
‖ use limited; if in doubt, see a dictionary

ant questionable

2 free from doubt or wavering < he had a *decided* manner >

syn bent, decisive, determined, intent, resolute, resolved, set, settled

rel certain, cocksure, positive, sure; iron=jawed; established, fixed; earnest, purposeful, serious; unfaltering, unhesitating, unwavering

con doubtful, dubious, irresolute, uncertain; faltering, hesitant, vacillating, wavering; undetermined, unresolved, unsettled, unsure

ant undecided

3 *syn* see POSITIVE 1

decidedness *n syn* see DECISION 2

decimate *vb* 1 *syn* see DESTROY 1

2 *syn* see SLAUGHTER 3

decipher *vb* 1 *syn* see DECODE

ant cipher, encipher

2 *syn* see SOLVE 2

rel paraphrase, translate; analyze, break down

idiom find the key of

con misconstrue, misinterpret, misunderstand; confuse, muddle; bewilder, confound, mystify; puzzle; jumble, mix, scramble

decision *n* 1 a position arrived at after consideration < the *decision* of the committee remains firm >

syn conclusion, determination, resolution, settlement

rel accord, agreement, understanding; accommodation, adjustment, arrangement; compromise, reconciliation; choice, preference, selection

con deadlock, draw, stalemate, standoff, tie

2 freedom from doubt or wavering < a man of unusual *decision* >

syn decidedness, determination, firmness, purposefulness, purposiveness, resoluteness, resolution, resolve

rel doggedness, obstinacy, obstinance, perseverance, persistence, stubbornness; earnestness, seriousness; backbone, fortitude, grit, pluck

con changeableness, indetermination, irresolution; uncertainty, unsureness; faltering, fluctuation, hesitation, vacillation, wavering

ant indecision

decisive *adj syn* see DECIDED 2

rel imperative, imperious, masterful, peremptory; assured, self-assured, self-confident; steadfast, unswerving, unwavering

con fluctuating, oscillating; hesitant, reluctant; doubtful, dubious, irresolute, uncertain, undecided

ant indecisive

deck *vb syn* see ADORN

rel apparel, array, attire, clothe, dress; accouter, appoint, furnish

con deface, disfigure; impair, mar, spoil; contort, deform, distort; dismantle, divest, strip

deck (out) *vb syn* see DRESS UP 1

declaim *vb syn* see ORATE

declamatory *adj syn* see RHETORICAL

declaration *n* the act of declaring, proclaiming, or publicly announcing < a *declaration* of war >

syn advertisement, announcement, broadcast, proclamation, promulgation, pronouncement; pronunciamento, publication

rel information, notice, notification; communication; disclosure, revelation; report, statement; acknowledgment, avowal

con concealment, hiding; denial, disaffirmation; recall, recantation, retraction, revocation

declare *vb* 1 to make known openly or publicly < *declared* his intention to run for the senate >

syn advertise, announce, annunciate, blaze (abroad), blazon, broadcast, bruit (about), disseminate, proclaim, promulgate, publish, sound, toot, vend

rel acquaint, advise, apprise, inform, notify; communicate, impart; pronounce; disclose, discover, divulge, reveal; report

idiom declare oneself, make public (or known)

con hold, hold back, keep back, reserve, withhold; recall, recant, retract, revoke

2 *syn* see ASSERT 1

rel air, broach, express, utter, vent, ventilate, voice; acknowledge, admit, own

idiom have one's say

con controvert; deny; repress, suppress; conceal, hide

3 *syn* see SAY 1

rel broach, express, voice

idiom speak one's piece

declare off *vb syn* see BACK DOWN

declass *vb syn* see DEGRADE 1

rel disbar, exclude, rule out; abash, discomfit, disconcert

con aggrandize, exalt, magnify

déclassé *adj syn* see INFERIOR 2

declension *n syn* see DETERIORATION 1

rel regression, regressiveness, retrogression, retrogressiveness; dilapidation, ruination

con ascension, ascent; rise, rising; advance, progress, progression; development, maturation

declination *n* 1 *syn* see DETERIORATION 1

2 *syn* see FAILURE 4

decline *vb* 1 *syn* see SET 12

ant ascend

2 *syn* see FAIL 1

rel backslide, lapse, relapse; slide; return, revert; recede, retrograde; abate, ebb, subside, wane

idiom go downhill, take a turn for the worse

con advance, progress; develop, mature; gain, recover

3 *syn* see DETERIORATE 1

4 to turn away by not accepting, receiving, or considering < he *declined* the invitation >

syn disapprove, dismiss, refuse, reject, reprobate, repudiate, spurn, turn down

rel balk, boggle, demur, jib, scruple, shy, stick, stickle; abstain, forbear, refrain; deny, gainsay; abjure, renounce; bypass

idiom send regrets

con receive, take; accede, acquiesce, assent, consent; choose, select; adopt, embrace, espouse

ant accept

decline *n* 1 *syn* see FAILURE 4

rel devitalization, weakening
con advancement, progress; recovery; development, maturation
2 *syn* see DETERIORATION 1
rel comedown, descent, drop, fall, falling off, slump; ebb, wane; backsliding, lapse, relapse
con development, evolution
3 a downward movement (as in price or value) <stocks suffered a *decline* in the market>
syn dip, downslide, downswing, downtrend, downturn, drop, falloff, sag, slide, slip, slump
rel lapse, loss, lowering; depression; decrease, drop-off, sell-off
con upswing, uptrend, upturn
4 *syn* see DESCENT 4

declivate *adj syn* see INCLINED 3

declivitous *adj syn* see INCLINED 3

declivity *n syn* see DESCENT 4
ant acclivity

decode *vb* to convert code into ordinary language <*decode* a message>
syn break, crack, cryptanalyze, decipher, decrypt
rel anagram; render; translate; ‖dope out, figure out, make out; resolve, solve, unfold, unravel, unriddle, work, work out; elucidate, explain, interpret
con cipher, codify, encipher; anagrammatize
ant code, encode, encrypt

decollate *vb syn* see BEHEAD

decolor *vb syn* see WHITEN 1
rel wash out; achromatize, fume, peroxide
con blacken; dye, imbue, stain, tinge, tint; paint, shade
ant color

decolorize *vb syn* see WHITEN 1
ant color

decompose *vb* **1** *syn* see ANALYZE
con combine, join, link, write; synthesize, unify; amalgamate, merge, mix
ant compound
2 *syn* see DECAY
rel deliquesce, liquefy, melt; break up, dissolve

decompound *vb syn* see ANALYZE
ant compound

decorate *vb syn* see ADORN
rel accouter, appoint, equip, furnish, outfit
con impair, injure, mar, spoil; blot, blotch, foul, mutilate, scar, uglify; dismantle, divest, strip

decorated *adj syn* see BEMEDALED

decoration *n syn* see HONOR 2

decorous *adj* **1** conforming to an accepted standard of propriety or good form <*decorous* behavior seems regrettably out of fashion>
syn au fait, becoming, befitting, Christian, civilized, comely, conforming, correct, decent, de rigueur, done, nice, proper, respectable, right, seemly
rel ceremonial, ceremonious, conventional, formal; dignified, elegant; appropri-

ate, fit, fitting, meet, seasonable, suitable; prim, punctilious, rigid, stiff, stuffy
con blatant, clamorous, obstreperous, strident; aggressive, assertive, pushing, pushy; coarse, gross, vulgar; easy, fast, loose; improper, incorrect, unbecoming
ant indecorous
2 *syn* see GOOD 13

decorously *adv syn* see WELL 1

decorousness *n syn* see ORDER 7
rel ceremoniousness, conventionality, formality, solemnity; convenance, convention, form, usage
con inappropriateness, incorrectness; unfitness, unsuitability, unsuitableness; disorder, misbehavior, misconduct, misdeed, misdemeanor
ant indecorousness

decorticate *vb syn* see SKIN 2
rel bark; scalp; denude, divest

decorum *n* **1** socially acceptable behavior or accepted standards of this <they found his conduct quite lacking in *decorum*>
syn decency, dignity, etiquette, propriety, seemliness
rel convenance, convention, form, usage
con laxity, laxness, license, slackness; carelessness, heedlessness, inconsiderateness, mannerlessness; inappropriateness, incorrectness
ant indecorum
2 *syn* see ORDER 7
rel ceremoniousness, conventionality, formality, solemnity; convenance, convention, form, usage
con inappropriateness, incorrectness; unfitness, unsuitability, unsuitableness; disorder, misbehavior, misconduct, misdeed, misdemeanor
ant indecorum; license
3 *usu* decorums *syn* see MANNER 3

decoy *n* **1** *syn* see LURE 2
rel chicane, chicanery, deception, trickery; drawing card
con rebuff, repellence, repellency, repellent, repugnance, repulse, repulsion
2 a person used as a lure <used the detective as a *decoy* to catch the pushers>
syn blind, ‖bonnet, ‖booster, capper, shill, shillaber, stick
rel lugger, roper, steerer; come-on, front, plant, stall

decoy *vb syn* see LURE
rel deceive, delude, mislead; ensorcell, wile
con disgust, repel, sicken; offend, repulse, revolt

decrease *vb* to grow less especially gradually <his influence *decreased* as a new generation grew up>
syn abate, bate, close, diminish, drain (away), dwindle, lessen, peak (out), peter (out), rebate, recede, reduce, taper, taper off
rel abbreviate, abridge, clip, curtail, retrench, shorten, trim; contract, shrink; allay, alleviate, ease, lighten, mitigate; ebb, subside; cut, cut back, cut down, lower; deduct, subtract
con augment, enlarge, multiply; elongate, extend, lengthen, prolong, protract; amplify, dilate, distend, expand, swell; accumulate, amass

---

syn synonym(s)   *rel* related word(s)
ant antonym(s)   *con* contrasted word(s)
idiom idiomatic phrase(s)
‖ use limited; if in doubt, see a dictionary

ant increase

decree *n* 1 *syn* see EDICT 1
2 *syn* see LAW 1
rel behest, bidding, injunction, order; charge, charging, direction, instruction; announcement, declaration, proclamation, promulgation, pronouncement

decree *vb* *syn* see DICTATE
rel compel, constrain, force, oblige; demand, require

decrepit *adj* 1 *syn* see WEAK 1
rel haggard, wasted, worn; aged, old, superannuated; creaky, quavering, shaking, tottering
con strong; lusty; hale, healthy, hearty, robust, sound, well
ant sturdy
2 *syn* see SHABBY 1
rel damaged, impaired, injured, marred, spoiled; cast-off, ragged, used; slipshod, sloppy, unkempt

decrepitude *n* *syn* see INFIRMITY 1
ant vigor

decretum *n* *syn* see LAW 1

decry *vb* 1 *syn* see DEPRECIATE 1
2 to indicate one's low opinion of something < *decrying* his opponent's character >
syn abuse, belittle, cry down, depreciate, derogate, detract (from), diminish, discount, disparage, dispraise, downcry, ‖low-rate, minimize, opprobriate, run down, take (from), take away, write off
rel deprecate, disapprove; censure, condemn, criticize, denounce, reprehend, reprobate; asperse, calumniate, defame, malign, traduce, vilify; discredit, disgrace
idiom bring into discredit, cast a slur upon, cast blame upon, throw stones at
con acclaim, eulogize, laud, praise; aggrandize, exalt, magnify; applaud, commend, compliment, recommend; endorse, sanction; approve, countenance, favor
ant extol, puff

decrypt *vb* *syn* see DECODE
decumbent *adj* *syn* see PRONE 4
decussate *vb* *syn* see INTERSECT
dedicate *vb* *syn* see DEVOTE 1
rel address, apply, direct, give, surrender; commit, confide, consign, entrust; allot, appropriate, assign, set (aside)
idiom give over to

dedition *n* *syn* see SURRENDER
deduce *vb* *syn* see INFER
rel cogitate; consider, deem, regard; conceive, fancy, imagine; assume, presume, presuppose; read (into)
idiom take to mean

deducible *adj* *syn* see DEDUCTIVE
deduct *vb* 1 to take away one quantity from another < *deduct* the cost from his bill >
syn discount, draw back, knock off, substract, subtract, take, take away, take off, take out
rel decrease, diminish, lessen, reduce; roll back
con cast, figure, sum, tot, total
ant add
2 *syn* see INFER

deduction *n* 1 an amount subtracted from a sum < *deductions* from gross income >
syn abatement, discount, rebate, reduction, subtraction

rel allowance, credit, cut; decrease, decrement, depreciation, diminution; charge-off, offtake, takeoff, write-off; dockage
con accession, accretion, augmentation, increase, increment, raise, rise; appreciation
ant addition
2 *syn* see INFERENCE 1
3 *syn* see INFERENCE 2
rel cogitation, deliberation, reasoning, reflection, speculation, thinking; consideration, contemplation; meditation, mulling, musing, pondering, rumination

deductive *adj* that can be deduced or developed from premises < *deductive* laws >
syn a priori, deducible, derivable, dogmatic, reasoned
rel illative, inferential, ratiocinative; conjectural, hypothetical, purported, putative, supposed, suppositious; academic, speculative, theoretical
con categorical, definite, explicit, express; instinctive, intuitive

deed *n* 1 *syn* see ACTION 1
2 *syn* see FEAT 2
rel gaining, securing, winning; adventure, enterprise, quest; cause, crusade
idiom bold stroke
3 a written, signed, and usually sealed instrument that spells out some bargain, transfer, or contract < the *deed* to the property >
syn charter, conveyance
rel bargain, compact, contract, covenant, pact

deed *vb* *syn* see TRANSFER 4
deem *vb* 1 *syn* see CONSIDER 3
rel conjecture, guess, surmise, suspect, ‖suspicion, understand; ‖allow, assume, believe, ‖calculate, daresay, divine, expect, presume, suppose
idiom hold to be true
2 *syn* see FEEL 3
idiom take for granted

de-emphasize *vb* *syn* see SOFT-PEDAL

deep *adj* 1 having great extension downward or inward < a *deep* well > < a *deep* closet >
syn abysmal, profound; *compare* BOTTOMLESS 2
con depthless, shallow, superficial, unprofound; flat, level, plain, plane
ant shallow
2 *syn* see INTENSIVE
3 *syn* see RECONDITE
rel complex, complicated, intricate; arcane, mysterious; concealed, hidden
con easy, facile, simple; apparent, clear, distinct, evident, manifest, obvious; lucid, perspicuous; depthless, shallow, superficial, unprofound
4 *syn* see SLY 2
rel shrewd; acute, keen, knowing, sharp; contriving, intriguing, plotting
con ingenuous, naive, simple, unsophisticated; aboveboard, forthright, straightforward
5 *syn* see INTENT
rel abstracted, concentrated; centered, fixed, focused, set
con distracted, diverted; detached, disinterested, indifferent, unconcerned, uninterested

deep *n syn* see OCEAN
deep–dyed *adj syn* see INVETERATE 1
deepen *vb syn* see INTENSIFY
deepness *n* 1 *syn* see DEPTH 1
   ant shallowness
   2 *syn* see DEPTH 2
deep–rooted *adj syn* see INVETERATE 1
deep–seated *adj* 1 *syn* see INHERENT
   2 *syn* see INVETERATE 1
   rel constitutional, immanent, indwelling, ingrained, inherent, intrinsic; deep, profound; inner, internal, inward; implanted; infixed
   con peripheral, shallow, superficial, surface; adventitious, casual, chance, incidental
   ant skin-deep
‖deep–six *vb syn* see DISCARD
deep water *n syn* see PREDICAMENT
deface *vb* to mar the appearance of < deface the wall with graffiti >
   syn disfashion, disfeature, disfigure
   rel blemish, damage, harm, impair, injure, mar, spoil; contort, deform, distort, misshape; batter, mangle, mutilate; demolish, destroy; dilapidate, ruin, wreck
   con mend, patch, repair; freshen, improve, refurbish, renew, restore; adorn, beautify, deck, decorate, embellish, ornament
defacer *n syn* see VANDAL
de facto *adv syn* see VERY 2
defalcation *n syn* see FAILURE 3
   rel laxness, negligence, remissness, slackness; failing, fault
   con discharge, effectuation, execution, fulfillment; completion, conclusion
defamation *n syn* see DETRACTION
   ant puffery
defamatory *adj syn* see LIBELOUS
defame *vb syn* see MALIGN
   rel belie, misrepresent
   idiom cast a slur on, throw mud at
   con applaud, commend, compliment; exalt, magnify; back, champion, support, uphold
   ant laud; puff
default *n* 1 *syn* see FAILURE 1
   rel deficiency, fault, imperfection, shortcoming; lapse, weakness; disregard, omission, overlooking, slight
   2 *syn* see ABSENCE
defeasance *n syn* see DEFEAT 1
defeat *vb* 1 *syn* see CONQUER 1
   rel bar, block, hinder, impede, obstruct; repress, suppress
   idiom beat all hollow, get the better of, grind into the dust, ‖have by the short hairs
   con capitulate, defer, give in, submit; back down, withdraw
   2 to win a victory over < defeated his opponent in the race >
   syn best, down, outdo, ‖pip, worst; *compare* CONQUER 1, WHIP 2
   rel outfight, outgame; nose out
   idiom get the better of
defeat *n* 1 an overthrow especially of an army in battle < the brigade suffered a defeat >

syn beating, debacle, defeasance, discomfiture, downcast, downthrow, drubbing, ‖dusting, licking, overthrow, rout, shellacking, thrashing, trouncing, vanquishment, warming
   rel bafflement, check, foil, frustration; rebuff, repulse, reversal, reverse, setback; ‖cleaning, ‖cleanup, clobbering, lambasting
   con conquest, triumph; gaining, securing, winning; ascendancy, supremacy
   ant victory
   2 *syn* see FAILURE 2
defeater *n syn* see VICTOR 1
   ant defeated
defect *n* 1 *syn* see BLEMISH
   rel failing, fault, foible, frailty; infirmity, weakness, deficiency, imperfection, shortcoming
   con excellence, faultlessness, impeccability; merit, perfection, virtue
   2 *syn* see ABSENCE
   rel scantiness, scarceness, scarcity, shortage
   con overage, overplus, superfluity, surplus, surplusage
   ant excess
defect *vb* to desert a cause or party often in order to espouse another < he defected from the Communist party >
   syn apostatize, desert, rat, renounce, repudiate, tergiversate, tergiverse, turn
   rel abandon, forsake; back out, renege, withdraw; depart, go, leave, quit; reject, spurn
   idiom change sides, go back on, go over, turn one's coat, walk (or run) out on
   con adhere (to), cling (to), hang on, stick (to or with); cherish, cultivate, foster
defection *n* conscious abandonment of allegiance or duty < defection from family responsibilities in times of trouble >
   syn apostasy, desertion, falseness, recreancy, tergiversation
   rel alienation, disaffection, estrangement; disloyalty, faithlessness; abandonment, forsaking; divorce, parting, runout, separation, sundering; disownment, rejection, repudiation
   idiom running out on, ‖taking a runout powder
   con constancy, faithfulness, loyalty, resoluteness, staunchness, steadfastness; allegiance, fealty, fidelity; dependability, reliability, trustworthiness
defective *adj* 1 *syn* see FAULTY
   rel broken, damaged, impaired, injured
   con faultless, flawless, impeccable, unblemished, undamaged
   ant defectless
   2 *syn* see DEFICIENT 1
   rel corrupted, debased, vitiated; deranged, disordered, disturbed, unsettled; unhealthy, unsound
   con entire, perfect, whole; complete, full, plenary; healthy, sound
   ant intact; defectless
defector *n syn* see RENEGADE
defend *vb* 1 to keep safe (as from danger or against attack) < defend the country from aggression >
   syn bulwark, cover, fend, guard, protect, safeguard, screen, secure, shield

---

syn synonym(s)   *rel* related word(s)
ant antonym(s)   *con* contrasted word(s)
idiom idiomatic equivalent(s)
‖ use limited; if in doubt, see a dictionary

rel avert, prevent, ward; oppose, resist, withstand; battle, contend, fight, war; conserve, preserve, save
idiom stand on the defensive, stave off from
con aggress, assail, assault, fall (on *or* upon); bombard, storm; beset, besiege, overrun; capitulate, cave, submit, yield
ant attack
2 *syn see* MAINTAIN 2
rel air, express, utter, vent, voice; account, explain, justify, rationalize; back, champion, support, uphold
idiom speak (*or* stand *or* stick) up for
con contradict, deny, gainsay, traverse; confute, controvert, disprove, rebut, refute
defendable *adj syn see* TENABLE 1
ant undefendable
defense *n* 1 means or method of defending < the skunk's powerful *defense* against attackers >
syn aegis, armament, armor, guard, protection, safeguard, security, shield, ward
rel arms, munitions, weaponry, weapons; fastness, fort, fortress, stronghold
con aggression, offense, offensive
ant attack
2 *syn see* APOLOGY 1
rel answer, rejoinder, reply, response, retort, return; exculpation, excuse, explanation, rationalization
con censure, condemnation, criticism, decrial, reprehension, reprobation, reproof; assault, attack, onset, onslaught
defenseless *adj syn see* HELPLESS 1
defensible *adj* 1 *syn see* TENABLE 1
ant indefensible
2 *syn see* JUSTIFIABLE
ant indefensible
defer *vb* to delay an action or proceeding < decided to *defer* voting until the next meeting >
syn adjourn, delay, hold off, hold over, hold up, intermit, lay over, postpone, prorogue, put off, put over, remit, shelve, stand over, stay, suspend, waive
rel detain, retard, slow; block, hinder, impede, obstruct; stall; extend, lengthen, prolong, protract
idiom hold up on, lay to one side, put on ice, set aside
con accelerate, hasten, hurry, speed; expedite, further, promote
ant advance
defer *vb syn see* YIELD 2
rel accede, acquiesce, agree, assent; accommodate, adapt, adjust, conform; cringe, fawn, truckle
con combat, fight, oppose, resist; object, remonstrate; balk, demur, stickle, strain
ant withstand
deference *n syn see* HONOR 1
rel acquiescence, compliance; submission, submissiveness
con insolence, irreverence; disesteem, disfavor; discourtesy, incivility, rudeness
ant disrespect
deferential *adj syn see* RESPECTFUL
2 *syn see* INGRATIATING
defi *n syn see* DEFIANCE 1
defiance *n* 1 the act or an instance of defying < presented a *defiance* to his rival >

syn cartel, challenge, dare, defi, defy, stump
rel call, muster, summons; command, enjoinder, order
con capitulation, submission, surrender
2 disposition to resist or unwillingness to brook opposition < exhibited *defiance* toward his teacher >
syn contempt, contumacy, despite, recalcitrance, stubbornness
rel factiousness, insubordination, insurgency, rebelliousness; headstrongness, intractableness, unruliness; boldness, bravado, brazenness, impudence, insolence; audacity, effrontery, hardihood, temerity; contrariness, perversity
con acquiescence, compliance; amenableness, docility, obedience, tractableness; submissiveness
deficiency *n* 1 *syn see* FAILURE 3
rel absence, default, defect, want
con copiousness, plenty; great deal, heap, lot, much
2 *syn see* IMPERFECTION
rel dearth, defect, lack, privation, want; default, dereliction, miscarriage, neglect
ant excess
deficient *adj* 1 showing lack of something necessary < *deficient* in judgment >
syn defective, ‖half-assed, inadequate, incomplete, insufficient, lacking, uncomplete, wanting
rel faulty, flawed, imperfect, unsound; damaged, impaired, injured, marred; amiss, bad, unsatisfactory
idiom in want of
con complete, entire, intact, whole; acceptable, adequate, sufficient
2 *syn see* SHORT 3
rel infrequent, rare, uncommon
idiom found wanting
con excessive, extravagant, immoderate, inordinate; enough, satisfactory, sufficing
ant adequate, sufficient
deficit *n syn see* FAILURE 3
con copiousness, plenty; excess, surplus, surplusage
defile *vb* 1 *syn see* CONTAMINATE 1
rel desecrate, profane; befoul, dirty, foul, sully, tarnish
con consecrate, hallow
ant cleanse; purify
2 *syn see* RAPE
rel dishonor, shame, soil, sully
3 *syn see* TAINT 1
defiled *adj syn see* IMPURE
define *vb* 1 *syn see* PRESCRIBE 2
rel circumscribe, limit, mark (off), mark (out); designate, delineate, describe
con confound, confuse, mistake
2 *syn see* BORDER 1
3 *syn see* ETCH 2
rel explain, expound, interpret
definite *adj* 1 having distinct or certain limits < *definite* dimensions >
syn circumscribed, determinate, fixed, limited, narrow, precise, restricted
rel assigned, defined, prescribed; established, set; decided, determined, settled
con ambiguous, obscure, vague; unconditional, unlimited, unqualified, unrestricted; indeterminate, uncircumscribed; imprecise, loose, undefined

ant indefinite
2 syn see EXPLICIT
rel complete, full; downright, forthright; incisive
con doubtful, dubious, questionable; ambiguous
ant indefinite; equivocal
3 syn see POSITIVE 1
4 syn see DECIDED 1
ant uncertain
definitely adv **1 syn** see EXPRESSLY 1
2 syn see EASILY 2
definiteness n **syn** see PRECISION
ant indefiniteness
definitive adj **1 syn** see CONCLUSIVE
rel determining, settling; concluding, final, last, terminal, ultimate; closing, completing, ending, finishing, terminating; absolute, categorical
con inconclusive, indecisive; temporary, transitory
ant provisional, tentative
2 syn see EXPLICIT
rel actual, real
con doubtful, dubious, questionable; ambiguous
ant indefinite
definitiveness n **syn** see PRECISION
ant indefinitiveness, indefinitude
definitude n **syn** see PRECISION
ant indefinitiveness, indefinitude
deflect vb **1 syn** see TURN 6
rel disperse, swerve; hook, skew
2 syn see WARD 1
rel hold off, keep off
deflection n **1 syn** see DEVIATION 1
rel bending, curving, twisting; departing, swerve, swerving, veer, veering
2 syn see TURN 2
deflorate vb **syn** see RAPE
deflower vb **1 syn** see RAPE
2 syn see RAVAGE
deform vb to mar or spoil by or as if by twisting <a face *deformed* by bitterness>
syn contort, distort, misshape, torture, warp, wind
rel batter, cripple, maim, mangle, mutilate; deface, disfigure; damage, impair, injure, mar, spoil; blemish, flaw; screw (up), squinch
deformity n a physical blemish or disfigurement <the dwarf's humpback *deformity*>
syn distortion, malconformation, malformation, misshape
rel defacement, deformation, disfigurement; damage, impairment, injury; aberration, abnormality; irregularity, unnaturalness
defraud vb **syn** see CHEAT
rel bamboozle, hoax, trick; circumvent, foil, outwit; fleece, milk, stick; take in
idiom do out of, put over a fast one, take to the cleaner's
defrauder n **syn** see SWINDLER
deft adj **syn** see DEXTEROUS 1
rel agile, brisk, fleet; apt, prompt, quick, ready; adept, crack, crackerjack; ingenious, neat

con heavy-handed, unskillful; blundering, bungling, butterfingered; rigid, stiff, wooden
ant awkward, unhandy
deftness n **syn** see ADDRESS 1
rel agility, fleetness, nimbleness; assuredness, confidence
con incompetence, inefficiency; clumsiness, heavy-handedness, maladroitness
ant awkwardness
defunct adj **1 syn** see DEAD 1
rel inactive, inert
ant alive; live
2 syn see EXTINCT 2
ant surviving
defunction n **syn** see DEATH 1
defy vb **syn** see FACE 3
rel deride, mock, ridicule; gibe, flout; scorn, scout, spurn; disregard, ignore
idiom fling (*or* throw) down the gauntlet, hurl defiance at
con blench, flinch, quail, shrink
ant recoil
defy n **syn** see DEFIANCE 1
dégagé adj **syn** see EASYGOING 3
ant mannered
degeneracy n **syn** see DETERIORATION 1
degenerate adj **1 syn** see EFFETE 3
rel deteriorating, retrograde, retrogressive, worsening; failing, sinking
2 syn see VICIOUS 2
rel degraded, demeaned
con ethical, moral, virtuous; honorable, just, upright
ant regenerate
degenerate vb **syn** see DETERIORATE 1
rel corrupt, deprave, vitiate; backslide, lapse; return, revert
con improve, upgrade; lift, uplift
degeneration n **syn** see DETERIORATION 1
rel regression, regressiveness, retrogression, retrogressiveness; depreciation; corruption, depravation, depravedness, depravity, perversion
con regeneracy, regenerateness; progress, progression
ant regeneration
degradation n **syn** see DEMOTION
ant advancement; elevation
degrade vb **1** to lower in station, rank, or grade <*degraded* in rank for misconduct>
syn break, bump, bust, declass, demerit, demote, disgrade, disrate, downgrade, put down, reduce
rel abase, debase, humble, humiliate, lower; disbar, rule out
con advance, further; boost, lift, raise; enhance, heighten
ant elevate
2 syn see HUMBLE
rel belittle, decry, derogate, detract, disparage; diminish, lessen, reduce
con elevate, raise; acclaim, extol, laud, praise
ant uplift
degree n **1** a unitary component of a process, course, or order of classification <advanced by *degrees*>
syn grade, notch, stage, step
2 relative size or character of the parts or components in a complex whole compared with other like things <the *degree* of

---

syn synonym(s)   **rel** related word(s)
ant antonym(s)   **con** contrasted word(s)
idiom idiomatic equivalent(s)
‖ use limited; if in doubt, see a dictionary

difference between the two jobs> <his work demands a high *degree* of intelligence>
syn proportion, rate, ratio, scale
rel dimension; extent, magnitude, measure, size

dégringolade *n syn* see DETERIORATION 1

dehydrate *vb syn* see DRY 1
ant hydrate; rehydrate

deific *adj* 1 *syn* see DIVINE 1
2 *syn* see DIVINE 2

deification *n syn* see APOTHEOSIS 2

deign *vb syn* see STOOP 1

deject *vb syn* see DISCOURAGE 1
ant exhilarate; cheer

dejected *adj syn* see DOWNCAST
idiom down in the dumps (*or* mouth), in the dumps
ant animated

dejection *n syn* see SADNESS
rel despair, desperation
ant exhilaration

‖**dekko** *vb syn* see SEE 2

delay *vb* 1 to cause to be late or behind in movement or progress <was *delayed* by traffic>
syn bog (down), decelerate, detain, embog, hang up, mire, retard, set back, slacken, slow (up *or* down)
rel block, hinder, impede, obstruct; defer, hold over, hold up, intermit, postpone, put off, stay, suspend; arrest, check, interrupt
idiom hang fire
con accelerate, hasten, hurry, precipitate, quicken, speed; advance, forward, further, promote
ant expedite
2 to move or act slowly so that progress or work is retarded <their landlord kept *delaying* in making repairs>
syn dally, dawdle, dilly, dillydally, drag, lag, linger, loiter, mull, poke, procrastinate, put off, tarry, trail
rel hang back, idle, wait; drone; falter, hesitate, vacillate, waver
idiom take one's own sweet (*or* good) time
ant hasten, hurry
3 *syn* see DEFER

delectable *adj syn* see DELIGHTFUL
rel choice, dainty, delicate, exquisite, rare; palatable, sapid, savory, tasty, toothsome
con loathsome, offensive, repulsive, revolting
ant distasteful

delectate *vb syn* see PLEASE 2

delectation *n* 1 *syn* see PLEASURE 2
rel gratification, gratifying, regalement, regaling; enjoyment, relish
ant distaste
2 *syn* see ENJOYMENT 1

‖**deleerit** *adj syn* see INTOXICATED 1

delegate *n* a person standing in the place of another or others <was a *delegate* to the convention>
syn catchpole, deputy, representant, representative; *compare* AGENT 2
rel agent, factor, proxy; alternate, replacement, stand-in, substitute, surrogate; mouthpiece, spokesman; emissary, envoy

delegate *vb* to appoint as one's representative <*delegated* her to watch the children>
syn commission, depute, deputize
rel ascribe, assign, charge; appoint, designate, name; choose, pick, select

delete *vb syn* see ERASE
rel eliminate, exclude, rule out; omit

deleterious *adj syn* see HARMFUL
rel destroying, destructive; ruining, ruinous
con advantageous, profitable; healthful, healthy, salubrious, wholesome
ant salutary

deliberate *adj* 1 arrived at after due thought <a *deliberate* judgment>
syn advised, aforethought, considered, designed, premeditated, prepense, studied, studious, thought-out
rel planned, projected, schemed; calculated; careful, meticulous, scrupulous; foresighted, forethoughtful, provident, prudent
con chance, chancy, desultory, haphazard, happy-go-lucky, hit-or-miss, random; aimless, designless, purposeless; hasty, hurried; abrupt, impetuous, sudden; automatic, instinctive, spontaneous
ant casual
2 *syn* see VOLUNTARY
rel intended, meant, meditated, purposed; determined, purposeful; aware, cognizant, conscious
con careless, heedless, inadvertent, thoughtless; unintended, unpurposed
ant impulsive
3 *syn* see SLOW 2
rel calculating, cautious, chary, circumspect, wary; careful, heedful; collected, composed, cool, imperturbable
con hasty, headlong, impetuous, sudden
ant abrupt, precipitate

deliberate *vb* 1 *syn* see PONDER 2
2 *syn* see THINK 5
rel excogitate, study, weigh; argue, debate, discuss, talk over

deliberately *adv syn* see INTENTIONALLY

deliberation *n* 1 *syn* see ATTENTION 1
2 *syn* see THOUGHT 1
3 *syn* see CONFERENCE 1

delicacy *n* something special and delicious to eat <fresh fruit in the winter was once an uncommon *delicacy*>
syn bonne bouche, dainty, goody, kickshaw, morsel, tidbit (*or* titbit), treat
rel banquet, feast, regale; cosseting, indulgence, luxury
idiom choice bit, dish fit for a king

delicate *adj* 1 *syn* see CHOICE
rel delectable, delicious, delightful; balmy, gentle, lenient, mild, soft; aerial, airy, ethereal
con coarse, crude, vulgar
ant gross
2 *syn* see FINE 1
3 *syn* see NICE 1
rel perceptive, sensitive
con insensitive, undiscriminating, unperceptive
4 *syn* see FRAGILE 1
5 lacking in strength or substance <a *delicate* constitution>
syn flimsy, slight

rel feeble, fragile, frail, weak; sickly; unhealthy; decrepit, infirm
con stalwart, stout, strong, sturdy, tenacious, tough; hale, healthy, robust, sound, well, wholesome
6 *syn* see TACTFUL
rel adept, expert, masterly, proficient; discreet, foresighted, prudent; careful, heedful; cautious, wary
con impolitic; imprudent, indiscreet; awkward, clumsy, gauche, inept, maladroit; unskillful
7 marked by or requiring tact < a *delicate* situation >
syn precarious, sensitive, ticklish, touchy, tricky
rel uncertain, unpredictable; hair-trigger, volatile; sticky
delicatesse *n* *syn* see TACT
ant indelicacy
delicious *adj* *syn* see DELIGHTFUL
rel appetizing, palatable, sapid, savory, toothsome; choice, dainty, delicate, exquisite, rare
con banal, flat, inane, insipid, jejune, wishy-washy
delight *vb* **1** *syn* see EXULT
2 *syn* see PLEASE 2
rel amuse, divert, entertain; allure, attract, charm, enchant, fascinate; enrapture, entrance, transport
con aggrieve, distress, pain, trouble; afflict, try; grieve; bother, irk; bore
delight (in) *vb* **1** *syn* see ADMIRE 1
rel enjoy, like, savor; eat up, luxuriate (in)
con abhor, abominate, hate, loathe
2 *syn* see LOVE 1
delight *n* *syn* see PLEASURE 2
rel glee, hilarity, jollity, mirth; ecstasy, rapture, transport; contentment, satisfaction; relish
con abhorrence, detestation, hate, hatred; dislike, distaste; discontent, dissatisfaction
ant aversion; disappointment
delightful *adj* highly pleasing to the senses or to aesthetic taste < a *delightful* view >
syn adorable, ambrosial, darling, delectable, delicious, heavenly, luscious, lush, scrumptious, yummy
rel charming, enchanting, fascinating; alluring, attractive; beautiful, fair, lovely; ineffable; agreeable, gratifying, pleasant, pleasing; satisfying
con miserable, wretched; distasteful, obnoxious, repellent, repugnant; abhorrent, detestable, hateful, odious; boring, irksome, tedious; distressing, troubling
ant abominable, horrid
delimit *vb* **1** *syn* see DEMARCATE 1
rel decide
2 *syn* see LIMIT 2
delimitate *vb* **1** *syn* see DEMARCATE 1
2 *syn* see LIMIT 2
delineate *vb* **1** *syn* see REPRESENT 1
rel design, plan; evoke, paint
2 *syn* see ETCH 2
delineation *n* **1** *syn* see REPRESENTATION

rel design, plan; evocation, painting; account, story, version
2 *syn* see OUTLINE
delinquency *n* *syn* see FAILURE 1
rel nonobservance; nonfulfillment; lapse, weakness
delinquent *adj* *syn* see NEGLIGENT
deliquesce *vb* *syn* see LIQUEFY
rel decay, decompose, disintegrate
con cake, harden, indurate, set, solidify
delirious *adj* **1** disordered in mind especially temporarily < *delirious* from the fever >
syn raving, wandering
rel deranged, disarranged, disordered, disturbed, unsettled; bewildered, confused, distracted; rambling; irrational, unreasonable; crazed, crazy, demented, insane, lunatic, mad, maniac
idiom out of one's head (*or* mind)
con rational, reasonable; sane, sensible; comatose, unconscious
2 *syn* see FURIOUS 2
rel overexcited, overwrought; ecstatic, rapturous, transported; delighted, enthused, thrilled
idiom all agog, beside oneself
con collected, composed, easy, relaxed; unexcited, unmoved, unstimulated
delirium *n* frenzied excitement or wild enthusiasm < in a *delirium* of patriotic feeling >
syn frenzy, furor
rel ardor, enthusiasm, fervor, passion, zeal; ecstasy, rapture, transport
con nonchalance, sangfroid; indifference, unconcern
ant apathy
deliver *vb* **1** *syn* see RESCUE
con immure, imprison, incarcerate, intern, jail; capture, catch, ensnare, entrap, snare, trap; condemn, damn, doom
2 *syn* see GIVE 3
rel relinquish, resign, surrender, yield
con keep, retain
3 *syn* see BEAR 5
4 *syn* see SAY 1
rel broach, express, vent, voice; communicate, impart
5 *syn* see GIVE 10
rel dispatch, send, transmit; fling, hurl, pitch, throw
delivery *n* *syn* see BIRTH 1
Delphian *adj* **1** *syn* see PROPHETIC
2 *syn* see CRYPTIC
delude *vb* *syn* see DECEIVE
idiom play tricks (*or* a trick) on
con enlighten, illume, illuminate, illustrate, light, lighten; elucidate, explain
deluding *adj* *syn* see MISLEADING
deluge *n* *syn* see FLOOD 2
rel flux; overrunning
deluge *vb* **1** to flow over so as to submerge or enclose < the lowlands were completely *deluged* >
syn drown, engulf, flood, inundate, overflow, overwhelm, submerge, swamp, whelm
rel overrun; flush, gush, pour, sluice, stream
2 *syn* see WET
con dehydrate, desiccate, dry, parch

3 to affect overwhelmingly as if by a deluge of water < he was *deluged* by telephone calls >
syn flood, overwhelm, swamp, whelm
rel overcome; oversupply; abound, teem

delusion *n* **1** something accepted as true that is actually false or unreal < people who suffer from *delusions* of persecution >
syn hallucination, ignis fatuus, illusion, mirage, phantasm
rel chicane, chicanery, deception, trickery; cheat, counterfeit, deceit, fake, fraud, humbug, imposture, sham; daydream, dream, fancy, fantasy, figment, vision; apparition, eidolon, ghost, phantom, shade
ant reality
2 *syn* see FALLACY 2
ant verity

delusive *adj syn* see MISLEADING
rel chimerical, fanciful, fantastic, imaginary, quixotic, visionary; apparent, illusory, ostensible, seeming
con authentic, bona fide, genuine, veritable; actual, real, true

delusory *adj syn* see MISLEADING

deluxe *adj syn* see LUXURIOUS 3
rel choice, dainty, delicate, elegant, exquisite, rare, recherché
con coarse, common, ordinary; inelegant

delve *vb* ||**1** *syn* see DIG 1
rel gouge (out), hollow (out), scoop (out), quarry (out); burrow, tunnel; comb, ferret out, search, seek
2 *syn* see MINE

delve (into) *vb syn* see EXPLORE

delve *n syn* see HOLE 1

delving *n syn* see INQUIRY 1

demagogue *n* a leader who makes use of popular prejudices and false claims especially for political advantage < *demagogues* who endanger the orderly processes of democratic government >
syn rabble-rouser
rel fomenter, inciter, instigator; agitator, firebrand, hothead, incendiary, inflamer; troublemaker

demand *n* **1** *syn* see REQUIREMENT 1
2 *syn* see NEED 3

demand *vb* **1** to ask for something as or as if one's right or due < the physician *demanded* payment of his bill >
syn call, challenge, claim, exact, postulate, require, requisition, solicit
rel ask, request; bid, charge, command, direct, enjoin, order; cite, summon, summons; coerce, compel, constrain, force, oblige; necessitate
con cede, relinquish, resign, waive; allow, concede, grant; give, offer, tender
2 to have as a need or requirement < it *demands* considerable practice to master the piano >
syn ask, call (for), crave, necessitate, require, take
rel fail, lack, need, want
idiom need (*or* want), doing, stand in need of

demanding *adj syn* see ONEROUS
rel rigid, rigorous, severe, stern, strict, stringent; crying, imperative, importunate, instant, pressing, urgent
ant undemanding

demarcate *vb* **1** to mark the limits of < *demarcate* the boundary between two countries >
syn bound, delimit, delimitate, determine, limit, mark (out), measure
rel establish, fix, set; assign, define, prescribe; circumscribe, confine, restrict
2 *syn* see DISTINGUISH
rel insulate, isolate, seclude, segregate, sequester

demean *vb syn* see BEHAVE 1

demean *vb syn* see HUMBLE
rel belittle, decry, derogate, detract, disparage; contemn, despise, scorn
con elevate, enhance, heighten

demeanor *n syn* see BEARING 1
rel behavior, conduct

dement *n syn* see LUNATIC 1

demented *adj syn* see INSANE 1
rel delirious, frenzied, hysterical

demerit *n syn* see IMPERFECTION

demerit *vb syn* see DEGRADE 1

demeritorious *adj syn* see BLAMEWORTHY
ant meritorious

demesne *n syn* see FIELD

demigod *n syn* see SUPERMAN

demimondaine *n syn* see HARLOT 1

demimonde *n syn* see HARLOT 1

demirep *n syn* see HARLOT 1

demise *vb syn* see DIE 1

demise *n syn* see DEATH 1
rel annihilation, ending, expiration, extinction

demit *vb syn* see ABDICATE 1

demit *vb syn* see LOWER 3

demiurgic *adj syn* see INVENTIVE

||demob *vb syn* see DISCHARGE 7
ant mobilize

demobilize *vb syn* see DISCHARGE 7
rel break up, disband, dispel, disperse, scatter; retire, withdraw
ant mobilize

democratic *adj* of or relating to a political system in which the supreme power is held and exercised by the people < a *democratic* government >
syn popular, self-governing, self-ruling
rel representative; libertarian
con totalitarian; absolute, arbitrary, autocratic, despotic; tyrannical, tyrannous; fascistic, nazi, patriarchal
ant authoritarian; undemocratic

démodé *adj syn* see OLD-FASHIONED
ant à la mode

demoded *adj syn* see OLD-FASHIONED
ant à la mode

demolish *vb syn* see DESTROY 1
rel dilapidate; crush, smash; break, burst, crack
con build, erect, frame, raise, rear
ant construct; rebuild
2 *syn* see TOTAL 3

demon *n syn* see DEVIL 2

demoniac *adj syn* see FIENDISH
rel crazed, crazy, insane, maniac; fired, inspired
con celestial, heavenly
ant angelic

demonian *adj syn* see FIENDISH
rel crazed, crazy, insane, maniac; fired, inspired
con celestial, heavenly

ant angelic

demonic *adj syn* see FIENDISH
rel crazed, crazy, insane, maniac; fired, inspired
con celestial, heavenly
ant angelic

demonstrate *vb* 1 *syn* see SHOW 2
rel display, exhibit, expose, flaunt, parade; explain, set forth
idiom go to show
con conceal, hide, secrete; camouflage, cloak, disguise, dissemble, mask
2 *syn* see PROVE 1
rel authenticate, validate
3 *syn* see ESTABLISH 6

demonstration *n syn* see EXHIBITION 1

demonstrative *adj* marked by display of feeling <was *demonstrative* in his welcome>
syn expansive, outgoing, unconstrained, unreserved, unrestrained
rel affectionate, loving; effusive, outpouring, profuse; candid, frank, open, outspoken, plain
con constrained, reserved, restrained, reticent, taciturn; bashful, shy; retiring, shrinking; introverted; aloof, detached, indifferent, unconcerned; chilly, cold, frigid, glacial, icy
ant undemonstrative

demoralize *vb* 1 *syn* see DEBASE 1
rel debilitate, undermine, weaken; damp, dampen
2 *syn* see DISCOURAGE 1
rel agitate, disturb, upset; disarrange, disorder, disorganize, unsettle; confuse, jumble, muddle, snarl; debilitate, undermine, weaken; unman, unnerve
con arrange, order, organize; energize, fortify, invigorate, strengthen

demote *vb syn* see DEGRADE 1
rel demean, lower
ant promote

demotion *n* the action or an instance of demoting <received a *demotion* from sergeant to corporal>
syn degradation, downgrading, reduction
rel debasement, humbling, humiliation; blackballing, disbarment, exclusion, suspension
con advancement, preferment, upgrading; aggrandizement; boost, elevation, lift, raise
ant promotion

demur *vb* to object or have scruples <he *demurred* at any horseplay>
syn balk, boggle, gag, jib, scruple, shy, stick, stickle, strain, stumble
rel falter, hesitate, vacillate, waver; combat, fight, oppose, resist; expostulate, object, protest, remonstrate; deprecate, disapprove
con accept, admit, receive, take; acquiesce, agree, assent, consent, subscribe, yes; concur; defer, relent, succumb, submit, yield
ant accede

demur *n* 1 *syn* see QUALM

syn synonym(s) *rel* related word(s)
ant antonym(s) *con* contrasted word(s)
idiom idiomatic equivalent(s)
‖ use limited; if in doubt, see a dictionary

rel faltering, hesitancy, hesitation; aversion, disinclination, loathness; expostulation, protest
con promptness, quickness, readiness
2 the act of objecting or taking exception <accepted without *demur*>
syn challenge, demurral, demurrer, difficulty, objection, protest, question, remonstrance, remonstration
rel reluctance, unwillingness; faltering, hesitancy, hesitation; deprecation, disapproval; protestation; difference, disagreement, dissent, variance
con acquiescence, agreement, assent, consent; concurrence; submission

demure *adj syn* see SHY 1
rel decent, decorous, nice, proper, seemly; prim; earnest, serious, solemn; close, reserved, reticent, silent
con impertinent, intrusive, meddlesome, obtrusive, officious; brash, forward, unbashful, unretiring

demurral *n syn* see DEMUR 2

demurrer *n syn* see DEMUR 2

den *n* 1 *syn* see LAIR 1
2 *syn* see HIDEOUT
3 *syn* see SINK 1

denaturant *n syn* see ADMIXTURE 1

denial *n* 1 refusal to satisfy a request or desire <*denial* of his visiting privileges>
syn disallowance, refusal, rejection
rel declination, nonacceptance
con allowing, conceding, grant, letting; leave, permission, sufferance
2 refusal to admit the truth <his *denial* that he took the money>
syn contradiction, gainsaying, negation
rel controversion, disproof, rebuttal, refutal, refutation; refusal, rejection, repudiation
con acknowledgment, avowal, confession; affirmation, assertion, confirmation
ant admission
3 *syn* see RENUNCIATION
rel abstaining, refraining
con indulgence, self-indulgence; overdoing, overindulgence

denigrate *vb syn* see MALIGN

denizen *n* 1 *syn* see INHABITANT
rel citizen, national, subject
2 *syn* see HABITUÉ 1

denominate *vb syn* see NAME 1

denomination *n* 1 *syn* see NAME 1
2 *syn* see RELIGION 2

denotative *adj syn* see INDICATIVE

denote *vb syn* see MEAN 2
rel insinuate; announce, argue, bespeak, prove

denotive *adj syn* see INDICATIVE

denounce *vb syn* see CRITICIZE
rel accuse, arraign, charge, impeach, incriminate, indict, tax; revile, vituperate; delate, inform
idiom cry harrow (*or* haro)
con panegyrize, praise
ant eulogize

de novo *adv syn* see OVER 7

dense *adj* 1 *syn* see CLOSE 4
rel heaped, massed, piled; crammed, crowded, jam-packed
con dispersed, dissipated, scattered; rare, thin; exiguous, meager, scant, scanty, spare

ant sparse; tenuous
2 *syn* see STUPID 1
rel obtuse; impassive, phlegmatic, stolid; lethargic, sluggish, torpid
ant subtle; bright

denticulate *adj syn* see SERRATE
denudate *vb syn* see STRIP 2
denude *vb* 1 *syn* see STRIP 1
2 *syn* see STRIP 2
denuded *adj syn* see OPEN 2
denunciate *vb syn* see CRITICIZE
rel delate, inform; menace, threaten
ant eulogize

deny *vb* 1 *syn* see DISCLAIM
rel abandon, desert, forsake
con adopt, embrace, espouse; recognize
ant acknowledge; admit
2 to refuse to grant <he was unwilling to *deny* the child's request>
syn disallow, keep back, refuse, withhold
idiom say no to, turn thumbs down on
con allow, concede, let, permit; afford, give
ant grant
3 to restrain (as oneself) from or forgo what is pleasant or satisfying <decided to *deny* himself a second piece of pie>
syn abstain, constrain, curb, hold back, refrain
rel eschew, forbear, forgo, sacrifice; inhibit, restrain; avoid, shun
con overdo, overindulge
ant indulge
4 to refuse to accept as true, valid, or worthy of consideration <*denying* the existence of witches>
syn contradict, contravene, cross, disaffirm, gainsay, impugn, negate, negative, traverse
rel decline, refuse, reject, repudiate; confute, controvert, disprove, rebut, refute; downface
con affirm, assert, aver; allow, grant; authenticate, corroborate, substantiate, validate, verify; avow, confess; claim, submit
ant concede; confirm

depart *vb* 1 *syn* see GO 2
rel set out, start, strike out, toddle
con linger, stay, tarry, wait; come; approach, near
ant arrive; abide, remain
2 *syn* see DIE 1
con exist, live, survive
3 *syn* see SWERVE 2
rel abandon, desert, forsake; reject, repudiate; cast, discard; differ, disagree, dissent, vary
4 *syn* see DIGRESS 2
departed *adj* 1 *syn* see DEAD 1
idiom called home, gone to a better land
2 *syn* see EXTINCT 1
departing *adj syn* see PARTING
departure *n* 1 the act of going, coming out, or leaving a place <the hasty *departure* of the refugees>
syn egress, egression, exit, exiting, exodus, offgoing, setting-out, withdrawal
rel going, leaving, quitting, retreat; decampment, flight; farewell, leave-taking
con coming, entering, ingress
ant arrival
2 *syn* see DEVIATION 1

rel rambling, straying, wandering
depend *vb syn* see HANG 1
depend (on *or* upon) *vb* 1 to rest or to be contingent upon something uncertain, variable, or indeterminable <our trip *depends* upon the weather>
syn hang (on *or* upon), hinge (on *or* upon), ‖pend, stand (on *or* upon), turn (on *or* upon)
rel base, bottom, found, ground, rest, stay
idiom hang in the balance
2 *syn* see RELY (on *or* upon)
rel incline, lean
dependable *adj* 1 *syn* see RELIABLE 1
rel assured, confident, sure; responsible; constant, faithful, loyal, staunch, steadfast, steady
idiom as good as one's word, to be counted on
con capricious, fickle, inconstant, mercurial, unstable; dishonest, lying, mendacious, untruthful
ant independable, undependable
2 *syn* see TRUE 9
3 *syn* see CERTAIN 3
dependence *n syn* see TRUST 1
dependent *adj* 1 determined or conditioned by another <a conclusion that is *dependent* on a premise>
syn conditional, contingent, relative, reliant
rel exposed, liable, open, subject, susceptible; iffy, provisional, provisory; uncertain; circumscribed, limited, restricted
con categorical, ultimate; boundless, eternal, illimitable, uncircumscribed; basal, basic, fundamental, primary, underived
ant absolute; infinite; original
2 *syn* see SUBORDINATE
rel counting, depending, reckoning, relying, trusting; accessory, ancillary, appurtenant; abased, debased, humbled
con principal; paramount, predominant, preponderant, preponderating, sovereign
ant independent
depict *vb syn* see REPRESENT 1
rel narrate, recite, recount, rehearse, relate, report, state; outline, sketch
depiction *n syn* see REPRESENTATION
deplete *vb* to bring to a low estate by depriving of something essential <an epidemic which *depletes* an army of manpower>
syn bankrupt, drain, draw, draw down, exhaust, impoverish, use up
rel cripple, debilitate, disable, enfeeble, sap, undermine, weaken; decrease, diminish, lessen, reduce; bleed, draw off, dry up, empty, milk; consume, expend, finish, spend, wash up
idiom dig into
con augment, enlarge, increase; bolster, fortify, strengthen; rebuild, repair, restore, revive
ant renew, replace
depleted *adj syn* see EFFETE 2
rel sapped, weakened
con augmented, enlarged, increased
deplorable *adj* of a kind to cause great distress <a *deplorable* loss of life>
syn afflictive, calamitous, dire, distressing, dolorous, grievous, heartbreaking, heart-

rending, lamentable, mournful, regrettable, unfortunate, woeful

rel awful, dreadful, terrible; horrifying, intolerable, overwhelming, sickening, unbearable; miserable, wretched; disastrous

idiom as bad as bad can be, as bad as can be

con beneficial, helpful, salutary; advantageous, favorable, propitious

deplore *vb* **1** to manifest grief or sorrow for something < *deplore* the death of a close friend >

  syn bemoan, bewail, grieve, lament, moan, weep

  rel deprecate, disapprove; mourn, sorrow; cry, keen, wail

  con boast, brag, crow, vaunt; rejoice

  2 *syn* see REGRET

depone *vb syn* see TESTIFY 2

deport *vb* **1** *syn* see BEHAVE 1

  2 *syn* see BANISH

deportation *n* **1** *syn* see EXILE 1

deportment *n* **1** *syn* see BEHAVIOR

  2 *syn* see BEARING 1

depose *vb* **1** to remove from a throne or other high position < trying to *depose* the king in favor of his brother > < *deposed* industrial leaders >

  syn dethrone, discrown, disenthrone, displace, disthrone, uncrown, unmake

  rel overthrow, subvert, upset; chuck, dismiss, eject, oust, throw out

  con inaugurate, induct, install, instate, invest; crown, enthrone, throne

  2 *syn* see ASSERT 1

  3 *syn* see TESTIFY 2

deposit *vb syn* see BANK

  rel put by, store, stow

deposit *n syn* see SEDIMENT

depository *n syn* see DEPOT 2

depot *n* **1** *syn* see ARMORY

  2 a place where something is deposited or stored < a gasoline *depot* >

  syn arsenal, depository, magazine, repository, store, storehouse

  rel storeroom, warehouse

  3 *syn* see RAILROAD STATION

  rel terminal, terminus

deprave *vb syn* see DEBASE 1

  con elevate, ennoble, exalt, raise, uplift

depraved *adj* **1** *syn* see DEBASED

  rel degenerate, infamous, vicious, villainous; degraded; twisted, warped

  con scrupulous, upright

  2 *syn* see VICIOUS 2

depravity *n syn* see VICE 1

deprecate *vb syn* see DISAPPROVE 1

  rel bemoan, bewail, deplore, lament; derogate, detract

  ant endorse

depreciate *vb* **1** to reduce the value of < *depreciate* the dollar >

  syn cheapen, decry, devalorize, devaluate, devalue, downgrade, lower, mark down, soften, underprize, underrate, undervalue, write down, write off

  rel depress; abate, decrease, diminish, dwindle, lessen, reduce; erode

con augment, increase; bloat, blow up, expand, inflate; amplify, magnify

  ant appreciate

  2 *syn* see DECRY 2

  rel underestimate, underrate, undervalue; discountenance, disfavor, disesteem

  con cherish, prize, treasure, value; comprehend, understand

  ant appreciate

depreciation *n syn* see DETRACTION

depreciative *adj syn* see DEROGATORY

  rel underestimating, underrating, undervaluing

  ant appreciative

depreciatory *adj syn* see DEROGATORY

  rel underestimating, underrating, undervaluing

  ant appreciative

depredate *vb syn* see RAVAGE

depredator *n syn* see MARAUDER

depress *vb* **1** *syn* see LOWER 3

  2 to lower in spirit or mood < the thought of all his debts *depressed* him >

  syn oppress, press, sadden, weigh down

  rel ail, distress, trouble; afflict, torment, try; contrist, deject, discourage, dishearten, dispirit; bother, disturb, perturb, upset

  con delight, gladden, gratify, please, rejoice; excite, inspire, stimulate; brighten, cheer up, encourage; buoy, elevate

  ant elate, exhilarate, cheer

depressant *adj syn* see GLOOMY 3

depressed *adj* **1** *syn* see DOWNCAST

  rel lugubrious, melancholy

  ant exhilarated; animated

  2 *syn* see UNDERPRIVILEGED

depressing *adj* **1** *syn* see GLOOMY 3

  con cheering, elevating, uplifting; exciting, inspiring

  ant exhilarating

  2 *syn* see SAD 2

depression *n* **1** *syn* see SADNESS

  rel boredom, doldrums, ennui, tedium

  con glee, hilarity, mirth

  ant buoyancy; elation

  2 a low spot < a *depression* in the land >

  syn basin, concavity, dip, hollow, sag, sink, sinkage, sinkhole; *compare* NOTCH 1

  rel cavity, hole, pocket, vacuity, vacuum, void; crater, pit; scoop

  3 a period of lowered economic activity and extensive unemployment < indicators that warn of a coming *depression* >

  syn recession, slump, stagnation

  rel crash, decline, dislocation, drop; sag; paralysis; ‖stagflation

  con expansion; booming, development, growth; advancement, progress

  ant boom

depressive *adj syn* see GLOOMY 3

deprivation *n syn* see PRIVATION 2

deprive *vb* **1** *syn* see STRIP 2

  2 to prevent one from possessing < to *deprive* a person of his civil rights >

  syn bereave, disinherit, dispossess, divest, lose, oust, rob; *compare* STRIP 2

  rel dock; denude, dismantle, strip

  con furnish, give, supply; clothe, endow, equip, fit (out), invest, outfit

  ant provide

deprived *adj syn* see UNDERPRIVILEGED

deprivement *n syn* see PRIVATION 2

---

syn synonym(s)   *rel* related word(s)
ant antonym(s)   *con* contrasted word(s)
idiom idiomatic equivalent(s)
‖ use limited; if in doubt, see a dictionary

depth *n* 1 the perpendicular extent or measurement downward from a surface < measured the *depth* of the river >
syn deepness, drop
rel profoundness, profundity; lowness; sounding; draft
con shallowness; altitude, elevation
2 the quality of being profound (as in insight) or full (as of knowledge) < her answer showed she had great *depth* in that subject >
syn abyss, deepness, profoundness, profundity
rel sense, wisdom, wiseness; brain, intellect, intelligence; keenness, sharpness
con shallowness, superficiality, unprofoundness; sciolism, smatter, smattering

depthless *adj syn see* SUPERFICIAL 2
depurate *vb syn see* PURIFY 1
depute *vb syn see* DELEGATE
deputize *vb syn see* DELEGATE
deputy *n* 1 *syn see* AGENT 2
rel substitute, surrogate; replacement
2 *syn see* DELEGATE
derange *vb* 1 *syn see* DISORDER 1
rel perturb; discommode, incommode, inconvenience
con compose, settle
ant arrange; adjust
2 *syn see* UPSET 5
3 *syn see* MADDEN 1
deranged *adj syn see* INSANE 1
rel disarranged, disordered, disturbed
derangement *n syn see* INSANITY 1
rel disarrangement, disorder; confusion; disturbance; unsoundness
derelict *adj* 1 given up especially by the owner or occupant < a *derelict* old home >
syn abandoned, deserted, desolate, forsaken, lorn, solitary, uncouth
rel dilapidated, dingy, faded, run-down, seedy, shabby, threadbare
con cherished, prized, treasured; attended, kept up, maintained
2 *syn see* NEGLIGENT
rel irresponsible, undependable, unreliable, untrustworthy
con dependable, reliable, responsible, trustworthy; careful, heedful, thoughtful
ant faithful
derelict *n* 1 *syn see* OUTCAST
2 *syn see* VAGABOND
dereliction *n syn see* FAILURE 1
rel abuse, misuse, outrage
ant faithfulness
deride *vb syn see* RIDICULE
rel banter, chaff, jolly, kid, rag, rib
de rigueur *adj syn see* DECOROUS 1
derision *n syn see* LAUGHINGSTOCK
derivable *adj syn see* DEDUCTIVE
derivate *adj syn see* SECONDARY 2
derivation *n syn see* SOURCE
derivational *adj syn see* SECONDARY 2
derivative *adj syn see* SECONDARY 2
ant underivative
derivative *n syn see* OUTGROWTH 2
derive *vb* 1 to reach (as a conclusion) as an end point of reasoning and observation < evidence from which he *derived* a startling new set of axioms >
syn educe, evolve, excogitate

rel conclude, deduce, gather, infer, judge; arrive (at), elicit, extract, reach; develop, elaborate, formulate, put (together), work out
2 *syn see* INFER
3 *syn see* TAKE 14
derive (from) *vb syn see* SPRING 1
derived *adj syn see* SECONDARY 2
dernier cri *n syn see* FASHION 3
dernier ressort *n syn see* RESOURCE 3
derogate *vb syn see* DECRY 2
rel decrease, lessen, reduce; discredit, disgrace
con enhance, heighten, intensify
derogatory *adj* designed or tending to belittle < *derogatory* comments about the actor's performance >
syn depreciative, depreciatory, detracting, disadvantageous, disparaging, dyslogistic, pejorative, slighting, uncomplimentary
rel belittling, decrying, minimizing; aspersing, calumnious, defamatory, maligning, vilifying; degrading, demeaning, humiliating; despiteful, malevolent, malicious, spiteful; contumelious, disdainful, scornful
con admiring, esteeming; acclaiming, laudatory, praising; appreciative
ant complimentary
derout *vb syn see* ROUT 1
derriere *n syn see* BUTTOCKS
descant *n* 1 *syn see* MELODY
2 *syn see* SONG 2
descant *vb syn see* DISCOURSE 1
descend *vb* 1 *syn see* FALL 1
ant rise
2 *syn see* STOOP 2
3 *syn see* DETERIORATE 1
descendant *n* 1 **descendants** *pl syn see* OFFSPRING
ant ascendants, ancestors
2 *syn see* OUTGROWTH 2
descent *n* 1 the act or process of passing from a higher to a lower level or state < a parachute *descent* > < his slow *descent* to the gutter >
syn drop, fall
rel plummeting, plunging, sinking
con rise, upswing, upturn; advance, headway, progress, progression; betterment, improvement
ant ascent
2 *syn see* COMEDOWN
3 *syn see* ANCESTRY
4 an inclination downward < the steep *descent* of the mountain >
syn decline, declivity, dip, drop, fall
rel downgrade, grade, gradient, incline, slope; drop, drop-off
con acclivity, upgrade, uphill
ant ascent, rise
describe *vb syn see* RELATE 1
rel communicate, impart; transmit; construe, elucidate, explain, explicate, expound; exemplify, illustrate; characterize, distinguish
2 *syn see* REPRESENT 1
description *n* 1 *syn see* REPRESENTATION
2 a descriptive statement < a fascinating *description* of his adventures >
syn narration, recital, recountal, recounting

rel anecdote, narrative, story, tale, yarn; account, chronicle, version; report, statement

3 *syn* see TYPE

descry *vb* 1 *syn* see SEE 1

2 *syn* see FIND 1

rel appreciate, comprehend, understand; realize

desecrate *vb syn* see RAVAGE

desecrated *adj syn* see IMPURE 3

desecration *n syn* see PROFANATION

ant consecration

desensitize *vb syn* see DEADEN 1

ant sensitize

desert *n syn* see WASTE 1

desert *n usu* deserts *pl syn* see DUE 1

rel chastening, chastisement, discipline, disciplining, punishment

idiom just deserts

desert *vb* 1 *syn* see ABANDON 1

rel depart, go, leave

con adhere, cohere

ant cleave (to), stick (to)

2 *syn* see DEFECT

rel abscond, decamp, escape, flee, fly

idiom go over the hill

con abide, remain, stay

deserted *adj syn* see DERELICT 1

rel empty, vacant; uninhabited, unoccupied; bare, barren

desertion *n syn* see DEFECTION

rel perfidiousness, perfidy, treacherousness, treachery

deserve *vb syn* see EARN 2

rel gain, get, win; demand

idiom have it coming

deserved *adj syn* see JUST 3

ant undeserved

deserving *n syn* see DUE 1

deserving *adj syn* see WORTHY 1

ant undeserving

desexualize *vb syn* see STERILIZE

desiccate *vb* 1 *syn* see DRY 1

2 to drain or be drained of emotional or intellectual vitality < this book is *desiccated* by undue concentration on statistics >

syn devitalize, dry up

rel deplete, drain, exhaust; divest; decay, fade, shrivel, wither, wizen

con brighten, enliven

desiderate *vb syn* see DESIRE 1

desight *n syn* see EYESORE

design *vb* 1 *syn* see INTEND 2

2 *syn* see PLAN 2

rel delineate, diagram; create, invent; construct, fashion, form, frame, produce; contrive

con accomplish, achieve, effect, execute, fulfill, perform

3 to work out the arrangement of the parts of < *design* an urban center >

syn arrange, lay out, map (out), plan, set out; *compare* PLAN 2

rel delineate, diagram, draft, outline, sketch

design *n* 1 *syn* see PLAN 1

rel delineation, diagram, draft, outline, sketch, tracing; creation, invention

---

con accomplishment, achievement, execution, fulfillment, performance

2 *syn* see INTENTION

rel conation, volition, will; deliberation, reflection, thinking, thought; intrigue, machination, plot

con accident, chance, fortuity, hap; impulse

3 *syn* see FIGURE 3

4 *syn* see MAKEUP 1

designate *vb* 1 *syn* see NAME 1

2 to declare a person one's choice < *designated* him to fill the position >

syn appoint, finger, make, name, nominate, tap

rel choose, elect, opt, pick, select, single; assign, delegate, depute; dictate

con disapprove, disfavor, object (to), oppose; disallow, reject, turn down

3 to set aside (as funds) for a specific use < *designated* the income to be used for charity >

syn allocate, earmark

rel specify; appropriate, reserve; stipulate; allot, apportion, mete (out)

designation *n syn* see NAME 1

rel identification, recognition; classification, pigeonhole, pigeonholing

designative *adj syn* see INDICATIVE

designed *adj syn* see DELIBERATE 1

rel decided, determined, resolved

con casual, chance, contingent, fluky, fortuitous, incidental; impulsive, spontaneous; natural, normal, regular, typical

ant accidental

designedly *adv syn* see INTENTIONALLY

designless *adj syn* see RANDOM

desire *n* 1 a longing for something that promises enjoyment or satisfaction < he had a strong *desire* for fame and fortune >

syn appetite, appetition, craving, itch, lust, passion, urge

rel hankering, hunger, hungering, longing, pining, thirst, thirsting, yearning; desideratum, desiderium; avarice, cupidity, greed, rapacity; concupiscence, eros

con abhorrence, repellency, repugnance, repulsion; aversion, disfavor, dislike

ant distaste

2 *syn* see LUST 2

desire *vb* 1 to have a longing for something < men who *desire* success >

syn ‖choose, covet, crave, desiderate, want, wish

rel hanker, hunger, long, pine, thirst, yearn; enjoy, fancy, like; aim, aspire, pant

idiom set one's eyes (*or* heart) upon

con abhor, abominate, detest, hate, loath; decline, refuse, reject, repudiate, spurn

2 *syn* see ASK 2

desired *adj syn* see TRUE 7

desirous *adj syn* see COVETOUS

desist *vb syn* see STOP 3

rel abstain, forbear; abandon, relinquish, resign, yield

idiom have done with

con continue; persevere

ant persist

desistance *n syn* see END 2

desk *n* a table, frame, or case with a sloping or horizontal surface especially for writing < sat meditating at her *desk* >

syn escritoire, secretaire, secretary, writing desk

---

rel lectern, reading desk
desolate *adj* 1 *syn* see DERELICT 1
rel empty, vacant; uninhabited, unoccupied
2 *syn* see INCONSOLABLE
3 *syn* see GLOOMY 3
rel bare, barren; destitute, poor, poverty-stricken; dark, murky
desolate *vb* *syn* see RAVAGE
despair *vb* to lose all hope or confidence
< *despaired* of winning >
syn despond, give up
rel abandon, drop, relinquish, renounce, resign, surrender, yield
idiom lose heart (*or* courage *or* faith *or* hope)
con await, count (on), depend (on), hope, look (for); trust (in *or* to)
ant expect
despairing *adj* *syn* see DESPONDENT
rel atrabilious, melancholy, melancholy; cynical, misanthropic, pessimistic; depressed, oppressed, weighed down
con optimistic, roseate, rose-colored; assured, confident, sanguine, sure
ant hopeful
desperado *n* *syn* see OUTLAW
rel convict, criminal, lawbreaker
desperate *adj* 1 *syn* see DESPONDENT
rel foolhardy, rash, reckless, venturesome; headlong, precipitate; baffled, balked, circumvented, foiled, frustrated, outwitted, thwarted
con collected, composed, cool, nonchalant; assured, confident, sanguine, sure
2 *syn* see ACUTE 6
3 *syn* see INTENSE 1
4 *syn* see OUTRAGEOUS 2
despicable *adj* 1 *syn* see CONTEMPTIBLE
rel disgraceful, disreputable, ignominious, infamous, loathsome
con applaudable, commendable
ant laudable, praiseworthy
2 *syn* see BASE 3
despisable *adj* *syn* see CONTEMPTIBLE
despisal *n* *syn* see DESPITE 1
despise *vb* to regard as beneath one's notice and unworthy of consideration or interest < he had always *despised* the weak >
syn abhor, contemn, disdain, look down, scorn, scout
rel abominate, detest, execrate, hate, loathe; reject, repudiate, spurn; avoid, eschew, renounce, shun; disregard, ignore, overlook, slight, snub
idiom have no use for, look down one's nose at
con apprize, cherish, prize, treasure, value; admire, regard, respect
ant appreciate, esteem
despisement *n* *syn* see DESPITE 1
despite *n* 1 the feeling or attitude of despising < felt *despite* toward the lowly >
syn contempt, despisal, despisement, disdain, disparagement, scorn
rel disdainfulness, insolence, superciliousness; abhorrence, abomination, detestation, hate, hatred, loathing; rejection, repudiation, spurning; aversion, disfavor, dislike, distaste; cold shoulder, rebuff, slight, snub; disgust, loathing
con admiration, esteem, honor, regard, respect; attraction, liking

2 *syn* see MALICE
rel contempt, disdain, scorn; abhorrence, abomination, detestation, hate, hatred, loathing
con admiration, esteem, respect; awe, fear, reverence
ant appreciation
3 *syn* see DEFIANCE 2
rel harm, hurt, injury
4 *syn* see AFFRONT
rel cut, discourtesy, incivility; rebuff, slight, snub
despite *prep* *syn* see AGAINST 4
despiteful *adj* *syn* see MALICIOUS
despitefulness *n* *syn* see MALICE
despoil *vb* *syn* see RAVAGE
despoiler *n* 1 *syn* see MARAUDER
2 *syn* see VANDAL
despond *vb* 1 *syn* see DESPAIR
rel droop, sag; languish
idiom reach the depths
con expect, hope, look
2 *syn* see MOPE 1
despondent *adj* having lost all or nearly all hope < *despondent* about his health >
syn despairing, desperate, desponding, forlorn, hopeless
rel grieving, mourning, sorrowful; dejected, depressed, melancholy, sad; disconsolate, dispirited, downcast, woebegone; discouraged, disheartened
con cheerful, glad, happy, joyful, joyous; buoyant, elastic, resilient, volatile; hopeful, optimistic
ant lighthearted
desponding *adj* *syn* see DESPONDENT
despot *n* *syn* see TYRANT
despotic *adj* *syn* see ABSOLUTE 4
despotism *n* *syn* see TYRANNY
despotize *vb* *syn* see TYRANNIZE
desquamate *vb* *syn* see SCALE 2
destine *vb* *syn* see PREDESTINE 1
destiny *n* *syn* see FATE
rel design, goal, intent, intention, objective
destitute *adj* 1 *syn* see DEVOID
rel deficient; bankrupt, bankrupted, depleted, drained, exhausted; divested, stripped
con complete, full, replete
2 *syn* see POOR 1
rel depleted, drained, exhausted
idiom on one's uppers, on the rocks
con comfortable, prosperous, well-fixed, well-off, well-to-do
ant opulent
destituteness *n* *syn* see POVERTY 1
rel absence, dearth, lack; adversity, misfortune
con competence, sufficiency
ant opulence
destitution *n* *syn* see POVERTY 1
rel absence, dearth, lack, privation, want; adversity, misfortune
con competence, sufficiency
ant opulence
destroy *vb* 1 to bring to ruin < the army *destroyed* the enemy village > < his health was finally *destroyed* by drink >
syn annihilate, atomize, decapitate, decimate, demolish, destruct, discreate, dismantle, dissolve, dynamite, pull down, pulverize, quench, raze, rub out, ruin, ‖ruinate, shatter, shoot, smash, tear down,

unbuild, undo, unframe, unmake, wrack, wreck; *compare* TOTAL 3

rel abolish, extinguish; devastate, pillage, ravage, sack, waste; eradicate, exterminate, extirpate, wipe; mangle, mutilate; rubble; doom

idiom blow to bits, bring to an end, dispose of, tear to shreds

con establish, found, institute, organize; fabricate, fashion, forge, form, make, manufacture, shape; conserve, preserve, protect, save

2 *syn* see KILL 1

destroyer *n* 1 *syn* see VANDAL

2 *syn* see DOWNFALL 2

destruct *vb syn* see DESTROY 1

destruction *n* 1 *syn* see DOWNFALL 2

2 *syn* see RUIN 3

destructive *adj* having the capability, property, or effect of destroying <a *destructive* windstorm> <his brother was a *destructive* influence in his life>

syn annihilative, ruinous, shattering, wrackful, wreckful

rel calamitous, disastrous, deadly, fatal, lethal, mortal; consumptive; internecine; baneful, deleterious, detrimental

con creative, formative; harmless, innocuous, inoffensive; helpful, improving

ant constructive

desuetude *n* 1 *syn* see END 2

2 *syn* see DISUSE

desultory *adj* 1 *syn* see FITFUL

rel erratic; shifting, vagrant, wavering

con constant, invariable, unchanging, unfailing

ant steady

2 *syn* see RANDOM

rel fitful, spasmodic; disorderly, unmethodical, unsystematic; capricious, fickle, inconstant, mercurial

con orderly, systematic

ant assiduous; methodical

detach *vb* to remove one thing from another with which it is in union or association <*detach* sheets from a loose-leaf book>

syn abstract, disassociate, disconnect, disengage, dissociate, uncouple, unfix

rel cut off, divorce, part, separate, sever, sunder; disjoin, disunite; disassemble, dismantle, dismember, dismount; disaffiliate

idiom take apart

con fasten, fix; bind, tie; combine, conjoin, unite

ant affix, attach

detached *adj* 1 *syn* see ALONE 1

rel separate, unconnected

con abutting, adjacent; connected, joined, linked

ant adjoining; attached

2 *syn* see INDIFFERENT 2

con anxious, concerned, solicitous; self-centered, selfish

ant interested

3 *syn* see NEUTRAL

rel distant, remote, removed

detachment *n syn* see SEPARATION 1

detail *n syn* see POINT 1

con anatomy, framework, skeleton, structure; bulk, mass; design, plan

detail *vb syn* see SPECIFY 3

detailed *adj syn* see CIRCUMSTANTIAL

rel abundant, copious; exhausting, exhaustive, thoroughgoing

detailedly *adv syn* see THOROUGHLY 2

detain *vb* 1 *syn* see ARREST 2

rel buttonhole, hold, restrain

2 *syn* see KEEP 5

3 *syn* see DELAY 1

rel check, curb, inhibit, restrain

detect *vb syn* see FIND 1

detectable *adj syn* see PERCEPTIBLE

detection *n syn* see DISCOVERY

detective *n* one employed or engaged in detecting lawbreakers or in getting information that is not readily or publicly accessible <used *detectives* to locate the missing witness>

syn dick, ||eye, gumshoe, hawkshaw, investigator, plainclothesman, Sherlock, Sherlock Holmes, sleuth, ||tec; *compare* INFORMER, PRIVATE DETECTIVE

rel G-man; roper; shoofly

detention *n syn* see ARREST

rel imprisonment, incarceration, internment

deter *vb* 1 *syn* see DISSUADE

rel prevent; block, hinder, impede, obstruct; debar, shut out; frighten, scare; inhibit, restrain

con abet, incite, instigate; excite, provoke, stimulate; actuate, motivate

2 *syn* see PREVENT 1

deteriorate *vb* 1 to pass from a higher to a lower type or condition <the road quickly *deteriorated* into a bumpy path>

syn decline, degenerate, descend, disimprove, disintegrate, retrograde, rot, sink, worsen

rel crumble, decay, decompose; impair, mar, spoil; debilitate, undermine, weaken; depreciate, lessen

idiom be the worse for wear, go downhill, go to pot (or the dogs)

con better, improve; advance, progress; enhance, heighten

ant ameliorate

2 *syn* see FAIL 1

deterioration *n* 1 a falling from a higher to a lower level (as of quality or character) <the *deterioration* of business during the depression>

syn atrophy, decadence, declension, declination, decline, degeneracy, degeneration, dégringolade, devaluation, devolution, downfall, downgrade, ruin

rel impairment, spoiling; crumbling, decay, decaying, decomposition, disintegration, dissolution, dry rot, rotting; debasement, degradation; depreciation, lessening; dislocation, disruption

con betterment, help; enhancement, heightening, improvement

ant amelioration

2 *syn* see FAILURE 4

con convalescence, recovering, recuperation

ant improvement

determinable *adj syn* see TERMINABLE

---

syn synonym(s)   *rel* related word(s)
ant antonym(s)   *con* contrasted word(s)
idiom idiomatic equivalent(s)
|| use limited; if in doubt, see a dictionary

determinant *n syn* see CAUSE 1
rel factor; authority, influence, weight

determinate *adj* 1 *syn* see INFLEXIBLE 3
2 *syn* see DEFINITE 1
ant indeterminate

determinate *vb syn* see IDENTIFY

determination *n* 1 *syn* see DECISION 1
2 *syn* see DECISION 2
ant indetermination

determine *vb* 1 *syn* see ESTABLISH 6
rel fix, set; settle
2 *syn* see PREDESTINE 1
3 *syn* see DEMARCATE 1
4 *syn* see DECIDE
rel bias, dispose, incline, predispose; actuate, drive, impel, move; induce, persuade
5 *syn* see CLOSE 3
6 *syn* see DISCOVER 3

determined *adj syn* see DECIDED 2
rel earnest, purposeful, serious; unfaltering, unhesitating, unwavering
con unresolved, unsettled; hesitating, hesitant, wavering
ant undetermined

detest *vb syn* see HATE
rel reject, repudiate, spurn
con love; appreciate, treasure, value
ant adore

detestable *adj syn* see HATEFUL 2
rel sorry; atrocious, heinous, monstrous, outrageous
ant adorable

detestation *n* 1 *syn* see ABOMINATION 2
rel antipathy, disgust
con affection, attachment, love; forbearance, indulgence, tolerance
ant adoration
2 *syn* see ABOMINATION 1
ant adoration

dethrone *vb syn* see DEPOSE 1
ant enthrone, throne

detonate *vb syn* see EXPLODE 1

detour *n* an indirect course often temporarily replacing part of a usual route <a *detour* around road construction> <took a *detour* to show him the lake>
syn roundabout, runaround
rel bypass

detour *vb syn* see SKIRT 2

detract (from) *vb syn* see DECRY 2
rel libel, slander; decrease, lessen, reduce
con enhance, heighten, intensify

detracting *adj* 1 *syn* see DEROGATORY
2 *syn* see LIBELOUS

detraction *n* the expression of damaging or malicious opinions <his persistent *detraction* of his rival's motives was wholly unfair>
syn backbiting, backstabbing, belittlement, calumny, character assassination, defamation, depreciation, disparagement, scandal, slander, sycophancy, tale
rel damage, harm, hurt, injury; injustice, wrong; aspersion, calumniation, libel, libeling, maligning, slandering, traducing, vilification
con enhancement, heightening, laudation, praise; approbation, approval
ant commendation

detractive *adj syn* see LIBELOUS

detractory *adj syn* see LIBELOUS

detriment *n syn* see DISADVANTAGE
rel damage, harm, hurt, injury, mischief; impairment, marring, spoiling

ant advantage, benefit

detrimental *adj syn* see HARMFUL
con aiding, helpful, helping; harmless
ant beneficial
2 *syn* see ADVERSE 2

de trop *adj syn* see SUPERFLUOUS

detruncate *vb syn* see TOP 1

deuced *adj syn* see UTTER

‖**deval** *vb syn* see STOP 3

devalorize *vb syn* see DEPRECIATE 1

devaluate *vb syn* see DEPRECIATE 1

devaluation *n syn* see DETERIORATION 1

devalue *vb syn* see DEPRECIATE 1

devast *vb syn* see RAVAGE

devastate *vb syn* see RAVAGE

devastation *n syn* see RUIN 3

‖**devel** *vb syn* see STRIKE 2

develop *vb* 1 *syn* see EXPAND 4
2 *syn* see UNFOLD 3
rel actualize, materialize, realize
3 *syn* see MATURE
rel dilate, expand; enroot, establish; flourish, prosper, thrive
con shrivel, wither, wizen
4 to come to have usually gradually <*develop* a taste for dry wine>
syn acquire, form
rel gain, get, obtain; achieve, attain, reach
5 *syn* see HAPPEN 1

development *n* progressive advance from a lower or simpler to a higher or more complex form <*development* of a seed into a plant> <*development* of an industry>
syn evolution, evolvement, flowering, growth, progress, progression, unfolding, upgrowth
rel advance, advancement, ongoing
con decadence, declension, degeneration, deterioration, devolution
ant decline

deviant *adj* 1 *syn* see ABNORMAL 1
con normal; natural
2 *syn* see IRREGULAR 1

deviate *vb* 1 *syn* see SWERVE 2
2 *syn* see ERR
idiom deviate from the path of virtue

deviation *n* 1 departure from a course or procedure or from a norm or standard <no *deviation* from traditional methods was permitted>
syn aberration, deflection, departure, divergence, diversion, turning
rel alteration, change, modification, variation; breach, transgression, violation; anomaly, failing, fault; blunder, error, lapse
con accordance, agreement, conformance, conformity, correspondence
2 *syn* see TURN 2

deviative *adj syn* see ABNORMAL 1

device *n* 1 *syn* see TRICK 1
2 something (as a mechanical device) that performs a function or effects a desired end <invented many handy household *devices*>
syn contraption, contrivance; *compare* GADGET 1
rel appliance, implement, instrument, tool, utensil; apparatus, machine, mechanism; expedient, makeshift, resort, resource, shift; creation, invention; dingus, doohickey, hickey, thingumbob
3 *syn* see FIGURE 3

rel attribute, emblem, symbol, type; insignia, motto

deviceful *adj syn* see INVENTIVE

devil *n* **1** *often cap* the personal supreme spirit of evil and unrighteousness in Jewish and Christian theology
syn Apollyon, Beelzebub, ‖Cloot(s), ‖Clootie, diablo, fiend, Lucifer, Old Gooseberry, Old Nick, Old Scratch, Satan, serpent
rel cacodemon; dybbuk
idiom Prince of Darkness
2 an extremely and malignantly wicked person < he was a *devil* who would stop at nothing to get what he wanted >
syn Archfiend, demon, fiend, Satan, Succubus; *compare* SCAMP, VILLAIN 1
rel blackguard, caitiff, knave; scoundrel, villain; beast, brute
3 *syn* see SCAMP

‖**devil–devil** *n syn* see SPELL

‖**devil–dodger** *n syn* see CLERGYMAN

deviling *n syn* see IMP 1

devilish *adj* **1** *syn* see FIENDISH
rel iniquitous, nefarious, villainous; accursed, cursed, damnable, execrable; bad, evil, wicked
ant angelic
2 *syn* see SATANIC 1

devilkin *n syn* see IMP 1

devil–may–care *adj syn* see WILD 7
rel rash, reckless
con careful, heedful, responsible, thoughtful

devilment *n syn* see MISCHIEVOUSNESS

devilry *n syn* see MISCHIEVOUSNESS

‖**devil's–bones** *n pl syn* see DICE

deviltry *n syn* see MISCHIEVOUSNESS

devious *adj* **1** *syn* see OBSCURE 2
2 *syn* see CROOKED 1
rel deviating, digressing, diverting
ant straightforward
3 *syn* see ERRATIC 1
4 *syn* see ERRANT 2
rel artful, crafty, cunning, foxy, insidious, sly, tricky
5 *syn* see UNDERHAND
ant straightforward

devise *n syn* see LEGACY 1

devise *vb* **1** *syn* see PLAN 2
2 *syn* see CONTRIVE 2
rel create, discover; forge, form, shape; design
3 *syn* see PLOT
4 *syn* see WILL

devitalize *vb syn* see DESICCATE 2
rel deprive; eviscerate, weaken
ant vitalize

devoid *adj* showing a want or lack < a poem *devoid* of worth >
syn destitute, empty, innocent, void
rel bare, barren; lacking, wanting; deficient
con filled, full; furnished, provided, supplied
ant replete

devoir *n* **1** *syn* see OBLIGATION 2
2 *syn* see TASK 1

devolution *n syn* see DETERIORATION 1
rel regression, regressiveness, retrogression, retrogressiveness; receding, recession, retrogradation, retrograding
con development; progress, progression
ant evolution

devote *vb* **1** to set apart for a particular and often a better or higher use or end < a woman who *devotes* her life to helping others >
syn consecrate, dedicate, hallow
rel sanctify, vow; commit, confide, consign, entrust
idiom set apart
2 *syn* see GIVE 1
3 *syn* see ADDRESS 3
rel attempt, endeavor, strive, struggle, try; employ, use, utilize

devote (to) *vb syn* see HABITUATE 2
rel attach, wrap (up)

devoted *adj syn* see LOVING
rel constant, faithful, loyal, true; thoughtful; fervid, zealous

devotee *n* **1** *syn* see ADDICT
2 *syn* see AMATEUR 1

devotion *n* **1** *syn* see FIDELITY 1
rel enthusiasm, fervor, passion, zeal; affection, attachment, love; consecration, dedication, devotement
2 *syn* see LOVE 1

devour *vb* **1** *syn* see EAT 1
2 *syn* see EAT UP 1
idiom eat like a horse, eat one's head off
3 *syn* see CONSUME 1
4 *syn* see RAVAGE
rel demolish, destroy; ruin, wreck; dissipate, squander
5 to exhibit avid interest in or enjoyment of < the crowd *devoured* the lurid scene >
syn ‖eat up
rel delight (in), enjoy, rejoice (in), relish, revel (in); feast (on), gloat (over *or* on)
con avoid, eschew, shun

devout *adj* showing fervor in the practice of religion < a *devout* churchgoer >
syn godly, holy, pietistic, pious, prayerful, religious
rel ardent, fervent, fervid, zealous; adoring, revering, venerating, worshiping
con impious, irreligious, ungodly, unholy; irreverent; apostate, backsliding
ant undevout

dexter *adj syn* see FAVORABLE 5
ant sinister

dexterity *n* **1** *syn* see ADDRESS 1
rel adeptness, skillfulness; effortlessness, smoothness
con awkwardness, maladroitness
ant clumsiness
2 *syn* see ART 1

dexterous *adj* **1** ready and skilled in physical movements < a *dexterous* worker >
syn adroit, clever, deft, handy, neat=handed, nimble
rel agile; adept, expert, masterly, proficient, skilled, skillful; easy, effortless, facile, smooth
con awkward, gauche, inept, maladroit
ant clumsy
2 *syn* see CLEVER 4

dexterousness *n syn* see ADDRESS 1
ant clumsiness

dextrorotatory *adj* *syn* see RIGHT=HANDED

---

syn synonym(s)   *rel* related word(s)
ant antonym(s)   *con* contrasted word(s)
idiom idiomatic equivalent(s)
‖ use limited; if in doubt, see a dictionary

ant levorotatory

diablerie *n* 1 *syn* see MISCHIEVOUSNESS
2 *syn* see EVIL 3

diablo *n syn* see DEVIL 1

diabolic *adj* 1 *syn* see SATANIC 1
2 *syn* see FIENDISH
rel evil, ill, wicked
ant angelic

diabolism *n syn* see SATANISM

diabolonian *adj syn* see FIENDISH

diacritic *adj syn* see CHARACTERISTIC

diagnose *vb syn* see IDENTIFY

diagnostic *adj syn* see CHARACTERISTIC

diagnosticate *vb syn* see IDENTIFY

diagonal *adj* between horizontal and vertical in direction < cloth with a *diagonal* stripe >
syn bevel, beveled, bias, biased, slanted, slanting; *compare* INCLINED 3

diagonally *adv* in a line running across from corner to corner < decided to place the couch *diagonally* at the end of the room >
syn catercorner (*or* catty-corner *or* kittycorner), cornerwise, slantingways, slantways, slantwise, ||slaunchways
idiom on the bias
con parallelly, square, straight

||**dial** *n syn* see FACE 1

dial *vb syn* see TUNE 3

dialect *n* 1 *syn* see LANGUAGE 1
2 a form of language that is not recognized as standard < the Doric *dialect* of ancient Greece >
syn argot, cant, jargon, lingo, patois, patter, slang, vernacular; *compare* TERMINOLOGY, VERNACULAR 3
rel localism, provincialism, regionalism

dialectic *n syn* see ARGUMENTATION

dialogue *n* 1 *syn* see CONVERSATION 1
2 *syn* see CONVERSATION 2

diametric *adj syn* see OPPOSITE

diapason *n syn* see MELODY

diaphanous *adj syn* see FILMY

diarrhea *n* abnormally frequent intestinal evacuations with more or less fluid stools < they were taken with severe *diarrhea* >
syn ||backdoor trots, dysentery, flux, ||runs, scour(s), ||squirts
idiom Montezuma's revenge, summer complaint

diatribe *n syn* see TIRADE

||**dibs** *n pl* 1 *syn* see MONEY
2 *syn* see CLAIM 1

dice *n pl, sing* **die** a pair or set of small cubes marked on each face with from one to six spots and used in various games and in gambling by being shaken and thrown to come to rest at random < staked everything on a cast of the *dice* >
syn ||African dominoes, bones, ||cubes, ||devil's-bones, ||ivory, ||tats

dice *vb syn* see DISCARD

dichotomize *vb syn* see SEPARATE 1

dick *n* 1 *syn* see DETECTIVE

dicker *vb syn* see HAGGLE 2

dickey *adj syn* see WEAK 2

dictate *vb* to promulgate expressly something to be followed, observed, obeyed, or accepted < the commission *dictated* the policies to be followed >
syn decree, impose, lay down, ordain, prescribe, set

rel control, direct, manage; guide, lead; govern, rule; say, tell, utter; bid, charge, command, enjoin, instruct, order

dictate *n syn* see COMMAND 1

dictative *adj syn* see DICTATORIAL

dictator *n syn* see TYRANT

dictatorial *adj* imposing one's will or opinions on others < the chief was inclined to be *dictatorial* with his subordinates >
syn authoritarian, authoritative, dictative, doctrinaire, dogmatic, magisterial; *compare* TOTALITARIAN 1
rel bossy, domineering, imperative, imperious, masterful, peremptory; absolute, arbitrary, autocratic, despotic, tyrannical; arrogant, haughty, overbearing, proud; firm, stern
con amenable, biddable, docile, obedient, tractable; menial, obsequious, servile, slavish, subservient

dictatorship *n syn* see TYRANNY

diction *n syn* see WORDING

dictionary *n syn* see TERMINOLOGY

dictum *n syn* see MAXIM

||**dicty** *adj syn* see SNOBBISH

didactic *adj* overburdened with instruction and the proprieties < his speech to the new freshmen was painfully *didactic* >
syn moral, moralizing, preachy, schoolmasterish, sermonic, sermonizing, teachy
rel advisory, exhortative, hortative; preceptive
ant undidactic

||**didder** *vb syn* see SHAKE 1

diddle *vb* 1 *syn* see IDLE
2 *syn* see CHEAT

diddle-daddle *vb syn* see IDLE

diddler *n syn* see SWINDLER

dido *n* 1 *usu* **didoes** *pl syn* see PRANK
2 *syn* see KNICKKNACK

die *vb* 1 to pass from physical life < he *died* at an advanced age >
syn cash in, ||check out, conk, ||cop out, ||croak, decease, demise, depart, drop, expire, go, ||kick in, ||kick off, pass, pass away, pass out, peg out, perish, pip, pop off, ||snuff (out), succumb, ||swelt
idiom be gathered to one's fathers, bite the dust (*or* ground), breathe one's last, cash in one's checks (*or* chips), give up the ghost, ||kick the bucket, ||kick up one's heels, meet one's end, shuffle off this mortal coil, ||snuff it, turn up one's toes (to the daisies)
con be, exist, subsist; flourish, thrive
ant live
2 *syn* see PERISH 2

die (down *or* away) *vb syn* see ABATE 4
rel recede; disappear
con ascend, mount, rise
ant come up

die *n* 1 *see* DICE
||2 *syn* see TOY 2

die-away *adj syn* see LANGUID

diehard *n* 1 an irreconcilable opponent of change < party *diehards* who would make no concessions >
syn bitter-ender, conservative, fundamentalist, old liner, praetorian, pullback, right, rightist, right wing, right-winger, standpat, standpatter, tory; *compare* REACTIONARY

rel mossback, old fogy, stick-in-the-mud; intransigent; true blue; right-center

con liberal, progressive, radical

2 *syn* see REACTIONARY

die-hard *adj syn* see CONSERVATIVE 1

differ *vb* 1 to be unlike or distinct in nature, form, or characteristics <the houses *differ* only in a few minor details>

syn disagree, vary

rel depart, deviate, diverge

con accord, conform, correspond

ant agree

2 to be of unlike or opposite opinion <men who *differ* on religious matters>

syn disaccord, disagree, discord, dissent, divide, vary

rel clash, conflict, jar; bicker, quarrel, squabble; argue, debate, dispute; oppose, protest (against)

idiom differ in opinion, hold opposite views

con coincide, concert, concur, harmonize; accord, conform, correspond

ant agree

difference *n* 1 *syn* see DISSIMILARITY

rel modification, variation

con equivalence, equivalency, sameness

ant resemblance

2 *syn* see DISCORD

rel clash, conflict

3 *syn* see VARIANCE 1

difference *vb syn* see KNOW 4

different *adj* 1 unlike in kind or character <could hardly be more *different*>

syn disparate, dissimilar, distant, divergent, diverse, other, otherwise, unalike, unequal, unlike, unsimilar, various

rel particular, single; distinctive, individual, peculiar; divers, sundry

con akin, analogous, comparable, like, parallel, similar, uniform; equal, equivalent, self-same

ant alike, identical, same

2 *syn* see DISTINCT 1

differential *adj syn* see DISCRIMINATORY

differentiate *vb syn* see KNOW 4

rel comprehend, understand

con confound, mistake

ant confuse

differently *adv syn* see OTHERWISE 1

difficile *adj syn* see HARD 6

difficult *adj syn* see HARD 6

rel problem, problematic

idiom easier said than done, no picnic, tough sledding

ant simple

difficultly *adv syn* see HARD 8

difficulty *n* 1 something obstructing one's course and demanding effort and endurance if one's end is to be attained <he encountered great *difficulties* on his way to success>

syn asperity, hardness, hardship, rigor, vicissitude

rel impediment, obstacle, obstruction, snag; dilemma, fix, jam, pickle, plight, predicament, quandary, scrape; emergency, exigency, pass, pinch, strait; bother, inconvenience, problem, trouble

---

syn synonym(s)   *rel* related word(s)
ant antonym(s)   *con* contrasted word(s)
idiom idiomatic equivalent(s)
‖ use limited; if in doubt, see a dictionary

idiom hard nut to crack, hard row to hoe, heavy sledding

2 *syn* see DEMUR 2

3 *syn* see QUARREL

diffident *adj syn* see SHY 1

rel blenching, flinching, shrinking; hesitant, reluctant

con assured, presumptuous, sanguine, sure; self-assured, self-confident, self-possessed, self-reliant; brazen, impudent, shameless

ant confident

difform *adj syn* see LOPSIDED

diffuse *adj syn* see WORDY

rel exuberant, lavish, profuse; casual, desultory, random; lax, loose, slack; lengthy, long

con concentrated; condensed

ant succinct

diffuse *vb* 1 *syn* see SPREAD 1

rel extend; expand

con compact, consolidate; center, centralize, focus

ant concentrate

2 *syn* see INTERFUSE 2

dig *vb* 1 to loosen and turn over or remove (as soil) with or as if with a spade <*dig* for potatoes> <*dug* through her drawer looking for the scarf>

syn ‖delve, excavate, grub, shovel, spade

rel quarry; enter, penetrate, pierce, probe; dig up, root, rootle, root out

2 to form by digging <*dig* a trench>

syn dig out, excavate, scoop, shovel, spade

3 *syn* see THRUST 2

‖4 *syn* see RESIDE 1

5 *syn* see POKE 1

‖6 *syn* see APPREHEND 1

7 *syn* see ENJOY 1

dig (into) *vb syn* see EXPLORE

dig *n* 1 *syn* see POKE 1

2 *syn* see SITE 3

digest *n syn* see COMPENDIUM 1

rel abridgment, synopsis

digest *vb* 1 *syn* see BEAR 10

2 *syn* see EPITOMIZE 1

digit *n syn* see NUMBER

dignification *n syn* see APOTHEOSIS 2

dignify *vb syn* see EXALT 1

con abase, debase

ant demean

dignitary *n syn* see NOTABLE 1

dignity *n* 1 *syn* see STATUS 2

2 *syn* see DECORUM 1

rel excellence, merit, perfection, virtue; ethicalness, ethics, morality, nobleness, nobility

con impropriety, indecency, indecorum, unseemliness

3 *syn* see ELEGANCE

rel augustness, grandeur, grandness, magnificence, majesty, nobleness, nobility; address, poise

dig out *vb* 1 *syn* see DIG 2

2 *syn* see RUMMAGE 3

digress *vb* 1 *syn* see SWERVE 2

2 to turn aside from the main subject of attention or course of argument <he *digressed* into too many side issues>

syn depart, divagate, diverge, excurse, ramble, stray, wander

rel drift, roam

idiom get off the subject, go off on a tangent

con advance, proceed, progress

digression *n* a departure from a subject or theme < a *digression* from the main point of the speech >

syn aside, discursion, divagation, excursion, excursus, parenthesis

rel episode, excurse, incident, underaction; deflection, deviation, divergence; departure; drifting, rambling, straying, wandering

||**dike** (out *or* up) *vb syn* see DRESS UP 1

dilapidate *vb syn* see RUIN 2

rel crumble, decay, decompose, disintegrate; disregard, forget, ignore, neglect, overlook, slight

con mend, rebuild, repair; rejuvenate, renew, renovate, restore

dilapidated *adj syn* see SHABBY 1

rel damaged, impaired, injured, marred; crumbled, decayed

dilate *vb syn* see EXPAND 3

rel augment, enlarge, increase; extend, lengthen, prolong, protract; broaden, widen

con compress, condense, contract, shrink; attenuate

ant circumscribe; constrict

dilate (on *or* upon) *vb syn* see DISCOURSE 1

rel describe, narrate, recite, recount, rehearse, relate

con abbreviate, abridge, curtail, shorten

dilatory *adj syn* see SLOW 2

rel lax, neglectful, negligent, remiss, slack

con assiduous, busy, industrious, sedulous; prompt, quick, ready; hasty, impetuous, precipitate

ant diligent

dilemma *n syn* see PREDICAMENT

rel bewilderment, mystification, perplexity

idiom horns of a dilemma

dilettante *n* 1 *syn* see CONNOISSEUR

2 *syn* see AMATEUR 2

dilettante *adj syn* see AMATEURISH

dilettantish *adj syn* see AMATEURISH

dilettantist *adj syn* see AMATEURISH

diligent *adj syn* see ASSIDUOUS

rel persevering, persistent, persisting; unflagging

con deliberate, laggard, leisurely, slow; desultory

ant dilatory

||**dilly** *adj syn* see FOOLISH 2

||**dilly** *n* one that is remarkable or extraordinary of its kind < came up with a *dilly* of an idea to sell the product >

syn ||corker, crackerjack, ||daisy, dandy, ||dinger, ||doozer, humdinger, jim-dandy, knockout, ||lalapalooza, ||lulu, nifty, peach, ||pip, pippin, ripper, ripsnorter, rouser

dilly *vb syn* see DELAY 2

dillydally *vb syn* see DELAY 2

dilute *vb* to make less strong or concentrated < *dilute* acid >

syn cut, thin, weaken

rel moderate, qualify, temper; deliquesce, liquefy; alter, modify

con enrich, fortify, richen, upgrade; condense, densify, evaporate, thicken

ant concentrate

dilute *adj* of relatively low strength or concentration < *dilute* acid >

syn diluted, thin, washy, watered-down, waterish, watery, weak

rel reduced; adulterated, sophisticated; impaired, impoverished, weakened

con condensed, densified, thickened

ant concentrated

diluted *adj syn* see DILUTE

ant concentrated

dim *adj* 1 *syn* see DARK 1

ant bright

2 *syn* see DULL 7

||3 *syn* see DULL 9

4 *syn* see FAINT 2

con manifest, plain

ant distinct

dim *vb* 1 *syn* see OBSCURE

2 *syn* see DULL 1

3 *syn* see DULL 4

dime novel *n* a usually paperback melodramatic novel < read mostly *dime novels* >

syn dreadful, penny dreadful, shilling shocker, shocker, yellowback

rel bloodcurdler, chiller, ||killer-diller; thriller; pulp

dimension *n* 1 *usu* dimensions *pl syn* see SIZE 1

2 *usu* dimensions *pl syn* see RANGE 2

dimensionality *n syn* see SIZE 1

diminish *vb* 1 *syn* see ABRIDGE 1

2 *syn* see DECREASE

rel ebb, subside, wane; moderate, temper; attenuate, extenuate

con aggravate, enhance, heighten, intensify

3 *syn* see DECRY 2

diminutive *adj syn* see TINY

||**dimmet** *n syn* see EVENING 1

dimple *vb syn* see RIPPLE

||**dimps** *n syn* see EVENING 1

dim-sighted *adj syn* see PURBLIND

||**dimpsy** *n syn* see EVENING 1

dimwit *n syn* see DUNCE

dim-witted *adj syn* see RETARDED

con alert, keen

din *n* a welter of discordant sounds < the *din* of a machine shop >

syn babel, brouhaha, ||chirm, clamor, hubbub, hullabaloo, jangle, music, pandemonium, racket, racketry, tintamarre, tumult, uproar; *compare* COMMOTION 4

rel blatancy, boisterousness, clamorousness, stridency; bedlam; clangor, clatter, rattle; clash, percussion; ||row; noise, sound

con calm, lull, quietude, stillness; concord, consonance, harmony; melody, musicality, tunefulness

diner *n syn* see EATING HOUSE

dinero *n syn* see MONEY

ding *vb* 1 *syn* see STRIKE 2

2 *syn* see SURPASS 1

||**ding** *n syn* see BLOW 1

ding-a-ling *n syn* see CRACKPOT

dingdong *adv syn* see HARD 3

dinge *n syn* see SADNESS

||**dinger** *n syn* ||DILLY, ||corker, crackerjack, ||daisy, dandy, humdinger, jim-dandy, knockout, ||lalapalooza, ||lulu

dingus *n syn* see DOODAD

dingy *adj syn* see SHABBY 1

rel grimed, smirched, soiled, sullied, tarnished; dull; dusky, gloomy, murky *con* bright, brilliant, luminous, shining; clean, cleanly

dining table *n syn* see TABLE 1

dinky *adj syn* see MINOR 2

‖**dinky-di** *adj syn* see FAITHFUL 1

dinner *n* a usually elaborate meal served to guests or a group often to mark an occasion or honor an individual < the annual club *dinner* >
syn banquet, feast, regale, spread
rel ‖blowout, festival, fete, junket; breakfast, collation, luncheon

dinner table *n syn* see TABLE 1

dinosauric *adj syn* see HUGE

‖**dinsome** *adj syn* see VOCIFEROUS

dint *n syn* see POWER 4

dip *vb* 1 to plunge or thrust momentarily or partially under the surface of a liquid < *dip* a dress in cleansing fluid >
syn douse, duck, dunk, immerse, souse, submerge, submerse
rel pitch, plunge
2 to lift a portion of by reaching below the surface with something shaped to hold liquid < *dip* drinking water from a spring >
syn bail, lade, ladle, scoop
rel dish, spoon; bucket (up *or* out), draw
‖3 *syn* see PAWN
4 *syn* see DUCK 2
5 *syn* see PLUMMET
6 *syn* see SET 12
7 *syn* see SWERVE 1

dip (into) *vb syn* see BROWSE

dip *n* 1 *syn* see DESCENT 4
2 *syn* see DECLINE 3
3 *syn* see DEPRESSION 2
‖4 *syn* see PICKPOCKET

diplomacy *n syn* see TACT

diplomatic *adj syn* see TACTFUL
rel bland, smooth; courteous, polite; astute, shrewd; artful, crafty, guileful, wily
ant undiplomatic

‖**dippy** *adj syn* see FOOLISH 2

‖**dipsy-doodle** *n syn* see DECEPTION 1

dire *adj* 1 *syn* see FEARFUL 3
rel depressing, oppressing
3 *syn* see OMINOUS
4 *syn* see PRESSING
5 *syn* see ACUTE 6

direct *vb* 1 *syn* see ADDRESS 6
2 to turn something toward its appointed or intended mark or goal < *directed* his eyes to the door >
syn address, aim, cast, head, incline, lay, level, point, present, set, train, turn, zero (in)
rel beam; divert; fasten, focus
3 *syn* see ADDRESS 3
rel fix, set, settle
con deflect, divert; deviate, digress, diverge, swerve
4 *syn* see GUIDE
ant misdirect
5 *syn* see GOVERN 3
6 *syn* see CONDUCT 3
7 *syn* see COMMAND

rel assign, define, prescribe

direct *adj* 1 being or passing in a straight line of descent from parent to offspring < *direct* ancestors >
syn lineal
2 admitting free or continuous passage < a *direct* route to the beach >
syn straight, straightforward, through, uninterrupted
rel linear; continuous, unbroken, undeviating, unswerving
con circuitous, roundabout
ant indirect
3 *syn* see FRANK
ant devious
4 marked by absence of an intervening agency, instrumentality, or influence < he had no *direct* knowledge of the crime >
syn firsthand, immediate, primary
rel contiguous, next, proximate
ant indirect

direct *adv* 1 *syn* see DIRECTLY 1
2 *syn* see VERBATIM

direction *n* 1 *syn* see VIEWPOINT 2

directive *n* 1 *syn* see EDICT 1
2 *syn* see MEMORANDUM 2
3 *syn* see MESSAGE 1

directly *adv* 1 without deviation of course < the turnpike runs *directly* east and west >
syn dead, direct, due, right, straight, straightly, undeviatingly
idiom as the crow flies, in a beeline
con circuitously, deviously, round about; discursively, ramblingly
ant indirectly
2 *syn* see VERBATIM
3 *syn* see IMMEDIATELY 1
4 *syn* see AWAY 3
5 *syn* see PRESENTLY 1

direful *adj* 1 *syn* see FEARFUL 3
2 *syn* see OMINOUS

dirt *n* 1 *syn* see EARTH 2
2 *syn* see DECEPTION 1

dirt poor *adj syn* see POOR 1

dirty *adj* 1 soiled or begrimed with dirt < wash those *dirty* hands >
syn black, dungy, filthy, foul, grubby, impure, mucky, murky, nasty, soily, sordid, squalid, unclean, uncleanly
rel contaminated, defiled, polluted, tainted; dreggy; draggled, draggletailed, draggly
idiom dirty as a pig
con immaculate, spotless; unsoiled, unspotted, unsullied
ant clean
2 *syn* see IMPURE 1
ant clean
3 *syn* see OBSCENE 2
4 *syn* see WILD 6

dirty *vb* 1 *syn* see SOIL 2
ant clean
2 *syn* see TAINT 1
idiom dirty one's hands

disability *n syn* see DISADVANTAGE

disable *vb* 1 *syn* see DISQUALIFY 1
2 *syn* see PARALYZE 1
3 *syn* see WEAKEN 1
rel harm, hurt, mar, spoil; batter, maim, mangle, mutilate; ruin, wreck
con restore, resuscitate, revive, revivify
ant rehabilitate

---

syn synonym(s)   *rel* related word(s)
ant antonym(s)   *con* contrasted word(s)
idiom idiomatic equivalent(s)
‖ use limited; if in doubt, see a dictionary

disabuse *vb* to set free from mistakes (as in reasoning or judgment) < he was *disabused* of his belief when the facts were presented >
syn purge, undeceive, undelude
rel amend, correct, emend, rectify, redress; disillude, disillusion, unblind; enlighten, illuminate; free, liberate, release
idiom open one's eyes, prick the (*or* one's) bubble, puncture one's balloon, set (*or* put) right (*or* straight)
con deceive, delude, mislead; dupe, gull

disaccord *vb* 1 *syn* see CLASH 2
2 *syn* see DIFFER 2
ant accord

disaccord *n syn* see DISCORD
ant accord

disacknowledge *vb syn* see DISCLAIM

disadvantage *n* an unfavorable or prejudicial quality or circumstance < the machine has two serious *disadvantages* >
syn detriment, disability, drawback, handicap
rel bar, impediment, obstacle, obstruction; blocking, hamper, hindrance, imposition
con aid, assistance, help; service, usefulness, utility, value, worth
ant advantage

disadvantaged *adj syn* see UNDERPRIVILEGED
ant advantaged

disadvantageous *adj syn* see DEROGATORY
ant advantage

disadvise *vb syn* see DISSUADE

disaffect *vb syn* see ESTRANGE
rel agitate, discompose, disquiet, disturb, upset
ant win (over)

disaffection *n syn* see ESTRANGEMENT

disaffirm *vb syn* see DENY 4

disagree *vb* 1 *syn* see DIFFER 1
ant agree
2 *syn* see DIFFER 2
ant agree

disagreeable *adj* 1 *syn* see BAD 8
rel annoying, distressing, disturbing, woeful
ant agreeable
2 *syn* see IRRITABLE
ant agreeable

disallow *vb* 1 *syn* see DENY 2
con accede, acquiesce, assent
ant allow
2 *syn* see DISCLAIM
rel debar, exclude, shut out
ant allow

disallowance *n syn* see DENIAL 1

disappear *vb syn* see VANISH
rel go, leave
ant appear

disappoint *vb syn* see FRUSTRATE 1

disapprove *vb* 1 to feel or express an objection < *disapprove* of his actions >
syn deprecate, discommend, discountenance, disesteem, disfavor, frown, object
rel blame, censure, condemn, criticize, denounce, reprehend, reprobate; decry, depreciate, detract, disparage, dispraise; expostulate, remonstrate
idiom look askance at, make a wry face at, not go for, take a dim view of, take exception to

con applaud, commend, compliment, recommend; accredit, certify, endorse, sanction; approbate, countenance, favor
ant approve
2 *syn* see DECLINE 4

disarm *vb* 1 *syn* see PARALYZE 1
2 to influence favorably by persuasive words or acts < *disarmed* by her smile >
syn unarm, unsteel, win (over)
rel allure, attract, bewitch, captivate, charm, enchant, fascinate
con alert, caution, tip (off), warn
ant arm

disarming *adj* ingratiating, deferential, ingratiatory, insinuating, insinuative, saccharine, silken, silky

disarrange *vb syn* see DISORDER 1
rel mislay, misplace; displace, replace; overturn
ant arrange

disarray *n syn* see CONFUSION 3
con arrangement, marshaling

disarray *vb syn* see DISORDER 1
ant array

disassemble *vb syn* see DISMOUNT

disassociate *vb syn* see DETACH

disaster *n* a sudden calamitous event bringing great damage, loss, or destruction < a flood *disaster* struck the valley >
syn calamity, cataclysm, catastrophe, misadventure, tragedy, woe(s)
rel accident, casualty, fatality, mishap; adversity, distress, misadventure, mischance, misfortune; rock(s)

disastrous *adj syn* see FATAL 2
rel hapless, luckless, unfortunate; destructive
con fortunate, happy, lucky, providential

disavow *vb syn* see DISCLAIM
rel impugn, negate, negative
con allow, concede, grant; assert, justify, maintain
ant avow

disband *vb* to cease to exist as a unit < the dance group *disbanded* after a farewell concert >
syn break up, disperse, dissolve
rel dispel, dissipate, scatter; dichotomize, disjoin, disjoint, dissect, dissever, disunite, divide, divorce, part, separate, sever, sunder
idiom go their several ways, part company
con combine, concur, conjoin, cooperate, unite; assemble, collect, congregate, gather; call up, summon
ant band

disbelief *n syn* see UNBELIEF
rel atheism, deism; rejection, repudiation, spurning
con credence, credit, faith
ant belief

disbelieve *vb* to hold not to be true or real < *disbelieved* his professions of sincerity >
syn discredit, unbelieve
rel distrust, doubt, mistrust, question, suspect; eschew, reject, scorn, scout
con accept, ‖buy, swallow
ant believe

disbelieving *adj syn* see INCREDULOUS

disbodied *adj syn* see IMMATERIAL 1

disburden *vb syn* see UNLOAD

disburse *vb* 1 *syn* see SPEND 1

2 *syn* see DISTRIBUTE 1

disbursement *n syn* see EXPENSE 1

discalceate *adj syn* see DISCALCED

discalced *adj* wearing only sandals on the feet < *discalced* monks >
syn barefoot, discalceate
con calced, shod

discard *vb* to get rid of < *discard* old clothes > < people who *discard* traditional values >
syn abdicate, cashier, cast, chuck, ‖deep= six, ‖dice, ditch, dump, jettison, junk, lay aside, reject, scrap, shed, ‖shoot, shuck (off), slough, throw away, throw out, wash out
rel abandon, desert, forsake; repudiate; spurn; dismiss, eject, oust
idiom do away with, let go by the board
con adopt, embrace, espouse, take on, take up; employ, use, utilize; hold, hold back, keep, retain; cherish, esteem, nurture

discarding *n syn* see DISPOSAL 2

discarnate *adj syn* see IMMATERIAL 1
ant carnate, incarnate

discept *vb syn* see DISCUSS 1

discern *vb* 1 *syn* see SEE 1
rel ascertain, discover; anticipate, apprehend, divine, foresee
2 *syn* see KNOW 4

discernible *adj syn* see PERCEPTIBLE
ant indiscernible

discerning *adj syn* see WISE 1
ant undiscerning

discernment *n syn* see WIT 3
rel intuition, reason; sagaciousness, sagacity
con crassness, density, slowness; blindness

discharge *vb* 1 *syn* see UNLOAD
2 *syn* see EXEMPT
3 *syn* see SHOOT 1
4 *syn* see FREE
rel dismiss, eject, expel, oust; eliminate, exclude
5 to give outlet to < the river *discharges* its waters into the bay >
syn disembogue, emit, flow, give off, pour, void
rel eject, exude, release
6 *syn* see DISMISS 3
rel displace, replace, supersede, supplant
con hire; contract
ant engage
7 to release from service with the armed forces < *discharged* from the army with the rank of sergeant >
syn ‖demob, demobilize, muster out, separate
rel disenroll; deactivate, inactivate; bounce, cashier, dismiss, drop, fire, sack
8 *syn* see CLEAR 5
9 *syn* see ANNUL 4

discinct *adj syn* see NEGLIGENT

disciple *n syn* see FOLLOWER
rel enthusiast, fanatic, zealot

disciplinary *adj syn* see PUNITIVE

discipline *n* 1 *syn* see PUNISHMENT
2 *syn* see WILL 3

discipline *vb* 1 *syn* see PUNISH 1

---

syn synonym(s)   *rel* related word(s)
ant antonym(s)   *con* contrasted word(s)
idiom idiomatic equivalent(s)
‖ use limited; if in doubt, see a dictionary

rel overcome, reduce, subdue, subjugate; bridle, check, curb, inhibit, restrain
2 *syn* see TEACH
rel guide, lead; conduct, control, direct, manage

disclaim *vb* to refuse to admit, accept, or approve < the senator *disclaimed* the comment attributed to him > < *disclaim* responsibility for a subordinate's mistake >
syn deny, disacknowledge, disallow, disavow, disown, repudiate
rel contradict, contravene, gainsay, traverse; refuse, reject, spurn; deprecate; belittle, disparage, minimize; abjure, forswear, recant, renounce, retract; challenge, criticize
idiom turn one's back on, wash one's hands of
con acknowledge, avow, own; accept, admit, receive, take
ant claim

disclose *vb* 1 *syn* see OPEN 2
2 *syn* see REVEAL 1
rel acknowledge, admit, avow, confess, own
idiom make public
con conceal, hide; camouflage, cloak, disguise, dissemble, mask

discolor *vb* 1 *syn* see TAINT 1
2 *syn* see STAIN 1

discolor *adj syn* see VARIEGATED

discombobulate *vb* 1 *syn* see DISCOMPOSE 1
2 *syn* see CONFUSE 2

discomfit *vb syn* see EMBARRASS
rel annoy, bother, irk, vex; disturb, perturb, upset

discomfiture *n* 1 *syn* see DEFEAT 1
2 *syn* see COMEDOWN
3 *syn* see EMBARRASSMENT
rel agitation, disquiet, perturbation, upset; commotion; prickles

discomforting *adj syn* see UNCOMFORTABLE
ant comforting

discommend *vb syn* see DISAPPROVE 1
rel admonish; criticize, reprehend; censure
con approve, endorse, sanction
ant commend; recommend

discommode *vb syn* see INCONVENIENCE
rel flurry, fluster, perturb, upset; bother, irk, vex

discommoding *adj syn* see INCONVENIENT

discommodious *adj syn* see INCONVENIENT

discompose *vb* 1 to destroy or impair one's capacity for collected thought or decisive action < *discomposed* by the rudeness of his friend >
syn agitate, bother, discombobulate, dismay, disquiet, disturb, flurry, fluster, perturb, unhinge, unsettle, untune, upset; compare EMBARRASS
rel disagree; annoy, irk, vex; harass, harry, pester, plague, worry
con calm, quiet, settle, soothe, tranquilize; allay, alleviate, assuage; appease, conciliate, mollify, pacify, placate, propitiate
ant compose
2 *syn* see DISORDER 1
ant compose

discomposure *n syn* see EMBARRASSMENT

ant composure

disconcert *vb syn* see EMBARRASS

rel bewilder, nonplus, perplex, puzzle

disconcertion *n syn* see EMBARRASS-MENT

disconcertment *n syn* see EMBARRASS-MENT

disconfirm *vb syn* see DISPROVE 1

disconnect *vb syn* see DETACH

ant connect

disconnected *adj syn* see INCOHERENT 2

ant connected

disconsolate *adj* 1 *syn* see DOWNCAST

rel comfortless, inconsolable; sorrowful, woeful; doleful, melancholy; unhappy

ant cheerful

2 *syn* see INCONSOLABLE

3 *syn* see GLOOMY 3

ant cheerful, cheery

disconsonant *adj syn* see INCONSONANT 1

discontent *adj syn* see DISCONTENTED

ant content

discontented *adj* showing or expressing a sense of grievance or thwarted aspirations or desires < *discontented* with his position >

syn discontent, disgruntled, dissatisfied, malcontent, malcontented, uncontent, uncontented, ungratified

rel disquieted, disturbed, perturbed, restless, upset; displeased; unhappy

con satisfied; gratified, pleased; happy; elated, exultant, jubilant, triumphant

ant contented

discontinuance *n syn* see END 2

ant continuance, continuation

discontinuation *n syn* see END 2

ant continuance, continuation

discontinue *vb syn* see STOP 3

ant continue

discontinuity *n syn* see GAP 1

ant continuity

discontinuous *adj syn* see INCOHERENT 2

ant continuous

‖**disconvenience** *n syn* see INCONVENIENCE

ant convenience

‖**disconvenience** *vb syn* see INCONVENIENCE

ant convenience

discord *n* the state of those who disagree and lack harmony < a household full of turmoil and *discord* >

syn conflict, contention, difference, disaccord, disharmony, dispeace, dissension, dissent, dissidence, dissonance, disunion, disunity, division, inharmony, mischief, strife, unpeace, variance

rel discrepancy, incompatibility, incongruity, inconsistency, inconsonance, uncongeniality; animosity, antagonism, antipathy, enmity, hostility, rancor; polarization; collision

con accord, consonance; agreement, concordance, concurrence

ant concord, harmony

discord *vb* 1 *syn* see CLASH 2

ant concord, harmonize

2 *syn* see DIFFER 2

ant accord

discordant *adj* 1 *syn* see INHARMONIOUS 2

2 *syn* see INCONSONANT 1

con according, agreeing, congenial, harmonious, harmonizing

ant concordant

3 *syn* see ANTIPATHETIC 1

ant concordant

4 *syn* see DISSONANT 1

discotheque *n syn* see NIGHTCLUB

discount *n syn* see DEDUCTION 1

discount *vb* 1 *syn* see DEDUCT 1

con boost, hike, increase, mark up, raise

2 *syn* see NEGLECT

3 *syn* see DECRY 2

discountenance *vb* 1 *syn* see EMBARRASS

idiom put out of countenance

2 *syn* see DISAPPROVE 1

rel reproach, reprove

con encourage, favor

ant countenance

discourage *vb* 1 to weaken the stamina, interest, or zeal of < the long winter and lack of fuel *discouraged* the settlers >

syn chill, deject, demoralize, dishearten, disparage, dispirit

rel depress, weigh; afflict, try; damp, dampen, droop; distress, trouble; bother, irk, vex

idiom take the heart out of

con cheer, embolden, hearten, inspirit, nerve, steel

ant encourage

2 *syn* see DISSUADE

rel check, inhibit, restrain; prevent; frighten, scare

idiom lay a wet blanket on, throw cold water on

con advocate, countenance, favor; approve, back, endorse

ant encourage

discouraging *adj syn* see GLOOMY 3

rel deterring; hindering

ant encouraging

discourse *n* 1 *syn* see SPEECH 1

2 a systematic, serious, and often learned exposition of a subject or topic < his *discourses* during the seminar were long remembered >

syn disquisition, dissertation, memoir, monograph, monography, thesis, tractate, treatise

rel article, essay, paper; lecture, sermon; rhetoric, speech, talk

discourse *vb* 1 to express oneself especially formally and at length < *discourses* knowledgeably about the laws of nature >

syn descant, dilate (on *or* upon), discuss, dissert, dissertate, expatiate, sermonize

rel converse, speak, talk, voice; argue, dispute; harangue, lecture, orate, perorate; amplify, develop, elaborate, enlarge, expand; explain, expound; comment, commentate, remark

2 *syn* see ACT 1

discourteous *adj syn* see RUDE 6

con chivalrous, civil, courtly, gallant

ant courteous

discover *vb* 1 *syn* see EXPOSE 4

2 *syn* see REVEAL 1

rel advertise, proclaim, publish

con repress, suppress

3 to become or be made aware of something not previously known < *discover* a secret >

syn ascertain, catch on, determine, find out, hear, learn, see, tumble, unearth

rel descry, detect, encounter, espy, hit (on or upon), meet (with), spot; discern, note, observe, perceive

idiom get wise to

con miss, overlook; disregard, ignore

discovery *n* the gaining knowledge of or ascertaining the existence of something previously unknown or unrecognized < the *discovery* of a new chemical element >

syn detection, espial, find, strike, unearthing

rel disclosure, exposition, exposure, revelation, uncovering

discreate *vb syn* see DESTROY 1

discredit *vb* 1 *syn* see DISBELIEVE

ant credit

2 to deprive of credibility < he *discredited* the rumor immediately >

syn blow up, disprove, explode, puncture, shoot

rel expose, show up; destroy, ruin

idiom bring to naught, knock the bottom out of, not leave a leg to stand on

con accept, believe, credit

discredit *n syn* see DISGRACE

ant credit

discreditable *adj syn* see DISREPUTABLE 1

discreet *adj* 1 *syn* see CAUTIOUS

con foolhardy

ant indiscreet

2 *syn* see PLAIN 1

3 *syn* see CONSERVATIVE 2

discreetness *n syn* see PRUDENCE 1

ant indiscreetness

discrepancy *n syn* see DISSIMILARITY

discrepant *adj syn* see INCONSONANT 1

rel different, disparate, divergent, diverse; disagreeing, varying

con agreeing, conforming, corresponding, jibing, squaring, tallying; alike, identical, like, parallel, similar, uniform

discrepate *vb syn* see KNOW 4

discrete *adj syn* see DISTINCT 1

con blended, fused, merged, mingled

ant indiscrete

discretion *n syn* see PRUDENCE 1

rel moderation, restraint; gumption, judgment, sense, wisdom

con asininity, fatuousness, foolishness, simplicity; foolhardiness, rashness, recklessness

ant indiscretion

discretionary *adj syn* see OPTIONAL

discriminate *vb syn* see KNOW 4

rel note, perceive, remark; collate, compare, contrast

ant confound

discriminating *adj syn* see ECLECTIC 1

rel careful; judicious, prudent, wise

ant undiscriminating

discrimination *n syn* see WIT 3

rel judgment, sense

con crassness, density, slowness

discriminative *adj syn* see DISCRIMINATORY

ant undiscriminative

discriminatory *adj* applying or favoring discrimination in treatment < *discriminatory* employment practices against women >

syn discriminative

rel biased, inequitable, partial, partisan, prejudiced, prepossessed, unfair, unjust

con dispassionate, equal, equitable, fair, impartial, just, objective, unbiased, uncolored, unprejudiced

ant nondiscriminatory

discrown *vb syn* see DEPOSE 1

disculpate *vb syn* see EXCULPATE

ant inculpate

discumber *vb syn* see EXTRICATE 2

discursion *n syn* see DIGRESSION

discuss *vb* 1 to exchange views about something in order to arrive at the truth or to convince others < met to *discuss* community needs >

syn agitate, argue, canvass, debate, discept, dispute, ‖kick around, moot, pro and con, thrash out, toss (around)

rel deliberate, hash over, reason (out), talk over; consider, weigh

idiom consider pro and con, go into, reason the point

2 *syn* see DISCOURSE 1

rel elucidate, explicate, interpret

discussion *n syn* see CONFERENCE 1

disdain 1 *syn* see DESPITE 1

rel antipathy, aversion; arrogance, haughtiness, insolence, superciliousness

con awe, fear, reverence

2 *syn* see PRIDE 3

disdain *vb syn* see DESPISE

con accept, receive, take; acknowledge, admit, own; esteem, respect

ant admire

disdainful *adj syn* see PROUD 1

rel rejecting, repudiating, spurning; contemning, despising, scorning, scouting; antipathetic, averse, unsympathetic

ant admiring; respectful

disdainfulness *n syn* see PRIDE 3

disease *n* 1 a kind or instance of impairment of a living being that interferes with normal bodily function < tuberculosis has become a controllable *disease* >

syn affection, ailment, complaint, condition, disorder, ill, infirmity, malady, sickness, syndrome; *compare* INFIRMITY 1, SICKNESS 1

rel bug, ‖epizootic, ‖misery, virus

2 *syn* see INFIRMITY 1

ant health

diseasedness *n syn* see SICKNESS 1

disedge *vb syn* see DULL 3

disembark *vb* to go ashore out of a ship < *disembark* at the next port >

syn debark, land

rel put in

con board, get on

ant embark

disembarrass *vb syn* see EXTRICATE 2

rel clear, rid, unburden

ant embarrass

disembodied *adj syn* see IMMATERIAL 1

disembogue *vb syn* see DISCHARGE 5

disembowel *vb syn* see EVISCERATE

disembroil *vb syn* see EXTRICATE 2

ant embroil

---

syn synonym(s)   **rel** related word(s)
ant antonym(s)   **con** contrasted word(s)
idiom idiomatic equivalent(s)
‖ use limited; if in doubt, see a dictionary

disemploy *vb syn* see DISMISS 3
disenable *vb syn* see DISQUALIFY
disenchanted *adj syn* see SOPHISTICATED 2
disencumber *vb syn* see EXTRICATE 2
  rel alleviate, lighten, relieve
  con depress, oppress, weigh
  ant encumber
disenfranchise *vb syn* see DISFRANCHISE
disengage *vb* 1 *syn* see DETACH
  rel free, liberate, release
  con associate, connect, join, link, unite
  ant engage
  2 *syn* see LOOSE 3
disentangle *vb* 1 *syn* see EXTRICATE 2
  rel detach, disengage; part, separate, sever, sunder
  con enmesh, involve
  ant entangle, tangle
disenthrall *vb syn* see FREE
disenthrone *vb syn* see DEPOSE 1
disentranced *adj syn* see SOPHISTICATED 2
disentwine *vb syn* see EXTRICATE 2
disesteem *vb syn* see DISAPPROVE 1
disesteem *n syn* see DISGRACE
  ant esteem
disfashion *vb syn* see DEFACE
disfavor *n* 1 *syn* see DISLIKE
  rel distrust, mistrust
  con approbation, approval; admiration, esteem, liking, regard, respect
  ant favor
  2 *syn* see DISGRACE
disfavor *vb syn* see DISAPPROVE 1
  con approve, accept, approbate, countenance, go (for), hold (with)
  ant favor
disfeature *vb syn* see DEFACE
disfigure *vb syn* see DEFACE
  ant adorn
disfranchise *vb* to deprive of a legal right and especially of the right to vote < people subtly *disfranchised* by community apathy >
  syn disenfranchise
  rel deprive, take away
  ant affranchise, enfranchise, franchise
disgorge *vb* 1 *syn* see VOMIT
  2 *syn* see ERUPT 1
disgrace *n* the state of one who has lost esteem and good repute < retired in *disgrace* after the scandal became public >
  syn contempt, discredit, disesteem, disfavor, dishonor, disrepute, ignominy, infamy, obloquy, odium, opprobrium, shame
  rel abasement, debasement, debasing, degradation, humbling, humiliation; black eye, blot, brand, spot, stain, stigma
  con admiration, regard; awe, fear, reverence; fame, glory, honor, renown, repute
  ant esteem, respect
disgraceful *adj syn* see DISREPUTABLE 1
  ant respectable; respectworthy
disgracious *adj syn* see RUDE 6
  ant gracious
disgrade *vb syn* see DEGRADE 1
disgruntled *adj syn* see DISCONTENTED
disguise *vb* to alter so as to hide the true appearance or character of < *disguised* herself with a wig > < *disguised* his anger behind a false geniality >
  syn camouflage, cloak, dissemble, dissimulate, dress up, mask

  rel conceal, hide; obfuscate, obscure; belie, falsify, garble, misrepresent; affect, assume, counterfeit, feign, pretend, sham, simulate
  con display, exhibit, expose, flaunt, parade, show; betray, disclose, discover, reveal
disguise *n* 1 *syn* see MASK 2
  rel deception, delusion; speciousness
  2 *syn* see PRETENSE 2
disguised *adj syn* see INTOXICATED 1
disguisement *n syn* see MASK 2
disgust *vb* to be offensive to the taste or sensibilities of < the sight of filth *disgusted* him >
  syn nauseate, reluct, repel, repulse, revolt, sicken
  rel offend, outrage
  idiom make one sick, stick in one's craw (or crop or gizzard), turn one's stomach
  con charm, entice, tempt; delight, gratify, please, rejoice, tickle
disgusted *adj syn* see FED UP
disgusting *adj syn* see OFFENSIVE
‖**dish** *vb syn* see CHAT 1
disharmonic *adj syn* see DISSONANT 1
  ant harmonic, harmonious
disharmonious *adj syn* see DISSONANT 1
  ant harmonic, harmonious
disharmonize *vb syn* see CLASH 2
  ant harmonize
disharmony *n syn* see DISCORD
  ant harmony
dishearten *vb syn* see DISCOURAGE 1
  ant hearten
disheartening *adj syn* see GLOOMY 3
  rel despondent, pessimistic
  con encouraging, optimistic
  ant heartening
disheveled *adj syn* see SLOVENLY 1
dishonest *adj* 1 unworthy of trust or belief < made a *dishonest* report on their progress >
  syn deceitful, knavish, lying, mendacious, roguish, shifty, unhonest, untruthful
  rel crooked, devious, furtive, oblique; faithless, false, perfidious, untrustworthy; cheating, cozening, ‖cronk, defrauding, double-dealing, fraudulent, swindling, two-faced; insidious, tricky
  con conscientious, honorable, just, scrupulous, upright; aboveboard, forthright, straightforward; candid, fair, frank, open, plain; dependable, reliable, sure, trustworthy, trusty
  ant honest
  2 *syn* see CROOKED 2
dishonesty *n syn* see DECEPTION 1
dishonor *n syn* see DISGRACE
  con reverence, veneration; authority, credit, influence, prestige, weight
  ant honor
dishonorable *adj syn* see DISREPUTABLE 1
  ant honorable
dish out *vb syn* see GIVE 3
disillusioned *adj syn* see SOPHISTICATED 2
  con beguiled, deceived, deluded, misled
disimpassioned *adj syn* see COOL 2
  ant heated, impassioned
disimprison *vb syn* see FREE
  ant imprison

disimprove *vb syn* see DETERIORATE 1
ant improve

disinclination *n syn* see DISLIKE
ant inclination

disinclined *adj* lacking the will or desire to do something < *disinclined* to accept his story >
syn afraid, averse, backward, hesitant, indisposed, loath, reluctant, shy, uneager, unwilling, unwishful
rel antipathetic, unsympathetic; doubtful, dubious; opposing, resisting; balking, boggling, shying, sticking, stickling; objecting, protesting
con anxious, avid, eager, keen; disposed, predisposed, ready, willing
ant inclined

disingenuous *adj* lacking in candor and often giving a false appearance of simple frankness < had a *disingenuous* way of asking for advice when he really wanted help >
syn uncandid, unfrank
rel false, feigned, insincere, left-handed; artful, crafty, cunning, foxy, guileful, insidious, sly, tricky, wily; devious, indirect, oblique
con artless, naive, natural, simple, unsophisticated; candid, frank, open, plain; sincere, unfeigned; aboveboard, direct, straightforward
ant ingenuous

disinherit *vb* 1 to deprive (an heir apparent) of the right to inherit < the father *disinherited* his wayward son in his will >
syn cut off
rel disown, repudiate; dispossess
idiom cut off without a cent
2 *syn* see DEPRIVE 2

disinhume *vb syn* see EXHUME
ant inhume

disintegrate *vb* 1 *syn* see DECAY
rel deliquesce; disperse, dissipate, scatter
con articulate, concatenate; blend, coalesce, fuse, merge; associate, combine, conjoin, connect, join, link, unite
2 *syn* see DETERIORATE 1

disinter *vb syn* see EXHUME
ant inter

disinterest *n syn* see APATHY 2
ant interest

disinterested *adj* 1 *syn* see INDIFFERENT 2
rel negative, neutral
con concerned, curious; fervent, impassioned, passionate
ant interested
2 *syn* see NEUTRAL
rel fair, just, impartial, unbiased
con biased, prejudiced; involved
ant concerned

disject *vb syn* see STREW 1

disjoin *vb syn* see SEPARATE 1

disjoint *vb* 1 *syn* see SEPARATE 1
2 *syn* see DISORDER 1

disjointed *adj syn* see INCOHERENT 2

dislike *n* a state of mind or feeling marked by an inner avoidance of something usually felt as unpleasant or repugnant < a pronounced *dislike* for mathematics >
syn aversion, bad books, disfavor, disinclination, disliking, displeasure, disrelish, dissatisfaction, distaste, indisposition
rel detestation, hate, hatred; deprecation, disapproval; prejudice, scunner
idiom ‖a derry on
con affection, attachment, love; partiality, predilection, preference
ant liking

disliking *n syn* see DISLIKE
ant liking

dislimb *vb syn* see MAIM

dislimn *vb syn* see OBSCURE

dislocate *vb* 1 *syn* see DISORDER 1
2 *syn* see MOVE 4

disloyal *adj syn* see FAITHLESS
rel alienated, disaffected, estranged
ant loyal

disloyalty *n* 1 *syn* see INFIDELITY
ant loyalty
2 *syn* see TREACHERY
ant loyalty

dismal *adj syn* see GLOOMY 3
con animated, gay, lively; cheerful

dismals *n pl, used with the syn* see SADNESS

dismantle *vb* 1 *syn* see STRIP 2
con appoint, equip, outfit
2 *syn* see DESTROY 1
3 *syn* see REVOKE 2
4 *syn* see DISMOUNT

dismay *n syn* see FEAR 1
con aplomb, assurance, confidence, self=possession; mettle, resolution, spirit

dismay *vb* 1 to unnerve and check by arousing fear, apprehension, or aversion < *dismayed* by the task that lay ahead >
syn appall, consternate, daunt, horrify, shake
rel bewilder, confound, dumbfound, mystify, nonplus, perplex, puzzle; abash, discomfit, disconcert, embarrass, faze, rattle; discourage, dishearten; affright, alarm, frighten, scare, terrify
idiom set one back on one's heels, take aback
con assure, ensure, secure; excite, galvanize, pique, provoke, quicken, stimulate
2 *syn* see DISCOMPOSE 1

dismayed *adj syn* see AGHAST 2
rel discomfited, disconcerted, fazed, rattled
ant undismayed

dismember *vb* 1 *syn* see MAIM
rel part, separate, sever, sunder
2 *syn* see DISMOUNT

dismiss *vb* 1 *syn* see DIVORCE 2
2 *syn* see DECLINE 4
3 to let go from one's employ or service < during the recession thousands of employees were *dismissed* >
syn ax, boot (out), bounce, ‖can, cashier, discharge, disemploy, drop, fire, kick out, let out, sack, terminate, turn off
rel depose, displace, furlough, lay off, remove, retire, suspend, unseat; reject, turn away; riff
idiom give one the gate (*or* one's walking papers), let go; give the ax (*or* the can) to
con hire; contract, engage; get, obtain, procure, secure

---

syn synonym(s)   *rel* related word(s)
ant antonym(s)   *con* contrasted word(s)
idiom idiomatic equivalent(s)
‖ use limited; if in doubt, see a dictionary

ant employ

4 *syn see* EJECT 1
rel cast, discard, shed, slough
idiom send one to Coventry
5 to refuse to consider seriously < *dismisses* the other performers as mere amateurs >
syn kiss off, pooh-pooh
rel deride, mock, rally, ridicule, taunt, twit; flout, gibe, gird, jeer, scoff; contemn, despise, disdain, scorn, scout; reject

dismissive *adj see* PROUD 1

dismount *vb* to take down or apart from an assembled position < *dismount* a revolver for cleaning >
syn disassemble, dismantle, dismember, take down
rel detach, disengage; disconnect, disjoin, disunite, separate
idiom take apart, take to pieces
con assemble, construct, put together; combine, unite

disobedient *adj* refusing or neglecting to obey < the *disobedient* child refused to come in >
syn naughty, obstreperous, unruly; *compare* CONTRARY 3, NAUGHTY 1
rel headstrong, recalcitrant, willful; contumacious, insubordinate, rebellious
con amenable, biddable, docile, tractable; decorous, good, well-behaved
ant obedient

disoblige *vb syn see* INCONVENIENCE
con accommodate, convenience, favor
ant oblige

disorder *n* **1** *syn see* CONFUSION 3
con orderliness; pattern, plan
ant order
2 breach of public order < the overthrow of the government caused *disorder* in the country >
syn anarchism, anarchy, distemper, misrule, riot
rel anomie; agitation, commotion, convulsion, tumult, turbulence, turmoil, upheaval
ant order
3 *syn see* DISEASE 1
4 *syn see* SICKNESS 1

disorder *vb* **1** to undo the fixed or proper order of something < *disorder* the carefully arranged contents of a drawer >
syn derange, disarrange, disarray, discompose, disjoint, dislocate, disorganize, disrupt, distemper, disturb, jumble, ‖mammock, mess (up), mix up, muddle, muss (up), ‖mux, rummage, shuffle, tumble, unsettle, upset; *compare* CONFUSE 5
rel ball up, embroil; dishevel, rumple
idiom make hay of
con arrange, marshal, methodize, organize, systematize; align, array, line, line up, range; adjust, fix, regulate
ant order
2 *syn see* UPSET 5

disordered *adj* **1** *syn see* INCOHERENT 2
2 *syn see* INSANE 1

disorderly *adj syn see* TURBULENT 1

disorderly house *n syn see* BROTHEL

disorganize *vb syn see* DISORDER 1
ant organize

disown *vb syn see* DISCLAIM
ant own

disparage *vb* **1** *syn see* DECRY 2

ant applaud
2 *syn see* DISCOURAGE 1

disparagement *n* **1** *syn see* DETRACTION
rel animadversion, aspersion, reflection, stricture
2 *syn see* DESPITE 1

disparaging *adj syn see* DEROGATORY
rel underestimating, underrating, undervaluing
con acclaiming, extolling, praising; exalting, magnifying

disparate *adj syn see* DIFFERENT 1
rel discordant, discrepant, incompatible, inconsistent, inconsonant; distinct, separate
ant analogous, comparable

disparity *n* the state of being different (as in degree, rank, excellence, or number) < the *disparity* between the rich and the poor > < their stories showed significant *disparity* >
syn disproportion, imparity, inequality, unevenness
rel alterity, difference, dissemblance, dissimilarity, dissimilitude, distinction, divergence, divergency, otherness, unlikeness
con adequation, equality, equatability, equivalence, equivalency, sameness; correlation, correspondence, likeness; evenness
ant parity

dispassionate *adj syn see* NEUTRAL
rel imperturbable, unflappable, unruffled
con fervent, vehement; intemperate
2 *syn see* FAIR 4
rel aloof, indifferent; frank, open; aboveboard, straightforward

dispatch *vb* **1** *syn see* SEND 1
rel hasten, quicken, speed
2 *syn see* KILL 1
3 *syn see* EAT UP 1

dispatch *n* **1** *syn see* HASTE 1
con dawdling, loitering, procrastination
ant delay
2 *syn see* ALACRITY
rel diligence, industriousness

dispeace *n syn see* DISCORD

dispel *vb syn see* SCATTER 1
rel dismiss, eject, expel, oust; crumble, disintegrate

dispensable *adj* capable of being dispensed with < many household gadgets are readily *dispensable* >
syn nonessential, unessential, unrequired
rel needless, unnecessary, unneeded; minor, trivial, unimportant
con essential, imperative, necessary, necessitous, required; vital
ant indispensable

dispensation *n syn see* FAVOR 4

dispense *vb* **1** *syn see* DISTRIBUTE 1
2 *syn see* GIVE 3
rel portion, prorate
3 *syn see* ADMINISTER 2
4 *syn see* HANDLE 2
5 *syn see* EXEMPT

disperse *vb* **1** *syn see* SCATTER 1
rel discharge, dismiss
con call, cite, convene, convoke, summon
ant assemble, congregate; collect
2 *syn see* DISTRIBUTE 1
3 *syn see* SPREAD 1
4 *syn see* DISBAND

dispirit *vb syn see* DISCOURAGE 1

idiom dampen (*or* lower) one's spirits
ant inspirit

dispirited *adj syn see* DOWNCAST
rel melancholy, sad
ant high-spirited, inspirited

dispiriting *adj syn see* GLOOMY 3
rel dejecting, distressing; oppressing
ant inspiriting

displace *vb* 1 *syn see* BANISH
2 *syn see* DEPOSE 1
3 *syn see* SUPPLANT 1

displaced person *n syn see* REFUGEE

displacement *n syn see* EXILE 1

display *vb* 1 *syn see* OPEN 2
rel demonstrate, evidence, evince, lay out,
manifest, show
con camouflage, cloak, disguise, dissemble, mask; conceal, hide, secrete
2 *syn see* SHOW 4
3 *syn see* SHOW 1

display *n* 1 *syn see* EXHIBITION 1
2 a striking or spectacular exhibition <a
parvenu's *display* of wealth>
syn array, fanfare, panoply, parade,
pomp, shine, show
rel ostentation, ostentatiousness, pretension, pretentiousness, showiness; setout

displeasing *adj syn see* BAD 8
rel annoying, bothersome, irksome, vexing
con agreeable, gratifying, pleasant
ant pleasing

displeasure *n syn see* DISLIKE
rel anger; vexation
con delight, enjoyment
ant pleasure

disponible *adj syn see* AVAILABLE 1

disport *n syn see* PLAY 1
rel jollity, merriment

disport *vb* 1 *syn see* SHOW 4
2 *syn see* BEHAVE 1
3 *syn see* PLAY 1

disposal *n* 1 *syn see* ORDER 3
2 the act of ridding oneself of something
<incinerators used for the *disposal* of
trash>
syn discarding, disposition, dumping,
jettison, junking, relegation, riddance,
scrapping, throwing away
rel chucking, clearance; demolishing,
demolition, destroying, destruction
con acquirement, acquisition; accumulation, collection, cumulation, deposit,
hoard, trove

dispose *vb* 1 *syn see* INCLINE 3
ant indispose
2 *syn see* ORDER 1

disposed *adj syn see* WILLING 1
ant indisposed

disposition *n* 1 *syn see* DISPOSAL 2
rel control, controlling, direction, management
2 *syn see* ORDER 3
3 the complex of especially mental and
emotional qualities that distinguish an
individual <a man of irritable *disposition*>

syn character, complexion, humor, individualism, individuality, makeup, nature,
personality, temper, temperament
rel mood, tone, vein; cast, stamp, tenor,
type; being; identity
idiom frame of mind
4 *syn see* LEANING 2

dispossess *vb syn see* DEPRIVE 2
con provide, supply

dispossession *n syn see* PRIVATION 2

dispraise *vb syn see* DECRY 2
ant praise

disproportion *n syn see* DISPARITY

disproportional *adj syn see* LOPSIDED

disproportionate *adj syn see* LOPSIDED
ant proportionate

disprove *vb* 1 to show by presenting evidence that something is not true <the
defendant's claims were *disproved* by the
testimony>
syn break, confound, confute, controvert,
disconfirm, evert, rebut, refute
rel contravene, impugn, negative,
traverse; overthrow, overturn
con evidence, show; demonstrate, display,
illustrate, manifest; argue, bespeak, tell
ant prove
2 *syn see* DISCREDIT 2

disputable *adj syn see* MOOT

disputation *n syn see* ARGUMENTATION

disputatious *adj syn see* CONTENTIOUS 2

dispute *vb* 1 *syn see* ARGUE 2
con give in, surrender
2 *syn see* DISCUSS 1
rel confute, controvert, disprove, rebut,
refute
con allow, grant
ant concede
3 *syn see* QUESTION 2
4 *syn see* RESIST

dispute *n* 1 *syn see* ARGUMENT 2
rel conflict, discord, dissension, strife
2 *syn see* QUARREL

disqualified *adj syn see* UNFIT 2
ant qualified

disqualify *vb* to deprive of a power, right,
or privilege <a conviction of perjury
disqualified him from being a witness>
syn disable, disenable, incapacitate
rel bar, bate, debar, eliminate, except,
exclude, rule out, suspend
con empower, enable
ant qualify

disquiet *vb syn see* DISCOMPOSE 1
rel distress, trouble
con calm, compose, lull, still
ant quiet, soothe, tranquilize

disquiet *n* 1 *syn see* CARE 2
ant quiet
2 *syn see* UNREST
ant quiet

disquietude *n* 1 *syn see* CARE 2
2 *syn see* UNREST
ant quietness, quietude

disquisition *n syn see* DISCOURSE 2
rel inquiry, investigation; argumentation,
debate, disputation

disquisitive *adj syn see* INQUISITIVE 1

disrate *vb syn see* DEGRADE 1

disregard *vb syn see* NEGLECT
con attend, mind, tend, watch; note, notice, observe, remark
ant regard

---

syn synonym(s)   *rel* related word(s)
ant antonym(s)   *con* contrasted word(s)
idiom idiomatic equivalent(s)
‖ use limited; if in doubt, see a dictionary

disregard *n syn* see APATHY 2
 rel forgetting, ignoring, neglecting, omission, omitting, overlooking, slighting
 con consideration, thoughtfulness
disregardful *adj syn* see NEGLIGENT
 ant regardful
disrelish *n syn* see DISLIKE
 ant :relish
disremember *vb syn* see FORGET 1
disreputable *adj* 1 not reputable or decent
 <was punished for his *disreputable* conduct>
 syn discreditable, disgraceful, dishonorable, ignominious, inglorious, shabby, shady, shameful, shoddy, unrespectable
 rel abject, mean, sordid; beggarly, cheap, contemptible, despicable, pitiable, scurvy, sorry
 con admirable, creditable, estimable, honorable, respectable
 ant reputable
 2 *syn* see SHABBY 1
disrepute *n syn* see DISGRACE
 ant repute
disrespect *n syn* see INSOLENCE
 ant respect
disrespectful *adj syn* see RUDE 6
 ant respectful
disrobe *vb* 1 *syn* see STRIP 1
 2 *syn* see STRIP 2
disrupt *vb* 1 *syn* see OPEN 3
 2 *syn* see DISORDER 1
dissatisfaction *n syn* see DISLIKE
 ant satisfaction
dissatisfactory *adj syn* see BAD 1
 ant satisfactory
dissatisfied *adj syn* see DISCONTENTED
 rel annoyed, bothered, irked, vexed
 con content, contented, gratified
 ant satisfied
dissect *vb* 1 *syn* see SEPARATE 1
 2 *syn* see CUT 5
 rel penetrate, pierce, probe
 3 *syn* see ANALYZE
dissection *n syn* see ANALYSIS 1
 rel examination, inspection, review, scrutiny; criticism, critique
dissemblance *n syn* see DISSIMILARITY
 ant resemblance, semblance
dissemblance *n syn* see DECEIT 1
dissemble *vb syn* see DISGUISE
 con demonstrate, evidence, evince, manifest, show
dissembler *n syn* see HYPOCRITE
disseminate *vb* 1 *syn* see SPREAD 1
 2 *syn* see DECLARE 1
 3 *syn* see STREW 1
dissension *n syn* see DISCORD
 rel altercation, bickering, quarrel, wrangle; argument, controversy, dispute
 con amity, friendship, goodwill
 ant accord; comity
dissent *vb syn* see DIFFER 2
 rel balk, boggle, demur, shy, stickle
 con accede, acquiesce, agree, subscribe
 ant assent; concur
dissent *n* 1 *syn* see DISCORD
 2 *syn* see HERESY
 rel disagreement, nonagreement, nonconcurrence
dissenter *n syn* see HERETIC
dissert *vb syn* see DISCOURSE 1
dissertate *vb syn* see DISCOURSE 1

dissertation *n syn* see DISCOURSE 2
 rel exposition; argumentation, disputation
dissever *vb* 1 *syn* see SEPARATE 1
 2 *syn* see CUT 5
dissidence *n* 1 *syn* see DISCORD
 2 *syn* see HERESY
dissident *adj syn* see HERETICAL
dissident *n syn* see HERETIC
dissimilar *adj syn* see DIFFERENT 1
 rel antithetical, antonymous, contradictory, contrary, opposite
 ant similar
dissimilarity *n* lack of agreement or correspondence or an instance of this <the *dissimilarities* in the cultures of the two countries>
 syn alterity, difference, discrepancy, dissemblance, dissimilitude, distance, distinction, divarication, divergence, divergency, otherness, unlikeness
 rel disparity, diversity; discordance, incongruity, inconsistency, inconsonance; discord, variance; severance; offset; margin
 con affinity, analogy, likeness, resemblance, similitude; accordance, congruity, consistency, consonance; agreement, conformity, correspondence
 ant similarity
dissimilitude *n syn* see DISSIMILARITY
 ant similitude
dissimulate *vb syn* see DISGUISE
dissimulation *n syn* see DECEIT 1
 rel camouflaging, cloaking, disguising, dissembling, masking; concealing, hiding, secreting; feigning, pretending, pretense, shamming; hypocrisy, pharisaism, sanctimony
dissimulator *n syn* see HYPOCRITE
dissipate *vb* 1 *syn* see SCATTER 1
 rel crumble, disintegrate
 ant accumulate; concentrate (*as efforts, thoughts*)
 2 *syn* see WASTE 2
 rel disappear, evanesce, evaporate, vanish
 ant absorb (*as time, attention*)
dissipation *n syn* see ENTERTAINMENT
dissociate *vb syn* see DETACH
 rel alienate, estrange
 ant associate
dissolute *adj syn* see ABANDONED 2
 rel lax, light, loose, slack, wanton, wayward; fast, raffish, rakish, wild
dissolution *n* 1 *syn* see SEPARATION 1
 2 *syn* see DEATH 1
dissolve *vb* 1 *syn* see DESTROY 1
 2 *syn* see ADJOURN 2
 3 *syn* see ANNUL 4
 4 *syn* see LIQUEFY
 5 *syn* see SOLVE 2
 6 *syn* see DISBAND
dissonance *n syn* see DISCORD
dissonant *adj* 1 marked by a mingling of discordant sounds <the two bands playing different pieces at the same time sounded *dissonant*>
 syn cacophonic, cacophonous, discordant, disharmonic, disharmonious, immusical, inharmonic, inharmonious, rude, unharmonious, unmusical
 rel grating, harsh, hoarse, jarring, raucous, rugged, strident
 con blending, chiming, concerted, harmonic, symphonious; euphonious, harmo-

nious, mellifluous, mellow, melodious,
musical; agreeable, pleasing
ant consonant
2 *syn* see INCONSONANT 1

dissuade *vb* to turn one aside from a purpose, a project, or a plan < they tried to
dissuade a friend from making a mistake >
syn deter, disadvise, discourage, divert
rel derail, throw off; advise, counsel;
exhort, prick, urge
idiom talk out of
con get, induce, prevail; affect, influence,
touch
ant persuade

distance *n* 1 an extent of areal or linear
measure < he did not know the *distance*
he had walked >
syn length, stretch
rel area, extent; ambit, compass, extension, orbit, purview, radius, range, reach,
scope, sweep
2 the length of a literal or figurative
course traversed or to be traversed < he
had come a long *distance* from his pitiful
beginnings >
syn way, ways
rel extent, size; piece, spell
3 *syn* see EXPANSE
4 *syn* see DISSIMILARITY

distance *vb* *syn* see OUTSTRIP 1

distant *adj* 1 not close in space, time, or
relationship < traveling to a more *distant*
place > < the *distant* days of the Pilgrim
fathers > < a *distant* cousin >
syn far, faraway, far-flung, far-off, off-
lying, outlying, remote, removed
rel apart, isolated, obscure, out-of-the-
way, retired, secret; secluded, sequestered
idiom at a distance
con close, near, nearby, next, nigh; adjacent, adjoining, contiguous
2 *syn* see DIFFERENT 1
3 *syn* see UNSOCIABLE
rel arrogant, haughty, proud; modest,
retiring, shy
con forward, presuming, ‖pushy, self-
assertive

distaste *n* *syn* see DISLIKE
rel abhorrence, repugnance, repulsion,
revulsion; antipathy, hostility
con relish, zest; appetite, desire; enjoyment
ant taste

distasteful *adj* 1 *syn* see UNPALATABLE 1
ant tasteful, tasty
2 *syn* see BITTER 2
rel obnoxious, repellent, repugnant, repulsive; abominable, detestable, hateful, odious
con agreeable, grateful, gratifying, pleasant, pleasing, welcome

distemper *vb* *syn* see DISORDER 1
distemper *n* *syn* see DISORDER 2
distend *vb* *syn* see EXPAND 3
rel augment, enlarge, increase; extend,
lengthen
ant constrict

disthrone *vb* *syn* see DEPOSE 1

distill *vb* *syn* see DRIP
distinct *adj* 1 capable of being distinguished as differing < the novel has two
related, but nevertheless *distinct*, plots >
syn different, discrete, diverse, separate,
several, various
rel distinctive, individual, peculiar; particular, single, sole; especial, individual, special, specific; disparate, dissimilar, divergent
con identical, same, selfsame; corresponding, equivalent, like, similar
ant indistinguishable
2 *syn* see CLEAR 5
rel defined, prescribed; categorical, definite, explicit, express, specific; lucid, perspicuous; clear-cut, incisive, trenchant
con faint, obscure
ant indistinct; nebulous

distinction *n* 1 *syn* see DISSIMILARITY
con affinity, analogy, likeness, similarity,
similitude
ant indistinction, resemblance
2 *syn* see EMINENCE 1
3 *syn* see HONOR 2

distinctive *adj* *syn* see CHARACTERISTIC
rel separate, single, unique; discrete, distinct, several
con common, familiar, ordinary, popular,
vulgar; alike, analogous, comparable, identical, like, parallel; equal, equivalent, same

distinctively *adv* *syn* see ESPECIALLY 1

distinctiveness *n* *syn* see INDIVIDUALITY
3

distingué *adj* *syn* see GENTEEL 1

distinguish *vb* *syn* see KNOW 4
rel divide, part; detach, disengage; demarcate, set off
con confuse, mistake
ant confound
2 *syn* see EXALT 1
3 *syn* see CHARACTERIZE 2
idiom set apart
4 *syn* see SEE 1
5 *syn* see IDENTIFY

distinguished *adj* *syn* see FAMOUS 2
rel courtly, dignified, grand, imposing,
stately
ant undistinguished

distort *vb* 1 *syn* see MISREPRESENT
rel misconstrue, misinterpret; alter,
change
2 *syn* see DEFORM
rel bend, curve, twist

distortion *n* *syn* see DEFORMITY

distract *vb* 1 *syn* see CONFUSE 2
2 *syn* see MADDEN 1

distracted *adj* *syn* see DISTRAUGHT

distraction *n* 1 *syn* see INSANITY 1
2 *syn* see ENTERTAINMENT

distrait *adj* 1 *syn* see ABSTRACTED
2 *syn* see DISTRAUGHT

distraught *adj* 1 agitated with doubt or
mental conflict < *distraught* over the
health of her child >
syn distracted, distrait, distressed, harassed, tormented, troubled, worried
rel agitated, concerned, discomposed,
flustered, perturbed, upset; addled, confused, muddled; bewildered, nonplussed
idiom beside oneself
con composed, cool, imperturbable, nonchalant, unflappable, unruffled; calm,

---

syn synonym(s)   *rel* related word(s)
ant antonym(s)   *con* contrasted word(s)
idiom idiomatic equivalent(s)
‖ use limited; if in doubt, see a dictionary

tranquil; unconcerned, undisturbed, unworried
ant collected
2 *syn* see INSANE 1
distress *n* the state of being in serious trouble or in mental or physical anguish <in great *distress* over the decision he had to make>
syn agony, dolor, misery, passion, suffering
rel affliction, cross, trial, tribulation, visitation; anguish, grief, heartbreak, sorrow, woe; exigency, pass, pinch, strait; difficulty, hardship, rigor, vicissitude; ache, pain, pang, throe, twinge
con comfort, comforting, consolation, solace, solacing; allaying, alleviation, assuagement, ease, relief, relieving; ease, peace, security
distress *vb* 1 *syn* see TRY 2
rel afflict, rack, torment, torture
con allay, alleviate, assuage, lighten, mitigate, relieve
2 to cause pain or suffering to <the death of his longtime friend *distressed* him deeply>
syn aggrieve, constrain, grieve, hurt, injure, pain
rel harass, strain, stress, try, trouble; depress, oppress, weigh
con comfort, console, solace; aid, assist, help
3 *syn* see TROUBLE 1
rel annoy, harry, pester, plague
distressed *adj syn* see DISTRAUGHT
distressing *adj syn* see DEPLORABLE
distribute *vb* 1 to give out, usually in shares, to each member of a group <*distributed* his possessions among his heirs>
syn deal, disburse, dispense, disperse, divide, ‖divvy, dole (out), lot (out), measure (out), partition
rel allocate, allot, apportion, assign, mete (out); parcel, portion, prorate, ration; administer; dribble; bestow, donate, give, present
con assemble, gather; accumulate, hoard
ant amass; collect
2 *syn* see SPREAD 1
distribution *n syn* see ORDER 3
district *n* 1 *syn* see QUARTER 2
2 *syn* see LOCALITY 1
rel division, parcel
distrust *vb* to have no trust or confidence in <he *distrusted* most politicians>
syn doubt, misdoubt, mistrust, suspect, ‖suspicion
rel disbelieve, discredit, unbelieve
con bank, count, depend, reckon, rely; commit, confide, consign, entrust
ant trust
distrustful *adj syn* see SUSPICIOUS 2
distrustfully *adv syn* see ASKANCE 2
disturb *vb* 1 *syn* see MOVE 4
2 *syn* see DISCOMPOSE 1
rel alarm, frighten, scare, terrify; bewilder, distract, perplex, puzzle; discommode, incommode, inconvenience, trouble
3 *syn* see DISORDER 1
rel displace, replace; move, remove, shift; interfere, intermeddle, meddle, tamper
con establish, fix, set, settle; adjust, regulate

disunify *vb syn* see ESTRANGE
disunion *n* 1 *syn* see SEPARATION 1
2 *syn* see DISCORD
disunite *vb* 1 *syn* see SEPARATE 1
2 *syn* see ESTRANGE
disunity *n syn* see DISCORD
disusage *n syn* see DISUSE
disuse *n* cessation of use, practice, or exercise <to keep the mind from falling into *disuse*, one must exercise one's reading abilities> <his muscles became atrophied from *disuse*>
syn desuetude, disusage
con appliance, application, employment, operation, play, usance; exercise
ant use
disused *adj syn* see OBSOLETE
ditch *n syn* see TRENCH
ditch *vb* 1 *syn* see DISCARD
‖2 *syn* see HIDE
‖**dite** *n syn* see PARTICLE
dither *vb* 1 *syn* see SHAKE 1
2 *syn* see HESITATE
3 *syn* see CHAT 1
dither *n* 1 *syn* see JITTERS
2 *syn* see COMMOTION 2
dithyrambic *adj syn* see IMPASSIONED
ditto *n syn* see REPRODUCTION
ditty *n syn* see SONG 1
diurnal *adj syn* see DAILY
ant nocturnal
diuturnal *adj syn* see LASTING
divagate *vb syn* see DIGRESS 2
divagation *n syn* see DIGRESSION
divarication *n syn* see DISSIMILARITY
dive *vb syn* see PLUNGE 2
rel bound, jump, leap, spring; impel, move
dive *n* a shabby or disreputable place for drinking or entertainment <got a schooner of beer at the *dive* down the street>
syn barrelhouse, hangout, honky-tonk, joint
rel dump, hole; bar, barroom, lounge, pothouse, pub, saloon, taproom, tavern
‖**diver** *n syn* see PICKPOCKET
diverge *vb* 1 *syn* see SWERVE 2
rel differ, disagree, vary; divide, part, separate
ant converge; conform
2 *syn* see DIGRESS 2
divergence *n* 1 *syn* see DISSIMILARITY
rel diversity, variety
con accord, concord, consonance, harmony
ant conformity, correspondence
2 *syn* see DEVIATION 1
rel division, parting, separation; differing, disagreeing, varying
con agreement, coincidence, concurrence
ant convergence
divergency *n syn* see DISSIMILARITY
divergent *adj* 1 *syn* see DIFFERENT 1
rel antithetical, contradictory, contrary, opposite; aberrant, abnormal, atypical
con alike, identical, parallel, same
ant convergent
2 *syn* see IRREGULAR 1
divers *adj syn* see SEVERAL 3
divers *pron, pl in constr syn* see SUNDRY
diverse *adj* 1 *syn* see DIFFERENT 1
rel contrasted, contrasting, contrastive; contradictory, contrary, opposite

con equal, equivalent, same
ant identical, selfsame
2 *syn* see DISTINCT 1
idiom of every description
3 *syn* see MANIFOLD
diversely *adv syn* see OTHERWISE 1
diverseness *n syn* see VARIETY 1
diversiform *adj syn* see MANIFOLD
diversion *n* **1** *syn* see DEVIATION 1
  2 *syn* see PLAY 1
  3 *syn* see ENTERTAINMENT
  rel frivolity, levity
  4 *syn* see ENJOYMENT 1
diversity *n syn* see VARIETY 1
  rel difference, dissimilarity, distinction, divergence, divergency, unlikeness
  ant uniformity; identity
divert *vb* **1** *syn* see TURN 6
  rel swerve; alter, change, modify
  con fix, set, settle
  2 *syn* see DISSUADE
  rel abstract, detach, disengage
  3 *syn* see AMUSE
  rel delight, gladden, please, regale, tickle
divertissement *n syn* see ENTERTAINMENT
divest *vb* **1** *syn* see STRIP 2
  ant invest, vest; apparel, attire, clothe
  2 *syn* see DEPRIVE 2
  rel despoil, plunder, spoil
  ant invest, vest
divestiture *n syn* see PRIVATION 2
divide *vb* **1** *syn* see SEPARATE 1
  rel carve, chop, cut
  ant unite
  2 *syn* see DISTRIBUTE 1
  3 *syn* see APPORTION 2
  rel allocate, allot, assign
  4 *syn* see DIFFER 2
  rel part, separate
  con combine, concur, conjoin, cooperate
  ant unite
dividend *n syn* see REWARD
divine *n syn* see CLERGYMAN
divine *vb syn* see FORESEE
divine *adj* **1** of or relating to God or a god < the *divine* will >
  syn deific, godly
  rel chthonian
  2 like or like that of God or a god < men who aspire to *divine* honors >
  syn deific, godlike
  rel extramundane, superhuman, superphysical, transmundane
  3 *syn* see MARVELOUS 2
division *n* **1** *syn* see PART 1
  2 *syn* see SEPARATION 1
  3 *syn* see DISCORD
divorce *n syn* see SEPARATION 1
divorce *vb* **1** *syn* see SEPARATE 1
  rel disaffect, wean
  2 to end a marriage by legal action < unable to agree, they decided to *divorce* > < *divorced* his wife >
  syn dismiss, put away, unmarry
  rel break up, separate, split; annul, cancel
divorcement *n syn* see SEPARATION 1
divulge *vb syn* see REVEAL 1

---

rel proclaim; gossip, tattle
‖**divvy** *vb* **1** *syn* see DISTRIBUTE 1
  2 *syn* see APPORTION 2
‖**dizzard** *n syn* see DUNCE
dizzy *adj* **1** *syn* see GIDDY 1
  rel asinine, fatuous, foolish; inane
  2 affected by a sensation of being whirled about or around < the speed with which she dispatched her tasks made the onlookers *dizzy* >
  syn giddy, light, light-headed, swimming, swimmy, vertiginous
  rel reeling, whirling; bewildered, confounded, distracted, puzzled; addled, befuddled, confused, dazed, dazzled, fuddled, muddled
  idiom with spots before one's eyes
  3 *syn* see EXCESSIVE 1
dizzy *vb syn* see CONFUSE 2
do *vb* **1** *syn* see PERFORM 2
  2 *syn* see CLOSE 3
  3 *syn* see ACT 1
  4 *syn* see CHEAT
  idiom do out of, sell one a bill of goods
  5 *syn* see COOK 1
  6 *syn* see BEHAVE 1
  7 *syn* see SHIFT 5
  8 *syn* see HAPPEN 1
  9 *syn* see TRAVEL 2
  10 *syn* see SERVE 3
  11 *syn* see SERVE 5
‖**do** *n syn* see SUCCESS
doable *adj syn* see POSSIBLE 1
doc *n syn* see PHYSICIAN
docile *adj syn* see OBEDIENT
  rel adaptable, pliable, pliant
  con obstinate, self-willed, stubborn, willful
  ant indocile; ungovernable, unruly
‖**docious** *adj syn* see OBEDIENT
dock *n syn* see WHARF
docket *n syn* see PROGRAM 1
doctor *n syn* see PHYSICIAN
doctor *vb* **1** *syn* see TREAT 4
  2 *syn* see MEND 2
  3 *syn* see ADULTERATE
doctrinaire *adj syn* see DICTATORIAL
  rel bullheaded, dogged, mulish, obstinate, pertinacious, pigheaded, stiff-necked, stubborn
  ant undoctrinaire
doctrine *n* a principle accepted as valid and authoritative < the *doctrine* of evolution >
  syn canon, dogma, tenet
  rel instruction, teaching; axiom, basic, fundamental, principle
  idiom article of belief (or faith)
document *n* something preserved and serving as evidence (as of an event, a situation, or the culture of a period) < ceramic and flint artifacts provide our only *document* of this ancient people >
  syn archive(s), monument, record
  rel evidence, testimony
doddering *adj syn* see SENILE
doddery *adj syn* see SENILE
dodge *vb* **1** to avoid or evade by some maneuver or shift < *dodging* in and out among the crowd > < *dodged* his pursuer with ease >
  syn duck, fence, parry, shirk, sidestep
  rel malinger; avoid, elude, escape, evade, skirt; slide, slip; short-circuit

---

idiom fight shy of
con ||banter, beard, brave, challenge, dare, defy, front, venture; confront, encounter, meet
ant face
2 *syn* see EQUIVOCATE 2
dodo *n syn* see DUNCE
||**dods** *n pl syn* see SULK
||**dodunk** *n syn* see DUNCE
doff *vb syn* see REMOVE 3
do for *vb syn* see HELP 1
dofunny *n syn* see DOODAD
dog *n* **1** a highly variable carnivorous domesticated mammal <many households have *dogs* as pets>
syn bowwow, canine, hound, ||pooch, tyke
rel pup, puppy; cur, ||feist, mongrel, mutt
2 *syn* see SNOT 1
3 *syn* see FRANKFURTER
4 *syn* see JALOPY
dog *vb syn* see TAIL
Dogberry *n syn* see POLICEMAN
dogfall *n syn* see DRAW 4
dogfight *n syn* see BRAWL 2
dogged *adj* **1** *syn* see INFLEXIBLE 2
2 *syn* see PERSISTENT 1
doggery *n syn* see RABBLE 2
doggish *adj syn* see DAPPER
doggone *adj* **1** *syn* see DAMNED 2
2 *syn* see UTTER
doggy *adj syn* see DAPPER
dogma *n syn* see DOCTRINE
rel belief, conviction, persuasion, view
dogmatic *adj* **1** *syn* see DICTATORIAL
2 *syn* see DEDUCTIVE
dog nap *n syn* see NAP
dog's age *n syn* see AGE 2
do in *vb* **1** *syn* see RUIN 2
2 *syn* see MURDER 1
3 *syn* see EXHAUST 4
doing *n syn* see ACTION 1
doit *n syn* see PARTICLE
doldrums *n pl* **1** *syn* see TEDIUM
rel blues, dejection, depression, dumps, gloom; apathy, disinterest, indifference, listlessness
con high spirits, spirits
2 *syn* see ABEYANCE
rel depression, retardation, slump, stagnation; inactivity
dole (out) *vb* **1** *syn* see ADMINISTER 2
2 *syn* see DISTRIBUTE 1
||**dole** *n* **1** *syn* see SORROW
2 *syn* see MISFORTUNE
doleful *adj* **1** *syn* see DOWNCAST
2 *syn* see WOEFUL 1
3 *syn* see MELANCHOLY 2
rel grieving, mourning, sorrowing; piteous, pitiful
con blithe, blithesome, radiant, sparkling, sunny
ant cheerful, cheery
dolefuls *n pl, used with the syn* see SADNESS
dolent *adj syn* see WOEFUL 1
dolesome *adj syn* see MELANCHOLY 2
dolittle *n syn* see SLUGGARD
dollar *n* a currency bill representing one hundred cents <had a single *dollar* left>
syn bill, ||bone, ||buck, ||fish, ||frogskin, ||ironman, oner, rock, ||skin, ||smacker, smackeroo
dollop *n syn* see DRAM 1

doll out *vb syn* see DRESS UP 1
doll up *vb syn* see DRESS UP 1
dolor *n syn* see DISTRESS
con blessedness, bliss, felicity, happiness
ant beatitude
dolorous *adj* **1** *syn* see DEPLORABLE
2 *syn* see WOEFUL 1
3 *syn* see MELANCHOLY 2
dolt *n syn* see DUNCE
dolthead *n syn* see DUNCE
doltish *adj syn* see STUPID 1
domain *n syn* see FIELD
||**dome** *n syn* see HEAD 1
domestic *adj* **1** of or relating to the household or family <*domestic* chores required to maintain a home>
syn family, home, household
con civic, public; personal, private; business, occupational, professional
2 of, relating to, or carried on within an indicated or implied country <charts of *domestic* as well as foreign waters>
syn home, ||inland, internal, intestine, municipal, national, native
ant foreign
3 *syn* see TAME
domesticate *vb* to adapt (an animal or plant) to life in intimate association with and to the advantage of man <the man who *domesticated* the first dog>
syn domesticize, domiciliate, master, tame
rel gentle, subdue; housebreak; break, bust, train
domesticated *adj syn* see TAME
domesticize *vb syn* see DOMESTICATE
domicile *n syn* see HABITATION 2
domicile *vb syn* see HARBOR 2
domiciliate *vb* **1** *syn* see HARBOR 2
2 *syn* see DOMESTICATE
dominance *n syn* see SUPREMACY
dominant *adj* **1** superior to all others in power, influence, or importance <the Sumerians were a *dominant* race of ancient times>
syn ascendant, master, outweighing, overbalancing, overbearing, overweighing, paramount, predominant, predominate, preponderant, prevalent, regnant, sovereign
rel prevailing; preeminent, supreme, surpassing, transcendent; chief, first, foremost, leading, main, principal; governing, ruling
con collateral, dependent, secondary, subject, tributary; unimportant
ant subordinate
2 *syn* see CHIEF 2
dominate *vb* **1** *syn* see GOVERN 3
2 *syn* see RULE 2
3 *syn* see OVERLOOK 2
domination *n* **1** *syn* see SUPREMACY
2 *syn* see POWER 1
dominator *n syn* see LEADER 2
domineer *vb syn* see RULE 2
domineering *adj syn* see MASTERFUL 1
rel arrogant, insolent, lordly
con obsequious, servile, slavish; bootlicking, groveling, sycophantic, toadying
ant subservient; fawning
||**dominie** *n syn* see CLERGYMAN
dominion *n* **1** *syn* see SUPREMACY
2 *syn* see FIELD
3 *syn* see OWNERSHIP

domino *n syn* see MASK 1
domitae naturae *adj syn* see TAME
don *vb* 1 to place on one's person (an article of clothing) < *donned* a raincoat for his trip >
  syn assume, draw on, get on, huddle (on), put on, slip (on), throw
  rel apparel, array, attire, clad, clothe, dress, enclothe, garb, garment, raiment
  con cast, pull (off), remove, take off, throw off; unclothe, undress; disrobe
  ant doff
  2 to clothe or envelop oneself in < able to *don* a new personality at will >
  syn assume, pull, put on, strike, take on
  rel camouflage, color, disguise; belie, falsify, garble, misrepresent
donate *vb syn* see GIVE 1
donation *n* a gift of money or its equivalent to a charity, humanitarian cause, or public institution < sought *donations* for victims of the flood >
  syn alms, benefaction, beneficence, charity, contribution, offering
  rel aid, assistance, help, relief; philanthropy; bequest, endowment; appropriation, grant, subsidy, subvention; allowance, dole, pittance, ration
donator *n syn* see DONOR
done *adj* 1 *syn* see DECOROUS 1
  2 *syn* see COMPLETE 4
  3 *syn* see EFFETE 2
  4 *syn* see THROUGH 4
done for *adj syn* see THROUGH 3
done in *adj syn* see EFFETE 2
||**doney** *n syn* see GIRL FRIEND 1
||**donicker** *n syn* see TOILET
Don Juan *n* 1 *syn* see GALLANT 2
  2 *syn* see WOLF
donk *n syn* see DONKEY 1
donkey *n* 1 the domestic ass < the *donkey*, a typical pack animal >
  syn ass, burro, donk, jackass, ||moke, ||neddy, ||Rocky Mountain canary
  rel ||dickey, jack; hinny, mule; jennet, jenny, jenny ass
  2 *syn* see FOOL 1
donkeyish *adj syn* see FOOLISH 2
donkey's years *n pl syn* see AGE 2
donkeywork *n syn* see WORK 2
donnybrook *n syn* see BRAWL 2
donor *n* one that gives something to another < a *donor* of funds to research foundations >
  syn bestower, conferrer, donator, giver, presenter
  rel contributor, subscriber
do–nothing *n syn* see SLUGGARD
||**donsie** *adj syn* see UNWELL
doodad *n* something trivial which is hard to classify or whose name is unknown < wondered what the little round *doodad* was for >
  syn business, dingus, dofunny, doohickey, gadget, gizmo, ||hootenanny, jigger, rigamajig, thingum, thingumajig, thingumbob, thingummy; *compare* GADGET 1, WHAT-DO-YOU-CALL-IT

doodle *n syn* see FOOL 1
||**doodle** *vb syn* see CHEAT
doodle *vb syn* see FIDDLE 2
doohickey *n syn* see DOODAD
doom *n syn* see FATE
  rel calamity, cataclysm, catastrophe, disaster, tragedy
doom *vb syn* see SENTENCE
doom (to) *vb syn* see PREDESTINE 1
doomed *adj syn* see DAMNED 1
doomful *adj syn* see OMINOUS
door *n* 1 an opening by which one can enter or leave a structure and especially a building < looked through the front *door* >
  syn doorway, entrance, entranceway, entry, entryway, portal
  2 a means or right of entering, approaching, or participating < viewed education as the *door* to success >
  syn access, adit, admission, admittance, entrance, entrée, entry, ingress, way
doormat *n syn* see WEAKLING
doorway *n syn* see DOOR 1
||**doozer** *n syn* ||DILLY, ||corker, ||daisy, dandy, ||dinger, humdinger, jim-dandy, ||lalapalooza, ||lulu, peach
dope *n* 1 *syn* see DRUG 2
  2 *syn* see DUNCE
dope (up) *vb syn* see ADULTERATE
doped *adj syn* see DRUGGED
||**dope out** *vb* 1 *syn* see SOLVE 2
  2 *syn* see INFER
  3 *syn* see PLAN 2
dopey *adj syn* see LETHARGIC
do–re–mi *n syn* see MONEY
dorm *vb syn* see DOZE
dormancy *n syn* see ABEYANCE
dormant *adj syn* see LATENT
  ant active
||**dort** *vb syn* see SULK
||**dorts** *n pl syn* see SULK
||**dorty** *adj syn* see SULLEN
||**doss** *n syn* see SLEEP 1
||**doss** *vb syn* see SLEEP
dot *n syn* see POINT 11
dot *vb syn* see SPECKLE 1
  2 *syn* see SPOT 2
dot *n syn* see DOWRY
dotage *n* advanced age accompanied by a decline of mental poise and alertness < a doddering eighty-year-old entering his *dotage*>
  syn second childhood, senility; *compare* OLD AGE
  rel decrepitude, feebleness, infirmity; age, elderliness, senectitude
  con adolescence, youth; maturity
||**doted** *adj syn* see SENILE
doting *adj* 1 *syn* see SENILE
  2 *syn* see LOVING
  rel asinine, fatuous, foolish, silly, simple
dottiness *n syn* see FOOLISHNESS
dotty *adj* 1 *syn* see INFATUATED
  2 *syn* see FOOLISH 2
double *adj* 1 *syn* see TWOFOLD 1
  2 *syn* see TWIN
  3 *syn* see TWOFOLD 2
  4 *syn* see INSINCERE

---

syn synonym(s)   *rel* related word(s)
ant antonym(s)   *con* contrasted word(s)
idiom idiomatic equivalent(s)
|| use limited; if in doubt, see a dictionary

double n 1 syn see MATE 5
  2 syn see IMAGE 1
  3 syn see TURN 2
  rel departure, digression, divergence, swerving, veering
double vb 1 to make twice as great or as many < *doubled* the amount of his salary >
  syn dualize, dupe, duplicate
  rel replicate; amplify, augment, enlarge, increase, magnify; supplement
  con decrease, lessen, minimize
  ant halve
  2 to make of two thicknesses by turning or bending usually in the middle < he *doubled* the towel for better absorbency >
  syn fold
  rel pleat, plicate, turn over
  3 syn see ESCAPE 2
  4 syn see DUB
double–barreled adj 1 syn see TWOFOLD 2
  2 syn see TWOFOLD 1
double–cross vb 1 syn see DECEIVE
  2 syn see BETRAY 2
double–dealer n syn see SWINDLER
double–dealing n syn see DECEPTION 1
double–dealing adj syn see INSINCERE
double–distilled adj syn see UTTER
‖**double–dog dare** vb syn see FACE 3
double–dome n syn see INTELLECTUAL 2
double–dyed adj syn see UTTER
double–edged adj syn see OBSCURE 3
double entendre n syn see AMBIGUITY
double–faced adj 1 syn see OBSCURE 3
  2 syn see INSINCERE
doublehearted adj syn see INSINCERE
double meaning n syn see AMBIGUITY
double–minded adj 1 syn see VACILLATING 2
  idiom of two minds
  2 syn see INSINCERE
doublet n syn see COUPLE
double–talk n 1 syn see NONSENSE 2
  2 syn see GOBBLEDYGOOK
double–tongued adj syn see INSINCERE
doubt vb 1 syn see QUESTION 2
  2 syn see DISTRUST
  con accredit, credit, trust; accept, believe, ‖buy, swallow
doubt n syn see UNCERTAINTY
  rel dubiousness, questionableness; disbelief, incredulity, unbelief
  con dependence, faith, reliance, trust
  ant certitude; confidence
doubtable adj syn see DOUBTFUL 1
  ant undoubtable
doubter n syn see SKEPTIC
doubtful adj 1 not having or affording assurance of the certainty or soundness of something or someone < their chance of success is *doubtful* >
  syn ambiguous, borderline, clouded, doubtable, dubious, dubitable, equivocal, fishy, impugnable, indecisive, open, precarious, problematic, queasy, shady, shaky, suspect, suspicious, uncertain, unclear, undecided, uneasy, unsettled, unstable, unsure; *compare* MOOT
  rel question-begging; touch-and-go; chancy, insecure, questionable, speculative; hazy, obscure; unlikely; contingent, iffy
  idiom at issue, in dispute, in doubt, in question

  con decisive, open-and-shut, positive, sure; inarguable, incontestable, unarguable, undeniable, undoubted, unquestionable
  ant indubitable
  2 syn see MOOT 1
  3 syn see IMPROBABLE 1
doubtfully adv syn see ASKANCE 2
doubtfulness n syn see UNCERTAINTY
doubting Thomas n syn see SKEPTIC
doubtless adv 1 syn see EASILY 2
  2 syn see PRESUMABLY
doubtlessly adv 1 syn see WELL 7
  ant doubtfully
  2 syn see EASILY 2
dough n syn see MONEY
doughface n syn see MASK 1
‖**doughhead** n syn see DUNCE
doughty adj syn see BRAVE 1
doughy adj syn see PALE 1
do up vb syn see MEND 2
dour adj 1 syn see GRIM 2
  rel rigid, rigorous, strict; implacable
  2 syn see SULLEN
‖**douse** n syn see BLOW 1
douse vb syn see REMOVE 3
douse vb 1 syn see DIP 1
  2 syn see WET
  con bake, dehydrate, desiccate, dry, parch
  3 syn see SPLASH
  4 syn see EXTINGUISH 1
‖**dout** vb syn see EXTINGUISH 1
dove n syn see PACIFIST
  ant hawk
dovecote n a small compartmented raised house or box for domestic pigeons < old countryseats with elaborate stone *dovecotes* >
  syn columbary, culverhouse, dovehouse, pigeon house, pigeonry
  rel aviary, birdhouse; perch, roost
dovehouse n syn see DOVECOTE
‖**dover** n syn see NAP
dovetail vb syn see AGREE 4
dowager n syn see MATRIARCH
dowd n syn see SLATTERN 1
dowdy n syn see SLATTERN 1
dowdy adj 1 syn see SLATTERNLY
  con chic, fashionable, modish, stylish; flashy, garish, gaudy
  ant smart
  2 syn see TACKY 2
  ant smart
  3 syn see OLD-FASHIONED
dower n syn see DOWRY
dower vb syn see ENDOW 1
  rel accouter, appoint, equip, furnish, outfit
‖**dowly** adj syn see OVERCAST
down adv 1 from a higher to a lower level < the land sloped *down* toward the sea >
  syn downward, downwardly, downwards, netherwards
  rel below, earthward, groundward; downgrade, downhill, downslope
  con aloft, upward, upwardly, upwards
  ant up
  2 to completion < wash *down* the car >
  syn completely, fully, through-and-through
  idiom from top to bottom
  3 syn see SERIOUSLY 1
down adj 1 syn see SLOW 3

2 *syn* see DOWNCAST
ant up
3 *syn* see SICK 1
4 *syn* see LOWER
ant up
5 *syn* see COMPLETE 4
down *n syn* see COMEDOWN
down *vb* 1 *syn* see SWALLOW 1
2 *syn* see DEFEAT 2
3 *syn* see FELL 1
4 *syn* see KILL 1
5 *syn* see OVERCOME 1
down *n* a soft fluffy material or covering
< the *down* on a peach >
syn floss, flue, fluff, fur, fuzz, lint, pile
down-and-out *n syn* see PAUPER
down-at-heel *adj syn* see SHABBY 1
downcast *n syn* see DEFEAT 1
downcast *adj* low in spirits < felt *downcast*
by the rejection >
syn bad, blue, cast down, chapfallen,
crestfallen, dejected, depressed, disconsolate, dispirited, doleful, down, downhearted, down-in-the-mouth, downthrown,
droopy, dull, heartsick, heartsore, hipped,
low, low-spirited, mopey, soul-sick, spiritless, sunk, woebegone; *compare* SAD 1
rel discouraged, disheartened; oppressed,
weighed down; distressed, troubled; despondent, forlorn; listless; broody, moody;
gloomy, glum, morose
idiom in the depths
con cheerful, happy, joyous, lighthearted;
excited, exhilarated, intoxicated; buoyed
up, gladdened; encouraged, heartened;
animated, gay, lively, sprightly, vivacious;
delighted, pleased
ant elated
downcry *vb syn* see DECRY 2
downfall *n* 1 *syn* see DETERIORATION 1
rel comedown, descent, discomfiture,
down
2 something that causes a downfall
< drink was his *downfall* >
syn bane, destroyer, destruction, ruin,
ruination, undoing
rel headache, problem, trouble
idiom road to ruin
con aid, help, support
downgrade *n syn* see DETERIORATION 1
ant upgrade
downgrade *vb* 1 *syn* see DEPRECIATE 1
ant upgrade
2 *syn* see DEGRADE 1
ant upgrade
downgrading *n syn* see DEMOTION
ant upgrading
downhearted *adj syn* see DOWNCAST
down-in-the-mouth *adj syn* see DOWN-
CAST
downright *adj* 1 *syn* see UTTER
2 being what is stated beyond any possibility of doubt < a *downright* lie >
syn flat, indubitable, unquestionable, up-
and-down; *compare* POSITIVE 3
rel out-and-out, sure-enough; absolute,
positive; certain, clear
downside-up *adj syn* see UPSIDE-DOWN 2

downslide *n syn* see DECLINE 3
downswing *n syn* see DECLINE 3
downthrow *n syn* see DEFEAT 1
downthrown *adj syn* see DOWNCAST
down-to-date *adj syn* see UP-TO-DATE
down-to-earth *adj syn* see REALISTIC
downtrend *n syn* see DECLINE 3
downtrodden *adj* oppressed by superior
power < the *downtrodden* peasants >
syn abject, underfoot
rel oppressed, persecuted; abused, mal-
treated, mistreated
downturn *n syn* see DECLINE 3
downward *adv syn* see DOWN 1
ant upward
downwardly *adv syn* see DOWN 1
ant upwardly
downwards *adv syn* see DOWN 1
ant upwards
‖**downy** *adj syn* see SLY 2
dowry *n* the money, goods, or estate that a
woman brings to her husband in marriage
< from a poor family, she came to her
marriage with no *dowry* >
syn dot, dower, marriage portion
con bride-price, bridewealth; settlement
doxy *n* 1 a usually young woman who
engages in promiscuous sexual intercourse
< a *doxy* who frequented singles bars >
syn ‖chippy, floozy, grisette, light-o'-love,
nymph, nymphet, party girl, roundheel,
tart, ‖tootsie; *compare* HARLOT 1, PROSTI-
TUTE, WANTON
idiom woman of easy virtue
‖2 *syn* see MISTRESS
doyen *n* 1 *syn* see LEADER 1
2 *syn* see EXPERT
doze *vb* to sleep lightly < he was inclined
to *doze* at his desk >
syn ‖dorm, drowse, ‖sloom, slumber,
‖snoozle, ‖sog; *compare* NAP, SLEEP
doze (off) *vb* to fall into a light sleep
< *dozed* off while sitting before the fire >
syn drop off, drowse (off)
idiom drift off
doze *n* a light sleep < was caught in a *doze*
at his desk >
syn drowse, ‖sloom, slumber; *compare*
NAP, SLEEP 1
dozy *adj syn* see SLEEPY 1
DP *n syn* see REFUGEE
drab *n* 1 *syn* see HAG 2
2 *syn* see SLATTERN 1
3 *syn* see PROSTITUTE
drab *adj* 1 *syn* see DULL 8
2 *syn* see COLORLESS 2
rel bleak, desolate, dismal, dispiriting,
dreary; dingy, faded
con bright, brilliant, luminous
draconian *adj syn* see RIGID 3
draffy *adj syn* see WORTHLESS 1
draft *n* DRINK 3, drag, drain, drench, ‖peg,
swig, swill
draft *vb* 1 to enroll in the armed forces by
compulsion < *drafted* when he was barely
eighteen >
syn conscribe, conscript; *compare* CALL
UP
rel induct; enlist, enroll, muster (in *or*
out); impress, press
2 *syn* see SKETCH
3 to formulate and produce < *drafting*
plans to meet an emergency >

---

syn synonym(s)   *rel* related word(s)
ant antonym(s)   *con* contrasted word(s)
idiom idiomatic equivalent(s)
‖ use limited; if in doubt, see a dictionary

syn draw up, formulate, frame, make, prepare

rel concoct, contrive, devise, invent; fabricate, fashion, forge, form, manufacture, shape; plan, project; outline, sketch

4 *syn* see DRAIN 1

drag *n* **1** *syn* see DRAW 1

2 *syn* see DRINK 3

‖**3** *syn* see PULL 2

‖**4** *syn* see WAY 1

drag *vb* **1** *syn* see PULL 2

con propel, push, shove, thrust; drive, impel, move

2 *syn* see DELAY 1

idiom drag one's feet (*or* heels)

con hasten, hurry

3 to hang down and be drawn behind < her dress *dragged* in the dust >

syn draggle, trail, traipse

rel droop, hang, sag

‖**drag down** *vb* *syn* see EARN 1

dragging *adj* *syn* see LONG 2

draggle *vb* *syn* see DRAG 3

draggle-tail *n* *syn* see SLATTERN 1

draggletailed *adj* *syn* see SLATTERNLY

dragoon *vb* *syn* see INTIMIDATE

drain *vb* **1** to draw off (liquid) by degrees < *drain* the water from the swimming pool >

syn draft, draw, draw off, pump, siphon, tap

rel milk; bleed; suck; empty, exhaust

2 *syn* see TIRE 1

3 *syn* see DEPLETE

idiom bleed white

drain (away) *vb* *syn* see DECREASE

drain *n* *syn* see DRINK 3

drained *adj* *syn* see EFFETE 2

dram *n* **1** a small quantity of something (as alcoholic liquor) to drink < a *dram* of brandy helped to break his chill >

syn ‖caulker, dollop, drop, jolt, nip, shot, slug, snifter, snort, snorter, spot, toothful, tot, ‖wet

rel draft, drink, ‖peg, potation, pull, swig, swill; finger; jigger; dash; ‖splash; snack; quick one

2 *syn* see PARTICLE

drama *n* dramatic art, literature, or affairs < was interested in *drama* during his college years >

syn boards, footlights, (the) stage, theater

rel show business

dramatic *adj* **1** of or relating to drama < made no objections to his son's *dramatic* ambitions >

syn dramaturgic, histrionic, theatral, theatric, theatrical, thespian

2 *syn* see THEATRICAL 2

ant undramatic

dramatist *n* *syn* see PLAYWRIGHT

dramatizer *n* *syn* see PLAYWRIGHT

dramaturge *n* *syn* see PLAYWRIGHT

dramaturgic *adj* *syn* see DRAMATIC 1

drape *vb* **1** *syn* see SWATHE

2 *syn* see SPRAWL 1

dratted *adj* *syn* see DAMNED 2

draw *vb* **1** *syn* see PULL 2

rel bring, fetch; educe, elicit, evoke, extract

con propel, push, shove, thrust; drive, impel, move

2 *syn* see DRAIN 1

3 *syn* see ATTRACT 1

4 *syn* see INDUCE 1

5 *syn* see TAKE 14

6 *syn* see INFER

7 *syn* see EXTEND 3

8 *syn* see DEPLETE

9 *syn* see EVISCERATE

draw *n* **1** a sucking pull on something (as a sipping straw or cigarette) < took a long *draw* on his pipe before answering >

syn drag, puff, pull

rel smoke; inhale

2 *syn* see ADVANTAGE 3

3 *syn* see ATTRACTION 1

4 an indecisive ending to a contest or competition < the prizefight ended in a *draw* >

syn deadlock, dogfall, stalemate, standoff, tie

rel dead heat, photo finish; standstill

con loss; win

draw back *vb* *syn* see DEDUCT 1

drawback *n* *syn* see DISADVANTAGE

rel evil, ill; inconvenience, trouble

con advantage, edge

draw down *vb* **1** *syn* see EARN 1

2 *syn* see DEPLETE

draw in *vb* *syn* see INDUCE 1

drawing *adj* *syn* see ATTRACTIVE 1

drawing power *n* *syn* see ATTRACTION 1

drawing room *n* *syn* see SALON 1

drawn *adj* *syn* see HAGGARD

con hale, robust

drawn-out *adj* *syn* see LONG 2

draw off *vb* *syn* see DRAIN 1

rel abstract; withdraw; move, remove, shift, transfer

draw on *vb* **1** *syn* see EFFECT 1

2 *syn* see INDUCE 1

3 *syn* see DON 1

draw out *vb* *syn* see EXTEND 3

draw up *vb* **1** *syn* see DRAFT 3

2 *syn* see STOP 4

dray horse *n* *syn* see SLAVE 2

dread *n* *syn* see FEAR 1

dreadful *adj* *syn* see FEARFUL 3

‖**dreadful** *adv* *syn* see VERY 1

dreadful *n* *syn* see DIME NOVEL

dreadfully *adv* *syn* see VERY 1

dream *n* **1** *syn* see FANCY 4

2 *syn* see PIPE DREAM

dream *vb* *syn* see LONG

dreamer *n* one whose conduct is guided more by ideals than practicalities < a *dreamer* proposing glorious plans impossible to make work >

syn castle-builder, idealist, ideologue, utopian, visionary

rel daydreamer, illusionist, lotus-eater, wishful thinker; Don Quixote; theorist

con pragmatist, realist; Babbitt, Philistine; pedant

dream up *vb* *syn* see CONTRIVE 2

dreamy *adj* **1** given to dreaming, reverie, or fancy < a *dreamy* and most impractical person >

syn astral, daydreaming, daydreamy, otherworldly, unworldly, visionary

rel fanciful, idealistic, romantic, whimsical

con down-to-earth, practical, pragmatic, realistic; actual, factual

2 *syn* see MARVELOUS 2

drear *adj* *syn* see GLOOMY 3

dreary *adj* **1** *syn* see GLOOMY 3
  2 *syn* see DULL 9
dreck *n syn* see REFUSE
dreg *n, usu* **dregs** *pl* **1** *syn* see SEDIMENT
  2 *syn* see RABBLE 2
‖**dreich** *adj syn* see LONG 2
drench *n syn* see DRINK 3
drench *vb* **1** *syn* see WET
  rel dip, duck, dunk, immerse, submerge
  2 *syn* see SOAK 1
  3 *syn* see POUR 3
drenched *adj syn* see WET 1
dress *vb* **1** *syn* see CLOTHE
  ant undress
  2 *syn* see BANDAGE
  3 to remove the entrails from < *dress* fish,
  fowl, or game >
  syn clean, gut
  rel butcher, slaughter
  4 *syn* see TILL
  rel fertilize, topdress
dress (up) *vb syn* see ADORN
dress *n* **1** *syn* see CLOTHES
  2 *syn* see COSTUME
dress down *vb syn* see SCOLD 1
dress up *vb* **1** to attire in best or formal
  clothes < *dressed up* to go to the theater >
  syn deck (out), ‖dike (out *or* up), doll
  out, doll up, ‖dude up, fix up, gussy up,
  prank, ‖prick (up), primp, prink (up),
  slick, smarten (up), smug, spiff, spruce
  (up), tog (out *or* up), ‖toggle, trick (off,
  out, *or* up)
  rel prettify, pretty (up); apparel, array,
  attire, clad, clothe, dress, enclothe, garb,
  garment, raiment; overdress; preen; prim
  (up)
  idiom dress fit to kill, dress to the nines,
  put on the dog
  2 *syn* see DISGUISE
drib *vb syn* see DRIP
drib *n syn* see DROP 1
dribble *vb* **1** *syn* see DRIP
  2 *syn* see DROOL 2
dribble (away) *vb syn* see WASTE 2
dribble *n syn* see PITTANCE
driblet *n* **1** *syn* see PITTANCE
  2 *syn* see DROP 1
drift *n* **1** *syn* see FLOW
  2 *syn* see PILE 1
  rel array, batch, bunch, bundle, clump,
  cluster, clutch, group, lot, parcel, set
  ‖**3** *syn* see DROVE 2
  4 *syn* see TENDENCY 1
  rel motion, movement, progress, progression; aim, intent, intention, purpose
  5 *syn* see LEANING 2
  6 *syn* see TENOR 1
  rel direction, line, set
drift *vb* **1** to become carried or floated
  along < cakes of ice *drifting* along the
  stream >
  syn float, ride, wash
  rel dart, fly, sail, scud, shoot, skim;
  dance, flicker, flit, flitter, flutter, hover
  2 *syn* see SAUNTER
  3 *syn* see WANDER 1
  4 *syn* see SLIDE 6

5 *syn* see HEAP 1
drifter *n* **1** *syn* see ROVER
  2 *syn* see VAGABOND
driftwood *n* vagrant impoverished people
  < the *driftwood* of skid row >
  syn flotsam, jetsam, wreckage
drill *vb* **1** *syn* see PERFORATE
  2 *syn* see EXERCISE 3
  rel accustom, habituate
drill *n syn* see EXERCISE 3
drilling *n syn* see EXERCISE 3
drink *vb* **1** to take in (potable liquid) < the
  boys *drank* all the soda >
  syn imbibe, quaff, sip, sup (off *or* up),
  swallow, toss
  rel drain, gulp, guzzle, slosh, slurp, swig,
  swill; wash down
  idiom wet one's whistle
  2 to salute and wish honor and health to
  (a person) by raising and then drinking
  from a vessel < *drink* to the bride and
  groom >
  syn pledge, toast
  rel honor, salute; wet
  3 to partake of alcoholic liquors especially
  habitually or to excess < he *drinks* but
  does not smoke >
  syn booze, guzzle, imbibe, liquor (up),
  ‖lush (up), nip, soak, swig, swill, swizzle,
  tank up, tipple, tope
  idiom bend the elbow, cheer the inner
  man, drink like a fish, go on a binge, hit
  the bottle, take a nip
drink *n* **1** liquid suitable for swallowing
  < able to make palatable *drink* from
  seawater >
  syn beverage, drinkable, liquor, potable
  rel liquid; brew; potion
  2 *syn* see LIQUOR 2
  3 a portion of potable liquid < took a
  drink from the cup >
  syn draft, drag, drain, drench, ‖peg, swig,
  swill
  rel draw, pull; finger, jigger; libation
  4 *syn* see OCEAN
drinkable *adj syn* see POTABLE
drinkable *n syn* see DRINK 1
drinkery *n syn* see BAR 5
drip *vb* to let fall drops of moisture or
  liquid < trees *dripping* after the rain >
  syn distill, drib, dribble, drop, trickle,
  trill, weep
  rel spatter, sprinkle, spurtle; gush, pour,
  sluice, stream
‖**drip** *n* **1** *syn* see NONSENSE 2
  2 *syn* see DUNCE
dripping *adj syn* see WET 1
drippy *adj syn* see SENTIMENTAL
drive *vb* **1** *syn* see MOVE 5
  rel coerce, compel, force; incite, instigate
  con check, curb, inhibit, restrain; guide,
  lead, pilot, steer
  2 *syn* see PUSH 1
  3 to urge along (as cattle) < cowboys
  driving the great herds north >
  syn ‖drove, herd, run
  rel shepherd; wrangle; egg, exhort, goad,
  prick, prod, punch, sic, spur, urge
  4 *syn* see THRUST 2
  5 to operate and steer (a motor vehicle)
  < *drive* a car >
  syn auto, charioteer, motor, pilot, tool,
  wheel

---

syn synonym(s)   *rel* related word(s)
ant antonym(s)   *con* contrasted word(s)
idiom idiomatic equivalent(s)
‖ use limited; if in doubt, see a dictionary

rel operate, run, work; guide, steer; roll; chauffeur

6 *syn* see IMPRESS 3

7 *syn* see PLUNGE 2

8 *syn* see LABOR 1

drive *n* **1** a short trip in a vehicle < took a *drive* around town >
    syn ride, spin, turn; *compare* TRIP 1
    rel whirl; joyride; excursion, outing

2 *syn* see DRIVEWAY

3 *syn* see ENTERPRISE 4

4 *syn* see VIGOR 2
    rel impetus, momentum, speed, velocity

drivel *vb* **1** *syn* see DROOL 2

2 *syn* see BABBLE 2

3 *syn* see WASTE 2

drivel *n* **1** *syn* see NONSENSE 2

2 *syn* see GIBBERISH 1

driveling *adj syn* see INSIPID 3

driver *n syn* see MOTORIST

driveway *n* a private road giving access from a public way < the *driveway* to a house >
    syn ‖avenue, drive
    rel court, place, row, street

driving *adj syn* see ENERGETIC 2

drizzle *vb syn* see SPRINKLE 5

drogher *n syn* see BEARER 2

drôlerie *n syn* see JOKE 1

droll *adj syn* see LAUGHABLE

droll *n syn* see HUMORIST 2

drollery *n* **1** *syn* see JOKE 1

2 *syn* see HUMOR 4

drollness *n syn* see HUMOR 4

drone *vb* **1** *syn* see HUM

2 *syn* see IDLE

drony *adj syn* see LAZY

drool *vb* **1** to secrete or become filled with saliva usually in anticipation of food < mouths *drooled* as we waited for dinner >
    syn water
    idiom water at the mouth

2 to let saliva or some other substance flow from the mouth < babies often *drool* uncontrollably >
    syn dribble, drivel, salivate, slabber, slaver, slobber

3 *syn* see ENTHUSE 2

4 *syn* see BABBLE 2

drool *n syn* see NONSENSE 2

droop *vb* **1** *syn* see SLOUCH

2 *syn* see LOWER 3

3 to become literally or figuratively limp through loss of vigor or freshness < he walked along, his shoulders *drooping* from exhaustion >
    syn flag, sag, swag, wilt
    rel drop, fall, sink, slump, subside; dangle, hang, loll, lop, sling, suspend; decline, deteriorate, ‖dwine, fade, fail, languish, weaken

droopy *adj syn* see DOWNCAST

drop *n* **1** the quantity of fluid that falls in one spherical mass < a *drop* of rain >
    syn drib, driblet, droplet, globule, gobbet
    rel dribble, drip, trickle

2 *syn* see PARTICLE

3 *syn* see DRAM

4 *syn* see DESCENT 4

5 *syn* see DESCENT 1

6 *syn* see DECLINE 3

7 *syn* see DEPTH 1

drop *vb* **1** *syn* see FALL 2

2 *syn* see FALL 1
    ant mount

3 *syn* see PLUMMET
    rel slide, slip
    con rally, rebound; ascend, climb; soar
    ant mount

4 *syn* see COLLAPSE 2
    rel backslide, lapse, relapse

5 *syn* see DIE 1

6 *syn* see DRIP

7 *syn* see FELL 1

8 *syn* see QUIT 6

9 *syn* see CANCEL 2

10 *syn* see DISMISS 3

11 *syn* see LOSE 2

12 *syn* see LOSE 1

drop (in *or* by) *vb syn* see VISIT 2

drop (off) *vb syn* see DOZE (off)

droplet *n syn* see DROP 1

drop off *vb syn* see DOZE (off)

dropsical *adj syn* see INFLATED

dropsied *adj syn* see INFLATED

drossy *adj syn* see WORTHLESS 1

droughty *adj syn* see DRY 1

‖drouk *vb syn* see SOAK 1

drove *n* **1** *syn* see CROWD 1

2 a group of domestic animals reared or handled as a unit < a *drove* of cattle >
    syn ‖drift, flock, herd
    rel drive; pack; school

‖drove *vb syn* see DRIVE 3

drown *vb* **1** *syn* see OVERWHELM 4

2 *syn* see DELUGE 1

3 *syn* see WET

drowse *vb syn* see DOZE

drowse (off) *vb syn* see DOZE (off)

drowse *n syn* see DOZE

drowsy *adj syn* see SLEEPY 1
    rel lackadaisical, languid, languorous
    con alert, vigilant, watchful; active, dynamic, live; animated, lively, vivacious

drub *vb* **1** *syn* see BEAT 1

2 *syn* see LAMBASTE 3

3 *syn* see WHIP 2

drubbing *n syn* see DEFEAT 1

drudge *vb* to perform hard, menial, or monotonous work < *drudged* all day washing floors >
    syn grind, grub, ‖muck, plod, slave, slog, toil
    rel hammer, peg (away *or* at *or* on), plow, plug, pound (away); perform, work
    idiom keep one's nose to the grindstone
    con idle, laze, loaf, lounge; dally, dawdle, potter, putter; cheat, chisel

drudge *n* **1** *syn* see SLAVE 2

2 *syn* see WORK 2

3 *syn* see HACK 2

drudgery *n syn* see WORK 2

drudging *adj syn* see IRKSOME

drug *n* **1** a substance used by itself or in a mixture in the treatment or diagnosis of disease < a life-sustaining *drug* >
    syn biologic, medicinal, pharmaceutic, pharmaceutical
    rel cure, medicament, medication, medicine, physic, remedy, specific; simple

2 a narcotic substance or preparation < depended on *drugs* to make life bearable >
    syn dope, ‖hop, narcotic, opiate

drugged *adj* being under the influence of a drug taken for nonmedical purposes < was *drugged* on LSD >
  syn doped, high, hopped-up, spaced-out, stoned, tripped out, turned on, ‖wiped out, zonked
  idiom on a trip
  ant straight

druggist *n* one who deals in medicinal drugs
  syn apothecary, ‖chemist, pharmacist
  rel pharmacologist

drum *vb syn see* SOLICIT 1

drumfire *n syn see* BARRAGE

drumhead *adj syn see* SUMMARY 2

drum up *vb syn see* SOLICIT 1

drunk *adj syn see* INTOXICATED 1
  rel drinking, drinky
  idiom roaring drunk
  con bone-dry, dry
  ant sober

drunk *n* 1 *syn see* BINGE 1
  2 *syn see* DRUNKARD

drunkard *n* one who drinks alcoholic liquors to excess < *drunkards* lurching homeward when the bar finally closes >
  syn bibber, ‖bloat, ‖blotter, boozehound, boozer, drunk, fuddler, guzzler, inebriate, lush, ‖lusher, rumdum, rummy, ‖rumpot, ‖shicker, soak, soaker, sot, sponge, stiff, swillbowl, swiller, tippler, toper, tosspot
  rel alcoholic, dipsomaniac; wino; drammer
  idiom elbow bender (*or* crooker)
  ant teetotaler

drunken *adj syn see* INTOXICATED 1

drunkery *n syn see* BAR 5

‖**druthers** *n syn see* CHOICE 1

dry *adj* 1 devoid of or deficient in moisture < preferred a *dry* climate >
  syn arid, bone-dry, droughty, moistureless, sere, thirsty, unwatered, waterless
  rel baked, dehydrated, desiccated, parched; bald, bare, barren; depleted, drained, exhausted, impoverished; juiceless, sapless, sapped
  con drenched, dripping, saturated, soaked, soaking, sodden, sopping, soppy, soused, wringing-wet; damp, dank, humid, moist; exuberant, lush, luxuriant, prodigal, profuse
  ant wet
  2 *syn see* THIRSTY 1
  3 marked by the absence of or abstention from alcoholic beverages < a *dry* party >
  syn bone-dry, teetotal
  ant wet
  4 *syn see* IMPASSIVE 1
  5 *syn see* ARID 2
  6 *syn see* PLAIN 1
  7 *syn see* SOUR 1
  ant sweet
  8 *syn see* HARSH 3

dry *vb* 1 to treat or affect so as to deprive of moisture < clothes *dried* in the wind >
  syn dehydrate, desiccate, exsiccate, parch, sear
  rel evaporate; anhydrate; deplete, drain, exhaust; shrivel, wither, wizen

---

  con deluge, douse, drench, soak, sop, souse; damp, dampen, moisten
  ant wet
  2 *syn see* HARDEN 1

dryasdust *adj syn see* ARID 2

dry land *n syn see* EARTH 2

‖**dry-shave** *vb syn see* CHEAT

dry up *vb* 1 *syn see* DESICCATE 2
  2 *syn see* WITHER
  3 *syn see* SHUT UP 2

dual *adj* 1 *syn see* TWOFOLD 1
  2 *syn see* TWIN

dualistic *adj syn see* TWOFOLD 1

dualize *vb syn see* DOUBLE 1

dub *vb* 1 *syn see* NAME 1
  2 *syn see* BOTCH

dub *vb* to provide (a motion-picture film) with a new sound track (as for substituting dialogue in a foreign language) < *dubbed* the Italian movie into English >
  syn double

dubiety *n syn see* UNCERTAINTY
  rel hesitancy; faltering, vacillation, wavering
  con decidedness, decisiveness
  ant decision

dubiosity *n syn see* UNCERTAINTY
  rel addlement, confusion, muddlement; faltering, vacillation, wavering
  con cocksureness, positiveness
  ant decidedness

dubious *adj* 1 *syn see* MOOT
  2 *syn see* DOUBTFUL 1
  rel skeptical; mistrustful; disinclined, hesitant, reluctant
  con dependable, tried, trustworthy, trusty; certain, positive, sure
  ant cocksure; reliable
  3 *syn see* IMPROBABLE 1
  4 *syn see* UNRELIABLE 1
  ant trustworthy

dubitable *adj syn see* DOUBTFUL 1
  ant indubitable

dubitancy *n syn see* UNCERTAINTY

duce *n syn see* TYRANT

‖**duck** *n syn see* ECCENTRIC

duck *vb* 1 *syn see* DIP 1
  2 to lower (as the head or body) quickly < had to *duck* his head to get through the door >
  syn dip, stoop
  rel bend; bow
  3 *syn see* DODGE 1
  rel avert, prevent, ward
  4 *syn see* ESCAPE 2

duck soup *n syn see* SNAP 1

duct *n syn see* CHANNEL 1

ductile *adj syn see* PLASTIC
  rel responsive; submitting; fluid, liquid
  con intractable, refractory; adamant, obdurate

ductus *n syn see* HANDWRITING

dud *n syn see* FAILURE 5

dude *n syn see* FOP

‖**dude up** *vb syn see* DRESS UP 1

dudgeon *n syn see* OFFENSE 2
  rel fury, ire, rage, wrath; humor, mood, temper

duds *n pl* 1 *syn see* CLOTHES
  ‖2 *syn see* RAGS 1

due *adj* 1 *syn see* JUST 3
  rel good, right; equitable, fair, just; coming, earned

---

syn synonym(s)   *rel* related word(s)
ant antonym(s)   *con* contrasted word(s)
idiom idiomatic equivalent(s)
‖ use limited; if in doubt, see a dictionary

con excessive, exorbitant, extravagant, immoderate, inordinate; deficient
ant undue
2 having reached the date at which payment is required <a note that would become *due* after eighteen months>
syn mature, payable
3 *syn* see UNPAID 2

due *n* **1** what one fairly has coming <the artist has finally been accorded his *due*>
syn comeuppance, desert(s), deserving, lumps, merit, right(s)
rel deservedness, dueness, entitlement; compensation, payment, recompense, recompensing, repayment, satisfaction; reprisal, retaliation, retribution, revenge, vengeance; guerdon, need, reward
idiom what is coming to one
2 *syn* see DEBT 3

due *adv syn* see DIRECTLY 1
duel *vb syn* see RESIST
due to *prep syn* see OVER 6
‖**duff** *vb syn* see CHEAT
‖**duff** *n syn* see BUTTOCKS
duffer *n* ‖**1** *syn* see PEDDLER
2 *syn* see DUNCE
dulcet *adj* **1** *syn* see MELODIOUS 1
con grinding, rasping, scraping, scratching
ant grating
2 *syn* see SWEET 1
dull *adj* **1** *syn* see STUPID 1
ant sharp
2 *syn* see RETARDED
con advanced, precocious
3 *syn* see INSENSIBLE 5
4 *syn* see DOWNCAST
5 *syn* see COLORLESS 2
ant bright
6 lacking sharpness of edge or point <a knife with a *dull* blade>
syn blunt, obtuse
rel blunted, dulled, unsharpened
con honed, keen, razor-sharp, unblunted, whetted
ant sharp
7 lacking warmth, luster, or brilliance <a smooth *dull* finish>
syn blind, dead, dim, flat, lackluster, lusterless, mat, muted
rel cold, dingy, drab, dun, leaden, somber; deadened, lifeless
con beaming, bright, brilliant, effulgent, fulgent, incandescent, lambent, lucent, lucid, luminous, lustrous, radiant, refulgent; burnished, polished, shiny
8 cloudy in color <a *dull* brown>
syn drab, muddy, murky, subfusc
rel blurry, cloudy, hazy; flat, lackluster, lifeless, lusterless; mousy
ant clear; rich
9 being so unvaried or uninteresting as to provoke boredom or tedium <any routine constantly repeated can become *dull*>
syn banausic, blah, ‖dim, dreary, humdrum, monotone, monotonous, pedestrian, plodding, poky, stodgy
rel boring, irksome, tedious, tiring, wearisome; brainless; exhausting, fagging, fatiguing
con animating, exciting, stimulating; gay, spritely
ant lively

10 *syn* see OVERCAST
11 *syn* see ARID 2
rel matter-of-fact, prosaic, prosy; bloodless
idiom dull as ditchwater
con exciting, stimulating
ant lively

dull *vb* **1** to make less clear, distinct, or bright <colors *dulled* by the sun>
syn dim, fade, muddy, pale, tarnish
rel discolor, wash out; blur
con brighten, freshen, intensify
2 *syn* see DEADEN 1
ant sharpen
3 to deprive of sharpness (as of edge or point) <*dull* a spade>
syn blunt, disedge, obtund, turn
idiom take the edge off
con edge, hone
ant sharpen
4 to impair one or more of the senses <age had *dulled* his hearing>
syn blear, blur, dim
rel debilitate, enfeeble, weaken; darken; retard, slow
ant sharpen
5 to make slow or obtuse <his mind had been *dulled* by drink>
syn blunt, hebetate, stupefy
rel becloud, befog, cloud, darken, dim; benumb, deaden, numb; retard, slow
con quicken, stimulate, whet
ant sharpen

dullard *n syn* see DUNCE
dullhead *n syn* see DUNCE
dullness *n syn* see LETHARGY 1
rel denseness, stupidity
con edge, incisiveness, keenness
ant sharpness

dumb *adj* **1** lacking the power to speak <deaf and *dumb* from birth>
syn inarticulate, mute, silent, speechless, unarticulate, voiceless; *compare* SILENT 2
ant articulate
2 *syn* see SILENT 2
rel incoherent, indistinct, maundering, tongue-tied
3 *syn* see SILENT 3
con speaking, talking; talkative, verbose
4 *syn* see STUPID 1
idiom dumb as an ox

dumb (up) *vb syn* see SHUT UP 2
dumbbell *n syn* see DUNCE
‖**dumb bunny** *n syn* see DUNCE
‖**dumb cluck** *n syn* see DUNCE
dumbfound *vb* **1** *syn* see SURPRISE 2
2 *syn* see STAGGER 5
dumbfounded *adj syn* see AGHAST 2
‖**dumbhead** *n syn* see DUNCE
‖**dummkopf** *n syn* see DUNCE
dummy *n* **1** *syn* see DUNCE
2 *syn* see STOOGE 1
dummy *adj syn* see ARTIFICIAL 2
‖**dummy** (up) *vb syn* see SHUT UP 2
dump *vb* **1** *syn* see DISCARD
‖**2** *syn* see BEAT 1
dump *n* **1** *syn* see ARMORY
2 *syn* see STY 1
dumping *n syn* see DISPOSAL 2
dumpling *n syn* see FATTY
dumps *n pl syn* see SADNESS
idiom low spirits
dumpy *adj syn* see STOCKY

rel formless, shapeless, unformed

dun *adj syn* see DARK 1

dun *vb syn* see WORRY 1

dunce *n* a dull-witted person < the traditional *dunce* in pointed cap >
syn beetlehead, blockhead, bonehead, boob, booby, ||bufflehead, cabbagehead, chowderhead, chucklehead, chump, clod, clodpate, clodpoll, ||cluck, dimwit, ||dizzard, dodo, ||dodunk, dolt, dolthead, dope, ||doughhead, ||drip, duffer, dullard, dullhead, dumbbell, ||dumb bunny, ||dumb cluck, ||dumbhead, ||dummkopf, dummy, dunderhead, dunderpate, fathead, featherweight, goof, ||goon, hammerhead, idiot, ignoramus, ironhead, knothead, knucklehead, lackwit, lame-brain, lunk, lunkhead, ||moonraker, moron, muddlehead, mug, muggins, mutt, muttonhead, nitwit, noddy, noodle, numskull, oaf, pinhead, poke, prune, pumpkin head, put, ||schnook, simp, simpleton, ||spoon, squarehead, ||stunpoll, ||stupe, stupid, thickhead, thickskull, turnip, wantwit, woodenhead, zombie
rel lightweight; ass, donkey, fool, imbecile, jackass, jerk, nincompoop, ninny, ||schmo, ||schmuck; birdbrain, featherbrain, scatterbrain
idiom dumb ox, Simple Simon
con brain, highbrow, intellectual, thinker, wit; pundit, sage, savant, scholar, wise man; prodigy, wizard; genius, mastermind

duncical *adj syn* see STUPID 1

dunderhead *n syn* see DUNCE

dunderpate *n syn* see DUNCE

dundrearies *n pl syn* see SIDE-WHISKERS

dungeon *n* a close dark prison or vault commonly underground < the prisoners were kept in lightless *dungeons* >
syn oubliette
rel vault; black hole; cell; jail, prison

dungy *adj syn* see DIRTY 1

dunk *vb syn* see DIP 1
rel saturate, soak, sop

duo *n syn* see COUPLE

dupe *n syn* see FOOL 3

dupe *vb* to delude by underhand methods < the public is easily *duped* by extravagant claims in advertising >
syn bamboozle, befool, catch, chicane, con, dust, flimflam, fool, gull, hoax, hoodwink, hornswoggle, job, kid, pigeon, ||rig, spoof, trick, victimize
rel beguile, betray, deceive, delude, double-cross, mislead; cheat, cozen, defraud, overreach; baffle, circumvent, outwit
idiom pull one's leg, put something over (or across)
con enlighten, inform, wise (up)

dupe *vb syn* see DOUBLE 1

dupery *n syn* see DECEPTION 1

duple *adj syn* see TWOFOLD 1

duplex *adj syn* see TWOFOLD 1

duplicate *adj syn* see SAME 2

duplicate *n* 1 *syn* see REPRODUCTION
rel analogue, counterpart, parallel
2 *syn* see MATE 5

duplicate *vb* 1 *syn* see DOUBLE 1
2 *syn* see COPY

duplicitous *adj syn* see UNDERHAND

duplicity *n syn* see DECEIT 1
rel faithlessness, perfidiousness, perfidy, treacherousness, treachery

durable *adj syn* see LASTING
rel stout, strong, tenacious
con feeble, fragile, frail, weak

duration *n* 1 *syn* see CONTINUATION 1
2 *syn* see RUN 2
3 *syn* see TERM 2

duress *n syn* see FORCE 4

during *prep* in the course of < *during* the disorder some men kept their heads >
syn amid, mid, midst, over, throughout

dusk *adj syn* see DARK 1

dusk *n syn* see EVENING 1

||**dusk dark** *n syn* see EVENING 1

dusky *adj* 1 *syn* see DARK 3
2 *syn* see DARK 1
3 *syn* see GLOOMY 3
4 *syn* see OBSCURE 3

dust *n* 1 *syn* see DUSTING
2 *syn* see QUARREL
||3 *syn* see REFUSE

dust *vb* 1 *syn* see SPRINKLE 1
2 *syn* see WHIP 2
3 *syn* see DUPE
idiom throw dust in one's eyes
||4 *syn* see HURRY 2

dusting *n* 1 a small quantity lightly applied to or sprinkled on < a *dusting* of sugar on the cake >
syn dust, powdering, sprinkling
2 *syn* see DEFEAT 1

||**dust off** *vb syn* see MURDER 1

dustup *n syn* see QUARREL

dusty *adj syn* see ARID 2

Dutch *n syn* see TROUBLE 3

duteous *adj syn* see RESPECTFUL

dutiful *adj syn* see RESPECTFUL

duty *n* 1 *syn* see OBLIGATION 2
rel accountability, amenability, answerability, liability
2 *syn* see FUNCTION 1
3 *syn* see LOAD 3
4 *syn* see TAX 1
5 *syn* see TASK 1
6 *syn* see USE 4

dwarf *n* a very small person < she was a tiny little thing, almost a *dwarf* >
syn homunculus, hop-o'-my-thumb, Lilliputian, manikin, midge, midget, peewee, pygmy, runt, Tom Thumb
rel ||ribe, ||shrimp, wart; dwarfling; minimus
ant giant

dwarf *vb syn* see STUNT

dwarf *adj syn* see TINY

dwarfish *adj syn* see TINY

dwell *vb* 1 *syn* see RESIDE 1
2 *syn* see CONSIST 1

dweller *n syn* see INHABITANT

dwelling *n syn* see HABITATION 2

dwindle *vb* 1 *syn* see DECREASE
rel ebb, subside, wane; attenuate, extenuate, thin; moderate; disappear
2 *syn* see FAIL 3

||**dwine** *vb syn* see FAIL 1

dyad *n syn* see COUPLE

dye *n syn* see COLOR 6

dyed-in-the-wool *adj syn* see INVETERATE 1

---

dyestuff *n syn* see COLOR 6
dying *adj syn* see MORIBUND
dynamic *adj* 1 *syn* see ACTIVE 1
 rel activating, energizing, vitalizing
 ant static
 2 *syn* see VIGOROUS
 rel forceful, forcible; intense, vehement, violent
 con idle, inactive, passive

 ant inert
dynamite *vb syn* see DESTROY 1
dynamo *n syn* see HUSTLER 1
dysentery *n syn* see DIARRHEA
dyslogistic *adj syn* see DEROGATORY
 ant eulogistic
dyspathy *n syn* see ANTIPATHY 2
dyspeptic *aaj syn* see ILL-TEMPERED
dysphoria *n syn* see SADNESS

E

each *adj syn* see ALL 2
 rel any, several, various; particular, respective, specific
each *adv syn* see APIECE
 idiom a shot, a throw, a whack
eager *adj* moved by a strong and urgent desire or interest < young executives *eager* to succeed >
 syn agog, anxious, appetent, ardent, athirst, avid, breathless, impatient, keen, raring, solicitous, thirsty
 rel enthusiastic, gung ho, heated, hot; ambitious, intent; acquisitive, covetous, craving, desirous, hankering, ‖honing, hungry, longing, pining, wishful, yearning; impatient, restive, restless
 idiom champing at the bit, ready and willing
 con aloof, disinterested, incurious, indifferent, unconcerned, uninterested; apathetic, detached, impassive, stolid
 ant listless
eagerness *n* a strong and urgent desire or interest < an *eagerness* to learn >
 syn ardor, enthusiasm, zing
 rel alacrity, avidity, keenness, quickness; ambition; gusto, ‖mustard, zest
 con lackadaisicality, languor, lethargy; aloofness, disinterest; apathy, deliberation; detachment, impassivity, stolidity
 ant listlessness
eagle eye *n syn* see EYE 3
eagle-eyed *adj syn* see SHARP-EYED
ear *n syn* see NOTICE 1
earlier *adv* 1 *syn* see BEFORE 2
 2 *syn* see HITHERTO 1
 3 *syn* see BEFORE 3
earliest *adj syn* see FIRST 2
 con final, terminal, ultimate
 ant latest
early *adv* 1 at or nearly at the beginning of a period, course, process, or series < it is much too *early* to guess the outcome >
 syn betimes, seasonably, soon, timely
 rel first
 2 in advance of the expected or usual time < these apples bear *early* and heavy >
 syn betimes, oversoon, prematurely
 rel beforehand
 idiom ahead of time, bright and early
early *adj* 1 of, relating to, or occurring near the beginning of a period of time, a development, or a series < *early* Renaissance > < *early* art forms >
 syn primitive, primordial

 rel original, pristine; ancient, antediluvian, antiquated, primal, primeval; antecedent, preceding, prevenient, prior
 con conclusive, final, last, terminal, ultimate; eventual; intermediate, middle, midmost
 ant late
 2 occurring before the expected or usual time < an *early* death > < an *early* peach >
 syn overearly, oversoon, premature, previous, ‖soon, untimely; *compare* PRECOCIOUS
 rel anticipative, anticipatory, precipitant, precocious; unanticipated, unexpected
 con slow, tardy; anticipated, expected
 ant late
earmark *vb syn* see DESIGNATE 3
earn *vb* 1 to receive as return for effort < *earn* a living wage >
 syn acquire, bring in, ‖drag down, draw down, gain, get, knock down, make, win
 rel attain, effect, obtain, procure, realize, receive, secure
 2 to be or make worthy of < his devotion to duty *earned* him a promotion >
 syn deserve, merit, rate
 rel bag, come by, harvest, net, reap, score
earnest *n syn* see EARNESTNESS
 rel attention, interest; enthusiasm, warmth, zeal
 ant jest, play
earnest *adj syn* see SERIOUS 1
 rel ardent, enthusiastic, passionate, pressing, warm, zealous; assiduous, busy, diligent, industrious, perseverant, sedulous; sincere, wholehearted, whole-souled
 con buoyant, effervescent, elastic, flippant, light
 ant frivolous
earnest *n syn* see PLEDGE 1
earnestly *adv* 1 *syn* see HARD 3
 rel seriously, soberly, solemnly, thoughtfully; zealously
 2 *syn* see SERIOUSLY 1
earnestness *n* a state of freedom from all jesting or trifling < he studied with great *earnestness* >
 syn earnest, intentness, serious-mindedness, seriousness
 rel doggedness, perseverance, persistence; decision, determination, firmness, purposefulness, resolve; absorption, attentiveness, concentration, engrossment; deliberation; gravity, sobriety

con levity, lightness; shallowness, superficiality; carelessness, slackness
ant frivolity

earnings *n pl syn* see PROFIT

earshot *n* the range within which something (as a voice) may be heard <the gossips were still within *earshot* of her>
syn hearing, sound
idiom carrying (*or* hearing) distance

earsplitting *adj syn* see LOUD 1
rel penetrating, shrill

earth *n* 1 the entire area in which man lives and acts <expect the destruction of the *earth*>
syn globe, (the) planet, world
rel orb, sphere; cosmos, creation, macrocosm, universe, vale
2 areas of land as distinguished from sea and air <clayey *earth*, difficult to drain>
syn dirt, dry land, ground, land, soil, terra firma
rel clay, gravel, humus, loam, mud, sand; fill, subsoil; terrain, turf; clod

earthlike *adj syn* see EARTHY 1

earthly *adj* 1 of, relating to, or characteristic of this earth or man's life on earth <*earthly* pursuits>
syn earthy, mundane, sublunary, tellurian, telluric, terrene, terrestrial, uncelestial, worldly
rel carnal, corporeal, earthbound, physical; material, temporal; unspiritual
con celestial, empyreal, empyrean, heavenly; ideal, utopian; divine, spiritual
2 *syn* see PROBABLE
rel imaginable, potential

earthquake *n* a shaking or trembling of the earth that is volcanic or tectonic in origin <homes destroyed by *earthquakes*>
syn quake, ‖quaker, shake, shock, temblor (*or* tremblor), tremor

earthy *adj* 1 consisting of, resembling, or suggesting earth <a stale *earthy* smell>
syn earthlike, terrene, terrestrial
rel clayey, dusty, muddy, sandy
2 *syn* see EARTHLY 1
3 *syn* see MATERIALISTIC
4 *syn* see REALISTIC
ant impractical

ease *n* 1 *syn* see REST 1
rel idleness, inactivity, inertia, inertness, passivity, supinity; calmness, security
con labor, toil, travail; adversity, difficulty; burden, care, worry
2 *syn* see UNCONSTRAINT
3 freedom from or mitigation of pain <medication brought him instant *ease*>
syn alleviation, easement, mitigation, relief
rel decrease, diminishment, moderation, reduction; calming, soothing
con discomfort, unrest; agony, pain
4 *syn* see READINESS 3
rel adroitness, artfulness, cleverness, deftness, effortlessness, expertise, expertness, fluency, knack, poise, skillfulness, smoothness; efficiency, grace

---

syn synonym(s)   *rel* related word(s)
ant antonym(s)   *con* contrasted word(s)
idiom idiomatic equivalent(s)
‖ use limited; if in doubt, see a dictionary

con awkwardness, clumsiness, maladroitness, stiffness, woodenness; constraint; inconvenience, pains; exertion
ant effort
5 *syn* see PROSPERITY 2

ease *vb* 1 *syn* see RELIEVE 1
rel deaden, dull; ameliorate, help
con afflict, torment
2 *syn* see LOOSE 5
rel disengage, free, release
con bind, restrain, tighten
3 to make less difficult <new laws that will *ease* voting requirements>
syn facilitate
rel aid, assist, better, help, improve; forward, further, promote, speed
idiom clear (*or* prepare) the way (for), grease the wheels, open the door (to *or* for)
con hinder, impede, retard

easeful *adj syn* see COMFORTABLE 2

easement *n syn* see EASE 3
rel allayment, appeasement, assuagement, mollification

ease off *vb* 1 *syn* see LOOSE 5
2 *syn* see ABATE 4
3 *syn* see RELAX 2

easily *adv* 1 without discomfort, difficulty, or reluctance <*easily* translated the document>
syn effortlessly, facilely, freely, lightly, readily, smoothly, well
rel competently, dexterously, efficiently, fluently, handily, simply
idiom hands down, slick as a whistle
con awkwardly, clumsily, ineptly, stiffly; arduously, wearily
ant laboriously
2 without question <this is *easily* the best course of action>
syn absolutely, definitely, doubtless, doubtlessly, positively, unequivocally, unquestionably
rel actually, assuredly, certainly, clearly, decidedly, indeed, really, truly, undoubtedly
idiom no doubt
con apparently, perhaps, probably, seemingly; doubtfully, equivocally, questionably
3 *syn* see WELL 7

easy *adj* 1 causing or involving little or no difficulty <an *easy* solution>
syn effortless, facile, light, royal, simple, smooth, untroublesome
rel apparent, clear, distinct, evident, manifest, obvious, plain; clear-cut, straightforward, uncomplicated, uncompounded, uninvolved
idiom easy as falling off a log, easy as pie, nothing to it
con arduous, difficult, troublesome; abstruse, complex, complicated, intricate, knotty
ant hard
2 *syn* see FORBEARING
rel compassionate, condoning, excusing, forgiving, pardoning, sympathetic; benign, kindly; lax, moderate, soft; humoring, mollycoddling, pampering, spoiling
con austere, exacting, rigid, severe, stern, strict, stringent
3 easily taken advantage of or imposed upon <he was *easy* prey to her wiles>

syn fleeceable, gullible, naive, susceptible

rel credulous, trusting, unmistrusting, unsuspicious; deceivable, deludable, dupable, exploitable; artless, dewy-eyed, green, simple, unsophisticated

con critical, cynical, disbelieving, mistrustful, scoffing, skeptical, suspicious, unbelieving

4 *syn* see FAST 7

5 *syn* see COMFORTABLE 2

rel secure

con discontented, dissatisfied; miserable

ant uncomfortable

6 *syn* see AMIABLE 1

rel familiar, gregarious, informal; courtly, diplomatic, pleasant, polite, sociable; smooth, suave, urbane

con brusque, curt, unfriendly, unpleasant; constrained, embarrassed, formal, restrained; discourteous, impolite, undiplomatic, ungracious; stiff, unsocial, withdrawn, wooden

ant ill at ease

7 *syn* see CALM 2

rel relaxed; lethargic, unambitious

con agitated, tense, troubled, uptight

8 *syn* see PROSPEROUS 3

rel successful, thriving

idiom in easy circumstances, on easy street

con straitened

9 marked by ready facility (as of expression) <an *easy* style of writing>

syn cursive, effortless, flowing, fluent, running, smooth

rel facile; graceful

con effortful, labored

ant difficult

easygoing *adj* **1** *syn* see CALM 2

con agitated, flurried, flustered, harassed; anxious, concerned, upset, worried

ant uptight

2 *syn* see LAZY

rel apathetic, careless, indifferent, unconcerned; unambitious

con active, ambitious, diligent, dynamic, energetic, industrious, live, vigorous

3 not constrained or bound by rigid standards <enjoyed the *easygoing* morality of a commune>

syn breezy, casual, ‖common, dégagé, informal, low-pressure, relaxed, ‖sonsy, unconstrained, unfussy, unreserved

rel affable, folksy; flexible, lax, moderate, offhand, off-handed, unaffected; carefree, devil-may-care, happy-go-lucky; outgoing; uninhibited

idiom free and easy

con ceremonious, decorous, formal, proper, stuffy; constrained, inflexible, inhibited, restrained, rigid, starchy, stiff

easy mark *n* **1** *syn* see FOOL 3

2 *syn* see SOFT TOUCH 1

‖**easy rider** *n* **1** *syn* see SYCOPHANT

2 *syn* see PIMP 1

easy street *n* *syn* see PROSPERITY 2

eat *vb* **1** to take in as food <they quickly *ate* a hearty breakfast>

syn consume, devour, feed (on), ingest, meal, partake (of), take; *compare* CONSUME 1

rel banquet, feast, gormandize; eat up, gobble (up *or* down), gorge (on), ‖mop (up), polish off, scoff; breakfast, dine,

lunch, snack, sup; mouth, ‖muckamuck, nibble, pick

idiom break bread, get away with, have (*or* take) a bite, take nourishment, ‖put on the feed bag

2 *syn* see CONSUME 1

3 to consume gradually <the acid *ate* the surface of the copper>

syn bite, corrode, eat away, erode, gnaw, scour, wear (away)

rel nibble (away); consume, decompose, disintegrate, dissolve

eatable *adj* *syn* see EDIBLE

eat away *vb* *syn* see EAT 3

eating house *n* a cheap often small restaurant <grabbed a quick sandwich at a local *eating house*>

syn beanery, ‖buffet, café, coffee shop, cookshop, diner, ‖greasy spoon, ‖hashery, ‖hash house, lunch counter (*or* bar), luncheonette, lunchroom, lunch wagon (*or* cart), quick-lunch, sandwich shop, snack bar (*or* counter)

rel cafeteria, eatery, tearoom; trattoria

‖**eats** *n pl syn* see FOOD 1

eat up *vb* **1** to eat completely and without delay <eat *up* your dinner before it gets cold>

syn devour, dispatch, polish off

rel down, eat; bolt, gobble (up *or* down), gorge (on), ‖mop (up), wolf

2 *syn* see CONSUME 1

‖**3** *syn* see DEVOUR 5

rel luxuriate (in), riot (in), wallow (in)

idiom be beside oneself over, be thrilled to death by, smack one's lips over, take delight in

‖**4** *syn* see LOVE 1

ebb *vb* *syn* see ABATE 4

rel decline, peter (out); recede, retreat, retrograde

con ascend, increase, mount, rise; advance, progress

ant flow

ebbing *n* *syn* see FAILURE 4

rel declining, sinking

ebon *adj* *syn* see BLACK 1

ebony *adj* *syn* see BLACK 1

ebullience *n* lively or enthusiastic expression of thoughts or feelings <her bubbling *ebullience* was infectious>

syn buoyancy, effervescence, exuberance, exuberancy

rel animation, enthusiasm, gaiety, high= spiritedness, liveliness, vitality, vivaciousness, vivacity; agitation, excitement, exhilaration, ferment

con apathy, impassivity, languor, lethargy, listlessness, passivity, sluggishness, stolidity, torpidity, torpor; enervation, inactivity, inertia, lifelessness; disinterest, unconcern, uninterest

ebullient *adj* *syn* see EXUBERANT 1

eccentric *adj* **1** not having the same center <*eccentric* spheres>

syn off-center

rel uncentered; off-balance, unbalanced

con centered; balanced

ant concentric

2 *syn* see STRANGE 4

rel anomalous, irregular, unnatural; exceptionable, exceptional, quirky, quizzical; beheaded, ‖dippy, wacky; fantastic, grotesque *con* customary, habitual; natural, normal, regular, typical

eccentric *n* one who deviates from established patterns especially in odd or whimsical ways <an *eccentric* who filled his house with statues of himself >
syn case, character, ‖duck, oddball, oddity, original, quiz, ‖spook, ‖wack, zombie
rel bohemian, maverick, nonconformist, unconformist; dissenter, heretic; caution, coot, ‖geezer; crackpot, crank, freak, kook, screwball
idiom queer duck (*or* potato)
con conformer, conformist, conventionalist, traditionalist; bore, bromide, dullard

ecclesiast *n syn* see CLERGYMAN

ecclesiastic *n syn* see CLERGYMAN

ecclesiastical *adj* of, relating to, or belonging to a church especially as an established institution < *ecclesiastical* law >
syn church, churchly, churchmanly, spiritual
rel apostolic, canonical, episcopal, episcopalian, evangelistic, theological; clerical, ministerial, papal, pastoral, patriarchal, pontifical, prelatial, priestly, rabbinical, sacerdotal; cathedralesque, churchlike, pantheonic, synagogal, synagogical, tabernacular, templelike
con lay, secular

ecdysiast *n syn* see STRIPTEASER

echelon *n syn* see LINE 5

echoic *adj syn* see ONOMATOPOEIC

éclat *n syn* see FAME 2
rel bang, brilliance, brilliancy, display, luster, notice- ableness, prominence, remarkableness; distinction, standing; kudos
con oblivion, obscurity; contempt, derision, scorn

eclectic *adj* 1 selecting what appears to be the best from various doctrines, methods, or styles <an *eclectic* taste in music >
syn discriminating, select, selective
rel elective, selecting; choosing, choosy, discerning, fastidious, finicky, fussy, particular, picky
2 composed of elements drawn from various sources <an *eclectic* art incorporating romanticism and impressionism >
syn catholic
rel broad, comprehensive, inclusive; assorted, mingled, mixed; diverse, diversified, heterogeneous, multifarious, multiform, varied; derived, unoriginal
con distinctive, narrow; new, original

eclipse *vb syn* see OBSCURE

economical *adj syn* see SPARING
rel careful, forehanded, prudent; economizing, penny-wise; cheeseparing, close, mean, miserly, niggardly, penny-pinching, penurious, scrimping, skimping, spare, stingy
con generous, lavish, wasteful
ant extravagant

economic poison *n syn* see PESTICIDE

economize *vb* to avoid unnecessary waste or expense < *economize* on food by using leftovers >

syn save
rel conserve; scrimp, skimp
con dissipate, scatter, waste
ant squander, throw away

economy *n* careful management of material resources < retired people often must learn to practice *economy* >
syn forehandedness, frugality, husbandry, providence, prudence, thrift, thriftiness
rel meanness, miserliness, niggardliness, parcity, parsimony, scrimping, skimping, stinginess; carefulness, discretion
con improvidence, lavishness, prodigality, squandering, thriftlessness, wastefulness
ant extravagance

ecstasy *n* intense exaltation of mind and feelings < was in *ecstasy* over flying >
syn heaven, rapture, rhapsody, seventh heaven, transport; *compare* EXHILARATION
rel beatitude, blessedness, bliss, blissfulness, felicity, gladness, happiness; delectation, delight, elation, joy, joyfulness, overjoyfulness, pleasure; enchantment, euphoria, intoxication, madness; exaltation, inspiration; paradise; afflatus, frenzy, fury
idiom cloud nine
con dejection, downheartedness, lowness, lowspiritedness, oppression; blues, dumps, melancholy
ant depression

ecumenical *adj syn* see UNIVERSAL 2
rel heaven-wide; all-comprehending, all≍comprehensive, all-covering, all-including, all-pervading; comprehensive, general, inclusive
con diocesan, local, parochial, provincial; circumscribed, insular, limited, narrow, restricted

edacious *adj syn* see VORACIOUS

eddy *n* a swirling mass especially of water < dark *eddies* in the flooded stream >
syn maelstrom, vortex, whirl, whirlpool
rel gurge, surge, swirl, twirl, whirl; back current, back stream, countercurrent, counterflow, counterflux; backwash, backwater

eddy *vb syn* see SWIRL

edge *n* 1 *syn* see BORDER 1
rel end, extremity; ledge, side
con area, surface
2 a cutting quality < there was an *edge* to his voice as he answered >
syn incisiveness, keenness, sharpness
rel bite, cut, sting; knife-edge, razor-edge; acerbity, acidity, acridity, causticity; astringency, stringency; acuteness, penetration, shrillness, thinness
3 *syn* see VERGE 2
4 *syn* see ADVANTAGE 3
con bar, encumbrance, obstacle; disadvantage

edge *vb* 1 *syn* see SHARPEN
2 *syn* see BORDER 1
3 *syn* see SIDLE

edge in *vb syn* see INSINUATE 3

edgy *adj* 1 *syn* see TENSE 2
rel skittish; excitable, excited, high≍strung, overstrung; irritable, touchy; impatient, restless
idiom on edge
con detached; peaceful, placid; patient
2 *syn* see EXCITABLE

---

syn synonym(s)   *rel* related word(s)
ant antonym(s)   *con* contrasted word(s)
idiom idiomatic equivalent(s)
‖ use limited; if in doubt, see a dictionary

edible *adj* suitable for use as food < *edible*
plant products >
syn comestible, eatable, esculent
rel digestible; nourishing, nutritious, nutritive; palatable, savory, succulent, tasty,
toothsome
ant inedible

edibles *n pl syn* see FOOD 1

edict *n* **1** a publicly proclaimed order or
rule of conduct by a competent authority
< a government *edict* regarding curfew
enforcement >
syn decree, directive, ruling, ukase
rel instrument; order; manifesto, proclamation, pronouncement, pronunciamento;
bull
2 *syn* see LAW 1

edifice *n* a large, magnificent, or massive
building < a marble *edifice* now used as a
museum >
syn erection, pile, structure; *compare*
BUILDING, HUT

edify *vb syn* see ILLUMINATE 2
rel better, enhance; elucidate; educate,
instruct, teach
con debase, deprave

edition *n* the total number of copies of the
same work printed during a stretch of
time < the initial *edition* of 50,000 copies
was exhausted in a month >
syn impression, printing, reissue, reprinting

educate *vb syn* see TEACH
rel cultivate, nurture; brief, explain, inform

education *n* **1** the act or process of educat-
ing < devoted himself to the *education* of
illiterate adults >
syn instruction, schooling, teaching, training, tuition, tutelage
rel coaching, pedagogy, tutorage, tutor-
ing, tutorship; direction, guidance
2 the product or result of being educated
< obtained his *education* in local schools
and in college >
syn erudition, knowledge, learning, scholarship, science
rel culture, edification, enlightenment,
learnedness, literacy
con ignorance, illiteracy

educational *adj syn* see INFORMATIVE

educative *adj syn* see INFORMATIVE

educe *vb* **1** to draw out something hidden,
latent, or reserved < *educed* important
information from the witness >
syn elicit, evince, evoke, extort, extract,
milk
rel drag, draw, draw out, pull, wrest,
wring; gain, get, obtain, procure, secure;
distill
con miss, overlook, pass over
2 *syn* see DERIVE 1
rel reason (out), think (out)

eerie *adj syn* see WEIRD 1
rel bizarre, fantastic, grotesque; arcane;
crawly

efface *vb syn* see ERASE
rel eradicate, extirpate; eliminate, exclude,
rule out

effect *n* **1** a condition or occurrence trace-
able to a cause < the *effect* of the medicine was dizziness >
syn aftereffect, aftermath, causatum, consequence, corollary, end product, event,

eventuality, issue, outcome, precipitate,
result, sequel, sequence, upshot
rel pursuance; development, fruit, outgrowth, ramification; denouement, reper-
cussion; conclusion, end; side effect
con antecedent, determinant, occasion,
reason; base, basis, foundation, ground,
groundwork
ant cause

2 effects *pl syn* see POSSESSION 2

effect *vb* **1** to induce to come into being
< specific genes *effect* specific bodily
characters >
syn bring about, cause, draw on, make,
produce, secure
rel conceive, create, generate; bring on,
induce; enact, render, turn out, yield
con impede, limit, restrict; repress, suppress
2 to carry to a successful conclusion
< found a pass that allowed them to *effect*
passage through the mountains >
syn bring off, carry out, carry through,
effectuate; *compare* FULFILL 1, PERFORM
2
rel actualize, realize; achieve, procure
con fail, fall down
3 *syn* see ENFORCE

effective *adj* producing or capable of producing a result < an *effective* rebuke >
syn effectual, efficacious, efficient, virtuous
rel adequate, capable, competent; cogent,
compelling, convincing, sound, telling,
valid; able, active, dynamic; operative,
useful; direct
con abortive, bootless, fruitless, futile,
vain; empty, hollow, idle, nugatory, otiose,
pointless; inoperative, useless, worthless
ant ineffective

effectiveness *n* **1** *syn* see POINT 3
rel forcefulness, potency, power, strength,
verve, vigor
con impotence, weakness
ant ineffectiveness
2 *syn* see EFFICIENCY 1
3 *syn* see EFFICACY 1

effectual *adj syn* see EFFECTIVE
rel accomplishing, achieving, effecting,
fulfilling; practicable, sound, useful, valid,
workable; conclusive, decisive, determinative, influential; authoritative, potent,
powerful, strong, toothy
con impotent, weak
ant ineffectual

effectuate *vb syn* see EFFECT 2

effeminate *adj* lacking manly strength and
purpose < an *effeminate* preoccupation
with trifles >
syn epicene, Miss-Nancyish, pansified,
prissy, sissified, sissy, unmanly
rel chichi, old-maidish, overnice, precious;
foppish, sappy, silken
ant manly, masculine

effervescence *n syn* see EBULLIENCE
rel bubbling, ebullition, fizzing, foaming
con deadness, flatness, staleness

effervescent *adj* **1** *syn* see EXUBERANT 1
2 *syn* see ELASTIC 2
rel animated, boiling, bubbly, excited,
gay, lively, sparkling, sprightly, vivacious;
gleeful, hilarious, jolly, mirthful
con lifeless, listless, subdued; earnest,
sedate, serious, solemn

effete *adj* **1** *syn* see STERILE 1

2 having lost energy or drive < *effete*, weary, burned out revolutionaries >

syn all in, bleary, depleted, done, done in, drained, exhausted, far-gone, spent, used up, washed-out, worn-out

rel consumed; debilitated, enfeebled, fatigued

idiom on one's last legs, out on one's feet

con alive, lively, vigorous, vital

3 having lost character < a soft, *effete* society >

syn decadent, decayed, degenerate, overripe

rel decaying, declining; soft, weak; dissolute, immoral

efficacious *adj syn* see EFFECTIVE

rel active, operative, productive; influential, potent, powerful, puissant, strong

con abortive; impotent, powerless, useless, vain, weak

ant inefficacious

efficacy *n* **1** the power to produce an effect < *efficacy* of the drug >

syn capability, effectiveness, efficiency, potency

rel capableness, productiveness, use; adequacy, capacity, sufficiency

con ineffectiveness, inefficiency; uselessness, worthlessness

ant inefficacy

2 *syn* see EFFICIENCY 1

efficiency *n* **1** the capacity to produce desired results with a minimum expenditure of energy, time, or resources < demands a high degree of *efficiency* on the job >

syn effectiveness, efficacy, performance

rel ability, address, adeptness, competence, expertise, know-how, proficiency, prowess, skill; capability, resourcefulness; productivity

con inadequacy, incompetence, ineffectiveness; unproductiveness

ant inefficiency

2 *syn* see EFFICACY 1

efficient *adj syn* see EFFECTIVE

rel able, capable, competent, fitted, qualified; adept, expert, masterly, proficient, skilled, skillful

con incapable, incompetent, inexpert, unadept, unproficient, unqualified, unsuitable; unproductive; ineffectual

ant inefficient

effloresce *vb syn* see BLOSSOM

effort *n* **1** the active use of energy in producing a result < thought the job wasn't worth the *effort* >

syn elbow grease, exertion, pains, trouble, while

rel labor, toil, travail, work; energy, force, might, power, puissance; attempt, endeavor, essay

idiom sweat of one's brow

con adroitness, facility, smoothness; do-nothingness, inaction, indolence, inertia, lackadaisicalness, languor, laziness

ant ease

2 *syn* see TASK 2

effortful *adj syn* see HARD 6

effortless *adj syn* see EASY 1

rel adept, expert, masterly, proficient, ready, skilled, skillful

con laborious, toilsome, trying

ant painstaking

2 *syn* see EASY 9

effortlessly *adv syn* see EASILY 1

rel adeptly, adroitly, efficiently, expertly, proficiently, skillfully

con painstakingly

ant arduously, laboriously

effrontery *n* flagrant disregard of courtesy or propriety and an arrogant assumption of privilege < had the *effrontery* to insult her father >

syn brashness, brass, cheek, confidence, ||crust, face, gall, nerve, presumption; *compare* INSOLENCE

rel audacity, hardihood, temerity; assurance, self-assurance, self-confidence; brazenness, impudence; impertinence, insolence

con courtesy, grace, propriety

effulgent *adj syn* see BRIGHT 1

rel vivid; glorious, resplendent, splendid

con dark, dusky, gloomy, murky

effusive *adj* unduly demonstrative < *effusive* assurances of undying love >

syn gushing, gushy, slobbering, slobbery, sloppy

rel expansive, fulsome, outpouring, profuse; demonstrative, unconstrained, unreserved, unrestrained; cloying, slushy; smarmy

con close, restrained, reticent, taciturn; bashful, modest, shy

ant reserved

egg (on) *vb syn* see URGE

rel agitate, excite, pique, stimulate; instigate; arouse, drive, rally, stir up, whip (on *or* up)

con arrest, bridle

egghead *n syn* see INTELLECTUAL 2

egocentric *adj* **1** concerned with the individual person rather than society < an *egocentric* approach to world problems >

syn individualist, individualistic

rel self-centered, selfish

2 concerned only with one's own activities or needs and usually tending to self-assertion or self-satisfaction < an *egocentric* man, lacking feeling for others >

syn egoistic, egomaniacal, egotistic, self=absorbed, self-centered, self-concerned, self-interested, self-involved, selfish, self=seeking, self-serving; *compare* POMPOUS 1

rel conceited, narcissistic, self-affected, self-applauding, self-conceited, self-concentered, self-indulgent, self-loving, stuck-up, vainglorious; megalomaniac

idiom wrapped up in oneself

egoism *n* **1** *syn* see EGOTISM 1

rel self-assurance, self-confidence, self=possession

ant altruism

2 *syn* see CONCEIT 2

rel self-satisfaction

con meekness, modesty

ant humility

egoistic *adj syn* see EGOCENTRIC 2

rel individualistic; self-satisfied, swell-headed

---

con humble, modest
ant altruistic

egomaniacal *adj syn* see EGOCENTRIC 2
rel self-exalting, self-glorifying, vainglorious

egotism *n* 1 an exaggerated sense of one's own importance <in believing that he was indispensable, he exhibited consummate *egotism* >
syn egoism, self-importance
rel conceit, conceitedness, narcissism, self-esteem, self-love, vainness; boastfulness, boasting, bragging, gasconade, gasconism, megalomania, vaunting
con humility, lowliness; bashfulness, diffidence, shyness; modesty
ant altruism
2 *syn* see CONCEIT 2
rel arrogance, superiority; contempt
con humbleness, self-effacement
ant humility

egotistic *adj syn* see EGOCENTRIC 2
rel boastful, cocky, inflated, pretentious, proud, puffed up, self-satisfied; conceited, stuck-up
idiom in love with oneself, stuck on oneself
con humble, modest; self-effacing, shy

egregious *adj* conspicuously bad or objectionable <an *egregious* mistake>
syn capital, flagrant, glaring, gross, rank
rel arrant, outright, stark; infamous, nefarious, notorious; atrocious, deplorable, heinous, monstrous, outrageous, preposterous
con measly, minor, petty, piddling, slender, slight, trifling, trivial

egress *n* 1 *syn* see DEPARTURE 1
rel emergence, emerging
con coming, entering; arrival
ant ingress
2 a place or means of going out <a gate providing *egress* from the pasture>
syn exit, outlet
rel opening, passage; escape
idiom way out
con entrance, entry, entryway
ant access, ingress

egression *n syn* see DEPARTURE 1
con entrance, entering
ant ingression

eidolon *n syn* see APPARITION

ejaculate *vb syn* see EXCLAIM
rel call (out), shout, vociferate, yell

eject *vb* 1 to drive or force (somebody) out <*eject* an intruder from one's home>
syn boot (out), chase, chuck, dismiss, evict, extrude, kick out, throw out;
compare BANISH
rel displace, dispossess; drive off, rout, run off; debar, disbar, eliminate, exclude, rule out, shut out; bump, cashier, discharge, fire, sack; discard, shed; reject, repudiate, spurn
idiom give one his walking papers, send packing, show one the door
con accept, admit, install, receive; entertain, harbor, house, lodge, shelter
2 *syn* see ERUPT 1

elaborate *adj* 1 *syn* see COMPLEX 2
2 marked by complexity of detail or ornament <an *elaborate* coiffure>
syn complicated, fancy, intricate

rel detailed, highly-wrought; decorated, dressy, embellished, ornate; elegant; busy, overdone, overworked, overwrought
con common, ordinary, plain, unpolished; inartificial, inornate, natural
ant simple

elaborate *vb* 1 *syn* see EXPAND 4
rel comment, discuss, dwell (upon); clarify, explain, expound, interpret
2 *syn* see UNFOLD 3

élan *n syn* see SPIRIT 5
rel impetus

élan vital *n syn* see SOUL 1

elapse *vb syn* see PASS 3
rel flow, glide, pass (by), slide, slip (by), lapse, run out

elastic *adj* 1 able to withstand strain without being permanently affected or injured <a rubber band is *elastic* >
syn flexible, resilient, springy, stretch, stretchy, supple, whippy
rel ductile, malleable, pliable, pliant, plastic, rubberlike, rubbery; adaptable, moldable, stretchable, yielding; bouncy, limber, lithe
con brittle; inflexible, stiff, tense
ant rigid
2 able to recover quickly from depression and maintain high spirits <had an *elastic* optimistic nature>
syn airy, bouncy, buoyant, effervescent, expansive, resilient, volatile
rel animated, gay, lively, sprightly, vivacious; ebullient, high-spirited, mettlesome, soaring, spirited; adaptable, recuperative
con blue, dejected, depressed, gloomy, melancholy, sad; flaccid, limp

elate *vb* to elevate the spirits of <the phenomenal sales record *elated* him>
syn commove, excite, exhilarate, inspire, set up, spirit (up), stimulate
rel brighten, cheer, cheer up, encourage; delight, gladden, gratify, overjoy; buoy, elevate, exalt, uplift
con distress; oppress, weigh; weary
ant depress

elated *adj syn* see INTOXICATED 2
rel enchanted, enraptured, exalted, transported; delighted, ecstatic, euphoric, exultant, jubilant, overjoyed
idiom in heaven, in seventh heaven, on cloud nine
con blue, deflated, unhappy

elation *n* 1 the quality or state of being elated <felt great *elation* when he won the presidential nomination>
syn euphoria, exaltation, exhilaration
rel buoyancy; happiness, joy; excitement; rapture, transport
idiom stars in one's eyes
con blues, depression; distress, misery, sadness, unhappiness
ant deflation
2 *syn* see EUPHORIA 2
ant depression

elbow *vb syn* see PUSH 2

elbowroom *n syn* see ROOM 3
rel space

elder *n* 1 *syn* see SENIOR 2
2 *syn* see OLDSTER
3 *syn* see SUPERIOR

elderliness *n syn* see OLD AGE

elderly *adj syn* see AGED 1

rel aging, declining
con juvenile, young
ant youthful

eldorado *n syn* see BONANZA

elect *adj syn* see SELECT 1
rel choice, rare; hand-picked, singled out; designated, destined, ordained; delivered, redeemed, saved
con refused, rejected, repudiated, spurned; disdained, scorned; damned, doomed, reprobate

elect *vb* 1 *syn* see CHOOSE 1
rel decide, determine, resolve, settle; conclude, judge; accept, admit, receive
con reject; dismiss, eject, expel, oust
ant abjure
2 to select by or as if by ballot < the board of directors *elected* a new chairman >
syn ballot, vote (in)
rel choose, designate, name, opt, pick, select, single; nominate; appoint
3 *syn* see WILL

election *n syn* see CHOICE 1

elective *adj syn* see OPTIONAL

electrify *vb syn* see THRILL
rel provoke; jar, stagger, stun

eleemosynary *adj syn* see CHARITABLE 1
rel beneficent, generous, liberal, munificent, openhanded
con close, parsimonious, tight

elegance *n* impressive beauty of form, appearance, or behavior < the sumptuous *elegance* of the furnishings >
syn dignity, grace
rel beauty, charm; cultivation, culture, polish, refinement, sophistication, style, taste, tastefulness; lushness, magnificence, ornateness, poshness, richness, splendor, sumptuousness
con grotesqueness, ugliness; clumsiness, crudeness, roughness, rudeness; austerity, bareness, inornateness, severity

elegant *adj syn* see CHOICE
rel august, grand, majestic, noble, stately; beautiful, graceful, handsome, lovely; cultivated, cultured, finished, polished, refined, tasteful; luxurious, opulent, sumptuous
con crude, rough, rude, uncouth; grotesque

element *n* 1 *syn* see ESSENTIAL 1
2 one of the parts, substances, or principles that make up a compound or complex whole < analyzed the various *elements* of the problem >
syn component, constituent, factor, ingredient; *compare* POINT 1
rel fundamental, principle; item, member, part, particle, piece, portion; detail, particular; aspect, facet, feature, view
con bulk, mass, volume; entirety, whole; sum, total, totality
ant composite, compound
3 **elements** *pl syn* see ALPHABET 2
rel basics, basis, foundations, groundwork; outlines
4 *syn* see POINT 1

rel division, member, section, sector, segment

elemental *adj* 1 of, relating to, or being an ultimate and irreducible element < such *elemental* aspects of life as sex and nutrition >
syn basic, elementary, essential, fundamental, primitive, substratal, underlying
rel primary, prime, primordial; inherent, intrinsic, radical
con secondary, subordinate; casual, incidental, trivial, unimportant
2 *syn* see ELEMENTARY 1
3 *syn* see INHERENT

elementary *adj* 1 of, relating to, or dealing with the simplest principles of something < can't handle the most *elementary* decision-making >
syn basal, beginning, elemental, rudimental, rudimentary, simplest
rel introductory, prefatory, preliminary; easy, simple; rude, unsubtle
con complex, complicated, elaborate, intricate, labyrinthine; sophisticated
ant advanced
2 *syn* see ELEMENTAL 1

elephantine *adj* 1 *syn* see HUGE
con slender, slight, slim, thin; dainty
2 *syn* see PONDEROUS 2
rel awkward, clumsy, graceless, maladroit, ungraceful
con graceful, nimble, quick

elevate *vb* 1 *syn* see LIFT 1
rel ensky, erect
con cut (down), deflate, depress, scale (down)
ant lower
2 *syn* see ADVANCE 2
rel boost; enhance, glorify, heighten
con demote, downgrade, lower, reduce; abase, debase, degrade

elevated *adj* 1 being positioned above a surface < an *elevated* monorail >
syn lifted, raised, upheaved, uplifted, upraised, uprisen
rel high; aerial
con ground-level, low, lowered, low-lying, unelevated
ant sunken
2 being on a high moral or intellectual plane < *elevated* ideas >
syn high-minded, moral, noble
rel ethical, honorable, righteous, upright, upstanding, virtuous
con base, ignoble, mean; immoral, low, unethical; intolerable, unacceptable
3 *syn* see GRAND 3
4 being exceedingly dignified in form, tone, or style < an *elevated* prose style >
syn eloquent, high, lofty
rel dignified, formal; grand, grandiloquent, grandiose, high-flown, majestic, stately, towering
con informal; lowly, unassuming

elevation *n* 1 *syn* see HEIGHT
rel acclivity, ascent, rise
con depression, descent; flatness, levelness
2 *syn* see ADVANCEMENT 1
rel advance, boost, raise; ennoblement, exaltation, glorification, lionization; apotheosis, deification, immortalization, magnification
con downgrading; depreciation, detraction, disparagement

---

ant degradation

elf *n syn* see FAIRY

elicit *vb syn* see EDUCE 1
rel bring, fetch
con eschew, forego; abandon

elide *vb syn* see NEGLECT

eligible *adj* qualified to be or worthy of being chosen < an *eligible* bachelor >
syn fit, suitable
rel acceptable, desirable, likely, preferable, seemly; capable, fitted, qualified, suited, worthy; marriageable, nubile; visitable
con undesirable; disqualified, unfit, unqualified, unsuitable, unworthy
ant ineligible

eliminate *vb* 1 *syn* see EXCLUDE
rel freeze out, shut out; dismiss, ∥dump, eject, evict, expel, oust; delete, erase, expunge
con accept, receive
2 *syn* see REMOVE 4
3 *syn* see PURGE 3

elite *n* 1 *syn* see BEST
rel elect, pink, select; ∥hoi polloi
idiom cream of the crop, crème de la crème, pick of the bunch
2 *syn* see ARISTOCRACY
rel drawing rooms; Four Hundred; beautiful people, jet set, smart set
idiom high society, horsey set
con hoi polloi, (the) masses, mob, peasantry, people, proletariat, rabble

elixir *n syn* see PANACEA
rel balm, cure, therapy, therapeutic

ell *n syn* see ANNEX

elocution *n syn* see ORATORY

elongate *vb syn* see EXTEND 3
rel drag (out); string
con contract, draw in; compress; curtail, retrench; shrink
ant abbreviate, shorten

elongate *adj syn* see LONG 1
rel lengthened
ant abbreviated, shortened

elongated *adj syn* see LONG 1
rel drawn (out), lengthened, prolonged, prolonged, protracted, stretched
con contracted, drawn (in), shrunken
ant shortened

elongation *n syn* see EXTENSION 1

elope *vb* to go away usually with the intention of marrying < decided to *elope* rather than endure a big wedding >
syn run away
idiom go to Gretna Green

eloquence *n* discourse marked by force and persuasiveness suggesting strong feeling < read the poem with *eloquence* >
syn expression, expressiveness, expressivity, facundity
rel meaningfulness, persuasiveness; fervor, force, forcefulness, passion, power, spirit, vigor

eloquent *adj* 1 *syn* see VOCAL 3
rel forceful, potent, powerful; ardent, fervent, fervid, impassioned, passionate; glib, silver-tongued, voluble
con inarticulate, ineffective, weak
2 *syn* see EXPRESSIVE
rel graphic, indicative, revealing, suggestive, telling; affecting, impressive, moving, poignant, touching

3 *syn* see ELEVATED 4

else *adv syn* see OTHERWISE 2

else *adj syn* see ADDITIONAL

∥**elseways** *adv syn* see OTHERWISE 2

elsewise *adv syn* see OTHERWISE 2

elucidate *vb syn* see CLARIFY 2
rel exemplify; demonstrate, prove; annotate, spell out; enlighten
con confuse; darken

elude *vb syn* see ESCAPE 2
rel baffle, circumvent, foil, frustrate, outwit, thwart; flee, fly
idiom give the slip
con accost; face; chase, follow, pursue, tag, tail, trail

elusion *n syn* see ESCAPE 2

elusive *adj* not easily perceived, grasped, comprehended, pinned down, or isolated < inspiration need not be forever *elusive* > < they finally isolated the *elusive* virus that caused the disease >
syn elusory, evasive, intangible
rel evanescent, fleeting, fugitive; baffling, imponderable, incomprehensible, mysterious; insubstantial, phantom

elusory *adj syn* see ELUSIVE
rel nebulous, vague

elvish *adj syn* see PLAYFUL 1

elysium *n syn* see HEAVEN 2

emaciated *adj* being very lean through loss of flesh (as from hunger or disease) < *emaciated* bony hands clutched at him >
syn cadaverous, gaunt, skeletal, wasted
rel bony, lean, scrawny, skinny, wizened; starved, underfed, undernourished
idiom all skin and bones, thin as a rail
con fit, husky, solid, well-fed, well-nourished; chubby, plump, portly, rotund, stocky, stout; corpulent, obese
ant fleshy

emanate *vb syn* see SPRING 1
rel initiate; emit, exude, radiate

emancipate *vb syn* see FREE
ant enslave

emasculate *vb syn* see UNNERVE
rel debilitate, devitalize
con energize, vitalize

emasculate *adj syn* see WEAK 4

embark *vb syn* see BOARD 1

embark (on *or* upon) *vb syn* see BEGIN 1

embarrass *vb* to throw into a state of self-conscious distress < bawdy stories *embarrassed* her >
syn abash, confound, confuse, discomfit, disconcert, discountenance, faze, rattle; *compare* DISCOMPOSE 1
rel agitate, bother, discompose, flurry, fluster, perturb; nonplus; chagrin, distress, vex; queer
idiom put on the spot, put to the blush
con calm, relieve, soothe

embarrassing *adj syn* see INCONVENIENT

embarrassment *n* the quality, state, or condition of being embarrassed < felt great *embarrassment* when she fell down >
syn abashment, confusion, discomfiture, discomposure, disconcertion, disconcertment, unease, uneasiness
rel constraint, stain; agitation, discombobulation, perturbation; chagrin, distress, vexation; humiliation, mortification; difficulty, Queer Street

con assurance, calm, imperturbability, savoir faire

embed *vb syn* see ENTRENCH 1

embellish *vb* 1 *syn* see ADORN
rel apparel, array, ‖doll up, dress up, emblaze, embroider, enrich, furbish
con bare, denude, divest, strip
2 *syn* see EMBROIDER

embellishment *n syn* see EXAGGERATION
rel floridity, ostentation

embezzle *vb* to appropriate dishonestly and fraudulently to one's own use < *embezzled* a trust fund >
syn misappropriate, peculate
rel loot, pilfer, steal, thieve

embitter *vb syn* see EXACERBATE
rel bitter, sour

emblem *n* 1 *syn* see SYMBOL 1
2 *syn* see INSIGNIA

emblematize *vb syn* see REPRESENT 2

embodiment *n* a concrete or actual entity in which something (as an idea, principle, or type) is embodied < he is the *embodiment* of all our hopes >
syn incarnation, personification; *compare* APOTHEOSIS 1
rel manifestation; prosopopoeia; archetype; apotheosis, epitome, quintessence

embody *vb* 1 to make an abstraction concrete or perceptible often by representation in human or animal form < Dickens *embodied* hypocrisy in his Uriah Heep >
syn exteriorize, externalize, incarnate, manifest, materialize, objectify, personalize, personify, personize, substantiate; *compare* REPRESENT 2
rel actualize, hypostatize, realize, reify, symbolize, typify; demonstrate, evince, exemplify, exhibit, illustrate, show (forth)
ant disembody
2 to cause to become a body or part of another body < *embodied* a revenue provision in the new law >
syn combine, incorporate, integrate
rel absorb, amalgamate, assimilate, blend, consolidate, fuse, merge, unify
3 *syn* see INCLUDE
rel compose, consist (of), constitute
4 *syn* see REPRESENT 2

embog *vb syn* see DELAY 1

embolden *vb syn* see ENCOURAGE 1
rel impel; inspire; chance, hazard, venture
con deter, discourage
ant abash

embouchement *n syn* see MOUTH 5

embouchure *n syn* see MOUTH 5

embowel *vb syn* see EVISCERATE

embrace *vb* 1 to gather into one's arms usually as a gesture of affection < *embraced* his wife >
syn clasp, ‖clinch, ‖clip, ‖coll, enfold, hug, press, squeeze
rel cling, grip, hold; encircle, entwine, envelop, enwind, fold, lock, twine, wrap; cuddle, fondle, nuzzle, snuggle; cradle, hold
idiom ‖go into a clinch

2 *syn* see ADOPT
rel accept, accommodate, admit, incorporate, receive, take (over), take in; seize (upon), welcome
con reject; abjure, deny, forswear, renounce
ant spurn
3 *syn* see INCLUDE
rel compose, cover, enclose, hold

embracement *n syn* see ESPOUSAL 4

embracing *n syn* see ESPOUSAL 4

embrangle *vb syn* see ENTANGLE 3

embroider *vb* to give an elaborate account of, often with florid language and fictitious details < *embroidered* the story of his adventures in the army >
syn color, embellish, exaggerate, fudge, magnify, overcharge, overdraw, overpaint, overstate, pad, stretch
rel aggrandize, amplify, build up, distend, elaborate, enhance, enlarge (upon), expand; dramatize, hyperbolize, overdo, overelaborate, overembellish, overemphasize, overestimate
idiom lay it on thick, stretch (or strain) the truth
con deemphasize, minimize, play (down), underestimate, understate

embroidering *n syn* see EXAGGERATION

embroil *vb syn* see INVOLVE 1

embroilment *n* 1 *syn* see QUARREL
2 *syn* see ENTANGLEMENT 1

embryo *n syn* see SEED 2

emend *vb syn* see CORRECT 1
rel alter, edit, emendate; polish, retouch

emerge *vb syn* see APPEAR 1
rel derive, originate, spring, stem; arise, materialize, rise; come (forth), come out, emanate, flow, issue (forth); proceed
idiom appear on the horizon, come on the scene, come out in the open, come to light, make its appearance
con disappear, fade, fade (out); evaporate, dissolve

emergency *n syn* see JUNCTURE 2
rel difficulty, extremity; clutch, fix, hole, pinch, push, squeeze, vicissitude; climax
idiom turn of events

emigrant *n* one that leaves one place to settle in another < a city teeming with *emigrants* from many lands >
syn immigrant, migrant
rel alien, displaced person, DP, émigré, evacuee, exile, expatriate, fugitive, refugee; migrator, migratory
con aborigine, native

emigrate *vb syn* see MIGRATE

émigré *n* 1 a person forced to immigrate usually for political reasons < a city filled with White Russian *émigrés* >
syn exile, expatriate, expellee
rel emigrant, immigrant; alien, displaced person, DP, evacuee, fugitive, refugee
2 *syn* see REFUGEE

eminence *n* 1 a condition, position, or state of great importance or superiority < the *eminence* of the presidency >
syn distinction, illustriousness, kudos, preeminence, prestige, prominence, prominency, renown
rel greatness, loftiness, prepotency, significance, superiority; authority, credit, dignity, importance, influence, power, weight;

---

syn synonym(s)   *rel* related word(s)
ant antonym(s)   *con* contrasted word(s)
idiom idiomatic equivalent(s)
‖ use limited; if in doubt, see a dictionary

fame, famousness, glory, honor, reputation, repute
con insignificance, unimportance; obscurity
2 *syn* see NOTABLE 1
3 a natural elevation < the house stood on an *eminence* overlooking the river >
syn projection, prominence
rel peak, raise, rise, uprise; altitude, elevation, height; highness, loftiness
con cavity, depression, dip
eminency *n syn* see FORTE
eminent *adj syn* see FAMOUS 2
rel well-known; august, dominant, exalted, important, lofty, noble, preeminent; big league, big-name, big-time
con uncelebrated, unremarkable, unrenowned; common, lowly
eminently *adv syn* see VERY 1
emissary *n syn* see MESSENGER
emit *vb* **1** *syn* see DISCHARGE 5
2 to discharge something such as moisture, vapor, or fumes < a smokestack *emitting* effluents >
syn give off, give out, issue, release, throw off, vent
rel discharge, evacuate, expel; let out, loose, pass (off); pour (out), reek; drip, emanate, excrete, extrude, exude, ooze, secrete; exhale, expire
emolument *n syn* see WAGE
rel guerdon
emote *vb* to give expression to emotion especially on or as if on the stage < she *emotes*, postures, and harangues at the slightest provocation >
syn emotionalize
rel gush, sentimentalize; carry on, rage, rant, storm, take on
emotion *n syn* see FEELING 3
rel excitability, responsiveness, sensibility, sensitiveness, sensitivity, susceptibilities; sensation
con coldness, detachment, reserve, unfeelingness
emotionable *adj syn* see EMOTIONAL 1
emotional *adj* **1** dominated by, prone to, or moved by emotion < an irritable *emotional* woman who was easily upset by trivialities >
syn emotionable, feeling, sensitive, sentient
rel responsive, susceptible, susceptive; softhearted, sympathetic; ardent, fervent, passionate; rhapsodic, rhapsodical
con cold, detached, insensitive, reserved, taciturn, unfeeling
ant emotionless, unemotional
2 appealing to or arousing emotion < an *emotional* sermon >
syn affective, emotive, moving; *compare* MOVING 2
rel affecting, stirring, touching
emotionalize *vb syn* see EMOTE
emotionless *adj* **1** *syn* see COLD 2
rel nonemotional, undemonstrative; cool, dispassionate, distant, immovable, impassive, remote, reserved; heartless, unfeeling
con emotional; softhearted, sympathetic; ardent, fervent, passionate
ant emotional
2 *syn* see MATTER-OF-FACT 3
emotive *adj syn* see EMOTIONAL 2

empathy *n syn* see SYMPATHY 2
rel accord, affinity, communion, compatibility, concord, congeniality, fellow feeling, rapport, responsiveness, warmth; appreciation, comprehension, understanding
idiom community of interests
con animosity, animus, antagonism, antipathy, enmity
emphasis *n* force brought to bear on something to bring out what is important < the school's *emphasis* on discipline >
syn accent, accentuation, stress
rel attention; force, insistence; weight
emphasize *vb* to give more emphasis to especially by displaying more or less prominently < the papers *emphasized* crime stories >
syn feature, italicize, play (up), stress, underline, underscore
rel accent, accentuate, charge, highlight, mark, pinpoint, point (up), punctuate, spotlight; assert, press
idiom bear down on (or upon)
con depreciate, minimize, play (down), shrug off, underrate, understate
ant de-emphasize
emphatic *adj* marked by, uttered with, or made prominent by stress or emphasis < made his point in an *emphatic* argument >
syn assertive, forceful, insistent, resounding
rel aggressive, energetic, insistive, vigorous; accented, accentuated, assertative, decided, emphasized, marked, pointed, stressed, underlined
con insipid, milk-and-water, unaggressive, unassertive, weak, wishy-washy; de-emphasized, played (down), understated
ant unemphatic
empirical *adj* originating in, relying on, or based on factual information, observation, or direct sense experience < an *empirical* basis for an ethical theory >
syn experient, experiential, experimental
rel observational; factual
con conjectural, speculative, unproved, unsubstantiated; ideal, imagined
ant theoretical
employ *vb* **1** *syn* see USE 2
rel avail, exert, practice, work; devote, engross, monopolize
2 to provide with a job that pays wages < *employed* a new draftsman >
syn engage, hire, put on, take on
rel add, contract (for); obtain, procure, retain, secure, sign (on or up)
employable *adj syn* see OPEN 5
employed *adj syn* see BUSY 1
employment *n* **1** *syn* see USE 1
rel purpose; disposition, exercise, exploitation, handling, utilization
2 *syn* see EXERCISE 1
3 *syn* see WORK 1
rel assignment, mission; office, position, post, situation; function
4 the act of employing for wages < handled the *employment* of new workers >
syn engagement, engaging, hiring
rel enlistment, enrollment, recruitment, signing on
empower *vb* **1** *syn* see INVEST 2

2 *syn* see AUTHORIZE 1

3 *syn* see ENABLE 2

rel endow, invest; authorize, charge, commission, entitle, entrust, license, privilege, sanction

con debar, disallow, disbar, exclude, rule out, shut out

emprise *n syn* see ADVENTURE

emptiness *n syn* see VACUITY 2

emptor *n syn* see PURCHASER

empty *adj* 1 lacking contents that could or should be present <an *empty* apartment> <the whole book is *empty* of meaning>

syn bare, clear, stark, vacant, vacuous, void

rel barren, blank; abandoned, deserted, emptied, forsaken, godforsaken, unfilled, unfurnished uninhabited, untenanted, vacated; destitute, devoid; depleted, drained, exhausted

con complete, replete; filled, occupied, packed, teeming

ant full

2 *syn* see VAIN 1

rel paltry, petty, trifling, trivial; banal, flat, inane, ineffectual, insipid, jejune, vapid; dumb, fatuous, foolish, ignorant, silly, simple

con meaningful, pregnant, significant; authentic, bona fide, genuine, veritable

3 *syn* see EXPRESSIONLESS

4 *syn* see DEVOID

empty *vb syn* see VACATE 2

empty–headed *adj* 1 *syn* see GIDDY 1

rel brainless, rattleheaded; ignorant, simple

2 *syn* see VACUOUS 2

3 *syn* see IGNORANT 1

empyreal *adj syn* see CELESTIAL

rel aerial, airy; extraterrestrial; divine, holy, spiritual, sublime

ant terrestrial

empyrean *adj syn* see CELESTIAL

empyrean *n* 1 *syn* see HEAVEN 2

2 *syn* see SKY

emulate *vb syn* see RIVAL 2

rel challenge, outvie

emulation *n syn* see CONTEST 1

emulative *adj syn* see SLAVISH 3

emulous *adj syn* see AMBITIOUS 1

rel aiming, striving; agog, athirst; competitive, vying

con unambitious, unaspiring; detached, disinterested, uninterested

enable *vb* 1 *syn* see AUTHORIZE 1

rel allow, let, permit, sanction

2 to render able often by giving power, strength, or competence to <his education *enabled* him to find an excellent job>

syn empower

rel allow, let, permit; condition, fit, prepare, qualify, ready

con inhibit, preclude, prevent; disallow, enjoin, forbid, prohibit

enact *vb* 1 to cause to be by legal and authoritative act <*enact* a law>

---

syn constitute, establish, make

rel bring about, institute; authorize, decree, proclaim; accomplish, carry (through), effect, effectuate, execute, legislate, pass, put (through), ratify

con abolish, abrogate, annul, cancel, invalidate, nullify, rescind, revoke; overturn

ant repeal

2 *syn* see ACT 1

rel depict, portray, represent

enamored *adj* 1 moved by intense sexual attraction <became more desperately *enamored* of the man every day>

syn mashed, smitten, soft (on), spoony (over *or* on)

rel infatuated; crazy (over *or* about), mad (about), nuts (about), silly (over *or* about), wild (about); amorous, devoted, loving

idiom head over heels in love, stuck on, sweet on

2 *syn* see INFATUATED

3 taking great pleasure in something <found herself *enamored* of those huge English teas>

syn bewitched, captivated, charmed, enchanted, entranced, fascinated

rel fond

encamp *vb syn* see CAMP

encampment *n syn* see CAMP 1

enceinte *adj syn* see PREGNANT 1

enchant *vb* 1 *syn* see BEWITCH 1

2 *syn* see ATTRACT 1

rel delight, enthrall, please, send, thrill; mesmerize

idiom carry away, knock dead

con disillusion, dissatisfy, let down

ant disenchant

enchanted *adj syn* see ENAMORED 3

rel delighted, pleased; pixilated

ant disenchanted

enchanter *n syn* see MAGICIAN 1

enchanting *adj syn* see ATTRACTIVE 1

rel attractive, pleasing; delectable, delightful; beguiling, enthralling, entrancing, intriguing, witching; exciting, sirenic

con repellent

enchantment *n syn* see MAGIC 1

enchantress *n syn* see WITCH 1

enchiridion *n syn* see HANDBOOK

rel book, text

encincture *vb syn* see BELT 1

encircle *vb syn* see SURROUND 1

rel band, cincture, circuit, enring; halo, wreathe

enclose *vb* 1 to shut up or confine by or as if by barriers <a valley *enclosed* by mountains>

syn cage, close in, coop, corral, envelop, fence, hedge, hem, immure, mew, mure, pen, shut in, wall

rel bound, circumscribe, confine, contain, limit, restrict; circle, compass, encircle, encompass, surround; environ; enlock

2 *syn* see ENFOLD 1

enclosure *n syn* see COURT 1

enclothe *vb syn* see CLOTHE

encomiastic *adj syn* see EULOGISTIC

encomium *n* a formal expression of praise <an unstinted *encomium* of a national hero>

syn citation, eulogy, panegyric, salutation, tribute

rel approval, kudos, laud, laudation, magnification, praise; acclaim, acclama-

---

tion, applause, plaudits; accolade, commendation, compliment

con abuse, invective, obloquy, vituperation; criticism, critique, faultfinding

encompass *vb* 1 *syn* see SURROUND 1

rel bound, delimit

2 *syn* see INCLUDE

encounter *vb* 1 *syn* see CONFRONT 1

rel clash, collide, conflict

2 *syn* see ENGAGE 5

3 *syn* see MEET 6

rel ‖bump (into), come (across), run (across), run (into)

idiom cross the path of, fall in with, meet up with

con miss, pass (by)

4 *syn* see FIND 1

encounter *n* a sudden, hostile, and usually brief confrontation or dispute between factions or persons <a sharp courtroom *encounter* between opposing lawyers>

syn brush, run-in, set-to, skirmish, velitation

rel conflict, contest; scrap; fray, fight; battle; argument, contention, quarrel

encourage *vb* 1 to fill with courage or strength of purpose especially in preparation for a hard task <the teacher's praise *encouraged* the student to try harder>

syn animate, cheer, chirk (up), embolden, enhearten, hearten, inspirit, nerve, ‖pearten (up), steel, strengthen; *compare* SUPPORT 5

rel assure, reassure; boost, excite, galvanize, pique, provoke, quicken, stimulate; buck up, buoy (up), energize, fortify, invigorate; rally, stir

idiom give a shot in the arm

con deject, depress, discourage, dishearten, dispirit; affright, caution, frighten

ant discourage

2 to give the support of one's approval to <the government openly *encouraged* East-West détente>

syn advocate, countenance, favor

rel approve, back, endorse, go (for), sanction, subscribe (to); abet, assist, reinforce, support, sustain; incite, instigate; induce, prevail

idiom lend one's countenance to, lend one's favor (or support) to, smile upon

con deter, dissuade, divert, hinder; inhibit, restrain; disapprove

ant discourage

3 *syn* see ADVANCE 1

rel patronize, push, support; develop, improve, subsidize

con weaken; check, retard, slow

ant discourage

encouraging *adj syn* see HOPEFUL 2

encroach *vb syn* see TRESPASS 2

rel barge (in), ‖bust (in), butt (in), chisel (in), horn (in), muscle (in), worm (in); interfere, interpose, intervene, meddle; overstep

idiom foist oneself upon, stick one's nose in (or into)

con ignore, let (alone), pass over; avoid

encrust (or **incrust**) *vb syn* see CAKE 1

encumber *vb syn* see BURDEN

rel freight; discommode, incommode, inconvenience; fetter, hamper, handicap; block, impede, obstruct; oppress, overburden

encumbrance *n* something that impedes and makes action difficult <told his story simply without the *encumbrance* of unnecessary details>

syn clog, cumbrance, hindrance, impedance, impediment

rel disadvantage, handicap, load; difficulty, hardship, inconvenience

con aid; catalyst, impetus, stimulus

ant assist, assistance

encyclopedic *adj* embracing, comprehensively treating, or informed in a wide range of subjects <an *encyclopedic* article on world history>

syn comprehensive, inclusive

rel all-comprehensive, all-embracing, all-inclusive, complete; extensive, general; discursive

end *n* 1 *syn* see LIMIT 1

rel borderline, tip; extreme, extremity

con center, hub, middle

2 ceasing of a course (as of action or activity) or the point at which something ceases <the *end* of the war>

syn cease, cessation, close, closing, closure, conclusion, desistance, desuetude, discontinuance, discontinuation, ending, finish, period, stop, termination, terminus; *compare* FINALE

rel consummation, culmination; expiration; coda, curtains, finale, finality, finis, terminal, windup

idiom cutoff point, end of the line, stopping point

con genesis, inception

ant beginning

3 *syn* see FINALE

4 something residual <melted down candle *ends*>

syn bit, fragment, scrap

rel butt end, fag end, leaving, remainder, remnant, residue; part, particle, piece

end *vb syn* see CLOSE 3

ant begin

endable *adj syn* see TERMINABLE

endanger *vb* to bring into peril (as of harm or disaster) <conspirators who were *endangering* the cause of freedom>

syn compromise, hazard, imperil, jeopard, jeopardize, jeopardy, menace, peril, risk

rel expose, lay (open); chance, venture

con guard, protect, shelter, shield; preserve, save

endeavor *vb syn* see TRY 5

rel determine, intend, purpose; address, apply, bid (for), drive (at), go (for); strain

endeavor *n syn* see ATTEMPT

rel exertion, push; labor, toil, travail, work

ended *adj syn* see COMPLETE 4

endemic *adj syn* see NATIVE 2

rel home-bred, native-born

con pandemic; extraneous, extrinsic

ant exotic

ending *n* 1 *syn* see END 2

ant beginning

2 *syn* see FINALE

endless *adj* 1 *syn* see LIMITLESS

2 *syn* see EVERLASTING 1

rel constant, continuous; deathless, immortal, undying; boundless, limitless, unbounded, unlimited; self-perpetuating

3 *syn* see CONTINUAL

rel overlong

endorse *vb syn* see APPROVE 2
  rel attest, authenticate, pass (on *or* upon), vouch, witness; command, recommend; advocate, back (up), champion, stand by, support, uphold
  con deprecate, disapprove; anathematize, denounce

endorsement *n syn* see SANCTION

endow *vb* **1** to furnish or provide with a gift, talent, or good quality < poets *endowed* with genius >
  syn crown (with), dower, endue
  rel bestow, confer; accord, award, grant; empower, enable; enhance, enrich, heighten
  con bare, denude, divest, strip; despoil, ravage, spoliate; deplete, drain, exhaust
  2 to furnish (as an institution) with a store of capital < *endowed* a hospital >
  syn finance, fund, subsidize
  rel found, organize; bequeath, contribute, donate, subscribe, support; award, grant; back, promote, sponsor; provide, supply
  con beggar, impoverish, pauperize; drain, draw (on)

end product *n syn* see EFFECT 1

endue *vb syn* see ENDOW 1
  rel clothe, invest, vest; accouter, equip, furnish

endurable *adj syn* see BEARABLE

endurance *n* **1** *syn* see CONTINUATION 1
  2 *syn* see TOLERANCE 1

endure *vb* **1** *syn* see CONTINUE 1
  rel bide, linger
  con crumble, decay, disintegrate; collapse, fall
  ant perish
  2 *syn* see ACCEPT 2
  rel stand, submit (to), suffer, sustain; undergo
  con break, collapse, give in, resign
  3 *syn* see BEAR 10

enduring *adj* **1** *syn* see LASTING
  ant fleeting
  2 *syn* see OLD 2
  3 *syn* see SURE 2
  rel durable, resolute, solid, sound, stable, staunch, sturdy, substantial
  con capricious, changeable, fickle, inconstant, mercurial, unstable, variable

endways *adv syn* see LENGTHWISE

endwise *adv syn* see LENGTHWISE

enemy *n* an individual or group that is hostile toward another < the senator was blackmailed by a political *enemy* >
  syn foe
  rel adversary, antagonist, opponent; assailant, attacker, combatant, invader; competitor, contender, emulator, rival
  con benefactor, friend, supporter; ally, collaborator, colleague, confederate, friendly; adherent, follower, partisan, upholder

energetic *adj* **1** *syn* see VIGOROUS
  rel aggressive, emphatic, vibrant; indefatigable
  con easygoing; faineant, idle, languorous, lethargic

  2 disposed to or having a capacity for action < an *energetic* campaign worker >
  syn active, driving, enterprising, lively
  rel animated, breezy, brisk, fresh, kinetic, peppy, spirited, sprightly, spry, vivacious, zippy
  idiom full of go (*or* life *or* pep *or* zip)
  con apathetic, inert; lethargic, limp, listless, passive, phlegmatic, spiritless, spunkless
  ant inactive

energetically *adv syn* see HARD 1
  rel firmly, strenuously; busily, industriously, zealously
  idiom at full tilt
  con idly, lazily, lethargically, listlessly; slowly
  ant unenergetically

energize *vb* **1** *syn* see VITALIZE
  idiom put pep (*or* zip) into
  con emasculate, enervate; debilitate, enfeeble
  2 *syn* see STRENGTHEN 2
  rel arm, empower, enable; build (up), sustain
  con daunt

energy *n* **1** *syn* see POWER 4
  rel activity, operativeness; forcefulness, mightiness, powerfulness
  con impotence; decrepitude, feebleness, weakness; powerlessness
  ant inertia
  2 vigorous and effectual application and operation of power < work with *energy* >
  syn birr, go, hardihood, ‖moxie, pep, potency, tuck, vigor; *compare* VIGOR 2
  rel application, effectiveness, efficacy; effort, operativeness; toughness
  con kef, languor, lethargy, listlessness, sluggishness; ergophobia

enervate *vb syn* see UNNERVE
  rel debilitate, devitalize, disable; exhaust, fatigue, jade, tire, weary
  con activate, energize, vitalize; galvanize, quicken, stimulate

enervated *adj syn* see LANGUID
  rel debilitated, devitalized, enfeebled, undermined, weakened; exhausted, fatigued, run-down, tired, weary; decadent, degenerate, degenerated, deteriorated
  con active, animated, energetic, lusty, strenuous, vigorous, vital; strong, sturdy, tenacious, tough

enfant terrible *n syn* see SCAMP

enfeeble *vb syn* see WEAKEN 1
  rel devitalize, exhaust
  con galvanize; harden, strengthen
  ant fortify

enfold *vb* **1** to surround or cover closely < a heavy fog *enfolded* the ships >
  syn enclose, enshroud, envelop, enwrap, invest, shroud, veil, wrap; *compare* SWATHE
  rel cover, drape; encase, ensheathe; encircle, encompass, environ, gird, girdle, surround
  2 *syn* see EMBRACE 1

enforce *vb* to put something into effect or operation < *enforce* a law >
  syn effect, implement, invoke
  rel accomplish, administer, carry (out *or* through), discharge, execute, fulfill, perform; compel, force, oblige

---

syn synonym(s)   *rel* related word(s)
ant antonym(s)   *con* contrasted word(s)
idiom idiomatic equivalent(s)
‖ use limited; if in doubt, see a dictionary

con disregard, forget, ignore, neglect; relax

enfranchise *vb* to admit to full political rights as a freeman or citizen < slaves were emancipated in 1863 but were not *enfranchised* until the fifteenth amendment went into effect in 1870 >
syn affranchise, franchise
rel emancipate, free, liberate, release; deliver, extricate, rescue
con enslave, oppress, subject
ant disenfranchise, disfranchise

engage *vb* 1 to come into contact and interlock with < the teeth of one gear wheel *engaging* those of another >
syn intermesh, mesh
rel interact, interlace, interlock, interplay
con free, release
ant disengage
2 *syn* see PROMISE 1
rel commit; bind, tie; affiance, betroth, troth
3 *syn* see EMPLOY 2
con dismiss, eject, fire
ant discharge
4 to hold the attention of < the puzzle *engaged* him all evening >
syn busy, engross, immerse, occupy, soak
rel absorb, imbue, involve; arrest, captivate, enthrall, fascinate, grip; monopolize, preengage, preoccupy
5 to enter into contest or conflict with < ordered to seek out and *engage* the enemy fleet >
syn encounter, face, meet, take on
rel assault, attack, strike; battle, fight
idiom do battle with, join battle with
con elude, escape, evade

engaged *adj* 1 *syn* see BUSY 1
ant unengaged
2 pledged in marriage < the *engaged* couple made a charming pair >
syn affianced, betrothed, contracted, intended, plighted, ‖promised
rel committed, pledged
con free, uncommitted, unpledged
ant unengaged
3 *syn* see INTENT

engagement *n* 1 *syn* see PROMISE
2 the act or state of being engaged to be married < the couple recently announced their *engagement* >
syn betrothal, betrothing, betrothment, espousal, troth
rel pledge, plight, promise
ant disengagement
3 a promise to be in an agreed place at a specified time, usually for a particular purpose < had an *engagement* with him for nine that evening >
syn appointment, assignation, date, rendezvous, tryst
rel arrangement, invitation; interview, get-together, meeting, visit
4 *syn* see EMPLOYMENT 4
5 *syn* see BATTLE

engaging *adj* 1 *syn* see ATTRACTIVE 1
2 *syn* see SWEET 1
rel alluring, appealing, attractive, captivating, charming, enchanting, entrancing, fetching; fascinating, interesting, intriguing
con repellent, repelling, repulsive; unappealing, unattractive, uninteresting

ant loathsome

engaging *n* *syn* see EMPLOYMENT 4

engender *vb* *syn* see GENERATE 3
rel develop; excite, stimulate; arouse, quicken, rouse, stir

engineer *vb* to contrive or plan out usually with subtle skill or craft < *engineered* an agreement between the two rival governments >
syn finagle, machinate, maneuver, wangle; *compare* MANIPULATE 2
rel arrange, contrive, devise, mastermind, plan (out), set up; intrigue, plot, scheme; manage, manipulate, negotiate; put (over), put (through), swing
idiom pull strings (*or* wires)

engird *vb* *syn* see BELT 1

engirdle *vb* *syn* see BELT 1

englut *vb* *syn* see GULP

engrave *vb* 1 to cut into a surface usually with a graving tool in order to form an inscription or a pictorial illustration < *engraved* a banknote design on the copper plate >
syn etch, grave, incise
rel chase, enchase; carve; inscribe
2 to impress deeply < the incident was *engraved* in his memory >
syn etch, impress, imprint, inscribe
rel carve; fix; instill; print; embed, entrench, infix, ingrain, root

engross *vb* 1 *syn* see WRITE
2 *syn* see MONOPOLIZE
rel apply, fill, occupy, preoccupy; assimilate, take up; arrest, engage, grip, ‖hog, hold, immerse, involve; attract, captivate, enthrall
con bewilder, distract; disperse, dissipate, scatter
3 *syn* see ENGAGE 4

engrossed *adj* *syn* see INTENT
rel consumed, monopolized, occupied; submerged; assiduous, busy, diligent, industrious, sedulous
idiom caught up in, lost in, taken up with
con detached, disinterested, indifferent, unconcerned, uninterested

engrossing *adj* gripping the attention completely so as to exclude everything else < the *engrossing* nature of his task made the time pass quickly >
syn absorbing, consuming, monopolizing
rel all-consuming, controlling, gripping; interesting, intriguing; exciting, provoking, stimulating; obsessing, preoccupying
con boring, drab, dull, monotonous; unentertaining, unexciting, uninteresting

engulf *vb* *syn* see DELUGE 1

enhance *vb* 1 *syn* see INTENSIFY
rel elevate, lift, raise; enlarge (upon), exaggerate, strengthen; augment, build (up), increase; adorn, beautify, embellish, embroider
con belittle, deprecate, detract, minimize
2 *syn* see FLATTER

enhancement *n* *syn* see ACCOMPANIMENT 1
rel improvement, intensification

enhearten *vb* *syn* see ENCOURAGE 1

enigma *n* *syn* see MYSTERY
rel crux, knot, puzzler, sticker; bewilderment, perplexity, question, question mark

idiom hard nut to crack

enigmatic *adj syn* see CRYPTIC

enisle *vb syn* see ISOLATE

enjewel *vb syn* see BEJEWEL

enjoin *vb* 1 *syn* see COMMAND
rel decree, dictate, impose, prescribe, rule; adjure, advise, counsel; admonish, caution, forewarn
con acquiesce, agree, comply, conform, obey, submit, yield
2 *syn* see FORBID
rel deny, disallow

enjoy *vb* 1 to take pleasure in or receive satisfaction from < *enjoyed* the meal >
syn ‖dig, go, like, ‖mind, relish
rel cotton (to); take (to); appreciate, dote (on *or* upon), fancy, love; delight (in), drink (in), eat up, luxuriate (in), savor
con abhor, abominate, detest, hate, loathe; condemn, despise, scorn
2 *syn* see HAVE 1
rel fill, occupy, maintain; boast, command

enjoyableness *n syn* see AMENITY 1
rel attractiveness, pleasingness, pleasurableness; niceness

enjoyment *n* 1 an attitude, circumstance, or favorable response to a stimulus that tends to make one gratified or happy < gave himself up to vigorous *enjoyment* of his pipe >
syn delectation, diversion, pleasure, relish; *compare* PLEASURE 2
rel delight, joy; amusement, entertainment; indulgence, savor; recreation, relaxation; gratification, satisfaction
con abhorrence, antipathy, aversion; repugnance, repulsion
2 *syn* see PLEASURE 2

enkindle *vb syn* see LIGHT 1

enlarge *vb* 1 *syn* see INCREASE 1
rel add (to), embroider, exaggerate; grow, stretch, widen
con attenuate; abridge; compress
2 *syn* see EXPAND 4
3 *syn* see INCREASE 2

enlargement *n syn* see EXPANSION 2

enlighten *vb syn* see ILLUMINATE 2
rel direct, educate, guide, inform, instruct, school, teach, train; acquaint, advise, apprise, inform
con bewilder, confuse, mystify, perplex, puzzle; addle, fuddle, muddle

enlightening *adj* tending to dissipate ignorance or increase knowledge and awareness < an *enlightening* glimpse of government in action >
syn illuminant, illuminating, illuminative, illumining
rel broadening, edifying, educational, instructive; clarifying, elucidative, explanatory
con unedifying, uninstructive; confusing, obfuscatory, obscuring

enlist *vb syn* see ENTER 3

enliven *vb syn* see QUICKEN 1
rel refresh, rejuvenate, renew, restore; excite, galvanize, invigorate, jazz (up), pep (up); provoke, stimulate; amuse, cheer,

divert, entertain, recreate; exhilarate, fire, inspire
idiom give (new) life to
con depress, oppress, weigh
ant subdue

en masse *adv syn* see ALTOGETHER 3

enmesh *vb syn* see ENTANGLE 3
rel drag (into), draw (in), hook, tangle; embarrass, implicate
idiom make party to
con disembarrass, disentangle
ant extricate

enmeshment *n syn* see ENTANGLEMENT 1

enmity *n* deep-seated dislike or ill will or a manifestation of such feeling < the country had experienced generations of racial *enmity* >
syn animosity, animus, antagonism, antipathy, hostility, rancor
rel uncordiality, unfriendliness; alienation, dead set, disaffection, estrangement; abhorrence, detestation, dislike, hate, hatred, loathing; aversion; bad blood, bitterness, daggers, gall, ill will, malevolence, malice, malignancy, malignity, spite, spleen
con amicability, cordiality, friendliness, neighborliness; comity, empathy, friendship, goodwill, sympathy, understanding
ant amity

ennoble *vb syn* see EXALT 1

ennui *n syn* see TEDIUM
rel blues, dejection, depression, dumps, melancholy, sadness; boredness; fatigue, languidness, languor, listlessness, spiritlessness, tiredness, weariness; satiety, surfeit

ennui *vb syn* see BORE
con enliven, stimulate, vitalize

enormity *n* 1 the quality or state of being abnormally, monstrously, or outrageously evil < the utter *enormity* of the crime >
syn atrociousness, atrocity, heinousness, monstrousness
rel grossness, outrage, outrageousness, rankness; depravity; flagrancy
con excusableness, remissibility, veniality; bearableness, tolerability
2 the quality or state of being huge < the *enormity* of the task confounded him >
syn enormousness, hugeness, immensity, magnitude, tremendousness, vastness
rel bigness, greatness, massiveness; graveness, seriousness, weightiness
con diminutiveness, minuteness, smallness, tininess; triviality, unimportance

enormous *adj syn* see HUGE
rel stupendous
ant tiny

enormousness *n syn* see ENORMITY 2
rel monstrousness, prodigiousness, stupendousness

enough *adj syn* see SUFFICIENT 1

enough *adv* 1 in or to a degree or quantity that satisfies some condition < unstable *enough* to react with water >
syn adequately, sufficiently
rel abundantly, amply; acceptably, admissibly, satisfactorily; commensurately, proportionately
2 in a tolerable degree < she sang well *enough* >

---

syn synonym(s)   *rel* related word(s)
ant antonym(s)   *con* contrasted word(s)
idiom idiomatic equivalent(s)
‖ use limited; if in doubt, see a dictionary

syn averagely, fairly, moderately, passably, rather, so-so, tolerably

rel acceptably, decently, satisfactorily

enough *n* as much as is needed or wanted < we have *enough* for all of our needs >

syn adequacy, competence, sufficiency, sufficient

rel abundance, ampleness, plenty

con inadequateness; deficiency, deficit, lack, shortage, want; outage, ullage, wantage

ant inadequacy, insufficiency

enounce *vb syn* see ENUNCIATE 1

enrage *vb syn* see ANGER 1

idiom make one's blood boil, work up into a passion

ant placate

enrapture *vb syn* see TRANSPORT 2

rel elate, gladden, gratify, please, rejoice; allure, attract, captivate, charm, enchant, enthrall, fascinate

enravish *vb syn* see TRANSPORT 2

enrich *vb* to make financially rich or richer < *enriched* himself through speculation >

syn richen

enrichment *n syn* see ACCOMPANIMENT 1

enroll *vb* 1 to take in (as a person) by entering identification in a list, catalog, or roll < the school *enrolls* about 800 students >

syn list, register

rel enter, insert; catalog, inscribe, record; enlist, line (up), recruit, sign (up); join, matriculate

con discard, omit, reject

2 *syn* see LIST 3

3 *syn* see ENTER 3

ensample *n* 1 *syn* see MODEL 2

2 *syn* see EXAMPLE 3

ensanguined *adj syn* see BLOODY 1

ensconce *vb* 1 *syn* see HIDE

2 to establish or place firmly, comfortably, or snugly < was happily *ensconced* on the sofa before the fire >

syn install, settle

rel establish, fix, locate, place, plant, seat, set, situate, station

ensepulcher *vb syn* see ENTOMB 1

enshroud *vb syn* see ENFOLD 1

rel cloak, conceal, curtain, hide

con disclose, display, illustrate, open (up), reveal, show, uncover, unveil

ensign *n syn* see FLAG

enslave *vb* to reduce to and hold in a state of servitude < free peasants reduced to serfdom or *enslaved* >

syn enthrall, subjugate

rel disenfranchise, disfranchise; subject; oppress, shackle, yoke

con affranchise, enfranchise; free, liberate

ant emancipate

enslavement *n syn* see BONDAGE

ensnare *vb syn* see CATCH 3

rel decoy, entice, inveigle, lure; hook, net, snag; bag, capture

ensnarl *vb* 1 *syn* see ENTANGLE 1

2 *syn* see ENTANGLE 3

ensorcell *vb syn* see BEWITCH 1

ensorcellment *n syn* see MAGIC 1

ensphere *vb syn* see BALL

ensue *vb syn* see FOLLOW 1

rel derive, emanate, issue, proceed, stem; attend, result

idiom be subsequent (to), come next

con antecede, forerun, preface

ensuing *adj* 1 *syn* see SUBSEQUENT 1

2 *syn* see NEXT

ensure *vb* to make something certain or sure < provisions *ensuring* that the rank and file have a voice in union policy-making >

syn assure, cinch, insure, secure

rel certify, guarantee, warrant; arrange, establish, provide, set out

enswathe *vb syn* see SWATHE

entangle *vb* 1 to twist or interweave so as to make separation difficult < *entangled* the yarn >

syn ensnarl, intertangle, perplex, snarl, tangle

rel intertwine, interweave, ||snirl, twist; ball up

2 *syn* see COMPLICATE

3 to catch or hold as if in a net from which escape is difficult < a firm hopelessly *entangled* in financial difficulties >

syn embrangle, enmesh, ensnarl, trammel; *compare* CATCH 3, INVOLVE 1

rel burden, clog, fetter, hamper, impede; bag, capture, catch, ensnare, entrap, snare, trap; discomfit, embarrass, embroil

con extricate, untangle; detach, disengage; clear, free; disburden, unfetter

ant disentangle

4 *syn* see CATCH 3

entanglement *n* 1 the condition of being deeply involved or closely linked often in an embarrassing or compromising way < *entanglements* with underworld figures tarnished his reputation >

syn embroilment, enmeshment, involvement; *compare* WEB 2

rel ensnarement; affair, intrigue, liaison; association, contact

2 *syn* see WEB 2

enter *vb* 1 to come or go into some place or thing < he *entered* the room >

syn come (in), go in, ingress, penetrate

rel pierce, probe

idiom set foot in

con egress, exit, go out, leave; come out, emerge, sally; escape, flee

ant issue

2 to cause or permit to go in or into < *enter* synonyms in a thesaurus >

syn admit, introduce

rel inject, insert, intercalate, interpolate, put (in), set down; docket, inscribe, list, post, record, register; enroll

3 to make or become a member of < decided to *enter* the army >

syn enlist, enroll, join (up), muster, sign on, sign up

rel come (into), go (into)

idiom get oneself into, take up (*or* out) membership (in)

4 *syn* see BEGIN 1

enterprise *n* 1 *syn* see ADVENTURE

rel attempt, effort, endeavor, striving, struggle; campaign, cause, project, pursuit, task, undertaking; deed

2 *syn* see PROJECT 2

rel speculation

3 a unit of economic or business organization or activity < an economy encouraging the expansion of small, privately owned *enterprises* >

syn business, company, concern, establishment, firm, house, outfit
rel interest; organization; corporation; industry
4 readiness to attempt or engage in what requires energy or daring <complained about his brother's lack of *enterprise* >
syn ambition, drive, get-up-and-go, initiative, push; *compare* VIGOR 2
rel ambitiousness, eagerness, energy, enthusiasm, ||hustle, vigor; boldness, courage, daring, venturesomeness; inventiveness, self-reliance
con languor, lethargy; indolence, laziness, sloth; apathy, inertia
enterprising *adj* **1** *syn* see ENERGETIC 2
rel aggressive, ambitious, busy, eager, hustling, pushing, up-and-coming; adventurous, venturesome
2 showing initiative, resolution, and determined effort (as in pursuing a course or a career) <an *enterprising* young man likely to go far>
syn go-ahead, gumptious, up-and-coming
rel aggressive, pushing; diligent, hard-working, industrious, zealous; ambitious, aspiring, craving, hungry, itching, lusting, yearning; audacious, daring, dashing, venturesome
idiom on one's toes
ant unenterprising
entertain *vb* **1** *syn* see HARBOR 2
rel invite; admit, receive; cherish, cultivate, foster; feed, nourish
con banish, eject, throw out; ignore, neglect
2 *syn* see AMUSE
rel delight, enliven, gladden, gratify, please, regale, rejoice
entertainment *n* something diverting, amusing, or entertaining <staged a floor show as *entertainment* for her guests>
syn amusement, dissipation, distraction, diversion, divertissement, recreation
rel disport, play, sport; enjoyment, gaiety, pleasure; relaxation, relief
enthrall *vb* **1** *syn* see ENSLAVE
rel master, subdue
con emancipate
2 to hold spellbound <told mystery stories that *enthralled* his playmates>
syn catch up, fascinate, grip, hold, mesmerize, spellbind
rel absorb, engage, preoccupy; charm, enchant, engross, intrigue
con bore, ennui, weary
enthuse *vb* **1** *syn* see THRILL
2 to show great enthusiasm <tourists *enthusing* over the medieval towns>
syn drool, rave, rhapsodize, rhapsody
con censure, criticize; belittle, depreciate, disparage, dispraise, knock, undervalue
enthusiasm *n* **1** *syn* see PASSION 6
rel craze, fascination, infatuation, mania
con impassivity, phlegm, stolidity; aloofness, detachment, indifference, unconcern
ant apathy
2 *syn* see EAGERNESS

---

rel earnest, interest; ebullience, élan
enthusiast *n* a person who manifests extreme and often uncritical ardor, fervor, or devotion in an attachment <an increasing number of ecology *enthusiasts* >
syn bigot, bug, fanatic, fiend, freak, maniac, nut, zealot
rel addict, aficionado, buff, bum, devotee, fan, habitué, lover, votary; partisan, supporter; bear, extremist
con depreciator, detractor, disparager, knocker
enthusiastic *adj* filled with or marked by enthusiasm <was *enthusiastic* about golf>
syn ||buggy, ||bugs, gung ho, keen, nutty, warm, zealous
rel ardent, devoted, eager, fervent, hearty, spirited; gaga, ||gone (on), hopped-up; hipped, obsessed; passionate, vascular; rabid
con apathetic, detached, indifferent, reluctant, uninterested
ant unenthusiastic
entice *vb* *syn* see LURE
con alarm, fright, frighten (off), terrify
ant scare (off)
enticement *n* *syn* see LURE 2
enticing *adj* being extremely and often dangerously attractive <she looked at him with an *enticing* smile>
syn Circean, fetching, luring, tempting
rel attractive, beguiling, bewitching, enchanting, fascinating, intriguing, inviting, siren, witching; captivating; likable, pleasant, pleasing
entify *vb* *syn* see MATERIALIZE 2
entire *adj* **1** *syn* see WHOLE 3
rel all, gross; plenary
con incomplete, unfinished; limited, qualified
ant partial
2 *syn* see WHOLE 1
rel concatenated, integrated; compacted, consolidated, unified
con broken (up); faulty
ant impaired
3 *syn* see WHOLE 4
entirely *adv* **1** *syn* see WELL 3
2 *syn* see ONLY 1
entireness *n* **1** *syn* see ENTIRETY 1
con incompleteness
2 *syn* see INTEGRITY 2
entirety *n* **1** the state of being complete <the striking *entirety* and self-sufficiency of the feudal community>
syn allness, completeness, entireness, oneness, totality, wholeness
rel collectiveness, unity; integrity, plenitude; comprehensiveness, omneity, universality
con disunity, division, separateness; fragmentation, incompleteness
2 *syn* see WHOLE 1
rel collectivity, complex, everything
con component, detail, element, item, part
ant particular
entitle *vb* **1** *syn* see NAME 1
2 to furnish with proper authority or grounds for seeking or claiming something <this ticket *entitles* the bearer to free admission>

---

syn synonym(s)   *rel* related word(s)
ant antonym(s)   *con* contrasted word(s)
idiom idiomatic equivalent(s)
|| use limited; if in doubt, see a dictionary

syn authorize, qualify
rel empower, license; allow, enable, let, permit

entity *n* 1 one that has real and independent existence <each *entity* of the series requires separate study>
syn being, existence, existent, individual, something, thing
rel body, object
2 *syn* see THING 4
3 *syn* see WHOLE 2

entomb *vb* 1 to deposit in or as if in a tomb <relics *entombed* in pyramids>
syn ensepulcher, sepulcher, sepulture, tomb; *compare* BURY 1
rel bury, inhume, inter, ‖plant; inurn; enshrine, shrine
con dig (up), disinhume, disinter, exhume, unbury
ant disentomb
2 *syn* see BURY 1

entombment *n syn* see BURIAL 2

entourage *n* one's attendants or subordinates <the queen's *entourage*>
syn following, retinue, suite, train
rel associates, attendants, courtiers, followers, retainers; hangers-on, sycophants, toadies

entrails *n pl* the internal organs of the body <some of the *entrails* are valued as food>
syn gut(s), innards, insides, internals, inwards, ‖pudding(s), stuffing, tripes, viscera
rel bowels, intestines; vitals; giblets, pluck, purtenance

entrammel *vb syn* see HAMPER
con assist, expedite, facilitate; extricate

entrance *n* 1 the act or fact of going in or coming in <awaited the *entrance* of the army into the city>
syn entry, ingress, ingression
rel arrival, coming, incoming, ingoing; penetration
con departure, egress, emergence, emerging, emigration, exit
ant egression, exiting
2 *syn* see DOOR 1
rel access, aperture, opening, threshold
ant exit
3 *syn* see DOOR 2
rel open door

entrance *vb syn* see TRANSPORT 2
rel gladden, please, rejoice; attract, bewitch, captivate, charm, enchant, fascinate; enthrall, hypnotize, spellbind
con disappoint, disgust, repel, repulse; bore

entranced *adj syn* see ENAMORED 3

entranceway *n syn* see DOOR 1

entrap *vb* 1 *syn* see CATCH 3
2 *syn* see LURE

entreat *vb syn* see BEG
rel blandish, coax, wheedle; pester, plague, press, urge

entreaty *n syn* see PRAYER

entrée *n syn* see DOOR 2
rel introduction; open door

entrench *vb* 1 to establish so solidly or strongly as to make dislodgment or change extremely difficult <prejudices *entrenched* for generations>
syn embed, fix, infix, ingrain, lodge, root

rel found, ground; implant; confirm, define, establish, settle, strengthen
con eliminate, eradicate, root out, uproot; banish, cast out, eject, expel; remove
ant dislodge
2 *syn* see TRESPASS 2
rel interfere, intervene
idiom break in upon, stick one's nose into

entrenched *adj syn* see INVETERATE 1

entrepreneur *n* 1 one who owns, launches, manages, and assumes the risks of an economic venture <theatrical *entrepreneurs* making fortunes from successful shows>
syn undertaker
rel organizer; backer, impresario; contractor; administrator, manager; producer; promoter
2 *syn* see GO-BETWEEN 2

entrust *vb* 1 to confer a trust upon <*entrusted* him with responsibility for completing the work>
syn charge, trust
rel confer, impose; delegate, relegate; allocate, allot, assign
2 *syn* see COMMIT 1
rel deliver, deposit, leave, trust; bank, count, depend, reckon, rely
idiom give in trust

entry *n* 1 *syn* see ENTRANCE 1
2 *syn* see DOOR 1
rel access, opening, threshold
con egress
ant exit
3 *syn* see DOOR 2

entryway *n syn* see DOOR 1
rel threshold
con egress
ant exit

entwine *vb syn* see WIND 2
rel entangle, entwist, interlace, interplait, intertwine, interweave; enmesh
con uncoil, undo, unravel, untwine, untwist, unwind, unwrap; straighten (out)

enumerate *vb* 1 *syn* see COUNT 1
2 to specify one after the other <*enumerated* the advantages of his position>
syn list, numerate, tick off
rel run (over), tell off; identify, mention, recite, recount, relate, specify
3 *syn* see ITEMIZE 1

enunciate *vb* 1 to make a definite or systematic statement of <was the first to *enunciate* the modern principle of inertia>
syn enounce, state
rel develop, formulate, outline, postulate; advance, lay down, submit; announce, declare, proclaim; affirm; show
idiom set forth
2 *syn* see ARTICULATE 2
rel express, intone, modulate, vocalize, voice

envelop *vb* 1 *syn* see ENFOLD 1
rel cloak, hide, mask
2 *syn* see SWATHE
3 *syn* see ENCLOSE 1
rel guard, protect, shield

envenom *vb syn* see EXACERBATE

envious *adj* maliciously grudging another's advantages <*envious* of her rival's charm>
syn envying, green-eyed, invidious, jealous

rel coveting, covetous, grasping, greedy; begrudging, grudging; appetent, desirous, longing, yearning; resentful, umbrageous
idiom green with envy
con benign, benignant; generous, kind; tolerant; unconcerned, uninterested

enviousness *n syn* see ENVY

environ *vb syn* see SURROUND 1
rel enclose, fence, go (around)

environment *n* surrounding or associated matters that influence or modify a course of development < the socioeconomic *environment* in Germany that produced Hitler >
syn ambience, ambient, atmosphere, climate, medium, milieu, mise-en-scène, surroundings
rel habitat; backdrop, background, context, setting; situation, status

environs *n pl* 1 an enclosing line or margin < several thousand businesses located within the *environs* of the city >
syn bound(s), boundary, compass, confine(s), limits, precinct(s), purlieus; *compare* LIMIT 1
rel fringes
2 the suburban areas or districts around a city or heavily populated area < a new system of parks for the national capital and its *environs* >
syn outskirt(s), purlieus, suburbs
rel locality, neighborhood, vicinity; surroundings

envisage *vb syn* see THINK 1
rel behold, grasp, look (upon), picture, regard, survey, view; externalize, materialize, objectify; foresee
idiom form a mental picture of, have a picture of, picture to oneself, view in the mind's eye

envision *vb syn* see THINK 1
rel call up, conjure up, summon up; picture, view; foresee
idiom have a mental picture of, picture to oneself, view in the mind's eye

envoy *n* 1 a representative with a rank between an ambassador and a minister resident who is accredited to a foreign government < the President received the *envoy* from Spain >
syn envoy extraordinary, minister plenipotentiary
rel ambassador, attaché, chargé d'affaires, consul, councillor, internuncio, legate, minister, nuncio; diplomat
2 *syn* see MESSENGER

envoy extraordinary *n syn* see ENVOY 1

envy *n* spiteful malice and resentment over another's advantage < his lavish life-style provoked *envy* among his colleagues >
syn enviousness, invidiousness, jealousy
rel covetousness; grudging; resentment

envy *vb* to experience envy < while she outwardly criticized her sister's looks, she secretly *envied* them >
syn begrudge, grudge
rel covet, crave, desire, hanker, long, want, yearn

idiom be green with envy

envying *adj syn* see ENVIOUS

enwrap *vb* 1 *syn* see SWATHE
2 *syn* see ENFOLD 1
rel enswathe, swaddle, swathe; sheathe

ephemeral *adj syn* see TRANSIENT
rel brief, short, temporary, unenduring; episodic
idiom here today and gone tomorrow
con endless, enduring, eternal, everlasting, lasting
ant perpetual

epicene *adj syn* see EFFEMINATE

epicure *n* one who takes great and fastidious pleasure in eating and drinking < was a real *epicure*, and his dinners were excellent >
syn bon vivant, gastronome, gastronomer, gastronomist, gourmand, gourmet
rel amateur, connoisseur, epicurean; glutton, ravener; high liver

epicurean *adj syn* see SENSUOUS

epidemic *n* the sudden widespread occurrence of something felt to resemble an epidemic disease < an *epidemic* of art forgeries >
syn outbreak, plague, rash; *compare* OUTBREAK 1

epigrammatic *adj syn* see PITHY

epilogue *n* 1 the final part that rounds out or completes the design of a nondramatic literary work < the author wrote an *epilogue* to his book explaining that some of his earlier impressions were wrong >
syn afterword
rel postlude; conclusion, ending
con prelude; foreword, introduction, preface
ant prologue
2 something that resembles an epilogue in rounding out or giving point to something else < an incident that can be regarded as an *epilogue* to the history of Roman Britain >
syn sequel
rel follow-up, postscript
ant prologue

episode *n syn* see OCCURRENCE

epistle *n syn* see LETTER 2
rel communication

epitaph *n* an inscription on a tombstone in memory of the one buried there
syn hic jacet

epitome *n* 1 *syn* see ABRIDGMENT
2 *syn* see SUMMARY
3 *syn* see APOTHEOSIS 2

epitomize *vb* 1 to make or give an epitome of < a report which *epitomizes* one of the most complex theories of all time >
syn condense, digest, inventory, nutshell, sum, summarize, summate, sum up, synopsize
rel boil down, capsulize; outline, tabulate
con elaborate, enlarge (on), expand
2 to serve as the typical representation or ideal expression of < he *epitomized* safe, dull conservatism >
syn exemplify, typify
rel embody, incarnate, incorporate, personify, represent, symbolize
3 *syn* see REPRESENT 2

epitomized *adj syn* see CONDENSED

epoch *n syn* see PERIOD 2

---

syn synonym(s)   *rel* related word(s)
ant antonym(s)   *con* contrasted word(s)
idiom idiomatic equivalent(s)
‖ use limited; if in doubt, see a dictionary

rel interval, term

epochal *adj* uniquely or highly significant < had to make an *epochal* decision: whether or not to declare war >
syn momentous
rel consequential, far-reaching, important; unmatched, unparalleled
con inconsequential, minor, petty, small-time, trivial, unimportant

equable *adj syn* see STEADY 2
rel methodical, orderly, regular, systematic; immutable, invariable, unchangeable; equal, equivalent, same
con variable; fitful, spasmodic
ant inequable, unequable

equal *adj 1 syn* see SAME 2
rel equable, even, uniform; alike, like; commensurate, corresponding, proportionate
idiom one and the same
con different, disparate, divergent, diverse, varied; un- alike, unequable, uneven; irregular
ant unequal
2 *syn* see FAIR 4
idiom without distinction
con discriminating, discriminative, unfair
ant inequitable
3 *syn* see EVEN 3
4 *syn* see EVEN 4
5 *syn* see PROPORTIONAL

equal *n* one that is equal to another in status, acquirement, value, meaning, or effect < he has no *equal* in common sense and honesty >
syn counterpart, equivalent, like, match; *compare* OPPOSITE NUMBER, PARALLEL
rel companion, fellow, mate, peer; alter ego, double, twin; competitor, rival; similar

equal *vb 1 syn* see AMOUNT 2
rel compare, parallel; accord, agree, square, tally; reach
idiom amount to the same thing
2 *syn* see EVEN 2
3 to make or produce something equal to (as in quality or value) < *equal* that if you can >
syn match, measure up, meet, rival, tie, touch
rel beat, top

equality *n syn* see EQUIVALENCE

equalize *vb 1* to make equal in amount, degree, or status < *equalize* educational opportunities >
syn equate, even
rel balance, level, square
2 *syn* see EVEN 2

equally *adv 1 syn* see EVENLY 1
2 *syn* see EVENLY 2

equanimity *n* the characteristic quality of one who is self-possessed and not easily disturbed or perturbed < faced disaster with bland *equanimity* >
syn ataraxy, calmness, composure, coolness, imperturbability, phlegm, sangfroid, self-possession; *compare* CONFIDENCE 2
rel balance, equilibrium, equipoise, poise; aplomb, assurance, confidence, self-assurance; detachment; placidity, serenity, tranquillity
con alarm, anxiety, apprehension; excitability, nervousness; agitation, discomposure, disquiet, disturbance, perturbation

equatability *n syn* see EQUIVALENCE
equate *vb 1 syn* see EQUALIZE 1
2 to treat, represent, or regard as equal, equivalent, or comparable < *equated* retreat with cowardice >
syn assimilate, compare, liken, match, paragon, parallel
rel associate, relate, similize; consider, hold, regard, represent, treat

equidistant *adj syn* see MIDDLE 1

equilibrium *n syn* see BALANCE 1
rel stabilization, steadiness, steadying; counterbalance, counterpoise
con top-heaviness

equip *vb syn* see FURNISH 1
rel provide, supply; fit (out), rig (up *or* out), turn (out); gear, prepare, qualify

equipment *n* items needed for the performance of a task or useful in effecting an end < the *equipment* for the polar expedition included ships, instruments, sleds, dogs, and supplies >
syn accoutrement(s), apparatus, gear, habiliments, machinery, material(s), matériel, outfit, paraphernalia, tackle, tackling
rel accessories, appurtenances, attachments, fittings, trappings; baggage, belonging(s), impedimenta, rig, things, traps; equipage, provisioning, provisions

equipoise *n syn* see BALANCE 1
rel counterbalance, counterpoise, counterweight

equiponderation *n syn* see BALANCE 1

equitable *adj 1 syn* see FAIR 4
rel level, stable; equivalent, identical, same
idiom fair and square
con discriminatory
ant inequitable, unfair
2 *syn* see EVEN 3

equity *n syn* see JUSTICE 1
rel equitableness, justness
con bias, discrimination, partiality, unfairness
ant inequity

equivalence *n* the state or property of being equivalent or the result of making equivalent < the *equivalence* of paper money and coins >
syn adequation, equality, equatability, equivalency, par, parity, sameness
rel likeness; compatibility, correlation, correspondence; exchangeability, interchangeability
con discrepancy, disparity, divergence, incompatibility, inequality, unlikeness
ant difference

equivalency *n syn* see EQUIVALENCE
equivalent *adj 1 syn* see SAME 2
rel commensurate, proportionate; convertible, correlative, corresponding, parallel, reciprocal, substitute
con disparate, divergent, diverse, various; discordant, discrepant, incompatible, inconsonant
ant different
2 *syn* see LIKE

equivalent *n syn* see EQUAL
rel obverse, reciprocal, substitute; parallel

equivocal *adj 1 syn* see OBSCURE 3
rel hazy, indistinct; doubtful, dubious, questionable; indeterminate, multivocal
idiom clear as mud

con clear, distinct, understandable; categorical, explicit, unambiguous, univocal; certain, conclusive
ant unequivocal
2 characterized by a mixture of opposing feelings <an *equivocal* attitude toward the expensive proposal>
syn ambivalent
rel uncertain, undecided
idiom having mixed (*or* divided) feelings
con assured, certain, decided, sure
3 *syn* see DOUBTFUL 1
rel disreputable
idiom open to question
con credible
equivocality *n syn* see AMBIGUITY
equivocate *vb* 1 *syn* see LIE
rel elude, escape, evade
2 to avoid committing oneself by speaking evasively <he'd rather be brutally frank with them than *equivocate* on that issue>
syn dodge, evade, hedge, pussyfoot, shuffle, sidestep, tergiversate, tergiverse, weasel; *compare* SKIRT 3
rel cavil, prevaricate, quibble; fence, parry; avoid, elude, eschew
idiom beat around (*or* about) the bush, beg the question, mince words
equivocating *adj syn* see EVASIVE 1
rel deceptive, delusive, misleading
equivocation *n* 1 *syn* see AMBIGUITY
rel hedging; coloring, distortion, misrepresentation; deceit, dissimulation, duplicity
ant explicitness
2 *syn* see FALLACY 2
rel haggling, quibbling; fib, fibbing, lie, lying
equivoque *n syn* see AMBIGUITY
era *n syn* see PERIOD 2
rel term; stage
eradicate *vb syn* see ANNIHILATE 2
rel demolish, destroy, raze; liquidate, purge
con establish, fix, set; implant, inculcate, instill; breed, engender, generate, propagate
erase *vb* to eliminate or neutralize with or as if with a stroke of the pen <time has *erased* their sad memories> <*erase* an error>
syn annul, black (out), blot out, cancel, delete, efface, expunge, obliterate, wipe (out), x (out)
rel disannul, negate, nullify; abolish, blank (out), cross (off *or* out), cut out, dele, eliminate, excise, extirpate, rub out, scrape (out), sponge (out), strike (out); neutralize; remove, take out, withdraw
con impress, imprint, print, stamp; insert; reinstate, renew, restore
ere *prep syn* see BEFORE 1
erect *adj* standing up straight <the dog's *erect* ears pricked forward>
syn arrect, raised, stand-up, straight-up, upright, upstanding
rel erectile; elevated, lifted, upraised; perpendicular, standing, vertical
con decumbent, flat, prostrate, recumbent; drooping, hanging, pendent

erect *vb* 1 *syn* see BUILD 1
2 *syn* see MAKE 3
rel compose, create; make up, run up
con demolish, destroy, tear up, unbuild, wreck
3 to fix in an upright position <*erected* a flagpole>
syn put up, raise, rear, set up; *compare* BUILD 1
rel elevate, heighten, hoist, lift, upraise, uprear; upend
4 *syn* see EXALT 1
idiom put on a pedestal
ant abase
5 to bring into existence as if by raising a building <*erect* social barriers along religious lines>
syn build up, construct, establish, hammer (out), set up
rel fabricate, fashion, forge, form, shape; bring about, effect
con break down, tear down; liquidate, purge; dispose (of), eliminate, remove
erection *n syn* see EDIFICE
eremitic *adj syn* see ANTISOCIAL
ergo *adv syn* see THEREFORE
erode *vb* 1 *syn* see EAT 3
rel crumble, decay, deteriorate, disintegrate; consume
2 *syn* see ABRADE 1
rel grate, rub (off *or* away), scrape (off *or* away)
erotic *adj* of, devoted to, affected by, or tending to arouse sexual love or desire <*erotic* art>
syn amative, amatory, amorous, aphrodisiac
rel ardent, fervent, fervid, impassioned, lovesome, passionate; earthy; carnal, epicurean, fleshly, voluptuous; bawdy, sexy, spicy; concupiscent, lecherous; lascivious, lewd, lickerish, prurient, salacious, sensual
eroticism *n syn* see LUST 2
err *vb* to depart from a standard (as of wisdom or morality) <the human tendency to *err*>
syn deviate, stray, wander
rel miscalculate; lapse, slip (up), stumble, trip; transgress, trespass; offend; sin
idiom go astray (*or* amiss *or* wrong), leave the straight and narrow
errable *adj syn* see FALLIBLE 1
errant *adj* 1 *syn* see ERRATIC 1
rel drifting, itinerant, meandering, rambling, ranging, roaming, roving, shifting, straying
con static, unmoving
2 deviating from an accepted pattern or standard <a parent scolding his *errant* child>
syn aberrant, devious, erring
rel deviating, straying, wandering; misbehaving, mischievous, naughty
idiom off the straight and narrow
3 *syn* see FALLIBLE
rel aberrant, erring; unreliable
con perfect, trustworthy
ant inerrant
erratic *adj* 1 moving about aimlessly or irregularly without a fixed course <an *erratic* breeze barely stirred the leaves of the tree>
syn devious, errant, stray, wandering

---

syn synonym(s) *rel* related word(s)
ant antonym(s) *con* contrasted word(s)
idiom idiomatic equivalent(s)
|| use limited; if in doubt, see a dictionary

rel curving, meandering, roundabout, winding; shifting, undirected

con fixed, stable, unmoving; active, animated, brisk, lively, sprightly

ant static

2 *syn* see UNCERTAIN 1

rel doubtful, dubious

ant stable

3 *syn* see ARBITRARY 1

rel changeable, inconsistent, inconstant, unpredictable, variable; mercurial, unstable, volatile

con consistent, conventional, predictable, stable

4 *syn* see STRANGE 4

rel anomalous, irregular, unnatural

con natural, normal, regular, typical; customary, usual

erring *adj syn* see ERRANT 2

erroneous *adj* **1** *syn* see FALSE 1

rel amiss, askew, awry, off; defective; mistaken

idiom all off, all wrong, way off the mark

con right, true

ant accurate, correct

2 *syn* see MISTAKEN

erroneousness *n syn* see FALLACY 1

rel inaccurateness, mistakenness

con accuracy, accurateness, rightness

ant correctness

error *n* **1** an often unintentional deviation from truth or accuracy < made an *error* in adding the figures >

syn mistake, x

rel inaccuracy; miscalculation, miscomputation; oversight, slip

2 something (as an act, statement, or belief) that departs from what is or is generally held to be acceptable < spying on the opposing party proved to be a grave *error* >

syn blooper, blunder, boner, bull, bungle, fluff, lapse, miscue, misstep, mistake, rock, slip, slipup, trip; *compare* FAUX PAS

rel bevue, fault, misdoing, misjudgment, stumble; ∥boo-boo, botch, fumble, muff; howler, screamer; impropriety, indecorum

3 *syn* see FALLACY 1

rel misreading, misunderstanding; delusion, illusion

errorless *adj syn* see IMPECCABLE 1

con imprecise, inaccurate, incorrect, unexact, wrong

ersatz *adj syn* see ARTIFICIAL 2

rel factitious, synthetic; fake

ersatz *n syn* see IMITATION

erstwhile *adv syn* see BEFORE 2

erstwhile *adj syn* see FORMER 2

eruct *vb* **1** *syn* see BELCH 1

idiom bring up gas

2 *syn* see ERUPT 1

eructate *vb syn* see BELCH 1

erudite *adj syn* see LEARNED

rel lettered, well-read; studious

ant illiterate

eruditeness *n syn* see ERUDITION 2

erudition *n* **1** *syn* see EDUCATION 2

2 the quality or state of being erudite < a scholar of great cultivation and *erudition* >

syn eruditeness, learnedness, scholarliness, scholarship

rel cultivation, culture, education, intellectuality, literacy; bookishness, pedantry, studiousness

ant illiteracy

erupt *vb* **1** to give off or release (as something pent up) forcefully < the volcano *erupted* gouts of lava >

syn belch, disgorge, eject, eruct, expel, irrupt, spew

rel cast (out *or* up), hurl, throw off; boil, discharge, emit; jet, spout, spurt; extravasate

2 to break away or burst from limits or restraint < riots *erupted* in the ghetto >

syn break out, burst (forth), explode

rel detonate, touch off; go off

eruption *n* **1** *syn* see OUTBURST 1

2 *syn* see OUTBREAK 1

escalade *vb syn* see ASCEND 1

con clamber (down), climb (down); go (down)

escalate *vb* **1** *syn* see ASCEND 1

2 to increase in extent, volume, amount, number, intensity, or scope < a little war threatens to *escalate* into a huge, ugly one >

syn expand, grow

rel broaden, enlarge, heighten, increase, intensify, spread, widen

con decrease, limit, minimize; constrict, contract, narrow; collapse, shrink, shrivel

ant de-escalate

escapade *n* a usually adventurous action that runs counter to approved or conventional conduct < childish *escapades* on Halloween >

syn caper, lark, rollick; *compare* PRANK

rel antic, frolic, vagary; prank; fling, spree; mischief, roguery

escape *vb* **1** to run away especially from something that limits one's freedom and threatens one's well-being < trying to *escape* from prison >

syn abscond, break, ∥bunk, decamp, flee, fly, scape

rel get away, make off, mosey, run away; bail out, ∥ditch, double, duck out, flit, jump, skip; depart; disappear, vanish

idiom cut and run, cut loose, fly the coop, take it on the lam

con come back, return; abide, remain, stay; chase, follow, pursue, tag, trail

2 to get away or keep away from what one does not wish to incur, endure, or encounter < made every effort to *escape* suspicion >

syn avoid, bilk, double, duck, elude, eschew, evade, shun, shy; *compare* SHAKE 5, SKIRT 3

rel burke, bypass, circumvent; dodge, shake, shun, skit; miss

idiom fight shy of, give the slip

con catch, contract, incur; abide, bear, brook, endure, stand, suffer, tolerate; dare, face, meet

escape *n* **1** the act or fact of escaping or having escaped physically < succeeded in making his *escape* from the prison >

syn breakout, escapement, escaping, flight, getaway, lam, ∥scape, slip

rel departure; deliverance, liberation, release

con return; grasp, grip, hold, retention; imprisonment, incarceration

2 the act or fact of escaping or having escaped what one does not wish to incur, encounter, or endure < sought *escape* from responsibility >
syn avoidance, come-off, elusion, escaping, eschewal, evasion, runaround, shunning
rel bypassing, circumvention, dodging, ducking, sidestepping; elusiveness, evasiveness
con abidance, abiding, bearing, endurance, enduring, submission, submitting, toleration; facing

escapement *n* *syn* see ESCAPE 1

escaping *n* 1 *syn* see ESCAPE 1
2 *syn* see ESCAPE 2

eschew *vb* 1 *syn* see ESCAPE 2
idiom shy away from, steer clear of
con adopt, embrace, espouse
ant choose
2 *syn* see FORGO
rel abstain, refrain
idiom let well enough alone

eschewal *n* *syn* see ESCAPE 2
rel shirking; shying

escort *n* 1 a boy or man who goes on a date with a girl or woman < had her pick of *escorts* to the dance >
syn date
rel beau, boyfriend, fellow; cavalier, gallant, squire, vis-à-vis
2 a person who leads or directs another or others in a way or course (as through difficult terrain) < served as our *escort* when we drove through the desert >
syn guide
rel attendant, companion, guard

escort *vb* 1 *syn* see ACCOMPANY
2 *syn* see GUIDE
rel bring; squire

escritoire *n* *syn* see DESK

esculent *adj* *syn* see EDIBLE

esoteric *adj* *syn* see RECONDITE

especial *adj* 1 *syn* see SPECIAL 1
rel preeminent, supreme, surpassing; dominant, paramount, predominant, preponderant; exceptional, notable, singular, unusual
con unexceptional, usual
ant general
2 *syn* see EXPRESS 2

especially *adv* 1 in a special way < was *especially* good at math >
syn distinctively, particularly, special, specially, specifically
rel remarkably, unusually; exceptionally, markedly, peculiarly, singularly, uniquely; eminently, notably, preeminently, supremely
idiom before all else
2 *syn* see EXPRESSLY 2

espial *n* *syn* see DISCOVERY

espionage *n* systematic secret observation in order to accumulate information < agents engaged in industrial *espionage* >
syn spying
rel observation, reconnaissance, sleuthing, surveillance, watching

espousal *n* 1 *syn* see ENGAGEMENT 2
2 *often* **espousals** *pl* *syn* see WEDDING
3 *syn* see MARRIAGE
rel mating; union
idiom getting hitched, taking on the ball and chain, tying the knot
con estrangement, separation
4 ready acceptance of or the taking up of a cause or belief < his wholehearted *espousal* of left-wing philosophies worried his family >
syn adoption, embracement, embracing
rel acceptance, approval; advocacy; aid, promotion, support
con denial, rejection; disapproval, dislike, distaste; antipathy, aversion, intolerance
ant repudiation

espouse *vb* 1 *syn* see MARRY 1
2 *syn* see ADOPT
rel accept, approve; advocate, back, champion, support, uphold
con abandon, desert, forsake; deny, reject; disapprove, dislike
ant repudiate

esprit *n* 1 *syn* see SPIRIT 5
rel acumen, acuteness, brains, brightness, cleverness, intelligence, mind, quick-wittedness, sharpness, wit; courage, mettle, tenacity; fervor, passion
2 *syn* see MORALE
rel camaraderie, fellowship; devotion, loyalty; enthusiasm, fervor, passion
3 *syn* see WIT 5

esprit de corps *n* *syn* see MORALE
rel camaraderie, comradeship, fellowship; partisanism, partisanship; devotion, loyalty; enthusiasm, spirit

espy *vb* 1 *syn* see SEE 1
rel recognize, take in; sight, spot, spy; witness
idiom catch sight of, get a load of
2 *syn* see FIND 1
rel spy; make out; notice

essay *vb* *syn* see TRY 5
rel venture; labor, toil, travail, work
idiom give it a try (*or* fling *or* go), have at it, make a stab at, take a crack (*or* whack) at

essay *n* 1 *syn* see ATTEMPT
rel exertion; labor, toil, travail, work; go, venture
2 a relatively brief discourse written for others' reading or consideration < an *essay* on free will >
syn article, composition, paper, theme
rel discourse, discussion, explication, exposition, study; piece; tract, treatise; dissertation, thesis

essence *n* 1 a basic underlying or constituting entity, substance, or form < succeeds in conveying completely the cruel *essence* of loneliness >
syn being, essentia, essentiality, nature, texture
rel entity, form, substance
2 the most basic, significant, and indispensable element, attribute, quality, property, or aspect of a thing < the very *essence* of Machiavellianism is the belief that in politics there is neither good nor evil >
syn be-all and end-all, bottom, essentiality, marrow, pith, quintessence, quintessential, rock bottom, root, soul, stuff,

---

syn synonym(s)　　*rel* related word(s)
ant antonym(s)　　*con* contrasted word(s)
idiom idiomatic equivalent(s)
‖ use limited; if in doubt, see a dictionary

substance, virtuality; *compare* BODY 3, CENTER 2, SUBSTANCE 2
rel timber; element, fiber, property; aspect, attribute, quality, spirit; inwardness, significance; crux, gist, kernel, nub, nubbin; distillate, distillation

essentia *n syn* see ESSENCE 1

essential *adj* 1 *syn* see INHERENT
con conditional, contingent, dependent
ant accidental
2 so important to the nature and essence of a thing as to be indispensable < the *essential* ingredient in this medicine is a new drug >
syn cardinal, constitutive, fundamental, vital
rel basal, basic, underlying; capital, chief, foremost, leading, main, principal; primal, primary, prime
con dependent, secondary, subordinate; accessory, auxiliary, contributory, subsidiary
3 *syn* see ELEMENTAL 1
4 urgently required < raw materials *essential* to industry >
syn imperative, indispensable, necessary, necessitous, prerequisite
rel needed, reedful; required, requisite, wanted; right-hand; vital
con dispensable, unnecessary, unneeded, unrequired, unwanted
ant nonessential

essential *n* 1 something that forms part of the minimal body, character, or structure of a thing < prosperity is an *essential* of the good life >
syn basic, element, fundamental, part and parcel, rudiment
rel essence, stuff, substance; must, necessary, prerequisite, sine qua non
2 something necessary, required, or unavoidable < work was an *essential* to survival >
syn condition, must, necessity, precondition, prerequisite, requirement, requisite, sine qua non
idiom name of the game

essentiality *n* 1 *syn* see ESSENCE 1
2 *syn* see ESSENCE 2

essentially *adv* 1 in regard to the essential points < *essentially* the problem is this: he is unreliable >
syn au fond, basically, fundamentally, in essence
rel actually, really
idiom at bottom
2 *syn* see ALMOST 2
rel substantially, virtually
idiom in the main

establish *vb* 1 *syn* see SET 1
rel enroot, entrench, implant, inculcate, infix, instill, root; set down, set up; moor, rivet, secure; found, ground
con eradicate, exterminate, extirpate, uproot, wipe (out)
ant abrogate
2 *syn* see BASE
idiom lay the foundation for (*or* of)
3 *syn* see ENACT 2
rel formulate; authorize, decree, legislate, prescribe
ant repeal
4 *syn* see FOUND 2

rel endow, provide; originate; build
con disestablish; demolish, tear down
ant abolish
5 *syn* see ERECT 5
6 to make clear beyond a reasonable doubt < *established* an alibi for the time of the crime >
syn demonstrate, determine, make out, prove, show
rel authenticate, confirm, corroborate, document, substantiate, verify; attest; clarify
idiom afford (*or* offer) proof of
con discredit, expose, show up; confute, invalidate, parry, rebut, refute
ant disprove

established *adj syn* see FIRM 3

establishment *n* 1 *syn* see ENTERPRISE 3
rel workplace; institute, institution; foundation
2 *often cap* a group of influential leaders who represent an established order of society < the literary *establishment* >
syn Old Guard
rel conservative(s), diehard(s)
con liberal(s)

estate *n* 1 *syn* see ORDER 9
rel form, state
2 a class of people in a community distinguishable by social or political duties or privileges < a party platform appealing to people of every *estate* >
syn grade, rank
rel bracket, category; footing, level, order, standing; place, position, station; caste, class
3 an extensive landed property < spent the weekend at his country *estate* >
syn acres, land, manor, quinta
rel farm, ranch; plantation; villa

esteem *n syn* see REGARD 4
rel approval, liking; appreciation, valuation
ant abomination

esteem *vb* 1 *syn* see APPRECIATE 1
rel idolize, revere, worship
idiom hold dear, think the world of
ant despise
2 *syn* see ADMIRE 2
rel revere, venerate
idiom hold in esteem (*or* high regard)
con abhor
ant abominate

estimable *adj* 1 *syn* see WORTHY 1
2 *syn* see RESPECTABLE 1
rel admired, esteemed, respected
con disreputable, unworthy; bad
3 *syn* see HONORABLE 1

estimate *vb* 1 to judge something with respect to its worth < *estimated* the value of the jewels >
syn appraise, assay, assess, evaluate, rate, set (at), survey, valuate, value
rel adjudge, adjudicate, judge; ascertain, determine, discover; price, prize; decide, settle
2 *syn* see CALCULATE
rel cast, sum; count, enumerate
3 to fix some value (as size, distance, or composition) more or less accurately < *estimated* the rainfall at over six inches >
syn approximate, call, judge, place, put, reckon

rel round, round off; conjecture, guess, suppose, surmise; fancy, imagine; deduce, infer

con calculate, compute; measure

estimate *n* **1** the act of appraising or valuing the nature, character, quality, status, or worth of something < his influence as President is beyond *estimate* >

syn appraisal, appraisement, assessment, estimation, evaluation, valuation

rel calculation, measurement, reckoning; sizing up; projection

2 *syn* see ESTIMATION 1

idiom point of view

estimation *n* **1** the result of evaluating something < his *estimation* of the man's ability proved incorrect >

syn appraisal, appraisement, assessment, estimate, evaluation, judgment, stock

rel impression; opinion

2 *syn* see COMPUTATION

3 *syn* see ESTIMATE 1

4 *syn* see REGARD 4

estrange *vb* to cause one to break a bond or tie of affection or loyalty < her arrogance *estranged* her children and friends >

syn alien, alienate, disaffect, disunify, disunite, wean

rel break up, divide, divorce, part, separate, sever, split, sunder

idiom see at odds

con appease, conciliate, pacify, propitiate; associate, espouse, join, link, unite

ant reconcile

estrangement *n* the act of estranging or the condition of being estranged < a petty dispute resulted in total *estrangement* >

syn alienation, disaffection

rel division, divorce, schism; withdrawal

con appeasement, conciliation, propitiation

ant reconciliation

etceteras *n pl syn* see SUNDRIES

etch *vb* **1** *syn* see ENGRAVE 1

2 to set forth in a sharp, clear-cut manner with minute attention to detail < the most sharply *etched* character in the novel >

syn define, delineate

rel outline, set forth; depict, describe, picture, portray, represent

3 *syn* see ENGRAVE 2

eternal *adj* **1** *syn* see INFINITE 1

rel endless, interminable, unceasing, unending; lasting, permanent, perpetual; deathless, immortal, undying

con ephemeral, evanescent, momentary, passing, short-lived, temporary, transient

ant mortal

2 *syn* see EVERLASTING 1

rel deathless, undying

3 *syn* see CONTINUAL

con interrupted, sporadic

4 valid or existing unaltered at all times < right and wrong are *eternal* verities that cannot be changed >

syn ageless, dateless, intemporal, timeless

rel immemorial, lasting, perdurable, permanent, perpetual; immutable, inalterable, unalterable, unchangeable, unchanging

con alterable, changeable, changing, fluctuating, varying; debatable, questionable, suspect

eternalize *vb syn* see PERPETUATE

eternally *adv syn* see EVER 2

eternity *n* **1** a totality of infinite time < in *eternity* there is no change or passing away >

syn infinity, sempiternity

rel endlessness, infiniteness, infinitude, perpetuity, timelessness

con ephemerality, impermanence, transience; limitedness, restrictedness

ant finiteness

2 unending existence after death < belief in the *eternity* of our spiritual nature >

syn afterlife, everlastingness, eviternity, immortality, world-without-end

3 *syn* see AGE 2

idiom forever and a day, forever and ever

eternize *vb syn* see PERPETUATE

ethereal *adj syn* see AIRY 3

rel celestial, empyreal, empyrean, heavenly; vaporish, vaporlike, unsubstantial; filmy, gossamer; delicate, fragile, light

con heavy, thick

ant substantial

ethic *n* **1 ethics** *pl but usu sing in constr* the discipline dealing with what is good and bad and with moral duty and obligation < *ethics* has been called the science of the ideal of human character >

syn morals

2 a group of moral principles or set of values < the Christian *ethic* >

syn morality, morals, mores

3 ethics *pl* the code of conduct or behavior governing an individual or a group (as the members of a profession) < medical *ethics* >

syn principles

rel moralities, morals, mores; criteria, standards

4 the complex of ideals, beliefs, or standards that characterizes or pervades a group, community, or people < the American work *ethic* >

syn ethos

rel belief, ideal, standard, value

ethical *adj syn* see MORAL 1

rel high-principled; elevated; upright, upstanding

con flagitious, iniquitous, nefarious; improper, indecent, indecorous, unbecoming, unseemly; immoral, low

ethnic *adj* **1** *syn* see HEATHEN

rel non-Christian, unchristian

2 of, relating to, or originating from the traits shared by members of a group as a product of their common heredity and cultural tradition < only a person thoroughly familiar with Yiddish can recognize the *ethnic* quality of the pun > < *ethnic* cookery >

syn racial

rel national; tribal

ethos *n syn* see ETHIC 4

etiquette *n* **1** *syn* see MANNER 5

2 *syn* see DECORUM 1

rel behavior, conduct, deportment, manners; amenities, civilities, formalities; convention, form, protocol

idiom social graces

---

eulogistic *adj* of, relating to, characterized by, or bestowing praise < the speaker made *eulogistic* remarks on the group's accomplishment >
syn encomiastic, laudative, laudatory, panegyrical, praiseful
rel approbatory, approving, commendatory, complimentary
con uncomplimentary; critical, disapproving, disparaging; abusive
ant dyslogistic

eulogize *vb syn* see PRAISE 2
rel applaud; belaud; bepraise
idiom praise to the skies, sing the praises of
ant vilify

eulogy *n syn* see ENCOMIUM
rel adulation, glorification
con calumny, slander
ant vilification

euphemism *n* an agreeable or inoffensive expression that is substituted for one that might offend or suggest unpleasantness < vandalism that goes under the *euphemism* of souvenir hunting >
syn nice Nelly, nice-nellyism
ant dysphemism

euphonic *adj syn* see MELODIOUS 1

euphonious *adj syn* see MELODIOUS 1

euphoria *n* 1 *syn* see ELATION 1
ant deflation, dysphoria
2 an often groundless or excessive feeling of well-being and happiness < drug-induced *euphoria* >
syn elation, exaltation, intoxication
rel ecstasy, frenzy; madness; glee
con anxiety, unease, uneasiness
ant depression

euphuistic *adj syn* see RHETORICAL
rel elaborate; colorful; verbose; elevated
con concise, simple, straightforward; lean

evacuee *n syn* see REFUGEE

evade *vb* 1 *syn* see ESCAPE 2
rel flee, fly, slip (away); foil, outwit, thwart
idiom keep (*or* know) one's distance
con accost, confront, dare, face
2 *syn* see EQUIVOCATE 1
rel bypass, circumvent, duck; parry, turn (aside)
idiom give (someone) the runaround
con confront, face; elucidate, explain

evaluate *vb* 1 *syn* see ESTIMATE 1
rel appreciate; class, gauge, rank; criticize
2 *syn* see CLASS 2

evaluation *n* 1 *syn* see ESTIMATE 1
rel interpreting; judging, rating
2 *syn* see ESTIMATION 1
rel appreciation; interpretation; decision

evanesce *vb syn* see VANISH
rel disintegrate, dispel, disperse, dissipate, dissolve, scatter
idiom go up in smoke, vanish into thin air
con appear; coalesce
ant materialize

evanescent *adj syn* see TRANSIENT
rel temporary; flying; dissolving, fading, melting; disappearing, vanishing

evangelical *adj* characterized by or reflecting a missionary, reforming, or redeeming impulse or purpose < a mood of *evangelical* nationalism >
syn crusading, evangelistic
rel ardent, fervid, impassioned, militant, zealous; missionary, propagandizing, proselytizing

evangelist *n syn* see MISSIONARY

evangelistic *adj syn* see EVANGELICAL
rel missionary, reforming

evangelize *vb syn* see PREACH 1
idiom pass out of the picture

evanish *vb syn* see VANISH
idiom pass out of the picture

evaporate *vb syn* see VANISH
rel escape, pass (away *or* off); weaken; vaporize
idiom go pouf

evasion *n syn* see ESCAPE 2
rel dodging, equivocating, equivocation, evading, excuse, subterfuge; haggling, quibbling; escapism
con confrontation, confronting; daring
ant facing

evasive *adj* 1 tending to evade or avoid confrontation < his answers were ambiguous and *evasive* >
syn equivocating, prevaricative, prevaricatory, shifty, shuffling
rel ambiguous, equivocal, unclear, vague; sliding, slippery, sly
con categorical, definite, explicit, unambiguous, univocal; candid, forthright
ant direct
2 *syn* see ELUSIVE

even *adj* 1 *syn* see LEVEL
con bent, crooked, curved, twisted
ant uneven
2 *syn* see STEADY 2
rel equal, identical, same; consistent, continual, continuous, undeviating, unvaried
3 giving no advantage to either side < an *even* exchange >
syn equal, equitable, fair
rel balanced, fair and square, square; honest, straightforward, unprejudiced
con inequitable, unequal, unfair
ant uneven
4 being nicely in balance < his chances for success or failure are *even* >
syn equal, even-up, fifty-fifty
rel balanced, comparable, proportionate
con disproportionate, unbalanced
ant uneven
5 being neither more nor less than the named or understood amount, extent, or number < an *even* mile >
syn exact, square
con approximate, imprecise, inaccurate

even *adv* 1 in a like manner < they can learn *even* as others do >
syn as well, exactly, expressly, just, precisely
2 at the very time < perhaps *even* now the moment has come to consider a retreat >
syn already
3 not this merely but also — used as an intensive to emphasize the identity or character of something < a huge, *even* monstrous animal >
syn indeed, nay, truly, verily, yea
rel absolutely, positively; quite, really
4 — used as an intensive to indicate an extreme, hypothetical, or unlikely case or instance < refused *even* to look at her > < *even* if this were so, it should not change our plans >

syn so much as
idiom even so much as
5 *syn* see YET 1

even *vb* **1** to make (as a surface) smooth, even, level, or flat < *even* the soil with a spade >
syn flatten, flush, lay, level, plane, smooth, smoothen
rel grade, roll; align; symmetrize; uniform; pancake
con rough, roughen
2 to make even or balanced in advantage < hoped to *even* the odds by training >
syn equal, equalize
rel balance, square
con unbalance, unequalize, upset; derange, disarrange
3 *syn* see EQUALIZE 1

evening *n* **1** the closing part of day and the early part of night < the last light of *evening* >
syn ∥dimmet, ∥dimps, ∥dimpsy, dusk, ∥dusk dark, eventide, gloaming, nightfall, owl-light, twilight
rel afternoon; sundown, sunset; duskiness, duskness
con sunrise; dawn
ant morning
2 a latter portion or a period of decline < in the *evening* of life >
syn sunset, twilight
3 a party taking place in the evening < their *evenings* were notable affairs >
syn soiree
rel reception; salon; party

evenly *adv* **1** in equal parts < a career divided *evenly* between stage and screen >
syn equally, fifty-fifty, squarely
rel commensurably, proportionately
con disproportionately, unequally
ant unevenly
2 in a just or fair manner < she was *evenly* polite to everyone >
syn equally, impartially
rel fairly, justly
con unfairly, unjustly
3 without variation or fluctuation < spread the paint *evenly* >
syn flatly, smooth, smoothly, uniformly
con irregularly, roughly
ant unevenly

event *n* **1** *syn* see OCCURRENCE
rel act, action, deed; achievement, exploit, feat; accident, chance, fortune
2 a matter worthy of remark < the trip was an *event* in their dull routine >
syn milepost, milestone, occasion
rel affair, landmark; delight, treat
idiom historic event
con insignificancy, trifle, triviality
3 *syn* see EFFECT 1
rel offshoot, outgrowth; product, resultant, sequent
idiom end result
4 a postulated outcome, condition, or contingency < in the *event* of rain, we will not meet >
syn case, eventuality

rel chance, fortuity, hap, happenstance
5 any of the contests in a sports program < track-and-field *events* >
syn match, meet
rel competition, contest
6 *syn* see FACT 2

eventide *n* *syn* see EVENING 1
eventual *adj* *syn* see LAST
rel consequent, ensuing, inevitable, succeeding; ending, endmost
con antecedent, beginning, inceptive, initial, original
eventuality *n* **1** *syn* see EVENT 4
rel contingency, possibility
2 *syn* see EFFECT 1
con antecedent, beginning, root
eventually *adv* *syn* see YET 2
idiom in the long run
even–up *adj* *syn* see EVEN 4
ever *adv* **1** *syn* see ALWAYS 1
2 through all or an indefinite time < a name that will *ever* be respected >
syn always, eternally, evermore, forever, forevermore, in perpetuum
3 in each and every case < war and suffering have *ever* gone hand in hand >
syn invariably
rel consistently, regularly, usually
4 at any time or on any occasion < he is seldom if *ever* absent >
syn anytime, at all
5 in any way < nor was it *ever* important >
syn anyway, anywise, at all, once
6 — used as an intensive after an inverted verb-subject construction < is he *ever* proud of himself >
syn confoundedly, consumedly, excessively, extremely, immensely, inordinately, over, overfull, overly, overmuch, super, too, unduly
rel annoyingly, plaguey; grievously, mortally; consummately
ever and again *adv* *syn* see SOMETIMES
ever and anon *adv* *syn* see SOMETIMES
everlasting *adj* **1** lasting or enduring through all time < *everlasting* laws governing the physical universe >
syn amaranthine, ceaseless, endless, eternal, immortal, never-ending, unending, world-without-end; *compare* IMMORTAL 1
rel lasting, perdurable, permanent, perpetual; boundless, infinite, limitless, termless
con ephemeral, evanescent, momentary, short-lived, transitory
2 *syn* see CONTINUAL
con off-and-on, interrupted, periodic, sporadic
everlastingness *n* *syn* see ETERNITY 2
evermore *adv* *syn* see EVER 2
evert *vb* *syn* see DISPROVE 1
every *adj* *syn* see ALL 2
everybody *pron* every person < *everybody* must do what his conscience dictates >
syn all, everyman, everyone
idiom all and sundry
ant nobody
everyday *adj* **1** *syn* see COMMON 4
con distinctive, singular, unique; uncommon, unusual
ant exceptional
2 *syn* see PROSAIC 3
3 *syn* see ORDINARY 1

---

syn synonym(s)   *rel* related word(s)
ant antonym(s)   *con* contrasted word(s)
idiom idiomatic equivalent(s)
∥ use limited; if in doubt, see a dictionary

everyman *pron syn* see EVERYBODY
idiom the man in the street

everyone *pron syn* see EVERYBODY
ant no one

everyplace *adv syn* see EVERYWHERE 1
idiom all over the place

everything *pron* the whole amount < lost *everything* in the fire >
syn all
idiom all in all, the lot, the whole bit (*or* shebang), the whole kit and kaboodle, the works

everywhere *adv* 1 in every place or in all places < poverty anywhere is a danger to peace and prosperity *everywhere* >
syn all over, all round (*or* all around), everyplace, far and near, far and wide, high and low, overall, throughout
idiom in all quarters, in every quarter
2 *syn* see WHEREVER

evict *vb syn* see EJECT 1
rel dislodge, dispossess, force (out), put out, shut out, turn out
idiom turn (*or* put) out bag and baggage, turn out of doors, turn out of house and home
con harbor, house, lodge, shelter

evidence *n* 1 *syn* see INDICATION 3
2 *syn* see TESTIMONY

evidence *vb syn* see SHOW 2
rel display, expose; attest, bespeak, betoken, confirm, indicate, prove, testify

evident *adj syn* see CLEAR 5
rel noticeable, prominent, pronounced
idiom as plain as the nose on one's face, plain as day
con inconspicuous; ambiguous, unapparent, unrecognizable; concealed, hidden
ant inevident

evidently *adv syn* see OSTENSIBLY

evil *n* 1 whatever is harmful, distressing, or disastrous < attempts to grasp the nature of *evil* >
syn ill
rel bad, badness, devilry, diablerie, diabolism, evilness, satanism, satanity, wickedness, wrong
con goodness, virtue
ant good
2 whatever is morally unacceptable < return good for *evil* >
syn debt, sin, wickedness, wrong
rel evildoing, misconduct, sinfulness, wrongdoing
con rectitude, righteousness, virtue
ant good
3 a particular thing (as an act) that is evil < choose the lesser of two *evils* >
syn crime, diablerie, iniquity, sin, tort, wrong, wrongdoing
rel badness, evilness, maleficence, vice, wickedness; misdeed, offense

evil *adj* 1 *syn* see WRONG 1
rel base, low, vile; flagitious, nefarious; baneful, pernicious; black, damnable, execrable
con high, noble; exemplary, salutary
ant good
2 *syn* see OFFENSIVE
rel distasteful, repellent; fetid, putrid, stinking
3 *syn* see MALICIOUS

rel angry, disagreeable, ugly, unpleasant, wrathful; harmful, hurtful, injurious, mischievous; destructive
4 *syn* see HARMFUL
rel calamitous, destructive, disastrous
con harmless, noninjurious
ant innocuous
5 reporting or predicting harm or misfortune < messengers bearing *evil* tidings >
syn bad, ill, unfavorable; *compare* OMINOUS
rel baleful, baneful, inauspicious; ill-boding, ill-omened, ominous
con auspicious, favorable
ant good
6 marked by misfortune or calamity < the family fell upon *evil* times >
syn bad, inauspicious
rel unfavorable, unfortunate, unlucky; difficult, hard, trying; calamitous, disastrous
con favorable; lucky; easy, prosperous; auspicious, halcyon, happy
ant good

evince *vb* 1 *syn* see SHOW 2
rel argue, attest, bespeak, betoken, confirm, indicate, prove; display, exhibit, expose, illustrate, signify
con repress, suppress; conceal, hide
2 *syn* see EDUCE 1
rel bring (about); cause; provoke, stimulate

eviscerate *vb* to take out the entrails of < *eviscerate* a turkey >
syn bowel, disembowel, draw, embowel, exenterate, gut, paunch

eviternity *n syn* see ETERNITY 2

evocative *adj* serving or tending to call something (as a mood) forth < conduct *evocative* of the utmost contempt >
syn evocatory, suggestive
rel meaningful, pregnant, weighty; arousing, moving, stimulating, stirring; causing, effecting, inducing, producing

evocatory *adj syn* see EVOCATIVE

evoke *vb syn* see EDUCE 1
rel excite, provoke, stimulate; arouse, awaken, rally, rouse, stir, waken; call forth, call up, conjure (up), raise, summon (forth *or* up)

evolution *n syn* see DEVELOPMENT
rel change, transformation

evolve *vb* 1 *syn* see DERIVE 1
rel get (at), obtain; advance
2 *syn* see UNFOLD 3
rel advance, progress; mature, open (up), ripen

evolvement *n syn* see DEVELOPMENT
rel metamorphosis, transformation

evulse *vb syn* see EXTRACT 1

exacerbate *vb* to cause to become increasingly bitter or severe < foolish words that only *exacerbated* the quarrel >
syn acerbate, embitter, envenom
rel annoy, exasperate, irritate, provoke; aggravate, heighten, intensify; inflame
idiom add fuel to the flame, fan the flames, feed the fire, pour oil on the fire
con appease, mollify, pacify, placate, quell; lessen, moderate
ant assuage

exact *vb* 1 *syn* see EXTORT 1
2 *syn* see LEVY

3 *syn* see DEMAND 1
  rel coerce, compel, constrain, force, oblige; extort, extract, squeeze, wrest, wring

exact *adj* **1** *syn* see CORRECT 2
2 *syn* see EVEN 5
  ant imprecise, inexact
3 *syn* see SAME 1
4 *syn* see CAREFUL 2
5 *syn* see PRECISE 4

exacting *adj syn* see ONEROUS
  rel rigid, rigorous, severe, stern, strict, stringent; finicky, fussy, particular; critical, hypercritical
  con laissez-faire, lenient
  ant unexacting

exactitude *n syn* see PRECISION

exactly *adv* **1** *syn* see JUST 1
  rel ‖plumb, plunk; specifically
  idiom on the dot (*or* nose), right on the nail
  con about, around, more or less, roughly
  ant approximately
2 *syn* see ALL 1
  rel absolutely, expressly, positively; completely
3 as you say or state — used to express agreement or concurrence <"You are accusing me of lying?" he asked. "*Exactly*," she replied.>
  syn precisely, yes
  idiom quite so, (that's) for sure (*or* certain)
4 *syn* see EVEN 1

exactness *n syn* see PRECISION

exaggerate *vb syn* see EMBROIDER
  rel hyperbolize, overcolor, romance, romanticize
  idiom blow up out of (all) proportion, draw the long bow, make the eagle scream
  ant understate

exaggeration *n* an overstepping of the bounds of truth <the passage shows the author's penchant for grotesque *exaggeration*>
  syn coloring, embellishment, embroidering, hyperbole, overstatement
  rel aggrandizement, amplification, enlargement; overcoloring, overdrawing, romance, stretching
  idiom flight of fancy, tall talk
  con minimizing, underestimation
  ant understatement

exalt *vb* **1** to enhance the status of <propaganda that *exalts* nationalism to the level of religion>
  syn aggrandize, dignify, distinguish, ennoble, erect, glorify, honor, magnify, pedestal, stellify, sublime, uprear
  rel boost, build up, elevate, lift, promote, raise, upgrade, uplift; enhance, heighten, intensify; acclaim, enhalo, extol, laud, praise; apotheosize
  con debase, degrade, demean, humble, humiliate; belittle, decry, depreciate, derogate, detract, disparage, downgrade, minimize

ant abase
2 *syn* see FIRE 2
  rel pique, stimulate, quicken; deepen, enhance, sharpen; encourage, inspirit, spirit (up), uplift

exaltation *n syn* see APOTHEOSIS 2
  rel upgrading, uplifting; extolment, laudation, praise
  con debasement, degradation, demeanment, humiliation; belittlement, depreciation, derogation, disparagement, downgrading
  ant abasement
2 *syn* see ELATION 1
  rel delectation, delight; bliss, joy, rapture
  ant deflation
3 *syn* see EUPHORIA 2
  ant depression

exalted *adj* **1** raised to or having high rank <moved in *exalted* circles> <Alexander was *exalted* to the papal throne in 1492>
  syn astral, highest, highest-ranking, top-drawer, top-ranking
  rel august, noble; eminent, illustrious, prominent; high, high-ranking; foremost, number one; first, leading, outstanding
  con low, lowly, low-ranking, unimportant; minor; humble, plebeian
  ant abject
2 *syn* see GRAND 3
  ant abject

examination *n* a careful, detailed, and often formal study designed to uncover pertinent information <the doctor gave him a physical *examination*>
  syn analysis, audit, check-over, checkup, inspection, perlustration, review, scan, scrutiny, survey, view
  rel assay, breakdown, diagnosis, dissection; sifting, winnowing; canvass, catechization, inquiry, questioning, quizzing, testing

examine *vb* **1** *syn* see SCRUTINIZE 1
  rel check (out), go (over), investigate, look (into); contemplate, look (at *or* over), observe
  idiom give a going over, give the once-over, go over with a fine-toothed comb
2 *syn* see TRY 1
3 *syn* see ASK 1
  rel cross-examine; grill; pump
  idiom give the third degree to, put to the question

example *n* **1** *syn* see INSTANCE
2 *syn* see MODEL 2
  idiom shining example
3 an instance that illustrates a rule or provides practice in its application <worked out his arithmetic *examples*>
  syn ensample, illustration, problem
  idiom case in point

exanimate *adj syn* see DEAD 1

exasperate *vb syn* see IRRITATE
  rel agitate, work up
  idiom try one's temper (*or* patience)
  ant appease; mollify

exasperation *n* **1** *syn* see ANNOYANCE 2
  rel irritation, vexation; displeasure; resentment
2 *syn* see ANNOYANCE 3

ex cathedra *adj syn* see OFFICIAL

excavate *vb* **1** *syn* see DIG 1
  rel gouge (out), hollow (out), scoop (out), scrape (out), quarry (out)

---

syn synonym(s)   *rel* related word(s)
ant antonym(s)   *con* contrasted word(s)
idiom idiomatic equivalent(s)
‖ use limited; if in doubt, see a dictionary

2 syn see DIG 2

exceed *vb* **1** to go or be beyond a natural or set limit <the policeman *exceeded* his authority> <this task *exceeds* my powers>
syn outstep, overrun, overstep, surpass
rel outreach, overreach; dare, presume, venture
2 syn see SURPASS 1

exceedingly *adv syn* see VERY 1

excel *vb syn* see SURPASS 1

excellence *n* something that gives especial worth or value <the particular *excellence* of this cake is its lightness>
syn arete, excellency, merit, perfection, quality, virtue
rel value, worth; distinction, fineness, superiority; goodness, niceness, superbness; class
con blemish, defect, flaw; failing, foible, frailty, vice
ant fault

excellency *n syn* see EXCELLENCE

excellent *adj* meritoriously near the standard or model and eminently good of its kind <an *excellent* restaurant specializing in French cuisine>
syn A1, bang-up, banner, blue-ribbon, ‖boss, bully, ‖bunkum, capital, champion, classic, classical, ‖dandy, famous, fine, first-class, first-rate, first-string, front-rank, Grade A, number one, par excellence, prime, quality, royal, skookum, ‖slap-up, sovereign, stunning, superior, ‖swingeing, top, top-notch, whiz-bang; *compare* MARVELOUS 2; SUPREME
rel high-class, high-grade, proper; ‖rum; distinguished, exceptional, premium; brag, incomparable, magnificent, nobby, sensational, smart, superb, superlative, terrific, tip-top, unsurpassed
idiom all wool and a yard wide, beyond compare, out of this world
con mediocre; bad, inadequate, inferior, low, low-grade, low-quality, substandard; fourth-rate, second-class, second-rate; poor, shoddy, sorry, unsatisfactory, wretched; commonplace, mediocre, ordinary
ant execrable

except *vb* **1** *syn* see EXCLUDE
rel omit, pass over; exempt; reject
con incorporate, receive, work in
ant admit
2 syn see OBJECT 1

except *prep* with the exclusion or exception of <*except* Christmas, we had no long holiday>
syn apart from, aside from, bar, barring, bating, beside, besides, but, ‖cep, except for, excluding, exclusive of, outside, outside of, save, saving

except *conj* **1** on any other condition than that <wouldn't go near that woman *except* I had to>
syn but, save, saving, unless, ‖without
2 syn see ONLY

except for *prep syn* see EXCEPT

exceptionable *adj syn* see OBJECTIONABLE
con unimpeachable; exemplary
ant unexceptionable

exceptional *adj* **1** being out of the ordinary <an *exceptional* opportunity>
syn extraordinary, phenomenal, rare, remarkable, singular, uncommon, uncustomary, unimaginable, unique, unordinary, unthinkable, unusual, unwonted; *compare* STRANGE 4
rel infrequent, scarce; distinct, exceptional, notable, noteworthy
con frequent; common, commonplace, familiar, ordinary, usual
ant unexceptional
2 syn see SUPERIOR 4
rel good; excellent, marvelous, outstanding, phenomenal, wonderful; extraordinary, singular, special
con common, ordinary, run-of-the-mill
ant average

exceptionally *adv syn* see VERY 1
rel especially, particularly; extraordinarily, unusually; marvelously, phenomenally, stupendously, wonderfully

excerpt *vb* to select (passages or details) as typical of a larger store <quotations *excerpted* from many authors>
syn extract
rel cull, glean; choose, pick, pick out, select, single; cite, quote

excess *n* **1** whatever exceeds a limit, measure, bound, or accustomed degree <the proper balance between sufficiency and *excess*>
syn fat, overabundance, overflow, overkill, overmuch, overplus, plethora, superfluity, surfeit, surplus, surplusage
rel overbalance, overspill; oversupply; profusion; superabundance
idiom enough and then some, enough and to spare, too much of a good thing
con insufficiency, lack, scarcity
ant deficiency; dearth
2 the amount or degree by which a thing or number exceeds another <an *excess* of 10 bushels over what was needed>
syn overage, overstock, oversupply, plus, surplus, surplusage
rel overproduction; overmeasure
ant deficit, shortfall
3 *often* **excesses** *pl* undue or immoderate personal indulgence especially in eating and drinking <*excess* at table is seldom healthful> <his *excesses* led to his failure in business>
syn immoderation, inordinateness, intemperance, overindulgence
rel extravagance, overdoing; indulgence, self-indulgence; immoderacy, immoderateness; dissipation, prodigality, Saturnalia
con moderation; sobriety, temperateness; restraint, self-discipline, self-restraint
ant temperance

excess *adj syn* see SUPERFLUOUS
rel redundant; unessential

excessive *adj* **1** going beyond a normal or acceptable limit <spend an *excessive* amount on clothes>
syn dizzy, exorbitant, extravagant, extreme, immoderate, inordinate, sky-high, steep, stiff, stratospheric, supernatural, towering, unconscionable, undue, unmeasurable
rel boundless, limitless, unbounded; over, overboard, overmuch, overweening; super
idiom out of bounds
con exiguous, meager, narrow, scant, scanty, skimpy, sparse, tight

ant deficient

2 given to personal excesses < an *excessive* drinker, often drunk and never quite sober >
syn immoderate, inordinate, intemperate, overindulgent, unrestrained, untempered
rel extravagant; indulgent, self-indulgent; dissipated, prodigal
con conservative, moderate, sober, temperate
ant restrained

excessively *adv syn* see EVER 6

exchange *vb* **1** *syn* see TRADE 1

2 to give up, taking in return something else < *exchanged* his uniform for civilian clothes >
syn change, substitute, swap, switch, trade; *compare* TRADE 1
rel displace, replace

3 to give and receive reciprocally < *exchanged* a few words with his neighbor >
syn bandy, interchange
rel pay back, reciprocate
idiom give as much as one takes, give tit for tat, return the compliment

exchangeable *adj syn* see INTERCHANGEABLE

exchequer *n syn* see TREASURY 2

excise *vb* to remove by or as if by dissecting < *excise* a tumor > < *excised* some wordy passages >
syn cut out, exsect, extirpate, resect
rel amputate, cut off; elide, remove, strike out; eradicate, root out; delete, expurgate, exscind, slash

excitable *adj* easily excited < an *excitable* child who needs a firm hand >
syn agitable, alarmable, combustible, edgy, skittery, skittish, startlish, volatile
rel high-strung, mercurial, temperamental, unstable; touchy
idiom like a bundle of nerves, likely to go off at half cock, on edge, on the ragged edge
con calm, collected, cool, easy, easygoing, phlegmatic, placid, quiet
ant unexcitable

excite *vb* **1** *syn* see PROVOKE 4
rel agitate, discompose, disquiet, disturb, perturb, stir up; impassion; charge (up), energize, touch off, turn on
idiom set astir, set on fire, stir the blood
con allay, placate, soothe
ant quiet

2 *syn* see ELATE
rel move; fire
con depress, dishearten

3 *syn* see INTEREST

excited *adj syn* see INTOXICATED 2
rel animated, atwitter; agitated, charged (up), inflamed, pink; delighted, enthusiastic
idiom all fired up, all of a twitter, beside oneself
con apathetic, unmoved; deflated
ant unexcited

exciting *adj* absorbingly interesting < the most *exciting* day of her life > < an *exciting* personality >

syn exhilarant, exhilarating, exhilarative, eye-popping, inspiring, intoxicating, rousing, stimulating, stirring
rel arresting, interesting, intriguing; moving, provocative; heady, thrilling
con blah, dull, uninteresting, unintriguing; humdrum, monotonous, tedious
ant unexciting

exclaim *vb* to speak or utter suddenly and usually sharply, vehemently, or passionately < *exclaimed* in delight at the sight of the toy >
syn blat, blurt (out), bolt, cry out, ejaculate
rel burst (out); roar, snort

exclude *vb* to prevent the participation, consideration, or inclusion of < *excluded* that subject from discussion >
syn bar, bate, count out, debar, eliminate, except, rule out, suspend
rel ban; close out, estop, obviate, preclude, prevent, prohibit, ward (off); blackball, blacklist, ostracize; block; disbar; lock out, put out, shut out
idiom close (*or* shut) the door on
con comprehend, involve; embrace, take in
ant admit; include

excluding *prep syn* see EXCEPT

exclusionary *adj syn* see EXCLUSIVE 1

exclusive *adj* **1** having or exercising the power to limit or exclude < a tangle of *exclusive* laws >
syn exclusionary, exclusory
rel barring, debarring, excluding; limitative, limiting, restrictive; preclusive, prohibitive
con free, unlimited, unrestricted, unrestrictive
ant admissive

2 *syn* see SELECT 1
rel aristocratic, elite, preferred, privileged, tony; aloof, clannish, cliquish, cliquy; high-hat, snobbish, standoffish
con catholic, cosmopolitan, universal; common, familiar, ordinary, popular, vulgar
ant inclusive

3 *syn* see STYLISH
con tasteless; frumpy, unfashionable

4 *syn* see SOLE 4
rel individual, lone, only
con common, general, public

5 *syn* see WHOLE 5
con divided, partial

exclusive *n syn* see SCOOP

exclusively *adv syn* see ONLY 1
rel completely, wholly; particularly

exclusive of *prep syn* see EXCEPT

exclusory *adj syn* see EXCLUSIVE 1

excogitate *vb* **1** *syn* see CONSIDER 1

2 *syn* see DERIVE 1
rel contrive, invent, think (up); develop, think (out)

excoriate *vb* **1** *syn* see CHAFE 3

2 *syn* see LAMBASTE 3
idiom tear into

excorticate *vb syn* see SKIN 2

excrescence *n syn* see OUTGROWTH 1

excrescency *n syn* see OUTGROWTH 1

excruciate *vb syn* see AFFLICT
rel inflame, irritate; hurt, pain, wound; convulse

idiom prolong the agony

excruciating *adj* intensely or unbearably painful < his suffering was *excruciating* >
syn agonizing, harrowing, racking, tearing, tormenting, torturing, torturous
rel acute, extreme; piercing, sharp, shooting, stabbing; consuming, rending

exculpate *vb* to free from alleged fault or guilt < the court *exculpated* him after a thorough investigation >
syn absolve, acquit, clear, disculpate, exonerate, vindicate
rel explain, justify, rationalize; condone, excuse, forgive, pardon, remit; amnesty, free, let off
idiom clear the (*or* one's) record, wipe the slate clean
con blame, censure, denounce, reprehend, reprobate; incriminate; accuse, charge; arraign, indict; impeach; convict
ant inculpate

excurse *vb syn see* DIGRESS 2

excursion *n* 1 a trip not involving a prolonged or definite separation from one's usual abode or way of life < an afternoon *excursion* to the city >
syn jaunt, junket, outing, roundabout, sally
rel expedition, journey, trek, trip, safari; circuit, tour; one-way trip, pleasure trip, round trip; ‖pasear, paseo, walk, ‖walkabout
2 *syn see* DIGRESSION

excursus *n syn see* DIGRESSION

excusable *adj* 1 *syn see* VENIAL
2 *syn see* JUSTIFIABLE

excuse *vb* 1 to exact neither punishment nor redress for or from < she was much too ready to *excuse* her children's faults >
syn condone, forgive, pardon, remit
rel alibi, apologize (for), explain, justify, pretext, rationalize; absolve, acquit, clear, exculpate, exonerate, vindicate; extenuate, gloss (over), gloze, overlook, palliate, pass over, shrug off, whitewash, wink (at)
con blame, censure, criticize, reprehend, reprobate; castigate, chasten, chastise, correct, discipline; admonish, chide, rebuke, reprimand
ant punish
2 *syn see* EXEMPT

excuse *n* 1 a justifying explanation of a fault or defect < what's your *excuse* for being late >
syn alibi, plea, pretext, ‖right; *compare* APOLOGY 1, 2
rel defense; explanation, justification, rationalization; reason
2 *syn see* APOLOGY 2
3 an inferior example of a specified kind < this heap is a sorry *excuse* for a car >
syn apology
rel makeshift, shift, stopgap, substitute
idiom a sorry specimen
con nonpareil, paragon; gem, jewel, treasure

exec *n syn see* EXECUTIVE

execrable *adj* 1 so odious as to be utterly detestable < an *execrable* crime >
syn accursed, cursed, damnable
rel atrocious, heinous, horrific, horrifying, monstrous; base, despicable, foul, low, vile; detestable, loathsome, nauseating, repulsive, revolting

idiom beneath (*or* below) contempt, not to be put up with (*or* endured)
2 *syn see* DAMNED 2

execrate *vb* 1 to denounce violently < *execrated* those responsible for the concentration camps >
syn anathematize, curse, damn, objurgate
rel censure, condemn, denounce, reprehend, reprobate, reprove; ban; revile; accurse, imprecate
con applaud, commend, compliment; acclaim, extol, laud, praise; admire
ant eulogize
2 *syn see* HATE
3 *syn see* SWEAR 3

execration *n syn see* BLASPHEMY 1

execute *vb* 1 *syn see* PERFORM 2
rel act; bring about, cause; carry out, complete, discharge, transact
2 *syn see* ADMINISTER 1
rel discharge, dispatch, transact; conduct, handle
3 *syn see* FULFILL 1
rel put through
4 *syn see* MURDER 1
rel eliminate, purge
idiom put to death

executive *n* one who holds an administrative or managerial position < a senior sales *executive* >
syn administrator, exec, manager, officer, official
rel businessman, businesswoman; entrepreneur; higher-up; director, leader, supervisor

exegesis *n syn see* EXPLANATION 1

exegetic *adj syn see* EXPLANATORY

exemplar *n syn see* MODEL 2
rel soul; exponent, illustration; prototype

exemplary *adj* 1 *syn see* GOOD 11
rel ideal, model; admirable, commendable, praiseworthy, worthy
con evil, corrupt; unworthy
2 *syn see* TYPICAL 1

exemplify *vb* 1 to use examples in order to clarify < a good teacher *exemplifies* each complex point >
syn illustrate, instance
rel clarify, clear up, spell out; cite, quote; enlighten, illuminate
2 *syn see* EPITOMIZE 2
rel demonstrate; illustrate
3 *syn see* REPRESENT 2

exempt *vb* to free from a liability or requirement < *exempt* a man from military service >
syn absolve, discharge, dispense, excuse, let off, privilege (from), relieve, spare
rel except; free
idiom give (one) exemption

exemption *n* freeing or the state of being free or freed from a charge or obligation to which others are subject < received a tax *exemption* >
syn immunity, impunity
rel exception; discharge, freedom, release

exenterate *vb syn see* EVISCERATE

exercise *n* 1 the act of bringing into play or realizing in action < one can usually avoid accidents by the *exercise* of foresight >
syn application, employment, exercising, exertion, operation, use; *compare* USE 1

con dereliction, disregard, neglect; carelessness, heedlessness, inattention, laxity

2 regular or repeated appropriate use of a faculty, power, or bodily organ < muscular atrophy from lack of *exercise* >
syn activity, exercising, exertion
rel action, movement; practice, use, workout
con inactiveness, inactivity; idleness, unemployment

3 something practiced or performed in order to develop, improve, or display a specific power or skill < spelling *exercises* >
syn drill, drilling, practice

4 a performance having a strongly marked secondary or ulterior aspect < his writing is an *exercise* in confusion >
syn lesson, study

exercise *vb* **1** *syn* see USE 2
idiom put into practice

2 *syn* see EXERT

3 to use repeatedly in order to master or strengthen < beginning swimmers *exercising* their new skill > < games that *exercise* the muscles >
syn drill, practice, rehearse
rel break in, condition, groom, prepare, train; cultivate, develop, foster, improve; fix, set

4 *syn* see ANNOY 1

exercising *n* **1** *syn* see EXERCISE 1
2 *syn* see EXERCISE 2

exert *vb* to bring to bear especially with sustained effort or lasting effect < *exerted* tremendous influence over his son's development >
syn exercise, ply, put out, throw, wield
rel apply, employ, use
idiom put forth

exertion *n* **1** *syn* see EXERCISE 1
2 *syn* see EFFORT 1
rel strain, striving, struggle
idiom hard (or long) pull
con ease, leisure, relaxation, repose, rest; inactivity, idleness
ant inertia

3 *syn* see EXERCISE 2

exfoliate *vb* *syn* see SCALE 2

exhale *vb* to let or force out of the lungs < *exhaled* a cloud of cigarette smoke >
syn breathe (out), expire, outbreathe
rel emit, let (out); blow
ant inhale, inspire

exhaust *vb* **1** *syn* see DEPLETE
rel dispel, disperse, dissipate, scatter; run out
idiom suck dry
con conserve, preserve, save; renew, restore

2 *syn* see CONSUME 1

3 *syn* see GO 4

4 to tire utterly < the 14-hour flight *exhausted* everyone >
syn ‖BUGGER *compare* TIRE 1
rel overdo, overdrive, overexert, overextend, overplay, overwork; debilitate, enfeeble, weaken

idiom run one ragged, tire to death
con relax, rest, unlax

exhausted *adj* *syn* see EFFETE 2
rel run-down, weak, weakened; ‖beat, dog-tired, tired, ‖tucked up; limp; dead
idiom all done in (or for)

exhaustion *n* *syn* see FATIGUE
rel collapse, prostration

exhaustive *adj* testing all possibilities or considering all the elements of < an *exhaustive* investigation was soon under way >
syn complete, full-dress, thorough, thoroughgoing, whole-hog
rel all-encompassing, all-out, comprehensive, full-blown, full-scale, out-and-out, profound, total; intensive, radical, sweeping
con cursory, shallow; incomplete, partial; slipshod, unthorough
ant superficial

exhaustively *adv* **1** *syn* see HARD 3
con cursorily, superficially; incompletely, partially

2 *syn* see THOROUGHLY 2

exhibit *vb* **1** *syn* see SHOW 2
2 *syn* see LOOK 4
3 *syn* see SHOW 4
idiom parade one's wares, strut one's stuff

exhibit *n* *syn* see EXHIBITION 2

exhibition *n* **1** an act or instance of showing, evincing, or showing off < she gave an incredible *exhibition* of bad manners >
syn demonstration, display, show, spectacle
rel manifestation, sight

2 a public display of objects of interest < a trade *exhibition* >
syn exhibit, exposition, fair, show
rel demonstration, display, offering, presentation, showing

exhibitive *adj* *syn* see INDICATIVE

exhilarant *adj* *syn* see EXCITING

exhilarate *vb* *syn* see ELATE
rel animate, enliven, invigorate, vitalize; boost, buoy, exhalt, inspirit, lift, pep (up), uplift; cheer, delight, gladden, ‖send, thrill
idiom send into ecstasies
con deject, dishearten, dispirit, weigh down
ant depress

exhilarated *adj* *syn* see INTOXICATED 2
rel buoyed up, exalted, gladdened, pepped up, uplifted
idiom in ecstasies, on cloud nine
con blue, dispirited, down, low, unhappy, weighed down
ant depressed

exhilarating *adj* **1** *syn* see EXCITING
rel animating, animative, enlivening, inspiriting, invigorating, quickening; cheering, elevating, uplifting; breathtaking, electric
con deflating, disheartening, dispiriting
ant depressing

2 *syn* see INVIGORATING

exhilaration *n* *syn* see ELATION 1 *compare* ECSTASY
rel animation, enlivenment, firing, invigoration, quickening, stimulation, vitalization, vivification; electrification, excitation, excitement, galvanization; elevation, inspiration, uplift

---

syn synonym(s)   *rel* related word(s)
ant antonym(s)   *con* contrasted word(s)
idiom idiomatic equivalent(s)
‖ use limited; if in doubt, see a dictionary

ant dejection

exhilarative *adj* 1 *syn* see EXCITING
2 *syn* see INVIGORATING

exhort *vb syn* see URGE
rel admonish, plead; call upon, insist; stimulate
con block, deter, discourage, impede

exhumate *vb syn* see EXHUME

exhume *vb* to take out of a place of burial < the body was *exhumed* and burned >
syn disinhume, disinter, exhumate, unbury, uncharnel
rel dig up, disentomb, unearth; disembalm
con bury, entomb, inter, ‖plant
ant inhume

exigency *n* 1 *syn* see JUNCTURE 2
rel difficulty, hardship, rigor, vicissitude; dilemma, fix, jam, pickle, scrape; pressure, urgency
2 *syn* see NEED 4
rel demand, imperativeness, insistence, requirement; coercion, compulsion, constraint; duress, pressure, urgency
idiom matter of life and death

exigent *adj* 1 *syn* see PRESSING
rel acute; necessary; menacing, threatening
2 *syn* see ONEROUS

exiguous *adj syn* see MEAGER 2
rel diminutive, little, small, tiny; slender, slight, tenuous, thin; confined, limited, narrow, restricted, straitened
ant ample

exile *n* 1 forced removal from one's native country < a deposed king living in *exile* in Rome >
syn banishment, deportation, displacement, expulsion, ostracism, relegation
rel exclusion; extradition; expatriation; diaspora, dispersion, migration, scattering
con recall, restoration
2 *syn* see ÉMIGRÉ
rel nonperson, outcast, unperson
idiom man without a country

exile *vb syn* see BANISH
rel dispossess; evacuate; extradite; drive out
idiom turn out of house and home
con recall, restore

exist *vb* 1 *syn* see BE
2 *syn* see CONSIST 1

existence *n* 1 the state or fact of having independent reality < customs that have recently come into *existence*>
syn actuality, being
rel life; presence; reality; perseity
ant nonexistence
2 *syn* see ENTITY 1
rel essence; individuality

existent *adj* 1 *syn* see ACTUAL 1
rel existing; present
2 *syn* see EXTANT 1
3 *syn* see PRESENT

existent *n syn* see ENTITY 1

existing *adj syn* see EXTANT 1

exit *n* 1 *syn* see DEPARTURE 1
ant entry
2 *syn* see EGRESS 2
ant entrance, entry

exit *vb syn* see GO 2
idiom make an (*or* one's) exit
con arrive, come

ant enter

exiting *n syn* see DEPARTURE 1
ant entering

exodus *n syn* see DEPARTURE 1
rel emigration, migration; flight
con immigration; ingress
ant influx

ex officio *adj syn* see OFFICIAL

exonerate *vb syn* see EXCULPATE
rel disburden, free
ant incriminate

exorbitant *adj syn* see EXCESSIVE 1
rel overboard, overmuch; unwarranted; outrageous, preposterous; exacting, extortionate
idiom out of sight
con equitable, fair, just; rational, reasonable

exordium *n syn* see INTRODUCTION
rel preliminary
con afterword, conclusion, epilogue, postscript

exotic *adj* 1 not native to the place where found < *exotic* fish >
syn foreign
rel imported, introduced, naturalized; alien, extrinsic, strange
con aboriginal, autochthonous, endemic, native; domestic, local
ant indigenous
2 excitingly or enticingly different or unusual < he was moved by her *exotic* beauty >
syn romanesque, romantic, strange
rel different, unusual; alluring, enticing, fascinating, glamorous, mysterious

expand *vb* 1 *syn* see OPEN 4
2 *syn* see INCREASE 1
3 to increase or become increased in bulk, volume, or size < water *expands* when heated >
syn amplify, dilate, distend, inflate, swell
rel grow; bulk (up), enlarge, fill (out); bolster; mushroom, ‖plim, puff (up)
con condense, decrease, deflate, shrink, shrivel; dwindle, lessen
ant contract
4 to express more fully and in greater detail < *expanded* his notes into an essay >
syn amplify, develop, elaborate, enlarge
rel detail, explicate; augment; discourse, expatiate
con compress, condense, contract
ant abridge
5 *syn* see INCREASE 2
6 *syn* see ESCALATE 2
rel prolong, protract
con de-escalate; circumscribe
ant limit, restrict

expanse *n* a significantly large area or range < a trackless *expanse* of moor >
syn amplitude, breadth, distance, expansion, space, spread, stretch
rel compass, extent, orbit, range, reach, scope, sweep; area, domain, field, sphere, territory; immensity, magnitude

expansion *n* 1 *syn* see EXPANSE
2 the act or process of increasing in some way < the recent *expansion* of science >
syn enlargement, extension, spread
con contraction, decrease, shrinking

expansive *adj* 1 *syn* see ELASTIC 2

rel communicative, demonstrative, extro-verted, gregarious, unconstrained, unre-served, unrestrained; effusive, gushy, lav-ish; generous, liberal, openhanded
con austere, severe, stern; reserved, reti-cent, silent, taciturn
2 *syn* see DEMONSTRATIVE
ant withdrawn
3 *syn* see COMMUNICATIVE
4 *syn* see EXTENSIVE 1
rel ample, large; big, great
ant limited
expatiate *vb syn* see DISCOURSE 1
rel narrate, recite, recount, rehearse, re-late; ramble
expatriate *vb syn* see BANISH
ant repatriate
expatriate *n syn* see ÉMIGRÉ
ant repatriate
expect *vb* **1** to anticipate in the mind < did not *expect* him for dinner >
syn await, count (on *or* upon), hope, look
rel anticipate, apprehend, divine, fore-know, foresee
idiom bargain on (*or* for), look for
ant despair (of)
2 *syn* see UNDERSTAND 3
rel feel, sense; presume, presuppose
expectancy *n* **1** the state of one who looks forward to something < had an air of wistful *expectancy* >
syn anticipation, expectation
rel presensation, presentiment
2 *syn* see EXPECTATION 2
expectant *adj* **1** characterized by expecta-tion < an *expectant* crowd >
syn anticipant, anticipative, anticipatory, atiptoe, expecting
rel open-eyed, openmouthed; hopeful; eager; alert, watchful
con apathetic, indifferent, uninterested; unconcerned, unimpressed, unmoved
2 *syn* see PREGNANT 1
idiom anticipating a blessed event, wait-ing for the stork
expectation *n* **1** *syn* see EXPECTANCY 1
2 something that is expected < each had his own dreams and *expectations* >
syn expectancy
rel design, hope, intention, motive, no-tion; prospect
expecting *adj* **1** *syn* see EXPECTANT 1
2 *syn* see PREGNANT 1
expediency *n* **1** *syn* see ORDER 11
rel propitiousness; convenience
2 *syn* see RESOURCE 3
rel design, strategy, tactic; measure, step
idiom card up one's sleeve, means to an end
expedient *adj* dictated by practical or prudential motives < decided it was not *expedient* to interfere yet >
syn advisable, politic, prudent, tactical, wise
rel advantageous, beneficial, convenient, practical, profitable, useful, utilitarian; opportune, seasonable, timely, well-timed; feasible, possible, practicable; appropriate, fit, fitting, suitable; judicious

con deleterious, detrimental; harmful, hurtful, injurious; fruitless, futile, vain; inappropriate, uncalled-for, unfitting, un-suitable; impolite, imprudent, inadvisable, injudicious, unwise
ant inexpedient
expedient *n syn* see RESOURCE 3
rel agency, instrument, instrumentality, means, medium
expedition *n* **1** *syn* see JOURNEY
rel campaign; entrada, exploration
2 *syn* see HASTE 1
rel alacrity, promptitude
con delay, retardation, slackening, slow-ing
ant procrastination
3 *syn* see ALACRITY
rel expeditiousness, speediness, swiftness; punctuality
con dawdling, delaying, faltering, hesita-tion
expeditious *adj syn* see FAST 3
rel effective, effectual, efficacious, effi-cient; prompt, ready
con ineffective, ineffectual, inefficacious, inefficient; dilatory, laggard, leisurely, slow
ant sluggish
expeditiously *adv syn* see FAST 2
rel effectively, efficaciously; punctually
con ineffectively; deliberately, dilatorily, leisurely, slowly
ant sluggishly
expeditiousness *n syn* see HASTE 1
expeditive *adj syn* see FAST 3
expel *vb* **1** *syn* see ERUPT 1
rel blow off, blow out, ejaculate, exhaust
2 *syn* see BANISH
rel drum out, read out; eliminate, turn out; ||bounce
idiom give (one) the boot, give the bum's rush, give the old heave-ho, send to Cov-entry, throw out on one's ear
ant admit
expellee *n syn* see ÉMIGRÉ
expend *vb* **1** *syn* see SPEND 1
rel dispense, distribute; blow, exhaust, use up
idiom loose (*or* untie) the purse strings, open one's purse
con hoard, lay up, save
2 *syn* see GO 4
expenditure *n syn* see EXPENSE 1
expense *n* **1** something expended to secure a benefit or bring about a result < spared no *expense* in furnishing their home >
syn cost, disbursement, expenditure, out-lay
2 a loss incurred in the course of gaining something < won the war at the *expense* of many lives >
syn cost, price, toll
rel decrement, forfeit, forfeiture, sacrifice; deprivation, loss
expensive *adj syn* see COSTLY 1
rel immoderate, uneconomical; big-ticket, high-priced
con economical, moderate; bargain, low-cost, low-priced, thrifty; cheap
ant inexpensive
experience *n syn* see ACQUAINTANCE 1
rel background; observation; know-how, practice, skill; savoir faire, sophistication; wisdom

---

syn synonym(s)   *rel* related word(s)
ant antonym(s)   *con* contrasted word(s)
idiom idiomatic equivalent(s)
|| use limited; if in doubt, see a dictionary

ant inexperience

experience *vb* **1** to meet with directly (as through participation or observation) < *experience* pain > < trying to *experience* the problems of a different culture >
syn have, know, see, suffer, sustain, undergo
rel encounter, meet; accept, receive
2 *syn* see FEEL 2
rel behold, see, survey, view

experienced *adj* made skillful or wise through practice < an *experienced* sales executive >
syn old, old-time, practical, practiced, seasoned, skilled, versed, vet, veteran; *compare* PROFICIENT
rel broken in; accomplished, skillful; expert, qualified; old-line, wise
idiom having been around, knowing the score (*or* the ropes)
con apprentice, beginning, freshman, green, new, novice, raw, untested, untried
ant experienceless, inexperienced

experient *adj syn* see EMPIRICAL

experiential *adj syn* see EMPIRICAL

experiment *n* an operation or process carried out to resolve an uncertainty < *experiments* that added much to our understanding of nutritional needs >
syn experimentation, test, trial, trial and error, trial run
rel probe, research, search; examination, investigation; analysis, study

experiment *vb* to engage in experimentation < *experimenting* with regional solutions to urban problems >
syn experimentalize, experimentize, test (out), try (out), try on
rel investigate, probe, research, search; analyze, scrutinize, study, weigh
idiom play around with

experimental *adj* **1** *syn* see EMPIRICAL
2 of, relating to, or having the characteristics of experiment < *experimental* missile flights >
syn experimentative, test, trial
rel preliminary, preparatory; developmental; provisional, temporary, tentative
con tested, tried; permanent, proved; accepted, established, standard

experimentalize *vb syn* see EXPERIMENT

experimentation *n syn* see EXPERIMENT

experimentative *adj syn* see EXPERIMENTAL 2

experimentize *vb syn* see EXPERIMENT

expert *adj syn* see PROFICIENT
rel schooled, trained; adroit, deft, dexterous; pro, professional
con unpracticed; unschooled
ant amateur, inexpert

expert *n* one who has acquired special skill in or knowledge and mastery of something < a fingerprint *expert* >
syn adept, artist, artiste, authority, ‖dab, ‖dabster, doyen, master, master-hand, maven, passed master, past master, pro, professional, proficient, swell, virtuoso, whiz, wiz, wizard
rel ‖darb; specialist
con dabbler, dilettante, tyro; apprentice, novice, probationer
ant amateur

expertise *n* **1** *syn* see ABILITY 2

rel readiness; competence; skillfulness
2 *syn* see ART 1
rel quickness; cleverness, ingeniousness; finesse; savvy

expertism *n syn* see ABILITY 2

expertness *n syn* see ABILITY 2
rel prowess; facility

expiate *vb* to make amends or give satisfaction for wrong done < *expiated* his crime with his life >
syn atone
rel amend, compensate (for), correct, rectify, redress, remedy
idiom make up for, put right

expiative *adj syn* see PURGATIVE

expiatory *adj syn* see PURGATIVE

expire *vb* **1** *syn* see DIE 1
idiom draw one's last breath; give up the breath of life
con live, thrive
2 *syn* see PASS 3
3 *syn* see EXHALE
ant inspire

explain *vb* **1** to make something comprehensible or more comprehensible < a commentary that *explains* the allegory >
syn construe, explicate, expound, interpret, spell out; *compare* CLARIFY 2
rel decipher, disentangle, undo, unravel, unriddle, unscramble, untangle; analyze, break down; clear up, resolve, solve
idiom put into plain English
con confound, confuse, puzzle
ant obfuscate
2 *syn* see CLARIFY 2
3 to give the reason for or cause of < unable to *explain* his strange conduct >
syn account, explain away, justify, rationalize
rel condone, excuse; absolve, acquit, exculpate, exonerate, vindicate

explain away *vb syn* see EXPLAIN 3

explanation *n* **1** something that makes clear what is obscure < sought some *explanation* of the difficult passage >
syn construal, construction, exegesis, explication, exposé, exposition, interpretation
rel disentanglement, unscrambling; enlightenment, illumination; definition, meaning; resolution, solution; demonstration, example, exemplification, illustration
2 a statement of causes, grounds, or motives < refused an *explanation* for his act >
syn account, justification, rationale, rationalization, reason
rel grounds; motive

explanative *adj syn* see EXPLANATORY

explanatory *adj* serving to explain < *explanatory* notes in a book >
syn exegetic, explanative, explicative, explicatory, expositional, expositive, expository, interpretive
rel enlightening, illuminating; discursive; demonstrative, illustrative
con baffling, bewildering, confusing, misleading, mystifying, puzzling
ant obfuscatory

expletive *n syn* see SWEARWORD

explicate *vb syn* see EXPLAIN 1
rel amplify, develop, dilate, enlarge (upon), expand, expatiate; demonstrate

idiom dot the *i*'s (and cross the *t*'s)
explication *n syn* see EXPLANATION 1
rel amplification, development, enlargement, expansion, expatiation
explicative *adj syn* see EXPLANATORY
rel annotative, exemplificative, scholastic
explicatory *adj syn* see EXPLANATORY
explicit *adj* characterized by full precise expression < gave the guard *explicit* orders about whom to admit >
syn categorical, clean-cut, clear-cut, definite, definitive, express, specific, unambiguous
rel certain, clear, distinct, lucid, perspicuous, plain, sure, understandable, unequivocal; accurate, correct, exact, precise
con cryptic, dark, enigmatic, equivocal, obscure, unclear, vague; implicit, implied, inferred; imprecise, inaccurate, incorrect, inexact
ant ambiguous
explicitly *adv syn* see EXPRESSLY 1
explode *vb* 1 to burst violently and noisily usually due to pressure within < the bomb *exploded* >
syn blow up, burst, detonate, go off, mushroom
rel blast, discharge
idiom blow sky-high, blow to kingdom come
con fail, fizzle, peter (out)
2 *syn* see ERUPT 2
rel flame (up), flare (up)
idiom blow a fuse (*or* gasket)
3 *syn* see DISCREDIT 2
rel invalidate; deflate
idiom shoot full of holes
exploit *n* 1 *syn* see ADVENTURE
rel effort, job; maneuver
2 *syn* see FEAT 2
rel do, performance, stunt; blow, coup, stroke
idiom bold stroke
exploit *vb* 1 *syn* see USE 2
rel cultivate, work
2 to take unfair advantage of < *exploits* his friend's good nature >
syn abuse, impose (on *or* upon), use
rel manipulate; bleed, fleece, skin, soak, stick
3 *syn* see MANIPULATE 2
explore *vb* to search through or into < *explored* the possibilities of reaching an agreement >
syn delve (into), dig (into), go (into), inquire (into), investigate, look (into), probe, prospect, sift
rel burrow, mouse (out); quarry, search; examine, test, try; inquisite, question
idiom nose around
explosion *n syn* see OUTBURST 1
exponent *n* one who actively promotes or backs something < an *exponent* of arbitration in labor disputes >
syn advocate, champion, expounder, proponent, supporter
rel backer, booster, partisan, promoter, protagonist; defender, upholder

---

syn synonym(s)   *rel* related word(s)
ant antonym(s)   *con* contrasted word(s)
idiom idiomatic equivalent(s)
‖ use limited; if in doubt, see a dictionary

con antagonist, enemy; opposition
ant opponent
expose *vb* 1 to make accessible to something detrimental or dangerous < he needlessly *exposed* his troops to enemy fire >
syn lay (open), subject, uncover
rel endanger, hazard, imperil, jeopard, jeopardize, jeopardy, peril, risk
idiom put (*or* leave) in harm's way
con cover, shelter; guard, protect
ant shield
2 *syn* see OPEN 2
rel unfold, unshroud
3 *syn* see SHOW 4
rel advertise, air, broadcast, publish
4 to reveal the faults, frailties, unsoundness, or pretensions of < the monograph *exposed* the theory as being pure myth >
syn debunk, discover, show up, uncloak, undress, unmask, unshroud
rel disclose, reveal, uncover
idiom lay bare
exposé *n syn* see EXPLANATION 1
exposed *adj* 1 *syn* see OPEN 2
rel apparent, evident, manifest; unconcealed, unhidden; revealed; visible
idiom laid bare
con covered, enveloped, sheathed
2 *syn* see LIABLE 2
rel likely; menaced, threatened
con defended, guarded, protected, safeguarded, shielded
exposition *n* 1 *syn* see EXPLANATION 1
rel presentation; discourse, discussion, disquisition, expounding; statement; delineation, enunciation
2 *syn* see EXHIBITION 2
rel display, production
expositional *adj syn* see EXPLANATORY
expositive *adj syn* see EXPLANATORY
rel depictive, descriptive, graphic; illuminative; delineative
expository *adj syn* see EXPLANATORY
rel disquisitional; critical
expostulate *vb syn* see OBJECT 1
rel combat, fight, oppose, resist; argue, debate, discuss, dispute
idiom raise one's voice against
exposure *n* the condition of being exposed to something detrimental < *exposure* to attack >
syn liability, openness, vulnerability, vulnerableness
rel susceptibility, susceptiveness, susceptivity; defenselessness, helplessness, unprotection; danger, jeopardy, peril, risk
con bulwark, cover, protection, safeguard, shelter, shield, shielding
expound *vb syn* see EXPLAIN 1
rel express, present, state; comment, discourse; clarify, delineate, describe, exemplify, illustrate
expounder *n syn* see EXPONENT
rel explainer, expositor
express *adj* 1 *syn* see EXPLICIT
rel expressed, uttered, voiced; out-and-out, unmistakable; unconditional, unqualified
con unexpressed, unsaid, unstated; ambiguous, equivocal; conditional, qualified
2 of a particular or exact sort < came for the *express* purpose of buying a car >
syn especial, set, special, specific

rel individual; definite, particular; explicit; intended, intentional, premeditated
ant vague

express *vb* **1** *syn* see WORD
2 to give expression to (as a thought, an opinion, or an emotion) < *expressed* his views freely >
syn air, give, put, state, vent, ventilate; *compare* SAY 1, WORD
rel broach, circulate, put about; disclose, tell; frame; enunciate, phrase; announce, declare, proclaim, pronounce; discharge, drain
con hint, insinuate, intimate, suggest
ant imply
3 *syn* see MEAN 2
rel communicate, convey, impart
4 *syn* see PRESS 3

expression *n* **1** an act, process, or instance of expressing in words < his anger found *expression* in a string of oaths >
syn statement, utterance, vent, voice
rel issue; manifestation, representation; observation, reflection
con hint, insinuation, intimation, suggestion
2 *syn* see PHRASE 2
rel word; verbalism; idiom; clause
3 one thing that calls to mind another often symbolically < sent flowers as an *expression* of sympathy >
syn gesture, indication, reminder, sign, token
rel embodiment, manifestation, representation, symbol; demonstration, show
4 *syn* see ELOQUENCE
rel graphicness, vividness
5 *syn* see LOOK 2

expressionless *adj* lacking expression < cold *expressionless* eyes >
syn blank, deadpan, empty, inexpressive, unexpressive, vacant
rel dull, lackluster, lusterless, vacuous; impassive, inscrutable, stolid, wooden; dead
con lustrous; responsive; alive, vital
ant expressive

expressive *adj* clearly conveying or manifesting something < a forceful and *expressive* word >
syn eloquent, facund, meaningful, pregnant, rich, sententious, significant
rel revealing, revelatory, suggestive; graphic, pictorial, vivid; alive, demonstrative, lively, responsive, senseful, spirited
con banal, commonplace, drab, dull, flat, jejune, inane, insipid, vacuous, vapid; impassive, indifferent; austere, severe, stern, stiff, wooden; blank, deadpan, empty, expressionless, vacant; dead
ant inexpressive, unexpressive

expressiveness *n* *syn* see ELOQUENCE
ant inexpressiveness

expressivity *n* *syn* see ELOQUENCE

expressly *adv* **1** in direct and unmistakable terms < his beliefs *expressly* repudiate the church's teachings >
syn categorically, definitely, explicitly, specifically
rel directly; unmistakably
con ambiguously, equivocally; conditionally; likely, possibly, probably

2 for the express purpose < programs designed *expressly* to serve immediate political objectives >
syn especially, in specie, specially, specifically
3 *syn* see EVEN 1

expropriate *vb* **1** *syn* see APPROPRIATE 1
rel dispossess; take (away)

expulse *vb* *syn* see BANISH
rel ‖bounce; eject
con admit, receive

expulsion *n* *syn* see EXILE 1
rel driving out, forcing out; ejection, ousting; removal
idiom the boot, the old heave-ho

expunge *vb* *syn* see ERASE
rel discard, drop, exclude, omit; annihilate, eradicate

expurgate *vb* **1** *syn* see PURIFY 2
2 *syn* see CENSOR

expurgation *n* *syn* see PURIFICATION
expurgatorial *adj* *syn* see PURGATIVE
expurgatory *adj* *syn* see PURGATIVE

exquisite *adj* **1** *syn* see CHOICE
rel consummate, finished; faultless, flawless, impeccable
2 *syn* see IMPECCABLE 1
rel superb, superlative
con faulty, flawed, imperfect
3 *syn* see INTENSE 1
rel acute, extreme; consummate, transcending

exquisite *n* *syn* see FOP

exsect *vb* *syn* see EXCISE

exsiccate *vb* *syn* see DRY 1

extant *adj* **1** that is in existence < the most talented writer *extant* >
syn alive, around, existent, existing, living
con dead, defunct, destroyed, exterminated; extinct; departed, gone, lost
ant nonextant
2 *syn* see ACTUAL 1
rel current, immediate, present
con possible, potential
3 *syn* see PRESENT

extemporaneous *adj* composed, devised, or done at the moment rather than beforehand < made an *extemporaneous* speech after the dinner >
syn autoschediastic, extemporary, extempore, impromptu, improvised, offhand, spur-of-the-moment, unrehearsed, unstudied; *compare* UNINTENTIONAL
rel casual, informal; unprepared, unthought-out; impulsive, snap, spontaneous
idiom off the cuff, on the spur of the moment
con designed, planned, prepared, projected, schemed, thought-out; considered, deliberated, premeditated, studied

extemporary *adj* *syn* see EXTEMPORANEOUS
extempore *adj* *syn* see EXTEMPORANEOUS
extemporization *n* *syn* see IMPROVISATION
extemporize *vb* *syn* see IMPROVISE
rel dash off, knock off, toss off
idiom do offhand, play (it) by ear
con cook up, plan, prepare, think out

extend *vb* **1** *syn* see OPEN 4
con close, fold
2 *syn* see OFFER 1

rel allocate, allot; accord, advance, award, bestow, confer, grant; donate
idiom place at one's disposal
3 to make or become longer < *extended* his visit by a week >
syn draw, draw out, elongate, lengthen, prolong, prolongate, protract, spin (out), stretch
rel amplify, enlarge, expand, increase
con abridge; curtail
ant shorten
4 *syn* see INCREASE 1
5 *syn* see RUN 8
rel advance, proceed; continue
6 *syn* see RANGE 3
7 to reach a certain point < his education doesn't *extend* beyond elementary school >
syn go
rel reach, run; advance; attain

extended *adj* **1** *syn* see LONG 1
rel prolonged, protracted, spread out, stretched out (*or* forth)
ant contracted
2 *syn* see EXTENSIVE 1
rel far-flung, widespread
con narrow; inextensive
ant unextended

extension *n* **1** the act or state of extending or being extended < a one-month *extension* of the price freeze seems likely >
syn elongation, lengthening, production, prolongation, prolongment, protraction
rel continuation, continuing; drawing out, stretch, stretch-out
con abridgment, shortening; contraction, curtailment, shrinking
2 *syn* see EXPANSION 2
rel augmentation, increase; spreading out
con abridgment, curtailment; reduction
ant contraction
3 *syn* see RANGE 2
rel magnitude, size, spread; comprehensiveness
4 *syn* see ANNEX

extensity *n* *syn* see RANGE 2

extensive *adj* **1** widely ranging in scope or application < *extensive* privileges >
syn broad, expansive, extended, scopic, scopious, wide
rel comprehensive, general, inclusive; far-reaching, far-spreading, spacious, wide-ranging; all-encompassing, all-inclusive, blanket, boundless, indiscriminate, unrestricted, wholesale
con circumscribed, constricted, limited, narrow, restricted; unextended
2 *syn* see BIG 1
con little, small

extent *n* **1** *syn* see RANGE 2
rel domain, field, province, sphere
2 *syn* see SIZE 1
rel compass, extension, orbit, radius, reach, scope, sweep
3 *syn* see ORDER 4

extenuate *vb* **1** *syn* see THIN 1
rel mitigate; moderate, qualify, temper
con aggravate, enhance, heighten

2 *syn* see PALLIATE
rel explain, justify, rationalize; apologize
idiom put a gloss on (*or* upon *or* over), put a good face upon

exterior *adj* *syn* see OUTER
rel outermost, outmost
con inner, ingrained, inherent, intrinsic
ant interior

exteriorize *vb* *syn* see EMBODY 1
ant interiorize

exterminate *vb* **1** *syn* see ANNIHILATE 2
rel finish off; execute; kill (off)
idiom do away with, put an end to, put out of the way
2 *syn* see SLAUGHTER 3
idiom wipe off the face of the earth, wipe off the map

external *adj* *syn* see OUTER
rel out, outermost, outmost, peripheral
con ingrained, inherent, intrinsic
ant internal

externalize *vb* *syn* see EMBODY 1
ant internalize

extinct *adj* **1** *syn* see DEAD 1
2 that has died out altogether < an *extinct* civilization >
syn bygone, dead, defunct, departed, gone, lost, vanished
rel nonexistent; collapsed, fallen, overthrown; disappeared
idiom gone from the face of the earth
con existent, existing, living; active; contemporary, current
ant extant
3 *syn* see OBSOLETE
rel antiquated, archaic, old-fashioned
con modern; contemporary
ant current

extinguish *vb* **1** to cause to cease burning < firemen *extinguishing* the blaze >
syn douse, ‖dout, out, put out, quench, ‖squench
rel blow out, snuff out; smother
con fire, kindle, start; torch
ant ignite
2 *syn* see ANNIHILATE 2
rel erase, expunge, obliterate
3 *syn* see CRUSH 5
rel check; smother, stifle; snuff (out); choke (out), trample (down)
idiom put the lid (*or* the kibosh) on
con encourage, fire (up)
ant inflame

extinguishment *n* *syn* see REPRESSION 1

extirpate *vb* **1** *syn* see ANNIHILATE 2
rel efface, erase, expunge, demolish, destroy, raze; kill off
con breed, engender, generate, propagate
2 *syn* see EXCISE

extol *vb* *syn* see PRAISE 2
idiom beat the drum for, make much of
ant decry

extort *vb* **1** to obtain something by pressure or intimidation < racketeers *extorting* protection money >
syn exact, gouge, pinch, screw, shake down, squeeze, wrench, wrest, wring; *compare* CHEAT, FLEECE 1
rel demand; coerce, force; extract, get, obtain, secure; bleed, fleece, skin
idiom bleed one white, make one pay through the nose, put the screws to
2 *syn* see EDUCE 1

---

syn synonym(s)   *rel* related word(s)
ant antonym(s)   *con* contrasted word(s)
idiom idiomatic equivalent(s)
‖ use limited; if in doubt, see a dictionary

extra *adj syn* see SUPERFLUOUS
rel added, additional, supplemental, supplementary

extra *adv* to a degree or extent beyond the usual < she was *extra* smart >
syn extremely, rarely, ‖uncommon, uncommonly, unusually
rel especially; particularly; considerably, markedly, noticeably
con barely, scarcely

extract *vb* 1 to draw out forcibly or with effort < *extract* a confession > < *extract* a tooth >
syn evulse, pull, tear, yank
rel pry; avulse
2 *syn* see EKE OUT 3
3 *syn* see GLEAN
4 *syn* see EDUCE 1
5 *syn* see EXCERPT
rel abridge, condense, shorten

extraction *n syn* see ANCESTRY

extraneous *adj* 1 *syn* see EXTRINSIC
rel accidental, adventitious, incidental
con constitutional, ingrained, inherent; germane, material, pertinent
2 *syn* see IRRELEVANT
rel incidental; unessential; unrelated; pointless; inappropriate
idiom beside the point
ant relevant

extraordinary *adj syn* see EXCEPTIONAL 1
rel amazing; stupendous, terrific, wonderful
idiom out of the ordinary
con customary, normal, regular, usual
ant ordinary

extravagance *n* 1 *syn* see LUXURY
2 the quality, state, fact, or an instance of being extravagant < by living simply and avoiding *extravagance* they saved enough for the trip >
syn extravagancy, lavishness, overdoing, prodigality, squander, unthrift, waste, wastefulness
rel improvidence, spendthriftness; excess, indulgence, overindulgence
con moderation, temperateness; care, forehandedness, frugality; austerity
ant economy

extravagancy *n syn* see EXTRAVAGANCE 2

extravagant *adj* 1 grossly exaggerated < *extravagant* accusations >
syn fantastic, preposterous, wild
rel unbalanced, unrestrained; absurd, foolish, ludicrous, nonsensical, ridiculous, silly; bizarre, crazy; exaggerated, implausible
con plausible, sensible; restrained
ant reasonable
2 *syn* see EXCESSIVE 1
rel exuberant, lavish, profuse; prodigal, profligate, wasteful
con economical, frugal, sparing
ant restrained

extreme *adj* 1 very great < the project demanded *extreme* secrecy >
syn utmost, uttermost
2 *syn* see ARDENT 2
rel deep, moving
3 departing sharply from the traditional or usual < *extreme* political views >

syn extremist, fanatic, rabid, radical, revolutional, revolutionary, revolutionist, ultra, ultraist; *compare* OUTLANDISH 3
rel excessive, immoderate; desperate, drastic; extravagant, unreasonable; violent, wild
con conservative, moderate, restrained; reasonable, sensible
4 *syn* see EXCESSIVE 1
rel intolerable, unwarranted
5 most distant from a center < the *extreme* edge of the city >
syn farthest, furthermost, furthest, outermost, outmost, remotest, utmost, uttermost

extreme *n* 1 an extreme state or condition < an *extreme* of poverty >
syn extremity
rel excess, inordinancy
2 something situated at or marking one end or the other of a range < *extremes* of heat and cold >
syn extremity, limit
rel climax, consummation, culmination; ceiling, crest, crown, height; peak, pinnacle, summit, top; maximum, utmost, uttermost

extremely *adv* 1 *syn* see EVER 6
2 *syn* see VERY 1
3 *syn* see EXTRA

extremism *n syn* see RADICAL

extremist *adj syn* see EXTREME 3

extremity *n* 1 *syn* see EXTREME 2
rel acme, apex, apogee, vertex, zenith
2 *syn* see EXTREME 1

extricate *vb* 1 *syn* see KNOW 4
2 to free from an undesirable situation or condition < *extricate* himself from financial difficulties >
syn clear, clear away, discumber, disembarrass, disembroil, disencumber, disentangle, disentwine, unentangle, unscramble, untangle, untie, untwine
rel unravel; abstract, detach, disengage; disburden, disemb/disen; deliver, disinvolve, free, liberate, release, rescue; resolve
con embroil, entangle, tangle; clog, fetter, hog-tie, manacle, shackle, trammel; block, hamper, hinder, impede, obstruct

extrinsic *adj* not properly part of a thing < a point *extrinsic* to his basic thesis >
syn alien, extraneous, foreign
rel acquired, gained; exterior, external, outer, outside, outward
con native; inner, inside, interior, internal, inward; individual, personal
ant intrinsic

extrude *vb syn* see EJECT 1

exuberance *n syn* see EBULLIENCE
rel gayness; friskiness, life, liveliness, sprightliness, zest, zestfulness; abandon, ardor

exuberancy *n syn* see EBULLIENCE

exuberant *adj* 1 joyously unrestrained and enthusiastic < his warm *exuberant* personality >
syn brash, ebullient, effervescent, high-spirited, vivacious
rel gay, lively, spirited, sprightly, zestful; frolicsome; ardent, passionate
con constrained, inhibited, repressed, restrained, subdued; calm, impassive, quiet
ant austere

2 *syn* see PROFUSE

rel fecund, fertile, fruitful, prolific; rampant, rank; diffuse

con scant, scanty, spare

exude *vb* to flow slowly out <a sticky resin *exuded* from the bark>

syn bleed, ooze, percolate, ‖screeve, seep, ‖sew, ‖sicker, strain, sweat, transude, weep

rel emanate; discharge, emit; trickle

exult *vb* to rejoice especially with feelings or display of triumph or self-satisfaction <the team were *exulting* in their victory>

syn delight, glory, jubilate, triumph

rel rejoice; celebrate; boast, brag, crow, show off

con lament, mourn

ant bemoan

exultance *n syn* see EXULTATION

exultant *adj* manifesting proud elation <*exultant* over his successes>

syn cock-a-hoop, cock-a-whoop, exulting, jubilant, triumphal, triumphant

rel happy, joyous, overjoyed; delighting, rejoicing; elated, flushed

idiom in high feather

con depressed, mournful, unhappy

exultation *n* the act of exulting or the state of being exultant <the *exultation* of victory and the thrill of power>

syn exultance, jubilance, jubilation, triumph

rel delight, elation, satisfaction; celebration, rejoicing; gloating

exulting *adj syn* see EXULTANT

exuviate *vb syn* see SHED 2

eye *n* **1** an organ of sight <turned his *eyes* to the view>

syn lamp, ocular, oculus, ‖ogle, orb, peeper, winker

2 the faculty of seeing with or as if with the eyes <had a keen *eye* for details>

syn eyesight, seeing, sight, vision

3 very close watching or observation <kept an *eye* on him>

syn eagle eye, scrutiny, surveillance, tab, watch

4 *often* eyes *pl* a way of looking at something <in the *eyes* of the law, a man is innocent until proven guilty>

syn view, viewpoint; *compare* VIEWPOINT 2

rel attitude, position, thinking; conception, grasp; conclusion, judgment

5 *syn* see OPINION

6 *syn* see LOOP 1

7 *syn* see LOOP 2

‖8 *syn* see DETECTIVE

eye *vb* **1** to fix the eyes on <the child *eyed* the presents with delight>

syn consider, contemplate, gaze (upon), look (at *or* upon), view; *compare* LOOK 7

rel regard; stare (at)

2 to keep a close watch on <the detective *eyed* the suspect>

syn eyeball, scrutinize, watch; *compare* TAIL

rel stare (at); size up

idiom keep a close (*or* an eagle) eye on

3 *syn* see LOOK 7

eyeball *vb syn* see EYE 2

eye-catching *adj syn* see NOTICEABLE

eyeful *n syn* see BEAUTY

eyeless *adj syn* see BLIND 1

eye-popping *adj syn* see EXCITING

eyesight *n syn* see EYE 2

eyesore *n* something offensive to the sight <the old abandoned house was a neighborhood *eyesore*>

syn desight, fright, mess, monstrosity, sight

eyewash *n syn* see NONSENSE 2

eyewitness *n syn* see SPECTATOR

F

fable *n* **1** *syn* see FICTION

2 *syn* see ALLEGORY 2

fabric *n* **1** *syn* see BUILDING

2 *syn* see TEXTURE 2

fabricate *vb syn* see MAKE 3

rel turn out; create, formulate, invent; concoct, contrive, devise

fabrication *n syn* see FICTION

rel creation; deceit, fib; artifact, opus, product, production, work

fabulous *adj syn* see MYTHICAL

rel amazing, astonishing, astounding, incredible, marvelous, unbelievable, wonderful; exorbitant, extravagant, inordinate, outrageous,. preposterous; monstrous, prodigious, stupendous

con believable, colorable, credible

facade *n syn* see MASK 2

face *n* **1** the front part of the head including the eyes, nose, mouth, cheeks, chin, and usually forehead <hid his *face* from the camera>

syn countenance, ‖dial, features, ‖kisser, ‖map, mug, ‖mush, muzzle, ‖pan, phiz, puss, visage

rel lineaments, physiognomy

2 *syn* see LOOK 2

3 *syn* see APPEARANCE 2

4 *syn* see MASK 2

5 *syn* see EFFRONTERY

6 a distortion of the face usually as an expression of contempt or distaste <the old man made a *face* at the flat beer>

syn grimace, moue, mouth, mouthing, mow, mug

rel frown, glower, lower, pout, scowl

idiom wry face, wry mouth

con grin, simper, smile, smirk

7 *syn* see MAKEUP 3

8 *syn* see TOP 2

---

syn synonym(s)   *rel* related word(s)
ant antonym(s)   *con* contrasted word(s)
idiom idiomatic equivalent(s)
‖ use limited; if in doubt, see a dictionary

face *vb* **1** to have the face or front in a specified direction <the house *faces* toward the river>
syn front, look
rel border, meet
ant back
2 *syn* see MEET 6
rel watch; gaze, glare, stare; await, expect, look (for)
3 to confront with courage or boldness <ready to *face* his accusers>
syn ‖banter, beard, brave, challenge, dare, defy, ‖double-dog dare, front, outdare, outface, venture
rel confront, encounter, meet; oppose, resist, withstand; contend, fight
idiom brazen it out, face the music, face up to, take the bull by the horns
con elude, escape, eschew, evade, shun
ant avoid
4 *syn* see CONFRONT 1
5 *syn* see ACCOST 2
rel beard, brave, challenge, dare, defy
idiom stand up to
6 *syn* see ENGAGE 5
7 *syn* see SHEATHE
facet *n syn* see PHASE
rel face, front
facetious *adj syn* see WITTY
rel jesting, joking, quipping, wisecracking; blithe, jocund, jolly, jovial, merry; comic, comical, droll, funny, laughable, ludicrous
con grave, serious, sober, solemn, somber
ant lugubrious
facile *adj syn* see EASY 1
rel adroit, deft, dexterous; fluent, glib, voluble; cursory, shallow, superficial, uncritical
con awkward, clumsy, constrained, cumbersome, labored, maladroit; tongue-tied; deep, profound, thorough
ant arduous
facilely *adv syn* see EASILY 1
ant arduously
facilitate *vb syn* see EASE 3
facility *n* **1** *syn* see READINESS 3
rel skill, wit; aptitude, bent, leaning, propensity, turn; abandon, spontaneity, unconstraint; address, poise, tact; effortlessness, lightness, smoothness
con awkwardness, clumsiness, ineptness, maladroitness, rigidity, stiffness, woodenness; effort, exertion, pains
2 *syn* see AMENITY 2
rel accommodation, advantage, aid, fitting
con difficulty, hardship, inconvenience
facing *prep* **1** *syn* see AGAINST 1
con side by side
2 *syn* see BEFORE 2
facsimile *n syn* see REPRODUCTION
con archetype, model, original, pattern, prototype, standard
fact *n* **1** the quality of being actual <the realm of *fact* is distinct from fancy>
syn actuality, reality
rel authenticity, genuineness, truth
con fancy, fantasy, fiction
2 something that has actual existence <stubborn *facts* that cannot be confuted>
syn event, phenomenon

rel circumstance, detail, episode, particular; happening, incident, occurrence; observable
con contingency, eventuality, hope, possibility, potentiality, probability
ant illusion
faction *n syn* see COMBINATION 2
rel camp, offshoot, wing
idiom splinter group
factious *adj syn* see INSUBORDINATE
rel contending, fighting, warring; belligerent, contentious, quarrelsome; alienated, disaffected, estranged
con companionable, gregarious, social; acquiescent, compliant; faithful, loyal, true
ant cooperative
factitious *adj syn* see SYNTHETIC
rel affected, assumed, counterfeited, false, feigned, forced, pretended, sham, shammed, simulated
con authentic, bona fide, genuine, veritable; artless, naive, simple, spontaneous
ant natural
factor *n* **1** *syn* see ELEMENT 2
rel antecedent, cause, determinant; agency, agent, instrument, instrumentality, means
2 *syn* see AGENT 2
rel bailiff, majordomo, seneschal, steward; adjutant, aid, assistant, coadjutor, helper
factory *n* an establishment for the manufacturing of goods <a shoe *factory*>
syn manufactory, mill, plant, works
factual *adj syn* see ACTUAL 2
rel certain, undoubted, veritable; authentic, legitimate, unquestionable, valid
con erroneous, false, questionable, wrong
ant illusory
facultative *adj syn* see OPTIONAL
faculty *n* **1** *syn* see GIFT 2
rel instinct; property, quality; leaning, penchant, proclivity, propensity; predilection
con inability, incapability, incapacity, ineptness
2 *syn* see POWER 3
facund *adj syn* see EXPRESSIVE
facundity *n syn* see ELOQUENCE
fad *n syn* see FASHION 3
rel caprice, conceit, fancy, vagary, whim, whimsy
con custom, habit, practice, usage
fade *vb* **1** *syn* see FAIL 1
2 *syn* see DULL 1
3 *syn* see VANISH
rel deliquesce, dissolve, melt; abate, diminish, dwindle, ebb, lessen, moderate, wane; attenuate, rarefy, thin
idiom fade like a shadow
con intensify; eternalize, immortalize, perpetuate
faded *adj syn* see SHABBY 1
rel haggard, washed-out, wasted, worn; dim, murky; achromatic, colorless; ashen, pale, pallid, wan
con energetic, lusty, vigorous; colorful; vivid
fag *n syn* see CIGARETTE
fag *vb syn* see EXHAUST 4
con refresh, relax, rest, restore
fag *n syn* see HOMOSEXUAL
faggot *n syn* see HOMOSEXUAL

fail *vb* **1** to lose strength, power, vitality, or intensity < his health *failed* and he retired early >
syn decline, deteriorate, ‖dwine, fade, flag, languish, weaken
rel jade, sink, slip, waste (away), worsen
idiom go downhill, hit the skids
con better, improve, strengthen
2 to become used up < food *failed* before they got back to civilization >
syn give out, run out
rel dwindle, shrink, wane
3 to be or become inadequate or deficient < the spring gradually *failed* as the drought persisted >
syn dwindle, shrink, wane, waste (away), weaken
rel decrease, diminish, lessen; give out, run out; short
idiom be found wanting
con appreciate, gain, grow, increase, wax
4 to be less than adequate or successful < the attack *failed* >
syn ‖flop, flummox, wash out
rel bankrupt, bomb, deplete, drain, exhaust, impoverish; bust out, flunk, ‖spin
idiom come to grief, fall flat (*or* short), go on the rocks, ‖lay an egg, ‖take the count
ant succeed
5 to be unable to meet financial engagements < the bank *failed* >
syn break, bust, crash, fold
rel gazette; close, end, finish, terminate
idiom be ruined, go bankrupt, go broke, go on the rocks, go to the wall, go under
con boom, prosper
6 *syn* see NEGLECT
idiom be found wanting, come (*or* fall) short of

failing *n syn* see FAULT 2
rel imperfection, shortcoming
idiom weak point

failing *adj syn* see SHORT 3

failure *n* **1** omission of performance of an action or task < the mechanic's *failure* to adjust the brakes >
syn default, delinquency, dereliction, neglect, oversight
rel laxity, negligence, remissness, slackness; indifference, unconcern
con accomplishment, achievement, discharge, effectuation, fulfillment
2 lack of satisfactory performance or effect < the *failure* of the candidate in the election >
syn defeat, insuccess, nonsuccess, unsuccess, unsuccessfulness
rel failing, fault, imperfection, shortcoming
idiom no go
ant success
3 the fact or state of being inadequate < the crop *failure* brought on a near famine >
syn defalcation, deficiency, deficit, inadequacy, insufficiency, insufficiency, lack, scantiness, shortage, underage; *compare* ABSENCE, SCARCITY

rel inferiority, meagerness, poorness, skimpiness; dearth, paucity
con abundance, adequacy, sufficiency
4 a marked weakening < felt a warning *failure* of physical strength >
syn declination, decline, deterioration, ebbing, waning
rel debilitation, enfeeblement, exhaustion, flagging, weakness
con improvement; invigoration, revitalization, strengthening
5 one that has failed < he is a *failure* in school because of inattention >
syn bomb, bust, dud, flop, lemon, loser
rel botch, fiasco, fizzle, hash, muddle, washout; might-have-been
ant success

fain *adj syn* see WILLING 1

faineant *n syn* see SLUGGARD

faineant *adj syn* see LAZY
rel apathetic, impassive, phlegmatic
con active, energetic, vigorous; busy, industrious

faint *adj* **1** *syn* see GENTLE 1
2 scarcely or imperfectly perceptible < he had only a *faint* idea of how he could help >
syn blear, bleary, dim, fuzzy, ill-defined, indistinct, obscure, shadowy, unclear, undefined, undetermined, undistinct, vague; *compare* OBSCURE 3
rel blurred, dusty, pale, wan, weak; hushed, inaudible, low, muffled, small, soft, stifled, thin
con bright, distinct, evident, obvious, patent, unmistakable; certain, sure
ant clear

faint *n* the act or condition of losing consciousness < was so frightened she fell into a *faint* >
syn blackout, coma, swoon, syncope
rel grayout, swim; dizziness, vertigo
idiom a dead faint

faint *vb* to lose consciousness < *fainted* at the sight of blood >
syn black out, ‖crap out, pass out, ‖swarf, ‖swelt, swoon
rel gray out
idiom faint dead away, fall in a faint, go out like a light, pass out cold

faintly *adv syn* see SOTTO VOCE

fair *adj* **1** *syn* see BEAUTIFUL
rel dainty, delicate, exquisite; charming, enchanting; chaste, pure
con ill-favored, ugly
ant foul
2 not stormy < a *fair* day >
syn clarion, clear, cloudless, fine, pleasant, rainless, sunny, sunshine, sunshining, sunshiny, unclouded, undarkened
rel calm, placid, tranquil, unthreatening; balmy, clement, mild, pretty
con overcast, stormy, threatening
3 of light complexion < *fair* people often sunburn badly >
syn blond, light
rel ruddy, tawny
con brunet, dark, swarthy
4 characterized by honesty, justice, and freedom from improper influence < a *fair* decision by the judge >
syn candid, dispassionate, equal, equitable, impartial, impersonal, indifferent, just, nondiscriminatory, nonpartisan, objective,

---

syn synonym(s)   *rel* related word(s)
ant antonym(s)   *con* contrasted word(s)
idiom idiomatic equivalent(s)
‖ use limited; if in doubt, see a dictionary

square, unbiased, uncolored, undistinctive, unprejudiced, unprepossessed
rel detached, disinterested; balanced, rational, reasonable, sane; open-minded, straight
con biased, inequitable, partial, partisan, prejudiced, prepossessed, unjust
ant unfair
5 observing the rules <a *fair* fight>
syn clean, sportsmanlike, sportsmanly
rel decent, honest, lawful
con dirty, dishonest, fixed
ant unfair
6 *syn* see EVEN 3
7 *syn* see MEDIUM
rel common, ordinary
con choice, good, prime, right; bad, poor, wrong
fair *n syn* see EXHIBITION 2
rel carnival, festival
fair–haired *adj syn* see FAVORITE 1
fairish *adj syn* see MEDIUM
fairly *adv* **1** *syn* see ENOUGH 2
2 *syn* see SOMEWHAT 2
fairy *n* a benevolent mythical being <children who believe in *fairies*>
syn brownie, elf, fay, nisse, pixie, sprite
rel gremlin, imp, leprechaun, puck; dwarf, gnome, goblin, kobold
con ogre, troll
fairyland *n syn* see UTOPIA
faith *n* **1** *syn* see BELIEF 1
con dubiety, dubiosity, skepticism, uncertainty
2 *syn* see TRUST 1
con disbelief, incredulity, unbelief; apprehension, misgiving
3 *syn* see RELIGION 1
4 *syn* see RELIGION 2
rel doctrines, dogmas, tenets
faithful *adj* **1** firm in adherence to whatever one is bound to by duty or promise <a *faithful* public official, conscientious and above reproach>
syn allegiant, ardent, constant, ‖dinky-di, fast, liege, loyal, resolute, staunch, steadfast, steady, true
rel dependable, reliable, tried, trustworthy; affectionate, devoted, loving; dyed-in-the-wool
con disloyal, false, perfidious, traitorous, treacherous; fickle, inconstant, unstable
ant faithless
2 *syn* see TRUE 3
idiom at one with, on all fours with
3 *syn* see AUTHENTIC 1
faithfulness *n* **1** *syn* see ATTACHMENT 1
2 *syn* see FIDELITY 1
faithless *adj* not true to allegiance or duty <a *faithless* husband>
syn disloyal, false, perfidious, recreant, traitorous, treacherous, unfaithful, unloyal, untrue
rel capricious, fickle, inconstant, unstable; fluctuating, wavering; changeable, changeful
con constant, loyal, resolute, staunch, steadfast, true
ant faithful
faithlessness *n* **1** *syn* see TREACHERY
2 *syn* see INFIDELITY 1
fake *vb syn* see ASSUME 4
fake *n* **1** *syn* see IMPOSTURE

2 *syn* see IMPOSTOR
fake *adj* **1** *syn* see COUNTERFEIT
rel fabricated, forged; concocted, framed, invented
con bona fide, genuine
2 *syn* see FICTITIOUS 2
faker *n syn* see IMPOSTOR
rel cheat, cheater, cozener, defrauder, swindler
fall *vb* **1** to pass downward <fruit *falling* off a tree> <the temperature *fell* sharply>
syn descend, drop, lower
rel decline, dip, plummet, sink; decrease, diminish, lessen; dangle, drag, droop, trail
ant rise
2 to come down suddenly and involuntarily <*fell* on the ice>
syn drop, go down, keel (over), pitch, plunge, slump, topple, tumble
rel slip, sprawl, stumble, trip
idiom come a cropper, take a header, take a spill
con ascend, climb
3 to suffer ruin, defeat, or failure <the city *fell* after a long siege>
syn go down, go under, submit, succumb, surrender
rel give up, yield
con endure, prevail, resist; conquer, triumph, vanquish, win
4 *syn* see ABATE 4
ant rise
5 *syn* see PLUMMET
fall (off *or* away) *vb syn* see SLIP 6
fall (on *or* upon) *vb syn* see ATTACK 1
fall *n* **1** *syn* see DESCENT 1
2 *syn* see DESCENT 4
3 *usu* falls *pl but sing or pl in constr syn* see WATERFALL
fallacious *adj* **1** *syn* see ILLOGICAL
ant valid, sound
2 *syn* see MISLEADING
ant veritable
fallaciousness *n syn* see FALLACY 1
rel ambiguity, equivocation; deception, deluding, misleading; faultiness, illogicality, unreasonableness
ant soundness, validity
fallacy *n* **1** a false or erroneous idea <his argument is based on a *fallacy*>
syn erroneousness, error, fallaciousness, falsehood, falseness, falsity, untruth
rel misconception, misconstrual, misinterpretation, misunderstanding
con comprehension, grasp, understanding; correctitude, correctness, truth
ant verity
2 unsound and misleading reasoning <the *fallacy* of his theory is clearly evident>
syn casuistry, deception, deceptiveness, delusion, equivocation, sophism, sophistry, speciousness, spuriousness
rel elusion, evasion, inconsistency, quibble, quibbling
fall back *vb* **1** *syn* see RETREAT 2
2 *syn* see RECEDE 1
fall flat *vb syn* see FAIL 4
fall guy *n* **1** *syn* see SCAPEGOAT
2 *syn* see FOOL 3
fallible *adj* liable or inclined to error <a *fallible* rule>
syn errable, errant

rel careless, faulty, heedless
con careful, heedful; inerrable, inerrant, unerring; exact, perfect, precise
ant infallible

falling-out *n syn* see QUARREL

falloff *n syn* see DECLINE 3

fall out *vb* 1 *syn* see HAPPEN 1
2 *syn* see QUARREL

fall to *vb syn* see PITCH IN 1

false *adj* 1 not in conformity with what is true < the information turned out to be *false* >
syn counterfactual, erroneous, inaccurate, incorrect, specious, unsound, untrue, wrong; *compare* ILLOGICAL
rel deceptive, delusive, delusory, distorted, fallacious, misleading; deceitful, dishonest, fraudulent, lying, mendacious, untruthful
idiom contrary to fact, off the mark
con accurate, correct, established, factual, truthful, veracious, veridical
ant true
2 *syn* see MISLEADING
3 *syn* see FAITHLESS
rel apostate, backsliding, renegade; crooked, devious; hollow
ant true
4 *syn* see COUNTERFEIT
rel apparent, ostensible, seeming
con bona fide, genuine
ant real
5 *syn* see ARTIFICIAL 2

false face *n syn* see MASK 1

false front *n syn* see MASK 2

falsehood *n* 1 *syn* see FALLACY 1
2 *syn* see LIE
rel fakery, feigning, pretense, sham; deceit, dissimulation, fraud
ant truth
3 *syn* see MENDACITY

falseness *n* 1 *syn* see FALLACY 1
2 *syn* see INFIDELITY
3 *syn* see DEFECTION

falsifier *n syn* see LIAR

falsify *vb* 1 *syn* see LIE
2 *syn* see MISREPRESENT
rel alter, change; cook, doctor; contort; contradict, contravene, deny, traverse

falsity *n* 1 *syn* see LIE
2 *syn* see FALLACY 1
rel bluff, fabrication, fake, sham; disingenuousness, hypocrisy, insincerity, uncandidness
ant verity
3 *syn* see INFIDELITY

falter *vb* 1 *syn* see TEETER
2 *syn* see HESITATE
rel blench, flinch, quail, recoil, shrink; quake, quaver, shake, shudder, tremble; tick over
con persevere, persist; decide, determine, resolve

faltering *adj syn* see VACILLATING 2

fame *n* 1 *syn* see REPUTATION 2
2 the state of being widely known for one's deeds < his *fame* was short-lived >
syn celebrity, éclat, notoriety, renown, ‖rep, reputation, repute

rel acclaim, acclamation, applause; acknowledgment, recognition; conspicuousness, prominence; distinction, eminence, glory, greatness, honor, illustriousness, note, preeminence
con disgrace, dishonor, disrepute, ignominy, obloquy, odium, opprobrium, shame
ant obscurity; infamy

famed *adj syn* see FAMOUS 2
ant obscure; ill-famed

familiar *n syn* see FRIEND

familiar *adj* 1 closely associated < time and interests have made them *familiar* >
syn chummy, close, confidential, intimate, thick
rel amicable, friendly, neighborly; affable, boon, cordial, genial, gracious, sociable; comfortable, cozy, easy, snug; forward, fresh, impertinent, intrusive, obtrusive, officious
con detached, disinterested, incurious, indifferent, remote, unconcerned; ceremonial, ceremonious, conventional, formal
ant aloof
2 *syn* see COMMON 4
rel accustomed, habitual, wonted; commonplace, prosaic
con new, newfangled, new-fashioned, novel; rare, strange, uncommon; chimerical, fantastic
ant unfamiliar
3 well-informed especially through study or experience < *familiar* with what is being taught in the schools >
syn abreast, acquainted, au courant, au fait, conversant, informed, up, versant, versed
rel aware, cognizant, conscious, mindful
con unacquainted, unconversant, uninformed, unversed; insensible, unaware, unconscious, unmindful; ignorant, unenlightened, unknowing
ant unfamiliar

familiarity *n syn* see ACQUAINTANCE 1
rel awareness, cognition, comprehension, knowledge, understanding
ant unfamiliarity

familiarize *vb syn* see ACCUSTOM
rel acquaint, adapt, adjust, condition, naturalize, season

family *n* 1 a group of persons of or regarded as of common ancestry < traditionally all men belong to the *family* of Noah >
syn clan, folk, house, kindred, lineage, race, stock, tribe
rel brood, dynasty, line, stirp; strain; issue, offspring, progeny
idiom kith and kin, one's own flesh and blood
2 a group of usually related persons living in one house and under one head < was the only child in her *family* >
syn folks, house, household, ménage

family *adj syn* see DOMESTIC 1

family tree *n syn* see GENEALOGY

famished *adj syn* see HUNGRY

famous *adj* 1 *syn* see WELL-KNOWN
2 widely known and honored for achievement < a *famous* physician >
syn celebrated, celebrious, distinguished, eminent, famed, great, illustrious, notable,

---

syn synonym(s)   *rel* related word(s)
ant antonym(s)   *con* contrasted word(s)
idiom idiomatic equivalent(s)
‖ use limited; if in doubt, see a dictionary

prestigious, prominent, redoubtable, renowned; *compare* WELL-KNOWN
  rel estimable, honorable, reputable, respectable, well-thought-of
  idiom held in esteem
  con humble, inconspicuous, undistinguished, unimportant, unknown
  ant obscure; infamous
  3 *syn* see EXCELLENT
  ant wretched
fan *n* 1 *syn* see ADDICT
  2 *syn* see AMATEUR 1
fan *vb* 1 *syn* see BLOW 1
  ‖2 *syn* see SEARCH 2
fan (out) *vb syn* see OPEN 4
fanatic *adj syn* see EXTREME 3
fanatic *n syn* see ENTHUSIAST
fancied *adj syn* see IMAGINARY 1
fancier *n syn* see AMATEUR 1
fanciful *adj* 1 *syn* see IMAGINARY 1
  rel apocryphal, fabulous, fictitious, legendary, mythical; bizarre, fantastic, grotesque; absurd, preposterous; false, wrong
  con matter-of-fact, prosaic; truthful, veracious
  ant realistic
  2 *syn* see FICTITIOUS 1
  ant veridical
fancy *n* 1 *syn* see WILL 1
  2 *syn* see CAPRICE
  rel idea; irrationality, unreasonableness;
contrariness, perverseness
  3 *syn* see IMAGINATION
  rel envisagement, envisioning, objectifica-
tion
  idiom flight of fancy
  con awareness, experience, perception
  4 an idea or image present in the mind
but having no concrete or objective reality
< unable to tell fact from *fancy* >
  syn daydream, dream, fantasy (*or* phantasy), nightmare, phantasm, vision
  rel fable, fabrication, fiction, figment,
invention; concept, conception, idea, notion; chimera, delusion, illusion; fata morgana, hallucination, mirage
  idiom figment of the imagination
  con actuality, fact, reality
fancy *vb* 1 *syn* see LIKE
  rel approve, endorse, sanction
  idiom have a fancy (*or* hankering) for;
have one's heart set on
  con deprecate, disapprove; abhor, abominate, detest, dislike, hate, loathe
  2 *syn* see THINK 1
  con demonstrate, prove, test, try
fancy *adj syn* see ELABORATE 1
fancy–free *adj syn* see FREE 6
fancy house *n syn* see BROTHEL
fancy man *n* 1 *syn* see LOVER 1
  2 *syn* see PIMP 1
fancy woman *n syn* see HARLOT 1
fanfare *n syn* see DISPLAY 2
fanny *n syn* see BUTTOCKS
fantastic *adj* 1 *syn* see FICTITIOUS 1
  rel implausible, incredible, unbelievable;
absurd, preposterous; irrational, unreasonable; deceptive, delusive, delusory, misleading
  con common, commonplace, everyday,
familiar, ordinary; customary, prevailing,
universal, usual
  2 conceived or made without reference to
reality < their explanation was *fantastic* >

  syn antic, bizarre, grotesque
  rel adroit, clever, ingenious; eccentric,
erratic, odd, queer, singular, strange; absurd, nonsensical, preposterous; ridiculous
  con factual, solid, sound, valid, well=
grounded; plausible, reasonable
  3 *syn* see FOOLISH 2
  4 *syn* see MONSTROUS 1
  5 *syn* see EXTRAVAGANT 1
fantasy (*or* **phantasy**) *n* 1 *syn* see IMAGI-
NATION
  rel conceiving, envisioning, fancying,
imagining; externalizing, objectifying
  2 *syn* see FANCY 4
  rel caprice, freak, vagary, whim, whimsy;
bizarrerie, grotesquerie
  con actuality, fact, reality
  3 *syn* see PIPE DREAM
far *adv syn* see WELL 8
far *adj syn* see DISTANT 1
  idiom a long day's journey
  ant near
far and away *adv* by a considerable margin < he was *far and away* the best man
for the job >
  syn by all odds, by a long shot, by far,
by long odds, by odds, out and away
  rel decidedly, definitely; doubtless, uncon-
ditionally, undoubtedly, unequivocally,
unquestionably; absolutely, positively;
just, quite, very
  con barely; slightly; possibly
far and near *adv syn* see EVERYWHERE 1
far and wide *adv syn* see EVERYWHERE 1
faraway *adj* 1 *syn* see DISTANT 1
  ant near-at-hand
  2 *syn* see ABSTRACTED
  rel disregardful, heedless, oblivious, star-
gazing, unheeding, unmindful
  idiom off one's guard
farce *n syn* see MOCKERY 2
farceur *n syn* see ZANY 2
farcical *adj syn* see LAUGHABLE
  rel absurd, extravagant, nonsensical, outrageous, preposterous
fare *vb* 1 *syn* see GO 1
  rel advance, progress
  idiom make headway
  con stay, stop
  2 *syn* see SHIFT 5
farewell *interj syn* see GOOD-BYE
farewell *n syn* see PARTING
farewell *adj syn* see PARTING
farfetched *adj syn* see FORCED
  rel bizarre, fantastic, grotesque; eccentric,
erratic, queer, strange
  con accustomed, usual, wonted
far–flung *adj syn* see DISTANT 1
far–gone *adj syn* see EFFETE 2
farming *n syn* see AGRICULTURE
  rel cultivation, tillage; agronomy, geopon-
ics, hydroponics
far–off *adj syn* see DISTANT 1
  idiom behind the farthest range
  ant nearby
far–out *adj syn* see OUTLANDISH 3
farther *adv syn* see BEYOND 1
farther *adj syn* see ADDITIONAL
farthest *adj syn* see EXTREME 5
  ant nearest
fascinate *vb* 1 *syn* see ENTHRALL 2
  2 *syn* see ATTRACT 1
  rel affect, impress, influence, strike, sway,
touch; delight, gladden, please, rejoice;

absorb, engage, engross, occupy, preoccupy
con disgust, horrify, repel; affront, insult,
offend, outrage, shame
3 *syn* see INTEREST
fascinated *adj syn* see ENAMORED 3
fascinating *adj syn* see ATTRACTIVE 1
rel delectable, delightful; seducing
fascination *n syn* see CHARM 3
fashion *n* **1** *syn* see METHOD 1
rel custom, habit, practice, usage, wont
2 *syn* see VEIN 1
3 the prevailing or accepted custom < follow the *fashion* >
syn bandwagon, chic, craze, cry, dernier
cri, fad, furore, mode, rage, style, thing,
ton, trend, ‖twig, vogue
rel drift, tendency; convention, form,
usage
idiom the in thing, the last word, the
latest thing
fashion *vb syn* see MAKE 3
rel contrive, devise; design, plan, plot;
turn out
fashionable *adj syn* see STYLISH
rel current, popular, prevalent, up-to-the-
minute
idiom all the rage
ant unfashionable
fast *adj* **1** *syn* see SURE 1
rel fixed, held, inextricable, stuck, wedged
con insecure, loose, shaky, unstable
2 *syn* see FAITHFUL 1
3 moving, proceeding, or acting with great
celerity < a *fast* horse >
syn breakneck, expeditious, expeditive,
fleet, harefooted, hasty, posthaste, quick,
raking, rapid, snappy, speedy, swift
rel active, alert, brisk, keen, lively
idiom quick as lightning, quick as
thought, swift as an arrow
con lethargic, logy, poky, sluggish, tardy,
torpid; languid, languorous; deliberate,
gradual
ant slow
4 persistent in adhering to something < a
fast grip >
syn firm, fixed, secure, set, tenacious,
tight; *compare* STABLE 4, SURE 1
idiom stuck fast
con insecure, loose, relaxed, unfirm, weak;
free, unattached, unfixed
5 *syn* see WILD 7
6 *syn* see LICENTIOUS 2
7 sexually promiscuous—usually used of a
woman < she's said to be *fast* >
syn easy, light, loose, ‖riggish, unchaste,
wanton, whorish
rel careless, heedless, lax, slack; bawdy,
indecent; lascivious, lecherous, lewd, libertine, licentious, lickerish, riotous
idiom no better than one should be, of
easy virtue
con chaste, decent, decorous, modest,
moral, pure, virtuous
fast *adv* **1** *syn* see HARD 7
2 in a rapid manner < run up the hill as
fast as you know how >

syn apace, chop-chop, expeditiously, flatout, fleetly, full tilt, hastily, lickety-split,
posthaste, presto, promptly, pronto,
quick, quickly, rapidly, soon, speedily,
swift, swiftly
idiom by leaps and bounds, in a flash, in
a twinkling, in nothing flat, in short order, like a bat out of hell, like a blue
streak, like a flash, like a house afire, like
a shot, like a streak, like greased lightning, like wildfire
con deliberately, leisurely; apathetically,
lethargically, sluggishly
ant slow, slowly
fasten *vb* **1** to cause one thing to hold to
another < *fasten* a feather to a hat >
syn affix, attach, fix, rivet
rel connect, join, link, unite; adhere,
cleave, cling, cohere, stick
con divide, divorce, part, separate, sever,
sunder; loose, loosen
ant unfasten
2 to fix in place or in a desired position
< *fasten* the door >
syn anchor, catch, fix, moor, secure
rel bed, implant, infix, lodge, set, settle;
embed, join, wedge; establish; bar, hitch,
hook
idiom make fast (*or* secure *or* sure)
con loose, undo, unloose, unloosen
ant unfasten
3 to direct (as attention or hope) directly
and steadily < *fastened* his whole mind on
the problem >
syn concenter, concentrate, fix, fixate,
focus, put, rivet
rel address, apply, devote, direct, train,
turn
con falter, vacillate, waver
fastidious *adj syn* see NICE 1
rel demanding, exacting; captious, critical,
hypercritical
con cursory, uncritical
fastigium *n syn* see TOP 1
fastness *n syn* see FORT
rel retreat, shelter; defense, guard, protection; adytum, sanctum
fat *adj* **1** *syn* see FATTY 1
2 having excess adipose tissue < a *fat*
woman overflowing her chair >
syn corpulent, fleshy, gross, heavy, obese,
overblown, overweight, porcine, portly,
pursy, stout, upholstered, weighty; *compare* ROTUND 2
rel beefy, bulky, chunky, dumpy, full-
bodied, heavyset, squat, stocky, stubby,
thick, thickset; paunchy, potbellied;
brawny, burly, husky
idiom broad in the beam, fat as a pig
con angular, gaunt, lank, lanky, rawboned, scrawny, skinny, spare; slender,
slight, slim, thin
ant lean
3 *syn* see LARGE 1
rel broad, deep, wide
con narrow, skinny
4 *syn* see RESONANT
‖**5** *syn* see REMOTE 4
fat *n* **1** *syn* see BEST
2 *syn* see EXCESS 1
fatal *adj* **1** *syn* see DEADLY 1
2 bringing on an adverse fate < to accept
his word was a *fatal* mistake >

syn calamitous, cataclysmic, catastrophic, disastrous, fateful, ruinous

rel baneful, pernicious; baleful, malefic, maleficent, malign, sinister; ill-fated, ill-starred, unlucky

con advantageous, beneficial, profitable; auspicious, benign, favorable, propitious

fatal *n syn* see FATALITY 2

fatality *n* **1** the condition of causing death <the tuberculosis *fatality* remains high>

syn deadliness, lethality, mortality

rel malignancy, noxiousness, perniciousness, poisonousness, virulence

2 an instance of dying especially as the result of accident or disaster <two *fatalities* over the weekend>

syn casualty, death, fatal

‖**fat cat** *n syn* see NOTABLE 1

fate *n* whatever is destined or inevitably decreed for one <the *fate* of the bill has not been decided>

syn circumstance, destiny, doom, kismet, lot, moira, portion, weird

rel consequence, effect, issue, outcome, result, upshot; end, ending, termination; ineluctability, inescapableness, inevitability, inevitableness, unavoidability

con accident, fortune, hazard, luck

fate *vb syn* see PREDESTINE 1

fateful *adj* **1** *syn* see OMINOUS

rel important, momentous, significant; conclusive, decisive, determinative; acute, critical, crucial

con inconclusive, insignificant, trivial, unimportant

2 *syn* see FATAL 2

fathead *n syn* see DUNCE

fatheaded *adj syn* see STUPID 1

father *n* **1** a male human parent <scarcely knew his *father*>

syn dad, dada, daddy, ‖governor, ‖old man, pa, ‖pap, papa, ‖pappy, ‖pater, pop, poppa; *compare* MOTHER 1

2 one that originates or institutes <the *father* of radiotelegraphy>

syn architect, author, creator, founder, generator, inventor, maker, originator, patriarch, sire

rel builder, encourager, motor, mover, organizer, prime mover, producer, promoter, promulgator, supporter; inaugurator, initiator, introducer

con disciple, follower

father *vb* **1** to be the male parent in reproduction <didn't know who *fathered* the child>

syn beget, breed, get, procreate, progenerate, sire

rel engender, generate, ingenerate; spawn

2 *syn* see GENERATE 1

fatherland *n syn* see COUNTRY

fatherless *adj syn* see ILLEGITIMATE 1

fathom *vb* **1** *syn* see SOUND

2 *syn* see KNOW 1

rel penetrate, pierce, probe; perceive, recognize; ‖dig, savvy

fathomable *adj syn* see UNDERSTANDABLE

fathomless *adj syn* see BOTTOMLESS 2

fatidic *adj syn* see PROPHETIC

fatigue *n* complete depletion of strength <suffering from *fatigue*>

syn exhaustion, lassitude, tiredness, weariness

rel enervation, ennui, languor, listlessness; debilitation, faintness, feebleness, weakness

con briskness, energy, liveliness, vigor, vitality; endurance, strength

fatigue *vb syn* see TIRE 1

rel deplete; exhaust, fag, tucker, wear out; debilitate, disable, weaken; annoy, bother, irk, vex

con refresh, rejuvenate, renew, restore; assuage, relieve

fatigued *adj syn* see TIRED 1

fatness *n syn* see OBESITY

‖**fatso** *n syn* see FATTY

fatty *adj* **1** containing fat especially in unusual amounts <a rather *fatty* steak>

syn adipose, fat

rel blubbery, lardy, suety

ant lean

2 having the qualities of fat <the constant frying left a *fatty* deposit on the kitchen woodwork>

syn greasy, oily, oleaginous, unctuous

fatty *n* a fat person <*fatties* trying to diet>

syn blimp, butterball, dumpling, ‖fatso, ‖tub

rel overweight; pudge, roly-poly, strapper; potbelly

idiom tons of fun

ant skinny

fatuous *adj syn* see SIMPLE 3

rel idiotic, imbecile, moronic; besotted, fond, infatuated, insensate; absurd, dumb, silly, stupid

con judicious, prudent, sage, sane, sapient, wise

ant sensible

faucet *n* a fixture for controlling the passage of fluid <turn off the *faucet*>

syn cock, gate, hydrant, petcock, spigot, stopcock, tap, valve

rel bung, spile

fault *n* **1** *syn* see IMPERFECTION

rel infirmity, weakness

con faultlessness, impeccability; meticulousness, preciseness, precision

2 an imperfection in character or an ingrained moral weakness <he has few *faults*>

syn failing, foible, frailty, vice

rel infirmity, weakness; blemish, defect, flaw

con excellence, perfection, virtue; desirability, goodness, rightness

ant merit

3 *syn* see BLAME

rel accountability, answerability, liability, responsibility; crime, error, offense, sin, transgression

faultfinder *n* **1** *syn* see CRITIC

2 *syn* see GROUCH

faultfinding *adj syn* see CRITICAL 1

rel particular, pernickety; ultracritical

con appreciative, cherishing, prizing, valuing

faultily *adv syn* see AMISS 1

rel erroneously, fallaciously, inaccurately, mistakenly, unfairly

con correctly, right

faultless *adj* **1** *syn* see IMPECCABLE 1

rel entire, intact, perfect, whole; blameless

con defective, deficient, imprecise, inaccurate, inexact, uncorrect
ant faulty

2 *syn* see INNOCENT 2

faulty *adj* marked by a fault or defect <a *faulty* mechanism>
syn amiss, defective, flawed, imperfect, sick
rel imprecise, inaccurate, inexact, uncorrect; deficient, inadequate, incomplete; erroneous, fallacious, fallible, specious, wrong; blemished, damaged, defaced, disfigured, marred
con accurate, correct, exact, nice, precise, right; complete, entire, intact, perfect, whole; excellent, good; unflawed, unimpaired
ant faultless

faux pas *n* a breach of etiquette or of social convention <hustled him out of the room before he could commit another *faux pas*>
syn blooper, boner, ‖boo-boo, break, gaffe, impropriety, indecorum, solecism; *compare* ERROR 2
rel bungle, misstep, stumble; howler, screamer; indiscretion, misjudgment, oversight, pratfall

favor *n* 1 *syn* see REGARD 4
ant disfavor

2 *syn* see APPROBATION 1
con depreciation, derogation, disparagement
ant disfavor

3 *syn* see GIFT 1
rel aid, assistance, backing, encouragement, help, support

4 a special privilege <willing to grant a *favor* to a good friend>
syn courtesy, dispensation, indulgence, kindness, service
rel aid, assistance, cooperation, help

favor *vb* 1 *syn* see APPROVE 1
rel endorse, OK (*or* okay), sanction; appreciate, prize, value
idiom set great store by
con decry, depreciate, disparage
ant disfavor

2 *syn* see OBLIGE 2
rel humor, indulge, pamper
idiom do one a favor (*or* service), do right by
con baffle, circumvent, foil, frustrate, thwart

3 *syn* see ENCOURAGE 2

4 *syn* see RESEMBLE
con contradict, differ

favorable *adj* 1 expressing approval <a *favorable* recommendation>
syn approbative, approbatory, approving
rel benignant, kind, kindly; recommendatory, well-disposed; commendatory, complimentary, laudatory, praiseful
idiom in one's favor
con depreciative, disapprobatory, disapproving, disparaging, uncomplimentary; censorious, condemnatory, critical, faultfinding

ant unfavorable

2 *syn* see PLEASANT 1

3 *syn* see GOOD 1
rel healthful, salutary, wholesome
con disadvantageous, unpropitious; damaging, hampering
ant unfavorable

4 *syn* see TIMELY 1

5 indicative of a successful outcome <*favorable* conditions for opening a new business>
syn auspicious, benign, bright, dexter, fortunate, propitious, white
rel advantageous, beneficial, profitable; happy, lucky, promising, providential; cheering, encouraging, reassuring
idiom full of promise
con calamitous, cataclysmic, catastrophic, disastrous, fatal, fateful, ruinous; baleful, malefic, maleficent, malign, sinister; ill=fated, ill-starred, unlucky; inauspicious, unpromising, unpropitious
ant unfavorable

favorably *adv* *syn* see WELL 5
favored *adj* *syn* see FAVORITE 2
favoring *adj* *syn* see GOOD 1
favorite *adj* 1 accorded special treatment or attention <a *favorite* daughter>
syn beloved, blue-eyed, darling, dear, fair-haired, loved, pet, precious, white-haired, white-headed
rel admired, adored, esteemed, revered; cherished, prized, treasured
idiom dear as the apple of one's eye, dear to one's heart, held dear
con contemned, despised, disdained; abhorrent, detested, hated

2 constituting a favorite <*favorite* melodies>
syn favored, popular, preferred, well-liked
rel laudable, pleasant, praiseworthy; cherished, prized, treasured
con despised, detested, disliked, hated, unpopular; eschewed, rejected

fawn *vb* to act or behave with abjectness in the presence of a superior <*fawn* on the master>
syn apple-polish, bootlick, ‖brownnose, cotton, cower, cringe, grovel, honey (up), kowtow, slaver, toady, truckle
rel blandish, cajole, coax, wheedle; butter (up), flatter, make up (to); cater (to), pander (to); crawl; abase, debase, demean; bow, cave, defer, submit, yield; court, invite, woo
idiom be at one's beck and call, curry favor, dance attendance, kiss one's feet, lick one's shoes (*or* boots), make a doormat of oneself, ‖suck up to
con contemn, despise, disdain, scorn, scout; reject, repudiate, spurn; flout, gibe, jeer, scoff; deride, mock, ridicule, taunt
ant domineer

fawning *adj* characteristic of one that fawns <sent *fawning* greetings>
syn bootlicking, cowering, cringing, groveling, kowtowing, parasitic, sycophant, sycophantic, sycophantical, sycophantish, toadying, toadyish, truckling
rel flunkyish, obsequious, servile, slavish, subservient; compliant, deferential, humble, submissive, yielding; ingratiating; adulatory, flattering, mealy-mouthed; crawling, spineless; abject, ignoble, mean

---

syn synonym(s)   *rel* related word(s)
ant antonym(s)   *con* contrasted word(s)
idiom idiomatic equivalent(s)
‖ use limited; if in doubt, see a dictionary

con arrogant, disdainful, haughty, insolent, lordly, overbearing, proud, supercilious; contemptuous, insulting, scathing, scornful; authoritative, imperious, magisterial, masterful
ant domineering

fay *n syn* see FAIRY

faze *vb syn* see EMBARRASS
rel confound, dumbfound, mystify, nonplus, perplex, puzzle; confuse, muddle; appall, daunt, dismay, horrify; annoy, bother, irritate, vex
con calm, compose, quiet, relax, soothe; ease, relieve

fealty *n syn* see FIDELITY 1
rel faith, trueness, truth; dependability, reliability, trustworthiness; devotedness, support
con disloyalty, traitorousness, treacherousness
ant perfidy

fear *n* **1** agitation or dismay in the anticipation of or in the presence of danger < living in *fear* of what the future might hold >
syn alarm, cold feet, consternation, dismay, dread, fright, horror, panic, terror, trepidation, trepidity
rel apprehension, foreboding, misgiving, presentiment; angst, anxiety, concern, worry; agitation, discomposure, disquietude, perturbation; chickenheartedness, cowardice, cowardliness, faintheartedness, timidity, timorousness; funk, scare
idiom cold sweat
con boldness, bravery, courage, courageousness, dauntlessness, fortitude, gallantry, intrepidity, prowess, valiancy, valor
ant fearlessness
2 *syn* see REVERENCE 2
rel esteem, respect
con contempt, scorn

fearful *adj* **1** *syn* see AFRAID 1
rel agitated, alarmed, discomposed, disquieted, disturbed, perturbed
con audacious, bold, brave, courageous, dauntless, unafraid, valiant
ant fearless
2 inspired or moved by fear < *fearful* of loud noises >
syn afraid, apprehensive; *compare* AFRAID 1
rel alarmed, disquieted, disturbed; aflutter, agitated, jittery, nervous, perturbed, uneasy; anxious, concerned, solicitous, worried
con assured, confident, sanguine, sure; collected, composed, cool, imperturbable, nonchalant, unflappable, unperturbed
ant unafraid
3 causing fear < a *fearful* sight >
syn appalling, awful, dire, direful, dreadful, formidable, frightful, horrible, horrific, redoubtable, shocking, terrible, terrific, tremendous
rel alarming, frightening, terrifying; ghastly, grim, grisly, gruesome, lurid, macabre; baleful, malign, sinister; overwhelming, sublime
con attractive, charming, delightful, enchanting, pleasant, pleasing
ant reassuring

fearless *adj syn* see BRAVE 1

rel assured, confident, sanguine, sure
con afraid, frightened, scared, terrified
ant fearful

feasible *adj syn* see POSSIBLE 1
rel practical; advantageous, beneficial, profitable; appropriate, fit, fitting, suitable
con impossible, impracticable, unachievable, unattainable, unworkable; ambitious, pretentious, utopian
ant infeasible, unfeasible

feast *n syn* see DINNER
rel entertainment, festivity; refreshment, repast; meal

feat *n* **1** *syn* see ADVENTURE
idiom bold stroke, deed of derring-do
2 a remarkable act or performance < Washington's *feat* of tossing a dollar across the river >
syn achievement, deed, exploit, tour de force
rel act, action; accomplishment, consummation, execution, performance; conquest, triumph, victory
3 *syn* see TRICK 3

feather *n syn* see TYPE

featherbrain *n syn* see SCATTERBRAIN

featherbrained *adj syn* see GIDDY 1
rel capricious, fickle, impulsive, whimsical; shallow, superficial, unprofound

featherhead *n syn* see SCATTERBRAIN

featherlight *adj syn* see LIGHT 1

featherweight *n syn* see DUNCE

featherweight *adj syn* see LIGHT 1

feature *n* **1** *syn* see QUALITY 1
2 *syn* see CHARACTERISTIC 1
rel article, detail, item, particular; component, constituent, element, factor, ingredient; individuality, particularity, peculiarity, speciality, specialty; attribute, property, quality
3 features *pl syn* see FACE 1

feature *vb* ‖ **1** *syn* see RESEMBLE
2 *syn* see THINK 1
3 *syn* see EMPHASIZE

febrile *adj syn* see FEVERISH 1

feckless *adj* **1** having no real worth or purpose < after years of *feckless* negotiations >
syn fustian, good-for-nothing, meaningless, purposeless, unpurposed, useless, worthless
rel bootless, fruitless, futile, unavailing, vain; ineffective, ineffectual, inefficacious
con meaningful, purposeful, worthwhile; fruitful; effective, effectual, efficacious; consequential, important, momentous, significant, weighty
ant efficient, ‖feckful
2 *syn* see CARELESS 1
rel carefree, easygoing, happy-go-lucky, lackadaisical, nonchalant; remiss; irresponsible, undependable, unreliable, untrustworthy
con attentive, considerate, thoughtful; meticulous, punctilious, punctual, scrupulous; dependable, reliable, responsible, trustworthy
3 *syn* see IRRESPONSIBLE
ant ‖feckful

fecund *adj syn* see FERTILE
rel breeding, generating, propagating, reproducing
con infertile, sterile

ant barren
fecundity *n* **1** *syn* see FERTILITY
rel productiveness, productivity; exuberance, lavishness, lushness, luxuriance, prodigality, profuseness, profusion
con infertility, sterility, unproductiveness
ant barrenness, infecundity
2 *syn* see ELOQUENCE
federation *n syn* see ALLIANCE 2
fed up *adj* disgusted and completely out of patience < *fed up* with her bad behavior >
syn disgusted, sick, tired, weary
rel bored; glutted, sated, satiated, surfeited
idiom fed to the gills (*or* teeth), full up to here with, sick and tired of, sick (*or* tired) to death
con enchanted, enraptured, enthralled; delighted, excited, exhilarated, pleased, thrilled
fee *n syn* see WAGE
rel consideration; charge, cost, expense, price
‖**feeb** *n syn* see FOOL 4
feeble *adj* **1** *syn* see WEAK 1
rel emasculated, enervated, unmanned, unnerved; helpless; aged, doddering, senile; ailing, sapless
con hale, healthy, sound; lusty, strenuous; strong
ant robust
2 *syn* see TENUOUS 3
feebleminded *adj syn* see RETARDED
ant strong-minded
feebleness *n syn* see INFIRMITY 1
feed *vb syn* see GIVE 3
feed (on) *vb syn* see EAT 1
idiom have (*or* take) a bite, ‖put on the feed bag (*or* nose bag)
feed *n* **1** *syn* see MEAL
2 *syn* see FOOD 1
rel banquet, feast, meal, repast
feel *vb* **1** *syn* see TOUCH 1
rel manipulate, ply, wield; explore, sound; fumble, grope
2 to have as an emotional response < *felt* pleasure in her company >
syn experience, know, savor, taste
rel apprehend; notice, observe, perceive; encounter, meet; endure, suffer, undergo
idiom be aware (*or* conscious) of, be sensible of
con disregard, ignore
3 to view as right or true < we *feel* that he should retire soon >
syn believe, consider, credit, deem, hold, sense, think; *compare* CONSIDER 3
rel assume, presume, suppose, suspect; conclude, deduce, gather, infer, judge; conjecture, guess, surmise; esteem; repute
idiom take (it) into one's head
con challenge, distrust, doubt, misdoubt, mistrust, question
4 *syn* see GROPE
feel (for) *vb syn* see COMPASSIONATE
feel *n* **1** *syn* see TOUCH 3
2 *syn* see TOUCH 4
3 *syn* see AIR 3

con basis, essence, reality
feeler *n* an attempt to ascertain opinion < the letter was a *feeler* to see how they would react >
syn trial balloon
rel query, question; inquiry, probe, test; leader, leading question; sounding board; intimation, representation; prospectus; kiteflying
feeling *n* **1** *syn* see SENSATION 1
rel action, behavior, reaction; responsiveness; palpability, palpableness, perceptibility, perceptibleness, tangibility, tangibleness
con apathy, indifference, insensibility, numbness
2 *syn* see TOUCH 4
3 subjective response or reaction (as to a person or situation) < a *feeling* of sadness >
syn affection, affectivity, emotion, passion, sentiment
rel humor, mood, temper, vein; attitude, outlook; belief, opinion, view; concept, idea, impression, notion, thought
4 *syn* see OPINION
5 *syn* see AIR 3
rel impress, impression, imprint
feeling *adj syn* see EMOTIONAL 1
con numb, unmoved, unresponsive
ant unfeeling
feel out *vb syn* see PROBE 2
feign *vb syn* see ASSUME 4
feigned *adj syn* see ARTIFICIAL 3
rel counterfeit, false, sham
con heartfelt, hearty, sincere, wholehearted, whole-souled
feint *n syn* see TRICK 1
rel make-believe, pretense, pretension; befooling, hoax, hoodwinking; cheat, counterfeit, deceit, fake, humbug, imposture, sham; expedient, resort, shift
felicitate *vb syn* see CONGRATULATE
rel commend, compliment, recommend; salute
con comfort, console, solace; commiserate, condole (with), pity; gibe, jeer, scoff; deride, mock, ridicule, taunt; contemn
felicitous *adj syn* see FIT 1
rel convincing, telling; opportune, pat, seasonable, timely, well-timed; apposite, apropos, germane, pertinent, relevant
con awkward, clumsy, gauche, inept, maladroit; unfortunate, unhappy, unlucky
ant infelicitous
feline *adj syn* see STEALTHY 2
fell *vb* **1** to force an opponent off his feet < *felled* the heckler with a single blow >
syn bowl (down *or* over), bring down, down, drop, flatten, floor, ground, knock down, knock over, lay low, level, mow (down), prostrate, throw down, tumble
rel shoot, shoot down
idiom lay level with the ground
con pick up, raise
2 to bring down by cutting < *felled* the great oak by the driveway >
syn chop, cut, hew
rel flatten, level, raze; cleave, rive, split; sever, sunder; gash, hack, mangle, slash
fell *adj syn* **1** *syn* see FIERCE 1
rel baleful, malefic, maleficent, malign, sinister; implacable, relentless, unrelenting; fearful, horrible, horrific, terrific

---

syn synonym(s)   *rel* related word(s)
ant antonym(s)   *con* contrasted word(s)
idiom idiomatic equivalent(s)
‖ use limited; if in doubt, see a dictionary

con compassionate, sympathetic, tender; clement, forbearing, lenient, merciful; humane

2 *syn* see GRAVE 3

fell *n syn* see HIDE

fellow *n* 1 *syn* see PARTNER

2 *syn* see ACCOMPANIMENT 2

3 *syn* see MATE 3

4 *syn* see MAN 3

fellow feeling *n syn* see SYMPATHY 2

fellowship *n* 1 *syn* see COMPANY 1

2 *syn* see ASSOCIATION 2

felo–de–se *n syn* see SUICIDE

felon *n syn* see CRIMINAL

femme fatale *n syn* see SIREN

fen *n syn* see SWAMP

fence *n syn* see BAR 2

fence *vb* 1 *syn* see ENCLOSE 1

2 *syn* see DODGE 1

rel feint, maneuver; baffle, foil, outwit

fend *vb* 1 *syn* see DEFEND 1

2 *syn* see WARD 1

fend (off) *vb* to give a sharp check to < tried to *fend* off his attentions >

syn hold off, keep off, rebuff, rebut, repel, repulse, stave off, ward (off)

rel refuse, reject; snub, spurn; avert, avoid

idiom hold (*or* keep) at bay, keep at a distance, keep at arm's length

con allure, attract, captivate, charm, enchant, fascinate; embolden, hearten

feral *adj* 1 *syn* see BRUTISH

rel barbaric, barbarous, ferocious, fierce, inhuman, savage, vicious

con gentle, mild, tame

2 *syn* see SAVAGE 1

ferine *adj syn* see BRUTISH

ferment *vb syn* see SEETHE 4

ferment *n* 1 *syn* see UNREST

2 *syn* see COMMOTION 1

ferocious *adj* 1 *syn* see FIERCE 1

rel rapacious, ravening, ravenous, voracious; implacable, relentless

ant tender

2 *syn* see SAVAGE

ferret out *vb syn* see SEEK 1

rel elicit, extract; nose out, pry (out); penetrate, pierce, probe; chase, follow, pursue, trail; ascertain, determine, discover, learn

con conceal, hide, screen, secrete; camouflage, disguise; cover (up), hush (up), suppress

ant squirrel (away)

ferry *vb syn* see CARRY 1

fertile *adj* marked by abundant productivity < *fertile* soil > < a *fertile* mind >

syn childing, fecund, fruitful, productive, proliferant, prolific, rich, spawning

rel bearing, producing, yielding; abundant, bountiful, copious, exuberant, generous, lush, luxuriant, plenteous, plentiful, teeming; creative, ingenious, inventive, pregnant, resourceful; exciting, galvanizing, provoking, quickening, stimulating

con barren, impotent, unfruitful; dull, imitative, stupid, unproductive

ant infertile, sterile

fertility *n* the quality or state of being fertile < insure the *fertility* of the soil >

syn fecundity, fruitfulness, prolificacy

rel abundance, copiousness, plentifulness; creativity, ingenuity, inventiveness, resourcefulness

con barrenness, impotence, unfruitfulness

ant infertility, sterility

fervent *adj syn* see IMPASSIONED

rel devout, pious, religious; responsive, tender, warm, warmhearted; heartfelt, hearty, sincere, unfeigned, wholehearted, whole-souled; earnest, serious; eager, enthusiastic

con apathetic, impassive, phlegmatic; aloof, detached, indifferent, unconcerned

fervid *adj* 1 *syn* see IMPASSIONED

con collected, composed, cool, imperturbable, nonchalant

ant gelid

2 *syn* see FEVERISH 2

fervor *n syn* see PASSION 6

rel devoutness, piety, piousness; earnestness, seriousness, solemnity; heartiness, sincerity, wholeheartedness; empressement, warmth

con apathy, impassiveness, impassivity; aloofness, detachment, indifference, unconcern; languor, lethargy, torpor

fescennine *adj syn* see OBSCENE 2

fess (up) *vb syn* see ACKNOWLEDGE 1

fester *vb syn* see RANKLE

festive *adj syn* see MERRY

festivity *n syn* see MERRYMAKING

fetch *vb syn* see SELL 4

fetching *adj syn* see ENTICING

fetch up *vb* ‖ 1 *syn* see BRING UP 1

2 *syn* see STOP 4

fetid *adj syn* see MALODOROUS 1

rel loathsome, repugnant, repulsive, revolting

con aromatic, balmy, odorous, redolent

ant fragrant

fetish *n* 1 *syn* see CHARM 2

2 irrational reverence or attachment < had a *fetish* for red hair >

syn fixation, mania, obsession, thing

rel preoccupation, prepossession; bias, partiality, predilection, prejudice; leaning, penchant, proclivity, propensity

con antipathy, aversion, repugnance, repulsion; dislike, disrelish, distaste

fetter *n, usu* fetters *pl syn* see SHACKLE

fetter *vb syn* see HAMPER

con disembarrass, disencumber, disentangle, extricate, untangle; detach, disengage

fettle *n syn* see ORDER 10

feud *n* 1 *syn* see VENDETTA

2 *syn* see QUARREL

rel argument; combat, contest

fevered *adj* 1 *syn* see FEVERISH 1

ant afebrile

2 *syn* see FEVERISH 2

feverish *adj* 1 abnormally heated by fever < the child's forehead felt *feverish* >

syn febrile, fevered, fiery

rel burning, flushed, hectic, hot, inflamed, pyretic

ant afebrile

2 marked by intense emotion or activity < a *feverish* imagination >

syn burning, fervid, fevered, heated, hectic

rel excited, high-strung, nervous, overwrought; frenzied, furious, passionate

idiom keyed up

con calm, composed, cool, serene, tranquil; apathetic, languid, lethargic, listless, phlegmatic

few *adj syn* see INFREQUENT

few *n* a small quantity or number <sold a *few* of the books>
syn handful, scattering, smatch, smatter, smattering, spatter, spattering, sprinkling
con abundance, many, multitude, numbers

fiat *n syn* see SANCTION

fib *n syn* see LIE
rel equivocation, evasiveness; mendacity, untruthfulness
idiom tall tale

fib *vb syn* see LIE
rel concoct, fabricate, make up, trump up
idiom draw the long bow, stretch the truth

fibber *n syn* see LIAR

fibbery *n syn* see MENDACITY

fiber *n syn* see TEXTURE 2

fibrous *adj syn* see MUSCULAR 1

fibster *n syn* see LIAR

fickle *adj syn* see INCONSTANT 1
rel unfaithful; undependable, unreliable
con stable, unchanging
ant constant, true

fiction *n* a story, account, explanation, or conception which is an invention of the human mind <his belief was based on a *fiction*>
syn fable, fabrication, figment
rel concoction, fantasy, invention; falsehood, lie, misrepresentation, untruth; anecdote, narrative, story, tale, yarn; fish story
con actuality, reality
ant fact

fictional *adj syn* see FICTITIOUS 1

fictitious *adj* 1 suggestive of fiction especially in lacking a sound factual basis <*fictitious* values in logic>
syn chimerical, fanciful, fantastic, fictional, fictive, illusory, imaginary, supposititious, suppositious, unreal
rel concocted, created, invented, made; fabricated, fashioned; cooked-up, false, made-up, trumped-up, untrue; romantic
con actual, real, true; authentic, genuine; factual, veritable; truthful, veracious, verisimilar
2 not genuine <the gigolo wooed the heiress with *fictitious* ardor>
syn fake, mock, sham, simulated; *compare* ARTIFICIAL 2
rel deceptive, delusive, delusory, misleading; dishonest, unreal, untrue; artificial, ersatz, factitious, synthetic
con authentic, bona fide, veritable; actual, honest, real, true
ant genuine

fictive *adj syn* see FICTITIOUS 1

fiddle *vb* 1 to handle something nervously or absently <always *fiddling* with his tie>
syn fidget, play, trifle, twiddle
rel feel, handle, touch

2 to work aimlessly, fruitlessly, or pointlessly <*fiddled* around with the engine for hours>
syn doodle, mess, mess around, potter, puddle, putter, tinker
rel dabble, fool, monkey

fiddle–faddle *n syn* see NONSENSE 2

fiddlesticks *n pl syn* see NONSENSE 2

fidelity *n* 1 constancy to something to which one is bound by a pledge or duty <we must practice *fidelity* to our word>
syn allegiance, ardor, devotion, faithfulness, fealty, loyalty, piety
rel constancy, staunchness, steadfastness; dependability, reliability, trustworthiness
con disloyalty, falseness, falsity, perfidiousness, traitorousness, treacherousness, treachery; undependableness, unreliability, untrustworthiness
ant perfidy; faithlessness
2 *syn* see ATTACHMENT 1
ant infidelity

fidget *vb syn* see FIDDLE 1

fidgety *adj syn* see NERVOUS

field *n* a limited area of knowledge or endeavor to which pursuits, activities, and interests are confined <a lawyer eminent in his *field*>
syn bailiwick, champaign, demesne, domain, dominion, precinct, province, region, sphere, terrain, territory, walk
rel bounds, confines, limits; area, department; compass, orbit, purview, range, reach, scope, sweep
con terra incognita

fiend *n syn* see DEVIL 1
2 *syn* see DEVIL 2
3 *syn* see ENTHUSIAST

fiendish *adj* having or manifesting qualities associated with devils, demons, and fiends <inflicted *fiendish* tortures on his captive>
syn demoniac, demonian, demonic, devilish, diabolic, diabolonian, satanic, serpentine, unhallowed
rel hellish, infernal; baleful, malefic, maleficent, malign, sinister; malevolent, malicious, malignant; atrocious, heinous, monstrous, outrageous; barbarous, cruel, ferocious, inhuman, savage, vicious
con benign, benignant, kind, kindly; gentle, mild; compassionate, sympathetic, tender

fierce *adj* 1 displaying fury or malignity in looks or actions <*fierce* native tribes>
syn barbarous, cannibalic, cruel, fell, ferocious, grim, inhuman, inhumane, savage, truculent, wolfish
rel menacing, threatening; enraged, infuriated, maddened; aggressive, bellicose, belligerent, pugnacious; brutal, merciless, pitiless, ruthless, vicious, wild
con benign, benignant, gentle, kind, kindly; peaceful; subdued, submissive, tame
ant mild
2 *syn* see INTENSE 1
rel excessive, extreme, inordinate; penetrating, piercing; superlative, supreme, transcendent
con gentle, mild, subdued

fiercely *adv syn* see HARD 2

fiery *adj* 1 *syn* see BURNING 1

---

2 *syn* see HOT 1
ant frigid, icy
3 *syn* see FEVERISH 1
4 *syn* see SPIRITED 2
rel headlong, hotheaded, impetuous, madcap, precipitate; fervid, impassioned, perfervid; fierce, intense, vehement, violent; enthusiastic, excitable, impulsive, unrestrained; irascible, irritable
con deliberate, leisurely, slow; apathetic, dull, impassive, lethargic, phlegmatic, sluggish; enervated, listless, spiritless
5 *syn* see IMPASSIONED
ant icy

fifty-fifty *adv syn* see EVENLY 1
fifty-fifty *adj syn* see EVEN 4
fight *vb* 1 *syn* see CONTEND 1
rel strive, struggle; rowdy, scuffle, tussle; debate, dispute; altercate, bicker, quarrel, scrap, spat, squabble, tiff, wrangle
idiom ‖mix it, mix it up, put up a fight
con bow, capitulate, submit, succumb, yield
2 *syn* see RESIST
con abide, bear, endure, suffer; advocate, back, champion, support, uphold; defend, guard, protect, shield

fight *n* 1 *syn* see BRAWL 2
2 *syn* see QUARREL
3 *syn* see ATTACK 2
fighter *n syn* see SOLDIER
fighting man *n syn* see SOLDIER
figment *n syn* see FICTION
rel daydream, dream, fancy, nightmare; bubble, chimera, illusion; creation
figurant *n syn* see DANCER
figurante *n syn* see DANCER
figuration *n* 1 *syn* see OUTLINE
2 *syn* see ALLEGORY 1
figure *n* 1 *syn* see NUMBER
rel character, symbol
2 *syn* see FORM 1
rel delineation; appearance, build, frame, physique
3 a unit in a decorative composition (as in a fabric) < a rug with geometrical *figures* in blue and red >
syn design, device, motif, motive, pattern
rel decoration, embellishment, ornamentation
figure *vb* 1 *syn* see CALCULATE
2 *syn* see ADD 2
rel count, enumerate, number
3 *syn* see DECIDE
figure out *vb syn* see SOLVE 2
rel disentangle, unscramble, untangle; crack, decode
con obfuscate, obscure; conceal, hide, screen
figuring *n syn* see COMPUTATION
filch *vb syn* see STEAL 1
filcher *n syn* see THIEF
file *n syn* see LINE 1
filius nullius *n syn* see BASTARD 1
filius populi *n syn* see BASTARD 1
fill *vb* 1 to make full in a way or to a degree that prevents further entry or passage < *fill* a cavity in a tooth >
syn block, choke, clog, close, congest, obstruct, occlude, plug, stop, stopper
rel bar, dam, jam; ‖bung, pug
con clear, free
2 *syn* see LOAD 3

3 *syn* see SATISFY 5
4 *syn* see SATIATE
rel overfeed, overfill, overstuff
fille de joie *n syn* see PROSTITUTE
fillet *n syn* see STRIP 1
fill in *vb* 1 *syn* see INTRODUCE 6
2 *syn* see INFORM 2
fill-in *n syn* see SUBSTITUTE
film *n* 1 *syn* see HAZE 1
2 *syn* see MOVIE
filmy *adj* characterized by fineness and delicacy of texture < *filmy* curtains >
syn diaphanous, flimsy, gauzy, gossamer, sheer, tiffany, transparent
rel dainty, delicate, fine
con coarse, heavy, opaque, rough
filthy *adj* 1 *syn* see DIRTY 1
rel disheveled, slipshod, sloppy, slovenly, unkempt; loathsome, offensive, repulsive, revolting, verminous; coarse, gross, obscene, ribald, vulgar
con cleaned, cleansed; clean, cleanly; neat, shipshape, tidy, trig, trim
ant immaculate, spick-and-span
2 *syn* see OBSCENE 2
filthy lucre *n syn* see MONEY
finagle *vb syn* see ENGINEER
final *adj syn* see LAST
rel crowning, ending, finishing; conclusive, decisive, definitive, determinative; irrefutable, unanswerable, unappealable
con earliest, maiden, original, primary; beginning, incipient, introductory; inaugural
ant initial
finale *n* a final part or element (as of a sequence, series, or action) < the solution of the mystery forms the *finale* of the play >
syn close, conclusion, end, ending, finish, windup; *compare* END 2
rel climax, consummation, culmination; denouement, payoff; cessation, termination
con beginning, genesis, initiation, rise, start; inception, origin, root, source
ant prologue
finally *adv syn* see YET 2
idiom at last, at length, at long last, in the long run, when all is said and done
finance *vb* 1 *syn* see CAPITALIZE
idiom put up the money, raise the dough
2 *syn* see ENDOW 2
rel back, bank, bankroll, grubstake, stake, underwrite; patronize, promote, sponsor, support
financial *adj* of or relating to finance < the *financial* interests of the country >
syn fiscal, monetary, pecuniary, pocket
rel business, commercial, economic
find *vb* 1 to come upon < they soon *found* what they needed >
syn catch, descry, detect, encounter, espy, hit (on or upon), meet (with), spot, turn up
rel discern, discover, note, sight; distinguish, identify, recognize; dig up, scare up
idiom bring to light, come up with, fall in with, lay one's finger (on or upon), lay one's hand (on or upon)
con miss, overlook, pass (over)
ant lose
2 *syn* see GIVE 3
find *n* 1 one of unexpected worth or merit obtained or encountered more or less by

chance <the young understudy proved to be a remarkable *find*>
syn treasure, treasure trove
rel boast, gem, jewel, pride
idiom one in a thousand (*or* million)
2 *syn* see DISCOVERY

find out *vb syn* see DISCOVER 3

fine *n* a pecuniary penalty exacted by an authority <paid a *fine* of ten dollars>
syn amercement, forfeit, mulct, penalty
rel damages, reparation; punishment; assessment

fine *vb syn* see PENALIZE
rel distrain, exact, levy, tax; confiscate, sequestrate

fine *adj* 1 marked by subtlety of perception or discrimination <I cannot follow these *fine* distinctions>
syn delicate, finespun, hairline, hairsplitting, nice, refined, subtle
rel abstruse, esoteric, recondite; cryptic, enigmatic, obscure; minute, petty, trifling
con definite, explicit, express, specific; clear, lucid, perspicuous; broad, extensive, general, generic, indefinite, wide
2 consisting of small particles <*fine* sand>
syn impalpable, powdery, pulverized
rel light, loose, porous
ant coarse
3 *syn* see EXCELLENT
rel beautiful, splendid; enjoyable, pleasant
idiom fine and dandy
con miserable, wretched; atrocious, awful, objectionable, unpleasant
4 *syn* see FAIR 2

finecomb *vb syn* see SCOUR 2

finery *n* dressy clothing <decked out in all her *finery*>
syn ‖best bib and tucker, bravery, frippery, full dress, ‖glad rags, regalia, Sunday best, war paint
rel apparel, clothes; foofaraw, frill, gewgaw, ornament, trimming
con rags, tatters

finespun *adj syn* see FINE 1

finesse *vb syn* see MANIPULATE 2

fine–tooth–comb *vb syn* see SCOUR 2

finger *vb* 1 *syn* see TOUCH 1
2 *syn* see DESIGNATE 2
3 *syn* see IDENTIFY

finical *adj syn* see NICE 1
con slipshod, sloppy, slovenly; blowsy, dowdy, frowzy, slatternly

finicking *adj syn* see NICE 1

finicky *adj syn* see NICE 1

finish *vb* 1 *syn* see CLOSE 3
rel accomplish, achieve, effect, fulfill
idiom have done with
2 *syn* see GO 4
3 *syn* see KILL 1
4 *syn* see MURDER 1

finish *n* 1 *syn* see END 2
2 *syn* see FINALE
3 *syn* see ACQUIREMENT
rel correctness, discrimination, propriety, refinement; elegance, grace, polish; cultivation, taste

finished *adj* 1 *syn* see COMPLETE 4
2 *syn* see THROUGH 3
3 *syn* see CONSUMMATE 1
rel cultivated, cultured, refined; smooth, suave, urbane; elegant, exquisite; all-around, many-sided, versatile
con imperfect, incomplete
ant crude; unfinished

finish off *vb syn* see CLIMAX

finite *adj* having definite or definable limits or boundaries <a *finite* thickness>
syn bound, bounded, limited
rel confined, restricted; definable, defined, definite, determinate, fixed, terminable; exact, precise, specific
con boundless, unbounded, unlimited; absolute, complete, total
ant infinite

‖**fink** *n syn* see INFORMER

fire *n* 1 a destructive burning <the house was destroyed by *fire*>
syn conflagration, holocaust, inferno
rel blaze, flame, flare, glare; burning, charring, scorching, searing
idiom sea of flames, sheet of fire
2 *syn* see PASSION 6
rel animation, exhilaration, liveliness; dash, drive, energy, ginger, gusto, heartiness, pep, punch, snap, spirit, starch, verve, vigor, vim, zest, zing, zip
con languor, lassitude, lethargy, listlessness, stupor, torpidity, torpor; apathy, impassivity, phlegm

fire *vb* 1 *syn* see LIGHT 1
idiom set fire to, set on fire
con extinguish, quench, smother
2 to stimulate (as mental powers) to higher or more intense activity <a painting that *fired* the viewer's imagination>
syn animate, exalt, inform, inspire; compare PROVOKE 4
rel arouse, enliven, rouse, stir; electrify, excite; heighten, intensify; enthuse, thrill
con appall, dismay; alarm, frighten, terrify
ant daunt
3 *syn* see DISMISS 3
rel eject, expel, oust
idiom give the pink slip, give the sack, strike off the rolls
con engage; appoint, designate, elect, name
ant hire
4 *syn* see SHOOT 1
5 *syn* see THROW 1
6 to dry or harden by subjecting to heat <*fire* bricks>
syn bake, burn, kiln

firebug *n syn* see INCENDIARY

fire–new *adj syn* see BRAND-NEW

firewater *n syn* see LIQUOR 2

firm *adj* 1 *syn* see FAST 4
2 *syn* see STABLE 4
3 having a texture or consistency that resists deformation by external force <*firm* flesh>
syn hard, solid
rel close, compact, dense, thick; inelastic, inflexible, rigid, stiff, unyielding; sturdy, substantial, tough
con flaccid, flimsy, floppy, limp, loose, slack, sleazy, soft, squishy
ant flabby

---

syn synonym(s)   *rel* related word(s)
ant antonym(s)   *con* contrasted word(s)
idiom idiomatic equivalent(s)
‖ use limited; if in doubt, see a dictionary

4 that has been established and is not
usually subject to change < a *firm* price>
syn certain, fixed, set, settled, stated,
stipulated
rel established, going, prevailing; consistent, stable, steady, unwavering; definite,
exact, explicit, specific, undeviating; flat
con changeable, fluctuating, shaky, shifting, unsteady, variable
5 *syn* see SURE 1
6 *syn* see SURE 2
firm *adv syn* see HARD 7
firm *n syn* see ENTERPRISE 3
firmament *n syn* see SKY
firmly *adv* **1** *syn* see HARD 7
2 *syn* see HARD 9
firmness *n* **1** *syn* see STABILITY
2 *syn* see DECISION 2
first *adj* **1** being number one in a series
< the *first* day of the week>
syn foremost, headmost, inaugural, initial,
leading
con final, terminal, ultimate; interjacent,
intermediary, intermediate, intervenient,
intervening
ant last
2 preceding all others < succeeded at his
first try>
syn earliest, initial, maiden, original, pioneer, primary, prime
rel early, pristine; primal, primogenial,
primordial
con derivative, imitative, secondary
ant final
3 exceeding all others < he was the *first*
statesman of his era>
syn arch, champion, chief, foremost,
head, leading, premier, principal
rel eminent, highest, preeminent, primary,
prime, supreme; dominant, paramount,
predominant, sovereign; main, outstanding
con ancillary, auxiliary, secondary, subsidiary
ant subordinate
4 most rudimentary < had not the *first*
chance of success>
syn least, slightest, smallest
rel measly, slight, slim, trifling, trivial
con considerable, goodly, significant,
substantial, tolerable, worthwhile
first *adv syn* see FIRSTLY
first-class *adj syn* see EXCELLENT
idiom in a class by itself
con fair, indifferent, middling; unexceptional, unnoteworthy, unremarkable
firsthand *adj syn* see DIRECT 4
firstly *adv* as the first thing to be mentioned < *firstly*, we wish to consider the
economic problem>
syn first, initially
rel incipiently, originally, primarily
idiom before all (*or* anything) else, first of
all, first off, to begin with
con ultimately
ant finally, lastly
first off *adv syn* see AWAY 3
first-rate *adj syn* see EXCELLENT
con fair, indifferent, middling, poor; unexceptional, unnoteworthy, unremarkable
first-string *adj syn* see EXCELLENT
firth *n syn* see INLET
fiscal *adj syn* see FINANCIAL
fish *n* **1** *syn* see FOOL 3

‖**2** *syn* see DOLLAR
fish *vb syn* see HINT 4
fishwife *n syn* see VIRAGO
fishy *adj syn* see DOUBTFUL 1
fissure *n* **1** *syn* see CRACK 3
rel abyss, chasm, gorge, ravine; breach,
rent, rupture; gash, hole, opening
2 *syn* see BREACH 3
fist *n syn* see HANDWRITING
fisticuffs *n pl syn* see BOXING
fit *n syn* see ATTACK 3
fit *adj* **1** adapted to an end or use by nature or art < food *fit* for a king>
syn applicable, appropriate, apt, befitting,
felicitous, fitting, happy, just, meet,
proper, right, rightful, suitable; *compare*
JUST 3
rel adapted, adjusted; congruous, consonant; decent, decorous; acceptable, adequate, tolerable
con improper, inadequate, inappropriate,
unsuitable; false, wrong
ant unfit
2 *syn* see ELIGIBLE
rel able, competent
3 *syn* see GOOD 2
4 *syn* see HEALTHY 1
idiom fit as a fiddle
ant unfit
fit *vb* **1** *syn* see SUIT 4
2 *syn* see BELONG 1
3 *syn* see PREPARE 1
4 *syn* see ADAPT
fit (in) *vb syn* see AGREE 4
fitful *adj* lacking steadiness or regularity in
course, movement, or succession < a *fitful*
breeze>
syn catchy, desultory, on-again-off-again,
spasmodic, sporadic, spotty
rel intermittent, interrupted, irregular,
periodic, recurrent; haphazard, hit-or-miss,
random; changeable, variable; capricious,
inconstant, unstable
con equable, even, steady, uniform; methodical, orderly, regular, systematic
ant constant
fitly *adv syn* see WELL 1
fitness *n* **1** *syn* see ORDER 10
2 *syn* see ORDER 11
rel decency, decorum, harmony
ant unfitness
3 *syn* see USE 3
fit out *vb syn* see FURNISH 1
fitted *adj syn* see ASSORTED 2
fitting *adj* **1** *syn* see FIT 1
rel apposite, apropos, germane, pertinent,
relevant, seemly; accordant, concordant,
harmonious
2 *syn* see TRUE 7
fittingly *adv* **1** *syn* see WELL 1
2 *syn* see WELL 4
fivefold *adj syn* see QUINTUPLE
five-star *adj syn* see EXCELLENT
fix *vb* **1** *syn* see SET 1
rel stabilize, steady; decide, determine,
rule; specify
con change, modify, vary
ant alter; abrogate
2 *syn* see ENTRENCH 1
rel inculcate, instill
con overthrow, overturn, subvert, upset
3 *syn* see FASTEN 1
4 *syn* see FASTEN 2

'con dislodge, displace
5 *syn* see FASTEN 3
6 *syn* see PREPARE 1
7 *syn* see MEND 2
8 *syn* see ADJUST 2
rel mend, patch, rebuild, repair; amend, emend, revise
con disorganize, unsettle
9 *syn* see SOLVE 1
10 *syn* see STERILIZE
11 *syn* see BRIBE
fix *n syn* see PREDICAMENT
fixate *vb syn* see FASTEN 3
fixation *n syn* see FETISH 2
rel craze, fascination, infatuation
idiom bee in one's bonnet
fixed *adj* 1 *syn* see FAST 4
2 *syn* see IMMOVABLE 1
3 *syn* see DEFINITE 1
4 *syn* see INFLEXIBLE 3
5 *syn* see FIRM 4
con changing, variable, varying
6 *syn* see SURE 1
7 *syn* see WHOLE 5
con distracted, erratic, wandering
fixedly *adv syn* see HARD 7
rel stubbornly, tenaciously
fixture *n syn* see INSTITUTION
fix up *vb syn* see DRESS UP 1
fizz *vb syn* see HISS
fizzle *vb syn* see HISS
flabbergast *vb syn* see SURPRISE 2
rel overwhelm, shock
flabby *adj syn* see LIMP 1
rel soft, yielding; impotent, powerless; enervated, languid, listless, spiritless
con taut, tense, tight; strong, sturdy, tenacious, tough; gritty, plucky
ant firm
flaccid *adj syn* see LIMP 1
rel emasculated, enervated, unnerved; debilitated, enfeebled, sapped, weakened
con elastic, flexible, springy, supple; limber, lithe; energetic, lusty, nervous, vigorous
ant resilient
flag *n* a piece of fabric that is used as a symbol (as of a nation) or as a signaling device < we respect the *flag* of our fathers >
syn banderole, banner, bannerol, burgee, color, ensign, gonfalon, gonfanon, jack, oriflamme, pendant, pennant, pennon, standard, streamer
flag *vb syn* see SIGNAL
flag *vb* 1 *syn* see FAIL 1
2 *syn* see DROOP 3
rel abate, ebb, wane
flagellate *vb syn* see WHIP 1
flagitious *adj syn* see VICIOUS 2
rel criminal, scandalous, sinful, wicked; disgraceful, shameful; flagrant, glaring, gross
con good, upstanding, virtuous
flagrant *adj syn* see EGREGIOUS
rel bold, conspicuous, obvious, striking; heinous; flagitious, wicked; disgraceful, scandalous, shameful, shocking

con hidden, inconspicuous, obscure; excusable, unimportant
flagrante delicto *adv syn* see RED-HANDED
flag-waver *n syn* see PATRIOTEER
flair *n syn* see GIFT 2
flake (off) *vb syn* see SCALE 2
‖**flake out** *vb syn* see COLLAPSE 2
flam *n syn* see IMPOSTURE
flamboyant *adj* 1 *syn* see ORNATE
2 *syn* see SHOWY
flame *n* 1 *syn* see SWEETHEART 1
2 *syn* see GIRL FRIEND 2
3 *syn* see BOYFRIEND 2
flame *vb syn* see BLAZE
rel coruscate, glint; fire, ignite, kindle, light
flaming *adj* 1 *syn* see BURNING 1
2 *syn* see IMPASSIONED
flammable *adj syn* see COMBUSTIBLE 1
ant incombustible, nonflammable
flap *n syn* see COMMOTION 2
flapdoodle *n syn* see NONSENSE 2
flare *vb syn* see BLAZE
rel dart, shoot; flicker, flutter
idiom burst into flame
ant gutter out
flare (up) *vb syn* see ANGER
idiom ‖blow one's stack (*or* top *or* lid), fly into a passion, fly off the handle
con calm (down), cool (off *or* down), simmer down
flare *n syn* see OUTBREAK 1
flare-up *n syn* see OUTBURST 1
flaring *adj syn* see BURNING 1
flash *vb* 1 to shoot forth light (as in rays or sparks) < lightning *flashed* in the sky >
syn coruscate, glance, gleam, glimmer, glint, glisten, glitter, scintillate, shimmer, spangle, sparkle, twinkle
rel dart, shoot; blare, blaze, burn, flame, flare, glare, glow, incandesce; blink, flicker, spark; dazzle; beam, radiate, shine
2 *syn* see BLINK 1
3 *syn* see SHOW 4
flash *n* 1 a sudden brief light < saw a *flash* sweep across the sky >
syn coruscation, glance, gleam, glimmer, glint, glisten, glitter, quiver, scintillation, shimmer, sparkle, twinkle
rel blare, blaze, flame, flare, glare, glow; flicker; beam, ray
2 *syn* see INSTANT 1
idiom half a second (*or* shake), twinkling of an eye
flashy *adj syn* see GAUDY
rel flamboyant, florid, ornate; flashing, glittering, sparkling
con dowdy, slatternly; natural, simple, unaffected; chic, modish, smart
flat *adj* 1 *syn* see LEVEL
idiom flat as a billiard table (*or* pancake)
con rugged, scabrous, uneven; hilly, mountainous
2 *syn* see PRONE 4
3 *syn* see DOWNRIGHT 2
4 *syn* see COLORLESS 2
5 *syn* see INSIPID 3
rel dull, lifeless; flavorless, stale, tasteless
6 *syn* see UNPALATABLE 1
7 *syn* see POOR 1
8 *syn* see DULL 7
flat *n syn* see APARTMENT 1

syn synonym(s)   *rel* related word(s)
ant antonym(s)   *con* contrasted word(s)
idiom idiomatic equivalent(s)
‖ use limited; if in doubt, see a dictionary

‖**flatfoot** *n syn* see POLICEMAN
flatly *adv syn* see EVENLY 3
flat–out *adj syn* see UTTER
flat–out *adv syn* see FAST 2
flatten *vb* 1 *syn* see EVEN 1
  2 *syn* see FELL 1
flatter *vb* to be becoming to < a neckline designed to *flatter* the stylishly stout >
  syn become, enhance, suit
  rel adorn, beautify, decorate, embellish, ornament; finish, perfect
  idiom put in the best light
  con deface, disfigure; distort; mar, spoil
flattery *n* flattering speech or attentions < *flattery* will get you nowhere >
  syn adulation, blandishment, blarney, incense, oil, soft soap
  rel compliments; laud, laudation, praise; cajolery, coaxing, wheedling; fulsomeness, unctuousness; bootlicking, fawning, ingratiation, obsequiousness, sycophancy, toadying, truckling
  idiom honeyed words
  con censure, condemnation, criticism, reprehension, reprobation; castigation, excoriation; aspersion, insult; contempt, disdain, scorn; belittling, depreciation, derogation, detraction, disparagement
flatulent *adj syn* see INFLATED
  rel empty, hollow, vain; shallow, superficial
  con weighty; cogent, compelling, convincing, telling; forceful, forcible, potent
flaunt *vb syn* see SHOW 4
  rel boast, brag, gasconade, vaunt; disclose, discover, divulge, reveal; advertise, broadcast, declare, proclaim, publish; flourish, wave
  idiom dangle before the (*or* one's) eyes
  con camouflage, cloak, disguise, dissemble, mask; bury, conceal, hide, screen, secrete
flavor *n syn* see TASTE 3
flavorless *adj syn* see UNPALATABLE 1
  ant flavorsome
flavorsome *adj syn* see PALATABLE 1
  con flat, insipid, vapid, wishy-washy; bland, mild; displeasing, tasteless, unflavored, unpalatable, unpleasant, unsavory
  ant flavorless
flaw *n syn* see BLEMISH
  rel cleavage, rent, rip, riving, split, tear
flawed *adj* 1 *syn* see DAMAGED
  ant flawless
  2 *syn* see FAULTY
  ant flawless
flawless *adj* 1 *syn* see WHOLE 1
  ant flawed
  2 *syn* see PERFECT 2
  3 *syn* see IMPECCABLE 1
  con defective, faulty, flawed, imperfect, unsound
  4 *syn* see IDEAL 3
flaxen *adj syn* see BLOND 1
flay *vb syn* see LAMBASTE 3
  rel assail, attack, berate, tongue-lash
fleckless *adj syn* see PERFECT 2
flection *n syn* see TURN 4
fledgling *n syn* see NOVICE
flee *vb* 1 *syn* see ESCAPE 1
  rel avoid, elude, evade, shun
  idiom take a (runout) powder
  2 *syn* see RUN 2

  con stand, stay
fleece *vb* 1 to obtain something valuable from by improper means < a corrupt mayor who *fleeced* the town treasury >
  syn bleed, milk, mulct, rook, stick, sweat; *compare* CHEAT, EXTORT 1
  rel cheat, cozen, defraud, do, hustle, ‖rope (in), swindle, take; pluck
  idiom sell one a bill of goods, take for a sucker, take to the cleaner's
  2 *syn* see OVERCHARGE 1
fleeceable *adj syn* see EASY 3
fleecy *adj syn* see HAIRY 1
fleer *vb* 1 *syn* see SNEER 1
  2 *syn* see SCOFF
  rel grin, smile, smirk
  idiom cast in one's teeth, curl one's lip at, laugh one out of court
fleet *vb* 1 *syn* see WHILE
  rel dally, fritter, idle, potter, squander, waste
  2 *syn* see FLY 4
  idiom go like the wind (*or* lightning), make (good) time
  3 *syn* see HURRY 2
fleet *adj syn* see FAST 3
  rel agile, brisk, nimble, spry; alert, animated, lively, spirited, sprightly, vivacious
fleeting *adj syn* see TRANSIENT
  con abiding, enduring, persistent
  ant lasting
fleetly *adv syn* see FAST 2
flesh *n syn* see MANKIND
fleshiness *n syn* see OBESITY
fleshliness *n syn* see ANIMALITY
fleshly *adj* 1 *syn* see BODILY
  2 *syn* see CARNAL 2
  rel epicurean, luxurious, sensuous, sybaritic, voluptuous; lay, profane, secular, temporal
  con divine, religious, spiritual; intellectual, mental, psychic
fleshy *adj syn* see FAT 2
  ant emaciated
flexible *adj syn* see ELASTIC 1
  rel amenable, docile, manageable, tractable; acquiescent, compliant
  con brittle, crisp, fragile, frangible; firm, hard, rigid, stiff, unyielding, wooden; intractable, recalcitrant, refractory, ungovernable; callous, hardened, indurated
  ant inflexible
flexuous *adj syn* see WINDING
flexure *n syn* see TURN 4
flibbertigibbet *n syn* see SCATTERBRAIN
flick *n syn* see MOVIE
flicker *vb* 1 *syn* see FLIT 2
  2 *syn* see BLINK 2
  rel fluctuate, oscillate, swing, vibrate, waver; blaze, flame, flare, glare; coruscate, glance, gleam, glint, glitter, sparkle; quaver, quiver, tremble
flier *n syn* see PILOT 2
flight *n syn* see ESCAPE 1
flightiness *n syn* see LIGHTNESS
  rel capriciousness, fickleness, inconstancy, instability, mercurialness
  con constancy, equableness, steadfastness
  ant steadiness
flighty *adj syn* see GIDDY 1
  rel changeable, inconstant, mercurial, unstable; buoyant, effervescent, volatile; gay, lively, sprightly; irresponsible

con constant, dependable, reliable, responsible, trustworthy; stable; sedate
ant steady

flimflam *n* 1 *syn* see IMPOSTURE
2 *syn* see NONSENSE 2

flimflam *vb* 1 *syn* see DUPE
2 *syn* see CHEAT

flimflammer *n syn* see SWINDLER

flimsy *adj* 1 *syn* see FILMY
2 *syn* see IMPLAUSIBLE
ant substantial
3 *syn* see DELICATE 5
4 *syn* see WEAK 1
ant sturdy
5 *syn* see LIMP 1

flinch *vb syn* see RECOIL
rel avoid, elude, escape, eschew, evade, shun; retire, withdraw; recede, retreat

fling *vb* 1 *syn* see RUSH 1
2 *syn* see THROW 1
con catch, grab, receive

fling *n* 1 a casual attempt < I'm willing to take a *fling* at almost any job>
syn crack, go, pop, shot, slap, stab, ‖stagger, try, whack, whirl
rel attempt, effort, essay, trial
con best, limit, maximum
ant utmost
2 *syn* see SPREE 1

flip (through) *vb syn* see BROWSE

flippancy *n syn* see LIGHTNESS
rel archness, pertness, sauciness; impishness, mischievousness, playfulness, roguishness, waggishness; cheekiness, cockiness, freshness
con earnestness, gravity, soberness, solemnity
ant seriousness

flirt *vb syn* see TRIFLE 1
rel disport, play, sport; caress, fondle, pet

flirt *n* a woman who trifles amorously < a charming girl but an outrageous *flirt*>
syn coquette, vamp

flit *vb* 1 *syn* see HURRY 2
2 to move briskly, irregularly, and usually intermittently < the hummingbird *flitted* from flower to flower>
syn dance, flicker, flitter, flutter, hover
rel dart, float, fly, scud, skim
3 *syn* see FLY 4

flitter *vb syn* see FLIT 2
rel quaver, quiver, teeter

float *vb* 1 *syn* see DRIFT 1
2 *syn* see HANG 3
3 *syn* see FLY 1
rel drift, waft

floater *n syn* see VAGABOND

flock *n* 1 *syn* see MULTITUDE 1
2 *syn* see DROVE 2

flog *vb syn* see WHIP 1

flood *n* 1 *syn* see FLOW
2 a great or overwhelming flow of or as if of water < a *flood* of messages>
syn cataclysm, cataract, deluge, flooding, inundation, niagara, overflow, pour, spate, torrent
rel current, flow, stream, tide; excess, superfluity, surplus; outgushing, outpouring—

con dribble, drip, dropping
ant trickle

flood *vb* 1 *syn* see DELUGE 1
2 *syn* see DELUGE 3

flooding *n syn* see FLOOD 2

floor *vb syn* see FELL 1

floozy *n syn* see DOXY 1

‖**flop** *vb* 1 *syn* see RETIRE 4
2 *syn* see FAIL 4
con come off, go over, succeed

flop *n syn* see FAILURE 5

floppy *adj syn* see LIMP 1

florid *adj* 1 *syn* see RHETORICAL
2 *syn* see ORNATE
rel ostentatious, pretentious, showy
con bald, bare, barren; austere, unadorned
3 *syn* see RUDDY
ant pallid

florilegium *n syn* see ANTHOLOGY

floss *n syn* see DOWN

flotsam *n syn* see DRIFTWOOD

flounce *vb syn* see SASHAY

flounder *vb syn* see WALLOW 2
rel strive, struggle; labor, toil, travail

flourish *vb syn* see SUCCEED 3
rel bloom, blossom, flower; augment, increase, multiply; amplify, expand; develop, grow, wax
con shrivel, wither; contract, shrink; abate, ebb, subside, wane
ant languish

flourishing *adj* enjoying a vigorous growth < a *flourishing* economy>
syn booming, prospering, prosperous, roaring, robust, thrifty, thriving; *compare* SUCCESSFUL
rel vigorous; rampant, rank; exuberant, lush, luxuriant, profuse
idiom going strong, in full swing
con decadent, declining, deteriorating; failing; decreasing, dwindling
ant languishing

flout *vb syn* see SCOFF
rel disregard, slight; repudiate, spurn; insult; defy
idiom thumb one's nose at
con admire, esteem, regard, respect
ant revere

flow *vb* 1 *syn* see POUR 2
rel cascade, jet, spout, spurt; well; course, ripple, run
2 *syn* see SPRING 1
3 *syn* see TEEM
4 *syn* see DISCHARGE 5

flow *n* something suggestive of running water < she expressed herself in a *flow* of words>
syn current, drift, flood, flux, rush, spate, stream, tide
rel progression, sequence, series, succession; continuance, continuation, continuity

flower *n* 1 the often showy part of a seed plant that bears reproductive organs < children picking *flowers* in the meadow>
syn bloom, blossom, posy
rel bud, floret; shoot, spray
2 *syn* see BEST
3 *syn* see ARISTOCRACY

flower *vb syn* see BLOSSOM

flowering *n syn* see DEVELOPMENT
ant fading

---

flowery *adj syn see* RHETORICAL
  rel diffuse, prolix, redundant, verbose, wordy
  con compendious, concise, laconic, pithy, succinct, summary, terse
flowing *adj syn see* EASY 9
flub *vb syn see* BOTCH
fluctuant *adj* 1 *syn see* WEAK 2
  2 *syn see* UNCERTAIN 1
flue *n syn see* DOWN
fluent *adj* 1 *syn see* VOCAL 3
  rel loquacious, talkative; easy, effortless, facile, smooth; apt, prompt, quick, ready
  con stammering, stuttering; tongue-tied; dumb; fettered, hampered, trammeled
  2 *syn see* EASY 9
fluff *n* 1 *syn see* DOWN
  2 *syn see* ERROR 2
fluff *vb syn see* BOTCH
fluid *adj syn see* CHANGEABLE 1
fluky *adj syn see* ACCIDENTAL
flummadiddle *n syn see* NONSENSE 2
flummox *vb syn see* FAIL 4
flurry *n syn see* STIR 1
  rel confusion, excitement, turbulence, turmoil; haste, hurry
flurry *vb syn see* DISCOMPOSE 1
  rel bewilder, distract, perplex; excite, galvanize, provoke, quicken, stimulate
flush *n* 1 *syn see* BLOOM 3
  2 *syn see* BLOOM 2
flush *vb* 1 *syn see* BLUSH
  2 *syn see* EVEN 1
flush *adj* 1 *syn see* RICH 1
  2 *syn see* RUDDY
  3 *syn see* LEVEL
flushed *adj syn see* RUDDY
fluster *vb* 1 *syn see* DISCOMPOSE 1
  rel bewilder, confound, distract, mystify, nonplus, perplex, puzzle; addle, confuse, fuddle, muddle
  ant steady
  2 *syn see* CONFUSE 2
flutter *vb syn see* FLIT 2
  rel quaver, quiver, shake, tremble, wobble; beat, palpitate, pulsate, throb; fluctuate, oscillate, swing, vibrate; flap
flux *n* 1 *syn see* DIARRHEA
  2 *syn see* FLOW
flux *vb syn see* LIQUEFY
fly *vb* 1 to pass lightly or quickly over or above a surface <clouds *flying* across the sky>
  syn dart, float, sail, scud, shoot, skim, skirr
  rel dance, flicker, flit, flitter, flutter, hover; arise, ascend, mount, rise, soar; glide, slide, slip
  2 *syn see* RUN 2
  rel hide; retreat, withdraw
  3 *syn see* ESCAPE 1
  4 to pass swiftly as if on wings <how time *flies* when we are happy>
  syn fleet, flit, sail, sweep, wing
  rel soar; hasten, hurry, speed; barrel, skim, whisk, whiz, zip; breeze, dart, dash, rush, tear
  idiom go like the wind (*or* lightning), outstrip the wind
  con dally, dawdle, dillydally, drift; lag, linger, loiter, trail; crawl, creep, poke
  ant drag
  5 *syn see* HURRY 2

fly-boy *n syn see* PILOT 2
fly-by-night *adj syn see* UNRELIABLE 1
flying colors *n pl syn see* SUCCESS
flyspeck *n syn see* POINT 11
foam *n* a mass of bubbles gathering in or on the surface of a liquid or something as insubstantial as such a mass <a *foam* of delicate lace at her throat>
  syn froth, lather, spume, suds, yeast
fob off *vb syn see* FOIST 3
focal point *n syn see* CENTER 2
focus *n syn see* CENTER 2
  idiom center of attraction (*or* interest), focus of attention
focus *vb* 1 *syn see* FASTEN 3
  2 *syn see* CONVERGE
  idiom come to a focus
foe *n syn see* ENEMY
  con associate, companion, comrade
  ant friend
fog *n syn see* HAZE 2
fog *vb* 1 *syn see* OBSCURE
  rel bewilder, distract, mystify, perplex, puzzle
  2 *syn see* CONFUSE 4
  rel addle, muddle
foggy *adj syn see* HAZY
  idiom in a fog
fogram *n syn see* FOGY
fogy *n* a person who is behind the times or overconservative <his father is an old *fogy*>
  syn antediluvian, fogram, fossil, fuddy-duddy, mid-Victorian, mossback, square, stick-in-the-mud
  rel conservative, diehard; back number
  idiom regular old fogy
  ant modern
fogyish *adj syn see* CONSERVATIVE 1
  ant up-to-the-minute
foible *n syn see* FAULT 2
  rel imperfection, shortcoming
foil *vb syn see* FRUSTRATE 1
  rel discomfit, disconcert, embarrass, faze, rattle; curb, restrain
foist *vb* 1 *syn see* INSINUATE 3
  2 *syn see* IMPOSE 4
  3 to pass or offer (something spurious) as genuine or worthy <his theory was far more reasonable than many *foisted* on the public>
  syn fob off, palm (on *or* upon), palm off, pass off, work off; *compare* IMPOSE 4
  rel beguile, deceive, delude, mislead; bamboozle, dupe, gull, hoax, hoodwink, trick; cheat, defraud, overreach, swindle; impose, inflict, wish
fold *n syn see* WRINKLE
fold *vb* 1 *syn see* DOUBLE 2
  2 *syn see* FAIL 5
fold up *vb* 1 *syn see* GIVE 12
  2 *syn see* RUIN 3
foliage *n* the leaves of plants <a tree with handsome *foliage*>
  syn leafage, umbrage, verdure
  rel greenness, herbage; growth, vegetation
folk *n* 1 *syn see* FAMILY 1
  2 **folks** *pl syn see* FAMILY 1
folklore *n syn see* LORE 2
follow *vb* 1 to come after in time <a juggling act *followed* the singer>
  syn ensue, succeed, supervene
  rel displace, replace, supersede, supplant; postdate

con herald, lead, preface, usher (in); antedate, predate
ant precede
2 to go after or on the track of < *followed*
the boys to their hiding place >
syn chase, chivy, pursue, trail; *compare*
TAIL
rel trace, track; hunt, search, seek; dog,
hound, tag; accompany, attend, convoy;
ape, copy, imitate; exercise, practice
con guide, lead, pilot, steer; elude, escape,
evade; abandon, desert
ant precede; forsake
3 *syn* see OBEY
4 *syn* see APPREHEND 1
follower *n* one who attaches himself to
another < he is a born *follower* >
syn adherent, cohort, disciple, henchman,
partisan, satellite, sectary, sectator, supporter
rel addict, devotee, freak, habitué, votary;
admirer, fan, fancier; advocate; bootlicker,
hanger-on, lickspittle, parasite, sycophant,
toady
ant leader
following *adj syn* see NEXT
following *n* **1** *syn* see ENTOURAGE
2 the body of persons who attach themselves to another especially as disciples,
patrons, or admirers < he has a strong
following in this country >
syn audience, clientage, clientele, public
following *prep syn* see AFTER 2
folly *n syn* see FOOLISHNESS
rel fatuity, stupidity
ant wisdom
foment *vb syn* see INCITE
rel goad, spur; cultivate, foster, nurse,
nurture
con repress, suppress
ant quell
fomenter *n syn* see INSTIGATOR
fond *adj* **1** *syn* see OPTIMISTIC
2 *syn* see LOVING
rel responsive, romantic, sentimental,
sympathetic, tender, warm; indulgent
idiom silly over
fondle *vb syn* see CARESS
rel clasp, embrace, hug; nestle, snuggle
fondness *n* **1** *syn* see LOVE 1
2 *syn* see APPETITE 3
rel partiality, predilection; relish
con disgust; hate
font name *n syn* see GIVEN NAME
food *n* **1** things that are edible < conserve
a nation's supply of *food* >
syn bread, ‖chow, comestibles, ‖eats,
edibles, feed, foodstuff, grub, meat,
‖muckamuck, nurture, provender, provisions, scoff, ‖tuck, viands, victuals, vivres
2 material which feeds and supports the
mind or spirit < *food* for thought >
syn aliment, nourishment, nutriment,
pabulum, pap, sustenance
foodstuff *n syn* see FOOD 1
foofaraw *n syn* see COMMOTION 3
fool *n* **1** a person lacking in judgment or
prudence < stop acting like a *fool* >

syn ass, asshead, donkey, doodle, idiot,
imbecile, jackass, jerk, madman, mooncalf, nincom, nincompoop, ninny, ninnyhammer, poop, ‖schmo, ‖schmuck, tomfool
rel blockhead, dimwit, dope, dumbbell,
dummy, nitwit, numskull, pinhead; birdbrain, featherbrain, featherhead, rattlebrain, scatterbrain; goose, silly
2 a retainer formerly kept to provide casual entertainment < a king's *fool* >
syn idiot, jester, motley
rel buffoon, clown, comedian, comic,
merry-andrew
3 one who is victimized or made to appear foolish < he's nobody's *fool* >
syn butt, chump, ‖come-on, ‖cull, dupe,
easy mark, fall guy, fish, gudgeon, gull,
mark, monkey, ‖mug, patsy, pigeon, sap,
saphead, ‖schlemiel, simple, sucker, victim
rel pushover; laughingstock; loser; instrument, tool
4 one who is mentally deficient < a badly
retarded child, little more than a *fool* >
syn ament, cretin, ‖feeb, half-wit, idiot,
imbecile, moron, natural, simpleton, softhead, underwit, zany
fool *vb* **1** *syn* see TRIFLE 1
2 *syn* see MEDDLE
3 *syn* see BANTER
4 *syn* see DUPE
fool (around) *vb syn* see PHILANDER
fool (away) *vb syn* see WASTE 3
foolhardy *adj syn* see ADVENTUROUS
rel headlong, impetuous, precipitate
con calculating, cautious, circumspect;
careful, prudent
ant wary
fooling *n syn* see HORSEPLAY
foolish *adj* **1** *syn* see SIMPLE 3
rel idiotic, imbecilic, moronic; daft, feebleminded, half-witted; ‖half-assed, half=
cocked; irrational
con bright, clever, intelligent, quick-witted
ant smart
2 felt to be ridiculous because not exhibiting good or conventional sense < a *foolish*
investment >
syn absurd, ‖balmy, crazy, ‖dilly, ‖dippy,
donkeyish, dotty, fantastic, harebrained,
idleheaded, insane, loony, loopy, lunatic,
mad, ‖potty, preposterous, sappy, silly,
tomfool, unearthly, wacky
rel laughable, ludicrous, ridiculous; half=
baked, headless, jerky, nonsensical;
offbeat, unacceptable, unconventional,
unorthodox
con judicious, sage, sapient; discreet,
foresighted, prudent; canny, shrewd, slick
ant sensible; wise
foolishness *n* the quality or state of being
foolish < the *foolishness* of so many of her
schemes >
syn absurdity, craziness, dottiness, folly,
inanity, insanity, lunacy, preposterousness,
senselessness, silliness, witlessness
rel imprudence, indiscretion, injudicious-
ness, insensibility, unwiseness; irrationality, unreasonableness; impracticality; ab-
surdness, ludicrousness, ridiculousness;
bull, bunk, nonsense
con discretion, judiciousness, prudence,
sensibility, wiseness; rationality, reason-

---

syn synonym(s)   *rel* related word(s)
ant antonym(s)   *con* contrasted word(s)
idiom idiomatic equivalent(s)
‖ use limited; if in doubt, see a dictionary

ableness; practicality; soundness; canniness, shrewdness
ant sense, wisdom

foot *n syn* see BOTTOM 3

foot *vb syn* see ADD 2

foot (it) *vb* 1 *syn* see DANCE 1
2 *syn* see WALK 1

footing *n* 1 *syn* see BASIS 1
2 *syn* see STATUS 1
3 *syn* see BASE 1
4 *syn* see TERM 5

footlicker *n syn* see SYCOPHANT

footlights *n pl syn* see DRAMA

footprint *n* the mark or impression made by a foot < *footprints* in the sand >
syn footstep, spoor, step, track, tract, vestige
rel sign, trace; pug, pugmark

footslog *vb syn* see PLOD 1

footstep *n syn* see FOOTPRINT

footstone *n syn* see TOMBSTONE

foozle *vb syn* see BOTCH

fop *n* a man who is conspicuously fashionable or elegant in dress or appearance < felt contempt for the mincing overdressed *fop* >
syn Beau Brummel, blood, buck, coxcomb, dandy, dude, exquisite, gallant, lounge lizard, macaroni, petit-maître, popinjay
rel fashion plate, silk stocking; blade, cavalier, man-about-town, spark, sport, swell; ladies' man, lady-killer, masher
idiom man of the world

for *prep* 1 *syn* see TO 5
2 on the side of < I'm *for* Smith all the way >
syn in favor of, pro, with
con anti, contra
ant against
3 *syn* see AFTER 1

for *conj syn* see BECAUSE

forage *vb syn* see SCOUR 2

forager *n syn* see MARAUDER

foray *vb* 1 *syn* see INVADE 1
2 *syn* see RAID 1

foray *n syn* see INVASION

forbear *vb* 1 *syn* see FORGO
rel bridle, curb, inhibit, restrain; avoid, escape, evade, shun; cease, desist
2 *syn* see REFRAIN 1
rel bear; endure, suffer, tolerate

forbearance *n* 1 *syn* see PATIENCE
rel restraint, temperance; endurance
2 the quality of being forbearing < she is known for her *forbearance* with children >
syn clemency, indulgence, lenience, leniency, mercifulness, tolerance, toleration; *compare* MERCY
rel longanimity, long-suffering; patience; charity, grace, lenity, mercy
con firmness, inflexibility, rigidity, sternness, strictness; austerity, harshness, inexorability
ant vindictiveness

forbearing *adj* disinclined to be severe or rigorous < *forbearing* toward her husband's weaknesses >
syn charitable, clement, easy, indulgent, lenient, merciful, tolerant
rel gentle, mild; longanimous, long-suffering, patient; considerate, thoughtful

con grim, implacable, merciless, relentless; impatient, nervous, restive; firm, inflexible, rigid, stern, strict; austere, harsh
ant unrelenting

forbid *vb* to debar one from using, doing, or entering or something from being used, done, or entered < smoking is *forbidden* here > < security regulations *forbid* the entry of unauthorized persons >
syn ban, enjoin, inhibit, interdict, outlaw, prohibit, taboo
rel debar, exclude, rule out, shut out; estop, obviate, preclude, prevent; forestall; proscribe, veto; check, curb, halt, restrain, stop; bar, block, hinder, impede, obstruct
con allow, let, suffer; authorize, license; approve, endorse, sanction; command, order; abide, bear, endure, tolerate
ant permit; bid

forbiddance *n syn* see TABOO

forbidden *adj* not permitted or allowed < accepting bribes is *forbidden* >
syn banned, prohibited, verboten
ant permitted

force *n* 1 *syn* see POWER 4
rel pressure, strain, stress, tension; headway, impetus, momentum, speed, velocity; vigor
2 *syn* see POINT 3
3 **forces** *pl syn* see TROOP 2
4 the exercise of power in order to impose one's will on a person or to have one's will with a thing < move a huge boulder by main *force* >
syn coercion, compulsion, constraint, duress, violence
rel fierceness, intensity, vehemence; effort, exertions, pains, trouble
con compliance, submission, yielding; impotence, powerlessness, weakness
ant forcelessness

force *vb* 1 *syn* see RAPE
2 to cause a person or thing to yield to pressure < hunger *forced* him to steal the food >
syn coerce, compel, concuss, constrain, make, oblige, shotgun
rel drive, impel, move; command, enjoin, order; demand, exact, require; press, pressure, sandbag; cause, occasion
con blandish, cajole, coax, wheedle; get, induce, persuade, prevail; entice, inveigle, lure, seduce, tempt

force (on *or* upon) *vb syn* see INFLICT 2

‖**force** *n syn* see WATERFALL

forced *adj* produced or kept up through effort < a *forced* laugh >
syn farfetched, labored, strained
rel coerced, compelled, constrained; artificial, factitious; unnatural; inflexible, rigid, stiff, wooden; exhausting, fatiguing
con easy, effortless, smooth; impulsive, instinctive, spontaneous; artless, natural, normal, unaffected, unsophisticated
ant unforced

forceful *adj* 1 *syn* see POWERFUL 2
rel compelling, constraining; manful, virile; cogent, telling
con decrepit, frail, infirm
ant feeble
2 *syn* see EMPHATIC

forcefully *adv syn* see HARD 1

forceless *adj syn* see WEAK 4

forcible *adj syn* see POWERFUL 2
  rel intense, vehement, violent; aggressive, assertive, militant, self-assertive; coercive
forcibly *adv syn* see HARD 1
forcing bed *n   syn   see* BREEDING GROUND
forcing house *n   syn   see* BREEDING GROUND
fore *adv syn* see BEFORE 1
forebear *n syn* see ANCESTOR 1
forebode *vb syn* see AUGUR 2
foreboding *n syn* see APPREHENSION 3
  rel augury, foretoken, omen, portent, prognostic; forewarning, warning
forecast *vb syn* see FORETELL
  rel conjecture, guess, surmise; conclude, gather, infer
forecast *n syn* see PREDICTION
forecaster *n syn* see PROPHET
foredestine *vb syn* see PREDESTINE 2
forefather *n syn* see ANCESTOR 1
forefeel *vb syn* see FORESEE
foregoer *n syn* see FORERUNNER 2
foregoing *adj syn* see PRECEDING
  ant following
forehandedness *n syn* see ECONOMY
forehead *n* the part of the face above the eyes < his broad noble *forehead* >
  syn brow, frons, front
foreign *adj* 1 *syn* see EXOTIC 1
  ant native
  2 *syn* see EXTRINSIC
  rel incompatible, incongruous, inconsistent, inconsonant; distasteful, obnoxious, repellent, repugnant; accidental, adventitious
  con applicable, apposite, apropos, material, pertinent, relevant; akin, alike, uniform
  ant germane
  3 *syn* see IRRELEVANT
foreigner *n syn* see STRANGER
foreknow *vb syn* see FORESEE
  rel conclude, gather, infer
foreland *n syn* see PROMONTORY
foremost *adj* 1 *syn* see FIRST 1
  2 *syn* see FIRST 3
forename *n syn* see GIVEN NAME
forenoon *n syn* see MORNING 2
forensic *n syn* see ARGUMENTATION
foreordain *vb* 1 *syn* see PREDESTINE 1
  2 *syn* see PREDESTINE 2
forerun *vb* 1 *syn* see PRECEDE 2
  2 *syn* see ANNOUNCE 2
forerunner *n* 1 one that goes before and in some way announces the coming of another < a coma is often a *forerunner* of death >
  syn harbinger, herald, outrider, precursor
  rel anticipator; advertiser, announcer; advertisement, announcement, augury, foretoken, omen, portent, presage, prognostic; forewarning, warning; mark, sign, symptom, token; foreshadow
  2 one belonging to an early developmental period of something contemporary or fully developed < the water-driven dynamo that was a *forerunner* of present-day giant atomic power plants >

  syn ancestor, antecedent, antecessor, foregoer, precursor, predecessor, prototype
  rel example, exemplar, model, pattern; pioneer; author, initiator, originator
  con consequence, result; effect, event, issue, outgrowth; conclusion, consummation, culmination
  ant end product
foresee *vb* to know or expect in advance that something will happen or come into existence or be made manifest < he had not *foreseen* his present problems >
  syn anticipate, apprehend, divine, forefeel, foreknow, preknow, previse, prevision, see, visualize
  rel forebode, forecast, foretell, predict, presage, prognosticate, prophesy; descry, discern, espy, perceive
  idiom look for, look forward to
foreseer *n syn* see PROPHET
foreshadow *vb* 1 *syn* see ADUMBRATE 1
  2 *syn* see AUGUR 2
foreshow *vb* 1 *syn* see AUGUR 2
  2 *syn* see ANNOUNCE 2
foresight *n syn* see PRUDENCE
  rel clairvoyance, discernment, perception
  ant hindsight
forest *n* a heavily wooded area
  syn timber, timberland, weald, wood(s), woodland
  rel coppice, copse, grove, thicket; wildwood, woodlot
  con field, meadow, plain, prairie
forestall *vb* 1 *syn* see PREVENT 2
  con court, invite, woo; advance, forward, further, promote
  2 *syn* see PREVENT 1
foretell *vb* to tell something before it happens through or as if through special knowledge or occult power < the prophet *foretold* the fall of the city >
  syn adumbrate, augur, call, forecast, portend, predict, presage, prognosticate, prophesy, soothsay, vaticinate
  rel anticipate, apprehend, divine, foreknow, foresee; announce, declare, proclaim; disclose, divulge, reveal; forewarn, warn; bode, forebode, foreshadow, foreshow, foretoken, promise; prefigure
foreteller *n syn* see PROPHET
foretelling *n syn* see PREDICTION
forethink *vb syn* see PREMEDITATE
forethought *n syn* see PRUDENCE 1
  rel deliberation, premeditation; gumption, judgment, sense
  ant rashness; impetuosity
foretime *n syn* see PAST
foretoken *n* something that serves as a sign of future happenings < they felt that his new job was a *foretoken* of good fortune >
  syn augury, bodement, boding, omen, portent, presage, prognostic
  rel badge, indication, mark, note, sign, symptom, token; forewarning, harbinger, herald, precursor; forerunner, shadow, warning; intimation, promise; ostent; hint, inkling, suggestion
foretoken *vb syn* see AUGUR 2
forever *adv syn* see EVER 2
forevermore *adv syn* see EVER 2
forewarn *vb syn* see WARN 1
forewarning *n syn* see WARNING

---

syn synonym(s)   *rel* related word(s)
ant antonym(s)   *con* contrasted word(s)
idiom idiomatic equivalent(s)
‖ use limited; if in doubt, see a dictionary

foreword n syn see INTRODUCTION
forfeit n syn see FINE
forfeit vb syn see LOSE 1
forfend vb syn see PREVENT 2
forgather vb syn see GATHER 6
forge vb syn see MAKE 3
 rel beat, pound, turn out; copy, imitate
forget vb 1 to lose the remembrance of < I soon *forgot* his name >
 syn disremember, ‖misremember, unknow
 rel misrecollect; blow up, fluff; unlearn
 idiom clean forget, draw a blank
 con recall, recollect
 ant remember
 2 syn see NEGLECT
 con bethink, mind, recall, recollect
 ant remember
forgetful adj tending to lose or let go from one's mind something once known or learned < she is growing *forgetful* >
 syn oblivious, unmindful, unwitting
 rel lax, neglectful, negligent, remiss, slack; careless, heedless, thoughtless; absent, absentminded, abstracted, bemused
 con alert, alive, awake, aware, cognizant, conscious, sensible; attentive, considerate, thoughtful
forgetfulness n syn see OBLIVION
forgivable adj syn see VENIAL
forgive vb syn see EXCUSE 1
 idiom forgive and forget
forgo vb to deny oneself something for the sake of an end < he vowed to *forgo* all luxuries until the debt was paid >
 syn eschew, forbear, sacrifice
 rel abandon, relinquish, surrender, waive; abdicate, renounce, resign; forsake, give up
fork (out) vb syn see SPEND 1
forlorn adj 1 dejected and saddened especially by reason of being alone < a *forlorn* lost child >
 syn lonely, lonesome, lorn
 rel abandoned, deserted, desolate, forgotten, forsaken; miserable, wretched; friendless, homeless; defenseless, helpless; depressed, oppressed, weighed down; alone, solitary
 2 syn see DESPONDENT
 rel cynical, pessimistic; fruitless, futile, vain
 con hopeful, optimistic, roseate, rose-colored
form n 1 outward appearance of something as distinguished from the substance of which it is made < the carefully graded *form* of the curves >
 syn cast, configuration, conformation, figure, shape
 rel contour, outline, profile, silhouette; anatomy, framework, skeleton; structure; economy, organism, scheme, system
 2 conduct regulated by an external control (as custom or a formal protocol of procedure) < observing the *forms* of polite society >
 syn ceremonial, ceremony, formality, liturgy, rite, ritual
 rel procedure, proceeding, process; custom, habit, practice, usage; canon, law, precept, regulation, rule; method, mode; decorum, etiquette, propriety

 3 a fixed or accepted way of doing or sometimes of expressing something < good *form* in swimming >
 syn convenance, convention, usage
 rel fashion, manner, mode, style, way
form vb 1 syn see MAKE 3
 rel devise; create, invent; turn out; design, plan, plot, project, scheme; establish, found, organize
 con demolish, destroy, ruin, wreck
 2 syn see DEVELOP 4
 3 syn see CONSTITUTE 1
formal adj 1 syn see CEREMONIAL
 rel methodical, orderly, regular, systematic; decorous, proper, seemly; prim, unbending; distant, reserved
 ant informal
 2 syn see NOMINAL
formality n 1 syn see FORM 2
 rel convenance, convention
 ant informality
 2 syn see RITE 2
formation n syn see MAKEUP 1
former adj 1 syn see PRECEDING
 con following, succeeding, supervening
 ant latter
 2 having been such at some previous time < *former* friends >
 syn bygone, erstwhile, late, old, once, onetime, past, quondam, sometime, whilom
 con current, present; future, prospective
formerly adv syn see BEFORE 2
formidable adj 1 syn see FEARFUL 3
 ant comforting
 2 syn see HARD 6
 ant simple
formless adj having no definite or recognizable form < a *formless* fear >
 syn amorphous, inchoate, shapeless, unformed, unshaped
 rel chaotic, orderless, unordered, unorganized; indistinct, obscure, unclear, vague; indefinite, indeterminate, undefined; crude, raw, rough, rude
 con distinct, formed; definite, explicit, express, specific; ordered, organized
formulate vb 1 syn see WORD
 2 syn see CONTRIVE 2
 3 syn see DRAFT 3
‖**fornent** prep syn see BESIDE 1
for real adv syn see SERIOUSLY 1
forsake vb syn see ABANDON 1
 rel spurn; leave; abdicate, resign
 ant return (to), revert (to)
forsaken adj syn see DERELICT 1
forswear vb 1 syn see ABJURE
 2 syn see PERJURE
fort n a structure or place offering resistance to a hostile force < settlers fled to the *fort* >
 syn citadel, fastness, fortress, redoubt, stronghold
forte n that in which one excels < cooking is her strongest *forte* >
 syn eminency, long suit, medium, métier, oyster, strong suit
 rel ableness, effectiveness, efficiency; ability, competence; bag, thing
 idiom cup of tea, dish of tea, strong point
 con inadequacy, incapability, incompetence, inefficiency; greenness, rawness
forth adv 1 syn see AHEAD 2

2 *syn* see ALONG 1

forthcome *vb syn* see LOOM 2

forthcoming *adj* being soon to appear or take place < the *forthcoming* holidays >
syn approaching, coming, nearing, on-coming, upcoming
rel future; imminent, impending, pending; anticipated, awaited, expected
con distant, far-off, remote; bygone, for-mer, gone, gone-by, past

forthright *adj* 1 *syn* see STRAIGHTFOR-WARD 2
con covert, secret, stealthy, surreptitious, underhand; deceitful, mendacious, un-truthful
ant furtive
2 *syn* see FRANK

forthwith *adv* 1 *syn* see AWAY 3
2 *syn* see SHORT 1

fortify *vb* 1 *syn* see STRENGTHEN 2
rel arouse, rally, rouse, stir; refresh, re-new, restore
con dilute, thin
ant enfeeble
2 *syn* see GIRD 3

fortitude *n* a quality of character combin-ing courage and staying power < she bore up under all her problems with admirable *fortitude* >
syn backbone, grit, guts, intestinal forti-tude, ‖moxie, nerve, sand, spunk; *compare* COURAGE
rel courage, mettle, pith, resoluteness, resolution, spirit, stick-to-itiveness, tenac-ity; boldness, bravery, courageousness, dauntlessness, fearlessness, intrepidity, valiancy, valor, valorousness; endurance, stamina, strength; constancy, determina-tion, perseverance; bottom
con cowardliness, fearfulness, timidity, timorousness; faintheartedness, milksoppi-ness, weakness; cowardice, yellowness
ant pusillanimity

fortress *n syn* see FORT

fortuitous *adj syn* see ACCIDENTAL
con activated, actuated, motivated; pro-jected, schemed
ant deliberate

fortuitously *adv syn* see INCIDENTALLY 1
ant deliberately

fortuity *n syn* see ACCIDENT 1
ant deliberation

fortunate *adj* 1 *syn* see FAVORABLE 5
ant disastrous
2 *syn* see LUCKY
ant unfortunate

fortunately *adv syn* see WELL 5

fortunateness *n syn* see LUCK 3
ant unfortunateness

fortune *n* 1 *syn* see CHANCE 2
rel destiny, doom, portion
con design, intent, intention
2 *syn* see LUCK 3
ant misfortune
3 *syn* see WEALTH 2
4 a very large amount of money < those furs must have cost a *fortune* >

syn ‖bomb, boodle, bundle, mint, packet, pile, pot, ‖roll, wad
idiom king's ransom, pretty penny, tidy sum

fortuneless *adj syn* see POOR 1

forty winks *n pl but sing or pl in constr*
syn see NAP

forward *adj* 1 *syn* see PRESUMPTUOUS
2 *syn* see WISE 5
ant bashful
3 *syn* see PRECOCIOUS
con regressive, retrograde, retrogressive
ant backward

forward *adv* 1 *syn* see BEFORE 1
2 *syn* see AHEAD 2
ant backward
3 *syn* see ALONG 1

forward *vb* 1 *syn* see ADVANCE 1
rel back, champion, support, uphold
con baffle, circumvent, foil, frustrate, outwit, thwart
ant balk
2 *syn* see SEND 1

fossil *n syn* see FOGY

foster *vb* 1 *syn* see NURSE 2
rel back, champion, support, uphold; entertain, harbor, house, lodge, shelter; accommodate, assist, favor, help, oblige
con combat, fight, oppose, resist, with-stand; curb, inhibit, restrain; ban, forbid, interdict, prohibit; abuse, disregard, ne-glect
2 *syn* see ADVANCE 1

foul *adj* 1 *syn* see OFFENSIVE
2 *syn* see DIRTY 1
rel fetid, malodorous, noisome, putrid, stinking; loathsome, offensive, repulsive, revolting
ant fair; undefiled
3 *syn* see OBSCENE 2

foul *vb* 1 *syn* see SOIL 2
rel contaminate, defile, pollute; desecrate, profane
2 *syn* see CONTAMINATE 2

foul play *n syn* see MURDER

foul up *vb syn* see CONFUSE 5

found *vb* 1 *syn* see BASE
rel support, sustain; erect, raise, rear
2 to set going or to bring into existence < *founded* a new school for graduate studies >
syn constitute, create, establish, institute, organize, set up, start
rel begin, commence, inaugurate, initiate; fashion, form
con close, conclude, end, finish, termi-nate; arrest, check, halt, stay, stop

foundation *n* 1 *syn* see BASIS 1
2 *syn* see BASIS 3
3 *syn* see BASE 1

foundational *adj syn* see FUNDAMENTAL 1

foundationless *adj syn* see BASELESS

founder *n syn* see FATHER 2

founder *vb syn* see SINK 1

fount *n syn* see SOURCE

fountain *n syn* see SOURCE

fountainhead *n syn* see SOURCE

four *n syn* see QUARTET

fourberie *n syn* see DECEPTION 1

four-flush *vb syn* see DECEIVE

foursome *n syn* see QUARTET

foursquare *adj syn* see SQUARE 1

---

syn synonym(s)   *rel* related word(s)
ant antonym(s)   *con* contrasted word(s)
idiom idiomatic equivalent(s)
‖ use limited; if in doubt, see a dictionary

fourth *n syn* see QUARTER 1

foxiness *n syn* see CUNNING 2

foxy *adj syn* see SLY 2
rel deceitful, dishonest
con aboveboard, forthright, straightforward

foyer *n syn* see VESTIBULE

fracas *n* 1 *syn* see QUARREL
2 *syn* see BRAWL 2

fractional *adj syn* see INCOMPLETE 1

fractious *adj* 1 *syn* see UNRULY 1
ant orderly
2 *syn* see IRRITABLE
ant peaceable

fracturable *adj syn* see FRAGILE 1

fracture *n syn* see BREACH 3

fragile *adj* 1 easily broken < a *fragile* dish of the finest porcelain >
syn breakable, delicate, fracturable, frail, frangible, shatterable, shattery
rel brittle, crisp, crumbly, crunchy, friable, short
con infrangible, unbreakable; elastic, flexible, resilient; stout, strong, sturdy, tenacious
ant tough
2 *syn* see WEAK 1
ant durable

fragment *n* 1 *syn* see PARTICLE
2 *syn* see END 4

fragment *vb syn* see SHATTER 1

fragmentary *adj syn* see INCOMPLETE 1

fragrance *n* a sweet or pleasant odor < the *fragrance* of flowers >
syn aroma, balm, bouquet, incense, perfume, redolence, scent, spice
rel odor, smell
con fetidness, fetor, malodor, noisomeness, rancidness, rankness
ant stench, stink

fragrant *adj syn* see SWEET 2
rel delectable, delicious, delightful
ant fetid

frail *adj* 1 *syn* see WEAK 1
rel slender, slight, slim, tenuous, thin; petty, puny
con hale, healthy, sound
ant robust
2 *syn* see FRAGILE 1
con solid, substantial

frailty *n syn* see FAULT 2

frame *vb* 1 *syn* see CONTRIVE 2
2 *syn* see DRAFT 3
3 *syn* see MAKE 3

framework *n syn* see STRUCTURE 3

franchise *n syn* see SUFFRAGE

franchise *vb syn* see ENFRANCHISE

frangible *adj syn* see FRAGILE 1

frank *adj* marked by free, forthright, and sincere expression < a *frank* answer >
syn candid, direct, forthright, man-to-man, open, openhearted, plain, plainspoken, single, single-eyed, single-hearted, single-minded, straightforward, unconcealed, undisguised, undissembled, undissembling, unmannered, unreserved, unvarnished; *compare* COMMUNICATIVE, STRAIGHTFORWARD 2
rel ingenuous, naive, natural, simple, unsophisticated; bluff, blunt; heart-to-heart, sincere; honest, scrupulous, upright; dispassionate, fair, impartial, just, unbiased; barefaced, brazen, outspoken, uninhibited

con reserved, reticent, secretive, silent, taciturn, uncommunicative; covert, furtive, secret, sneaking, underhand; deceitful, deceptive, dishonest, evasive, false, lying, mendacious, tricky, untruthful; insincere
ant reticent

frank *n syn* see FRANKFURTER

frankfurter *n* a seasoned beef or beef and pork sausage
syn dog, frank, hot dog, wiener, wienerwurst, ‖wienie

frantic *adj syn* see FURIOUS 2

frantically *adv syn* see HARD 2

fraternity *n syn* see ASSOCIATION 2

fraud *n* 1 *syn* see DECEPTION 1
2 *syn* see IMPOSTURE
rel bamboozlement, bamboozling, dupery, duping, hoodwinking
3 *syn* see IMPOSTOR

fray *n* 1 *syn* see BRAWL 2
rel contention, discord, dissension, strife
2 *syn* see CLASH 2

frayed *adj syn* see RAGGED

frazzle *vb syn* see EXHAUST 4

frazzled *adj syn* see RAGGED

freak *n* 1 *syn* see CAPRICE
2 one that is physically abnormal < pitiful *freaks* displayed in sideshows >
syn abortion, lusus, miscreation, monster, monstrosity
rel aberration, chimera, malconformation, malformation, misshape, mosaic, mutation, sport; abnormality, anomaly, curiosity, oddity; rara avis, rarity; androgyne, hermaphrodite
idiom freak of nature
3 *syn* see ENTHUSIAST

freakish *adj syn* see ARBITRARY 1

freckle *vb syn* see SPECKLE 1

free *adj* 1 not subject to the rule or control of another < a *free* country >
syn autarchic, autarkic, autonomous, independent, separate, sovereign
rel free-born, unenslaved; delivered, emancipated, enfranchised, freed, liberated, released; democratic, self-directing, self-governing, self-ruling; sui juris; individualistic, unregimented
con coerced, compelled, constrained, forced, obliged; dependent, restricted, subject; inferior, subordinate, subservient; captive, enslaved, enthralled, subjugated
ant bond
2 not bound, confined, or detained by force < the prisoner was now *free* >
syn loose, unconfined, unrestrained
rel unbound, unchained, unfettered, unshackled, untied; clear, loose, scot-free; emancipated, freed, liberated; independent
idiom at liberty, free as a bird, free as air, free to come and go
con confined, restrained; impounded, imprisoned, incarcerated, interned, jailed; bound, chained, fettered, shackled, tied
3 *syn* see LIBERAL 1
ant close
4 *syn* see OUTSPOKEN
5 not costing or charging anything < a *free* public school >
syn chargeless, complimentary, costless, gratis, gratuitous
rel unpaid, unrecompensed, unremunerated

idiom for free, for love, for nothing, on the cuff, on the house

con charged, paid; costly, dear, expensive, high, high priced

6 not having the affections fixed on a particular object < she was happy to be *free* and in no hurry to fall in love again >

syn fancy-free, heart-whole

free *vb* to relieve from constraint or restraint < *free* an oppressed people >

syn discharge, disenthrall, disimprison, emancipate, liberate, loose, loosen, manumit, redeem, release, ||spring, unbind, unchain, unshackle

rel clear, detach, disencumber, disengage, disentangle, extricate; deliver, ransom, redeem, rescue; affranchise, enfranchise

idiom cut loose

con fetter, hamper, hog-tie, manacle, shackle, trammel; immure, imprison, incarcerate, intern, jail; circumscribe, confine, limit, restrict; curb, inhibit, restrain; enslave, enthrall, subjugate

freebooter *n* **1** *syn* see MARAUDER
2 *syn* see PIRATE

freedom *n* the power or condition of acting without compulsion < *freedom* of the press >

syn liberty, license

rel exemption, immunity; prerogative, privilege, right; compass, latitude, scope, sweep

con coercion, compulsion, constraint; restraint

ant necessity

free-for-all *n* *syn* see BRAWL 2
free hand *n* *syn* see CARTE BLANCHE
freehanded *adj* *syn* see LIBERAL 1
freeloader *n* *syn* see PARASITE
freely *adv* EASILY 1, effortlessly, facilely, lightly, readily, smoothly, well
free-minded *adj* *syn* see HAPPY-GO-LUCKY
free-spoken *adj* *syn* see OUTSPOKEN
freezer *n* *syn* see JAIL
freezing *adj* *syn* see COLD 1
ant scorching
freight *n* *syn* see LOAD 1
frenetic *adj* *syn* see FURIOUS 2
frenzied *adj* *syn* see FURIOUS 2
frenziedly *adv* *syn* see HARD 2
frenzy *n* *syn* see DELIRIUM
frenzy *vb* *syn* see MADDEN 1
frequent *adj* *syn* see COMMON 4
ant infrequent, rare
frequent *vb* to go to or to be in often < he *frequents* the bar down the street >

syn affect, hang around, hang out, haunt, resort

rel attend, go (to), visit; infest, overrun

con avoid, miss, sidestep

ant shun

frequenter *n* *syn* see HABITUÉ 1
frequently *adv* **1** *syn* see OFTEN
ant infrequently
2 *syn* see USUALLY 2
fresh *adj* **1** *syn* see NEW 1

---

rel gleaming, glistening, sparkling; striking, vital, vivid; virginal, youthful; crude, green, raw, uncouth; artless, naive, natural, unsophisticated

con hackneyed, shopworn, stereotyped, threadbare, trite

ant stale

2 *syn* see ADDITIONAL
3 *syn* see INEXPERIENCED
4 *syn* see WISE 5

freshman *n* *syn* see NOVICE
freshness *n* *syn* see INEXPERIENCE
fret *vb* **1** *syn* see WORRY 3

rel chafe, fume; brood, mope

idiom eat one's heart out

2 *syn* see ANNOY 1
3 *syn* see CHAFE 3
4 *syn* see RIPPLE

fretful *adj* **1** *syn* see IRRITABLE

rel captious, carping, caviling, critical, faultfinding; contrary, perverse

con forbearing, long-suffering, patient, resigned; subdued, submissive, tame

2 *syn* see IMPATIENT 1

friable *adj* *syn* see SHORT 6
fribble *adj* *syn* see GIDDY 1
fribbling *adj* *syn* see GIDDY 1
fried *adj* *syn* see INTOXICATED 1
friend *n* a person with whom one is on good and, usually, familiar terms < he is one of my closest *friends* >

syn acquaintance, amigo, cater-cousin, confidant, familiar, intimate, mate; *compare* ASSOCIATE 3

rel alter ego, best friend, bosom friend; ally, colleague, partner; nodding acquaintance

con enemy; adversary, antagonist, opponent; competitor, rival

ant foe

friendliness *n* *syn* see GOODWILL 1

rel affability, amiability, congeniality, cordiality, neighborliness, sociability

ant unfriendliness

friendly *adj* **1** *syn* see AMICABLE 1

rel close, familiar, intimate; affectionate, devoted, loving

ant unfriendly; belligerent

2 *syn* see HARMONIOUS 3
3 *syn* see SYMPATHETIC 2
ant unfriendly

friendship *n* *syn* see GOODWILL 1

rel affinity, attraction; empathy; accord, concord, consonance, harmony; alliance, coalition, federation, fusion, league

con antagonism, antipathy, hostility, rancor; hate

ant animosity

fright *n* **1** *syn* see FEAR 1
2 *syn* see EYESORE

fright *vb* *syn* see FRIGHTEN
frighten *vb* to strike or to fill with fear or dread < the puppy was *frightened* by the unfamiliar noises >

syn affright, alarm, awe, fright, scare, ||spook, startle, terrify, terrorize

rel appall, astound, daunt, disconcert, dismay, faze, horrify, shock; demoralize, unman, unnerve; browbeat, bulldoze, cow, intimidate; agitate, discompose, disquiet, perturb, upset

idiom curdle the blood, curl the hair, frighten one out of one's wits, freeze the blood, give one a scare, give one a turn,

---

make one's blood run cold, make one's flesh creep, make one's hair stand on end, make one's heart in one's mouth, make one tremble, put one's heart in one's mouth, scare hell out of, scare one spitless, scare one stiff, scare the life out of, scare the pants off of, scare to death, strike terror into, take one's breath away
con embolden, encourage, hearten, reassure

frightened *adj syn* see AFRAID 1
idiom in a fright
ant unfrightened

frightful *adj syn* see FEARFUL 3

frigid *adj* 1 *syn* see COLD 1
2 *syn* see COLD 2
3 free from or deficient in passion <claimed his wife was a *frigid* woman>
syn cold, inhibited, passionless, undersexed, unresponsive
idiom as cold as an iceberg
con affectionate, demanding, loving
ant ardent; amorous

frill *n syn* see LUXURY

fringe *n syn* see BORDER 1

fringe *vb syn* see BORDER 1

frippery *n syn* see FINERY

frisk *vb* 1 *syn* see GAMBOL
2 *syn* see SEARCH 2

frisky *adj syn* see PLAYFUL 1

fritter *vb syn* see WASTE 2

frivol away *vb syn* see WASTE 2

frivolity *n syn* see LIGHTNESS
rel coquetting, dallying, flirting, toying, trifling; fun, game, jest, play, sport
ant seriousness; staidness

frivolous *adj syn* see GIDDY 1
rel shallow, superficial, unprofound; gay, light, playful
ant serious

‖**frogskin** *n syn* see DOLLAR

frolic *vb* 1 *syn* see REVEL 1
2 *syn* see GAMBOL

frolic *n syn* see PRANK

frolicsome *adj* 1 *syn* see ANTIC 2
2 *syn* see PLAYFUL 1

from *prep* 1 *syn* see AFTER 1
2 in the face of <protect them *from* exploitation>
syn against

frondeur *n syn* see REBEL

frons *n syn* see FOREHEAD

front *n* 1 *syn* see FOREHEAD
2 *syn* see MASK 2
3 a person, group, or thing used to mask the identity or true character of a controlling agent <the export company was a *front* for illegal activities>
syn blind
rel disguise, facade, mask

front *vb* 1 *syn* see FACE 1
2 *syn* see FACE 3
3 *syn* see MEET 6
4 *syn* see ACCOST 2

frontier *n* 1 a region between two countries <lived on the *frontier* between Mexico and the U.S.>
syn border, borderland, march, marchland
2 a rural region that forms the margin of settled or developed territory <settlers found living on the *frontier* was a hard life>

syn backcountry, backland, ‖backveld, backwash, backwater, backwoods, ‖boondocks, ‖boonies, bush, hinterland, ‖outback, sticks, up-country
idiom the back of beyond

frontier *adj syn* see BACK 1

fronting *prep syn* see AGAINST 1

front-rank *adj syn* see EXCELLENT

frore *adj syn* see COLD 1

frosty *adj syn* see COLD 1

froth *n syn* see FOAM
rel flippancy, frivolity, levity, lightness

froward *adj syn* see CONTRARY 3

frown *vb* 1 to put on a dark or malignant countenance or aspect <he *frowned* at the naughty child>
syn gloom, glower, lower, scowl
rel glare; grimace; pout, sulk
idiom look black, look daggers
con grin, laugh
ant smile
2 *syn* see DISAPPROVE 1

frowsy *adj* 1 *syn* see SLATTERNLY
rel lax, neglectful, negligent, remiss, slack
ant trim; smart
2 *syn* see MALODOROUS 1

frugal *adj syn* see SPARING
rel careful, meticulous; discreet, prudent; conserving, preserving; cheeseparing, penny-pinching, scrimping, stinting
ant wasteful

frugality *n syn* see ECONOMY

‖**fruit** *n syn* see HOMOSEXUAL

fruitage *n syn* see HARVEST 2

fruitful *adj syn* see FERTILE
rel breeding, propagating, reproducing; abounding
con abortive, bootless, futile, vain
ant unfruitful; fruitless

fruitfulness *n syn* see FERTILITY

fruition *n syn* see PLEASURE 2
rel actualization, materialization, realization; accomplishment, fulfillment; achievement, attainment

fruitless *adj syn* see FUTILE
rel barren, infertile, sterile, unfruitful; foiled, frustrated, thwarted; infructuous, unprofitable
con fecund, fertile, prolific
ant fruitful

‖**fruity** *adj syn* see INSANE 1

frumpish *adj syn* see TACKY 2

frumpy *adj syn* see TACKY 2

frustrate *vb* 1 to come between a person and his aim or desire or to defeat another's plan <my efforts are *frustrated* at every turn>
syn baffle, balk, beat, bilk, buffalo, circumvent, dash, disappoint, foil, ruin, thwart; *compare* OUTWIT
rel annul, cancel, counteract, negative, neutralize, nullify; anticipate, forestall; conquer, defeat, lick, overcome; forbid, inhibit, prohibit; obviate, preclude, prevent; bar, block, hinder, impede, obstruct; arrest, check, halt, interrupt
idiom cut the ground from under one, dash one's hope, defeat expectation, throw a monkey wrench into the works, upset one's applecart
con accomplish, achieve, bring about, effect, perform; advance, forward, further, promote; abet, foment, incite, instigate

ant fulfill
2 syn see NEUTRALIZE

frying pan *n* a pan with a handle used for frying food <some still prefer the sturdy cast-iron *frying pan*>
syn skillet, spider

fuddle *vb syn* see CONFUSE 2
ant clarify, clear

fuddler *n syn* see DRUNKARD

fuddy-duddy *n* **1 syn** see FOGY
2 syn see STUFFED SHIRT
3 syn see FUSSBUDGET

fudge *vb syn* see EMBROIDER

fudge *n syn* see NONSENSE 2

fugacious *adj syn* see TRANSIENT

fugitive *adj syn* see TRANSIENT

fugitive *n syn* see REFUGEE

fulfill *vb* **1** to do what is required by the terms of so as to make effective <found themselves unable to *fulfill* their contract>
syn complete, execute, implement, perform; *compare* EFFECT 2
rel effect, effectuate; discharge
2 syn see SATISFY 5

fulgent *adj syn* see BRIGHT 1

full *adj* **1** containing as much as is possible <the hamper is *full*>
syn awash, big, block and block, brimful, brimming, bung-full, chockablock, chock-full, cram-full, crammed, crowded, jam-full, jammed, jam-packed, loaded, packed, ||packed out, replete, stuffed, ||trig
rel abounding, teeming
idiom full to bursting (*or* overflowing), ready to burst
con blank, vacant, void; bare, barren
ant empty
2 syn see CIRCUMSTANTIAL
ant incomplete
3 syn see WHOLE 2
con denuded, dismantled, divested, stripped
4 syn see SATIATED

full-blooded *adj* **1 syn** see PUREBRED
2 syn see RUDDY

full-blown *adj* **1 syn** see MATURE 1
2 syn see TOTAL 5

full-bosomed *adj syn* see BUXOM

full-bodied *adj syn* see STRONG 3

full dress *n syn* see FINERY

full-dress *adj syn* see EXHAUSTIVE

full-fledged *adj syn* see MATURE 1

full-grown *adj syn* see MATURE 1

full-mouthed *adj syn* see LOUD 1

fullness *n syn* see BREADTH 2

full-out *adj syn* see TOTAL 5

full-scale *adj syn* see TOTAL 5

full tilt *adv syn* see FAST 2

fully *adv* **1 syn** see DOWN 2
2 syn see WELL 3

fulsome *adj* too obviously extravagant or ingratiating to be accepted as genuine or sincere <offering sickeningly *fulsome* praise>
syn oily, oleaginous, slick, smarmy, soapy, unctuous, unctuous
rel canting, holier-than-thou, hypocritical, pecksniffian, pharisaical, sanctimonious;

bland, glib, honey-mouthed, honey-tongued, ingratiating, mealy-mouthed, oily-tongued, smooth, smooth-tongued, suave; buttery, flattering, wheedling; excessive, extravagant, exuberant, lavish, profuse; cloying, satiating, sating; bombastic, grandiloquent, magniloquent
con earnest, genuine, heartfelt, hearty, sincere, true, truthful, unfeigned, whole-hearted, whole-souled

fumble *vb* **1 syn** see GROPE
2 syn see BOTCH
rel flounder, stumble
3 syn see MUMBLE

fume *n syn* see SNIT

fume *vb syn* see ANGER 2

fun *vb syn* see BANTER

fun *n* **1** action or speech intended to amuse or arouse laughter <you know he only said it in *fun*>
syn game, jest, joke, play, sport
rel amusement, diversion, entertainment, recreation; blitheness, jocundity, joviality, merriment; glee, hilarity, jollity, mirth; mischief, teasing
con soberness, thoughtfulness
ant earnestness, seriousness
2 syn see PLAY 1

function *n* **1** the acts or operations expected of a person or thing <fulfill one's *function* as a mother>
syn business, duty, office, province, role
rel affair, concern; job, task, work
2 syn see USE 4
3 syn see POWER 3
rel action, behavior, operation

function *vb* **1 syn** see ACT 4
2 syn see ACT 5
3 to operate in the proper or expected manner <finally succeeded in getting the motor to *function*>
syn act, go, run, work
rel do, operate, perform

functional *adj syn* see PRACTICAL 2

functioning *adj syn* see ACTIVE 1

fund *n syn* see SUPPLY

fund *vb syn* see ENDOW 2

fundament *n syn* see BUTTOCKS

fundamental *adj* **1** forming or affecting the groundwork, roots, or lowest part of something <the *fundamental* rules of poetry>
syn basal, basic, bottom, foundational, primary, radical, underlying
rel primal, prime, primordial; elemental, elementary
con incidental
2 syn see ELEMENTAL 1
3 syn see ESSENTIAL 2
rel indispensable, necessary, needful, requisite; dominant, paramount

fundamental *n* **1 syn** see PRINCIPLE 1
rel component, constituent, factor, element
2 syn see ESSENTIAL 1
3 *usu* **fundamentals** *pl syn* see ALPHABET 2

fundamentalist *n syn* see DIEHARD 1

fundamentally *adv syn* see ESSENTIALLY 1
ant superficially

funeral director *n syn* see MORTICIAN

funereal *adj syn* see GLOOMY 3

---

syn synonym(s)   *rel* related word(s)
ant antonym(s)   *con* contrasted word(s)
idiom idiomatic equivalent(s)
|| use limited; if in doubt, see a dictionary

rel grave, solemn
con animated, gay, lively, sprightly, vivacious; blithe, jocund, jolly, jovial, merry
ant festive

fungible *adj syn* see INTERCHANGEABLE

funk *vb 1 syn* see SMELL 3

funk *n syn* see COWARD

funker *n syn* see COWARD

funky *adj syn* see MALODOROUS 1

funnel *vb syn* see CONDUCT 4

funniness *n syn* see HUMOR 4

funny *adj syn* see LAUGHABLE
rel antic, bizarre, fantastic, grotesque
idiom too funny for words
con doleful, dolorous, lugubrious, melancholy, plaintive
ant unfunny

funnyman *n syn* see HUMORIST 2

fur *n 1 syn* see HIDE
2 *syn* see DOWN

furbish *vb syn* see POLISH 1

furious *adj 1 syn* see WILD 6
2 marked by uncontrollable excitement often under the stress of a powerful emotion < in a state of *furious* activity >
syn corybantic, delirious, frantic, frenetic, frenzied, mad, rabid, wild
rel excited, provoked, stimulated; enthusiastic, fanatic; desperate, feverish, hasty, impetuous; fierce, intense, vehement, violent; excessive, extravagant, extreme, inordinate; enraged, incensed, infuriated, maddened; hysterical, irrational, unreasonable; bewildered, distracted, upset; crazed, demented, insane, mad, maniac
con calm, composed, peaceful, placid, quiet, serene, subdued, tranquil; apathetic, impassive, imperturbable, inexcitable
3 *syn* see INTENSE 1

furiously *adv syn* see HARD 2

furl *vb syn* see ROLL 3

furnish *vb 1* to supply one with what is needed (as for daily living or a particular activity) < *furnished* him the papers for his application >
syn accouter, appoint, arm, equip, fit out, gear, outfit, rig, turn out
rel dower, endow, endue; apparel, array, clothe; mount; give, provide, supply
con denude, dismantle, divest, strip; despoil, spoliate; relieve (of), take away
2 *syn* see GIVE 3

furor *n syn* see DELIRIUM

furore *n 1 syn* see STIR 1
2 *syn* see FASHION 3
3 *syn* see COMMOTION 3

furrow *n syn* see WRINKLE
rel channel, groove, rut

further *adv 1 syn* see BEYOND 1
2 *syn* see AGAIN 4

further *adj syn* see ADDITIONAL

further *vb syn* see ADVANCE 1
rel engender, generate, propagate
con bar, block, impede, obstruct; forestall, prevent
ant hinder; retard

furthermore *adv syn* see ALSO 2

furthermost *adj syn* see EXTREME 5

furthest *adj syn* see EXTREME 5

furtive *adj 1 syn* see SECRET 1
rel artful, crafty, cunning, foxy, guileful,

insidious, scheming, shifty, sly, sneaky, tricky, wily; calculating, cautious, circumspect, wary; cloaked, disguised, masked
con brash, impudent, presumptuous
ant forthright; barefaced, brazen
2 *syn* see STEALTHY 2
ant open

furtively *adv syn* see SECRETLY
ant openly

furuncle *n syn* see ABSCESS

fury *n syn* see ANGER
rel passion; furor; acerbity, acrimony, asperity

fuse *vb 1 syn* see LIQUEFY
2 *syn* see MIX 1
rel compact, consolidate, unify

fusillade *n syn* see BARRAGE

fusion *n syn* see MIXTURE

fuss *n 1 syn* see STIR 1
rel fluster, perturbation; bother, flap, stew; racket, rumpus; haste, hurry, speed
2 *syn* see COMMOTION 3
3 *syn* see QUARREL

fuss *vb 1 syn* see WORRY 3
idiom fret and fume
2 *syn* see COMPLAIN
3 *syn* see GRIPE
4 *syn* see NAG

fussbudget *n* one who becomes upset over trifles < he is the biggest *fussbudget* I know, always going into a tizzy over nothing >
syn fuddy-duddy, fusser, fusspot, granny, old lady, old maid
rel perfectionist, precisionist, stickler

fusser *n syn* see FUSSBUDGET

fusspot *n syn* see FUSSBUDGET

fussy *adj 1 syn* see BUSTLING
2 *syn* see CAREFUL 2
3 *syn* see NICE 1
rel fretful, irritable, querulous

fustian *n syn* see BOMBAST

fustian *adj syn* see FECKLESS 1

fusty *adj 1 syn* see MALODOROUS 1
rel close, moldy; dirty, filthy, squalid; disheveled, slipshod, sloppy, slovenly, unkempt
2 *syn* see OLD-FASHIONED

futile *adj* barren of results < efforts to convince him were *futile* >
syn abortive, bootless, fruitless, ineffective, ineffectual, unavailable, unavailing, unprevailing, unproductive, useless, vain
rel empty, hollow, idle, nugatory, otiose; inadequate, inefficacious, inefficient, insufficient; unsatisfactory, unsuccessful
idiom in vain, no dice, of no avail, to no effect
con effectual, efficacious, fruitful; advantageous, beneficial, profitable
ant effective

future *n* time that is to come < you must try to do better in the *future* >
syn aftertime, afterward, by-and-by, hereafter, offing, to-be; *compare* PRESENT
idiom time to come
ant past

fuzz *n 1 syn* see DOWN
‖2 *syn* see POLICEMAN

fuzzy *adj syn* see FAINT 2

G

gab *vb syn* see CHAT 1
gab *n syn* see CHATTER
gabber *n syn* see CHATTERBOX
gabble *vb* 1 *syn* see GIBBER
  2 *syn* see BABBLE 2
  3 *syn* see CHAT 1
gabble *n syn* see CHATTER
gabby *adj syn* see TALKATIVE
gad *vb syn* see WANDER 1
gadget *n* 1 a usually small and often novel mechanical or electronic device or contrivance <a new kitchen *gadget* for separating egg whites>
  syn concern, gimmick, gizmo, jigger, widget; *compare* DEVICE 2, DOODAD, WHAT-DO-YOU-CALL-IT
  rel apparatus, appliance, contraption, tool, utensil
  2 *syn* see DOODAD
gaffe *n syn* see FAUX PAS
gaffer *n* a man of advanced years <doddering *gaffers* on the park benches>
  syn graybeard, patriarch; *compare* BELDAM 1, OLDSTER
  rel duffer, geezer, grandfather, old boy, veteran
gag *vb* 1 *syn* see RETCH
  2 *syn* see DEMUR
gag *n syn* see JOKE 1
  rel ruse, trick, wile
gaiety *n* 1 *syn* see MERRYMAKING
  2 *syn* see MIRTH
  rel cheerfulness, gladness, happiness, geniality, pleasantness, winsomeness; animation, conviviality, entertainment, exhilaration, liveliness, merrymaking, radiance, spiritedness, vivacity
  con blues, cheerlessness, dismalness, dreariness, gloom, grief, infelicity, joylessness, misery, moodiness, moroseness, pensiveness, solemnity, somberness, sorrow, sullenness, uncheerfulness, wistfulness, woe
gain *n syn* see PROFIT
  rel cut, rake-off, share, take, winnings
  ant loss
gain *vb* 1 to arrive at a goal, point, or end <*gained* success in the theater>
  syn accomplish, achieve, attain, rack up, reach, realize, score, win
  rel complete, consummate, fulfill, perfect, produce; succeed
  con falter, flop, flounder, flunk, lose
  2 *syn* see IMPROVE 3
  rel invigorate, renew, strengthen; cure, heal, remedy
  3 *syn* see EARN 1
  4 *syn* see GET 1
  ant lose

  5 *syn* see CLEAR 6
  ant lose
gainful *adj syn* see ADVANTAGEOUS 1
  rel fat, fruitful, generous, lush, productive, rich; satisfying, substantial
gainsay *vb syn* see DENY 4
  rel combat, fight, oppose, resist, withstand
  ant admit
gainsaying *n syn* see DENIAL 2
  ant admission; admitting
gait *n syn* see SPEED 2
gal *n* 1 *syn* see GIRL 1
  2 *syn* see GIRL FRIEND 1
gall *n syn* see EFFRONTERY
  rel arrogance, conceit, haughtiness, loftiness, lordliness, overbearance, pomposity, pride, priggishness, self-importance, smugness
  con bashfulness, humbleness, humility, lowliness, modesty, shyness
  ant meekness
gall *vb* 1 *syn* see ABRADE 1
  rel bark, burn, file, fray, frazzle, grate, graze, scrape, scratch, scuff, skin
  2 *syn* see CHAFE 3
  rel distress, pain; cut, score, wound
  3 *syn* see ANNOY 1
  4 *syn* see IRRITATE
  rel chide, disturb, harass, harry, torment, worry; bedevil, needle, trouble
gallant *n* 1 *syn* see FOP
  2 an individual who is amorously attracted to the opposite sex <his fiancee accused him of being a trifling *gallant*>
  syn amorist, Casanova, Don Juan, lothario, paramour, Romeo
  rel dirty old man, lecher, libertine, rake, satyr; admirer, adorer, beau, date, escort, lover, sparker, suitor, swain, wooer
  idiom gay blade
gallant *adj* 1 *syn* see COURTLY
  rel urbane, suave; attentive, considerate, thoughtful
  con heedless, inattentive, indifferent, thoughtless, unconcerned
  ant ungallant
  2 *syn* see BRAVE 1
  ant dastardly
gallantry *n* 1 *syn* see COURTESY 1
  rel deference, duty, homage, honor; reverence, suavity, urbanity; address, poise, savoir faire, tact
  con boorishness, churlishness, clownishness, loutishness; discourteousness
  ant discourtesy
  2 *syn* see HEROISM
  rel bravery, dauntlessness; mettle, resolution, spirit
  ant dastardliness
gallery *n syn* see MUSEUM
galley slave *n syn* see SLAVE 2
gallimaufry *n syn* see MISCELLANY 1
galling *adj syn* see BITTER 2

---

syn synonym(s)   *rel* related word(s)
ant antonym(s)   *con* contrasted word(s)
idiom idiomatic equivalent(s)
‖ use limited; if in doubt, see a dictionary

gallivant *vb syn* see WANDER 1

‖**gallows** *n pl syn* see SUSPENDERS

galluptious *adj syn* see MARVELOUS 2

‖**galluses** *n pl syn* see SUSPENDERS

galoot *n syn* see MAN 3

galumph *vb syn* see LUMBER

galvanize *vb syn* see PROVOKE 4
  rel activate, energize, vitalize

gambit *n syn* see TRICK 1
  rel design, plan, plot

gamble *vb* 1 to engage in a game of chance
  for something of value <swore he would
  never *gamble* for high stakes again>
  syn bet, game, lay, play, put (on), set,
  stake, wager
  rel chance, hazard, lot, risk, speculate,
  venture
  idiom buck the odds, take a flyer (on),
  try one's luck
  2 to take a chance on something <*gam-
  bled* on the train being late>
  syn chance, hazard, risk, venture; *compare*
  VENTURE 1
  rel brave, challenge, dare, defy, face;
  endanger, imperil, jeopardize
  idiom go it blind, take a chance (*or* one's
  chances), tempt fortune, trust to luck

gambol *vb* to leap or tumble about play-
  fully <young lambs *gamboling* in the
  meadow>
  syn caper, cavort, frisk, frolic, rollick,
  romp
  rel lark, revel, roister; bound, leap, spring
  idiom kick up one's heels, let off steam

game *n* 1 *syn* see FUN 1
  con business, duty, labor, study, toil
  2 **games** *pl syn* see ATHLETICS
  3 animals under pursuit <hunting big
  game is a risky and expensive sport>
  syn chase, prey, quarry
  rel kill, ravin, victim

game *vb syn* see GAMBLE 1

game *adj syn* see BRAVE 1

game plan *n syn* see PLAN 1

gamesome *adj syn* see PLAYFUL 1

gamin *n syn* see URCHIN

gamine *n syn* see TOMBOY

gammer *n syn* see BELDAM 1

gamy *adj syn* see MALODOROUS 1

‖**gander** *n syn* see PEEP

gangling *adj* being tall, thin, and usually
  loose-jointed <a *gangling* high-school
  boy>
  syn gangly, lanky, rangy, spindling, spindly
  rel bony, gaunt, lank, lean, scrawny,
  skinny, spare, tall, thin
  con low, low-set, low-statured, short,
  squat, stocky, sturdy, thickset

gangly *adj syn* see GANGLING

‖**gangrel** *n syn* see VAGABOND

gap *n* 1 an open space in a barrier <the
  sheep got through a *gap* in the fence>
  syn breach, break, discontinuity, hole,
  opening
  rel fracture, rupture; chink, cleavage,
  cleft, crack, crevice, fissure, slit, slot; division, interspace, interval, separation; aperture, cranny, orifice
  2 *syn* see RAVINE
  3 a period of discontinuity <a *gap* of an
  hour between speakers>
  syn breach, break, hiatus, interim, interruption, interval, lacuna; *compare* PAUSE

  rel caesura, intermission, lull, pause, respite, rest

gape *vb* 1 *syn* see GAZE 1
  2 *syn* see LOOK 7
  3 *syn* see YAWN

gaping *adj syn* see CAVERNOUS 1

garb *vb syn* see CLOTHE

garbage *n syn* see REFUSE
  rel dregs, rubble; filth, sewage, slop

garble *vb syn* see MISREPRESENT
  rel becloud, conceal, hide, obfuscate,
  obscure

garden house *n syn* see SUMMERHOUSE

gargantuan *adj syn* see HUGE
  ant lilliputian

garish *adj syn* see GAUDY
  rel overdone, overwrought
  con dark, dim, dreary, dull, dusky,
  murky; quiet, unpretentious
  ant somber

garland *n* 1 *syn* see WREATH
  2 *syn* see ANTHOLOGY

garment *vb syn* see CLOTHE

garner *vb* 1 *syn* see REAP
  2 *syn* see GLEAN
  3 *syn* see ACCUMULATE
  rel gather, glean, harvest, reap; hoard,
  store
  con disseminate, spread

garnish *vb syn* see ADORN

garrulous *adj syn* see TALKATIVE
  rel blabbing, prattling, prolix, verbose,
  windy, wordy
  con concise; terse; blunt, brusque, curt
  ant taciturn

‖**gas** *n syn* see NONSENSE 2

‖**gas** *vb syn* see CHAT 1

‖**gasbag** *n syn* see BRAGGART

gasconade *vb syn* see BOAST

gash *vb syn* see CUT 1
  rel carve, split; injure, wound; furrow,
  mark, notch; lance, nip

gasp *vb syn* see PANT 1

‖**gasper** *n syn* see CIGARETTE

gastronome *n syn* see EPICURE
  rel aesthete, connoisseur, dilettante

gastronomer *n syn* see EPICURE

gastronomist *n syn* see EPICURE

gate *n syn* see FAUCET

gather *vb* 1 *syn* see GROUP 1
  rel choose, cull, pick, select; accumulate,
  amass
  idiom separate the wheat from the chaff
  (*or* the sheep from the goats)
  con dispel, disperse, dissipate
  ant scatter
  2 *syn* see REAP
  rel cull, pick, pluck; heap, mass, pile,
  stack
  3 *syn* see GLEAN
  4 *syn* see INFER
  rel catch, fathom, follow, grasp, take in
  idiom put two and two together
  5 *syn* see UNDERSTAND 3
  6 to bring or come together <a crowd
  gathered to watch the fight>
  syn assemble, collect, congregate, congress, forgather, muster, raise, rendezvous;
  compare GROUP 1
  rel aggregate, troop; affiliate, ally, associate, league; encounter, meet
  con break up, disband, disperse, part,
  separate; disintegrate, disorganize, dissolve

ant scatter
7 *syn* see LOOM 2

gathering *n* **1** *syn* see CONCOURSE
2 a number of individuals come or brought together <a *gathering* in the town park>
syn aggregation, assemblage, assembly, collection, company, congeries, congregation, crowd, group, muster, ruck; *compare* GROUP 1
rel bunch, crew, crush, flock, gang, horde, mass, press, rout, swarm, turnout
3 *syn* see HARVEST 1

gauche *adj* *syn* see AWKWARD 2
rel crude, green, unpolished
con bland, smooth, suave, urbane
ant adroit

gaudy *adj* cheaply or vulgarly showy <*gaudy* sideshow posters>
syn blatant, brazen, chintzy, flashy, garish, glaring, loud, meretricious, tawdry, tinsel
rel obtrusive, ostentatious, pretentious, showy, tasteless; coarse, crude, gross, vulgar; brummagem, fake, phony, sham
con restrained, tasteful, unobtrusive; factual, illuminating, informative
ant quiet

gauge *n* *syn* see STANDARD 3
rel check, mark, model, norm, pattern, rule, type

gauge *vb* *syn* see MEASURE 2
‖**gaum** *n* *syn* see OAF 2

gaunt *adj* **1** *syn* see LEAN
2 *syn* see EMACIATED
ant bloated

‖**gaup** (*or* gawp) *vb* **1** *syn* see LOOK 7
2 *syn* see GAZE 1

gauzy *adj* *syn* see FILMY

gawk *vb* *syn* see GAZE 1

gawk *n* *syn* see OAF 2

gawky *adj* *syn* see CLUMSY 1

gay *adj* **1** *syn* see MERRY
2 *syn* see LIVELY 1
rel frolicsome, playful, sportive
con earnest, sedate, serious, solemn, somber, staid; quiet, silent, still
ant grave, sober
3 *syn* see COLORFUL
4 *syn* see WILD 7
5 *syn* see HOMOSEXUAL
6 *syn* see PRESUMPTUOUS

gaze *vb* **1** to look long and usually attentively <*gazed* out the window>
syn bore, gape, ‖gaup (*or* gawp), gawk, glare, gloat, goggle, peer, stare; *compare* LOOK 7
rel look, see, watch; peek, peep; contemplate, inspect, observe, scrutinize, survey; admire, ogle, regard
con glance, skim, skip
2 *syn* see LOOK 7

gaze (upon) *vb* *syn* see EYE 1

gazebo *n* *syn* see SUMMERHOUSE

gear *n* *syn* see EQUIPMENT
rel accessories, adjuncts, appendages, appurtenances; belongings, effects, means, possessions

gear *vb* *syn* see FURNISH 1
‖**gee** *n* *syn* see MAN 3
‖**gee** *vb* *syn* see AGREE 4

Gehenna *n* *syn* see HELL

gel *vb* *syn* see COAGULATE

gelastic *adj* *syn* see LAUGHABLE

gelate *vb* *syn* see COAGULATE

gelatinize *vb* *syn* see COAGULATE

geld *vb* *syn* see STERILIZE

gelid *adj* *syn* see COLD 1
con ardent, burning, fervent, scorching, sweltering, torrid
ant fervid

‖**gelt** *n* *syn* see MONEY

gem *vb* *syn* see BEJEWEL

gendarme *n* *syn* see POLICEMAN

genealogy *n* an account often in chart form recording a line of ancestors <decided to prepare a *genealogy* of his family>
syn ‖begats, family tree, pedigree, stemma

general *adj* **1** conforming to what is expected in the ordinary course of events <the *general* problems of everyday life>
syn common, commonplace, matter-of-course, natural, normal, prevalent, regular, run-of-the-mill, typic, typical, usual
rel everyday, popular; familiar, universal; habitual, humdrum, routine, uneventful
con abnormal, extraordinary, irregular, novel, strange, unexpected, unforeseeable, unusual
2 belonging or relating to the whole <a *general* change in the weather>
syn common, generic, universal
rel natural, normal, regular, typical; broad, inclusive, wide
con individual, particular, special; characteristic, distinctive, peculiar
3 *syn* see ALL-AROUND 1
4 *syn* see PUBLIC 4

generally *adv* **1** in a reasonably inclusive manner <the forest was *generally* coniferous>
syn chiefly, largely, mainly, mostly, overall, predominantly, primarily, principally
rel about, approximately, practically, roughly, roundly
con altogether, totally, wholly
2 *syn* see ALTOGETHER 3
3 *syn* see USUALLY 2

generate *vb* **1** to bring into existence <*generate* new business>
syn create, father, hatch, make, originate, parent, procreate, produce, sire, spawn
rel bring about, effect, impose, occasion; introduce; cause; found, inaugurate, institute, set up; develop, induce, whip (up)
idiom bring to pass, give birth to, give rise to
con demolish, destroy, extinguish, ruin; degenerate, deteriorate, impair, worsen
2 *syn* see PROCREATE 1
3 to be the cause or source of something immaterial <actions that *generated* a good deal of suspicion>
syn breed, cause, engender, get up, hatch, induce, muster (up), occasion, produce, provoke, work up
rel accomplish, achieve, perform
idiom give birth to, give rise to

generator *n* *syn* see FATHER 2

generic *adj* *syn* see GENERAL 2

---

ant specific

generous *adj* **1** marked by a noble or for-bearing spirit < *generous* toward the weak-ness of others >

syn benevolent, big, chivalrous, consider-ate, greathearted, lofty, magnanimous

rel altruistic, charitable, kindhearted, kindly, thoughtful, ungrudging, unselfish; fair, honest; long-suffering, tolerant; help-ful, willing

con base, ignoble, mean, self-centered, selfish; grim, hard, harsh, intolerant

ant ungenerous

2 *syn* see LIBERAL 1

ant stingy

3 *syn* see PLENTIFUL

rel lavish; luxuriant; affluent, wealthy

con scant, scanty, sparse

generously *adv syn* see WELL 2

genesis *n syn* see BEGINNING

rel provenance, provenience

con cessation, conclusion, culmination, end, finish, termination

genial *adj* **1** *syn* see GRACIOUS 1

rel amicable, friendly, neighborly; blithe, cheerful, jocund, jolly, jovial, merry

con discourteous, rude, uncivil, ungra-cious; crabbed, morose, sullen; ironic, sarcastic, sardonic, satiric

ant caustic (*remarks, comments*); satur-nine (*manner, disposition, aspect*)

2 *syn* see GENTLE 2

geniality *n syn* see AMENITY 1

genitalia *n pl* the external components of the reproductive system < the gradual adolescent differentiation of the *genita-lia* >

syn genitals, parts, private parts, privates, privities, privy parts, pudendum (*usu* pu-denda *pl*), secrets

genitals *n pl syn* see GENITALIA

genius *n syn* see GIFT 2

rel creativity, ingenuity, inventiveness, originality; astuteness, brains, grasp, intel-lect, intelligence, understanding

gent *n syn* see MAN 3

genteel *adj* **1** having characteristics or qualities befitting the upper classes < in those days croquet was a very *genteel* sport > < his manner was perfectly gen-teel >

syn cultivated, cultured, distingué, pol-ished, refined, urbane, well-bred

rel elegant, fashionable, graceful, stylish; chivalrous, gentlemanly, knightly, ladylike, noble; mannerly, well-mannered

con coarse, common, crude, ill-bred, rough, rude, uncouth, uncultured, unpol-ished, vulgar

ant ungenteel

2 *syn* see CIVIL 2

rel well-behaved; aristocratic, cultured

con crude, discourteous, inconsiderate, rough, rude

3 involving or excessively preoccupied with the airs and forms of middle-class or upper-class proprieties < a shy *genteel* girl terrified of blundering socially >

syn affected, la-di-da, ||lardy-dardy, minc-ing, pretentious, stilted, too-too; *compare* PRECIOUS 4, PRIM 1

rel artificial, formal, high-falutin

con cultured, genuine, honest, refined; gracious, polished; gentlemanly, ladylike

4 *syn* see PRIM 1

rel narrow; intolerant, uncharitable; con-fined, insular, parochial, provincial

idiom nasty nice

con charitable, tolerant, understanding; broad-minded, easy, relaxed

gentile *adj syn* see HEATHEN

gentility *n syn* see ARISTOCRACY

gentle *adj* **1** free from all harshness, rough-ness, or intensity < a *gentle* summer breeze >

syn balmy, bland, faint, lenient, mild, smooth, soft

rel delicate, mellow, tender; hushed, low, soothing; calm, halcyon, peaceful, placid, quiet, serene, tranquil

con coarse, harsh, rough; exquisite, fierce, intense, savage, vehement, violent; force-ful, forcible, powerful

2 having a pleasant easygoing nature < a *gentle* person in everything she does >

syn affable, amiable, genial

rel kind, pleasant, pleasing, tender; agree-able, benign, mild; compassionate, kindly, softhearted, sympathetic, warmhearted

con belligerent, cantankerous, conten-tious, ill-natured, petty, quarrelsome; aggressive, demanding, overbearing

ant harsh, stern

gentleman *n* **1** a person of good or noble birth < the contributions of the country *gentleman* to social stability >

syn aristo, aristocrat, blue blood, patri-cian

rel Brahmin; chevalier; nob, swell

con churl, clown, lout

ant boor

2 *syn* see MAN 3

gentleman friend *n syn* see BOYFRIEND 1

gentry *n syn* see ARISTOCRACY

genuine *adj* **1** *syn* see AUTHENTIC 2

con artificial, ersatz, factitious; counter-feited, sham, simulated; sophisticated

ant fraudulent

2 *syn* see ACTUAL 2

con uncommon, unordinary, unusual; alleged, apocryphal, apparent, fabulous, fictitious, mythical

3 free from hypocrisy or pretense < a *genuine* love for his fellowman >

syn heart-whole, honest, real, sincere, true, undesigning, undissembled, un-feigned; *compare* NATURAL 5, SINCERE 1

rel reliable, trustworthy, unaffected, un-impeachable, veritable

con affected, hyprocritical

ant insincere

genuinely *adv syn* see VERY 2

germ *n syn* see SEED 2

germane *adj syn* see RELEVANT

con incompatible, incongruous, inconso-nant

ant foreign

gest *n syn* see ADVENTURE

gestapo *adj syn* see TERRORISTIC

gestation *n syn* see PREGNANCY

gesture *n syn* see EXPRESSION 3

gesture *vb syn* see SIGNAL

get *vb* **1** to come into possession of < hoped to *get* a fortune from his inven-tion >

syn acquire, annex, chalk up, compass, gain, have, land, obtain, pick up, procure, pull, secure, win

rel educe, elicit, evoke, extort, extract, ‖promote; accept, receive; clutch, grab, grasp, take; accomplish, achieve, effect; capture, carry; draw

idiom come by

con abnegate, eschew, forbear, forgo, give up, sacrifice; abandon, forsake, renounce

2 *syn* see EARN 1

3 *syn* see BECOME 1

rel achieve, attain, effect, realize

idiom get to be, turn out to be

4 *syn* see CONTRACT 1

5 *syn* see FATHER 1

6 *syn* see PREPARE 1

rel arrange, order, right; adjust, coordinate, organize

7 *syn* see CATCH 1

8 *syn* see AFFECT

rel bend, bias, dispose, predispose, prompt

con benumb, deaden, numb; blunt, dull, harden

9 *syn* see NONPLUS 1

rel bother, distress, disturb, perturb, upset; discomfit, disconcert, embarrass

10 *syn* see IRRITATE

idiom try one's temper

con calm, compose, cool, lull, soothe, subdue

11 *syn* see LEARN 1

idiom get into one's head

12 *syn* see MEMORIZE

13 *syn* see INDUCE 1

rel provoke; beg, coax, press, pressure, urge

14 *syn* see REACH 4

15 *syn* see COME 1

get along *vb* 1 *syn* see ADVANCE 5

rel depart, go

con recede, regress, retreat, retrogress, reverse, revert

2 *syn* see SHIFT 5

rel flourish, prosper, succeed, thrive

get away *vb syn* see GO 2

getaway *n syn* see ESCAPE 1

get back *vb syn* see RECOVER 1

get by *vb syn* see SHIFT 5

get in *vb syn* see COME 1

get off *vb* 1 *syn* see GO 2

rel advance, progress

2 *syn* see BEGIN 1

get on *vb* 1 *syn* see DON 1

2 *syn* see ADVANCE 5

3 *syn* see SHIFT 5

get out *vb* 1 to go away quickly, immediately, and often secretly < had to *get out* before the police arrived >

syn begone, clear out, decamp, hightail, kite, scram, skedaddle, skiddoo, take off, ‖vamoose

rel depart, duck (out), egress, exit, go, leave, split

idiom beat it, be off, make tracks, take a powder, take a runout powder

con abide, remain, reside, stay

2 to become known < we can't let this story *get out* >

syn break, come out, leak, out, transpire

3 *syn* see PUBLISH 2

gettable *adj syn* see AVAILABLE 1

get up *vb* 1 *syn* see ROLL OUT

2 *syn* see RISE 1

3 *syn* see GENERATE 3

getup *n* 1 *syn* see COSTUME

2 *syn* see VIGOR 2

get–up–and–go *n* 1 *syn* see VIGOR 2

2 *syn* see ENTERPRISE 4

gewgaw *n syn* see KNICKKNACK

ghastly *adj* 1 disturbingly frightening or repellent in appearance or aspect < the *ghastly* sight of burned and rotting bodies >

syn grim, grisly, gruesome, hideous, horrible, horrid, horrifying, lurid, macabre, terrible, terrifying

rel appalling, awful, dreadful, frightening, frightful, shocking; disgustful, disgusting, nauseant, nauseating, sickening

con appealing, attractive, charming, pleasant, touching; acceptable, bearable; trivial, unimportant

2 resembling or suggestive of a ghost < a *ghastly* form slightly visible through the fog >

syn cadaverous, corpselike, deathlike, ghostlike, ghostly, shadowy, spectral

rel ashen, livid, lurid, pale; uncanny, weird; gruesome, haggard, macabre; dim, faint, weak; charnel, mortuary, sepulchral

ghost *n syn* see APPARITION

rel demon, devil

ghost *vb syn* see GHOSTWRITE

ghostlike *adj syn* see GHASTLY 2

ghostly *adj syn* see GHASTLY 2

ghostwrite *vb* to write for and in the name of another < a *ghostwritten* autobiography >

syn ghost, ‖spook

GI *n syn* see SOLDIER

giant *n* something of monstrous size, appearance, or power < a *giant* of a tractor >

syn behemoth, leviathan, mammoth, monster, whale

rel cyclops, polypheme

giant *adj syn* see HUGE

rel gross, hulking

con paltry, petty, puny, trifling, trivial

ant dwarf

gibber *vb* to utter or speak rapidly, inarticulately, and usually unintelligibly < a *gibbering* idiot >

syn babble, chatter, gabble, jabber

rel blather, blither, prate, prattle, yammer; stammer, stutter; mumble, mutter; mow

idiom run off at the mouth

con articulate, enunciate, pronounce

gibberish *n* 1 unintelligible or meaningless talk < the *gibberish* of an imbecile >

syn babble, drivel, Greek, jabber, jabberwocky, nonsense, skimble-skamble; compare GIBBERISH 3

rel blather, bunkum, claptrap, twaddle; blabber, gabble, palaver, prattle

2 *syn* see GOBBLEDYGOOK

3 speech or actions that are esoteric in nature and suggest the magical, strange, or unknown < the shaman's strange *gibberish* >

---

syn synonym(s)   *rel* related word(s)
ant antonym(s)   *con* contrasted word(s)
idiom idiomatic equivalent(s)
‖ use limited; if in doubt, see a dictionary

syn abracadabra, hocus-pocus, mumbo jumbo, mummery
rel magic, sorcery, thaumaturgy

gibbet vb syn see HANG 2

gibble–gabble n syn see CHATTER

gibe vb syn see SCOFF
rel rail, rally, revile, scold, twit

giddy adj 1 having a lightheartedly silly nature <tried to teach a bunch of giddy Girl Scouts how to make a fire>
syn bird-witted, dizzy, empty-headed, featherbrained, flighty, fribble, fribbling, frivolous, harebrained, hoity-toity, light, lightheaded, rattlebrained, scatterbrained, silly, skittish, volage, yeasty
rel capricious, fickle, impulsive, whimsical; brainless, exuberant, thoughtless, witless
idiom giddy as a goose
con earnest, pensive, sedate, serious, sober, solemn, staid, thoughtful
2 syn see DIZZY 2
rel bemused, flustered
idiom going around in circles, like a chicken with its head cut off, seeing double

gift n 1 something freely given by one person to another for his benefit or pleasure <the watch was a graduation gift>
syn benevolence, boon, ‖compliment, favor, largess, present
rel alms, benefaction, contribution, donation; award, bestowal, grant, presentation; legacy; offering, reward, tip; remembrance, souvenir, token
2 a natural or special facility or capableness <has a gift for electronics>
syn aptness, bent, bump, faculty, flair, genius, head, knack, nose, set, talent, turn; compare LEANING 2
rel ability, aptitude, capability; accomplishment, acquirement, attainment; instinct, numen, power; forte, leaning, propensity, specialty
con awkwardness, clumsiness, maladroitness

gigantean adj syn see HUGE

gigantesque adj syn see HUGE

gigantic adj syn see HUGE
rel hulking, stupendous
con paltry, petty, puny, trifling, trivial

giggle vb syn see LAUGH

gill n syn see CREEK 2

gimcrack n syn see KNICKKNACK

gimmick n 1 syn see GADGET 1
2 syn see TRICK 1
rel cheat, counterfeit, deceit, dodge, fake, humbug, imposture; fun, game, jest, method, sport

gimp n syn see SPIRIT 5

gingerly adj syn see CAUTIOUS

gingery adj syn see SPIRITED 2
con lethargic, listless, poky, slow; dead, dull, flat, insipid, stuffy; dreary; blasé, lackadaisical, nonchalant

‖**gin mill** n syn see BAR 5

gird vb 1 syn see BELT 1
ant ungird
2 syn see SURROUND 1
rel wrap, wreathe
3 to prepare oneself for action <girded himself for the coming trial>
syn brace, fortify, prepare, ready, steel, strengthen

rel bolster, buttress, support, sustain; harden, reinforce, shore (up); invigorate; dispose, forearm, prepare
idiom gird one's loins, whet the knife

gird vb syn see SCOFF

girdle n syn see BELT 1

girdle vb 1 syn see BELT 1
2 syn see SURROUND 1

girl n 1 a young unmarried female person <hired a girl to babysit>
syn damsel, gal, lass, lassie, maid, maiden, miss, missy, ‖quail, ‖quiff, wench
rel hoyden, tomboy; deb, debutante, subdeb, subdebutante; bobby-soxer; schoolgirl; gamine
2 syn see MAID 2
3 syn see GIRL FRIEND 1

girl Friday n syn see RIGHT-HAND MAN

girl friend n 1 a woman who is a man's usual or preferred companion <took his girl friend out every weekend>
syn best girl, ‖chick, ‖doney, gal, girl, lady friend, lass, mouse, popsy
2 a woman who shares with a man a strong and usually sexually oriented mutual attraction <his wife caught him with his girl friend>
syn ‖baby, beloved, flame, honey, inamorata, ladylove, steady, sweetheart, sweetie, truelove
3 syn see MISTRESS

gist n syn see SUBSTANCE 2
rel sap, soul, spirit; subject, theme, topic; bearing, drift, tenor

give vb 1 to provide gratuitously <gave their labor to rebuild the burned church>
syn bestow, devote, donate, give away, hand out, present; compare CONTRIBUTE 1
rel accord, award, confer, grant, hand; afford, contribute, furnish, provide; aid, assist, benefact, help
con keep, retain, withhold; lease, sell
2 to provide by or as if by formal action <he was given a diploma>
syn accord, award, confer, grant; compare GRANT 1
rel bestow, hand over, present; allocate, appropriate, assign
con decline, refuse; hold back, withhold
3 to put into the possession of another usually for use or consumption <gave the dog a drink of water>
syn deliver, dish out, dispense, feed, find, furnish, hand, hand over, provide, supply, transfer, turn over
rel administer, commit, offer; deal, disburse, disperse, distribute, divide, dole (out), lot (out); afford, lend
con have, hold, hold back, keep, keep back, reserve, retain, withhold
4 syn see OFFER 1
rel bestow, confer, render; administer, dispense, issue
5 syn see EXPRESS 2
6 syn see ALLOT
7 to furnish as a result or product <6 +6 gives 12>
syn produce, yield
rel be, equal, make; afford, furnish, offer, supply
8 syn see SPEND 1
9 syn see SELL 2

10 to bestow or dispense by some action
< *gave* him a punch in the nose >
syn administer, deal, deliver, inflict, strike
rel bestow, dispense; fetch
11 *syn* see ADDRESS 3
12 to fail in response to physical stress
< the bridge *gave* under the heavy load >
syn bend, break, cave, collapse, crumple,
fold up, go, yield
rel fail, relax, relent, slacken, weaken
idiom cave in, give way
13 *syn* see HAPPEN 1
give away *vb* 1 *syn* see GIVE 1
2 *syn* see REVEAL 1
give back *vb* 1 *syn* see RETREAT 2
rel back out, backtrack, backwater; crumble, fail, falter, weaken
2 *syn* see RESTORE 5
given *adj syn* see APT 1
given name *n* the name that precedes
one's surname < arguing over the baby's
given name >
syn baptismal name, Christian name, font
name, forename, personal name, prename
rel first name, middle name; appellation,
appellative, compellation, denomination,
style; praenomen; epithet, label, tag
give off *vb* 1 *syn* see EMIT 2
2 *syn* see DISCHARGE 5
give out *vb* 1 *syn* see EMIT 2
2 *syn* see COLLAPSE 2
3 *syn* see FAIL 2
give over *vb syn* see STOP 3
giver *n syn* see DONOR
give up *vb* 1 *syn* see RELINQUISH
2 *syn* see DESPAIR
gizmo *n* 1 *syn* see DOODAD
2 *syn* see GADGET
glabrous *adj syn* see HAIRLESS
rel beardless, shaven, smooth-shaven
con bristled, bristly, hairy, hirsute, stubbled, stubbly
glacial *adj* 1 *syn* see COLD 1
2 *syn* see COLD 2
rel aloof, distant, remote, reserved, standoffish, withdrawn; exclusive, inaccessible,
seclusive, unapproachable
con affable, gregarious, sociable
glad *adj* 1 characterized by or expressing
the mood of one who is pleased or delighted < he was *glad* to be on vacation >
syn happy, joyful, joyous, lighthearted
rel delighted, gratified, pleased, rejoiced,
tickled; blithe, exhilarated, jocund, jolly,
jovial, merry; gleeful, hilarious, mirthful
idiom filled with (*or* full of) delight
con blue, dejected, depressed, downcast,
melancholy; despondent, dispirited, heavyhearted, sadhearted, unhappy; forlorn,
joyless, sorrowful, woeful
ant sad
2 full of brightness and cheerfulness < a
glad spring morning >
syn bright, cheerful, cheery, radiant
rel beaming, sparkling; beautiful; genial,
pleasant
con dark, dim, dull, gloomy, somber
gladden *vb syn* see PLEASE 2

rel comfort, console, solace; animate,
enliven, exhilarate, invigorate, liven,
quicken, vivify
con depress, oppress, weigh; discourage,
dishearten, dispirit; damp, dampen;
bother, irk
ant sadden
gladiatorial *adj syn* see BELLIGERENT
‖**glad rags** *n pl syn* see FINERY
glamorous *adj syn* see ATTRACTIVE 1
glamour *n syn* see CHARM 3
glance *vb* 1 to strike a surface obliquely so
as to go off at an angle < the bullet
glanced off the stone wall >
syn carom, dap, graze, ricochet, skim,
skip
rel brush, kiss, scrape, shave, slant;
contact, hit, strike, touch; bounce, careen,
rebound
con center, focus
2 *syn* see BRUSH
3 *syn* see FLASH 1
glance (at *or* over) *vb syn* see BROWSE
glance *n* 1 *syn* see FLASH 1
2 *syn* see PEEP
glance *vb syn* see POLISH 1
glare *vb* 1 *syn* see BLAZE
rel dazzle, flash, gleam, glisten, glitter
2 *syn* see GAZE 1
rel frown, glower, lower, scowl
glaring *adj* 1 *syn* see EGREGIOUS
rel conspicuous, noticeable, outstanding;
excessive, extreme, inordinate; obtrusive
ant unnoticeable
2 *syn* see GAUDY
rel cheap, coarse, crude, gross
con elegant, tasteful
glass *n syn* see MIRROR 1
glass *vb syn* see REFLECT 1
‖**glasshouse** *n syn* see GREENHOUSE
glassy *adj syn* see SLEEK
glaze *vb syn* see POLISH 1
glaze *n syn* see LUSTER
gleam *n syn* see FLASH 1
gleam *vb* 1 *syn* see SHINE 1
2 *syn* see FLASH 1
rel burn
gleaming *adj syn* see LUSTROUS 1
glean *vb* to gather by effort and usually bit
by bit < evidence *gleaned* from various
testimonies >
syn cull, extract, garner, gather, pick up
rel sift, winnow; ascertain, conclude,
deduce, learn
con amass, heap, pile
glee *n syn* see MIRTH
rel delectation, delight, enjoyment, joy,
pleasure; blitheness; joyousness
ant gloom
gleeful *adj syn* see MERRY
glen *n syn* see VALLEY
glib *adj* characterized by very fluent often
superficial address toward others < *glib*
chatter >
syn silver-tongued, vocative, voluble,
well-hung; *compare* TALKATIVE
rel articulate, eloquent, facile, fluent,
vocal
con inarticulate, unfluent
glide *vb* 1 *syn* see SLIDE 1
rel float, fly, sail, scud, shoot, skim
2 *syn* see STEAL 3
3 *syn* see SNEAK

---

syn synonym(s)   *rel* related word(s)
ant antonym(s)   *con* contrasted word(s)
idiom idiomatic equivalent(s)
‖ use limited; if in doubt, see a dictionary

glimmer *vb syn* see FLASH 1

glimmer *n syn* see FLASH 1

glimpse *n syn* see PEEP

glint *vb syn* see FLASH 1

glint *n* 1 *syn* see FLASH 1

  2 *syn* see LUSTER

glissade *vb syn* see SLIDE 1

  rel float, fly, sail, scud, shoot, skim

glisten *vb syn* see FLASH 1

glisten *n syn* see FLASH 1

glistening *adj syn* see LUSTROUS 1

glitter *vb* 1 *syn* see FLASH 1

  2 *syn* see SPANGLE 1

glitter *n syn* see FLASH 1

gloaming *n syn* see EVENING 1

gloat *vb syn* see GAZE 1

  con begrudge, covet, envy, grudge

global *adj* 1 *syn* see UNIVERSAL 2

  ant parochial

  2 *syn* see ALL-ROUND 2

  rel all-inclusive, blanket, catholic, grand, universal

globe *n* 1 *syn* see BALL

  2 *syn* see EARTH 1

globule *n syn* see DROP 1

gloom *vb* 1 *syn* see FROWN 1

  rel brood, mope

  con smile; bubble, effervesce, enthuse, sparkle

  2 *syn* see OBSCURE

gloom *n syn* see SADNESS

  con hilarity, jollity, mirth; gaiety, gladness

  ant glee

gloomy *adj* 1 *syn* see DARK 1

  rel bleak, dismal, dreary

  ant brilliant

  2 *syn* see SULLEN

  rel cheerless, dejected, depressed, downcast, joyless, melancholy, oppressed, solemn, unhappy, weary

  con glad, happy, joyful, joyous, lighthearted; blithe, jocund, jovial, merry

  ant cheerful

  3 causing or marked by gloom < the *gloomy* atmosphere of the dungeon >

  syn acheronian, acherontic, black, bleak, cheerless, cold, depressant, depressing, depressive, desolate, disconsolate, discouraging, disheartening, dismal, dispiriting, drear, dreary, dusky, funereal, joyless, lugubrious, morne, oppressive, somber, tenebrific, unhappy, woebegone

  rel despondent, mirthless, pessimistic; melancholy, mournful, sad; drab, dull, muzzy

  con bright, cheerful, happy; cheering, emboldening, encouraging, heartening, optimistic

  ant gloomless

glorification *n syn* see APOTHEOSIS 2

glorify *vb* 1 *syn* see PRAISE 2

  2 *syn* see EXALT 1

glorious *adj* 1 *syn* see SPLENDID 2

  rel brilliant, effulgent, lustrous, radiant; imposing, impressive; majestic, noble; ravishing, stunning; beautiful

  ant inglorious

  2 *syn* see MARVELOUS 2

glory *vb syn* see EXULT

gloss *n syn* see LUSTER

  rel glossiness, silkiness, sleekness, slickness; burnish

gloss *vb syn* see POLISH 1

gloss (over) *vb syn* see PALLIATE

  rel account, explain, justify, rationalize; belie, falsify, miscolor, misrepresent

gloss *vb syn* see ANNOTATE

glossy *adj* 1 *syn* see LUSTROUS 1

  2 *syn* see SLEEK

glow *vb* 1 *syn* see BLAZE

  rel burn; ignite, kindle, light

  2 *syn* see BLUSH

glow *n syn* see BLOOM 3

glower *vb syn* see FROWN 1

  rel stare; look, watch

glowing *adj* 1 *syn* see RUDDY

  2 *syn* see IMPASSIONED

  rel enthusiastic; avid, desirous, eager, fierce, keen; burning, heated

gloze (over) *vb syn* see PALLIATE

  rel account, explain, justify, rationalize; belie, falsify, miscolor, misrepresent

gluey *adj syn* see STICKY 1

glum *adj syn* see SULLEN

  rel close-lipped, silent, taciturn, tight-lipped; depressed, oppressed, weighed down

  con glad, happy, joyful, joyous, lighthearted

  ant cheerful

glut *vb syn* see SATIATE

  rel cram, feast, stuff

  idiom make a pig of (oneself)

  con scant, skimp

  ant stint

glutted *adj syn* see SATIATED

gluttonous *adj syn* see VORACIOUS

  rel hoggish, piggish; indulgent, intemperate

  con sober, temperate; ascetic, austere; sparing

  ant abstemious

gnaw *vb* 1 *syn* see WORRY 1

  rel haunt, irritate, rankle

  2 *syn* see EAT 3

  rel abrade, fret; consume, crumble

gnome *n syn* see MAXIM

gnostic *adj syn* see WISE 1

go *vb* 1 to move on a course < they were glad to be *going* toward home >

  syn ‖cruise, fare, hie, journey, pass, proceed, ‖process, push on, repair, travel, wend

  rel advance; approach, near

  idiom gain ground, get over the ground, make one's way

  ant stay; stop

  2 to move out of and away from where one is < it's time to *go* now >

  syn ‖blow, depart, exit, get away, get off, leave, ‖mog, move, pop off, pull out, push off, quit, retire, run along, shove off, take off, withdraw

  rel abscond, decamp, escape, flee, fly, hightail

  idiom take a powder

  con abide, remain, stay; arrive

  ant come

  3 *syn* see RUN 8

  4 to be brought to or toward an end < his money will soon be *gone* >

  syn consume, exhaust, expend, finish, run through, spend, use up, wash up

  rel deplete, devour, dissipate, fritter (away), overspend, squander, waste

260   **go**

con conserve, preserve, save
5 *syn* see DIE 1
6 *syn* see PASS 3
7 *syn* see GIVE 12
8 *syn* see HAPPEN 1
9 *syn* see BECOME 1
10 *syn* see RANGE 3
11 *syn* see SUCCEED 3
12 *syn* see SUCCEED 2
13 *syn* see RESORT 2
14 *syn* see FUNCTION 3
15 *syn* see EXTEND 7
16 *syn* see AGREE 4
17 *syn* see BELONG 1
18 *syn* see BEAR 10
19 *syn* see ENJOY 1
go (for) *vb syn* see APPROVE 1
go (into) *vb syn* see EXPLORE
go (together *or* with) *vb syn* see SUIT 4
go *n* 1 *syn* see OCCURRENCE
2 *syn* see VIGOR 2
3 *syn* see ENERGY 2
4 *syn* see FLING 1
5 *syn* see SPELL 1
6 *syn* see SIEGE
7 *syn* see SUCCESS
goad *n syn* see STIMULUS
rel compulsion, drive, impulsion; desire,
lust, passion, urge, zeal
ant curb
goad *vb syn* see URGE
rel impel, move; coerce, compel, force;
instigate
go–ahead *adj syn* see ENTERPRISING 2
goal *n* 1 *syn* see AMBITION 2
2 *syn* see USE 4
goat *n syn* see SCAPEGOAT
goatish *adj syn* see LUSTFUL 2
gob *n* 1 *syn* see LUMP 1
2 *usu* gobs *pl syn* see SCAD
gob *n syn* see MOUTH 1
gobbet *n syn* see DROP 1
gobble *vb syn* see GULP
gobbledygook *n* wordy unintelligible language < *gobbledygook* of bureaucrats >
syn double-talk, gibberish
rel double Dutch, Greek, jabberwocky;
‖bull, bunkum, claptrap, drivel, garbage,
malarkey, nonsense, poppycock, twaddle
go–between *n* 1 *syn* see MARRIAGE BRO-
KER
2 an intermediate agent between individuals or groups < served as *go-between* in
the labor dispute >
syn broker, entrepreneur, interagent,
interceder, intercessor, intermediary, intermediate, intermediator, mediator, middleman
rel agent, attorney, deputy, factor, proxy;
emissary, envoy, messenger; delegate,
representative; arbitrator, negotiator
godless *adj syn* see IRRELIGIOUS
rel agnostic, atheistic, infidel
ant godly
godlike *adj syn* see DIVINE 1
godly *adj* 1 *syn* see DIVINE 1
2 *syn* see SAINTLY
3 *syn* see DEVOUT

ant godless
go down *vb* 1 *syn* see FALL 2
rel droop, sag, sink; cave (in), collapse,
crumple, fold
2 *syn* see SET 12
3 *syn* see SINK 1
4 *syn* see FALL 3
God's acre *n syn* see CEMETERY
godsend *n syn* see GOOD 1
go–getter *n syn* see HUSTLER 1
goggle *vb* 1 *syn* see LOOK 7
2 *syn* see GAZE 1
go in *vb syn* see ENTER 1
Golconda *n syn* see BONANZA
goldarn *adj* 1 *syn* see DAMNED 2
2 *syn* see UTTER
goldbrick *n syn* see SLACKER
goldbrick *vb syn* see IDLE
golden *adj* 1 *syn* see BLOND 1
2 *syn* see MELLIFLUOUS
golden–ager *n syn* see OLDSTER
gold mine *n syn* see BONANZA
golem *n syn* see ROBOT 2
gone *adj* 1 *syn* see EXTINCT 2
2 *syn* see ABSENT 1
3 *syn* see LOST 2
4 *syn* see PREGNANT 1
gonfalon *n syn* see FLAG
gonfanon *n syn* see FLAG
goo *n* 1 a sticky substance < slipped on a
patch of greasy *goo* on the walk >
syn gook, goop, gumbo, gunk, muck;
compare CRUD
rel dope
2 *syn* see CRUD
good *adj* 1 having a helpful or auspicious
character < a *good* wind >
syn advantageous, benefic, beneficial,
brave, favorable, favoring, helpful, propitious, toward, useful
rel convenient, suitable; desirable, needed;
appropriate, proper, right
con disadvantageous, unfavorable; damaging, hampering, harmful; unwanted
ant ill
2 adapted to the end in view < they
doubted that the fruit was *good* to eat >
syn appropriate, convenient, fit, meet,
proper, suitable, useful
rel all right, apt, becoming, conformable,
congruous, fitting, seemly
con inadequate, inappropriate, undesirable, unfit, unsuitable, useless
3 *syn* see WHOLE 1
con blemished, damaged, defective,
flawed, impaired, imperfect, unsound
ant bad
4 *syn* see ADVANTAGEOUS 1
5 *syn* see PLEASANT 1
6 *syn* see HEALTHFUL
7 *syn* see CLEVER 5
8 *syn* see CONSIDERABLE 2
9 *syn* see WELL-FOUNDED
10 *syn* see DECENT 4
11 conforming to a high standard of morality or virtue < if you can't be *good*, be
careful >
syn blameless, exemplary, guiltless, inculpable, innocent, irreprehensible, irreproachable, lily-white, pure, righteous,
unblamable, virtuous
rel incorrupt, sound, uncorrupted, untainted

---

syn synonym(s)   *rel* related word(s)
ant antonym(s)   *con* contrasted word(s)
idiom idiomatic equivalent(s)
‖ use limited; if in doubt, see a dictionary

con blameworthy, impure, unrighteous; evil, iniquitous, reprobate, sinful

ant bad

12 *syn* see CHARITABLE 1

13 behaving in an acceptable or desirable manner < a *good* child >

syn decorous, well-behaved

rel polite, proper; considerate, kindly, thoughtful

con ill-behaved, indecorous, naughty; careless, heedless, inconsiderate, mischievous, thoughtless

ant bad

14 *syn* see SKILLFUL 2

ant bad

15 *syn* see ABLE

good *n* **1** something that is desirable or beneficial < it's an ill wind that blows no *good* >

syn advantage, benediction, benefit, blessing, boon, godsend

con bane, harm, misfortune; detriment, jinx

ant evil, ill

2 *syn* see RIGHT 1

3 *syn* see WELFARE

4 goods *pl syn* see POSSESSION 2

5 goods *pl syn* see MERCHANDISE

good-bye *interj* — used as a conventional expression of good wishes at parting < the party was over; the time had come to say *good-bye* >

syn adieu, by, bye-bye, ‖cheerio, farewell, so long, ‖toodle-oo

rel good day, good evening, good morning, good night

idiom be good, be seeing you, fare you well, keep in touch, see you (later)

con hello, how do, howdy, hullo

good-bye *n syn* see PARTING

good-bye *adj syn* see PARTING

good faith *n* a state of mind characterizing one free from fraud, deceit, or misconduct < determined to act in *good faith* >

syn bona fides, sincereness, sincerity, uberrima fides

rel decency, decorum, propriety, seemliness; ethicality, morality, virtuousness

good-fellowship *n syn* see CAMARADERIE

good-for-nothing *n syn* see WASTREL 1

good-for-nothing *adj* **1** *syn* see FECKLESS 1

2 *syn* see WORTHLESS 1

ant precious

good-hearted *adj syn* see KIND

good-humored *adj syn* see AMIABLE 1

rel buoyant, cheerful, cheery, genial, smiling

ant ill-humored

good-looking *adj syn* see BEAUTIFUL

ant ill-looking

good-natured *adj syn* see AMIABLE 1

rel altruistic, benevolent, charitable; acquiescent, compliant

con choleric, cranky, cross, irascible, splenetic, touchy; crabbed, gloomy, glum, morose, splenetic

ant contrary; ill-natured

goodness *n* the quality or state of being morally excellent < that eternal *goodness* that burns away evil >

syn morality, probity, rectitude, righteousness, rightness, uprightness, virtue

rel honesty, honor, integrity; grace, merit, quality, superiority

ant badness, evil

good sense *n syn* see SENSE 6

good-tasting *adj syn* see PALATABLE

good-tempered *adj syn* see AMIABLE 1

con crabbed, surly; snappish, touchy; irascible

ant bad-tempered, ill-tempered

goodwill *n* **1** benevolent interest or concern < trying to promote interracial *goodwill* >

syn amity, benevolence, comity, friendliness, friendship, kindliness

rel altruism, charity, favor, generosity, helpfulness, kindness, rapport, sympathy, tolerance

con animus, disfavor, enmity, hatred, intolerance, malevolence

ant animosity, ill will

2 *syn* see ALACRITY

goody *n syn* see DELICACY

goody-goody *n syn* see PRUDE

gooey *adj* **1** *syn* see STICKY 1

2 *syn* see SENTIMENTAL

goof *n syn* see DUNCE

‖**goof (off)** *vb syn* see IDLE

goof (up) *vb syn* see BOTCH

go off *vb syn* see EXPLODE 1

gook *n* **1** *syn* see GOO

2 *syn* see CRUD

3 *syn* see NONSENSE 2

go on *vb* **1** *syn* see PERSEVERE

2 *syn* see BEHAVE 1

‖**goon** *n syn* see DUNCE

goop *n syn* see GOO 1

goose egg *n syn* see ZERO 1

goosey *adj* **1** *syn* see STUPID 1

2 *syn* see NERVOUS

go over *vb syn* see SUCCEED 1

gordian *adj syn* see COMPLEX 2

gore *n syn* see BLOOD 1

gorge *n syn* see RAVINE

gorge *vb syn* see SATIATE

rel bolt, devour, gobble, guzzle, raven, wolf; overeat, overindulge, stuff

idiom eat like a horse, eat one out of house and home

gorged *adj syn* see SATIATED

gorgeous *adj* **1** *syn* see SPLENDID 2

rel elegant, luxurious, opulent, plush, sumptuous; flamboyant, garish, gaudy, ostentatious, pretentious, showy; beautiful, colorful

2 *syn* see GRAND 2

‖**gorilla** *n syn* see THUG 1

gory *adj syn* see BLOODY 1

gospel *n syn* see VERACITY 2

gossamer *adj syn* see FILMY

gossip *n* **1** a person who habitually retails private, scandalous, or sensational and often inaccurate information < her life ruined by a vicious old *gossip* >

syn carrytale, circulator, clack, gossiper, gossipmonger, ‖long tongue, mumblenews, newsmonger, quidnunc, rumorer, rumormonger, scandalizer, scandalmonger, sieve, tabby, talebearer, telltale; *compare* BUSYBODY, INFORMER

2 *syn* see REPORT 1

rel account, chronicle, conversation, story, tale; babble, banter, chatter, prate

gossip *vb* to disclose something, often of questionable veracity, that is better kept

to oneself < *gossiped* about his neighbor's business >
syn blab, noise (about *or* abroad), rumor, talk, tattle
rel babble, chat, chatter, prate, prattle; hint, imply, insinuate, intimate, suggest
idiom dish the dirt, spill the beans, tell idle tales, tell tales out of school

gossiper *n syn see* GOSSIP 1

gossipmonger *n syn see* GOSSIP 1

Gothic *adj syn see* BARBARIAN 1
rel brutal, coarse, crude

gouge *vb syn see* EXTORT 1
rel cheat, con, swindle; overcharge

go under *vb* 1 *syn see* FALL 3
2 *syn see* SINK 1

gourmand *n syn see* EPICURE

gourmet *n syn see* EPICURE

govern *vb* 1 to exercise sovereign authority < a dictator may *govern* in a thoroughly enlightened manner >
syn overrule, reign, rule, sway
rel captain, command, head; administer, conduct, control, direct, manage, master; regulate, supervise
2 *syn see* ADMINISTER 1
3 to exercise a decisive role in influencing the actions and conduct of < parents who *govern* their children wisely >
syn control, direct, dominate, handle, manage
rel directionalize, guide, lead, shepherd, steer; boss, oversee, supervise
idiom be at the helm (*or* wheel), be in the driver's seat, hold the reins

‖**governor** *n syn see* FATHER 1

grab *vb syn see* SEIZE 2

grabble *vb syn see* GROPE

grabby *adj syn see* COVETOUS

grace *n* 1 a short prayer either asking a blessing before or giving thanks after a meal < taught each child a *grace* of his own >
syn benediction, blessing, thanks, thanksgiving
rel invocation, petition
2 *syn see* MERCY
rel compassionateness, responsiveness, tenderness; forbearance, indulgence, leniency; goodness
3 *syn see* ELEGANCE

graceless *adj* 1 *syn see* BARBARIC 1
2 *syn see* INFELICITOUS
ant graceful

gracious *adj* 1 marked by kindly courtesy < her *gracious* attitude toward those around her >
syn affable, congenial, cordial, genial, sociable, ‖sonsy
rel amiable, complaisant, easy, obliging; benign, benignant, kind, kindly; chivalrous, courteous, courtly; approachable, bonhomous, clubby, forthcoming, forthgoing, outgoing
con boorish, churlish; blunt, brusque, crabbed, crusty, curt, gruff, short, sullen, surly
ant ungracious

---

syn synonym(s)   *rel* related word(s)
ant antonym(s)   *con* contrasted word(s)
idiom idiomatic equivalent(s)
‖ use limited; if in doubt, see a dictionary

2 *syn see* COURTLY
rel mannered, starchy

gradation *n* the difference or variation between two things that are nearly alike < the *gradations* were too small to be seen with the unaided eye >
syn nuance, shade
rel difference, distinction, divergence; change, modification, variation

grade *n* 1 *syn see* DEGREE 1
2 *syn see* ESTATE 2
3 *syn see* CLASS 1
4 *syn see* QUALITY 3
5 *syn see* SLOPE

grade *vb syn see* CLASS 2
rel arrange, order; assort, sort

Grade A *adj syn see* EXCELLENT

gradient *n syn see* SLOPE

gradual *adj* proceeding slowly usually by minute or imperceptible steps or degrees < his health showed *gradual* improvement >
syn piecemeal, step-by-step
rel deliberate, dilatory, lagging, poky, sluggish
con acute, sharp, sudden
ant abrupt

gradually *adv* by small degrees or amounts < *gradually* he learned the new job >
syn bit by bit, little by little, piecemeal
idiom a little at a time, by degrees
con quickly, rapidly, speedily; at once, immediately, suddenly

grain *n syn see* PARTICLE

grainy *adj syn see* COARSE 1

grammar *n syn see* ALPHABET 2

grand *adj* 1 large and impressive in size, scope, extent, or conception < the platform provided a *grand* view of the canyon >
syn august, baronial, grandiose, imposing, lordly, magnific, magnificent, majestic, noble, princely, royal, stately; *compare* HUGE
rel monumental, prodigious, stupendous, tremendous; towering; gorgeous, splendid, sublime, superb
con measly, paltry, petty, puny, trifling, trivial
2 marked by great magnificence, display, and usually ceremony or formality < delighted to attend the *grand* presidential fete >
syn gorgeous, impressive, lavish, luxurious, splendid, sumptuous
rel magnificent, majestic; flashy, garish, gaudy, ornate, ostentatious, showy
con crude, meretricious, obtrusive, vulgar; flimsy, tawdry
3 noble in character or spirit < a *grand* outlook on life >
syn elevated, exalted, lofty, sublime, superb
rel magnificent, splendid
con average, common, commonplace, ordinary; base, lowly, mean, poor

grandam *n syn see* BELDAM 1

grande dame *n syn see* MATRIARCH

grandiloquent *adj syn see* RHETORICAL

grandiose *adj* 1 *syn see* GRAND 1
rel ostentatious, pretentious, showy; cosmic, overwhelming, unfathomable, vast

2 *syn* see AMBITIOUS 2
granny *n syn* see FUSSBUDGET
grant *vb* 1 to give as a favor or right
< *granted* him an extension of payments >
syn accord, award, concede, vouchsafe
rel bestow, confer, donate, give, present;
allow, permit; cede, relinquish, yield
con decline, refuse, turn down
2 *syn* see ACKNOWLEDGE 1
con differ, disagree, dissent; challenge,
dispute, object, protest
3 *syn* see GIVE 2
grant *n syn* see APPROPRIATION
rel gift; assistance, benefaction, contribution, donation; alms, charity, dole, hand-
out
granular *adj syn* see COARSE 1
grapevine *n syn* see REPORT 1
graph *n syn* see CHART 1
rel diagram, outline, sketch
graphic *adj* 1 giving a clear visual impression especially in words < gave a *graphic*
description of the whole incident >
syn photographic, pictorial, picturesque,
vivid
rel clear, lucid, perspicuous; clear-cut,
incisive; cogent, compelling, convincing,
telling; definite, explicit, precise, realistic,
striking, visual
con confused, hazy, indistinct, obscure
2 *syn* see PICTORIAL 1
grapple *n syn* see HOLD
grapple *vb* 1 *syn* see SEIZE 2
2 *syn* see WRESTLE
grasp *vb* 1 *syn* see TAKE 4
2 *syn* see APPREHEND 1
rel envisage, fathom, perceive
3 *syn* see KNOW 1
grasp *n syn* see HOLD
graspable *adj syn* see UNDERSTANDABLE
ant ungraspable
grasping *adj syn* see COVETOUS
rel extorting, extortionate
grass *n syn* see MARIJUANA
grate *vb* 1 *syn* see SCRAPE 1
rel abrade, bark, chafe, fray, gall, scuff,
skin
2 *syn* see IRRITATE
grateful *adj* 1 feeling or expressing gratitude < was *grateful* for the gift >
syn obliged, thankful
rel appreciative, beholden; gratified,
pleased
idiom filled with gratitude
ant ungrateful
2 *syn* see PLEASANT 1
rel comforting, consoling, solacing; refreshing, rejuvenating, renewing, restorative, restoring; delectable, delicious, delightful
ant obnoxious
gratefulness *n syn* see AMENITY 1
gratify *vb* 1 *syn* see PLEASE 2
rel appease, baby, cater (to), coddle,
favor, humor, indulge, oblige, pamper
con bother, irk; aggravate, exasperate,
irritate, nettle, rile; agitate, disturb, perturb, upset
2 *syn* see SATISFY 3
3 *syn* see INDULGE 1
idiom do one proud
gratifying *adj syn* see PLEASANT 1
rel contenting, satisfying; delighting, glad-
dening, regaling, rejoicing

con invidious, obnoxious; offensive, revolting
grating *adj syn* see HARSH 3
gratis *adj syn* see FREE 5
gratuitous *adj* 1 *syn* see FREE 5
rel voluntary, willing
2 *syn* see SUPEREROGATORY
3 *syn* see BASELESS
rel indefensible, reasonless, unsupportable
gratuity *n* something given over and above
what is due, generally in return for or
expectation of good service < he found
that an occasional *gratuity* smoothed his
path >
syn cumshaw, lagniappe, largess, ||palm
grease, ||palm oil, ||perk(s), perquisite,
pourboire, tip
rel alms, benefaction, contribution, donation; offering, reward
grave *vb* 1 *syn* see ENGRAVE 1
2 *syn* see IMPRESS 3
grave *n* a place of interment < his *grave* is
in the church burial ground >
syn burial, ||pit, sepulcher, sepulture,
tomb
rel catacomb, crypt, vault; mausoleum;
ossuary; cinerarium
idiom final resting place
grave *adj* 1 *syn* see SERIOUS 2
2 *syn* see SERIOUS 1
rel heavy, ponderous; grim, sad, saturnine; awful, dreadful, horrible, terrible
con flippant, light, light-minded
ant gay
3 involving marked risk of impairment or
destruction < a *grave* illness >
syn dangerous, fell, grievous, major, serious, ugly; *compare* DANGEROUS 1
rel deadly, destructive, dire, fatal, killing,
murderous; frightening, ghastly, terrible;
afflictive, severe
con paltry, petty, trivial; harmless, innocuous; temporary, transitory
gravely *adv syn* see SERIOUSLY 2
grave marker *n syn* see TOMBSTONE
gravestone *n syn* see TOMBSTONE
graveyard *n syn* see CEMETERY
gravid *adj syn* see PREGNANT 1
gravidity *n syn* see PREGNANCY
graybeard *n syn* see GAFFER
gray matter *n syn* see MIND 1
graze *vb* 1 *syn* see BRUSH
2 *syn* see GLANCE 1
3 *syn* see ABRADE 1
rel harm, hurt, injure; bruise, contuse,
wound
greasy *adj* 1 *syn* see FATTY 2
2 *syn* see SLICK 1
||**greasy spoon** *n syn* see EATING HOUSE
great *adj* 1 *syn* see LARGE 1
con measly, paltry, petty, puny, trifling,
trivial
ant little
2 *syn* see FAMOUS 2
rel superlative, supreme, surpassing, transcendent
great deal *n syn* see MUCH
greater *adj* 1 *syn* see BEST
2 *syn* see SUPERIOR 1
great gun *n syn* see NOTABLE 1
greathearted *adj* 1 *syn* see BRAVE 1
2 *syn* see GENEROUS 1
greatly *adv syn* see VERY 1

greatness *n syn* see SIZE 2
greed *n syn* see CUPIDITY
  rel gluttonousness, gluttony, rapaciousness, ravenousness, voraciousness
greedy *adj syn* see COVETOUS
  con bounteous, bountiful, generous, liberal, munificent, openhanded; exuberant, lavish, prodigal, profuse
Greek *n syn* see GIBBERISH 1
green *adj* 1 *syn* see YOUNG 1
  2 *syn* see INEXPERIENCED
  con grown-up, ripe, mature, matured; educated, instructed, trained; proficient, skilled, skillful
  ant experienced
green *n syn* see COMMON 2
‖**greenbacks** *n pl syn* see MONEY
green-eyed *adj syn* see ENVIOUS
greenhorn *n syn* see RUSTIC
greenhouse *n* a glass-enclosed structure for the cultivation and protection of tender plants <a small window *greenhouse* full of bloom>
  syn conservatory, ‖glasshouse
  rel coolhouse, hotbed, hothouse
greenness *n* 1 *syn* see YOUTH 1
  2 *syn* see INEXPERIENCE
greet *vb syn* see ADDRESS 7
greeting *n* the ceremonial words or acts of one who meets, welcomes, or formally addresses another <after the *greeting* the chairman called the roll>
  syn salutation, salute
  rel address, hail, hello, welcome
  con farewell, good-bye
  ant valediction
gregarious *adj syn* see SOCIAL 2
grief *n syn* see SORROW
  rel bemoaning, bewailing, deploring, lamenting
  con comfort, comforting, consolation, solace, solacing
  ant joy
grievance *n syn* see INJUSTICE 2
  rel hardship, rigor; affliction, cross, trial, tribulation
grieve *vb* 1 *syn* see DISTRESS 2
  2 to feel or express deep distress <*grieved* at the loss of so many lives>
  syn mourn, sorrow
  rel bear, endure, suffer; bemoan, bewail, deplore, lament; cry, keen, wail, weep
  ant rejoice
  3 *syn* see DEPLORE 1
grievous *adj* 1 *syn* see ONEROUS
  2 *syn* see BITTER 2
  3 *syn* see GRAVE 3
  4 *syn* see DEPLORABLE
‖**grifter** *n syn* see SWINDLER
grill *n syn* see CROSS-EXAMINATION
grilling *n syn* see CROSS-EXAMINATION
grim *adj* 1 *syn* see FIERCE 1
  rel foreboding, ominous
  2 forbidding in action or appearance <had a *grim* and determined expression on his face>
  syn austere, bleak, dour, hard, harsh, severe, stringent

---

  rel cold, forbidding, ‖off-putting; fixed, rigid, set; determined, firm, stern
  con calm, mellow, mild, soft, warm; attractive, beautiful, pleasing
  ant pleasant
  3 being extremely obdurate or firm in action or purpose <fought with *grim* determination>
  syn implacable, ironfisted, merciless, mortal, relentless, ruthless, unappeasable, unflinching, unrelenting, unyielding
  rel adamant, inexorable, inflexible, obdurate, resolute, stubborn, unforgiving, vindictive; certain, inevitable; determined, dogged
  con considerate, gentle, mild; clement, forbearing, indulgent
  ant lenient
  4 *syn* see GHASTLY 1
  rel loathsome, offensive, repugnant, repulsive, revolting
grimace *n syn* see FACE 6
grimace *vb* to distort one's face by way of expressing a feeling <*grimaced* with pain>
  syn mop, mouth, mow, mug, ‖mump
  rel contort, deform, distort, misshape
  idiom make a face (*or* mouth), make a wry face (*or* mouth), pull a face, screw up one's face
grime *vb syn* see SOIL 2
grim reaper *n syn* see DEATH 1
grin *vb syn* see SMILE
  con frown, gloom
  ant grimace
grind *vb syn* see DRUDGE
grind *n* 1 *syn* see WORK 2
  2 *syn* see ROUTINE
grip *vb* 1 *syn* see TAKE 4
  2 *syn* see ENTHRALL 1
grip *n syn* see HOLD
  rel coercion, constraint, duress, restraint
gripe *vb* to complain emphatically and often petulantly <students *griping* about the cafeteria food>
  syn ‖beef, bellyache, ‖bitch, bleat, ‖blow off, crab, ‖crib, fuss, squawk, yammer, yawp (*or* yaup); *compare* COMPLAIN
  rel brawl, kick, take on; croak, grouch, grouse, grumble, murmur, mutter
  con applaud, approve, cheer; rejoice; accept, bear, endure, tolerate
gripe *n* 1 *syn* see HOLD
  2 *usu* **gripes** *pl syn* see stomachache, bellyache, colic, collywobbles
griper *n syn* see GROUCH
grisette *n syn* see DOXY 1
grisly *adj syn* see GHASTLY 1
  rel eerie, uncanny, weird
grit *n syn* see FORTITUDE
  con faltering, hesitation, vacillation, wavering
  ant faintheartedness
grobian *n syn* see BOOR 2
grog *n syn* see LIQUOR 2
‖**groggery** *n syn* see BAR 5
‖**grogshop** *n syn* see BAR 5
groove *n syn* see ROUTINE
groovy *adj syn* see MARVELOUS 2
grope *vb* to reach out or about blindly (as in testing or searching) <*groped* along the wall in search of a door>
  syn feel, fumble, grabble

rel poke, pry, root; examine, explore, search

gross *adj* **1** *syn* see EGREGIOUS
rel excessive, exorbitant, extreme, immoderate, inordinate
con paltry, trifling, trivial
ant petty
2 *syn* see UTTER
3 *syn* see FAT 2
4 *syn* see WHOLE 4
ant net
5 *syn* see MATERIAL 1
6 *syn* see COARSE 3
7 *syn* see OBSCENE 2
rel animal, carnal, fleshy, sensual; loathsome, offensive, repulsive, revolting; improper, unrefined
con decent, decorous, proper, refined
gross *n* *syn* see WHOLE 1
grotesque *adj* *syn* see FANTASTIC 2
rel baroque, flamboyant, rococo; eerie, uncanny, weird; extravagant, extreme; comic, comical, droll, ludicrous
grotto *n* *syn* see CAVE
grouch *n* an habitually irritable or complaining person <it's hard to live with a *grouch*>
syn ‖bellyacher, complainer, crab, crabber, crank, crosspatch, faultfinder, griper, grouser, growler, grumbler, grump, kicker, malcontent, sorehead, sourpuss
con optimist, Pollyanna
grouch *vb* *syn* see GRUMBLE 1
ground *n* **1** *syn* see BASIS 1
2 *syn* see BASE 1
3 *syn* see REASON 3
rel evidence, testimony; antecedent, cause, determinant; demonstration, test, trial
4 grounds *pl* *syn* see SEDIMENT
5 *syn* see EARTH 2
ground *vb* **1** *syn* see FELL 1
2 *syn* see BASE
rel buttress, support, sustain
grounded *adj* *syn* see AGROUND
groundless *adj* *syn* see BASELESS
ant well-founded, well-grounded
groundwork *n* **1** *syn* see BASIS 1
2 *syn* see BASE 1
group *n* **1** a usually comparatively small assemblage of individuals <people gathered in *groups* about the hall>
syn assembly, band, bevy, bunch, cluster, covey, crew, party; *compare* COMPANY 1, GATHERING
rel circle, clique, cotery, set
con crowd, crush, horde, mob, press, rout, throng
2 *syn* see GATHERING 2
3 an assemblage of things constituting a unit <a *group* of houses behind the church>
syn array, batch, battery, body, bunch, bundle, clot, clump, cluster, clutch, lot, parcel, passel, platoon, set, sort, suite
rel assemblage, collection, mess, shooting match
4 *syn* see SET 5
5 *syn* see SYNDICATE
6 *syn* see CLASS 1
group *vb* **1** to make into or bring together in a group <*grouped* the children according to age>
syn assemble, cluster, collect, gather, round up; *compare* GATHER 6

rel adjust, arrange, harmonize, organize, systematize; allocate, dispose, distribute, place; bunch, crowd, huddle
idiom bring together, get together
con disband, disperse, scatter, separate
2 *syn* see ASSORT
grouping *n* *syn* see CLASS 1
grouse *vb* *syn* see GRUMBLE 1
grouser *n* *syn* see GROUCH
grovel *vb* *syn* see FAWN
idiom lick the dust (*or* one's boots)
groveler *n* *syn* see SYCOPHANT
groveling *adj* *syn* see FAWNING
grow *vb* **1** to cause (something living) to exist or flourish <*grew* a crop of wheat>
syn breed, cultivate, produce, propagate, raise
rel care (for), foster, nurse, nurture, rear, tend
2 *syn* see MATURE
3 *syn* see ESCALATE 2
4 *syn* see BECOME 1
growl *vb* *syn* see RUMBLE
growler *n* *syn* see GROUCH
grown *adj* **1** *syn* see MATURE 1
2 *syn* see OVERGROWN
grown-up *adj* *syn* see MATURE 1
ant childish; callow
growth *n* *syn* see DEVELOPMENT
grow up *vb* *syn* see MATURE
grub *vb* **1** *syn* see DIG 1
rel burrow, poke, root
2 *syn* see SCOUR 2
3 *syn* see DRUDGE
grub *n* **1** *syn* see HACK 2
2 *syn* see FOOD 1
grubber *n* *syn* see HACK 2
grubby *adj* *syn* see DIRTY 1
ant immaculate
grubstake *vb* *syn* see CAPITALIZE
grudge *vb* *syn* see ENVY
rel deny; refuse
grudge *n* *syn* see MALICE
rel grievance, injury, injustice
gruesome *adj* *syn* see GHASTLY 1
rel appalling, daunting; horrendous, horrific; baleful, sinister
gruff *adj* **1** *syn* see BLUFF
rel crabbed, dour, morose, saturnine, sullen, surly; boorish, churlish; fierce, truculent
con bland, smooth, suave, urbane; fulsome, oily, slick, soapy, unctuous
2 *syn* see HOARSE 1
grumble *vb* **1** to complain in a low harsh voice and often in a surly manner <workers *grumbling* about the low wages>
syn croak, grouch, grouse, ‖grunt, murmur, mutter, scold; *compare* COMPLAIN
rel ‖beef, ‖bellyache, ‖bitch, brawl, crab, fuss, gripe, holler, squawk, whine; groan, moan; complain, kick
con applaud, cheer; rejoice
2 *syn* see RUMBLE
grumbler *n* *syn* see GROUCH
grump *n* **1 grumps** *pl* *syn* see SULK
2 *syn* see GROUCH
grump *vb* *syn* see SULK
Grundy *n* *syn* see PRUDE
‖**grunt** *vb* *syn* see GRUMBLE 1
guarantee *n* **1** an assurance for the fulfillment of a condition <gave him a *guarantee* that the work would be done according to specifications>

syn bail, bond, guaranty, security, surety, warranty; *compare* PLEDGE 1
rel earnest, pledge, promise, token, undertaking, word; oath, vow
2 *syn* see WORD 8
guarantee *vb syn* see WARRANT 2
guarantor *n syn* see SPONSOR
guaranty > *n syn* see GUARANTEE 1
rel bargain, contract
guaranty *vb syn* see WARRANT 2
guard *n* 1 *syn* see DEFENSE 1
2 a person or group on sentinel duty < posted six *guards* around the diamond necklace > < turned out the *guard* >
syn lookout, picket, sentinel, sentry, ward, watch, watchman
rel guardian, jailer, keeper, turnkey, warden, warder; patrolman; outguard, patrol
guard *vb syn* see DEFEND 1
rel attend, mind, tend, watch; accompany, chaperon, conduct, convoy, escort
guarded *adj* 1 *syn* see ULTERIOR
2 *syn* see CAUTIOUS
ant unguarded
guardian *n syn* see CUSTODIAN
guardianship *n syn* see CUSTODY
guardroom *n syn* see JAIL
gudgeon *n syn* see FOOL 3
guerdon *n syn* see REWARD
guerdon *vb syn* see PAY 1
guerrilla *n syn* see PARTISAN 2
guess *vb* 1 *syn* see CONJECTURE
rel reason, speculate; deduce; estimate, reckon
idiom venture a guess
2 *syn* see PREDICT 1
guest *n* 1 *syn* see VISITOR 1
2 guests *pl syn* see COMPANY 2
guff *n* 1 *syn* see NONSENSE 2
2 *syn* see BACK TALK
guffaw *vb syn* see LAUGH
guide *vb* to put or lead on a course or into the way to be followed < *guided* them safely through the minefields >
syn conduct, direct, escort, lead, pilot, route, see, shepherd, show, steer
rel accompany, chaperon, convoy; control, manage; contrive, engineer, maneuver
idiom set one on one's way
con bewilder, distract, mystify, perplex, puzzle; beguile, deceive, delude, mislead
ant misguide
guide *n* 1 *syn* see LEADER 1
2 *syn* see ESCORT 2
rel conductor, director, leader, pilot
3 *syn* see HANDBOOK
guidebook *n syn* see HANDBOOK
guild *n syn* see ASSOCIATION 2
guile *n syn* see DECEIT 1
ant ingenuousness; candor
guileful *adj* 1 *syn* see SLY 2
ant guileless
2 *syn* see UNDERHAND
guileless *adj syn* see NATURAL 5
ant guileful
guillotine *vb syn* see BEHEAD
guilt *n syn* see BLAME
rel crime, offense, sin; responsibility

ant innocence; guiltlessness
guiltless *adj* 1 *syn* see GOOD 11
2 *syn* see INNOCENT 2
ant guilty
guilty *adj syn* see BLAMEWORTHY
rel accountable, answerable, responsible; impeached, incriminated, indicted
ant innocent; guiltless
guise *n* 1 *syn* see COSTUME
2 *syn* see APPEARANCE 2
3 *syn* see MASK 2
gulch *n syn* see RAVINE
gulf *n* 1 *syn* see INLET
2 a hollow place of vast width and depth < a *gulf* extending deep into the earth >
syn abysm, abyss, chasm
rel cave, cavity, hollow; crevasse, gulch, ravine; pit, shaft, well
gull *vb syn* see DUPE
gull *n syn* see FOOL 3
gullible *adj syn* see EASY 3
ant astute
gulp *vb* to swallow hurriedly or greedily or in one swallow < *gulped* his lunch and ran off >
syn bolt, cram, englut, gobble, guzzle, ingurgitate, slop, slosh, wolf
rel devour, glut, stuff
con nibble, pick
gum (up) *vb syn* see BOTCH
gumbo *n syn* see GOO 1
gummy *adj syn* see STICKY 1
gumption *n syn* see SENSE 6
rel astuteness, perspicaciousness, perspicacity, sagaciousness, sagacity, shrewdness
gumptious *adj syn* see ENTERPRISING 2
gumshoe *n* 1 *syn* see DETECTIVE
2 *syn* see POLICEMAN
gumshoe *vb syn* see SNEAK
gun *n syn* see ASSASSIN
gung ho *adj syn* see ENTHUSIASTIC
gunk *n* 1 *syn* see GOO 1
2 *syn* see CRUD
gunman *n syn* see ASSASSIN
‖**gunsel** *n syn* see ASSASSIN
gunslinger *n syn* see ASSASSIN
gurge *vb syn* see SWIRL
gurgle *vb syn* see SLOSH 1
gush *vb syn* see POUR 2
rel flood, flush; emanate, issue, spring
gushing *adj syn* see EFFUSIVE
gushy *adj syn* see EFFUSIVE
gussy up *vb syn* see DRESS UP 1
gust *n syn* see OUTBURST 1
gusto *n syn* see TASTE 4
rel delectation, delight, enjoyment, pleasure; ardor, enthusiasm, fervor, passion, zeal
gusty *adj syn* see WINDY 1
‖**gusty** *adj syn* see PALATABLE
gut *n* 1 *usu* guts *pl syn* see ENTRAILS
‖2 *syn* see ABDOMEN
3 guts *pl syn* see COURAGE
4 guts *pl syn* see FORTITUDE
gut *vb* 1 *syn* see EVISCERATE
2 *syn* see DRESS 3
gut *adj syn* see INNER 2
gutless *adj syn* see COWARDLY
ant ‖gutsy
‖**gutsy** *adj syn* see BRAVE 1
guy *n syn* see MAN 3
guzzle *vb* 1 *syn* see DRINK 3
2 *syn* see GULP

---

syn synonym(s)   *rel* related word(s)
ant antonym(s)   *con* contrasted word(s)
idiom idiomatic equivalent(s)
‖ use limited; if in doubt, see a dictionary

guzzler *n syn* see DRUNKARD
gyp *n* 1 *syn* see SWINDLER
   2 *syn* see IMPOSTURE
gyp *vb syn* see CHEAT
gypper *n syn* see SWINDLER
gyrate *vb* 1 *syn* see TURN 1

   2 *syn* see SPIN 1
gyration *n syn* see REVOLUTION 1
gyre *vb* 1 *syn* see TURN 1
   2 *syn* see SPIN 1
gyre *n syn* see REVOLUTION 1
gyve *n, usu* **gyves** *pl syn* see SHACKLE

H

habiliment *n* 1 **habiliments** *pl syn* see EQUIPMENT
   2 *usu* **habiliments** *pl syn* see CLOTHES
habit *n* 1 a mode of behaving or doing fixed by constant repetition <it was his *habit* to rise early>
   syn consuetude, custom, habitude, manner, practice, praxis, trick, usage, use, way, wont
   rel bent, disposition, inclination, proclivity, tendency, turn; convention, fashion, form, mode, pattern, style; addiction; groove, rote, routine, rut, set
   2 *syn* see PHYSIQUE
   rel carcass; framework; contour, outline
habitable *adj syn* see LIVABLE 1
   ant unhabitable, uninhabitable
habitant *n syn* see INHABITANT
habitat *n* the physical environment natural to a kind of being <the watery *habitat* of the eel>
   syn haunt, home, locality, range, site, stamping ground
   rel environment, locale, surroundings, territory
habitation *n* 1 the act of inhabiting or the state of being inhabited <places suitable for *habitation*>
   syn inhabitancy, inhabitation, occupancy, occupation, residence, settlement
   rel colonization, domiciliation, peopling; sojourning
   2 the place where one lives <*habitations* unfit for human occupancy>
   syn abode, commoracy, domicile, dwelling, home, house, residence, residency
   rel apartment, flat, tenement; housing, lodging, lodgment, quarters; haunt, haven, homeplace, homestead, place, seat; ||digs, nest, nook, ||pad, ||roost; astre, fireside, hearth, hearthside, hearthstone, roof, rooftree
   idiom roof over one's head, where one hangs one's hat
habitual *adj* 1 *syn* see USUAL 1
   rel constant, established, ingrained, inveterate, persistent, steady
   con infrequent, irregular, sporadic, uncommon
   ant occasional
   2 acting by force of habit <*habitual* smokers who blue the air>
   syn accustomed, chronic, confirmed, habituated
   rel continual, inveterate, persistent, regular, steady; automatic, instinctive, involuntary; addicted; customary, wonted
   con conscious, deliberate, premeditative, purposive, witting
habitually *adv syn* see USUALLY 1

   ant occasionally
habituate *vb* 1 *syn* see ACCUSTOM
   2 to make acceptable or desirable (as to oneself) through use <*habituate* oneself to poverty>
   syn addict, adjust, confirm (in), devote (to), take (to)
   rel bear, endure, inure, support, tolerate; condition, familiarize, season
   con balk (at), object (to), resist
habituated *adj syn* see HABITUAL 2
habitude *n syn* see HABIT 1
   rel attitude, position, stand; condition, situation, state
   con humor, mood, temper; caprice, freak, vagary, whim
habitué *n* 1 one who frequents a place <an *habitué* of libraries>
   syn denizen, frequenter, haunter
   rel customer, devotee, patron, sojourner; employer, user
   2 *syn* see ADDICT
habitus *n syn* see PHYSIQUE
hack *vb* to cut with repeated crude or ruthless blows <*hack* a path through the jungle>
   syn hackle, haggle, slash
   rel gash, mangle; chop, cut, fell, hew
hack *n* 1 *syn* see TAXICAB
   2 one who surrenders intellectual or personal integrity for an assured reward (as a regular income) <party *hacks* and hangers-on>
   syn drudge, grub, grubber, hireling, mercenary, slavey
   rel grind, lackey, servant, slave; machine, plodder; potboiler
hack *adj* 1 *syn* see INFERIOR 2
   rel commonplace, dull, ordinary, trite, usual; inconsequential, petty, trivial
   con individual, original, uncommon, unusual
   2 *syn* see TRITE
   rel antiquated, old, outmoded, outworn
   con lively; unfamiliar
hackle *vb syn* see HACK
hackneyed *adj syn* see TRITE
   rel antediluvian, antiquated, archaic, obsolete, outmoded, out-of-date; conventional, everyday, quotidian, stock; motheaten
   ant unhackneyed
Hadean *adj syn* see INFERNAL 1
   rel gloomy, murky, stygian
hades *n syn* see HELL
hag *n* 1 *syn* see WITCH 1
   2 an ugly or evil-looking old woman <a pitiful homeless *hag*>

syn ‖bag, ‖bat, beldam, biddy, crone, drab, trot, witch

rel gammer, grandam; ‖battle-ax, fishwife, gorgon, harpy, harridan, shrew, slattern, virago, vixen

haggard *adj* thin and contracted by or as if by fatigue or inner distress < *haggard* from their long vigil >

syn careworn, drawn, pinched, worn

rel angular, gaunt, lank, lean, scraggy, scrawny, skinny, spare; ashen, faded, pale, pallid, wan; exhausted, fagged, fatigued, tired, wearied, worn-down

con energetic, lusty, strenuous, vigorous; easy, relaxed

haggle *vb* 1 *syn* see HACK

2 to argue as to terms < *haggle* over prices >

syn bargain, chaffer, dicker, higgle, huckster, palter

rel barter, deal, horse-trade; trade; bicker, cavil, dispute, quibble, squabble, stickle, wrangle

hagridden *adj syn* see OBSESSED

hagride *vb syn* see WORRY 1

hail *n syn* see BARRAGE

hail *vb* 1 *syn* see ADDRESS 7

rel hallo, hallow, holler, shout

2 *syn* see COMMEND 2

con belittle, depreciate, disparage, downgrade; berate, censure, condemn, libel, rap; dismiss, reject

hail (from) *vb syn* see ORIGINATE 5

hair *n* a minute distance, degree, or margin < won the election by a *hair* >

syn ace, hairbreadth, whisker; *compare* HINT 2

rel bit, fraction, jot, mite, particle, trace, trifle

hairbreadth *n syn* see HAIR

haircutter *n syn* see BARBER

hairless *adj* lacking hair < he had a shining *hairless* head >

syn bald, glabrous, smooth

rel baldish; shaved, shaven, shorn, tonsured

ant hairy

hairline *adj syn* see FINE 1

hairsplitting *adj syn* see FINE 1

hair-trigger *adj syn* see INSTANTANEOUS

hairy *adj* 1 covered with or as if with hair < wore a *hairy* overcoat >

syn fleecy, hirsute, pileous, pilose, whiskered, woolly

rel bristly, bushy, downy, fluffy, fuzzy, lanate, nappy, pubescent, rough, shaggy, tomentose, tufted, unshorn, villous

con bald, barefaced, beardless, glabrous, shaved, shaven, shorn, smooth

ant hairless

2 *syn* see DANGEROUS 1

3 *syn* see ROUGH 1

halcyon *adj syn* see CALM 1

con blustery, fevered, foul, raging, rough, stormy, tempestuous, troubled, tumultuous, wild

hale *adj syn* see HEALTHY 1

rel husky, stout, strapping

idiom hale and hearty

ant infirm

haleness *n syn* see HEALTH

‖**half-assed** *adj syn* see DEFICIENT 1

half-blind *adj syn* see PURBLIND

half blood *n syn* see HYBRID

ant full blood

half-breed *n syn* see HYBRID

ant full blood

halfhearted *adj syn* see TEPID 2

‖**half-seas over** *adj syn* see INTOXICATED 1

halfway *adj syn* see MIDDLE 1

half-wit *n syn* see FOOL 4

half-witted *adj syn* see RETARDED

hall *n syn* see PASSAGE 4

hallo *vb syn* see CALL 1

hallow *vb* 1 *syn* see BLESS 1

2 *syn* see DEVOTE 1

con defile, desecrate, pollute, profane

hallowed *adj syn* see HOLY 1

hallucination *n syn* see DELUSION 1

rel apparition, fata morgana, phantom, wraith

hallway *n syn* see PASSAGE 4

halt *vb syn* see LIMP 1

halt *vb* 1 *syn* see STOP 4

ant proceed

2 *syn* see STOP 3

3 *syn* see ARREST 1

4 *syn* see HESITATE

5 *syn* see CLOSE 2

halting *adj syn* see AWKWARD 2

2 *syn* see VACILLATING 2

ham-handed *adj syn* see AWKWARD 2

hammer *vb* 1 to strike or shape with or as if with a hammer < brass *hammered* into bowls and trays >

syn beat, malleate, pound

rel elaborate, fashion, form, shape

2 *syn* see BEAT 1

3 *syn* see IMPRESS 3

‖4 *syn* see STAMMER 1

hammer (out) *vb syn* see ERECT 5

hammerhead *n syn* see DUNCE

hammerheaded *adj syn* see STUPID 1

hamper *vb* to impede in moving, progressing, or acting freely < the long dress *hampered* her escape >

syn clog, curb, entrammel, fetter, hobble, hog-tie, leash, shackle, tie, tie up, trammel; *compare* HINDER, RESTRAIN 1

rel cumber, encumber, handicap, hinder, impede, lumber, obstruct; baffle, balk, bar, block, foil, frustrate, thwart; restrain, restrict, retard; discomfit, embarrass; check, inconvenience, inhibit

idiom tie one's hands

con free, liberate, loose, release, unfetter, unleash, unshackle

ant aid, facilitate

hamper *n syn* see OBSTACLE 1

hams *n pl syn* see BUTTOCKS

hand *n* 1 *syn* see SIDE 1

2 *syn* see PHASE

3 *syn* see HANDWRITING

4 *syn* see HELP 1

5 *syn* see WORKER

6 *syn* see TOUCH 6

hand *vb* 1 *syn* see GIVE 3

2 *syn* see PASS 9

handbill *n syn* see POSTER

handbook *n* a concise reference book < a *handbook* of wild flowers >

---

syn synonym(s)   *rel* related word(s)
ant antonym(s)   *con* contrasted word(s)
idiom idiomatic equivalent(s)
‖ use limited; if in doubt, see a dictionary

syn Baedeker, compendium, enchiridion, guide, guidebook, manual, vade mecum
con cyclopedia, encyclopedia

hand down *vb* to convey in succession <a skill *handed down* from father to son>
syn bequeath, hand on, pass (on), transmit
con get, obtain, receive

handful *n syn* see FEW

handicap *n* 1 *syn* see DISADVANTAGE
rel burden, encumbrance, load; embarrassment
ant asset
2 *syn* see ADVANTAGE 3

handicraft *n syn* see TRADE 1

hand in *vb syn* see SUBMIT 2

handkerchief *n* a small usually square piece of cloth used especially for blowing the nose <carry a pocket *handkerchief*>
syn hankie, kerchief, ‖wipe, ‖wiper

‖**handle** *n* 1 *syn* see NAME 1
2 *syn* see NICKNAME

handle *vb* 1 *syn* see TOUCH 1
rel test, try; manipulate
2 to deal with or manage usually with dexterity or efficiency < *handles* his tools with great skill>
syn dispense, maneuver, manipulate, ply, swing, wield
rel direct, guide, manage, operate, run, work; brandish, flourish, shake, wave; aim, lay, level, point
3 *syn* see OPERATE 3
4 *syn* see TREAT 2
rel conduct, control, direct, manage
5 *syn* see GOVERN 3
6 *syn* see USE 2

handling *n syn* see OVERSIGHT 1

handmaid *n syn* see MAID 2

hand on *vb syn* see HAND DOWN

hand out *vb syn* see GIVE 1

hand over *vb* 1 *syn* see RELINQUISH
2 *syn* see GIVE 3
3 *syn* see COMMIT 1

hand running *adv syn* see TOGETHER 2

handsome *adj* 1 *syn* see LIBERAL 1
con economical, frugal, sparing; scrimpy, skimpy
2 *syn* see BEAUTIFUL
rel august, majestic, noble, stately; chic, dashing, fashionable, modish, smart, stylish
con inelegant, unsightly
ant unhandsome

handwriting *n* writing in which the letters are formed by a hand-guided implement (as a pen) <legible *handwriting*>
syn calligraphy, chirography, ductus, fist, hand, penmanship, script
rel longhand

handy *adj* 1 *syn* see CONVENIENT 2
idiom at one's hand (*or* elbow), ready to hand
ant unhandy
2 *syn* see PRACTICAL 2
rel adaptable, advantageous, beneficial, wieldy
con clumsy, cumbersome, cumbrous, unwieldy
ant unwieldy
3 *syn* see DEXTEROUS 1

hang *vb* 1 to place or be placed so as to be supported at one point or side usually at the top <*hang* the washing on the line>
syn dangle, depend, sling, suspend
rel attach, hook; fix, pin, tack (up); adhere, cling, stick
2 to put to death by suspending by the neck <was *hanged* for stealing a sheep>
syn gibbet, noose, scrag, string (up), turn off
rel execute, lynch
idiom bring to the gallows, hang by the neck, make dance on air (*or* nothing)
3 to remain poised or stationary as if suspended in midair <clouds *hanging* in the west>
syn float, hover, poise
4 to project outward or incline downward <children *hanging* out the windows to watch a parade>
syn beetle, bend (over), jut, lean (over), overhang
rel drape, droop, loll, lop, sag, trail

hang (on *or* upon) *vb syn* see DEPEND (on *or* upon) 1

hang *n* the special method of doing, using, or dealing with something <can't get the *hang* of this gadget>
syn knack, swing, trick
rel art, craft, skill

hang around *vb syn* see FREQUENT

hanger-on *n syn* see PARASITE
rel bystander, follower, spectator, sycophant

hanging *adj syn* see SUSPENDED

hang on *vb syn* see PERSEVERE

hang out *vb* 1 *syn* see RESIDE 1
2 *syn* see FREQUENT

hangout *n* 1 *syn* see RESORT 2
2 *syn* see DIVE

hang up *vb syn* see DELAY 1

hanker *vb syn* see LONG
rel covet, desire, wish

hankie *n syn* see HANDKERCHIEF

hanky-panky *n syn* see DECEPTION 1

hap *n syn* see ACCIDENT 1
rel destiny, fate, lot, portion

hap *vb syn* see HAPPEN 1

‖**hap** *vb syn* see BUNDLE UP

haphazard *adj syn* see RANDOM
rel accidental; careless, helter-skelter, slipshod; unorganized, unsystematic
con deliberate, designed, intentional, voluntary, willful
ant planned

haphazard *adv syn* see ABOUT 4
rel accidentally, aimlessly, carelessly, casually, promiscuously

haphazardly *adv syn* see ABOUT 4
rel accidentally, aimlessly, carelessly, casually, promiscuously

hapless *adj syn* see UNLUCKY
rel infelicitous; miserable, woeful, wretched

happen *vb* 1 to take place or come about <the incident *happened* at midnight>
syn befall, betide, break, chance, come, come off, develop, do, fall out, give, go, hap, occur, pass, rise, transpire
rel go off, turn out
idiom come to pass
2 to come by chance <he unexpectedly *happened* on a new method>
syn bump, chance, hit, light, luck, meet, stumble, tumble
rel befall

happening *n syn* see OCCURRENCE
happify *vb syn* see PLEASE 2
happily *adv syn* see WELL 5
happiness *n* a state of well-being or plea-surable satisfaction <felt *happiness* at her husband's success>
  syn beatitude, blessedness, bliss, blissful-ness
  rel content, contentedness, satisfaction; cheer, cheerfulness, felicity, gladness; gai-ety, jollity, joy; delectation, delight, enjoy-ment, pleasure
  con discontent, dissatisfaction, vexation; cheerlessness, despair, desperation, de-spondency, hopelessness; distress, misery, wretchedness
  ant unhappiness
happy *adj* 1 *syn* see LUCKY
  rel accidental, casual, fortuitous, inciden-tal; opportune, seasonable, timely
  ant unhappy
  2 *syn* see FIT 1
  rel effective, effectual, efficacious, effi-cient; cogent, convincing, telling; pat, seasonable, well-timed; correct, nice, right
  ant unhappy
  3 *syn* see GLAD 1
  rel content, contented, satisfied
  ant unhappy; disconsolate
happy–go–lucky *adj* disposed to accept cheerfully whatever happens <enjoyed a *happy-go-lucky* existence without need-lessly worrying>
  syn carefree, free-minded, insouciant, lighthearted, lightsome; *compare* COOL 2
  rel casual, easy, easygoing; blithe, care-less, cheerful, feckless, heedless, lackadaisi-cal; debonair, nonchalant, unconcerned; devil-may-care, reckless
  con careful, cautious, circumspect, dis-creet, guarded, prudent
happy hunting ground *n syn* see HEAVEN 2
hara–kiri *n syn* see SUICIDE
harangue *n syn* see TIRADE
harangue *vb syn* see ORATE
harass *vb* 1 *syn* see RAID 1
  2 *syn* see WORRY 1
  rel badger, bait, bullyrag, chivy, devil, heckle, hector, hound, ride
  idiom give a bad (*or* hard) time
  3 *syn* see TRY 2
harassed *adj syn* see DISTRAUGHT
harasser *n syn* see BULLY 1
harassment *n syn* see ANNOYANCE 1
  rel aggravation, disturbance, exasperation, irritation, perturbation
harbinger *n syn* see FORERUNNER 1
harbinger *vb syn* see ANNOUNCE 2
harbor *n* 1 *syn* see SHELTER 1
  2 *syn* see INLET
  3 a place where seacraft may ride secure <a yacht *harbor*>
  syn anchorage, ‖chuck, harborage, haven, port, riding, road(s), roadstead
harbor *vb* 1 to provide with shelter or a refuge <*harbored* the refugees in our homes>

  syn chamber, haven, house, roof, shelter, shield
  rel cherish, foster, nurse, nurture; conceal, hide, secrete; guard, protect, safeguard, screen
  idiom give shelter (*or* asylum) to
  con eject, evict, expel, oust; banish, de-port, exile; eliminate, exclude, shut out
  2 to provide with a usually temporary place to live <the miners were *harbored* in camps>
  syn accommodate, bestow, billet, board, bunk, domicile, domiciliate, entertain, house, hut, lodge, put up, quarter, room, roost
  rel cabin, camp, encamp
harborage *n syn* see SHELTER 1
  2 *syn* see REFUGE 1
  3 *syn* see HARBOR 3
hard *adj* 1 *syn* see FIRM 2
  rel compacted, compressed, concentrated, consolidated, packed; callous, hardened, indurate, indurated; set; adamantine, flinty, granitic, iron, ironhard
  con fluid, liquid; flabby, limp; ductile, malleable, pliable, pliant, plastic; elastic, flexible, limber, resilient, supple
  ant soft
  2 *syn* see SPIRITUOUS
  ant soft
  3 *syn* see REALISTIC
  4 *syn* see INSENSIBLE 5
  5 *syn* see INTENSIVE
  6 demanding great toil and effort <a *hard* but rewarding task>
  syn arduous, difficult, difficult, effortful, formidable, heavy, knotty, labored, labori-ous, operose, rough, rugged, serious, se-vere, slavish, sticky, strenuous, terrible, toilful, toilsome, tough, uphill
  rel burdensome, exacting, onerous; com-plex, complicated, intricate, involved, scabrous; backbreaking, distressing, ex-hausting, fatiguing, grinding, tiring, wear-ing, wearisome, wearying; bothersome, demanding, irksome, rocky, straining, troublesome, trying; merciless, unsparing
  con effortless, facile, light, simple, smooth
  ant easy
  7 *syn* see ACTUAL 2
  8 *syn* see GRIM 2
  9 *syn* see SEVERE 3
hard *adv* 1 with great or utmost force <hit the nail *hard*>
  syn energetically, forcefully, forcibly, hardly, might and main, mightily, power-fully, strongly, vigorously
  rel actively, animatedly, briskly, snappily, spiritedly, sprightly, vivaciously; earnestly, intensely, keenly, seriously, urgently, wholeheartedly
  idiom with all one's might
  con faintly, feebly, nervelessly, softly, strengthlessly, unenergetically, weakly
  ant easily, easy
  2 in a violent manner <the wind blew *hard* all the next day>
  syn fiercely, frantically, frenziedly, furi-ously, hardly, madly, stormily, tumultu-ously, turbulently, violently, wildly
  rel boisterously, exuberantly, rowdily, uproariously; angrily, brutally, ferociously, savagely, viciously

---

syn synonym(s)   *rel* related word(s)
ant antonym(s)   *con* contrasted word(s)
idiom idiomatic equivalent(s)
‖ use limited; if in doubt, see a dictionary

idiom like a house afire, like fury, like mad

con gently, mildly, softly

3 with intentness and determination <made up his mind to study *hard*>

syn assiduously, dingdong, earnestly, exhaustively, intensely, intensively, painstakingly, thoroughly, unremittingly

rel conscientiously, meticulously, punctiliously

con carelessly, casually, desultorily, fitfully, haphazardly

4 in a fixed and intensive manner <stared *hard* at the offender>

syn closely, intently, searchingly, sharply

con casually, cursorily, idly, offhand

5 in such manner as to cause hardship, difficulty, or defeat <things will go *hard* with him if he doesn't reform>

syn badly, hardly, harshly, painfully, rigorously, roughly, severely; *compare* AMISS 2

rel cruelly; relentlessly; meanly, shabbily, unfairly

con comfortably, pleasantly, smoothly; acceptably, satisfactorily, satisfyingly

ant easily, easy

6 with great or excessive resentment or grief <don't take your setback so *hard*>

syn bitterly, hardly, keenly, rancorously, resentfully, sorely

con casually, lightly, nonchalantly, offhandedly

7 in a firm manner <hold on *hard*>

syn fast, firm, firmly, fixedly, solidly, steadfastly, tight, tightly

con easily, easy, loose, loosely, slackly

8 with difficulty <breathing *hard* after the climb>

syn arduously, burdensomely, difficultly, hardly, laboriously, onerously, toilsomely

rel exhaustingly, gruelingly, painfully, tiredly; awkwardly, cumbersomely, cumbrously, inconveniently, ponderously, unhandily, unwieldily

con effortlessly, evenly, handily, readily, smoothly

ant easily, easy

9 to the point of hardness <the pond is frozen *hard*>

syn firmly, hardly, solid, solidly

10 *syn* see CLOSE

hard–boiled *adj* **1** *syn* see UNFEELING 2

rel coarse, crude, rough; seasoned, sophisticated, worldly-wise

idiom not born yesterday

con artless, guileless, naive, simplehearted, unsophisticated; kindly, mild, soft

2 *syn* see REALISTIC

harden *vb* **1** to make or become physically hard or solid <this substance *hardens* immediately on exposure to air>

syn cake, concrete, congeal, dry, indurate, set, solidify

rel compact, consolidate, densify, firm, stiffen; anneal, caseharden, temper; calcify, fossilize, lithify, ossify, petrify

con deliquesce, dissolve, fuse, liquefy, melt

ant soften

2 to make proof against hardship, strain, or exposure <frontier life *hardened* most men quickly to rough conditions>

syn acclimate, acclimatize, climatize, season, toughen

rel accustom, habituate, indurate, inure; accommodate, adapt, adjust, conform

con emasculate, enervate; debilitate, devitalize, enfeeble, sap, undermine, weaken

ant soften

hardened *adj* *syn* see UNFEELING 2

hardfisted *adj* *syn* see STINGY

ant openhanded

hardhanded *adj* *syn* see STINGY

ant openhanded

hardheaded *adj* **1** *syn* see OBSTINATE

2 *syn* see REALISTIC

hardhearted *adj* *syn* see UNFEELING 2

hardihood *n* **1** *syn* see TEMERITY

rel boldness, intrepidity; brazenness, cockiness; fortitude, grit, guts, pluck, sand

ant cowardice; timidity

2 *syn* see INSOLENCE

3 *syn* see ENERGY 2

hardiness *n* *syn* see TEMERITY

ant cowardice; timidity

hard–line *adj* *syn* see TOUGH 3

hardly *adv* **1** *syn* see HARD 1

2 *syn* see HARD 2

3 *syn* see HARD 5

4 *syn* see HARD 6

5 *syn* see HARD 8

6 *syn* see JUST 2

7 *syn* see HARD 9

hardly ever *adv* *syn* see SELDOM

hardness *n* *syn* see DIFFICULTY 1

ant easiness

hardpan *n* *syn* see BASE 1

hardscrabble *adj* *syn* see BARREN 2

hard–shell *adj* *syn* see INVETERATE 1

hardship *n* *syn* see DIFFICULTY 1

rel adversity, mischance, misfortune; danger, hazard, peril; affliction, trial, tribulation; drudgery, toil, travail; discomfort, distress

con comfort, ease

hardy *adj* *syn* see TOUGH 4

ant tender

harebrain *n* **1** *syn* see SCATTERBRAIN

2 *syn* see CRACKPOT

harebrained *adj* **1** *syn* see GIDDY 1

2 *syn* see FOOLISH 2

harefooted *adj* *syn* see FAST 3

hark *vb* *syn* see LISTEN

rel mark, mind, note, notice, remark

idiom be all ears, not miss a trick

harlequin *n* *syn* see CLOWN 3

harlot *n* **1** a woman who engages in unlawful or socially unacceptable sexual intercourse often for material gain <ply the trade of a *harlot*>

syn blowen, courtesan, demimondaine, demimonde, demirep, fancy woman, hetaera, kept woman, paphian, whore; *compare* DOXY, MISTRESS, PROSTITUTE, WANTON

2 *syn* see PROSTITUTE

harlotry *n* *syn* see PROSTITUTION

harm *n* *syn* see INJURY 1

rel deleteriousness; banefulness, noxiousness, perniciousness; mischance, misfortune, misuse; impairment, marring

con aid, help; accommodation, benefaction; charity, favor, service

ant benefit

harm *vb* *syn* see INJURE 1

rel abuse, ill-use, maltreat, mistreat, misuse, molest; dilapidate, ruin; discommode, incommode, inconvenience; sabotage, sap, undermine
idiom do violence to
con ameliorate, better, improve; avail, profit
ant benefit

harmful *adj* inflicting or capable of inflicting injury < a *harmful* drug >
syn bad, damaging, deleterious, detrimental, evil, hurtful, ill, injurious, mischievous, nocent, nocuous, prejudicial, prejudicious
rel baleful, baneful, malefic, malign, malignant, noisome, noxious, pernicious, toxic; insalubrious, unhealthful, unhealthy, unwholesome; dangerous, hazardous, risky, unsafe
con innocuous, inoffensive, nontoxic; beneficent, beneficial, benign, benignant, favorable, helpful, salutary, useful; safe, unhazardous
ant harmless

harmless *adj* not having hurtful or injurious qualities < *harmless* pastimes >
syn innocent, innocuous, innoxious, inobnoxious, inoffensive, unoffending, unoffensive; *compare* SAFE 3
rel guiltless; nontoxic, painless, safe
con baneful, dangerous, malignant, noxious, pernicious, toxic, virulent; damaging, detrimental, destructive, hurtful, injurious; deadly, fell, ruinous; improper, unsuitable, wrong
ant harmful

harmonic *adj syn* see HARMONIOUS 1

harmonious *adj* 1 musically concordant < a *harmonious* morning chorus of birds >
syn blending, chiming, consonant, harmonic, musical, symphonic, symphonious
rel canorous, dulcet, euphonious, melodious, mellifluous, mellisonant, musical, silvery, sonorous, sweet, tuneful; chordal, contrapuntal, counterpointed, polyphonic
idiom in concert, in tune
con clashing, discordant, dissonant, grating, harsh, jangling, jarring, raucous, shrill, strident, tuneless, unmusical, untuneful; atonal
ant disharmonious, inharmonious, unharmonious

2 having the parts agreeably related < a building with *harmonious* proportions >
syn accordant, concordant, congruous; *compare* CONSONANT 1
rel agreeable, pleasing, satisfying; concinnate, symmetrical
con clashing, incongruous, unsymmetrical; askew, distorted, skewed
ant inharmonious, unharmonious

3 marked by accord in sentiment or action < a *harmonious* effort to reach a practicable agreement >
syn amicable, amical, congenial, friendly
rel coactive, collaborative, cooperative; empathetic, empathic, simpatico, sympathetic; calm, irenic, pacific, peaceful

idiom of one accord
con incompatible, uncongenial, uncooperative, unfriendly, unsympathetic; belligerent, contentious, pugnacious
ant inharmonious, unharmonious

harmonize *vb* 1 *syn* see AGREE 3
rel cooperate, match, unite
con differ, disagree
ant clash; conflict

2 *syn* see AGREE 4
ant differ (from)

3 to bring into consonance or accord < *harmonize* the factions of a political party >
syn accommodate, attune, conform, coordinate, integrate, proportion, reconcile, reconciliate, tune
rel adapt, adjust, correlate; coapt, relate
con alienate, disrupt, estrange
ant disharmonize

4 to combine or adapt so as to achieve a desired effect < *harmonize* the elements of a story >
syn arrange, blend, integrate, orchestrate, symphonize, synthesize, unify
rel coordinate, correlate

harmonizing *n syn* see RECONCILIATION

harmony *n* 1 musical agreement of sounds < singing in *harmony* >
syn accord, chorus, concert, concord, consonance, tune
rel mellifluousness, melodiousness, melody, musicality, sonority, tunefulness; diapason, polyphony
con cacophony, discord, discordance, discordancy, dissonance, harshness, inharmoniousness, jangle, stridency, tunelessness, unharmoniousness, unmusicalness, untunefulness; atonality
ant disharmony, inharmony

2 the effect produced when different things come together without clashing or disagreement < goals that are in *harmony* with our capabilities >
syn accord, agreement, chime, concord, concordance, consonance, tune; *compare* CONSISTENCY
rel conformance, conformity, correspondence; articulation, coaptation, compatibility, congruity; concatenation, concurrence, integration, oneness, togetherness, unity
con disagreement, discord, disparity, dissidence, disunity, variance
ant conflict

3 the state of persons who are in full and perfect agreement < friends who live in *harmony* >
syn concord, rapport, unity
rel affinity, empathy, fellow-feeling, kinship; peace, tranquillity
idiom meeting of minds
con contention, dissension, strife
ant discord

4 *syn* see SYMMETRY
rel concinnity, consonance; dignity, elegance, grace; integrity, unity
con asymmetry, discordance, discordancy, imbalance
ant inharmony

harness *vb syn* see HITCH 2

‖**harness bull** (*or* cop) *n syn* see POLICEMAN

harpy *n syn* see VIRAGO

---

syn synonym(s)   *rel* related word(s)
ant antonym(s)   *con* contrasted word(s)
idiom idiomatic equivalent(s)
‖ use limited; if in doubt, see a dictionary

harrier *n syn* see BULLY 1
harrow *vb syn* see AFFLICT
  rel fret, irritate, pester; badger, bait, bedevil, devil, heckle, hector, needle, tantalize, tease
harrowing *adj syn* see EXCRUCIATING
harry *vb* 1 *syn* see RAVAGE
  2 *syn* see RAID 1
  3 *syn* see WORRY 1
  rel disturb, irk, perturb, upset; badger,
  irritate
harsh *adj* 1 *syn* see ROUGH 1
  rel coarse, granular, loose; bristly, scrag-
  gly, scratchy, shaggy, stubbly
  con glossy, satiny, silken, silky, sleek,
  slick, velvety
  2 *syn* see ACRID
  rel acerb, acerbic, biting, burning, mordant; pungent, tangy; dry, sour, tart
  con mild, smooth, sweet; velvety
  3 disagreeable to the ear <many birds
  have *harsh* cries>
  syn dry, grating, hoarse, jarring, rasping,
  raucous, rough, rugged, rusty, squawky,
  strident, stridulent, stridulous
  rel discordant, dissonant, immelodious,
  ineuphonious, inharmonious, unmelodious,
  unmusical; grinding, jangling, scraping;
  blaring, brassy; ear-piercing, piercing,
  shrill, squeaky
  con euphonious, harmonious, mellow,
  melodic, melodious, musical, sonorous,
  sweet; low, soft; agreeable, pleasing
  4 *syn* see UNCOMFORTABLE
  5 *syn* see GRIM 2
  6 *syn* see SEVERE 3
  ant mild
harshly *adv syn* see HARD 5
  con considerately; gently, lightly, well;
  famously
  ant smoothly
haruspex *n syn* see PROPHET
harvest *n* 1 the act, process, or occasion of
  gathering a crop <the time of *harvest*>
  syn cropping, gathering, harvesting, ingathering, reaping
  rel garnering, storing
  con planting, seedtime, sowing
  2 the gathered produce of land <a
  bountiful *harvest* saved the settlers>
  syn crop, fruitage
  rel yield; bearing, vintage
harvest *vb syn* see REAP
  rel assemble, collect; accumulate, amass,
  bin, store (up), stow (away); cache, hide,
  hoard, squirrel, stash
harvesting *n syn* see HARVEST 1
hash *vb syn* see CHOP 2
hash *n* 1 *syn* see MISCELLANY 1
  2 *syn* see CLUTTER 2
  3 *syn* see MESS 3
‖**hashery** *n syn* see EATING HOUSE
‖**hash house** *n syn* see EATING HOUSE
hassle *n* 1 *syn* see QUARREL
  2 *syn* see COMMOTION 4
  3 *syn* see ATTEMPT
hassle *vb syn* see ARGUE 2
  rel cavil; brawl, fight, spar, struggle
haste *n* 1 rapidity of motion or action
  <we finished our job with great *haste*>
  syn celerity, dispatch, expedition, expeditiousness, hurry, hustle, rustle, speed,
  speediness, swiftness

  rel fastness, fleetness, quickness, rapidity;
  pace, velocity; dash, drive
  con languidness, languor, leisureliness,
  reluctance, slowness; lethargy, sluggishness, torpor
  ant deliberateness, deliberation
  2 rash or headlong action <oversights
  due to *haste*>
  syn hastiness, hurriedness, precipitance,
  precipitancy, precipitateness, precipitation,
  rush
  rel impetuosity, impetuousness, impulsiveness
  con care, carefulness, circumspection,
  hastelessness, unhurriedness
  ant deliberateness, deliberation
haste *vb syn* see HURRY 2
hasten *vb syn* see SPEED 3
  2 *syn* see HURRY 2
hastily *adv syn* see FAST 2
  rel agilely, nimbly; impetuously, impul-
  sively, unpremeditatedly; carelessly, reck-
  lessly, thoughtlessly; precipitately, prematurely, suddenly
  con carefully, designedly, studiedly,
  thoughtfully; gradually, leisurely, slowly,
  sluggishly
  ant deliberately
hastiness *n syn* see WASTE 2
hasty *adj* 1 *syn* see FAST 3
  rel agile, brisk, nimble; hurried, quickened
  con dilatory, laggard, leisured, leisurely
  2 *syn* see PRECIPITATE 1
  ant deliberate
  3 *syn* see RASH 1
  rel devil-may-care, slambang, slapdash
hatch *vb* 1 *syn* see GENERATE 3
  2 *syn* see GENERATE 1
hatch (up) *vb syn* see CONTRIVE 2
hatchet man *n syn* see ASSASSIN
hate *n* 1 *syn* see ABOMINATION 2
  rel animosity, animus, antipathy, hostility, ill will, rancor; disgust, scorn, spite
  con affection; toleration; adoration, veneration
  ant love
  2 *syn* see ABOMINATION 1
  rel bother, grievance, gripe, irritant, nuisance, ‖pain, trouble
  ant delight
hate *vb* to feel extreme enmity or dislike
  <Cain *hated* his brother> <*hate* to meet
  strangers>
  syn abhor, abominate, detest, execrate,
  loathe
  rel contemn, despise, disdain, dislike,
  scorn; deprecate, disapprove; resent
  con cherish, enjoy, fancy, like, relish;
  favor, prefer, prize; esteem, respect, revere;
  dote; idolize, worship
  ant love
hateable *adj syn* see HATEFUL 2
  ant lovable
hateful *adj* 1 *syn* see MALICIOUS
  rel acrimonious, ill-natured; bitter, resentful; mean
  con benevolent, charitable, cordial, genial,
  good-humored, good-natured, kind,
  kindly, pleasant
  2 deserving of or arousing hate <found
  himself in a *hateful* situation>
  syn abhorrent, abominable, detestable,
  hateable, horrid, odious

rel distasteful, distressing, obnoxious, repellent, repulsive; contemptible, despicable, execrable, opprobrious, reprehensible, scurvy; foul, infamous, vile; accursed, blasphemous, damnable, unspeakable
con compatible, congenial, consonant; alluring, appealing, attractive, charming, enchanting; agreeable, delectable, delightful, likable, pleasant, pleasing
ant lovable; sympathetic

hatred *n syn* see ABOMINATION 2
rel antipathy, dislike; animosity, enmity, hostility, rancor
con affability, benevolence, benignity, charitableness, cordiality
ant love; admiration

haughtiness *n syn* see PRIDE 3
ant lowliness

haughty *adj syn* see PROUD 1
rel aloof, detached, distant, indifferent, reserved; egotistic; contemptuous, scornful
con humble; obsequious, servile, subservient
ant lowly

haul *vb syn* see PULL 2
rel move, remove, shift; boost, elevate, hoist, lift, raise

haul *n syn* see LOAD 1

haul up *vb syn* see STOP 4

haunches *n pl syn* see BUTTOCKS

haunt *vb syn* see FREQUENT

haunt *n* 1 *syn* see RESORT 2
2 *syn* see HABITAT
3 *syn* see APPARITION

haunter *n syn* see HABITUÉ 1

hauteur *n syn* see PRIDE 3
ant lowliness

haut monde *n syn* see ARISTOCRACY

have *vb* 1 to keep, control, or experience as one's own < can't *have* your cake and eat it too >
syn enjoy, hold, own, possess, retain
idiom to be possessed of, have in hand
con lack, need, want
2 *syn* see INCLUDE
rel admit, compose, comprise
3 *syn* see BEAR 3
4 *syn* see GET 1
5 *syn* see EXPERIENCE 1
6 *syn* see LET 2
7 *syn* see KNOW 1
8 *syn* see OUTWIT
9 *syn* see BRIBE
10 *syn* see MUST 2

haven *n* 1 *syn* see HARBOR 3
2 *syn* see SHELTER 1

haven *vb syn* see HARBOR 1

haversack *n syn* see BACKPACK

havoc *n syn* see RUIN 3
rel calamity, cataclysm, catastrophe; despoiling, pillaging, ravaging; vandalism

havoc *vb syn* see RAVAGE

hawk *vb syn* see PEDDLE 2

hawker *n syn* see PEDDLER

hawk-eyed *adj syn* see SHARP-EYED

hawkshaw *n syn* see DETECTIVE

haymaker *n syn* see CUFF

hayseed *n syn* see RUSTIC

ant city slicker, slicker

hazard *n* 1 *syn* see CHANCE 2
2 *syn* see DANGER

hazard *vb* 1 *syn* see VENTURE 1
2 *syn* see GAMBLE 2
3 *syn* see ENDANGER

hazardous *adj syn* see DANGEROUS 1
ant safe; unhazardous

haze *vb syn* see OBSCURE

haze *n* 1 an atmospheric condition that is characterized by the presence of fine particulate material in the air and that deprives the air of its transparency < *haze* obscured the distant hills >
syn brume, film, mist, smaze
rel cloud, ‖drisk, fog, murk, ‖smeech, smog, smoke, vapor; cloudiness, mistiness, murkiness, smokiness
2 a state of mental vagueness or obtuseness < lived in a *haze* of pleasant memories >
syn befuddlement, daze, fog, ‖maze, muddledness, muddleheadedness, muddlement
rel dream, reverie, stupor, trance; absentmindedness, abstraction, bemusement, preoccupation, woolgathering
con alertness, attentiveness, awareness

hazy *adj* obscured or made dim by or as if by haze < had only a *hazy* idea of where they were >
syn cloudy, foggy, misty, mushy, vague, vaporous, vapory
rel blurred, clouded, dim, indefinite, indistinct, murky, nebulous, obscure; bemused, dreamy, tranced, stuporous; dazed, ‖mazed, muzzy

he *n syn* see MAN 3

head *n* 1 the upper division of the body that contains the brain, the chief sense organs, and the mouth < put your hat on your *head* >
syn ‖bean, ‖belfry, ‖chump, ‖coco, ‖coconut, ‖conk, ‖dome, headpiece, noddle, noggin, noodle, ‖nut, ‖pallet, pate, poll, sconce
rel brainpan, cranium, crown, scalp
2 *syn* see MIND 1
3 *syn* see GIFT 2
4 *syn* see LEADER 2
con subordinate; aide, assistant, helper
5 *syn* see PROMONTORY
6 *syn* see TOILET
7 *syn* see HEADLINE
8 *syn* see SUBJECT 2

head *adj syn* see FIRST 3

head *vb* 1 *syn* see BEHEAD
2 *syn* see DIRECT 2
3 to commence to go in an indicated direction < the cowboys *headed* for town >
syn bear, light out, make, set out, strike out, take off
rel go, proceed, start
idiom make a beeline for
4 *syn* see SPRING 1

heading *n syn* see HEADLINE

headland *n syn* see PROMONTORY

headline *n* a word or group of words usually in large type introducing and summarizing a newspaper story < *headlines* that screamed the news of the president's death >
syn head, heading
rel banner, banner head, bannerline, scarehead, screamer, spreadhead

---

syn synonym(s)   *rel* related word(s)
ant antonym(s)   *con* contrasted word(s)
idiom idiomatic equivalent(s)
‖ use limited; if in doubt, see a dictionary

headlong *adj syn* see PRECIPITATE 1
  rel daredevil, daring, foolhardy, rash, reckless
headman *n syn* see LEADER 2
headmost *adj syn* see FIRST 1
headpiece *n syn* see HEAD 1
headshaker *n syn* see SKEPTIC
head start *n syn* see ADVANTAGE 3
headstone *n syn* see TOMBSTONE
headstrong *adj syn* see OBSTINATE
  con subdued, tame; amenable, biddable, docile, meek, obedient, tractable
headway *n* 1 *syn* see ADVANCE 2
heady *adj syn* see SHREWD
heal *vb syn* see CURE
healing *adj syn* see CURATIVE
health *n* the state of being sound in body or mind <the patient was nursed back to *health*>
  syn haleness, healthiness, soundness, wholeness
  rel stamina, vitality, well-being; euphoria
  con debility, decrepitude, feebleness; ill health, illness, sickliness
  ant disease, infirmity
healthful *adj* 1 conducive or beneficial to the health or soundness of body or mind <regular exercise is a *healthful* practice>
  syn good, healthy, hygienic, salubrious, salutary, salutiferous, wholesome
  rel advantageous, beneficial, profitable, useful; corrective, curative, remedial; aiding, alleviating, helpful, mitigative, restorative, sanative
  con insalubrious, unhealthy, unhygienic, unwholesome; damaging, deleterious, detrimental, harmful, injurious, mischievous, pernicious
  ant unhealthful
healthiness *n syn* see HEALTH
  ant unhealthiness
healthy *adj* 1 enjoying or manifesting health <a *healthy* baby>
  syn ‖bunkum, fit, hale, right, sane, sound, well, well-conditioned, well-liking, whole, wholesome
  rel hearty, iron, lusty, robust, thriving, vigorous, rugged, stalwart, strong, sturdy, tough; agile, chipper, spry; blooming, rosy, thriving
  idiom fit as a fiddle, in (top) condition, in fine fettle, in shape, in trim, sound as a dollar, up to snuff
  con decrepit, delicate, feeble, fragile, frail, weak; infirm, ‖poorly, sickly
  ant unhealthy
  2 *syn* see HEALTHFUL
  ant unhealthful
  3 *syn* see SAFE 3
heap *n* 1 *syn* see PILE 1
  rel congeries, gathering
  2 *syn* see MUCH
  3 *syn* see SCAD
  4 *syn* see JALOPY
heap *vb* 1 to throw or collect in a pile <*heap* up leaves for a bonfire>
  syn bank, cock, drift, hill, mound, pile, stack
  rel cord, ‖dess, rick, shock; bunch, clump, lumber, lump, mass; deposit, dump; accumulate, amass, assemble, collect, gather, group
  con broadcast, disperse, distribute, scatter, separate, spread, strew

  2 *syn* see LOAD 3
hear *vb* 1 *syn* see LISTEN
  idiom get wind of
  2 *syn* see DISCOVER 3
hearing *n* 1 *syn* see EARSHOT
  2 an opportunity to be heard <they finally obtained a *hearing* on their complaints>
  syn audience, audition
  rel conference, interview, meeting, parley; test, tryout; discussion, negotiation
hearken *vb syn* see LISTEN
hearsay *n syn* see REPORT 1
heart *n* 1 the seat or center of secret thoughts and emotions <in his *heart* he knew he was seriously in the wrong>
  syn bosom, breast, soul
  idiom bottom of the heart, cockles of the heart
  2 *syn* see COURAGE
  3 *syn* see TASTE 4
  4 *syn* see CENTER 2
  5 *syn* see CENTER 3
heartache *n syn* see SORROW
  idiom aching heart, heavy heart
heartbreak *n* 1 *syn* see SORROW
  rel agony, bale, torment
  idiom bleeding heart
heartbreaking *adj syn* see DEPLORABLE
hearten *vb syn* see ENCOURAGE 1
  rel energize, enliven; arouse, rally, rouse, stir
  con damp, dampen; weigh
  ant dishearten
heartfelt *adj syn* see SINCERE 1
  rel bona fide, genuine, honest, true, unfeigned; deep, profound
  con hypocritical, insincere; false, pretended
heartless *adj syn* see UNFEELING 2
heartrending *adj syn* see DEPLORABLE
heart-searching *n syn* see INTROSPECTION
heartsick *adj syn* see DOWNCAST
heartsore *adj syn* see DOWNCAST
heartthrob *n syn* see SWEETHEART 1
heart-whole *adj* 1 *syn* see FREE 6
  2 *syn* see GENUINE 3
hearty *adj syn* see SINCERE 1
  rel responsive, warm, warmhearted; deep, profound; exuberant, profuse
  con cold, dispassionate, emotionless
  ant hollow
‖**heat** *n syn* see POLICEMAN
heated *adj* 1 *syn* see HOT 1
  ant chilled
  2 *syn* see FEVERISH 2
  3 *syn* see ANGRY
heathen *adj* of or relating to people who do not acknowledge the God of the Bible <ancient *heathen* sacrificial rites>
  syn ethnic, gentile, infidel, infidelic, pagan, profane
  rel heathenish, paganish
heave *vb* 1 *syn* see THROW 1
  2 *syn* see TOSS 2
  3 *syn* see PANT 1
  4 *syn* see RETCH
  ‖5 *syn* see VOMIT
heaven *n* 1 *usu* **heavens** *pl syn* see SKY
  2 an abode of blissful spiritual life after death <the religious conceptions of *heaven* and hell>

syn Abraham's bosom, bliss, Canaan, Civitas Dei, elysium, empyrean, happy hunting ground, kingdom come, New Jerusalem, nirvana, paradise, Zion
rel afterworld, eternity, glory, hereafter, promised land; everlastingness, immortality
idiom Beulah Land (*or* Land of Beulah), City of God, Kingdom of God, Kingdom of Heaven
con earth, world; Gehenna, hades, inferno, netherworld, perdition, pit, Sheol, Tartarus, Tophet, underworld
ant hell
3 *syn* see UTOPIA
4 *syn* see ECSTASY
heavenly *adj* **1** *syn* see CELESTIAL
con hadean, Tartarean
ant hellish
2 *syn* see DELIGHTFUL
heavy *adj* **1** having great or relatively great weight < a *heavy* load >
syn hefty, massive, ponderous, weighty; *compare* UNWIELDY
rel awkward, bulky, clumsy, lumbering, lumbersome; unhandy, unmanageable, unwieldy; cumbersome, cumbrous
con airy, buoyant, weightless; handy, manageable, wieldy
ant light
2 *syn* see FAT 2
3 *syn* see SERIOUS 2
4 *syn* see RECONDITE
5 *syn* see PREGNANT 1
6 *syn* see LETHARGIC
7 *syn* see OVERCAST
8 *syn* see HARD 6
9 *syn* see RICH 3
heavy–footed *adj* *syn* see PONDEROUS 2
heavy–handed *adj* **1** *syn* see AWKWARD 2
2 *syn* see PONDEROUS 2
heavyhearted *adj* *syn* see SAD 1
ant lighthearted
heavyheartedness *n* *syn* see SADNESS
ant lightheartedness
heavyset *adj* *syn* see STOCKY
heavyweight *n* *syn* see NOTABLE 1
con lightweight
hebetate *vb* *syn* see DULL 5
hebetude *n* *syn* see LETHARGY 1
hebetudinous *adj* *syn* see LETHARGIC
heckle *vb* **1** *syn* see BAIT 2
rel plague, worry; discomfit, disconcert, embarrass, faze, rattle; tease, torment
2 *syn* see MOLEST
hectic *adj* *syn* see FEVERISH 2
hector *n* *syn* see BULLY 1
hector *vb* **1** *syn* see INTIMIDATE
2 *syn* see BAIT 2
hedge *vb* **1** *syn* see EQUIVOCATE 2
2 *syn* see ENCLOSE 1
hedonist *n* one given to the zealous pursuit of pleasure < lead the life of a *hedonist* >
syn carpet knight, pleasuremonger, sybarite
rel bon vivant, man-about-town; epicure, epicurean, gourmand, gourmet; debauchee,

libertine, rake; sensualist, voluptuary; pleasure-seeker
ant ascetic
hedonistic *adj* *syn* see SYBARITIC
con austere, self-denying, self-disciplined, self-restricted
ant ascetic
heebie–jeebies *n pl* *syn* see JITTERS
heed *vb* *syn* see LISTEN
rel mark, mind, note; observe, see, watch
idiom give (*or* pay) heed to
heed *n* **1** *syn* see NOTICE 1
rel awareness, interest, mindfulness; audience, hearing
2 *syn* see ATTENTION 1
rel concern, interest
con inattention, unconcern
3 *syn* see CARE 4
heedful *adj* **1** *syn* see ATTENTIVE 1
ant heedless, unheeding
2 *syn* see MINDFUL 2
ant heedless, unheeding
3 *syn* see CAREFUL 2
heedfully *adv* *syn* see WELL 2
ant heedlessly, unheeding
heedfulness *n* *syn* see CARE 4
ant heedlessness
heedless *adj* *syn* see CARELESS 1
ant heedful, heeding
heedlessness *n* *syn* see APATHY 2
ant heedfulness
hee–haw *vb* *syn* see LAUGH
heel *n* **1** *syn* see REMAINDER
2 *syn* see VILLAIN 1
heel *vb* *syn* see SLANT 1
hefty *adj* **1** *syn* see HEAVY 1
2 *syn* see HUSKY 1
3 *syn* see BIG 1
height *n* the distance a thing rises above the level on which it stands < the *height* of a building >
syn altitude, elevation
rel highness, loftiness, rise, tallness, stature
con lowness, profundity
ant depth
heighten *vb* **1** *syn* see INCREASE 1
2 *syn* see INCREASE 2
rel elevate, lift, raise; better, improve; enlarge, increase
con diminish, lessen, shrink
3 *syn* see INTENSIFY
heinie (*or* hiney) *n* *syn* see BUTTOCKS
heinous *adj* *syn* see OUTRAGEOUS 2
con paltry, petty, trifling, trivial
ant venial
heinousness *n* *syn* see ENORMITY 1
heir *n* one who inherits < died without *heirs* >
syn heritor, inheritor
‖**heist** *vb* *syn* see STEAL 1
hell *n* a place or state of the dead or of the damned < went to *hell* for his sins >
syn abyss, barathrum, blazes, Gehenna, hades, inferno, netherworld, Pandemonium, perdition, pit, Sheol, Tophet
rel limbo, Styx, Tartarus
idiom the hot place, infernal regions, place of torment
ant heaven
hell *vb* *syn* see REVEL 1
hell–fired *adj* *syn* see UTTER
hellish *adj* *syn* see INFERNAL 2

helotry *n syn* see BONDAGE

help *n* **1** an act or instance of giving what will benefit or assist < the stranded travelers received *help* from passersby >
syn aid, assist, assistance, comfort, hand, lift, relief, secours, succor, support
rel benefit, cooperation, service
ant hindrance
2 something that is beneficial < the rain was a real *help* to late crops >
syn aid, support
rel benefit, use
3 *syn* see HELPER

help *vb* **1** to give assistance or support < *help* the children with their lessons >
syn abet, aid, assist, benefact, do for, help out, stead
rel back, bolster, boost, champion, second, support, uphold; avail, benefit, profit; advance, facilitate, forward, further, promote, serve; befriend, succor
idiom give a lift, lend a hand (*or* a helping hand), stand back of (*or* behind)
con bar, block, impede, obstruct, oppose; baffle, balk, foil, frustrate, thwart; discomfit, embarrass; damage, harm, hurt, injure
ant hinder
2 *syn* see IMPROVE 1
rel alleviate, mitigate, palliate, relieve
con harm, impair, worsen

helper *n* one that helps < was made boss and assigned a dozen *helpers* >
syn aid, ancilla, assistant, attendant, help, striker
rel helpmate, helpmeet; auxiliary, deputy, subordinate; associate, follower; employee, laborer, servant, worker
idiom helping hand, right-hand man

helpful *adj* **1** of service or assistance < *helpful* suggestions >
syn aidant, aiding, assistive, serviceable
rel beneficial, effective, profitable, salutary, usable; constructive, practical, useful
con timeserving, uncooperative, unreliable; impractical, ineffectual
ant unhelpful
2 *syn* see GOOD 1

helpless *adj* **1** lacking protection or support < *helpless* nestlings >
syn defenseless, unprotected
rel abandoned, desolate, forlorn, forsaken, friendless; feeble, weak
2 *syn* see POWERLESS

helplessly *adv syn* see WILLY-NILLY

help out *vb syn* see HELP 1

helter-skelter *adv* **1** *syn* see PELL-MELL
2 *syn* see ABOUT 4

hem *n syn* see BORDER 1

hem *vb* **1** *syn* see BORDER
2 *syn* see ENCLOSE 1
3 *syn* see SURROUND 1

hence *adv* **1** *syn* see AWAY 1
2 *syn* see THEREFORE

henceforth *adv* from this time forward < made up his mind to keep out of trouble *henceforth* >
syn henceforward, hereafter; *compare* THENCEFORTH
idiom from now on

henceforward *adv syn* see HENCEFORTH

henchman *n syn* see FOLLOWER
rel attendant; lackey, minion, stooge

henpeck *vb syn* see NAG

hep *adj syn* see WISE 4

herald *n syn* see FORERUNNER 1
rel courier, crier, messenger

herald *vb* **1** *syn* see ANNOUNCE 2
2 *syn* see TOUT

Herculean *adj syn* see HUGE

herd *n syn* see DROVE 2

herd *vb syn* see DRIVE 3

here *adv syn* see HITHERTO 2

hereafter *adv syn* see HENCEFORTH

hereafter *n* **1** *syn* see FUTURE
2 an existence or place of existence after this life < buried pots and tools with the dead for use in the *hereafter* >
syn afterlife, afterworld, beyond, otherworld
idiom great beyond (*or* hereafter), life after death, next world (*or* life), world beyond the grave, world to come
con here and now

here and there *adv syn* see SOMETIMES

heresy *n* defection from a dominant belief or ideology < the *heresy* of the flat-earth theory >
syn dissent, dissidence, heterodoxy, misbelief, nonconformism, nonconformity, schism, unorthodoxy
rel impiety, infidelity; apostasy, defection, revisionism; error, fallacy

heretic *n* one who is not orthodox in his beliefs < a *heretic* in religion >
syn dissenter, dissident, misbeliever, nonconformist, schismatic, schismatist, sectary, separatist
rel apostate, defector, iconoclast, recreant, recusant, renegade; infidel, unbeliever; deviationist, revisionist
ant orthodox

heretical *adj* of, relating to, or characterized by heresy < *heretical* beliefs >
syn dissident, heterodox, nonconformist, schismatic, sectarian, unorthodox
rel apostate, infidel, miscreant, revisionist; differing, disagreeing, dissentient, dissenting, dissentive, misbelieving, unbelieving
con conventional, established; agreeing, conforming, conformist
ant orthodox

heretofore *adv syn* see BEFORE 2

heritage *n* **1** something that one receives or is entitled to receive by succession (as from a parent) < the *heritage* of freedom >
syn birthright, heritance, inheritance, legacy, patrimony
2 *syn* see TRADITION 1

heritance *n syn* see HERITAGE 1

heritor *n syn* see HEIR

hermaphrodite *adj syn* see BISEXUAL

hermaphroditic *adj syn* see BISEXUAL

hermetic *adj* **1** *syn* see RECONDITE
2 *syn* see SECLUDED

hermit *n syn* see RECLUSE

heroic *adj* **1** *syn* see BRAVE 1
ant pusillanimous
2 *syn* see HUGE

heroism *n* conspicuous courage or bravery < received an award for *heroism* >
syn gallantry, prowess, valiance, valiancy, valor, valorousness
rel boldness, bravery, courage, doughtiness, fearlessness, intrepidity, spirit; chivalry, nobility

con cowardice, spiritlessness, timidity, timorousness, weakness
ant pusillanimity

hesitancy *n syn* see HESITATION

hesitant *adj* 1 *syn* see DISINCLINED
con resolute, staunch, steadfast
2 *syn* see VACILLATING 2

hesitate *vb* to show irresolution or uncertainty < *hesitate* to buy a new car just now >
syn dither, falter, halt, shilly-shally, stagger, vacillate, waver, whiffle, wiggle-waggle
rel balk, boggle, demur, scruple, stick, stickle; fluctuate, oscillate, swing; dawdle, delay, dillydally, hang back, procrastinate, stall, temporize; pause

hesitating *adj syn* see VACILLATING 2

hesitation *n* the act or action of hesitating < several persons volunteered without *hesitation* >
syn hesitancy, indecision, indecisiveness, irresolution, shilly-shally, to-and-fro, vacillation, wavering
rel doubt, dubiety, dubiosity, mistrust, uncertainty; dawdling, delay, procrastination; averseness, indisposition, reluctance
con alacrity, eagerness; courage, mettle, resolution, spirit, tenacity; aplomb, assurance, confidence

hetaera *n syn* see HARLOT 1

heteroclite *adj syn* see ABNORMAL 1

heterodox *adj syn* see HERETICAL
ant orthodox

heterodoxy *n syn* see HERESY
ant orthodoxy

heterogeneous *adj syn* see MISCELLANEOUS
ant homogeneous

hew *vb syn* see FELL 2

hex *vb syn* see BEWITCH 1

hex *n* 1 *syn* see JINX
2 *syn* see WITCH 1

hiatus *n syn* see GAP 3

hic jacet *n syn* see EPITAPH

hick *n syn* see RUSTIC

hick town *n syn* see BURG

hidden *adj syn* see ULTERIOR
ant open

hide *vb* to withdraw or withhold from sight or observation < they *hid* their loot in a cave >
syn bury, ‖bush up, cache, conceal, cover, ‖ditch, ensconce, occult, plant, screen, secrete, stash
rel mantle, mask, obscure, shade, shield; entomb, inter; cloak, curtain, shroud, veil; harbor, lodge, seclude, shelter
con bare, disclose, discover, display, exhibit, expose, reveal, show; uncover, unmask, unveil, unwrap; flaunt, parade, show off

hide *n* an animal skin < tanned *hides* for shoe leather >
syn fell, fur, jacket, pelt, skin

hide *vb syn* see WHIP 1

hideaway *n syn* see HIDEOUT

hidebound *adj syn* see ILLIBERAL

hideous *adj* 1 *syn* see UGLY 2
ant lovely
2 *syn* see OFFENSIVE
3 *syn* see GHASTLY 1

hideout *n* a place of retreat or concealment < a gangsters' *hideout* >
syn den, hideaway, lair
rel covert, haven, hermitage, refuge, retreat, sanctuary, shelter; robbers' roost

hie *vb syn* see GO 1

hierarch *n syn* see LEADER 2

hieratic *adj syn* see SACERDOTAL

higgle *vb syn* see HAGGLE 2

higgler *n syn* see PEDDLER

high *adj* 1 having a relatively great upward extension < a *high* building >
syn altitudinous, tall; *compare* LOFTY 6
rel aerial, eminent, lofty, soaring, towering; big, gigantic, grand, large, prominent
idiom tall (*or* high) as a steeple
con little, short, squat
ant low
2 *syn* see COSTLY 1
ant low
3 *syn* see MALODOROUS 1
4 *syn* see ELEVATED 4
5 *syn* see ACUTE 4
6 *syn* see DRUGGED

high and low *adv syn* see EVERYWHERE 1

high-and-mighty *adj syn* see PROUD 1

highball *vb syn* see HURRY 2

highbinding *n syn* see DECEPTION 1

highbrow *n syn* see INTELLECTUAL 2

highbrow *adj syn* see INTELLECTUAL 2

highbrowed *adj syn* see INTELLECTUAL 2
ant lowbrow, low-browed

higher *adj syn* see SUPERIOR 1

higher-up *n syn* see SUPERIOR

highest *adj* 1 *syn* see TOP 1
ant lowest
2 *syn* see EXALTED 1

highest-ranking *adj syn* see EXALTED 1

highfalutin *adj syn* see RHETORICAL
con down-to-earth, matter-of-fact

highfalutin *n syn* see BOMBAST

high-flown *adj syn* see RHETORICAL

high-handed *adj syn* see MASTERFUL 1

high hat *n syn* see SNOB

high-hat *adj syn* see SNOBBISH

high-hearted *adj syn* see SPIRITED 2

high jinks *n pl* 1 *syn* see HORSEPLAY
2 *syn* see REVELRY 2

highly *adv syn* see VERY 1

high-minded *adj syn* see ELEVATED 2
ant low-minded

high-muck-a-muck *n syn* see NOTABLE 1

high-principled *adj syn* see HONORABLE 1

high roller *n syn* see SPENDTHRIFT

high sign *n* 1 *syn* see SIGN 1
2 a private usually covert signal, warning, or cue < I gave him the *high sign* when I saw the police approaching >
syn ‖office
rel tip, tip-off, wink; nod; alarm, SOS, warning

high-sounding *adj syn* see PRETENTIOUS 3

high-spirited *adj* 1 *syn* see SPIRITED 2
rel jolly, lighthearted, merry, mirthful
ant low-spirited

---

syn synonym(s)   *rel* related word(s)
ant antonym(s)   *con* contrasted word(s)
idiom idiomatic equivalent(s)
‖ use limited; if in doubt, see a dictionary

2 *syn* see EXUBERANT 1
high–strung *adj* 1 *syn* see TENSE 3
2 *syn* see NERVOUS
hightail *vb syn* see GET OUT 1
highway *n syn* see WAY 1
high yellow *n syn* see MULATTO
hike *vb* 1 *syn* see RAISE 9
2 to travel about or through on foot
< *hiked* through the woods>
syn tramp, tromp
rel footslog; stroll, walk; ramble, rove,
wander; explore
hike *n* 1 *syn* see TRAMP 3
2 *syn* see RISE 3
hilarity *n syn* see MIRTH
hill *n syn* see PILE 1
hill *vb syn* see HEAP 1
hillbilly *n syn* see RUSTIC
hillman *n syn* see RUSTIC
hind *adj syn* see POSTERIOR 2
hind end *n syn* see BUTTOCKS
hinder *vb* to put obstacles in the way of
< their cause was *hindered* by the excesses
of overzealous supporters>
syn bar, block, brake, dam, impede, obstruct, overslaugh; *compare* HAMPER
rel arrest, check, interrupt, retard; clog,
entrammel, fetter, hamper, hog-tie, manacle, shackle, trammel; curb, deter, hamstring, inhibit, restrain, tie (down); embog,
mire; burden, handicap, lumber; baffle,
balk, frustrate, thwart
idiom bog down
con abet, advance, aid, assist, ease, encourage, facilitate, forward, promote; accelerate, hasten, quicken, speed
ant further, help
hinder *adj syn* see POSTERIOR 2
ant fore, front
‖**hinder** *n syn* see BUTTOCKS
hindmost *adj* 1 *syn* see POSTERIOR 2
con foremost, headmost
2 *syn* see LAST
hindrance *n syn* see ENCUMBRANCE
ant help
hinge (on *or* upon) *vb syn* see DEPEND (on
or upon) 1
hint *n* 1 a slight or indirect pointing out of
something and especially of the way to an
end < give me a *hint* on how you would
deal with the matter>
syn clue, cue, indication, inkling, intimation, notion, suggestion, telltale, wind
rel innuendo, insinuation; inspiration,
prompting; aiming, direction, pointing;
key, pointer, tip; advice, assistance
con command, directive, instruction, order
2 a very small amount or admixture
< add a *hint* of garlic to the salad>
syn breath, cast, dash, intimation, lick,
shade, shadow, smack, smatch, smell,
soupçon, spice, sprinkling, strain, streak,
suggestion, suspicion, taste, tincture, tinge,
touch, trace, trifle, twang, vein, whiff,
whisper, wink; *compare* HAIR
rel adumbration, taint, vestige; particle,
scintilla
con abundance, heap, lot
ant oodles
3 *syn* see ASSOCIATION 4
hint *vb* 1 *syn* see SUGGEST 1
2 *syn* see POINT 2

3 *syn* see ADUMBRATE 1
4 to seek to obtain by sly or indirect
means < kept *hinting* for an invitation to
the party>
syn angle, fish
rel beg, coax, plead; importune, press;
seek, solicit
con ask (for), demand, insist (on *or* upon)
hinterland *n syn* see FRONTIER 2
hipped *adj* 1 *syn* see DOWNCAST
2 *syn* see OBSESSED
hire *n syn* see WAGE
hire *vb* 1 to take or engage something or
grant the use of something for a stipulated
price or rate < *hire* a conveyance>
syn charter, lease, let, rent
rel contract (for); engage; sublease, sublet, subrent
2 *syn* see EMPLOY 1
ant fire
hired girl *n syn* see MAID 2
hireling *n syn* see HACK 2
hiring *n syn* see EMPLOYMENT 4
hirsute *adj syn* see HAIRY 1
ant hairless
hiss *vb* to make a sibilant sound < he
thought he heard a snake *hiss*>
syn buzz, fizz, fizzle, sibilate, sizz, sizzle,
swish, wheeze, whish, whisper, whiz,
whoosh
hiss *n syn* see RASPBERRY
history *n* 1 *syn* see ACCOUNT 7
2 a chronological record of events < a
history of the American Revolution>
syn annals, chronicle
rel account, recital, relation, report; diary,
journal, memoir; epic, saga, tale
histrionic *adj syn* see DRAMATIC 1
hit *vb* 1 *syn* see STRIKE 2
rel buffet, pound, stroke
idiom give one a clip
2 *syn* see OCCUR 2
3 *syn* see HAPPEN 2
hit (on *or* upon) *vb syn* see FIND 1
hit *n* 1 a stroke delivered with a part of the
body or an instrument < gave the disobedient boy a *hit* on the head with her ru-
ler>
syn ‖conk, knock, lick, rap, swat, swipe,
wipe; *compare* BLOW 1, CUFF
2 *syn* see SMASH 6
hitch *vb* 1 *syn* see LIMP 1
2 to attach as a means of motive power
< *hitched* the team to a wagon>
syn couple, harness, yoke
idiom make fast
con free, release, unfasten; uncouple, un-
harness, unyoke
ant unhitch
‖3 *syn* see MARRY 2
4 *syn* see HITCHHIKE
hitchhike *vb* to travel by securing free
rides < *hitchhiked* to California>
syn hitch, thumb
idiom bum (*or* hook) a ride
hitherto *adv* 1 up to this particular point
or time < imposed order upon what was
hitherto haphazard>
syn as yet, earlier, so far, thus far, yet
rel before, formerly, heretofore, once,
previously
idiom up to now (*or* then)
2 to this place < the appointed delegate
shall come *hitherto*>

syn here

hit man *n syn* see ASSASSIN

hit-or-miss *adj syn* see RANDOM

hive *vb syn* see ACCUMULATE

hoard *n* 1 *syn* see ACCUMULATION

2 *syn* see DUPE

hoard *vb* to store up beyond one's present or reasonable need < *hoarding* sugar during war>

syn squirrel, stash; *compare* ACCUMULATE, SAVE 4

rel ‖sock away; garner, lay by, lay up

idiom take all one can lay one's hands on

hoarse *adj* 1 rough or dry in sound <developed a *hoarse* cough>

syn croaking, croaky, gruff, husky

rel coarse, dry, guttural, thick

2 *syn* see HARSH 3

con honeyed, mellifluent, mellifluous, smooth

hoary *adj syn* see ANCIENT 1

hoax *vb syn* see DUPE

hoax *n syn* see IMPOSTURE

hobble *vb* 1 *syn* see LIMP 1

2 *syn* see HAMPER

hobo *n syn* see VAGABOND

hoboism *n syn* see VAGRANCY

hock *vb syn* see PAWN

hocus-pocus *n syn* see GIBBERISH 3

‖**hodge** *n syn* see RUSTIC

hodgepodge *n syn* see MISCELLANY 1

hogback *n syn* see RIDGE 1

hogshead *n syn* see CASK

hog-tie *vb syn* see HAMPER

hogwash *n syn* see NONSENSE 2

hoi polloi *n syn* see RABBLE 2

hoist *vb syn* see LIFT 1

hoity-toity *adj syn* see GIDDY 1

hokum *n syn* see NONSENSE 2

hold *vb* 1 *syn* see KEEP 5

2 *syn* see ENTHRALL 2

3 *syn* see HAVE 1

4 *syn* see CONTAIN 2

5 *syn* see FEEL 3

hold (with) *vb syn* see APPROVE 1

hold *n* the act or manner of grasping or holding <lost his *hold* on the side of the boat>

syn clamp, clasp, clench, clinch, clutch, grapple, grasp, grip, gripe, tenure

rel handclasp, handhold; purchase

hold back *vb* 1 *syn* see RESTRAIN 1

2 *syn* see KEEP 5

3 *syn* see DENY 3

hold down *vb syn* see RESTRAIN 1

holder *n syn* see OWNER

hold in *vb syn* see RESTRAIN 1

hold off *vb* 1 *syn* see FEND (off)

2 *syn* see DEFER

hold out *vb syn* see OFFER 1

hold over *vb syn* see DEFER

hold up *vb syn* see DEFER

hole *n* 1 *syn* see APERTURE

2 *syn* see GAP 1

3 a space within the substance of a body or mass <buried their trash in a *hole* in the ground>

syn cavity, hollow, vacuity, void

hole *vb syn* see OPEN 3

hole-and-corner *adj syn* see SECRET 1

holiday *n syn* see VACATION

holiness *n* a state of spiritual soundness and unimpaired virtue <the *holiness* of the saints>

syn saintliness, sanctity

rel blessedness, divineness, divinity, sacredness; consecration, devotion, devoutness, piety, piousness, spirituality

holler *vb syn* see CALL 1

hollo *vb syn* see CALL 1

hollow *adj* 1 having a muffled or reverberating quality <had a deep *hollow* gloomy voice>

syn cavernous, reverberant, sepulchral

rel echoing, resonant, resounding, reverberating, sounding

con dead, dull, flat, toneless

2 *syn* see VAIN 1

hollow *n* 1 *syn* see DEPRESSION 2

2 *syn* see HOLE 3

holocaust *n syn* see FIRE 1

holy *adj* 1 dedicated to the service of or set apart by religion <pilgrimages to *holy* places>

syn blessed, consecrated, hallowed, sacred, sanctified, unprofane; *compare* SACRED 2

rel adored, glorified, revered, reverenced, venerated, worshiped; divine, religious, spiritual

2 *syn* see SAINTLY

ant unholy

3 *syn* see DEVOUT

‖**Holy Joe** *n syn* see CLERGYMAN

holy place *n syn* see SHRINE

Holy Writ *n syn* see BIBLE

homage *n syn* see HONOR 1

home *n* 1 *syn* see HABITATION 2

2 *syn* see HABITAT

3 *syn* see COUNTRY

home *adj* 1 *syn* see DOMESTIC 1

2 *syn* see DOMESTIC 2

homeland *n syn* see COUNTRY

homely *adj* 1 *syn* see PLAIN 1

rel commonplace, familiar, intimate

2 *syn* see PLAIN 5

idiom homely as a mud (*or* hedge) fence, homely enough to sour milk

ant comely

homicidal *adj syn* see MURDEROUS

homicide *n* 1 *syn* see MURDERER

2 *syn* see MURDER

homilize *vb syn* see PREACH 1

hominine *adj syn* see HUMAN

hominoid *n syn* see ANTHROPOID

homo *n syn* see HOMOSEXUAL

homoerotic *adj syn* see HOMOSEXUAL

homophile *adj syn* see HOMOSEXUAL

Homo sapiens *n syn* see MANKIND

homosexual *adj* relating to or exhibiting sexual desire toward a member of one's own sex < *homosexual* acts between consenting adults>

syn gay, homoerotic, homophile, inverted, queer, uranian

rel androgynous, bisexual, epicene; transvestite; lesbian, sapphic; effeminate, swishy

---

syn synonym(s)	*rel* related word(s)
ant antonym(s)	*con* contrasted word(s)
idiom idiomatic equivalent(s)	
‖ use limited; if in doubt, see a dictionary	

homosexual *n* one who is inclined to or practices homosexuality <a bar frequented by *homosexuals*>
syn fag, faggot, ||fruit, homo, invert, queer, uranian, uranist
rel transvestite; fairy, nance, nancy, pansy, queen, ||swish; dike, lesbian, sapphist; pederast, sodomite

homunculus *n syn* see DWARF

honcho *n syn* see LEADER 2

hone *vb syn* see SHARPEN

honed *adj syn* see SHARP 1

honest *adj* 1 *syn* see GENUINE 3
rel reliable, unaffected, unimpeachable
2 *syn* see UPRIGHT 2
rel candid, forthright, frank, open, plain; dispassionate, objective; truthful, veracious
ant dishonest

honestness *n syn* see HONESTY
ant dishonesty

honesty *n* uprightness as evidenced in character and actions <he was generally known as a person of scrupulous *honesty*>
syn honestness, honor, honorableness, incorruption, integrity
rel conscientiousness, justness, probity, scrupulousness, uprightness; dependability, reliability, trustworthiness; goodness, morality, rectitude, virtue
con deceitfulness, mendaciousness, mendacity, untruthfulness; deceit, duplicity, guile
ant dishonesty

honey *n* 1 *syn* see SWEETHEART 1
2 *syn* see GIRL FRIEND 2

honey *vb syn* see SUGARCOAT 1

honey (up) *vb syn* see FAWN

honeybunch *n syn* see SWEETHEART 1

honeyed *adj syn* see MELLIFLUOUS

honky-tonk *n syn* see DIVE

honor *n* 1 respect or esteem shown one as his due or claimed by one as a right <received the *honor* due his rank>
syn deference, homage, obeisance, reverence
rel admiration, esteem; adoration, adulation, devotion, veneration, worship; acknowledgment, compliment, recognition, regard, respect
con contempt, despite, disdain, scorn; disregard, neglect, slighting
ant dishonor
2 an evidence or symbol of distinction <received many *honors* for his devoted public service>
syn accolade, award, badge, bays, decoration, distinction, kudos, laurels
rel deference, esteem, respect; admiration, approval
3 *syn* see HONESTY
con disgrace, ignominy, shame
ant dishonor, dishonorableness

honor *vb syn* see EXALT 1
ant dishonor

honorable *adj* 1 deserving of or entitled to honor (as because of rank, achievements, or service) <medicine is an *honorable* profession>
syn estimable, high-principled, noble, sterling, worthy; *compare* VENERABLE 1
rel august, illustrious, reverend, venerable, worshipful

ant dishonorable
2 *syn* see UPRIGHT 2
ant dishonorable

honorableness *n syn* see HONESTY
ant dishonor, dishonorableness

||**hooch** *n* 1 *syn* see LIQUOR 2
2 *syn* see MOONSHINE 2

||**hood** *n syn* see THUG 1

hoodlum *n syn* see THUG 1

hoodoo *n syn* see JINX

hoodwink *vb syn* see DUPE

hooey *n syn* see NONSENSE 2

hoof *vb syn* see WALK 1

hoof (it) *vb syn* see DANCE 1

hoofer *n syn* see DANCER

hook *vb syn* see STEAL 1

||**hooker** *n syn* see PROSTITUTE

||**hookshop** *n syn* see BROTHEL

hookup *n syn* see ASSOCIATION 1

hooligan *n syn* see THUG 1

||**hoosegow** *n syn* see JAIL

hoosier *n syn* see RUSTIC

hoot *n* 1 *syn* see RASPBERRY
2 *syn* see PARTICLE

||**hootenanny** *n syn* see DOODAD

hop *vb* 1 *syn* see SKIP 1
2 *syn* see JUMP 1

||**hop** *n syn* see DRUG 2

hope *vb syn* see EXPECT 1

hope *n syn* see TRUST 1

hopeful *adj* 1 full of hope or inclined to hope <the candidate was *hopeful* of winning>
syn hoping; *compare* CONFIDENT 1, EXPECTANT 1, OPTIMISTIC
rel anticipative, assured, satisfied, secure; cheerful, content, easy, undisturbed; fond, optimistic, Pollyannaish, rose-colored, sanguine, upbeat
con doubtful, insecure, pessimistic, uncertain; discouraged, disheartened, gloomy, glum
ant hopeless
2 exhibiting qualities that inspire hope <a *hopeful* prospect for improvement>
syn couleur de rose, encouraging, likely, promiseful, promising, roseate, rose-colored, rosy
rel advantageous, auspicious, propitious; bright, cheering, cheery, golden, halcyon, happy, sunny; budding, up-and-coming
con discouraging, disheartening, dismal, dreary, gloomy, pessimistic
ant hopeless

hopeful *n syn* see CANDIDATE

hopeless *adj* 1 *syn* see DESPONDENT
rel gloomy, glum, morose
con cheerful; assured, confident, optimistic, sanguine, sure
ant hopeful
2 offering no prospect of change for the better <his case was *hopeless* and beyond all human aid>
syn cureless, immedicable, impossible, incurable, insanable, irremediable, irreparable, uncorrectable, uncurable, unrecoverable
rel insoluble; incorrigible, irredeemable
idiom beyond hope (*or* remedy *or* repair), beyond human aid
con correctable, curable, medicable, remediable, reparable
ant hopeful

hoper *n syn* see OPTIMIST
hoping *adj syn* see HOPEFUL 1
hop-o'-my-thumb *n syn* see DWARF
hopped–up *adj syn* see DRUGGED
hopping *adj syn* see BUSTLING
horde *n syn* see CROWD 1
horizon *n syn* see KEN
horn in *vb* 1 *syn* see MEDDLE
  2 *syn* see INTRUDE 1
‖**horning** *n syn* see SHIVAREE
hornswoggle *vb syn* see DUPE
horrible *adj* 1 *syn* see GHASTLY 1
  rel abhorrent, abominable, detestable, hateful; loathsome, obnoxious, offensive, repulsive, revolting
  con gratifying, pleasing, soothing
  2 *syn* see FEARFUL 3
  3 *syn* see OFFENSIVE
horrid *adj* 1 *syn* see GHASTLY 1
  2 *syn* see HATEFUL 2
  3 *syn* see OFFENSIVE
horrific *adj syn* see FEARFUL 3
horrify *vb syn* see DISMAY 1
horrifying *adj syn* see GHASTLY 1
horror *n* 1 *syn* see FEAR 1
  rel distress, pain, shock, throe, wrench
  2. *syn* see ABOMINATION 2
hors d'oeuvre *n syn* see APPETIZER
horse *n syn* see SAWHORSE
horse *vb syn* see CUT UP 2
‖**horsefeathers** *n pl syn* see NONSENSE 2
horse opera *n syn* see WESTERN
horseplay *n* rough or boisterous play < their friendly *horseplay* almost ended in tragedy >
  syn fooling, high jinks, roughhouse, roughhousing, rowdiness, skylarking
  rel buffoonery, clowning
horseplay *vb syn* see CUT UP 2
horse sense *n syn* see SENSE 6
hospice *n syn* see HOTEL
hospitable *adj syn* see SOCIAL
  ant inhospitable
host *n syn* see MULTITUDE 1
hostage *n syn* see PLEDGE
  rel guaranty, security, surety
hostel *n syn* see HOTEL
hostelry *n syn* see HOTEL
hostile *adj* 1 marked by lack of friendliness or by opposition < takes a *hostile* view of a tax increase > < *hostile* tribes >
  syn ill, inimicable, inimical, unfriendly
  rel argumentative, competitive, contrary, dim, disaffected, disapproving, opposed, opposite, unfavorable; dour; sour; bellicose, belligerent, contentious, pugnacious; militant, warlike
  con amicable, benign, friendly
  ant unhostile
  2 *syn* see BITTER 3
hostility *n syn* see ENMITY
hot *adj* 1 marked by a notable amount of heat < a *hot* day >
  syn ardent, baking, blistering, boiling, broiling, burning, fiery, heated, red-hot, scalding, scorching, sizzling, sultry, sweltering, sweltry, torrid, white-hot

  rel febrile, fevered, feverish, feverous, hectic; summery, tropic, tropical; mild, warm
  idiom hot as a firecracker (*or* furnace), hot as an oven, hot as hell
  con chilly, cool, frigid, icy
  ant cold
  2 *syn* see LUSTFUL 2
  3 *syn* see MARVELOUS 2
  4 *syn* see CONTRABAND
hot air *n syn* see NONSENSE 2
hotbed *n syn* see BREEDING GROUND
hot–blooded *adj syn* see IMPASSIONED
  con callous, hard, unfeeling
  ant cold-blooded
hotchpotch *n syn* see MISCELLANY 1
hot dog *n syn* see FRANKFURTER
hotel *n* an establishment for the lodging and entertainment especially of transients < spent their vacation at a resort *hotel* >
  syn auberge, caravansary, hospice, hostel, hostelry, inn, lodge, public house, roadhouse, tavern
  rel boardinghouse, lodging house, pension, rooming house, spa; boatel, motel, motor inn; ‖fleabag, ‖flophouse
hotfoot *adv syn* see PELL-MELL
hotfoot *vb syn* see HURRY 2
hotheaded *adj syn* see RASH 1
  ant cool
hothouse *n syn* see BREEDING GROUND
hot spot *n syn* see NIGHTCLUB
hot–tempered *adj* 1 *syn* see ILL-TEMPERED
  2 *syn* see IRASCIBLE
hot water *n* 1 *syn* see PREDICAMENT
  2 *syn* see TROUBLE 3
hound *n* 1 *syn* see DOG 1
  2 *syn* see ADDICT
hound *vb syn* see BAIT 2
house *n* 1 *syn* see HABITATION 2
  2 *syn* see FAMILY 2
  3 *syn* see FAMILY 1
  4 *syn* see ENTERPRISE 3
house *vb* 1 *syn* see HARBOR 1
  2 *syn* see HARBOR 2
housebreak *vb* to commit an act of breaking open and entering with a felonious purpose the dwelling of another by day or night < was arrested again in September for *housebreaking* >
  syn break in; *compare* BURGLARIZE, ROB 1
  rel knock over, rob; ransack, rifle
  idiom break and enter
household *n syn* see FAMILY 2
household *adj syn* see DOMESTIC 1
housemaid *n syn* see MAID 2
houseman *n syn* see BOUNCER 2
house of God *syn* see HOUSE OF WORSHIP
house of prayer *syn* see HOUSE OF WORSHIP
house of worship a building for religious exercises < there are many *houses of worship* in this city >
  syn church, house of God, house of prayer, tabernacle, temple
  rel abbey, basilica, bethel, cathedral, chantry, chapel, conventicle, ‖fane, ‖kirk, masjid, meetinghouse, minster, mosque, oratory, pagoda, sanctuary, shrine, stupa, synagogue

---

syn synonym(s)	**rel** related word(s)
ant antonym(s)	**con** contrasted word(s)
idiom idiomatic equivalent(s)	
‖ use limited; if in doubt, see a dictionary	

idiom the Lord's house

housing *n syn* see SHELTER 2

hovel *n* a small wretched dwelling place < migrants forced to live in *hovels* >
syn burrow, hole; *compare* HUT
rel hut, hutch, shack, shanty; pigpen, pigsty, sty

hover *vb* 1 *syn* see FLIT 2
2 *syn* see HANG 3

howbeit *adv syn* see HOWEVER

howbeit *conj syn* see THOUGH

however *conj syn* see ONLY

however *adv* in spite of that < I accept your decision; I cannot, *however*, approve of it >
syn after all, howbeit, nevertheless, nonetheless, notwithstanding, per contra, still, still and all, though, withal, yet
idiom all the same, be that as it may, for all that, on the other hand

howl *vb* 1 to utter or emit a loud sustained doleful sound or outcry < the dogs *howled* through the night >
syn bay, quest, ululate, wail
rel bark, growl, yelp; blubber, cry, keen, weep, whimper; bawl, squall, yowl
2 *syn* see YELL 2
3 *syn* see BAWL 2

howl *n syn* see RIOT 2

hoyden *n syn* see TOMBOY

hub *n syn* see CENTER 2

hubbub *n* 1 *syn* see DIN
2 *syn* see COMMOTION 4

‖**hubby** *n syn* see HUSBAND

hubristic *adj syn* see PROUD 1

huckster *n syn* see PEDDLER

huckster *vb* 1 *syn* see HAGGLE 2
2 *syn* see PEDDLE 2

huddle *vb* 1 *syn* see CROUCH
2 *syn* see CONFER 2

huddle (on) *vb syn* see DON 1

huddle *n syn* see CONFUSION 3

hue *n syn* see COLOR 1

huff *vb* 1 *syn* see PANT 1
2 *syn* see IRRITATE

huff *n syn* see OFFENSE 2

huffy *adj* 1 *syn* see PROUD 1
2 *syn* see IRRITABLE

hug *vb syn* see EMBRACE 1

huge *adj* exceedingly or excessively large < *huge* corporations > < ate a *huge* dinner >
syn Antaean, behemothic, Brobdingnagian, Bunyanesque, colossal, cyclopean, dinosauric, elephantine, enormous, gargantuan, giant, gigantean, gigantesque, gigantic, Herculean, heroic, immense, jumbo, leviathan, lusty, mammoth, massive, massy, mastodonic, mighty, monster, monstrous, monumental, mountainous, planetary, prodigious, pythonic, ‖swapping, Titan, titanic, tremendous, unfathomed, untold, vast, walloping, whacking, whaling, whopping; *compare* GRAND 1
rel bulky, extensive, great, immeasurable, magnificent, towering; outsize, oversize
con diminutive, little, miniature, minute, petite, small, teeny, tiny, wee, weeny

hugely *adv syn* see VERY 1

hugeness *n syn* see ENORMITY 2

hugger-mugger *n* 1 *syn* see SECRECY
2 *syn* see CLUTTER 2

hugger-mugger *adv syn* see SECRETLY

hugger-mugger *adj syn* see SECRET 1

hugger-muggery *n syn* see SECRECY

hull *n* an outer covering of a fruit or seed < peanut *hulls* >
syn case, husk, pod, shell, shuck, skin, ‖slough
rel chaff; bark, peel, rind

hull *vb syn* see SHUCK

hullabaloo *n syn* see DIN

hum *vb* to make a low prolonged sound < the wind *hummed* in the chimney >
syn bombinate, ‖bum, bumble, buzz, drone, ‖sowf, strum, thrum
rel moan, murmur, purr, vibrate, whisper
con howl, roar, shriek

human *adj* of, relating to, or characteristic of mankind < problems of *human* relationships >
syn hominine, mortal
rel anthropological, ethnologic, ethological; anthropoid, hominid, hominoid
con angelic, divine, superhuman; animal, brute, subhuman

human *n* a member of the human race < every *human* has a right to live >
syn being, body, ‖character, creature, individual, life, man, mortal, party, person, personage, soul, wight; *compare* MAN 3, MANKIND

humane *adj syn* see CHARITABLE 1
rel chickenhearted, compassionate, kindhearted, soft-hearted; benevolent, gentle, kind, kindly, mild
ant inhuman, inhumane

humanitarian *adj syn* see CHARITABLE 1

humanity *n syn* see MANKIND

humankind *n syn* see MANKIND

humanoid *adj syn* see ANTHROPOID

humble *adj* 1 lacking all signs of pride, aggressiveness, or self-assertiveness < accepted his success with *humble* appreciation >
syn lowly, meek, modest, unassuming
rel simple, unobtrusive, unostentatious, unpretentious; acquiescent, compliant, resigned; quiet, subdued, submissive
con ostentatious, pretentious, showy; vain, vainglorious; arrogant, disdainful, haughty, lordly, overbearing, proud, toplofty
ant conceited
2 *syn* see IGNOBLE 1

humble *vb* to make lower in status, prestige, or esteem < his devotion to duty *humbled* his critics >
syn abase, bemean, cast down, debase, degrade, demean, humiliate, lower, sink
rel chagrin, mortify; abash, discomfit, embarrass
idiom bring low, take down a peg or two
con aggrandize, exalt, magnify

humbug *n* 1 *syn* see IMPOSTURE
2 *syn* see IMPOSTOR
3 *syn* see NONSENSE 2

humbug *vb syn* see DECEIVE

humdinger *n syn* ‖DILLY, ‖corker, crackerjack, ‖daisy, dandy, jim-dandy, ‖lulu, nifty, peach, ‖pip

humdrum *adj syn* see DULL 9

humdrum *n syn* see MONOTONY

humid *adj* containing or characterized by an uncomfortable amount of atmospheric warmth and moisture < a *humid* climate >

syn mucky, muggy, soggy, sticky, sultry; *compare* STIFLING 1, STUFFY 1

rel clammy, dank, sodden; close, oppressive, stuffy; sweltering

con arid, dry; cool, crisp, fresh

humiliate *vb syn* see HUMBLE

humming *adj syn* see BUSTLING

humor *n* **1** *syn* see DISPOSITION 3

2 *syn* see MOOD 1

3 *syn* see CAPRICE

4 that quality or element which appeals to a sense of the ludicrous or incongruous < see the *humor* in a situation >

syn comedy, comicality, comicalness, drollery, drollness, funniness, humorousness, wittiness

rel jocosity, jocularity, jocundity, jocundness; flippancy, levity, lightness; banter, chaffing, jesting, joking, kidding

con earnestness, seriousness, solemnity; depth, profundity

5 something that is or is designed to be humorous < his heavy *humor* fell flat >

syn wit

rel banter, chitchat, pleasantry, repartee

6 *syn* see WIT 5

ant humorlessness

humor *vb* **1** *syn* see INDULGE 1

2 *syn* see BABY

humorist *n* **1** *syn* see WAG 1

2 a person noted for or specializing in humor < a writer best known as a *humorist* >

syn comedian, comic, droll, funnyman, jester, joker, jokester, quipster, wag, wit

rel buffoon, card, clown, cutup, gagman, gagster, jokesmith, merry-andrew, prankster, punster, zany; banterer, kidder

humorous *adj syn* see WITTY

humorousness *n syn* see HUMOR 4

humorsome *adj syn* see MOODY

‖**hump** *vb syn* see CARRY 1

hunch *vb syn* see CROUCH

hunch *n syn* see LUMP 1

hunger *vb syn* see LONG

hungry *adj* feeling distressed from lack of food < a group of *hungry* children >

syn famished, ‖peckish, ravenous, starved, starving

rel rapacious, voracious

con full, glutted, gorged, sated, satiated

ant surfeited

hunk *n syn* see LUMP 1

hunker (down) *vb syn* see SQUAT

hunkers *n pl syn* see BUTTOCKS

hunks *n pl but sing or pl in constr syn* see MISER

hunky–dory *adj syn* see MARVELOUS 2

Hunnic *adj syn* see BARBARIAN 1

Hunnish *adj syn* see BARBARIAN 1

hunt *vb* **1** to search for or pursue (game or prey) for the purpose of capturing or killing < *hunted* deer in bow-and-arrow season only >

syn chase, run

rel dog, ferret, hawk, hound; course, drive, stalk, start, still-hunt, track; capture, kill, snare; gun, shoot

idiom go hunting

2 *syn* see SEEK 1

hunt (down *or* out *or* up) *vb syn* see RUMMAGE 3

hunting *n* the act or practice of seeking and taking wild and especially game animals < lived by *hunting* and fishing >

syn chase, venery

rel angling, coursing, falconry, fishing, gunning, hawking, shooting

hurdle *n syn* see OBSTACLE

hurdle *vb* **1** *syn* see CLEAR 8

2 *syn* see JUMP 1

3 *syn* see OVERCOME 1

hurl *vb syn* see THROW 1

hurly–burly *n syn* see COMMOTION 4

hurrah *n* **1** *syn* see PASSION 6

2 *syn* see COMMOTION 3

3 *syn* see ARGUMENT 2

hurricane *n* a violent rotating storm or system of winds originating in the tropics and often moving into temperate latitudes < the *hurricane* struck the coast early today >

syn tropical cyclone, tropical storm, typhoon, ‖willy-willy; *compare* TORNADO, WHIRLWIND 1

rel williwaw

hurried *adj syn* see PRECIPITATE 1

ant unhurried

hurriedness *n syn* see HASTE 2

hurry *vb* **1** *syn* see SPEED 3

2 to proceed or move with dispatch < *hurry* home after school >

syn barrel, barrelhouse, beeline, bucket, bullet, bustle, ‖dust, fleet, flit, fly, haste, hasten, highball, hotfoot, hustle, ‖nip, pelt, rock, rocket, run, rush, scoot, scour, ‖skeet, skin, smoke, speed, stave, ‖tatter, whirl, whish, whisk, whiz, zip; *compare* RUSH 1

rel jog, peg, skelp, trot; bowl (along), breeze; dig in; post

idiom get a move on, go (*or* move) like lightning, make tracks, step on it, step on the gas

con creep, dally, dawdle, drag, lag, linger, loiter, poke, saunter, stroll

hurry *n syn* see HASTE 1

hurry–scurry *adv syn* see PELL-MELL

hurt *vb* **1** *syn* see INJURE 1

rel abuse, afflict, mistreat, misuse

ant benefit

2 *syn* see INJURE 3

3 *syn* see DISTRESS 2

4 to experience or be the seat of sharp physical distress < my arm still *hurts* >

syn ache, pain, ‖suffer; *compare* SMART

hurt *n syn* see INJURY 1

hurtful *adj* **1** *syn* see HARMFUL

con harmless, innocuous

2 *syn* see PAINFUL 1

hurting *adj syn* see PAINFUL 1

husband *n* the male partner in a marriage < neglected his responsibilities as a *husband* >

syn ‖hubby, lord, man, ‖master, mister, Mr., ‖old man

rel consort, helpmate, helpmeet, mate, other half, spouse; benedict, bridegroom

husbanding *n syn* see CONSERVATION 1

ant squandering

husbandry *n* **1** *syn* see ECONOMY

---

syn synonym(s)   *rel* related word(s)
ant antonym(s)   *con* contrasted word(s)
idiom idiomatic equivalent(s)
‖ use limited; if in doubt, see a dictionary

2 syn see AGRICULTURE

hush vb syn see SILENCE

hush (up) vb syn see SUPPRESS 3

hush adj syn see STILL 3

hush n 1 syn see QUIET 1
2 syn see SECRECY

hushed adj 1 syn see CALM 1
2 syn see PRIVATE 2

hushful adj syn see STILL 3

hush–hush adj syn see SECRET 1

hush–hush n syn see SECRECY

husk n syn see HULL

husk vb syn see SHUCK

husky adj syn see HOARSE 1

husky adj 1 big and muscular <a *husky* man carried in the trunks>
syn beefy, burly, hefty
rel brawny, muscular, well-built; stalwart, stout, strapping, strong, sturdy; Herculean, mighty, powerful; Bunyanesque, gigantic
con delicate, fragile, frail; puny, scrawny, slight; elfin; mousey
2 syn see LARGE 1

hussy n 1 syn see WANTON
2 syn see MINX

hustle vb 1 syn see PUSH 2
2 syn see HURRY 2

hustle n syn see HASTE 1

hustler n 1 an alert enterprising individual <he's a *hustler*, eager to get ahead in the world>
syn dynamo, go-getter, live wire, peeler, rustler, self-starter
rel humdinger, hummer; new broom; doer, powerhouse
idiom busy bee
con dawdler, idler; slow coach, slowpoke, stick-in-the-mud
2 syn see PROSTITUTE

hustling adj syn see BUSTLING

hut n a small, simply constructed dwelling often for temporary or intermittent occupancy <the shepherds lived in *huts* in the summer>
syn ‖box, cabin ‖caboose, camp, cot, cottage, lodge, shack, shanty; compare BUILDING, EDIFICE, HOVEL
rel cabana, chalet, crib, dacha, hovel, hutch, lean-to, shed, summer house

hut vb syn see HARBOR 2

Hyblaean adj syn see MELLIFLUOUS

hybrid n an offspring produced by parents of different strains, breeds, varieties, species, or genera <the mule is a *hybrid* of the ass and the horse>
syn bastard, cross, crossbred, crossbreed, half blood, half-breed, mongrel, mule
rel incross, incrossbred, outcross; combination, composite, mixture
con pureblood, purebred, thoroughbred

hybridize vb syn see CROSS 4

hydrant n syn see FAUCET

‖**hydro** n syn see SPA 1

hydroponics n the growing of plants in nutrient solution and without soil <tomatoes grown by *hydroponics*>
syn aquiculture, nutriculture
idiom soilless agriculture

hygienic adj syn see HEALTHFUL
ant unhygienic

hymeneal adj syn see MATRIMONIAL

hymn n syn see SONG 2

hymn vb 1 syn see PRAISE 2
2 syn see SING

hypaethral adj syn see OUTDOOR

hyperbole n syn see EXAGGERATION
con depreciation, minimization, understatement
ant litotes

hypercritical adj syn see CRITICAL 1

hypercriticize vb syn see QUIBBLE 1

hypnotic adj syn see SOPORIFIC 1

hypocorism n syn see NICKNAME

hypocrisy n the pretense or affectation of having virtues, principles, or beliefs that one does not actually have <political *hypocrisy*>
syn cant, hypocriticalness, pecksniffery, pharisaicalness, pharisaism, sanctimoniousness, sanctimony, sham, Tartuffery, Tartuffism
rel pietism, religiosity; casuistry, glibness, insincerity, self-righteousness, unctuousness; charlatanry, humbug, quackery
con candidness, fairness, openness; honesty, probity, truthfulness
ant sincerity

hypocrite n one who affects virtues, qualities, or attitudes he does not have <don't be a *hypocrite*—if you don't approve, say so>
syn dissembler, dissimulator, lip server, pharisee, Tartuffe, whited sepulcher
rel pietist; actor, attitudinizer, bluffer, charlatan, faker, four-flusher, fraud, humbug, impostor, masquerader, phony, poser, poseur, pretender, quack, sham

hypocritical adj 1 characterized by hypocrisy <*hypocritical* compliments>
syn canting, pecksniffian, pharisaic, pharisaical, sanctimonious, self-righteous
rel goody-goody, holier-than-thou, moralistic, pietistic, religiose; casuistic; affected, insincere; bland, glib, mealymouthed, oily, smooth, smooth-spoken, smooth-tongued, unctuous
con honest, open, straightforward
ant sincere
2 syn see INSINCERE

hypocriticalness n syn see HYPOCRISY
ant sincerity

hypostatize vb syn see MATERIALIZE 2

hypothesis n syn see THEORY 1

hypothetical adj 1 syn see SUPPOSED 1
rel doubtful, problematic
2 syn see ABSTRACT 1

I

icky *adj syn* see OFFENSIVE

iconographic *adj syn* see PICTORIAL 1

icy *adj* **1** *syn* see COLD 1
ant fiery
2 *syn* see COLD 2
ant fiery

idea *n* what exists in the mind as a representation (as of something comprehended) or as a formulation (as of a plan) < that's not my *idea* of a good time >
syn apprehension, conceit, concept, conception, image, impression, intellection, notion, perception, thought
rel assumption, belief, conclusion, conviction, estimation, feeling, inclination, judgment, opinion, persuasion, presumption, reaction, reflection, sentiment, view; conjecture, guess, hypothesis, speculation, supposition, surmise, suspicion, theory; caprice, fancy, fantasy, vagary, whim, whimsy; brainstorm, inspiration

ideal *adj* **1** *syn* see ABSTRACT 1
ant actual
2 *syn* see CONCEPTUAL
3 constituting a standard (as of perfection or excellence) < the *ideal* man of letters >
syn flawless, indefectible, model
rel archetypal, archetypical, prototypal, prototypical
con average, normal, representative, typical
4 *syn* see PERFECT 3
5 *syn* see TYPICAL 1

ideal *n* **1** *syn* see MODEL 2
2 *syn* see PARAGON

idealist *n syn* see DREAMER

idealist *adj syn* see IDEALISTIC

idealistic *adj* characterized by idealism < made an *idealistic* speech on human rights >
syn idealist, utopian, visionary
rel impractical, poetical, quixotic, romantic, starry, starry-eyed, unrealistic
con empirical, matter-of-fact, practical, pragmatic, rational, realistic
ant unidealistic

ideational *adj syn* see CONCEPTUAL

identic *adj syn* see SAME 2
ant nonidentical

identical *adj* **1** *syn* see SAME 1
2 *syn* see SAME 2
ant nonidentical

identicalness *n syn* see IDENTITY 1

identification *n syn* see RECOGNITION 1

identify *vb* to establish the identity of < the culprit was *identified* by his fingerprints >
syn determinate, diagnose, diagnosticate, distinguish, finger, pinpoint, place, recognize, spot

rel find; determine, establish, make out, pick out, select, separate (out)

identity *n* **1** the quality of being the same in all that constitutes the objective reality of separate things < the *identity* of the two texts is exact >
syn identicalness, oneness, sameness, selfsameness
rel agreement, likeness, resemblance, semblance, similarity, similitude; correspondence, equality, equivalence; uniformity
con dissimilarity, dissimilitude, unlikeness, unsimilarity
ant nonidentity
2 *syn* see INDIVIDUALITY 4

ideologue *n syn* see DREAMER

ideology *n* an overall view of or attitude toward life < an *ideology* based on tolerance >
syn credo, creed, weltanschauung
rel outlook, philosophy, view

idiom *n syn* see LANGUAGE 1

idiosyncratic *adj* **1** *syn* see CHARACTERISTIC
2 *syn* see STRANGE 4

idiot *n* **1** *syn* see FOOL 1
2 *syn* see FOOL 2
3 *syn* see FOOL 4
4 *syn* see DUNCE

idle *adj* **1** *syn* see VAIN 1
2 *syn* see VACANT 4
3 *syn* see INACTIVE
ant busy

idle *vb* to spend time in idleness < people *idling* in the park >
syn ‖brogue, bum, dawdle, diddle, diddle-daddle, drone, goldbrick, ‖goof (off), ‖lallygag, laze, lazy, loaf, loiter, loll, lounge
rel relax, repose, rest; amble, linger, mooch, mosey, saunter, stroll, tarry; hang around, sit around, sit back, sit by
idiom dog it, kill time, lie around, mark time

idleheaded *adj syn* see FOOLISH 2

idleness *n syn* see SLOTH 1

idler *n syn* see SLUGGARD

idolatry *n syn* see ADORATION

idolization *n syn* see ADORATION

idolize *vb syn* see ADORE 3
idiom worship the ground one walks on

iffy *adj syn* see UNCERTAIN 1

ignis fatuus *n syn* see DELUSION 1

ignitable *adj syn* see COMBUSTIBLE 1

ignite *vb syn* see LIGHT 1

ignited *adj syn* see BURNING 1

ignoble *adj* **1** belonging to or characteristic of socially or economically inferior classes < a person of *ignoble* antecedents >
syn base, baseborn, humble, low, lowborn, lowly, mean, plebeian, unennobled, unwashed

---

syn synonym(s)   *rel* related word(s)
ant antonym(s)   *con* contrasted word(s)
idiom idiomatic equivalent(s)
‖ use limited; if in doubt, see a dictionary

rel coarse, common, homely, inferior, inglorious, modest, ordinary, peasant, plain, poor, popular, simple, vulgar

con highborn, highbred, wellborn, wellbred; eminent, high, lofty, proud, superior

ant noble

2 *syn* see BASE 3

ant noble

ignominious *adj syn* see DISREPUTABLE 1

ignominy *n syn* see DISGRACE

rel contempt, despite, disdain, scorn; chagrin, mortification

con glory, honor; esteem, respect

ignoramus *n syn* see DUNCE

ignorance *n* 1 the state of being unlearned < the blight of *ignorance* >

syn benightedness, illiteracy

rel callowness, greenness, inexperience, naiveté, rawness, simpleness, simplicity, uncouthness, uncultivation, unsophistication; empty-headedness, unintelligence, witlessness; know-nothingism, philistinism

con education, enlightenment, erudition, learning, literacy

2 the state of being unaware or uninformed < *ignorance* of the law >

syn innocence, inscience, nescience, unacquaintance, unacquaintedness, unawareness, unfamiliarity, unknowingness

con acquaintance, acquaintanceship, experience; awareness, familiarity, knowledgeableness

ignorant *adj* 1 lacking knowledge or education < an *ignorant* boy with no taste for school >

syn benighted, empty-headed, illiterate, know-nothing, rude, uneducated, uninstructed, unlettered, unschooled, untaught, untutored

rel lowbrow, uncultured, unintellectual; callow, green, inexperienced; crude, gross, raw, uncouth; ingenuous, naive, simple, unsophisticated

con educated, erudite, learned, literate

2 lacking information on or awareness of something < was *ignorant* of the circumstances surrounding the affair >

syn incognizant, inconversant, oblivious, unacquainted, unaware, unfamiliar, uninformed, uninstructed, unknowing, unwitting

idiom in the dark

con aware, conscious, conversant, informed, knowing, knowledgeable

3 *syn* see BACKWARD 5

ignore *vb syn* see NEGLECT

rel avoid, evade

ilk *n syn* see TYPE

ill *adj* 1 *syn* see EVIL 5

ant good

2 *syn* see HARMFUL

3 *syn* see SICK 1

4 *syn* see RUDE 6

5 *syn* see HOSTILE 1

ill *n* 1 *syn* see EVIL 1

ant benefit

2 *syn* see DISEASE 1

ill-adapted *adj syn* see UNFIT 1

ill-advised *adj* 1 *syn* see RASH 1

2 *syn* see INADVISABLE

ant well-advised

3 *syn* see UNWISE

ant well-advised

illation *n* 1 *syn* see INFERENCE 1

2 *syn* see INFERENCE 2

ill-behaved *adj syn* see NAUGHTY 1

ill-boding *adj syn* see OMINOUS

ill-bred *adj* 1 *syn* see BOORISH

ant well-bred

2 *syn* see RUDE 6

ant well-bred, well-mannered

ill-chosen *adj syn* see INFELICITOUS

ill-defined *adj syn* see FAINT 2

ant well-defined

illegal *adj syn* see UNLAWFUL

rel banned, forbidden, interdicted, prohibited, proscribed, outlawed, unauthorized, unlicensed, unwarranted; felonious; contraband, hot; actionable, irregular

con authorized, lawful, licensed, licit, permitted, regular, right

ant legal

illegality *n* the quality or state of being illegal < the *illegality* of an act >

syn illegitimacy, illicitness, unlawfulness

rel badness, impropriety, wrongness

con lawfulness, legitimacy, licitness; propriety

ant legality

illegible *adj* incapable of being read or deciphered < an *illegible* signature >

syn indecipherable, undecipherable, unreadable

rel faint, indistinct, obscure, unclear

ant legible, readable

illegitimacy *n* 1 the state or condition of being born out of wedlock < he accepted the fact of his *illegitimacy* >

syn bastardy, illegitimateness, supposititiousness

rel bar sinister

ant legitimacy, legitimateness

2 *syn* see ILLEGALITY

ant legitimacy, legitimateness

illegitimate *adj* 1 not recognized by law as lawful offspring < an *illegitimate* child >

syn baseborn, bastard, fatherless, misbegotten, natural, spurious, supposititious, unfathered

rel birthless; adulterine

ant legitimate

2 *syn* see UNLAWFUL

ant legitimate

illegitimate *n syn* see BASTARD 1

ant legitimate

illegitimateness *n syn* see ILLEGITIMACY 1

ant legitimacy, legitimateness

ill-famed *adj syn* see INFAMOUS 1

ill-fated *adj syn* see UNLUCKY

ill-favored *adj* 1 *syn* see UGLY 2

ant well-favored

2 *syn* see OBJECTIONABLE

ill-flavored *adj syn* see UNPALATABLE 1

ill-humored *adj syn* see ILL-TEMPERED

ant good-humored, good-natured

illiberal *adj* unwilling or unable to grasp the point of view of others < the *illiberal* outlook of an old-time schoolmaster >

syn bigoted, brassbound, hidebound, intolerant, narrow, narrow-minded, smallminded, unenlarged

rel biased, jaundiced, one-sided, opinionated, partial, partisan, prejudiced; grudging, little, mean, paltry, petty, small, un-

charitable, ungenerous; insular, parochial, provincial; rigid, rigorous, stringent
con broad-minded, open-minded, tolerant, unbigoted; advanced, progressive, radical
ant liberal

illicit *adj syn* see UNLAWFUL
ant licit

illicitness *n syn* see ILLEGALITY

illimitable *adj syn* see INFINITE 1
rel endless, interminable
ant limitable; limited

illiteracy *n syn* see IGNORANCE 1

illiterate *adj syn* see IGNORANT 1
ant literate; erudite

illiterate *n* one who cannot read or write < the training of adult *illiterates* >
syn analphabet
rel functional illiterate, semiliterate, subliterate
ant literate

ill-judged *adj syn* see UNWISE

ill-kempt *adj syn* see SLOVENLY 1

ill-looking *adj syn* see UGLY 2
ant good-looking, ‖well-looked

ill-mannered *adj syn* see RUDE 6
ant well-bred, well-mannered

ill-natured *adj syn* see ILL-TEMPERED
ant good-humored, good-natured

illness *n syn* see SICKNESS 1
ant health

illogical *adj* contrary to or devoid of logic < came to an *illogical* conclusion from the facts presented >
syn fallacious, invalid, irrational, mad, nonrational, reasonless, sophistic, unreasonable, unreasoned; *compare* FALSE 1
rel inconsistent; plausible, specious; unscientific, unsound; absurd, meaningless, senseless
idiom without rhyme or reason
con rational, reasonable, sensible; sane, sound, valid
ant logical

ill-omened *adj syn* see OMINOUS
ant auspicious

ill-seasoned *adj syn* see UNSEASONABLE 1
ant seasonable

ill-starred *adj syn* see UNLUCKY
rel bodeful, fateful, foreboding, ominous, portentous; baleful, malefic, malign, sinister; unfavorable, unpromising, unpropitious

ill-suited *adj syn* see UNFIT 1

ill-tempered *adj* having a bad temper < an *ill-tempered* old man >
syn bad-tempered, dyspeptic, hot-tempered, ill-humored, ill-natured, ‖rusty, tempersome
rel crabbed, surly; fractious, huffy, irritable, peevish, petulant, querulous, snappish, sour, waspish; shrewish, vixenish
con calm, easy, placid, serene, tranquil; amiable, complaisant, considerate, good-natured, kindly, obliging, tolerant
ant good-tempered, sweet-tempered, well-tempered

ill-timed *adj syn* 1 see UNSEASONABLE 1

---

syn synonym(s)   *rel* related word(s)
ant antonym(s)   *con* contrasted word(s)
idiom idiomatic equivalent(s)
‖ use limited; if in doubt, see a dictionary

---

ant seasonable
2 *syn* see IMPROPER 1

ill-treat *vb syn* see ABUSE 4
rel aggrieve, harass, harry, molest
con befriend, relieve, succor; countenance, encourage, favor, patronize

illude *vb syn* see DECEIVE

illume *vb* 1 *syn* see ILLUMINATE 1
2 *syn* see ILLUMINATE 2

illuminant *adj syn* see ENLIGHTENING

illuminate *vb* 1 to supply with physical light < a room dimly *illuminated* by firelight >
syn illume, illumine, light, lighten
rel brighten; irradiate; floodlight, highlight, spotlight; fire, ignite, kindle
con blur, cloud, darken, dim, dull, obscure, pale
2 to supply with spiritual or intellectual light < the worth of a truly *illuminating* book >
syn edify, enlighten, illume, illumine, improve, irradiate, uplift
rel better, improve; ennoble, exalt, refine; finish, mature, perfect, polish
con becloud, cloud, darken, obfuscate, obscure, overshadow, shadow
3 *syn* see CLARIFY 2
rel construe, define, dramatize, expound, express, gloss, interpret
idiom shed light on (*or* upon)
con baffle, confound, confuse, mystify, pose, puzzle, stump

illuminati *n pl syn* see INTELLIGENTSIA

illuminating *adj syn* see ENLIGHTENING

illuminative *adj syn* see ENLIGHTENING

illumine *vb* 1 *syn* see ILLUMINATE 1
2 *syn* see ILLUMINATE 2

illumining *adj syn* see ENLIGHTENING

ill-use *vb syn* see ABUSE 4
con befriend, relieve, succor; countenance, encourage, favor, patronize

illusion *n* 1 *syn* see DELUSION 1
rel invention; bubble, chimera, dream, will-o'-the-wisp; appearance, seeming, semblance
2 *syn* see PIPE DREAM

illusionist *n syn* see MAGICIAN 2

illusive *adj syn* see APPARENT 2

illusory *adj* 1 *syn* see FICTITIOUS 1
ant factual
2 *syn* see APPARENT 2
rel chimerical, fanciful, fantastic, imaginary, unreal, visionary; deceptive, delusive, delusory, misleading
con actual, real, veritable; authentic, true, valid
ant factual

illustrate *vb* 1 *syn* see CLARIFY 2
rel display, exhibit, expose, show; disclose, discover, reveal
con cloak, conceal, enshroud, mask, screen, shroud, veil
2 *syn* see EXEMPLIFY 1
rel elucidate, explain, expound, interpret; demonstrate, manifest, show; enliven, vivify
3 *syn* see REPRESENT 2
4 *syn* see SHOW 2

illustration *n* 1 *syn* see EXAMPLE 3
2 *syn* see INSTANCE

illustrational *adj syn* see PICTORIAL 1

illustrative *adj syn* see PICTORIAL 1

illustratory *adj syn* see PICTORIAL 1

illustrious *adj syn* see FAMOUS 2
rel glorious, resplendent, splendid, sublime; conspicuous, lofty, outstanding, signal, striking
con abject, inglorious, mean; disgraceful, dishonorable, ignoble, ignominious, shameful
ant infamous

illustriousness *n syn* see EMINENCE 1
ant infamy

ill will *n syn* see MALICE
rel hostility, rancor, venom
ant goodwill

image *n* 1 one strikingly like another especially in appearance or manner < she was the *image* of her mother >
syn double, picture, portrait, ringer, simulacrum, spit, spitting image
rel counterpart, equal, equivalent, match
idiom chip off the old block, dead ringer, speaking likeness, spit and image
2 *syn* see IDEA

image *vb* 1 *syn* see REPRESENT 1
2 *syn* see THINK 1
3 *syn* see REFLECT 1

imaginable *adj syn* see THINKABLE 2
ant unimaginable

imaginary *adj* 1 having no real existence but existing in imagination < elves are *imaginary* beings >
syn fancied, fanciful, imagined, notional, shadowy
rel imaginative; abstract, hypothetical, ideal, visionary; apparitional, chimerical, fantastic, figmental, hallucinatory, illusory, phantasmal, phantasmic, quixotic, spectral; unreal, unsubstantial
con genuine, true, valid
ant actual, real
2 *syn* see FICTITIOUS 1
ant actual, real

imagination *n* the power or function of the mind by which mental images are formed or the exercise of that power < children have great *imagination* >
syn fancy, fantasy (*or* phantasy), imaginativeness
rel creativity, inspiration, invention, inventiveness, visualization
con literalness, matter-of-factness, prosaism, unimaginativeness

imaginativeness *n syn* see IMAGINATION
ant unimaginativeness

imagine *vb* 1 *syn* see THINK 1
2 *syn* see UNDERSTAND 3

imagined *adj syn* see IMAGINARY 1
con known, recognized, seen

imbecile *adj syn* see RETARDED

imbecile *n* 1 *syn* see FOOL 4
2 *syn* see FOOL 1

imbibe *vb* 1 *syn* see ABSORB 1
2 *syn* see DRINK 1
3 *syn* see DRINK 3

imbricate *vb syn* see OVERLAP

imbroglio *n syn* see QUARREL

imbrued *adj syn* see BLOODY 1

imbue *vb syn* see INFUSE 1

imitate *vb* 1 *syn* see COPY
2 *syn* see MIMIC

imitation *adj syn* see ARTIFICIAL 2
ant real

imitation *n* something made or produced as an often inferior likeness of something

else < usually wore *imitations* of her costly jewels >
syn copy, ersatz, simulacrum
rel counterfeit, fake, forgery, phony, sham, simulation; counterpart, duplicate, replica, reproduction; likeness, semblance
ant original

imitative *adj* 1 *syn* see ONOMATOPOEIC
2 *syn* see SLAVISH 3

immaculate *adj* 1 *syn* see CHASTE
ant maculate
2 *syn* see IMPECCABLE 1
3 *syn* see CLEAN 1

immalleable *adj syn* see STIFF 1
ant malleable

immaterial *adj* 1 not composed of matter < *immaterial* forces >
syn asomatous, bodiless, disbodied, discarnate, disembodied, incorporeal, insubstantial, metaphysical, nonmaterial, nonphysical, spiritual, unbodied, ‖uncorporal, unembodied, unfleshly, unmaterial, unphysical, unsubstantial
rel impalpable, imponderable; psychic, subjective; aerial, airy, ethereal; insensible, unearthly, unworldly; supernatural; celestial, heavenly; apparitional, ghostly, shadowy
con bodily, corporeal, fleshly, incarnate; material, objective, palpable, physical, substantial; mundane, terrestrial, worldly
ant material
2 *syn* see IRRELEVANT
ant material

immature *adj* 1 *syn* see YOUNG 1
rel premature, precocious
ant mature
2 *syn* see CHILDISH
ant mature

immeasurable *adj* 1 *syn* see INCALCULABLE 1
2 *syn* see LIMITLESS

immediacy *n syn* see PROXIMITY

immediate *adj* 1 *syn* see DIRECT 4
ant distant (*of relatives*)
2 *syn* see INSTANTANEOUS
3 *syn* see CLOSE 6

immediately *adv* 1 in direct connection without intermediary < *immediately* in front of the viewers >
syn contiguously, directly
2 *syn* see AWAY 3
rel anon, shortly, soon
idiom right now

immedicable *adj syn* see HOPELESS 2
ant medicable

immense *adj syn* see HUGE

immensely *adv syn* see EVER 6

immensity *n syn* see ENORMITY 2

immerse *vb* 1 *syn* see DIP 1
rel saturate, soak
2 *syn* see BAPTIZE
3 *syn* see ENGAGE 4

immersed *adj syn* see INTENT

immigrant *n syn* see EMIGRANT

imminent *adj* 1 about to take place < their departure is *imminent* >
syn impending, proximate
rel approaching, coming, nearing, upcoming; brewing, gathering; pending; likely, possible, probable; ineluctable, inescapable, inevasible, inevitable, unavoidable, unescapable

idiom in prospect, in store, in the cards, in the offing, in the wind, in view
con distant, far-off, remote
2 menacingly near < a thunderstorm was *imminent* >
syn lowering (*or* louring), lowery (*or* loury), menacing, overhanging, threatening
rel alarming, ominous, sinister; brewing, gathering; minatory

immingle *vb syn* see MIX 1

immix *vb syn* see MIX 1

immixture *n syn* see MIXTURE

immobile *adj* **1** *syn* see IMMOVABLE 1
ant mobile, movable
2 *syn* see STATIC

immobilize *vb syn* see PARALYZE 1

immoderate *adj* **1** *syn* see EXCESSIVE 1
ant moderate
2 *syn* see EXCESSIVE 2
ant moderate

immoderation *n syn* see EXCESS 3
ant moderation

immolate *vb syn* see SACRIFICE 1

immoral *adj* **1** *syn* see IMPURE 1
ant moral
2 *syn* see WRONG 1
ant moral

immorality *n syn* see VICE 1
ant morality

immortal *adj* **1** not subject to death < the *immortal* gods >
syn deathless, undying; *compare* EVERLASTING 1
rel endless, enduring, imperishable, indestructible, perpetual, sempiternal, timeless
con ephemeral, evanescent, fleeting, fugitive, passing, short-lived, transient, transitory
ant mortal
2 *syn* see EVERLASTING 1

immortality *n syn* see ETERNITY 2
ant mortality

immortalize *vb syn* see PERPETUATE

immotile *adj syn* see IMMOVABLE 1
ant motile

immotive *adj syn* see IMMOVABLE 1

immovable *adj* **1** incapable of moving or being moved < an *immovable* rock >
syn fixed, immobile, immotile, immotive, irremovable, ‖sitfast, steadfast, unmovable
rel adamant, fast, rooted, stable, stationary, stuck, unmoving, unyielding
con portable, removable, transferable, transportable
ant movable
2 *syn* see INFLEXIBLE 3

immunity *n syn* see EXEMPTION
ant susceptibility

immure *vb* **1** *syn* see ENCLOSE 1
2 *syn* see IMPRISON

immusical *adj syn* see DISSONANT 1
ant musical

immutable *adj syn* see INFLEXIBLE 3
ant mutable

imp *n* **1** a small demon, devil, or wicked spirit < the *imps* of hell >
syn deviling, devilkin

rel elf, gnome, goblin, gremlin, ‖hob, hobgoblin, kobold, ouph, pixie, puck, sprite, troll
2 *syn* see URCHIN

impact *n* a forcible or enforced contact between two or more things < a crater formed by the *impact* of a meteorite >
syn appulse, blow, bump, clash, collision, concussion, crash, impingement, jar, jolt, jounce, percussion, shock, smash, wallop
rel brunt; buffet, hit, pound, punch, rap, slap, smiting, strike, stroke; bounce, quake, quiver, rock, shake, tremble, tremor; encounter, meeting

impair *vb syn* see INJURE 1
rel sap, undermine, weaken
con ameliorate, better
ant improve; repair

impaired *adj syn* see DAMAGED

impale *vb* to pierce or fix with or as if with something pointed < an insect *impaled* on a pin >
syn lance, skewer, skiver, spear, spike, spit, transfix, transpierce
rel perforate, pierce, prick, punch, puncture, stab

impalpable *adj* **1** *syn* see IMPERCEPTIBLE
ant palpable
2 *syn* see FINE 2

imparity *n syn* see DISPARITY
ant parity

impart *vb syn* see COMMUNICATE 1

impartial *adj syn* see FAIR 4
ant partial

impartially *adv syn* see EVENLY 2

impassable *adj* **1** not allowing passage < an *impassable* barrier >
syn impenetrable, impermeable, impervious, unpierceable
con penetrable, permeable, pervious
ant passable
2 *syn* see INSUPERABLE

impasse *n* **1** *syn* see DEAD END
2 *syn* see PREDICAMENT

impassible *adj syn* see INSENSIBLE 5
rel cold, emotionless, passionless, unemotional, unfeeling, inert, unresponsive
ant passible

impassioned *adj* actuated by or showing intense feeling < *impassioned* oratory >
syn ardent, blazing, burning, dithyrambic, fervent, fervid, fiery, flaming, glowing, hot-blooded, overheated, passionate, perfervid, red-hot, torrid, white-hot
rel feverish, fierce, furious, intense, vehement, violent; deep, profound, warm, zealous; gushing, gushy, maudlin, melodramatic, mushy, overemotional, romantic, sentimental
con cold, cool, dispassionate, frigid, icy, unemotional; objective
ant unimpassioned

impassive *adj* **1** unresponsive to what might normally excite interest or emotion < *impassive* endurance of pain >
syn apathetic, dry, matter-of-fact, phlegmatic, stoic, stolid
rel calm, cold, cool; collected, composed, dispassionate, emotionless, imperturbable, inexcitable, unexcitable, unflappable; inexpressive, reserved, reticent, taciturn, unemotional, unexpressive; bovine, placid, passionless, spiritless, unconcerned, wooden; callous, hardened, indurated,

insensible; cold-blooded, coldhearted, heartless

con compassionate, sympathetic, tender, warm, warmhearted

ant responsive

2 *syn* see INSUSCEPTIBLE

impassivity *n syn* see APATHY 1

impatient *adj* 1 lacking power to endure hardship, distress, or opposition < married to an *impatient* self-centered man >

syn chafing, fretful, unpatient

rel abrupt, hasty, headlong, impetuous; anxious, edgy, itchy, nervous; irascible, irritable

idiom all of a stew

con enduring, forbearing, tolerant; self-controlled, Spartan, stoic

ant patient

2 *syn* see INTOLERANT 1

rel demanding, harsh

3 *syn* see EAGER

ant patient

impeach *vb syn* see ACCUSE

impeccable *adj* 1 absolutely correct and beyond criticism < *impeccable* manners >

syn errorless, exquisite, faultless, flawless, immaculate, irreproachable

rel accurate, clean, correct, exact, nice, perfect, precise, right; infallible, unerring

con defective, deficient, faulty; blameworthy, censurable, criticizable, culpable; cursory, shallow, superficial, uncritical

ant peccant

2 *syn* see PERFECT 2

impecunious *adj syn* see POOR 1

ant affluent; flush

impecuniousness *n syn* see POVERTY 1

ant affluence; flushness

impedance *n syn* see ENCUMBRANCE

impede *vb syn* see HINDER

rel discomfit, disconcert, embarrass, faze, rattle

ant aid, assist

impediment *n* 1 *syn* see ENCUMBRANCE

ant aid, assistance

2 *syn* see OBSTACLE

impel *vb syn* see MOVE 5

rel compel, constrain, force; foment, incite, instigate; goad, spur; inspire, motivate

con check, curb, inhibit

ant restrain

impend *vb syn* see LOOM 2

impending *adj syn* see IMMINENT 1

impenetrable *adj* 1 *syn* see IMPASSABLE 1

rel firm, solid, substantial

ant penetrable

2 *syn* see INCOMPREHENSIBLE 1

ant penetrable

3 *syn* see MYSTERIOUS

impenetrate *vb syn* see PERMEATE

impenitent *adj syn* see REMORSELESS

ant penitent

imperative *adj* 1 *syn* see MASTERFUL 1

rel bidding, commanding, ordering; harsh, stern

con begging, entreating, imploring; lenient, mild, soft

2 *syn* see PRESSING

rel acute, critical, crucial

3 *syn* see ESSENTIAL 4

rel basic, fundamental; claimed, demanded, exacted

4 *syn* see MANDATORY

imperceptible *adj* incapable of being apprehended by the senses or intellect < *imperceptible* changes in temperature >

syn impalpable, imponderable, inappreciable, indiscernible, insensible, intangible, invisible, unapparent, unappreciable, undiscernible, unobservable, unperceivable

rel faint, inconspicuous, indistinct, indistinguishable, insignificant, obscure, undistinguishable, unnoticeable, vague; ephemeral, evanescent, fugitive, momentary; slight, trivial

con apparent, appreciable, discernible, observable, palpable, ponderable, sensible, visible

ant perceptible, perceivable

imperceptive *adj* lacking perception or insight < *imperceptive* criticism >

syn impercipient, unperceiving, unperceptive

rel unappreciative, undiscerning, unobservant; cursory, shallow, slapdash, superficial

con astute, discerning, discriminating, judicious, perspicacious; delicate, nice, refined, sensitive, subtle

ant perceiving, perceptive, percipient

impercipient *adj syn* see IMPERCEPTIVE

ant perceiving, perceptive, percipient

imperfect *adj syn* see FAULTY

ant perfect

imperfection *n* an instance of failure to reach a standard of excellence or perfection < watch for *imperfections* in the cloth >

syn deficiency, demerit, fault, shortcoming, sin

rel blemish, defect, flaw; failing, foible, frailty

ant perfection

imperial *adj syn* see MASTERFUL 1

imperil *vb syn* see ENDANGER

imperious *adj* 1 *syn* see MASTERFUL 1

rel heavy-handed, oppressive, strict, stringent; absolute, arbitrary

con considerate, easy, gentle, kindly

2 *syn* see MANDATORY

imperishable *adj syn* see INDESTRUCTIBLE

impermanent *adj syn* see TRANSIENT

ant permanent

impermeable *adj syn* see IMPASSABLE 1

ant permeable

impersonal *adj* 1 *syn* see NEUTRAL

2 *syn* see FAIR 4

3 *syn* see MATTER-OF-FACT 3

impersonate *vb syn* see ACT 1

impersonator *n syn* see ACTOR 1

impertinence *n syn* see INSOLENCE

impertinent *adj* 1 *syn* see IRRELEVANT

ant pertinent

2 going beyond what is proper or acceptable in thrusting oneself into the affairs of others < *impertinent* interference with her sister's family >

syn busy, intrusive, meddlesome, ‖nebby, obtrusive, officious, polypragmatic

rel arrogant, bold, brash, brazen, fresh, impudent, pert, presumptuous, saucy; inquisitive, interfering, meddling, nosy, prying; offensive, rude *con* decent, decorous, proper, seemly; reserved, reticent, silent; apposite, germane, pertinent, relevant

3 *syn* see RUDE 6

4 *syn* see INSOLENT 2

imperturbability *n syn* see EQUANIMITY

imperturbable *adj syn* see COOL 2
rel complacent, self-satisfied, smug; unaffected, unmoved, untouched
con discomfited, disconcerted, fazed, rattled; irascible, splenetic, testy
ant choleric; touchy

impervious *adj syn* see IMPASSABLE 1

impervious *adj syn* see IMPASSABLE 1
ant pervious

impetuous *adj syn* see PRECIPITATE 1
rel spontaneous; restive; ardent, fervid, impassioned, passionate
con equable, even, steady; advised, considered, deliberate, planned, premeditated

impetuously *adv syn* see PELL-MELL

impetus *n syn* see STIMULUS

impignorate *vb syn* see PAWN

impingement *n syn* see IMPACT

impious *adj* 1 lacking reverence for holy or sacred matters < made *impious* remarks about the church >
syn irreverent, irreverential, profane, ungodly, unhallowed, unholy
rel godless, iconoclastic, irreligious, sacrilegious, scandalous, undevout
con devout, godly, religious, spiritual
ant pious

2 lacking due respect (as toward one's parents) < an *impious* son >
syn unduteous, undutiful
rel disobedient, froward, unfaithful, wayward; contrary, perverse, wrongheaded
con duteous, dutiful

impish *adj syn* see PLAYFUL 1
rel arch, pert, saucy; flippant, fresh, giddy; casual, devil-may-care, free and easy, offhand

impishness *n syn* see MISCHIEVOUSNESS

implacable *adj syn* see GRIM 3
con peaceable, tractable; kindly, tolerant
ant placable

implant *vb* to introduce into the mind < *implanted* worthy ideals in their children >
syn inculcate, infix, inseminate, instill
rel imbue, infuse, ingrain, inoculate, leaven, root; impenetrate, impregnate, penetrate, permeate, pervade, saturate; inspire

implausible *adj* not plausible or readily believable < an *implausible* explanation >
syn flimsy, improbable, inconceivable, incredible, thick, thin, unbelievable, unconceivable, unconvincing, unsubstantial, weak; *compare* TENUOUS 3
rel doubtful, dubious, fishy; problematic, puzzling, suspect
idiom a bit thick
con meaty, pithy; solid, sound, substantial; believable, conceivable, credible; likely, probable
ant plausible

implement *n* a usually relatively simple device for performing a mechanical or manual operation < spades, hoes, and other gardener's *implements* >
syn instrument, tool, utensil
rel apparatus, appliance; contrivance, device; contraption, gadget

implement *vb* 1 *syn* see FULFILL 1

2 *syn* see ENFORCE
rel actualize, materialize, realize

implemental *adj syn* see INSTRUMENTAL

impliable *adj syn* see STIFF 1
ant pliable

implicate *vb syn* see INVOLVE 1
rel affect, concern; incriminate
con absolve, acquit, exculpate, exonerate

implicated *adj syn* see INTERESTED

implication *n syn* see ASSOCIATION 4

implicit *adj* 1 *syn* see TACIT 1
idiom taken for granted
ant explicit

2 being such in essential character < our *implicit* freedom is better than your nominal liberty >
syn constructive, practical, virtual
rel absolute, complete, unqualified, wholehearted; genuine, real
ant spelled out

implied *adj syn* see TACIT 1

imploration *n syn* see PRAYER

implore *vb syn* see BEG

imply *vb* 1 *syn* see POINT 2

2 *syn* see SUGGEST 1
con state; express; affirm, assert, declare

impolite *adj syn* see RUDE 6
ant polite

impolitic *adj* 1 *syn* see UNWISE
ant politic

2 *syn* see INADVISABLE
ant politic

3 *syn* see TACTLESS

imponderable *adj syn* see IMPERCEPTIBLE
ant appreciable, ponderable

imponderous *adj syn* see LIGHT 1
ant ponderous

import *vb* 1 *syn* see MEAN 2

2 *syn* see MATTER

import *n* 1 *syn* see MEANING 1
rel construction, interpretation

2 *syn* see IMPORTANCE
rel value, worth; design, intent, object, objective, purpose; emphasis, stress

importance *n* the quality or state of being of notable worth or influence < persons of national and worldwide *importance* >
syn consequence, import, magnitude, moment, momentousness, pith, significance, ‖signification, weight, weightiness
rel conspicuousness; distinction, eminence, mark, prominence, salience; notability, note, noteworthiness, reputation, standing; substance, value, worth, worthiness; gravity, seriousness
con inconsequence, insignificance, paltriness, pettiness, triviality
ant unimportance

important *adj* 1 marked by or indicative of notable worth or consequence < an *important* discovery > < his manner was grave and *important* >
syn big, consequential, considerable, material, meaningful, momentous, significant, substantial, ‖weighty

---

syn synonym(s)   *rel* related word(s)
ant antonym(s)   *con* contrasted word(s)
idiom idiomatic equivalent(s)
‖ use limited; if in doubt, see a dictionary

rel conspicuous, distinctive, exceptional, impressive, marked, memorable, notable, noteworthy, noticeable, outstanding, prominent, remarkable, salient, unusual; essential; valuable, worthwhile; worthy; effective, potent, powerful, telling; bigtime, first-class, first-rate, front-page, topnotch; distinguished, eminent, famous, noted

con inconsiderable, little, minor, paltry, petty, slight, trivial

ant unimportant

2 *syn* see POMPOUS 1

importunate *adj syn* see PRESSING

rel persevering, persistent; dogged, pertinacious

importune *vb syn* see BEG

impose *vb* 1 *syn* see DICTATE

rel charge, command, enjoin, order; demand, exact, require; compel, constrain, oblige

2 *syn* see LEVY

3 *syn* see INFLICT 2

4 to force another to accept < *imposed* all the dirty jobs on her sister >

syn foist, wish; *compare* FOIST 3, INFLICT 2

rel burden, lade, saddle; fob, fob off, palm off

idiom take advantage of

5 to take usually unwarranted advantage < did not wish to *impose* by turning up unannounced >

syn infringe, intrude, obtrude, presume

rel encroach, trespass

idiom make free, take liberties

impose (on *or* upon) *vb syn* see EXPLOIT 2

imposing *adj* 1 *syn* see GRAND 1

rel impressive, moving; imperial, regal

ant unimposing

2 *syn* see PRETENTIOUS 3

impossible *adj* 1 not capable of being realized or attained < *impossible* goals >

syn impracticable, impractical, infeasible, irrealizable, unattainable, unfeasible, unrealizable, unworkable

rel absurd, inexecutable, unobtainable, unreasonable, unthinkable

idiom out of the question

con attainable, feasible, realizable; practicable, practical, rational, reasonable

ant possible

2 *syn* see HOPELESS 2

impost *n syn* see TAX 1

impostor *n* one who passes himself off as something or someone he is not < the presumed heir was discovered to be an *impostor* >

syn fake, faker, fraud, humbug, phony, pretender; *compare* CHARLATAN

rel imitator, mimic; beguiler, deceiver, misleader; cheat, pettifogger, shyster, trickster; hypocrite; charlatan, mountebank, quack; bluffer, dissembler, fourflusher, shammer

idiom wolf in sheep's clothing

imposture *n* the act, practice, or an instance of imposing on another by use of an assumed character or name < his claims were based on *imposture* >

syn cheat, counterfeit, deceit, deception, fake, flam, flimflam, fraud, gyp, hoax, humbug, mare's nest, phony, put-on, ‖rig, sell, sham, spoof, swindle

rel copy, imitation; fabrication, forgery; artifice, feint, gambit, maneuver, ploy, ruse, sleight, stratagem, trick, wile; makebelieve, pretense, pretension

impotent *adj* 1 *syn* see POWERLESS

rel crippled, disabled, enfeebled

con able, capable, competent

ant potent

2 *syn* see WEAK 4

con forceful, powerful, puissant, strenuous, vigorous

ant potent

3 *syn* see STERILE 1

impoverish *vb* 1 *syn* see DEPLETE

ant enrich

2 *syn* see RUIN 3

impoverished *adj syn* see POOR 1

impoverishment *n syn* see POVERTY 1

impracticable *adj* 1 *syn* see IMPOSSIBLE 1

ant feasible, practicable

2 incapable of being successfully used or turned to account < a route through the mountains that is *impracticable* in winter >

syn impractical, nonfunctional, unfunctional, unserviceable, unusable, unworkable, useless

rel disadvantageous, unacceptable, undesirable, unsatisfactory; awkward, inconvenient, troublesome

con functional, practical, serviceable, usable, useful, workable

ant practicable

impractical *adj* 1 incapable of dealing prudently with practical matters < a very *impractical* person whose checkbook never balanced >

syn ivory-tower, ivory-towered, ivorytowerish, nonrealistic, unpractical, unrealistic, viewy

rel idealistic, otherworldly, quixotic, romantic, starry-eyed, visionary

con commonsensible, commonsensical, realistic, sensible, worldly-wise

ant practical

2 *syn* see IMPRACTICABLE 2

ant practical

3 *syn* see IMPOSSIBLE 1

imprecate *vb syn* see SWEAR 3

imprecation *n* 1 *syn* see BLASPHEMY 1

2 *syn* see PRAYER

3 *syn* see CURSE 1

con blessing

impregnable *adj syn* see INVINCIBLE 1

rel safe, secure; defended, guarded, protected, safeguarded, shielded

con exposed, open, susceptible

impregnate *vb* 1 *syn* see PERMEATE

rel inoculate, leaven

2 *syn* see SOAK 1

impress *vb* 1 *syn* see ENGRAVE 2

2 *syn* see AFFECT

rel enthuse, electrify, thrill; excite, galvanize, pique, provoke, stimulate

idiom make (*or* leave) one's mark

3 to fix in the mind or memory by emphasis or repetition < the speaker *impressed* his principal thesis upon his audience >

syn drive, grave, hammer, pound, stamp

rel establish, fix, set

idiom drive home to one, fix in one's mind, get into one's head

impress *n syn* see IMPRESSION 1
impressible *adj syn* see SENTIENT 3
impression *n* **1** the perceptible trace or traces left by pressure < the *impression* made by a die >
syn impress, imprint, indentation, print, stamp
rel dent, dint, hollow; trace, track, vestige; mark, sign
2 *syn* see IDEA
3 *syn* see EDITION
impressionable *adj syn* see SENTIENT 3
rel affectable, influenceable
impressive *adj* **1** *syn* see MOVING 2
rel august, grand, imposing, majestic, noble; splendid, superb; arresting, notable, striking
ant unimpressive
2 *syn* see GRAND 2
imprint *vb syn* see ENGRAVE 2
imprint *n syn* see IMPRESSION 1
imprison *vb* to shut up closely so that escape is impossible or unlikely < the offender was quickly sentenced and *imprisoned* >
syn bastille, confine, constrain, immure, incarcerate, intern, jail, jug, ||prison, ||quod
rel circumscribe, limit, restrict; check, curb, restrain
idiom put under lock and key
con free, liberate, release
improbable *adj* **1** not likely to be true or to occur < the immediate success of their plan is *improbable* >
syn doubtful, dubious, questionable, unlikely
ant probable
2 *syn* see IMPLAUSIBLE
impromptu *n syn* see IMPROVISATION
impromptu *adj syn* see EXTEMPORANE-OUS
rel prompt, quick
improper *adj* **1** unsuited to the circumstances or the occasion < wore quite *improper* dress for such a formal reception >
syn ill-timed, inadmissible, inappropriate, inapt, inept, intempestive, malapropos, unapt, unbecoming, unbefitting, uncomely, undue, unfitting, unseasonable, unseemly, unsuitable, untimely
rel infelicitous, unhappy; inapplicable, inapposite; fresh, impertinent, sassy; crude, gauche, tactless
idiom out of place, out of season
con apposite, appropriate, apropos, apt, becoming, befitting, felicitous, fitting, germane, happy, opportune, pat, pertinent, seasonable, suitable, timely, well-timed
ant proper
2 *syn* see INDECOROUS
rel informal, unceremonious, unconventional
con correct, right
ant proper
impropriety *n* **1** the quality or state of being improper (as in social behavior) < was shocked by the *impropriety* of their actions >

---

syn synonym(s)   *rel* related word(s)
ant antonym(s)   *con* contrasted word(s)
idiom idiomatic equivalent(s)
|| use limited; if in doubt, see a dictionary

syn incorrectness, indecorousness, indecorum, inelegance, unbecomingness, unmeetness, unseemliness, untowardness
rel inadmissibility, objectionableness, unacceptableness
con becomingness, decency, decorousness, decorum, meetness
ant propriety, seemliness
2 *syn* see FAUX PAS *compare* ERROR 2
3 *syn* see BARBARISM
improve *vb* **1** to make more acceptable or bring nearer to some standard < studied hard to *improve* his chances of success >
syn ameliorate, amend, better, help, meliorate
rel cultivate, develop, perfect; correct, emend, rectify, reform, remedy; edit, revise; enhance, enrich, refine, rub up, upgrade
con diminish, downgrade, lessen, lower
2 *syn* see ILLUMINATE 2
3 to grow or become better (as in health or well-being) < the invalid is steadily *improving* >
syn ameliorate, convalesce, gain, look up, mend, perk (up), recuperate
rel advance, better, progress; recover; rally, revive, strengthen
idiom gain ground, make progress
con decline, deteriorate, fail, flag, languish, run down, sink, weaken
improvident *adj* not foreseeing or providing for the future < an *improvident* way of life >
syn thriftless, unthrift, unthrifty
rel careless, heedless, imprudent; extravagant, prodigal, profligate, spendthrift; lavish, profuse, reckless; uneconomical, wasteful
con careful, economical, frugal, parsimonious, prudent, saving, sparing
ant provident, thrifty
improvisate *vb syn* see IMPROVISE
improvisation *n* something that is improvised < the pianist played several clever *improvisations* >
syn autoschediasm, extemporization, impromptu
improvise *vb* to perform or provide on the spur of the moment < *improvise* an excuse for being late >
syn ad-lib, extemporize, improvisate
rel concoct, contrive, devise, invent
improvised *adj syn* see EXTEMPORANEOUS
imprudent *adj* **1** *syn* see UNWISE
ant prudent
2 *syn* see INADVISABLE
ant prudent
impudence *n syn* see INSOLENCE
impudent *adj* **1** *syn* see WISE 5
2 *syn* see INSOLENT 2
3 *syn* see SHAMELESS
impugn *vb syn* see DENY 4
rel assail, attack
idiom call in (*or* into) question (*or* doubt), throw doubt on
con back, support, uphold
ant advocate; authenticate
impugnable *adj syn* see DOUBTFUL 1
impulse *n syn* see STIMULUS
rel excitant; lust, passion, urge; actuation, drive, impulsion

impulsive *adj syn see* SPONTANEOUS
  rel abrupt, hasty, headlong, impetuous, precipitate, sudden
  con considered, designed, premeditated; calculating, cautious, circumspect
  ant deliberate
impulsiveness *n syn see* ABANDON 2
impunity *n syn see* EXEMPTION
impure *adj* 1 morally or mentally unclean < *impure* thoughts >
  syn dirty, immoral, unchaste, unclean, uncleanly
  rel belowstairs, carnal, immodest, indecent, indecorous, lascivious, lewd, lustful, prurient, scarlet, sensual; filthy, vile
  con chaste, clean, cleanly, decent, decorous, immaculate, modest, virtuous; moral
  ant pure
  2 *syn see* DIRTY 1
  3 made unfit for ceremonial purposes < altars overturned and sacred vessels made *impure* by the touch of profane hands >
  syn common, defiled, desecrated, polluted, profaned, unclean
  rel unhallowed, unholy
  con clean, consecrated, undefiled
  ant pure
  4 *syn see* UNREFINED 3
impute *vb syn see* ASCRIBE
  rel accuse, indict; adduce; hint, insinuate, intimate
in *adj syn see* STYLISH
in *n syn see* PULL 2
inability *n* lack of sufficient power, resources, or capacity to perform < suffered from an *inability* to make quick decisions >
  syn inadequacy, incapability, incapacity, incompetence, ineffectiveness, ineffectualness, inefficacy
  rel inadeptness, inaptitude, inaptness, inefficiency, ineptitude, ineptness
  con adequacy, capability, capacity; competence, efficiency
  ant ability
inaccessible *adj* not capable of being achieved < an *inaccessible* goal >
  syn inapproachable, unapproachable, unattainable, un-come-at-able, ungetatable, unobtainable, unreachable
  rel distant, far, faraway, far-off, out-of-the-way, remote
  ant accessible
inaccurate *adj syn see* FALSE 1
  con right, true
  ant accurate
inaction *n* lack of action or activity < the delay was due to the committee's *inaction* >
  syn inactiveness, inactivity
  rel drift, idleness, indolence, inertness, lethargy, quiescence, slackness, slothfulness, torpidity
  con activeness, activity
inactive *adj* not characterized by or engaged in usual or normal activity < forced by illness to lead an *inactive* life >
  syn asleep, idle, inert, passive, quiet, sleepy
  rel abeyant, dormant, inoperative, latent, quiescent; do-nothing, indolent, lethargic, lymphatic, slack, slothful, sluggish, torpid; motionless, sedentary, static; disengaged,

jobless, unemployed, unoccupied, unworking; ossified
  con busy, employed, engaged, occupied; energetic, strenuous, vigorous; animated, brisk, lively
  ant active
inactiveness *n syn see* INACTION
inactivity *n syn see* INACTION
  ant activity
in addition *adv syn see* AGAIN 4
inadept *adj syn see* UNSKILLFUL 1
  ant adept
inadequacy *n* 1 *syn see* INABILITY
  2 *syn see* FAILURE 3
  ant adequacy
inadequate *adj* 1 *syn see* DEFICIENT 1
  ant adequate
  2 *syn see* SHORT 3
  ant adequate
  3 *syn see* MEAGER
  ant adequate
  4 *syn see* WEAK 4
  ant adequate
inadmissible *adj* 1 *syn see* IMPROPER 1
  2 *syn see* OBJECTIONABLE
  ant admissible
in advance *adv syn see* BEFORE 1
in advance of *prep* 1 *syn see* BEFORE 1
  2 *syn see* UNTIL
inadvertent *adj* 1 *syn see* CARELESS 1
  ant advertent
  2 *syn see* UNINTENTIONAL
inadvisable *adj* not likely to have a satisfactory outcome < it seemed *inadvisable* to go any farther because of threatening weather >
  syn ill-advised, impolitic, imprudent, inexpedient, unadvisable, unexpedient
  rel careless, inappropriate, incautious, rash, undesirable, unsensible; foolish, indiscreet, pointless, unwise; foolhardy, harebrained
  con expedient, judicious, politic, prudent, sensible, wise
  ant advisable
in all *adv syn see* ALTOGETHER 2
in all probability *adv syn see* PRESUMABLY
inalterable *adj syn see* INFLEXIBLE 3
  ant alterable
inamorata *n* 1 *syn see* GIRL FRIEND 2
  2 *syn see* MISTRESS
inamorato *n syn see* BOYFRIEND 2
in and out *adv syn see* THOROUGHLY 2
inane *adj syn see* INSIPID 3
  rel asinine, fatuous, foolish, silly; idle, vain; blank, empty, hollow
  con expressive, meaningful, pregnant, significant, weighty
  ant deep, profound
inanimate *adj* 1 *syn see* INSENSATE 1
  ant animate
  2 *syn see* DEAD 1
  ant animate; living
inanity *n syn see* FOOLISHNESS
inapplicable *adj syn see* IRRELEVANT
  ant applicable
inapposite *adj syn see* IRRELEVANT
  ant apposite
inappreciable *adj* 1 *syn see* IMPERCEPTIBLE
  ant appreciable
  2 *syn see* MEAGER

inapproachable *adj syn* see INACCESSI-
BLE
  ant approachable
inappropriate *adj* **1** *syn* see UNFIT 1
  rel indecorous, unseemly; inconsonant
  con felicitous, fitting, happy, meet,
proper; fit, suitable
  ant appropriate
  2 *syn* see IMPROPER 1
inapt *adj* **1** *syn* see UNFIT 1
  rel awkward, clumsy, gauche, maladroit;
banal, flat, insipid, jejune
  con apposite, germane, pertinent, relevant
  ant apt
  2 *syn* see IMPROPER 1
  ant apt
  3 *syn* see UNSKILLFUL 1
  ant adept
inarguable *adj syn* see POSITIVE 3
  ant arguable
inarticulate *adj* **1** *syn* see DUMB 1
  ant articulate
  2 *syn* see TACIT 1
  3 failing to give or incapable of giving
clear or effective verbal expression to
one's ideas or feelings <made some *inarticulate* explanation for being late> <was
completely *inarticulate* when it came to
expressing affection>
  syn incoherent, maundering, tongue-tied,
unvocal
  rel faltering, halting, hesitating, mum-
bling, stammered, stammering; blurred,
indistinct
  con facile, glib, smooth
  ant articulate
inartificial *adj syn* see NATURAL 5
  ant artificial
inasmuch as *conj syn* see BECAUSE
inattentive *adj* not paying proper attention <an *inattentive* pupil dozing at his
desk>
  syn inobservant, unheeding, unnoticing,
unobservant, unobserving, unperceiving,
unwatchful
  rel distracted, distrait; distraught; careless, heedless, thoughtless, undiscerning,
unmindful, unthinking; bored, ennuyé
  ant attentive; observant
inaugural *adj syn* see FIRST 1
inaugural *n syn* see INITIATION
inaugurate *vb* **1** *syn* see INITIATE 3
  2 *syn* see BEGIN 1
  3 *syn* see INTRODUCE 3
inauguration *n syn* see INITIATION
inauspicious *adj* **1** *syn* see OMINOUS
  ant auspicious
  2 *syn* see EVIL 6
in between *prep syn* see BETWEEN 2
inborn *adj* **1** *syn* see INNATE 1
  ant acquired
  2 *syn* see INHERENT
inbred *adj syn* see INHERENT
in brief *adv syn* see BRIEFLY
incalculable *adj* **1** being great beyond
calculation <*incalculable* damage>
  syn immeasurable, inestimable, measureless, uncountable, unmeasurable, unmeasured, unreckonable

  rel countless, innumerable, unnumbered,
untold; boundless, enormous, infinite,
limitless, vast
  con minimal, slight, trivial
  ant infinitesimal
  2 *syn* see UNCERTAIN 1
  ant calculable
in camera *adv syn* see SECRETLY
incandescent *adj syn* see BRIGHT 1
incantation *n* **1** *syn* see SPELL
  2 *syn* see MAGIC 1
incapability *n syn* see INABILITY
  ant capability
incapable *adj* **1** *syn* see UNFIT 2
  ant capable
  2 *syn* see INEFFICIENT 2
  ant capable
incapacitate *vb* **1** *syn* see PARALYZE 1
  2 *syn* see DISQUALIFY
  ant capacitate
incapacity *n syn* see INABILITY
  ant capacity
incarcerate *vb syn* see IMPRISON
incarnadine *vb syn* see REDDEN 1
incarnate *vb syn* see EMBODY 1
incarnation *n syn* see EMBODIMENT
incautious *adj* **1** lacking in caution
<made an *incautious* prediction>
  syn unalert, unguarded, unvigilant, unwary, unwatchful; *compare* CARELESS 1
  rel imprudent, indiscreet, injudicious;
bold, brash, impetuous, rash, reckless;
neglectful, negligent, regardless, thoughtless, unmindful; hasty
  idiom caught napping, off one's guard
  con careful, circumspect, judicious, wary,
watchful; discreet, judicious, prudent;
sensible, thoughtful, wise
  ant cautious
  2 *syn* see RASH 1
  ant cautious
  3 *syn* see IRRESPONSIBLE
incendiary *n* a person who deliberately
and unlawfully sets fire to a building or
other property <a fire set by an *incendiary*>
  syn arsonist, firebug, torch
  rel pyromaniac
incendiary *adj syn* see INFLAMMATORY
incense *n* **1** *syn* see FRAGRANCE
  2 *syn* see FLATTERY
incense *vb syn* see ANGER 1
  ant placate
incentive *n syn* see STIMULUS
inception *n syn* see SOURCE
  con closing, completion, conclusion
  ant termination
inceptive *adj syn* see INITIAL 1
  ant terminal
incertitude *n syn* see UNCERTAINTY
  ant certitude
incessant *adj syn* see CONTINUAL
  ant intermittent
inchoate *adj* **1** *syn* see FORMLESS
  2 *syn* see INCOHERENT 2
incident *n syn* see OCCURRENCE
incident *adj* **1** *syn* see CONCOMITANT
  ant essential, fundamental
  2 *syn* see RELATED
incidental *adj syn* see ACCIDENTAL
  ant essential
incidentally *adv* **1** by chance <in this
discussion grave questions were brought
up *incidentally*>

---

syn synonym(s)   *rel* related word(s)
ant antonym(s)   *con* contrasted word(s)
idiom idiomatic equivalent(s)
‖ use limited; if in doubt, see a dictionary

syn accidentally, casually, fortuitously
ant deliberately
2 by way of interjection or digression
<another leading industry, *incidentally*,
has quadrupled its business in four
years>
syn by the bye, by the way, in passing,
obiter, parenthetically
idiom in the bygoing

incipient *adj syn* see INITIAL 1
incise *vb* 1 *syn* see CUT 1
2 *syn* see ENGRAVE 1
incisive *adj* having, manifesting, or suggesting a keen alertness of mind <a man
well known for his *incisive* wit>
syn biting, clear-cut, crisp, cutting, ingoing, penetrating, trenchant
rel acute, drilling, keen, sharp; acerb,
acerbic, caustic, mordant, scathing, slashing, tart; concise, laconic, succinct, terse
con diffuse, prolix, verbose, wordy; feeble,
limp, pithless, sapless
ant unincisive

incisiveness *n syn* see EDGE 2
incitation *n syn* see STIMULUS
incite *vb* to aid or promote the activity or
development of <*incite* a riot>
syn abet, foment, instigate, provoke, raise,
set, set on, stir (up), whip (up)
rel forward, further, promote, stimulate;
set off, trigger; agitate, solicit; encourage,
motivate, motive; excite, inflame, rouse
con check, curb, discourage, inhibit, restrain; calm, quiet, subdue

incitement *n syn* see STIMULUS
ant restraint; inhibition
inciter *n syn* see INSTIGATOR
incivil *adj syn* see RUDE 6
ant civil
inclement *adj syn* see SEVERE 3
ant clement
inclination *n* 1 *syn* see LEANING 2
ant disinclination
2 *syn* see WILL 1
ant disinclination
3 *syn* see APPETITE 3
ant disinclination
4 *syn* see SLOPE
incline *vb* 1 *syn* see TEND 1
2 *syn* see SLANT 1
rel deflect, turn
3 to have an attitude toward or to influence one to take an attitude <*inclined* to
believe the story> <his argument *inclined*
me to share his view>
syn bend, bias, dispose, predispose; *compare* PREJUDICE 2, TEND 1
rel affect, influence, prompt, sway; drive,
impel, induce, move, persuade
ant disincline, indispose
4 *syn* see DIRECT 2
incline *n syn* see SLOPE
inclined *adj* 1 *syn* see WILLING 1
ant disinclined
2 *syn* see APT 1
ant disinclined
3 sloping from the horizontal or perpendicular <cars running on an *inclined*
track>
syn declivate, declivitous, inclining, leaning, oblique, pitched, pitching, sloped,
sloping, tilted, tilting, tipped; *compare*
DIAGONAL

rel dipping, graded, raked
inclining *n syn* see LEANING 2
inclining *adj syn* see INCLINED 3
include *vb* to possess as an integral part of
a whole <the park *includes* a zoo and a
botanical garden>
syn comprehend, contain, embody, embrace, encompass, have, involve, subsume,
take in
rel comprise, cover, encircle, enclose,
hold; number; admit, receive
con leave out, omit; preclude, reject;
debar; eliminate, rule out
ant exclude
inclusive *adj* 1 *syn* see ALL-AROUND 2
2 *syn* see ENCYCLOPEDIC
incogitable *adj syn* see INCREDIBLE 1
ant cogitable
incogitant *adj syn* see RASH 1
incognizable *adj syn* see INCOMPREHEN-
SIBLE 1
ant cognizable
incognizant *adj syn* see IGNORANT 2
ant cognizant
incoherent *adj* 1 *syn* see LOOSE 3
2 lacking cohesion or continuity <an
incoherent presentation>
syn disconnected, discontinuous, disjointed, disordered, inchoate, incohesive,
muddled, unconnected, uncontinuous,
unorganized
rel discordant, incompatible, incongruous,
inconsistent, inconsonant, inharmonious
con ordered, orderly; connected; organized, planned, plotted
ant coherent
3 *syn* see INARTICULATE 3
incohesive *adj syn* see INCOHERENT 2
ant cohesive
incombustible *adj syn* see NONCOMBUS-
TIBLE
ant combustible
income *n syn* see REVENUE
incommode *vb syn* see INCONVENIENCE
rel block, hinder, impede, obstruct; annoy, bother, irk, vex
con favor, oblige; humor, indulge; gratify,
please
ant accommodate
incommodious *adj* 1 *syn* see INCONVE-
NIENT
ant commodious
2 *syn* see CRAMPED
ant commodious
incommunicable *adj* 1 *syn* see UNUTTER-
ABLE
ant communicable
2 *syn* see RESERVED 1
ant communicable, communicative
incomparable *adj syn* see SUPREME
rel matchless
con common, commonplace, ordinary;
indifferent, mediocre, medium, middling
ant average
incompatible *adj syn* see INCONSONANT
1
rel adverse, antagonistic, counter; antipathetic; antipodal, antipodean, antithetical,
contradictory, contrary, opposite; irreconcilable, unadaptable, unconformable
ant compatible
2 *syn* see IRRECONCILABLE
ant compatible

incompetence *n syn* see INABILITY
incompetent *adj* **1** *syn* see UNFIT 2
　ant competent
　2 *syn* see INEFFICIENT 2
　ant competent
incomplete *adj* **1** lacking a part or parts
< an *incomplete* text of a speech >
　syn fractional, fragmentary, part, partial
　rel broken, deficient, incoherent, lacking,
short, wanting; bitty, composite, scrappy
　con intact, undamaged, whole
　ant complete
　2 *syn* see DEFICIENT 1
　ant complete
incompliant *adj* **1** *syn* see OBSTINATE
　ant compliant
　2 *syn* see STIFF 1
incomprehensible *adj* **1** lying above or
beyond the reach of the human mind
< the *incomprehensible* universe >
　syn impenetrable, incognizable, uncomprehensible, unfathomable, ungraspable,
unintelligible, unknowable
　rel inscrutable, mysterious, mystifying,
unsearchable; cryptic, enigmatic, obscure,
unclear; imperceptible, indistinguishable
　con cognizable, fathomable, graspable,
intelligible, knowable; clear, lucid, plain,
simple, straightforward; rational, reasonable
　ant comprehensible, understandable
　2 *syn* see INCONCEIVABLE 1
　ant comprehensible, graspable
inconceivable *adj* **1** impossible to comprehend in the absence of actual experience
or knowledge < color is *inconceivable* to
those born blind >
　syn incomprehensible, unimaginable,
unknowable, unununderstandable
　idiom beyond one's grasp
　con comprehensible, imaginable, knowable, understandable
　ant conceivable
　2 *syn* see INCREDIBLE 1
　ant conceivable
　3 *syn* see IMPLAUSIBLE
　con believable, convincing, credible, plausible
　ant conceivable
inconclusive *adj* leading to no conclusion
or definite result < the report was *inconclusive* >
　syn indecisive
　rel open, uncertain, undecided, unsettled;
incomplete, unfinished
　con clarifying, illuminating; decisive
　ant conclusive
incondite *adj syn* see RUDE 6
inconformable *adj syn* see IRRECONCIL-
ABLE
　ant conformable
incongruent *adj syn* see INCONSONANT 1
　ant congruent, congruous
incongruous *adj syn* see INCONSONANT 1
　rel alien, extraneous, foreign; bizarre,
fantastic, grotesque
　idiom out of place
　con appropriate, fit, fitting, meet, seemly,
suitable

　ant congruent, congruous
inconnu *n syn* see STRANGER
inconquerable *adj* **1** *syn* see INVINCIBLE
1
　2 *syn* see INSUPERABLE
inconscient *adj syn* see ABSTRACTED
　ant conscient, conscious
inconscious *adj syn* see INSENSIBLE 2
　ant conscious
inconsequent *adj syn* see PETTY 2
inconsequential *adj syn* see PETTY 2
　ant consequential
inconsiderable *adj* **1** *syn* see LITTLE 3
　ant considerable
　2 *syn* see MEAGER
　ant considerable
　3 *syn* see PETTY 2
　ant considerable
inconsiderate *adj* **1** *syn* see RASH 1
　ant considerate
　2 *syn* see SHORT 5
　ant considerate
inconsistent *adj* **1** *syn* see INCONSTANT 1
　ant consistent
　2 *syn* see INCONSONANT 1
　ant consistent
　3 *syn* see IRRECONCILABLE
　ant consistent
inconsolable *adj* incapable of being con-
soled < she was *inconsolable* over the loss
of her child >
　syn desolate, disconsolate, unconsolable
　rel comfortless, dejected, forlorn, heartsick
　ant consolable
inconsonant *adj* **1** not in agreement with
one another or not agreeable one to the
other < his actions are *inconsonant* with
his words >
　syn conflicting, disconsonant, discordant,
discrepant, dissonant, incompatible, incongruent, incongruous, inconsistent, unmixable
　rel ill-matched, ill-suited, mismated, uncongenial; inappropriate, unsuitable
　con accordant, compatible, congenial,
congruous, consistent
　ant consonant
　2 *syn* see INHARMONIOUS 2
　ant consonant
inconspicuous *adj* not readily noticeable
< occupied an *inconspicuous* position >
　syn obscure, unconspicuous, unemphatic,
unnoticeable
　rel indistinct, insignificant, unnoticeable,
unobtrusive, vague
　con eye-catching, showy, striking; distinct, noticeable
　ant conspicuous, prominent
inconstant *adj* **1** lacking firmness or
steadiness (as in purpose or devotion)
< depended too much on an *inconstant*
friend >
　syn capricious, changeable, fickle, inconsistent, lubricious, mercurial, temperamental, ticklish, uncertain, unstable, variable,
volatile; *compare* CHANGEABLE 1, MUTA-
BLE 2, UNCERTAIN 1
　rel changeful, mutable, protean, unsettled,
unsteady; elusive, erratic, vacillating, vagrant, wavering, wayward; irresolute,
shifty, shilly-shally; undependable, unreliable; disloyal, faithless, false, perfidious,

---

syn synonym(s)　　*rel* related word(s)
ant antonym(s)　　*con* contrasted word(s)
idiom idiomatic equivalent(s)
‖ use limited; if in doubt, see a dictionary

traitorous, treacherous, untrue; frivolous, light, light-minded
con dependable, reliable, trustworthy, trusty; faithful, loyal, resolute, staunch, steadfast, true
ant constant
2 *syn* see MUTABLE 2
ant constant

incontestable *adj syn* see POSITIVE 3
ant contestable

incontinent *adj syn* see LICENTIOUS 2
ant continent

incontinently *adv syn* see PELL-MELL

incontrovertible *adj syn* see POSITIVE 3
ant controvertible

inconvenience *n* the quality or state of being inconvenient < he hated the *inconvenience* of not having a telephone >
syn bother, bothersomeness, ‖disconvenience, troublesomeness
rel annoyance, aggravation, exasperation, trial; fuss, pother, stew
ant convenience

inconvenience *vb* to subject to disturbance or discomfort < was not seriously *inconvenienced* by the bad weather >
syn discommode, ‖disconvenience, disoblige, incommode, put about, put out, trouble
rel discompose, disturb; interfere, intermeddle, meddle; aggravate, exasperate, try
idiom put to trouble
ant convenience

inconvenient *adj* not conducive to physical, mental, or social ease and comfort < he came at an *inconvenient* time >
syn awkward, discommoding, discommodious, embarrassing, incommodious
rel bothersome, pestiferous, troublesome; inexpedient; detrimental, disadvantageous, prejudicial
con appropriate, becoming, fitting, suitable; acceptable, bearable, tolerable; advantageous, desirable, helpful
ant convenient

inconversable *adj syn* see SILENT 3
ant conversable

inconversant *adj syn* see IGNORANT 2
ant conversant

incorporate *vb* **1** *syn* see ABSORB 1
2 *syn* see EMBODY 2

incorporeal *adj syn* see IMMATERIAL 1
ant corporeal

incorrect *adj syn* see FALSE 1
ant correct

incorrectly *adv syn* see AMISS 1
ant correctly

incorrectness *n syn* see IMPROPRIETY 1
ant correctitude, correctness

incorruptible *adj syn* see INDESTRUCTIBLE
ant corruptible

incorruption *n syn* see HONESTY
ant corruption

increase *vb* **1** to make greater or more numerous < *increase* crops by good cultural practices >
syn aggrandize, augment, beef (up), boost, build, compound, enlarge, expand, extend, heighten, magnify, manifold, multiply, plus, push
rel aggravate, enhance, intensify; amplify, dilate, distend, inflate, swell; elongate,

lengthen, prolong, protract; reinforce, strengthen
con abate, abbreviate, condense, contract; depreciate, diminish, lessen, lower, reduce; curtail, shorten, shrink; minimize
ant decrease

2 to become greater or more numerous < his wealth *increased* over the years >
syn augment, build, burgeon, enlarge, expand, heighten, mount, multiply, rise, run up, snowball, upsurge, wax
rel dilate, distend, inflate, intensify, lengthen, strengthen, swell; pullulate, swarm, teem
con abate, condense, contract, diminish, lessen, lower, reduce, shorten, shrink; die off, die (out), end, terminate
ant decrease

3 *syn* see RAISE 9

increase *n* **1** *syn* see ADDITION
ant decrease

2 *syn* see RISE 3

increate *adj syn* see SELF-EXISTENT
ant created

incredible *adj* **1** too extraordinary or improbable to admit of belief < an *incredible* story of privations overcome >
syn incogitable, inconceivable, insupposable, unbelievable, unimaginable, unthinkable
rel absurd, outlandish, preposterous, ridiculous; impossible, untenable
idiom beyond belief, out of the question
con acceptable, believable, conceivable, likely, plausible, reasonable
ant credible

2 *syn* see IMPLAUSIBLE
ant credible

incredulity *n syn* see UNBELIEF
con gullibility, naiveté
ant credulity, credulousness

incredulous *adj* unwilling to admit or accept what is offered as true < his explanation met an *incredulous* response from his listeners >
syn aporetic, disbelieving, questioning, quizzical, show-me, skeptical, unbelieving
rel hesitant, suspicious, uncertain, wary; distrustful, distrusting, mistrustful; doubting, dubious, unconvinced, unsatisfied
con trustful, trusting; unsuspecting, unsuspicious, unwary; gullible, naive
ant credulous

increment *n syn* see ADDITION

incriminate *vb syn* see ACCUSE
rel implicate, involve
ant exonerate

incrustate *vb syn* see CAKE 1

inculcate *vb syn* see IMPLANT
rel educate, instruct, teach; communicate, impart

inculpable *adj* **1** *syn* see GOOD
ant culpable

2 *syn* see INNOCENT 2
ant culpable

inculpate *vb syn* see ACCUSE
ant exculpate

incult *adj syn* see COARSE 3

incur *vb* to bring (something usually unpleasant) upon oneself < he foolishly *incurred* debts beyond his ability to pay >
syn contract
rel acquire, get; bring on, induce

idiom bring down on (*or* upon)
con avoid, elude, escape, eschew, evade, shun; discharge, pay, settle

incurable *adj syn* see HOPELESS 2
ant curable

incurious *adj syn* see INDIFFERENT 2
rel absent, absentminded, abstracted, distraught, preoccupied
con nosy, prying, snoopy; impertinent, intrusive, meddlesome; observant, observing
ant curious, inquisitive

incursion *n syn* see INVASION

indebted *adj* owing gratitude or recognition (as for a favor or service rendered) <was *indebted* to the book for most of his information>
syn beholden, obligated, obliged
rel duty-bound, honor-bound

indebtedness *n* **1** a state of owing something <unable to escape from *indebtedness*>
syn arrearage, debt, liability, obligation; compare DEBT 3
rel delinquency, nonpayment; bankruptcy, failure, insolvency
con discharge, liquidation, satisfaction; exoneration, freeing, release
2 *syn* see DEBT 3

indecent *adj* **1** *syn* see INDECOROUS
ant decent
2 *syn* see OBSCENE 2
ant decent

indecipherable *adj syn* see ILLEGIBLE
ant decipherable

indecision *n syn* see HESITATION
ant decision, decisiveness

indecisive *adj* **1** *syn* see INCONCLUSIVE
ant decisive
2 *syn* see DOUBTFUL 1
con certain, incontrovertible, undebatable, unequivocal
ant decisive
3 *syn* see VACILLATING 2
rel undecided, unsettled
idiom of two minds
con decided, determined, firm, positive, resolved, settled, unfaltering, unhesitant, unhesitating, unwavering
ant decisive

indecisiveness *n syn* see HESITATION
ant indecision, decisiveness

indecorous *adj* not conforming with accepted standards of propriety or good taste <they regarded argument in public as *indecorous*>
syn improper, indecent, indelicate, malodorous, ridiculous, rough, unbecoming, undecorous, ungodly, unseemly, untoward
rel inappropriate, incorrect, unbefitting, unfit, unfitting; immodest, inelegant, undignified; coarse, gross, loose, offensive, shameful, tasteless, vulgar; discourteous, ill-mannered, impolite, rude, uncivil; irregular, unlawful
idiom in bad form
con becoming, courteous, decent, nice, proper, seemly; conventional, formal

syn synonym(s)   *rel* related word(s)
ant antonym(s)   *con* contrasted word(s)
idiom idiomatic equivalent(s)
‖ use limited; if in doubt, see a dictionary

ant decorous

indecorousness *n syn* see IMPROPRIETY 1
ant decorousness

indecorum *n* **1** *syn* see FAUX PAS
2 *syn* see IMPROPRIETY 1
ant decorum

indeed *adv* **1** *syn* see WELL 7
2 *syn* see EVEN 3

indefatigable *adj* capable of prolonged and arduous effort <a teacher who has *indefatigable* patience with slow learners>
syn inexhaustible, tireless, unflagging, untiring, unwearirable, unwearying, weariless
rel assiduous, diligent, painstaking, sedulous; determined, dogged, patient, persevering, persistent, pertinacious, relentless, steadfast, stubborn, tenacious, unfaltering, unflinching, unrelenting, unwavering; energetic, strenuous, vigorous
con dawdling, dilatory, laggard, lagging, procrastinating; faineant, indolent, lackadaisical, lazy, slothful, sluggish
ant fatigable

indefectible *adj* **1** *syn* see PERFECT 2
2 *syn* see IDEAL 3

indefensible *adj syn* see INEXCUSABLE
ant defensible

indefinable *adj syn* see UNUTTERABLE
ant definable

indefinite *adj* **1** having no exact limits <a region with *indefinite* boundaries>
syn indeterminate, indistinct, inexact, undeterminable
rel unclear, undefined, unfixed, unspecific; broad, loose, wide; general, obscure, vague
con exact, measured; known
ant definite
2 *syn* see LIMITLESS
ant definite

indelible *adj* that cannot be removed or erased <made an *indelible* impression on his hearers>
syn ineffaceable, ineradicable, inerasable, inexpungible, inextirpable, uneradicable, unerasable
rel indestructible, undestroyable; enduring, permanent
con eradicable, effaceable, erasable, removable; ephemeral, evanescent, passing, temporary, transitory
ant delible

indelicate *adj syn* see INDECOROUS
rel callow, crude, rude, uncouth; lewd, wanton
con chaste, modest, pure
ant delicate

indemnification *n syn* see REPARATION

indemnify *vb syn* see COMPENSATE 3

indemnity *n syn* see REPARATION

indentation *n* **1** *syn* see NOTCH 1
2 *syn* see IMPRESSION 1

indenture *n syn* see NOTCH 1

indentured *adj syn* see BOUND 2

independent *adj* **1** *syn* see FREE 1
2 *syn* see SELF-SUFFICIENT
ant dependent

independently *adv syn* see APART 1
idiom on one's own

indescribable *adj syn* see UNUTTERABLE
ant describable

indestructible *adj* incapable of being destroyed <*indestructible* idealism>

syn imperishable, incorruptible, inexterminable, inextinguishable, inextirpable, irrefragable, irrefrangible, quenchless, undestroyable, unperishable

rel changeless, immutable, unalterable, unchangeable; deathless, immortal, perpetual, undying; durable, enduring, lasting, permanent; indelible, ineradicable; unextinguishable, unquenchable

con alterable, changeable, corruptible, impermanent, temporary, transient, unlasting; mortal, temporal; evanescent

ant destroyable, destructible, perishable

indeterminate *adj syn* see INDEFINITE 1
   ant determinate

index *n syn* see INDICATION 3

Indian sign *n syn* see JINX

indicate *vb* 1 *syn* see POINT 2

2 to give evidence of or serve as ground for a valid or reasonable inference < several polls *indicate* a landslide for the incumbent >
syn announce, argue, attest, bespeak, betoken, testify, witness
rel denote, import, mean, signify; demonstrate, prove; evidence, evince, manifest, show; display, exhibit, express, illustrate; connote, hint, imply, suggest
3 *syn* see SHOW 5

indication *n* 1 *syn* see HINT 1

2 *syn* see EXPRESSION 3

3 something that is an outward manifestation of something else < such *indications* of prosperity as second cars and color TVs >
syn evidence, index, indicia, mark, sign, significant, symptom, token; *compare* SYMBOL 1, TESTIMONY
rel expression, manifestation; hint, suggestion; proof; prefiguration, type

indicative *adj* serving to indicate < the roar of the crowd was *indicative* of its approval >
syn denotative, denotive, designative, exhibitive, indicatory, indicial, significative
rel characteristic, demonstrative, evidential, evincive, expressive, suggestive, symbolic, symptomatic, testatory

indicatory *adj syn* see INDICATIVE

indicia *n pl syn* see INDICATION 3

indicial *adj syn* see INDICATIVE

indict *vb syn* see ACCUSE

indifference *n syn* see APATHY 2

indifferent *adj* 1 *syn* see FAIR 4

2 marked by a lack of interest or concern < was *indifferent* to suffering and poverty >
syn aloof, by-the-way, casual, detached, disinterested, incurious, numb, pococurante, remote, unconcerned, uncurious, uninterested, withdrawn; *compare* UNSOCIABLE
rel apathetic, impassive, insensible; dispassionate; careless, heedless, negligent, regardless, uncaring, unmindful; inattentive, unobserving
con attentive, considerate, heedful, interested, mindful, regardful, sympathetic
ant concerned
3 *syn* see COLD 2
4 *syn* see MEDIUM

indigence *n syn* see POVERTY 1
   ant affluence, opulence

indigency *n syn* see POVERTY 1
   ant affluence, opulence

indigenous *adj* 1 *syn* see NATIVE 2
con alien, extraneous, foreign
ant exotic; naturalized
2 *syn* see INNATE 1

indigent *adj syn* see POOR 1
   ant affluent, opulent

indignant *adj syn* see ANGRY
   ant gratified

indignation *n syn* see ANGER
   ant gratification

indignity *n syn* see AFFRONT
rel grievance, injury, injustice, wrong

indirect *adj* 1 deviating from a direct line or straightforward course < made *indirect* inquiries about the new neighbor >
syn circuitous, circular, collateral, oblique, roundabout
rel circumlocutory, crooked, devious; meandering, serpentine, sinuous, tortuous, twisting, winding; errant, vagrant, wandering
ant direct; forthright, straightforward
2 *syn* see UNDERHAND
   ant straight

indirection *n syn* see DECEPTION 1

indiscernible *adj syn* see IMPERCEPTIBLE
   ant discernible, distinguishable

indiscreet *adj syn* see UNWISE
   ant discreet

indiscriminate *adj* 1 including all or nearly all within the range of choice, operation, or effectiveness < her charity was *indiscriminate* but generous >
syn indiscriminating, indiscriminative, sweeping, undiscriminated, undiscriminating, undistinguishing, wholesale
rel assorted, heterogeneous, miscellaneous, promiscuous; shallow, superficial, uncritical; broad, extensive, wide
con discretionary, discriminative; choosy, picky; critical, perfectionist
ant selective; discriminate, discriminated
2 *syn* see RANDOM
3 *syn* see MISCELLANEOUS

indiscriminating *adj syn* see INDISCRIMINATE 1
   ant discriminating

indiscriminative *adj syn* see INDISCRIMINATE 1
   ant discriminative

indispensable *adj syn* see ESSENTIAL 4
rel cardinal, fundamental
ant dispensable

indisposed *adj* 1 *syn* see UNWELL
2 *syn* see DISINCLINED
rel antagonistic, antipathetic, hostile, inimical
con amicable, neighborly; responsive, sympathetic
ant disposed

indisposition *n* 1 *syn* see DISLIKE
2 *syn* see SICKNESS 1

indisputable *adj* 1 *syn* see POSITIVE 3
   ant disputable
2 *syn* see REAL 3

indistinct *adj* 1 *syn* see INDEFINITE 1
   ant distinct
2 *syn* see FAINT 2
   ant distinct

indistinguishable *adj syn* see SAME 2
   ant distinguishable

indite *vb syn* see WRITE

individual *adj* **1** *syn* see PERSONAL 1
ant common, popular
2 *syn* see SPECIAL 1
rel separate, single, sole
con generic, universal
ant general
3 *syn* see CHARACTERISTIC
ant common
4 *syn* see SEVERAL 1

individual *n* **1** *syn* see ENTITY 1
2 *syn* see THING 4
3 *syn* see HUMAN

individualism *n* **1** *syn* see DISPOSITION 3
2 *syn* see INDIVIDUALITY 3

individualist *adj syn* see EGOCENTRIC 1

individualistic *adj syn* see EGOCENTRIC 1

individuality *n* **1** *syn* see DISPOSITION 3
2 *syn* see UNITY 1
3 distinctive character < a person of marked *individuality* >
syn distinctiveness, individualism, particularity, singularity
rel character, personality
4 individual identity < a teacher who respects children's *individualities* >
syn identity, ipseity, personality, seity, selfdom, selfhood, selfness, singularity
rel independence, separateness, uniqueness; difference, dissimilarity, unlikeness
con likeness, resemblance, similarity

individualize *vb syn* see CHARACTERIZE 2

individually *adv syn* see APART 1

individuate *vb syn* see CHARACTERIZE 2

indocile *adj syn* see UNRULY 1
ant docile

indolence *n syn* see SLOTH 1
ant industry

indolent *adj syn* see LAZY
con active, diligent, energetic, vigorous
ant industrious

indomitable *adj* **1** *syn* see INVINCIBLE 1
ant domitable
2 *syn* see INSUPERABLE
rel dogged, pertinacious, stubborn; resolute, staunch, steadfast
ant domitable
3 *syn* see UNRULY 1

indoors *adv* in or into a building < stayed *indoors* during the storm >
syn inside, within, withindoors, withinside
con outdoors, outside, without, withoutdoors
ant outdoors

indubitable *adj* **1** *syn* see POSITIVE 3
ant dubitable, questionable
2 *syn* see AUTHENTIC 2
ant doubtful, dubious
3 *syn* see DOWNRIGHT 2

induce *vb* **1** to move another to do or agree to something < *induced* him to give up smoking for the sake of his health >
syn argue (into), bring around, convince, draw, draw in, draw on, get, oversway, persuade, prevail (on *or* upon), procure, prompt, talk (into), win (over)

rel influence, sway; abet, incite, lead; actuate, impel, move; activate, motivate
con check, curb, hold back, restrain
2 *syn* see GENERATE 3

inducible *adj syn* see INDUCTIVE

induct *vb syn* see INITIATE 3

induction *n syn* see INITIATION

inductive *adj* **1** derived or derivable by reasoning from a part to a whole, from particulars to generals, or from the individual to the universal < used an *inductive* approach to the problem >
syn a posteriori, inducible
rel Baconian, epagogic
2 *syn* see PRELIMINARY

indulge *vb* **1** to give free rein to (as curiosity or a desire) < *indulged* their taste for gourmet foods >
syn cater (to), gratify, humor
rel favor, oblige, satisfy; delight, please, regale
idiom give rein to
con bridle, check, constrain, curb, restrain
2 *syn* see BABY
3 *syn* see WALLOW 3

indulgence *n* **1** *syn* see FORBEARANCE 2
rel benignancy, benignity, benignness, kindliness, kindness; gentleness, mildness
con rigor, severity, sternness; rigidity, rigorousness; harshness
ant strictness
2 *syn* see FAVOR 4

indulgent *adj syn* see FORBEARING
rel cosseting, pampering, permissive; condoning, excusing, forgiving, pardoning; benign, benignant, kind, kindly
con severe, stern; harsh, rigorous, stringent
ant strict

indurate *vb syn* see HARDEN 1

industrious *adj syn* see ASSIDUOUS
rel active, busy, live, dynamic; persevering, persistent
con idle, inactive; lethargic, sluggish
ant indolent, slothful; unindustrious

industry *n syn* see BUSINESS 4

indwell *vb syn* see BELONG 3

indweller *n syn* see INHABITANT

indwelling *adj syn* see INHERENT

inebriant *n syn* see LIQUOR 2

inebriate *n syn* see DRUNKARD

inebriated *adj syn* see INTOXICATED 1

inebrious *adj syn* see INTOXICATED 1

inedible *adj* not fit for food < an *inedible* plant >
syn inesculent, uneatable
rel indigestible, unwholesome; insipid, unappetizing; baneful, noxious, poisonous
con eatable, esculent; digestible, wholesome; appetizing, savory, tasty; harmless, innocuous, innoxious, nonpoisonous
ant edible

ineffable *adj syn* see UNUTTERABLE
rel celestial, empyreal, empyrean, heavenly; ethereal; divine, holy, sacred, spiritual; abstract, ideal, transcendent, transcendental
con expressible; utterable

ineffaceable *adj syn* see INDELIBLE

ineffective *adj* **1** *syn* see FUTILE
ant effective
2 *syn* see WEAK 4

3 not producing or not capable of producing a required result < *ineffective* remedies >
syn ineffectual, inefficacious, inefficient
rel inadequate, incompetent, inferior; useless, worthless
con active, effectual, efficacious; esteemed, valuable
ant effective

ineffectiveness *n syn* see INABILITY
ant effectiveness

ineffectual *adj* **1** *syn* see FUTILE
ant effectual
2 *syn* see INEFFECTIVE 3
ant effectual
3 *syn* see WEAK 4
4 *syn* see LITTLE 2

ineffectualness *n syn* see INABILITY
ant effectualness

inefficacious *adj syn* see INEFFECTIVE 3
ant efficacious

inefficacy *n syn* see INABILITY
ant efficacy

inefficient *adj* **1** *syn* see INEFFECTIVE 3
ant efficient
2 incapable of the proper performance of duties < *inefficient* workmen >
syn incapable, incompetent, inept, inexpert, unexpert, unskilled, unskillful, unworkmanlike
rel careless, slipshod, slovenly; unfitted, unprepared, unqualified, untrained; unskilled, unskillful
con able, adept, capable, competent, expert, proficient, qualified, skilled, skillful, workmanlike
ant efficient

inelaborate *adj syn* see PLAIN 1
ant elaborate

inelastic *adj syn* see STIFF 1
ant elastic

inelegance *n syn* see IMPROPRIETY 1
ant elegance

inelegant *adj syn* see COARSE 3

ineligible *adj syn* see UNFIT 2
ant eligible

ineluctable *adj syn* see INEVITABLE
con doubtful, dubious, questionable; likely, possible, probable

ineludible *adj syn* see INEVITABLE

inenarrable *adj syn* see UNUTTERABLE

inept *adj* **1** *syn* see IMPROPER 1
ant apt
2 *syn* see INFELICITOUS
ant apropos, apt
3 *syn* see AWKWARD 2
ant apt; adept
4 *syn* see UNSKILLFUL 1
ant able
5 *syn* see INEFFICIENT 2
ant competent, efficient

inequable *adj syn* see INEQUITABLE
ant equable

inequality *n* **1** the quality of being uneven < hampered by the *inequality* of the ground >
syn asperity, irregularity, roughness, unevenness
rel cragginess, jaggedness, ruggedness, rugosity
con equality, evenness, levelness, smoothness
2 *syn* see DISPARITY

ant equality

inequitable *adj* not fair or just < an *inequitable* tax burden >
syn inequable, unequitable, unfair, unjust, unrighteous
rel undeserved, undue, unmerited; bad, wrong, wrongful; arbitrary, high-handed, oppressive
con fair, just
ant equitable

inequitableness *n syn* see INJUSTICE 1
ant equitableness

inequity *n syn* see INJUSTICE 1
ant equity

ineradicable *adj syn* see INDELIBLE
ant eradicable

inerasable *adj syn* see INDELIBLE
ant erasable

inerrable *adj syn* see INFALLIBLE 1
ant errable

inerrant *adj syn* see INFALLIBLE 1
rel accurate, correct, exact, precise; dependable, reliable, trustworthy
ant errant

inert *adj syn* see INACTIVE
rel impotent, powerless; apathetic, impassive, phleg- matic, stolid; dead, inanimate, lifeless
con animated, awake; alert, vigilant, watchful; live, operative
ant animated; dynamic

inerudite *adj syn* see UNSCHOLARLY
ant erudite, learned

inescapable *adj syn* see INEVITABLE
ant escapable

inescapably *adv syn* see WILLY-NILLY

inesculent *adj syn* see INEDIBLE
ant esculent

in essence *adv* **1** *syn* see ESSENTIALLY 1
2 *syn* see VIRTUALLY

inessential *adj syn* see UNNECESSARY
ant crucial, essential

inestimable *adj* **1** *syn* see INCALCULABLE 1
2 *syn* see PRECIOUS 1

inevasible *adj syn* see INEVITABLE

inevitable *adj* incapable of being avoided or escaped < the effect of the scandal on the election was *inevitable* >
syn certain, ineluctable, ineludible, inescapable, inevasible, necessary, returnless, unavoidable, unescapable, unevadable
rel ineliminable, sure, unpreventable; decided, settled; destined, foreordained; inexorable, inflexible
idiom as sure to follow as night follows day, in the cards
con eludible, escapable, evadable
ant avoidable, evitable

inevitably *adv syn* see WILLY-NILLY

inexact *adj syn* see INDEFINITE 1
ant exact

inexcusable *adj* being without excuse or justification < an *inexcusable* blunder >
syn indefensible, inexpiable, unforgivable, unjustifiable, unpardonable, untenable
rel blamable, blameworthy, censurable, criticizable; impermissible, unallowable, unpermissible; intolerable, reprehensible
con allowable, blameless, defensible, forgivable, justifiable, pardonable, venial
ant excusable

inexhaustible *adj syn* see INDEFATIGABLE

inexorable *adj syn* see INFLEXIBLE 2
  rel resolute; immobile, immovable
  con compassionate, responsive, sympathetic, tender; clement, forbearing, indulgent, lenient

inexpedient *adj syn* see INADVISABLE
  ant expedient

inexpensive *adj syn* see CHEAP 1
  ant expensive

inexperience *n* lack or serious deficiency of practical wisdom < his failure was due to his *inexperience* >
  syn callowness, freshness, greenness, rawness
  rel ignorance, naiveté; amateurishness; unfamiliarity; unsophistication; verdancy
  con grasp, understanding; polish, sophistication; skill, training
  ant experience

inexperienced *adj* lacking knowledge, skill, or practice based on direct observation and participation < hired *inexperienced* help >
  syn callow, fresh, green, inexpert, raw, rude, unconversant, unexperienced, unfleshed, unpracticed, unseasoned, untried, unversed, young
  rel ignorant, immature, inept, naive; prentice, unacquainted, unfamiliar, unskilled, untrained
  con expert, old, practiced, seasoned, skilled, versed, veteran
  ant experienced

inexpert *adj* 1 *syn* see INEXPERIENCED
  ant expert
  2 *syn* see UNSKILLFUL 1
  ant expert
  3 *syn* see INEFFICIENT 2
  ant expert
  4 *syn* see CRUDE 5

inexpiable *adj syn* see INEXCUSABLE
  ant expiable

inexplainable *adj syn* see INEXPLICABLE
  ant explainable, explicable

inexplicable *adj* not capable of being explained or accounted for < an *inexplicable* discrepancy in the accounts >
  syn inexplainable, unaccountable, unexplainable; *compare* MYSTERIOUS
  rel indecipherable, indescribable, inscrutable, undefinable, unfathomable, unsolvable; mysterious, odd, peculiar, strange
  con clear, obvious, plain; comprehensible, graspable, intelligible
  ant explainable, explicable

inexpressible *adj syn* see UNUTTERABLE
  ant expressible

inexpressive *adj syn* see EXPRESSIONLESS
  ant expressive

inexpugnable *adj syn* see INVINCIBLE 1
  rel irresistible, unopposable
  con assailable, attackable
  ant expugnable

inexpungible *adj syn* see INDELIBLE

inexterminable *adj syn* see INDESTRUCTIBLE

inextinguishable *adj syn* see INDESTRUCTIBLE

  ant extinguishable

inextirpable *adj* 1 *syn* see INDESTRUCTIBLE
  2 *syn* see INDELIBLE

inextricable *adj syn* see INSOLUBLE
  ant extricable

infallible *adj* 1 incapable of being in error < an *infallible* ear for pitch in music >
  syn inerrable, inerrant, sure, unerring
  rel faultless, flawless, impeccable, undeceivable; correct, exact, perfect
  con deceivable, faulty, unsure; doubtful, dubious, questionable
  ant fallible
  2 not liable to mislead, deceive, or disappoint < an *infallible* remedy >
  syn certain, sure, surefire, unfailing
  rel effective, efficacious, efficient; handy, helpful, useful; acceptable, agreeable, satisfying; satisfactory
  con doubtful, questionable, uncertain, unsure; useless, worthless; unacceptable, unsatisfying; unsatisfactory
  ant fallible

infamous *adj* 1 having an extremely and deservedly bad reputation < one of the most *infamous* of the dictator's henchmen >
  syn ill-famed, notorious, opprobrious
  rel abominable, atrocious, evil, hateful, heinous, iniquitous, odious, scandalous, vile, villainous; contemptible, despicable, scurvy, sorry
  con distinguished, eminent, esteemed, honored, illustrious, notable, prestigious, reputable
  2 *syn* see VICIOUS 2
  rel disgraceful, disreputable, ignominious, shameful
  con glorious, splendid, sublime
  ant illustrious

infamy *n syn* see DISGRACE
  rel notoriety, notoriousness

infancy *n* 1 early childhood < the helplessness of *infancy* >
  syn babyhood, infanthood
  rel childhood, immaturity, juvenility, nonage
  con adulthood, maturity, old age, senescence
  2 the state or period of being under the age established by law for the attainment of full civil rights < his heirs were still in *infancy* >
  syn minority, nonage
  rel immaturity, juniority, juvenility
  con adulthood, adultness, maturity, seniority
  ant majority

infant *n syn* see BABY 1

infant *adj syn* see YOUNG 1

infanthood *n syn* see INFANCY 1

infantile *adj syn* see CHILDISH
  ant adult

infantine *adj syn* see CHILDISH
  ant adult

infatuate *adj syn* see INFATUATED

infatuated *adj* possessed with or marked by a strong attachment or foolish or unreasoning love or desire < *infatuated* with a woman he can't have >
  syn besotted, dotty, enamored, infatuate
  rel bewitched, captivated, enraptured, obsessed; foolish, silly

---

syn synonym(s)   *rel* related word(s)
ant antonym(s)   *con* contrasted word(s)
idiom idiomatic equivalent(s)
‖ use limited; if in doubt, see a dictionary

con detached, dispassionate, objective, undazzled, unprepossessed

infatuation *n* a strong and unreasoning but transitory attachment < went through a series of *infatuations* before he settled down >
syn béguin, crush, ||pash, passion
rel ardor, craze, devotion, fascination, obsession, rage

in favor of *prep syn* see FOR 1

infeasible *adj syn* see IMPOSSIBLE 1
ant feasible

infectious *adj* 1 capable of causing infection < viruses and other *infectious* agents >
syn infective
rel mephitic, miasmic, noxious, pestilent, pestilential, poisonous, toxic, virulent
con healthful, hygienic, salutary, wholesome
2 transmissible by infection < *infectious* diseases >
syn catching, communicable, contagious
3 easily communicated or diffused < her enthusiasm was *infectious* >
syn catching, contagious, taking
rel irresistible, sympathetic

infective *adj syn* see INFECTIOUS 1
infecund *adj syn* see STERILE 1

infelicitous *adj* marked by a lack of appropriateness and grace of expression < made a very *infelicitous* remark >
syn awkward, graceless, ill-chosen, inept, unfortunate, unhappy
rel inappropriate, inapropos, inapt, malapropos, unapt; deplorable, gauche, regrettable
con fortunate, graceful, happy
ant felicitous

infer *vb* to arrive at by reasoning from evidence or from premises < we *inferred* from his questions that he was a stranger in the vicinity >
syn collect, conclude, deduce, deduct, derive, ||dope out, draw, gather, judge, make, make out; *compare* CONJECTURE
rel induce; conjecture, glean, guess, reckon, speculate, surmise, think; ascertain, construe, interpret, reason, understand
idiom come to (or draw or reach) a conclusion; read between the lines

inference *n* 1 the deriving of a conclusion by reasoning < the answer was obtainable by *inference* >
syn deduction, illation, judgment, ratiocination
rel conjecture, guessing, reckoning, supposition, surmise
2 a determination arrived at by reasoning < a wrong *inference* based on incomplete evidence >
syn conclusion, deduction, illation, judgment, ratiocination, sequitur
rel assumption, conjecture, guess, presumption, reckoning, supposition, surmise

inferior *adj* 1 being or regarded as being below the level of another thing < the *inferior* latitudes of the northern hemisphere >
syn lesser, low, lower, nether, subjacent, under

rel junior, minor, secondary, subaltern, subordinate
con greater, higher, over, overlying
ant superior
2 of little or less importance, value, or merit < sold *inferior* goods at high prices >
syn common, déclassé, hack, low-grade, mean, poor, second-class, second-drawer, second-rate; *compare* CHEAP 2
rel average, fair, indifferent, mediocre, middling, ordinary; bad, base, paltry, punk, shoddy, sleazy, sorry, tawdry, tinpot, wretched; good-for-nothing, lousy, ||no-account, no-good, unworthy, valueless, worthless
con choice, excellent, first-class, first-rate, high-grade, prime
ant superior

inferior *n* one lower than another (as in station or worth) < a man inclined to be disdainful of his social *inferiors* >
syn poor relation, scrub, secondary, subaltern, subordinate, underling, understrapper
rel attendant, auxiliary, deputy; retainer, satrap, subject, vassal; hanger-on, heeler, henchman, hireling, minion, satellite, sycophant; adherent, disciple, follower
con chief, head, leader, master, principal
ant superior

infernal *adj* 1 of or relating to a nether world of the dead < the *infernal* regions >
syn chthonian, chthonic, Hadean, plutonian, plutonic, sulphurous, Tartarean
con celestial, elysian, Hesperidean, paradisaic, paradisal, paradisiacal
ant supernal
2 resembling or appropriate to hell or its inhabitants < an *infernal* glow in the sky >
syn avernal, cimmerian, hellish, pandemoniac, plutonian, plutonic, stygian
rel demonic, devilish, diabolic, fiendish; sulphurous
ant celestial, heavenly
3 *syn* see DAMNED 2
4 *syn* see UTTER

inferno *n* 1 *syn* see HELL
2 *syn* see FIRE 1

inferred *adj syn* see TACIT 1

infertile *adj* 1 *syn* see STERILE 1
rel depleted, drained, exhausted, impoverished
con breeding, generating, propagating, reproducing
ant fertile
2 *syn* see BARREN 2
ant fertile

infest *vb* 1 to spread or swarm over in a troublesome manner < lawns *infested* with weeds >
syn beset, overrun, overspread, overswarm
rel abound, crawl, swarm, teem; annoy, harass, harry, pester, plague, worry
2 to live in or on as a parasite < a dog *infested* by fleas >
syn parasite, parasitize

infidel *adj syn* see HEATHEN
infidelic *adj syn* see HEATHEN
infidelity *n* betrayal of a moral obligation < a leader guilty of *infidelity* to the responsibilities he had accepted >

syn disloyalty, faithlessness, falseness, falsity, perfidiousness, perfidy, unfaithfulness; *compare* TREACHERY

rel fickleness, inconstancy; treacherousness, treachery, treason

idiom bad faith

con devotion, faithfulness, fealty; constancy, loyalty, steadfastness

ant fidelity

infiltrate *vb syn see* INSINUATE 3

infinite *adj* 1 being without known limits < the idea of an *infinite* universe >

syn eternal, illimitable, perdurable, sempiternal, supertemporal

rel everlasting, perpetual

con bounded, circumscribed, limited, restricted

ant finite

2 *syn see* LIMITLESS

ant finite

infinity *n syn see* ETERNITY 1

infirm *adj syn see* WEAK 1

ant hale

infirmity *n* 1 the quality or state of being enfeebled and weakened in health < suffering from old age and attendant physical *infirmity* >

syn debility, decrepitude, disease, feebleness, infirmness, malaise, sickliness, unhealthiness; *compare* DISEASE 1, SICKNESS 1

rel debilitation, decay, enfeeblement, failing, frailty, weakening, weakness; diseasedness, unwellness; illness, indisposition, sickness, unhealth

ant haleness

2 *syn see* DISEASE 1

3 *syn see* SICKNESS 1

infirmness *n syn see* INFIRMITY 1

infix *vb* 1 *syn see* ENTRENCH 1

2 *syn see* IMPLANT

inflame *vb* 1 *syn see* LIGHT 1

ant extinguish

2 *syn see* IRRITATE

inflammable *adj syn see* COMBUSTIBLE 1

ant nonflammable, noninflammable

inflammatory *adj* exciting or tending to excite anger, animosity, or disorder < *inflammatory* speeches designed to spark rebellion >

syn incendiary

rel exciting, incitive, instigative, provocative; revolutionary, seditionary, seditious

con calming, moderating, soothing, temperate

inflate *vb syn see* EXPAND 3

ant deflate

inflated *adj* swollen with or as if with something insubstantial < had an *inflated* idea of his own importance >

syn dropsical, dropsied, flatulent, overblown, tumescent, tumid, turgid, windy

rel aureate, bombastic, flowery, grandiloquent, magniloquent, rhetorical; ostentatious, pretentious, showy; fustian, ranting, rhapsodical; diffuse, prolix, verbose, wordy

con compendious, concise, laconic, pithy, succinct, summary, terse

inflatus *n syn see* INSPIRATION

inflection *n* a particular manner of employing the sounds of the voice in speech < questions end on a rising *inflection* >

syn accent, intonation, tone

rel articulation, enunciation, pronunciation; timbre, tonality

idiom tone of voice

inflexible *adj* 1 *syn see* STIFF 1

rel immobile, immovable

con elastic, resilient, springy, supple; ductile, malleable, plastic, pliable, pliant; fluid, liquid

ant flexible

2 rigidly firm in will or purpose < a person of *inflexible* resolution >

syn adamant, adamantine, brassbound, dogged, inexorable, iron, obdurate, relentless, rigid, rockbound, rock-ribbed, single-minded, steadfast, stubborn, unbendable, unbending, uncompliant, uncompromising, unswayable, unyielding; *compare* STIFF 1

rel intractable, obstinate; indomitable, invincible, unconquerable; grim, hard, implacable, unrelenting; dyed-in-the-wool, fixed, set, ‖sot

con agreeable, amenable, compliant, docile, pliant, responsive, swayable, yielding; mild, open

ant flexible

3 incapable of changing or being changed < *inflexible* rules >

syn constant, determinate, fixed, immovable, immutable, inalterable, invariable, ironclad, unalterable, unchangeable, unmodifiable, unmovable

rel strict; rigorous; established, set, settled; changeless, unchanging

con adaptable, adjustable, alterable, changeable, mutable, variable

ant flexible

4 *syn see* TOUGH 3

inflict *vb* 1 *syn see* GIVE 10

2 to cause one to endure (something damaging or painful) < *inflict* retribution >

syn force (on *or* upon), impose, visit, wreak, wreck; *compare* IMPOSE 4

rel expose, subject

idiom lay open to, put on the spot

con guard, protect, shelter, shield

inflow *n syn see* INFLUX

ant outflow, outflux

influence *n* 1 power exerted over the minds or behavior of others < a person of great *influence* in national politics >

syn authority, credit, prestige, weight; *compare* PULL 2

rel command, domination, dominion, mastery; ascendancy, dominance, eminence, predominance; consequence, importance, moment; ‖drag, in, pull

2 *syn see* PULL 2

influence *vb* 1 *syn see* AFFECT

2 *syn see* PREJUDICE 2

influenceable *adj syn see* RECEPTIVE 1

influx *n* a flowing in < anticipated an *influx* of immigrants >

syn inflow, influxion, inpour, inpouring, inrush

rel accession, augmentation, increase; illapse

con outpour, outpouring, outrush; efflux, effluxion, exodus

---

syn synonym(s)   *rel* related word(s)
ant antonym(s)   *con* contrasted word(s)
idiom idiomatic equivalent(s)
‖ use limited; if in doubt, see a dictionary

ant outflow, outflux

influxion *n syn* see INFLUX
ant effluxion

inform *vb* 1 *syn* see FIRE 2
rel imbue, infuse, leaven, permeate; enlighten, illuminate; endow, endue
2 to make aware or cognizant of something < was kept *informed* of developments >
syn acquaint, advise, apprise, clue (*or* clew), fill in, notify, post, tell, warn, wise (up)
rel educate, enlighten, instruct, teach; familiarize; caution, forewarn
idiom keep posted
3 to give information about someone especially as an informer < his suspicions aroused, he *informed* on his neighbor to the police >
syn ‖nark, peach, ‖pimp, rat, ‖sing, snitch, squeak, squeal, ‖stool; *compare* TALK 6
rel blab, tattle, tell; betray, give away, turn in

informal *adj* 1 conducted or carried out without rigidly prescribed procedure < carried on an *informal* investigation >
syn irregular, unceremonious, unofficial
rel casual, spontaneous; unauthorized; unconventional; private, special
con authorized, ceremonious, conventional, official, regular
ant formal
2 *syn* see EASYGOING 3
rel familiar, natural, simple
con affected, mannered, prim, rigid, stiff, stilted
ant formal

information *n* 1 *syn* see KNOWLEDGE 2
2 *syn* see NEWS

informational *adj syn* see INFORMATIVE

informative *adj* imparting information < gave an *informative* talk >
syn educational, educative, informational, informatory, instructional, instructive
rel edifying, elucidative, enlightening, explanatory, illuminating
ant uninformative

informatory *adj syn* see INFORMATIVE

informed *adj syn* see FAMILIAR 3
ant uninformed

informer *n* one who informs against another < his arrest was brought about by an *informer* >
syn betrayer, ‖canary, ‖fink, ‖nark, ‖pimp, snitch, squawker, ‖squeaker, squealer, stool, stoolie, stool pigeon, talebearer, tattler, tattletale, tipster; *compare* BUSYBODY, DETECTIVE, GOSSIP 1, SPY

infra *adv* 1 *syn* see BELOW 2
ant above, supra
2 *syn* see AFTER

infract *vb syn* see VIOLATE 1

infraction *n syn* see BREACH 1
rel crime, offense, sin; error, faux pas, lapse, slip

infrastructure *n* 1 *syn* see BASE 1
ant superstructure
2 *syn* see BASIS 1

infrequent *adj* appearing, happening, or met with so seldom as to attract attention < held only *infrequent* press conferences >

syn few, occasional, rare, scarce, seldom, semioccasional, sporadic, uncommon, unfrequent
rel isolated, scattered; meager, scant, scanty, sparse; exceptional, limited, unusual; odd, spasmodic, stray
idiom few and far between
con abundant, common, numerous, regular; ordinary, routine
ant frequent

infrequently *adv* 1 *syn* see SELDOM
ant frequently
2 *syn* see OCCASIONALLY
ant frequently

infringe *vb* 1 *syn* see TRESPASS 2
2 *syn* see VIOLATE 1
3 *syn* see IMPOSE 5

infringement *n syn* see BREACH 1

infuriate *vb syn* see ANGER 1

infuse *vb* 1 to introduce one thing into another so as to change or affect it < a teacher who *infused* her pupils with the desire to learn >
syn imbue, ingrain, inoculate, invest, leaven, steep, suffuse
rel animate, fire, inform, inspire; implant, inculcate, instill; impregnate, permeate, pervade, saturate; indoctrinate
2 *syn* see INTERFUSE 2

ingather *vb syn* see REAP

ingathering *n syn* see HARVEST 1

ingeminate *vb syn* see REPEAT

ingenerate *adj syn* see INHERENT

ingenious *adj* 1 *syn* see INVENTIVE
2 *syn* see CLEVER 4

ingenuous *adj syn* see NATURAL 5
con covert, furtive, stealthy, surreptitious, underhand; artful, crafty, foxy, guileful, insidious, sly, tricky, wily
ant disingenuous

ingest *vb syn* see EAT 1

inglorious *adj syn* see DISREPUTABLE 1
ant glorious

ingoing *adj syn* see INCISIVE

ingot *n syn* see BAR 1

ingrain *vb* 1 *syn* see ENTRENCH 1
rel engrave, etch, grave, incise
2 *syn* see INFUSE 1

ingrained *adj syn* see INHERENT
rel chronic, confirmed, deep-rooted, inveterate
con exterior, external, outer, outside, outward

ingratiating *adj* intended or designed to gain favor < an *ingratiating* smile >
syn deferential, disarming, ingratiatory, insinuating, insinuative, saccharine, silken, silky
rel adulatory; fawning, sycophantic

ingratiatory *adj syn* see INGRATIATING

ingredient *n syn* see ELEMENT 2

ingress *n* 1 *syn* see ENTRANCE 1
ant egress
2 *syn* see DOOR 2
ant egress

ingress *vb syn* see ENTER 1
ant egress

ingression *n syn* see ENTRANCE 1
ant egression

ingroup *n syn* see CLIQUE
ant outgroup

ingurgitate *vb syn* see GULP

inhabit *vb* to dwell in as a place of settled residence <islands *inhabited* by Polynesians>
syn occupy, people, populate, tenant
rel settle; abide, dwell, live
inhabitable *adj syn see* LIVABLE 1
ant uninhabitable
inhabitancy *n syn see* HABITATION 1
inhabitant *n* one that occupies a particular place regularly <*inhabitants* of large cities>
syn denizen, dweller, habitant, indweller, liver, occupant, resident, ||residenter, resider
rel aborigine, autochthon, indigene, native
inhabitation *n syn see* HABITATION 1
inhale *vb* to draw (as air) into the lungs <*inhaling* smoke>
syn breathe (in), inspire
ant exhale, expire
inharmonic *adj syn see* DISSONANT 1
ant harmonic
inharmonious *adj* 1 *syn see* DISSONANT 1
ant harmonious
2 lacking harmony especially in sentiment <the committee meeting was singularly *inharmonious*>
syn discordant, inconsonant, uncongenial, unharmonious
rel antagonistic, cat-and-dog, conflicting, conflictive, differing, disagreeing, incompatible, incongruous, quarrelsome
con concordant, congenial, consonant; amiable, compatible; collaborative
ant harmonious
inharmony *n syn see* DISCORD
ant harmony
inhere *vb* 1 *syn see* CONSIST 1
2 *syn see* BELONG 3
inherent *adj* being a part, element, or quality of a thing's inmost being <*inherent* rights of every citizen>
syn born, built-in, congenital, connate, constitutional, deep-seated, elemental, essential, inborn, inbred, indwelling, ingenerate, ingrained, innate, intimate, intrinsic
rel inner, internal, inward, resident; basic, elementary, fundamental, immanent, integral; characteristic, distinctive, individual, peculiar; natural, normal, regular, typical; bred-in-the-bone
con shallow, superficial; accidental, fortuitous, incidental; alien, extraneous, extrinsic, foreign
ant adventitious
inheritance *n* 1 *syn see* HERITAGE 1
2 *syn see* LEGACY 1
inherited *adj syn see* INNATE 1
inheritor *n syn see* HEIR
inhibit *vb* 1 *syn see* FORBID
rel avert, ward
ant allow
2 *syn see* RESTRAIN 1
ant activate; animate
inhibited *adj syn see* FRIGID 3
ant uninhibited

inhuman *adj syn see* FIERCE 1
rel malicious, malign, malignant; implacable, relentless, unrelenting; devilish, diabolical, fiendish
con altruistic, benevolent, charitable, eleemosynary, humanitarian, philanthropic; compassionate, tender
ant humane
inhumane *adj syn see* FIERCE 1
ant humane
inhumation *n syn see* BURIAL 2
ant exhumation
inhume *vb syn see* BURY 1
ant disinhume, exhume
inimicable *adj syn see* HOSTILE 1
inimical *adj syn see* HOSTILE 1
iniquitous *adj syn see* WRONG 1
iniquity *n syn see* EVIL 3
initial *adj* 1 marking a commencement or constituting a start <*initial* symptoms of the disease>
syn beginning, inceptive, incipient, initiative, initiatory, introductory, nascent
rel basic, elementary, first, fundamental; embryonic, germinal; early, infant; antecedent; earliest, introductory, primary
con closing; concluding, conclusive; terminal, terminative; last, ultimate
ant final
2 *syn see* FIRST 2
3 *syn see* FIRST 1
ant final
initially *adv* 1 in the beginning <*initially* we were confused but soon enough we fully understood>
syn originally, primarily, primitively
rel first, firstly, incipiently
idiom at first, at the first go-off, from the word go
con lastly, ultimately
ant finally
2 *syn see* FIRSTLY
initiate *vb* 1 *syn see* BEGIN 1
ant terminate
2 *syn see* INTRODUCE 3
3 to put through the formalities for becoming a member or official <the club *initiated* four new members>
syn inaugurate, induct, install, instate, invest
rel institute; admit, enter, introduce, take in
initiation *n* the process or an instance of being formally introduced into an office or made a member of an organization <a fraternity *initiation*>
syn inaugural, inauguration, induction, installation, investiture
rel baptism; institution, introduction
initiative *adj syn see* INITIAL 1
initiative *n syn see* ENTERPRISE 4
initiatory *adj syn see* INITIAL 1
injudicious *adj syn see* UNWISE
ant judicious
injunction *n syn see* COMMAND 1
injure *vb* 1 to deplete the soundness, strength, effectiveness, or perfection of something <*injured* his prestige by making rash statements>
syn blemish, damage, harm, hurt, impair, mar, prejudice, spoil, tarnish, vitiate
rel disserve; disadvantage; endamage, weaken; blight, queer; foul up, louse up; contort, deface, deform, disfigure, distor⸱

bespatter, foul, smirch; disable, incapacitate

con assist, help, succor; better, enhance, improve; benefit; strengthen

ant aid

2 *syn* see DISTRESS 2

idiom do dirt to

3 to inflict bodily hurt on <was *injured* in an auto accident>

syn hurt, wound

rel damage, harm; afflict, torment, torture; batter, cripple, maim, mangle, mutilate

idiom draw blood

injurious *adj syn* see HARMFUL

injury *n* 1 an act or the result of inflicting something that causes loss or pain <we cannot forgive his *injury* of the painting> <his falsehood caused grave *injury* to his brother's reputation>

syn damage, harm, hurt, mischief, outrage, ruin

rel agony, discomfiture, distress, misery, suffering; pain, pang; detriment, disservice, loss; bad, evil, ill

2 *syn* see INJUSTICE 2

injustice *n* 1 absence of justice <preached against *injustice*>

syn inequitableness, inequity, unfairness, unjustness, wrong

rel crime, malfeasance, malpractice, villainy, wrongdoing; favoritism, inequality, partiality, partisanship

con equity, fairness, right

ant justice, justness

2 an act or instance of unjustness <pointed out various *injustices* in the law> <you do him an *injustice* when you call him lazy>

syn grievance, injury, wrong

rel damage, harm, hurt, mischief, outrage, ruin; breach, infraction, infringement, tort, transgression, trespass, violation

ink *vb syn* see SIGN 1

inkling *n syn* see HINT 1

inky *adj syn* see BLACK 1

‖**inland** *adj syn* see DOMESTIC 2

ant foreign

inlet *n* a recess in the shores of a body of water <*inlets* of lakes and rivers>

syn arm, bay, bayou, bight, cove, ‖creek, firth, gulf, harbor, ‖loch, ‖lough, slough

inn *n syn* see HOTEL

innards *n pl syn* see ENTRAILS

innate *adj* 1 existing in or belonging to an individual inherently <*innate* vigor>

syn congenital, connate, connatural, inborn, indigenous, inherited, native, natural, unacquired

rel constitutional, deep-seated, essential, ingrained, inherent, intrinsic; hereditary; normal, regular, standard, typical

con accidental, adventitious, fortuitous, incidental; affected, assumed, feigned, simulated; cultivated, fostered, nurtured

ant acquired

2 *syn* see INHERENT

inner *adj* 1 situated further in <the *inner* layers were less worn>

syn ‖innermore, inside, interior, internal, intestine, inward

rel central, focal, middle, nuclear; close, familiar, intimate; constitutional, essential, inherent, intrinsic

con exterior, external, outside, outward

ant outer

2 arising from one's inmost self <*inner* thoughts and feelings>

syn gut, interior, internal, intimate, visceral, viscerous

rel individual, personal, private; concealed, hidden, secret

con exterior, outer; open, public

‖**innermore** *adj syn* see INNER 1

innervate *vb syn* see PROVOKE 4

innerve *vb syn* see PROVOKE 4

innholder *n syn* see SALOONKEEPER

innkeeper *n syn* see SALOONKEEPER

innocence *n syn* see IGNORANCE 2

innocent *adj* 1 *syn* see GOOD 11

rel unstained, unsullied, white, whitehanded

2 free from legal guilt or fault <the defendant was found *innocent*>

syn blameless, clean, crimeless, faultless, guiltless, inculpable, unguilty

idiom in the clear

ant guilty

3 *syn* see LAWFUL

4 *syn* see DEVOID

5 *syn* see NATURAL 5

6 *syn* see HARMLESS

con harmful, injurious, mischievous

innocuous *adj* 1 *syn* see HARMLESS

con harmful, injurious; evil; troublesome

ant pernicious

2 *syn* see INSIPID 3

innominate *adj syn* see ANONYMOUS

innovation *n syn* see CHANGE 2

rel deviation, introduction, wrinkle

innovational *adj syn* see INVENTIVE

innovative *adj syn* see INVENTIVE

innovator *n* one who introduces something new <an *innovator* of bold ideas in the field of computers>

syn introducer, inventor, original, originator

rel author, creator, maker, producer; architect, builder, developer

innovatory *adj syn* see INVENTIVE

innoxious *adj syn* see HARMLESS

ant noxious

innuendo *n syn* see INSINUATION

innumerable *adj* too many to be counted <received *innumerable* requests for help>

syn countless, innumerous, numberless, uncountable, uncounted, unnumberable, unnumbered, untold

ant numberable, numerable

innumerous *adj syn* see INNUMERABLE

inobnoxious *adj syn* see HARMLESS

ant obnoxious

inobservant *adj syn* see INATTENTIVE

ant observant

inobtrusive *adj syn* see QUIET 4

ant obtrusive

inoculate *vb syn* see INFUSE 1

rel admit, enter, introduce

inodorous *adj syn* see ODORLESS

ant odorous; smelly

inoffensive *adj syn* see HARMLESS

con loathsome, repulsive, revolting; distasteful, obnoxious, repellent, repugnant

ant offensive

inopportune *adj syn* see UNSEASONABLE 1

ant opportune

inordinate *adj* **1** *syn* see EXCESSIVE 1
  rel irrational, unreasonable; gratuitous, supererogatory, uncalled-for, wanton; extra, superfluous, surplus
  con moderate, temperate; checked, curbed, inhibited, restrained
  2 *syn* see EXCESSIVE 2
inordinately *adv syn* see EVER 6
inordinateness *n syn* see EXCESS 3
in passing *adv syn* see INCIDENTALLY 2
in perpetuum *adv syn* see EVER 2
inpour *n syn* see INFLUX
  ant outpour, outpouring
inpouring *n syn* see INFLUX
  ant outpour, outpouring
inquest *n syn* see INQUIRY 1
inquietude *n syn* see UNREST
  rel anxiety, uneasiness
  ant quiet, quietness, quietude
inquire *vb syn* see ASK 1
  rel investigate, probe, search; scrutinize, study
inquire (into) *vb syn* see EXPLORE
inquiring *adj syn* see INQUISITIVE 1
inquiry *n* **1** the act or an instance of seeking truth, information, or knowledge about something <an exhaustive *inquiry* revealed no evidence of a conspiracy>
  syn delving, inquest, inquisition, investigation, probe, probing, quest, research
  rel catechizing, interrogation, questioning; audit, check, examination, inspection, scrutiny; hearing; inquirendo
  2 a request for information <addressed his *inquiry* to the personnel director>
  syn interrogation, interrogatory, query, question, questioning
inquisition *n syn* see INQUIRY 1
inquisitive *adj* **1** given to examination or investigation <an *inquisitive* child who was interested in everything around him>
  syn curious, disquisitive, inquiring, investigative, questioning
  rel nosy, prying, snoopy
  con indifferent, unconcerned, uninquisitive, uninterested
  ant incurious
  2 *syn* see CURIOUS 2
  ant incurious, uninquiring
inquisitorial *adj syn* see CURIOUS 2
inquisitory *adj syn* see CURIOUS 2
in re *prep syn* see APROPOS
in respect to *prep syn* see APROPOS
in reverse *adv syn* see ABOUT 6
inroad *n syn* see INVASION
inroad *vb syn* see INVADE 1
inrush *n syn* see INFLUX
  ant outrush
insalubrious *adj syn* see UNWHOLESOME 1
  ant salubrious, salutary
insalutary *adj syn* see UNWHOLESOME 1
  ant salubrious, salutary
insanable *adj syn* see HOPELESS 2
ins and outs *n pl* characteristic peculiarities or technicalities <soon learned the *ins and outs* of his job>
  syn minutiae, ropes

---

syn synonym(s)	*rel* related word(s)
ant antonym(s)	*con* contrasted word(s)
idiom idiomatic equivalent(s)	
‖ use limited; if in doubt, see a dictionary	

  rel details, incidentals, particulars; ramifications; oddities, peculiarities, quirks
insane *adj* **1** being afflicted by or manifesting unsoundness of mind or an inability to control one's rational processes <adjudged *insane* after a period of observation>
  syn ‖batty, bedlamite, ‖bonkers, brainsick, ‖buggy, ‖bughouse, ‖bugs, crackbrained, cracked, ‖crackers, ‖cracky, ‖cranky, crazed, crazy, cuckoo, daffy, daft, demented, deranged, disordered, distraught, ‖fruity, ‖loco, lunatic, mad, maniac, ‖mental, mindless, non compos mentis, nuts, nutsy, nutty, reasonless, screwy, teched, unbalanced, unsane, unsound, wacky, witless, wrong
  rel irrational, unreasonable; bewildered, distracted; dotty, eccentric, off, rocky, strange, touched; ‖dippy
  idiom around the bend, crazy as a coot, not all there, not right in one's head, ‖off one's dot, off one's nut (*or* rocker), ‖off one's onion, out of (*or* off) one's head, out of one's mind, touched in the head
  con judicious, sapient, sensible, wise; rational, reasonable; balanced; logical, subtle; healthy, sound; clear, lucid
  ant sane
  2 *syn* see FOOLISH 2
  rel fanciful, fantastic, imaginary, visionary; impractical, unrealistic
  con feasible, possible, practicable, usable; rational, reasonable, sane, sensible; practical, realistic
insaneness *n syn* see INSANITY 1
  ant saneness, sanity
insanity *n* **1** grave disorder of mind that impairs one's capacity to function safely or normally in society <his *insanity* required confinement in a mental institution>
  syn aberration, alienation, derangement, distraction, insaneness, lunacy, madness, psychopathy, unbalance
  rel acromania; delirium, frenzy, hysteria; delusion, hallucination, illusion; irrationality, unreasonableness; dotage
  con judiciousness, sageness, sensibility, wiseness; rationality, reasonableness; healthiness, soundness, wholesomeness
  ant saneness, sanity
  2 *syn* see FOOLISHNESS
  rel asininity, fatuousness, stupidity; impracticality
insatiable *adj* incapable of being satisfied or appeased <an *insatiable* lust for glory>
  syn insatiate, quenchless, unappeasable, unquenchable, unsatiate, unsatisfiable
  rel unsatiated, unsatisfied; demanding, exigent, importunate, insistent, urgent; clamorous, crying, pressing, yearning
  con appeasable, quenchable, satisfiable; satiate, satiated, satisfied; controlled, curbed, restrained
  ant satiable
insatiably *adv syn* see VERY 1
insatiate *adj syn* see INSATIABLE
  ant satiate, satiated
inscience *n syn* see IGNORANCE 2
inscribe *vb* **1** *syn* see WRITE
  rel engrave, enscroll

2 *syn* see LIST 3
3 *syn* see ENGRAVE 2
inscrutable *adj syn* see MYSTERIOUS
insecure *adj* 1 not confident or sure
<feels very *insecure* about his future>
syn unassured, unconfident, unsure
rel hesitant, questioning, uncertain
idiom in suspense, up in the air
con assured, confident, self-assured, self=
confident, sure
ant secure
2 *syn* see WEAK 2
ant secure
inseminate *vb syn* see IMPLANT
insensate *adj* 1 lacking animate awareness
or sensation <would often talk to stones
and other *insensate* objects>
syn inanimate, insensible, insentient,
senseless, unfeeling
rel exanimate, unanimated; anesthetic,
insensitive
con aware, cognizant, conscious; feeling,
sensible, sentient
ant sensate
2 *syn* see SIMPLE 3
3 *syn* see INSENSIBLE 5
insensibility *n syn* see APATHY 1
ant sensibility
insensible *adj* 1 *syn* see INSENSATE 1
ant sensible
2 deprived of consciousness <knocked
insensible by a sudden punch>
syn cold, comatose, inconscious, sense=
less, unconscious
idiom out cold
3 *syn* see NUMB 1
4 *syn* see IMPERCEPTIBLE
ant sensible
5 devoid or insusceptible of emotion or
passion <*insensible* to love or compas=
sion>
syn anesthetic, bloodless, dull, hard, im=
passible, insensate, insensitive, rocky
rel blunt, obtuse; apathetic, impassive,
phlegmatic, stoic, stolid; callous, hard=
ened, indurated, pachydermatous, thick=
skinned; absorbed, engrossed, intent, rapt
con alert, alive, awake, aware, cognizant,
conscious; affected, impressed, influenced,
touched
ant sensible
insensitive *adj* 1 *syn* see INSENSIBLE 5
rel aloof, incurious, indifferent, uncon=
cerned
con compassionate, responsive, tender
ant sensitive
2 *syn* see NUMB 1
ant sensitive
3 *syn* see INSUSCEPTIBLE
ant sensitive
insentient *adj* 1 *syn* see INSENSATE 1
ant sentient
2 *syn* see INSUSCEPTIBLE
insert *vb syn* see INTRODUCE 6
rel interlope, intrude, obtrude; implant,
inculcate, instill; admit, enter
con detach, disengage
ant abstract, extract
in short *adv syn* see BRIEFLY
inside *n* 1 *syn* see INTERIOR
ant outside
2 insides *pl syn* see ENTRAILS
inside *adj* 1 *syn* see INNER 1

ant outside
2 *syn* see PRIVATE 2
inside *adv syn* see INDOORS
ant outside
inside out *adv syn* see THOROUGHLY 2
insidious *adj syn* see SLY 2
rel perfidious, treacherous; dangerous,
perilous; gradual, subtle
insight *n* 1 *syn* see SAGACITY
2 *syn* see INTUITION
insighted *adj syn* see WISE 1
insightful *adj syn* see WISE 1
rel discriminating, penetrating; inseeing
insignia *n* a distinguishing mark of author=
ity, office, or honor <wore a coronet with
the strawberry leaf *insignia* of his ducal
rank>
syn badge, emblem
rel decoration; regalia
insignificancy *n syn* see NONENTITY
insignificant *adj* 1 *syn* see SENSELESS 5
ant significant
2 *syn* see MINOR 2
3 *syn* see LITTLE 3
ant significant
insincere *adj* not being or expressing what
one appears to be or express <an *insin=
cere* person who could not be trusted>
syn ambidextrous, double, double-dealing,
double-faced, doublehearted, double=
minded, double-tongued, hypocritical, left=
handed, mala fide
rel deceitful, dishonest, lying, menda=
cious, untruthful; shifty, slippery, tricky
con candid, frank, open, plain; direct,
forthright, straight, straightforward
ant sincere
insinuate *vb* 1 *syn* see INTRODUCE 6
2 *syn* see SUGGEST 1
rel ascribe, impute
con affirm, assert, aver, avouch, avow,
declare, profess; air, broach, express, state,
voice
3 to introduce (as oneself) by stealthy,
smooth, or artful means <*insinuated* him=
self into the confidence of others>
syn edge in, foist, infiltrate, work in,
worm
rel insert, intercalate, interject, interpo=
late, interpose, introduce
insinuating *adj syn* see INGRATIATING
insinuation *n* a stealthy or indirect hinting
or suggestion <*insinuations* about his
opponent's probity>
syn innuendo, insinuendo
rel hint, hinting, implication, implying,
intimation, suggestion; animadversion,
aspersion, reflection; ascription, imputa=
tion
insinuative *adj syn* see INGRATIATING
insinuendo *n syn* see INSINUATION
insipid *adj* 1 *syn* see UNPALATABLE 1
rel bland, mild
con appetizing, flavorable, tasty
ant sapid, savory
2 *syn* see ARID 2
rel commonplace, ordinary, plain; mun=
dane, prosaic, unimaginative
3 devoid of qualities that make for spirit
and character <an *insipid* little story of
teenage puppy love>
syn banal, bland, driveling, flat, inane,
innocuous, jejune, milk-and-water, namby=

pamby, sapless, swashy, vapid, waterish, watery, wishy-washy
rel slight, tenuous, thin; feeble, weak; subdued, tame; mild, soft; pointless
con piquant, poignant, pungent, racy, spicy; fiery, gingery, high-spirited, mettlesome, peppery, spirited, spunky; exciting, piquing, provocative, provoking
ant sapid

insistent *adj* 1 *syn* see PERSISTENT 1
2 *syn* see EMPHATIC
rel persevering, persistent, pressing; obtrusive
3 *syn* see PRESSING

insociable *adj syn* see UNSOCIABLE
ant sociable

insolate *vb syn* see SUN

insolence *n* the quality, state, or an instance of being insulting or grossly lacking in respect <court-martialed because of *insolence* to an officer>
syn boldness, disrespect, hardihood, impertinence, impudence, insolency, insolentness; *compare* EFFRONTERY
rel brazenness; presumption; arrogance; rudeness; contempt
con deference; correctness, decency, decorum, decorousness, properness, seemliness
ant respect, respectfulness

insolency *n syn* see INSOLENCE
ant respect, respectfulness

insolent *adj* 1 *syn* see PROUD 1
rel imperative, peremptory; dictatorial, magisterial
ant deferential
2 exhibiting boldness or effrontery <an *insolent* child with no respect or regard for anyone>
syn audacious, bold, ‖boldacious, brazen, contumelious, impertinent, impudent, procacious, saucy
rel arrogant, disdainful, overbearing; discourteous, impolite, rude, uncivil, ungracious
con humble, lowly, meek, modest, unassertive; civil, courteous, polite
ant deferential

insolentness *n syn* see INSOLENCE
ant respect, respectfulness

insoluble *adj* admitting of no solution <seemingly *insoluble* problems faced the city council>
syn inextricable, insolvable, irresoluble, irresolvable, unsoluble, unsolvable
rel inexplicable, unexplainable; inconceivable, unaccountable; mysterious
con answerable, explicable, understandable; resolvable; clear, plain, straightforward
ant soluble, solvable

insolvable *adj syn* see INSOLUBLE
ant soluble, solvable

insomnia *n* prolonged inability to obtain adequate sleep <sleeping pills failed to relieve his *insomnia*>
syn insomnolence, sleeplessness
rel restlessness, wakefulness; stress, tension

syn synonym(s)   *rel* related word(s)
ant antonym(s)   *con* contrasted word(s)
idiom idiomatic equivalent(s)
‖ use limited; if in doubt, see a dictionary

insomnolence *n syn* see INSOMNIA
insorb *vb syn* see ABSORB 1
insouciance *n syn* see APATHY 2
insouciant *adj syn* see HAPPY-GO-LUCKY
inspect *vb syn* see SCRUTINIZE 1
rel notice, observe; catechize, inquire, interrogate, question; review
inspection *n syn* see EXAMINATION
rel inquest, inquiry, inquisition, investigation, probe, research; oversight, supervision, surveillance
inspiration *n* a divine or seemingly divine imparting of knowledge or power <*inspiration* is the only plausible explanation for his exquisite work>
syn afflation, afflatus, inflatus
rel animus, genius, muse, vision; enlightenment, illumination; brainstorm, brain wave
inspire *vb* 1 *syn* see INHALE
ant expire
2 *syn* see FIRE 2
rel quicken, stimulate; infect, infuse; endow, endue
3 *syn* see ELATE
4 *syn* see AFFECT
inspiring *adj syn* see EXCITING
ant uninspiring
inspirit *vb syn* see ENCOURAGE 1
rel exalt, fire, inform, inspire
ant dispirit
in spite of *prep syn* see AGAINST 4
instability *n* the state or quality of not being firm or fixed <the *instability* of the economy>
syn precariousness, shakiness, unfixedness, unsettledness, unstability, unstableness, unsteadfastness, unsteadiness
rel undependability, unreliability; inconstancy, insecurity
con firmness, soundness, stoutness, sturdiness; fixity, solidity
ant stability, stableness
install *vb* 1 *syn* see INITIATE 3
2 *syn* see ENSCONCE 2
installation *n syn* see INITIATION
instance *n* an individual that clearly belongs to an indicated class <their rescue was an *instance* of great courage>
syn case, case history, example, illustration, representative, sample, sampling, specimen
rel ground, proof, reason; detail, item, particular; exponent
instance *vb* 1 *syn* see EXEMPLIFY 1
2 *syn* see MENTION
rel exemplify, illustrate
instant *n* 1 an infinitesimal space of time <came not an *instant* too soon>
syn breathing, crack, flash, ‖jiff, jiffy, minute, moment, second, shake, split second, ‖tick, trice, twinkle, twinkling, wink
2 *syn* see POINT 7
3 *syn* see OCCASION 5
instant *adj* 1 *syn* see PRESSING
2 *syn* see PRESENT
3 *syn* see INSTANTANEOUS
instantaneous *adj* done, occurring, or acting without any perceptible duration of time <*instantaneous* answers to tough questions>
syn hair-trigger, immediate, instant; *compare* QUICK 2

rel spontaneous; fast, quick, rapid; momentary, transitory
con late, tardy; slow, sluggish

instanter *adv syn* see AWAY 3

instantly *adv syn* see AWAY 3
idiom in a flash, on a dime, on the spot

instate *vb syn* see INITIATE 3

instead *adv* as an alternative to something expressed or implied <longed *instead* for a quiet country life>
syn alternately, alternatively, in lieu, rather

insteep *vb syn* see SOAK 1

instigate *vb syn* see INCITE
rel activate, actuate; hint, insinuate, suggest; plan, plot, scheme; goad, urge; fire, inflame

instigation *n syn* see STIMULUS

instigator *n* one that goads or urges forward <the *instigator* of the riot>
syn agitator, fomenter, inciter, mover
rel firebrand, incendiary, inflamer, rabble-rouser

instill *vb syn* see IMPLANT

instinctive *adj* 1 prompted by natural instinct or propensity <was quite unable to control her *instinctive* fear of snakes>
syn instinctual, intuitive, visceral
rel congenital, inborn, innate; ingrained, inherent, intrinsic; natural
ant reasoned
2 *syn* see SPONTANEOUS
rel natural, normal, regular, typical
ant intentional

instinctual *adj syn* see INSTINCTIVE 1

institute *vb* 1 *syn* see FOUND 2
ant abrogate
2 *syn* see INTRODUCE 3

institute *n syn* see LAW 1

institution *n* something or someone well established in a customary relationship <he's been in the office so long that he has become an *institution*>
syn fixture
rel custom, habit; establishment, rite

instruct *vb* 1 *syn* see TEACH
rel acquaint, apprise, inform; engineer, guide, lead, pilot, steer
2 *syn* see COMMAND
rel assign, define, prescribe

instruction *n syn* see EDUCATION 1

instructional *adj syn* see INFORMATIVE

instructive *adj syn* see INFORMATIVE
rel didactic, moralistic, moralizing

instrument *n* 1 *syn* see MEAN 2
2 *syn* see IMPLEMENT
rel equipment, gear, machinery, paraphernalia, tackle

instrumental *adj* serving as a means, agent, or tool <was *instrumental* in organizing the strike>
syn implemental, ministerial
rel conducive, helpful; serviceable, useful

instrumentality *n syn* see MEAN 2
rel energy, force, might, power

instrumentation *n syn* see MEAN 2

insubordinate *adj* unwilling to submit to authority <*insubordinate* soldiers are court-martialed>
syn contumacious, factious, insurgent, mutinous, rebellious, seditious
rel intractable, recalcitrant, refractory, ungovernable, unruly; indocile, uncompliant, uncomplying; disaffected, dissentious

con amenable, biddable, docile, obedient, tractable; subdued, submissive, tame
ant subordinate

insubstantial *adj* 1 *syn* see IMMATERIAL 1
ant substantial
2 *syn* see WEAK 1
ant substantial
3 *syn* see TENUOUS 3
ant substantial

insuccess *n syn* see FAILURE 2
ant success, successfulness

insufferable *adj* incapable of being endured <that man is an *insufferable* bore>
syn insupportable, intolerable, unbearable, unbrookable, unendurable, unsufferable, unsupportable
rel distressing, painful; unacceptable
ant sufferable

insufficience *n* 1 *syn* see FAILURE 3
ant sufficiency
2 *syn* see SCARCITY
ant sufficiency

insufficiency *n* 1 *syn* see FAILURE 3
ant sufficiency
2 *syn* see SCARCITY
ant sufficiency

insufficient *adj* 1 *syn* see DEFICIENT 1
ant sufficient
2 *syn* see SHORT 3
ant sufficient

insular *adj* having the narrow and limited outlook characteristic of geographic isolation <the *insular* thinking of peasant communities>
syn local, ‖parish-pump, parochial, provincial, sectarian, small-town
rel regional, sectional; insulated, isolated, secluded; circumscribed, confined, limited, restricted; illiberal, narrow, narrow-minded
con broad-minded, liberal; cosmopolitan, metropolitan, urban

insulate *vb syn* see ISOLATE

insult *vb syn* see OFFEND 3
rel abase, debase, degrade, humble, humiliate; fleer, flout, gibe, gird, jeer, scoff, sneer; deride, mock, ridicule, taunt; rump
con admire, esteem, respect
ant honor

insult *n syn* see AFFRONT
rel abuse, invective, obloquy, vituperation; disgrace, ignominy, opprobrium, shame; disdainfulness, insolence, superciliousness; contempt, disdain, scorn; unpleasantry
con deference, homage, honor, obeisance, reverence

insuperable *adj* incapable of being surmounted, overcome, or passed over <they met with *insuperable* difficulties>
syn impassable, inconquerable, indomitable, insurmountable, invincible, unconquerable, unsurmountable
rel unachievable, unattainable; unsurpassable; impregnable, impenetrable, invulnerable
con surmountable; achievable, negotiable
ant superable

insupportable *adj syn* see INSUFFERABLE
ant bearable, supportable

insupposable *adj syn* see INCREDIBLE 1

ant supposable

insuppressible *adj syn* see IRREPRESS-
IBLE
ant suppressible

insuppressive *adj syn* see IRREPRESSIBLE

insure *vb syn* see ENSURE
rel guard, protect, safeguard, shield

insurgent *n syn* see REBEL

insurgent *adj syn* see INSUBORDINATE

insurmountable *adj syn* see INSUPER-
ABLE
ant surmountable

insurrect *vb syn* see REVOLT 1

insurrectionist *n syn* see REBEL

insusceptible *adj* incapable of being
moved, affected, or impressed < *insusceptible* to flattery>
syn impassive, insensitive, insentient,
unimpressible, unimpressionable, unresponsive, unsusceptible
con impressible, impressionable, responsive, sensitive, sentient
ant susceptible

intact *adj* 1 *syn* see WHOLE 1
ant defective
2 *syn* see VIRGIN 1
ant deflowered

intangible *adj* 1 *syn* see IMPERCEPTIBLE
rel rare, tenuous, thin; slender, slight;
aerial, aeriform, airy, ethereal; eluding,
elusive, evading, evasive; touchless
ant tangible
2 *syn* see ELUSIVE

integer *n syn* see NUMBER

integral *adj syn* see WHOLE 3

integral *n syn* see WHOLE 2

integrate *n syn* see WHOLE 2

integrate *vb* 1 *syn* see HARMONIZE 4
2 *syn* see HARMONIZE 3
3 to join together systematically < an
economic system that successfully *inte-
grates* private gain with public respon-
sibility>
syn articulate, concatenate
rel combine, conjoin, link, unite; compact, concentrate, consolidate, unify;
blend, coalesce, fuse, merge; organize,
systematize
con disperse, dissipate, scatter; analyze,
break down, resolve
ant disintegrate
4 *syn* see UNIFY 1
5 *syn* see EMBODY 2

integrative *adj* tending to integrate < *integrative* forces in a fragmented society>
syn centralizing, centripetal, compacting,
concentrating, consolidating, unifying
ant disintegrative

integrity *n* 1 *syn* see HONESTY
rel forthrightness, straightforwardness
2 the quality or state of being complete or
undivided < trying to maintain the *integrity* of the empire>
syn completeness, entireness, perfection,
wholeness
rel soundness, stability; absoluteness,
purity, simplicity

intellect *n* 1 *syn* see REASON 5

rel comprehension; intuition
2 a person with great intellectual powers
< one of the great *intellects* of his time>
syn brain, intellectual, intelligence
rel genius; egghead, pundit; thinker

intellection *n syn* see IDEA

intellective *adj syn* see MENTAL 1

intellectual *adj* 1 *syn* see MENTAL 1
con animal, fleshly, sensual
ant carnal
2 devoted to or engaged in the creative
use of the intellect < the play appealed to
the *intellectual* members of the audience>
syn cerebral, highbrow, highbrowed,
intellectualistic

intellectual *n* 1 *syn* see INTELLECT 2
2 a person who possesses or has pretensions of strong intellectual interest or
superiority < accused of being an *intellectual* and a snob>
syn Brahmin, double-dome, egghead,
highbrow
3 **intellectuals** *pl syn* see INTELLIGENTSIA

intellectualistic *adj syn* see INTELLEC-
TUAL 2

intelligence *n* 1 the ability to learn and to
cope < what he lacked in education, he
made up in *intelligence* >
syn brain(s), brainpower, mentality,
mother wit, sense, wit
rel acumen, discernment, insight, judgment; perspicacity, sagacity, wisdom
2 *syn* see INTELLECT 2
3 *syn* see NEWS

intelligent *adj* 1 *syn* see RATIONAL
con irrational, unreasonable
ant unintelligent
2 mentally keen or quick < quite *intelligent* for his age>
syn alert, brainy, bright, brilliant, clever,
knowing, knowledgeable, quick-witted,
ready-witted, sharp, smart; *compare* WISE
4
rel astute, perspicacious, sagacious,
shrewd; acute, keen; adroit, cunning, ingenious
con foolish, idiotic, imbecilic, moronic;
crass, dense, dull, dumb, slow, stupid
ant unintelligent

intelligentsia *n* a class of articulate persons devoted to intellectual, cultural, and
social matters < the *intelligentsia* posed a
threat to the new regime>
syn clerisy, illuminati, intellectuals, literati
rel avant-garde, vanguard

intelligible *adj syn* see UNDERSTAND-
ABLE
ant unintelligible

intemperance *n syn* see EXCESS 3
rel drunkenness, insobriety; debauchery
ant temperance

intemperate *adj* 1 *syn* see EXCESSIVE 2
rel bibacious, bibulous, crapulous,
drunken; gluttonous
ant temperate, tempered
2 *syn* see SEVERE 3
ant temperate

intempestive *adj syn* see IMPROPER 1

intemporal *adj syn* see ETERNAL 4
ant temporal

intend *vb* 1 *syn* see MEAN 2
2 to have in mind as a purpose < *intended*
to read the book>

syn synonym(s)   *rel* related word(s)
ant antonym(s)   *con* contrasted word(s)
idiom idiomatic equivalent(s)
‖ use limited; if in doubt, see a dictionary

interest 315

syn aim, contemplate, design, mean, ||mind, plan, propose, purpose

rel attempt, endeavor, essay, strive, try; plot, scheme; assign, designate, destine

idiom figure on, have in mind to, look forward to

intendance *n syn* see OVERSIGHT 1

intended *adj syn* see ENGAGED 2

intended *n syn* see BETROTHED

intendment *n* 1 *syn* see INTENTION
2 *syn* see MEANING 1

intensate *vb syn* see INTENSIFY

intense *adj* 1 extreme in degree, power, or effect < *intense* hatred >
syn concentrated, desperate, exquisite, fierce, furious, terrible, vehement, vicious, violent
rel aggravated, enhanced, heightened, intensified; accentuated, emphasized, stressed
ant subdued
2 *syn* see INTENSIVE
3 *syn* see ARDENT 2
ant slight

intensely *adv* 1 *syn* see HARD 3
rel fiercely, furiously, vehemently, viciously, violently
2 *syn* see SERIOUSLY 2

intensify *vb* to increase markedly in measure or degree < both companies *intensified* their efforts to win the contract > < the pain *intensified* sharply >
syn aggravate, deepen, enhance, heighten, intensate, magnify, mount, redouble, rise, rouse
rel accent, accentuate, emphasize, stress; aggrandize, exalt; sharpen
con moderate, qualify; alleviate, ease, lighten, relieve; decrease, diminish, lessen, reduce
ant abate; allay, mitigate; temper

intensive *adj* highly concentrated < an *intensive* study of the causes of the war >
syn blood-and-guts, deep, hard, intense, profound
con casual, shallow, superficial

intensively *adv syn* see HARD 3

intent *n* 1 *syn* see INTENTION
rel conation, volition, will
con chance, fortune, hap, hazard, luck
ant accident
2 *syn* see MEANING 1

intent *adj* 1 having one's mind or attention deeply fixed < the student was too *intent* on his work to hear the phone >
syn absorbed, deep, engaged, engrossed, immersed, preoccupied, rapt, wrapped, wrapped up
rel attending, attentive, minding, watching; concentrated, riveted
con absent, absent-minded, abstracted, bemused, faraway, preoccupied; daydreaming, napping, oblivious
ant distracted
2 *syn* see DECIDED 2

intention *n* what one purposes to accomplish or do < his *intention* was to finish by noon >
syn animus, design, intendment, intent, meaning, plan, purpose; *compare* AMBITION 2
rel project, scheme; desire, hope, wish

intentional *adj syn* see VOLUNTARY

rel intended, meant, proposed, purposed; advised, considered, designed, designful, premeditated, studied
con accidental, casual, fortuitous; careless, heedless, inadvertent, thoughtless
ant unintentional

intentionally *adv* with intention < hurt her *intentionally* >
syn ||apurpose, deliberately, designedly, on purpose, prepensely, purposedly, purposely, purposively
ant unintentionally

intentive *adj syn* see ATTENTIVE 1

intently *adv syn* see HARD 4

intentness *n syn* see EARNESTNESS

inter *vb syn* see BURY 1
ant disinter

interact *vb* to act upon one another < humor and pathos *interacted* to make a moving drama >
syn coact, interplay, interreact
rel collaborate, cooperate; combine, join, merge, unite

interagent *n syn* see GO-BETWEEN 2

interblend *vb syn* see MIX 1

interbreed *vb syn* see CROSS 4

intercalate *vb syn* see INTRODUCE 6

intercede *vb syn* see INTERPOSE 2

interceder *n syn* see GO-BETWEEN 2

intercept *vb* to stop, seize, or interrupt in progress or course < *intercept* a forward pass >
syn block, catch, cut off
rel grab, seize, take; check, curb
con fumble, miss; loose, release

intercessor *n syn* see GO-BETWEEN 2

interchange *vb syn* see EXCHANGE 3
rel reverse, transpose

interchangeable *adj* permitting mutual substitution < *interchangeable* parts >
syn commutable, exchangeable, fungible, interconvertible, substitutable
rel changeable, convertible; reciprocal, reciprocative

interchurch *adj syn* see NONSECTARIAN

intercommunication *n* 1 *syn* see COMMUNICATION 3
2 *syn* see CONTACT 2

intercomparable *adj syn* see LIKE

interconnect *vb syn* see INTERJOIN

interconvertible *adj syn* see INTERCHANGEABLE

intercourse *n* 1 *syn* see COMMERCE 2
2 *syn* see COMMUNICATION 3
3 *syn* see CONTACT 2

intercreedal *adj syn* see NONSECTARIAN

intercross *vb* 1 *syn* see INTERSECT
2 *syn* see CROSS 4

interdenominational *adj syn* see NONSECTARIAN

interdict *vb syn* see FORBID
ant sanction

interdiction *n syn* see TABOO
ant sanction

interest *n* 1 participation in advantage, profit, and responsibility < he owned a half *interest* in a furniture store >
syn claim, share, stake
2 *syn* see WELFARE
3 readiness to be concerned with or moved by something < had an *interest* in art >
syn concern, curiosity, interestedness, regard

rel enthusiasm, excitement, passion; attention, care, concernment; absorption, engrossment

con apathy, indifference, unconcern

ant disinterest

interest *vb* to engage the attention and interest of <his appeal failed to *interest* his listeners>

syn appeal, attract, excite, fascinate, intrigue

rel arouse, tantalize, titillate; lure, pull, snare, tempt; pique

ant bore

interested *adj* having a share or concern in some affair <all *interested* parties met for the reading of the will>

syn affected, concerned, implicated, involved

rel biased, partial, partisan, prejudiced

con aloof, incurious, indifferent, unconcerned; apathetic, bored, ennuyé

ant detached, disinterested

interestedness *n syn* see INTEREST 3

interfere *vb* 1 *syn* see INTERPOSE 2

rel bar, block, hinder, impede, obstruct

2 *syn* see MEDDLE

rel discommode, incommode, inconvenience, trouble; baffle, balk, foil, frustrate, thwart

interflow *vb syn* see MIX 1

interfuse *vb* 1 *syn* see MIX 1

2 to cause to pass into or through <*interfused* illuminating anecdotes with the informative text>

syn diffuse, infuse, interlard, intersow, intersperse, intersprinkle

rel impenetrate, impregnate, interpenetrate, penetrate, pervade, saturate

3 *syn* see PERMEATE

interfusion *n syn* see MIXTURE

interim *n syn* see GAP 3

interim *adj syn* see TEMPORARY

interior *adj* 1 *syn* see INNER 1

con extraneous, extrinsic, foreign

ant exterior

2 *syn* see INNER 2

interior *n* the internal or inner part <the *interior* of the house>

syn inside, inward(s), within

rel center, heart; belly, bosom; innards, internals

ant exterior, outside

interject *vb syn* see INTRODUCE 6

interjoin *vb* to join mutually <*interjoined* several stations into a new system>

syn anastomose, interconnect, interlink, intertie

rel interdigitate, interlace, interlock, interrelate

con disunite, part, separate, sunder

ant disjoin

interknit *vb syn* see INTERWEAVE

interlace *vb syn* see INTERWEAVE

interlard *vb syn* see INTERFUSE 2

interlink *vb syn* see INTERJOIN

interlope *vb* 1 *syn* see INTRUDE

2 *syn* see MEDDLE

interlude *n* an intervening or interruptive period or space <an *interlude* of happiness in a tragic story> <woodland broken by *interludes* of meadow>

syn break, intermission, interregnum, interval, parenthesis

rel breather, lull, pause, respite, rest; episode, idyll; meantime, meanwhile, spell; entr'acte

intermeddle *vb syn* see MEDDLE

rel encroach, entrench, invade, trespass

intermeddler *n syn* see BUSYBODY

intermediary *adj syn* see MIDDLE 2

intermediary *n* 1 *syn* see GO-BETWEEN 2

2 *syn* see MEAN 2

intermediate *adj syn* see INTERPOSE 2

intermediate *adj* 1 *syn* see MIDDLE 2

2 *syn* see MEDIUM

intermediate *n syn* see GO-BETWEEN 2

intermediator *n syn* see GO-BETWEEN 2

interment *n syn* see BURIAL 2

ant disinterment

intermesh *vb syn* see ENGAGE 1

interminable *adj syn* see CONTINUAL

rel eternal, infinite; lasting, permanent

con intermittent, periodic; discontinued, stopped; closed, completed, ended, finished, terminated

intermingle *vb syn* see MIX 1

intermission *n* 1 *syn* see ABEYANCE

2 *syn* see INTERLUDE

intermit *vb syn* see DEFER

rel arrest, check, interrupt

con continue, persist; iterate, reiterate, repeat

intermittent *adj* occurring or appearing in interrupted sequence <they predict *intermittent* rain throughout the day>

syn alternate, isochronal, isochronous, periodic, periodical, recurrent, recurring

rel cyclic, cyclical, iterant, iterative, metrical, rhythmic, rhythmical, seasonal, serial; arrested, checked, interrupted; fitful, spasmodic; infrequent, occasional, sporadic; discontinuing, discontinuous

con constant, perpetual; everlasting, interminable

ant continual, continuous; incessant, unceasing

intermix *vb syn* see MIX 1

intermixture *n syn* see MIXTURE

intermutual *adj syn* see COMMON 1

intern *vb syn* see IMPRISON

internal *adj* 1 *syn* see INNER 1

ant external

2 *syn* see INNER 2

3 *syn* see DOMESTIC 2

ant external

internals *n pl syn* see ENTRAILS

internuncio *n syn* see MESSENGER

interpenetrate *vb syn* see PERMEATE

interplay *vb syn* see INTERACT

interpolate *vb syn* see INTRODUCE 6

rel admit, enter; interlope, intrude; add, annex, append, superadd

con cancel, delete, erase, expunge

interpose *vb* 1 *syn* see INTRODUCE 6

rel cast, throw, toss; push, shove, thrust

2 to come between disagreeing elements <forced to *interpose* when the argument grew heated>

syn intercede, interfere, intermediate, intervene, mediate, step in

rel butt in, interlope, intrude, obtrude; intermeddle, meddle; arbitrate, moderate, negotiate

interpret *vb* **1** *syn* see EXPLAIN 1
rel exemplify, illustrate; annotate, gloss; comment, commentate
con contort, deform, distort; garble, misrepresent; misconstrue, misunderstand
2 *syn* see REPRESENT 1
interpretation *n* **1** *syn* see EXPLANATION 1
2 manner of artistic presentation in performance or adaptation or an instance of this < *interpretation* involves a re-creative effort by the performer >
syn reading, rendering, rendition, version
interpretive *adj syn* see EXPLANATORY
interreact *vb syn* see INTERACT
interregnum *n syn* see INTERLUDE
interrogate *vb syn* see ASK 1
interrogation *n* **1** *syn* see CROSS-EXAMINATION
2 *syn* see INQUIRY 2
interrogatory *n syn* see INQUIRY 2
interrupt *vb* **1** *syn* see ARREST 1
rel defer, intermit, postpone, suspend
2 to ask questions or make remarks while another is speaking < a chatterbox who habitually *interrupts* everyone >
syn break in, chime in, chip in
rel cut in, put in
idiom break in on (*or* upon)
interruption *n* **1** *syn* see GAP 3
rel rent, rift, rupture, split
2 *syn* see ABEYANCE
intersect *vb* to divide by passing through or across < parallel lines can never *intersect* >
syn crisscross, cross, crosscut, decussate, intercross
rel traverse; bisect
intersow *vb syn* see INTERFUSE 2
intersperse *vb syn* see INTERFUSE 2
intersprinkle *vb syn* see INTERFUSE 2
intertangle *vb syn* see ENTANGLE 1
intertie *vb syn* see INTERJOIN
intertrude *vb syn* see INTRUDE 1
intertwine *vb syn* see INTERWEAVE
intertwist *vb syn* see INTERWEAVE
interval *n* **1** *syn* see PAUSE
2 *syn* see INTERLUDE
3 *syn* see GAP 3
intervene *vb syn* see INTERPOSE 2
rel divide, part, separate, sever
intervolve *vb syn* see INTERWEAVE
interweave *vb* to blend or unite intimately < joy and melancholy are often closely *interwoven* >
syn interknit, interlace, intertwine, intertwist, intervolve, interwind, interwork, interwreathe, inweave
rel associate, join, link; blend, fuse, mix
interwind *vb syn* see INTERWEAVE
interwork *vb syn* see INTERWEAVE
interwreathe *vb syn* see INTERWEAVE
intestinal fortitude *n syn* see FORTITUDE
intestine *adj* **1** *syn* see DOMESTIC 2
2 *syn* see INNER 1
intimacy *n syn* see ACQUAINTANCE 1
intimate *vb syn* see SUGGEST 1
rel attest, bespeak, betoken, indicate
con air, express, utter, vent, voice; affirm, assert, aver, avouch, declare, profess
intimate *adj* **1** *syn* see INHERENT
2 *syn* see INNER 2

3 *syn* see FAMILIAR 1
rel nearest, next; affectionate, devoted, fond, loving; privy, secret
con distant, remote
4 having or marked by a warm personal relation < *intimate* friends for many years > < an *intimate* friendship >
syn ||buddy-buddy, chummy, cozy, pally, ||palsy-walsy
idiom thick as thieves
intimate *n syn* see FRIEND
rel associate, companion, comrade, crony
con outsider, stranger
intimation *n* **1** *syn* see HINT 1
2 *syn* see HINT 2
intimidate *vb* to frighten or coerce into submission or obedience < refused to be *intimidated* by the manager >
syn bludgeon, bluster, ||bounce, browbeat, bulldoze, bully, bullyrag, cow, dragoon, hector, ||ruffle, strong-arm, terrorize
rel alarm, disquiet, frighten, scare, terrify; badger, bait, chivy, hound, ride; coerce, compel, constrain, force, oblige; ||ruffianize
con blandish, cajole, coax, wheedle; induce, persuade, prevail
intimidator *n syn* see BULLY 1
into *prep syn* see TO 1
intolerable *adj syn* see INSUFFERABLE
ant tolerable
intolerant *adj* **1** unwilling or unable to endure with composure < he was inclined to be very *intolerant* of interruption >
syn impatient, unforbearing, unindulgent
rel contemptuous, disdainful; fractious, irritable, snappish, waspish; indignant, irate, outraged, stuffy, upset, worked up
con forbearing, indulgent, long-suffering, patient; resigned, uncomplaining
ant tolerant
2 *syn* see ILLIBERAL
rel inflexible, obdurate; antipathetic, averse, unsympathetic
con forbearing, indulgent, lenient
ant tolerant
intonation *n syn* see INFLECTION
in toto *adv syn* see ALL 1
intoxicant *n syn* see LIQUOR 2
intoxicated *adj* **1** significantly under the influence of alcoholic liquor < some people become *intoxicated* more easily than others >
syn alcoholized, ||bagged, blind, ||blotto, ||boiled, ||bombed, ||boozed, ||boozy, ||buffy, ||buzzed, ||canned, ||capernoited, cockeyed, ||crocked, cut, ||deleerit, disguised, drunk, drunken, fried, ||half-seas over, inebriated, inebrious, ||jagged, ||juiced, ||lit, ||lit up, ||loaded, ||looped, ||lushed, muddled, ||oiled, ||organized, ||pickled, ||pie-eyed, ||pipped, ||pissed, ||pixilated, ||plastered, polluted, ||potted, rum-dum, ||screwy, ||shick, ||shicker, ||shot, slewed, slopped, sloppy, ||smashed, soshed, sozzled, ||spifflicated, ||squiffed, ||stewed, stiff, ||stinking, ||stinko, stoned, ||swacked, tanked, ||tiddly, tight, unsober, wet, zonked
rel befuddled, bemused, besotted, dazed, dopey, fuddled, loopy, maudlin, sodden, soppy, sotted, tipsy
idiom disguised with drink, full as a tick, in drink (*or* liquor), in one's cups, in the bag, stewed to the gills, the worse for drink, three sheets in (*or* to) the wind,

under the table, under the weather, with drink taken

con abstemious, abstinent, moderate, temperate

ant sober

2 profoundly and usually pleasantly moved < *intoxicated* with the beauty of the scene >

syn elated, excited, exhilarated, turned-on

rel affected, concerned, interested, moved; galvanized, piqued, quickened, stimulated

con disinterested, unconcerned; depressed, disheartened, distressed, saddened

intoxicating *adj syn* see EXCITING

intoxication *n syn* see EUPHORIA 2

intractable *adj* 1 *syn* see UNRULY 1

ant tractable

2 *syn* see OBSTINATE

ant tractable

intransigent *adj syn* see OBSTINATE

intrepid *adj syn* see BRAVE 1

ant craven

intricate *adj* 1 *syn* see COMPLEX 2

rel arduous, difficult, hard

2 *syn* see ELABORATE 2

intrigue *vb* 1 *syn* see INTEREST

2 *syn* see PLOT

intrigue *n* 1 *syn* see PLOT 2

2 *syn* see AMOUR 2

intrinsic *adj syn* see INHERENT

con added, annexed, appended, super-added

ant extrinsic

intrinsically *adv syn* see PER SE

introduce *vb* 1 *syn* see ENTER 2

rel inaugurate, induct, install; bring forward

2 *syn* see BROACH

3 to bring into practice or use < *introduce* reforms in the welfare system >

syn inaugurate, initiate, institute, launch, originate, set up, usher in

rel establish, found, organize; innovate, invent; unveil; pioneer

4 to cause to know each other personally < planned to *introduce* her to his mother >

syn acquaint, present, ||quaint

5 *syn* see PRECEDE 3

6 to put among or between others < *introduced* several new lines of dialogue >

syn fill in, insert, insinuate, intercalate, interject, interpolate, interpose, throw in

rel inlay, inlet, inset; inject, instill; work in

con eject, evict, oust; eliminate, exclude

ant abstract; withdraw

introducer *n syn* see INNOVATOR

introduction *n* something that serves as a preliminary or antecedent < the crisis could be the *introduction* to a general war >

syn exordium, foreword, overture, preamble, preface, prelude, prelusion, proem, prolegomenon, prologue

introductory *adj* 1 *syn* see PRELIMINARY

ant closing, concluding

2 *syn* see INITIAL 1

introspection *n* the examination of one's own thought and feeling < a man much given to *introspection* >

syn heart-searching, self-contemplation, self-examination, self-observation, self-questioning, self-reflection, self-scrutiny, self-searching, soul-searching

rel contemplation, meditation, reflection; self-analysis

ant extrospection

intrude *vb* 1 to thrust or force in without permission, welcome, or fitness < constantly *intruded* himself into his sister's affairs >

syn butt in, chisel (in), cut in, horn in, intertrude, obtrude

rel encroach, entrench, infringe, invade, muscle, trespass; insinuate, intercalate, interject, interpolate, interpose, introduce; interfere, intervene; intermeddle, meddle; bother, disturb, pester

con retire, stand off, withdraw

2 *syn* see IMPOSE 5

intrusive *adj syn* see IMPERTINENT 2

rel butting in, intruding, obtruding

con bashful, coy, diffident, modest, retiring, shy

ant unintrusive

intuition *n* immediate apprehension or cognition < skeptical of the traditional woman's *intuition* >

syn anschauung, insight, intuitiveness

rel second sight, sixth sense

ant ratiocination

intuitive *adj syn* see INSTINCTIVE 1

rel direct, immediate, presentative

ant ratiocinative

intuitiveness *n syn* see INTUITION

inumbrate *vb syn* see SHADE

inundate *vb syn* see DELUGE 1

inundation *n syn* see FLOOD 2

inurbane *adj syn* see RUDE 6

ant urbane

inure *vb syn* see ACCUSTOM

rel discipline, train

inutile *adj syn* see WORTHLESS 1

ant utile

invade *vb* 1 to enter for conquest or plunder < the Danes *invaded* England >

syn foray, inroad, overrun, overswarm, raid

rel loot, pillage, plunder, ravage

2 *syn* see TRESPASS 2

rel impenetrate, interpenetrate, permeate, pervade

invalid *adj* 1 *syn* see ILLOGICAL

ant valid

2 *syn* see NULL

invalidate *vb syn* see ABOLISH 1

rel counteract, counterbalance, negative, neutralize, offset; discredit

ant validate

invaluable *adj syn* see PRECIOUS 1

ant worthless

invariable *adj* 1 *syn* see INFLEXIBLE 3

ant variable

2 *syn* see SAME 3

ant variable, varying

invariably *adv* 1 *syn* see ALWAYS 1

2 *syn* see EVER 3

invasion *n* a hostile entrance into the territory of another < Hitler's *invasion* of Poland >

---

syn foray, incursion, inroad, irruption, raid

rel aggression, attack, offense, offensive; breach, infraction, infringement, transgression, trespass, violation; encroachment, entrenchment

invective *adj syn see* ABUSIVE

rel censorious, condemnatory, damnatory, denunciatory, reproachful

invective *n syn see* ABUSE

rel diatribe, jeremiad, philippic, tirade

inveigh (against) *vb syn see* OBJECT 1

inveigle *vb syn see* LURE

inveiglement *n syn see* LURE 2

invent *vb syn see* CONTRIVE 2

rel conceive, envision, imagine; create, mint, produce, turn out; inaugurate, initiate

invention *n* a product of creative imagination < his most famous *invention* is the electric light bulb >

syn brainchild, coinage, contrivance

rel concoction, contraption, innovation, novelty; creation, opus, original

inventive *adj* adept or prolific at producing new things and ideas < had a very *inventive* turn of mind > < he was an *inventive* genius >

syn creative, demiurgic, deviceful, ingenious, innovational, innovative, innovatory, original, originative

rel fertile, fruitful, productive, teeming; causative, constructive, formative

con sterile, uncreative, unproductive

ant uninventive

inventor *n* 1 *syn see* INNOVATOR

2 *syn see* FATHER 2

inventory *n* 1 *syn see* SUPPLY

2 *syn see* RESERVE

inventory *vb* 1 to make an itemized report or record of < will *inventory* all office supplies >

syn catalog, itemize, tally

rel list, record, register; enumerate, tabulate

idiom take account (*or* stock) of

2 *syn see* ITEMIZE 1

3 *syn see* EPITOMIZE 1

inveracity *n syn see* LIE

ant veracity

inverse *vb syn see* REVERSE 1

inversion *n syn see* REVERSAL 1

invert *vb syn see* REVERSE 1

rel flip, turn down, turn over

invert *n syn see* HOMOSEXUAL

invertebrate *n syn see* WEAKLING

invertebrate *adj syn see* WEAK 4

rel disorganized, structureless

inverted *adj* 1 *syn see* UPSIDE-DOWN 1

2 *syn see* HOMOSEXUAL

invest *vb* 1 *syn see* INITIATE 3

rel endow, endue; consecrate, honor

ant divest, strip

2 to make a formal grant of power or authority < the Constitution *invests* the Congress with taxation powers >

syn authorize, empower, vest

rel bequeath, endow

con hold back, keep back, reserve, withhold

ant divest

3 *syn see* ENFOLD 1

4 *syn see* BESIEGE

5 *syn see* INFUSE 1

investigate *vb syn see* EXPLORE

rel muckrake, poke, pry

investigation *n syn see* INQUIRY 1

rel observation, observing; sounding, survey, surveying

investigative *adj syn see* INQUISITIVE 1

investigator *n syn see* DETECTIVE

investiture *n syn see* INITIATION

inveterate *adj* 1 firmly established or having something firmly established < the *inveterate* tendency to overlook the obvious >

syn bred-in-the-bone, confirmed, deep-dyed, deep-rooted, deep-seated, dyed-in-the-wool, entrenched, hard-shell, irradicable, settled, sworn

rel accustomed, addicted, chronic, habituated; customary, habitual, usual; hardened, indurated; established, fixed, set; inbred, innate; abiding, enduring, persistent, persisting

2 *syn see* OLD 2

invidious *adj* 1 *syn see* LIBELOUS

2 *syn see* ENVIOUS

rel bitter; hateful

3 *syn see* REPUGNANT 1

rel abominable, detestable, hateful, odious

con agreeable, grateful, gratifying, pleasant, pleasing

invidiousness *n syn see* ENVY

invigorate *vb syn see* STRENGTHEN 2

rel refresh, rejuvenate, renew, restore; rally, rouse, stir; activate, animate, stimulate, vitalize, vitaminize

ant debilitate

invigorating *adj* having an enlivening effect < an *invigorating* discussion >

syn animating, bracing, exhilarating, exhilarative, quickening, stimulating, stimulative, tonic, vitalizing

rel brisk, lively; fascinating, interesting

con anesthetic, numbing, somniferous

ant deadening

invincible *adj* 1 incapable of being conquered < the team proved to be *invincible* >

syn impregnable, inconquerable, indomitable, inexpugnable, invulnerable, unassailable, unbeatable, unconquerable, undefeatable

rel inviolable, untouchable; unattackable

con conquerable, subduable, surmountable, vanquishable

ant vincible

2 *syn see* INSUPERABLE

ant vincible

inviolable *adj syn see* SACRED 3

rel consecrated, hallowed; blessed, divine, holy; chaste, pure

ant violable

inviolate *adj syn see* SACRED 3

rel intact, perfect; faultless, flawless

con desecrated, profaned; defiled, polluted

invisible *adj syn see* IMPERCEPTIBLE

rel hidden, unseeable

ant visible

invitation *n syn see* PROPOSAL

invite *vb* to request the presence or participation of < *invited* guests to dinner > < *invited* the major nations to confer >

syn ask, bid

rel call, call in, summon; court, solicit, woo; entice, inveigle, lure, tempt

invoice *n syn* see BILL 1

invoke *vb* 1 *syn* see BEG
  2 *syn* see ENFORCE

involuntary *adj syn* see SPONTANEOUS
  rel unintended, unintentional, unwitting
  ant voluntary

involve *vb* 1 to bring a person or thing into circumstances or a situation from which extrication is difficult < nations *involved* in war >
  syn embroil, implicate, mire, tangle; *compare* ENTANGLE 3
  rel catch up; draw (into)
  2 *syn* see INCLUDE

involved *adj* 1 *syn* see COMPLEX 2
  rel confused, muddled
  con easy, facile, simple
  2 *syn* see INTERESTED
  rel enmeshed, entangled
  ant uninvolved

involvement *n syn* see ENTANGLEMENT 1

invulnerable *adj syn* see INVINCIBLE 1
  ant vulnerable

inward *adj syn* see INNER 1
  con alien, extraneous, extrinsic, foreign
  ant outward

inward *n* 1 *often* **inwards** *pl syn* see INTERIOR
  2 **inwards** *pl syn* see ENTRAILS

inwardness *n syn* see ACQUAINTANCE 1

inweave *vb syn* see INTERWEAVE

iota *n syn* see PARTICLE

ipseity *n syn* see INDIVIDUALITY 4

irascible *adj* easily aroused to anger < an *irascible* fellow and hard to get along with >
  syn choleric, cranky, cross, hot-tempered, ireful, passionate, peppery, quick-tempered, ratty, ‖stomachy, temperish, testy, tetchy, touchy; *compare* CANTANKEROUS, IRRITABLE
  rel fractious, huffy, irritable, peevish, petulant, querulous, snappish, waspish; impatient, jittery, jumpy, nervous, restive; bristly, crabbed, surly
  con amiable, complaisant, good-natured, obliging; calm, quiet, relaxed; long-suffering, patient, tolerant

irate *adj syn* see ANGRY

ire *n syn* see ANGER

ire *vb syn* see ANGER 1

ireful *adj* 1 *syn* see ANGRY
  2 *syn* see IRASCIBLE

irenic *adj syn* see PACIFIC
  ant acrimonious

irk *vb* 1 *syn* see ANNOY 1
  rel discommode, incommode, inconvenience, trouble
  2 *syn* see TRY 2

irking *n syn* see ANNOYANCE 1

irksome *adj* tending to cause boredom or tedium < an *irksome* task >
  syn boresome, boring, drudging, tedious, tiresome, tiring
  rel dull, stupid; exhausting, fagging, fatiguing, wearisome
  con exciting, inspiring, provocative, stimulative, stirring

  ant absorbing, engrossing

iron *n, usu* **irons** *pl syn* see SHACKLE

iron *adj syn* see INFLEXIBLE 2

ironbound *adj syn* see ROUGH 1

ironclad *adj syn* see INFLEXIBLE 3

ironfisted *adj* 1 *syn* see STINGY
  2 *syn* see GRIM 3

ironhanded *adj syn* see RIGID 3

ironhead *n syn* see DUNCE

ironhearted *adj syn* see UNFEELING 2
  ant softhearted

ironic *adj syn* see SARDONIC
  rel biting, cutting, incisive, trenchant; caustic, mordant, scathing

‖**ironman** *n syn* see DOLLAR

irradiate *vb syn* see ILLUMINATE 2

irradicable *adj syn* see INVETERATE 1

irrational *adj syn* see ILLOGICAL
  rel crazy, demented, insane
  con logical, reasonable, sensible
  ant rational

irrealizable *adj syn* see IMPOSSIBLE 1
  ant realizable

irrebuttable *adj syn* see POSITIVE 3
  ant rebuttable

irreclaimable *adj syn* see IRRECOVERABLE
  ant reclaimable

irreconcilable *adj* incapable of being made consistent < the two versions of the story are completely *irreconcilable* >
  syn incompatible, inconformable, inconsistent
  rel discordant, discrepant, dissonant, inaccordant, incongruent, incongruous, inharmonious
  ant reconcilable

irrecoverable *adj* not capable of being recovered, regained, remedied, or rectified < suffered an *irrecoverable* loss in the fire >
  syn irreclaimable, irredeemable, irremediable, irreparable, irretrievable
  ant recoverable

irredeemable *adj syn* see IRRECOVERABLE
  ant redeemable

irreflective *adj syn* see CARELESS 1
  ant reflective

irrefragable *adj syn* see INDESTRUCTIBLE

irrefrangible *adj syn* see INDESTRUCTIBLE

irrefutable *adj syn* see POSITIVE 3
  ant refutable

irregular *adj* 1 not according with or explainable by law, rule, or custom < unusual problems require *irregular* solutions >
  syn abnormal, anomalous, deviant, divergent, off-key, unnatural, unregular
  rel aberrant, atypical; exceptional, odd, peculiar, queer, singular, strange, unique
  con natural, normal, typical; accustomed, customary, habitual, usual, wonted
  ant regular
  2 *syn* see INFORMAL 1
  3 *syn* see LOPSIDED
  ant regular
  4 *syn* see RANDOM
  rel occasional, sporadic; erratic, fitful, spasmodic; inconstant, uneven, unsteady
  5 *syn* see SPOTTY 1

irregular *n syn* see PARTISAN 2

---

syn synonym(s)   *rel* related word(s)
ant antonym(s)   *con* contrasted word(s)
idiom idiomatic equivalent(s)
‖ use limited; if in doubt, see a dictionary

irregularity *n syn* see INEQUALITY 1
ant regularity
irregularly *adv syn* see OCCASIONALLY
ant regularly
irrelative *adj syn* see IRRELEVANT
ant relative
irrelevant *adj* not applicable or pertinent
< *age* should be *irrelevant* to employability >
syn extraneous, foreign, immaterial, impertinent, inapplicable, inapposite, irrelative
rel inconsequential, insignificant, unimportant
idiom beside the point, neither here nor there, out of the question
con applicable, appurtenant, germane, material, pertinent, significant
ant relevant
irreligious *adj* lacking religious emotions, doctrines, or practices < an *irreligious* person but not openly hostile to organized religion >
syn godless, nonreligious, unreligious
rel indevout, undevout; ungodly, unholy, unsanctimonious; blasphemous, impious, profane, sacrilegious; amoral, unmoral
con devout, pious
ant religious
irremediable *adj* 1 *syn* see IRRECOVERABLE
ant remediable
2 *syn* see HOPELESS 2
irremovable *adj syn* see IMMOVABLE 1
ant removable
irreparable *adj* 1 *syn* see IRRECOVERABLE
ant reparable
2 *syn* see HOPELESS 2
irreprehensible *adj syn* see GOOD 11
ant reprehensible
irrepressible *adj* impossible to repress, restrain, or control < an *irrepressible* joy over his brother's good fortune >
syn insuppressible, insuppressive, irrestrainable, uncontainable, uncontrollable, unrestrainable
rel bubbling over, effervescent, enthusiastic, rhapsodical
ant repressible
irreproachable *adj* 1 *syn* see GOOD 11
2 *syn* see IMPECCABLE 1
irresoluble *adj syn* see INSOLUBLE
ant resoluble
irresolute *adj syn* see VACILLATING 2
ant resolute
irresolution *n syn* see HESITATION
ant resolution
irresolvable *adj syn* see INSOLUBLE
ant resolvable
irresponsible *adj* lacking in responsibility
< *irresponsible* behavior >
syn carefree, careless, feckless, incautious, reckless, uncareful, wild
rel undependable, unreliable, untrustworthy; unaccountable, unanswerable
con careful, cautious, discreet, heedful; dependable, reliable, trustworthy
ant responsible
irrestrainable *adj syn* see IRREPRESSIBLE
ant restrainable
irretrievable *adj syn* see IRRECOVERABLE

ant retrievable
irreverent *adj syn* see IMPIOUS 1
ant reverent
irreverential *adj syn* see IMPIOUS 1
ant reverential
irreversible *adj syn* see IRREVOCABLE
ant reversible
irrevocable *adj* incapable of being recalled or revoked < an *irrevocable* decision of the Supreme Court >
syn irreversible, nonreversible, unrepealable
rel constant, established, fixed; immutable, unchangeable, unmodifiable
con repealable, reversible; alterable, changeable, modifiable
ant revocable
irritable *adj* easily exasperated < the miserable weather made us all *irritable* >
syn disagreeable, fractious, fretful, huffy, peevish, pettish, petulant, ‖pindling, prickish, prickly, querulent, querulential, querulous, raspish, raspy, snappish, snappy, twitty, waspish, waspy, whiny; *compare* CANTANKEROUS, IRASCIBLE
rel cranky, cross, testy, touchy; choleric, irascible, splenetic
con amiable, complaisant, good-natured, obliging; affable, cordial, genial, gracious, sociable
ant easygoing
irritant *n syn* see ANNOYANCE 3
irritate *vb* to excite to angry annoyance
< his rude interruptions really *irritated* her >
syn aggravate, burn (up), exasperate, gall, get, grate, huff, inflame, nettle, peeve, pique, provoke, put out, rile, roil; *compare* ANNOY 1
rel abrade, bother, ‖bug, chafe, exercise, fret, irk, ruffle, try, vex; anger, enrage, incense, infuriate, madden; affront, offend
con appease, conciliate, mollify, pacify, placate, propitiate; delight, gladden, gratify, please
irrupt *vb syn* see ERUPT 1
irruption *n syn* see INVASION
Ishmael *n syn* see OUTCAST
Ishmaelite *n syn* see OUTCAST
island *vb syn* see ISOLATE
isochronal *adj syn* see INTERMITTENT
isochronous *adj syn* see INTERMITTENT
isolate *vb* to set apart from others < the jury was *isolated* for several days >
syn close off, cut off, enisle, insulate, island, segregate, separate, sequester
rel quarantine; block (off); abstract, detach, disengage, remove; divide, part, sever, sunder
con associate, connect, join, link, unite
isolate *adj syn* see ALONE 1
isolated *adj syn* see ALONE 1
rel retired, secluded, withdrawn; abandoned, deserted, forsaken, stranded
isolation *n syn* see SOLITUDE
issue *n* 1 *syn* see OFFSPRING
2 *syn* see EFFECT 1
3 *syn* see PROBLEM 2
rel matter; subject, topic
issue *vb* 1 *syn* see SPRING 1
2 *syn* see EMIT 2
3 *syn* see PUBLISH 2
italicize *vb syn* see EMPHASIZE

itch *n* **1** *syn* see DESIRE 1
  2 *syn* see LUST 2
itch *vb* *syn* see LONG
itchy *adj* *syn* see COVETOUS
item *adv* *syn* see ALSO 2
item *n* *syn* see POINT 1
  rel component, piece; incidental, minutia
itemize *vb* **1** to set down in detail or by
  particulars < *itemize* deductions on a tax
  form >
  syn enumerate, inventory, list, particularize, specialize, specify; *compare* SPECIFY 3
  rel circumstantiate, document; count,
  number; cite, instance, mention; spell out
  ant summarize
  2 *syn* see INVENTORY
itemized *adj* *syn* see CIRCUMSTANTIAL
  ant summarized
iterate *vb* *syn* see REPEAT

itinerant *adj* traveling from place to place
  < *itinerant* preachers >
  syn ambulant, ambulatory, deambulatory,
  itinerate, nomadic, perambulant, perambulatory, peripatetic, roving, vagabond, vagrant, wandering, wayfaring
  rel rambling, ranging, roaming; moving,
  shifting
itinerate *adj* *syn* see ITINERANT
itsy–bitsy *adj* *syn* see TINY
itty–bitty *adj* *syn* see TINY
‖**ivory** *n* *often* **ivories** *pl* *syn* see DICE
ivory–tower *adj* *syn* see IMPRACTICAL 1
  ant down-to-earth
ivory–towered *adj* *syn* see IMPRACTICAL
  1
ivory–towerish *adj* *syn* see IMPRACTI-
  CAL 1

J

jab *vb* *syn* see POKE 1
jab *n* **1** *syn* see POKE 1
  2 *syn* see PRICK 1
jabber *vb* *syn* see GIBBER
jabber *n* **1** *syn* see GIBBERISH 1
  2 *syn* see CHATTER
jabberer *n* *syn* see CHATTERBOX
jabberwocky *n* *syn* see GIBBERISH 1
jack *n* **1** *syn* see MARINER
  2 *syn* see FLAG
  ‖**3** *syn* see MONEY
jack (up) *vb* *syn* see RAISE 9
jackass *n* **1** *syn* see DONKEY 1
  2 *syn* see FOOL 1
jacket *n* *syn* see HIDE
jackleg *adj* *syn* see AMATEURISH
jackleg lawyer *n* *syn* see PETTIFOGGER
jackpot *n* *syn* see POT 3
jack–tar *n* *syn* see MARINER
jade *n* **1** *syn* see WANTON
  2 *syn* see MINX
jade *vb* **1** *syn* see TIRE 1
  rel cloy, pall, sate, satiate, surfeit; emasculate, enervate, unman, unnerve; depress,
  oppress, weigh
  con rejuvenate, renew, restore
  ant refresh
  2 *syn* see SATIATE
jaded *adj* **1** *syn* see TIRED 1
  ant refreshed
  2 *syn* see SATIATED
‖**jag** *n* *syn* see PRICK 1
jag *n* *syn* see BINGE 1
‖**jag** *vb* *syn* see CARRY 1
jagged *adj* *syn* see ROUGH 1
‖**jagged** *adj* *syn* see INTOXICATED 1
jail *n* a building or institution for the confinement of persons held in lawful custody
  < sent to *jail* for perjury >
  syn bastille, ‖big house, bridewell, ‖brig,

‖bucket, ‖caboose, ‖calaboose, ‖can, ‖car-
cel, ‖chokey, ‖clink, ‖college, cooler, coop,
freezer, guardroom, ‖hoosegow, jug, keep,
lockup, pen, penitentiary, ‖pokey, prison,
reformatory, rock pile, skookum-house,
slammer, ‖stir, stockade
  idiom house of correction
jail *vb* *syn* see IMPRISON
  ant release
jailbird *n* *syn* see CONVICT
jake *n* *syn* see RUSTIC
jakes *n pl* but *sing or pl in constr* *syn* see
  PRIVY 1
jalopy *n* a dilapidated old automobile
  < bought a *jalopy* for $50 >
  syn clunker, crate, dog, heap, junker,
  wreck
jam *vb* **1** *syn* see PRESS 1
  rel tamp, wad
  2 *syn* see CRAM 1
  3 *syn* see PRESS 7
jam *n* *syn* see PREDICAMENT
jam *n* a rich spread prepared by boiling
  fruit and sugar until the mixture thickens
  < enjoyed his mother's tasty berry *jams* >
  syn confiture, conserve, preserve
  rel jelly, marmalade
jam–full *adj* *syn* see FULL 1
jammed *adj* *syn* see FULL 1
jam–pack *vb* *syn* see CRAM 1
jam–packed *adj* *syn* see FULL 1
jangle *vb* *syn* see CLASH 2
jangle *n* *syn* see DIN
jape *n* *syn* see JOKE 1
jar *vb* **1** *syn* see CLASH 2
  2 *syn* see SHAKE 2
jar *n* *syn* see IMPACT
  rel fluctuation, sway, vibration; agitation,
  disturbance, upset
jargon *n* **1** *syn* see TERMINOLOGY
  2 *syn* see DIALECT 2
  rel idiom, speech; abracadabra, gibberish
jarring *adj* *syn* see HARSH 3
  ant soothing
jaundiced *adj* *syn* see BIASED 2
jaunt *n* *syn* see EXCURSION 1

---

syn synonym(s)   *rel* related word(s)
ant antonym(s)   *con* contrasted word(s)
idiom idiomatic equivalent(s)
‖ use limited; if in doubt, see a dictionary

‖**jaw** *n syn* see BACK TALK
jaw *vb* 1 *syn* see SCOLD 1
  2 *syn* see CHAT 1
jay *n syn* see RUSTIC
jazz *n syn* see NONSENSE 2
jealous *adj* 1 intolerant of rivalry or un-faithfulness <her husband was *jealous* of her flirting with other men>
  syn possessive, possessory
  rel covetous, demanding; grasping, grudg-ing; envious, green-eyed, invidious; mis-trustful, suspicious; doubting, questioning
  con tolerant, trusting, understanding
  2 *syn* see ENVIOUS
  3 *syn* see SUSPICIOUS 2
jealousy *n syn* see ENVY
jeer *vb syn* see SCOFF
  con fawn, toady, truckle; approve, en-dorse, OK, sanction
jejune *adj syn* see INSIPID 3
  rel slight, slim, tenuous, thin; arid, dry
jell *vb syn* see COAGULATE
  rel stiffen, thicken; cohere, stick
jellify *vb syn* see COAGULATE
jelly *vb syn* see COAGULATE
jellyfish *n syn* see WEAKLING
jeopard *vb syn* see ENDANGER
jeopardize *vb syn* see ENDANGER
jeopardous *adj syn* see DANGEROUS 1
jeopardy *n syn* see DANGER
  rel exposure; liability, openness, sensitive-ness, susceptibility; accident, chance, hap
  ant safety
jeopardy *vb syn* see ENDANGER
jeremiad *n syn* see TIRADE
jerk *vb* to act on with or make a sudden sharp quick movement <*jerked* to one side> <*jerk* a root from the ground>
  syn lug, lurch, snap, twitch, vellicate, yank
  rel drag, pull; fling, sling, throw, toss; wrench, wrest, wring
jerk *n syn* see FOOL 1
jerkwater town *n syn* see BURG
jerry–build *vb syn* see THROW UP 1
jest *n* 1 *syn* see JOKE 1
  rel banter, chaff, jolly; derision, ridicule, twit
  2 *syn* see FUN 1
  con gravity, seriousness, soberness
  ant earnest
  3 *syn* see LAUGHINGSTOCK
jest *vb* 1 *syn* see SCOFF
  2 *syn* see BANTER
jestee *n syn* see LAUGHINGSTOCK
jester *n* 1 *syn* see FOOL 2
  2 *syn* see HUMORIST 2
jet *adj syn* see BLACK 1
jet *vb syn* see SQUIRT
jetsam *n syn* see DRIFTWOOD
jet set *n syn* see SMART SET
jettison *n syn* see DISPOSAL 2
jettison *vb syn* see DISCARD
  ant salvage
jetty *n syn* see WHARF
jetty *adj syn* see BLACK 1
jewel *n syn* see PARAGON
jewel *vb syn* see BEJEWEL
jezebel *n syn* see WANTON
jib *vb syn* see DEMUR
jibe *vb syn* see AGREE 4
‖**jiff** *n syn* see INSTANT 1
jiffy *n syn* see INSTANT 1

jig *n syn* see TRICK 1
jigger *n* 1 *syn* see DOODAD
  2 *syn* see GADGET 1
‖**jiggery–pokery** *n syn* see NONSENSE 2
jiggle *vb syn* see SHAKE 3
jillion *n syn* see SCAD
jim–dandy *n syn* see ‖DILLY
‖**jimjams** *n syn* see JITTERS
‖**jimmies** *n syn* see JITTERS
jimmy *vb syn* see PRY
jingle *vb* to make a repeated sharp light ringing sound <the coins *jingled* in his pocket>
  syn chink, chinkle, clink, tingle, tinkle
  rel clack, clatter, rattle
jinx *n* something that is felt or meant to bring bad luck <his continual bad luck seemed due to a *jinx*>
  syn hex, hoodoo, Indian sign, voodoo, whammy
  rel charm, enchantment, spell; curse, evil eye
jitters *n pl* a sense of panic or extreme nervousness <got the *jitters* whenever he thought of the money he had lost>
  syn ‖all-overs, dither, heebie-jeebies, ‖jim-jams, ‖jimmies, jumps, shakes, shivers, whim-whams, willies
jittery *adj syn* see NERVOUS
‖**jive** *vb syn* see BANTER
job *n* 1 *syn* see TASK 1
  rel affair, concern, matter, thing
  2 a regular remunerative employment <held two *jobs* to make ends meet>
  syn appointment, berth, billet, connec-tion, office, place, position, post, situation, spot; *compare* WORK 1
  rel assignment, engagement, posting; calling, employment, occupation, pursuit; profession, trade, vocation; niche, opening, slot
  3 *syn* see WORK 1
  4 *syn* see TASK 2
job *vb syn* see DUPE
jobless *adj syn* see UNEMPLOYED
jockey *vb syn* see MANIPULATE 2
jocose *adj syn* see WITTY
  rel playful, roguish, sportive, waggish, whimsical; comic, comical, droll, laugh-able, ludicrous; blithe, jocund, jolly, jovial
  con demure, earnest, grave, sedate, seri-ous, sober, solemn, staid
  ant lugubrious
jocular *adj syn* see WITTY
  rel jolly, jovial, merry; playful, sportive; comic, comical, droll, laughable, ludicrous
  con earnest, grave, serious, sober, solemn
jocularity *n syn* see MIRTH
jocund *adj syn* see MERRY
  rel mischievous, playful, sportive
  con dour, gloomy, glum, morose, satur-nine, sullen; grave, sedate, serious, solemn, somber, staid
jocundity *n syn* see MIRTH
jog *vb syn* see POKE 1
  rel agitate, shake
joggle *vb syn* see SHAKE 3
john *n syn* see TOILET
John Law *n syn* see POLICEMAN
johnny *n syn* see TOILET
join *vb* 1 to bring or come together into some manner of union <the couple were *joined* in marriage soon thereafter>

syn associate, bracket, coadunate, coagment, coalesce, combine, compound, concrete, conjoin, conjugate, connect, couple, link, marry, one, relate, unite, wed, yoke

rel agree, concur, cooperate; articulate, concatenate, integrate; affix, attach, fasten; knit, weave; bind, tie, tie up

con separate, sever, sunder; detach, disengage; disembarrass, disentangle, untangle

ant disjoin, part

2 *syn see* ADJOIN

join (up) *vb syn see* ENTER 3

joining *n syn see* JOINT 1

joint *n* 1 a place where two or more things are united < the leak was found at a *joint* in the pipeline >

syn connection, coupling, joining, junction, juncture, seam, union

rel crux, link, tie; interconnection; abutment, articulation, suture; concourse, confluence, meeting

2 *syn see* DIVE

joint *adj syn see* COMMON 1

jointly *adv syn see* TOGETHER 3

joke *n* 1 a remark, story, or action intended to evoke laughter < had a good memory for *jokes* >

syn crack, drôlerie, drollery, gag, jape, jest, quip, sally, waggery, wisecrack, witticism, ‖yak

rel antic, caper, dido, monkeyshine, prank; bijouterie, bon mot; burlesque, caricature, parody, quiz, rib; badinage, persiflage, raillery; facetiousness, humorousness, jocoseness, jocularity, wittiness; humor, repartee, sarcasm, wit

2 *syn see* FUN 1

3 *syn see* LAUGHINGSTOCK

joke *vb syn see* BANTER

joker *n* 1 *syn see* WAG 1

2 *syn see* HUMORIST 2

3 *syn see* ZANY 2

jokester *n* 1 *syn see* HUMORIST 2

2 *syn see* ZANY 2

jollity *n* 1 *syn see* MIRTH

rel blitheness; disport, frolic, gambol, play, rollick, romp, sport

con earnestness, gravity, sedateness, seriousness, solemnity, staidness

ant somberness

2 *syn see* MERRYMAKING

jolly *adj syn see* MERRY

rel frolicsome, mischievous, playful, roguish, sportive, waggish

con earnest, grave, sedate, serious, solemn, staid; doleful, dolorous, lugubrious, rueful

ant somber

jolly *vb syn see* BANTER

rel blandish, cajole

jolt *vb syn see* SHOCK 2

jolt *n* 1 *syn see* IMPACT

2 *syn see* DRAM

jongleur *n syn see* BARD 1

josh *vb syn see* BANTER

joskin *n syn see* RUSTIC

jostle *vb syn see* PUSH 2

jot *n syn see* PARTICLE

jounce *n syn see* IMPACT

journal *n* a publication that appears at regular intervals < a monthly scientific *journal* >

syn magazine, newspaper, organ, periodical, review

journey *n* passing or a passage from one place to another < at that time it was a four day *journey* from Boston to New York > < she was tired though their *journey* was barely begun >

syn expedition, peregrination(s), travel(s), trek, trip; compare TRIP 1

rel excursion, jaunt, junket, sally, tour; cruise, voyage; pilgrimage, progress, safari

journey *vb syn see* GO 1

jovial *adj syn see* MERRY

rel facetious, humorous, jocose, jocular; affable, genial, sociable; amiable, good=natured; bantering, chaffing, jollying, joshing

con dour, gloomy, glum, morose, saturnine, sullen; grave, sedate, serious, solemn, staid

joviality *n syn see* MIRTH

joy *n syn see* PLEASURE 2

rel ecstasy, rapture, transport

ant sorrow; misery

joyance *n syn see* PLEASURE 2

joyful *adj syn see* GLAD 1

rel buoyant, effervescent, expansive

con despairing, desperate, despondent, forlorn, hopeless; depressed, oppressed, weighed down

ant joyless

joy girl *n syn see* PROSTITUTE

joyhouse *n syn see* BROTHEL

joy–juice *n syn see* LIQUOR 2

joyless *adj* 1 *syn see* SAD 2

2 *syn see* GLOOMY 3

joyous *adj syn see* GLAD 1

rel ecstatic, rapturous, transported

con doleful, dolorous, melancholy; miserable, wretched

ant lugubrious

jubilance *n syn see* EXULTATION

jubilant *adj syn see* EXULTANT

jubilate *vb syn see* EXULT

jubilation *n syn see* EXULTATION

judge *n* 1 a person who impartially decides unsettled questions or controversial issues < the *judge* declared the ruling invalid >

syn arbiter, artitrator, referee, umpire

rel intermediary, mediator, negotiator; conciliator, peacemaker, reconciler

2 an official entrusted with administration of laws < the *judge* gave the defendant a suspended sentence >

syn ‖beak, court, justice, magistrate

judge *vb* 1 to decide something in dispute or controversy upon its merits and upon evidence < the committee will *judge* the truth of the testimony >

syn adjudge, adjudicate, arbitrate, referee, umpire

rel decide, determine, rule, settle

2 *syn see* INFER

rel demonstrate, prove, show; check, test, try

3 *syn see* ESTIMATE 3

judgmatic *adj syn see* WISE 2

judgment *n* 1 *syn see* INFERENCE 1

rel decision, determination, ruling; belief, conviction, opinion, persuasion, view

---

syn synonym(s)   *rel* related word(s)
ant antonym(s)   *con* contrasted word(s)
idiom idiomatic equivalent(s)
‖ use limited; if in doubt, see a dictionary

2 *syn* see INFERENCE 2

3 *syn* see ESTIMATION 1

4 *syn* see SENSE 6

rel astuteness, perspicacity, sagacity, shrewdness; acumen, discernment, insight, penetration

judicious *adj syn* see WISE 2

rel rational, reasonable; dispassionate, equitable, fair, objective

con irrational, thoughtless, unreasonable; ill-considered

ant injudicious; asinine

jug *n syn* see JAIL

jug *vb syn* see IMPRISON

juggle *vb syn* see DECEIVE

juice *n syn* see LIQUOR 2

‖**juiced** *adj syn* see INTOXICATED 1

juicy *adj syn* see SUCCULENT

juju *n syn* see CHARM 2

jumble *vb* 1 *syn* see CONFUSE 5

2 *syn* see DISORDER 1

jumble *n* 1 *syn* see CLUTTER 2

2 *syn* see MISCELLANY 1

jumbo *adj syn* see HUGE

jump *vb* 1 to move suddenly through space by or as if by muscular action < *jumped* across the open trench >

syn bounce, bound, hop, hurdle, leap, lop, saltate, spring, vault

2 *syn* see START 1

3 *syn* see RAISE 9

jump (in *or* into) *vb syn* see PITCH IN 1

jump (off) *vb syn* see BEGIN 1

jumps *n pl syn* see JITTERS

jumpy *adj syn* see NERVOUS

idiom on pins and needles

junction *n* 1 *syn* see CONCOURSE

2 *syn* see JOINT 1

juncture *n* 1 *syn* see JOINT 1

2 a critical or crucial time or state of affairs < was at a *juncture* where he had to make a decision >

syn contingency, crisis, crossroad(s), emergency, exigency, pass, pinch, strait, turning point, zero hour

rel condition, posture, situation, state, status; plight, predicament, quandary

3 *syn* see POINT 7

jungle *n* 1 *syn* see CLUTTER 2

2 *syn* see MAZE 1

junk *n syn* see REFUSE

junk *vb syn* see DISCARD

junker *n syn* see JALOPY

junket *n syn* see EXCURSION 1

junking *n syn* see DISPOSAL 2

Junoesque *adj syn* see CURVACEOUS

jurisdiction *n syn* see POWER 1

rel bounds, confines, limits; compass, range, reach, scope; bailiwick, domain, field, province, sphere, territory

just *adj* 1 *syn* see WELL-FOUNDED

2 *syn* see TRUE 3

3 being what is called for by circumstances or accepted standards < punishments once considered fair and *just* are now held to be cruel, excessive, and unreasonable >

syn appropriate, condign, deserved, due, merited, requisite, rhadamanthine, right, rightful, suitable; *compare* FIT 1

rel fit, fitting, meet, proper

con farfetched, irrelevant, remote, unconnected; improper, inapplicable, inapposite, inappropriate; abusive, cruel, harsh

ant unjust

4 *syn* see UPRIGHT 2

rel rigid, strict; dependable, reliable, tried, trustworthy

5 *syn* see FAIR 4

rel aloof; condign, due, rightful

ant unjust

6 *syn* see FIT 1

just *adv* 1 as stated or indicated without deviation < *just* six inches long >

syn accurately, bang, exactly, precisely, right, sharp, ‖smack-dab, spang, square, squarely

rel definitely, directly, expressly, unmistakably

con almost, nearly; approximately, imprecisely, inaccurately, inexactly, loosely

2 by a very small margin < *just* enough food for one meal >

syn barely, hardly, scarce, scarcely

rel almost, approximately, nearly

con copiously, fully, generously, lavishly, unstintedly, unstintingly

3 no more than < *just* a note to remind you >

syn but, merely, only, simply

idiom nothing but

4 *syn* see ALL 1

5 *syn* see EVEN 1

just about *adv syn* see NEARLY

justice *n* 1 the action, practice, or obligation of awarding each his just due < his *justice* was stern but absolutely fair >

syn equity

rel evenness, fairness, impartiality

con foul play, inequity, unjustness; bias, leaning, one-sidedness, partiality

ant injustice

2 *syn* see JUDGE 2

justifiable *adj* capable of being justified < thought her absence was not *justifiable* >

syn condonable, defensible, excusable, tenable, vindicable, warrantable

rel admissible, allowable, legitimate, reasonable; forgivable, pardonable, remissible

ant unjustifiable

justification *n* 1 *syn* see EXPLANATION 2

2 *syn* see APOLOGY 1

justified *adj syn* see WELL-FOUNDED

ant unjustified

justify *vb* 1 *syn* see MAINTAIN 2

rel demonstrate, prove; back, support, uphold

con confute, disprove, refute

2 *syn* see CONFIRM 2

3 *syn* see EXPLAIN 3

rel extenuate, gloss, gloze, palliate, whitewash

con accuse, arraign, incriminate, indict; blame, condemn, denounce

4 to constitute sufficient grounds < thought the storm warning *justified* his leaving early >

syn warrant

rel allow, permit; approve, authorize, sanction

justly *adv syn* see WELL 1

jut *vb* 1 *syn* see BULGE

rel elongate, extend, lengthen

2 *syn* see HANG 4

jut *n syn* see PROJECTION 1

juvenile *adj syn* see YOUNG 1

ant adult
juvenile *n syn* see CHILD 1

juvenility *n syn* see YOUTH 1
juxtaposed *adj syn* see ADJACENT 3

K

‖**kale** *n syn* see MONEY
keck *vb syn* see RETCH
keel (over) *vb syn* see FALL 2
keen *adj* 1 *syn* see SHARP 1
  2 *syn* see ENTHUSIASTIC
  3 *syn* see EAGER
  rel fervent, fervid, perfervid; fierce, intense, vehement; fired
  con apathetic, impassive, phlegmatic, stolid; languid, listless
  4 *syn* see SHARP 4
  5 *syn* see ACUTE 3
  con dull, obtuse
  6 *syn* see LIVELY 1
  ‖7 *syn* see MARVELOUS 2
keenly *adv syn* see HARD 6
keenness *n* 1 *syn* see EDGE 2
  2 *syn* see WIT 3
keep *vb* 1 *syn* see OBEY
  ant neglect
  2 to notice or honor a day, occasion, or deed < remember the Sabbath and *keep* it rightly>
  syn celebrate, commemorate, observe, solemnize
  rel regard, respect; bless, consecrate, sanctify; honor, laud, praise
  idiom keep the faith
  con disregard, forget, ignore, neglect, omit, overlook, slight; contravene, infringe, transgress, violate
  ant break
  3 *syn* see STOCK
  4 *syn* see RESTRAIN 1
  ant release
  5 to hold in one's possession or under one's control < *kept* all the money for himself>
  syn detain, hold, hold back, keep back, keep out, reserve, retain, withhold
  rel conserve, preserve, save; enjoy, have, own, possess; conduct, control, direct, manage
  con cast, discard, junk; refuse, reject, repudiate, spurn; abandon, resign, surrender, yield
  ant relinquish
  6 *syn* see REFRAIN 1
  7 *syn* see CONDUCT 3
keep *n* 1 *syn* see LIVING
  2 *syn* see JAIL
keep back *vb* 1 *syn* see KEEP 5
  2 *syn* see DENY 2
keeper *n syn* see CUSTODIAN
keeping *n* 1 *syn* see CUSTODY
  2 *syn* see PRESERVATION 1

keep off *vb syn* see FEND (off)
keep out *vb syn* see KEEP 5
keepsake *n syn* see REMEMBRANCE 3
keep up *vb syn* see MAINTAIN 1
keg *n syn* see CASK
‖**keister** *n syn* see BUTTOCKS
kelter *n syn* see REFUSE
ken *n* the extent of one's recognition, comprehension, perception, understanding, or knowledge < abstractions that are beyond the *ken* of small children>
  syn horizon, purview, range, reach
  rel comprehension, grasp, perception, understanding
kept woman *n syn* see HARLOT 1
kerchief *n* 1 a square of cloth used as a head covering or scarf < wore a *kerchief* around his neck>
  syn babushka, bandanna
  2 *syn* see HANDKERCHIEF
kernel *n syn* see SUBSTANCE 2
key *n syn* see PASSPORT
kibitzer *n syn* see BUSYBODY
kick *vb* 1 *syn* see OBJECT 1
  rel combat, fight, oppose, resist, withstand; anathematize, condemn, curse, damn, execrate
  idiom put up a fight (against)
  2 *syn* see COMPLAIN
kick *n syn* see THRILL
‖**kick around** *vb syn* see DISCUSS 1
kick back *vb syn* see BACKFIRE
kicker *n syn* see GROUCH
‖**kick in** *vb* 1 *syn* see CONTRIBUTE 1
  2 *syn* see DIE 1
kick off *vb* 1 *syn* see BEGIN 1
  ‖2 *syn* see DIE 1
kick out *vb* 1 *syn* see DISMISS 3
  2 *syn* see EJECT 1
kickshaw *n syn* see DELICACY
kid *n syn* see CHILD 1
kid *vb* 1 *syn* see DUPE
  2 *syn* see BANTER
kidnap *vb* to carry off a person surreptitiously for an illegal purpose < an ex-convict *kidnapped* the child for ransom>
  syn abduct, ‖snatch, spirit (away)
  rel shanghai, waylay; coax, decoy, entice, inveigh, lure, seduce
  idiom make off with
  con deliver, ransom, redeem, rescue; bring (back), give back, restore, return
kidney *n syn* see TYPE
kid stuff *n syn* see SNAP 1
kill *vb* 1 to deprive of life < found it hard to *kill* animals>
  syn carry off, cut off, destroy, dispatch, down, finish, lay low, put away, scrag, slay, take off; *compare* MURDER 1
  rel butcher, choke, drown, massacre, poison, shoot, slaughter, suffocate; knife, sacrifice, stifle; annihilate, exterminate, ruin

---

syn synonym(s)   *rel* related word(s)
ant antonym(s)   *con* contrasted word(s)
idiom idiomatic equivalent(s)
‖ use limited; if in doubt, see a dictionary

idiom do (*or* make) away with, do for, put out of the way, put (*or* do) to death, put to sleep, take one's life

2 *syn* see VETO

killer *n syn* see MURDERER

killing *n syn* see MURDER

kiln *vb syn* see FIRE 6

kilter *n syn* see ORDER 10

kin *n* 1 *syn* see FAMILY

2 the members of one's immediate or extended family < all our *kin* gathered to celebrate great grandma's birthday>

syn cousinage, cousinhood, kinfolk, kinsmen

3 *syn* see RELATIVE

kind *n syn* see TYPE

kind *adj* showing or having a gentle considerate nature < mother was a *kind* person, always willing to help others>

syn benign, benignant, good-hearted, kindly

rel altruistic, benevolent, charitable, eleemosynary, humane, humanitarian, open-hearted, philanthropic, propitious; compassionate, kindhearted, responsive, sympathetic, tender, warm, warmhearted; clement, forbearing, indulgent, lenient, merciful, tolerant; affable, amiable, cordial, genial, good-humored, good-natured, good-tempered, sweet-tempered; complaisant, obliging; gentle, good

con cruel, fell, fierce, inhuman, savage; hard, harsh, rough; grim, implacable, merciless, unrelenting

ant unkind

kindhearted *adj syn* see TENDER

kindle *vb* 1 *syn* see LIGHT 1

rel blaze, flame, flare, glow; excite, provoke, stimulate; arouse, foment, incite, instigate, rouse, stir

ant smother

2 *syn* see STIR 1

ant stifle

kindless *adj syn* see ANTIPATHETIC 2

kindliness *n syn* see GOODWILL 1

ant unkindliness

kindly *adj syn* see KIND

rel gracious, sociable; friendly, neighborly; attentive, considerate, thoughtful

con malevolent, malicious, malign, spiteful

ant unkindly; acrid (*of temper, attitudes, comments*)

kindly *adv syn* see WELL 2

kindness *n syn* see FAVOR 4

kind of *adv syn* see SOMEWHAT 2

kindred *n syn* see FAMILY 1

kindred *adj syn* see RELATED

ant alien

kinfolk *n pl syn* see KIN 2

king *n syn* see MAGNATE

kingdom come *n syn* see HEAVEN 2

kinglike *adj syn* see KINGLY

kingly *adj* of, relating to, or befitting a king < a *kingly* entourage>

syn kinglike, majestic, monarchal, monarchial, monarchical, regal, royal, sovereign

rel imperious, lordly, masterful, powerful, puissant; imperial, princely, queenly

kinky *adj syn* see OUTLANDISH 3

kinsman *n* 1 *syn* see RELATIVE

2 kinsmen *pl syn* see KIN 2

kinswoman *n syn* see RELATIVE

kismet *n syn* see FATE

kiss *vb* 1 to touch with the lips especially as a sign of affection < *kissed* his mother good night>

syn buss, lip, osculate, peck, smack, smooch, ‖smoodge, ‖smouch

2 *syn* see BRUSH

‖**kisser** *n syn* see FACE 1

kiss off *vb syn* see DISMISS 5

kite *vb syn* see GET OUT 1

kittenish *adj syn* see PLAYFUL 1

kitty *n syn* see POT 3

klutz *n syn* see OAF 2

knack *n* 1 *syn* see GIFT 2

rel quickness, readiness

ant ineptitude

2 *syn* see ABILITY 2

3 *syn* see HANG

knapsack *n syn* see BACKPACK

knave *n syn* see VILLAIN 1

knavish *adj syn* see DISHONEST

knell *vb syn* see RING

knickknack *n* a small or trivial ornamental article < a collection of pretty *knickknacks* was displayed on the mantel>

syn bauble, bibelot, curio, dido, gewgaw, gimcrack, novelty, objet d'art, pretty-pretty, rattletrap(s), toy, trifle, trinket, whatnot, whigmaleerie

rel souvenir; bric-a-brac, virtu; miniature; kickshaw, notion; trumpery

knifelike *adj syn* see SHARP 8

ant dull

knobkerrie *n syn* see CUDGEL

knock *vb* 1 *syn* see TAP 1

2 *syn* see CRITICIZE

ant boost

knock *n syn* see HIT 1

knock about *vb syn* see MANHANDLE

knock down *vb* 1 *syn* see FELL 1

2 *syn* see EARN 1

knock-down-and-drag-out *n* 1 *syn* see BRAWL

2 *syn* see QUARREL

knocker *n syn* see CRITIC

knock off *vb* 1 *syn* see STOP 3

2 *syn* see DEDUCT 1

3 *syn* see MURDER 1

‖**4** *syn* see ROB 1

knock out *vb syn* see EXHAUST 4

knockout *n* 1 *syn* see ‖DILLY

2 *syn* see BEAUTY

knock over *vb* 1 *syn* see FELL 1

2 *syn* see OVERTURN 1

3 *syn* see OVERWHELM 4

4 *syn* see ROB 1

knot *n* 1 *syn* see BOND 3

2 *syn* see BUMP 2

3 *syn* see MAZE 1

knothead *n syn* see DUNCE

knotty *adj* 1 *syn* see COMPLEX 2

2 *syn* see HARD 6

know *vb* 1 to possess an intellectual hold of < *knows* several languages>

syn appreciate, apprehend, cognize, comprehend, fathom, grasp, have, understand

rel apperceive; differentiate, discern, discriminate, distinguish, realize

idiom have at one's fingertips, see through

2 *syn* see EXPERIENCE 1

3 *syn* see FEEL 2

4 to recognize the differences between < *know* right from wrong>

syn difference, differentiate, discern, discrepate, discriminate, distinguish, extricate, separate, sever, severalize

con confound, mingle, mix

ant confuse, mix up

5 *syn* see RECOGNIZE 1

knowable *adj syn* see UNDERSTANDABLE

ant unknowable

know-how *n* 1 *syn* see ABILITY 2

2 *syn* see ART 1

knowing *adj* 1 *syn* see INTELLIGENT 2

rel vigilant, watchful; discerning, observant, perceptive

con blunt, obtuse

2 *syn* see WISE 1

3 *syn* see WISE 4

4 *syn* see AWARE

5 *syn* see SOPHISTICATED 2

know-it-all *n syn* see SMART ALECK

knowledge *n* 1 *syn* see EDUCATION 2

ant ignorance

2 the body of things known about or in science < made major contributions to scientific *knowledge* >

syn information, lore, science, wisdom

rel advice, intelligence, news; data, evidence, facts

knowledgeable *adj* 1 *syn* see INTELLIGENT 2

2 *syn* see WISE 1

know-nothing *adj syn* see IGNORANT 1

know-nothing *n syn* see DUNCE

knuckle *vb syn* see YIELD 2

knucklehead *n syn* see DUNCE

knuckle under *vb syn* see YIELD 2

kook *n syn* see CRACKPOT

kowtow *vb syn* see FAWN

kowtowing *adj syn* see FAWNING

kudize *vb syn* see COMMEND 2

kudo *n syn* see COMPLIMENT 1

kudos *n* 1 *syn* see EMINENCE 1

2 *syn* see HONOR 2

L

laager *vb syn* see CAMP

label *n syn* see TICKET 1

rel mark, marker

labor *n* 1 *syn* see WORK 2

rel endeavor, struggle

con ease, leisure, relaxation, repose, rest; amusement, diversion, entertainment, recreation; idleness, inactivity, inertia, inertness, passiveness

2 the physical activities involved in parturition < first *labors* are sometimes difficult >

syn birth pang(s), childbearing, childbirth, travail

labor *vb* 1 to exert one's powers of mind or body especially with painful or strenuous effort < *labored* all day to make a living >

syn drive, moil, strain, strive, toil, tug, work

idiom break one's neck

con idle, laze, loaf, lounge; goof (off), shirk; dawdle, poke, putter

|| 2 *syn* see TILL

labored *adj* 1 *syn* see HARD 6

2 *syn* see FORCED

rel heavy, ponderous, weighty; awkward, clumsy, inept, maladroit

laborer *n syn* see WORKER

laborious *adj syn* see HARD 6

ant easy, effortless

laboriously *adv syn* see HARD 8

ant easily, effortlessly

labyrinth *n syn* see MAZE 1

labyrinthine *adj syn* see COMPLEX 2

lacerated *adj* having jagged cuts or breaks < the *lacerated* area was badly swollen >

syn mangled, rent, torn

rel gashed, mutilated, ripped, slashed; jagged, ragged, saw-toothed, scalloped, scored; serrated

lachrymose *adj syn* see TEARFUL

lack *vb* to be without something and especially something essential or greatly needed < the building *lacks* a fire escape >

syn need, require, want

con enjoy, have, hold, own, possess

lack *n* 1 *syn* see ABSENCE

2 *syn* see FAILURE 3

lackadaisical *adj syn* see LANGUID

rel incurious, indifferent, unconcerned; faineant, indolent, lazy, slothful; idle, passive; emasculated; romantic, sentimental

con energetic, lusty, strenuous, vigorous; active, dynamic, live

lacking *adj* 1 *syn* see ABSENT 1

2 *syn* see DEFICIENT 1

lacking *prep syn* see WITHOUT 2

lackluster *adj* 1 *syn* see DULL 7

2 *syn* see COLORLESS 2

rel dead, leaden, rusty, tarnished

con lustrous

lackwit *n syn* see DUNCE

laconic *adj syn* see CONCISE

rel brusque

con garrulous, glib, loquacious, talkative

ant verbose, wordy

laconically *adv syn* see BRIEFLY

lacuna *n syn* see GAP 3

lad *n syn* see BOY 1

laddie *n syn* see BOY 1

lade *vb* 1 *syn* see BURDEN

2 *syn* see DIP 2

la-di-da *adj* 1 *syn* see PRECIOUS 4

2 *syn* see GENTEEL 3

ladies' man *n syn* see WOLF

lading *n syn* see LOAD 1

ladle *vb syn* see DIP 2

lady *n syn* see WIFE

lady friend *n syn* see GIRL FRIEND 1

---

syn synonym(s)   *rel* related word(s)

ant antonym(s)   *con* contrasted word(s)

idiom idiomatic equivalent(s)

|| use limited; if in doubt, see a dictionary

lady–killer *n syn* see WOLF

ladylove *n syn* see GIRL FRIEND 2

lag *vb syn* see DELAY 2
 rel retard, slacken, slow; stay

lag *adj syn* see LAST

||**lag** *vb syn* see BANISH

||**lag** *n syn* see CONVICT

laggard *adj syn* see SLOW 2
 rel dawdling, delaying, loitering, procrastinating; comatose, lethargic, sluggish; apathetic, impassive, phlegmatic
 con alert, vigilant, watchful, wide-awake; expeditious, fast, fleet, speedy
 ant prompt, quick

laggard *n* one that delays unnecessarily or falls behind <no room for *laggards* on the expedition>
 syn dawdler, lingerer, loiterer, slow coach, slowpoke, straggler
 rel lazybones, loafer
 con dynamo, go-ahead, go-getter, hustler, live wire, rustler; eager beaver

lagniappe *n syn* see GRATUITY

lair *n* 1 a resting or living place of a wild animal <photographed the wolf at the entrance to his *lair*>
 syn burrow, couch, den, lodge
 2 *syn* see HIDEOUT

||**lalapalooza** *n syn* ||DILLY, ||corker, crackerjack, ||daisy, dandy, humdinger, jim-dandy, ||lulu, peach, ||pip

||**lallygag** *vb syn* see IDLE

lam *vb syn* see BEAT 1

lam *n syn* see ESCAPE 1

lambaste *vb* 1 *syn* see BEAT 1
 2 *syn* see WHIP 2
 3 to assail with withering oral or written denunciation <the senator has been publicly *lambasted* for taking bribes>
 syn blister, castigate, ||crawl, drub, excoriate, flay, lash (into), roast, scarify, scathe, scorch, score, scourge, slam, slap, slash, ||slate; *compare* CRITICIZE, REPROVE, SCOLD 1
 rel censure, criticize, denounce, pan; berate, scold, tongue-lash; assail, attack, squabash
 idiom burn one's ears, ||crawl all over, give (one) a roasting, pin one's ears back, rake (one) over the coals, read the riot act, rip into
 con applaud, extol, praise; approve, countenance, endorse

lambent *adj syn* see BRIGHT 1

lame–brain *n syn* see DUNCE

lament *vb syn* see DEPLORE 1
 ant exult; rejoice

lamentable *adj* 1 *syn* see DEPLORABLE
 2 *syn* see MELANCHOLY 2

lamia *n syn* see WITCH 1

lamp *n syn* see EYE 1

lampoonery *n syn* see SATIRE

lampooning *adj syn* see SATIRIC

lance *vb syn* see IMPALE

land *n* 1 *syn* see EARTH 2
 2 *syn* see COUNTRY
 3 *syn* see ESTATE 3

land *vb* 1 *syn* see DISEMBARK
 2 *syn* see ALIGHT
 3 *syn* see GET 1

||**lang syne** *n syn* see PAST

language *n* 1 a body or system of words and phrases used by a large community or by a people, a nation, or a group of nations <the English and French *languages*>
 syn dialect, idiom, speech, tongue, vernacular
 rel argot, cant, jargon, lingo, patois, slang
 2 *syn* see TERMINOLOGY

languid *adj* lacking in vim or energy <doing the job in a slow and *languid* manner>
 syn die-away, enervated, lackadaisical, languishing, languorous, limp, listless, spiritless
 rel comatose, lethargic, sluggish, torpid; apathetic, impassive, phlegmatic; inactive, inert, supine
 con alert, awake, ||fly, keen, lively, wide-awake
 ant vivacious; chipper

languish *vb syn* see FAIL 1
 ant flourish

languishing *adj syn* see LANGUID
 rel debilitated, enfeebled, weakened; faineant, indolent; longing, pining, yearning
 con hale, healthy, robust, sound; energetic, lusty, vigorous
 ant flourishing, thriving; unaffected

languor *n syn* see LETHARGY 1
 rel exhaustion, fatigue, weariness; blues, depression, dumps; doldrums, ennui, tedium
 con celerity, legerity; gusto, zest
 ant alacrity

languorous *adj syn* see LANGUID
 rel dilatory, laggard, leisurely, slow; faineant, indolent, slothful; passive; lax, loose, relaxed, slack; indulged, pampered
 ant vigorous; strenuous (*of times, seasons*)

lank *adj syn* see LEAN
 rel attenuated, extenuated
 con chubby
 ant burly

lanky *adj* 1 *syn* see GANGLING
 2 *syn* see LEAN

lap *vb syn* see OVERLAP

lap *vb* 1 *syn* see SLOSH 1
 2 *syn* see BATHE 2

lapse *n* 1 *syn* see ERROR 2
 rel crime, offense, sin, vice; failing, foible, frailty; breach, transgression, trespass, violation
 2 a temporary deviation or fall especially from a higher to a lower state <a *lapse* into nonproductiveness> <ashamed of his *lapse* from grace>
 syn backsliding, relapse
 rel decadence, declension, decline, degeneration, deterioration, devolution; recession, retrogradation; regression, retrogression
 con advance, progress; development, maturation; amendment; betterment, improvement

lapse *vb* to fall from a better or higher state into a lower or poorer one <*lapsed* into his old vulgar ways>
 syn backslide, recidivate, relapse
 rel return, revert; slide, slip; decline, degenerate, deteriorate; subside; descend; recede, retrograde; apostatize
 con advance, progress; develop, mature; amend, mend; better, improve

larcener *n syn* see THIEF

larcenist *n* *syn* see THIEF

larcenous *adj* prone to committing larceny < *larcenous* employees were robbing the company blind >
  syn sticky-fingered, thieving, thievish
  rel burglarious; light-fingered

larceny *n* *syn* see THEFT

‖**lardy–dardy** *adj* *syn* see GENTEEL 3

lares and penates *n* *pl* *syn* see POSSESSION 2

large *adj* 1 above the average of its kind in magnitude < a *large* increase in the tax rate >
  syn big, bull, fat, great, husky, oversize
  rel colossal, enormous, gigantic, huge, immense, mammoth, vast, voluminous; monstrous, monumental, prodigious, stupendous, tremendous; excessive, exorbitant, extravagant, extreme, immoderate, inordinate
  con diminutive, little, minute, tiny, wee; slender, slight, slim, thin
  ant small
  2 *syn* see BIG 1

largely *adv* *syn* see GENERALLY 1

largeness *n* *syn* see SIZE 2

large–scale *adj* *syn* see BIG 1

largess *n* 1 *syn* see GIFT 1
  2 *syn* see GRATUITY

largest *adj* *syn* see BEST

lark *n* 1 *syn* see ESCAPADE
  2 *syn* see PRANK

larkish *adj* *syn* see PLAYFUL 1

‖**larrup** *vb* 1 *syn* see WHIP 1
  2 *syn* see WHIP 2

‖**larruping** *adv* *syn* see VERY 1

lascivious *adj* 1 *syn* see LICENTIOUS 2
  rel coarse, gross, obscene
  2 *syn* see LUSTFUL 2

lash *vb* 1 *syn* see RUSH 1
  2 *syn* see POUR 3
  3 *syn* see WHIP 1
  4 *syn* see WAG
  5 *syn* see SCOLD 1

lash (into) *vb* *syn* see LAMBASTE 3

lashings *n* *pl* *syn* see MUCH

lass *n* 1 *syn* see GIRL 1
  2 *syn* see GIRL FRIEND 1

lassie *n* *syn* see GIRL 1

lassitude *n* 1 *syn* see FATIGUE
  2 *syn* see APATHY 2
  3 *syn* see LETHARGY 1
  rel doldrums, ennui, tedium; blues, depression, dumps; impotence, powerlessness
  con energy, force, might, power, strength
  ant vigor

last *vb* *syn* see CONTINUE 1

last *adj* following all relevant others (as in time, order, or importance) < he was the *last* one in line >
  syn closing, concluding, eventual, final, hindmost, lag, latest, latter, rearmost, terminal, terminating, ultimate
  rel bottommost, end, extreme, furthest, outermost, remotest, utmost, uttermost
  con beginning, inaugural, initial, introductory, original, primary, prime
  ant first

lasting *adj* existing or continuing for so long a time as to seem fixed or established < his reading made a *lasting* impression on him >
  syn diuturnal, durable, enduring, perdurable, perduring, permanent, stable; *compare* OLD 2
  rel abiding, continuing, persisting; endless, everlasting, unceasing; continual, continuous, incessant, perennial, unremitting; eternal, sempiternal; indelible, indissoluble, inexhaustible, inexpugnable, inexpungible
  con ephemeral, evanescent, fugitive, momentary, passing, short-lived, transient, transitory
  ant fleeting

last word *n* *syn* see APOTHEOSIS 1

late *adj* 1 *syn* see TARDY
  con opportune, seasonable, well-timed
  ant early; prompt, punctual
  2 *syn* see DEAD 1
  3 *syn* see FORMER 2
  4 *syn* see MODERN 1

lated *adj* *syn* see TARDY

lately *adv* *syn* see NEW

latency *n* *syn* see ABEYANCE

latent *adj* not now manifest or showing signs of existence or activity < a *latent* infection >
  syn abeyant, dormant, lurking, potential, prepatent, quiescent
  rel concealed, hidden; idle, inactive, inert; immature, unmatured, unripe
  con active, dynamic, live, operative; activated, energized, vitalized
  ant patent

later *adj* *syn* see SUBSEQUENT 1

later *adv* *syn* see AFTER
  ant earlier

laterally *adv* *syn* see SIDEWAYS 1

latest *adj* *syn* see LAST
  ant earliest

lather *n* 1 *syn* see FOAM
  2 *syn* see COMMOTION 4
  3 *syn* see COMMOTION 2

lather *vb* *syn* see WHIP 1

latitude *n* *syn* see ROOM 3

latrine *n* *syn* see TOILET

latter *adj* *syn* see LAST
  ant former

latterly *adv* *syn* see AFTER

laud *vb* *syn* see PRAISE 2
  rel adore, revere, reverence, venerate, worship; admire; flatter
  con blame, condemn; anathematize, curse, damn, execrate, objurgate
  ant revile

laudable *adj* *syn* see WORTHY 1
  ant illaudable

laudative *adj* *syn* see EULOGISTIC

laudatory *adj* *syn* see EULOGISTIC

laugh *vb* to show mirth, joy, or scorn with a smile and a usually explosive sound < *laughed* at all the funny things that happened >
  syn chortle, chuckle, giggle, guffaw, hee‗haw, snicker, ‖sniggle, tehee, titter
  rel cachinnate, cackle, crow, roar, whoop; beam, grin, simper, smile, smirk

laughable *adj* provoking laughter or mirth < the *laughable* antics of the clowns >
  syn comic, comical, droll, farcical, funny, gelastic, ludicrous, ridiculous, risible

---

syn synonym(s)   *rel* related word(s)
ant antonym(s)   *con* contrasted word(s)
idiom idiomatic equivalent(s)
‖ use limited; if in doubt, see a dictionary

rel amusing, diverting, entertaining, rich; facetious, humorous, jocose, jocular, witty; derisive, derisory, mocking
con grave, serious, solemn; boring, irksome, tedious, tiresome, wearisome; affecting, impressive, moving, pathetic, poignant, touching

laughingstock *n* an object of ridicule < totally unaware that he was the *laughingstock* of the entire office >
syn butt, derision, jest, jestee, joke, mock, mockery, pilgarlic, sport
rel gazingstock; mark, target

launch *vb* 1 *syn* see THROW 1
2 *syn* see BEGIN 1
3 *syn* see INTRODUCE 3

laurels *n pl syn* see HONOR 2

lavatory *n syn* see TOILET

lave *vb syn* see BATHE 2

lavish *adj* 1 *syn* see PROFUSE
con scant, scanty; economical, frugal, thrifty; discreet, provident, prudent; miserly, niggardly, parsimonious, penurious, stingy
ant sparing
2 *syn* see GRAND 2

lavishness *n syn* see EXTRAVAGANCE 2
ant sparingness

law *n* 1 a principle governing conduct, action, or procedure < found it hard to live by outdated *laws* >
syn assize, canon, decree, decretum, edict, institute, ordinance, precept, prescript, prescription, regulation, rule, statute
rel command, dictate, mandate
2 *syn* see PRINCIPLE 1
rel exigency, necessity
ant chance

lawbreaker *n syn* see CRIMINAL

lawcourt *n syn* see COURT 2

lawful *adj* being in accordance with law < obtained *lawful* custody of the child >
syn innocent, legal, legitimate, licit
rel condign, due, rightful; allowable, permissible; justifiable, warrantable; bona fide
idiom of right
con flagitious, iniquitous, nefarious; improper, unjustifiable, wrong; criminal, guilty, peccant; illegitimate, illicit
ant lawless, unlawful

lawless *adj syn* see UNLAWFUL
ant lawful

lawlessness *n syn* see ANARCHY 1
rel conflict, contention, difference, discord, dissension, strife, variance

lawsuit *n syn* see SUIT 1

lawyer *n* a person authorized to practice law in the courts or to serve clients in the capacity of legal agent or adviser < took the problem to his family *lawyer* >
syn attorney, attorney-at-law; *compare* PETTIFOGGER
rel advocate, ‖barrister, counsel, counselor, ‖mouthpiece, pleader, ‖solicitor; jurisconsult, jurisprudent, jurist; legist

lax *vb syn* see LOOSE 1

lax *adj* 1 *syn* see LOOSE 5
con firm, hard, solid; elastic, resilient, springy
ant rigid
2 *syn* see NEGLIGENT
rel forgetful, oblivious, unmindful
con austere, severe, stern; rigid, rigorous; conscientious, honest, upright, scrupulous

ant strict, stringent

lay *vb* 1 *syn* see SET 1
2 *syn* see GAMBLE 1
3 *syn* see EVEN 1
4 *syn* see ASCRIBE
5 *syn* see DIRECT 2
6 *syn* see SET 5
7 *syn* see ADDUCE

lay (for) *vb syn* see SURPRISE 1

lay (open) *vb syn* see EXPOSE 1

lay *n* 1 *syn* see MELODY
2 *syn* see SONG 2

lay *adj syn* see PROFANE 1
con professional

lay aside *vb* 1 *syn* see DISCARD
2 *syn* see SAVE 4

lay away *vb* 1 *syn* see SAVE 4
2 *syn* see BURY 1

lay by *vb syn* see SAVE 4

lay down *vb* 1 *syn* see RELINQUISH
2 *syn* see PRESCRIBE 2
3 *syn* see DICTATE

layer *n syn* see BOOKMAKER

lay in *vb syn* see SAVE 4

lay low *vb* 1 *syn* see FELL 1
2 *syn* see KILL 1

lay off *vb syn* see REST 3

lay out *vb* 1 *syn* see DESIGN 3
2 *syn* see SPEND 1

lay over *vb syn* see DEFER

lay up *vb* 1 *syn* see ACCUMULATE
2 *syn* see SAVE 4

laze *vb syn* see IDLE
con drudge, grind, labor, toil, travail, work

laze *n syn* see SLOTH 1

laziness *n syn* see SLOTH 1
ant industriousness

lazy *adj* not easily aroused to action or activity < the hot humid weather made them *lazy* >
syn drony, easygoing, faineant, indolent, slothful, slowgoing, work-shy
rel idle, inactive, inert, passive, supine, trifling; comatose, lethargic, sluggish, torpid; lackadaisical, languid, languorous, listless, unenergetic, unindustrious; lax, neglectful, negligent, remiss, shiftless, slack
con diligent, hardworking; brisk, chipper, energetic, vigorous; active, animated, lively, spry, vivacious; prompt, quick, ready
ant industrious

lazy *vb syn* see IDLE

lazybones *n syn* see SLUGGARD

lead *vb* 1 *syn* see GUIDE
rel get, induce, persuade, prevail
con drive, impel; coerce, compel, constrain, force, oblige
ant follow
2 *syn* see PRECEDE 3
3 *syn* see CONVERT 1

lead *n syn* see LEADER 1

leader *n* 1 one that takes the lead or initiative < each group selected its own *leader* for the tour >
syn ‖bell cow, bellwether, dean, doyen, guide, lead, pilot
rel pacemaker, pacesetter; forerunner, harbinger, herald, precursor; conductor, director, rector
con adherent, dependent, hanger-on, henchman, satellite

ant follower
2 a person in whom resides authority or ruling power < the company had only one *leader* >
syn boss, chief, chieftain, cock, dominator, head, headman, hierarch, honcho, master
rel captain, commander, general; director, principal, superintendent, superior; foreman, manager, straw boss
con inferior, subaltern, subordinate, underling, understrapper
3 *syn* see NOTABLE 1
leading *adj* 1 *syn* see FIRST 1
2 *syn* see FIRST 3
ant subordinate
3 *syn* see WELL-KNOWN
lead off *vb syn* see BEGIN 1
lead on *vb* 1 *syn* see LURE
2 *syn* see TRIFLE 1
leaf (through) *vb syn* see BROWSE
leafage *n syn* see FOLIAGE
league *n* 1 *syn* see ALLIANCE 2
2 *syn* see ASSOCIATION 2
3 *syn* see CLASS 1
4 a group of sports clubs or teams that play one another competitively < the new baseball *league* >
syn association, circuit, conference, loop, wheel
rel division
league *vb syn* see UNITE 2
leak *vb syn* see GET OUT 2
lean *vb* 1 *syn* see SLANT 1
rel bend, curve; deflect, divert, sheer, turn
2 *syn* see TEND 1
lean (over) *vb syn* see HANG 4
lean *n syn* see SLOPE
lean *adj* thin because of absence of superfluous flesh < a *lean* strong horse >
syn angular, bony, gaunt, lank, lanky, meager, rawboned, scraggy, scrawny, skinny, spare; *compare* THIN 1
rel slender, slight, slim, spare-set, stringy, thin; cadaverous, haggard, pinched, wasted, worn; wizened
con brawny, burly, husky, muscular, sinewy; stalwart, stout, strong, sturdy; corpulent, fat, fatty, flabby, obese, plump, portly, rotund
ant fleshy
leaning *n* 1 *syn* see SLOPE
2 an attraction to a particular activity, thing, or end < a strong *leaning* toward liberal views >
syn bent, bias, disposition, drift, inclination, inclining, lurch, partiality, penchant, predilection, predisposition, proclivity, propensity, sentiment, tendency; *compare* GIFT 2, PREJUDICE
rel favor, favoritism, odds
con avoidance, evasion, shunning; disdaining, scorning, scouting, spurning; disinterest, dislike, distaste
leaning *adj syn* see INCLINED 3
leap *vb* 1 *syn* see JUMP 1
rel arise, ascend, mount, rise, soar
con drop, fall, sink, slump

---

syn synonym(s)   rel related word(s)
ant antonym(s)   con contrasted word(s)
idiom idiomatic equivalent(s)
‖ use limited; if in doubt, see a dictionary

2 *syn* see CLEAR 8
learn *vb* 1 to acquire knowledge of or skill in by study and experience < *learn* a trade >
syn get, master, pick up
rel con, peruse, study
idiom make oneself master of
2 *syn* see MEMORIZE
3 *syn* see DISCOVER 3
learned *adj* possessing or manifesting unusually wide and deep knowledge < a most *learned* scholar in his field >
syn erudite, scholarly, scholastic
rel cultivated, cultured; academic, bookish, pedantic, professorial; abstruse, esoteric, polymath, recondite
con ignorant, illiterate, uneducated, unlearned, unlettered, untutored
learnedness *n syn* see ERUDITION 2
learning *n syn* see EDUCATION 2
lease *vb syn* see HIRE 1
leash *vb syn* see HAMPER
least *adj syn* see FIRST 4
leave *vb* 1 *syn* see WILL
rel commit, confide, consign, entrust; allot, apportion, assign
2 *syn* see LET 2
3 *syn* see GO 2
4 *syn* see QUIT 6
5 *syn* see RELINQUISH
leave *n* 1 *syn* see PERMISSION
rel assent
con refusal, rejection; forbiddance, interdiction, prohibition
2 *syn* see VACATION
leaven *vb syn* see INFUSE 1
rel moderate, qualify, temper; enliven, quicken, vivify
leave off *vb syn* see STOP 3
leave-taking *n syn* see PARTING
leaving *n*, *usu* **leavings** *pl syn* see REMAINDER
rel fragments, pieces, portions; discards, junk, scrap
lecherous *adj syn* see LICENTIOUS 2
lecture *n syn* see SPEECH 2
lecture *vb syn* see TALK 7
ledger *n syn* see TOMBSTONE
leech *n syn* see PARASITE
leer *vb syn* see SNEER 1
lees *n pl syn* see SEDIMENT
leeway *n syn* see ROOM 3
left-handed *adj syn* see INSINCERE
legacy *n* 1 a gift by will especially of money or personal property < received a *legacy* of $5,000 from her late uncle >
syn bequest, devise, inheritance
2 *syn* see HERITAGE 1
legal *adj syn* see LAWFUL
ant illegal
legal tender *n syn* see MONEY
legate *vb syn* see WILL
legend *n* 1 *syn* see MYTH 1
2 *syn* see CAPTION
3 *syn* see LORE 2
legendary *adj syn* see MYTHICAL
legerdemain *n syn* see MAGIC 2
legion *n syn* see MULTITUDE 1
legion *adj syn* see MANY
legitimate *adj* 1 *syn* see LAWFUL
rel cogent, sound, valid; acknowledged, recognized; customary, usual; natural, normal, regular, typical

ant illegitimate

2 *syn* see TRUE 8
ant arbitrary

leisure *n syn* see REST 1
con drudgery, grind, labor
ant toil

leisurely *adj syn* see SLOW 2
rel lax, relaxed, slack; delayed, retarded, slackened; comfortable, easy, restful
con fast, hasty, quick, rapid, speedy; headlong, impetuous, precipitate
ant hurried; abrupt

leitmotiv *n* a dominant recurring thematic element or feature (as in a work of art) <the *leitmotiv* of man against nature often appears in his paintings>
syn motif
rel motive, theme

lemon *n syn* see FAILURE 5

lend *vb* to give into another's keeping for temporary use on condition that the borrower return the same or its equivalent <I do not have another copy of the book to give, but I can *lend* you mine>
syn advance, loan
rel lease-lend, lend-lease; allow, furnish, give; accommodate, oblige

length *n* **1** *syn* see DISTANCE 1

2 *syn* see RANGE 2

lengthen *vb syn* see EXTEND 3
ant shorten; abbreviate

lengthening *n syn* see EXTENSION 1
ant shortening

lengthways *adv syn* see LENGTHWISE
ant widthways, widthwise

lengthwise *adv* in the direction of the length <the students folded their papers *lengthwise*>
syn endways, endwise, lengthways, longitudinally, longways, longwise
con latitudinally, widthways; broadside, broadway, broadwise
ant widthways, widthwise

lengthy *adj* **1** *syn* see LONG 2
ant short

2 *syn* see LONG 1

lenience *n syn* see FORBEARANCE 2

leniency *n syn* see FORBEARANCE 2

lenient *adj* **1** *syn* see GENTLE 1
ant caustic

2 *syn* see FORBEARING
rel condoning, excusing, forgiving, pardoning; benign, benignant, kindly; compassionate, tender; humoring, indulging, pampering, mollycoddling, spoiling
con rigid, rigorous, stringent; austere, severe
ant stern; exacting

3 *syn* see AMIABLE 1

lenity *n syn* see MERCY
rel tenderness; benevolence, charitableness, humaneness
con rigidity, rigorousness, strictness, stringency; austerity, sternness
ant severity

leper *n syn* see OUTCAST

lessen *vb* **1** *syn* see ABRIDGE 1
rel amputate, clip, crop, truncate

2 *syn* see DECREASE
rel attenuate, dilute, thin, weaken

lesser *adj* **1** *syn* see INFERIOR 1

2 *syn* see MINOR 2

lesson *n syn* see EXERCISE 4

lesson *vb syn* see REPROVE

let *vb* **1** *syn* see HIRE 1

2 to neither forbid nor prevent <*let* the boy go to the movies>
syn allow, have, leave, permit, suffer
rel accredit, approve, certify, endorse, sanction; authorize, commission, license; concede, grant
con ban, enjoin, forbid, inhibit, interdict, prohibit; bar, block, hinder, impede, obstruct; circumvent, foil, frustrate, thwart

let down *vb syn* see LOWER 3

lethal *adj syn* see DEADLY 1
con renewing, restorative, restoring

lethality *n syn* see FATALITY 1

lethargic *adj* deficient in alertness or activity <became *lethargic* after taking the drug>
syn comatose, dopey, heavy, hebetudinous, sluggish, slumberous, stupid, torpid
rel dormant, idle, inactive, inert, passive, supine; apathetic, impassive, phlegmatic, spiritless, stolid; lackadaisical, languid, languorous, listless; dilatory, laggard, slow
con alert, aware, responsive; apt, prompt, quick, ready; brisk, gingery, peppery, spirited
ant energetic

lethargy *n* **1** physical and mental inertness <disgusted, he sank into a state of *lethargy*>
syn coma, dullness, hebetude, languor, lassitude, sleep, slumber, stupor, torpidity, torpidness, torpor
rel comatoseness, sluggishness; indolence, laziness, sloth, slothfulness; idleness, inactivity, inertia, inertness, passiveness, supineness; apathy, impassivity, inanition, phlegm
con aptness, promptness, quickness, readiness; alertness, quick-wittedness
ant vigor

2 *syn* see APATHY 2

lethe *n syn* see OBLIVION

let off *vb syn* see EXEMPT

let on *vb* **1** *syn* see ACKNOWLEDGE 1

2 *syn* see REVEAL 1

let out *vb* ‖ **1** *syn* see REVEAL 1

2 *syn* see DISMISS 3

letter *n* **1** letters *pl syn* see ALPHABET 1

2 a direct or personal written or printed message addressed to a person or organization <wrote several *letters* to his friends>
syn epistle, missive, note
rel dispatch, memorandum, message, report

‖**lettuce** *n syn* see MONEY

let up *vb syn* see ABATE 4

levee *n* **1** *syn* see WHARF

2 *syn* see RED-LIGHT DISTRICT

level *vb* **1** *syn* see EVEN 1

2 *syn* see DIRECT 2

3 *syn* see FELL 1

level *adj* having a surface without bends, curves, or irregularities <looked for a *level* spot to land the plane>
syn even, flat, flush, planate, plane, smooth
rel akin, alike, identical, like, parallel, similar, uniform; aligned; regular; equal, equivalent, same
con bumpy, irregular, lumpy, uneven; unaligned, unparallel; changing, varying;

fluctuating, rolling, swaying, undulating; coarse, rough

lever *vb syn* see PRY

leviathan *n syn* see GIANT

leviathan *adj syn* see HUGE

levity *n syn* see LIGHTNESS
 rel absurdity, folly, foolishness, silliness
 con collection, quietude, sobriety
 ant gravity

levy *n syn* see TAX 1

levy *vb* to determine and require satisfaction of (as a tax or obligation) <several broad-based taxes were *levied* >
 syn assess, exact, impose, put (on *or* upon)
 rel extort, wrest, wring; charge, lay (on *or* upon), place, set
 con remit; abate, diminish, lessen

lewd *adj syn* see LICENTIOUS 2
 rel coarse, gross, obscene; improper, indecent, indelicate
 con modest, proper, self-restrained; temperate
 ant chaste

lexicon *n* 1 *syn* see VOCABULARY 1
 2 *syn* see TERMINOLOGY

lexiphanicism *n syn* see BOMBAST

liability *n* 1 *syn* see DEBT 3
 ant asset
 2 *syn* see INDEBTEDNESS 1
 3 *syn* see EXPOSURE

liable *adj* 1 *syn* see RESPONSIBLE
 rel bound, tied
 con exempt, immune; free, independent
 2 being likely to be affected by some usually adverse contingency or action <without the heat shield he was *liable* to be burned>
 syn exposed, obnoxious, open, prone, sensitive, subject, susceptible
 rel assailable, penetrable, vulnerable; attackable, beatable, conquerable, vincible
 ant unliable
 3 *syn* see APT 1
 ant unliable

liaison *n syn* see AMOUR 2

liar *n* one that tells lies <he is a compulsive *liar* >
 syn Ananias, falsifier, fibber, fibster, perjurer, prevaricator, storyteller

libel *vb syn* see MALIGN
 rel burlesque, caricature, travesty

libelous *adj* injurious to reputation <the campaign degenerated into an exchange of *libelous* statements>
 syn backbiting, calumnious, defamatory, detracting, detractive, detractory, invidious, maligning, scandalous, slanderous, traducing, vilifying
 rel depreciative, depreciatory, derogative, disparaging, pejorative; contumelious, debasing, malevolent, vituperative
 con adulating, adulatory, applauding, commendatory, eulogistic, eulogizing, laudatory, praising

liberal *adj* 1 marked by generosity and openhandedness <a *liberal* allowance for his son>

 syn bounteous, bountiful, free, free-handed, generous, handsome, munificent, openhanded, unsparing
 rel exuberant, lavish, prodigal, profuse; benevolent, charitable, eleemosynary, philanthropic
 con closefisted, miserly, niggardly, parsimonious, penurious, stingy, tight, tightfisted; meager, scanty
 ant close
 2 *syn* see PLENTIFUL
 3 not bound by authoritarianism, orthodoxy, or traditional forms <modern young people usually have a *liberal* attitude toward sex>
 syn advanced, broad, broad-minded, progressive, radical, tolerant, wide
 rel forbearing, indulgent, lenient
 con rigid, rigorous, strict, stringent; dictatorial, doctrinaire, dogmatic, oracular; conservative, reactionary
 ant authoritarian

liberate *vb syn* see FREE
 rel detach, unhook; untangle; disembarrass
 con bind, tie; ensnare, entrap, snare, trap; constrain, restrain, restrict

libertine *adj syn* see LICENTIOUS 2
 con ethical; continent, sober, temperate
 ant straitlaced

liberty *n syn* see FREEDOM
 rel autonomy, independence; delivery, emancipation, enfranchisement, liberation
 con circumscription, confinement, limitation, restriction
 ant restraint

libidinous *adj* 1 *syn* see LICENTIOUS 2
 rel coarse, gross, obscene
 2 *syn* see LUSTFUL 2

library *n* a place in which literary, musical, artistic, or reference materials (as books or films) are kept for use but not for sale <planned to study all evening in the *library*>
 syn archive(s), athenaeum
 rel reading room

license *n syn* see FREEDOM
 rel laxity, looseness, relaxation, slackness
 con duty, obligation; decency, propriety; continence, sobriety, temperance
 ant decorum

license *vb syn* see AUTHORIZE 1
 rel allow, let, permit, suffer; certify, sanction
 con check, curb, restrain
 ant ban

licentious *adj* 1 *syn* see ABANDONED 2
 2 disregarding sexual restraints <a coarse *licentious* man>
 syn fast, incontinent, lascivious, lecherous, lewd, libertine, libidinous, lustful, randy, salacious, satyric
 rel animal, carnal, fleshly, oversexed, sensual; abandoned, dissolute, profligate, reprobate; corrupt, debauched, depraved, scabrous; amoral, immoral, unmoral; lax, loose, relaxed
 con chaste, decent, pure; moral, virtuous; rigid, strict; ascetic, austere, severe
 ant continent

licit *adj syn* see LAWFUL
 rel approved, sanctioned; authorized, licensed

---

con banned, forbidden, inhibited, interdicted, prohibited
ant illicit
lick *vb* 1 *syn* see WHIP 2
2 *syn* see OVERCOME 1
lick *n* 1 *syn* see HINT 2
2 *syn* see HIT 1
lickerish *adj syn* see LUSTFUL 2
lickerishness *n syn* see LUST 2
lickety–split *adv syn* see FAST 2
licking *n syn* see DEFEAT 1
lickspit *n syn* see SYCOPHANT
lickspittle *n syn* see SYCOPHANT
lie *vb* 1 *syn* see REST 1
2 *syn* see CONSIST 1
lie *vb* to be untruthful directly or indirectly < *lying* under oath is a crime >
syn equivocate, falsify, fib, palter, prevaricate
rel beguile, deceive, delude, misguide, misinform, misinstruct, mislead; distort, exaggerate, misstate
lie *n* a statement or declaration that is not true < was sued for printing *lies* about the candidate >
syn ‖bouncer, canard, cock-and-bull story, falsehood, falsity, fib, inveracity, misrepresentation, misstatement, prevarication, ‖rapper, story, tale, taradiddle, untruism, untruth
rel deceitfulness, dishonesty, distortion, fraudulence, inaccuracy, mendacity; fable, flam, myth; falsification, forgery, libel, perjury; fish story, song and dance
con veracity, verisimilitude, verity
ant truth
lie by *vb syn* see REST 3
lied *n syn* see SONG 2
lie down *vb syn* see REST 1
liege *adj syn* see FAITHFUL 1
lieutenant *n syn* see ASSISTANT 2
life *n* 1 *syn* see BIOGRAPHY
2 *syn* see HUMAN
3 *syn* see SPIRIT 5
lifeless *adj* 1 *syn* see DEAD 1
ant living
2 *syn* see COLORLESS 2
ant lifeful
lifelong *adj syn* see OLD 2
lifework *n syn* see MISSION
lift *vb* 1 to remove from a lower to a higher place or position < *lifted* the sack to his shoulder >
syn elevate, hoist, pick up, raise, rear, take up, uphold, uplift, upraise, uprear
rel arise, ascend, levitate, mount, rise, rocket, soar, surge, tower; aggrandize, exalt, magnify
con decrease, diminish, lessen, reduce; abase, debase, degrade, demean, humble, humiliate; depress, oppress, weigh
ant lower
2 *syn* see REVOKE 2
ant invoke
3 *syn* see STEAL 1
4 *syn* see RISE 4
lift *n* 1 *syn* see THEFT
2 *syn* see HELP 1
lifted *adj syn* see ELEVATED 1
ligament *n syn* see BOND 3
ligature *n syn* see BOND 3
light *n syn* see DAWN 1
light *adj syn* see FAIR 3

light *vb* 1 to cause something to start burning < *lighted* the fuse on the dynamite >
syn enkindle, fire, ignite, inflame, kindle
con douse, ‖dout, put out, quench, snuff; damp (down), smother, stamp (out)
ant extinguish
2 *syn* see ILLUMINATE 1
light *adj* 1 having little weight < the package was *light* >
syn featherlight, featherweight, imponderous, lightweight, unheavy, weightless
rel inconsequential, trifling, trivial; little, petty, small; flimsy, meager, slender, slight
idiom light as a feather
con bulky, burdensome, cumbersome, huge, massive, overweight, ponderous, portly, unwieldy, weighty
ant heavy
2 *syn* see EASY 1
ant arduous
3 *syn* see FAST 7
4 *syn* see GIDDY 1
5 *syn* see LITTLE 3
6 *syn* see DIZZY 2
light *vb* 1 *syn* see ALIGHT
2 *syn* see HAPPEN 2
lighted *adj syn* see BURNING 1
ant unlighted, unlit
lighten *vb syn* see ILLUMINATE 1
ant darken
lighten *vb syn* see RELIEVE 1
rel attenuate, dilute, extenuate, thin
con depress, oppress, weigh
light–headed *adj* 1 *syn* see GIDDY 1
2 *syn* see DIZZY 2
lighthearted *adj* 1 *syn* see HAPPY-GO≈ LUCKY
ant heavyhearted
2 *syn* see GLAD 1
rel buoyant, effervescent, expansive, resilient, volatile; high-spirited, spirited; gay, lively, sprightly, vivacious
con gloomy, glum, morose, sullen
ant despondent
3 *syn* see MERRY
ant heavyhearted
lighthouse *n* a building equipped to guide sea navigators by means of a powerful light < rowed out to the *lighthouse* >
syn beacon, pharos
rel direction, guidance
lightless *adj syn* see DARK 1
ant bright, ‖lightful
lightly *adv syn* see EASILY 1
light–mindedness *n syn* see LIGHTNESS
lightness *n* gaiety or indifference where seriousness and attention are called for < a crisis that allowed no room for *lightness* >
syn flightiness, flippancy, frivolity, levity, light-mindedness, volatility
rel buoyancy, effervescence, elasticity, expansiveness, resiliency; gaiety, liveliness, vivacity; cheerfulness, lightheartedness
con earnestness, gravity, sedateness, soberness, somberness, staidness
ant seriousness
light–o'–love *n syn* see DOXY 1
light out *vb syn* see HEAD 3
lightsome *adj* 1 *syn* see CHEERFUL 1
2 *syn* see HAPPY-GO-LUCKY
lightweight *adj syn* see LIGHT 1
like *vb* 1 *syn* see ENJOY 1

rel choose, elect, prefer, select; admire, esteem, regard, respect; approve, endorse; appreciate, comprehend, understand
ant dislike
2 *syn* see WILL

like *adj* being so similar as to appear to be the same or nearly the same (as in appearance, character, or quantity) <shirts of *like* design>
syn agnate, akin, alike, analogous, comparable, consonant, corresponding, equivalent, intercomparable, parallel, similar, such, suchlike, undifferenced, undifferentiated, uniform; *compare* SAME 2
rel equal, equivalent, identical, same, selfsame; allied, cognate, close, related, resembling; coextensive, commensurate
idiom of that ilk, on the order of
con different, disparate, divergent, diverse, various; dissimilar, distinct; discordant, discrepant, inconsistent, inconsonant
ant unlike

like *n* *syn* see EQUAL

likely *adj* **1** *syn* see PROBABLE
con problematic; certain, inevitable, necessary
ant unlikely
2 *syn* see APT 1
ant unlikely
3 *syn* see HOPEFUL 2

likely *adv* *syn* see PRESUMABLY

liken *vb* *syn* see EQUATE 2

likeness *n* agreement or correspondence in details (as of appearance, structure, or quality) <the remarkable *likeness* of the two cousins>
syn affinity, alikeness, analogy, comparison, resemblance, semblance, similarity, simile, similitude
rel equality, equivalence, identicalness, identity, sameness; agreement, conformity, correspondence; analogousness, comparableness, parallelism, uniformity
con difference, dissimilarity, distinction, divergence, divergency; disaffinity, opposition
ant unlikeness

likewise *adv* **1** *syn* see ALSO 1
2 *syn* see ALSO 2

liking *n* **1** *syn* see APPETITE 3
ant disliking
2 *syn* see WILL 1

lilliputian *adj* *syn* TINY, diminutive, minute, teensy, teensy-weensy, teenty, teeny, teeny-weeny, wee, weeny
ant Brobdingnagian

lilliputian *n* *syn* see DWARF

lily–livered *adj* *syn* see COWARDLY

lily–white *adj* *syn* see GOOD 11

limb *n* **1** a member of a woody plant that is an outgrowth from a main stem or from one of its divisions <hung the swing from a tree's *limb*>
syn bough, branch
rel shoot, spray, sprig, switch, twig; arm
2 *syn* see SCAMP

limber *adj* *syn* see SUPPLE 3
rel plastic, pliable, pliant; elastic, flexible, resilient, springy

con inflexible, rigid, stark, stiff, tense, wooden

limit *n* **1** a material or immaterial point beyond which something does not or cannot extend <there seemed no *limit* to the problems they faced>
syn bound, confine(s), end, limitation, term; *compare* ENVIRONS 1
rel circumscription, confinement, restriction, termination; border, brim, brink, edge, margin, rim, verge
2 limits *pl* *syn* see ENVIRONS 1
3 *syn* see EXTREME 2

limit *vb* **1** *syn* see DEMARCATE 1
2 to prescribe or serve as a restricting boundary <*limited* the naughty child to the house for three days> <ignorance that *limits* spiritual growth>
syn bar, circumscribe, confine, delimit, delimitate, prelimit, restrict
rel constrict, contract, lessen, narrow, pinch; check, curb, hinder, inhibit, restrain; appoint, assign, define, prescribe, set
con enlarge, expand, extend, increase, widen; develop, grow
ant broaden

limitation *n* **1** *syn* see LIMIT 1
2 *syn* see RESTRICTION 1

limited *adj* **1** *syn* see DEFINITE 1
rel inexhaustive, inextensive
con boundless, infinite
ant unlimited
2 *syn* see FINITE
3 *syn* see QUALIFIED 2
4 *syn* see LITTLE 2

limitless *adj* having no limits <the *limitless* black of deep space>
syn boundless, endless, immeasurable, indefinite, infinite, measureless, unbounded, unlimited, unmeasured
rel bottomless, countless, incalculable, incomprehensible, inexhaustible, innumerable, undrainable, unfathomable, vast, wasteless
con bound, bounded, finite, fixed, limited, measurable; comprehensible, fathomable; confined, restricted
ant limited

limn *vb* *syn* see REPRESENT 1

limp *vb* **1** to walk lamely <*limped* across the floor after his fall>
syn halt, hitch, hobble
rel toddle, totter, waddle; falter, stagger, stumble, wobble
2 *syn* see STUMBLE 6

limp *adj* **1** deficient in firmness of texture, substance, or structure <plants going *limp* from lack of water>
syn flabby, flaccid, flimsy, floppy, sleazy
rel lax, loose, relaxed, slack; limber, supple
con inflexible, rigid, stark, stiff, tense, wooden; firm, hard, solid; brittle, crisp
2 *syn* see LANGUID

limpid *adj* *syn* see TRANSPARENT 1

limpidity *n* *syn* see CLARITY

line *n* **1** *syn* see WAY 2
2 *syn* see COURSE 3
3 *syn* see WORK 1
‖**4** *syn* see SPIEL
5 a series of things arranged in continuous or uniform order <a *line* of cars waiting at the light>

---

syn synonym(s)   *rel* related word(s)
ant antonym(s)   *con* contrasted word(s)
idiom idiomatic equivalent(s)
‖ use limited; if in doubt, see a dictionary

syn echelon, file, queue, rank, row, string, tier

rel column, progression, succession, train; sequence, series

6 *syn see* OUTLINE

7 *syn see* MERCHANDISE

line *vb* **1** to arrange in a line or lines < *lined* the bottles along the shelf >

syn align, allineate, line up, range

rel arrange, array, marshal, order, ordinate

con derange, disarrange, disorder, disturb; disperse, dissipate, scatter

2 *syn see* ADJOIN

lineage *n* **1** *syn see* ANCESTRY

2 *syn see* FAMILY 1

lineal *adj syn see* DIRECT 1

lineament *n syn see* OUTLINE

lineation *n syn see* OUTLINE

line up *vb syn see* LINE 1

linger *vb* **1** *syn see* STAY 2

2 *syn see* DELAY 2

3 *syn see* SAUNTER

lingerer *n syn see* LAGGARD

lingo *n syn see* DIALECT 2

link *n syn see* BOND 3

link *vb syn see* JOIN 1

lint *n syn see* DOWN

lion *n syn see* NOTABLE 1

lionhearted *adj syn see* BRAVE 1

‖**lip** *n syn see* BACK TALK

lip *vb* **1** *syn see* KISS 1

2 *syn see* BATHE 2

lip server *n syn see* HYPOCRITE

liquefy *vb* to convert or to become converted to a liquid state < *liquefy* a block of ice by heating >

syn deliquesce, dissolve, flux, fuse, liquesce, melt, run, thaw

rel soften; thin

con clot, coagulate, congeal; harden, set; gel, jellify, jelly; condense, inspissate, thicken

ant solidify

liquesce *vb syn see* LIQUEFY

liquid *adj syn see* MELLIFLUOUS

liquidate *vb* **1** *syn see* CLEAR 5

2 *syn see* PURGE 3

3 *syn see* MURDER 1

liquor *n* **1** *syn see* DRINK 1

2 an intoxicating beverage usually distilled after being fermented < belted down a slug of *liquor* >

syn alcohol, aqua vitae, booze, ‖budge, drink, firewater, grog, ‖hooch, inebriant, intoxicant, ‖joy-juice, ‖juice, ‖lush, ‖sauce, spirit(s), ‖strunt, tipple

idiom Demon Rum, the bottle

liquor (up) *vb syn see* DRINK 3

lissome *adj syn see* SUPPLE 3

list *n* a series of items (as names) written down or printed expecially as a memorandum or record < all the people on the *list* were present >

syn catalog, register, roll, roll call, roster, schedule

rel checklist, handlist; index; inventory

list *vb* **1** *syn see* ENUMERATE 2

2 *syn see* ITEMIZE 1

3 to enter in a list < his name was not *listed* in the telephone book >

syn book, catalog, enroll, inscribe

rel file, index, note, post, schedule, tabulate; record, register, roster

4 *syn see* ENROLL 1

list *vb syn see* SLANT 1

listen *vb* to perceive by ear usually with careful or responsive attention < now hear me; *listen* to my words >

syn attend, hark, hear, hearken, heed

idiom give a hearing to, give ear to, hang upon the lips (*or* words) of, keep one's ears open, lend one's (*or* an) ear, prick up one's ears, strain one's ears

listless *adj syn see* LANGUID

rel careless, heedless, thoughtless

con agog, anxious, avid, keen; alert, vigilant, watchful; energetic, lusty, vigorous; prompt, quick, ready

ant eager

listlessness *n syn see* APATHY 2

‖**lit** *adj syn see* INTOXICATED 1

literal *adj syn see* VERBATIM

literally *adv syn see* VERBATIM

literati *n pl syn see* INTELLIGENTSIA

literatim *adv syn see* VERBATIM

lithe *adj syn see* SUPPLE 3

rel slender, slight, slim, thin; lean, spare

con awkward, clumsy, gauche, inept, maladroit; inflexible, stiff, tense, wooden

lithesome *adj syn see* SUPPLE 3

litigious *adj syn see* CONTENTIOUS 2

litter *n* **1** *syn see* REFUSE

2 *syn see* CLUTTER 2

little *adj* **1** *syn see* SMALL 1

ant big

2 contemptibly limited < men with *little* minds picking at flaws in a great leader >

syn borné, ineffectual, limited, mean, narrow, paltry, set, small

rel bigoted, hidebound, illiberal, narrow=minded, provincial; contemptible; niggard, niggardly, self-centered, selfish

ant great

3 lacking importance < the nagging *little* details of a job >

syn casual, inconsiderable, insignificant, light, minor, minute, petty, ‖potty, shoestring, small, small-beer, trivial, unimportant; *compare* PETTY 2

rel fortuitous; incidental; collateral, secondary, subordinate, subsidiary

con consequential, meaningful, significant, substantial, weighty; basal, basic, essential, foundational, fundamental

ant important

little *adv syn see* SELDOM

ant much

little by little *adv syn see* GRADUALLY

‖**little woman** *n syn see* WIFE

lit up *adj syn see* INTOXICATED 1

liturgy *n* **1** *syn see* FORM 2

2 *syn see* RITE 2

livable *adj* **1** suitable for living < a very *livable* apartment >

syn habitable, inhabitable, lodgeable, occupiable, tenantable

rel cozy, homelike, homey, snug; acceptable, bearable, tolerable

ant unlivable

2 *syn see* BEARABLE

live *vb* **1** *syn see* BE

2 *syn see* RESIDE 1

live *adj syn see* ACTIVE 1

rel effective, effectual, efficacious, efficient

ant inactive, inert; dormant (*as a volcano*); defunct (*as an institution, journal*)

livelihood *n syn* see LIVING
  rel art, craft, handicraft, profession, trade; emolument, fee, pay, salary, stipend, wage

lively *adj* 1 keenly alive and brisk < always thought of as a *lively* teacher >
  syn alert, animate, animated, bright, ‖cant, ‖canty, chipper, ‖chirk, dashing, gay, keen, ‖peart, peppy, pert, rousing, spirited, ‖spirity, sprightful, sprightly, unpedantic, vivacious; *compare* CHEERFUL 1
  rel agile, brisk, nimble, spry; buoyant, effervescent, elastic, expansive, resilient, volatile; blithe, cock-a-hoop, jocund, jolly, merry; gleeful, hilarious, mirthful; chirping, chirpy, chirrupy
  con lethargic, sluggish, torpid; lackadaisical, languid, languorous, listless; apathetic, impassive, phlegmatic, stolid; boring, irksome, tedious
  ant dull, unlively
  2 *syn* see AGILE
  idiom full of pep
  3 *syn* see ENERGETIC 2
  4 *syn* see BUSTLING
  ant unanimated

liven *vb syn* see QUICKEN 1
liver *n syn* see INHABITANT
live wire *n syn* see HUSTLER 1
livid *adj* 1 *syn* see PALE 1
  rel grisly; dusky, gloomy, murky
  con bright, brilliant, effulgent, lucent, luminous, lustrous, radiant
  2 *syn* see SENSATIONAL 2

living *adj* 1 having or showing life < the *living* things of a locality >
  syn alive, animate, animated, vital, zoetic
  rel being, existing, subsisting; active, dynamic, live, operative
  con dead, deceased, defunct, demised, departed, gone, inanimate
  ant lifeless
  2 *syn* see EXTANT 1

living *n* supplies or resources needed to live < kept trying to earn a *living* the honest way >
  syn alimentation, alimony, bread, bread and butter, keep, livelihood, maintenance, salt, subsistence, support, sustenance
  rel sustainment, sustentation

load *n* 1 something which is carried, conveyed, or transported from one place to another < a *load* of grain just arrived >
  syn burden, cargo, freight, haul, lading, payload
  rel bale, pack, parcel, shipment
  2 something heavy < could not lift the *load* >
  syn weight
  3 a burdensome or laborious responsibility < considered taking care of the children a heavy *load* >
  syn burden, charge, deadweight, duty, millstone, onus, task, tax, weight
  rel care, liability, obligation, responsibility; drag, drain, pressure
  idiom millstone around one's neck
  con breeze, child's play, cinch, duck soup, picnic, ‖pipe, pushover, snap

---

syn synonym(s)   *rel* related word(s)
ant antonym(s)   *con* contrasted word(s)
idiom idiomatic equivalent(s)
‖ use limited; if in doubt, see a dictionary

---

  ant sinecure
  4 *usu* loads *pl syn* see SCAD

load *vb* 1 *syn* see BURDEN
  rel bear, carry, convey, transport
  ant unload
  2 *syn* see ADULTERATE
  3 to make full or overfull < a basket *loaded* with fresh fruit >
  syn charge, choke, fill, heap, pack, pile; *compare* CRAM 1
  rel glut, gorge, surfeit; flood, oversupply, swamp

loaded *adj* 1 *syn* see FULL 1
  ‖2 *syn* see INTOXICATED 1
loaf *vb syn* see IDLE
  con labor, toil, travail, work
loafer *n syn* see SLUGGARD
loan *vb syn* see LEND
loan shark *n* one who lends money to individuals at exorbitant rates of interest < got involved with *loan sharks* >
  syn Shylock, usurer
  rel lender, loaner, moneylender; shark
loath *adj syn* see DISINCLINED
  ant anxious
loathe *vb syn* see HATE
  rel decline, refuse, reject, repudiate, spurn
  con covet, crave, desire, want, wish
  ant tolerate
loathing *n syn* see ABOMINATION 2
  ant tolerance
loathsome *adj syn* see OFFENSIVE
  rel hateful, invidious, obnoxious
  con bearable, endurable, sufferable, supportable; engaging, inviting; alluring, bewitching, charming, enchanting, fascinating
  ant tolerable

lobby *n syn* see VESTIBULE
lobster *n syn* see OAF 2
local *adj syn* see INSULAR
  ant cosmopolitan
locale *n syn* see SCENE 3
  rel area, district, neighborhood, vicinage, vicinity
locality *n* 1 a more or less definitely circumscribed place or region < searched for the child in the *locality* of the waterfront >
  syn area, district, neighborhood, vicinage, vicinity
  rel belt, region, tract, zone; section, sector; bailiwick, domain, field, province, sphere, territory
  idiom neck of the woods
  2 *syn* see HABITAT
located *adj syn* see SITUATED
location *n syn* see PLACE 1
‖**loch** *n syn* see INLET
‖**lockup** *n syn* see JAIL
‖**loco** *adj syn* see INSANE 1
locum tenens *n syn* see SUBSTITUTE
locus *n syn* see PLACE 1
locution *n syn* see PHRASE 2
lodge *vb* 1 *syn* see HARBOR 2
  rel accept, admit, receive, take; accommodate, contain, hold
  2 *syn* see ENTRENCH 1
lodge *n* 1 *syn* see HUT
  2 *syn* see HOTEL
  3 *syn* see LAIR 1
lodgeable *adj syn* see LIVABLE 1
lodging *n* 1 *syn* see ACCOMMODATIONS

2 usu **lodgings** pl syn see APARTMENT 1

lodgment n syn see ACCOMMODATIONS

loftiest adj syn see TOP 1

loftiness n syn see PRIDE 3

lofty adj 1 syn see PROUD 1
2 syn see AMBITIOUS 2
3 syn see GRAND 3
4 syn see GENEROUS 1
5 syn see ELEVATED 4
6 extending or rising high in the air so as to have great or imposing height < a *lofty* monument to human aspiration>
syn aerial, airy, skyscraping, soaring, spiring, topless, towering, towery; compare HIGH 1
rel elevated, lifted, raised; aggrandized, exalted, magnified; august, imposing, majestic, stately
con humble, low, modest

logical adj 1 syn see RATIONAL
ant illogical
2 having or showing skill in thinking or reasoning < a *logical* argument>
syn analytic, analytical, ratiocinative, subtle
rel cogent, compelling, convincing, sound, telling, valid; clear, lucid, perspicuous; rational, reasonable; discriminating
con instinctive, intuitive; irrational, unreasonable; casuistical, sophistical
ant illogical

logo n syn see MARK 7

logotype n syn see MARK 7

loiter vb 1 syn see DELAY 2
2 syn see IDLE

loiterer n syn see LAGGARD

loll vb 1 syn see SLOUCH
2 syn see IDLE

‖**lollop** vb syn see SLOUCH

lone adj 1 having no company < a *lone* figure walking through the snow>
syn alone, lonely, lonesome, solitary
rel single, sole, unique; abandoned, deserted, forsaken; isolated, secluded
con attended, chaperoned, companioned, convoyed, escorted
ant accompanied
2 syn see ONLY 2
3 syn see SINGLE 2

lonely adj 1 syn see LONE 1
2 syn see FORLORN 1

loneness n syn see SOLITUDE

lonesome adj 1 syn see LONE 1
2 syn see FORLORN 1
3 syn see OBSCURE 2

long adj 1 having considerable extension in space or time < a *long* road > < it has been a *long* time since we have seen you>
syn elongate, elongated, extended, lengthy
rel extensive, longish, outstretched
con brief, curtailed
ant short
2 unduly extended < went through many *long* days of misery>
syn dragging, drawn-out, ‖dreich, lengthy, long-drawn-out, longsome, overlong, prolonged, protracted
rel diffuse, diffusive, long-winded, prolix; flatulent, verbose, wordy
con ephemeral, evanescent, fleeting, fugacious, fugitive, impermanent, passing, short-lived, transient, transitory; abbreviated, abridged, curtailed, shortened

ant brief

long n syn see AGE 2

long vb to desire urgently < *long* for peace>
syn ache, crave, dream, hanker, hunger, itch, lust, pine, sigh, suspire, thirst, yearn, yen
rel aim, aspire, want; miss
idiom have an appetite (or a longing) for
con abhor, detest, dread, fear, loathe

longanimity n syn see PATIENCE

long-drawn-out adj syn see LONG 2
ant short; curtailed

‖**long green** n syn see MONEY

longitudinally adv syn see LENGTHWISE
ant horizontally

long-lasting adj syn see OLD 2
ant ephemeral

long-lived adj syn see OLD 2
ant short-lived

longsome adj syn see LONG 2

long-suffering n syn see PATIENCE
rel subduedness; humility, lowliness, meekness
con impatience, uneasiness; irksomeness, tediousness, wearisomeness; boredom, ennui, tedium

long suit n syn see FORTE
rel specialism, specialization, specialty

longtimer n syn see VETERAN
con apprentice, neophyte, novice; newcomer, rookie, tenderfoot

‖**long tongue** n syn see GOSSIP 1

longways adv syn see LENGTHWISE

long-winded adj syn see WORDY
rel extended, lasting, lengthy, long, long-drawn-out, prolonged, protracted
con brief, close, compact

longwise adv syn see LENGTHWISE

loo n syn see TOILET

looby n syn see OAF 2

look vb 1 to make sure or take care (that something is or is not done) < *look* that you accuse no one unjustly>
syn mind, see, watch
rel attend, heed, tend; note, notice, observe; beware
2 syn see SEE 2
rel note, notice, observe, spot
idiom get a load of, take a gander at
3 syn see EXPECT 1
rel divine, forecast, foretell
ant despair (of)
4 to make apparent by the expression of the eyes or countenance < *looked* her annoyance at this interruption>
syn exhibit, show; compare SHOW 2
rel display, express, indicate, manifest
5 syn see SEEM
idiom strike one as
6 syn see FACE 1
7 to gaze in wonder or surprise < you should have seen them *look*>
syn eye, gape, ‖gaup (or gawp), gaze, goggle, ogle, rubberneck, stare; compare GAZE 1
rel gawk; glare, gloat, glower; peer
8 syn see TEND 1

look (at or upon) vb syn see EYE 1

look (into) vb syn see EXPLORE

look n 1 the directing of one's eyes in order to see < he wanted one last *look* before departing>

syn sight, view

rel glance, glimpse, peek, peep, squint; cast, slant; eye, ‖gander, ‖look-see, regard; eyeful, gaze, stare, survey

2 facial aspect especially as indicative of mood or feeling <you should have seen the *look* on her face>

syn cast, countenance, expression, face, visage

rel mug, physiognomy, ‖puss

3 *syn* see APPEARANCE 1

look down *vb* **1** *syn* see OVERLOOK 2

2 *syn* see DESPISE

3 *syn* see STARE DOWN

looker *n syn* see BEAUTY

looker-on *n syn* see SPECTATOR

look in *vb syn* see VISIT 2

look-in *n syn* see OPPORTUNITY

looking glass *n syn* see MIRROR 1

look out *vb syn* see BEWARE

lookout *n* **1** *syn* see GUARD 2

2 an elevated place affording a wide view for observation <guards posted at a *lookout* to watch for enemy troops entering the valley>

syn observatory, outlook, overlook

rel watchtower; crow's nest; cupola, widow's walk; firetower

3 a careful looking or watching <kept a constant *lookout* for new developments>

syn surveillance, tout, vigil, vigilance, watch, watch and ward

rel observance, observation

4 *syn* see VISTA

5 *syn* see BUSINESS 8

look up *vb* **1** *syn* see IMPROVE 3

2 *syn* see VISIT 2

loom *vb* **1** *syn* see APPEAR 1

2 to take shape as an impending occurrence <an international economic crisis *looms* ahead>

syn brew, forthcome, gather, impend

rel approach, come on, make up, near

con disappear, fade, pass, vanish; die (down *or* away), diminish, dwindle, wane; recede, retreat, withdraw

3 to appear in an impressively great or exaggerated form <the power of the enemy *loomed* in the soldiers' imagination>

syn bulk, stand out

rel lower, rear, threaten, tower

con die (down *or* away), diminish, dwindle, wane

loon *n syn* see LUNATIC 1

loony *adj syn* see FOOLISH 2

loony *n syn* see LUNATIC 1

loony bin *n syn* see ASYLUM 3

loop *n* **1** a curving or doubling of a line so as to form a closed or partly open curve <the transit makes a *loop* around town>

syn eye, ring

rel circlet, circuit, circumference, hoop, wreath; curve

2 a circular or curved piece used often to form a fastening or a handle <one of his belt *loops* is broken>

syn eye, ring, staple

rel hook

---

syn synonym(s)   *rel* related word(s)

ant antonym(s)   *con* contrasted word(s)

idiom idiomatic equivalent(s)

‖ use limited; if in doubt, see a dictionary

---

3 *syn* see LEAGUE 4

loop *vb syn* see SURROUND 1

rel arc, arch, bend, coil, curve

looped *adj syn* see INTOXICATED 1

loopy *adj syn* see FOOLISH 2

loose *adj* **1** not tightly bound, held, restrained, or stretched <*loose* rope>

syn lax, relaxed, slack

rel detached, free; flabby, flaccid, limp; desultory, negligent, remiss

con rigid, rigorous, stringent, taut, tense; exact, precise; bound, checked, curbed, inhibited, restrained, tied

ant strict; tight

2 *syn* see FREE 2

rel clear; disconnected, unattached, unconnected, undone, unfastened

con fast

3 not dense, close, or compact in structure <*loose* soil>

syn incoherent, nonadhesive

rel disconnected, disjointed, separate, unconnected

con compressed, condensed, contracted; concentrated, crammed, crowded, localized; close, compact, dense, thick

4 *syn* see FAST 7

rel capricious, extravagant, free, inconstant, reckless, unrestrained

loose *vb* **1** *syn* see FREE

2 *syn* see TAKE OUT (on)

3 to set free from a fastened or fixed condition <*loose* a knot>

syn disengage, unbind, undo, unfasten, unfix, unloose, unloosen

rel unbandage, unbar, unbolt, unbuckle, unbutton, unchain, unclasp, unglue, unhitch, unhook, unlace, unlash, unlatch, unlock, unpin, unscrew, unsnap, unstick, unstrap, untie

con bind, engage, fasten, fix, secure

4 *syn* see SHOOT 1

5 to make less rigid or tight <exercise *loosed* his muscles>

syn ease, ease off, lax, loosen, relax, slack, slacken, untighten

rel abate, alleviate, bate, lessen, let up, mitigate

con anchor, cement, clamp, clinch, fasten, knit, secure, set, tauten

ant tighten

loose-lipped *adj syn* see TALKATIVE

ant closemouthed

loosen *vb* **1** *syn* see LOOSE 5

ant tighten

2 *syn* see FREE

loosen up *vb syn* see RELAX 2

ant tighten (up)

loose-tongued *adj syn* see TALKATIVE

ant closemouthed

loot *n* **1** *syn* see SPOIL

rel lift, pillage, seizure

2 *syn* see MONEY

loot *vb syn* see ROB 1

looter *n syn* see MARAUDER

lop *vb* **1** *syn* see SLOUCH

2 *syn* see JUMP 1

lope *vb syn* see SKIP 1

rel run, sprint; romp, trip

‖**lopper** *vb syn* see CURDLE

lopsided *adj* lacking in balance, symmetry, or proportion <the arrangement of the furniture was *lopsided*>

syn asymmetric, difform, disproportional, disproportionate, irregular, nonsymmetrical, off-balance, overbalanced, proportionless, unbalanced, unequal, uneven, unproportionate, unsymmetrical

rel cockeyed, crooked, top-heavy, unsteady

con balanced, even, regular, symmetrical

loquacious *adj syn see* TALKATIVE

rel jabbering, overtalkative; prolix, verbose, wordy

con breviloquent, concise, succinct, taciturn, terse; abrupt, brusque, curt

lord *n syn see* HUSBAND

lord *vb* to affect an air of superiority and authority < nouveau riche love to *lord* it >

syn cock, peacock, pontificate, swagger, swank, swell

rel affect, pretend, put on; boss, order (about *or* around), overawe, overbear; tyrannize

idiom put on airs

lordly *adj* 1 *syn see* GRAND 1

2 *syn see* PROUD 1

rel egotistic, puffed; affected, snobbish, swollen; authoritarian, dictatorial, magisterial

con humble; abject, mean; subdued, submissive

lore *n* 1 *syn see* KNOWLEDGE 2

2 a body of traditions relating to a person, institution, or place < the Scottish highlands are rich in local *lore*>

syn folklore, legend, myth, mythology, mythos, tradition

rel custom, folkway, traditionalism; fable, old wives' tale, saga, superstition, tale

Lorelei *n syn see* SIREN

lorn *adj* 1 *syn see* DERELICT 1

2 *syn see* FORLORN 1

lose *vb* 1 to suffer deprivation of < *lost* all his savings in a poor investment >

syn drop, forfeit, sacrifice

rel mislay, misplace, miss; give up, relinquish, surrender, yield

con cash in, profit; clear, make, realize, take in; obtain, win

ant gain

2 to fail to win, gain, or obtain < *lost* every contest she entered >

syn drop, lose out

rel decline, fall, succumb, yield

ant win

3 *syn see* DEPRIVE 2

4 *syn see* SHAKE 5

5 *syn see* RID

lose out *vb syn see* LOSE 2

loser *n* 1 *syn see* FAILURE 5

rel also-ran, underdog

ant winner

2 *syn see* CONVICT

losing *n syn see* LOSS 1

loss *n* 1 the action of having something go out of one's control or possession < took precautions against *loss* or theft of his property >

syn losing, mislaying, misplacement, misplacing; *compare* PRIVATION 2

rel forfeit, forfeiture, sacrifice; bereavement, deprivation, deprivement, dispossession, divestiture, divestment, privation

2 *syn see* PRIVATION 2

3 *syn see* RUIN 3

lost *adj* 1 *syn see* DAMNED 1

rel incorrigible, irreclaimable, irredeemable, irreformable, unconverted, unregenerate; graceless

2 no longer possessed < earned his *lost* reputation by his outrageous behavior >

syn gone, missing

rel absent, lacking; passed; irrecoverable, irretrievable, irrevocable

con cherished, protected, treasured

3 *syn see* EXTINCT 2

4 *syn see* ABSTRACTED

rel absorbed; daydreamy, musing, unconscious

lot *n* 1 *syn see* SHARE 1

2 *syn see* FATE

rel decree, fortune; foreordination, predestination, predestination

3 a measured portion of land having fixed boundaries < building *lots* >

syn parcel, plat, plot, tract

rel clearing, field, patch; part, plottage; block, frontage, real estate

4 *syn see* GROUP 3

rel aggregate, aggregation, conglomerate, conglomeration

5 *syn see* SET 5

6 *syn see* TYPE

7 *syn see* MUCH

lot *vb syn see* ALLOT

‖**lot** (on *or* upon) *vb syn see* RELY (on *or* upon)

lot (out) *vb syn see* DISTRIBUTE 1

lothario *n syn see* GALLANT 2

loud *adj* 1 marked by intensity or volume of sound < a *loud* blast on a trumpet >

syn blaring, earsplitting, full-mouthed, piercing, roaring, stentorian, stentorious, stentorophonic

rel booming, deafening, ear-piercing, fulminating, pealing, ringing, thunderous; resonant, resounding, sonorous; harsh, hoarse, raucous, stertorous, strident

con dulcet, gentle, mellifluous, mellow, quiet, smooth

ant low, soft

2 *syn see* GAUDY

rel brassy, vulgar; obnoxious, offensive; obtrusive

loudmouthed *adj syn see* VOCIFEROUS

‖**lough** *n syn see* INLET

lounge *vb syn see* IDLE

rel drift, vegetate; dally, slack; lie, lie down, recline

lounge *n syn see* BAR 5

lounge car *n syn see* PARLOR CAR

lounge lizard *n* 1 *syn see* FOP

2 *syn see* PARASITE

louse *n syn see* SNOT 1

louse up *vb syn see* BOTCH

lout *n syn see* OAF 2

rel boor, bumpkin, churl, clodhopper, hayseed, hick, peasant, rube, rustic, yokel; dolt

lout *vb syn see* RIDICULE

loutish *adj syn see* BOORISH

rel awkward, bungling, clumsy, inept, maladroit, rusty; callow, crude, gauche, raw, rough, uncouth

lovable *adj* gifted with traits and qualities that attract affection < a *lovable* child >

syn adorable, lovesome

rel admirable, agreeable, attractive, desirable, genial, likable, pleasing, winning, winsome; alluring, appealing, bewitching, captivating, charming, enchanting, engaging, enthralling, entrancing, fetching, ravishing, seductive
con dislikable, displeasing, distasteful, unattractive, unlikable, unpleasing; odious, offensive; abhorrent, abominable, obnoxious, repellent; contemptible, despicable, detestable
ant hateful; unlovable

love *n* **1** the feeling which animates a person who is genuinely fond of someone or something < a mother's *love* for her child >
syn affection, attachment, devotion, fondness
rel like(s), liking, regard; adoration, idolatry, piety, worship; allegiance, fealty, fidelity, loyalty; emotion, sentiment; crush, infatuation, passion, yearning; ardency, ardor, enthusiasm, fervor, zeal
con antipathy, aversion; animosity, animus, enmity, hostility, rancor; abhorrence, detestation, hatred
ant hate
2 the affection and tenderness felt by lovers < the ability to distinguish between *love* and lust was the mark of her maturity >
syn amorousness, amour, passion
rel crush, infatuation; desire, lust, yearning; ardency, ardor, fervor
idiom (the) tender passion
3 *syn* see LOVE AFFAIR
4 *syn* see SWEETHEART 1

love *vb* **1** to like or desire actively < she *loves* her material possessions all too dearly >
syn adore, delight (in), ‖eat up
rel appreciate, cherish, prize, treasure, value; dote (on or upon), fancy
idiom hold dear
con abjure, give up, reject, relinquish
2 to feel a lover's passion, devotion, or tenderness for < in spite of all their misfortunes, they continued to *love* each other devotedly >
syn adore, affection, worship
rel deify, exalt, idolize, revere, venerate; cherish, dote (on or upon); admire, fancy, like
con avoid, disregard, ignore, neglect, overlook, shun, slight
3 *syn* see CARESS

love affair *n* a romantic attachment or episode between lovers < saddened by the end of a summer *love affair* >
syn affair, amour, love, romance
rel flirtation, intrigue; triangle, ménage à trois

love child *n syn* see BASTARD 1
loved *adj syn* see FAVORITE 1
love letter *n* a letter expressing a lover's affection < she had never received a *love letter* >
syn billet-doux, mash note

rel valentine
loveling *n syn* see SWEETHEART 1
lovely *adj syn* see BEAUTIFUL
rel alluring, bewitching, captivating, charming, enchanting, engaging, entrancing, lovesome; delectable, delightful; dainty, delicate, exquisite, rare; graceful
ant hideous; unlovely
lovely *n syn* see BEAUTY
lover *n* **1** a man who is a woman's regular partner in nonmarital sexual activity
syn boyfriend, fancy man, man, master, paramour
rel cavalier servente, sugar daddy
2 *syn* see BOYFRIEND 2
3 *syn* see ADDICT
4 *syn* see MISTRESS
lovesome *adj* **1** *syn* see LOVABLE
2 *syn* see LOVING
lovey-dovey *adj syn* see SENTIMENTAL
loving *adj* feeling or expressing love < his *loving* son unfailingly waited upon him during his last years >
syn affectionate, dear, devoted, doting, fond, lovesome
rel adoring, attached, benevolent, cordial, kind, tender, warmhearted; attentive, caring, considerate, solicitous; amatory, amorous, erotic; enamored, infatuated; ardent, fervent, impassioned, passionate; faithful; bound up
con aloof, detached, indifferent, unconcerned; chilly, cold, frigid
ant unloving
low *adj* ‖**1** *syn* see SHORT 2
rel squatty; unelevated
2 *syn* see INFERIOR 1
3 *syn* see POOR 1
4 *syn* see IGNOBLE 1
rel lowbred, rude
5 *syn* see BASE 3
rel scrubby, scruffy; miserable, woebegone, woeful
con decent, decorous, proper, seemly; ethical, moral, noble; high, lofty
6 *syn* see COARSE 3
7 *syn* see UNWELL
rel declining, weak; dizzy, faint, feverish
8 *syn* see DOWNCAST
9 of lesser degree, size, or amount than average or ordinary < the energy crisis resulted in *lower* speed limits for all vehicles >
syn subaverage, subnormal
rel fallen, reduced; brief, short; mediocre, moderate; atypical
10 *syn* see CHEAP 1
rel economical; moderate, nominal; cut, cut-rate, marked down, slashed
con elevated, enhanced, increased; raised
lowborn *adj syn* see IGNOBLE 1
ant highborn
lowbred *adj syn* see BOORISH
ant highbred
low-cost *adj syn* see CHEAP 1
low-down *adj syn* see BASE 3
lower *vb syn* see FROWN 1
rel peer, stare; intimidate, menace, threaten
lower *adj syn* see INFERIOR 1
ant higher
lower *vb* **1** *syn* see FALL 1
ant rise

---

2 *syn* see DEPRECIATE 1
rel demote; de-escalate, deflate
con raise

3 to cause or allow to descend < *lowered* the landing gear of the aircraft>
syn couch, demit, depress, droop, let down, sink
rel detrude, submerge; debase, reduce
con elevate, hoist, lift, pull up, raise

4 *syn* see REDUCE 2
ant raise

5 *syn* see HUMBLE
ant elevate

lowering (*or* **louring**) *adj* 1 *syn* see IMMINENT 2
rel frowning, gloomy, sullen; black, dark; foreboding, impending, portentous
2 *syn* see OVERCAST

lowermost *adj syn* see BOTTOMMOST
ant uppermost

lowery (*or* **loury**) *adj syn* see IMMINENT 2

lowest *adj syn* see BOTTOMMOST
ant highest

low-grade *adj syn* see INFERIOR 2

low-key *adj syn* see SUBDUED 2

low-keyed *adj syn* see SUBDUED 2

lowlife *n* 1 *syn* see WRETCH 1
2 *syn* see VILLAIN 1

lowly *adj* 1 *syn* see HUMBLE 1
rel retiring, withdrawing; deferential, obeisant, reverential; obsequious, servile
ant haughty
2 *syn* see IGNOBLE 1
3 *syn* see PROSAIC 3

low-pressure *adj syn* see EASYGOING 3
ant high-pressure

low-priced *adj syn* see CHEAP 1

||**low-rate** *vb syn* see DECRY 2

low-set *adj syn* see SHORT 2

low-spirited *adj syn* see DOWNCAST
ant high-spirited

low-statured *adj syn* see SHORT 2

loyal *adj syn* see FAITHFUL 1
con faithless; alienated, disaffected, estranged; contumacious, factious, insubordinate, mutinous, rebellious, seditious
ant disloyal

loyalist *n syn* see PATRIOT 1

loyalty *n* 1 *syn* see FIDELITY 1
rel trueness, truth
ant disloyalty
2 *syn* see ATTACHMENT 1

lubber *n syn* see OAF 2

lubberland *n syn* see UTOPIA

lubberly *adj syn* see BOORISH

||**lubricate** *vb syn* see BRIBE

lubricious *adj* 1 *syn* see INCONSTANT 1
2 *syn* see SLICK 1

lucent *adj* 1 *syn* see BRIGHT 1
2 *syn* see CLEAR 4

lucid *adj* 1 *syn* see BRIGHT 1
2 *syn* see SANE 2
3 *syn* see UNDERSTANDABLE
4 *syn* see CLEAR 4
con dusky, gloomy, murky; muddy, turbid

lucidity *n* 1 *syn* see CLARITY
rel comprehensibility, intelligibility, understandability; distinctness, explicitness
ant ambiguity
2 *syn* see WIT 2

Lucifer *n syn* see DEVIL 1

luck *n* 1 *syn* see CHANCE 2

rel break, occasion, opportunity
2 *syn* see ACCIDENT 1

3 success dependent on chance < he had all the *luck* in the world and was greatly envied by every one of his associates>
syn fortunateness, fortune, luckiness
rel advantage, break, fluke, godsend, opportunity, windfall; weal; hap, kismet
ant ill-fortune

4 *syn* see CHARM 2

luck *vb syn* see HAPPEN 2

luckiness *n syn* see LUCK 3

luckless *adj syn* see UNLUCKY
rel miserable, wretched
ant lucky

lucky *adj* having a favorable outcome or an unforeseen or unpredictable success < he can only be described as *lucky*, as his success and fame are unearned>
syn fortunate, happy, providential, ||sonsy, well
rel auspicious, benign, favorable, propitious; advantageous, beneficial, profitable; felicitous
idiom in luck
con baleful, malefic, maleficent, malign, sinister
ant luckless, unlucky

lucrative *adj syn* see ADVANTAGEOUS 1

lucre *n* 1 *syn* see PROFIT
2 *syn* see MONEY

luculent *adj syn* see CLEAR 4

ludicrous *adj syn* see LAUGHABLE
rel absurd, foolish, preposterous, silly; antic, bizarre, fantastic, grotesque
con doleful, dolorous, lugubrious, melancholy

lug *vb* 1 *syn* see PULL 2
2 *syn* see CARRY 1
3 *syn* see JERK

||**lug** *n syn* see OAF 2

||**lugs** *n pl syn* see POSE 2

lugubrious *adj* 1 *syn* see MELANCHOLY 2
rel depressing, oppressing, oppressive; dour, glum, morose, saturnine, sullen
con blithe, jocund, jolly, jovial, merry; cheerful, glad, joyful
ant facetious
2 *syn* see GLOOMY 3

lukewarm *adj* 1 *syn* see TEPID 1
2 *syn* see TEPID 2
rel irresolute, irresolved, uncommitted, unresolved; hesitant, indecisive, uncertain, undecided; cool; wishy-washy
ant icy; boiling

lull *vb* 1 *syn* see CALM
rel moderate, qualify, temper
ant agitate
2 *syn* see ABATE 4

lull *n* 1 *syn* see QUIET 1
2 *syn* see PAUSE
rel abeyance, quiescence

lullaby *n* a song to quiet children or lull them to sleep < sang a *lullaby* to the baby every night>
syn berceuse, cradlesong

||**lulu** *n syn* see ||DILLY

lumber *vb* to tread heavily or clumsily < the tired old man slowly *lumbered* home>
syn barge, clump, galumph, stumble, stump
rel plod, trudge; shamble, slog

lumber *vb syn* see BURDEN
lumbering *adj* 1 *syn* see CLUMSY 1
rel cumbersome, cumbrous, ponderous; hulking, hulky
2 *syn* see AWKWARD 2
luminary *n* 1 *syn* see CELEBRITY 2
rel leading light
2 *syn* see NOTABLE 1
luminous *adj* 1 *syn* see BRIGHT 1
2 *syn* see CLEAR 4
3 *syn* see UNDERSTANDABLE
lummox *n syn* see OAF 2
lump *n* 1 a compact mass of indefinite size and shape <dropped a large *lump* of butter into the steaming chowder>
syn chunk, clod, clump, gob, hunch, hunk, nugget, wad
rel particle, piece, portion; batch, bunch, ‖swad; bit, chip, crumb, morsel, scrap; wedge; block, bulk
2 *syn* see MUCH
3 *syn* see BUMP 2
rel bulge, protuberance, swelling
4 *syn* see OAF 2
5 **lumps** *pl syn* see DUE 1
lump *vb syn* see BEAR 10
lumpish *adj* 1 *syn* see BOORISH
2 *syn* see CLUMSY 1
lumpkin *n syn* see OAF 2
lumpy *adj syn* see RUDE 1
lunacy *n* 1 *syn* see INSANITY 1
rel absurdity, folly, foolery, foolishness; asininity, fatuity, inanity, ineptitude, stupidity
2 *syn* see FOOLISHNESS
lunatic *adj* 1 *syn* see INSANE 1
2 *syn* see FOOLISH 2
lunatic *n* 1 a person who is insane or of unsound mind <Bedlam was a famous old English asylum for *lunatics*>
syn bedlamite, dement, loon, loony, madling, madman, maniac, non compos, nut, Tom o' Bedlam
rel demoniac, energumen; raver; neuropath, neurotic, paranoid, psycho, psychoneurotic
2 *syn* see CRACKPOT
lunch counter (*or* bar) *n syn* see EATING HOUSE
luncheonette *n syn* see EATING HOUSE
lunchroom *n syn* see EATING HOUSE
lunch wagon (*or* cart) *n syn* see EATING HOUSE
lunge *vb syn* see PLUNGE 2
lunk *n syn* see DUNCE
lunkhead *n syn* see DUNCE
lupanar *n syn* see BROTHEL
lurch *n syn* see LEANING 2
lurch *vb* 1 *syn* see SEESAW
2 to move forward unsteadily while swaying from side to side <the sodden drunk *lurched* uncertainly toward the door>
syn careen, stagger, ‖stoit, ‖stoiter, ‖stot, sway, swing, weave, wobble; *compare* TEETER
rel reel, rock, roll, swag, toss, totter, whirl; bob; wave, waver
con march, stride

3 *syn* see TEETER
rel pitch, plunge
4 *syn* see JERK
5 *syn* see WALLOW 2
6 *syn* see STUMBLE 3
lure *n* 1 *syn* see ATTRACTION 1
2 something that leads an individual into a place or situation from which escape is difficult <used her charm as a *lure* to trap the unsuspecting youth>
syn allurement, bait, come-on, decoy, enticement, inveiglement, seducement, siren song, snare, ‖stale, temptation, trap
rel appeal, attraction, incentive, inducement; con game, gimmick, suck-in, trick; ambush, blind, camouflage, delusion, fake, illusion
con caution, caveat, warning
lure *vb* to draw from a usual, desirable, or proper course or situation into one felt as unusual, undesirable, or wrong <the promise of money *lured* him away from his steady job>
syn allure, bait, decoy, entice, entrap, inveigle, lead on, seduce, tempt, toll, train
rel bag, capture, catch, draw in, ensnare, rope, snare, suck in; attract, beguile, bewitch, captivate, charm, enchant, fascinate, invite; draw, draw on; blandish, cajole, wheedle
idiom bait the hook, give the come-on
con drive (away *or* off), rebuff, repulse
ant repel
lurid *adj* 1 *syn* see PALE 1
2 *syn* see GHASTLY 1
rel ashen, ashy, livid, pale, pallid, wan; baleful, malefic, maleficent, malign, sinister
3 *syn* see SENSATIONAL 2
luring *adj syn* see ENTICING
ant repellent, repelling
lurk *vb syn* see SNEAK
lurking *adj syn* see LATENT
luscious *adj* 1 *syn* see DELIGHTFUL
rel appetizing, flavorsome, nectarious, palatable, piquant; choice, distinctive, exquisite, rare, rich
ant austere
2 *syn* see LUXURIOUS 3
3 *syn* see SENSUOUS
4 *syn* see ORNATE
lush *adj* 1 *syn* see PROFUSE
rel luxurious, sumptuous
2 *syn* see DELIGHTFUL
3 *syn* see SENSUOUS
4 *syn* see LUXURIOUS 3
lush *n* ‖1 *syn* see LIQUOR 2
2 *syn* see DRUNKARD
lush (up) *vb syn* see DRINK 3
‖**lushed** *adj syn* see INTOXICATED 1
‖**lusher** *n syn* see DRUNKARD
lust *n* 1 *syn* see DESIRE 1
rel coveting, yearning, yen
2 sexual appetency <they mistakenly thought that *lust* was lasting love>
syn aphrodisia, concupiscence, desire, eroticism, itch, lickerishness, lustfulness, passion, prurience, pruriency
rel nymphomania, priapism, satyriasis, satyrism; excitement, heat, hunger, libido, rut; fervor; carnality, lasciviousness, lecherousness, lechery, lubricity, salacity
lust *vb syn* see LONG

---

rel desire, wish

luster *n* the quality or condition of shining by reflected light < the satiny *luster* of fine pearls >
syn glaze, glint, gloss, polish, sheen, shine
rel iridescence, opalescence; brilliance, brilliancy, effulgence, luminosity, radiance, refulgence; afterglow, gleam, glow; candescence, incandescence

lusterless *adj* 1 *syn* see DULL 7
ant lustrous
2 *syn* see COLORLESS 2

lustful *adj* 1 *syn* see LICENTIOUS 2
2 sexually excited < *lustful* old man >
syn concupiscent, goatish, hot, lascivious, libidinous, lickerish, passionate, prurient, ruttish, rutty, satyric
rel burning, hot-blooded, itching; lecherous, salacious

lustfulness *n* *syn* see LUST 2

lustral *adj* *syn* see PURGATIVE

lustrate *vb* *syn* see PURIFY 2

lustration *n* *syn* see PURIFICATION

lustratory *adj* *syn* see PURGATIVE

lustrous *adj* 1 having a high gloss or shine < a *lustrous* star sapphire >
syn burnished, gleaming, glistening, glossy, polished, sheeny, shining, shiny
rel gleamy, glimmering, glinting, sparkling; radiant
con dull, flat, lackluster, mat
ant lusterless
2 *syn* see BRIGHT 1
rel glorious, resplendent, splendid

lusty *adj* 1 *syn* see VIGOROUS
rel hale, healthy
ant effete
2 *syn* see STRONG 3
3 *syn* see HUGE

lusus *n* *syn* see FREAK 2

luxuriant *adj* 1 *syn* see PROFUSE
rel fecund, fertile, fruitful, prolific; rampant, rank

con barren, infertile, sterile, unfruitful
2 *syn* see LUXURIOUS 3

luxuriate *vb* *syn* see WALLOW 3
rel overindulge, overdo; eat up, enjoy, feast, love, riot

luxurious *adj* 1 *syn* see SENSUOUS
rel self-indulging, self-pampering; languishing, languorous
con self-abnegating, self-denying; austere, severe, stern
ant ascetic
2 *syn* see GRAND 2
rel imposing, majestic, stately
3 ostentatiously rich or magnificent < the robber barons built *luxurious* homes which rivaled the palaces of Europe >
syn Capuan, deluxe, luscious, lush, luxuriant, opulent, palace, palatial, plush, plushy, sumptuous, upholstered
rel extravagant, grandiose, ostentatious, posh, pretentious, showy; awful, grand, imposing, magnificent, majestic, stately; Lucullan; elaborate, fancy; costly, expensive, precious
con economical, frugal, sparing, thrifty; exiguous, meager, scant, scanty, scrimpy, skimpy, spare

luxury *n* something adding to pleasure but not absolutely necessary < the poor cannot even afford the essentials, let alone occasional *luxuries* >
syn amenity, extravagance, frill, luxus, superfluity
rel comfort; embellishment, redundancy, self-indulgence; dainty, delicacy
con basics, essential(s), fundamental(s)

luxus *n* *syn* see LUXURY

lying *adj* *syn* see DISHONEST
rel false, wrong; deceptive, delusive, delusory, misleading

lying–in *n* *syn* see CONFINEMENT 2

lyncean *adj* *syn* see SHARP-EYED

lynx–eyed *adj* *syn* see SHARP-EYED

M

ma *n* *syn* see MOTHER 1

macabre *adj* *syn* see GHASTLY 1
rel deadly, deathlike, deathly; ghostlike, ghostly

macaroni *n* *syn* see FOP

mace *n* *syn* see CUDGEL

||**mace** *n* *syn* see SWINDLER

||**mace** *vb* *syn* see CHEAT

machinate *vb* 1 *syn* see ENGINEER
2 *syn* see PLOT

machination *n* *syn* see PLOT 2

machine *n* 1 *syn* see CAR
2 *syn* see ROBOT 2

machinery *n* *syn* see EQUIPMENT
rel agency, agent, channel, instrument, instrumentality, means, medium, organ, vehicle; contraption, contrivance, device, gadget; appliance, implement, instrument, tool, utensil

||**mack** *n* *syn* see PIMP 1

macquereau *n* *syn* see PIMP 1

macrocosm *n* *syn* see UNIVERSE
ant microcosm

macrocosmos *n* *syn* see UNIVERSE
ant microcosm

mad *adj* 1 *syn* see INSANE 1
rel delirious, frantic, frenetic, furious, rabid, wild
2 *syn* see FOOLISH 2
3 *syn* see ILLOGICAL
4 *syn* see ANGRY
rel sore, worked up; affronted, offended, outraged
5 *syn* see FURIOUS 2

mad *vb* *syn* see ANGER 1

mad *n* *syn* see ANGER

mad–brained *adj* *syn* see RASH 1

madcap *adj* *syn* see RASH 1

madden *vb* 1 to make insane < prolonged solitary confinement had *maddened* the prisoners >
syn craze, derange, distract, frenzy, unbalance, unhinge

rel shatter; possess
idiom drive insane (*or* mad *or* crazy)
2 *syn* see ANGER 1
con allay, assuage, mitigate, relieve
made-to-order *adj syn* see CUSTOM-MADE
madhouse *n syn* see ASYLUM 3
madid *adj syn* see WET 1
madling *n syn* see LUNATIC 1
madly *adv syn* see HARD 2
rel foolishly, insanely, irrationally; hastily, rashly
madman *n* **1** *syn* see LUNATIC 1
2 *syn* see FOOL 1
madness *n syn* see INSANITY 1
maelstrom *n syn* see EDDY
rel commotion, confusion, fury, storm, turmoil
magazine *n* **1** *syn* see DEPOT 2
rel cache, lumber room
2 *syn* see ARMORY
3 *syn* see JOURNAL
rel publication; digest, gazette; annual, bimonthly, biweekly, daily, monthly, quarterly, semiweekly, weekly
mage *n syn* see MAGICIAN 1
maggot *n syn* see CAPRICE
magian *n syn* see MAGICIAN 1
magian *adj syn* see MAGIC
magic *n* **1** the use of means (as charms or spells) believed to have supernatural power over natural forces <the practice of *magic*>
syn bewitchment, conjuring, conjury, enchantment, ensorcellment, incantation, magicking, necromancy, sorcery, thaumaturgy, witchcraft, witchery, witching, wizardry
rel abracadabra, alchemy, augury, charm, divining, exorcism, fortune-telling, mumbo jumbo, occultism, soothsaying, sortilege, voodooism; devilry, deviltry, diablerie, diabolism, satanism; wicca
2 the art of producing mysterious effects by illusion and sleight of hand <the club presented a program of clever *magic* to raise funds>
syn conjuring, legerdemain
idiom sleight of hand
magic *adj* having seemingly supernatural qualities or powers <modern medicine has developed a host of *magic* drugs>
syn magian, magical, mystic, necromantic, sorcerous, thaumaturgic, witchy, wizardly
rel extraordinary, marvelous, prodigious, remarkable, stupendous, unbelievable, unprecedented
magical *adj syn* see MAGIC
magician *n* **1** one who practices magical arts <a *magician* cast a spell over the child>
syn archimage, charmer, conjurer, enchanter, mage, magian, magus, necromancer, sorcerer, voodoo, voodooist, warlock, wizard; compare WITCH 1
rel augurer, brujo, diviner, exorciser, exorcist, invocator, thaumaturge, thaumaturgist; medicine man, shaman; prophet,

seer, soothsayer; fortune-teller, medium; diabolist, satanist
2 one who practices tricks of illusion and sleight of hand <a *magician* performed tricks for the children at the party>
syn conjurer, illusionist, trickster
magicking *n syn* see MAGIC 1
magisterial *adj* **1** *syn* see DICTATORIAL
rel disdainful, insolent, lordly, supercilious
2 *syn* see MASTERFUL 1
3 *syn* see POMPOUS 1
magistrate *n syn* see JUDGE 2
magnanimous *adj syn* see GENEROUS 1
rel altruistic, liberal, unselfish; great, highminded, knightly, noble, nobleminded, princely
con measly, paltry, petty, picayunish, picayune
magnate *n* a businessman of exceptional wealth, influence, or power <the oil and steel *magnates* who controlled whole nations>
syn baron, czar, king, merchant prince, mogul, prince, tycoon
rel figure, name, personage; ‖biggie, big gun, big-timer, ‖big wheel, fat cat, lion, nabob; plutocrat
idiom captain of industry
magnetic *adj syn* see ATTRACTIVE 1
rel arresting, irresistible; charismatic
con repellent, repugnant, repulsive
magnetism *n syn* see CHARM 3
magnetize *vb syn* see ATTRACT 1
magnific *adj syn* see GRAND 1
magnificent *adj* **1** *syn* see GRAND 1
rel glorious, resplendent, splendid, sublime, superb; luxurious, opulent, sumptuous
con abject, ignoble, mean, sordid; humble, lowly, meek; paltry
ant modest
2 *syn* see SPLENDID 2
3 *syn* see SUPERB 3
magnify *vb* **1** *syn* see PRAISE 2
2 *syn* see EXALT 1
rel augment, enlarge, increase; amplify, dilate, distend, expand, inflate, swell
ant belittle, minimize
3 *syn* see INCREASE 1
ant minify
4 *syn* see INTENSIFY
5 *syn* see OVERPLAY 2
6 *syn* see EMBROIDER
magniloquent *adj syn* see RHETORICAL
magnitude *n* **1** *syn* see ENORMITY 2
2 *syn* see SIZE 1
3 *syn* see SIZE 2
4 *syn* see ORDER 4
5 *syn* see IMPORTANCE
magnum opus *n syn* see MASTERPIECE 1
magpie *n syn* see CHATTERBOX
magus *n syn* see MAGICIAN 1
mahogany *n syn* see TABLE 1
maid *n* **1** *syn* see GIRL 1
2 a woman hired to do housework <in addition to her other duties the *maid* was expected to care for the baby>
syn biddy, girl, handmaid, hired girl, housemaid, maidservant
rel au pair girl; chambermaid, nursemaid, parlormaid; handmaiden; domestic, factotum, ‖muchacha, servant

---

syn synonym(s)   *rel* related word(s)
ant antonym(s)   *con* contrasted word(s)
idiom idiomatic equivalent(s)
‖ use limited; if in doubt, see a dictionary

idiom maid of all work
maiden *n syn* see GIRL 1
maiden *adj* 1 *syn* see VIRGIN 1
rel husbandless; old-maidish, spinsterish, spinsterly
2 *syn* see FIRST 2
maidenhead *n syn* see VIRGINITY
maidenhood *n syn* see VIRGINITY
maiden lady *n syn* see SPINSTER
maidservant *n syn* see MAID 2
maim *vb* to wound so severely as to deprive of the use of or to cause loss of a limb or member <an arm hanging useless, *maimed* in an auto accident>
syn cripple, dislimb, dismember, mayhem, mutilate; *compare* PARALYZE 1
rel disable, disfigure, hamstring; batter, break, ‖bung up, mangle, massacre, maul
con rehabilitate, restore, salvage; cure, fix, heal, mend, remedy, repair
main *n syn* see OCEAN
main *adj syn* see CHIEF 2
rel foremost, head, leading, paramount; cardinal, controlling, essential, fundamental, vital; prevailing
‖**main** *adv syn* see VERY 1
mainline *vb syn* see SHOOT UP 2
mainly *adv syn* see GENERALLY 1
mainstay *n* a chief reliance <the *mainstay* of the organization held things together>
syn backbone, pillar, sinew(s)
rel brace, buttress, crutch, maintainer, prop, staff, standby, stay, support, supporter, sustainer, upholder
maintain *vb* 1 to keep in a state of repair, efficiency, or validity <he followed a careful regimen to *maintain* his good health>
syn keep up, preserve, save, sustain; *compare* SAVE 3
rel husband, manage; care (for), cultivate; guard, protect
con disregard, ignore, neglect, omit, overlook, slight
2 to uphold as true, right, proper, or acceptable often in the face of challenge or indifference <I *maintain* that his actions were justified by the circumstances>
syn argue, assert, claim, contend, defend, justify, vindicate, warrant
rel affirm, aver, avouch, avow, declare, profess, protest; emphasize, insist, persist, stress; correct, rectify, right
con contradict, deny, gainsay, traverse; challenge, query, question
3 *syn* see SUPPORT 3
maintenance *n syn* see LIVING
majestic *adj* 1 *syn* see GRAND 1
rel courtly, dignified; ceremonious; imperial
2 *syn* see KINGLY
major *adj* 1 *syn* see CHIEF 2
rel better, greater, higher, superior
2 *syn* see BIG 1
3 *syn* see GRAVE 3
make *vb* 1 *syn* see EFFECT 1
rel initiate, originate, start
2 *syn* see GENERATE 1
rel brew
3 to bring something into being by forming, shaping, combining, or altering materials <*made* a dress from odd bits of material>

syn assemble, build, construct, erect, fabricate, fashion, forge, form, frame, manufacture, mold, produce, put together, shape; *compare* BUILD 1
4 *syn* see DRAFT 3
5 *syn* see CONSTITUTE 1
6 *syn* see PREPARE 1
7 *syn* see DESIGNATE 2
8 *syn* see ENACT 1
9 *syn* see RUN 3
10 *syn* see EARN 1
rel harvest, reap
11 *syn* see CLEAR 6
12 *syn* see FORCE 2
13 *syn* see HEAD 3
rel break (for)
‖14 *syn* see MEDDLE
15 *syn* see RUN 8
make–believe *n syn* see PRETENSE 2
make off *vb syn* see RUN 2
rel depart, go, leave, quit, retire, withdraw; abscond, decamp, escape
make out *vb* 1 *syn* see APPREHEND 1
2 *syn* see ESTABLISH 6
3 *syn* see INFER
‖4 *syn* see SHIFT 5
5 *syn* see SUCCEED 3
make over *vb syn* see TRANSFER 4
make–peace *n syn* see PEACEMAKER
maker *n syn* see FATHER 2
rel executor, operator; manufacturer
makeshift *n syn* see RESOURCE 3
makeshift *adj* serving as a temporary expedient <forced to make *makeshift* plans>
syn provisional, rough-and-ready, rough–and-tumble, stopgap
make up *vb* 1 *syn* see CONTRIVE 2
2 *syn* see MIX 1
3 *syn* see PREPARE 1
4 *syn* see CONSTITUTE 1
5 *syn* see COMPENSATE 1
make up (to) *vb syn* see ADDRESS 8
makeup *n* 1 the way in which parts or constituents are related in an organized whole <the complex *makeup* of the eye>
syn architecture, composition, constitution, construction, design, formation
rel arrangement, ordering, organization, plan, setup; form, shape, style
2 *syn* see DISPOSITION 3
rel cast, fiber, grain, mold, stamp, stripe, vein; constitution, frame
3 cosmetics used to color and beautify the face or body <with *makeup* on, she didn't look bad>
syn face, maquillage, paint, war paint
rel powder; blackface, grease paint
maladroit *adj* 1 *syn* see AWKWARD 2
rel blundering, floundering, stumbling, ungraceful; left-handed, unskilled
con deft, dexterous, handy; clever, cunning, ingenious
ant adroit
2 *syn* see TACTLESS
malady *n syn* see DISEASE 1
mala fide *adj syn* see INSINCERE
ant bona fide
malaise *n syn* see INFIRMITY 1
malapert *adj syn* see SAUCY 1
malapert *n syn* see MINX
malapropos *adj* 1 *syn* see IMPROPER 1
ant apropos

2 *syn* see UNSEASONABLE 1

malarkey *n syn* see NONSENSE 2

malconformation *n syn* see DEFORMITY

malcontent *n* 1 *syn* see GROUCH

   2 *syn* see REBEL

malcontent *adj syn* see DISCONTENTED

   rel alienated, disaffected, estranged; disobedient, ungovernable, unruly; restless; contumacious, factious, insubordinate, mutinous, rebellious, seditious

malcontented *adj syn* see DISCONTENTED

male *adj syn* see VIRILE 2

malediction *n syn* see CURSE 1

   ant benediction

malefactor *n syn* see CRIMINAL

   rel blackguard, knave, miscreant, rascal, rogue, scoundrel; evildoer, sinner, wrongdoer

malefic *adj syn* see SINISTER

   ant benefic

maleficent *adj syn* see SINISTER

   ant beneficent

malevolence *n syn* see MALICE

   rel antagonism, hostility; abhorrence, abomination, detestation

   ant benevolence

malevolent *adj syn* see MALICIOUS

   rel baleful, malefic, maleficent, sinister

   con benign, benignant, kind, kindly

   ant benevolent

malformation *n syn* see DEFORMITY

malice *n* a desiring or wishing pain, injury, or distress to another < they sought to ruin his reputation out of pure *malice* >

   syn despite, despitefulness, grudge, ill will, malevolence, maliciousness, malignancy, malignity, spite, spitefulness, spleen

   rel bane, poison, venom; bile; animosity, animus, antipathy, down, enmity; hate, hatefulness, hatred, invidiousness, meanness; bitterness, resentment, unbrage

   con benevolence, benignancy, benignity, charity, kindliness, kindness

malicious *adj* having, showing, or indicative of intense often vicious ill will < the helpless victim of *malicious* rumors >

   syn bitchy, catty, despiteful, evil, hateful, malevolent, malign, malignant, nasty, rancorous, spiteful, spitish, vicious, wicked

   rel poisonous, poison-pen, venomous, virulent; baneful, deleterious, detrimental, noxious, pernicious; envious, green, green-eyed, jealous; mean, petty

   con benevolent, charitable, friendly, kind, kindly; considerate, thoughtful

maliciousness *n syn* see MALICE

malign *adj* 1 *syn* see SINISTER

   rel baneful, deleterious, detrimental, injurious, noxious, pernicious

   con auspicious, favorable, propitious; fortunate, happy, lucky, providential

   ant benign

   2 *syn* see MALICIOUS

   rel antagonistic, antipathetic, hostile, inimical

   con benignant, kind, kindly

   ant benign

malign *vb* to speak evil of for the purpose of injuring and without regard for the truth < the candidates increasingly *maligned* each other as the campaign degenerated >

   syn asperse, befoul, bespatter, blacken, calumniate, defame, denigrate, libel, ‖scandal, scandalize, slander, slur, smear, spatter, tear down, traduce, vilify, villainize

   rel decry, depreciate, derogate, detract, disparage; opprobriate, revile, vituperate; backbite, besmirch, defile, pollute, smirch, soil, stain, sully, taint, tarnish

   idiom blow upon, cast aspersion(s) on (*or* upon)

   con acclaim, applaud, eulogize, extol, laud, praise; defend, justify, maintain, vindicate

malignancy *n syn* see MALICE

malignant *adj syn* see MALICIOUS

   rel devilish, diabolical, fiendish

   con altruistic, benevolent, charitable, humane

   ant benignant

maligning *adj syn* see LIBELOUS

malignity *n syn* see MALICE

   rel revengefulness, vengefulness, vindictiveness

   ant benignity

malison *n syn* see CURSE 1

   ant benison

‖**malkin** *n syn* see SLATTERN 1

malleable *adj syn* see PLASTIC

   rel governable, manageable; transformable

   con intractable, recalcitrant, ungovernable, unmanageable, unruly

   ant refractory

malleate *vb syn* see HAMMER 1

malodorous *adj* 1 having an unpleasant smell < *malodorous* cheeses >

   syn fetid, frowsy, funky, fusty, gamy, high, mephitic, musty, nidorous, noisome, olid, putrid, rancid, rank, reeking, reeky, ‖smellful, smelly, stale, stenchful, stenchy, stinking, stinky, strong, whiffy; *compare* ODOROUS

   rel bad, foul, offensive, nauseating, vile; decayed, decomposed, fuggy, off, rotten, spoiled, tainted; nasty, noxious, pestilential, poisonous, polluted

   con clean, deodorized, fresh

   ant fragrant, sweet

   2 *syn* see INDECOROUS

maltreat *vb syn* see ABUSE 4

‖**mam** *n syn* see MOTHER 1

mama (*or* **mamma**) *n syn* see MOTHER 1

‖**mammock** *vb syn* see DISORDER 1

mammoth *n syn* see GIANT

mammoth *adj syn* see HUGE

mammy *n syn* see MOTHER 1

man *n* 1 *syn* see HUMAN

   2 *syn* see MANKIND

   3 a male human being < just an average *man* trying to get by >

   syn ‖bloke, boy, buck, ‖cat, chap, cuss, fellow, galoot, ‖gee, gent, gentleman, guy, he, ‖mun, skate, snap, ‖stirra; *compare* HUMAN

   4 *syn* see HUSBAND

   5 *syn* see LOVER 1

   6 *syn* see POLICEMAN

manage *vb* 1 *syn* see CONDUCT 3

   rel superintend; guide

   2 *syn* see GOVERN 3

   3 *syn* see SHIFT 5

---

syn synonym(s)   *rel* related word(s)

ant antonym(s)   *con* contrasted word(s)

idiom idiomatic equivalent(s)

‖ use limited; if in doubt, see a dictionary

rel bring about, carry out, contrive, effect, execute; accomplish, achieve, succeed
idiom sink or swim on one's own
con collapse, fail, fall down; give up, poop (out)

management *n syn* see OVERSIGHT 1

manager *n syn* see EXECUTIVE
rel handler, impresario, producer

man-at-arms *n syn* see SOLDIER

mancipium *n syn* see SLAVE 1

mandarin *n syn* see BUREAUCRAT

mandate *n syn* see COMMAND 1
rel decree, fiat, imperative; authority, authorization

mandatory *adj* containing or constituting a command < *mandatory* entrance examinations >
syn compulsatory, compulsory, imperative, imperious, obligatory, required
rel essential, indispensable, irremissible, necessary, needful, requisite; binding, commanding, compelling, de rigueur; forced, involuntary
con discretionary, elective, voluntary
ant optional

maneuver *n* 1 *syn* see MEASURE 7
2 *syn* see TRICK 1
rel contrivance, device; intrigue, machination, manipulation, plot; demarche, movement, plan; finesse, subterfuge

maneuver *vb* 1 *syn* see ENGINEER
rel navigate; finesse; design
2 *syn* see HANDLE 2
rel navigate
3 *syn* see MANIPULATE 2

man Friday *n syn* see RIGHT-HAND MAN

manful *adj syn* see BRAVE 1

mangle *vb syn* see BATTER 1
rel damage, impair, injure, mar; deface, disfigure; contort, deform, distort; butcher, hack

mangled *adj syn* see LACERATED

mangy *adj syn* see SHABBY 1

manhandle *vb* to treat roughly < riot police *manhandled* innocent bystanders >
syn knock about, mishandle, rough (up), roughhouse, slap around
rel abuse, maltreat, mistreat; batter, ‖bung up, mangle, maul

mania *n syn* see FETISH 2
rel craze, enthusiasm, fancy, fascination, infatuation, passion; compulsion, fixed idea, hangup, idée fixe

maniac *adj syn* see INSANE 1
rel berserk, delirious, frantic, frenetic, frenzied, furious, rabid, raging, ranting, violent, wild

maniac *n* 1 *syn* see LUNATIC 1
2 *syn* see ENTHUSIAST

manifest *adj syn* see CLEAR 5
rel disclosed, divulged, revealed, told; evidenced, evinced, shown; noticeable, prominent
con implicit; obscure

manifest *vb* 1 *syn* see EMBODY 1
2 *syn* see SHOW 2
rel display, expose; express, utter, vent, voice
con adumbrate, shadow
ant suggest

manifold *adj* comprehending or uniting various features < a *manifold* operation >

syn diverse, diversiform, multifarious, multifold, multiform, multiplex, multivarious
rel multiphase, polymorphic, polymorphous
con homogeneous, pure, uniform; plain, simple, straightforward, uncomplex, uncomplicated

manifold *vb syn* see INCREASE 1

manikin *n syn* see DWARF

manipulate *vb* 1 *syn* see HANDLE 2
2 to control or play upon by artful, unfair, or insidious means < the sycophant cleverly *manipulated* his master >
syn beguile, exploit, finesse, jockey, maneuver, play; *compare* ENGINEER
rel machinate, use; conduct, control, direct, engineer, manage

mankind *n* the human race < all *mankind* will benefit from this new discovery >
syn flesh, Homo sapiens, humanity, humankind, man, mortality; *compare* HUMAN

manlike *adj* 1 *syn* see ANTHROPOID
2 *syn* see VIRILE 2

manly *adj* 1 *syn* see VIRILE 2
2 *syn* see BRAVE 1

man-made *adj syn* see SYNTHETIC

manner *n* 1 *syn* see HABIT 1
2 *syn* see METHOD 1
rel custom, habit, habitude, practice, usage, use, wont; form, style
3 *syn* see STYLE 4
4 *syn* see VEIN 1
rel form, turn; affectation, affectedness, mannerism; idiosyncrasy, peculiarity
5 **manners** *pl* habitual conduct or deportment in social intercourse evaluated according to some conventional standard of politeness or civility < a person with impeccable *manners* >
syn amenities, civilities, decorum(s), etiquette, mores, proprieties
rel formalities, protocol; elegancies; bearing, behavior, demeanor, deportment, mien, p's and q's; mannerliness
idiom conduct becoming a gentleman
con mannerlessness, unmannerliness

mannered *adj syn* see SELF-CONSCIOUS

mannerism *n syn* see POSE 2
rel eccentricity, idiosyncrasy; oddness, peculiarity, queerness, singularity

mannerless *adj syn* see RUDE 6
ant mannerly

mannerly *adj syn* see CIVIL 2
ant mannerless, unmannerly

manor *n* 1 *syn* see MANSION
2 *syn* see ESTATE 3

mansion *n* a large imposing residence < the governor's *mansion* >
syn castle, chateau, manor, villa
rel estate, hall, house

manslaughter *n syn* see MURDER

manslayer *n syn* see MURDERER

mantic *adj syn* see PROPHETIC

mantle *vb syn* see BLUSH

man-to-man *adj syn* see FRANK

manual *n syn* see HANDBOOK
rel abecedarium, hornbook, primer; text, textbook

manufactory *n syn* see FACTORY

manufacture *vb syn* see MAKE 3

manumit *vb syn* see FREE

ant enslave

many *adj* consisting of a goodly but indefinite number < *many* lives were lost in the flood >
syn legion, multifarious, multitudinal, multitudinous, numerous, populous, ‖several, sundry, various, voluminous
rel divers, manifold, multiple, multiplicate, multiplied, myriad; abounding, abundant, bounteous, bountiful, copious, plentiful
con meager, scant, scanty, sparse; only, sole
ant few

many *pron syn* see SUNDRY

many–sided *adj* 1 *syn* see MULTILATERAL
2 *syn* see VERSATILE

map *n* 1 *syn* see CHART 1
rel picture, portrayal; delineation, design, diagram, draft, outline, sketch, tracing
‖2 *syn* see FACE 1

map (out) *vb syn* see DESIGN 3

maquillage *n syn* see MAKEUP 3

mar *vb syn* see INJURE 1
rel bruise, scar, scratch, warp; ruin, wreck
con adorn, beautify, decorate, embellish; mend, patch, repair; amend, correct, emend, rectify, reform, revise

maraud *vb syn* see RAID 1

marauder *n* one who raids in search of plunder < *marauders* sacked village after village>
syn bandit, brigand, bummer, cateran, depredator, despoiler, forager, freebooter, looter, pillager, plunderer, raider, ravager, ravisher, sacker, spoiler, spoliator
rel buccaneer, desperado, pirate; wrecker

marblehearted *adj syn* see UNFEELING 2
ant softhearted

marbles *n pl syn* see WIT 2

march *n syn* see FRONTIER 1
rel boundary, periphery; territory; outlands, provinces

march *vb syn* see ADJOIN
rel fringe, hem, rim, skirt; extend; parallel

march *vb* 1 *syn* see AGREE 4
2 *syn* see STRIDE 1
3 *syn* see ADVANCE 5

march *n syn* see ADVANCE 2

marchland *n syn* see FRONTIER 1

mare's nest *n syn* see IMPOSTURE
rel babel, clamor, din, hubbub, hullabaloo, racket, uproar

margin *n* 1 *syn* see BORDER 1
rel frame, trimming; shore; side
2 *syn* see ROOM 3
3 *syn* see MINIMUM

margin *vb syn* see BORDER 1
rel abut, connect, join, line, neighbor, touch

marijuana *n* the dried leaves and flowering tops of the pistillate hemp plant sometimes smoked for their intoxicating effect < *marijuana* was smoked by several students at the party>
syn boo, cannabis, grass, ‖Mary Jane, moocah, pot, ‖tea, weed

rel joint, reefer; hash, hashish

marine *adj* 1 of or relating to the sea < *marine* biology >
syn maritime, oceanic, thalassic
rel hydrographic oceanographic; abyssal, bathyal, bathybic, bathysmal, benthic, dipsey, neritic, pelagic; aquatic, fluvial, fluviatile, lacustrine
2 of or relating to the navigation of the sea < *marine* charts and maps>
syn maritime, nautical, navigational
rel naval; seamanlike, seamanly; deep-sea, ocean-going, seafaring, seagoing

mariner *n* one engaged in sailing or handling a ship < the tanker crew was made up mostly of experienced *mariners*>
syn jack, jack-tar, sailor, sailorman, salt, seaman, tar, tarpaulin
rel bluejacket, gob, rating, ‖swab, ‖swabbie; ‖lascar, ‖limey; old salt, sea dog, shellback

marital *adj syn* see MATRIMONIAL

maritime *adj* 1 *syn* see MARINE 2
2 *syn* see MARINE 1

mark *n* 1 *syn* see AMBITION 2
2 *syn* see TARGET 1
3 *syn* see USE 4
4 *syn* see FOOL 3
5 *syn* see INDICATION 3
rel attribute, emblem, symbol, type; character, property, quality
6 *syn* see QUALITY 1
7 a device (as a word) pointing distinctly to the origin or ownership of merchandise to which it is applied and legally reserved to the exclusive use of the owner < the company was brought to court for illegally using the *mark* of its rival>
syn brand, logo, logotype, trademark
rel label, stamp
idiom brand name
8 *syn* see CHARACTER 1
9 *syn* see NOTICE 1

mark *vb* 1 *syn* see CHOOSE 1
2 *syn* see SHOW 5
3 *syn* see SHOW 2
4 *syn* see CHARACTERIZE 2
rel bespeak, betoken, denote, signify
idiom set apart
5 *syn* see SEE 1
rel record, register; attend, heed, regard

mark (out) *vb syn* see DEMARCATE 1
rel lay off, mark off; chart, lay out, map

mark down *vb* 1 *syn* see REDUCE 2
ant mark up
2 *syn* see DEPRECIATE 1

marked *adj syn* see NOTICEABLE
rel distinguished, noted; considerable

market *n syn* see STORE 4

market *vb* 1 *syn* see SELL 3
rel wholesale
2 *syn* see SELL 2

marketable *adj* capable of being sold < *marketable* commodities >
syn merchandisable, merchantable, salable, sellable, trafficable, vendible
rel commercial; profitable, selling; fit, good, sound, wholesome
con unmerchantable, unsalable
ant unmarketable

‖**maroon** *vb syn* see CAMP

marred *adj syn* see DAMAGED
rel banged-up, battered, bruised, mutilated; ruined, wrecked

---

syn synonym(s) *rel* related word(s)
ant antonym(s) *con* contrasted word(s)
idiom idiomatic equivalent(s)
‖ use limited; if in doubt, see a dictionary

ant unmarried

marriage *n* 1 the state of being united to a person of the opposite sex as husband or wife < *marriage* was not in the plans of this couple >
syn conjugality, connubiality, matrimony, wedlock
rel match, union
2 *syn* see WEDDING

marriage broker *n* one who arranges marriages < the old widow served as the town's *marriage broker* >
syn go-between, matchmaker
rel shadchan

marriage portion *n syn* see DOWRY

married *adj syn* see MATRIMONIAL

marrow *n syn* see ESSENCE 2
rel core, heart, kernel, meat

marrowy *adj syn* see PITHY

marry *vb* 1 to take as spouse < he *married* her for her money >
syn catch, espouse, wed
rel wive
idiom get hitched, get married, tie the knot
con annul, divorce, separate
2 to join in wedlock < the minister *married* all three daughters in one ceremony >
syn ‖hitch, mate, splice, tie, wed
idiom tie the knot, unite in marriage
3 *syn* see JOIN 1

marsh *n syn* see SWAMP

marshal *vb* 1 *syn* see ORDER 1
rel distribute, space; escort, guide, shepherd, usher
2 *syn* see MOBILIZE 3

marshland *n syn* see SWAMP

martial *adj* belonging to, engaged in, or appropriate to the affairs of war < the reviewing officer saw the company standing in *martial* array >
syn military, warlike
rel bellicose, belligerent, combative, pugnacious; aggressive, militant; high-spirited, mettlesome, spirited
con civil, civilian; irenic, pacific, peaceable, peaceful
ant unmartial

martyr *vb syn* see AFFLICT

martyrize *vb syn* see AFFLICT

marvel *n syn* see WONDER 1

marveling *n syn* see WONDER 2
rel surprise

marvelous *adj* 1 causing or exciting wonder < the way in which he could bring together opposing forces was truly *marvelous* >
syn amazing, astonishing, astounding, miraculous, prodigious, spectacular, staggering, strange, stupendous, surprising, wonderful, wondrous
rel awe-inspiring, awesome, awful, awing; incomprehensible, inconceivable, incredible, unimaginable; fabulous, phenomenal, supernatural; exceptional, extraordinary; bewildering, confounding, striking, stunning
con commonplace, ordinary, routine; blah, unexciting, uninteresting
2 superior or outstanding of its kind < had a *marvelous* weekend >
syn ‖cool, ‖dandy, divine, dreamy, ‖galluptious, glorious, groovy, hot, hunky‡dory, ‖keen, ‖neat, nifty, peachy, ripping,

sensational, super, swell, terrific, wonderful; *compare* EXCELLENT, SUPERIOR 4, SUPREME
rel agreeable, enjoyable, pleasant, pleasurable; rewarding, satisfying
con dreary, dull, humdrum, monotonous, tedious; inferior, low-grade, mean, poor, punk

‖**Mary Jane** *n syn* see MARIJUANA

mascot *n syn* see CHARM 2

masculine *adj syn* see VIRILE 2
ant effeminate, unmasculine

mash *n syn* see CLUTTER 2

mash *vb* 1 *syn* see CRUSH 2
‖2 *syn* see PRESS 1

mashed *adj syn* see ENAMORED 1

masher *n syn* see WOLF

mash note *n syn* see LOVE LETTER

mask *n* 1 a cover or partial cover for the face that has openings for the eyes and is used especially for disguise < on Halloween he wore a pirate's *mask* >
syn domino, doughface, false face, visor, vizard
rel disguise, masquerade; veil
2 an outward appearance that seeks to obscure an underlying true character < he was able to maintain a *mask* of dignity and tranquillity in his time of anxiety >
syn cloak, color, coloring, cover, disguise, disguisement, facade, face, false front, front, guise, masquerade, muffler, pretense, pretext, put-on, semblance, show, veil, veneer, window dressing; *compare* APPEARANCE 2
rel affectation, air, pose, posture; fakery, sham; dissembling, dissimulation, seeming, simulation; appearance, aspect

mask *vb syn* see DISGUISE
rel screen, secrete, veil; blur; defend, guard, protect, safeguard, shield

masquerade *n syn* see MASK 2

masquerade *vb syn* see POSE 4

mass *n* 1 *syn* see BODY 4
2 *syn* see PILE 1
3 *syn* see BULK 1
rel aggregate, aggregation, conglomerate, conglomeration; sum, whole
4 *syn* see BODY 3
5 *syn* see MUCH
6 *usu* **masses** *pl syn* see RABBLE 2

massacre *vb syn* see SLAUGHTER 3

massacre *n* the act or an instance of killing a considerable number of human beings under circumstances of atrocity or cruelty < the *massacre* of the Indians by the soldiers and settlers >
syn bloodbath, bloodshed, butchery, carnage, slaughter
rel blood purge, decimation, genocide, pogrom; internecion; assassination, killing, murder, slaying

massive *adj* 1 *syn* see HEAVY 1
rel hulking, hulky, massy
2 *syn* see HUGE
3 *syn* see MONSTROUS 1

massy *adj syn* see HUGE

master *n* 1 *syn* see EXPERT
rel maestro, savant; genius, mastermind; guru, swami
2 *syn* see LEADER 2
rel overlord, overman, overseer
3 *syn* see VICTOR 1

‖4 *syn* see HUSBAND
  5 *syn* see LOVER 1
master *vb 1 syn* see OVERCOME 1
  2 *syn* see DOMESTICATE
  rel dominate, govern, predominate, rule
  3 *syn* see CONQUER 2
  4 *syn* see LEARN 1
master *adj 1 syn* see DOMINANT 1
  2 *syn* see PROFICIENT
masterdom *n syn* see SUPREMACY
masterful *adj* 1 disposed to exercise or flaunt dictatorial authority in a way to override any protestation < the royal favorite was pompous and *masterful* when dealing with subordinates >
  syn bossy, domineering, high-handed, imperative, imperial, imperious, magisterial, overbearing, peremptory
  rel absolute, arbitrary, authoritarian, authoritative, dictative, dictatorial, doctrinaire, dogmatic; autocratic, despotic, tyrannical; high-and-mighty, self-willed
  con humble, modest, unpretentious; indecisive, irresolute; submissive, yielding; feeble, weak
  2 *syn* see PROFICIENT
  rel adroit, deft, dexterous; preeminent, superlative, supreme, transcendent
master–hand *n syn* see EXPERT
masterly *adj syn* see PROFICIENT
  rel preeminent, superlative, supreme, transcendent
masterpiece *n* 1 something done or made with extraordinary skill or brilliance < his latest work is unquestionably a *masterpiece* >
  syn chef d'oeuvre, classic, magnum opus, masterwork, tour de force
  rel objet d'art, masterstroke
  con botch, disaster, fiasco
  2 *syn* see SHOWPIECE
mastership *n syn* see ABILITY 2
masterwork *n syn* see MASTERPIECE 1
mastery *n* 1 *syn* see POWER 1
  2 *syn* see ABILITY 2
masticate *vb syn* see CHEW 1
  rel bruise, crush, macerate, mash, pulp, pulpify, smash, squash
mastodonic *adj syn* see HUGE
mat *adj syn* see DULL 7
matador *n syn* see BULLFIGHTER
match *n* 1 *syn* see OPPONENT
  2 *syn* see EQUAL
  rel analogue, parallel
  3 *syn* see MATE 5
  4 *syn* see PARALLEL
  5 *syn* see EVENT 5
  rel bout, engagement, game
match *vb* 1 *syn* see OPPOSE 1
  2 *syn* see EQUATE 2
  3 *syn* see AMOUNT 2
  rel complement, supplement
  4 *syn* see EQUAL 3
  rel compare, stack up
  idiom hold a candle to
matched *adj syn* see ASSORTED 2
  rel balanced, equated, evened, similar; coordinated, harmonized; coupled, joined, mated, paired, yoked

ant unmatched
matchless *adj syn* see ALONE 3
  ant matchable
matchmaker *n*   *syn* see MARRIAGE BROKER
mate *n* 1 *syn* see PARTNER
  2 *syn* see ACCOMPANIMENT 2
  3 *syn* see FRIEND
  rel bedmate, classmate, co-mate, helpmate, playmate, roommate, schoolmate, teammate
  4 *syn* see SPOUSE
  rel match, parti
  5 one of a pair matched in one or more qualities < the *mate* of a shoe >
  syn companion, coordinate, double, duplicate, fellow, match, reciprocal, twin
  rel alter ego, complement, sosie; compeer, equal, equivalent, peer
mate *vb syn* see MARRY 2
  rel breed, crossbreed, pair; generate, procreate
‖**mater** *n syn* see MOTHER 1
material *adj* 1 of or belonging to actuality < for him the *material* world is the only world >
  syn corporeal, gross, objective, phenomenal, physical, sensible, substantial, tangible
  rel actual, real, true; appreciable, palpable, perceptible; earthly, worldly; animal, carnal, fleshly, sensual
  con impalpable, imperceptible, intangible, unsubstantial; spiritual
  ant immaterial, nonmaterial
  2 *syn* see IMPORTANT 1
  ant immaterial
  3 *syn* see RELEVANT
  rel consequential, important, momentous, significant; cardinal, essential, fundamental, vital
  ant immaterial
material *n* 1 *syn* see THING 4
  rel component, constituent, element, ingredient; apparatus, equipment, machinery
  2 *usu* **materials** *pl syn* see EQUIPMENT
materialistic *adj* of or relating to a preoccupation with or stress upon material rather than intellectual or spiritual things < *materialistic* values characterize the modern age >
  syn banausic, earthy, mundane, sensual, temporal, worldly
  rel carnal, profane; earthly, terrestrial; secular, unspiritual
  con intellectual, mental; spiritual, unfleshly, unworldly; heavenly
materiality *n syn* see ACTUALITY 2
materialize *vb* 1 *syn* see EMBODY 1
  rel appear, emerge, loom, show; issue, rise, spring
  2 to convert mentally into something concrete < with the help of graphs and figures abstract ideas can be *materialized* >
  syn entify, hypostatize, reify
  rel actualize, pragmatize, realize; corporealize; symbolize, typify
matériel *n syn* see EQUIPMENT
matriarch *n* a dignified, usually elderly woman of some rank or authority < the local *matriarchs* controlled the town's social functions >
  syn dame, dowager, grande dame, matron

---

syn synonym(s)   *rel* related word(s)
ant antonym(s)   *con* contrasted word(s)
idiom idiomatic function(s)
‖ use limited; if in doubt, see a dictionary

rel materfamilias, mother

matrimonial *adj* of, relating to, or characteristic of marriage <the *matrimonial* bond between husband and wife>
syn conjugal, connubial, hymeneal, marital, married, nuptial, spousal, wedded
rel bridal, epithalamic

matrimony *n syn* see MARRIAGE 1

matron *n syn* see MATRIARCH

matter *n* 1 *syn* see SUBJECT 2
2 *syn* see AFFAIR 1
rel complication, grievance, to-do, worry; circumstance, predicament
3 *syn* see SUBSTANCE 2
4 *syn* see THING 4
5 *syn* see ORDER 4

matter *vb* to be of importance <being your own self is what really *matters*>
syn count, import, mean, signify, weigh
idiom carry weight

matter-of-course *adj syn* see GENERAL 1

matter-of-fact *adj* 1 *syn* see REALISTIC
rel objective, sound
2 *syn* see PROSAIC 1
3 involving no display of emotion <the *matter-of-fact* reading of the judge masked his inner anguish>
syn cold, cold-blooded, emotionless, impersonal, unimpassioned
rel unaffected, unsentimental; prosaic
con emotional, impassioned, personal
4 *syn* see IMPASSIVE 1

maturate *vb syn* see MATURE

mature *adj* 1 having attained the normal peak of natural growth and development <*mature* plants ready to bear fruit>
syn adult, full-blown, full-fledged, full‑grown, grown, grown-up, matured, ripe, ripened
rel developed, ready
idiom of age
con childish, childlike; boyish, green, juvenile, maiden, puerile, youthful
ant immature
2 *syn* see DUE 2
3 *syn* see UNPAID 2

mature *vb* to become fully developed or ripe <she *matured* as an actress after several years of summer stock>
syn age, develop, grow, grow up, maturate, mellow, ‖ripe, ripen
rel blossom, flower; advance, progress, round; season; decline, deteriorate, olden, wane
idiom come of age

matured *adj* 1 *syn* see MATURE 1
rel completed, finished; advised, considered, deliberate, designed, premeditated, studied
con callow, crude, green, raw, rough, rude, uncouth
ant premature, unmatured
2 *syn* see RIPE 3

maudlin *adj syn* see SENTIMENTAL
rel addled, befuddled, confused, fuddled, muddled; silly

maul *n syn* see BRAWL 2

maul *vb syn* see BATTER 1
rel flagellate, flail, lash, whip; bang, bash, buffet, pound; abuse, maltreat, manhandle, molest, rough (up)

maunder *vb syn* see WANDER 1

maundering *adj syn* see INARTICULATE 3

maven *n syn* see EXPERT

maverick *n syn* see BOHEMIAN

mawkish *adj syn* see SENTIMENTAL
rel banal, flat; cloying, nauseating, sickening

maxim *n* a general truth or fundamental principle usually expressed sententiously <Francis Bacon is noted for his fondness for *maxims*>
syn aphorism, apothegm, axiom, brocard, dictum, gnome, moral, rule, truism
rel commonplace, motto, platitude; law, precept, prescript; theorem; proverb
idiom rule of thumb

maximal *adj syn* see MAXIMUM
ant minimal

maximize *vb syn* see OVERPLAY 2
ant minimize

maximum *adj* greatest in quantity or highest in degree attainable or attained <apply *maximum* pressure above the point of injury>
syn maximal, outside, top, topmost, utmost; *compare* SUPREME
rel greatest, highest, largest
con least, lowest, slightest, smallest
ant minimum

maybe *adv syn* see PERHAPS

mayhem *vb syn* see MAIM

maze *n* 1 something intricately or confusingly elaborate or complicated <the landscape soon became a *maze* of superhighways>
syn jungle, knot, labyrinth, mesh, miz‑maze, morass, skein, snarl, tangle, web
rel fog, haze; gordian knot; conglomeration, hodgepodge, miscellany, mishmash
‖2 *syn* see HAZE 2

‖**mazuma** *n syn* see MONEY

MD *n syn* see PHYSICIAN

meager *adj* 1 *syn* see LEAN
2 being smaller than what is normal, necessary, or desirable <the remains of dinner provided only a *meager* meal that evening>
syn exiguous, poor, scant, scanty, scrimp, scrimpy, skimp, skimpy, spare, sparse; *compare* SHORT 3
rel deficient, inadequate, insufficient; inappreciable, inconsiderable, slight; bare, mere, minimum; miserable, shabby
con adequate, enough, sufficient; appreciable, considerable; copious, plentiful
ant ample

meal *n* the portion of food taken at one time to satisfy appetite <the noonday dinner was the big *meal* of the day in those times>
syn ‖chow, feed, refection, repast
rel feast, spread; refreshment, regalement; collation, snack; fare, grub, meat, mess, victuals; board, table

meal *vb syn* see EAT 1

mean *adj* 1 *syn* see IGNOBLE 1
ant wellborn
2 *syn* see INFERIOR 2
3 *syn* see LITTLE 2
4 *syn* see CONTEMPTIBLE
5 *syn* see CHEAP 2
6 *syn* see STINGY
7 *syn* see TROUBLESOME

rel difficult, formidable, rough, rugged, tough

8 *syn* see UNWELL

mean *vb* **1** *syn* see INTEND 2

rel desire, want, wish

2 to convey (as an idea) to the mind <your answer *means* nothing to me>

syn add up (to), connote, denote, express, import, intend, signify, spell

rel designate, name; attest, betoken, indicate; hint, intimate, suggest

3 *syn* see MATTER

mean *n* **1** *syn* see AVERAGE

2 *usu* **means** *sing or pl in constr* one by which work is accomplished or an end effected <careful planning is a major *means* of improving output> <use any *means* to secure peace>

syn agency, agent, channel, instrument, instrumentality, instrumentation, intermediary, medium, ministry, organ, vehicle

rel fashion, manner, method, mode, system, way; apparatus, equipment, machinery, paraphernalia

3 *means* *pl* one's total property including real property and intangibles <people of moderate *means* are feeling the effects of inflation worse>

syn assets, capital, resources, wealth

rel finances, fortune, funds, moneybags, pocket, purse; ||bundle, nest egg, pile, reserves, savings; estate, holdings, possessions; intangibles

mean *adj* **1** *syn* see MIDDLE 2

2 *syn* see MEDIUM

meander *vb* *syn* see WANDER 1

rel snake, turn, twist, wind

meanderer *n* *syn* see ROVER

meandering *adj* *syn* see WINDING

meandrous *adj* *syn* see WINDING

meaning *n* **1** the idea that something conveys to the mind <critics have endlessly debated the *meaning* of the poem>

syn acceptation, import, intendment, intent, message, purport, sense, significance, significancy, signification, sum and substance, understanding; *compare* SUBSTANCE 2, TENOR 1

rel drift, effect, essence, tenor; force, point, value; hint, implication, intimation, suggestion; connotation, denotation, definition

2 *syn* see INTENTION

meaningful *adj* **1** *syn* see EXPRESSIVE

ant meaningless

2 *syn* see IMPORTANT 1

meaningless *adj* **1** *syn* see SENSELESS 5

rel blank, empty, vacant

ant meaningful

2 *syn* see FECKLESS 1

measly *adj* *syn* see PETTY 2

measure *n* **1** *syn* see RATION

2 *syn* see TEMPERANCE 1

3 *syn* see SIZE 1

4 *syn* see MELODY

5 *syn* see RHYTHM

6 *syn* see STANDARD 3

7 an action planned or taken toward the accomplishment of a purpose <developed a new set of safety *measures*>

syn maneuver, move, procedure, proceeding, step

rel effort, project, proposal, proposition; expedient, makeshift, resort, resource, shift, stopgap

measure *vb* **1** *syn* see DEMARCATE 1

2 to ascertain the quantity, mass, extent, or degree of in terms of a standard unit or fixed amount <*measure* the depth of the water>

syn gauge, scale

rel size, size up; calculate, compute, estimate, figure, reckon

measure (out) *vb* *syn* see DISTRIBUTE 1

measureless *adj* **1** *syn* see INCALCULABLE 1

ant measurable

2 *syn* see LIMITLESS

ant measurable

measure up *vb* *syn* see EQUAL 3

meat *n* **1** *syn* see FOOD 1

2 *syn* see SUBSTANCE 2

meathead *n* *syn* see OAF 2

meaty *adj* *syn* see PITHY

mechanical *adj* *syn* see PERFUNCTORY

meddle *vb* to concern oneself with officiously, impertinently, or indiscreetly <continually *meddling* in other people's affairs>

syn busybody, butt in, fool, horn in, interfere, interlope, intermeddle, ||make, mess around, monkey (with), tamper (with)

rel intervene, intrude, invade, obtrude; pry, snoop, trespass

idiom put (*or* shove *or* stick) one's oar in, stick one's nose into

con disregard, ignore, neglect, omit, overlook, slight; avoid, eschew, shun

meddler *n* *syn* see BUSYBODY

meddlesome *adj* *syn* see IMPERTINENT 2

Meddlesome Mattie *n* *syn* see BUSYBODY

medial *adj* **1** *syn* see MIDDLE 1

2 *syn* see MIDDLE 2

3 *syn* see MEDIUM

median *n* *syn* see AVERAGE

rel center, middle

median *adj* **1** *syn* see MIDDLE 1

2 *syn* see MIDDLE 2

mediate *vb* *syn* see INTERPOSE 2

mediator *n* **1** *syn* see GO-BETWEEN 2

rel arbitrator, judge; conciliator, peacemaker; negotiator, troubleshooter

2 *syn* see MODERATOR

medical *n* *syn* see PHYSICIAN

medicament *n* *syn* see REMEDY 1

medicant *n* *syn* see REMEDY 1

medication *n* *syn* see REMEDY 1

medicinal *n* *syn* see DRUG 1

medicine *n* *syn* see REMEDY 1

mediciner *n* *syn* see PHYSICIAN

medico *n* *syn* see PHYSICIAN

mediocre *adj* *syn* see MEDIUM

rel bad, inferior, poor; common, commonplace, ordinary, unexceptional

idiom no great shakes, nothing to write home about

meditate *vb* *syn* see PONDER 1

meditative *adj* **1** *syn* see THOUGHTFUL 1

---

syn synonym(s)   *rel* related word(s)
ant antonym(s)   *con* contrasted word(s)
idiom idiomatic equivalent(s)
|| use limited; if in doubt, see a dictionary

rel musing, ruminant; wistful

2 *syn* see PENSIVE 2

medium *adj* midway between the extremes of a scale, measurement, or evaluation < bought a suit of *medium* quality >
syn average, fair, fairish, indifferent, intermediate, mean, medial, mediocre, middle‑rate, middling, moderate, run-of-mine, run-of-the-mill, so-so
rel median, par; passable, tolerable; neutral; popular, vulgar; normal, standard
idiom fair to middling
con inferior, low-grade, poor; excellent, first-class, high-grade, prime, superior

medium *n* **1** *syn* see MEAN 2
rel intermediate, intermedium

2 *syn* see ENVIRONMENT

3 *syn* see FORTE

medley *n* *syn* see MISCELLANY 1

‖**meech** *vb* *syn* see SNEAK

meed *n* **1** *syn* see REWARD
rel recompensing, satisfaction

2 *syn* see RATION
rel desert, due, merit

meek *adj* *syn* see HUMBLE 1
rel gentle, mild; tame; forbearing, lenient, tolerant; long-suffering, patient
con high-spirited, mettlesome, spirited, spunky; contumacious, insubordinate, rebellious
ant arrogant

meet *vb* **1** *syn* see HAPPEN 2

2 *syn* see CONFRONT 1

3 *syn* see ENGAGE 5
rel brave, oppose

4 *syn* see EQUAL 3

5 *syn* see SATISFY 5
rel approach, equal, match, rival, tie, touch

6 to come together face-to-face or as if face-to-face < the two leaders agreed to *meet* in a series of summit talks >
syn close, encounter, face, front; *compare* CONFRONT 1
rel accost, greet, salute; bump, clash, collide, cross; grapple, tussle, wrestle; experience, suffer, sustain, undergo
con elude, escape, evade, shun
ant avoid

7 *syn* see CONVERGE

8 *syn* see CONVENE 1

meet (with) *vb* *syn* see FIND 1

meet *n* **1** *syn* see EVENT 5

2 *syn* see CONTEST 2

meet *adj* **1** *syn* see FIT 1
rel accommodated, conformed, reconciled; good, right; equitable, fair, just
ant unmeet

2 *syn* see GOOD 2
ant unmeet

meeting *n* **1** *syn* see CONTEST 2

2 *syn* see CONCOURSE

3 *syn* see TALK 4
rel congress, moot

meetness *n* *syn* see ORDER 11
ant unmeetness

megacosm *n* *syn* see UNIVERSE
ant microcosm

megrim *n* *syn* see CAPRICE
rel impulse, urge

melancholic *adj* *syn* see SAD 2

melancholy *n* *syn* see SADNESS

rel miserableness, misery, wretchedness; despair, desperation; boredom, ennui, tedium
con hopefulness, optimism
ant exhilaration

melancholy *adj* **1** *syn* see SAD 1

2 expressing or suggesting sorrow or mourning < the gloomy day led him to a *melancholy* train of thought >
syn doleful, dolesome, dolorous, lamentable, lugubrious, moanful, mournful, plaintive, rueful, sighful, sorrowful, wailful, woeful; *compare* SAD 1, SAD 2
rel pensive, reflective, thoughtful; discomposing, disquieting, disturbing, perturbing; dismal, dreary, funereal, gloomy, lachrymose, somber, sombrous
con cheerful, glad, happy, joyful, joyous, lighthearted; gay, lively, vivacious

3 *syn* see SAD 2

mélange *n* *syn* see MISCELLANY 1

meld *vb* *syn* see MIX 1

melding *n* *syn* see UNIFICATION

melee *n* **1** *syn* see CLASH 2
rel dogfight, scuffle

2 *syn* see BRAWL 2

3 *syn* see MISCELLANY 1

meliorate *vb* *syn* see IMPROVE 1

melisma *n* *syn* see MELODY

mellay *n* **1** *syn* see BRAWL 2

2 *syn* see CLASH 2

mellifluent *adj* *syn* see MELLIFLUOUS

mellifluous *adj* having a smooth rich flow < his *mellifluous* voice held his audience in a trance >
syn golden, honeyed, Hyblaean, liquid, mellifluent, mellow; *compare* MELODIOUS 1
rel accordant, canorous, euphonic, euphonious, harmonious, mellisonant, silvery; golden-tongued, silver-tongued; dulcet, sweet; resonant, sonorous
con blatant, boisterous, clamorous, obstreperous, strident, vociferous; discordant, grating, harsh

mellisonant *adj* *syn* see MELODIOUS 1

mellow *adj* **1** *syn* see RIPE 3

2 *syn* see MELLIFLUOUS

mellow *vb* *syn* see MATURE

melodia *n* *syn* see MELODY

melodic *adj* **1** *syn* see MELODIOUS 2

2 *syn* see MELODIOUS 1

melodious *adj* **1** pleasing to the ear < *melodious* sounds of the forest >
syn dulcet, euphonic, euphonious, mellisonant, melodic, sweet, tuneful; *compare* MELLIFLUOUS
rel canorous, harmonious
con discordant, grating, harsh
ant unmelodious

2 containing, constituting, or characterized by melody < his voice shows marked improvement and a new richly *melodious* quality >
syn melodic, musical, songful, tuned, tuneful
rel cantabile, lyric, melic

melody *n* a rhythmic succession of single tones organized as an aesthetic whole < took out his flute and played a simple *melody* >
syn air, descant, diapason, lay, measure, melisma, melodia, strain, tune, warble; *compare* SONG 2

rel song; bel canto, canto, vocalise; lyrics

melt *vb 1 syn* see LIQUEFY
rel heat, warm
con coagulate, harden, set
ant freeze; solidify
2 *syn* see BURN 3
rel perspire, sweat

member *n syn* see PART 1

memento *n 1 syn* see REMEMBRANCE 3
2 *syn* see VESTIGE 1

memo *n 1 syn* see NOTE 2
2 *syn* see MEMORANDUM 2

memoir *n 1 syn* see BIOGRAPHY
rel anecdote; memory, recollection, remembrance, reminiscence
2 *syn* see DISCOURSE 2

memoirist *n syn* see BIOGRAPHER

memorable *adj syn* see NOTEWORTHY
rel momentous, rememberable; deathless,
unfadable, unforgettable
ant unmemorable

memorandum *n 1 syn* see NOTE 2
2 a communication that contains directive,
advisory, or informative matter < the
memorandum announced the holiday
schedule >
syn directive, memo, notice
rel announcement, dispatch, minute; epistle, letter, missive, note; reminder, tickler;
message; diary

memorial *adj* serving to preserve remembrance < a *memorial* plaque >
syn commemorative, commemoratory
rel celebrative, consecrative, dedicatory,
enshrining

memorial *n 1 syn* see REMEMBRANCE 3
2 *syn* see MONUMENT 2

memorialize *vb 1 syn* see ADDRESS 4
2 to record or honor the memory of by or
as if by a monument < the new library
memorializes the late President >
syn commemorate, monument, monumentalize
rel etch, grave, impress, imprint; jog,
nudge, remind
idiom bring to mind, fix in the (*or* one's)
mind (*or* memory), impress on one's mind,
treasure in one's heart
con forget, neglect, overlook

memorial park *n syn* see CEMETERY

memorize *vb* to commit to memory < the
actors hadn't even *memorized* their lines >
syn con, get, learn
rel study
idiom get (*or* learn) by heart, get (*or*
learn) word for word
con forget

memory *n 1* the power or process of reproducing or recalling what has been
learned < blessed with a good *memory* >
syn recollection, remembrance, reminiscence
rel reflection, retrospection; retention,
retentiveness; mind, recall; mind's eye;
awareness, cognizance, consciousness
con forgetfulness, obliviousness, unmindfulness; lethe, oblivion
2 a particular act of recalling < her *memory* of her wedding day remains vivid >

syn anamnesis, recall, recollection, remembrance, reminiscence
rel memento, souvenir

menace *vb 1 syn* see THREATEN
rel alarm, frighten, scare; endanger, torment; loom, lower
2 *syn* see ENDANGER

menacing *adj syn* see IMMINENT 2

ménage *n syn* see FAMILY 2
rel ménage à trois

mend *vb 1 syn* see CORRECT 1
2 to put into good shape or working order again < *mends* garments in her spare
time >
syn doctor, do up, fix, overhaul, patch,
rebuild, recondition, reconstruct, repair,
revamp, ||right, ||rightle, vamp
rel condition, ready, service; refurbish,
rejuvenate, renew, renovate, restore; correct, emend, rectify, redress, reform; heal
3 *syn* see IMPROVE 3

mendacious *adj syn* see DISHONEST
rel false, wrong; erroneous, fallacious,
spurious; equivocating, fibbing, paltering,
prevaricating
ant veracious

mendaciousness *n syn* see MENDACITY
ant veraciousness, veracity

mendacity *n* the practice or an instance of
lying < he was ultimately caught by his
own outrageous *mendacity* >
syn falsehood, fibbery, mendaciousness,
truthlessness, untruthfulness, unveracity
rel boggling, caviling, dodging, equivocation, hedging, quibbling, shifting, sidestepping
ant veraciousness, veracity

mendicancy *n* the practice or act of begging < the city passed an ordinance
against *mendicancy* >
syn beggary, bumming, cadging, mendicity, mooching, panhandling
rel sponging

mendicity *n syn* see MENDICANCY

menial *adj syn* see SUBSERVIENT 2

mental *adj 1* of or relating to the mind
< the *mental* aspects of the problem >
syn cerebral, intellective, intellectual,
psychic, psychical, psychological
rel immaterial, inner, spiritual; telepathic;
intelligent, rational, reasoning, thinking;
ideological
con bodily, corporal, corporeal, physical,
somatic; perceptive; sensual, sensuous
||2 *syn* see INSANE 1

mentality *n syn* see INTELLIGENCE 1

mention *vb* to refer to someone or something in a clear unmistakable manner
< several donors were *mentioned* in the
article >
syn cite, instance, name, specify
rel denominate, designate; detail; advert,
allude, refer; quote
idiom make mention of
con disregard, ignore, neglect, overlook,
pass by, pass over, slight

menu *n* a list of the dishes that may be
ordered (as at a restaurant) or that are to
be served (as at a banquet) < hoped to
find something tasty on the *menu* > < he
saved the elaborate *menu* as a souvenir of
the awards banquet >
syn card, carte du jour

---

syn synonym(s)   *rel* related word(s)
ant antonym(s)   *con* contrasted word(s)
idiom idiomatic equivalent(s)
|| use limited; if in doubt, see a dictionary

idiom bill of fare

Mephistophelian *adj syn* see SATANIC 1

mephitic *adj* **1** *syn* see MALODOROUS 1
2 *syn* see POISONOUS

mercenary *n syn* see HACK 2

mercenary *adj syn* see CORRUPT 2
ant unmercenary

merchandisable *adj syn* see MARKET-
ABLE
ant unmerchantable, unsalable

merchandise *n* the products that are
bought and sold in business < *merchandise* of inferior quality>
syn commodities, goods, line, vendible(s),
wares
rel effects; job lot, stock; staples

merchandise *vb syn* see SELL 3
rel advertise, publicize

merchandiser *n syn* see MERCHANT

merchant *n* a buyer and seller of commodities for profit < a *merchant* of dry
goods>
syn businessman, dealer, merchandiser,
trader, tradesman, trafficker
rel jobber, retailer, wholesaler

merchantable *adj syn* see MARKETABLE
ant unmerchantable, unsalable

merchant prince *n syn* see MAGNATE

merciful *adj syn* see FORBEARING
rel compassionate, pitiful, softhearted;
benign, kind, kindly; condoning, forgiving,
pardoning
ant merciless, unmerciful

mercifulness *n syn* see FORBEARANCE 2
rel commiseration, pity, ruth
con severeness, severity, sternness
ant mercilessness, unmercifulness

merciless *adj* **1** *syn* see PITILESS
ant merciful
2 *syn* see GRIM 3
rel compassionless, cutthroat, pitiless;
gratuitous, uncalled-for, wanton
con charitable, lenient, tolerant; easy,
easygoing
ant merciful

mercurial *adj syn* see INCONSTANT 1
rel buoyant, effervescent, elastic, expansive, resilient; mobile, movable; adroit,
clever, cunning, ingenious
ant saturnine

mercy *n* a show of or a disposition to
show kindness or compassion < the *mercy*
of the Lord knows all seasons>
syn caritas, charity, clemency, grace,
lenity; *compare* FORBEARANCE 2
rel commiseration, compassion, pity,
ruth; benevolence, benignancy, benignity,
kindliness, kindness; generosity, goodwill
con reprisal, retaliation, retribution, revenge, vengeance; castigation, chastening,
chastisement, punishment

mere *adj syn* see VERY 4

merely *adv syn* see JUST 3

meretricious *adj syn* see GAUDY
rel deceptive, delusive, delusory, misleading, spurious; insincere

meretrix *n syn* see PROSTITUTE

merge *vb syn* see MIX 1

mergence *n syn* see UNIFICATION

merger *n* **1** *syn* see CONSOLIDATION 2
2 *syn* see UNIFICATION

merging *n syn* see UNIFICATION

meridian *n syn* see APEX 2

merit *n* **1** *syn* see EXCELLENCE
ant fault
2 *syn* see QUALITY 2
3 *syn* see DUE 1
rel gaining(s), winning(s)

merit *vb syn* see EARN 2
rel award, reward; recompense, repay,
requite; entitle, justify, warrant

meritable *adj syn* see WORTHY 1
ant meritless

merited *adj syn* see JUST 3
rel entitled, justified, warranted
ant unmerited

meritorious *adj syn* see WORTHY 1

merriment *n* **1** *syn* see MIRTH
2 *syn* see MERRYMAKING

merry *adj* indicative of or marked by high
spirits or lightheartedness < the *merry* life
of the town folk was a joy to see>
syn blithe, blithesome, boon, festive, gay,
gleeful, jocund, jolly, jovial, lighthearted,
mirthful, riant
rel animated, lively, sprightly, vivacious;
cheerful, glad, happy, joyful, joyous; hilarious, mad, unconstrained, wild
con gloomy, glum, melancholy; grave,
sober, somber; earnest, sedate, serious,
staid

merry–andrew *n syn* see CLOWN 3

merrymaking *n* gay or festive activity < a
night of *merrymaking*>
syn festivity, gaiety, jollity, merriment,
revel, reveling, revelment, revelry,
whoopee
rel enjoyment, indulgence, pleasure, self=
indulgence

mesh *n* **1** *usu* **meshes** *pl syn* see WEB 2
2 *syn* see MAZE 1
rel net, network

mesh *vb syn* see ENGAGE 1

meshuggaas *n syn* see NONSENSE 2

mesmeric *adj syn* see ATTRACTIVE 1

mesmerize *vb syn* see ENTHRALL 2
rel entrance, hypnotize

mess *n* ‖**1** *syn* see MUCH
2 *syn* see EYESORE
3 a confused or disordered state, condition, or situation < upon becoming president, he proceeded to make a *mess* of the
government>
syn botch, botchery, hash, mess-up, mix=
up, muddle, mull, muss, shambles; *compare* MISCELLANY 1
rel confusion, disorder; wreck, wreckage
idiom kettle of fish

mess *vb* **1** *syn* see BOTCH
rel confuse, disorder, jumble
idiom make a mess of
2 *syn* see FIDDLE 2

mess (up) *vb syn* see DISORDER 1
rel damage, mar, ruin, spoil; ‖muck,
mucker, muff

message *n* **1** something (as information)
conveyed by writing, speech, or signals
< left a *message* before he went out>
syn communication, directive, word
rel communiqué, dispatch, report; memo,
memorandum; epistle, letter, missive, note
2 *syn* see MEANING 1

mess around *vb* **1** *syn* see FIDDLE 2
2 *syn* see MEDDLE
3 *syn* see PHILANDER

messenger *n* one who bears a message or does an errand < blamed the *messenger* for the bad news he brought >
syn bearer, carrier, courier, emissary, envoy, internuncio
rel herald; go-between, intermediary, mediator; dispatcher, post

mess–up *n syn see* MESS 3

messy *adj* 1 *syn see* SLOVENLY 1
rel dirty, grimy, grubby
con clean
ant neat
2 *syn see* SLIPSHOD 3

metagrobolize *vb syn see* PUZZLE

metamorphize *vb syn see* TRANSFORM

metamorphose *vb syn see* TRANSFORM
rel age, develop, mature, ripen

metanoia *n syn see* CONVERSION 1

metaphor *n syn see* ANALOGY 2
rel comparison, trope; allegory, personification
idiom figure of speech

metaphysical *adj* 1 *syn see* IMMATERIAL 1
rel supernatural, transcendent, transcendental
2 *syn see* SUPERNATURAL 1

mete (out) *vb* 1 *syn see* ADMINISTER 2
rel measure
2 *syn see* ALLOT

meter *n syn see* RHYTHM

method *n* 1 the means or procedures used in attaining an end < he claimed that his ends justified his *methods* >
syn fashion, manner, mode, modus, system, technique, way, wise
rel design, plan, schema, scheme; form, style; course, line; modus operandi, practice, procedure, process, routine; wrinkle
2 *syn see* ORDER 8

methodic *adj syn see* ORDERLY 1
ant desultory, unmethodical

methodical *adj syn see* ORDERLY 1
rel methodized, organized, systematized; analytical, logical; careful, meticulous, scrupulous
con casual, hit-or-miss, random; confused, jumbled
ant desultory, unmethodical

methodize *vb syn see* ORDER 1
rel establish, fix, set, settle

meticulous *adj syn see* CAREFUL 2
rel fastidious, pernickety, picky; cautious, strict, thorough; microscopic

métier *n* 1 *syn see* TRADE 1
2 *syn see* FORTE

metropolitan *adj syn see* COSMOPOLITAN 1

mettle *n syn see* COURAGE

mettlesome *adj syn see* SPIRITED 2
rel edgy, excitable, high-strung, skittish, startlish

mew *vb syn see* ENCLOSE 1

Mickey Mouse *adj syn see* PETTY 2

mid *adj* 1 *syn see* MIDDLE 2
2 *syn see* MIDDLE 1

mid *prep* 1 *syn see* AMID 1
2 *syn see* AMONG 1

3 *syn see* DURING

middle *adj* 1 equally distant from the extremes < the *middle* finger >
syn center, centermost, equidistant, halfway, medial, median, mid, middlemost, midmost
2 being at neither extreme < paid a *middle* price for it >
syn center, central, intermediary, intermediate, mean, medial, median, mid

middle *n syn see* CENTER 1

middlebrow *n syn see* PHILISTINE

middleman *n syn see* GO-BETWEEN 2

middlemost *adj syn see* MIDDLE 1

middle–of–the–road *adj syn see* MODERATE 4

middle–rate *adj syn see* MEDIUM

middle–road *adj syn see* MODERATE 4

middling *adj syn see* MEDIUM
rel inferior, poor, second-rate

midge *n syn see* DWARF

midget *n syn see* DWARF

midget *adj syn see* TINY

midmost *adj syn see* MIDDLE 1

midpoint *n syn see* CENTER 1

midst *n syn see* CENTER 1

midst *prep* 1 *syn see* AMID 1
2 *syn see* AMONG 1
3 *syn see* DURING

mid–Victorian *n syn see* FOGY
rel bluenose, goody-goody, Mrs. Grundy, prig, prude, puritan; Victorian

mien *n* 1 *syn see* BEARING 1
rel expression, manner, mannerism
2 *syn see* APPEARANCE 1

miff *n* 1 *syn see* OFFENSE 2
rel conniption, fit
2 *syn see* QUARREL

might *n* 1 *syn see* POWER 1
2 *syn see* POWER 4
rel energeticness, lustiness, strenuousness, vigor, vigorousness; forcefulness, forcibleness, powerfulness
3 *syn see* ABILITY 1
4 *syn see* MUSCLE 1

might and main *adv syn see* HARD 1

mightily *adv* 1 *syn see* HARD 1
rel arduously, laboriously, strenuously, toilsomely
2 *syn see* VERY 1

mighty *adj* 1 *syn see* POWERFUL 2
2 *syn see* STRONG 1
3 *syn see* HUGE
rel eminent, illustrious, renowned; august, grand, imposing, impressive, moving

mighty *adv syn see* VERY 1

migrant *adj syn see* MIGRATORY

migrant *n syn see* EMIGRANT
rel in-migrant, out-migrant; drifter, mover, nomad, traveler, wanderer

migrate *vb* to move from one country, place, or locality to another < his father had *migrated* to the Far West years before >
syn emigrate, transmigrate
rel immigrate, in-migrate, out-migrate, remigrate; drift, trek; nomadize, range, roam, rove, wander

migrative *adj syn see* MIGRATORY
ant nonmigratory

migratorial *adj syn see* MIGRATORY
ant nonmigratory

---

syn synonym(s)   *rel* related word(s)
ant antonym(s)   *con* contrasted word(s)
idiom idiomatic equivalent(s)
‖ use limited; if in doubt, see a dictionary

migratory adj moving habitually or occasionally from one region or climate to another <the study of *migratory* birds>
syn migrant, migrative, migratorial, mobile, transmigratory
rel errant, nomad, nomadic, ranging, roving, wandering
ant nonmigratory

mild adj 1 *syn* see GENTLE 1
rel choice, dainty, delicate, exquisite; moderate, temperate; benign, benignant
con intense, severe, sharp, vehement
ant fierce, harsh
2 *syn* see AMIABLE 1
rel docile, meek; subdued, submissive; deferential, obeisant, subservient

milepost n *syn* see EVENT 2
milestone n *syn* see EVENT 2
milieu n *syn* see ENVIRONMENT
militant adj 1 *syn* see BELLIGERENT
rel martial, military
2 *syn* see AGGRESSIVE
military adj *syn* see MARTIAL
rel chauvinistic, jingoistic, militaristic, warmongering; soldierlike, soldierly
ant unmilitary
military n *syn* see TROOP 2
militate vb *syn* see WEIGH 3
milk vb 1 *syn* see FLEECE 1
rel exact, exploit, extort; drain, empty, exhaust, pump, suck, wring
2 *syn* see EDUCE 1
milk-and-water adj *syn* see INSIPID 3
milk-livered adj *syn* see COWARDLY
milksop n *syn* see WEAKLING
rel effeminate; coward
milk-warm adj *syn* see TEPID 1
mill n *syn* see FACTORY
million n *syn* see SCAD
millstone n *syn* see LOAD 3
Milquetoast n *syn* see WEAKLING
mime n *syn* see ACTOR 1
mimic n *syn* see ACTOR 1
mimic vb to copy or exaggerate (as manner or gestures) often by way of mockery <*mimicked* her halting speech>
syn ape, burlesque, imitate, mock, parody, take off, travesty
rel hit off, mime, mum; act, do, enact, impersonate, perform, personate, play; copycat; pantomime
mimicry n the art or practice of closely imitating another in speech, gestures, or manners <engaged in *mimicry* of café society>
syn apery
rel imitation, mimesis, mimetism; mock, mockery; caricature, parody
miminy-piminy adj *syn* see NICE 1
mince vb 1 *syn* see CHOP 2
2 *syn* see SASHAY
mincing adj *syn* see GENTEEL 3
rel dainty, delicate, fastidious, finical, finicking, finicky, fussy, nice, particular, pernickety, persnickety, squeamish
‖**mincy** adj *syn* see NICE 1
mind n 1 the element or complex of elements in an individual that feels, perceives, thinks, wills, and especially reasons <sad to see such a *mind* dulled by drink and drugs>
syn brain, gray matter, head, ‖upper story, ‖upperworks, wit

rel brainpower, intellect, intelligence; consciousness, mentality; faculty, function, power
2 *syn* see WILL 1
rel disposition, temper, temperament
con aversion, disinclination, indisposition
3 *syn* see WIT 2
4 *syn* see OPINION
5 *syn* see MOOD 1
‖6 *syn* see NOTICE 1
mind vb ‖1 *syn* see REMEMBER
‖2 *syn* see ENJOY 1
3 *syn* see SEE 1
‖4 *syn* see INTEND 2
5 *syn* see OBEY
6 *syn* see LOOK 1
7 *syn* see BEWARE
8 *syn* see TEND 2
rel oversee, superintend, supervise; discipline, govern
con forget, slight
9 *syn* see CONSIDER 1
minded adj *syn* see WILLING 1
rel contemplating, intending, planning, purposing
mindful adj 1 *syn* see AWARE
ant unmindful
2 inclined to be aware <*mindful* of the ever-changing social scene>
syn heedful, observant, observative, observing, regardful, thoughtful
rel attentive, conscientious; aware, cognizant, conscious, conversant, sensible; alert, vigilant, watchful
con heedless, inattentive
ant mindless, unmindful
mindless adj 1 *syn* see SIMPLE 3
2 *syn* see INSANE 1
mine n *syn* see BONANZA
rel lode, quarry, vein; spring, well, wellspring
mine vb to dig into for the purpose of obtaining items of use or value <*mined* manuscripts looking for undiscovered masterpieces>
syn delve, quarry
rel burrow, drill, excavate, sap, scoop; work
mingle vb 1 *syn* see MIX 1
2 *syn* see SOCIALIZE
mingle-mangle n *syn* see MISCELLANY 1
mingy adj *syn* see STINGY
miniature n *syn* see MODEL 1
miniature adj *syn* see TINY
rel small-scale, subminiature
con large-scale
minify vb *syn* see ABRIDGE 1
rel dwarf, miniaturize, shrink
minikin adj *syn* see TINY
minim n *syn* see PARTICLE
minimal adj constituting the least possible <*minimal* differences of opinion>
syn minimum
rel littlest, lowest, slightest, smallest; basal, basic, essential, fundamental
con maximum, topmost, utmost; greatest, highest, largest, most
ant maximal
minimize vb *syn* see DECRY 2
rel dwarf, reduce
ant magnify, maximize
minimum n the least quantity assignable, admissible, or possible <testing the use of a *minimum* of security at the prison>

syn margin

rel dab, hair, iota, jot, modicum, particle, pittance, smidgen, speck, whit

con abundance, bushel(s), gob(s), ‖lashings, load(s), lot(s), mass(es), much, oodles, profusion, scads, slather(s), ton(s), world(s)

ant maximum

minimum *adj syn* see MINIMAL

ant maximum

minion *n syn* see SYCOPHANT

minister *n syn* see CLERGYMAN

minister (to) *vb* to attend to the wants and comforts of someone < *minister* to the sick and dying >

syn care (for), mother, nurse, serve, wait (on)

rel cure, heal, remedy; doctor, treat; pander

ministerial *adj syn* see INSTRUMENTAL

minister plenipotentiary *n syn* see ENVOY 1

ministry *n syn* see MEAN 2

minor *adj* 1 *syn* see LITTLE 3

rel dependent; inferior, piddling, trifling; junior, lower

con meaningful, significant

ant major

2 lower in standing or reputation than others of the same class < a *minor* poet of the late eighteenth century >

syn dinky, insignificant, lesser, minor-league, secondary, small, small-fry, small-time

rel average, fair, indifferent, mediocre, medium, middling, second-rate, undistinguished, unnoticeable; trivial, unimportant

con chief, foremost, leading, principal

ant major

minor *n syn* see INFANT 2

minority *n syn* see INFANCY 2

ant majority

minor–league *adj syn* see MINOR 2

minstrel *n syn* see BARD 1

rel balladist, singer, wait

mint *n syn* see FORTUNE 4

mint *adj syn* see BRAND-NEW

rel intact, original, perfect, unmarred

minus *prep syn* see WITHOUT 2

ant plus

minute *n syn* see INSTANT 1

minute *adj* 1 *syn* see TINY

2 *syn* see LITTLE 3

3 *syn* see CIRCUMSTANTIAL

rel careful, meticulous, punctilious, scrupulous

con abstract; general, universal; comprehending, comprehensive, embracing, embracive, including, inclusive

minutely *adj syn* see CONTINUAL

minutia *n, usu* **minutiae** *pl* 1 *syn* see INS AND OUTS

2 *syn* see TRIVIA

minx *n* a pert girl < her rivals called her a brazen *minx* >

syn hussy, jade, malapert, saucebox, slut, snip

rel broad, brat, upstart; baggage, chippy, drab, floozy, strumpet, tart, trollop, trull

miracle *n syn* see WONDER 1

miraculous *adj* 1 *syn* see SUPERNATURAL 1

2 *syn* see MARVELOUS 1

con natural, normal

mirage *n syn* see DELUSION 1

mire *n syn* see SWAMP

rel muck

mire *vb* 1 *syn* see DELAY 1

rel bemire, sink; adhere, cleave, cling, cohere, stick; enmesh, ensnare, entangle, entrap, involve, snare, trap

2 *syn* see INVOLVE 1

mirror *n* 1 a polished or smooth surface (as of glass) that forms images by reflection < spent hours looking at herself in the *mirror* >

syn glass, looking glass, ‖seeing glass

rel cheval glass, pier glass, reflector, speculum

2 *syn* see MODEL 2

mirror *vb* 1 *syn* see REFLECT 1

2 *syn* see REPRESENT 2

mirth *n* a mood or temper characterized by joy and high spirits and usually manifested in laughter and merrymaking < a man of contentment, but seldom of *mirth* >

syn glee, hilarity, jocularity, jocundity, jollity, joviality, merriment

rel cheer, cheerfulness, joyfulness, light-heartedness; gladness, happiness; frivolity, levity

con blues, dejection, depression, dumps, gloom, sadness; boredom, ennui, tedium; anguish, misery, woe; infelicity, wretchedness

ant melancholy

mirthful *adj syn* see MERRY

ant mirthless

miry *adj syn* see MUDDY 1

misadventure *n* 1 *syn* see DISASTER

2 *syn* see ACCIDENT 2

rel blunder, boner, bull, error, faux pas, howler, lapse, slip

misanthropic *adj syn* see ANTISOCIAL

rel misogynic

con altruistic, benevolent, charitable, humane, humanitarian

ant philanthropic

misapply *vb syn* see ABUSE 2

rel misappropriate, misdirect, mismanage

misapprehend *vb* 1 *syn* see MISUNDERSTAND 1

ant apprehend

2 *syn* see MISUNDERSTAND 2

ant apprehend

misappropriate *vb syn* see EMBEZZLE

misbegotten *adj syn* see ILLEGITIMATE 1

misbehaving *adj syn* see NAUGHTY 1

ant well-behaved

misbehavior *n syn* see MISCONDUCT

misbelief *n syn* see HERESY

misbeliever *n syn* see HERETIC

miscalculate *vb* to calculate wrongly < *miscalculate* the distance > < he seriously *miscalculated* the effect of his remark >

syn misestimate, misjudge, misreckon

rel discount, disregard, overlook; misconstrue, misinterpret, misunderstand; overestimate, overprize, overrate, overvalue; understimate, underprize, underrate, undervalue

miscarry *vb* to go wrong or amiss < his plans *miscarried* almost from the start >
syn misfire, miss
rel abort; fail, flop
idiom fall through, miss fire, miss the mark
con come off, prevail, succeed

miscellaneous *adj* consisting of diverse things or members < gathered together a *miscellaneous* lot of books for sale >
syn assorted, chowchow, conglomerate, heterogeneous, indiscriminate, mixed, motley, multifarious, promiscuous, unassorted, unsorted, varied
rel different, disparate, divergent, diverse, various; divers, many, sundry; odd; commingled, jumbled, mingled, scrambled
con akin, alike, identical, like, parallel, similar, uniform

miscellany *n* 1 an unorganized mixture of various dissimilar items or elements < sold a *miscellany* of old household effects >
syn assortment, brew, chowchow, colluvies, gallimaufry, hash, hodgepodge, hotchpotch, jumble, medley, mélange, melee, mingle-mangle, mishmash, mixed bag, motley, odds and ends, olio, olla podrida, omnium-gatherum, pasticcio, pastiche, patchwork, porridge, potpourri, rumble-bumble, salad, salmagundi, smorgasbord, stew
rel mess, muddle; accumulation, aggregation, congeries, conglomeration, cumulation; combination, mix, mixture
2 *syn* see ANTHOLOGY

mischance *n* 1 *syn* see MISFORTUNE
2 *syn* see ACCIDENT 2

mischief *n* 1 *syn* see INJURY 1
rel difficulty, hardship, trouble
2 *syn* see SCAMP
3 *syn* see MISCHIEVOUSNESS
4 *syn* see DISCORD

||**mischieful** *adj syn* see PLAYFUL 1

mischief–maker *n* *syn* see TROUBLEMAKER

mischievous *adj* 1 *syn* see HARMFUL
rel dangerous, hazardous, perilous, precarious, risky
2 *syn* see NAUGHTY 1
rel annoying, bothering, bothersome, irking, irksome, vexatious, vexing
3 *syn* see PLAYFUL 1
rel artful, foxy, insidious, sly, tricky

mischievousness *n* action or conduct that annoys or irritates without causing or meaning serious harm < a wag who was forever engaging in *mischievousness* >
syn devilment, devilry, deviltry, diablerie, impishness, mischief, roguery, roguishness, sportiveness, waggery, waggishness
rel doggery, odiousness, offensiveness; evil, harm, hurt, injury; annoying, pestering, teasing

miscolor *vb syn* see MISREPRESENT

miscomprehend *vb syn* see MISUNDERSTAND 1

misconceive *vb syn* see MISUNDERSTAND 2

misconduct *n* improper behavior < was charged with *misconduct* >
syn misbehavior, misdoing, wrongdoing
rel impropriety; malfeasance, malversation, misfeasance

misconstrue *vb syn* see MISUNDERSTAND 2

miscreant *adj syn* see VICIOUS 2

miscreant *n syn* see VILLAIN 1

miscreation *n syn* see FREAK 2
rel deformation, deformity

miscue *n syn* see ERROR 2

misdate *n syn* see ANACHRONISM 1

misdating *n syn* see ANACHRONISM 1

misdeed *n syn* see CRIME 1

misdeem *vb* 1 *syn* see MISJUDGE 2
2 *syn* see MISTAKE 1

misdoing *n syn* see MISCONDUCT

misdoubt *vb syn* see DISTRUST
rel apprehend, dread, fear

mise–en–scène *n* 1 *syn* see SCENE 1
2 *syn* see SCENE 3
3 *syn* see ENVIRONMENT

misemploy *vb syn* see ABUSE 2

miser *n* a mean grasping person < an old *miser* who loved only his bank account >
syn cheapskate, cheeseparer, chuff, hunks, moneygrubber, muckworm, nabal, niggard, ||nipcheese, penny pincher, piker, scrooge, skin, skinflint, stiff, tightwad
rel glutton, hog, pig

miserable *adj syn* see WOEFUL 1
rel despairing, despondent, forlorn, hopeless; piteous, pitiable, pitiful; melancholy
con cheerful, glad, happy, joyful, joyous, lighthearted

miserly *adj syn* see STINGY
rel avaricious, covetous, grasping, greedy; abject, ignoble, sordid
con bounteous, generous; altruistic, benevolent, charitable

misery *n* 1 a state of suffering and want that is the result of poverty or conditions beyond one's control < the poor learn to live with *misery* > < the utter *misery* in which the flood victims survived >
syn unhappiness, woe, wretchedness
rel agony, anguish; despondency, grief, sorrow; desolation, squalor
con beatitude, blessedness, bliss, felicity, happiness; content, ease, satisfaction
2 *syn* see DISTRESS
rel adversity, misfortune; dejection, depression, melancholy, sadness
ant blessedness
||3 *syn* see PAIN 1

misesteem *vb syn* see MISJUDGE 2

misestimate *vb syn* see MISCALCULATE

misfire *vb syn* see MISCARRY

misfortunate *adj syn* see UNLUCKY
ant fortunate

misfortune *n* adverse fortune or an instance of this < his hopes and dreams soon ended in *misfortune* > < unable to grasp why he had been struck by such a *misfortune* >
syn adversity, contretemps, ||dole, mischance, mishap, tragedy, ||unluck
rel calamity, cataclysm, catastrophe, disaster; accident, casualty; affliction, cross, trial, tribulation, visitation
con break, chance, luck, opportunity
ant fortune

misgiving *n syn* see APPREHENSION 3
rel doubt, fear, qualm, suspicion; distrust, mistrust

misguided *adj syn* see MISTAKEN

mishandle *vb* 1 *syn* see MANHANDLE

2 *syn* see ABUSE 2
mishap *n* 1 *syn* see MISFORTUNE
2 *syn* see ACCIDENT 2
mishmash *n* 1 *syn* see MISCELLANY 1
2 *syn* see CLUTTER 2
misidentify *vb syn* see MISTAKE 1
misimprove *vb syn* see ABUSE 2
misinterpret *vb syn* see MISUNDERSTAND 2
misjudge *vb* 1 *syn* see MISCALCULATE
2 to have a mistaken opinion of <her first impression led her to *misjudge* the girl>
syn misdeem, misesteem, mistake
rel misapprehend, miscomprehend, misconceive, misconstrue, misinterpret, misunderstand
con catch on (to), penetrate, tumble (to), wise (up)
misknow *vb syn* see MISUNDERSTAND 1
mislaying *n syn* see LOSS 1
mislead *vb syn* see DECEIVE
rel lie, misguide, misinform; entice, inveigle, lure, seduce, tempt
misleading *adj* having an appearance or character that leads one astray or into error <the president made several *misleading* statements to the people>
syn beguiling, deceiving, deceptive, deluding, delusive, delusory, fallacious, false
rel casuistical, sophistical, specious; wrong; bewildering, confounding, distracting, perplexing, puzzling; deceitful, inaccurate
con clarifying, elucidative, explanatory, illuminating
‖**mismannered** *adj syn* see RUDE 6
mismatch *vb syn* see CLASH 2
misorder *n syn* see CONFUSION 3
misplacement *n syn* see LOSS 1
misplacing *n syn* see LOSS 1
misread *vb syn* see MISUNDERSTAND 2
misreckon *vb syn* see MISCALCULATE
‖**misremember** *vb syn* see FORGET 1
misrepresent *vb* to give a false, imperfect, or misleading representation of <the summary totally *misrepresents* the facts of the case>
syn belie, color, confuse, distort, falsify, garble, miscolor, misstate, pervert, twist, warp, wrench, wrest
rel dress, embellish, embroider, gild, gloss, varnish; camouflage, cloak, disguise, dissemble, mask; counterfeit, feign, simulate; equivocate, lie, palter, prevaricate, weasel
idiom give a false coloring, put a false construction (*or* appearance) on
misrepresentation *n syn* see LIE
misrule *n syn* see DISORDER 2
miss *vb* 1 *syn* see NEGLECT
2 *syn* see MISUNDERSTAND 1
3 *syn* see MISCARRY
‖**miss** *n syn* see ABSENCE
miss *n syn* see GIRL 1
misshape *vb syn* see DEFORM
misshape *n syn* see DEFORMITY
missing *adj* 1 *syn* see ABSENT 1

2 *syn* see LOST 2
mission *n* a continuing task or responsibility that one is destined or fitted to do or specially called upon to undertake <his *mission* in life was to serve humanity>
syn calling, lifework, vocation
rel goal, purpose; business, profession, trade
missionary *n* one who attempts to convert others to a specific way of life, set of ideas, or course of action <served as a *missionary* for the feminist cause>
syn apostle, colporteur, evangelist, missioner, propagandist
rel revivalist; promoter
missioner *n syn* see MISSIONARY
missish *adj syn* see PRIM 1
missive *n syn* see LETTER 2
Miss–Nancyish *adj syn* see EFFEMINATE
misstate *vb syn* see MISREPRESENT
misstatement *n syn* see LIE
misstep *n syn* see ERROR 2
‖**missus** *n syn* see WIFE
missy *n syn* see GIRL 1
mist *n syn* see HAZE 1
mist *vb syn* see OBSCURE
mistake *vb* 1 to take one thing to be another <he *mistakes* sarcasm for wit>
syn confound, confuse, misdeem, misidentify, mix, mix up
rel misconceive, misknow; addle, jumble, muddle, tumble
con discern, distinguish, grasp, perceive; differentiate, separate
ant recognize
2 *syn* see MISUNDERSTAND 2
3 *syn* see MISJUDGE 2
mistake *n* 1 *syn* see ERROR 2
rel confounding, confusion, mistaking; inadvertence; disregarding, neglect, neglecting, omission, omitting, slight, slighting
2 *syn* see ERROR 1
mistaken *adj* acting, thinking, or judging in a manner at variance with truth or the facts <he is *mistaken* in his evaluation of the crisis>
syn erroneous, misguided, wrong
rel confounded, confused; deceived, deluded, misinformed
idiom all wet, off base, off the track
con accurate, correct, right, unerring; exact, precise
mister *n syn* see HUSBAND
mistimed *adj syn* see UNSEASONABLE 1
ant well-timed
mistiming *n syn* see ANACHRONISM 1
mistreat *vb syn* see ABUSE 4
mistress *n* a woman who is a man's regular partner in nonmarital sexual activity <gave up his *mistress* when he married>
syn ‖doxy, girl friend, inamorata, lover, paramour, woman; *compare* HARLOT 1
rel bedmate; concubine; kept woman; dulcinea
mistrust *n syn* see UNCERTAINTY
rel apprehension, foreboding, misgiving, presentiment
con dependence, faith, reliance
ant assurance, trust
mistrust *vb* 1 *syn* see DISTRUST
rel anticipate, apprehend, foresee; alarm, frighten, scare; appall, dismay

---

syn synonym(s)   *rel* related word(s)
cnt antonym(s)   *con* contrasted word(s)
idiom idiomatic equivalent(s)
‖ use limited; if in doubt, see a dictionary

ant trust
2 *syn* see QUESTION 2

mistrustful *adj syn* see SUSPICIOUS 2
ant trustful, trusting

mistrustfully *adv syn* see ASKANCE 2
ant trustfully, trustingly

misty *adj syn* see HAZY

misunderstand *vb* 1 to fail to understand < he *misunderstood* the full meaning of the novel >
syn misapprehend, miscomprehend, misknow, miss
rel misconceive, misconstrue, misinterpret, misread, mistake
con apprehend, conceive, know, realize; fathom, follow, grasp, seize, take in
ant comprehend, understand
2 to interpret incorrectly < *misunderstood* the instructions >
syn misapprehend, misconceive, misconstrue, misinterpret, misread, mistake
rel misexplain, mistranslate; miscomprehend, misknow
con fathom, follow, take in
ant understand

misuse *vb* 1 *syn* see ABUSE 2
2 *syn* see ABUSE 4

mite *n syn* see PARTICLE

mitigate *vb syn* see RELIEVE 1
rel extenuate, palliate
con aggravate, enhance, heighten; augment, increase
ant intensify

mitigation *n syn* see EASE 3

mix *vb* 1 to combine or be combined into a more or less uniform whole < *mixed* the ingredients to make a thick sauce >
syn admix, amalgamate, blend, comingle, commingle, commix, compound, fuse, immingle, immix, interblend, interflow, interfuse, intermingle, intermix, make up, meld, merge, mingle
rel associate, combine, conjoin, inosculate, join, link, unite; braid, lump, work in; coalesce; blunge
con divide, part, separate, sever, sunder
2 *syn* see MISTAKE 1

mix *n syn* see MIXTURE

mixed *adj syn* see MISCELLANEOUS
rel amalgamated, blended, fused, merged, mingled

mixed bag *n syn* see MISCELLANY 1

mixologist *n syn* see BARTENDER

mixture *n* a product formed by the combination of two or more things < the tea is actually a *mixture* of several varieties >
syn admixture, alloy, amalgam, amalgamation, blend, commixture, composite, compost, compound, fusion, immixture, interfusion, intermixture, mix, mix-up
rel brew, concoction, confection, mélange

mix up *vb* 1 *syn* see CONFUSE 2
ant straighten (out)
2 *syn* see CONFUSE 5
3 *syn* see MISTAKE 1
4 *syn* see DISORDER 1
ant straighten (out *or* up)

mix-up *n* 1 *syn* see MESS 3
2 *syn* see MIXTURE

mizmaze *n syn* see MAZE 1

‖**mizzle** *vb syn* see SPRINKLE 5

‖**mizzle** *vb syn* see CONFUSE 2

moan *vb syn* see DEPLORE 1

moanful *adj syn* see MELANCHOLY 2

mob *n* 1 *syn* see RABBLE
2 a large disorderly crowd of people usually bent on riotous or destructive action < the *mob* screamed for a lynching >
syn rabble, rout
rel posse; crowd, crush, horde, press, push, throng; herd, swarm
3 *syn* see CLIQUE

‖**mob** *vb syn* see SCOLD 1

mobile *adj* 1 *syn* see MOVABLE
rel fluid, liquid; protean; capricious, fickle, inconstant, mercurial
con immutable, invariable, unchangeable
ant immobile
2 *syn* see CHANGEABLE 1
rel immobile, stable
3 *syn* see VERSATILE
4 *syn* see MIGRATORY

mobilize *vb* 1 to put into movement or circulation < an increase in prices *mobilizes* the whole cycle of inflation >
syn actuate, circulate, set off
rel activate; impel, propel
idiom set in motion
con inactivate, slow (down *or* up)
ant immobilize
2 *syn* see MOVE 5
3 to assemble (as resources) and make ready for use or action < the president tried to *mobilize* support for the new proposal >
syn marshal, muster, organize, rally

mobocracy *n syn* see ANARCHY 1

mock *vb* 1 *syn* see RIDICULE
rel buffoon, burlesque, caricature, parody, travesty
2 *syn* see DECEIVE
3 *syn* see MIMIC
rel affect, assume, counterfeit, feign, simulate

mock *n* 1 *syn* see LAUGHINGSTOCK
2 *syn* see MOCKERY 2

mock *adj* 1 *syn* see ARTIFICIAL 2
rel pseudo, quasi, so-called
2 *syn* see FICTITIOUS 2
rel bogus, phony

mockery *n* 1 *syn* see LAUGHINGSTOCK
2 an insincere, contemptible, or impertinent imitation of something worthwhile < arbitrary methods that make a *mockery* of justice >
syn burlesque, caricature, farce, mock, sham, travesty
rel derision, ridicule, sport; parody, satire, take-off; joke, laughingstock

mode *n* 1 *syn* see VEIN 1
2 *syn* see METHOD 1
3 *syn* see STATE 1

mode *n syn* see FASHION 3

model *n* 1 a miniature representation of something < a *model* of the dam that was accurate down to the last detail >
syn miniature, pocket edition
rel copy, mock-up, replica, reproduction; dummy, effigy
2 something set or held before one for guidance or imitation < Samuel Johnson's literary style is often used as a *model* for writers seeking precision and clarity >
syn archetype, beau ideal, ensample, example, exemplar, ideal, mirror, paradigm, pattern, standard; *compare* PARAGON

rel apotheosis, nonesuch, nonpareil, paragon; emblem, symbol, type; embodiment, epitome, quintessence; criterion, gauge, touchstone

model *adj* **1** *syn* see IDEAL 3
 rel commendable, exemplary
 2 *syn* see PERFECT 3
 3 *syn* see TYPICAL 1

moderate *adj* **1** *syn* see SOBER 3
 2 not excessive in degree, amount, or intensity < the new proposals were met with only *moderate* enthusiasm > < the snowfall is expected to be no more than *moderate*>
 syn modest, reasonable, temperate
 rel bland, gentle, mild, soft; inconsequential, inconsiderable, slight, small; paltry, piddling, trifling, trivial
 con excessive, extreme, inordinate, intemperate, radical, unreasonable
 ant immoderate
 3 *syn* see MEDIUM
 rel constant, equable, even, steady
 4 avoiding extreme political or social measures < party policy became increasingly *moderate* >
 syn middle-of-the-road, middle-road, softshell
 con conservative, right, tory; left, radical, red; extremist, fanatical, ultra
 5 *syn* see CONSERVATIVE 2

moderate *vb* **1** to modify as to avoid an extreme or keep within bounds < actors *moderate* their voices and gestures to fit the size of the theatre >
 syn modulate, restrain, temper
 rel abate, decrease, diminish, lessen, reduce; alleviate, cushion, lighten, mitigate, mollify, relieve, slacken, slow; constrain, control, qualify; chasten, cool, subdue, tone (down)
 con aggravate, enhance, heighten, intensify; augment, increase
 2 *syn* see ABATE 4

moderately *adv* **1** *syn* see ENOUGH 2
 2 *syn* see SOMEWHAT 2
 ant extremely, immoderately

moderateness *n syn* see TEMPERANCE 1
 ant immoderateness, immoderation

moderation *n syn* see TEMPERANCE 1
 ant immoderateness, immoderation

moderator *n* one who arbitrates < the labor dispute was finally referred to a *moderator* >
 syn arbitrator, mediator
 rel arbiter, judge; conciliator, negotiator, peacemaker

modern *adj* **1** having taken place, existed, or developed in times close to the present < *modern* concepts of engineering made the bridge possible >
 syn late, recent
 rel contemporary, present-day; latter
 con antiquated, old-fashioned, old hat, outdated, outmoded, outworn
 ant old-time
 2 *syn* see NEW 1

modernistic *adj syn* see NEW 1
 rel futuristic
 ant antiquated

modernize *vb syn* see RENEW 1

modest *adj* **1** *syn* see HUMBLE 1
 rel moderate, temperate; retiring, withdrawing; unboastful; unpresuming, unpresumptuous, unpretending
 con barefaced, brazen, impudent, shameless
 ant ambitious
 2 *syn* see SHY 1
 rel reticent, silent; nice, proper, seemly
 3 *syn* see CHASTE
 rel priggish, prim, prissy, prudish, puritanical, straitlaced, stuffy
 con improper, indecent, indecorous, indelicate, unseemly
 ant immodest
 4 *syn* see MODERATE 2
 5 *syn* see PLAIN 1

modicum *n syn* see PARTICLE

modification *n syn* see CHANGE 1
 rel conversion, metamorphosis, transformation, transmogrification; qualification, tempering

modified *adj syn* see QUALIFIED 2

modify *vb syn* see CHANGE 1
 rel modulate, restrain, temper; qualify

modish *adj syn* see STYLISH
 rel voguish

modulate *vb syn* see MODERATE 1

modus *n syn* see METHOD 1

‖**mog** *vb syn* see GO 2

mogul *n syn* see MAGNATE

moiety *n syn* see PART 1

moil *vb* **1** *syn* see LABOR 1
 ‖**2** *syn* see SEETHE 4

moil *n* **1** *syn* see WORK 2
 2 *syn* see COMMOTION 4

moira *n syn* see FATE

moist *adj* **1** *syn* see DAMP
 2 *syn* see SENTIMENTAL

moistureless *adj syn* see DRY 1
 ant moist

moisty *adj syn* see DAMP

‖**moke** *n syn* see DONKEY 1

mold *n syn* see TYPE

mold *vb syn* see MAKE 3

moldable *adj syn* see PLASTIC

molder *vb syn* see DECAY

moldy *adj syn* see OLD-FASHIONED

mole *n syn* see BIRTHMARK 1

molecule *n syn* see PARTICLE

molest *vb* to annoy or disturb with hostile intent or injurious effect < he was specifically warned by the court not to *molest* his former wife >
 syn bait, heckle, persecute, torment
 rel annoy, badger, bother, irk, pester; pother, tease; bedevil, beset, devil, trouble; harass, harry, vex

moll *n syn* see PROSTITUTE

mollify *vb* **1** *syn* see PACIFY
 rel lighten; temper; abate, decrease, lessen, reduce
 ant exasperate
 2 *syn* see RELIEVE 1

‖**molly** *n syn* see WEAKLING

---

syn synonym(s) *rel* related word(s)
ant antonym(s) *con* contrasted word(s)
idiom idiomatic equivalent(s)
‖ use limited; if in doubt, see a dictionary

mollycoddle *n syn* see WEAKLING
rel ‖mollycot

mollycoddle *vb syn* see BABY
ant neglect; abuse

molt *vb syn* see SHED 2

mom *n syn* see MOTHER 1

‖**momble** *vb syn* see CONFUSE 2

moment *n* 1 *syn* see INSTANT 1
ant eternity
2 *syn* see POINT 7
3 *syn* see OCCASION 5
4 *syn* see IMPORTANCE
rel advantage, avail, profit, use

momentaneous *adj syn* see TRANSIENT

momentary *adj syn* see TRANSIENT
rel brief, quick, short; impulsive
ant agelong

momentous *adj* 1 *syn* see IMPORTANT 1
ant trivial
2 *syn* see EPOCHAL

momentousness *n syn* see IMPORTANCE
ant triviality

mommy *n syn* see MOTHER 1

momus *n syn* see CRITIC

monarchal *adj syn* see KINGLY

monarchial *adj syn* see KINGLY

monarchical *adj syn* see KINGLY

mondaine *adj syn* see SOPHISTICATED 2

monetary *adj syn* see FINANCIAL
rel numismatic

money *n* something (as pieces of stamped metal or paper certificates) customarily and legally used as a medium of exchange < the only thing that he liked about his job was the *money* >
syn ‖blunt, ‖brass, ‖bread, ‖cabbage, cash, chink, ‖chips, ‖coin, currency, ‖dibs, dinero, ‖do-re-mi, dough, filthy lucre, gelt, ‖greenbacks, ‖jack, ‖kale, legal tender, ‖lettuce, ‖long green, loot, lucre, ‖mazuma, ‖moolah, ‖mopus, needful, ooftish, pelf, rhino, rocks, ‖scratch, ‖shekels, ‖smash, stuff, ‖stumpy, ‖sugar, swag, ‖wampum
rel bankroll, capital, coinage, finances, funds, mammon, resources, riches, treasure, wealth, wherewithal; boodle, hay; ‖stiff

moneyed *adj syn* see RICH 1
ant penniless, unmoneyed

moneygrubber *n syn* see MISER

moneymaking *adj syn* see ADVANTAGEOUS 1

monger *n syn* see PEDDLER

monger *vb syn* see PEDDLE 2

mongerer *n syn* see PEDDLER

mongrel *n syn* see HYBRID

‖**moniker** *n* 1 *syn* see NAME 1
2 *syn* see NICKNAME

monish *vb syn* see REPROVE

monition *n syn* see WARNING

monitorial *adj syn* see MONITORY

monitory *adj* giving a warning < the parents wrote their son a *monitory* letter >
syn admonishing, admonitory, cautionary, cautioning, monitorial, warning
rel advisory, counseling; critical, expostulatory, remonstratory; exhortatory, hortatory; moralistic, moralizing, preachy

monkey *n* 1 *syn* see FOOL 3
2 *syn* see URCHIN

monkey *adj syn* see SMALL 1

monkey (with) *vb syn* see MEDDLE

monkeyshine *n syn* see PRANK

monocratic *adj syn* see ABSOLUTE 4
con democratic

monogram *n* a sign of identity usually formed of the combined initials of a name < everything he owned had his *monogram* on it >
syn cipher
rel device, initials; John Hancock, signature

monograph *n syn* see DISCOURSE 2

monography *n syn* see DISCOURSE 2

monopolize *vb* to take up completely < he would attempt to *monopolize* every conversation >
syn absorb, consume, engross, sew up
rel corner, hog; devour; have, hold, own, possess; employ, use, utilize; control, manage
con contribute, participate, share

monopolizing *adj syn* see ENGROSSING

monopoly *n* exclusive possession < neither party has a *monopoly* on morality >
syn corner
rel cartel, consortium, pool, syndicate, trust; copyright; ownership, possessorship, proprietorship

monotone *n syn* see MONOTONY

monotone *adj syn* see DULL 9

monotonous *adj syn* see DULL 9
rel samely, uniform, unvaried; repetitious; jogtrot, singsong
con changing, varying; fresh, new, novel; absorbing, engrossing, interesting

monotonousness *n syn* see MONOTONY

monotony *n* a tedious sameness or reiteration < the *monotony* of his job finally got to him >
syn humdrum, monotone, monotonousness
rel ennui, boredom, tedium; dryness, flatness, uniformity
con variability, variation; diversification, diversity, multifariousness, variety

monster *n* 1 *syn* see FREAK 2
rel demon, devil, fiend, hellhound; bandersnatch
2 *syn* see GIANT

monster *adj syn* see HUGE

monstrosity *n* 1 *syn* see FREAK 2
2 *syn* see EYESORE

monstrous *adj* 1 extremely impressive < the traditional burial ceremonies turned into a *monstrous* spectacle >
syn cracking, fantastic, massive, monumental, mortal, prodigious, stupendous, towering, tremendous
rel grandiose, impressive, magnificent, showy, splendid, superb; colossal, enormous, huge, immense, mammoth, vast
con mean, petty, picayune, poky, small-time
2 *syn* see HUGE
3 *syn* see OUTRAGEOUS 2
rel glaring, rank; fateful, ominous, portentous; flagitious, infamous

‖**monstrous** *adv syn* see VERY 1

monstrousness *n syn* see ENORMITY 1

monument *n* 1 *syn* see DOCUMENT 2
2 a lasting evidence or reminder of someone or something notable < the whole body of students who learned from him form his *monument* >

syn memorial, testimonial
rel memento, tribute
3 *syn* see TOMBSTONE
monument *vb syn* see MEMORIALIZE 2
monumental *adj* **1** *syn* see HUGE
2 *syn* see MONSTROUS 1
3 *syn* see TOWERING 4
monumentalize *vb syn* see MEMORIALIZE
2
moocah *n syn* see MARIJUANA
mooch *vb syn* see WANDER 1
moocher *n syn* see BEGGAR 1
mooching *n syn* see MENDICANCY
mood *n* **1** a state of mind in which an
emotion or set of emotions gains ascendancy <a melancholy *mood* induced by
the sight of ancient ruins>
syn humor, mind, strain, temper, tone,
vein
rel character, disposition, individuality,
personality, temperament; soul, spirit;
affection, emotion, feeling, response
2 *syn* see TEMPER 1
3 *syn* see AIR 3
moody *adj* subject to moods <a *moody*
person whose behavior was erratic and
whose actions were unpredictable>
syn humorsome, temperamental
rel capricious, fickle, inconstant, mercurial, unstable, whimsical; broody
con calm, dispassionate, stable, steady,
unexcitable; bovine, impassive, stolid
‖**moolah** *n syn* see MONEY
mooncalf *n syn* see FOOL 1
‖**moonraker** *n syn* see DUNCE
moonshine *n* **1** *syn* see NONSENSE 2
2 illegally distilled liquor <his death was
caused by bad *moonshine*>
syn bathtub gin, ‖blockade, bootleg,
‖busthead, ‖hooch, mountain dew, white
lightning
rel homebrew; ‖bug juice, grappa, ‖jake,
smoke, squareface
moor *vb syn* see FASTEN 2
moot *vb* **1** *syn* see BROACH
2 *syn* see DISCUSS 1
moot *adj* open to question <it is a *moot*
point whether he would have been tried
and convicted>
syn arguable, debatable, disputable,
doubtful, dubious, mootable, problematic,
questionable, uncertain; *compare* DOUBT-
FUL 1
rel controversial, suspect; unsettled
con confirmed, established, settled; inarguable, indisputable, undebatable, unproblematic, unquestionable; certain, sure
mooting *n syn* see ARGUMENTATION
mootable *adj syn* see MOOT
mop *vb syn* see GRIMACE
mop (up) *vb syn* see WHIP 2
mope *vb* **1** to become listless or dejected
<*moped* for several days after the di-
vorce>
syn brood, despond
rel ache, grieve, grump, pout, sulk
2 *syn* see SAUNTER
mopes *n pl syn* see SADNESS

mopey *adj syn* see DOWNCAST
moppet *n syn* see CHILD 1
‖**mopus** *n syn* see MONEY
moral *adj* **1** conforming to a standard of
what is right and good < *moral* goodness
may be distinguished from intellectual
goodness>
syn ethical, moralistic, noble, principled,
righteous, right-minded, virtuous
rel good, right; conscientious, honest,
honorable, just, scrupulous, upright;
chaste, decent, modest, pure
con amoral, nonmoral, unmoral
ant immoral
2 *syn* see DIDACTIC
3 *syn* see ELEVATED 2
moral *n syn* see MAXIM
morale *n* a sense of common purpose or a
degree of dedication to a common task
regarded as characteristic of or dominant
in a group < *morale* was high among the
troops>
syn esprit, esprit de corps
rel drive, spirit, vigor; assurance, confidence, self-confidence, self-possession
con enervation; aimlessness, purposelessness; egoism, egotism, self-centeredness
moralistic *adj syn* see MORAL 1
rel didactic
morality *n* **1** *syn* see GOODNESS
rel godliness, saintliness
2 *syn* see ETHIC 2
moralize *vb* to make moral reflections
usually in an officious or tiresome manner
<people avoided him as he was always
moralizing>
syn preach, preachify, sermonize
rel lecture, pontificate
moralizing *adj syn* see DIDACTIC
morally *adv syn* see VIRTUALLY
morals *n pl* **1** *syn* see ETHIC 1
2 *syn* see ETHIC 2
rel conduct, habits, standards
morass *n* **1** *syn* see SWAMP
2 *syn* see MAZE 1
rel dunghill
moratorium *n syn* see SUSPENSION 2
morbid *adj* abnormally susceptible to or
characterized by gloomy or unwholesome
feelings <his *morbid* poetry is the product
of his lifelong frustrations>
syn morose, sick, sickly
rel gloomy, melancholic; psychotic; dark,
moody, saturnine, sullen
con healthy, sound, well, wholesome;
solid, stable, stolid, sturdy
mordacious *adj syn* see CAUSTIC 1
mordancy *n syn* see ACRIMONY
rel incisiveness, pungency, trenchancy;
acidity, acridity, causticity, mordacity
mordant *adj syn* see CAUSTIC 1
more *adj syn* see ADDITIONAL
more *adv syn* see ALSO 2
2 to a greater or higher degree <were
more evenly matched>
syn better
more or less *adv* **1** *syn* see SOMEWHAT 2
2 *syn* see NEARLY
moreover *adv syn* see ALSO 2
mores *n pl* **1** *syn* see ETHIC 2
2 *syn* see MANNER 5
morgue *n syn* see PRIDE 3

---

syn synonym(s)   *rel* related word(s)
ant antonym(s)   *con* contrasted word(s)
idiom idiomatic equivalent(s)
‖ use limited; if in doubt, see a dictionary

moribund *adj* approaching death or a final end < found lying *moribund* in her bed > < fox hunting is a *moribund* sport >
syn dying
rel expiring, fading, going; decadent, deteriorating, regressing
idiom at death's door, on one's last legs, with one foot in the grave
con booming, flourishing, prospering, thriving; lively, viable
morn *n* 1 *syn* see DAWN 1
2 *syn* see MORNING 2
morne *adj* *syn* see GLOOMY 3
morning *n* 1 *syn* see DAWN 1
con sundown, sunset
2 the time before noon < it rained most of the *morning*>
syn forenoon, morn
con afternoon, evening; day, night
moron *n* 1 *syn* see FOOL 4
2 *syn* see DUNCE
moronic *adj* *syn* see RETARDED
morose *adj* 1 *syn* see SULLEN
rel choleric, cranky, irascible, splenetic, testy; irritable, waspish; brusque, gruff
con jocund, jolly, jovial, merry
ant blithe
2 *syn* see MORBID
morsel *n* 1 a small piece or quantity of food < tossed a *morsel* of meat to the dog >
syn bit, bite, mouthful
rel taste; tidbit; crumb, ort, scrap
2 *syn* see SNACK
3 *syn* see DELICACY
mort *n* *syn* see CORPSE
‖**mortacious** *adv* *syn* see VERY 1
mortal *adj* 1 *syn* see DEADLY 1
rel implacable, relentless, unrelenting
2 *syn* see GRIM 3
3 *syn* see MONSTROUS 1
4 *syn* see HUMAN
rel finite, temporal; frail, weak
5 *syn* see PROBABLE
mortal *n* *syn* see HUMAN
mortality *n* 1 *syn* see FATALITY 1
2 *syn* see MANKIND
mortally *adv* *syn* see VERY 1
mortgage *vb* *syn* see PAWN
mortician *n* one whose business is to prepare the dead for burial and to arrange and manage funerals < *morticians* must be certified >
syn funeral director, undertaker
rel embalmer
mortiferous *adj* *syn* see DEADLY 1
mortified *adj* 1 *syn* see SEVERE 1
2 *syn* see ASHAMED
rel annoyed, harassed, harried, worried
mortuary *adj* *syn* see SEPULCHRAL 1
mosey *vb* *syn* see SAUNTER
‖**moss** *n* *syn* see SWAMP
mossback *n* 1 *syn* see RUSTIC
2 *syn* see FOGY
most *adj* *syn* see BEST
rel greatest, highest, maximum, utmost, uttermost
most *adv* *syn* see VERY 1
most *adv* *syn* see NEARLY
mostly *adv* *syn* see GENERALLY 1
idiom for the most part
mote *n* *syn* see POINT 11
moth–eaten *adj* 1 *syn* see SHABBY 1

2 *syn* see OLD-FASHIONED
mother *n* 1 a female human parent < the *mother* of seven children >
syn ma, ‖mam, mama (*or* mamma), mammy, ‖mater, mom, mommy, ‖mum, mummy, ‖old lady, ‖old woman; *compare* FATHER 1
2 *syn* see SOURCE
mother *vb* *syn* see MINISTER (to)
mother country *n* *syn* see COUNTRY
motherland *n* *syn* see COUNTRY
mother–naked *adj* *syn* see NUDE 2
mother wit *n* *syn* see INTELLIGENCE 1
motif *n* 1 *syn* see LEITMOTIV
2 *syn* see SUBJECT 2
3 *syn* see FIGURE 3
motion *n* 1 the act or an instance of moving < the *motion* of the planets >
syn move, movement, stir, stirring
rel agitation, fluctuation, oscillation, sway, swing, wavering; locomotion
con inertia, inertness, passivity
2 an impulse or inclination of the mind or will < a *motion* of the will toward what appears good >
syn movement
rel goad, impulse, incentive, inducement, motive, spring, spur
con inertia, stagnation, vegetation
motion *vb* *syn* see SIGNAL
motionless *adj* being without motion < stood *motionless* so that he would remain undiscovered >
syn still, stock-still, stone-still
rel stagnant, static, stationary, unmoving; fixed, immobile, immotile, immotive, immovable, irremovable, ‖sitfast, steadfast, unmovable
con active, changing, mobile, moving
motion picture *n* *syn* see MOVIE
motivate *vb* *syn* see PROVOKE 4
motivation *n* *syn* see STIMULUS
motive *n* 1 the object influencing a choice or prompting an action < trying to discover what was his *motive* in killing the girl >
syn cause, consideration, reason, spring; *compare* STIMULUS
rel antecedent, determinant; emotion, feeling, passion; aim, end, intent, intention, purpose
2 *syn* see FIGURE 3
3 *syn* see SUBJECT 2
motley *adj* 1 *syn* see VARIEGATED
2 *syn* see MISCELLANEOUS
rel discrepant, incompatible, incongruous, uncongenial
motley *n* 1 *syn* see FOOL 2
2 *syn* see MISCELLANY 1
motor *n* *syn* see CAR
motor *vb* 1 *syn* see RIDE 1
2 *syn* see DRIVE 5
motorcar *n* *syn* see CAR
motorist *n* a person who travels by automobile < the roads were crowded with *motorists* going to work >
syn autoist, automobilist, driver, operator
mottle *vb* *syn* see SPLOTCH
motto *n* *syn* see BATTLE CRY
rel byword, catchphrase, catchword, shibboleth, slogan, watchword, word
moue *n* *syn* see FACE 6
mound *vb* *syn* see HEAP 1

mound *n syn* see PILE 1
mount *n syn* see MOUNTAIN 1
mount *vb* 1 *syn* see INCREASE 2
2 *syn* see ASCEND 1
con descend, fall, lower
ant drop
3 *syn* see RISE 4
ant drop
4 *syn* see INTENSIFY
5 to get on (something) as a means of conveyance < *mount* a horse >
syn back, bestride
rel seat, settle
ant dismount
‖6 *syn* see TESTIFY 2
7 *syn* see STAGE
mountain *n* 1 a relatively steep and high elevation of land < why are *mountains* in New England considered no more than hills in Colorado >
syn alp, mount, peak
rel butte, mesa; bald, dome; hill; bluff; volcano; sierra
con bottom, bottomland, dale, dell, vale, valley
2 *syn* see PILE 1
3 *syn* see MUCH
4 *syn* see OBSTACLE
mountain dew *n syn* see MOONSHINE 2
mountaineer *n syn* see RUSTIC
mountainous *adj syn* see HUGE
mountebank *n* 1 *syn* see CHARLATAN
2 *syn* see SWINDLER
mourn *vb syn* see GRIEVE 2
con delight, gladden, please, rejoice
mournful *adj* 1 *syn* see SAD 1
2 *syn* see SAD 2
3 *syn* see MELANCHOLY 2
4 *syn* see DEPLORABLE
mournfulness *n syn* see SADNESS
mouse *n* 1 *syn* see GIRL FRIEND 1
2 *syn* see BLACK EYE 1
mouse *vb* 1 *syn* see SNOOP
2 *syn* see STEAL 3
mousehole *n syn* see CUBBYHOLE
mousetrap *n syn* see PITFALL
mouth *n* 1 the opening through which food passes into the body of an animal < the *mouth* in vertebrates is one of the features of the face >
syn ‖bazoo, gob, ‖mush, ‖row, ‖trap, ‖yap
rel mug, muzzle
2 *syn* see FACE 6
3 *syn* see SPOKESMAN
4 *syn* see BACK TALK
5 the place where a tributary enters a larger stream or body of water < the *mouth* of the Mississippi river is in the Gulf of Mexico >
syn embouchement, embouchure
rel estuary; delta
mouth *vb* 1 *syn* see ORATE
2 *syn* see BOAST
3 *syn* see REVEAL 1
4 *syn* see GRIMACE
mouthful *n syn* see MORSEL 1
mouthing *n syn* see FACE 6
mouthpiece *n syn* see SPOKESMAN

---

syn synonym(s)   *rel* related word(s)
ant antonym(s)   *con* contrasted word(s)
idiom idiomatic equivalent(s)
‖ use limited; if in doubt, see a dictionary

mouth–watering *adj syn* see PALATABLE
‖**mouthy** *adj* 1 *syn* see TALKATIVE
2 *syn* see RHETORICAL
movable *adj* capable of moving or of being moved < a device with a *movable* attachment >
syn mobile, moving, unstable, unsteadfast, unsteady
rel remotive, removable; motile; changeable, changeful, mutable, variable; roving
con immobile, immotile, immotive, irremovable, steadfast; established, fixed, set, settled; stagnant, static, unmoving
movables *n pl syn* see POSSESSION 2
move *vb* 1 *syn* see GO 2
2 *syn* see ADVANCE 5
3 *syn* see BE
4 to change or cause to change from one place to another < he *moved* quickly down the staircase > < *move* the chair across the room >
syn dislocate, disturb, remove, shift, ship, transfer
rel displace, replace, supersede, supplant; bear, carry, convey, transmit, transport
5 to set or keep in motion or action < the mechanism that *moves* the locomotive >
syn actuate, drive, impel, mobilize, propel
rel activate, motivate
con bring up, draw up, fetch up, halt, haul up, pull up, stop
6 *syn* see PROVOKE 4
7 *syn* see AFFECT
rel induce, persuade, prevail
8 *syn* see CONVERT 1
9 *syn* see BEHAVE 1
move *n* 1 *syn* see MEASURE 7
2 *syn* see MOTION 1
rel alteration, change, modification, variation
movement *n* 1 *syn* see MOTION 1
rel action, act, deed; activity, dynamism, liveness, operation, operativeness
2 *syn* see MOTION 2
mover *n syn* see INSTIGATOR
movie *n* a representation (as of a story) by means of motion pictures < tired old *movies* that appear on TV >
syn cine, ‖cinema, film, flick, motion picture, moving picture, photoplay, picture, picture show, show
rel cinematics, cinematography
moving *adj* 1 *syn* see MOVABLE
2 having the power to excite deep and usually somber emotion < made a *moving* appeal for help for the orphaned children >
syn affecting, impressive, poignant, touching; compare EMOTIONAL 2
rel eloquent, expressive, facund, meaningful, pregnant, sententious, significant; arousing, awakening, rallying, rousing, stirring; exciting, provoking, quickening, stimulating; breathless, gripping
con unaffecting, unimpressive, untouching; casual, cold, formal
ant unmoving
3 *syn* see EMOTIONAL 2
moving picture *n syn* see MOVIE
mow *n syn* see PILE 1
mow *vb* to cut down standing grass or grain with a tool or a machine < *mowed* the lawn every week >

syn clip, crop, cut
  rel reap; pare, trim
mow (down) *vb syn* see FELL 1
mow *n syn* see FACE 6
mow *vb syn* see GRIMACE
moxie *n* 1 *syn* see ENERGY 2
  2 *syn* see COURAGE
  3 *syn* see FORTITUDE
‖**mozo** *n syn* see WORKER
Mr. *n syn* see HUSBAND
Mrs. *n syn* see WIFE
Mrs. Grundy *n syn* see PRUDE
much *adv* 1 *syn* see VERY 1
  2 *syn* see OFTEN
  3 *syn* see NEARLY
much *n* a great quantity, amount, extent,
  or degree <learned *much* worth remem-
  bering from his experiences in the army>
  syn barrel, great deal, heap, lashings, lot,
  lump, mass, ‖mess, mountain, multiplicity,
  pack, peck, pile, plenty, ‖power, ‖sight;
  compare MULTITUDE 1, SCAD
  rel excess, overage, oversupply, plethora,
  superfluity
  idiom all kinds of
  con bit, crumb, modicum, trifle; deficiency, inadequacy, insufficiency, undersupply
  ant little
‖**much** *vb syn* see BABY
much as *conj syn* see THOUGH
muck *n* 1 *syn* see SLIME
  2 *syn* see REFUSE
  3 *syn* see GOO 1
muck *vb* 1 *syn* see SOIL 2
  ‖2 *syn* see BOTCH
  ‖3 *syn* see COMPLICATE
  4 *syn* see DRUDGE
  ‖5 *syn* see SAUNTER
‖**muckamuck** *n syn* see FOOD 1
muckamuck *n syn* see NOTABLE 1
mucker *vb syn* see BOTCH
mucker *n* 1 *syn* see BOOR
  2 *syn* see WRETCH 1
  3 *syn* see TOUGH
mucking *adj syn* see DAMNED 2
muckworm *n syn* see MISER
mucky *adj* 1 *syn* see DIRTY 1
  2 *syn* see MURKY 3
  3 *syn* see HUMID
‖**mucky** *vb syn* see SOIL 2
mucronate *adj syn* see POINTED 1
mud *vb syn* see ROIL 1
muddle *vb* 1 *syn* see ROIL 1
  2 *syn* see MUMBLE
  3 *syn* see CONFUSE 2
  4 *syn* see DISORDER 1
  5 *syn* see CONFUSE 5
  6 *syn* see COMPLICATE
  7 *syn* see STUMBLE 6
muddle (away) *vb syn* see WASTE 2
muddle *n* 1 *syn* see CONFUSION 3
  2 *syn* see MESS 3
  3 *syn* see CLUTTER 2
muddled *adj* 1 *syn* see INCOHERENT 2
  2 *syn* see INTOXICATED 1
muddledness *n syn* see HAZE 2
muddlehead *n syn* see DUNCE
muddleheadedness *n syn* see HAZE 2
muddlement *n syn* see HAZE 2
muddle through *vb syn* see SHIFT 5
muddy *adj* 1 having a great deal of mud
  <playing in the wet field, he got his
  shoes all *muddy*>

  syn bemired, ‖claggy, ‖clarty, miry, oozy
  rel black, dirty, dungy, filthy, foul,
  grubby, impure, nasty, soily, sordid,
  squalid, unclean, uncleanly; bedraggled,
  draggled
  con clean, cleanly, immaculate, spotless,
  taintless, unsoiled, unsullied
  ant mudless
  2 *syn* see TURBID
  rel gloomy, murky; addled, confused,
  muddled
  3 *syn* see DULL 8
muddy *vb* 1 *syn* see SOIL 2
  2 *syn* see ROIL 1
  3 *syn* see DULL 4
  4 *syn* see CONFUSE 4
  rel conceal, hide, screen
  con illuminate, illumine, light, lighten
mudhole *n* 1 *syn* see POTHOLE
  2 *syn* see BURG
muff *vb syn* see BOTCH
muffle *vb* 1 *syn* see BUNDLE UP
  rel cover, envelop, overspread, shroud,
  veil
  2 to dull the sound of <closed the door
  to *muffle* the outside noises>
  syn dampen, deaden, mute, stifle
  rel mellow, soften, soft-pedal, subdue,
  tone (down); smother
  con amplify, enhance, heighten, magnify,
  reinforce, strengthen
  3 *syn* see SUPPRESS 2
muffler *n syn* see MASK 2
mug *n* 1 *syn* see FACE 1
  2 *syn* see FACE 6
  3 *syn* see DUNCE
  ‖4 *syn* see FOOL 3
  5 *syn* see TOUGH
mug *vb syn* see GRIMACE
‖**mug** (up) *vb syn* see CRAM 4
muggins *n syn* see DUNCE
muggy *adj syn* see HUMID
  rel damp, dampish, moist, moisty, wettish
  con dry
mughouse *n syn* see ALEHOUSE
mug–up *n syn* see SNACK
mugwump *n syn* see NOTABLE 1
mulatto *n* a person of mixed Caucasian
  and Negro ancestry <the special conflicts
  faced by *mulattoes* with both whites and
  blacks>
  syn high yellow
  rel mulatta, mulattress; octoroon, qua-
  droon; sambo, zambo; mustee; half-breed
mulct *n syn* see FINE
mulct *vb* 1 *syn* see PENALIZE
  rel claim, demand, exact, require
  2 *syn* see FLEECE 1
mule *n syn* see HYBRID
muleheaded *adj syn* see OBSTINATE
muley *adj syn* see OBSTINATE
mulish *adj syn* see OBSTINATE
  rel ungovernable, unruly; fixed, set
mull *n syn* see MESS 3
mull *vb* 1 *syn* see DEADEN 1
  2 *syn* see CONFUSE 2
  3 *syn* see DELAY 2
mull (over) *vb syn* see PONDER 2
mulligrubs *n pl syn* see SULK
  rel blues, dejection, depression, (the)
  dismals, dumps, gloom, heavyheartedness,
  melancholy, mournfulness, sadness, unhappiness

||**mullock** *n* 1 *syn* see REFUSE
 2 *syn* see CONFUSION 3
multeity *n syn* see VARIETY 1
multicolor *adj syn* see VARIEGATED
 ant monotone
multicolored *adj syn* see VARIEGATED
 ant monotone
multifarious *adj* 1 *syn* see MANY
 2 *syn* see MANIFOLD
 3 *syn* see MISCELLANEOUS
multifariousness *n syn* see VARIETY 1
multifold *adj syn* see MANIFOLD
multiform *adj syn* see MANIFOLD
 ant uniform
multiformity *n syn* see VARIETY 1
 ant uniformity
multihued *adj syn* see VARIEGATED
 ant monotone
multilateral *adj* having many sides < *multilateral* figures >
 syn many-sided
 ant one-sided, unilateral
multiloquent *adj syn* see TALKATIVE
multiloquious *adj syn* see TALKATIVE
multiplex *adj syn* see MANIFOLD
multiplicity *n* 1 *syn* see VARIETY 1
 ant unity
 2 *syn* see MUCH
multiply *vb* 1 *syn* see INCREASE 1
 2 *syn* see INCREASE 2
 3 *syn* see PROCREATE 1
multitude *n* 1 a very large number of
 individuals or things < that child always
 asks a *multitude* of questions >
 syn army, cloud, crowd, flock, host, legion, rout, scores; *compare* CROWD 1,
 MUCH, SCAD
 rel numbers, oodles, quantities
 con few, handful, scattering, smatter,
 smattering, sprinkling
 ant none
 2 *syn* see CROWD 1
multitudinal *adj syn* see MANY
 rel countless, innumerable, innumerous,
 numberless, uncountable, uncounted, unnumberable, unnumbered, untold
multitudinous *adj syn* see MANY
 rel countless, innumerable, innumerous,
 numberless, uncountable, uncounted, unnumberable, unnumbered, untold
multivarious *adj syn* see MANIFOLD
multivocal *adj syn* see VOCIFEROUS
mum *adj syn* see SILENT 2
||**mum** *n syn* see MOTHER 1
mumble *vb* to utter with a low inarticulate
 voice < embarrassed, he *mumbled* an
 apology >
 syn ||chunter, fumble, muddle, ||mump,
 murmur, mutter, swallow
 rel maunder; limp, shuffle, stumble;
 ||hammer, stammer, ||stut, stutter; speak,
 talk, utter, verbalize, vocalize, voice
 idiom speak with mush in one's mouth
 con speak out, speak up; clamor, cry out,
 shout, vociferate
mumble *n syn* see MURMUR 1
mumblenews *n pl but sing or pl in constr*
 syn see GOSSIP 1

mumbo jumbo *n syn* see GIBBERISH 3
||**mumchance** *adj syn* see SILENT 2
mummer *n syn* see ACTOR 1
mummery *n syn* see GIBBERISH 3
mummify *vb syn* see WITHER
mummy *n syn* see MOTHER 1
mummy *vb syn* see WITHER
||**mump** *vb* 1 *syn* see MUMBLE
 2 *syn* see GRIMACE
 3 *syn* see SULK
||**mump** *vb syn* see CHEAT
mumpish *adj syn* see SULLEN
mumps *n pl syn* see SULK
||**mun** *vb syn* see MUST 2
||**mun** *n syn* see MAN 3
munch *vb syn* see CHEW 1
mundane *adj* 1 *syn* see EARTHLY 1
 rel profane, secular, temporal
 ant eternal
 2 *syn* see MATERIALISTIC
 rel animal, carnal, fleshly
 3 *syn* see PROSAIC 3
municipal *adj* 1 *syn* see DOMESTIC 2
 2 *syn* see URBAN
munificent *adj syn* see LIBERAL 1
 con close, mean, niggard, ungiving
murder *n* the crime of killing a person < a
 murder occurred during a gang shoot=
 out >
 syn blood, ||bump-off, foul play, homi-
 cide, killing, manslaughter
murder *vb* 1 to kill (a human being) unlawfully and with premeditated malice
 < planned a safe way to *murder* his rival >
 syn assassinate, ||bump off,\ cool, do in,
 ||dust off, execute, finish, knock off, liqui-
 date, put away, rub out, scrag, slay; *compare* KILL 1
 rel asphyxiate, behead, decapitate, elec-
 trocute, garrote, guillotine, /hang, lynch,
 smother, strangle
 idiom take for a ride
 2 *syn* see ANNIHILATE 2
murderer *n* one who kills a human being
 < a *murderer* who wouldn't hesitate to
 kill in cold blood >
 syn homicide, killer, manslayer, slayer;
 compare ASSASSIN
 rel butcher, slaughterer
murdering *adj syn* see MURDEROUS
murderous *adj* characterized by or of a
 kind to cause murder or bloodshed
 < made a *murderous* assault on his former
 friend >
 syn bloodthirsty, bloody, homicidal, murdering, sanguinary, sanguine, sanguineous
 rel deadly; destructive, devastating, ruinous
 con harmless, innocuous, trivial
mure *vb syn* see ENCLOSE 1
murk *vb* 1 *syn* see OBSCURE 1
 2 *syn* see SOIL 2
murky *adj* 1 *syn* see DARK 1
 rel glooming, glowering, lowering
 con bright, brilliant, effulgent, radiant
 2 *syn* see OBSCURE 3
 3 having visible material in suspension < a
 murky liquid >
 syn cloudy, mucky
 rel muddy, roily, turbid
 con clear, limpid, lucent, translucent,
 transparent; clean, fresh, pure, unpolluted

---

syn synonym(s)   *rel* related word(s)
ant antonym(s)   *con* contrasted word(s)
idiom idiomatic equivalent(s)
|| use limited; if in doubt, see a dictionary

4 *syn* see DULL 8

5 *syn* see DIRTY 1

murmur *n* 1 a low indistinct but often continuous sound (as of voices) <could hear the *murmur* of the audience throughout the entire performance>

syn mumble, mutter, rumor, susurration, undertone, whisper

rel murmuration; buzz, drone, hum, purr; brool

2 *syn* see REPORT 1

murmur *vb* 1 *syn* see GRUMBLE 1

2 *syn* see COMPLAIN

3 *syn* see MUMBLE

muscle *n* 1 muscular strength <loading cargo calls for real *muscle*>

syn beef, brawn, might, sinew, thew

rel power, strength

con impotence

2 *syn* see POWER 4

muscle–bound *adj syn* see STIFF 4

muscular *adj* 1 marked by good well-developed musculature <his arms were lean but *muscular*>

syn fibrous, ropy, sinewy, stringy, wiry

rel flexible, elastic, resilient, springy, supple

con flabby, flaccid, flimsy, floppy, limp, sleazy; feeble, weak

2 strong and powerful in build or action <a *muscular* lad who could wield an ax like a man>

syn athletic, brawny, sinewy; compare STRONG 1

rel stalwart, stout, strong, sturdy; well-built, well-knit, well-set; beefy, burly, husky; Herculean, mighty, powerful

con faint, fragile, frail; delicate, feeble, weak; ∥pindling, puny, slight

muse *vb syn* see PONDER 2

rel excogitate, study

muse *n syn* see REVERIE

muse *n syn* see POET

museum *n* a room, building, or locale where a collection of objects is put on exhibition <an art *museum* with a famous collection of jade>

syn gallery

rel salon; picture gallery, pinacotheka

∥**mush** *n* 1 *syn* see MOUTH 1

2 *syn* see FACE 1

∥**mush** (up) *vb syn* see CRUSH 2

mushroom *vb syn* see EXPLODE 1

mushy *adj* 1 *syn* see SOFT 6

2 *syn* see HAZY

3 *syn* see SENTIMENTAL

music *n syn* see DIN

musical *adj* 1 *syn* see HARMONIOUS 1

ant unmusical; musicless

2 *syn* see MELODIOUS 2

ant unmusical; musicless

musician *n* one skilled in music <the one playing the sax is a real *musician*>

syn musicianer, ∥musicker, musico, virtuoso

rel performer, player

musicianer *n syn* see MUSICIAN

∥**musicker** *n syn* see MUSICIAN

musico *n syn* see MUSICIAN

muskeg *n syn* see SWAMP

muss *n* ∥1 *syn* see BRAWL 2

2 *syn* see MESS 3

muss (up) *vb syn* see DISORDER 1

rel dishevel, rumple, wrinkle

mussy *adj syn* see SLOVENLY 1

must *verbal auxiliary* 1 *syn* see WANT 3

2 — used to indicate requirement by immediate or future need or purpose <we *must* hurry if we want to catch the bus>

syn have, ∥mun, need

rel ought, should want

idiom have got to, must needs

must *n* 1 *syn* see OBLIGATION 2

2 *syn* see ESSENTIAL 2

muster *vb* 1 *syn* see ENTER 3

2 *syn* see MOBILIZE 3

3 *syn* see GATHER 6

muster (up) *vb syn* see GENERATE 3

muster *n* 1 *syn* see GATHERING 2

2 *syn* see ROSTER 1

muster out *vb syn* see DISCHARGE 7

ant call up, draft

muster roll *n syn* see ROSTER 1

musty *adj* 1 *syn* see MALODOROUS 1

rel dirty, filthy, squalid

2 *syn* see TRITE

mutable *adj* 1 *syn* see CHANGEABLE 1

rel fluctuating, swaying, swinging, wavering; fickle, inconstant, unstable

con equable, even, steady, uniform; durable, lasting, permanent, stable

ant immutable

2 liable to change or to be changed <a flexible and perhaps too *mutable* policy>

syn changeable, inconstant, shifty, slippery, uncertain, unstable, unsteady, variable; compare CHANGEABLE 1, INCONSTANT 1

rel changeful, protean, unsettled; capricious, fickle, inconsistent, lubricious, mercurial, temperamental, ticklish, volatile; fluctuating, shilly-shally, vacillating, wavering

con constant, established, fixed, immovable, inalterable, invariable, set, unalterable, unchangeable, unmodifiable, unmovable

ant immutable

mutate *vb* 1 *syn* see TRANSFORM

2 *syn* see CHANGE 1

mutation *n* 1 *syn* see CHANGE 1

2 *syn* see CHANGE 2

mute *adj* 1 *syn* see DUMB 1

2 *syn* see SILENT 2

con articulate, eloquent, fluent, glib, vocal, voluble

mute *vb syn* see MUFFLE 2

muted *adj syn* see DULL 7

mutedly *adv syn* see SOTTO VOCE

mutilate *vb* 1 *syn* see MAIM

rel damage, hurt, injure, mar, spoil; deface

2 *syn* see STERILIZE

mutineer *n syn* see REBEL

mutinous *adj syn* see INSUBORDINATE

rel alienated, disaffected

mutiny *vb syn* see REVOLT 1

mutt *n syn* see DUNCE

mutter *vb* 1 *syn* see MUMBLE

2 *syn* see GRUMBLE 1

rel repine, wail

mutter *n syn* see MURMUR 1

muttonchops *n pl syn* see SIDE-WHISKERS

muttonhead *n syn* see DUNCE

mutual *adj syn* see COMMON 1

rel partaken, participated; associated, connected, related, united

mutually adv syn see TOGETHER 3

||**mux** vb syn see DISORDER 1

muzzle n syn see FACE 1

myopic adj affected by a condition in which the visual images come to a focus in front of the retina of the eye resulting especially in defective vision of distant objects < so *myopic* that he used glasses even to read >
  syn nearsighted, shortsighted
  rel presbyopic; astigmatic
  ant farsighted, hyperopic, longsighted

myriad-minded adj syn see VERSATILE

mysterial adj syn see MYSTERIOUS

mysterious adj being beyond one's powers to discover, understand, or explain < he had a *mysterious* sense of humor, laughing when other people did not >
  syn arcane, cabalistic, impenetrable, inscrutable, mysterial, mystic, numinous, unaccountable, unexaminable, unguessed, unknowable; *compare* INEXPLICABLE, STRANGE 4
  rel impenetrable, incognizable, incomprehensible, uncomprehensible, ungraspable, unintelligible, unknowable; abstruse, esoteric, occult, recondite; ambiguous, cryptic, enigmatic, equivocal, obscure
  con explainable, explicable; apprehensible, comprehendible, comprehensible, fathomable, graspable, intelligible, knowable, lucid, scrutable; candid, frank, honest, straightforward
  ant unmysterious

mystery n something which baffles or perplexes < the *mystery* of his disappearance has never been solved >
  syn Chinese puzzle, closed book, conundrum, enigma, mystification, puzzle, puzzlement, riddle, why
  rel poser, problem, stumper; perplexity; brainteaser, brain twister
  con open book

mystic adj 1 syn see MYSTICAL 1
  rel imaginary, visionary; quixotic
  2 syn see MYSTERIOUS
  3 syn see MAGIC

mystical adj 1 having a spiritual meaning or reality that is neither apparent to the senses nor obvious to the intelligence < the *mystical* food of the sacrament >
  syn anagogic, mystic, telestic
  rel abysmal, deep, profound; absolute, categorical, ultimate; divine, holy, sacred, spiritual; miraculous, supernatural, supranatural
  2 syn see SECRET 1

mystification n syn see MYSTERY

mystifying adj syn see CRYPTIC

myth n 1 a traditional story of ostensibly historical content whose origin has been lost < the various Greek *myths* that have come down to us >
  syn legend, mythos, mythus; *compare* ALLEGORY 2
  rel saga; fable, fabrication, fiction, figment; creation, invention
  2 syn see ALLEGORY 2
  3 syn see LORE 2

mythical adj lacking factual basis or historical validity < a *mythical* account attributes the founding of the city to Noah >
  syn fabulous, legendary, mythological
  rel fictional, fictitious, fictive, imaginary, supposititious, unreal; fanciful, fantastic, visionary; created, invented
  con actual, real, true; authentic, genuine, veritable; truthful, veracious, verisimilar
  ant historical

mythological adj syn see MYTHICAL

mythology n syn see LORE 2

mythos n 1 syn see MYTH 1
  2 syn see LORE 2

mythus n syn see MYTH 1

N

nab vb 1 syn see ARREST 2
  2 syn see SEIZE 2
  3 syn see STEAL 1

||**nab** n 1 syn see POLICEMAN
  2 syn see ARREST

nabal n syn see MISER

nabob n syn see NOTABLE 1

nada n syn see NOTHINGNESS

nadir n syn see BOTTOM 3
  con acme, climax, culmination; peak, summit
  ant apex, zenith

nag vb to find fault incessantly < stop *nagging* her over nothing >
  syn carp (at), fuss, henpeck, peck (at)
  rel annoy, harass, harry, pester, plague,

tease, worry; bother, irk, vex; badger, bait, chivy, heckle, hector, hound, ride; egg, goad, needle, prod, urge
  idiom give a bad (or hard) time, pick at (or on), take it out on
  con commend, compliment, praise; acclaim, applaud, hail

nail vb 1 syn see CATCH 1
  ||2 syn see SEIZE 2
  ||3 syn see STEAL 1
  ||4 syn see STRIKE 2

naive adj 1 syn see NATURAL 5
  rel fresh, original
  ant sophisticated
  2 syn see EASY 3

naked adj 1 syn see BARE 1
  2 syn see NUDE 2
  3 syn see OPEN 2
  rel disclosed, discovered, revealed; evident, manifest, obvious, palpable; colorless, uncolored; pure, sheer, simple

namby-pamby adj 1 syn see INSIPID 3
  2 syn see CHARACTERLESS

---

syn synonym(s)   **rel** related word(s)
ant antonym(s)   **con** contrasted word(s)
idiom idiomatic equivalent(s)
|| use limited; if in doubt, see a dictionary

namby–pamby n syn see WEAKLING

name n 1 the word or combination of words by which something is called and by means of which it can be distinguished or identified <the *name* always given to the eldest son> <what is the *name* of that bird?>
syn appellation, appellative, cognomen, compellation, denomination, designation, ‖handle, ‖moniker, nomen, rubric, style, title
rel baptismal name, Christian name, font name, forename, personal name, prename; byname, byword, hypocorism, nickname, pet name, sobriquet; epithet, label, tag; alias, incognito, nom de guerre, nom de plume, pen name, pseudonym
2 *syn* see REPUTATION 2
3 *syn* see CELEBRITY 2

name vb 1 to give a name to <*named* the child for his grandfather>
syn baptize, call, christen, denominate, designate, dub, entitle, style, term, title
rel label, tag, ticket; nickname
idiom give a handle, pin a moniker on
2 *syn* see DESIGNATE 2
rel advertise, announce, declare, publish
3 *syn* see MENTION
rel identify, recognize

nameable adj syn see NOTEWORTHY

nameless adj 1 syn see OBSCURE 5
2 *syn* see ANONYMOUS
ant named

namely adv that is to say <understandably his wife disapproves of his bad habits, *namely* gambling and fornication>
syn scilicet, to wit, videlicet
rel especially, expressly, particularly, specially, specifically

nana n syn see NURSEMAID

‖**nanny** n syn see NURSEMAID

nap n a short sleep <generally took an hour's *nap* after lunch>
syn catnap, dog nap, ‖dover, forty winks, siesta, snooze; compare DOZE, SLEEP 1
rel dogsleep; break, interlude, intermission, let up, pause, respite, rest

nap vb to sleep briefly <*napped* for an hour after lunch>
syn catnap, ‖caulk (off), siesta, snooze; compare DOZE, SLEEP
rel drowse; relax, rest, unlax
idiom catch a wink of sleep, catch forty winks, take a nap (or siesta or snooze)

narcissism n syn see CONCEIT 2

narcissistic adj syn see VAIN 3

narcotic n 1 syn see DRUG 2
2 *syn* see ANODYNE 2

narcotic adj syn see SOPORIFIC 1

‖**nark** n syn see INFORMER

‖**nark** vb syn see INFORM 3

narrate vb syn see RELATE 1
rel descant, dilate, discourse, expatiate

narration n 1 syn see DESCRIPTION 2
2 *syn* see STORY 2

narrative n 1 syn see STORY 2
2 *syn* see ACCOUNT 7

narrow adj 1 syn see DEFINITE 1
2 *syn* see LITTLE 2
3 *syn* see ILLIBERAL
rel inexorable, inflexible, obdurate
con forbearing, indulgent, lenient, tolerant
ant broad

‖4 *syn* see STINGY

narrow vb syn see CONSTRICT 2

narrow–fisted adj syn see STINGY
ant openhanded

narrowhearted adj syn see STINGY
ant openhearted

narrow–minded adj syn see ILLIBERAL
ant broad-minded

nascent adj syn see INITIAL 1

nasty adj 1 syn see DIRTY 1
rel coarse, gross, obscene, ribald, vulgar; improper, indecent, indecorous, indelicate, unseemly
2 *syn* see OFFENSIVE
3 *syn* see OBSCENE 2
4 *syn* see MALICIOUS

nates n pl syn see BUTTOCKS

national adj 1 syn see PUBLIC 1
2 *syn* see DOMESTIC 2

national n syn see CITIZEN 2

native adj 1 syn see INNATE 1
2 belonging to a locality by birth or origin <a *native* tradition> <delighted with the tasty *native* fruits>
syn aboriginal, autochthonous, endemic, indigenous
rel domestic, local
con adopted, introduced, naturalized
ant alien, foreign, nonnative
3 *syn* see DOMESTIC 2
4 *syn* see WILD 1
5 *syn* see UNREFINED 3

Nativity n syn see CHRISTMAS

‖**natter** vb syn see CHAT 1

natty adj syn see DAPPER

natural adj 1 syn see ILLEGITIMATE 1
2 *syn* see INNATE 1
ant abnormal, unnatural
3 *syn* see GENERAL 1
4 *syn* see WILD 1
5 free from pretension or calculation <he spoke in a perfectly *natural* manner>
syn artless, guileless, inartificial, ingenuous, innocent, naive, simple, simplehearted, unaffected, unartful, unartificial, unschooled, unsophisticated, unstudied, untutored, unworldly; compare GENUINE 3
rel impulsive, instinctive, spontaneous; easy, unlabored; constitutional, ingrained, inherent; folksy, homespun, unpretentious; ignorant, primitive, undesigning; unconstrained, unembarrassed; candid, frank, open, plain; sincere, unfeigned; provincial, rustic
con ceremonial, ceremonious, conventional, formal; ostentatious, pretentious, showy; assumed, contrived, counterfeited, feigned, pretended; artful, sophisticated, studied
ant affected; artificial, unnatural

natural n syn see FOOL 4

natural child n syn see BASTARD 1

naturalness n syn see UNCONSTRAINT
ant unnaturalness

nature n 1 syn see TYPE
rel anatomy, framework, structure; conformation, figure, shape
2 *syn* see ESSENCE 1
3 *syn* see DISPOSITION 3
4 *syn* see UNIVERSE

naught (or **nought**) n 1 syn see NOTHING 1

2 *syn* see ZERO

naughty *adj* 1 guilty of misbehavior < a *naughty* boy who teased the cat and upset the milk >
syn bad, ill-behaved, misbehaving, mischievous, paw; *compare* DISOBEDIENT
rel contrary, froward, perverse, wayward; headstrong, intractable, recalcitrant, refractory, ungovernable, unruly, willful; disorderly, rowdy, ruffianly; evil, indecorous, wicked
con decorous, good, well-behaved; amenable, docile, obedient, tractable; amiable, complaisant, good-natured, obliging; polite, proper; considerate, kindly, thoughtful

2 *syn* see DISOBEDIENT

nausea *n* a stomach distress with an urge to vomit < overcome with *nausea* as the boat continued to pitch and wallow >
syn qualmishness, queasiness, squeamishness

nauseate *vb syn* see DISGUST

nauseated *adj* affected with nausea < was *nauseated* after taking the drug >
syn nauseous, squeamish; *compare* SQUEAMISH 1
rel choking, gagging; heaving; barfing, upchucking, vomiting
idiom ready (*or* about) to lose one's cookies

nauseating *adj syn* see OFFENSIVE
ant appetizing

nauseous *adj syn* see NAUSEATED

nautical *adj syn* see MARINE 2

navigable *adj syn* see PASSABLE
ant unnavigable

navigational *adj syn* see MARINE 2

nawob *n syn* see NOTABLE 1

nay *adv* 1 *syn* see NO

2 *syn* see EVEN 3

naze *n syn* see PROMONTORY

neanderthal *adj syn* see OLD-FASHIONED

near *adv* 1 *syn* see CLOSE
ant far

2 *syn* see ABOUT 3

near *prep* 1 *syn* see ABOUT 1

2 not far distant from < kept the boy *near* him >
syn ‖aside, beside, by, nearby, nigh, round
idiom close to, hard by, within earshot, within reach, within sight

near *adj* 1 *syn* see CLOSE 6
ant far

2 *syn* see COMPARATIVE

near *vb syn* see APPROACH 1
rel equal, match, rival, touch
con alter, change, modify, vary; differ

‖**nearabout** *adv syn* see NEARLY

near-at-hand *adj* 1 *syn* see NEIGHBORING

2 *syn* see CLOSE 6

3 *syn* see CONVENIENT 2

near-at-hand *adv syn* see ABOUT 5

nearby *adv* 1 *syn* see CLOSE

2 *syn* see ABOUT 5

nearby *prep* 1 *syn* see NEAR 2

nearby *adj* 1 *syn* see CLOSE 6

2 *syn* see NEIGHBORING

3 *syn* see CONVENIENT 2

nearing *adj syn* see FORTHCOMING

nearly *adv* very close to < our work is *nearly* done for today >
syn about, all but, almost, approximately, as good as, just about, more or less, most, much, ‖nearabout, nigh, practically, roughly, round, roundly, rudely, say, some, somewhere, well-nigh
rel virtually
idiom as near as never mind(s), in effect, in essence, in substance, in the main, nigh on (*or* onto *or* upon), to all (practical) intents and purposes

nearsighted *adj syn* see MYOPIC

neat *adj* 1 *syn* see STRAIGHT 3

2 manifesting care and orderliness < always kept a *neat* house >
syn chipper, orderly, prim, shipshape, snug, spick-and-span, tidy, trig, trim, uncluttered, well-groomed; *compare* DAPPER
rel clean, immaculate, spotless; dainty, fastidious, finicky, nice; methodical, regular, systematic; accurate, correct, exact, precise
idiom in good order, neat as a pin (*or* bandbox), neat as can be, neat as wax
con disheveled, disordered, slipshod, sloppy, slovenly, unkempt, untidy; dirty, filthy, foul, nasty; lax, negligent, remiss, slack
ant disorderly, messy

‖3 *syn* see MARVELOUS 2

neat-handed *adj syn* see DEXTEROUS 1

neb *n syn* see BILL 1

‖**nebby** *adj syn* see IMPERTINENT 2

‖**necessary** *n syn* see PRIVY 1

necessary *adj* 1 *syn* see ESSENTIAL 4
rel compelling, compulsory, constraining, mandatory, obligatory; important, momentous, significant; cardinal, fundamental
con insignificant, unessential, unimportant
ant unnecessary

2 *syn* see INEVITABLE
rel inerrable, inerrant, infallible, unerring

necessitate *vb syn* see DEMAND 2

necessitous *adj* 1 *syn* see POOR 1
rel depleted, drained, exhausted

2 *syn* see ESSENTIAL 4

necessity *n* 1 *syn* see NEED 4
rel coercion, compulsion, constraint, duress, obligation; indispensableness, needfulness, requisiteness

2 *syn* see OCCASION 3

3 *syn* see ESSENTIAL 2

neck *vb syn* see BEHEAD

necrology *n syn* see OBITUARY

necromancer *n syn* see MAGICIAN 1

necromancy *n syn* see MAGIC 1

necromantic *adj syn* see MAGIC

necropolis *n syn* see CEMETERY

necropsy *n syn* see AUTOPSY

‖**neddy** *n syn* see DONKEY 1

need *n* 1 *syn* see OBLIGATION 2

2 *syn* see REQUIREMENT 1

3 opportunity or requirement to employ < found little *need* for his rifle >
syn demand, occasion, use

---

syn synonym(s)   *rel* related word(s)
ant antonym(s)   *con* contrasted word(s)
idiom idiomatic equivalent(s)
‖ use limited; if in doubt, see a dictionary

rel call, claim, exaction

4 a pressing lack of something essential <he is in *need* of food>

syn exigency, necessity

rel deficiency, deficit, lack, shortage, want

con adequacy, enough, sufficiency

5 *syn* see POVERTY 1

need *vb* 1 *syn* see LACK

rel claim, demand, exact; hanker, hunger, long, pine, thirst, yearn; covet, crave, desire, wish

2 *syn* see MUST 2

needed *adj syn* see NEEDFUL

needful *adj* necessary for supply or relief <provided them with everything *needful*>

syn needed, required, requisite

rel essential, imperative, indispensable, necessary; lacked, wanted; cardinal, fundamental, vital

con excess, redundant, superfluous; nonessential, unessential; uncalled-for, unnecessary, unneeded

ant needless

needful *n syn* see MONEY

neediness *n syn* see POVERTY 1

needle *vb syn* see WORRY 1

needless *adj syn* see UNNECESSARY

ant needful

needy *adj syn* see POOR 1

ne'er *adv syn* see NEVER

ne'er-do-well *n syn* see WASTREL 1

nefarious *adj syn* see VICIOUS 2

rel atrocious, heinous, monstrous, outrageous; flagrant, glaring, gross, rank

ant exemplary

negate *vb* 1 *syn* see DENY 4

ant affirm

2 *syn* see ABOLISH 1

3 *syn* see NEUTRALIZE

negation *n syn* see DENIAL 2

ant affirmation

negative *adj syn* see ADVERSE 2

negative *vb* 1 *syn* see VETO

2 *syn* see DENY 4

ant affirm

3 *syn* see NEUTRALIZE

rel abrogate, invalidate, nullify

neglect *vb* to pass over without giving due attention <*neglected* his family for the sake of his mistress>

syn blink (at *or* away), discount, disregard, elide, fail, forget, ignore, miss, omit, overleap, overlook, overpass, pass, pass by, pass over, pretermit, slight, slough over, slur (over)

rel brush (off *or* aside), disdain, dismiss, reject, scant, scorn, shrug away, shrug off

idiom pay no attention to, pay no heed (*or* mind), think little of

con appreciate, prize, treasure, value; cultivate, foster, nurse, nurture

ant cherish

neglect *n syn* see FAILURE 1

neglected *adj* not properly or sufficiently attended to or cared for <the whole property had a *neglected* appearance>

syn run-down, uncared-for, untended

rel disregarded, ignored, overlooked, slighted, unheeded

con prized, treasured; fostered, tended; guarded, supervised, watched

ant cherished

neglectful *adj syn* see NEGLIGENT

ant attentive

negligent *adj* failing to give proper attention or care <*negligent* in taking care of the children> <a *negligent* man, prone to forgetfulness>

syn behindhand, careless, delinquent, derelict, discinct, disregardful, lax, neglectful, regardless, remiss, slack

rel heedless, inadvertent, inattentive, inconsiderate, thoughtless, unheedful, unthinking; incurious, indifferent, unconcerned; slipshod, slovenly

con rigid, rigorous, strict; attentive, considerate, heedful, thoughtful; careful, exact, fussy, meticulous, punctilious, punctual, scrupulous

ant attentive

negligible *adj syn* see REMOTE 4

ant significant

negotiable *adj syn* see PASSABLE

ant nonnegotiable

negotiate *vb* 1 to bring about by mutual agreement <*negotiate* a treaty>

syn arrange, concert, settle

rel adjust, compose, transact; agree, bargain, contract, covenant

con break off, intermit, interrupt, suspend; differ, disagree, dissent

2 *syn* see CLEAR 8

neigh *vb* tc make the cry typical of a horse <the frightened horse *neighed* and stamped>

syn nicker, whicker, ‖whinner, whinny

neighbor *vb syn* see ADJOIN

neighborhood *n* 1 *syn* see LOCALITY 1

2 *syn* see ORDER 4

neighboring *adj* not distant <the need for understanding between *neighboring* countries>

syn adjacent, close-at-hand, close-by, contiguous, near-at-hand, nearby; *compare* CLOSE 6

rel abutting, adjoining, bordering, conterminous, touching; close, near

con distant, far, faraway, far-off, remote, removed; parted, separated

neighborly *adj syn* see AMICABLE

rel cooperative, gregarious, hospitable, social; cordial, gracious, sociable

ant unneighborly; ill-disposed

neonate *n syn* see BABY 1

neophyte *n syn* see NOVICE

neoteric *adj syn* see NEW 1

nepenthe *n syn* see ANODYNE 2

ne plus ultra *n syn* see APEX 2

nerve *n* 1 *syn* see FORTITUDE

2 *syn* see TEMERITY

3 *syn* see EFFRONTERY

nerve *vb syn* see ENCOURAGE 1

nerve center *n syn* see CENTER 2

nervous *adj* easily upset or irritated <a *nervous* fretful woman>

syn fidgety, goosey, high-strung, jittery, jumpy, nervy, spooky, twittery, unrestful

rel agitated, edgy, excitable, skittish, volatile; fretful, irritable, querulous, snappish, waspish

con calm, placid, serene, steady, tranquil; collected, composed, cool, imperturbable, inexcitable, poised, unflappable, unruffled

ant nerveless

nervous breakdown *n* an emotional disorder often characterized by depression, tenseness, irritability, headache, and susceptibility to fatigue < worked and worried himself into a *nervous breakdown* >
syn breakdown, collapse, crack-up, nervous prostration
rel neurasthenia; prostration

nervous prostration *n syn* see NERVOUS BREAKDOWN

nervy *adj* 1 *syn* see WISE 5
2 *syn* see NERVOUS
rel excitable, fidgety, jerky, tense, twitchy
idiom tied up in knots
con composed, easy, relaxed
ant phlegmatic
3 *syn* see TENSE 2

nescience *n syn* see IGNORANCE 2

nest egg *n syn* see RESERVE

nestle *vb syn* see SNUGGLE

net *vb syn* see CLEAR 6

nether *adj syn* see INFERIOR 1

nethermost *adj syn* see BOTTOMMOST
ant uppermost

netherwards *adv syn* see DOWN 1
ant upwards

netherworld *n syn* see HELL

nettle *vb syn* see IRRITATE
rel agitate, discompose, disturb, perturb, upset

nettlesome *adj syn* see THORNY

neuter *vb syn* see STERILIZE

neutral *adj* not experiencing or generating a strong emotional commitment or response < made a *neutral* response to his challenge >
syn abstract, colorless, detached, disinterested, dispassionate, impersonal, poker=faced, unpassioned
rel clinical, collected, composed, cool, nonchalant; calm, easy, relaxed; aloof, indifferent
con intemperate, loaded; fervent, impassioned, passionate, vehement

neutralize *vb* to make inoperative or ineffective usually by means of an opposite force, influence, or effect < attacked by the kind of propaganda that is difficult to *neutralize* >
syn annul, cancel (out), counteract, countercheck, frustrate, negate, negative, redress
rel balance, compensate, counterbalance, counterpoise, countervail, offset; abrogate, invalidate, nullify; conquer, defeat, overcome, subdue; override, overrule
con activate, animate, dynamize, vitalize

never *adv* not at any time < they had *never* seen him before >
syn ne'er
idiom never in all one's born days, never in one's life, never in the world, never on earth
con constantly, continuously, ever, invariably, perpetually
ant always

never-ending *adj syn* see EVERLASTING 1

ant ended; transitory

never-failing *adj syn* see SURE 2

nevertheless *adv syn* see HOWEVER

nevus *n syn* see BIRTHMARK 1

new *adj* 1 recently come into existence or use or a particular state or relation < *new* styles that flatter stout figures >
syn fresh, modern, modernistic, neoteric, newfangled, new-fashioned, new-sprung, novel, recent
rel first-hand, independent, primary
con dated, outdated, outmoded, out-of=date; shabby, worn; hackneyed, old hat, trite
ant old
2 *syn* see UNFAMILIAR 1
3 *syn* see ADDITIONAL
4 *syn* see REFRESHED

new *adv* within recent time < the scent of *new*-mown grass >
syn afresh, anew, lately, newly, of late, recently
con aforetime, before, earlier, formerly; heretofore, hitherto
ant once

newborn *n syn* see BABY 1

newcomer *n syn* see NOVICE

newfangled *adj syn* see NEW 1
ant oldfangled

new-fashioned *adj syn* see NEW 1
ant old-fashioned

New Jerusalem *n syn* see HEAVEN 2

newly *adv syn* see NEW

news *n pl but sing in constr* a report of events or conditions not previously known < her friend gave her the bad *news* >
syn advice, information, intelligence, speerings, tidings, word
rel announcement, report; dope, low-down, ‖poop; gossip, rumor, tattle

newsmonger *n syn* see GOSSIP 1

newspaper *n syn* see JOURNAL

new-sprung *adj syn* see NEW 1

next *adj* being the one that comes immediately after another < the *next* day >
syn coming, ensuing, following; *compare* CONSECUTIVE
rel proximate

next *adv syn* see AFTER

next *prep syn* see AFTER 2

next to *prep syn* see BESIDE 1

nexus *n syn* see BOND 3

niagara *n syn* see FLOOD 2

nib *n syn* see BILL 1

‖**nibby** *adj syn* see CURIOUS 2

nice *adj* 1 having or displaying exacting standards < too *nice* about his food to like camp cooking >
syn ‖choicy, choosy, clerkish, dainty, delicate, fastidious, finical, finicking, finicky, fussy, miminy-piminy, ‖mincy, nimi-ny-piminy, old-maidish, old-womanish, particular, pernickety, persnickety, picksome, picky, precious, squeamish, squeamy
rel discerning, discriminating, penetrating; overparticular; queasy; careful, meticulous, punctilious, scrupulous, judicious, sage, sapient, wise
con coarse, gross, vulgar; callow, crude, green, raw, uncouth; lax, neglectful, negligent, remiss, slack; careless, sloppy, slovenly

---

syn synonym(s)   *rel* related word(s)
ant antonym(s)   *con* contrasted word(s)
idiom idiomatic equivalent(s)
‖ use limited; if in doubt, see a dictionary

2 *syn* see FINE 1

3 *syn* see PLEASANT 1

4 *syn* see CORRECT 2
  rel rigid, strict, stringent; exquisite, rare
  con haphazard, happy-go-lucky, hit-or-
  miss, random; careless, heedless, inadvertent

5 *syn* see DECOROUS 1

nicely *adv syn* see WELL 1

nice Nelly *n* **1** *syn* see PRUDE

2 *syn* see EUPHEMISM

nice–nellyism *n syn* see EUPHEMISM

niche *n syn* see NOOK

nick *n syn* see NOTCH 1

‖**nick** *vb syn* see STEAL 1

nicker *vb syn* see NEIGH

nickname *n* a descriptive or familiar name
  that is used instead of or in addition to
  one's proper name <because he was a
  redhead his friends gave him the *nickname*
  "Red">
  syn byname, byword, ‖handle, hypocorism, ‖moniker, sobriquet
  rel first name, middle name; appellation,
  appellative, compellation, denomination,
  style; epithet, label, tag

nictate *vb syn* see WINK

nictitate *vb syn* see WINK

nidorous *adj syn* see MALODOROUS 1

nifty *adj syn* see MARVELOUS 2

nifty *n syn* see ‖DILLY

niggard *n syn* see MISER

niggard *adj syn* see STINGY

niggardly *adj syn* see STINGY
  ant bounteous, bountiful

niggling *adj syn* see PETTY 2

nigh *adv* **1** *syn* see CLOSE

2 *syn* see NEARLY

nigh *adj syn* see CLOSE 6

nigh *prep* **1** *syn* see NEAR 2

2 *syn* see ABOUT 1

nigh *vb syn* see APPROACH 1

night *n* the time from dusk to dawn
  <stayed up all *night* >
  syn nighttide, nighttime
  con day, daytime

night *adj syn* see NIGHTLY

night and day *adv syn* see TOGETHER 2

nightclub *n* a restaurant serving liquor and
  providing entertainment <Las Vegas
  nightclubs >
  syn bistro, cabaret, café, discotheque, hot
  spot, nightery, night spot, nitery, supper
  club, watering hole, watering place

nightery *n syn* see NIGHTCLUB

nightfall *n syn* see EVENING 1

nightly *adj* of, relating to, or associated
  with the night < *nightly* noises >
  syn night, nocturnal
  con daily, diurnal; matutinal, morning;
  evening, twilight, vespertine

nightmare *n syn* see FANCY 4

night spot *n syn* see NIGHTCLUB

nightstick *n syn* see CUDGEL

nighttide *n syn* see NIGHT

nighttime *n syn* see NIGHT

nightwalker *n syn* see PROSTITUTE

nihility *n syn* see NOTHINGNESS

nil *n syn* see NOTHING 1

nim *vb syn* see STEAL 1

nimble *adj* **1** *syn* see AGILE
  rel light, lightsome; alert, vigilant, watchful, wide-awake

2 *syn* see DEXTEROUS 1

nimble-witted *adj syn* see WISE 4
  ant slow-witted

niminy–piminy *adj syn* see NICE 1

nimmer *n syn* see THIEF

nincom *n syn* see FOOL 1

nincompoop *n syn* see FOOL 1

ninny *n syn* see FOOL 1

ninnyhammer *n syn* see FOOL 1

nip *vb* **1** *syn* see BLAST 1
  rel arrest, check; press, squeeze; balk,
  frustrate, thwart

2 *syn* see STEAL 1

‖3 *syn* see HURRY 2

nip *n syn* see DRAM

nip *vb syn* see DRINK 3

‖**nipcheese** *n syn* see MISER

‖**nipper** *n syn* see CHILD 1

nipping *adj syn* see COLD 1

nippy *adj syn* see COLD 1

nirvana *n syn* see HEAVEN 2

nisse *n syn* see FAIRY

‖**nit** *adv syn* see NO

nitery *n syn* see NIGHTCLUB

nitwit *n syn* see DUNCE

nitwitted *adj syn* see SIMPLE 3

‖**nix** *n syn* see NOTHING 1

‖**nix** *adv syn* see NO

nix *vb syn* see VETO

no *adv* — used as a function word to express negation, dissent, denial, or refusal
  < *no*, you can't come with me>
  syn nay, ‖nit, ‖nix, ‖nope
  idiom by no manner of means, by no
  means, in no case, no dice, not at any
  price, not for love or money, not for the
  life of me, not for the world, nothing
  doing, not on your life, on no account, on
  no condition, under no circumstances
  ant yes

‖**no-account** *adj syn* see WORTHLESS 1

Noachian *adj syn* see ANCIENT 1

noble *adj* **1** *syn* see GRAND 1
  rel eminent, illustrious
  con beggarly, contemptible, despicable,
  scurvy, sorry
  ant cheap, ignoble, unnoble

2 *syn* see ELEVATED 2
  ant base

3 *syn* see HONORABLE 1
  ant ignoble

4 *syn* see MORAL 1

nobody *pron syn* see NO ONE
  ant everybody; somebody

nobody *n syn* see NONENTITY
  ant somebody

nocent *adj syn* see HARMFUL
  ant innocent

nocturnal *adj syn* see NIGHTLY
  con daily, diurnal

nocuous *adj syn* see HARMFUL
  ant innocuous

nodding *adj syn* see SLEEPY 1

noddle *n syn* see HEAD 1

noddy *n syn* see DUNCE

noel *n syn* see CHRISTMAS

noggin *n syn* see HEAD 1

no–good *adj syn* see WORTHLESS 1

no–good *n* **1** *syn* see WASTREL 1

2 *syn* see WRETCH 1

noise *n syn* see SOUND 1
  rel babel, clamor, din, hubbub, pandemonium, racket, uproar

con quiet, silence, stillness

noise (about *or* abroad) *vb syn see* GOSSIP

noiseful *adj syn see* NOISY
ant noiseless, silent

noiseless *adj syn see* STILL 3
con boisterous, clamorous, strident, vociferous
ant noiseful, noisy

noiselessness *n syn see* SILENCE 1
ant noisiness

noisome *adj* 1 *syn see* UNWHOLESOME 1
ant wholesome

2 *syn see* MALODOROUS 1
rel dirty, filthy, squalid; loathsome, revolting
ant balmy

3 *syn see* OFFENSIVE

noisy *adj* making noise <the *noisiest* car you ever heard>
syn clangorous, clattery, noiseful, rackety, sonorous, uproarious
rel blatant, boisterous, clamorous, obstreperous, strepitous, strident, vociferous; tumultuous, turbulent
con quiet, silent, still, stilly
ant noiseless

nomadic *adj syn see* ITINERANT

no man *pron syn see* NO ONE
ant everybody, everyman

nom de guerre *n syn see* PSEUDONYM

nomen *n syn see* NAME 1

nominal *adj* being something in name or form only <the *nominal* head of his party>
syn formal, so-called, titular
rel apparent, ostensible, seeming; alleged, pretended, professed
idiom in name only
con genuine, real, true
ant actual

nominate *vb syn see* DESIGNATE 2
rel intend, mean, propose, purpose; offer, present, proffer, tender

nonadhesive *adj syn see* LOOSE 3

nonage *n syn see* INFANCY 2
ant age

nonchalant *adj syn see* COOL 2
rel cheerful, glad, lighthearted; easy, effortless, light, smooth
con anxious, careful, concerned, solicitous, worried

noncombustible *adj* incapable of being burned < *noncombustible* material was used whenever possible>
syn apyrous, incombustible, nonflammable, noninflammable, uninflammable
rel fireproof, fire-resistant, fire-resistive, fire-retardant, flameproof
con flammable, inflammable
ant combustible

noncommittal *adj syn see* RESERVED 1

noncompos *n syn see* LUNATIC 1

non compos mentis *adj syn see* INSANE 1

nonconformism *n syn see* HERESY
ant conformism

nonconformist *n* 1 *syn see* HERETIC
ant conformist

2 *syn see* BOHEMIAN
ant conformist

nonconformist *adj syn see* HERETICAL

nonconformity *n syn see* HERESY
ant conformity

noncreative *adj syn see* UNORIGINAL
ant creative

nondiscriminatory *adj syn see* FAIR 4
ant discriminatory

none *pron syn see* NO ONE

nonentity *n* an utterly insignificant person <tired of dealing with subordinates and *nonentities*>
syn cipher, insignificancy, nobody, nothing, nullity, rushlight, whiffet, whippersnapper, whipster, zero, zilch
rel lightweight, obscurity, sad sack, small beer, small fry
idiom blank space in the rear rank, man in the street, no great shakes

nonesuch *n syn see* PARAGON
idiom one in a million

nonessential *adj syn see* DISPENSABLE
ant essential

nonetheless *adv syn see* HOWEVER

nonexistence *n syn see* NOTHINGNESS
ant existence; reality

nonflammable *adj syn see* NONCOMBUSTIBLE
ant flammable, inflammable

nonfunctional *adj syn see* IMPRACTICABLE 2
ant functional

noninflammable *adj syn see* NONCOMBUSTIBLE
ant flammable, inflammable

nonliterate *adj syn see* PRIMITIVE 6

nonmaterial *adj syn see* IMMATERIAL 1
ant material

nonobligatory *adj syn see* OPTIONAL
ant obligatory

no-nonsense *adj syn see* SERIOUS 1

nonpareil *n syn see* PARAGON

nonpartisan *adj syn see* FAIR 4
ant partisan

nonphysical *adj syn see* IMMATERIAL 1
ant physical

non-placet *vb syn see* VETO

nonplus *vb* 1 to cause to be at a total loss as to how to act or decide <was totally *nonplussed* by the economic problems>
syn beat, buffalo, get, stick, stump; *compare* PUZZLE
rel baffle, frustrate, stymie, thwart; confound, perplex; mystify; dumbfound; overcome, throw; paralyze; confuse, flurry, fluster, muddle, rattle
idiom put (*or* drive) to one's wit's end, put up a tree (*or* stump), throw on one's beam end

2 *syn see* STAGGER 5
rel faze, rattle; baffle, balk, frustrate

nonprofessional *n syn see* AMATEUR 2
ant professional

nonrational *adj syn see* ILLOGICAL
ant rational

nonrealistic *adj syn see* IMPRACTICAL 1
ant realistic

nonreligious *adj syn see* IRRELIGIOUS
rel lay, profane, secular, temporal
ant religious

nonresistant *adj syn see* PASSIVE 2
ant resistant, resisting

---

syn synonym(s)   *rel* related word(s)
ant antonym(s)   *con* contrasted word(s)
idiom idiomatic equivalent(s)
‖ use limited; if in doubt, see a dictionary

nonresisting *adj syn* see PASSIVE 2
ant resistant, resisting

nonreversible *adj syn* see IRREVOCABLE
ant reversible

nonsectarian *adj* not affiliated with or restricted to a particular religious group <the problems facing *nonsectarian* colleges>
syn interchurch, intercreedal, interdenominational, undenominational, unsectarian
con denominational
ant sectarian

nonsense *n* 1 *syn* see GIBBERISH 1
2 something uttered or proposed that seems senseless or absurd <his theories are mere *nonsense*>
syn ‖applesauce, balderdash, ‖baloney, bilge, blague, blah, blather, blatherskite, bosh, ‖bull, ‖bunk, bunkum, bushwa, claptrap, ‖cock, ‖crap, double-talk, ‖drip, drivel, drool, eyewash, fiddle-faddle, fiddlesticks, flapdoodle, flimflam, flummadiddle, fudge, ‖gas, gook, guff, hogwash, hokum, hooey, ‖horsefeathers, hot air, humbug, jazz, ‖jiggery-pokery, malarkey, meshuggaas, moonshine, piffle, pishposh, poppycock, punk, rot, rubbish, slipslop, tomfoolery, tommyrot, tosh, trash, trumpery, twaddle, whangdoodle, windbaggery
idiom stuff and nonsense

nonsuccess *n syn* see FAILURE 2
ant success, successfulness

nonsymmetrical *adj syn* see LOPSIDED
ant symmetrical

nonviolent *adj syn* see PACIFIC
ant violent

noodle *n* 1 *syn* see DUNCE
2 *syn* see HEAD 1

nook *n* a secluded or sheltered place <resting in a shady *nook*>
syn byplace, cranny, niche
rel alcove, recess; cubbyhole, hole

noon *n syn* see APEX 2

no one *pron* no person <*no one* will be allowed to leave early>
syn nobody, no man, none
idiom never a one, nobody on earth, nobody under the sun, not a blessed soul, not a soul
con all, everyman; many, some
ant everybody, everyone

noontide *n syn* see APEX 2

noose *vb syn* see HANG 2

‖nope *adv syn* see NO
ant ‖yep, ‖yup

norm *n syn* see AVERAGE

normal *adj* 1 *syn* see SANE 2
2 *syn* see GENERAL 1

nose *n* 1 the prominent part of the human face that bears the nostrils and covers the nasal passage <had a large *nose*>
syn beak, ‖beezer, ‖boko, ‖conk, pecker, proboscis, ‖schnozzle, smeller, ‖sneezer, ‖snitch, snoot, snout
2 *syn* see BUSYBODY
3 *syn* see GIFT 2

nose *vb* 1 *syn* see SMELL 1
2 *syn* see SNOOP

nose-dive *vb syn* see PLUMMET

nosegay *n syn* see BOUQUET 1

nosey Parker *n syn* see BUSYBODY

Nostradamus *n syn* see PROPHET

nostrum *n syn* see PANACEA

nosy *adj syn* see CURIOUS 2

notability *n* 1 *syn* see NOTABLE 1
2 *syn* see CELEBRITY 2

notable *adj* 1 *syn* see NOTEWORTHY
2 *syn* see FAMOUS 2

notable *n* 1 a person of consequence or prominence <*notables* of Congress and the diplomatic corps>
syn big, big boy, ‖big bug, ‖big cheese, ‖big chief, ‖biggie, big gun, ‖big noise, big shot, big-timer, ‖big wheel, bigwig, character, chief, dignitary, eminence, ‖fat cat, great gun, heavyweight, high-muck-a-muck, leader, lion, luminary, muckamuck, mugwump, nabob, nawob, notability, personage, personality, pooh-bah, pot, somebody, VIP
rel figure; baron, czar, king, magnate, mogul, prince; light, star; power
idiom big-time operator, his nibs, Mr. Big
con cipher, nobody, nonentity; functionary, underling
2 *syn* see CELEBRITY 2

notably *adv syn* see VERY 1

notandum *n syn* see NOTE 2

notation *n syn* see NOTE 2

notch *n* 1 a usually V-shaped depression in an edge or surface <a *notch* in the table>
syn indentation, indenture, nick; *compare* DEPRESSION 2
rel cut, gash, incision, score, scratch; cleft, gap, nock
2 *syn* see DEGREE 1

note *vb syn* see SEE 1

note *n* 1 *syn* see CALL 1
2 a written reminder <made a *note* to return the call>
syn chit, memo, memorandum, notandum, notation
3 *syn* see REMARK 2
rel reminder
4 *syn* see LETTER 2
5 *syn* see NOTICE 1

noted *adj syn* see WELL-KNOWN
ant unnoted

note-perfect *adj syn* see PERFECT 2

noteworthy *adj* having a quality that attracts one's attention <a *noteworthy* event>
syn ‖bodacious, memorable, nameable, notable, observable, red-letter, rubric
rel conspicuous, noticeable, outstanding, prominent, remarkable; evident, manifest, patent; exceptional, extraordinary
con blah, common, commonplace, inconsequential, insignificant, ordinary, quotidian, unimportant, unremarkable
ant unnoteworthy

nothing *n* 1 something that does not exist <his hopes were based on *nothing*>
syn naught (*or* nought), nil, ‖nix, wind
idiom nothing at all, nothing whatever
con something
2 *syn* see ZERO 1
3 *syn* see NONENTITY
idiom (the) little end of nothing whittled down to a point

nothing *adj syn* see WORTHLESS 1

nothingness *n* the quality or state of being nothing <the house was blown into *nothingness* by the force of the explosion>
syn nada, nihility, nonexistence, nullity, vacuity

rel emptiness; vacuum, void

con concreteness, solidity, substantiality; materiality, reality

ant somethingness

notice *n* **1** a noting of or concerning oneself with something <take *notice* of the gathering clouds>

syn attention, cognizance, ear, heed, mark, ‖mind, note, observance, observation, regard, remark

rel care, concern, consideration, thought; apprehension, grasp, understanding

con disinterest, disregard, indifference, unconcern; carelessness, heedlessness, unmindfulness; insouciance, negligence, recklessness

2 *syn* see MEMORANDUM 2

3 *syn* see CRITICISM

notice *vb syn* see SEE 1

rel acknowledge, recognize; advert, allude, refer

con disregard, ignore, neglect, overlook, slight

noticeable *adj* attracting or compelling notice or attention <they both showed a *noticeable* aversion to his company>

syn arresting, arrestive, conspicuous, eye-catching, marked, outstanding, pointed, prominent, remarkable, salient, sensational, signal, striking

rel notable, noteworthy; evident, manifest, obvious, palpable, patent; spectacular

con obscure, vague; concealed, hidden, shrouded; insignificant, undistinguished

ant unnoticeable

notify *vb syn* see INFORM 2

rel announce, broadcast, declare, proclaim, promulgate, publish; disclose, discover, divulge, reveal

notion *n* **1** *syn* see IDEA

2 *syn* see CAPRICE

3 *syn* see HINT 1

notional *adj* **1** *syn* see CONCEPTUAL

2 *syn* see IMAGINARY 1

ant real

notoriety *n syn* see FAME 2

rel ballyhoo, promotion, propaganda, publicity

notorious *adj* **1** *syn* see WELL-KNOWN

2 *syn* see INFAMOUS 1

notwithstanding *prep syn* see AGAINST 4

notwithstanding *adv syn* see HOWEVER

nourish *vb* **1** *syn* see NURSE 1

2 *syn* see NURSE 2

nourishing *adj syn* see NUTRITIOUS

ant unnourishing

nourishment *n syn* see FOOD 2

rel keep, living, maintenance, support

nouveau riche *n syn* see UPSTART

novel *adj syn* see NEW 1

rel different, odd, peculiar, singular, special, strange, uncommon, unfamiliar, unique, unusual

con customary, habitual, usual; common, familiar, ordinary

novelty *n* **1** *syn* see CHANGE 2

con old story

2 *syn* see KNICKKNACK

novice *n* one who is just entering a field in which he has no previous experience <a *novice* in the theater —had never even had a walk-on role>

syn apprentice, beginner, boot, colt, fledgling, freshman, neophyte, newcomer, novitiate, prentice, punk, recruit, rookie, tenderfoot, tyro

rel amateur; cub; postulant, probationer; greenhorn, greeny; learner, student, trainee, undergraduate

con expert, pro, professional

ant doyen, old hand, old-timer, veteran

novitiate *n syn* see NOVICE

now *adv* **1** *syn* see TODAY

ant then

2 *syn* see AWAY 3

now *conj syn* see BECAUSE

now *n syn* see PRESENT

nowadays *adv syn* see TODAY

now and again *adv syn* see SOMETIMES

now and then *adv syn* see SOMETIMES

noxious *adj* **1** *syn* see UNWHOLESOME 1

ant wholesome; sanitary

2 *syn* see PERNICIOUS

rel fetid, putrid, noisome, stinking

ant innocuous, innoxious

nuance *n syn* see GRADATION

rel dash, soupçon, suggestion, suspicion, tinge, touch; nicety, subtlety

nub *n syn* see SUBSTANCE 2

nubbin *n syn* see SUBSTANCE 2

nubilous *adj* **1** *syn* see OVERCAST

2 *syn* see OBSCURE 3

nucleus *n syn* see SEED 2

nude *adj* **1** *syn* see BARE 1

con covered

2 not wearing any clothes <all the boys liked to swim *nude*>

syn au naturel, buff-bare, mother-naked, naked, raw, stark, stark-naked, stripped, unclad, unclothed, undressed

rel peeled, uncovered; dishabille, garment-less, unattired, unrobed

idiom ‖buck naked, in a state of nature, in one's birthday suit, in one's skin, in the altogether, in the buff, in the raw, stripped to the buff, without a stitch on, without a stitch to one's name

con attired, robed; decent; covered

ant clad, clothed, dressed

nudge *vb syn* see POKE 1

nudnick *n syn* see PEST 2

nugatory *adj syn* see VAIN 1

nugget *n syn* see LUMP 1

nuisance *n* **1** *syn* see PEST 2

2 *syn* see ANNOYANCE 3

null *adj* having no legal or binding force or validity <a *null* ballot>

syn bad, invalid, null and void, void

rel ineffective, ineffectual, inefficacious, useless, worthless

con acceptable, good, valid

null and void *adj syn* see NULL

nullify *vb syn* see ABOLISH 1

rel counteract, neutralize; compensate, counterbalance, countervail, offset; confine, limit, restrict

nullity *n* **1** *syn* see NOTHINGNESS

2 *syn* see NONENTITY

numb *adj* **1** devoid of sensation or feeling <my arm is *numb*>

---

syn synonym(s)   *rel* related word(s)
ant antonym(s)   *con* contrasted word(s)
idiom idiomatic equivalent(s)
‖ use limited; if in doubt, see a dictionary

syn anesthetized, asleep, benumbed, dead, deadened, insensible, insensitive, numbed, senseless, unfeeling

rel insensate, insentient, stupefied; comatose, unconscious

con alert; aware, conscious; sensitive

2 *syn* see INDIFFERENT 2

numb *vb syn* see DEADEN 1

rel chill, freeze, frost

numbed *adj syn* see NUMB 1

number *n* a character by which an arithmetical value is designated < you must add the *numbers* of the first column >

syn chiffer, cipher, digit, figure, integer, numeral, whole number

number *vb* **1** *syn* see COUNT 1

2 *syn* see AMOUNT 1

numberless *adj syn* see INNUMERABLE

ant numberable

number one *adj* **1** *syn* see CHIEF 2

2 *syn* see EXCELLENT

numeral *n syn* see NUMBER

numerate *vb* **1** *syn* see ENUMERATE 2

2 *syn* see COUNT 1

numerous *adj syn* see MANY

rel big, great, large

numinous *adj* **1** *syn* see SUPERNATURAL 1

2 *syn* see SACRED 2

3 *syn* see SPIRITUAL 4

4 *syn* see MYSTERIOUS

numskull *n syn* see DUNCE

numskulled *adj syn* see STUPID 1

nuptial *adj syn* see MATRIMONIAL

nuptial *n, usu* **nuptials** *pl syn* see WEDDING

nurse *n syn* see NURSEMAID

nurse *vb* **1** to feed from the breast < decided to *nurse* her baby >

syn breast-feed, nourish, suckle

rel bottle-feed

2 to promote the growth, development, or progress of < *nursed* the flame into a blaze >

syn cherish, cultivate, foster, nourish, nursle, nurture

rel feed; advance, forward, further, promote; humor, indulge, pamper

con check, hold back, retard, slow

3 *syn* see MINISTER (to)

nursemaid *n* one who is regularly employed to look after children < the *nursemaid* had three children in her charge >

syn ‖amah, ‖ayah, nana, ‖nanny, nurse, nurserymaid

rel babysitter, ‖minder, sitter; chaperon; governess

nurserymaid *n syn* see NURSEMAID

nursle *vb syn* see NURSE 2

nurture *n syn* see FOOD 1

nurture *vb syn* see NURSE 2

rel bring up, raise, rear; discipline, educate, school, train; back, bolster, support, sustain, uphold

con disregard, ignore, neglect, overlook, pass over, slight

nut *n* **1** *syn* see PROBLEM 2

‖**2** *syn* see HEAD 1

3 *syn* see CRACKPOT

4 *syn* see LUNATIC 1

5 *syn* see ENTHUSIAST

‖**nuthouse** *n syn* see ASYLUM 3

nutriculture *n syn* see HYDROPONICS

nutrient *adj syn* see NUTRITIOUS

nutriment *n syn* see FOOD 2

rel bread, bread and butter, keep, livelihood, living, maintenance, subsistence, support

nutrimental *adj syn* see NUTRITIOUS

nutritional *adj syn* see NUTRITIVE 1

nutritious *adj* promoting growth and repairing natural waste < *nutritious* food >

syn nourishing, nutrient, nutrimental, nutritive

rel good, healthful, salubrious, salutary, wholesome; balanced

con indigestible; bad, insalubrious, unhealthful, unwholesome

ant innutritious

nutritive *adj* **1** relating to or concerned with nutrition < *nutritive* organs of the body >

syn alimentary, alimentative, nutritional

rel digestive, metabolic; constructive, creative, formative, productive

2 *syn* see NUTRITIOUS

nuts *adj syn* see INSANE 1

nutshell *vb syn* see EPITOMIZE 1

nutsy *adj syn* see INSANE 1

nutty *adj* **1** *syn* see ENTHUSIASTIC

2 *syn* see INSANE 1

nuzzle *vb syn* see SNUGGLE

nymph *n syn* see DOXY 1

nymphet *n syn* see DOXY 1

O

oaf *n* **1** *syn* see DUNCE
2 a big clumsy, usually slow-witted person < an *oaf* who bumped into everything he passed >
syn bohunk, ‖gaum, gawk, klutz, lobster, looby, lout, lubber, ‖lug, lummox, lump, lumpkin, meathead, palooka, slouch
rel ‖baboon, beast, bruiser, brute, bull, gorilla, hulk, missing link, ox; clod, clown, dub, galoot, slob; blunderbuss, blunderer, blunderhead

oar *vb syn* see ROW

oater *n syn* see WESTERN

oath *n syn* see SWEARWORD

obdurate *adj* **1** *syn* see UNFEELING 2
con tender
2 *syn* see INFLEXIBLE 2
rel mulish, stiff-necked; immovable
con relenting, submitting

obedient *adj* submissive to the will, guidance, or control of another < children should always be *obedient* to their parents >
syn amenable, biddable, docile, ‖docious, tractable
rel acquiescent, compliant, sheeplike, submissive, yielding; duteous, dutiful, loyal; law-abiding; obeisant, subservient
con insubordinate, rebellious; contrary, froward, perverse, wayward, willful; headstrong, intractable, recalcitrant, refractory, uncontrollable, ungovernable, unruly
ant contumacious, disobedient

obeisance *n syn* see HONOR 1
rel allegiance, fealty, loyalty

obeisant *adj syn* see SUBSERVIENT 2

obese *adj syn* see FAT 2
ant skinny

obesity *n* a condition characterized by excessive bodily fat < could barely walk because of his *obesity* >
syn adiposity, corpulence, fatness, fleshiness
rel chubbiness, chunkiness, embonpoint, grossness, plumpness, portliness, pudginess, rotundity, stockiness, stoutness, tubbiness
con lankiness, leanness, scrawniness, slenderness, slimness
ant skinniness

obey *vb* to act or behave in conformity with (as an order) or in duty to (as a parent) < *obey* a superior's order >
syn comply, conform, follow, keep, mind, observe
rel bow, defer, submit, yield; accede, acquiesce, agree, assent; fulfill, satisfy; carry out; heed, regard
idiom abide by

---

syn synonym(s)   *rel* related word(s)
ant antonym(s)   *con* contrasted word(s)
idiom idiomatic equivalent(s)
‖ use limited; if in doubt, see a dictionary

con break, disregard, transgress, violate; command, order
ant disobey

obfuscate *vb syn* see OBSCURE
ant clarify

obit *n syn* see OBITUARY

obiter *adv syn* see INCIDENTALLY 2

obiter dictum *n syn* see REMARK 2

obituary *n* a notice of a person's death usually with a short biographical account < always read the *obituaries* in the paper >
syn necrology, obit

object *n* **1** *syn* see THING 3
rel doodad; gadget
2 *syn* see THING 4
3 *syn* see BODY 4
4 *syn* see VIEW 6
5 *syn* see USE 4

object *vb* **1** to oppose by arguing against < *objecting* because the evidence was unclear >
syn except, expostulate, inveigh (against), kick, protest, remonstrate
rel balk, boggle, demur, dissent, jib, stickle; complain; criticize; challenge; spurn; rail, rant, rave, storm
con accede, agree, assent, consent; accredit, approve, sanction
ant acquiesce
2 *syn* see DISAPPROVE 1

objectify *vb syn* see EMBODY 1

objection *n syn* see DEMUR 2

objectionable *adj* arousing or likely to arouse objection < the language in that movie is *objectionable* >
syn exceptionable, ill-favored, inadmissible, unacceptable, undesirable, unwanted, unwelcome
rel abhorrent, loathsome, offensive, repellent, repugnant, repulsive, revolting; disagreeable, distasteful, invidious, obnoxious, unpleasant; unfit, unsuitable; censurable, reprehensible
con acceptable, agreeable, gratifying, pleasant, pleasing, welcome
ant unobjectionable

objective *adj* **1** *syn* see MATERIAL 1
rel external, outer, outside, outward
ant subjective
2 *syn* see FAIR 4
ant subjective

objective *n* **1** *syn* see AMBITION 2
2 *syn* see USE 4

objectless *adj syn* see RANDOM

objet d'art *n syn* see KNICKKNACK

objurgate *vb syn* see EXECRATE 1
rel castigate, censure

obligated *adj syn* see INDEBTED

obligation *n* **1** *syn* see OCCASION 3
2 something one is bound to do or forbear < it is our *obligation* to obey the law >
syn charge, commitment, committal, devoir, duty, must, need, ought, ‖right

rel compulsion, constraint, restraint; burden, requirement, responsibility; business, part, place
con choice, discretion, free will, option; decision, determination, pleasure, will
3 *syn* see INDEBTEDNESS 1

obligatory *adj syn* see MANDATORY
ant nonobligatory

oblige *vb* 1 *syn* see FORCE 2
2 to do a service or courtesy < you will *oblige* me greatly if you will get there on time >
syn accommodate, convenience, favor
rel gratify, please; avail, benefit, profit; aid, assist, contribute, help
con bother, discommode, incommode, inconvenience, trouble
ant disoblige

obliged *adj* 1 *syn* see GRATEFUL 1
2 *syn* see INDEBTED

obliging *adj syn* see AMIABLE 1
ant disobliging

oblique *adj* 1 *syn* see INCLINED 3
2 *syn* see INDIRECT 1
ant straight

obliquely *adv syn* see ASIDE 1
ant straight

obliterate *vb syn* see ERASE

oblivion *n* a state of forgetting or the fact of having forgotten < the *oblivion* of sleep >
syn forgetfulness, lethe, obliviousness
rel nirvana; insensibleness
con alertness, awareness, consciousness; memory, recall, recalling, recollection, remembrance

oblivious *adj* 1 *syn* see FORGETFUL 1
rel absorbed, unaware, unconscious
idiom turned off
2 *syn* see IGNORANT 2

obliviousness *n syn* see OBLIVION

obloquy *n* 1 *syn* see ABUSE
2 *syn* see ANIMADVERSION
3 *syn* see DISGRACE

obnoxious *adj* 1 *syn* see LIABLE 2
ant unobnoxious
2 *syn* see REPUGNANT 1
con congenial, likable, simpatico
ant grateful; unobnoxious

obscene *adj* 1 *syn* see OFFENSIVE
2 marked by the use of words regarded as taboo in polite usage < knew all the *obscene* expressions for the genitalia >
syn barnyard, coarse, crude, crusty, dirty, fescennine, filthy, foul, gross, indecent, nasty, paw, profane, rank, raunchy, ||raw, rocky, scatological, scurrilous, smutty, vulgar; *compare* RISQUÉ
rel bawdy, ribald, smoking-room; impure, lascivious, lewd, warm; lurid, pornographic, salacious, scabrous, sultry; earthy, rich; unprintable; foulmouthed
con acceptable, proper, tolerable; appropriate, fit, suitable; clean, decent, decorous, seemly

obscure *adj* 1 *syn* see DARK 1
rel clouded, cloudy, fuliginous, shadowy, shady, umbrageous
con clear, lucid; bright, brilliant, luminous
2 withdrawn from the main centers of human activity < was exiled to an *obscure* Siberian village >

syn devious, lonesome, out-of-the-way, remote, removed, retired, secret
rel distant, far, far-off; close, hidden, odd, secluded, sequestered, solitary; blind; inaccessible
idiom back of beyond, off the beaten track (*or* path), in the boondocks (*or* sticks)
con central; urban; populous
3 not readily understood or grasped < an *obscure* textual reference >
syn ambiguous, amphibological, double-edged, double-faced, dusky, equivocal, murky, nubilous, opaque, sibylline, tenebrous, uncertain, unclear, unexplicit, unintelligible, vague; *compare* CRYPTIC, FAINT 2
rel difficult, incomprehensible, inexplicable, puzzling, unfathomable; illegible; abstruse, Delphian, enigmatic, esoteric, inscrutable, mysterious, mystic, mystical; inconclusive, indecisive, indefinite
con definite, explicit, obvious; clear, express, unambiguous, unequivocal
ant lucid
4 *syn* see INCONSPICUOUS
rel humble, lowly, minor, unimportant
5 lacking the prominence, showiness, or worth by which attention might be attracted < an *obscure* Roman poet >
syn nameless, uncelebrated, unfamed, unheard-of, unknown, unnoted, unrenowned
rel inconspicuous; minor, undistinguished, unimportant
con celebrated, distinguished, named, notable, noted, noteworthy, renowned, well-known
ant famed, famous
6 *syn* see FAINT 2
ant clear

obscure *vb* to make dark, dim, or indistinct < fog *obscured* our view >
syn adumbrate, becloud, bedim, befog, cloud, darken, dim, dislimn, eclipse, fog, gloom, haze, mist, murk, obfuscate, overcast, overcloud, overshadow, shadow
rel blear, blur, fuzz; blind, conceal, dim out, hide, screen, shade, shroud; bemask, camouflage, cloak, cover, disguise, mask, veil; belie, falsify, misrepresent
con brighten, light (up), lighten; clarify, enlighten; elucidate, exemplify, explain
ant illuminate, illumine

obscured *adj syn* see ULTERIOR

obsequious *adj syn* see SUBSERVIENT 2
rel deferential; parasitic, sycophantic, toadying
con self-assertive

observable *adj* 1 *syn* see PERCEPTIBLE
ant unobservable
2 *syn* see NOTEWORTHY

observance *n* 1 *syn* see RITE 2
2 *syn* see NOTICE 1
ant nonobservance, unobservance

observant *adj* 1 *syn* see ATTENTIVE 1
rel awake
ant unobservant
2 *syn* see MINDFUL 2

observation *n* 1 *syn* see NOTICE 1
2 *syn* see REMARK 2

observative *adj syn* see MINDFUL 2

observatory *n syn* see LOOKOUT 2

observe vb 1 syn see OBEY
2 syn see KEEP 2
rel revere, reverence, venerate
ant break, violate
3 syn see SEE 1
4 syn see REMARK 2
observer n syn see SPECTATOR
observing adj syn see MINDFUL 2
ant unobserving
obsessed adj preoccupied intensely or
abnormally < *obsessed* with cleanliness >
syn hagridden, hipped, queer
rel bewitched, dominated, gripped, held,
possessed, prepossessed; bedeviled, beset,
dogged, harassed, haunted, plagued, troubled; overcome
idiom have on the brain
con detached, unconcerned, uninterested;
indifferent, neutral; cool, easy-going
obsession n syn see FETISH 2
obsolesce vb syn see OUTDATE
obsolete adj no longer active or in use
< *obsolete* social customs >
syn dead, disused, extinct, outmoded,
outworn, passé, superseded; *compare* AN-
CIENT 1
rel old-fashioned, old hat, old-time, old≠
timey, out-of-date, unfashionable; dusty,
fusty, moldy, moth-eaten, musty, stale,
timeworn
idiom behind the times
con contemporary, modern, new-fashioned, up-to-date, up-to-the-minute; novel,
original, unique
ant current
obsolete vb syn see OUTDATE
obstacle n something that seriously ham-
pers action or progress < lack of education is an *obstacle* to advancement >
syn bar, Chinese wall, crimp, hamper,
hurdle, impediment, mountain, obstruction, rub, snag, stumbling block, traverse
rel clog, encumbrance, handicap, hindrance; bump, difficulty, hardship, vicissitude; catch, hitch; disincentive
con aid, assist, assistance, help
ant advantage
obstinate adj unwilling to submit (as to
reason or control) < he had an *obstinate*
determination to live as he pleased >
syn bullheaded, closed-minded, deaf,
hardheaded, headstrong, incompliant,
intractable, intransigent, muleheaded,
muley, mulish, pertinacious, perverse,
pervicacious, pigheaded, stubborn, self≠
willed, ‖sot, stiff, stiff-necked, stubborn,
tough, unpliable, unpliant, unyielding,
willful, wrongheaded; *compare* UNRULY 1
rel resistant, unsubmissive, withstanding;
contrary, crabbed, recalcitrant, renitent;
inexorable, inflexible, obdurate; opinionated; resolute, staunch, steadfast, unbudg-
ing
con acquiescent, complaisant, compliant;
submissive, yielding; agreeable, cooperative, willing
ant pliable, pliant
obstipated adj syn see CONSTIPATED

obstreperous adj 1 syn see VOCIFEROUS
2 syn see DISOBEDIENT
obstruct vb 1 syn see FILL 1
2 syn see HINDER
3 syn see SCREEN 3
obstruction n syn see OBSTACLE
obtain vb syn see GET 1
obtainable adj 1 syn see AVAILABLE 1
rel derivable
2 syn see PURCHASABLE 1
obtrude vb 1 syn see IMPOSE 5
2 syn see INTRUDE 1
obtrusive adj syn see IMPERTINENT 2
ant unobtrusive
obtund vb syn see DULL 3
obtuse adj syn see DULL 6
obviate vb syn see PREVENT 2
rel anticipate; interfere, interpose, intervene
obvious adj syn see CLEAR 5
ant abstruse, obscure; unobvious
occasion n 1 syn see OPPORTUNITY
2 syn see CAUSE 1
3 something that provides a reason for
something else < there is no *occasion* for
alarm >
syn call, cause, necessity, obligation
rel basis, foundation, ground, warrant;
justification, right; excuse
4 syn see OCCURRENCE
5 a particular point of time at which
something takes place < we always spoke,
but on that *occasion* we didn't >
syn instant, moment, time, while
idiom point in time
6 syn see NEED 3
7 occasions pl syn see BUSINESS 8
8 syn see EVENT 2
occasion vb syn see GENERATE 3
occasional adj syn see INFREQUENT
rel incidental; casual, random
con accustomed, habitual, usual; constant,
continual, continuous
ant customary
occasionally adv on a few occasions < oc-
casionally she'll walk instead of drive >
syn infrequently, irregularly, on occasion,
sporadically, uncommonly; *compare* SOME-
TIMES
rel off and on, once or twice
idiom every now and then, from time to
time, ‖once in a way, once in a while
con continually, continuously, frequently;
commonly, customarily, habitually, often;
hardly ever, rarely, scarcely, seldom; never
ant constantly
occlude vb syn see FILL 1
occult vb syn see HIDE
occult adj syn see RECONDITE
rel arcane, mysterious; cabalistic, mystical, supernatural; eerie, unearthly, weird
occupancy n syn see HABITATION 1
occupant n syn see INHABITANT
occupation n 1 syn see WORK 1
2 syn see HABITATION 1
occupiable adj syn see LIVABLE 1
occupied adj syn see BUSY 1
ant unoccupied
occupy vb 1 syn see ENGAGE 4
2 syn see INHABIT
occur vb 1 syn see HAPPEN 1
2 to enter one's mind < it just *occurred* to
me: she can't drive >

---

syn synonym(s)   rel related word(s)
ant antonym(s)   con contrasted word(s)
idiom idiomatic equivalent(s)
‖ use limited; if in doubt, see a dictionary

syn hit, strike

idiom come into one's head, come to mind, cross one's mind, flash across one's head, go through one's head

occurrence *n* something that happens or takes place < the chance encounter turned out to be a fortunate *occurrence* >
syn circumstance, episode, event, go, happening, incident, occasion, thing
rel contingency, emergency, exigency, juncture, pass; condition, situation, state; adventure, experience

ocean *n* the body of water that covers nearly three-fourths of the earth < pulled the downed pilot from the *ocean* >
syn blue, brine, ‖briny, deep, drink, main, sea

oceanic *adj syn see* MARINE 1

ochlocracy *n syn see* ANARCHY 1

ocular *adj* 1 *syn see* VISUAL 2
2 *syn see* VISUAL 1

ocular *n syn see* EYE 1

oculus *n syn see* EYE 1

odd *adj* 1 being without a corresponding mate < had only an *odd* glove; the other was lost >
syn unmatched, unpaired
rel lone, only, single
con matched, paired
2 *syn see* ACCIDENTAL
3 *syn see* STRANGE 4

oddball *n syn see* ECCENTRIC

oddball *adj syn see* STRANGE 4

oddity *n* 1 *syn see* ECCENTRIC
2 *syn see* CURIOSITY 2

oddments *n pl syn see* SUNDRIES

odds *n pl syn see* ADVANTAGE 3

odds and ends *n pl* 1 *syn see* SUNDRIES
2 *syn see* MISCELLANY 1

odiferous *adj syn see* ODOROUS

odious *adj syn see* HATEFUL 2

odium *n* 1 *syn see* DISGRACE
rel hate, hatred
ant honor
2 *syn see* STIGMA

odor *n syn see* SMELL 1

odoriferous *adj syn see* ODOROUS

odorize *vb syn see* SCENT 2

odorless *adj* having no odor < *odorless* castor oil >
syn inodorous, scentless, smell-less
rel deodorant, deodorizing; unscented
con scented, smelly
ant odorous

odorous *adj* having or emitting an odor < *odorous* chemicals are often malodorous >
syn odiferous, odoriferous, scented; *compare* MALODOROUS 1, SWEET 2
rel redolent, reeking, smelling, smelly; heady, pungent, strong; olfactive, olfactory
ant inodorous, odorless, scentless

o'er *prep syn see* OVER 1

oeuvre *n* a substantial body of work constituting the lifework of a writer, composer, or artist < one of the more popular operas in the Mozart *oeuvre* >
syn corpus, opera omnia
rel output

off *adv syn see* AWAY 2

off *adj* 1 *syn see* REMOTE 4
2 *syn see* SLOW 3

offal *n syn see* REFUSE

off-balance *adj syn see* LOPSIDED

off-center *adj syn see* ECCENTRIC 1

off-color *adj* 1 *syn see* UNWELL
2 *syn see* RISQUÉ

offend *vb* 1 *syn see* TRESPASS 1
2 *syn see* VIOLATE 1
3 to cause hurt feelings or deep resentment < *offended* her by his cruel remark >
syn affront, insult, outrage
rel aggrieve, hurt, sting, wound; exasperate, gall, irritate, nettle; excite, provoke; appall, horrify, scandalize, shock; disoblige, displease, distress, disturb, miff, pique, upset
idiom hurt one's feelings, ruffle one's feathers, step (*or* tread) on one's toes
con delight, gratify, please, tickle; captivate, charm, enchant; flatter

offender *n syn see* CRIMINAL

offense *n* 1 *syn see* ATTACK 1
2 an emotional response to a slight or indignity < he is so sensitive that he takes *offense* at the slightest criticism >
syn dudgeon, huff, miff, pique, resentment, ‖snuff, umbrage
rel affront, indignity, insult; anger, indignation; displeasure; catfit, conniption, fit, tantrum; pet, tizzy; explosion, flare-up, outburst, scene
con delight, pleasure
3 *syn see* CRIME 1

offensive *adj* utterly unpleasant or distasteful to the senses or sensibilities < the *offensive* odor of stale garbage > < her arrogant assurance was more than a little *offensive* >
syn atrocious, disgusting, evil, foul, hideous, horrible, horrid, icky, loathsome, nasty, nauseating, noisome, obscene, repellent, repugnant, repulsive, revolting, sickening, ungrateful, unwholesome, vile
rel abhorrent, bad, disagreeable, objectionable, uncongenial, unpleasant; abominable, detestable, fulsome, odious; rank; appalling, awful, beastly, dreadful, frightful, ghastly, grim, grisly, gruesome, lurid, shocking, terrible; unappetizing, unpalatable, unsavory
con agreeable, appealing, attractive, pleasant, pleasing; favorable, unobjectionable, welcome; appetizing, palatable, savory; divine
ant inoffensive, unoffensive

offensive *n syn see* ATTACK 1

offer *vb* 1 to put something before another for acceptance or consideration < he was soon *offered* another job >
syn extend, give, hold out, pose, present, proffer, tender
rel display, exhibit, show
con accept, receive, take; decline, refuse, reject
2 *syn see* ADDUCE
3 *syn see* TRY 5
4 *syn see* SHOW 1

offering *n* 1 *syn see* VICTIM 1
2 *syn see* DONATION

offgoing *n syn see* DEPARTURE 1

offhand *adj syn see* EXTEMPORANEOUS

office *n* 1 *syn see* JOB 2
2 *syn see* FUNCTION 1
‖3 *syn see* PRIVY 1

‖4 *syn* see HIGH SIGN 2
officer *n* 1 *syn* see POLICEMAN
2 *syn* see EXECUTIVE

official *n syn* see EXECUTIVE

official *adj* derived from the proper office, officer, or authority < the mayor's office issued an *official* statement >
syn authoritative, ex cathedra, ex officio
rel approved, authorized, certified, cleared, endorsed, OK'd, sanctioned; canonical, cathedral
ant officious (*in diplomatic use*), unofficial

officially *adv syn* see OSTENSIBLY

officiate *vb syn* see ACT 4

officious *adj syn* see IMPERTINENT 2

offing *n syn* see FUTURE

offish *adj* 1 *syn* see UNSOCIABLE
2 *syn* see UNWELL

off-key *adj syn* see IRREGULAR 1

off–load *vb syn* see UNLOAD

off–lying *adj syn* see DISTANT 1

offscouring *n syn* see OUTCAST

offset *vb syn* see COMPENSATE 1
rel check, stop

offshoot *n syn* see OUTGROWTH 2

offspring *n pl* those who follow in direct parental line < a mother of numerous *offspring* >
syn ‖begats, brood, children, descendants, issue, posterity, progeniture, progeny, scions, seed
rel hatch, swarm; produce, spawn, young
con antecedents, ascendants, forebears, forefathers, progenitors
ant ancestors

offstage *adj or adv syn* see BACKSTAGE
ant onstage

of late *adv syn* see NEW

oft *adv syn* see OFTEN

often *adv* many times < we called *often* but still could not reach you >
syn again and again, frequently, much, oft, oftentimes, ofttimes, over and over, repeatedly, time and again
idiom a number of times, many a time, many times over, time and time again
con infrequently, rarely; now and then, occasionally
ant seldom

oftentimes *adv syn* see OFTEN

ofttimes *adv syn* see OFTEN

ogle *vb syn* see LOOK 7

‖**ogle** *n syn* see EYE 1

ogress *n syn* see VIRAGO

oil *n syn* see FLATTERY

‖**oiled** *adj syn* see INTOXICATED 1

oily *adj* 1 *syn* see FATTY 2
2 *syn* see FULSOME

ointment *n* a semisolid medicinal or cosmetic preparation for application to the skin < put *ointment* on the burned skin >
syn balm, cerate, chrism, cream, salve, unction, unguent
rel embrocation, liniment; demulcent, emollient; lotion; dressing

OK (*or okay*) *adv syn* see YES 1

OK (*or okay*) *vb syn* see APPROVE 2

OK (*or okay*) *n syn* see APPROBATION

‖**okeydoke** *adv syn* see YES 1

old *adj* 1 *syn* see ANCIENT 1
con contemporary, current, recent; advanced
ant new
2 of long standing < the ending of such an *old* friendship was tragic >
syn continuing, enduring, inveterate, lifelong, long-lasting, long-lived, perennial; *compare* LASTING
rel constant, perpetual, staying; established, firm, solid, steady
con newfound, recent; brief, short-lived; casual, temporary, transitory, weak
ant new
3 *syn* see OLD-FASHIONED
rel primitive; traditional
con newish
ant modern, new
4 *syn* see AGED 1
idiom along in years, getting on
con juvenile, young
ant youthful
5 *syn* see EXPERIENCED
con young
ant new
6 *syn* see FORMER 2

old age *n* the final stage of the normal life span < spent his *old age* in a nursing home >
syn age, caducity, elderliness, senectitude, senescence, years; *compare* DOTAGE
rel decrepitude, feebleness; infirmity
idiom advanced years, declining years, winter of life
ant youth

olden *adj* 1 *syn* see ANCIENT 1
2 *syn* see AGED 1

oldest profession *n syn* see PROSTITUTION

oldfangled *adj syn* see OLD-FASHIONED
ant newfangled

old–fashioned *adj* typical of an earlier time and often replaced by something more modern or fashionable < *old-fashioned* high-buttoned shoes >
syn antiquated, antique, archaic, belated, bygone, dated, démodé, demoded, dowdy, fusty, moldy, moth-eaten, neanderthal, old, oldfangled, old hat, old-time, old=timey, outdated, outmoded, out-of-date, passé, rococo, unmodern, vintage
rel aged, ancient; discarded, disused, obsolete; outworn, unfashionable; crusty, fogyish, fuddy-duddy, fusty, moss-backed, moss-grown, mossy, stodgy; Victorian; old-line
con modernistic, modish, newfangled, stylish, ‖trendy; current, recent, timely; new-fashioned, up-to-date, up-to-the-minute
ant contemporary; modern

Old Gooseberry *n syn* see DEVIL 1

Old Guard *n syn* see ESTABLISHMENT 2

old hand *n syn* see VETERAN

old hat *adj* 1 *syn* see OLD-FASHIONED
2 *syn* see TRITE

old lady *n* ‖1 *syn* see WIFE
‖2 *syn* see MOTHER 1
3 *syn* see FUSSBUDGET

old–line *adj syn* see CONSERVATIVE 1

old liner *n syn* see DIEHARD 1

old maid *n* 1 *syn* see SPINSTER

---

syn synonym(s)   *rel* related word(s)
ant antonym(s)   *con* contrasted word(s)
idiom idiomatic equivalent(s)
‖ use limited; if in doubt, see a dictionary

2 *syn* see FUSSBUDGET

old–maidish *adj syn* see NICE 1

‖**old man** *n* 1 *syn* see HUSBAND

2 *syn* see FATHER 1

Old Nick *n syn* see DEVIL 1

Old Scratch *n syn* see DEVIL 1

oldster *n* a person of advanced years < an *oldster* long retired from the business world >

syn ancient, elder, golden-ager, old-timer, senior, senior citizen; *compare* BELDAM 1, GAFFER

ant youngster, youth

old–time *adj* 1 *syn* see OLD-FASHIONED

2 *syn* see EXPERIENCED

old–timer *n* 1 *syn* see VETERAN

2 *syn* see OLDSTER

old–timey *adj syn* see OLD-FASHIONED

‖**old woman** *n* 1 *syn* see WIFE

2 *syn* see MOTHER 1

old–womanish *adj syn* see NICE 1

oleaginous *adj* 1 *syn* see FATTY 2

2 *syn* see FULSOME

olid *adj syn* see MALODOROUS 1

olio *n syn* see MISCELLANY 1

olla podrida *n syn* see MISCELLANY 1

omen *n syn* see FORETOKEN

omen *vb syn* see AUGUR 2

ominous *adj* indicative of future misfortune or calamity < dark *ominous* clouds preceded the storm >

syn apocalyptic, baleful, baneful, dire, direful, doomful, fateful, ill-boding, ill-omened, inauspicious, threatening, unlucky, unpropitious; *compare* EVIL 5, SINISTER

rel portentous; malefic, maleficent, malign, sinister; comminatory, forbidding, grim, lowering, menacing; hostile, inhospitable, unfriendly

con auspicious, benign, favorable, promising, propitious; beneficial

omission *n* something omitted or missing < several *omissions* in the list >

syn blank, chasm, overlook, oversight, preterition, pretermission, skip

rel inadvertence, inadvertency, lapse, slip; break, gap, hiatus, lacuna

con inclusion; accession, addition, augmentation, increase, reinforcement; superaddition

omit *vb syn* see NEGLECT

omitted *adj syn* see ABSENT 1

ant included

omnibus *n syn* see ANTHOLOGY

omnipotent *adj* having virtually unlimited authority or influence < an *omnipotent* leader >

syn all-powerful, almighty

rel divine, godlike; unlimited, unrestricted

con impotent, powerless; limited, restricted

omnipresent *adj* present at all places at all times < *omnipresent* God >

syn allover, ubiquitous, universal

rel boundless, endless, immeasurable, infinite, limitless, unending

con bounded, finite, limited, restricted; cramped, straitened; narrow, strait

omnium–gatherum *n syn* see MISCELLANY 1

on *prep* 1 *syn* see OVER 4

2 *syn* see OVER 3

on *adv syn* see ALONG 1

on–again–off–again *adj syn* see FITFUL

onanism *n syn* see SELF-GRATIFICATION

onanistic *adj syn* see SYBARITIC

once *adv* 1 *syn* see EVER 5

2 *syn* see BEFORE 2

once *adj syn* see FORMER 2

once and again *adv syn* see SOMETIMES

once more *adv syn* see OVER 7

oncoming *adj syn* see FORTHCOMING

on–dit *n syn* see REPORT 1

one *adj syn* see SINGLE 2

one *vb syn* see JOIN 1

one by one *adv syn* see APART 1

one–horse town *n syn* see BURG

oneness *n* 1 *syn* see UNITY 1

ant multiplicity

2 *syn* see UNIQUENESS

3 *syn* see ENTIRETY 1

4 *syn* see IDENTITY 1

oner *n syn* see DOLLAR

onerous *adj* imposing great hardship or strain < found the care of his old mother an *onerous* burden >

syn burdensome, demanding, exacting, exigent, grievous, oppressive, superincumbent, taxing, tough, trying, weighty

rel arduous, difficult, hard, laborious; heavy, hefty, ponderous; cumbersome, unruly, unwieldy; driving, heavy-handed

con easy, effortless; facile, light, simple, smooth, unexacting, untaxing

onerously *adv syn* see HARD 8

one–sided *adj syn* see BIASED 2

rel lopsided, weighted

con many-sided

one–sidedness *n syn* see PREJUDICE

con manysidedness

onetime *adj syn* see FORMER 2

onfall *n syn* see ATTACK 1

ongoing *n syn* see ADVANCE 2

rel development, growth

onlooker *n syn* see SPECTATOR

only *adj* 1 *syn* see ALONE 3

2 being one or more of which there exist no others < the *only* survivors of the wreck >

syn alone, lone, singular, sole, solitary, solo, unexampled, unique, unrepeatable

rel incomparable, inimitable, matchless, peerless, transcendent, unequaled, unparalleled, unrivaled; companionless, separate, unaccompanied, unattended, uncompanied, uncompanioned

con divers, many, multifarious, numerous, sundry, various

3 *syn* see SINGLE 2

only *adv* 1 to the exclusion of any alternative or competitor < he will confess *only* to you >

syn alone, but, entirely, exclusively, solely

2 *syn* see JUST 3

only *conj* in spite of which < it looks delicious, *only* I'm not hungry >

syn but, except, however, save, yet

on occasion *adv syn* see OCCASIONALLY

on offer *adj syn* see PURCHASABLE 1

onomatopoeic *adj* formed in imitation of a natural sound < *buzz* is an *onomatopoeic* word to describe the sound of bees >

syn echoic, imitative, onomatopoetic

rel emulative, simulative; mimetic, mimic, mimical

onomatopoetic *adj syn see* ONOMATOPO-
EIC

on purpose *adv syn see* INTENTIONALLY

onset *n* 1 *syn see* ATTACK 1
  2 *syn see* BEGINNING

onslaught *n syn see* ATTACK 1

on the whole *adv syn see* ALTOGETHER 3

onus *n* 1 *syn see* LOAD 3
  2 *syn see* BLAME
  3 *syn see* STIGMA

onward *adv* 1 *syn see* AHEAD 2
  2 *syn see* ALONG 1

onyx *adj syn see* BLACK 1

oodles *n pl but sometimes sing in constr*
  syn see SCAD

‖**ooftish** *n syn see* MONEY

‖**oofy** *adj syn see* RICH 1

ooid *adj syn see* OVAL

oomph *n syn see* SPIRIT 5

ooze *vb syn see* EXUDE

oozy *adj syn see* MUDDY 1

opaque *adj syn see* OBSCURE 3
  ant transparent, transpicuous

ope *vb syn see* OPEN 1

open *adj* 1 not closed or obstructed <es-
caped through the *open* gate>
  syn patent, unclosed, unobstructed
  rel agape, dehiscent, gaping, patulous,
ringent, wide, yawning; ajar; unbarred,
unbolted, unfastened, unlocked, unsealed;
clear, unimpeded
  con blocked, obstructed; constricted,
cramped, narrow, strait
  ant closed, shut
  2 lacking a cover or covering <an *open*
wound that continued to ooze blood>
<his chest *open* to the sun>
  syn bare, denuded, exposed, naked,
peeled, stripped, uncovered
  3 *syn see* LIABLE 2
  ant closed
  4 not restricted to a particular group or
situation <favored *open* enrollment in the
schools>
  syn accessible, open-door, public, unrestricted
  rel attainable, available, obtainable,
reachable, securable
  idiom to be had, within reach
  con limited, restricted; inaccessible, private
  ant closed
  5 available for use or consideration or
decision <there are only two courses *open*
to us>
  syn accessible, employable, operative,
practicable, usable
  rel appropriate, fit, proper, suitable; acceptable, agreeable, pleasing
  idiom within reach
  con inaccessible, inoperative, unusable
  ant closed
  6 *syn see* DOUBTFUL 1
  7 *syn see* FRANK
  ant close; clandestine

open *vb* 1 to change from a closed to an
open condition <*open* the window>
  syn ope, unblock, unclose, undo, unshut,
unstop

rel clear, free, release; bare, disclose,
expose, reveal
  idiom lay open, swing open, throw open
  con block, occlude, stop
  ant close, shut
  2 to make physically or mentally visible
<dawn *opened* a surprising scene to his
startled eyes>
  syn disclose, display, expose, reveal, unclothe, uncover, unveil
  rel adumbrate, hint, shadow, suggest
  idiom bring to light, bring to (or into)
view, lay bare, make plain, show forth
  con cloak, conceal, hide, screen, secrete,
shroud
  3 to make an opening in <decided to
open a can of beans>
  syn breach, disrupt, hole, rupture
  rel break, broach, tap, undo; cut, gash,
slash; perforate, pierce
  idiom lay open
  con occlude, shut; fasten, secure
  ant close
  4 to spread out <the falcon slowly
opened her mighty wings>
  syn expand, extend, fan (out), outspread,
outstretch, spread, unfold
  rel billow, dilate, distend, swell; cover,
mantle, overspread
  con collect, concentrate, contract, gather
(in)
  ant close
  5 *syn see* BEGIN 1
  ant close
  6 *syn see* CONVENE 1

open *n syn see* OUTDOORS

open air *n syn see* OUTDOORS

open-air *adj syn see* OUTDOOR
  con indoor, inside; enclosed

open-and-shut *adj syn see* CLEAR 5

open-door *adj syn see* OPEN 4

open-eyed *adj syn see* WATCHFUL

openhanded *adj* 1 *syn see* LIBERAL 1
  ant closefisted, tightfisted
  2 *syn see* CLEAR 5

openhearted *adj syn see* FRANK

opening *n* 1 *syn see* BEGINNING
  ant closing
  2 *syn see* APERTURE
  3 *syn see* GAP 1
  4 *syn see* OPPORTUNITY

opening gun *n syn see* BEGINNING

openmouthed *adj syn see* VOCIFEROUS

openness *n syn see* EXPOSURE

open sesame *n syn see* PASSPORT

open up *vb syn see* OPERATE 2

opera omnia *n syn see* OEUVRE

operate *vb* 1 *syn see* ACT 5
  2 to perform surgery <*operated* on him to
remove a brain tumor>
  syn cut, open up
  3 to cause to function <knew how to
operate earth-moving equipment>
  syn handle, run, use, work
  rel play; manage, maneuver; drive, pilot,
steer; ply, wield
  idiom make go
  4 *syn see* CONDUCT 3

operation *n* 1 *syn see* EXERCISE 1
  2 *syn see* USE 1

operative *adj* 1 *syn see* ACTIVE 1
  ant inoperative
  2 *syn see* OPEN 5

---

syn synonym(s)   *rel* related word(s)
ant antonym(s)   *con* contrasted word(s)
idiom idiomatic equivalent(s)
‖ use limited; if in doubt, see a dictionary

operative n 1 syn see WORKER
  2 syn see PRIVATE DETECTIVE
operator n syn see MOTORIST
operose adj 1 syn see HARD 6
  2 syn see ASSIDUOUS
opiate adj syn see SOPORIFIC 1
opiate n 1 syn see DRUG 2
  2 syn see ANODYNE 2
opine vb to form or express an opinion
  < he *opined* that the story was true >
  syn ||opinion, opinionate
  rel accept, believe, consider, hold, judge,
  regard, think, view; speculate
  con deny, disclaim, disown, reject, repudiate; disbelieve, discredit, doubt
opinion n an idea or judgment held as true
  or valid < seek an expert *opinion* on the
  authenticity of the painting >
  syn belief, conviction, eye, feeling, mind,
  persuasion, sentiment, view
  rel attitude, impression, notion, think,
  thought; conclusion, estimate, estimation,
  judgment, reaction; assumption, conjecture, speculation, supposition, theory
  idiom point of view
  con disbelief, discredit, doubt, unbelief;
  distrust, mistrust, questioning, skepticism
||opinion vb syn see OPINE
opinionate adj syn see OPINE
opponent n one who expresses or manifests opposition < his *opponent* in the
  debate >
  syn adversary, antagonist, anti, con,
  match, opposer, oppugnant
  rel enemy, foe; competitor, rival; assailant, combatant; counteragent
  con ally, colleague, comrade, confederate,
  partner; advocate, champion
  ant exponent, pro, proponent
opportune adj syn see TIMELY 1
  rel appropriate, felicitous, happy
  ant inopportune
opportunity n a state of affairs or combination of circumstances favorable to some
  end < all he asked was an *opportunity* to
  show what he could do >
  syn break, chance, look-in, occasion,
  opening, shot, show, squeak, time
  rel room, space; leisure, liberty; relief,
  spell, turn; juncture, pass; dog's chance,
  hope, prayer
oppose vb 1 to place over against something to provide resistance or counterbalance < *oppose* one military force to another >
  syn counter, match, pit, play (off), vie
  rel array, confront, face
  idiom set over against
  2 syn see RESIST
opposed adj syn see ADVERSE 1
opposer n syn see OPPONENT
opposing adj syn see ADVERSE 1
opposite n something that is exactly opposed or contrary < virtue and vice are
  opposites >
  syn antipode, antipole, antithesis, contra,
  contradictory, contrary, converse, counter,
  counterpole, reverse
  rel contrast, counterpoint, foil; contrapositive, inverse, obverse; antonym
  idiom the other extreme, the other side of
  the coin
  con analogon, analogue, counterpart, like,
  parallel, similar; equal, equivalent; corre-

late, correlative; carbon copy, duplicate,
replica
  ant same
opposite adj being so far apart as to be or
  to seem irreconcilable < held *opposite*
  views on the solution of the problem >
  syn antipodal, antipodean, antithetical,
  contradictory, contrary, converse, counter,
  diametric, polar, reverse
  rel contrasting; contrapositive, inverse,
  obverse; antonymous; different, dissimilar,
  divergent, opposed, unalike, unlike, unsimilar; independent, separate, unconnected, unrelated
  con alike, analogous, equivalent, like,
  parallel, similar; equal; correlative
  ant same
opposite prep syn see TO 6
oppositely adv syn see AGAIN 5
opposite number n one holding an equivalent or parallel position < the Secretary
  of State and his *opposite number*, the Foreign Minister >
  syn coordinate, counterpart, vis-à-vis;
  compare EQUAL
  rel complement, cousin, equal, equivalent,
  like, match, tally
opposition n syn see ANTAGONISM 2
opposure n syn see ANTAGONISM 2
oppress vb 1 syn see WRONG
  rel harass, harry; afflict, torment, torture;
  conquer, overcome, overthrow, subjugate
  2 syn see DEPRESS 2
  rel burden, distress, trouble
oppressive adj 1 syn see ONEROUS
  ant unoppressive
  2 syn see GLOOMY 3
oppressor n syn see TYRANT
opprobriate vb syn see DECRY 2
opprobrious adj 1 syn see ABUSIVE
  2 syn see INFAMOUS 1
opprobrium n syn see DISGRACE
  rel abuse, scurrility, vituperation
  con credit, prestige
oppugn vb syn see CONTEND 1
oppugnant adj syn see ADVERSE 1
oppugnant n syn see OPPONENT
opt (for) vb syn see CHOOSE 1
optate vb syn see CHOOSE 1
optic adj syn see VISUAL 1
optical adj syn see VISUAL 1
optimacy n syn see ARISTOCRACY
optimism n an inclination to put the most
  favorable construction on actions and
  events or to anticipate the best possible
  outcome < was a practitioner of *optimism*
  in his everyday life >
  syn Pollyannaism, rose-colored spectacles,
  sanguineness, sanguinity
  rel brightness, buoyancy, happiness; idealism, positivism
  con hopelessness; despair, gloom, melancholy; malism; defeatism, fatalism; cyni-
  cism
  ant pessimism
optimist n one given to optimism < was a
  jaunty *optimist* >
  syn hoper, Pollyanna
  rel dreamer, idealist, positivist
  con defeatist, fatalist; cynic, doubter,
  skeptic
  ant pessimist
optimistic adj anticipating only the best to
  happen and minimizing all other possibili-

ties < was *optimistic* about book sales that year >

syn fond, Pollyannaish, sanguine, upbeat; *compare* HOPEFUL 1

rel bright, cheerful, merry, sunny; hopeful, hoping; assured, confident

idiom feeling on top of the world, looking on the bright side, riding (*or* sitting) on cloud nine

con cynical; doubtful, uncertain

ant pessimistic

option *n syn* see CHOICE 1

rel prerogative, privilege, right

optional *adj* not compulsory < attendance at the meeting is *optional* >

syn discretionary, elective, facultative, nonobligatory

rel free, voluntary; alternative

con demanded, imperative; enforced, involuntary; essential, necessary

ant compulsory, mandatory, obligatory, required

opulent *adj* **1** *syn* see RICH 1

rel lavish, prodigal, profuse; extravagant, ostentatious, pretentious, showy; plush, swank

con modest, simple, unpretentious

2 *syn* see LUXURIOUS 3

3 *syn* see PROFUSE

oracle *n syn* see REVELATION

oracular *adj syn* see PROPHETIC

oral *adj* **1** *syn* see VOCAL 1

2 expressed or transmitted vocally < stories of folk heroes kept alive in *oral* tradition >

syn spoken, traditional, unwritten, verbal, word-of-mouth

rel narrated, recounted, related, told

con chronicled, recorded, written, written down

orate *vb* to talk in a declamatory, grandiloquent, or impassioned manner < *orated* to the crowd about the flag and patriotism >

syn bloviate, declaim, harangue, mouth, perorate, rant, rave, soapbox

rel elocute; bombast, rodomontade, sermonize, speechify; blah-blah

oratorical *adj syn* see RHETORICAL

oratory *n* the art of speaking in public eloquently and effectively < a politician who was a master at *oratory* >

syn elocution, rhetoric, speechcraft

orb *n* **1** *syn* see BALL

2 *syn* see EYE 1

orbit *n syn* see RANGE 2

orchestra *n* a usually large group of musicians who perform together < a string *orchestra* played at the reception >

syn band, philharmonic, symphony

rel combo, ensemble

orchestrate *vb syn* see HARMONIZE 4

orchidaceous *adj syn* see SHOWY

orchids *n pl syn* see COMPLIMENT 1

ordain *vb* **1** *syn* see CONDUCT 3

2 *syn* see DICTATE

ordeal *n syn* see TRIAL 1

order *n* **1** *syn* see ASSOCIATION 2

2 *syn* see TYPE

rel bracket, branch, pigeonhole, set; estate, grade, rank, status

3 sequential occurrence in space or time < changed the *order* of the books on the shelf >

syn arrangement, disposal, disposition, distribution, ordering, sequence

rel array, arrayal, collocation; allocation, allotment, apportionment, arrayment, proration

con disarrangement, disordering; chaos, confusion, disorder, mix-up, muddle

4 general or approximate size or amount < a loss on the *order* of seven million dollars >

syn extent, magnitude, matter, neighborhood, range, tune, vicinity

rel approach, approximation, closeness, nearness, proximity

5 manner of being arranged in space or of occurring in time < tell everything in the *order* in which it happened >

syn consecution, procession, sequence, succession

rel consecutiveness, following, successiveness; chain, progression, series, train

6 *syn* see SUCCESSION 2

7 orderly conduct < about to call the meeting to *order* when the interruption occurred >

syn correctitude, correctness, decorousness, decorum, orderliness, properness, propriety, seemliness

rel goodness, niceness, rightness; fitness, suitability; integrity, probity, rectitude, uprightness

con impropriety, indecorousness, indecorum, unseemliness

ant disorder

8 orderly arrangement or disposition < troubled by the lack of *order* in their daily lives >

syn method, orderliness, pattern, plan, system

con anarchy, chaos, confusion, muddle, ∥snafu

ant disorder

9 state with respect to quality, functioning, or status < the equipment was in very poor *order* >

syn case, condition, estate, repair, shape

rel fettle, fitness, kilter, trim

10 a state of soundness < had his car put in *order* for spring >

syn condition, fettle, fitness, kilter, repair, shape, trim

rel adjustment, amendment, correction, gear, rectification

idiom working order

con disrepair

11 the state of being appropriate to or required by the circumstances < that remark is definitely out of *order* >

syn appositeness, appropriateness, aptness, expediency, fitness, meetness, propriety, rightness, suitability, suitableness

rel opportuneness, seasonableness, timeliness; auspiciousness, favorableness; felicity, grace

con inappropriateness, unfitness, unsuitability, unsuitableness

12 *syn* see COMMAND 1

rel authorization, permission

---

syn synonym(s)   **rel** related word(s)
ant antonym(s)   **con** contrasted word(s)
idiom idiomatic equivalent(s)
∥ use limited; if in doubt, see a dictionary

order *vb* 1 to bring about an orderly disposition of individuals, units, or elements <*ordered* his affairs in preparation for marriage>
syn arrange, array, dispose, marshal, methodize, organize, systematize
rel adjust, fix, regulate, right; align, line, line up, range; classify, codify, hierarchize; regiment, routine, routinize; streamline
idiom put (*or* set) in order, put in shape, put (*or* set) to rights, reduce to order, whip into shape (*or* order)
ant disorder
2 *syn* see COMMAND

ordering *n syn* see ORDER 3

orderliness *n* 1 *syn* see ORDER 7
ant disorderliness
2 *syn* see ORDER 8
ant disorderliness

orderly *adj* 1 following a set arrangement, design, or pattern <work out an *orderly* procedure and stick to it> <an *orderly* row of houses surrounded the village green>
syn methodic, methodical, regular, systematic
rel accurate, correct, exact, precise; alike, uniform; businesslike; conventional, formal
idiom in apple-pie order
con haphazard, irregular, unmethodical, unsystematic; careless, casual, free and easy
ant chaotic, disorderly
2 *syn* see NEAT 2
rel picked up
ant disordered; disorderly

order up *vb syn* see CALL UP

ordinance *n syn* see LAW 1

ordinarily *adv syn* see USUALLY 2

ordinary *adj* 1 of the customary or common type encountered in the normal course of events <*ordinary* traffic had been stopped to let the marchers pass>
syn everyday, plain, plain Jane, quotidian, routine, unremarkable, usual, workaday
rel commonplace, natural, normal, regular; customary, familiar, frequent
con infrequent, rare, uncommon; accidental, casual, chance, fortuitous
ant extraordinary
2 *syn* see COMMON 6

organ *n* 1 *syn* see MEAN 2
2 *syn* see JOURNAL

organize *vb* 1 *syn* see FOUND 2
rel construct, put together
2 *syn* see ORDER 1
rel coordinate, integrate
3 *syn* see MOBILIZE 3

‖organized *adj syn* see INTOXICATED 1

orgulous *adj syn* see PROUD 1

orgy *n* 1 *syn* see BINGE 1
2 an act or occasion of excessive indulgence in sex <the house detective investigated an *orgy* in the penthouse suite>
syn bacchanal, bacchanalia, debauch, party, saturnalia
3 *syn* see SPREE 1

orifice *n syn* see APERTURE

oriflamme *n syn* see FLAG

origin *n* 1 *syn* see ANCESTRY
rel maternity, parentage, paternity
2 *syn* see SOURCE

original *n* 1 a first form from which copies or reproductions can be produced <students copying the da Vinci *original*>
syn archetype, protoplast, prototype
rel forerunner, mother, precursor; model, pattern; precedent
con dummy, imitation, simulacrum; counterfeit, fake, forgery
ant copy, reproduction
2 *syn* see INNOVATOR
3 *syn* see ECCENTRIC

original *adj* 1 *syn* see FIRST 2
rel archetypal, prototypal
2 *syn* see PRIMARY 5
3 *syn* see INVENTIVE
con banal, trite; derivative, initative
ant unoriginal

originally *adv syn* see INITIALLY 1

originate *vb* 1 *syn* see GENERATE 1
2 *syn* see INTRODUCE 3
3 *syn* see SPRING 1
4 *syn* see BEGIN 2
5 to have one's origin or home base in <he *originates* from Ohio>
syn come (from), hail (from)
rel derive (from), spring (from), stem (from)

originative *adj syn* see INVENTIVE
ant unoriginative

originator *n* 1 *syn* see FATHER 2
2 *syn* see INNOVATOR

orison *n syn* see PRAYER

ornament *vb syn* see ADORN
rel enrich; embroider

ornate *adj* elaborately and often pretentiously decorated or designed <a very *ornate* room—all marble, gilt, and brocade>
syn baroque, flamboyant, florid, luscious, rich, rococo
rel elaborate, high-wrought, resplendent; labored, overdone, overelaborated, overembellished, overworked, overwrought; luxuriant, luxurious, opulent, sumptuous; aureate, gilded
con natural, plain, quiet, simple; severe, unembellished, unornamented, unostentatious, unpretentious; restrained, subdued
ant austere; chaste

ornery *adj* ‖1 *syn* see CHEAP 2
2 *syn* see CANTANKEROUS
3 *syn* see CONTRARY 3

orotund *adj* 1 *syn* see RESONANT
rel loud, stentorian
2 *syn* see RHETORICAL

orphan *adj* deprived by death of one and usually both parents <seeking homes for the countless *orphan* children from the disaster area>
syn orphaned, parentless, unparented
rel alone, solitary; abandoned, cast-off, forsaken, lost; disregarded, ignored, neglected, slighted

orphaned *adj syn* see ORPHAN

orphic *adj syn* see RECONDITE

orthodox *adj* 1 conforming to doctrines or practices that are held to be right or true by an authority, standard, or tradition <those who still hold an *orthodox* view about evolution>
syn accepted, authoritative, canonical, received, sanctioned, sound

rel acknowledged, admitted, approved; customary, official, recognized, standard, traditional; correct, proper, right
con heretical, heterodox, unauthoritative, uncanonical
ant unorthodox
2 *syn* see CONVENTIONAL 1
3 *syn* see CONSERVATIVE 1
ant unorthodox

oscillate *vb syn* see SWING 2

osculate *vb syn* see KISS 1

ostend *vb syn* see SHOW 2

ostensible *adj* 1 *syn* see APPARENT 2
2 *syn* see ALLEGED

ostensibly *adv* to all outward appearances < *ostensibly* it was a business trip but actually it was all pleasure >
syn apparently, evidently, officially, outwardly, professedly, seemingly
rel externally, superficially; sensibly
idiom on the face of it, on the surface, to the eye
con genuinely, really, truly; au fond, basically

ostentatious *adj syn* see SHOWY
ant unostentatious

ostracism *n syn* see EXILE 1

ostracize *vb* 1 *syn* see BANISH
con accept, entertain, receive, welcome; harbor, haven, refuge, shelter
2 *syn* see CUT 7

other *adj* 1 *syn* see DIFFERENT 1
2 *syn* see ADDITIONAL

‖**othergates** *adv syn* see OTHERWISE 1

other half *n syn* see RABBLE 2

otherness *n syn* see DISSIMILARITY

‖**otherways** *adv syn* see OTHERWISE 2

‖**otherwhile** *adv syn* see SOMETIMES

otherwise *adv* 1 in a different way or manner < he could not act *otherwise* >
syn differently, diversely, ‖othergates, variously
ant likewise
2 under different conditions < might *otherwise* have left >
syn else, ‖elseways, elsewise, ‖otherways

otherwise *adj syn* see DIFFERENT 1

otherworld *n syn* see HEREAFTER 2

otherworldly *adj* 1 of or relating to a world other than the actual world < believed in the existence of *otherworldly* phenomena >
syn transcendental, transmundane
rel exterrestrial, extramundane, extraterrestrial; unearthly, unworldly
2 *syn* see DREAMY 1

otiose *adj syn* see VAIN 1
rel purposeless, useless; inexcusable; superfluous, supernumerary, surplus

oubliette *n syn* see DUNGEON

ought *vb syn* see WANT 3

ought *n syn* see OBLIGATION 2

ounce *n syn* see PARTICLE

oust *vb* 1 *syn* see DEPRIVE 2
2 *syn* see BANISH

out *adv syn* see OUTDOORS

out *vb* 1 *syn* see EJECT 1
2 *syn* see EXTINGUISH 1

3 *syn* see GET OUT 2

out *n syn* see SHOWING 1

out and away *adv syn* see FAR AND AWAY

out–and–out *adj syn* see UTTER

outback *n syn* see FRONTIER 2

outbalance *vb syn* see OUTWEIGH 1

outbloom *vb syn* see BLOSSOM

outbreak *n* 1 a sudden or violent beginning of activity < an *outbreak* of new housing starts >
syn burst, eruption, flare, outburst; *compare* EPIDEMIC
rel beginning, commencement, dawn, onset, outset
2 *syn* see EPIDEMIC

outbreathe *vb syn* see EXHALE

outburst *n* 1 a violent expression of emotion < an *outburst* of anger >
syn access, burst, eruption, explosion, flare-up, gust, sally
rel scene, storm, tantrum; frenzy, rapture, transport(s)
2 *syn* see OUTBREAK 1

outcast *n* one who is cast out by society < a political *outcast* >
syn castaway, derelict, Ishmael, Ishmaelite, leper, offscouring, pariah, untouchable
rel hobo, tramp, vagabond, vagrant; displaced person; exile, expatriate; reprobate
con big name, bigwig, celebrity, lion, luminary, name, notable, personage, somebody

outcome *n syn* see EFFECT 1

outcomer *n syn* see STRANGER

out–country *adj syn* see RURAL

outcrier *n syn* see PEDDLER

outcry *n syn* see COMMOTION 1

outdare *vb syn* see FACE 3

outdate *vb* to make obsolete or out-of-date < the automobile *outdated* the horse and buggy >
syn antiquate, obsolesce, obsolete, outmode, superannuate
rel age, date, fossilize; replace, supersede

outdated *adj syn* see OLD-FASHIONED
ant up-to-the-minute

outdistance *vb syn* see OUTSTRIP 1

outdo *vb* 1 *syn* see SURPASS 1
idiom out-Herod Herod, steal (*or* get) a march on
2 *syn* see DEFEAT 2

outdoor *adj* taking place, done, or existing in the open air < an *outdoor* restaurant >
syn alfresco, hypaethral, open-air, out-of-door, outside
ant indoor, inside

outdoors *adv* in or into the open air < went *outdoors* for some fresh air >
syn out, out of doors, outside, without, withoutdoors
ant indoors, inside, withindoors

outdoors *n pl but sing in constr* the space where air is unconfined < every night he let the dog run in the *outdoors* >
syn open, open air, out-of-doors, outside, without
idiom God's good (*or* green) earth

outer *adj* being or located outside something < the sheep's thick *outer* coat of wool >
syn exterior, external, outside, outward, over

---

rel extraneous, extrinsic, superficial, surface; outlying, remote
con inside, interior, internal, inward
ant inner

outermost *adj syn* see EXTREME 5
ant inmost, innermost

outface *vb syn* see FACE 3

outfit *n* 1 *syn* see EQUIPMENT
2 *syn* see COSTUME
3 *syn* see COMPANY 4
4 *syn* see ENTERPRISE 3

outfit *vb syn* see FURNISH 1

outfox *vb syn* see OUTWIT

outgeneral *vb syn* see OUTWIT
rel outfight, outflank, outgame
idiom steal a march

outgo *vb syn* see SURPASS 1

outgoing *adj syn* see DEMONSTRATIVE
ant aloof

outgrowth *n* 1 a projecting part of an organism <a warty *outgrowth* on the skin>
syn excrescence, excrescency, process, processus
rel enlargement, prolongation, swelling; offshoot, shoot
2 something that develops or grows directly out of something else <the new TV series was an *outgrowth* of a popular play>
syn by-product, derivative, descendant, offshoot, spin-off
rel branch, member; child, offspring, product; aftereffect, consequence, effect, issue, outcome, result
con origin, root, source; antecedent, cause, determinant

outhouse *n syn* see PRIVY 1

outing *n syn* see EXCURSION 1

outjockey *vb syn* see OUTWIT

outland *adj syn* see RURAL

outlander *n syn* see STRANGER

outlandish *adj* 1 *syn* see BARBARIC 1
rel foreign, strange
2 *syn* see STRANGE 4
rel monstrous; outré
con commonplace, everyday
3 marked by sharp departure from the traditional or usual <men who wear beads, feathers, and other *outlandish* gear>
syn far-out, kinky, outré, ultra; *compare* EXTREME 3
rel bizarre, extravagant, outrageous, wild; unconventional, unorthodox
con conservative, conventional; compliant, conformable; moderate
4 *syn* see BACK 1

outlast *vb syn* see OUTLIVE

outlaw *n* a criminal of the American western frontier <*outlaws* held up stagecoaches>
syn badman, ‖bandido, bandit, desperado
rel gunman, gunslinger
idiom bad guy

outlaw *vb syn* see FORBID

outlay *vb syn* see SPEND 1

outlay *n syn* see EXPENSE 1

outlet *n* 1 *syn* see APERTURE
2 *syn* see EGRESS 2
rel escape; release
3 *syn* see STORE 4

outline *n* the line that gives form or shape to a body or a figure <saw only a dark *outline* of the house through the gloom>
syn contour, delineation, figuration, line, lineament, lineation, profile, silhouette
rel configuration, conformation, figure, form, shape; skyline
con bulk, hulk, mass

outline *vb* 1 *syn* see BORDER 1
2 *syn* see SKETCH

outlive *vb* to remain in existence longer than <the committee has *outlived* its usefulness>
syn outlast, outwear, survive
rel outstand, outstay

outlook *n* 1 *syn* see LOOKOUT 2
2 *syn* see VISTA
3 *syn* see VIEW 4
4 *syn* see VIEWPOINT 2

outlying *adj syn* see DISTANT 1

outmaneuver *vb syn* see OUTWIT
idiom steal a march (on)

outmatch *vb syn* see SURPASS 1

outmode *vb syn* see OUTDATE

outmoded *adj* 1 *syn* see OLD-FASHIONED
2 *syn* see OBSOLETE
3 *syn* see TACKY 2

outmost *adj syn* see EXTREME 5
ant inmost, innermost

out-of-date *adj* 1 *syn* see OLD-FASHIONED
ant up-to-date
2 *syn* see TACKY 2

out-of-door *adj syn* see OUTDOOR

out-of-doors *n pl but sing in constr syn* see OUTDOORS

out of doors *adv syn* see OUTDOORS

out-of-the-way *adj syn* see OBSCURE 2

outpace *vb syn* see OUTSTRIP 1

outplace *vb syn* see REPLACE 3

output *n* the amount of something produced <an annual *output* of 3,000,000 units>
syn outturn, product, production, turnout, yield
rel gain, get, profit, take; crop, harvest
con input; raw material

outrage *n syn* see INJURY 1

outrage *vb* 1 *syn* see RAPE
2 *syn* see ABUSE 4
3 *syn* see WRONG
4 *syn* see OFFEND 3

outrageous *adj* 1 exceeding the limits of what is normal or tolerable <*outrageous* prices that threaten our way of life>
syn barbarous, unchristian, uncivilized, unconscionable, ungodly, unholy, wicked
rel abominable, awful, beastly, dreadful, ghastly, horrible, horrid, impossible, intolerable, terrible, unreasonable; scandalous, shocking
con normal, reasonable, tolerable; acceptable, bearable, endurable, supportable
2 enormously or flagrantly bad or horrible <*outrageous* treatment of prisoners>
syn atrocious, crying, desperate, heinous, monstrous, scandalous, shocking
rel enormous, flagrant, gross; egregious, nefarious, notorious, villainous
con condonable, excusable, forgivable, pardonable; defensible, justifiable; legitimate, reasonable; comprehensible, plausible, understandable

outrank *vb syn* see PRECEDE 1
outré *adj syn* see OUTLANDISH 3
outreach *vb syn* see OUTWIT
outrecuidance *n syn* see CONCEIT 2
outrider *n syn* see FORERUNNER 1
outright *adj* 1 *syn* see UTTER
  2 *syn* see WHOLE 4
outrun *vb syn* see OUTSTRIP 1
outset *n syn* see BEGINNING
outshine *vb syn* see SURPASS 1
outside *n syn* see OUTDOORS
outside *adj* 1 *syn* see OUTER
  rel alien, foreign
  ant inside
  2 *syn* see OUTDOOR
  3 *syn* see MAXIMUM
  4 *syn* see REMOTE 4
outside *adv syn* see OUTDOORS
outside *prep* 1 *syn* see BEYOND 1
  2 *syn* see EXCEPT
outside of *prep syn* see EXCEPT
outsider *n syn* see STRANGER
  con insider
outskirt *n usu* **outskirts** *pl syn* see ENVI-
RONS 2
outslick *vb syn* see OUTWIT
outsmart *vb syn* see OUTWIT
outspeed *vb syn* see OUTSTRIP 1
outspoken *adj* speaking without fear or
reserve <quite *outspoken* in her views on
child rearing>
  syn free, free-spoken, round, vocal
  rel candid, direct, forthright, frank, open,
plain, plainspoken, straightforward, unreticent; bluff, blunt; explicit, point-blank,
unequivocal; strident
  con reserved, restrained, reticent; private,
retiring, shrinking; unassertive
outspread *vb syn* see OPEN 4
  ant folded (*of wings or a fan*)
outstanding *adj* 1 *syn* see UNPAID 2
  2 *syn* see NOTICEABLE
  3 *syn* see CHIEF 2
  4 *syn* see SUPERB 3
outstare *vb syn* see STARE DOWN
outstart *n syn* see BEGINNING
outstep *vb syn* see EXCEED 1
outstretch *vb syn* see OPEN 4
outstrip *vb* 1 to go faster than <could
outstrip even the fastest horse>
  syn distance, outdistance, outpace, outrun, outspeed
  rel outfly, outsoar, outwing; outfoot,
outrace, outride; outsail; outtravel; lose,
shake off
  con follow, trail; drag, hang back, lag
  2 *syn* see SURPASS 1
outsweepings *n pl syn* see REFUSE
outthink *vb syn* see OUTWIT
outthrust *n syn* see PROJECTION 1
outtire *vb syn* see EXHAUST 4
outturn *n syn* see OUTPUT
outward *adj syn* see OUTER
  ant inward
outwardly *adv syn* see OSTENSIBLY
  ant inwardly
outwear *vb* 1 *syn* see EXHAUST 4
  2 *syn* see OUTLIVE

  rel endure, hold up
outweigh *vb* 1 to exceed in weight, value,
or importance <her brother *outweighed*
her by nearly fifty pounds> <the facts
outweigh his argument>
  syn outbalance, overbalance, overweigh,
overweight
  rel overbear
  2 *syn* see COMPENSATE 1
outweighing *adj syn* see DOMINANT 1
outwit *vb* to defeat or get the better of by
superior cleverness or ingenuity <*outwitted* the enemy by taking a different
route>
  syn have, outfox, outgeneral, outjockey,
outmaneuver, outreach, outslick, outsmart,
outthink, overreach, undo; *compare* FRUS-
TRATE 1
  rel bamboozle, befool, dupe, gull, hoax,
hoodwink, outtrick, outtrump, trick;
outdo; outguess
outworn *adj syn* see OBSOLETE
oval *adj* having the shape of a longitudinal
section of an egg <an *oval* pond>
  syn ooid, ovate, oviform, ovoid
  rel ovaloid; ellipsoidal, elliptic
ovate *adj syn* see OVAL
over *adv* 1 from one point to another
across intervening space <sailed *over* to
the island>
  syn across, athwart, beyond, transversely
  2 *syn* see AWAY 2
  3 *syn* see EVER 6
  4 at a higher point <the plane was directly *over*>
  syn above, aloft, overhead
  idiom on high
  ant under
  5 at or to an end <it's all *over* between
them>
  syn by, through
  6 *syn* see THROUGH 1
  7 yet another time <do the work *over*>
  syn afresh, again, anew, de novo, once
more
  idiom over again
over *prep* 1 at a higher level <clouds hung
over the town>
  syn above, o'er
  ant under
  2 *syn* see ACROSS
  3 with respect to <children squabbling
over toys>
  syn about, on, upon, with
  4 so as to make contact with <hit him
over the head>
  syn on, upon
  5 *syn* see DURING
  6 as the result of <quarreled *over* money
matters>
  syn because of, due to, owing to, through
over *adj* 1 *syn* see SUPERIOR 1
  ant under
  2 *syn* see OVER
over *vb syn* see CLEAR 8
overabounding *adj syn* see SUPERABUN-
DANT
overabundance *n syn* see EXCESS 1
overabundant *adj syn* see SUPERABUN-
DANT
overact *vb* to exaggerate in acting especially on the stage or screen <was criticized for *overacting* the part>

---

syn synonym(s)   *rel* related word(s)
ant antonym(s)   *con* contrasted word(s)
idiom idiomatic equivalent(s)
|| use limited; if in doubt, see a dictionary

syn overplay

rel ham, mug; declaim, rant, spout

idiom chew the scenery

ant underact, underplay

over against *prep* 1 *syn* see AGAINST 1

2 *syn* see VERSUS 2

overage *n syn* see EXCESS 2

ant shortage, underage

overall *adv* 1 *syn* see EVERYWHERE 1

2 *syn* see GENERALLY 1

overall *adj syn* see ALL-AROUND 2

over and above *prep syn* see BESIDES 1

over and over *adv syn* see OFTEN

overbalance *vb syn* see OUTWEIGH 1

overbalanced *adj syn* see LOPSIDED

overbalancing *adj syn* see DOMINANT 1

overbearing *adj* 1 *syn* see MASTERFUL 1

2 *syn* see DOMINANT 1

3 *syn* see PROUD 1

rel absolute, autocratic, despotic, tyrannical

con passive, unassertive; acquiescent, compliant, unresisting

ant subservient

overblown *adj* 1 *syn* see FAT 2

2 *syn* see INFLATED

3 *syn* see RHETORICAL

4 *syn* see PRETENTIOUS 3

overbold *adj syn* see SHAMELESS

overbrim *vb syn* see OVERFLOW 2

overburden *vb syn* see OVERLOAD

overcast *vb* 1 *syn* see OBSCURE

2 *syn* see COVER 3

overcast *adj* clouded over <a gray *overcast* March day>

syn cloudy, ‖dowly, dull, heavy, lowering (*or* louring), nubilous, overclouded

rel brooding, dirty, oppressive, sullen

ant clear, cloudless

overcharge *vb* 1 to charge excessively for service or goods <a clip joint well known for *overcharging* customers>

syn clip, fleece, skin, soak, stick

ant undercharge

2 *syn* see OVERLOAD

3 *syn* see EMBROIDER

overcloud *vb syn* see OBSCURE

overclouded *adj syn* see OVERCAST

overcome *vb* 1 to get the better of <*overcome* a bad habit>

syn conquer, down, hurdle, lick, master, surmount, throw; *compare* CONQUER 2

rel beat, defeat; outlive, prevail

con adopt, embrace, take up; indulge

2 *syn* see CONQUER 2

3 *syn* see OVERWHELM 4

4 *syn* see WIN 1

overconfident *adj   syn*   see PRESUMPTUOUS

overcritical *adj syn* see CRITICAL 1

overdo *vb* to make excessive use or application of <he has *overdone* that joke to the point that it is no longer funny>

syn overplay, overuse, overwork

idiom go overboard, go to extremes, run into the ground

overdoing *n syn* see EXTRAVAGANCE 2

overdraw *vb syn* see EMBROIDER

overdue *adj* 1 *syn* see UNPAID 2

2 *syn* see TARDY

ant early

overearly *adj syn* see EARLY 2

overemphasize *vb syn* see OVERPLAY 2

ant underemphasize

overesteem *vb syn* see OVERVALUE

overestimate *vb syn* see OVERVALUE

ant underestimate

overfill *vb syn* see OVERFLOW 2

overflow *vb* 1 *syn* see DELUGE 1

2 to flow over the brim <the river *overflowed* its banks>

syn overbrim, overfill, overrun, run over, spill, well over

rel brim, cascade, slop, slosh

con drop, recede, withdraw

overflow *n* 1 *syn* see FLOOD 2

2 *syn* see EXCESS 1

overflowing *adj syn* see ALIVE 5

2 *syn* see SUPERABUNDANT

overfull *adv syn* see EVER 6

overgrown *adj* covered with growth or herbage <a vacant lot *overgrown* with weeds>

syn grown, rank

rel braky, brambly, brushy, copsy, jungly, thicketed, thickety; dense, overrun, thick; lush

‖**overhand** *n syn* see ADVANTAGE 3

overhang *vb* 1 *syn* see BULGE

2 *syn* see HANG 4

overhanging *adj syn* see IMMINENT 2

overhaul *vb* 1 *syn* see MEND 2

2 *syn* see CATCH 7

overhead *adv syn* see OVER 4

ant underfoot

overheated *adj syn* see IMPASSIONED

overindulgence *n syn* see EXCESS 3

overindulgent *adj syn* see EXCESSIVE 2

overkill *n syn* see EXCESS 1

overlade *vb syn* see OVERLOAD

overlap *vb* to extend over and cover a part of <each course of shingles should *overlap* the preceding course by several inches>

syn imbricate, lap, overlie, override, ride, shingle

overlay *vb syn* see COVER 3

overleap *vb* 1 *syn* see CLEAR 8

2 *syn* see NEGLECT

overlie *vb syn* see OVERLAP

overload *vb* to load to excess <*overload* a ship>

syn overburden, overcharge, overlade, overtax, overweigh, overweight

con lighten

overlong *adj syn* see LONG 2

overlook *vb* 1 *syn* see SURVEY 3

2 to rise above and afford a view of <the tower *overlooks* the city>

syn dominate, look down, overtop, tower (above *or* over)

rel oversee

3 *syn* see NEGLECT

4 *syn* see SUPERVISE

overlook *n* 1 *syn* see OMISSION

2 *syn* see LOOKOUT 2

overly *adv syn* see EVER 6

overlying *adj syn* see SUPERIOR 1

ant underlying

overmuch *n syn* see EXCESS 1

overmuch *adv syn* see EVER 6

overnice *adj syn* see PRECIOUS 4

overnice *vb syn* see EMBROIDER

overpass *vb syn* see NEGLECT

overpeopled *adj   syn*   see OVERPOPULATED

ant underpeopled

overplay *vb* **1** *syn* see OVERACT
ant underact, underplay
2 to give undue attention or emphasis to < *overplaying* the ephemeral at the expense of the significant>
syn magnify, maximize, overemphasize, overstress
rel accent, accentuate, point up; dramatize, exaggerate, hyperbolize, overdraw, overstate, stretch; overvalue
idiom lay it on thick
con downgrade, downplay; minimize
3 *syn* see OVERDO

overplus *n* *syn* see EXCESS 1

overpopulated *adj* populated too densely < *overpopulated* cities>
syn overpeopled
rel congested, dense, overcrowded
con empty, vacant, void; unpopulated
ant underpopulated

overpower *vb* **1** *syn* see CONQUER 1
2 *syn* see OVERWHELM 4

overpress *vb* *syn* see PRESSURE

overprize *vb* *syn* see OVERVALUE
ant underprize, undervalue

overrate *vb* *syn* see OVERVALUE
ant underrate

overreach *vb* **1** *syn* see CHEAT
2 *syn* see OUTWIT

overreckon *vb* *syn* see OVERVALUE

overrefined *adj* *syn* see PRECIOUS 4

override *vb* *syn* see OVERLAP

overriding *adj* *syn* see CENTRAL 1
rel primary, principal

overripe *adj* *syn* see EFFETE 3

overrule *vb* *syn* see GOVERN 1

overruling *adj* *syn* see CENTRAL 1

overrun *vb* **1** *syn* see WHIP 2
2 *syn* see INVADE 1
3 *syn* see INFEST 1
4 *syn* see EXCEED 1
5 *syn* see OVERFLOW 2

oversea *adj* *syn* see OVERSEAS

overseas *adv* beyond or across the sea < served *overseas* for two years>
syn abroad
con stateside

overseas *adj* situated, originating in, or relating to lands overseas < attempting to tap the potential of *overseas* markets>
syn oversea, transmarine, ultramarine
rel alien, exotic, foreign, strange
con domestic, home; stateside

oversee *vb* **1** *syn* see SURVEY 3
2 *syn* see SUPERVISE

overset *vb* **1** *syn* see OVERTURN 1
2 *syn* see OVERTHROW 2

overshadow *vb* *syn* see OBSCURE

oversight *n* **1** the function or duty of watching or guarding for the sake of proper direction or control < had *oversight* of the children as they played>
syn care, charge, conduct, handling, intendance, management, running, superintendence, superintendency, supervision
rel custody, guard, guardianship; keeping, maintenance; surveillance; aegis, tutelage; ciceronage; chaperonage; check, control

2 *syn* see FAILURE 1
3 *syn* see OMISSION

oversize *adj* *syn* see LARGE 1
ant undersized

overslaugh *vb* *syn* see HINDER

oversoon *adj* *syn* see EARLY 2

oversoon *adv* *syn* see EARLY 2

overspread *vb* **1** *syn* see COVER 3
2 *syn* see INFEST 1

overstate *vb* *syn* see EMBROIDER
ant understate

overstatement *n* *syn* see EXAGGERATION
ant understatement

overstep *vb* *syn* see EXCEED 1
rel infringe, transgress, trespass

overstock *n* *syn* see EXCESS 2
ant understock

overstress *vb* *syn* see OVERPLAY 2

oversupply *n* *syn* see EXCESS 2
ant undersupply

overswarm *vb* **1** *syn* see INFEST 1
2 *syn* see INVADE 1

oversway *vb* *syn* see INDUCE 1

overtake *vb* *syn* see CATCH 7

overtax *vb* *syn* see OVERLOAD

overthrow *vb* **1** *syn* see OVERTURN 1
2 to cause the downfall of < *overthrow* the government>
syn overset, overturn, topple, tumble, unhorse; *compare* CONQUER 1
rel depose, dethrone, oust, remove, unseat; liquidate, purge; conquer, defeat, destroy, ruin
con create, establish, found, set up

overthrow *n* *syn* see DEFEAT 1

overtone *n* *syn* see ASSOCIATION 4

overtop *vb* *syn* see OVERLOOK 2

overture *n* **1** action intended to attract favorable attention < made friendly *overtures* to the new member of the class>
syn advance, approach
rel bid, proposal, proposition, tender
2 *syn* see INTRODUCTION

overturn *vb* **1** to turn from an upright or level position < the embarrassed boy backed into the table and *overturned* a lamp>
syn knock over, overset, overthrow, tip (over), topple, turn over, upset
rel capsize, keel (over *or* up), upend, upturn; prostrate; down; roll (over)
con erect, right, set up, straighten (up)
2 *syn* see OVERTHROW 2

overturn *n* *syn* see SHAKE-UP

overuse *vb* *syn* see OVERDO
ant underuse

overvalue *vb* to set too high a value on < inclined to *overvalue* his own charm>
syn overesteem, overestimate, overprize, overrate, overreckon
rel cherish, prize, treasure, adore, idolize, worship
con belittle, depreciate
ant underprize, undervalue

overweening *adj* *syn* see PRESUMPTUOUS

overweigh *vb* **1** *syn* see OUTWEIGH 1
2 *syn* see OVERLOAD

overweighing *adj* *syn* see DOMINANT 1

overweight *vb* **1** *syn* see OUTWEIGH 1
2 *syn* see OVERLOAD

overweight *adj* *syn* see FAT 2
ant underweight

overwhelm *vb* **1** *syn* see DELUGE 1

---

syn synonym(s)   *rel* related word(s)
ant antonym(s)   *con* contrasted word(s)
idiom idiomatic equivalent(s)
|| use limited; if in doubt, see a dictionary

2 *syn* see DELUGE 3

3 *syn* see WHIP 2

4 to subject to the grip of something overpowering and usually distressing or damaging < *overwhelmed* by the death of his only child > < human wants that tend to *overwhelm* environmental realities >
syn drown, knock over, overcome, overpower, prostrate, whelm
rel demoralize, devastate, dumbfound, shatter; floor, sink; disturb, upset; destroy, ruin, wreck; downgrade, lower, subordinate

overwhelmed *adj syn* see AGHAST 2

overwhelming *adj syn* see TOWERING 4

overwork *vb syn* see OVERDO

oviform *adj syn* see OVAL

ovoid *adj syn* see OVAL

owing *adj syn* see UNPAID 2

owing to *prep syn* see OVER 6

owl-light *n syn* see EVENING 1

own *vb* 1 *syn* see HAVE 1
2 *syn* see ACKNOWLEDGE 1
con deny, disclaim
ant disown, repudiate

owner *n* one that has the legal or rightful title < *owner* of the shop >
syn holder, possessor, proprietor
rel lord, master
con lessee, renter, tenant; squatter; interloper, intruder, trespasser

ownership *n* lawful claim or title < would soon have *ownership* of the house >
syn dominion, possession, possessorship, property, proprietary, proprietorship
rel hand

own up *vb syn* see ACKNOWLEDGE 1

oyster *n syn* see FORTE 1

P

pa *n syn* see FATHER 1

pablum *n syn* see PAP 2

pabulum *n syn* see FOOD 2

pace *n* 1 *syn* see TEMPO
2 *syn* see SPEED 2
3 *syn* see ROUTINE

pace *vb* 1 *syn* see WALK 1
2 *syn* see PRECEDE 2

pacific *adj* affording or promoting peace < a *pacific* policy >
syn irenic, nonviolent, pacificatory, pacifist, peaceable, peaceful
rel appeasing, conciliating, conciliatory, pacifying, propitiating, propitiatory; dovelike, gentle, inoffensive
con belligerent, combative, contentious, pugnacious, quarrelsome; unpeaceable, unpeaceful; hawkish, violent, warlike
ant bellicose, unpacific

pacificator *n syn* see PEACEMAKER

pacificatory *adj syn* see PACIFIC

pacificist *n syn* see PACIFIST
idiom man of peace

pacifist *n* one who opposes war or violence as a means of settling disputes < *pacifists* who fight war with argument and propaganda >
syn dove, pacificist
rel satyagrahi; ‖conchie, conscientious objector; peacemonger
con belligerent, combatant; chauvinist, hawk; jingo, jingoist, warmonger
ant bellicist

pacifist *adj syn* see PACIFIC
ant combative

pacify *vb* to allay anger or agitation < saw his mounting rage and tried to *pacify* him >
syn appease, assuage, conciliate, mollify, placate, propitiate, sweeten
rel dulcify, soften; allay, alleviate, mitigate, relieve; moderate, qualify, smooth (over), temper
idiom pour balm into, pour oil on (the) troubled waters
con arouse, stir (up)

ant anger

pack *n* 1 *syn* see BACKPACK
2 *syn* see MUCH

pack *vb* 1 *syn* see STOW
2 *syn* see LOAD 3
3 *syn* see CARRY 1

packed *adj syn* see FULL 1
idiom packed like sardines (*or* herrings)

‖**packed out** *adj syn* see FULL 1

packet *n syn* see FORTUNE 4

packman *n syn* see PEDDLER

packsack *n syn* see BACKPACK

pact *n* 1 *syn* see CONTRACT
rel settlement
2 *syn* see TREATY

‖**pad** *n syn* see PROTECTION 2

pad *vb syn* see EMBROIDER

paddle *vb syn* see ROW

‖**paddy** *n syn* see POLICEMAN

pagan *adj syn* see HEATHEN

pageant *n syn* see PRETENSE 2

pagoda *n syn* see SUMMERHOUSE

pain *n* 1 a bodily sensation that causes acute discomfort or suffering < suffering from chest *pains* >
syn ache, ‖misery, pang, stitch, throe, twinge
rel discomfort, distress, hurt, suffering; agony, torment, torture
2 **pains** *pl syn* see EFFORT 1
rel assiduousness, diligence, industry, sedulousness

pain *vb* 1 *syn* see HURT 4
rel agonize, convulse, crucify, excruciate, harrow, lacerate
2 *syn* see DISTRESS 2
rel afflict; distress, upset; wound; anguish
idiom ‖hit one where one lives
3 *syn* see TRY 2

painful *adj* 1 causing, marked by, or affected with pain < a *painful* wound >
syn aching, afflictive, algetic, hurtful, hurting, sore
rel raw; acute, piercing, sharp, shooting, stabbing, stinging; agonizing, excruciating, harrowing, racking, tormenting, torturous

ant painless, unpainful

2 *syn* see BITTER 2

   rel unappetizing, unsavory

   ant painless

painfully *adv syn* see HARD 5

   ant painlessly

pain–killer *n syn* see ANODYNE 1

painstaking *adj syn* see CAREFUL 2

painstakingly *adv syn* see HARD 3

   rel carefully, meticulously; lovingly

paint *n syn* see MAKEUP 3

pair *n syn* see COUPLE

paired *adj syn* see TWIN

pal *n syn* see ASSOCIATE 3

palace *adj syn* see LUXURIOUS 3

palace car *n syn* see PARLOR CAR

palatable *adj* agreeable or pleasant especially to the sense of taste <a *palatable* meal>

   syn aperitive, appetizing, flavorsome, good-tasting, ‖gusty, mouth-watering, relishing, sapid, saporous, savorous, savorsome, savory, tasteful, tasty, toothsome, toothy

   rel delectable, delicious, delightful, luscious, scrumptious, yummy; tempting; saporific

   con bad-tasting, disagreeable, distasteful, ill-flavored, unappetizing

   ant unpalatable

palate *n syn* see TASTE 4

palatial *adj syn* see LUXURIOUS 3

   rel noble, regal; monumental; impressive; rich, splendid

palaver *n* 1 *syn* see CONFERENCE 2

   rel dialogue, discussion; parley

2 *syn* see CHATTER

   rel gas, guff, hot air

3 *syn* see TERMINOLOGY

4 *syn* see BUSINESS 8

palaverous *adj syn* see WORDY

pale *adj* 1 deficient in color or in intensity of color <a *pale* face>

   syn ashen, ashy, blanched, colorless, complexionless, doughy, livid, lurid, pallid, paly, wan, waxen

   rel sallow, sick, sickly; gray, pasty, pasty-faced, waxlike; white, whitened; deathlike, ghastly

   con flushed, ruddy; bright, colorful, florid

2 being weak and thin in substance or in vital qualities <a *pale*, inadequate foreign policy>

   syn anemic, bloodless, pallid, waterish, watery

   rel inane, insipid, jejune, wishy-washy; insubstantial, unsubstantial; ineffective, ineffectual; faint, feeble, weak

   con strong, substantial; effective, effectual; bright, colorful

   ant brilliant

pale *vb syn* see DULL 1

Pale Horse *n*, used with the *syn* see DEATH 1

palinode *vb syn* see ABJURE

pall *vb* 1 *syn* see BORE

2 *syn* see SATIATE

   rel disgust, weary

‖**pallet** *n syn* see HEAD 1

palliate *vb* to give a speciously fine appearance to what is erroneous, base, or evil <did not try to conceal or *palliate* his errors>

   syn blanch (over), extenuate, gloss (over), gloze (over), prettify, sugarcoat, varnish, veneer, white, whiten, whitewash

   rel alleviate, lighten, mitigate; condone, excuse; moderate, qualify, soften, temper; camouflage, cloak, conceal, cover up, disguise, dissemble, mask; hush (up)

   idiom paper over the cracks, put a good face on (*or* upon)

pallid *adj* 1 *syn* see PALE 1

2 *syn* see PALE 2

pally *adj syn* see INTIMATE 4

palm (on *or* upon) *vb syn* see FOIST 3

‖**palm grease** *n syn* see GRATUITY

palm off *vb syn* see FOIST 3

‖**palm oil** *n syn* see GRATUITY

palooka *n syn* see OAF 2

palpable *adj* 1 *syn* see TANGIBLE 1

2 *syn* see PERCEPTIBLE

   rel apparent, ostensible, seeming; believable, colorable, credible, plausible

3 *syn* see CLEAR 5

   rel certain, positive, sure; arresting, noticeable, remarkable, striking

   con doubtful, dubious, problematic, questionable

   ant impalpable

palpate *vb syn* see TOUCH 1

palpation *n syn* see TOUCH 2

palpitate *vb syn* see PULSATE

   rel pitter-patter

‖**palsy–walsy** *adj syn* see INTIMATE 4

palter *vb* 1 *syn* see LIE

   rel evade, fence

   idiom play false, play fast and loose

2 *syn* see HAGGLE 2

paltry *adj* 1 *syn* see CHEAP 2

   rel beggarly, shabby; pitiful

2 *syn* see LITTLE 3

   rel base, low, low-down, vile

3 *syn* see PETTY 2

   rel insignificant, unimportant

paly *adj syn* see PALE 1

pamper *vb syn* see BABY

   rel regale, tickle; caress, dandle, fondle, pet; overindulge

pan *n syn* see FACE 1

pan *vb syn* see CRITICIZE

panacea *n* a remedy for all ills or difficulties <bicycles are not a *panacea* for the traffic problem>

   syn catholicon, cure-all, elixir, nostrum

   rel relief; remedy

   idiom universal (*or* sovereign) remedy

pandect *n syn* see COMPENDIUM 1

pandemoniac *adj syn* see INFERNAL 2

pandemonium *n* 1 *cap* **Pandemonium** *syn* see HELL

2 *syn* see SINK 1

3 *syn* see DIN

pander *n syn* see PIMP 1

panegyric *n syn* see ENCOMIUM

panegyrical *adj syn* see EULOGISTIC

panegyrize *vb syn* see PRAISE 2

pang *n syn* see PAIN 1

   rel prick, stab, ‖stang

‖**pang** *vb syn* see CRAM 1

panhandler *n syn* see BEGGAR 1

---

syn synonym(s)   *rel* related word(s)

ant antonym(s)   *con* contrasted word(s)

idiom idiomatic equivalent(s)

‖ use limited; if in doubt, see a dictionary

panhandling *n syn* see MENDICANCY
panic *n* 1 *syn* see FEAR 1
 rel frenzy, hysteria; stampede
 con composure, equanimity, sangfroid, self-possession
 ‖2 *syn* see RIOT 2
‖**pank** *vb syn* see PANT 1
panoply *n syn* see DISPLAY 2
panorama *n syn* see RANGE 2
pan out *vb syn* see SUCCEED 2
pansified *adj syn* see EFFEMINATE
pant *vb* 1 to breathe quickly, spasmodically, or in a labored manner <was *pant­ing* after running up the stairs>
 syn blow, gasp, heave, huff, ‖pank, ‖pegh, puff
 rel gulp; wheeze; wind; chuff
 idiom be out of breath
 2 *syn* see AIM 2
 rel hunger, long, pine, thirst; desire, want, wish
 idiom be consumed with desire (for)
pantywaist *n syn* see WEAKLING
pantywaist *adj syn* see CHARACTERLESS
pap *n* 1 *syn* see FOOD 2
 2 something (as reading matter) lacking in solid value or substance <the sentimental *pap* that he offered his readers>
 syn pablum, rubbish, slop
 rel garbage, trash
‖**pap** *n syn* see FATHER 1
papa *n syn* see FATHER 1
paper *n syn* see ESSAY 2
paphian *n syn* see HARLOT 1
pappy *adj syn* see SOFT 6
‖**pappy** *n syn* see FATHER 1
par *n* 1 *syn* see EQUIVALENCE
 2 *syn* see AVERAGE
 rel standard
parable *n syn* see ALLEGORY 2
 rel comparison, similitude
parachronism *n syn* see ANACHRONISM 1
parade *n syn* see DISPLAY 2
 rel exhibition
parade *vb syn* see SHOW 4
 rel disclose, divulge, reveal; advertise, declare, proclaim, publish; boast, brag, gasconade
 idiom parade one's wares
 con camouflage, cloak, disguise, dissemble, mask
paradigm *n syn* see MODEL 2
paradigmatic *adj syn* see TYPICAL 1
paradise *n* 1 *syn* see HEAVEN 2
 idiom the next world (*or* life)
 2 *syn* see UTOPIA
paragon *n* an individual of unequaled excellence often serving as a model <she is a *paragon* of a housewife>
 syn ideal, jewel, nonesuch, nonpareil, phoenix; *compare* MODEL 2
 rel apotheosis, epitome, last word, quintessence, ultimate; archetype, beau ideal, exemplar, pattern; ‖beaut, beauty, crackerjack, gem, love, lovely, peach, trump; champ, champion; cream, pick, tops
paragon *vb syn* see EQUATE 2
parallel *adj syn* see LIKE
 ant nonparallel, unparallel
parallel *n* one that corresponds to or closely resembles another <we seek in vain a *parallel* for this situation>

syn analogue, correlate, correspondent, counterpart, countertype, match; *compare* COUNTERPART 1, EQUAL
 rel equivalent; double, duplicate, duplication
parallel *vb syn* see EQUATE 2
 2 to place (something) so as to be parallel with another <machines that combed and *paralleled* the fibers>
 syn collimate, collocate, parallelize
 rel align, line up
parallelize *vb syn* see PARALLEL 2
paralyze *vb* 1 to render completely powerless, ineffective, or inert <a general strike that *paralyzed* the nation>
 syn cripple, disable, disarm, immobilize, incapacitate, prostrate; *compare* MAIM, WEAKEN 1
 rel deaden, enfeeble, weaken; close, shut (down); freeze; demolish, destroy, knock out
 idiom bring to a grinding halt, tie hand and foot
 2 *syn* see DAZE 2
 rel appall, daunt, dismay, horrify; cripple, disable, enfeeble, weaken; astound, flabbergast, nonplus
 con animate, enliven, pep (up), stimulate
 ant galvanize
paramount *adj syn* see DOMINANT 1
 rel capital, headmost; commanding, controlling; cardinal, crowning
paramour *n* 1 *syn* see GALLANT 2
 2 *syn* see LOVER 1
 3 *syn* see MISTRESS
parapet *n syn* see BULWARK
paraphernalia *n pl but sometimes sing in constr syn* see EQUIPMENT 1
paraphrase *n syn* see VERSION 1
paraphrase *vb* to express or interpret something (as a text or passage) in other words <*paraphrased* the complicated document>
 syn rephrase, restate, reword, translate (into)
 rel summarize; transcribe
 con quote, reproduce
parasite *n* a person who is supported or seeks support from another without making an adequate return <lived as a *para­site* in his father's house>
 syn barnacle, bloodsucker, freeloader, hanger-on, leech, lounge lizard, ‖spiv, sponge, sponger, sucker; *compare* SYCOPHANT
 rel dependent; smell-feast; deadbeat, idler, laze
parasite *vb syn* see INFEST 2
parasitic *adj syn* see FAWNING
 rel freeloading, leechlike, sponging
parasitize *vb syn* see INFEST 2
parboil *vb syn* see BOIL 2
parcel *n* 1 *syn* see PART 1
 2 *syn* see LOT 3
 3 *syn* see GROUP 3
parcel *vb syn* see APPORTION 2
 rel allocate, allot, assign; deal, disburse, disperse; dole (out), lot (out)
parch *vb syn* see DRY 1
‖**pard** *n syn* see PARTNER
pardon *n* a remission of penalty or punishment <the governor granted the prisoner a *pardon*>

syn absolution, amnesty
rel acquittal, exculpation, exoneration, indemnification, indemnity; forgiveness, remission; justification, vindication
con conviction; condemnation
ant punishment

pardon *vb syn* see EXCUSE 1
rel justify; accept, tolerate; free, liberate, release
idiom let bygones be bygones, wipe the slate clean
con amerce, fine, mulct, penalize
ant punish

pardonable *adj syn* see VENIAL
ant unpardonable

pare *vb* 1 *syn* see CUT 6
rel flay, scalp, skin, strip
2 *syn* see REDUCE 2

parent *vb syn* see GENERATE 1

parenthesis *n* 1 *syn* see DIGRESSION
2 *syn* see INTERLUDE

parenthetically *adv syn* see INCIDENTALLY 2

parentless *adj syn* see ORPHAN
ant parented

par excellence *adj syn* see EXCELLENT

pariah *n syn* see OUTCAST
rel déclassé

‖**parish–pump** *adj syn* see INSULAR

parity *n syn* see EQUIVALENCE
rel analogy, parallelism, similitude; approximation, closeness, nearness
ant disparity, imparity

parlance *n syn* see WORDING

parley *vb* 1 *syn* see SPEAK 3
2 *syn* see CONFER 2

parley *n* 1 *syn* see TALK 4
rel rap session
2 *syn* see CONVERSATION 1

parlor car *n* a railroad passenger car equipped with individual revolving and reclining chairs and providing the services of an attendant
syn chair car, club car, lounge car, palace car, tavern car

parlor house *n syn* see BROTHEL
idiom flesh factory

parlous *adj syn* see DANGEROUS 1

parlous *adv syn* see VERY 1

Parnassian *n syn* see POET

parochial *adj syn* see INSULAR
rel prejudiced; bigoted
con unprejudiced; uncircumscribed, unlimited; cosmic, universal
ant catholic

parody *n syn* see CARICATURE 2
rel spoof, spoofery, rib, ridicule

parody *vb syn* see MIMIC

paronomasia *n syn* see PUN

parous *adj syn* see PREGNANT 1

parry *vb* 1 *syn* see DODGE 1
rel preclude, prevent; anticipate, forestall
2 *syn* see WARD 1

parsimonious *adj syn* see STINGY
idiom penny-wise and pound-foolish
ant prodigal

parson *n syn* see CLERGYMAN

---

syn synonym(s)   *rel* related word(s)
ant antonym(s)   *con* contrasted word(s)
idiom idiomatic equivalent(s)
‖ use limited; if in doubt, see a dictionary

part *n* 1 something less than the whole to which it belongs <a *part* of the road was paved>
syn cut, division, member, moiety, parcel, piece, portion, section, segment
rel component, constituent, element, ingredient; detail, fraction, fragment; bit, chip, scrap
con aggregate, total; combination, complex; entirety, entity, totality, unity
ant whole
2 **parts** *pl syn* see GENITALIA
3 *syn* see RATION
4 *syn* see SHARE 1
rel chunk
5 *syn* see SIDE 4

part *vb syn* see SEPARATE 1
ant unite

part *adj syn* see INCOMPLETE 1

partage *n syn* see SHARE 1

partake *vb syn* see SHARE 2
rel accept, receive, take
idiom take part in

partake (of) *vb* 1 *syn* see EAT 1
2 *syn* see AMOUNT 2
idiom bear resemblance (to)

partaker *n syn* see PARTICIPANT

part and parcel *n syn* see ESSENTIAL 1

partial *adj* 1 *syn* see BIASED 2
ant impartial
2 *syn* see INCOMPLETE 1
rel halfway
ant whole

partiality *n* 1 *syn* see PREJUDICE
2 *syn* see LEANING 2

participant *n* one that takes part in something <were *participants* in the uprising>
syn actor, partaker, participator, party, sharer
rel aide, assistant, helper; colleague, confrere, fellow, partner
con bystander, looker-on, nonparticipant, observer, onlooker, spectator, watcher

participate *vb syn* see SHARE 2
rel enter (into), join (in)
idiom be a party to, be in on, be (*or* get) in the act, have to do with
con observe, watch; retire, withdraw

participator *n syn* see PARTICIPANT

particle *n* a tiny or insignificant amount, part, or piece <not a *particle* of sense>
syn ace, atom, bit, crumb, damn, ‖dite, doit, dram, drop, fragment, grain, hoot, iota, jot, minim, mite, modicum, molecule, ounce, ray, ‖rissom, scrap, scruple, shred, smidgen, smitch, snap, speck, spot, syllable, tittle, whit, whoop
rel morsel; snip; dribbet, dribble; dot

parti–color *adj syn* see VARIEGATED

parti–colored *adj syn* see VARIEGATED
ant unicolor, unicolorous

particular *adj* 1 *syn* see SINGLE 2
ant general
2 *syn* see CIRCUMSTANTIAL
rel careful, meticulous, punctilious, scrupulous
3 *syn* see SPECIAL 1
rel appropriate; distinct; singular
ant universal
4 *syn* see SEVERAL 1
5 *syn* see NICE 1

particular *n syn* see POINT 1
rel speciality, specific

con entirety
ant universal
particularity *n syn see* INDIVIDUALITY 3
particularize *vb* 1 *syn see* SPECIFY 3
idiom draw it fine
2 *syn see* ITEMIZE 1
particularized *adj syn see* CIRCUMSTAN-TIAL
ant generalized
particularly *adv syn see* ESPECIALLY 1
parting *n* a mutual separation of two or more persons <saddened by their approaching *parting*>
syn adieu, congé, farewell, good-bye, leave-taking
rel separation; departure
con joining, meeting; return
ant reunion
parting *adj* given, taken, or performed during leave-taking <remembered his father's *parting* advice>
syn departing, farewell, good-bye, valedictory
rel final, last
partisan *n* 1 *syn see* FOLLOWER
rel backer, champion, upholder; die-hard, stalwart
con adversary, antagonist, opponent
2 an irregular soldier who operates behind enemy lines <a train blown up by *partisans*>
syn guerrilla, irregular, patriot
partisan *adj syn see* BIASED 2
rel denominational, factional, sectarian; blind, devoted, die-hard, fanatic, unreasoning
con impartial, indifferent, unbiased, unprejudiced
ant nonpartisan
partition *n syn see* SEPARATION 1
partition *vb syn see* DISTRIBUTE 1
partner *n* one that is associated in any action with another <*partners* in crime>
syn associate, cohort, confrere, consociate, copartner, fellow, mate, ‖pard
rel assistant, helper, sidekick; bedfellow, buddy, chum, companion, comrade, crony, pal
partnership *n syn see* ASSOCIATION 1
rel consociation, fellowship
parturient *adj syn see* PREGNANT 1
parturition *n syn see* BIRTH 1
party *n* 1 *syn see* COMBINATION 2
rel alliance, union; side
2 *syn see* PARTICIPANT
3 *syn see* HUMAN
4 *syn see* GROUP 1
5 *syn see* COMPANY 4
6 *syn see* ORGY 1
party girl *n* 1 *syn see* DOXY 1
2 *syn see* PROSTITUTE
parvenu *n syn see* UPSTART
idiom codfish aristocrat, pig in clover
‖**pash** *vb syn see* SHATTER 1
‖**pash** *n syn see* INFATUATION
pass *vb* 1 *syn see* GO 1
rel jog, ‖mog
2 *syn see* DIE 1
idiom pass on to the Great Beyond
con linger
3 to move or come to a termination or end <as time *passes*, the pain too will *pass*>

syn see ELAPSE
rel slip (by); roll (on); fade (away), peter (out); cease, close, discontinue, end, stop, terminate
con continue; linger
4 *syn see* HAPPEN 1
idiom come to pass
5 *syn see* SURPASS 1
idiom leave way behind, shoot ahead of
6 *syn see* SPEND 3
7 *syn see* NEGLECT
8 *syn see* PROMISE 1
9 to transfer by hand from one person to another <*pass* the salt>
syn buck, hand, reach, ‖shoot
rel give; fork (over)
pass (as *or* for) *vb syn see* POSE 4
pass (on) *vb syn see* HAND DOWN
pass (over) *vb syn see* TRAVEL 2
pass *n syn see* JUNCTURE 2
passable *adj* capable of being passed, crossed, or traveled <*passable* roads>
syn navigable, negotiable, travelable
rel open, unblocked; ‖motorable; accessible, attainable, reachable
con blocked, closed; unnavigable; inaccessible, unattainable, unreachable
ant impassable
passably *adv syn see* ENOUGH 2
passage *n* 1 movement or transference from one place or point to another <air *passage* from New York to London> <the *passage* of current through a wire>
syn transit, travel
rel traject, trajet, traverse, traversing; transfer, transference, transmission, transmittal, transmitting
2 *syn see* TRANSITION
3 *syn see* WAY 2
4 a typically long narrow way connecting parts of a building <the office building contained endless *passages*>
syn corridor, couloir, hall, hallway, passageway
rel areaway
passageway *n syn see* PASSAGE 3
pass away *vb* 1 *syn see* DIE 1
2 *syn see* PASS 3
pass by *vb syn see* NEGLECT
passé *adj* 1 *syn see* OBSOLETE
2 *syn see* OLD-FASHIONED
ant a la mode
passed master *n syn see* EXPERT
passel *n syn see* GROUP 3
passing *n syn see* DEATH 1
passing *adj syn see* TRANSIENT
con lingering
passion *n* 1 *syn see* DISTRESS
2 *syn see* DESIRE 1
rel coveting; aiming, aspiring, panting
3 *syn see* FEELING 3
ant dispassion
4 *syn see* TEMPER 4
rel outbreak, outburst
5 *syn see* LOVE 2
rel heartthrob
6 intense, high-wrought emotion that compels to action <the *passion* of an evangelist>
syn ardor, calenture, enthusiasm, fervor, fire, hurrah, zeal
rel dedication, devotion; eagerness, lust; lyricism; ecstasy, rapture, transport; fury, rage

7 *syn* see LUST 2
rel amorousness; sensuality, sensuousness
8 *syn* see INFATUATION
passionate *adj* 1 *syn* see IRASCIBLE
2 *syn* see IMPASSIONED
rel excited, quickened, stimulated; high-powered, high-pressure, steamed up; headlong, impetuous, precipitate
ant dispassionate
3 *syn* see LUSTFUL 2
rel steamy, sultry
ant passionless
passionless *adj* *syn* see FRIGID 3
rel detached, impassive, unsusceptible; unaffected, unmoved; apathetic, indifferent, uncaring, unconcerned, unfeeling; cold-blooded, coldhearted, frozen, heartless
ant passionate, passionful
passive *adj* 1 *syn* see INACTIVE
rel apathetic, impassive, phlegmatic, stolid
ant active
2 receiving or enduring without resistance < a *passive* acceptance of her fate >
syn acquiescent, nonresistant, nonresisting, resigned, submissive, unresistant, unresisting, yielding
rel bearing, enduring, patient; compliant, docile, tractable; nonviolent
con resistant, resisting, unresigned, unsubmissive, unyielding
pass off *vb* 1 *syn* see FOIST 3
2 *syn* see POSE 4
pass on *vb* *syn* see COMMUNICATE 1
pass out *vb* 1 *syn* see FAINT
2 *syn* see DIE 1
pass over *vb* *syn* see NEGLECT
passport *n* a means of entry into a desirable group, society, or condition of life < his skill at sports was a *passport* to fame and fortune >
syn key, open sesame, password, ticket
password *n* 1 a word or phrase that must be spoken by a person before he may pass a guard < give the *password* before entering the fort >
syn countersign, watchword, word
rel tessera
2 *syn* see PASSPORT
3 something (as a short phrase) used as a sign of recognition among members of the same society, class, or group < a fraternity that has secret handshakes and *passwords* >
syn watchword, word
past *adj* 1 *syn* see PRECEDING
2 *syn* see FORMER 2
rel bypast, gone-by; late, previous
ant present
past *prep* 1 *syn* see BEYOND 1
rel by
ant before
2 *syn* see BEYOND 2
past *n* former time < reminisced about the *past* >
syn foretime, ‖lang syne, yesterday, yesteryear, yore; *compare* PRESENT

syn synonym(s)   *rel* related word(s)
ant antonym(s)   *con* contrasted word(s)
idiom idiomatic equivalent(s)
‖ use limited; if in doubt, see a dictionary

rel antiquity
idiom bygone days (*or* times), days gone by, the good old days
con here and now; tomorrow
ant present; future
paste *vb* *syn* see BEAT 1
idiom give one a pasting
‖**paste** *n* *syn* see CUFF
pasticcio *n* *syn* see MISCELLANY 1
pastiche *n* *syn* see MISCELLANY 1
past master *n* *syn* see EXPERT
pastoral *adj* *syn* see RURAL
rel agrarian
patch *vb* *syn* see MEND 2
patchwork *n* *syn* see MISCELLANY 1
patchy *adj* *syn* see SPOTTY 1
pate *n* *syn* see HEAD 1
patent *adj* 1 *syn* see OPEN 1
2 *syn* see CLEAR 5
rel prominent; flagrant, glaring, gross, rank
idiom patently obvious
con impalpable, imperceptible, insensible; concealed, hidden, secreted
ant latent
‖**pater** *n* *syn* see FATHER 1
path *n* 1 *syn* see TRAIL
2 *syn* see WAY 1
3 *syn* see WAY 2
pathetic *adj* *syn* see PITIFUL 1
pathos *n* a quality that moves one to pity and sorrow < the *pathos* of the play was rarely offset by moments of comedy >
syn poignance, poignancy
rel bathos
pathway *n* *syn* see TRAIL
patience *n* the power or capacity to endure without complaint something difficult or disagreeable < it took a lot of *patience* to put up with him >
syn forbearance, longanimity, long-suffering, patientness, resignation, uncomplainingness
rel composure, cool, equanimity, imperturbability, self-control; endurance, sufferance, suffering, tolerance, toleration; nonresistance, passiveness, passivity, submission, submissiveness
con fretfulness; restiveness, restlessness; hastiness; rebellion, resistance
ant impatience
patientness *n* *syn* see PATIENCE
patois *n* 1 *syn* see VERNACULAR 3
2 *syn* see DIALECT 2
patriarch *n* 1 *syn* see FATHER 2
2 *syn* see GAFFER
patriarchal *adj* *syn* see VENERABLE 1
patrician *n* *syn* see GENTLEMAN
ant plebeian
patriciate *n* *syn* see ARISTOCRACY
ant plebs
patrimony *n* *syn* see HERITAGE 1
patriot *n* 1 a person who loves his country and supports its interests < *patriots* who asked what they could do for their country >
syn loyalist
rel nationalist
ant traitor
2 *syn* see PATRIOTEER
3 *syn* see PARTISAN 2
patrioteer *n* one who is ostentatiously and chauvinistically patriotic < bloodthirsty

patrioteers immersed in political witch-hunts >
  syn flag-waver, patriot, superpatriot
  rel jingo, jingoist
patrolman *n syn see* POLICEMAN
patron *n* 1 *syn see* PATRON SAINT
  2 *syn see* SPONSOR
  ant client; protégé
  3 *syn see* CUSTOMER
patronage *n* 1 *syn see* BACKING
  rel benefaction, guardianship, protection; subsidy
  2 commercial transactions of customers and patrons <developed a large *patronage* by offering fair prices and courteous service>
  syn business, custom, trade, traffic
  rel clientage, clientele
  3 the power to make appointments to government jobs on a basis other than merit alone <ousted his enemies from office and used *patronage* to support his policies>
  syn pork-barreling
  rel cronyism
patron saint *n* a saint to whose protection and intercession a person, society, church, or place is dedicated <Saint Christopher is the *patron saint* of travelers>
  syn avowry, patron
  rel titular; guardian angel
patsy *n* 1 *syn see* SCAPEGOAT
  2 *syn see* FOOL 3
patter *vb syn see* CHAT 1
patter *n syn see* DIALECT 2
pattern *n* 1 *syn see* MODEL 2
  rel original
  2 *syn see* FIGURE 3
  rel patterning
  3 *syn see* ORDER 8
  rel arrangement, constellation
paucity *n syn see* SCARCITY
  rel fewness
Paul Pry *n syn see* BUSYBODY
paunch *n* 1 *syn see* ABDOMEN
  2 *syn see* POTBELLY
paunch *vb syn see* EVISCERATE
pauper *n* a person having no financial resources except those derived from charity
  syn beggar, down-and-out
  rel have-not, indigent; ||casual; almsman, lazarus
  con millionaire, plutocrat
pauper *vb syn see* RUIN 3
pauperism *n syn see* POVERTY 1
pauperize *vb syn see* RUIN 3
pausation *n syn see* PAUSE
pause *n* a temporary cessation of activity or of an activity <a *pause* in the conversation>
  syn comma, interval, lull, pausation; *compare* BREAK 4, GAP 3
  rel caesura, hush, lapse, letup, suspension; interlude, intermission; recess, respite; wait; break, gap, interruption; cessation, ||deval
  con continuation, progression
paw *vb syn see* TOUCH 1
paw *adj* 1 *syn see* NAUGHTY 1
  2 *syn see* OBSCENE 2
pawn *n syn see* PLEDGE 1
pawn *vb* to give or deposit as security for the payment of a loan or debt or for the

fulfillment of an obligation <had to *pawn* all her jewels>
  syn ||dip, hock, impignorate, mortgage, pledge, ||pop, ||spout
  ant redeem
pawn *n syn see* TOOL 2
pay *vb* 1 to discharge an obligation to usually with money <*paid* the doctor for his services>
  syn compensate, guerdon, remunerate
  rel indemnify, recompense, satisfy; cough (up), plunk down, pony (up), pungle (up), remit, render, tender; pay off
  2 *syn see* CLEAR 5
  3 *syn see* SPEND 1
  4 *syn see* COMPENSATE 3
  idiom make up for
  5 *syn see* YIELD 5
pay *n syn see* WAGE
payable *adj* 1 *syn see* DUE 2
  ant unpayable
  2 *syn see* UNPAID 2
pay envelope *n syn see* WAGE
paying *adj syn see* ADVANTAGEOUS 1
  rel productive; sound; solvent
payload *n syn see* LOAD 1
pay up *vb syn see* CLEAR 5
PDQ *adv syn see* AWAY 3
peaceable *adj syn see* PACIFIC
  rel amicable, friendly, neighborly; amiable, complaisant
  ant acrimonious; contentious; warlike
peaceful *adj syn see* PACIFIC
  rel collected, composed, cool, unruffled; constant, equable, steady
  con agitated, discomposed, disquieted, disturbed, perturbed, upset
peacemaker *n* one that makes or seeks to make peace <a president who was remembered as a great *peacemaker*>
  syn make-peace, pacificator
  rel arbitrator, mediator, negotiator; placater; appeaser, peacemonger; peacekeeper
  con chauvinist, jingo, jingoist, militarist, war dog, warmonger; peacebreaker
peace officer *n syn see* POLICEMAN
peach *n syn* ||DILLY, crackerjack, ||daisy, dandy, humdinger, jim-dandy, ||lalapalooza, ||lulu, nifty, ||pip
  rel pearl
peach *vb syn see* INFORM 3
peachy *adj syn see* MARVELOUS 2
peacock *vb syn see* LORD
peacockish *adj syn see* SHOWY
peacocky *adj syn see* SHOWY
peak *n* 1 *syn see* VISOR 1
  2 *syn see* TOP 1
  3 *syn see* MOUNTAIN 1
  4 *syn see* APEX 2
peak (out) *vb syn see* DECREASE
peaked *adj syn see* POINTED 1
peaked *adj syn see* SICKLY 2
||peaking *adj syn see* SICKLY 2
peaky *adj syn see* POINTED 1
peaky *adj syn see* SICKLY 2
peal *vb syn see* RING
peanut *adj syn see* PETTY 2
||peart *adj syn see* LIVELY 1
||pearten (up) *vb syn see* ENCOURAGE 1
peasant *n syn see* RUSTIC
peck *n syn see* MUCH
peck *vb* 1 to strike at or pick up with the beak <a hen *pecking* the scattered grain from the ground>

syn beak, pick
2 *syn* see KISS 1

peck (at) *vb syn* see NAG

pecker *n* 1 *syn* see BILL 1
2 *syn* see NOSE 1

‖**peckish** *adj syn* see HUNGRY

pecksniffery *n syn* see HYPOCRISY

pecksniffian *adj syn* see HYPOCRITICAL

peculate *vb syn* see EMBEZZLE

peculiar *adj* 1 *syn* see CHARACTERISTIC
rel unique
2 *syn* see STRANGE 4
rel uncustomary
con normal

peculiarity *n syn* see QUALITY 1

pecuniary *adj syn* see FINANCIAL

pedantic *adj* too narrowly concerned with scholarly matters < intellectual life that was *pedantic* rather than broad and humane >
syn academic, bookish, book-learned, booky, quodlibetic, scholastic
rel erudite, learned; didactic, donnish, inkhorn, schoolish, schoolteacherish; arid, dry, dryasdust, dull
ant unpedantic

peddle *vb* 1 *syn* see PUSH 6
2 to sell or offer for sale from place to place < *peddled* fish from a pushcart >
syn hawk, huckster, monger, vend
rel sell; push

peddler *n* one who travels about with merchandise to sell < *peddlers* were once common in rural areas >
syn ‖arab, cheap-jack (*or* cheap-john), ‖duffer, hawker, higgler, huckster, monger, mongerer, outcrier, packman, piepoudre, roadman, vendor
rel colporteur, costermonger; pusher

peddling *adj syn* see PETTY 2

pedestal *vb syn* see EXALT 1

pedestrian *adj syn* see DULL 9
rel commonplace, platitudinous, truistic; banal, inane, jejune, wishy-washy; heavy

pedigree *n* 1 *syn* see GENEALOGY
2 *syn* see ANCESTRY

pedigree *adj syn* see PUREBRED

pedigreed *adj syn* see PUREBRED

peek (in *or* out) *vb syn* see PEEP

peek *n syn* see PEEP

peel *vb* 1 *syn* see SKIN 2
2 *syn* see SCALE 2

peeled *adj syn* see OPEN 2

peeler *n* 1 *syn* see STRIPTEASER
2 *syn* see HUSTLER

‖**peeler** *n syn* see POLICEMAN

peep *vb syn* see CHIRP
rel pip

peep *vb* to peer through or as if through a hole or crevice < *peeped* cautiously under the bed >
syn peek (in *or* out)
rel glance; look; peer, stare
idiom take a peep (*or* peek)

peep *n* a brief and sometimes furtive look < take a *peep* at the new neighbors >
syn ‖gander, glance, glimpse, peek
rel look-over, look-see; oeillade, ogle; stare

peeper *n* 1 *syn* see PEEPING TOM
2 *syn* see EYE 1

peeping tom *n* a pruriently prying person < a *peeping tom* spying on the couple >
syn peeper, voyeur
rel prowler, snoop, snooper
idiom porch climber, window (*or* transom) peeper

‖**peepy** *adj syn* see SLEEPY 1

peer *vb syn* see GAZE 1
rel eye, rubberneck; pry, snoop

peerless *adj syn* see ALONE 3
rel dominant, paramount, predominant, sovereign

peery *adj syn* see CURIOUS 2

peeve *vb syn* see IRRITATE
rel disturb; miff
idiom make one hot under the collar

peevish *adj syn* see IRRITABLE
rel captious, carping, caviling, critical, faultfinding
idiom being in a peeve

peewee *n syn* see DWARF

peewee *adj syn* see TINY

‖**peg** *n syn* see DRINK 3

‖**pegh** *vb syn* see PANT 1

peg out *vb* 1 *syn* see COLLAPSE 2
2 *syn* see DIE 1

pejorative *adj syn* see DEROGATORY
con acclaiming, extolling, lauding, praising; aggrandizing, exalting, magnifying

pelf *n* 1 *syn* see MONEY
‖2 *syn* see REFUSE

pell-mell *adv* in or as if in confused haste < barged in *pell-mell* without thinking >
syn helter-skelter, hotfoot, hurry-scurry, impetuously, incontinently
rel hurriedly; indiscreetly; carelessly, heedlessly, rashly, thoughtlessly
idiom on the spur of the moment

pell-mell *n syn* see CONFUSION 3

pell-mell *vb syn* see STAMPEDE 2

pellucid *adj* 1 *syn* see TRANSPARENT 1
rel sheer
con muddy, roily, turbid
2 *syn* see CLEAR 4

pelt *n syn* see HIDE

pelt *vb* 1 *syn* see BEAT 1
2 *syn* see HURRY 2

pen *vb syn* see ENCLOSE 1
ant unpen

pen *n syn* see JAIL

penalize *vb* to inflict a penalty on < *penalize* a delinquent taxpayer with a stiff fine >
syn amerce, fine, mulct
rel castigate, chasten, chastise, correct, discipline, punish; condemn; judge

penalty *n syn* see FINE

penance *n syn* see PENITENCE

penchant *n syn* see LEANING 2

‖**pend** *vb syn* see DEPEND (on *or* upon) 1

pendant *n* 1 *syn* see FLAG
2 *syn* see COUNTERPART 1

pendent *adj* 1 *syn* see SUSPENDED
2 *syn* see PENDING

pending *adj* not yet settled or decided < a claim still *pending* >
syn pendent, undecided, undetermined, unsettled
idiom hanging in the balance, in suspense, up in the air
con decided, determined, settled

---

syn synonym(s) *rel* related word(s)
ant antonym(s) *con* contrasted word(s)
idiom idiomatic equivalent(s)
‖ use limited; if in doubt, see a dictionary

ant closed

pendulant *adj syn* see SUSPENDED

pendulate *vb syn* see SWING 2

pendulous *adj* 1 *syn* see SUSPENDED
2 *syn* see VACILLATING 2

penetrable *adj syn* see PERMEABLE
ant impenetrable

penetrate *vb* 1 *syn* see ENTER 1
rel encroach, invade, trespass
2 to enter or go through by or as if by overcoming resistance < the icy wind *penetrated* the heavy parka >
syn pierce
rel bore, perforate, prick, puncture; jab, knife, stab; drill, drive
3 *syn* see PERMEATE
rel insert, insinuate, interpolate, introduce

penetrating *adj* 1 *syn* see INCISIVE
rel penetrant, penetrative
2 *syn* see SHARP 4

penetration *n syn* see WIT 3
rel penetrativeness

penetrative *adj syn* see SHARP 4

penitence *n* regret for sin or wrongdoing < forgiveness following true *penitence* >
syn attrition, compunction, contriteness, contrition, penance, penitency, remorse, remorsefulness, repentance, rue, ruth
rel qualm, scruple; self-accusation, self-castigation, self-punishment, self-reproach, self-reproof; anguish, distress, grief, regret, sadness, sorrow; debasement, degradation, humbling, humiliation
con adamancy, inexorableness, obduracy, obdurateness, stubbornness

penitency *n syn* see PENITENCE

penitent *adj syn* see REMORSEFUL

penitential *adj syn* see REMORSEFUL

penitentiary *n syn* see JAIL
idiom correctional institution

penmanship *n syn* see HANDWRITING

pennant *n syn* see FLAG

pennilessness *n syn* see POVERTY 1

pennon *n syn* see FLAG

penny dreadful *n syn* see DIME NOVEL

penny pincher *n syn* see MISER

penny–pinching *adj syn* see STINGY

penny–wise *adj syn* see STINGY

pennyworth *n syn* see BARGAIN

pensile *adj syn* see SUSPENDED

pension (off) *vb syn* see RETIRE 2

pensive *adj* 1 *syn* see THOUGHTFUL 1
rel musing, ruminating
2 being musingly sad and thoughtful < gazed out the window with a *pensive* expression on her face >
syn meditative, ‖pensy, wistful
rel absorbed, abstracted, contemplative, musing, preoccupied, thoughtful, withdrawn; blue, melancholy, sad, saddened
con alert, aware, interested, outgoing

‖**pensy** *adj* 1 *syn* see PENSIVE 2
2 *syn* see THOUGHTFUL 1
3 *syn* see SQUEAMISH 1

penumbra *n syn* see SHADE 1

penurious *adj* 1 *syn* see POOR 1
2 *syn* see STINGY

penury *n syn* see POVERTY 1
ant luxury

peon *n syn* see SLAVE 2

peonage *n syn* see BONDAGE

people *n* 1 *syn* see SOCIETY 3
2 *syn* see COMMONALTY

people *vb syn* see INHABIT

pep *n* 1 *syn* see ENERGY 2
2 *syn* see VIGOR 2

pepper *vb syn* see SPECKLE 1

peppery *adj* 1 *syn* see PUNGENT
2 *syn* see IRASCIBLE
3 *syn* see SPIRITED 2
rel pepperish; alert, keen, lively, peppy

peppy *adj syn* see LIVELY 1

per *prep syn* see VIA 2

‖**per** *adv syn* see APIECE

perambulant *adj syn* see ITINERANT

perambulate *vb syn* see TRAVERSE 5

‖**perambulator** *n* *syn* see BABY CARRIAGE

perambulatory *adj syn* see ITINERANT

per capita *adv syn* see APIECE

per caput *adv syn* see APIECE

perceive *vb syn* see SEE 1
rel divine, identify, realize, recognize; grasp, seize, take; apprehend

perceptible *adj* apprehensible as real or existent < a *perceptible* change in attitude >
syn appreciable, detectable, discernible, observable, palpable, sensible, tangible; *compare* TANGIBLE 1
rel distinguishable, recognizable; cognizable, understandable; clear, lucid, perspicuous; conspicuous, noticeable, signal
con impalpable, indiscernible, intangible, invisible, unappreciable, undetectable, undiscernible, unnoticeable, unobservable
ant imperceptible

perception *n syn* see IDEA

perceptive *adj* 1 *syn* see ACUTE 3
rel responsive
ant imperceptive, unperceptive
2 *syn* see WISE 1
rel prehensile, prehensive, prehensorial
ant imperceptive, unperceptive

perch *vb syn* see ALIGHT

perchance *adv syn* see PERHAPS

percipience *n syn* see WIT 3

percolate *vb* 1 *syn* see PERMEATE
2 *syn* see EXUDE

percussion *n syn* see IMPACT
rel percussiveness

per contra *adv syn* see HOWEVER

perdition *n syn* see HELL

perdurable *adj* 1 *syn* see LASTING
ant fleeting
2 *syn* see INFINITE 1

perdure *vb syn* see CONTINUE 1

perduring *adj syn* see LASTING
ant fleeting

peregrination *n, usu* peregrinations *pl syn* see JOURNEY

peremptory *adj syn* see MASTERFUL 1
rel certain, positive; decided, decisive; absolute, fixed, uncompromising; obstinate

perennial *adj syn* see OLD 2
rel durable, perdurable

perfect *adj* 1 *syn* see WHOLE 1
ant imperfect
2 being entirely without flaw and meeting supreme standards of excellence < a ballerina whose technique was *perfect* >
syn absolute, flawless, fleckless, impeccable, indefectible, note-perfect, unflawed; *compare* CONSUMMATE 1
rel excellent; consummate; expert, finished, masterful, masterly

con defective, faulty, flawed; deficient, inadequate, wanting; unfinished, unpolished; unsound
ant imperfect
3 precisely appropriate or right <found the *perfect* gift for him>
syn ideal, model, very
rel needed, required, requisite; appropriate, fit, proper, right, suitable; exact, express, precise
idiom being just the thing
con foolish, inappropriate, undesirable, unsuitable
4 *syn* see PURE 2
5 *syn* see WHOLE 3
rel consummate
6 *syn* see UTTER
perfect *vb syn* see POLISH 2
perfected *adj syn* see CONSUMMATE 1
ant unperfected
perfectibilian *n syn* see PERFECTIONIST
perfectibilist *n syn* see PERFECTIONIST
perfection *n* **1** *syn* see INTEGRITY 2
2 *syn* see EXCELLENCE
ant imperfection
perfectionist *n* one that demands or works to achieve perfection <a *perfectionist* who rehearsed one scene fifty times>
syn perfectibilian, perfectibilist, perfectist
rel precisian, precisionist, stickler
perfectist *n syn* see PERFECTIONIST
perfectly *adv syn* see WELL 3
perfervid *adj syn* see IMPASSIONED
rel enhanced, heightened, intensified
perfidious *adj syn* see FAITHLESS
rel mercenary, venal; alienated, estranged, disaffected; deceitful, dishonest
perfidiousness *n* **1** *syn* see INFIDELITY 1
2 *syn* see TREACHERY
perfidy *n* **1** *syn* see TREACHERY
rel foul play
idiom Judas' kiss
ant fealty
2 *syn* see INFIDELITY 1
rel betrayal, sellout
perforate *vb* to pierce through so as to leave a hole <*perforate* a sheet of postage stamps>
syn bore, drill, prick, ‖pritch, punch, puncture
rel pit; probe; drive, penetrate, pierce
perforce *adv syn* see WILLY-NILLY
perform *vb* **1** *syn* see FULFILL 1
2 to carry something (as a process) to a successful conclusion <*perform* a surgical procedure>
syn achieve, do, execute; *compare* EFFECT 2
rel accomplish, bring off; complete, end, finish, wind up
idiom carry to completion (*or* a successful conclusion), do to a turn, do up brown
3 *syn* see ACT 1
4 *syn* see ACT 5
performance *n syn* see EFFICIENCY 1
performer *n syn* see ACTOR 1
perfume *n syn* see FRAGRANCE

---

syn synonym(s)   *rel* related word(s)
ant antonym(s)   *con* contrasted word(s)
idiom idiomatic equivalent(s)
‖ use limited; if in doubt, see a dictionary

perfume *vb syn* see SCENT 2
perfumed *adj syn* see SWEET 2
perfumy *adj syn* see SWEET 2
perfunctory *adj* characterized by routine and often done merely as a duty <gave her his usual *perfunctory* nod>
syn automatic, mechanical
rel cursory, superficial; involuntary, unaware; routine, usual; standard, stock; cool, impersonal, indifferent; wooden; unconcerned, uninterested
con cordial, friendly, genial, hearty, warm
pergola *n syn* see ARBOR
perhaps *adv* conceivably but not certainly so <*perhaps* this is true, but I think it's debatable>
syn maybe, perchance, possibly
rel conceivably, feasibly, imaginably
idiom as it may be, as the case may be, for all one knows
con certainly, definitely, doubtlessly, surely, undoubtedly, unquestionably
perhaps *n syn* see THEORY 2
periapt *n syn* see CHARM 2
peril *n syn* see DANGER
rel exposure, liability, openness, subjection; endangerment
idiom cause for alarm, rocks (*or* breakers) ahead
peril *vb syn* see ENDANGER
perilous *adj syn* see DANGEROUS 1
rel shaky, tottery, unstable, unsteady; delicate, ticklish, touchy
perimeter *n* **1** *syn* see CIRCUMFERENCE
2 *syn* see BORDER 1
period *n* **1** *syn* see END 2
2 an extent of time set off or typified by someone or something <the Victorian *period*> <a *period* of expansion>
syn age, day(s), epoch, era, time
periodic *adj syn* see INTERMITTENT
rel on-again-off-again
periodical *adj syn* see INTERMITTENT
periodical *n syn* see JOURNAL
peripatetic *adj syn* see ITINERANT
periphery *n* **1** *syn* see CIRCUMFERENCE
2 *syn* see BORDER 1
periphrase *n syn* see VERBIAGE 1
periphrasis *n syn* see VERBIAGE 1
perish *vb* **1** *syn* see DIE 1
ant survive
2 to suffer spiritual or moral death <nations *perishing* for lack of true leaders>
syn die
rel decline; collapse, go under; expire, succumb; disappear, vanish; cease, end
con flourish, prosper, thrive
ant endure
‖**3** *syn* see DECAY
perishing *adj syn* see DAMNED 2
perjure *vb* to make a false swearer of oneself by violating one's oath to tell the truth <a *perjured* witness>
syn forswear
rel equivocate; deceive, delude, mislead, trick; lie, prevaricate
idiom commit perjury, lie under oath, swear falsely
perjurer *n syn* see LIAR
perk (up) *vb syn* see IMPROVE 3
‖**perk** *n, usu* perks *pl syn* see GRATUITY
perlustrate *vb syn* see SCRUTINIZE 1
perlustration *n syn* see EXAMINATION

permanent *adj syn see* LASTING
rel imperishable, invariable
ant temporary

permeable *adj* capable of being permeated
especially by fluids < a *permeable* membrane >
syn penetrable, pervious, porose, porous
rel passable
con impassable, impenetrable, impervious
ant impermeable

permeate *vb* to pass or cause to pass
through every part of a thing < air *permeated* with cigar smoke >
syn charge, compenetrate, impenetrate,
impregnate, interfuse, interpenetrate, penetrate, percolate, pervade, saturate, transfuse
rel invade; imbrue, imbue, infiltrate, infuse, ingrain; diffuse, suffuse; drench,
soak, steep; fill

permissible *adj* that may be permitted < a
permissible error >
syn admissible, allowable
rel unforbidden, unprohibited; allowed,
permitted, tolerated; approved, authorized,
endorsed, sanctioned; acceptable, bearable,
tolerable
con banned, forbidden, disallowed, prohibited, unpermitted, verboten; unacceptable, unbearable
ant impermissible

permission *n* a sanctioning to act or do
something that is granted by one in authority < received *permission* to leave
work early >
syn allowance, authorization, consent,
leave, permit, sanction, sufferance
rel acceptance, acquiescence; approbation,
approval; endorsement
ant prohibition

permit *vb syn see* LET 2
rel tolerate
idiom give one his head
ant forbid, prohibit

permit *n syn see* PERMISSION

permutation *n syn see* CHANGE 2
rel alteration, modification

pernicious *adj* exceedingly harmful or
destructive < *pernicious* gossip >
syn baneful, deadly, noxious, pestiferous,
pestilent, pestilential; *compare* DEADLY 1
rel damaging, deleterious, detrimental,
harmful, hurtful; baleful, malefic, maleficent, malign, sinister; miasmatic, miasmic,
poisonous, toxic, venomous; malignant,
swart, virulent; destructive, devastating,
ruinous; fatal, killing, lethal, mortal
con harmless, uninjurious; nonmalignant,
nonpoisonous, nontoxic
ant innocuous

pernickety *adj syn see* NICE 1
perorate *vb syn see* ORATE
perpend *vb syn see* CONSIDER 1
perpendicular *adj syn see* VERTICAL
rel stand-up, straight
ant horizontal

perpendicularity *n syn see* VERTICALITY
rel erectness, uprightness
ant horizontality

perpetrate *vb syn see* COMMIT 2
rel effect; inflict, wreak
idiom ‖up and do

perpetual *adj syn see* CONTINUAL

ant ephemeral, transient

perpetually *adv syn see* ALWAYS 1

perpetuate *vb* to make perpetual or cause
to last indefinitely < *perpetuate* his memory for future generations >
syn eternalize, eternize, immortalize
rel bolster, conserve, keep, maintain,
preserve, secure, support, sustain
con annihilate, blot out, erase, expunge
ant obliterate

perplex *vb* 1 *syn see* PUZZLE
rel discompose, perturb; balk, thwart;
astonish, astound, surprise
idiom put (*or* drive) to one's wit's end
2 *syn see* COMPLICATE
3 *syn see* ENTANGLE 1

perquisite *n* 1 *syn see* GRATUITY
2 *syn see* RIGHT 2

per se *adv* by, of, or in itself or oneself or
themselves < a lover of language *per se* >
syn as such, intrinsically
rel alone, independently, solely

persecute *vb* 1 *syn see* WRONG
rel dragoon, rack, torment, torture
con back, champion, support, uphold
2 *syn see* MOLEST
rel worry; hound, ride
con humor, indulge, pamper; accommodate, favor, oblige

perseverant *adj syn see* PERSISTENT 1
perseverative *adj syn see* PERSISTENT 1

persevere *vb* to continue in a state, enterprise, or undertaking in spite of counter
influences, opposition, or discouragement
< *persevered* in his unpopular economic
policy >
syn carry on, go on, hang on, persist
rel continue, get on, press (on), proceed
idiom ‖hang in there, keep at it, keep
driving, never say die, stick (*or* tough) it
out
con falter, hesitate, vacillate, waver; renounce, surrender, yield
ant give up

persevering *adj syn see* PERSISTENT 1
persiflage *n syn see* BANTER
persist *vb* 1 *syn see* PERSEVERE
con cease, discontinue, quit, stop
ant desist
2 *syn see* CONTINUE 1
rel go on; linger; obtain, prevail
ant desist

persistence *n* 1 *syn see* CONTINUATION 1
2 *syn see* RUN 2
rel course

persistent *adj* 1 continuing in a course of
action without regard to discouragement,
opposition, or previous failure < a *persistent* suitor >
syn dogged, insistent, perseverant, perseverative, persevering, persisting, persistive
rel determined, steadfast, tenacious, unshakable; relentless, unremitting
con malleable, pliant, tractable, yielding;
infirm, invertebrate, spineless; vacillating,
wavery, wobbling
2 *syn see* PRIMITIVE 3

persisting *adj syn see* PERSISTENT 1
persistive *adj syn see* PERSISTENT 1
persnickety *adj syn see* NICE 1
person *n syn see* HUMAN
rel chap, ‖cookie, coot, fellow, galoot,
guy, specimen, stick

personage *n* **1** *syn* see NOTABLE 1
2 *syn* see HUMAN
personal *adj* **1** of, relating to, or affecting
a particular person < owed his *personal*
allegiance to his wife >
syn individual
rel particular, peculiar, special
con general, universal; common, joint,
mutual, shared; commonplace, everyday,
ordinary
2 *syn* see PRIVATE 1
personal effects *n pl* privately owned
items (as clothing and toilet articles) normally worn or carried on the person
< packed his *personal effects* in a small
bag >
syn ‖plunder, stuff, things, traps, tricks
rel belongings, goods, possessions
idiom personal belongings
personality *n* **1** *syn* see INDIVIDUALITY 4
2 *syn* see DISPOSITION 3
3 *syn* see NOTABLE 1
personalize *vb* **1** *syn* see EMBODY 1
rel anthropomorphize
2 *syn* see REPRESENT 2
personal name *n syn* see GIVEN NAME
personate *vb* **1** *syn* see ACT 1
2 *syn* see REPRESENT 2
personification *n syn* see EMBODIMENT
personify *vb* **1** *syn* see EMBODY 1
rel reincarnate
2 *syn* see REPRESENT 2
personize *vb syn* see EMBODY 1
perspective *n syn* see VISTA
perspicacious *adj syn* see SHREWD
rel quick-sighted, sharp-sighted, sharp-
witted
perspicacity *n syn* see WIT 3
perspicuity *n syn* see CLARITY
rel intelligibility; explicitness
perspicuous *adj syn* see CLEAR 4
perspiring *adj syn* see SWEATY
perspiry *adj syn* see SWEATY
persuadable *adj syn* see RECEPTIVE 1
ant unpersuadable
persuade *vb* **1** *syn* see INDUCE 1
rel affect, impress, touch; reason; convert
con discourage, hinder, prevent
ant dissuade
2 *syn* see CONVERT 1
3 *syn* see ASSURE 2
ant dissuade
persuasible *adj syn* see RECEPTIVE 1
ant unpersuasible
persuasion *n* **1** *syn* see OPINION
rel bias, partiality, predilection, prejudice,
prepossession
2 *syn* see RELIGION 1
3 *syn* see RELIGION 2
rel affiliation; order
4 *syn* see TYPE
pert *adj* **1** *syn* see SAUCY 1
rel bold, daring; audacious, brazen
con shy
ant coy
2 *syn* see WISE 5
rel disrespectful, rude
3 *syn* see LIVELY 1

syn synonym(s)   *rel* related word(s)
ant antonym(s)   *con* contrasted word(s)
idiom idiomatic equivalent(s)
‖ use limited; if in doubt, see a dictionary

pertain *vb* **1** *syn* see BELONG 2
2 *syn* see BEAR (on *or* upon)
rel associate, combine, connect, join
idiom be pertinent (*or* relevant) to
pertinacious *adj syn* see OBSTINATE
rel fixed, unshakable; dogged, tenacious
pertinent *adj syn* see RELEVANT
rel pertaining
ant impertinent
perturb *vb syn* see DISCOMPOSE 1
rel trouble; unsettle
ant compose
pervade *vb syn* see PERMEATE
idiom spread through and through
perverse *adj* **1** *syn* see VICIOUS 2
2 *syn* see OBSTINATE
rel cranky, irritable, unreasonable
3 *syn* see CONTRARY 3
pervert *vb* **1** *syn* see DEBASE 1
rel abuse, maltreat, mistreat, misuse,
outrage; ruin
2 *syn* see ABUSE 2
rel ill-treat
3 *syn* see MISREPRESENT
perverted *adj syn* see DEBASED
rel defiled, polluted, tainted; contorted,
distorted, warped; abused, misused, outraged
pervicacious *adj syn* see OBSTINATE
pervious *adj syn* see PERMEABLE
ant impervious
pesky *adj syn* see TROUBLESOME
pesky *adv syn* see VERY 1
pessimist *n* one who emphasizes adverse
aspects or conditions and expects the
worst < *pessimists* predicting another depression >
syn calamity howler, Cassandra, crepehanger, worrywart
rel fussbudget; Job's comforter; defeatist;
killjoy; cynic, misanthrope
con positivist; idealist; Pollyanna
ant optimist
pest *n* **1** *syn* see ANNOYANCE 3
rel bane, trouble, vexation, worry
idiom pain in the neck, pea in the shoe,
thorn in the flesh
2 one who pesters or annoys < a little *pest*
who constantly asked questions >
syn nudnick, nuisance, pesterer
rel badgerer, heckler, tormentor
idiom pain in the neck
pester *vb syn* see WORRY 1
rel ride
idiom drive (one) crazy, drive (one) up
the wall, pester to death
pester *n syn* see ANNOYANCE 3
pesterer *n syn* see PEST 2
‖**pesterment** *n syn* see ANNOYANCE 3
pesticide *n* a chemical agent used to destroy pests < the need to control indiscriminate use of *pesticides* >
syn biocide, economic poison
rel bactericide, fungicide, germicide, in-
secticide, microbicide, rodenticide, vermi-
cide
pestiferous *adj syn* see PERNICIOUS
pestilence *n syn* see PLAGUE 1
pestilent *adj* **1** *syn* see DEADLY 1
2 *syn* see PERNICIOUS
pestilential *adj* **1** *syn* see DEADLY 1
2 *syn* see PERNICIOUS
pet *adj syn* see FAVORITE 1

pet *vb syn* see CARESS
rel embrace, hug

pet *vb syn* see SULK

petcock *n syn* see FAUCET

peter (out) *vb syn* see DECREASE

Peter Funk *n syn* see SWINDLER

petite *adj syn* see SMALL 1
rel diminutive, dwarf, lilliputian, miniature, wee

petition *n syn* see PRAYER
rel request

petition *vb* to make an earnest, formal, and often written request < *petitioned* for a hearing before the labor board>
syn appeal, sue (for *or* to)
rel ask, request; beg, beseech, entreat, implore, plead, pray, supplicate
con claim, demand, exact, press (for)

petitioner *n syn* see SUPPLIANT

petit-maître *n syn* see FOP

petrify *vb syn* see DAZE 2
rel alarm, frighten, startle, terrify; appall, dismay, horrify; numb
idiom turn to stone

pettifogger *n* an unscrupulous lawyer < done out of his rights by a slick *pettifogger*>
syn jackleg lawyer, shyster; *compare* LAWYER
rel ambulance chaser, Philadelphia lawyer; ‖bush lawyer

pettifogging *adj syn* see PETTY 2

pettish *adj syn* see IRRITABLE

petty *adj* 1 *syn* see LITTLE 3
2 being often contemptibly insignificant or unimportant < *petty* quarrels and intrigues>
syn inconsequent, inconsequential, inconsiderable, measly, Mickey Mouse, niggling, paltry, peanut, peddling, pettifogging, picayune, picayunish, piddling, piffling, pimping, puny, small, trifling, trivial, unconsequential, unconsidered, ungenerous, unvital; *compare* LITTLE 3
rel negligible, unimportant; hair-drawn, hairsplitting; impertinent, irrelevant
con consequential, considerable; big, gross; significant, vital
ant important, momentous

petulant *adj syn* see IRRITABLE
rel grouchy, sulky

phantasm *n* 1 *syn* see DELUSION 1
rel fabrication, fiction, invention
2 *syn* see APPARITION
3 *syn* see FANCY 4

phantom *n syn* see APPARITION

pharisaic *adj syn* see HYPOCRITICAL

pharisaical *adj syn* see HYPOCRITICAL

pharisaicalness *n syn* see HYPOCRISY

pharisaism *n syn* see HYPOCRISY

pharisee *n syn* see HYPOCRITE

pharmaceutic *n syn* see DRUG 1

pharmaceutical *n syn* see DRUG 1

pharmacist *n syn* see DRUGGIST

pharmacon *n syn* see REMEDY 1

pharos *n syn* see LIGHTHOUSE

phase *n* one of the possible ways of viewing or being presented to view < the moral *phase* of the problem>
syn angle, aspect, facet, hand, side
rel condition, situation, state; position, posture, view, viewpoint; appearance, look, semblance; color, complexion

phenomenal *adj* 1 *syn* see MATERIAL 1
con ontic
ant noumenal
2 *syn* see EXCEPTIONAL 1

phenomenon *n* 1 *syn* see FACT 2
rel experience; actuality, reality
2 *syn* see WONDER 1
rel abnormality; anomaly, paradox; peculiarity, singularity, uniqueness, unusualness

philander *n syn* see WOLF
idiom ‖skirt chaser

philander *vb* to have many love affairs < his reputation for *philandering* with married women>
syn fool (around), mess around, play (around), wolf, womanize
rel dally, flirt, trifle; chase, pursue; ‖tomcat (around)
idiom ‖chase skirts, play Don Juan, play the femmes

philanderer *n syn* see WOLF

philanthropic *adj syn* see CHARITABLE 1
rel bighearted, freehearted, greathearted, kindhearted, largehearted, openhearted; contributing, donating, freehanded, giving, magnanimous; civic-minded, public-spirited
ant misanthropic

philharmonic *n syn* see ORCHESTRA

philippic *n syn* see TIRADE

philistine *n* a crass, prosaic, often priggish individual guided by material rather than artistic or intellectual values < *philistines* who opposed everything new and creative in art>
syn Babbitt, boeotian, boob, middlebrow
rel bourgeois; capitalist; materialist; boor, clown, lout, vulgarian
ant aesthete

phiz *n syn* see FACE 1

phlegm *n* 1 *syn* see APATHY 1
2 *syn* see EQUANIMITY
rel nonchalance, unconcern

phlegmatic *adj syn* see IMPASSIVE 1
rel calm, undemonstrative; aloof, incurious, indifferent, unconcerned; lethargic, sluggish

phoebus *n syn* see SUN 1

phoenix *n syn* see PARAGON

phonate *vb syn* see ARTICULATE 2

phone *vb syn* see TELEPHONE

phony *adj syn* see COUNTERFEIT

phony *n* 1 *syn* see IMPOSTURE
2 *syn* see IMPOSTOR

photo *vb syn* see PHOTOGRAPH
idiom take a photo (of)

photog *n syn* see PHOTOGRAPHER

photograph *vb* to use a camera to make a picture, image, or likeness of < *photographed* the whole family>
syn photo, shoot
rel cinematize, ‖cinematograph, cinemize, film, filmize, picture; kodak, snap, snapshoot, snapshot; mug
idiom capture on film, take a picture (*or* photograph)

photographer *n* one who takes photographs < a newspaper *photographer*>
syn cameraman, camerist, photog, photographist, photoist
rel snapshooter, ‖snapshotter; shutterbug

photographic *adj syn* see GRAPHIC 1

rel accurate, detailed, exact

photographist *n syn* see PHOTOGRAPHER

photoist *n syn* see PHOTOGRAPHER

photoplay *n syn* see MOVIE

phrase *n* **1** *syn* see WORDING
  rel styling
  2 a group of words which, taken together, express a notion and may constitute part of a sentence < an adverbial *phrase* > < a trite *phrase* >
  syn expression, locution
  rel phrasing; idiom; catchword, slogan
  3 *syn* see CATCHWORD

phrase *vb syn* see WORD

phraseology *n syn* see WORDING
  idiom choice of words

phrasing *n syn* see WORDING

phthisis *n syn* see TUBERCULOSIS

phylactery *n syn* see CHARM 2

physic *n syn* see REMEDY 1

physical *adj* **1** *syn* see MATERIAL 1
  rel natural; elemental, elementary
  ant spiritual
  2 *syn* see BODILY
  rel visceral; lusty; brute
  ant mental

physician *n* a doctor of medicine < the shortage of *physicians* in rural areas >
  syn ‖croaker, doc, doctor, MD, medical, mediciner, medico, ‖sawbones
  rel medic; general practitioner, practitioner; surgeon; specialist
  idiom medical doctor, medical man

physique *n* bodily makeup or type < a muscular *physique* >
  syn build, constitution, habit, habitus
  rel anatomy, structure; configuration, shape; body, figure, form, frame

picaroon *n syn* see PIRATE

picayune *adj syn* see PETTY 2

picayunish *adj syn* see PETTY 2

pick *vb* **1** *syn* see CHOOSE 1
  idiom pick and choose
  ant reject
  2 *syn* see PECK 1

pick *n syn* see BEST

pick *adj syn* see SELECT 1

picked *adj syn* see SELECT 1

picket *n syn* see GUARD 2

pickle *n syn* see PREDICAMENT
  idiom pretty pickle, ‖sticky wicket, tight spot

‖pickled *adj syn* see INTOXICATED 1

pick out *vb syn* see CHOOSE 1

pickpocket *n* one who steals from pockets < his wallet was lifted by a *pickpocket* >
  syn ‖cannon, cutpurse, ‖dip, ‖diver, purse cutter, ‖wire
  rel ‖ganef, thief; ‖mobsman, ‖swell-mobsman
  idiom ‖pocket prowler

picksome *adj syn* see NICE 1

pick up *vb* **1** *syn* see LIFT 1
  2 *syn* see GLEAN
  3 *syn* see GET 1
  4 *syn* see LEARN 1
  5 *syn* see ARREST 2
  rel book

idiom ‖take (someone) downtown
  6 *syn* see RESUME 2
  idiom pick up the thread again

pickup *n syn* see ARREST
  rel booking

picky *adj syn* see NICE 1

picnic *n syn* see SNAP 1

pictorial *adj* **1** consisting of or relating to pictures < a collection of *pictorial* materials >
  syn graphic, iconographic, illustrational, illustrative, illustratory, pictoric
  rel photographic, pictographic
  2 *syn* see GRAPHIC 1

pictoric *adj syn* see PICTORIAL 1

picture *n* **1** *syn* see REPRESENTATION
  2 *syn* see IMAGE 1
  3 *syn* see MOVIE

picture *vb syn* see REPRESENT 1
  rel draw

picture show *n syn* see MOVIE

picturesque *adj syn* see GRAPHIC 1

piddling *adj syn* see PETTY 2

pie *n syn* see SNAP 1

piece *n* **1** *syn* see PART 1
  ‖ **2** *syn* see SNACK

pièce de résistance *n syn* see SHOWPIECE

piecemeal *adv syn* see GRADUALLY

piecemeal *adj syn* see GRADUAL

‖pie-eyed *adj syn* see INTOXICATED 1

piepoudre *n syn* see PEDDLER

pier *n* **1** *syn* see WHARF
  rel pierage, wharfage
  2 *syn* see PILLAR 1

pierce *vb* **1** *syn* see CUT 1
  rel penetrate, perforate
  2 *syn* see PENETRATE 2
  rel run through

piercing *adj* **1** *syn* see SHARP 8
  2 *syn* see LOUD 1
  3 *syn* see ACUTE 4

pietistic *adj syn* see DEVOUT
  rel reverencing, reverential

piety *n syn* see FIDELITY 1
  rel docility, obedience; enthusiasm, fervor, passion, zeal; holiness, sanctity

piffle *n syn* see NONSENSE 2

piffling *adj syn* see PETTY 2

‖pig *n* **1** *syn* see WANTON
  2 *syn* see POLICEMAN

pigeon *n syn* see FOOL 3

pigeon *vb syn* see DUPE

pigeonhole *n* **1** *syn* see CUBBYHOLE
  2 *syn* see CLASS 1
  rel niche, slot

pigeonhole *vb syn* see ASSORT
  rel identify, label, name; place, rank, rate; catalog; break down, subdivide

pigeon house *n syn* see DOVECOTE

pigeonry *n syn* see DOVECOTE

pigheaded *adj syn* see OBSTINATE
  idiom not to be moved (*or* budged)

pigment *n syn* see COLOR 6

pigpen *n syn* see STY 1

pigsty *n syn* see STY 1

piked *adj syn* see POINTED 1

piker *n syn* see VAGABOND

piker *n syn* see MISER

pilaster *n syn* see PILLAR 1

pile *n* **1** a quantity of things heaped or stacked together < a *pile* of dirty clothes >

---

syn synonym(s)   *rel* related word(s)
ant antonym(s)   *con* contrasted word(s)
idiom idiomatic equivalent(s)
‖ use limited; if in doubt, see a dictionary

syn bank, ‖bing, cock, drift, heap, hill, mass, mound, mountain, mow, pyramid, rick, ‖rickle, ‖ruck, shock, stack, stockpile, windrow

rel barrow, pyre, tumulus; ‖dess, haycock, hayrick, haystack; accumulation, aggregate, aggregation, amassment, assemblage, collection, conglomeration, glomeration, hoard, jumble

2 *syn* see MUCH

3 *syn* see EDIFICE

4 *syn* see FORTUNE 4

idiom a pile of money

pile *vb* 1 *syn* see HEAP 1

2 *syn* see LOAD 3

pile (in) *vb syn* see RETIRE 4

pile (out) *vb syn* see ROLL OUT

idiom ‖get the lead out, ‖shake it out

pile *n syn* see DOWN

pileous *adj syn* see HAIRY 1

con bare; pileless

pile up *vb syn* see SHIPWRECK 1

pileup *n syn* see CRASH 3

pilfer *vb syn* see STEAL 1

pilferer *n syn* see THIEF

pilgarlic *n syn* see LAUGHINGSTOCK

‖pill *n syn* see CIGARETTE

pillage *vb* 1 *syn* see RAVAGE

rel encroach, invade, trespass; appropriate, arrogate, confiscate, usurp

idiom lay waste

2 *syn* see STEAL 1

pillager *n syn* see MARAUDER

pillar *n* 1 a firm upright support for a superstructure <stone *pillars* supported the ceiling>

syn column, pier, pilaster

rel prop; pedestal; post

2 *syn* see MAINSTAY

pilose *adj syn* see HAIRY 1

pilot *n* 1 *syn* see LEADER 1

2 one who flies or is qualified to fly an airplane <jet *pilots*>

syn airman, aviator, birdman, flier, flyboy

rel aerialist

pilot *vb* 1 *syn* see GUIDE

2 *syn* see DRIVE 5

pimp *n* 1 a man who solicits for a prostitute, lives off her earnings, and often lives with her <after dark, the *pimp* appeared on the street seeking clients for his girls>

syn bully, cadet, ‖easy rider, fancy man, ‖mack, macquereau, pander

rel procurer; white slaver

‖2 *syn* see INFORMER

‖pimp *vb syn* see INFORM 3

pimping *adj syn* see PETTY 2

pimple *n syn* see ABSCESS

rel ‖plouk

pimple *vb syn* see SPOT 2

pin *n syn* see BROOCH

pinch *vb* 1 *syn* see EXTORT 1

2 *syn* see STEAL 1

3 *syn* see ARREST 2

4 *syn* see SCRIMP

pinch *n* 1 *syn* see JUNCTURE 2

2 *syn* see THEFT

3 *syn* see ARREST

pinchbeck *adj syn* see COUNTERFEIT

pinched *adj syn* see HAGGARD

con stalwart, stout, strong, sturdy; healthy, robust

pinching *adj syn* see STINGY

pinch hitter *n syn* see SUBSTITUTE

pinchpenny *adj syn* see STINGY

‖pindling *adj syn* see IRRITABLE

pine *vb syn* see LONG

rel brood, fret, mope; grieve, mourn; agonize

pinhead *n syn* see DUNCE

pinhead *adj syn* see STUPID 1

pinheaded *adj syn* see STUPID 1

pink *n syn* see BLUSH

pinken *vb syn* see BLUSH

Pinkerton *n syn* see PRIVATE DETECTIVE

pin money *n syn* see POCKET MONEY

pinnacle *n syn* see APEX 2

pinpoint *vb syn* see IDENTIFY

pint-size *adj syn* see TINY

pioneer *adj syn* see FIRST 2

rel pilot

pious *adj syn* see DEVOUT

rel priestlike, priestly

ant impious

pip *vb* ‖1 *syn* see DEFEAT 2

2 *syn* see DIE 1

‖pip *n syn* ‖DILLY, ‖corker, crackerjack, ‖daisy, dandy, humdinger, jim-dandy, ‖lalapalooza, ‖lulu, nifty

pipe *n* 1 *syn* see CASK

‖2 *syn* see PIPE DREAM

‖3 *syn* see SNAP 1

pipe *vb* ‖1 *syn* see CRY 2

2 *syn* see CONDUCT 4

pipe down *vb syn* see SHUT UP 2

pipe dream *n* an illusory or fantastic plan or hope <*pipe dreams* of universal peace>

syn bubble, chimera, dream, fantasy (*or* phantasy), illusion, ‖pipe, rainbow

rel expectation, hope, prospect

pipeline *n* a person through whom information is transmitted <she was his news *pipeline* from the mayor's office>

syn channel, conduit

rel grapevine; origin, source, wellspring; supplier; connection, contact

piping *adj syn* see ACUTE 4

‖pipped *adj syn* see INTOXICATED 1

pippin *n syn* ‖DILLY, ‖corker, crackerjack, dandy, ‖dinger, ‖doozer, humdinger, jim-dandy, ‖lalapalooza, ‖pip

piquant *adj syn* see PUNGENT

rel high-flavored, well-flavored; appetizing, sparkling

con inane, jejune

ant banal

pique *n syn* see OFFENSE 2

rel annoyance, irk, irking, vexation; exasperation, irritation, provocation

pique *vb* 1 *syn* see IRRITATE

2 *syn* see PROVOKE 4

rel prick, punch; ignite

3 *syn* see PRIDE

pirate *n* a robber on the high seas <little boys dreaming of sailing as *pirates*>

syn buccaneer, corsair, freebooter, picaroon, rover, sea dog, sea robber, sea rover, sea wolf

rel viking; privateer; looter, marauder, pillager, plunderer, raider

‖pirl *vb syn* see SPIN 1

‖piroot *vb syn* see SNOOP

pirouette *vb syn* see SPIN 1

pishposh *n syn* see NONSENSE 2

||**piss away** vb syn see WASTE 2
||**pissed** adj 1 syn see ANGRY
2 syn see INTOXICATED 1
||**pissed off** adj syn see ANGRY
pit n ||1 syn see GRAVE
2 syn see HELL
pit vb syn see OPPOSE 1
pitch vb 1 syn see THROW 1
rel hoist, raise; move
2 syn see THROW 2
||3 syn see PLANT 1
4 syn see FALL 2
idiom take a pitch
5 syn see PLUNGE 2
rel drop, fall, sink
6 syn see TOSS 2
7 syn see SEESAW
pitch n syn see SPIEL
rel persuasion
pitch–black adj syn see BLACK 1
pitch–dark adj syn see BLACK 1
pitched adj syn see INCLINED 3
pitch in vb 1 to set about doing something
energetically < had a lot to do and decided to pitch in >
syn buckle (down), fall to, jump (in or
into), set to, wade (in or into)
rel attack, tackle; launch, tee off; begin,
commence, start (off or out or up)
idiom fall to it, fall to work, get busy (or
cracking), get down to it, get going, get
(or have) with it, go to it, hop (or jump)
to it
con dally, dawdle, procrastinate, stall;
vacillate
2 syn see CONTRIBUTE 1
pitching adj syn see INCLINED 3
pitchy adj syn see BLACK 1
piteous adj syn see PITIFUL 1
rel beseeching, entreating, imploring,
supplicating; doleful, dolorous, melancholy, plaintive; ruined
pitfall n a hidden or obscure source of
danger, error, or harm < pitfalls that trap
the unwary investigator >
syn booby trap, deadfall, mousetrap,
springe, trapfall
rel danger, hazard, peril, risk; cobweb,
entanglement, mesh(es), toil(s), web; bait,
lure, snare, trap
pith n 1 syn see ESSENCE 2
rel center, focus, nucleus; meaning, meaningfulness
2 syn see SUBSTANCE 2
idiom the long and (the) short
3 syn see CENTER 3
rel fulcrum; hub
4 syn see IMPORTANCE
pithy adj being rich in meaning and tersely
cogent in expression < a pithy summary >
syn compact, epigrammatic, marrowy,
meaty; compare CONCISE
rel brief, concise, lean, short, short and
sweet, succinct; crisp, curt, terse; effective,
forceful; meaningful, significant, substantial
idiom brief and to the point, down to
brass tacks, right to the point

syn synonym(s)   rel related word(s)
ant antonym(s)   con contrasted word(s)
idiom idiomatic equivalent(s)
|| use limited; if in doubt, see a dictionary

con flatulent, inflated, tumid, turgid;
prolix, verbose, wordy
ant diffuse
pitiable adj 1 syn see PITIFUL 1
2 syn see CONTEMPTIBLE
rel miserable, wretched; deplorable, lamentable
pitiful adj 1 arousing or deserving pity
< pitiful refugees driven from their
homes >
syn commiserable, pathetic, piteous, pitiable, poor, rueful
rel affecting, moving, touching; miserable,
woeful, wretched; heartrending
2 syn see CONTEMPTIBLE
pitiless adj devoid of or unmoved by pity
< a pitiless concentration camp guard >
syn merciless, unmerciful, unpitying;
compare UNFEELING 2
rel coldhearted, hardhearted, heartless,
ironhearted, marblehearted, stony, stonyhearted, uncompassionate, unfeeling; barbarous, brutal, cruel, cutthroat, inhumane,
savage
idiom lacking bowels of compassion,
without an ounce of pity
con compassionate, humane, sympathetic;
clement, merciful; tender, warmhearted
ant pitying
pittance n a small, often barely sufficient
amount or allowance < a pittance of an
education > < worked for a mere pittance >
syn dribble, driblet, ||scrimption
rel bit, mite, scrap, smidgen, trace; inadequacy, insufficiency
idiom a drop in the bucket, cheeseparings
and candle ends, ||pinchgut money
con abundance, opulence, plenty, wealth
pity n sympathetic feeling for one suffering,
distressed, or unhappy < felt the deepest
pity for the prisoners >
syn commiseration, compassion, rue, ruth,
sympathy
rel dejection, distress, melancholy, sadness, sorrow; charity, clemency, lenity,
mercy
con contempt, disdain, disgust, scorn
pity vb syn see COMPASSIONATE
pivot vb syn see TURN 6
pivotal adj syn see CENTRAL 1
rel essential, vital; momentous; capital,
principal
pixie n 1 syn see FAIRY
2 syn see SCAMP
pixie adj syn see PLAYFUL 1
pixieish adj syn see PLAYFUL 1
pixilated adj 1 syn see PLAYFUL 1
2 syn see INTOXICATED 1
placard n syn see POSTER
placard vb syn see POST
placate vb syn see PACIFY
rel comfort; tranquilize
idiom lay the dust
con anger, incense, infuriate, madden;
excite, pique, provoke, stimulate
ant enrage
place n 1 the portion of space occupied by
or chosen for something < the place where
we'll meet >
syn location, locus, point, position, site,
situation, spot, station, where
rel district, locality, vicinity; area, region,
tract, zone; field, province, territory

2 *syn* see STATUS 1

3 *syn* see JOB 2

place *vb* 1 *syn* see SET 1

2 *syn* see ESTIMATE 3

3 *syn* see IDENTIFY

rel know, tell; nail, peg

idiom put one's finger on

placed *adj syn* see SITUATED

ant displaced

placid *adj* 1 *syn* see CALM 1

rel irenic, peaceful, serene, unagitated, unstirring

ant roiled

2 *syn* see CALM 2

rel detached, inexcitable, unmoved

con fidgety, jittery, jumpy, skittery; agitated

ant choleric

plague *n* 1 an epidemic disease causing a high mortality rate <smallpox finally ceased to be a *plague* in those nations>

syn curse, pestilence, scourge

rel infestation, invasion; affliction, disease; epidemic; ravage

2 *syn* see ANNOYANCE 3

rel bane, curse

3 *syn* see EPIDEMIC

plague *vb syn* see WORRY 1

rel chafe, gall; badger, bait, hassle, hector, hound, ride; afflict, torment

plain *adj* 1 free from all ostentation or superficial embellishment <just give the *plain* facts>

syn discreet, dry, homely, inelaborate, modest, simple, unadorned, unbeautified, undecorated, unelaborate, unembellished, unembroidered, ungarnished, unornamented, unostentatious, unpretentious

rel muted, restrained; austere, bald, bare, severe, spartan, stark, unluxurious; homespun

con adorned, beautified, elaborate, embellished, embroidered, exaggerated; high-flown, ostentatious, pretentious; flamboyant, rococo

ant rich

2 *syn* see STRAIGHT 3

3 *syn* see CLEAR 5

rel broad, unmistakable; legible

ant abstruse

4 *syn* see FRANK

rel unfeigned; abrupt

idiom plain and open

5 lacking allure without being positively ugly <a *plain* woman, drably dressed>

syn homely, unalluring, unattractive, unbeauteous, unbeautiful, uncomely, unhandsome, unpretty

rel plain-featured; inelegant; ordinary, plain Jane, unremarkable; ill-favored

idiom not much for looks, not much to look at, short on looks

con alluring, attractive, beautiful, comely, handsome; elegant; striking; knockout, sensational

6 *syn* see ORDINARY 1

plainclothesman *n syn* see DETECTIVE

plain dealing *adj syn* see STRAIGHTFORWARD 2

plain Jane *adj syn* see ORDINARY 1

plainness *n syn* see CLARITY

ant abstruseness

plainspoken *adj syn* see FRANK

plaintive *adj syn* see MELANCHOLY 2

rel deploring, lamenting, wailing; piteous, pitiful; sad, saddening

plan *n* 1 a method devised for making or doing something or attaining an end <each company had a *plan* for increasing profits>

syn blueprint, design, game plan, project, scheme, strategy

rel conception, idea, notion; ground plan, projection; projet; intent, intention, platform, purpose; means, method, way

idiom course (*or* plan) of action

2 *syn* see INTENTION

rel policy

3 *syn* see ORDER 8

plan *vb* 1 *syn* see DESIGN 3

2 to formulate a plan for arranging, realizing, or achieving something <*planned* next year's program>

syn arrange, blueprint, cast, chart, design, devise, ||dope out, project; compare DESIGN 3

rel contemplate, meditate; cut out, draft, outline, sketch; figure (out), think (out); formulate, work out; organize

3 *syn* see INTEND 2

idiom be planning (*or* counting) on, have all intentions of, have every intention of

planate *n syn* see LEVEL

plane *vb syn* see EVEN 1

plane *adj syn* see LEVEL

planet *n,* used with the *syn* see EARTH 1

planetary *adj* 1 *syn* see HUGE

2 *syn* see UNIVERSAL 2

plangent *adj syn* see RESONANT

plant *vb* 1 to put or set into the ground for growth <*plant* corn>

syn ||pitch, put in, seed, sow

rel drill; broadcast, dust, scatter; seed down

con crop, gather, harvest, reap

2 *syn* see HIDE

3 *syn* see BURY 1

plant *n syn* see FACTORY

plash *vb syn* see SPLASH

plaster *vb syn* see SMEAR 1

||**plastered** *adj syn* see INTOXICATED 1

plastic *adj* susceptible of being modified in form or nature <the *plastic* quality of modeling clay> <the *plastic* affections of children>

syn adaptable, ductile, malleable, moldable, pliable, pliant, supple

rel elastic, flexible, resilient, supple, workable; impressionable, influenceable, suggestible, susceptible; amenable, bending, giving, tractable, yielding

con inflexible, rigid, stiff; accepted, customary, prevailing, set, standard, wonted

plat *n syn* see LOT 3

plateau *n* a usually extensive level land area raised sharply above adjacent land on at least one side <the *plateaus* of central Bolivia>

syn table, tableland, upland

rel mesa

con dale, glen, vale, valley; bottom, bottomland, lowland

platitude *n syn* see COMMONPLACE

rel inanity, insipidity, vapidity; mawkishness, sentimentality

platoon *n syn* see GROUP 3

plaudit n, usu **plaudits** pl syn see AP-
PLAUSE
rel kudos
plausibility n syn see VERISIMILITUDE
plausible adj syn see BELIEVABLE
rel likely, possible, probable; presumable
con impossible, improbable, unlikely
ant implausible
play n 1 activity engaged in for amusement
< children need periods of work and
play >
syn disport, diversion, fun, recreation,
sport
rel amusement, entertainment; frolic,
gambol, romp; delectation, delight, enjoyment, pleasure
con business, duty, obligation; labor;
drudgery
ant work
2 syn see FUN 1
rel sportiveness
ant earnest
3 syn see TRICK 1
4 syn see USE 1
5 syn see ROOM 3
play vb 1 to engage in an activity for
amusement or recreation < played outside
for hours >
syn disport, recreate, sport
rel amuse, divert, engage, entertain; frolic,
gambol, rollick, romp
con labor, toil, travail; drudge, fag, slave
ant work
2 syn see FIDDLE 1
3 syn see TREAT 2
4 syn see MANIPULATE 2
5 syn see ACT 1
6 syn see GAMBLE 1
play (around) vb syn see PHILANDER
play (down) vb syn see SOFT-PEDAL
rel restrain; mute, soften
ant play (up)
play (off) vb syn see OPPOSE 1
play (up) vb syn see EMPHASIZE
idiom make a (big) production of
ant play (down)
playact vb syn see ACT 1
playactor n syn see ACTOR 1
player n syn see ACTOR 1
playful adj 1 given to or characterized by
play, jests, or tricks < in a playful
mood >
syn antic, coltish, elvish, frisky, frolicsome, gamesome, impish, kittenish, lark-
ish, ||mischiefful, mischievous, pixie, pixie-
ish, pixilated, prankful, prankish, pranky,
puckish, roguish, sportive, waggish,
wicked
rel gay, lighthearted, whimsical; dashing,
larking, lively, sprightly; blithe, jocund,
jolly, jovial, merry; gleeful, hilarious,
mirthful
idiom as playful as a kitten (or colt),
feeling one's oats
con grim, stern, stolid; grave, serious
2 syn see ANTIC 2
||**play-pretty** n syn see TOY 2
plaything n syn see TOY 2

playwright n one who writes plays < a
famous Broadway playwright >
syn dramatist, dramatizer, dramaturge
rel librettist; scenarist
plaza n syn see COMMON 2
plea n 1 syn see EXCUSE 1
rel extenuation, mitigation, palliation;
apology; out; vindication
2 syn see PRAYER
rel overture; call, cry
idiom solemn entreaty (or plea)
plead vb syn see BEG
pleasance n syn see AMENITY 1
pleasant adj 1 highly acceptable to the
mind or senses < a pleasant personality > < a pleasant respite >
syn agreeable, congenial, favorable, good,
grateful, gratifying, nice, pleasing, pleasurable, pleasureful, welcome
rel cheerful, cheering, cheery, glad, joyful,
joyous; alluring, attractive, charming,
pretty; convivial, engaging
con displeasing, distasteful; harsh; obnoxious, repellent, repelling, repugnant, repulsive
ant unpleasant
2 syn see FAIR 2
pleasantness n syn see AMENITY 1
rel goodness, niceness
ant unpleasantness
please vb 1 syn see WILL 1
2 to give or be a source of pleasure to
< her work pleased him >
syn arride, delectate, delight, gladden,
gratify, happify, pleasure
rel content, satisfy, suit; amuse, tickle,
titillate; regale, rejoice; overjoy
con vex; annoy; anger
ant displease
3 syn see SUIT 6
pleasing adj syn see PLEASANT 1
rel satisfactory, suitable; enchanting,
winning; adorable, darling, delightful
ant displeasing, repellent
pleasurable adj syn see PLEASANT 1
ant unpleasurable
pleasure n 1 syn see WILL 1
2 the agreeable emotion accompanying the
expectation, acquisition, or possession of
something good or desirable < the pleasures and pains of growing up >
syn delectation, delight, enjoyment, fruition, joy, joyance; compare ENJOYMENT 1
rel bliss, felicity, happiness; kick, thrill
con vexation; annoyance; anger; affliction,
distress, sorrow, trouble
ant displeasure
3 syn see ENJOYMENT 1
ant displeasure
pleasure vb syn see PLEASE 2
pleasure dome n syn see RESORT 3
pleasureful adj syn see PLEASANT 1
pleasuremonger n syn see HEDONIST
pleb n plebs pl syn see COMMONALTY
plebeian adj syn see IGNOBLE 1
ant patrician
plebeians n pl syn see COMMONALTY
ant patricians
plebs n plebes pl syn see COMMONALTY
rel peasantry, peasants
ant patricians, patriciate
pledge n 1 something given or held as a
sign of another's good faith or intentions

< the new school is the *pledge* given by the community to its children >

syn earnest, pawn, security, token, warrant; *compare* GUARANTEE 1, PROMISE

rel bail, bond, guarantee, guaranty, surety, warranty; promise, word; oath, vow

2 *syn* see WORD 8

pledge *vb* 1 *syn* see PAWN

2 *syn* see DRINK 2

3 *syn* see PROMISE 1

rel bind, tie; commit, confide, consign, entrust

idiom give (*or* make) a solemn pledge, pledge one's honor

4 *syn* see VOW

plenteous *adj syn* see PLENTIFUL

rel full, hearty; fruitful, galore, prolific; luxurious, opulent, sumptuous; lavish, prodigal, profuse, profusive, rampant, rife

plentiful *adj* being more than sufficient without being excessive < a *plentiful* harvest >

syn abundant, ample, bounteous, bountiful, copious, generous, liberal, plenteous, plenty

rel enough, sufficient; fulsome, rich, unstinted; excessive, extravagant, overabundant, overflowing, superabundant; abounding, bumper, bursting, swarming, swimming, teeming

con deficient, exiguous, meager, skimpy; inadequate, insufficient

ant scant, scanty

plenty *n syn* see MUCH

rel abundance, cornucopia

plenty *adj syn* see PLENTIFUL

pleonasm *n syn* see VERBIAGE 1

plethora *n syn* see EXCESS 1

rel much, plenty; many; deluge, flood

pliable *adj syn* see PLASTIC

rel manipulable, manipulatable

con unadaptable, unflexible, unmalleable, unpliant

ant unpliable

pliant *adj syn* see PLASTIC

rel spongy

ant unpliant

plica *n syn* see WRINKLE

plight *vb syn* see VOW

idiom plight one's honor

plight *n syn* see PROMISE

plight *n syn* see PREDICAMENT

rel quandary

plighted *adj syn* see ENGAGED 2

plink *vb syn* see TINKLE 1

plod *vb* to walk laboriously and heavily < slowly *plodded* across the sodden field >

syn footslog, ||plodge, plunther, slog, slop, stodge, toil, ||trash, trudge; *compare* TRAMP 1

rel tramp, trample, tromp; stamp, stomp, stump; flounder, wallow

2 *syn* see DRUDGE

idiom plug away at it

plodding *adj syn* see DULL 9

||**plodge** *vb syn* see PLOD 1

plot *n* 1 *syn* see LOT 3

2 a secret plan for accomplishing a usually evil or unlawful end < an assassination *plot* >

syn cabal, conspiracy, covin, intrigue, machination, practice, scheme

rel design, plan; connivance, conniving; collusion, complicity; contraption, contrivance, device; artifice, maneuver, ruse, stratagem, trick

plot *vb* to work out a plan especially for something unlawful or wrong < *plotted* the overthrow of the government >

syn cogitate, ||collogue, collude, conspire, contrive, devise, intrigue, machinate, scheme (out)

rel lay; brew, concoct, cook (up), hatch, set up; finagle, maneuver

plow *vb* to cut into and work the surface of (soil) < *plow* a field >

syn break, plow up, turn, turn over

rel cultivate, till; fallow; ||backset; furrow, list, ridge, trench; harrow, rake

plow up *vb syn* see PLOW

rel plow out

ploy *n syn* see TRICK 1

pluck *n syn* see COURAGE

||**plucked** *adj syn* see BRAVE 1

plucky *adj syn* see BRAVE 1

idiom full of pluck (*or* spunk)

con feeble, weak

ant pluckless

plug *n syn* see PUFF 3

plug *vb* 1 *syn* see FILL 1

rel pack; cork

2 *syn* see PROMOTE 3

plugging *n syn* see WORK 2

plug-ugly *n syn* see TOUGH

plum *n syn* see REWARD

rel catch, find

||**plumb** *adv syn* see WELL 3

plumb *vb syn* see SOUND

plumb *adj syn* see VERTICAL

plumbless *adj syn* see BOTTOMLESS 2

con plumbable

plumb-line *vb syn* see SOUND

plumbness *n syn* see VERTICALITY

plume *vb syn* see PRIDE

plummet *vb* to decrease suddenly and sharply in financial value or price < the stock *plummeted* 60 points when the story broke >

syn dip, drop, fall, nose-dive, plunge, skid, tumble

rel decline, decrease, descend, sink; dump; precipitate; collapse, crash

idiom take a sudden downturn (*or* downtrend)

con increase; rise; shoot up

ant skyrocket, soar

plummetless *adj syn* see BOTTOMLESS 2

plump *adj syn* see ROTUND 2

rel fleshy, portly

idiom plump as a partridge

ant skinny

plumpish *adj syn* see ROTUND 2

idiom like a butterball

plumpy *adj syn* see ROTUND 2

plunder *vb syn* see ROB 1

plunder *n* 1 *syn* see SPOIL

||2 *syn* see PERSONAL EFFECTS

plunderage *n syn* see SPOIL

plunderer *n syn* see MARAUDER

plunge *vb* 1 *syn* see THRUST 2

2 to thrust or cast oneself or something into or as if into deep water < *plunged* into the crowd >

syn burst, dive, drive, lunge, pitch, ||splunge; *compare* RUSH 1

rel dip, immerse, submerge; plump, plunk; propel, push, shove, thrust; boil, charge, fling, rush, tear
idiom plunge headlong
con ease, glide, slide, slip
3 *syn* see FALL 2
idiom take a plunge
4 *syn* see PLUMMET
idiom drop like a rock, take a downward plunge

plunther *vb syn* see PLOD 1
plus *n syn* see EXCESS 2
plus *vb syn* see INCREASE 1
plush *adj syn* see LUXURIOUS 3
idiom fit for the gods
plushy *adj syn* see LUXURIOUS 3
plutonian *adj* 1 *syn* see INFERNAL 1
2 *syn* see INFERNAL 2
plutonic *adj* 1 *syn* see INFERNAL 1
2 *syn* see INFERNAL 2
ply *vb* 1 *syn* see HANDLE 2
rel exercise; function
2 *syn* see EXERT
pneuma *n syn* see SOUL 1
pneumatic *adj syn* see AIRY 1
pocket *n syn* see DEAD END
pocket *vb* 1 *syn* see STEAL 1
2 *syn* see ACCEPT 2
pocket *adj* 1 *syn* see TINY
2 *syn* see CONDENSED
3 *syn* see FINANCIAL
pocket edition *n syn* see MODEL 1
pocket money *n* money for small personal expenses or incidentals < he had spent all his *pocket money* on candy and snacks >
syn pin money, spending money
rel petty cash; change, small change
con fortune, resources; income
pocket–size *adj syn* see TINY
pococurante *adj syn* see INDIFFERENT 2
pod *n* 1 *syn* see HULL
2 *syn* see POTBELLY
podex *n syn* see BUTTOCKS
podgy *adj syn* see ROTUND 2
Podunk *n syn* see BURG
poem *n* a particular example of metrical writing < recited a *poem* by Robert Frost >
syn poesy, poetry, rhyme, rune, verse
poesy *n* 1 *syn* see POEM
2 *syn* see POETRY 1
poet *n* a writer of verse < a *poet* to stir men's souls >
syn bard, muse, Parnassian
rel jongleur, rhapsodist, trouvère, trouveur; balladist, elegist, idyllist, lyricist, lyrist, odist, satirist, sonneteer, sonnetist
poetaster *n* a writer of mediocre or inferior verse < *poetasters* who churn out tasteless verse >
syn balladmonger, bardlet, bardling, poeticule, poetling, rhymer, rhymester, verseman, versemonger, verser, versesmith, versificator, versifier
poeticule *n syn* see POETASTER
poetling *n syn* see POETASTER
poetry *n* 1 metrical language or writing < studied the *poetry* of Milton >

syn poesy, rhyme, song, verse
2 *syn* see POEM
poignance *n syn* see PATHOS
poignancy *n syn* see PATHOS
poignant *adj* 1 *syn* see PUNGENT
ant dull
2 *syn* see MOVING 2
rel agitating, disturbing, perturbing
point *n* 1 one unitary part of a whole made up of two or more parts < listened to each *point* of his opponent's argument >
syn article, detail, element, item, particular, thing; *compare* ELEMENT 2
rel characteristic, feature, trait; constituent, material, part; circumstantial, circumstantiality
con aggregate, sum, total, whole
2 *syn* see CHARACTERISTIC 1
3 the quality of an utterance that arouses interest and produces an effect < a book that lacks *point* >
syn cogency, effectiveness, force, punch, validity, validness
rel appositeness, convincement, significance, suggestiveness; appeal, attraction, charm, fascination, interest
4 *syn* see SUBJECT 2
5 *syn* see TIP
6 *syn* see PLACE 1
7 a particular limited and often critical interval of time < at that *point* he was interrupted >
syn instant, juncture, moment
rel brink, threshold, verge
8 *syn* see VERGE 2
9 a sharp or slender and tapering terminal part < the *point* of a sword >
syn apex, cusp, tip
rel awn, barb, jag, nib, prong, snag, spike, tag, tine
10 *syn* see PROMONTORY
11 a tiny mark or spot < saw a distant *point* of light >
syn dot, flyspeck, mote, speck
rel bit, fleck, iota, minim, mite, particle, scrap, tittle, trace
point *vb* 1 *syn* see PUNCTUATE
2 to tend to show something as probable < all signs *point* to an economic recovery >
syn hint, imply, indicate, suggest; *compare* SUGGEST 1
idiom make (*or* give) promise of, lead one to expect, offer a good prospect of
3 *syn* see DIRECT 2
point (out) *vb syn* see REFER 3
point (to) *vb syn* see TESTIFY 1
pointed *adj* 1 tapering to a thin tip < a *pointed* rock >
syn acicular, aciculate, acuminate, acuminous, acute, cuspidate, mucronate, peaked, peaky, piked, pointy, sharp
con dull, rounded
ant blunt
2 *syn* see NOTICEABLE
pointer *n syn* see TIP
pointful *adj syn* see RELEVANT
pointless *adj syn* see SENSELESS 5
∥**pointsman** *n syn* see POLICEMAN
pointy *adj syn* see POINTED 1
poise *vb* 1 *syn* see STABILIZE
rel back, support, uphold
con agitate, disturb, upset; overthrow, overturn, subvert

---

syn synonym(s)   *rel* related word(s)
ant antonym(s)   *con* contrasted word(s)
idiom idiomatic equivalent(s)
∥ use limited; if in doubt, see a dictionary

2 *syn* see HANG 3

poise *n* 1 *syn* see BALANCE 1

2 *syn* see TACT

rel aplomb, assurance, confidence, self=possession; calmness, serenity, tranquillity; dignity, elegance, grace

poised *adj syn* see CALM 2

poison *n* something that harms, interferes with, or destroys the activity, progress, or welfare of something else < the publicity was *poison* to them >

syn bane, contagion, venom, virus

rel adulteration, contamination, corruption, sophistication

con catholicon, elixir, panacea

ant antidote

poison *vb syn* see DEBASE 1

poison *adj syn* see POISONOUS

poisonous *adj* having the properties or effect of poison < *poisonous* propaganda >

syn mephitic, poison, toxic, toxicant, venomous, virulent

rel miasmal, miasmatic, miasmic, pestilent, pestilential; deadly, fatal, lethal, mortal; baneful, deleterious, detrimental, nocuous, noxious, pernicious

con corrective, countervailing, emendatory, healing, remedial

ant antidotal

‖**poke** *n syn* see BAG 1

poke *vb* 1 to thrust something into so as to stir up, urge on, or attract attention < he *poked* the man in front of him to get his attention >

syn dig, jab, jog, nudge, prod, punch

rel push, shove, thrust; arouse, awaken, rouse, stir; excite, galvanize, provoke, quicken, stimulate

2 *syn* see SNOOP

3 *syn* see DELAY 2

4 *syn* see BULGE

poke *n* 1 a quick thrust with or as if with the hand < gave him a *poke* in the ribs with my finger >

syn dig, jab, punch, stab

rel bunt, butt; boost, push, shove

2 *syn* see CUFF

3 *syn* see DUNCE

poker–faced *adj* 1 *syn* see SERIOUS 1

2 *syn* see NEUTRAL

‖**pokey** *n syn* see JAIL

poky *adj syn* see DULL 9

polar *adj syn* see OPPOSITE

polemical *adj syn* see CONTENTIOUS 2

polestar *n syn* see CENTER 2

police *n syn* see POLICEMAN

‖**police constable** *n syn* see POLICEMAN

policeman *n* a member of a police force < ask the *policeman* for directions >

syn ‖bluebottle, bluecoat, ‖bobby, ‖bull, ‖constable, cop, ‖copper, Dogberry, ‖flatfoot, ‖fuzz, ‖gendarme, gumshoe, ‖harness bull (*or* cop), ‖heat, John Law, man, ‖nab, officer, ‖paddy, patrolman, peace officer, ‖peeler, ‖pig, ‖pointsman, police, ‖police constable, police officer, ‖rozzer, ‖trap

police officer *n syn* see POLICEMAN

policy *n syn* see COURSE 3

polish *vb* 1 to make smooth or glossy usually by friction < *polished* the silver >

syn buff, burnish, furbish, glance, glaze, gloss, rub, shine

rel brighten, scour, scrub

con roughen

2 to give an elegant finish to < attended classes to *polish* his manners >

syn perfect, refine, round, sleek, slick, smooth

rel better, improve, mend; brush up, furbish, touch up; mature, perfect

polish *n* 1 *syn* see LUSTER

2 *syn* see CULTURE

polished *adj* 1 *syn* see LUSTROUS 1

2 *syn* see SLEEK

3 *syn* see GENTEEL 1

polish off *vb* 1 *syn* see CONSUME 5

2 *syn* see EAT UP 1

polite *adj syn* see CIVIL 2

rel attentive, considerate, thoughtful

ant impolite

politic *adj* 1 *syn* see EXPEDIENT

rel astute, perspicacious, sagacious, shrewd

2 *syn* see TACTFUL

rel judicious, wise

polity *n syn* see COURSE 3

poll *n syn* see HEAD 1

pollard *vb syn* see TOP 1

polloi *n syn* see RABBLE 2

pollute *vb* 1 *syn* see CONTAMINATE 1

2 *syn* see CONTAMINATE 2

polluted *adj* 1 *syn* see IMPURE 3

2 *syn* see INTOXICATED 1

Pollyanna *n syn* see OPTIMIST

rel daydreamer, wishful thinker

Pollyannaish *adj syn* see OPTIMISTIC

Pollyannaism *n syn* see OPTIMISM

‖**polly–fox** *vb syn* see SKIRT 3

poltroon *n syn* see COWARD

poltroon *adj syn* see COWARDLY

poltroonish *adj syn* see COWARDLY

polyandrium *n syn* see CEMETERY

polychromatic *adj syn* see VARIEGATED

polychrome *adj syn* see VARIEGATED

polypragmatic *adj syn* see IMPERTINENT 2

polypragmatist *n syn* see BUSYBODY

pomp *n syn* see DISPLAY 2

rel ceremonial, ceremony, form, formality, liturgy, ritual

pom–pom girl *n syn* see PROSTITUTE

pompous *adj* characterized by or exhibiting self-importance < a *pompous* old fool >

syn arrogant, bloated, important, magisterial, pontifical, puffy, self-important, stuffy, wiggy; *compare* EGOCENTRIC 2, PROUD 1

rel conceited, narcissistic, self-conceited, stuck-up, vain, vainglorious; affected, highfalutin, hoity-toity, pretentious; presumptuous, self-centered, selfish; flaunting, flossy, ostentatious

con natural, unaffected, unpretentious; humble, meek, plain, simple; modest, unassuming

2 *syn* see RHETORICAL

ponder *vb* 1 *syn* see CONSIDER 1

rel appraise, evaluate

2 to consider or examine attentively or deliberately < *ponder* the best way to do it >

syn ‖chaw, deliberate, meditate, mull (over), muse, revolve, roll, ruminate, turn over

rel cogitate, reason, reflect, speculate, think; brood, debate, dwell

pondering *adj syn see* THOUGHTFUL 1
ponderous *adj* 1 *syn see* HEAVY 1
 rel substantial; burdensome, onerous, oppressive
 2 lacking all lightness and grace < a *ponderous* prose style>
 syn elephantine, heavy-footed, heavy-handed, uninspired
 rel dreary, dry, dull, humdrum, lifeless, monotonous, pedestrian, plodding, stodgy, stuffy; arid, barren; flat, insipid, savorless, vapid; buckram, cardboard, muscle-bound, stiff, stilted, wooden
 con sparkling, vivid; easy, natural, relaxed, supple, unlabored
 3 *syn see* UNWIELDY
pontifical *adj syn see* POMPOUS 1
pontificate *vb syn see* LORD
pony *n* a literal translation of a foreign language text used especially surreptitiously by students in rendering a lesson < had his *pony* hidden in his lap>
 syn crib, trot
‖**pooch** *n syn see* DOG 1
pooh *n syn see* RASPBERRY
pooh-bah *n syn see* NOTABLE 1
pooh-pooh *n syn see* RASPBERRY
pooh-pooh *vb syn see* DISMISS 5
pool *n* a small body of standing liquid < saw the *pool* of blood on the floor>
 syn puddle
pool *n* 1 *syn see* POT 3
 2 *syn see* SYNDICATE
poop *n syn see* FOOL 1
‖**poop** *vb syn see* EXHAUST
poor *adj* 1 lacking money or material possessions < they were so *poor* that the children had no winter coats>
 syn beggared, broke, destitute, dirt poor, flat, fortuneless, impecunious, impoverished, indigent, low, necessitous, needy, penurious, poverty-stricken, stone-broke, stony, strapped, unprosperous
 rel distressed, embarrassed, pinched, reduced, straitened; bankrupt, bankrupted, insolvent; hardscrabble; moneyless, penceless, penniless, unmoneyed; beggarly, down-and-out, pauperized; underprivileged
 idiom down to one's bottom dollar, flat broke, hard up, in need, in penury, in rags, in want, on one's beam-ends, on one's uppers, out at elbows, out of pocket, poor as a church mouse, unable to keep the wolf from the door, unable to make ends meet
 con affluent, comfortable, moneyed, ‖oofy, opulent, pecunious, prosperous, wealthy, well-fixed, well-heeled, well-off, well-to-do
 ant rich
 2 *syn see* MEAGER 2
 3 *syn see* PITIFUL 1
 4 *syn see* CHEAP 2
 5 *syn see* INFERIOR 2
 6 *syn see* BAD 1
poorly *adj syn see* UNWELL
poorness *n syn see* POVERTY 1
poor relation *n syn see* INFERIOR

poor-spirited *adj syn see* COWARDLY
pop *vb* 1 *syn see* STRIKE 2
 ‖2 *syn see* PAWN
pop *n syn see* FLING 1
pop *n syn see* FATHER 1
pop (in) *vb syn see* VISIT 2
popinjay *n syn see* FOP
pop off *vb* 1 *syn see* GO 2
 2 *syn see* DIE 1
poppa *n syn see* FATHER 1
popping *adj syn see* BUSTLING
poppycock *n syn see* NONSENSE 2
popsy *n syn see* GIRL FRIEND 1
populace *n syn see* COMMONALTY
popular *adj* 1 *syn see* PUBLIC 4
 2 *syn see* DEMOCRATIC
 3 *syn see* CHEAP 1
 4 *syn see* PREVAILING
 5 *syn see* FAVORITE 2
  ant unpopular
 6 *syn see* WELL-KNOWN
  ant unpopular
populate *vb syn see* INHABIT
populous *adj syn see* MANY
porcine *adj syn see* FAT 2
pork-barreling *n syn see* PATRONAGE 3
porky *adj syn see* FATTY 2
porose *adj syn see* PERMEABLE
porous *adj syn see* PERMEABLE
porridge *n syn see* MISCELLANY 1
port *n* 1 *syn see* HARBOR 3
 2 *syn see* SHELTER 1
port *n syn see* BEARING 1
portable *adj* capable of being carried or moved about < a *portable* TV>
 syn carriageable, portative, transportable
 rel convenient, handy, manageable, wieldy
 con fixed, stationary
portal *n syn see* DOOR 1
portative *adj syn see* PORTABLE
portend *vb* 1 *syn see* AUGUR 2
 2 *syn see* FORETELL
portent *n* 1 *syn see* FORETOKEN
 2 *syn see* WONDER 1
porter *n syn see* BEARER 2
portion *n* 1 *syn see* SHARE 1
 2 *syn see* FATE
 3 *syn see* PART 1
 4 *syn see* RATION
portion *vb syn see* APPORTION 2
portion (out) *vb syn see* ADMINISTER 2
portly *adj syn see* FAT 2
portrait *n syn see* IMAGE 1
portraiture *n syn see* REPRESENTATION
portray *vb syn see* REPRESENT 1
 rel photograph; copy, duplicate, reproduce
portrayal *n syn see* REPRESENTATION
pose *vb* 1 *syn see* OFFER 1
 2 *syn see* PROPOSE 1
 rel ask, query, question; confound, puzzle; baffle
 3 to assume a particular physical posture < they *posed* for a family portrait>
 syn posture, sit
 rel peacock, strut
 4 to assume an artificial or pretended attitude or character usually to deceive or impress < *posed* as a salesman>
 syn attitudinize, masquerade, pass (as *or* for), pass off, posture
 rel fake, feign, pretend, sham; profess, purport; grandstand, show off

---

syn synonym(s) *rel* related word(s)
ant antonym(s) *con* contrasted word(s)
idiom idiomatic equivalent(s)
‖ use limited; if in doubt, see a dictionary

pose *n* **1** *syn* see POSTURE 1
2 an adopted way of speaking or acting <his reticence is just a *pose*>
syn affectation, air(s), lugs, mannerism, prettyism
rel dog, prettiness; fake, pretense, pretension

pose *vb syn* see OFFER 1
pose *vb syn* see PUZZLE
posh *adj syn* see STYLISH
posit *vb syn* see PRESUPPOSE
posit *n syn* see ASSUMPTION 2
position *n* **1** a firmly held point of view or way of regarding something <took a conservative *position* on educational issues>
syn attitude, color, stance, stand; *compare* SIDE 4
rel belief, judgment, opinion, view; angle, slant, standpoint, viewpoint
2 *syn* see PLACE 1
3 *syn* see STATUS 1
4 *syn* see STATUS 2
5 *syn* see JOB 2
positioned *adj syn* see SITUATED
positive *adj* **1** expressed clearly and usually peremptorily <her answer was a *positive* no>
syn categorical, decided, definite, unequivocal
rel clear, unmistakable; decisive, emphatic, energetic, firm, forceful, forcible; explicit, express, specific, unambiguous
con irresolute, uncertain, undecided, unsure
2 *syn* see SURE 5
ant doubtful
3 not subject to being disputed or called in question <gave *positive* proof that he had been there>
syn certain, inarguable, incontestable, incontrovertible, indisputable, indubitable, irrebuttable, irrefutable, sure, uncontestable, uncontrovertible, undeniable, undisputable, undoubtable, unequivocal, unquestionable; *compare* DOWNRIGHT 2
rel assured, clear, decisive
con contestable, controvertible, debatable, disputable, doubtful, dubious, inconclusive, questionable, unconvincing
4 *syn* see UTTER
5 *syn* see ACTUAL 2
6 capable of being constructively applied <*positive* proposals for improving the city>
syn affirmative
rel practical, reasonable, sound
con impractical, unsound, unusable
ant negative
7 *syn* see RIGHT-HANDED
positively *adv syn* see EASILY 2
posture *n syn* see POSTURE 1
possess *vb* **1** *syn* see HAVE 1
2 *syn* see BEAR 3
possessed *adj syn* see CALM 2
possession *n* **1** *syn* see OWNERSHIP
2 **possessions** *pl* things one owns usually excluding real property and intangibles <lost all their *possessions* in the fire>
syn belongings, chattels, effects, goods, lares and penates, movables, things,
rel appointments, fixtures, furnishings, furniture; accessories, appurtenances, baggage, ‖duds, duffle, equipment, impedi-

menta, paraphernalia, trappings, tricks; havings; tangibles
possessive *adj syn* see JEALOUS 1
possessor *n syn* see OWNER
possessorship *n syn* see OWNERSHIP
possessory *adj syn* see JEALOUS 1
possibilities *n pl syn* see POTENTIAL
possible *adj* **1** capable of being realized <a cure is still *possible*>
syn doable, feasible, practicable, viable, workable
rel advisable, expedient; achievable, attainable, available
con futile, hopeless, impracticable
ant impossible
2 *syn* see PROBABLE
rel dormant, latent, potential
3 *syn* see POTENTIAL 1
possibly *adv syn* see PERHAPS
post *vb* to affix to a usual place (as a wall) for public notices <*posted* the notice on the bulletin board>
syn placard, poster
post *vb syn* see INFORM 2
post *n syn* see JOB 2
post *vb syn* see STATION
‖**post** *n syn* see AUTOPSY
poster *n* a notice or announcement for posting in a public place <nailed the *poster* to the side of the building>
syn affiche, bill, handbill, placard
rel advertisement, announcement, banner, broadside, notice, sign; billboard, signboard
poster *vb syn* see POST
posterior *adj* **1** *syn* see SUBSEQUENT 1
2 situated at or toward the back <the *posterior* part of the animal>
syn after, back, hind, hinder, hindmost, rear, retral
con fore, front
ant anterior
posterior *n* **1** *syn* see BACK 1
2 *syn* see BUTTOCKS
posterity *n syn* see OFFSPRING
ant ancestry
posthaste *adv syn* see FAST 2
posthaste *adj syn* see FAST 3
posthumous *adj* occurring after one's death <*posthumous* fame>
syn postmortal, postmortem, post-obit, post-obituary
rel delayed, late, retarded
con opportune, seasonable, timely
ant antemortem
postliminary *adj syn* see SUBSEQUENT 1
postmortal *adj syn* see POSTHUMOUS
postmortem *adj syn* see POSTHUMOUS
ant antemortem
postmortem *n syn* see AUTOPSY
postmortem examination *n syn* see AUTOPSY
post-obit *adj syn* see POSTHUMOUS
post-obituary *adj syn* see POSTHUMOUS
postpone *vb syn* see DEFER
postulate *vb* **1** *syn* see DEMAND 1
2 *syn* see PRESUPPOSE
rel affirm, assert, aver, predicate
postulate *n syn* see ASSUMPTION 2
postulation *n syn* see ASSUMPTION 2
posture *n* **1** the position or bearing of the body <erect *posture*>
syn attitude, carriage, pose, positure, stance

rel bearing, deportment, mien
2 *syn* see STATE 1
rel promptness, quickness, readiness
posture *vb* 1 *syn* see POSE 3
2 *syn* see POSE 4
posy *n* 1 *syn* see FLOWER 1
2 *syn* see BOUQUET 1
3 *syn* see ANTHOLOGY
pot *n* 1 *syn* see FORTUNE 4
2 *syn* see BET
3 the total of the bets at stake at one time
< lost track of how much was in the
pot >
syn jackpot, kitty, pool
4 *syn* see POTSHOT
‖5 *syn* see POTBELLY
6 *syn* see NOTABLE 1
7 *syn* see MARIJUANA
‖8 *syn* see TOILET
potable *adj* suitable for drinking < *potable*
water >
syn drinkable
rel clean, fresh, pure, uncontaminated,
unpolluted
con dirty, foul, impure, polluted, unclean
ant impotable
potable *n syn* see DRINK 1
potbelly *n* an enlarged, swollen, or pro-
truding abdomen < he had the biggest
potbelly we had ever seen >
syn bay window, corporation, paunch,
pod, ‖pot
potency *n* 1 *syn* see POWER 4
ant impotence
2 *syn* see EFFICACY 1
3 *syn* see ENERGY 2
ant impotence
potent *adj* 1 *syn* see POWERFUL 2
ant impotent
2 *syn* see STRONG 3
3 able to copulate < a *potent* male >
syn virile
ant impotent
potential *adj* 1 existing in possibility < a
potential site for the new factory >
syn possible
rel conceivable, imaginable, likely, plausible, probable, thinkable
idiom within the realm (*or* range) of possibility
con existent, extant; doubtful, impossible,
questionable; impracticable, unsuitable
ant actual
2 *syn* see LATENT
potential *n* something that can develop or
become actual < industrial *potential* >
syn possibilities, potentiality
ant actuality, reality
potentiality *n syn* see POTENTIAL
ant actuality
pother *n* 1 *syn* see COMMOTION 4
2 *syn* see STIR 1
3 *syn* see ANNOYANCE 2
4 *syn* see COMMOTION 2
pother *vb syn* see WORRY 3
pothole *n* a hole, depression, or rut in
a road surface < *potholes* all over that
stretch of highway >

syn chuckhole, mudhole
pothouse *n syn* see BAR 5
potpourri *n syn* see MISCELLANY 1
potshot *n* a critical remark made in a random or sporadic manner < took a few
potshots at his neighbor's argument >
syn pot, shy, sideswipe
rel cut, crack, dig; gibe, jeer; aspersion,
criticism, insult
potted *adj* 1 *syn* see CONDENSED
‖2 *syn* see INTOXICATED 1
potter *vb syn* see FIDDLE 2
potter (away) *vb syn* see WASTE 2
potter's field *n syn* see CEMETERY
potty *adj* ‖1 *syn* see LITTLE 3
‖2 *syn* see FOOLISH 2
3 *syn* see SNOBBISH
‖**potty** *n syn* see TOILET
pouch *n syn* see BAG 1
pouch *vb syn* see BULGE
pouf *n syn* see QUILT
poule *n syn* see PROSTITUTE
poultice *n* a soft, usually heated, and
sometimes medicated mass spread on
cloth and applied to sores or other lesions
< slapped a bread *poultice* over the boil >
syn cataplasm
rel plaster; compress; dressing
pound *vb* 1 *syn* see HAMMER 1
2 *syn* see BEAT 1
3 *syn* see IMPRESS 3
pound *n syn* see BLOW 1
pour *vb* 1 *syn* see DISCHARGE 5
2 to send forth or come forth abundantly
< medical supplies *poured* into the
stricken area >
syn flow, gush, roll, sluice, stream, surge
rel issue, proceed, spring; course, rill, run,
rush, swarm; cascade, cataract; deluge,
flood, inundate
3 to rain heavily < it *poured* for two solid
days >
syn drench, lash, teem
rel beat; deluge, flood, stream
idiom come down in buckets (*or* torrents),
rain cats and dogs
pour *n syn* see FLOOD 2
pourboire *n syn* see GRATUITY
pout *vb* 1 *syn* see SULK
2 *syn* see BULGE
pouts *n pl syn* see SULK
poverty *n* 1 the state of one with insufficient resources < repeated crop failures
had reduced the farmers to *poverty* >
syn beggary, borasca, destituteness, destitution, impecuniousness, impoverishment,
indigence, indigency, need, neediness,
pauperism, pennilessness, penury, poorness, privation, unprosperousness, want
rel exigency, necessity; juncture, pass,
pinch, strait; difficulty, distress, embarrassment; hardship, suffering; mendicancy
idiom hand-to-mouth existence, straitened
circumstances
con affluence, comfort, luxury, opulence,
prosperity, richness, wealth
ant riches
2 *syn* see SCARCITY
poverty–stricken *adj syn* see POOR 1
powder *vb* 1 *syn* see SPRINKLE 1
2 *syn* see PULVERIZE 1
powdering *n syn* see DUSTING
powdery *adj syn* see FINE 2

---

syn synonym(s)   *rel* related word(s)
ant antonym(s)   *con* contrasted word(s)
idiom idiomatic equivalent(s)
‖ use limited; if in doubt, see a dictionary

power *n* **1** the right or prerogative of determining, ruling, or governing or the exercise of that right or prerogative < party in *power* >
syn authority, command, control, domination, jurisdiction, mastery, might, strings, sway
rel birthright, prerogative, privilege, right; direction, management; ascendancy, dominance, dominion, masterdom, sovereignty, supremacy; superiority; influence, prestige, weight; force, strength
con forcelessness, impotence, weakness
ant impuissance, powerlessness
‖**2** *syn* see MUCH
3 the ability of a living being to perform in a given way or a capacity for a particular kind of performance < the *power* to think clearly >
syn faculty, function
rel ability, capability, capacity; aptitude, bent, turn; endowment, gift, talent
con inability, incapability, incapacity; inaptness, ineptitude
4 the ability to exert effort for a purpose < raised the productive *power* of the nation >
syn arm, beef, dint, energy, force, might, muscle, potency, puissance, sinew, steam, strength, strong arm, vigor, virtue
rel ability, capability, capacity; effectiveness; dynamism, powder, voltage; dynamis, potentiality; competence, qualification
con inability, incapability, incapacity; ineffectiveness; incompetence

powerful *adj* **1** *syn* see STRONG 1
2 having or manifesting power to effect great or striking results < a *powerful* leader >
syn forceful, forcible, mighty, potent, puissant
rel able, capable, competent; effective, effectual, efficacious, efficient; dynamic, energetic, strenuous, vigorous; convincing, great, invincible; authoritative, dominant, influential, weighty
con faulty, feeble, flawed; impotent, inadequate, incompetent, weak
ant powerless

powerfully *adv* *syn* see HARD 1

powerless *adj* unable to effect one's purpose, intention, or end < *powerless* to leave >
syn helpless, impotent
rel inactive, inert, passive, supine; decrepit, feeble, infirm, weak; incapable, incompetent, ineffective, unfit
con effective, effectual, efficient; able, capable, competent; potent, puissant
ant powerful

powwow *n syn* see TALK 4
powwow *vb syn* see CONFER 2
‖**prabble** *n syn* see QUARREL
practic *adj syn* see REALISTIC
practicable *adj* **1** *syn* see POSSIBLE 1
ant impracticable
2 *syn* see PRACTICAL 2
3 *syn* see OPEN 5
ant impracticable
practical *adj* **1** *syn* see IMPLICIT 2
2 capable of being turned to use or account < had a *practical* rather than a theoretical acquaintance with mechanics >
syn functional, handy, practicable, serviceable, useful, utile
con abstract, academic, theoretical
ant impractical, unpractical
3 *syn* see REALISTIC
ant impractical, unpractical
4 *syn* see EXPERIENCED

practically *adv* **1** *syn* see VIRTUALLY
2 *syn* see ALMOST 2
3 *syn* see NEARLY

practice *vb syn* see EXERCISE 3
rel execute, fulfill, perform; follow, pursue; iterate, repeat

practice *n* **1** *syn* see HABIT 1
rel procedure, proceeding, process; method, mode, system
2 *syn* see PLOT 2
3 *syn* see EXERCISE 3
rel use, usefulness, utility; convenance, convention, form, usage
ant theory; precept

practiced *adj syn* see EXPERIENCED
ant unpracticed

praetorian *adj syn* see CORRUPT 2
praetorian *n syn* see DIEHARD 1
pragmatic *n syn* see BUSYBODY
pragmatic *adj syn* see REALISTIC
pragmatical *adj syn* see REALISTIC
pragmatist *n syn* see BUSYBODY
praisable *adj syn* see WORTHY 1
praise *vb* **1** *syn* see COMMEND 2
ant censure, criticize
2 to glorify and exalt especially in song or writing < *praised* God for all his blessings >
syn bless, celebrate, cry up, eulogize, extol, glorify, hymn, laud, magnify, panegyrize, psalm, psalmody, resound
rel aggrandize, dignify, distinguish, ennoble, erect, exalt, honor, sublime, uprear; enhance, heighten, intensify; apotheosize; proclaim
idiom sing the praises of
con asperse, calumniate, defame, libel, malign, traduce, vilify; belittle, decry, depreciate, derogate, detract (from), discount, disparage, minimize, opprobriate; censure, criticize, denounce, reprehend, reprobate; abuse, reproach, revile
ant dispraise; blame

praiseful *adj syn* see EULOGISTIC
praiseworthy *adj syn* see WORTHY 1
ant despicable
‖**pram** *n syn* see BABY CARRIAGE
prance *vb* **1** *syn* see SASHAY
2 *syn* see DANCE 1
‖**prang** *vb syn* see BUMP 1
‖**prang** *n syn* see CRASH 3
prank *n* a mischievous or roguish act < he was always playing *pranks* on his sister >
syn antic, caper, dido(es), frolic, lark, monkeyshine, ‖rig, shenanigan, shine(s), ‖skite, tomfoolery, trick, wheeze; *compare* ESCAPADE, TRICK 1
rel fooling, high jinks, horseplay, roughhouse, roughhousing, rowdiness, skylarking; gambol, play, rollick, sport; frivolity, levity, lightness; caprice, conceit, fancy, freak, vagary, whim, whimsy

prank *vb* **1** *syn* see ADORN
2 *syn* see DRESS UP 1
prankful *adj syn* see PLAYFUL 1
prankish *adj syn* see PLAYFUL 1

pranky *adj syn* see PLAYFUL 1

‖**prat** *n syn* see TRICK 1

prate *vb* 1 *syn* see CHAT 1
  2 *syn* see BOAST
  3 *syn* see BABBLE 2

prate *n syn* see CHATTER

prater *n syn* see CHATTERBOX

prattle *vb* 1 *syn* see CHAT 1
  2 *syn* see BABBLE 2

prattle *n syn* see CHATTER

prattler *n syn* see CHATTERBOX

praxis *n syn* see HABIT 1

pray *vb syn* see BEG

prayer *n* an earnest and usually a formal request for something < the *prayer* in a bill in equity is the part that specifies the kind of relief sought >
  syn appeal, application, entreaty, imploration, imprecation, orison, petition, plea, suit, supplication
  rel begging, beseeching, imploring, pleading; adoration, worship
  con claim, demand, exaction

prayer *n syn* see SUPPLIANT

prayerful *adj syn* see DEVOUT

preach *vb* 1 to discourse publicly on a religious subject < *preached* at Sunday services >
  syn evangelize, homilize, sermonize
  rel minister, mission, missionary; prophesy; address, lecture, speak, talk
  2 *syn* see MORALIZE

preach *n syn* see SERMON

preacher *n syn* see CLERGYMAN

preachify *vb syn* see MORALIZE

preaching *n syn* see SERMON

preachment *n syn* see SERMON

preachy *adj syn* see DIDACTIC

preamble *n syn* see INTRODUCTION

precarious *adj* 1 *syn* see DOUBTFUL 1
  2 *syn* see DELICATE 7

precariousness *n syn* see INSTABILITY

precaution *n syn* see PRUDENCE 1

precede *vb* 1 to go before in rank, dignity, or importance < the small countries at the conference were *preceded* by the large wealthy ones > < those who still feel that age should *precede* beauty >
  syn outrank, rank
  2 to go before in time < all-out war was *preceded* by many small raids >
  syn antecede, antedate, forerun, pace, predate
  rel announce, herald, foreshadow, harbinger, presage
  con ensue, supervene
  ant follow, succeed
  3 to cause to be preceded < *preceded* his address with a welcome to the visitors >
  syn introduce, lead, preface, usher
  ant follow

precedence *n syn* see PRIORITY

precedency *n syn* see PRIORITY

precedent *adj syn* see PRECEDING

precedently *adv syn* see BEFORE 1

preceding *adj* being before especially in time or in arrangement < the *preceding* day >

  syn antecedent, anterior, foregoing, former, past, precedent, previous, prior
  rel other; preexistent; precursive, precursory; erstwhile, heretofore, hitherto
  con coming, ensuing, next, sequent, sequential, subsequent, successive
  ant following, succeeding

preceding *prep syn* see BEFORE 1

precept *n syn* see LAW 1
  rel axiom, fundamental, principle; doctrine, dogma, tenet; behest, bidding, injunction
  con practice; counsel

précieux *adj syn* see PRECIOUS 4

precinct *n* 1 *syn* see QUARTER 2
  2 *syn* see FIELD
  3 **precincts** *pl syn* see ENVIRONS 1

precious *adj* 1 of such great value that a suitable price is hard to estimate < a *precious* twelfth century painting >
  syn costly, inestimable, invaluable, priceless, valuable; *compare* COSTLY 1
  rel choice, exquisite, rare, recherché; treasurable; rich; prizable
  idiom of price
  con base, common, mean, paltry, poor, rubbishy, shabby, trashy; contemptible, despicable, miserable; claptrap, gimcrack, trumpery
  ant cheap; worthless
  2 *syn* see FAVORITE 1
  3 *syn* see NICE 1
  4 excessively refined < too *precious* to mingle with the common people >
  syn affected, alembicated, chichi, la-di-da, overnice, overrefined, précieux; *compare* GENTEEL 3
  rel ostentatious, pretentious, showy; artful, sophisticated, studied
  con artless, ingenuous, naive, natural, simple, unaffected, unartful, unschooled, unsophisticated, unstudied, untutored; down-to-earth, matter-of-fact, practical, pragmatic, rational

precipitance *n syn* see HASTE 2

precipitancy *n syn* see HASTE 2

precipitant *adj syn* see PRECIPITATE 1

precipitate *n* 1 *syn* see SEDIMENT
  2 *syn* see EFFECT 1

precipitate *adj* 1 characterized by impetuous or unexpected haste < beat a *precipitate* retreat >
  syn abrupt, hasty, headlong, hurried, impetuous, precipitant, precipitous, rushing, subitaneous, sudden
  rel breakneck, headstrong, hotheaded, impatient, impulsive, madcap, refractory, uncontrolled, willful; unanticipated, unexpected, unforeseen, unlooked-for; overhasty
  con leisurely, slow, unhurried
  ant deliberate
  2 *syn* see STEEP 1

precipitateness *n syn* see HASTE 2

precipitation *n* 1 *syn* see HASTE 2
  2 *syn* see SEDIMENT

precipitous *adj* 1 *syn* see PRECIPITATE 1
  2 *syn* see STEEP 1

précis *n syn* see COMPENDIUM 1

precise *adj* 1 *syn* see DEFINITE 1
  2 *syn* see CORRECT 2
  rel rigid, stringent
  con careless, heedless; lax, slack

---

syn synonym(s)   *rel* related word(s)
ant antonym(s)   *con* contrasted word(s)
idiom idiomatic equivalent(s)
‖ use limited; if in doubt, see a dictionary

ant imprecise; loose
3 *syn* see PRIM 1
4 distinguished from every other <arrived just at the *precise* moment when he was needed>
syn exact, very
rel specific; individual; particular
con general, inexact, nonspecific
ant imprecise
precisely *adv* **1** *syn* see JUST 1
idiom on the button
ant imprecisely; approximately
2 *syn* see EVEN 1
3 *syn* see EXACTLY 3
preciseness *n syn* see PRECISION
ant impreciseness
precisian *n syn* see PURIST
precision *n* the quality or character of what is precise <the *precision* involved in close-tolerance machining>
syn accuracy, correctness, definiteness, definitiveness, definitude, exactitude, exactness, preciseness
rel care, carefulness; attention, heed
con inaccuracy, incorrectness, indefiniteness, inexactness, obscurity, unclearness, vagueness; unreliability, untrustworthiness
ant imprecision
precisionist *n syn* see PURIST
preclude *vb syn* see PREVENT 2
rel cease, discontinue, quit, stop
precocious *adj* exceptionally early in development <a *precocious* child, smart beyond his years>
syn advanced, forward; *compare* EARLY 2
rel ahead, early, overearly, oversoon, premature, previous, ‖soon; developed, mature
con backward, undeveloped; dull, slow, slow-witted, sluggish
ant retarded
precogitate *vb syn* see PREMEDITATE
preconception *n* an attitude, belief, or impression formed beforehand <had a lot of *preconceptions* about a man she'd never met>
syn prejudgment, prepossession; *compare* PREJUDICE
rel illusion; delusion
idiom preconceived notion (*or* idea *or* opinion)
precondition *n syn* see ESSENTIAL 2
precursor *n* **1** *syn* see FORERUNNER 1
2 *syn* see FORERUNNER 2
predacious *adj syn* see RAPACIOUS 1
predate *vb syn* see PRECEDE 2
predative *adj syn* see RAPACIOUS 1
predatorial *adj syn* see RAPACIOUS 1
predatory *adj syn* see RAPACIOUS 1
predecessor *n syn* see FORERUNNER 2
predestinate *vb syn* see PREDESTINE 2
predestine *vb* **1** to fix the future of in advance <his treasured scribblings were *predestined* to light a kitchen fire>
syn destine, determine, doom (to), fate, foreordain, predetermine, preform, preordain
rel predecide; prejudge; preestablish
2 to determine by or as if by divine decree or eternal purpose <some believe that God *predestines* individuals to eternal life or to eternal death>
syn fordestine, foreordain, predestinate, predetermine, preordain

predetermine *vb* **1** *syn* see PREDESTINE 2
2 *syn* see PREMEDITATE
3 *syn* see PREDESTINE 1
predicament *n* a difficult, perplexing, or trying situation <was in a *predicament*, trying to decide whether or not to take the job>
syn box, corner, deep water, dilemma, fix, hole, hot water, impasse, jam, pickle, plight, quagmire, scrape, soup, spot
rel emergency, exigency, juncture, pass, pinch, strait; asperity, difficulty, hardness, hardship, rigor, vicissitude; Dutch, trouble; condition, posture, situation, state
idiom ‖in a bind
predicate *vb* **1** *syn* see ASSERT 1
2 *syn* see BASE
predict *vb* **1** *syn* see FORETELL
2 to conjecture correctly <*predicted* the turn of the market months in advance>
syn call, guess
rel conjecture, presume, suppose, surmise, think; conclude, gather, infer, judge
idiom hazard a conjecture (*or* guess)
prediction *n* something that is predicted <the *prediction* was for a good outcome>
syn cast, forecast, foretelling, prevision, prognosis, prognostication, prophecy, weird
rel conjecture, guess, surmising
predictor *n syn* see PROPHET
predilection *n syn* see LEANING 2
predispose *vb syn* see INCLINE 3
rel impress, strike, sway
con disaffect, disincline, disinterest, indispose
predisposed *adj syn* see WILLING 1
ant indisposed
predisposition *n syn* see LEANING 2
ant indisposition
predominant *adj* **1** *syn* see DOMINANT 1
ant subordinate
2 *syn* see CHIEF 2
predominantly *adv syn* see GENERALLY 1
predominate *adj syn* see DOMINANT 1
predominate *vb syn* see RULE 2
preeminence *n* **1** *syn* see SUPREMACY
2 *syn* see EMINENCE 1
preeminent *adj* **1** *syn* see SUPREME
2 *syn* see CHIEF 2
preempt *vb* **1** *syn* see APPROPRIATE 1
2 *syn* see ARROGATE 1
preen *vb syn* see PRIDE
preengage *vb* **1** *syn* see RESERVE 2
2 *syn* see PREPOSSESS 1
preface *n syn* see INTRODUCTION
preface *vb syn* see PRECEDE 3
prefatial *adj syn* see PRELIMINARY
prefatorial *adj syn* see PRELIMINARY
prefatory *adj syn* see PRELIMINARY
prefer *vb* **1** *syn* see ADVANCE 2
2 *syn* see CHOOSE 1
3 *syn* see PROPOSE 1
preferable *adj syn* see BETTER 2
preference *n* **1** *syn* see CHOICE 1
rel partiality, predilection, prepossession
2 *syn* see ADVANCEMENT 1
preferment *n syn* see ADVANCEMENT 1
preferred *adj syn* see FAVORITE 2
prefigurate *vb syn* see ADUMBRATE 1
prefigure *vb syn* see ADUMBRATE 1

preform *vb syn* see PREDESTINE 1

pregnance *n syn* see PREGNANCY

pregnancy *n* the condition of containing unborn young within the body <she was in the last trimester of her *pregnancy*>
syn gestation, gravidity, pregnance, situation

pregnant *adj* 1 containing unborn young within the body <she was *pregnant* with her second child>
syn big, childing, enceinte, expectant, expecting, gone, gravid, heavy, parous, parturient
idiom in an interesting condition, in the family way, with child (or young)
con barren, infertile; delivered; postpartum
2 *syn* see EXPRESSIVE
rel consequential, important, momentous, significant, weighty

prehend *vb syn* see CATCH 1

prehensile *adj syn* see COVETOUS

preindicate *vb syn* see ANNOUNCE 2

prejudgment *n syn* see PRECONCEPTION

prejudice *n* the inclination to take a stand (as in a conflict) usually without just grounds or sufficient information <could not review his competitor's work without *prejudice*>
syn bias, one-sidedness, partiality; *compare* LEANING 2, PRECONCEPTION
rel partisanship
idiom jaundiced eye
con detachment, dispassion, impartiality, indifference, neutrality
ant objectivity

prejudice *vb* 1 *syn* see INJURE 1
2 to cause to have opinions formed without due knowledge or examination <*prejudice* a man against his neighbor by innuendo>
syn bias, influence, prepossess; *compare* INCLINE 3, SLANT 3
rel bend, dispose, incline, predispose; angle, skew, slant; prejudge

prejudiced *adj syn* see BIASED 2
ant unprejudiced; disinterested

prejudicial *adj* 1 *syn* see HARMFUL
2 *syn* see DISCRIMINATORY

prejudicious *adj syn* see HARMFUL

prekindergarten *adj syn* see CHILDISH

preknow *vb syn* see FORESEE

prelation *n syn* see ADVANCEMENT 1

prelect *vb syn* see TALK 7

‖prelim *adj syn* see PRELIMINARY

preliminary *adj* serving to make ready the way for something that follows <held a *preliminary* discussion to set up the agenda of the conference>
syn inductive, introductory, prefatial, prefatorial, prefatory, ‖prelim, preludial, prelusive, preparative, preparatory, proemial
rel primal, primary; elemental, elementary; basic, fundamental; fitting, preparing, readying
ant postliminary

prelimit *vb syn* see LIMIT 2

---

preliterate *adj syn* see PRIMITIVE 6

prelude *n syn* see INTRODUCTION

preludial *adj syn* see PRELIMINARY

prelusion *n syn* see INTRODUCTION

prelusive *adj syn* see PRELIMINARY

premature *adj syn* see EARLY 2

prematurely *adv syn* see EARLY 2

premeditate *vb* to think on and revolve in the mind beforehand <carefully *premeditating* each step of his plan of campaign>
syn forethink, precogitate, predetermine
rel prearrange, preplan, set up; predecide; prepare

premeditated *adj syn* see DELIBERATE 1
ant unpremeditated; spontaneous

premier *adj syn* see FIRST 3

premise *n syn* see ASSUMPTION 2

premise *vb syn* see PRESUPPOSE

premium *n syn* see REWARD

premium *adj syn* see SUPERIOR 4

premonition *n syn* see APPREHENSION 3

prename *n syn* see GIVEN NAME

prenotion *n syn* see APPREHENSION 3

prentice *n syn* see NOVICE

prentice *adj syn* see CRUDE 5

preoccupied *adj* 1 *syn* see INTENT
2 *syn* see ABSTRACTED
rel absorbed; forgetful
ant unpreoccupied

preoccupy *vb syn* see PREPOSSESS 1

preordain *vb* 1 *syn* see PREDESTINE 1
2 *syn* see PREDESTINE 2

preparative *adj syn* see PRELIMINARY

preparatory *adj syn* see PRELIMINARY

prepare *vb* 1 to make ready in advance usually for a particular use or disposition <*prepared* rooms for the expected guests>
syn fit, fix, get, make, make up, ready
rel furnish, provide, supply; dower, endow, endue; equip, outfit; dispose, incline, predispose; prime
idiom set the stage (for)
ant unprepare
2 *syn* see DRAFT 3
3 *syn* see GIRD 3

prepared *adj syn* see READY 1
ant unprepared

prepatent *adj syn* see LATENT

prepense *adj syn* see DELIBERATE 1

prepensely *adv syn* see INTENTIONALLY

preponderance *n syn* see SUPREMACY

preponderancy *n syn* see SUPREMACY

preponderant *adj syn* see DOMINANT 1

preponderate *vb syn* see RULE 2

preponderation *n syn* see SUPREMACY

prepossess *vb* 1 to influence or affect strongly beforehand <was *prepossessed* with the notion of his own superiority>
syn preengage, preoccupy
rel busy, engage, engross, immerse, occupy, soak; absorb, imbue, involve
2 *syn* see PREJUDICE 2

prepossessed *adj syn* see BIASED 2
ant unprepossessed

prepossessing *adj syn* see ATTRACTIVE 1

prepossession *n syn* see PRECONCEPTION

preposterous *adj* 1 *syn* see FOOLISH 2
rel irrational, unreasonable
2 *syn* see EXTRAVAGANT 1

preposterousness *n syn* see FOOLISHNESS

prepotence *n syn* see SUPREMACY

---

syn synonym(s)   *rel* related word(s)
ant antonym(s)   *con* contrasted word(s)
idiom idiomatic equivalent(s)
‖ use limited; if in doubt, see a dictionary

prepotency *n syn* see SUPREMACY
prerequisite *n syn* see ESSENTIAL 2
prerequisite *adj syn* see ESSENTIAL 4
prerogative *n syn* see RIGHT 2
  rel exemption, immunity
presage *n* 1 *syn* see FORETOKEN
  2 *syn* see APPREHENSION 3
presage *vb* 1 *syn* see AUGUR 2
  rel bespeak, indicate
  2 *syn* see ANNOUNCE 2
  3 *syn* see FORETELL
prescribe *vb* 1 *syn* see DICTATE
  2 to fix arbitrarily or authoritatively for
  the sake of order or of a clear understanding < the Constitution *prescribes* the conditions under which it may be amended >
  syn assign, define, lay down
  rel establish, fix, set, settle; decide, determine; choose, pick out, select
prescript *n syn* see LAW 1
prescription *n syn* see LAW 1
presence *n syn* see BEARING 1
  rel appearance, aspect, look, seeming
present *n syn* see GIFT 1
present *vb* 1 *syn* see INTRODUCE 4
  2 *syn* see GIVE 1
  3 *syn* see OFFER 1
  4 *syn* see ADDUCE
  5 *syn* see DIRECT 2
present *adj* now existing or in progress
  < the *present* state of the economy seems
  to be shaky from all reports >
  syn contemporary, current, existent, extant, instant, present-day, todayish
  rel contemporaneous, modern; newfash-
  ioned, up-to-date, up-to-the-minute
  con bygone, erstwhile, late, old, once,
  onetime, quondam, sometime, whilom
  ant past
present *n* the present time < the course
  covers U.S. history from 1900 to the *present* >
  syn now, today; *compare* FUTURE, PAST
  idiom here and now, this day and age
  ant past; future
presentable *adj syn* see RESPECTABLE 5
present-day *adj syn* see PRESENT
presenter *n syn* see DONOR
presentiment *n syn* see APPREHENSION 3
  rel discomposing, discomposure, disquietude, disturbance, perturbation
presently *adv* 1 without undue time lapse
  < the results will be evident *presently* >
  syn anon, by and by, directly, shortly,
  soon
  2 *syn* see TODAY
presentment *n syn* see REPRESENTATION
preserval *n syn* see CONSERVATION 1
preservation *n* 1 the act of preserving or
  the state of being preserved < the *preservation* of peace in the world >
  syn conservation, keeping, safekeeping,
  salvation, saving, sustentation
  rel defense, guard, protection, safeguard,
  shield; care, guardianship, ward
  2 *syn* see CONSERVATION 1
preserve *vb* 1 *syn* see SAVE 3
  2 *syn* see MAINTAIN 1
preserve *n syn* see JAM
preside *vb* to occupy the place of authority
  (as in an assembly) < the chief justice
  presides over the supreme court > < the
  presiding elders of the church >

  syn chair
  rel carry on, conduct, control, direct,
  keep, manage, operate, ordain, run; administer, handle, head, oversee, supervise
press *n syn* see CROWD 1
press *vb* 1 to act upon through steady
  pushing or thrusting force exerted in
  contact < *pressed* his nose against the
  window >
  syn bear, compress, constrain, crowd,
  crush, jam, ∥mash, push, ∥squab, squash,
  squeeze, squish, squush
  rel propel, shove, thrust; drive, impel,
  move
  2 *syn* see DEPRESS 1
  3 to squeeze out the juice or contents of < *press* grapes >
  syn crush, express
  rel compress, squeeze
  4 *syn* see PUSH 2
  5 *syn* see PRESSURE
  6 *syn* see EMBRACE 1
  7 to crowd closely against or around
  someone or something < hundreds *pressed*
  around the performer after the show >
  syn cram, crowd, crush, jam, squash,
  squeeze; *compare* CRAM 1
  rel pack, ram, stuff, tamp; mass, pile;
  assemble, collect, congregate, gather
  8 to force or push one's way (as through
  a crowd or against obstruction) < had to
  press through the traffic to get to the
  other side of town >
  syn bear, squeeze
  rel force, push, shove
press-agent *vb syn* see PUBLICIZE
press-agentry *n syn* see PUBLICITY
pressing *adj* demanding or claiming especially immediate attention < he was barely
  able to pay his most *pressing* debts >
  syn burning, clamant, clamorous, crying,
  dire, exigent, imperative, importunate,
  insistent, instant, urgent
  rel direct, immediate; claiming, demanding, exacting, requiring; compelling, constraining, forcing, obliging; acute, critical,
  crucial
pressure *n syn* see STRESS 1
pressure *vb* to insist upon unduly < *pres-
  sured* him into making the wrong move >
  syn overpress, press, push
  rel drive, impel; rush
prestige *n* 1 *syn* see STATUS 2
  2 *syn* see INFLUENCE 1
  rel power, sway
  3 *syn* see EMINENCE 1
prestigious *adj syn* see FAMOUS 2
presto *adv syn* see FAST 2
presumably *adv* by reasonable assumption
  < *presumably* the best qualified for the job
  should get it >
  syn assumably, doubtless, likely, presumptively, probably
  con indubitably, surely, undoubtedly,
  unquestionably
presume *vb* 1 *syn* see CONJECTURE
  2 *syn* see PRESUPPOSE
  3 *syn* see IMPOSE 5
presuming *adj syn* see PRESUMPTUOUS
  ant unassuming, unpresuming
presumption *n* 1 *syn* see EFFRONTERY
  2 *syn* see PRESUPPOSITION 1
  3 *syn* see ASSUMPTION 2

presumptively *adv syn* see PRESUMABLY

presumptuous *adj* marked by or based on bold and excessive self-confidence < in such company his demand for attention was utterly *presumptuous* >
syn brash, brassbound, confident, forward, gay, overconfident, overweening, presuming, pushful, pushing, ‖pushy, self=asserting, self-assertive, uppish, uppity
rel pretentious, self-assured, self-conceited; lofty, pompous, supercilious; complacent, self-satisfied, smug; inexcusable, outrageous
idiom above one's britches
con deferential, dutiful, respectful, submissive; appropriate, proper

presuppose *vb* to take something for granted or as true or existent especially as a basis for action or reasoning < a lecturer who talks above the heads of his listeners *presupposes* too extensive a knowledge on their part >
syn assume, posit, postulate, premise, presume
rel conjecture, guess, surmise; deduce, infer, judge; believe, expect, gather, imagine, reckon, suppose, suspect, take, think, understand; preconceive

presupposition *n* 1 an act of presupposing < going on his *presupposition* that they would succeed >
syn assumption, presumption
rel conjecture, guess, surmise; deduction, inference, judgment; belief, conviction, opinion, view
2 *syn* see ASSUMPTION 2

pretend *vb* 1 *syn* see ASSUME 4
rel beguile, deceive, delude, mislead; profess, purport
idiom make believe
2 *syn* see CONJECTURE

pretended *adj syn* see ALLEGED

pretender *n syn* see IMPOSTOR

pretense *n* 1 *syn* see CLAIM 1
2 the offering of something false as real or true < there is too much *pretense* in his piety >
syn charade, disguise, make-believe, pageant, pretension, pretentiousness
rel deceit, deception, fake, fraud, humbug, imposture, sham; affectation, air, mannerism, pose
con sincereness; reality, soundness, substantiality, validity; fairness, honesty
ant sincerity
3 *syn* see MASK 2

pretension *n* 1 *syn* see CLAIM 1
2 *syn* see AMBITION 2
3 *syn* see PRETENSE 2

pretentious *adj* 1 *syn* see SHOWY
ant unpretentious
2 *syn* see GENTEEL 3
ant unpretentious
3 flamboyant, turgid, or bombastic in manner or content < a *pretentious* literary style >
syn arty, arty-crafty, big, high-sounding, imposing, overblown

rel affected, feigned, put-on; pompier; aureate, bombastic, euphuistic, flowery, grandiloquent, magniloquent, rhetorical; inflated, tumid, turgid
con heartfelt, hearty, sincere, unfeigned, wholehearted, whole-souled; artless, genuine, natural, simple, unaffected
ant unpretentious
4 *syn* see AMBITIOUS 2

pretentiousness *n syn* see PRETENSE 2
ant unpretentiousness

preterition *n syn* see OMISSION

pretermission *n syn* see OMISSION

pretermit *vb syn* see NEGLECT

preternatural *adj* 1 *syn* see SUPERNATURAL 1
rel anomalous, unnatural; nonnatural
2 *syn* see ABNORMAL 1
ant natural

pretext *n* 1 *syn* see EXCUSE 1
2 *syn* see MASK 2

prettify *vb syn* see PALLIATE

pretty *adj* 1 *syn* see SKILLFUL 2
2 *syn* see BEAUTIFUL
rel darling, ducky; cunning, cute
ant unpretty

pretty *adv syn* see SOMEWHAT 2
idiom pretty much

‖**pretty** *n syn* see TOY 2

prettyism *n syn* see POSE 2

pretty–pretty *n syn* see KNICKKNACK

preux *adj syn* see COURTLY

prevail *vb* 1 *syn* see CONQUER 2
2 *syn* see WIN 1
3 *syn* see RULE 2

prevail (on *or* upon) *vb syn* see INDUCE 1
rel affect, impress

prevailing *adj* general (as in circulation, acceptance, or use) in a given place or at a given time < the *prevailing* point of view among farmers >
syn current, popular, prevalent, rampant, regnant, rife, ruling, widespread
rel dominant, predominant, preponderant; common, familiar, ordinary; general, universal
con exceptional, uncommon, unusual

prevalent *adj* 1 *syn* see DOMINANT 1
2 *syn* see PREVAILING
3 *syn* see GENERAL 1
rel accustomed, customary, wonted

prevaricate *vb syn* see LIE
rel belie, garble, misrepresent

prevarication *n syn* see LIE

prevaricative *adj syn* see EVASIVE 1

prevaricator *n syn* see LIAR

prevaricatory *adj syn* see EVASIVE 1

prevent *vb* 1 to be or get ahead of or to deal with beforehand < many problems are *prevented* easily if one plans wisely >
syn anticipate, forestall
rel baffle, balk, foil, frustrate, thwart; arrest, check, interrupt
2 to stop from advancing or occurring < take steps to *prevent* war > < measures designed to *prevent* the spread of disease >
syn avert, deter, forestall, forfend, obviate, preclude, rule out, stave off, ward
rel bar, block, dam, hinder, impede, obstruct; debar, shut out; forbid, inhibit, interdict, prohibit
con allow, leave, let, suffer
ant permit

syn synonym(s)   *rel* related word(s)
ant antonym(s)   *con* contrasted word(s)
idiom idiomatic equivalent(s)
‖ use limited; if in doubt, see a dictionary

previous *adj* 1 *syn* see PRECEDING
  ant subsequent; consequent
  2 *syn* see EARLY 2
previous *adj* *syn* see BEFORE 1
previously *adv* *syn* see BEFORE 2
  ant subsequently; consequently
previousness *n* *syn* see PRIORITY
previse *vb* *syn* see FORESEE
prevision *n* *syn* see PREDICTION
prevision *vb* *syn* see FORESEE
prey *n* 1 *syn* see GAME 3
  2 *syn* see VICTIM 2
∥pribble *n* *syn* see QUARREL
price *n* 1 the quantity of one thing that is
  exchanged or demanded in barter or sale
  for another <what is the *price* of this
  book>
  syn charge, cost, price tag, rate, tab, tariff
  2 *syn* see EXPENSE 2
priceless *adj* *syn* see PRECIOUS 1
  rel cherished, prized, treasured, valued
  idiom without price
price tag *n* *syn* see PRICE 1
prick *n* 1 a mark or shallow hole made by
  or as if by a pointed tool <a needle *prick*
  in his arm>
  syn jab, ∥jag, puncture, stab
  rel prickle; hole
  ∥2 *syn* see SNOT 1
prick *vb* 1 *syn* see PERFORATE
  rel enter; cut, slash, slit
  2 *syn* see URGE
  rel excite, pique, stimulate
∥prick (up) *vb* *syn* see DRESS UP 1
prickish *adj* *syn* see IRRITABLE
prickly *adj* 1 *syn* see THORNY
  rel annoying, bothersome
  2 *syn* see IRRITABLE
pride *n* 1 *syn* see CONCEIT 2
  rel bighead, cockiness, overconfidence,
  self-assurance
  idiom overweening pride
  ant humility
  2 a reasonable or justifiable sense of one's
  worth or position <inhumane treatment
  in prison caused him to lose his *pride*>
  syn amour propre, self-esteem, self-regard,
  self-respect
  rel dignity, face, pridefulness, self-confidence, self-trust
  con humiliation, mortification; shame-
  facedness
  ant shame
  3 proud or disdainful behavior or actions
  <her snobbishness and overbearing *pride*
  were offensive>
  syn arrogance, disdain, disdainfulness,
  haughtiness, hauteur, loftiness, morgue,
  superbity, superciliousness
  rel condescension, snobbishness; contempt, scorn; insolence; smugness; pretentiousness
  idiom haughty airs
  con humbleness, modesty, unpretentiousness
  ant humility
  4 *syn* see BEST
  idiom pride of the herd
pride *vb* to congratulate (oneself) for something one is, has, or has done or achieved
  <he *prides* himself on his ancestry>
  syn pique, plume, preen
  rel boast, brag, crow, gasconade, vaunt;
  congratulate, felicitate

  ant efface
∥pridy *adj* *syn* see PROUD 1
prier (*or* **pryer**) *n* *syn* see BUSYBODY
priestal *adj* *syn* see SACERDOTAL
priestish *adj* *syn* see SACERDOTAL
priestlike *adj* *syn* see SACERDOTAL
priestly *adj* *syn* see SACERDOTAL
∥prig *vb* *syn* see STEAL 1
prig *n* *syn* see THIEF
prig *n* *syn* see PRUDE
prig *adj* *syn* see PRIM 1
priggish *adj* 1 *syn* see COMPLACENT
  rel self-righteous; self-esteeming, self-
  loving
  2 *syn* see PRIM 1
prim *adj* 1 excessively concerned with what
  one regards as proper or right <a *prim*
  woman, easily shocked by vulgar lan-
  guage>
  syn bluenosed, genteel, missish, precise,
  prig, priggish, prissy, proper, prudish,
  puritanical, straitlaced, stuffy, tight-laced,
  Victorian; *compare* GENTEEL 3
  rel correct, nice, precise; decorous; rigid,
  stiff, wooden; ceremonial, ceremonious,
  conventional, formal, straight
  idiom prim and proper
  con lax, loose, slack; easy, easygoing, free
  2 *syn* see NEAT 2
prima facie *adj* *syn* see SELF-EVIDENT
primarily *adv* 1 *syn* see GENERALLY 1
  2 *syn* see INITIALLY 1
primary *adj* 1 *syn* see FIRST 2
  2 *syn* see PRIMITIVE 4
  3 *syn* see FUNDAMENTAL 1
  4 *syn* see DIRECT 4
  5 not based on or derived from something
  else <the *primary* studies in nuclear phys-
  ics>
  syn original, prime, primitive, underivative, underived
  rel first, firsthand; basic, foundational,
  fundamental, principal, underlying
  con derivate, derivational, derivative,
  derived; borrowed, secondhand
  ant secondary
prime *n* 1 *syn* see MORNING 1
  2 *syn* see YOUTH 1
  3 *syn* see BEST
prime *adj* 1 *syn* see FIRST 2
  2 *syn* see EXCELLENT
  3 *syn* see PRIMARY 5
prime *vb* *syn* see PROVOKE 4
primeval *adj* *syn* see PRIMITIVE 4
primevous *adj* *syn* see PRIMITIVE 4
primitial *adj* *syn* see PRIMITIVE 4
primitive *adj* 1 *syn* see PRIMARY 5
  2 *syn* see EARLY 1
  3 closely approximating an early ancestral type <the opossums are *primitive*
  mammals>
  syn archaic, persistent, undeveloped, unevolved
  ant advanced
  4 of or relating to earlier ages of the
  world or of human history <archaeology
  is concerned especially with the study of
  primitive man>
  syn primary, primeval, primevous, primitial
  ant unprimitive
  5 *syn* see ELEMENTAL 1

6 characterized by a lack of written language, simple technology, and a relatively simple social organization
syn nonliterate, preliterate
rel barbarian, uncivilized, uncultivated
con advanced, civilized, cultivated
primitively *adv syn see* INITIALLY 1
primogenitor *n syn see* ANCESTOR 1
primordial *adj* 1 *syn see* EARLY 1
2 *syn see* FIRST 1
primp *vb syn see* DRESS UP 1
primrose *n syn see* BEST
prince *n syn see* MAGNATE
princely *adj syn see* GRAND 1
principal *adj* 1 *syn see* CHIEF 2
2 *syn see* FIRST 3
principally *adv syn see* GENERALLY 1
principium *n syn see* PRINCIPLE 1
principle *n* 1 a comprehensive and fundamental rule, doctrine, or assumption < the *principle* of free speech >
syn axiom, fundamental, law, principium, theorem
rel basis, foundation, ground; canon, precept, rule; convention, form, usage
2 **principles** *pl syn see* ETHIC 3
3 **principles** *pl syn see* ALPHABET 2
principled *adj syn see* MORAL 1
ant unprincipled
‖**prink** *vb syn see* SASHAY
prink (up) *vb syn see* DRESS UP 1
print *n* 1 *syn see* IMPRESSION 1
2 printed state or form < to see his name in *print* >
syn black and white, writing
printing *n syn see* EDITION
prior *adj syn see* PRECEDING
rel ahead, before, forward
con after, behind
priority *n* the act, the fact, or the right of preceding another < the right to inherit a title is dependent mainly on *priority* of birth >
syn antecedence, precedence, precedency, previousness
rel arrangement, order, ordering; ascendancy, supremacy; preeminence, transcendence
prior to *prep* 1 *syn see* BEFORE 1
2 *syn see* UNTIL
prison *n syn see* JAIL
‖**prison** *vb syn see* IMPRISON
prison bird *n syn see* CONVICT
prissy *adj* 1 *syn see* PRIM 1
rel fastidious, finicky, squeamish
2 *syn see* EFFEMINATE
‖**pritch** *vb syn see* PERFORATE
private *adj* 1 belonging to or concerning an individual person, company, or interest < *private* property >
syn personal, privy
rel intimate
con common, general, shared
ant public
2 known only to a select few < the group had *private* information about the strike >
syn closet, confidential, hushed, inside
rel secret; discreet; concealed, hidden

con common, general, open
ant public
private detective *n* a person concerned with the maintenance of lawful conduct or the investigation of crime either as a regular employee of a private interest (as a hotel) or as a contractor for fees < obtained a *private detective* to report on his wife's associates >
syn operative, Pinkerton, ‖private eye, ‖shamus; *compare* DETECTIVE
‖**private eye** *n syn see* PRIVATE DETECTIVE
privately *adv syn see* SECRETLY
private parts *n pl syn see* GENITALIA
privates *n pl syn see* GENITALIA
privation *n* 1 *syn see* ABSENCE
2 the state of one deprived of something previously or normally possessed < suffered great *privation* during the famine >
syn deprivation, deprivement, dispossession, divestiture, loss; *compare* LOSS 1
rel distress, misery, suffering; losing, mislaying, misplacement, misplacing
3 *syn see* POVERTY 1
privilege *n syn see* RIGHT 2
rel allowance, concession; boon, favor
privilege (from) *vb syn see* EXEMPT
privities *n pl syn see* GENITALIA
privy *adj* 1 *syn see* PRIVATE 1
2 *syn see* ULTERIOR
privy *n* 1 an outdoor toilet < in less settled areas, *privies* often take the place of indoor plumbing >
syn backhouse, ‖biffy, ‖closet, jakes, ‖necessary, ‖office, outhouse
2 *syn see* TOILET
privy parts *n pl syn see* GENITALIA
prize *n* 1 *syn see* REWARD
2 *syn see* BEST
prize *vb syn see* APPRECIATE 1
prize *n syn see* SPOIL
prize *vb syn see* PRY
prizefighting *n syn see* BOXING
pro *prep syn see* FOR 2
ant anti, con
pro *n syn see* EXPERT
pro and con *vb syn see* DISCUSS 1
probable *adj* being such as may become true or actual < seems to be a *probable* candidate >
syn conceivable, earthly, likely, mortal, possible
rel believable, colorable, credible, plausible; rational, reasonable; apparent, illusory, ostensible, seeming
con doubtful, dubious, questionable, unlikely
ant improbable, unprobable
probably *adv syn see* PRESUMABLY
ant improbably
probe *n syn see* INQUIRY 1
probe *vb* 1 *syn see* EXPLORE
2 to try to find out (as by discreet questioning) the views or intentions of < *probed* the neighbors on the subject of political reform >
syn feel out, sound (out)
rel ask, catechize, examine, inquire, interrogate, query, quiz
idiom feel the pulse, put out a feeler, see how the land lies, see which way the wind blows

---

syn synonym(s) *rel* related word(s)
ant antonym(s) *con* contrasted word(s)
idiom idiomatic equivalent(s)
‖ use limited; if in doubt, see a dictionary

3 *syn* see SCOUT
probing *n syn* see INQUIRY 1
probity *n syn* see GOODNESS
problem *n* 1 *syn* see EXAMPLE 3
2 something requiring thought and skill to arrive at a proper conclusion or decision < what to do now is a *problem* >
syn issue, nut, question
rel enigma, mystery, puzzle; bugaboo, bugbear; count, point
idiom a hard nut to crack
problematic *adj* 1 *syn* see DOUBTFUL 1
ant unproblematic
2 *syn* see MOOT
ant unproblematic
proboscis *n syn* see NOSE 1
procacious *adj* 1 *syn* see INSOLENT 2
2 *syn* see WISE 5
procedure *n* 1 *syn* see COURSE 3
2 *syn* see MEASURE 7
3 *syn* see PROCESS 1
proceed *vb* 1 *syn* see SPRING 1
2 *syn* see GO 1
3 *syn* see ADVANCE 5
ant recede
proceeding *n* 1 *syn* see MEASURE 7
2 *syn* see PROCESS 1
proceeds *n pl syn* see PROFIT
process *n* 1 the series of actions, operations, or motions involved in the accomplishment of an end < the *process* of making sugar from sugarcane >
syn procedure, proceeding
rel fashion, manner, method, mode, modus, system, technique, way, wise; routine; operation
2 *syn* see OUTGROWTH 1
‖**process** *vb syn* see GO 1
procession *n syn* see ORDER 5
processus *n syn* see OUTGROWTH 1
proclaim *vb* 1 *syn* see DECLARE 1
rel utter, vent, ventilate, voice
2 *syn* see SHOW 2
proclamation *n syn* see DECLARATION
proclivity *n syn* see LEANING 2
procrastinate *vb syn* see DELAY 2
rel defer, postpone, stay, suspend; prolong, protract
procreate *vb* 1 to produce offspring < *procreate* children >
syn bear, beget, breed, generate, multiply, produce, propagate, reproduce
rel mother; engender; hatch, spawn; proliferate
idiom give birth to, multiply the earth
2 *syn* see GENERATE 1
3 *syn* see FATHER 1
procumbent *adj syn* see PRONE 4
procurable *adj syn* see AVAILABLE 1
procure *vb* 1 *syn* see GET 1
2 *syn* see INDUCE 1
prod *vb* 1 *syn* see POKE 1
2 *syn* see URGE
rel instigate; excite, pique, provoke, stimulate
prodigal *adj syn* see PROFUSE
ant parsimonious; frugal
prodigal *n syn* see SPENDTHRIFT
prodigality *n syn* see EXTRAVAGANCE 2
ant parsimoniousness
prodigalize *vb syn* see WASTE 2
prodigious *adj* 1 *syn* see MARVELOUS 1
2 *syn* see MONSTROUS 1

3 *syn* see HUGE
prodigy *n syn* see WONDER 1
produce *vb* 1 *syn* see PROCREATE 1
2 *syn* see STAGE
3 *syn* see EFFECT 1
4 *syn* see GENERATE 1
5 *syn* see GENERATE 3
6 *syn* see MAKE 3
7 *syn* see BEAR 9
8 *syn* see GIVE 7
9 *syn* see GROW 1
produce *n syn* see PRODUCT 1
product *n* 1 something produced by physical labor or intellectual effort < the literary *products* of the Age of Reason >
syn produce, production
rel handiwork; consequence, effect, offshoot, outcome, outgrowth, result; fruit, harvest
2 *syn* see OUTPUT
production *n* 1 *syn* see PRODUCT 1
2 *syn* see EXTENSION 1
3 *syn* see OUTPUT
productive *adj syn* see FERTILE
ant unproductive
proem *n syn* see INTRODUCTION
proemial *adj syn* see PRELIMINARY
profanation *n* a violation or misuse of something normally held sacred < the *profanation* of a religious ritual >
syn blasphemy, desecration, sacrilege, violation
rel contamination, defilement, pollution; corruption, debasement, perversion, vitiation; transgression, trespass
con glorification, hallowing, sanctification
ant purification; consecration
profane *adj* 1 not concerned with religion or religious purposes < he was speaking of *profane* history, not the history found in the Bible >
syn lay, secular, temporal, unsacred
rel earthly, mundane, terrestrial, worldly
con consecrated, hallowed, holy, sanctified; divine, religious, spiritual
ant sacred
2 *syn* see HEATHEN
3 *syn* see IMPIOUS 1
4 *syn* see SACRILEGIOUS
5 *syn* see OBSCENE 2
profaned *adj syn* see IMPURE 3
ant unprofaned
profanity *n syn* see BLASPHEMY 1
profess *vb syn* see ASSERT 1
professed *adj syn* see ALLEGED
professedly *adv syn* see OSTENSIBLY
profession *n syn* see TRADE 1
professional *n syn* see EXPERT
ant amateur
proffer *vb syn* see OFFER 1
proffer *n syn* see PROPOSAL
proficiency *n syn* see ADVANCE 2
proficient *adj* having or manifesting the knowledge, skill, and experience needed for success in a particular field or endeavor < a *proficient* glider pilot >
syn adept, crack, crackerjack, expert, master, masterful, masterly, skilled, skillful; *compare* EXPERIENCED, SKILLFUL 2
rel checked-out, drilled, exercised, practiced; effective, effectual, efficient; able, capable, competent, qualified; accomplished, consummate, finished

con ignorant, untaught, untrained; inexperienced; unskilled
ant incompetent

proficient *n syn* see EXPERT

profile *n syn* see OUTLINE

profit *n* the excess of returns over expenditure in a transaction or a series of transactions < his *profits* from the business venture were rewarding >
syn earnings, gain, lucre, proceeds, return
rel cleaning, cleanup, killing; receipt(s); output, outturn, product, production, turnout, yield
con cost, expenditure, expense, outgo
ant loss

profit *vb syn* see BENEFIT
ant lose

profitable *adj syn* see ADVANTAGEOUS 1
ant profitless, unprofitable

profligate *adj syn* see ABANDONED 2

profligate *n* 1 *syn* see WASTREL 1
2 *syn* see SPENDTHRIFT

profound *adj* 1 *syn* see RECONDITE
2 *syn* see DEEP 1
3 *syn* see INTENSIVE

profoundness *n syn* see DEPTH 2

profundity *n syn* see DEPTH 2

profuse *adj* proffered in or characterized by great abundance < *profuse* apologies > < a *profuse* flow of blood >
syn exuberant, lavish, lush, luxuriant, opulent, prodigal, profusive, riotous
rel abundant, copious; abounding, swarming, teeming; excessive, extravagant, immoderate; bounteous, bountiful, generous, liberal, munificent, openhanded
con exiguous, meager, scrimpy, skimpy, slight, small, sparse
ant scant, scanty

profusive *adj syn* see PROFUSE

progenerate *vb syn* see FATHER 1

progenitor *n syn* see ANCESTOR 1

progeniture *n syn* see OFFSPRING

progeny *n syn* see OFFSPRING

prognosis *n syn* see PREDICTION

prognostic *n syn* see FORETOKEN

prognosticate *vb syn* see FORETELL

prognostication *n syn* see PREDICTION

prognosticator *n syn* see PROPHET

program *n* 1 a formulated plan listing things to be done or to take place especially in their time order < the *program* of a concert >
syn agenda, calendar, card, docket, programma, schedule, sked, timetable
rel bill; slate; plan
idiom order of the day
2 *syn* see COURSE 3

programma *n syn* see PROGRAM 1

progress *n* 1 *syn* see ADVANCE 2
ant regression, retrogression
2 a movement onward (as in time or space) < the *progress* of a disease > < they made slow *progress* toward their destination >
syn advance, course, progression
rel passage
3 *syn* see DEVELOPMENT

progress *vb syn* see ADVANCE 5
ant retrogress

progression *n* 1 *syn* see PROGRESS 2
2 *syn* see SUCCESSION 2
3 *syn* see DEVELOPMENT
ant regression, retrogression

progressive *adj syn* see LIBERAL 3
ant reactionary

prohibit *vb syn* see FORBID
ant permit

prohibited *adj syn* see FORBIDDEN

prohibition *n syn* see TABOO
ant permission

project *n* 1 *syn* see PLAN 1
2 something (as a business operation) that one engages in or attempts < large-scale *projects* involving large sums of money >
syn enterprise, undertaking
rel affair, business, concern, matter, proposition, thing; adventure, emprise, exploit, feat, gest, venture

project *vb* 1 *syn* see PLAN 2
rel intend, propose, purpose; delineate, diagram
2 *syn* see THINK 1
‖3 *syn* see WANDER 1
4 *syn* see BULGE
rel extend, lengthen, prolong

projection *n* 1 something which extends beyond a level or a normal outer surface < buttresses are *projections* which serve to support a wall >
syn bulge, jut, outthrust, protrusion, protuberance
rel bump, bunch, swelling; extension, prolongation; hook, knob, point, spine, spur
ant depression
2 *syn* see EMINENCE 3

prolegomenon *n syn* see INTRODUCTION

proletariat *n syn* see RABBLE 2

proliferant *adj syn* see FERTILE

prolific *adj syn* see FERTILE
rel abounding, swarming; breeding, generating, propagating, reproducing, reproductive
ant barren, unfruitful

prolificacy *n syn* see FERTILITY
ant barrenness, unfruitfulness

prolix *adj syn* see WORDY
rel irksome, tedious, tiresome, wearisome; prolonged, protracted

prolixity *n syn* see VERBOSITY

prolixness *n syn* see VERBOSITY

prologue *n syn* see INTRODUCTION
ant epilogue

prolong *vb syn* see EXTEND 3
rel continue, endure, last, persist
con abbreviate, retrench, shorten
ant curtail

prolongate *vb syn* see EXTEND 3

prolongation *n syn* see EXTENSION 1

prolonged *adj syn* see LONG 2
ant curtailed

prolongment *n syn* see EXTENSION 1

prominence *n* 1 *syn* see EMINENCE 1
2 *syn* see EMINENCE 3

prominency *n syn* see EMINENCE 1

prominent *adj* 1 *syn* see NOTICEABLE
ant inconspicuous
2 *syn* see FAMOUS 2
3 *syn* see WELL-KNOWN

promiscuous *adj* 1 *syn* see MISCELLANEOUS

---

syn synonym(s)   *rel* related word(s)
ant antonym(s)   *con* contrasted word(s)
idiom idiomatic equivalent(s)
‖ use limited; if in doubt, see a dictionary

·2 *syn* see RANDOM

promise *vb* 1 to give one's word to do, bring about, or provide <*promised* to render all possible assistance to the flood victims>
syn engage, pass, pledge, undertake; *compare* VOW
rel accede, agree, assent, consent; bargain, compact, contract; covenant, plight, swear, vow; assure, ensure, insure; guarantee
idiom give (*or* make) a promise, pass one's word
2 *syn* see AUGUR 2

promise *n* a declaration that one will do or refrain from doing something specified <never gave a *promise* that he did not intend to keep>
syn engagement, plight, word; *compare* PLEDGE 1, WORD 8
rel earnest, guarantee, pawn, pledge, security, token; covenant, swear, vow; assurance, warrant
idiom word of honor

‖**promised** *adj syn* see ENGAGED 2
promised land *n syn* see UTOPIA
promiseful *adj syn* see HOPEFUL 2
promising *adj syn* see HOPEFUL 2
ant unpromising

promontory *n* a high point of land or rock projecting into a body of water beyond the line of coast <stood on the *promontory* watching boats come in with the tide>
syn beak, bill, cape, foreland, head, headland, naze, point

promote *vb* 1 *syn* see ADVANCE 2
con break, bust, declass, degrade, demerit, disgrade, disrate, downgrade, reduce
ant bump, demote
2 *syn* see ADVANCE 1
3 to encourage public acceptance of (as a policy or merchandise) through publicity <official attempts to *promote* energy conservation> <television helped *promote* the new smaller cars>
syn advertise, boost, plug, push; *compare* PUBLICIZE
rel ballyhoo, propagandize; build up, cry, press-agent, publicize, puff; communicate, impart
idiom make much of
con belittle, decry, depreciate, discredit, knock, run down
ant disparage

promotion *n* 1 *syn* see ADVANCEMENT 1
ant demotion
2 *syn* see PUBLICITY
rel advertisement

prompt *vb* 1 *syn* see INDUCE 1
2 *syn* see URGE

prompt *adj* 1 *syn* see QUICK 2
rel alert, vigilant, watchful, wide-awake; expeditious, speedy, swift
con lax, remiss, slack; dilatory
2 *syn* see PUNCTUAL 2

promptitude *n syn* see ALACRITY
promptly *adv syn* see FAST 2
promulgate *vb syn* see DECLARE 1
promulgation *n syn* see DECLARATION
prone *adj* 1 *syn* see WILLING 1
2 *syn* see LIABLE 2

3 *syn* see APT 1
4 lying down <lying *prone* on the floor>
syn decumbent, flat, procumbent, prostrate, reclining, recumbent
rel resupine, supine; level
con arrect, raised, stand-up, straight-up, upright, upstanding
ant erect

pronounce *vb syn* see ARTICULATE 2
pronounced *adj syn* see DECIDED 1
pronouncement *n syn* see DECLARATION
‖**pronto** *adv syn* see FAST 2
pronunciamento *n syn* see DECLARATION

proof *n* 1 *syn* see REASON 3
2 *syn* see TESTIMONY

prop *n syn* see SUPPORT 3
prop *vb* 1 *syn* see SUPPORT 4
2 *syn* see SUPPORT 5

propagandist *n syn* see MISSIONARY
propagate *vb* 1 *syn* see PROCREATE 1
2 *syn* see GROW 1
3 *syn* see SPREAD 1

propel *vb* 1 *syn* see PUSH 1
2 *syn* see MOVE 5
3 *syn* see URGE

propellant *n syn* see STIMULUS
propensity *n syn* see LEANING 2
ant antipathy

proper *adj* 1 *syn* see FIT 1
ant improper
2 *syn* see TRUE 7
ant improper
3 *syn* see DECOROUS 1
ant improper
4 *syn* see ABLE
5 *syn* see GOOD 2
ant improper
6 *syn* see CHARACTERISTIC
‖7 *syn* see UTTER
8 *syn* see CORRECT 2
9 *syn* see PRIM 1

properly *adv* 1 *syn* see WELL 4
ant improperly
2 *syn* see WELL 1
idiom by rights
ant improperly

properness *n syn* see ORDER 7
ant improperness

property *n* 1 *syn* see QUALITY 1
2 *syn* see WEALTH 2
3 *syn* see OWNERSHIP

prophecy *n* 1 *syn* see REVELATION
2 *syn* see PREDICTION

prophesier *n syn* see PROPHET
prophesy *vb syn* see FORETELL

prophet *n* one who predicts events or developments <there have been many *prophets* foretelling the end of the world>
syn augur, auspex, forecaster, foreseer, foreteller, haruspex, Nostradamus, predictor, prognosticator, prophesier, seer, soothsayer

prophetic *adj* of, relating to, or characteristic of a prophet or prophecy <the old woman seemed to have *prophetic* powers>
syn apocalyptic, Delphian, fatidic, mantic, oracular, prophetical, sibylline, vatic, vaticinal
rel revelatory; interpretive; mysterious, mystic, strange, unexplainable
ant unprophetic

prophetical *adj syn* see PROPHETIC

propinquity *n syn* see PROXIMITY
propitiate *vb syn* see PACIFY
 rel adapt, adjust, conform, reconcile;
 content, satisfy; intercede, mediate
propitiatory *adj syn* see PURGATIVE
propitious *adj* 1 *syn* see FAVORABLE 5
 ant unpropitious; adverse
 2 *syn* see TIMELY 1
 ant unpropitious
 3 *syn* see GOOD 1
 ant unpropitious; adverse
‖**propone** *vb syn* see PROPOSE 1
proponent *n syn* see EXPONENT
 ant opponent
proportion *n* 1 *syn* see DEGREE 2
 2 *syn* see SYMMETRY
 ant disproportion
 3 *syn* see SIZE 1
proportion *vb syn* see HARMONIZE 3
proportional *adj* being in proportion < his
 weight is *proportional* to his size >
 syn commensurable, commensurate,
 equal, symmetrical
 rel correlative, corresponding, reciprocal;
 contingent, dependent, relative
 con asymmetrical, disproportionate, irregular, lopsided, nonsymmetrical, off-balance, overbalanced, unbalanced, unequal,
 uneven, unsymmetrical
 ant disproportional
proportionless *adj syn* see LOPSIDED
proposal *n* something which is proposed to
 another for consideration < his *proposal*
 for a new bussing plan >
 syn invitation, proffer, proposition, suggestion
 rel motion; recommendation; idea, plan,
 project; outline, scheme
propose *vb* 1 to set before the mind for
 consideration < he *proposed* Mr. Smith for
 secretary of the club >
 syn pose, prefer, ‖propone, proposition,
 propound, put, suggest
 rel move (for); offer, present, submit,
 tender; ask, request, solicit
 idiom put forth (*or* forward)
 ant withdraw
 2 *syn* see INTEND 2
proposition *n syn* see PROPOSAL
proposition *vb syn* see PROPOSE 1
propound *vb syn* see PROPOSE 1
proprietary *n syn* see OWNERSHIP
proprietor *n syn* see OWNER
proprietorship *n syn* see OWNERSHIP
propriety *n* 1 *syn* see ORDER 11
 2 *syn* see DECORUM 1
 ant impropriety
 3 *syn* see ORDER 7
 ant impropriety
 4 **proprieties** *pl syn* see MANNER 5
prorate *vb syn* see APPORTION 2
prorogate *vb syn* see ADJOURN 2
prorogue *vb* 1 *syn* see DEFER
 2 *syn* see ADJOURN 2
prosaic *adj* 1 belonging to or characteristic
 of prose as distinguished from poetry
 < his poetry is far more fanciful than his
 prosaic writings >

---

 syn matter-of-fact, prose, prosing, prosy
 rel actual, factual; literal
 con figurative, metaphorical, symbolic;
 fanciful, florid, flowery, ornate
 ant poetic
 2 *syn* see COLORLESS 2
 3 belonging to or suitable to the everyday
 world < the *prosaic* business of day-to-day
 housekeeping >
 syn commonplace, everyday, lowly, mundane, workaday, workday
 rel practicable, practical; boring, irksome,
 tedious
 4 *syn* see COMMON 6
prosaicism *n syn* see COMMONPLACE
prosaism *n syn* see COMMONPLACE
proscribe *vb syn* see SENTENCE
proscription *n syn* see TABOO
prose *n syn* see CHAT 2
prose *adj syn* see PROSAIC 1
prosing *adj syn* see PROSAIC 1
prospect *n syn* see VISTA
prospect *vb syn* see EXPLORE
prosper *vb syn* see SUCCEED 3
 rel augment, increase, multiply; bear,
 produce, turn out, yield
prospering *adj syn* see FLOURISHING
prosperity *n* 1 *syn* see SUCCESS
 2 a state of good fortune and especially of
 financial success < his wise investments
 finally brought him a life of *prosperity* >
 syn abundance, ease, easy street, prosperousness, thriving, well-being
 rel affluence, riches, wealth
 idiom bed of roses, comfortable (*or* easy)
 circumstances, life of ease, the good life
 con misery, suffering; distress, embarrassment, indigence, poverty, straits
 ant adversity
 3 *syn* see WELFARE
 4 a state of high general economic activity
 marked by relatively full employment < a
 war economy often generates *prosperity* >
 syn boom, prosperousness
 rel expansion; growth; inflation
 con recession, slump, stagnation; bust
 ant depression
prosperous *adj* 1 *syn* see TIMELY 1
 rel appropriate, convenient, desirable;
 felicitous, fortunate, happy, lucky
 con ill-seasoned, ill-timed, inauspicious,
 inopportune, unpropitious, unseasonable,
 untimely
 ant unpropitious
 2 *syn* see SUCCESSFUL
 3 enjoying or marked by economic well-
 being < in *prosperous* circumstances >
 syn comfortable, easy, ‖snug, substantial,
 well, well-fixed, well-heeled, well-off, well-
 to-do
 rel affluent, opulent, rich, wealthy; halcyon
 idiom comfortably off, comfortably situated, in (the) clover, in good case
 con impecunious, necessitous, needy,
 poor; failing, unfortunate, unsuccessful
 ant unprosperous
 4 *syn* see FLOURISHING
 rel lusty, strong
 con decrepit, feeble, spindling, weak
prosperously *adv syn* see WELL 5
 ant unprosperously
prosperousness *n* 1 *syn* see PROSPERITY
 2

---

syn synonym(s)   *rel* related word(s)
ant antonym(s)   *con* contrasted word(s)
idiom idiomatic equivalent(s)
‖ use limited; if in doubt, see a dictionary

ant unprosperousness
2 *syn* see PROSPERITY 4
prostitute *vb syn* see ABUSE 2
  rel corrupt, debase, debauch, deprave,
vitiate
prostitute *n* a woman who engages in
promiscuous sexual intercourse especially
for money < streets haunted by *prostitutes* >
  syn bawd, ‖callet, call girl, camp follower,
cocotte, ‖cruiser, drab, fille de joie, harlot,
‖hooker, hustler, ‖joy girl, meretrix, moll,
nightwalker, party girl, pom-pom girl,
poule, quean, sporting girl, street girl,
streetwalker, ‖tomato, whore; *compare*
DOXY, HARLOT 1, WANTON
  rel bar girl, B-girl, pickup; V-girl, victory
girl; cocodette
  idiom lady of pleasure, lady of the evening, woman of the street (*or* streets),
woman of the town
prostitution *n* the act or practice of engaging in promiscuous sexual intercourse
especially for money < the problem of
prostitution around military installations >
  syn harlotry, oldest profession, (the) social evil, streetwalking, whoredom
prostrate *adj syn* see PRONE 4
prostrate *vb 1 syn* see FELL 1
  2 *syn* see PARALYZE 1
  3 *syn* see OVERWHELM 4
  4 *syn* see EXHAUST 4
prosy *adj 1 syn* see PROSAIC 1
  2 *syn* see COLORLESS 2
protean *adj syn* see CHANGEABLE 1
protect *vb syn* see DEFEND 1
  rel conserve, preserve, save; harbor, shelter
protection *n 1 syn* see DEFENSE 1
  2 money paid under threat of depredation
< offered *protection* to keep his store from
being vandalized >
  syn ‖pad
  rel extortion, shakedown, squeeze; graft;
bribe
pro tem *adj syn* see TEMPORARY
pro tempore *adj syn* see TEMPORARY
protest *n syn* see DEMUR 2
protest *vb 1 syn* see ASSERT 1
  2 *syn* see OBJECT 1
  rel demonstrate; combat, fight, oppose,
resist
  ant agree
protoplast *n syn* see ORIGINAL 1
prototypal *adj syn* see TYPICAL 1
prototype *n 1 syn* see ORIGINAL 1
  2 *syn* see FORERUNNER 2
prototypical *adj syn* see TYPICAL 1
protract *vb syn* see EXTEND 3
  ant curtail
protracted *adj syn* see LONG 2
  ant curtailed
protraction *n syn* see EXTENSION 1
  rel dallying, dawdling, delay, lag; stay,
suspension
  ant curtailment
protrude *vb syn* see BULGE
protrusion *n syn* see PROJECTION 1
protuberance *n syn* see PROJECTION 1
protuberate *vb syn* see BULGE
proud *adj 1* showing or feeling superiority
toward others < a woman who was too
proud to do her share of menial tasks >

syn arrogant, cavalier, disdainful, dismissive, haughty, high-and-mighty, hubristic,
huffy, insolent, lofty, lordly, orgulous,
overbearing, ‖pridy, proudhearted, supercilious, superior, toploftical, toplofty;
compare POMPOUS 1, VAIN 3
  rel contemptuous, scornful; misproud;
ostentatious, pretentious; bloated, important, pompous, self-important, stuffy,
wiggy; conceited, narcissistic, self-conceited, stuck-up, vain, vainglorious; domineering, high-handed, imperious, masterful
  con lowly, meek, modest, unassuming;
chagrined, mortified
  ant humble
  2 *syn* see SPLENDID 2
proudhearted *adj syn* see PROUD 1
prove *vb 1* to establish a point by appropriate objective means < gathered evidence that *proved* the need for better controls >
  syn demonstrate, test, try
  rel confirm, corroborate, substantiate,
verify; argue, attest, bespeak, betoken,
indicate
  ant disprove; refute
  2 *syn* see TRY 1
  3 *syn* see ESTABLISH 6
provenance *n syn* see SOURCE
provender *n syn* see FOOD 1
provenience *n syn* see SOURCE
prove out *vb syn* see SUCCEED 2
proverb *n syn* see SAYING
provide *vb syn* see GIVE 3
provide (for) *vb syn* see SUPPORT 3
providence *n 1 syn* see ECONOMY
  ant improvidence
  2 *syn* see PRUDENCE 1
  ant improvidence
provident *adj syn* see SPARING
  ant improvident
providential *adj syn* see LUCKY
  rel benignant, kind, kindly
province *n 1 syn* see FUNCTION 1
  rel calling, pursuit, work
  2 *syn* see FIELD
provincial *n syn* see RUSTIC
provincial *adj 1 syn* see RURAL
  2 *syn* see INSULAR
  rel bigoted, hidebound
  con cosmic, universal; progressive
  ant catholic
provision *n syn* see CONDITION 1
provisional *adj 1 syn* see CONDITIONAL 1
  rel temporary; contingent, dependent
  ant definitive
  2 *syn* see MAKESHIFT
provisionary *adj syn* see CONDITIONAL 1
provisions *n pl syn* see FOOD 1
proviso *n syn* see CONDITION 1
provisory *adj syn* see CONDITIONAL 1
provocation *n syn* see ANNOYANCE 1
provocative *n syn* see STIMULUS
provoke *vb 1 syn* see IRRITATE
  rel insult, outrage
  ant gratify
  2 *syn* see ANNOY 1
  rel anger, incense, madden
  3 *syn* see INCITE
  rel perturb, upset
  4 to lead one into doing or feeling or to
produce by so leading a person < was
provoked into finding a solution to the

problem > < this foolish answer *provoked* an outburst of rage >
syn excite, galvanize, innervate, innerve, motivate, move, pique, prime, quicken, rouse, ||roust, stimulate, suscitate; *compare* FIRE 2, STIR 1
rel arouse, awaken, bestir, build up, challenge, kindle, rally, stir, wake, waken, whet; animate, exalt, fire, inform, inspire; electrify, enthuse, thrill; titillate, titivate
idiom bring (one) to one's feet
con calm, relax, soothe
5 *syn* see GENERATE 3

provoking *n syn* see ANNOYANCE 1

prowess *n* 1 *syn* see HEROISM
2 *syn* see ADDRESS 1

proximate *adj* 1 *syn* see CLOSE 6
2 *syn* see IMMINENT 1
3 *syn* see RUDE 3
ant exact

proximity *n* the quality or state of being near < the two houses are in close *proximity* >
syn appropinquity, contiguity, contiguousness, immediacy, propinquity
rel togetherness; closeness, nearness; adjacency, juxtaposition
con farness, remoteness
ant distance

proxy *n syn* see AGENT 2

prude *n* a person who is excessively or priggishly attentive to propriety or decorum < in that narrow atmosphere she hardened into a rigid, inhibited, censorious person—a thorough *prude* >
syn bluenose, comstock, goody-goody, Grundy, Mrs. Grundy, nice Nelly, prig, puritan, ||wowser
rel spoilsport, stick-in-the-mud, wet blanket; fuddy-duddy, old fogy, stuffed shirt; fussbudget, old maid
con freethinker, latitudinarian, libertarian

prudence *n* 1 a quality in a person that allows him to choose the sensible course < displayed *prudence* in setting up his business >
syn canniness, caution, discreetness, discretion, foresight, forethought, precaution, providence; *compare* WIT 3
rel acumen, astucity, astuteness, clearsightedness, discrimination, keenness, penetration, percipience, perspicacity, shrewdness, wit; insight, sagaciousness, sagacity, sageness, sapience, wisdom; advisableness, expediency; calculation, circumspection
con indiscretion, unreasonableness, unwiseness
ant imprudence
2 *syn* see ECONOMY

prudent *adj* 1 *syn* see WISE 2
ant imprudent
2 *syn* see EXPEDIENT

prudish *adj syn* see PRIM 1
rel strict; austere, severe, stern

prune *n syn* see DUNCE

prune *vb syn* see CUT 6
rel brash, lop; thin; eliminate, exclude

prurience *n syn* see LUST 2
pruriency *n syn* see LUST 2
prurient *adj syn* see LUSTFUL 2
rel bawdy, erotic, lewd; sensual

pry *vb syn* see SNOOP
idiom nose into

pry *vb* to raise, move, or pull apart with or as if with a pry < *pry* up a floorboard >
syn jimmy, lever, prize
rel elevate, hoist, lift, pick up, raise, rear, take up, uphold, uplift, upraise, uprear; turn, twist; disengage, disjoin, divide, separate

prying *adj syn* see CURIOUS 2
rel obtrusive, officious

psalm *vb syn* see PRAISE 2

psalmody *vb syn* see PRAISE 2

pseudo *adj syn* see COUNTERFEIT
rel wrong

pseudonym *n* a fictitious or assumed name < used a *pseudonym* in many of his adventures >
syn alias, anonym, nom de guerre
rel ananym; nom de plume, pen name; stage name; incognito

psychal *adj syn* see PSYCHIC 1

psyche *n syn* see SOUL 1

psychic *adj* 1 sensitive to nonphysical forces and influences < because he foretold many things correctly, people regarded him as *psychic* >
syn psychal, psychical, supersensible, supersensory
rel telepathic; spiritual; impressible, impressionable, responsive, sensible, sensile, sensitive, sentient, susceptible, susceptive
2 *syn* see MENTAL 1

psychical *adj* 1 *syn* see PSYCHIC 1
2 *syn* see MENTAL 1

psychological *adj syn* see MENTAL 1

psychopathy *n syn* see INSANITY 1

pub *n syn* see BAR 5

puberty *n syn* see YOUTH 1

pubescence *n syn* see YOUTH 1

public *adj* 1 of, relating to, or affecting the people as an organized community < *public* affairs >
syn civic, civil, national
rel government, governmental; community; state; municipal, urban
2 *syn* see OPEN 4
rel common, general, universal
con private
3 *syn* see COMMON 1
con private
4 held by or applicable to the majority of the people < *public* opinion >
syn general, popular, vulgar
rel prevalent, usual, widespread
ant private

public *n* 1 *syn* see SOCIETY 3
2 *syn* see FOLLOWING 2
rel hangers-on, suite

||**publican** *n syn* see SALOONKEEPER

publication *n syn* see DECLARATION 1
rel dissemination

public house *n* 1 *syn* see HOTEL
||2 *syn* see BAR 5

publicity *n* information with news value issued to gain public attention or support < $100,000 was allocated for new-product *publicity* >
syn advertising, buildup, press-agentry, promotion, puffery

---

syn synonym(s)   *rel* related word(s)
ant antonym(s)   *con* contrasted word(s)
idiom idiomatic equivalent(s)
|| use limited; if in doubt, see a dictionary

rel broadcasting, promulgation, skywriting; réclame; announcement, write-up; blurb, commercial, plug, puff; ballyhoo, hoopla; propaganda; hard sell

publicize *vb* to give publicity to < *publicize* a new book >
syn advertise, build up, cry, press-agent, puff; *compare* PROMOTE 3
rel announce, broadcast, headline, promulgate, skywrite; advance, boost, plug, push; extol; bruit, tout, trumpet; propagandize
idiom bring into the limelight, throw the spotlight on

publish *vb* 1 *syn* see DECLARE 1
rel broach, express, utter, vent, ventilate
idiom bring to public notice, lay before the public, publish (*or* noise *or* spread) abroad, put forth
2 to produce for publication and allow to be distributed and sold < *published* a newspaper >
syn get out, issue, put out
rel produce; bring out; market; distribute

puckfist *n syn* see BRAGGART
puckish *adj syn* see PLAYFUL 1
‖**pudding** *n, usu* puddings *pl syn* see ENTRAILS
puddle *n syn* see POOL
puddle *vb syn* see FIDDLE 2
puddy *adj syn* see ROTUND 2
pudendum *n, usu* pudenda *pl syn* see GENITALIA
pudgy *adj syn* see ROTUND 2
rel ‖chuffy, ‖chumpy, squab, squdgy, ‖stuggy, stumpy, thick-bodied
puerile *adj syn* see CHILDISH
puff *vb* 1 *syn* see PANT 1
idiom huff and puff, pant and blow
2 *syn* see BOAST
3 *syn* see PUBLICIZE
puff *n* 1 *syn* see DRAW 1
rel inhalation, inhaling
2 *syn* see QUILT
3 a commendatory and often extravagant publicity notice or review < this book fails to deliver what the *puff* promises >
syn blurb, plug, puffing, write-up
rel boost, buildup, push; laudation, praise
puffery *n syn* see PUBLICITY
puffing *n syn* see PUFF 3
puffy *adj syn* see POMPOUS 1
‖**puggy** *adj syn* see SWEATY
pugilism *n syn* see BOXING
pugnacious *adj syn* see BELLIGERENT
rel pushing, pushy, self-assertive; defiant, rebellious; brawling
idiom itching for a fight, itching (*or* ready) to fight, ready to fight at the drop of a hat
con bland, easygoing, mild; calm, peaceful; quiet
ant pacific
pugnacity *n syn* see ATTACK 2
puissance *n syn* see POWER 4
rel clout, influence, sway
con powerlessness, weakness
ant impuissance
puissant *adj syn* see POWERFUL 1
rel influential; commanding, ruling
con ineffectual, inefficacious, powerless
ant impuissant
puke *n syn* see SNOT 1

pukka *adj syn* see AUTHENTIC 2
pulchritudinous *adj syn* see BEAUTIFUL
pule *vb syn* see WHIMPER
pull *vb* 1 *syn* see EXTRACT 1
2 to cause to move toward or after an applied force < *pull* a trunk across the floor >
syn drag, draw, haul, lug, tow, tug
rel strain; heave; jerk, wrench, yank; drive, impel, push, shove
3 *syn* see STRAIN 1
4 *syn* see ROW
idiom pull on the oar (*or* oars)
5 *syn* see COMMIT 2
idiom ‖go and do
6 *syn* see DON 2
7 *syn* see GET 1
pull *n* 1 *syn* see DRAW 1
2 the power or ability to secure special favor or partiality < had lots of *pull* with the government >
syn clout, ‖drag, in, influence; *compare* INFLUENCE 1
rel persuasion; wire-pulling
idiom backstairs influence
3 *syn* see ATTRACTION 1
pullback *n syn* see DIEHARD 1
pull down *vb syn* see DESTROY 1
pull in *vb* 1 *syn* see RESTRAIN 1
2 *syn* see ARREST 2
pull out *vb syn* see GO 2
ant pull in
pull through *vb syn* see SURVIVE 2
pullulate *vb syn* see TEEM
pull up *vb syn* see STOP 4
pulp *vb syn* see CRUSH 2
pulpitarian *n syn* see CLERGYMAN
pulpiteer *n syn* see CLERGYMAN
pulpiter *n syn* see CLERGYMAN
pulpous *adj syn* see SOFT 6
pulpy *adj syn* see SOFT 6
pulsate *vb* to course or move with or as if with rhythmic strokes < blood *pulsating* through his veins >
syn beat, palpitate, pulse, throb
rel fluctuate, oscillate, vibrate; pump; drum, pound, roar, thrum
pulse *vb syn* see PULSATE
pulverize *vb* 1 to reduce (as by crushing, beating, or grinding) to minute particles < *pulverized* the ore in a stamp mill >
syn bray, buck, comminute, contriturate, crush, powder, triturate; *compare* SHATTER 1
rel break up; abrade, grate, grind; crumble, crunch, mull; levigate; atomize, fragment, fragmentalize, fragmentize, micronize; beat, shatter, smash, smatter, splinter; flour, mill
2 *syn* see DESTROY 1
pulverized *adj syn* see FINE 2
rel pulverous, pulverulent; dusty, granular, splintery
ant unpulverized
pummel *vb syn* see BEAT 1
pump *vb syn* see DRAIN 1
pumpkin head *n syn* see DUNCE
‖**pumpknot** *n syn* see BUMP 2
pun *n* the humorous use of a word so as to suggest different meanings, or of words having the same or similar sound but different meanings < "mourning shall come with approaching day" is a *pun* >

syn calembour, paronomasia
rel double entendre
idiom play on words

punch *vb* **1** *syn* see POKE 1
rel hit, slap, strike
2 *syn* see PERFORATE

punch *n* **1** *syn* see CUFF
2 *syn* see POKE 1
3 *syn* see POINT 3
4 *syn* see VIGOR 2

punctilious *adj syn* see CAREFUL 2
rel conventional, formal, observant; over-conscientious, overscrupulous

punctual *adj* **1** *syn* see CAREFUL 2
ant unpunctual
2 marked by exact adherence to an appointed time <a *punctual* arrival>
syn prompt, timely
rel quick, ready
idiom on the dot, on time
con late, tardy
ant unpunctual

punctuate *vb* to mark or divide (written matter) with punctuation marks <*punctuated* the sentence>
syn point
rel divide, separate

puncture *n syn* see PRICK 1
rel perforation

puncture *vb* **1** *syn* see PERFORATE
rel riddle
2 *syn* see DISCREDIT 2
idiom shoot full of holes

pungent *adj* sharp and stimulating to the mind or senses <his *pungent* wit>
syn peppery, piquant, poignant, racy, snappy, spicy, zesty
rel acute, keen, salt, salty, sharp; biting, bitter, cutting, hot, incisive, trenchant; exciting, provocative, stimulating; rich
con banal, corny, dull, flat, hackneyed, insipid, old hat, platitudinous, prosaic, prosy, stale, stodgy, tasteless, unimaginative, uninteresting
ant bland

punish *vb* **1** to inflict a penalty on in requital for a wrongdoing <*punished* the child for misbehaving>
syn castigate, chasten, chastise, correct, discipline
rel criticize, reprove; amerce, fine, mulct, penalize; avenge, fix, revenge; lambaste, scourge
con overlook; absolve, acquit, exculpate, exonerate, vindicate; let off, release
ant excuse, pardon
2 *syn* see CONSUME 5

punishing *adj syn* see PUNITIVE

punishment *n* the act or an instance of punishing <a spanking was his *punishment*>
syn castigation, chastisement, correction, discipline, punition, rod
rel criticism, reproof; amercement, fine, mulct, penalty; avengement, revenge
idiom carrot-and-stick treatment, disciplinary action, dose of strap oil, what for
con overlooking; acquittal, exculpation, exoneration, vindication

punition *n syn* see PUNISHMENT
idiom punitive measures

punitive *adj* inflicting, involving, or constituting punishment <took *punitive* action against him>
syn castigating, disciplinary, punishing, punitory
rel correctional, penal

punitory *adj syn* see PUNITIVE

punk *n* **1** *syn* see NONSENSE 2
2 *syn* see NOVICE
3 *syn* see TOUGH

‖**punk** *adj syn* see BAD 1

puny *adj* **1** *syn* see PETTY 2
rel feeble, weak
2 *syn* see WEAK 1

pup *n syn* see TWERP

puppet *n syn* see TOOL 2
rel dupe; slave

puppy *n syn* see TWERP

purblind *adj* partly blind <*purblind* with cataracts>
syn dim-sighted, half-blind
rel myopic, nearsighted, shortsighted; dim; blind, dark, sightless

purchasable *adj* **1** capable of being bought <*purchasable* goods>
syn available, obtainable, on offer
rel marketable, salable
idiom on (*or* for) sale, on the market, to be had
con rare; unavailable, unobtainable
ant unpurchasable
2 *syn* see VENAL 1
rel undependable, unreliable; slippery, tricky; treacherous

purchase *vb syn* see BUY 1
idiom make a purchase
ant sell

purchaser *n* one to whom something is sold <instruction booklets for new-car *purchasers*>
syn buyer, emptor, vendee
rel marketer, shopper; client, customer, patron; consumer, user
con seller, vendor

pure *adj* **1** *syn* see STRAIGHT 3
ant impure
2 being such and no other <his solution of the problem was *pure* genius>
syn absolute, perfect, pure and simple, sheer, simple, unadulterated, unalloyed, undiluted, unmitigated, unmixed, unqualified; *compare* UTTER
rel complete, plenary, total; authentic, genuine; classic; out-and-out, plain, utter
con mixed, qualified; doubtful, dubious, questionable, uncertain
3 *syn* see UTTER
4 *syn* see GOOD 11
ant impure
5 *syn* see CHASTE
rel fresh, inviolate, unblighted, unprofaned
idiom as pure as the driven snow
con contaminated, dirty, sullied
ant immoral, impure

‖**pure** *adv syn* see VERY 1

pure and simple *adj syn* see PURE 2

pureblood *adj syn* see PUREBRED

purebred *adj* being of unmixed ancestry <a *purebred* collie>

---

syn synonym(s)   *rel* related word(s)
ant antonym(s)   *con* contrasted word(s)
idiom idiomatic equivalent(s)
‖ use limited; if in doubt, see a dictionary

syn full-blooded, pedigree, pedigreed, pureblood, thoroughbred
rel registered
con bastard, hybrid, lowbred, mixed
ant mongrel

‖**puredee** (or **pure–D**) *adj syn see* UTTER
purely *adv syn see* ALL 1
purgation *n syn see* PURIFICATION
purgative *adj* cleansing or purifying especially from sin <confession as a *purgative* ritual>
syn expiative, expiatory, expurgatorial, expurgatory, lustral, lustratory, propitiatory, purgatorial
purgatorial *adj syn see* PURGATIVE
‖**purgatory** *n syn see* SWAMP
purge *vb* 1 *syn see* DISABUSE
rel absolve, cleanse; clear, rid
2 *syn see* PURIFY 2
3 to get rid of often by exile, imprisonment, or murder <Stalin *purged* all the Party dissidents>
syn eliminate, liquidate, remove
rel debar, exclude, shut out; dismiss, eject, expel, oust; erase, expunge, wipe (out); exterminate
con rehabilitate; reinstate; repatriate; accept, bear (with), tolerate
ant depurge
purification *n* a freeing from something morally harmful, offensive, or sinful <sought *purification* through repentance>
syn catharsis, cleansing, expurgation, lustration, purgation
rel atonement, expiation; absolution, forgiveness; grace, redemption, salvation; rebirth, regeneration; sanctification
con contamination; defilement
purify *vb* 1 to free from material impurities or noxious matter <*purify* the water for drinking>
syn clarify, clean, cleanse, depurate
rel elutriate; filter; refine
con dirty, foul, soil
ant contaminate, pollute
2 to free from guilt or moral blemish (often ceremonially) <*purify* one's heart through confession>
syn cleanse, expurgate, lustrate, purge
rel atone, expiate; absolve, remit
con defile, sully, tarnish
purist *n* one who adheres strictly and often excessively to a tradition <*purists* who believe in prescriptive grammar>
syn precisian, precisionist, traditionalist
rel Atticist, classicist; bitter-ender, conservative, diehard, Puritan
con liberal, radical, young Turk
ant revisionist
puritan *n syn see* PRUDE
puritanical *adj syn see* PRIM 1
rel rigorous, strict; bigoted, hidebound, illiberal, intolerant, narrow, narrow-minded
con liberal, tolerant; modern
purl *vb syn see* SWIRL
‖**purl** *vb syn see* SPIN 1
purlieu *n* 1 *syn see* RESORT 2
2 **purlieus** *pl syn see* ENVIRONS 1
3 **purlieus** *pl syn see* ENVIRONS 2
purloin *vb syn see* STEAL 1
purloiner *n syn see* THIEF

purloining *n syn see* THEFT
purple *adj* 1 *syn see* RISQUÉ
2 *syn see* RHETORICAL
purport *n* 1 *syn see* MEANING 1
2 *syn see* TENOR 1
rel connotation; implication
3 *syn see* SUBSTANCE 2
purported *adj syn see* ALLEGED
rel postulated, presupposed; suppositional, suppositive; academic, speculative, theoretical; reputed, rumored; suspected
purportless *adj syn see* SENSELESS 5
purpose *n* 1 *syn see* INTENTION
rel destination, direction; aim, goal, mission, objective, point; ambition, aspiration; proposal, proposition
2 *syn see* USE 4
rel mission
purpose *vb syn see* INTEND 2
rel meditate, ponder; consider; conclude, decide, determine, resolve
purposedly *adv syn see* INTENTIONALLY
purposefulness *n syn see* DECISION 2
rel certainty, confidence, sureness
con indecision, irresoluteness, irresolution, vacillation, waffling, wavering, weakness; aimlessness, indirection
ant purposelessness
purposeless *adj* 1 *syn see* FECKLESS 1
rel unhelpful, unprofitable; purportless, senseless; nonsensical
con helpful, profitable
ant purposeful
2 *syn see* RANDOM
ant purposeful
purposely *adv syn see* INTENTIONALLY
rel expressly; explicitly
con unintentionally
ant accidentally
purposively *adv syn see* INTENTIONALLY
purposiveness *n syn see* DECISION 2
purse cutter *n syn see* PICKPOCKET
pursual *n syn see* PURSUIT 2
pursuance *n syn see* PURSUIT 2
pursue *vb* 1 *syn see* FOLLOW 2
rel persevere, persist; oppress, persecute; badger, bait, hound, ride
idiom go in pursuit (of)
2 *syn see* ADDRESS 8
pursuing *n syn see* PURSUIT 2
pursuit *n* 1 *syn see* WORK 1
2 a following with a view to reach, accomplish, or obtain <the *pursuit* of happiness>
syn pursual, pursuance, pursuing, quest, search, seeking
rel following; reaching; obtaining; accomplishing, accomplishment
idiom a going all out (after)
pursy *adj syn see* FAT 2
purview *n* 1 *syn see* RANGE 2
2 *syn see* KEN
push *vb* 1 to use force so as to cause to move ahead or aside <*push* a wheelbarrow across the yard>
syn drive, propel, shove, thrust
rel launch; impel, move; force, ram
con brake, check, stay
ant pull
2 to do, effect, or accomplish by forcing aside obstacles or opposition <*pushed* his way through the crowd> <*pushed* the measure through congress>

syn bulldoze, elbow, hustle, jostle, press, ‖shog, shoulder, shove
rel dig, nudge; hunch; drive, force, thrust; bump, butt, ram
con ease, facilitate, slide (by), slip (through); expedite, help (along)
3 *syn* see INCREASE 1
4 *syn* see PRESSURE
5 *syn* see PROMOTE 3
rel oversell
6 to engage in the illicit sale of (narcotics) < *pushing* drugs to teenagers >
syn peddle, shove
7 *syn* see PRESS 1
push *n* **1** *syn* see ENTERPRISE 4
2 *syn* see VIGOR 2
3 *syn* see STIMULUS
4 *syn* see CROWD 1
5 *syn* see SET 5
push around *vb* see BAIT 2
pushful *adj* **1** *syn* see AGGRESSIVE
2 *syn* see PRESUMPTUOUS
rel imposing, intrusive, obtruding, obtrusive, officious; assured, confident, self‑confident
pushing *adj* **1** *syn* see AGGRESSIVE
idiom ‖not backward in going forward
2 *syn* see PRESUMPTUOUS
push off *vb* *syn* see GO 2
push on *vb* *syn* see GO 1
pushover *n* *syn* see SNAP 1
pushy *adj* **1** *syn* see AGGRESSIVE
‖**2** *syn* see PRESUMPTUOUS
pusillanimous *adj* *syn* see COWARDLY
puss *n* *syn* see CHILD 1
‖**puss** *n* *syn* see FACE 1
pussyfoot *vb* **1** *syn* see SNEAK
2 *syn* see EQUIVOCATE 2
pustule *n* *syn* see ABSCESS
put *vb* **1** *syn* see SET 1
2 *syn* see FASTEN 3
3 *syn* see PROPOSE 1
4 *syn* see WORD
5 *syn* see TRANSLATE 1
6 *syn* see EXPRESS 2
7 *syn* see ESTIMATE 3
put (back) *vb* *syn* see RESTORE 5
put (on) *vb* *syn* see GAMBLE 1
put (on *or* **upon)** *vb* *syn* see LEVY
put *n* *syn* see DUNCE
put about *vb* *syn* see INCONVENIENCE
putative *adj* *syn* see SUPPOSED 1
put away *vb* **1** *syn* see DIVORCE 2
2 *syn* see CONSUME 5
3 *syn* see MURDER 1
4 *syn* see BURY 1
5 *syn* see KILL 1
put by *vb* *syn* see SAVE 4
put down *vb* **1** *syn* see CRUSH 5
2 *syn* see DEGRADE 1
3 *syn* see CONSUME 5
put in *vb* *syn* see PLANT 1
put off *vb* **1** *syn* see DELAY 2
idiom drag one's feet
2 *syn* see DEFER

idiom lay on the table, let the matter stand
3 *syn* see REMOVE 3
ant put on
put on *vb* **1** *syn* see DON 1
ant put off
2 *syn* see DON 2
rel affect, feign, sham, simulate; masquerade, pose
idiom make as if (*or* as though)
3 *syn* see ASSUME 4
idiom put on a (false) front, put on an act
4 *syn* see EMPLOY 2
5 *syn* see STAGE
put–on *adj* *syn* see ARTIFICIAL 3
rel mannered, posed; faked, sham
put–on *n* **1** *syn* see IMPOSTURE
2 *syn* see MASK 2
put out *vb* **1** *syn* see EXERT
2 *syn* see EXTINGUISH 1
3 *syn* see PUBLISH 2
4 *syn* see IRRITATE
5 *syn* see INCONVENIENCE
rel displease, dissatisfy; annoy, irritate
idiom put out of the way, put to it
put over *vb* *syn* see DEFER
putrefy *vb* *syn* see DECAY
putresce *vb* *syn* see DECAY
putrid *adj* **1** *syn* see BAD 5
2 *syn* see MALODOROUS 1
3 *syn* see VICIOUS 2
putter *vb* *syn* see FIDDLE 2
rel boondoggle; dawdle
‖**put to** *vb* *syn* see CLOSE 1
put together *vb* *syn* see MAKE 3
put up *vb* **1** *syn* see HARBOR 2
2 *syn* see BUILD 1
rel forge, make, put together, shape
3 *syn* see ERECT 3
4 *syn* see RAISE 9
rel elevate, escalate
‖**puxy** *n* *syn* see SWAMP
puzzle *vb* to baffle and disturb mentally < a persistent fever that *puzzled* her doctor >
syn befog, bewilder, ‖cap, confound, confuse, metagrobolize, perplex, pose, stumble; *compare* NONPLUS 1
rel baffle, foil, frustrate; befuddle, ‖bumfuzzle, fuddle; disconcert, distract, disturb, upset; addle, muddle; mystify; amaze, dumbfound, flabbergast
con enlighten, inform
puzzle *n* *syn* see MYSTERY
puzzlement *n* *syn* see MYSTERY
puzzle out *vb* *syn* see SOLVE 2
idiom find the key to, pick the lock
pygmy *n* *syn* see DWARF
ant giant
pygmy *adj* *syn* see TINY
pyramid *n* *syn* see PILE 1
Pyrrhonian *n* *syn* see SKEPTIC
Pyrrhonist *n* *syn* see SKEPTIC
pythonic *adj* *syn* see HUGE

---

syn synonym(s)   *rel* related word(s)
ant antonym(s)   *con* contrasted word(s)
idiom idiomatic equivalent(s)
‖ use limited; if in doubt, see a dictionary

quarrel 439

Q

quack *n syn* see CHARLATAN
rel counterfeiter, pretender, shammer, simulator
‖**quackle** *vb syn* see SUFFOCATE
quacksalver *n syn* see CHARLATAN
quackster *n syn* see CHARLATAN
quad *n syn* see COURT 1
quadrangle *n syn* see COURT 1
quadrate *adj syn* see SQUARE 1
quadrate *vb* 1 *syn* see AGREE 4
2 *syn* see ADAPT
quadratic *adj syn* see SQUARE 1
quadratical *adj syn* see SQUARE 1
quaesitum *n syn* see AMBITION 2
quaff *vb syn* see DRINK 1
quag *n syn* see SWAMP
quaggy *adj syn* see SOFT 6
quagmire *n* 1 *syn* see SWAMP
2 *syn* see PREDICAMENT
quail *n syn* see GIRL 1
quail *vb syn* see RECOIL
rel cower, cringe
quaint *adj syn* see STRANGE 4
rel droll, funny, laughable; antiquated, antique, archaic
‖**quaint** *vb syn* see INTRODUCE 4
quake *vb* 1 *syn* see SHAKE 2
rel fluctuate, waver
2 *syn* see SHAKE 1
quake *n syn* see EARTHQUAKE
‖**quaker** *n syn* see EARTHQUAKE
quaking *adj syn* see TREMULOUS
quaky *adj syn* see TREMULOUS
qualification *n syn* see ABILITY 1
qualified *adj* 1 *syn* see ABLE
rel disciplined, instructed, trained; catechized, examined, quizzed; proved, tested, tried
con incapable, incompetent, unequipped, unfit
ant disqualified, unqualified
2 not unlimited and complete <gave only a *qualified* endorsement to the project>
syn limited, modified, reserved
rel circumscribed, definite, determined, fixed, restricted; partial
con complete, entire, full, total, utter, whole; unlimited, unrestricted
ant absolute, absolute
qualifiedness *n syn* see ABILITY 1
qualify *vb* 1 *syn* see CHARACTERIZE 2
rel ascribe, assign, attribute, impute; predicate
2 *syn* see ENTITLE 2
quality *n* 1 something inherent and distinctive <learned the special *qualities* of the native herbs>
syn affection, attribute, character, characteristic, feature, mark, peculiarity, property, savor, trait, virtue; *compare* CHARACTERISTIC 1
rel individuality; affirmation, predication; element, factor, parameter
2 a usually high level of merit or superiority <merchandise of *quality*>

syn caliber, merit, stature, value, virtue, worth
rel arete, excellence, excellency, perfection, superbness, superiority
con inferiority, meanness, mediocrity, poorness; inadequacy; deficiency
3 degree of excellence <upgrading the *quality* of incoming students>
syn caliber, class, grade
rel capacity, character, footing, place, position, rank, situation, standing, state, station, status
4 *syn* see STATUS 1
5 *syn* see ARISTOCRACY
6 *syn* see EXCELLENCE
quality *adj syn* see EXCELLENT
qualm *n* a misgiving about what one is going to do <had *qualms* about the secret meeting>
syn compunction, conscience, demur, scruple, squeam
rel apprehension, foreboding, misgiving, presentiment; doubt, mistrust, suspicion, uncertainty; agitation, insecurity, perturbation; objection, remonstrance; reluctance, unwillingness; impatience, nervousness, unease, uneasiness
con aplomb, assurance, confidence, self-assurance, self-confidence, self-possession; certainty, certitude, conviction
qualmish *adj syn* see SQUEAMISH 1
qualmishness *n syn* see NAUSEA
qualmy *adj syn* see SQUEAMISH 1
quantity *n* 1 *syn* see BODY 5
2 **quantities** *pl syn* see SCAD
quantum *n* 1 *syn* see BODY 5
2 *syn* see RATION
quarrel *n* a usually verbal dispute marked by anger or discord <a *quarrel* over who would drive the car>
syn altercation, ‖barney, beef, bickering, brabble, brannigan, brawl, controversy, difficulty, dispute, dust, dustup, embroilment, falling-out, feud, fight, fracas, fuss, hassle, imbroglio, knock-down-and-dragout, miff, ‖prabble, ‖pribble, rhubarb, row, ruckus, run-in, set-to, spat, squabble, squall, tiff, to-and-fro, word(s), wrangle; *compare* BRAWL 2
rel battle royal, catfight; affray, bobbery, broil, donnybrook, fray, free-for-all, melee, ruction, rumpus, scrap, scrimmage, scuffle; conflict, contention, difference, discord, dissension, strife, variance; disagreement, misunderstanding
idiom ‖pribbles and prabbles
con accord, concord, harmony; agreement, likemindedness, understanding, unity
quarrel *vb* to contend noisily or captiously <with his belligerent personality he was always *quarreling* with someone>
syn altercate, bicker, brabble, brawl, ‖cast out, caterwaul, fall out, row, scrap, ‖spat, squabble, tiff, wrangle; *compare* ARGUE 2

rel differ, disaccord, dissent, divide, vary; bump, clash, collide, conflict, thwart; battle, contend, fight, war
idiom have words with, pull caps
con agree, coincide, concur

quarrelsome *adj* 1 *syn* see BELLIGERENT
rel adverse, antagonistic, counter; antipathetic, hostile, inimical, rancorous
idiom having a chip on one's shoulder
2 apt or disposed to quarrel < when he's in a bad mood he becomes so *quarrelsome* >
syn battlesome, brawling, brawlsome, brawly, scrappy; *compare* BELLIGERENT
rel argumentative; disputatious; cankered, crabbed, irascible, irritable
con conciliatory, propitiatory

quarry *n syn* see GAME 3
quarry *vb syn* see MINE
quarter *n* 1 one of four equal parts < ate one *quarter* of the pie >
syn fourth, quartern
rel quadrant
2 a division or part of a town or city < the market *quarter* in Paris >
syn district, precinct, section, sector
rel division, part; area; locality; barrio
quarter *vb* 1 *syn* see HARBOR 2
2 *syn* see BILLET 1
quarterage *n syn* see SHELTER 2
quarterback *vb syn* see SUPERVISE
quartern *n syn* see QUARTER 1
quarter-witted *adj syn* see RETARDED
quartet *n* a group consisting of four individuals < a singing *quartet* >
syn four, foursome, quartetto, quaternion, quatuor, tetrad
rel quadruplet
quartetto *n syn* see QUARTET
quash *vb* 1 *syn* see ANNUL 4
2 *syn* see ABOLISH 1
3 *syn* see CRUSH 5
quashing *n syn* see REPRESSION 1
‖**quat** *vb syn* see SQUAT
quaternion *n syn* see QUARTET
quatuor *n syn* see QUARTET
quaver *vb syn* see SHAKE 1
rel falter, hesitate, vacillate, waver
‖**quawk** *vb syn* see SQUALL 1
quay *n syn* see WHARF
‖**queak** *vb syn* see SQUEAK 1
quean *n syn* see PROSTITUTE
queasiness *n syn* see NAUSEA
queasy *adj* 1 *syn* see DOUBTFUL 1
2 *syn* see SQUEAMISH 1
queer *adj* 1 *syn* see STRANGE 4
rel doubtful, dubious, questionable; droll, funny, laughable
2 *syn* see OBSESSED
3 *syn* see HOMOSEXUAL
4 *syn* see SQUEAMISH 1
queer *n syn* see HOMOSEXUAL
‖**quelch** *vb syn* see SUPPRESS 2
quell *vb syn* see CRUSH 5
rel conquer, overcome, subjugate, vanquish
con abet, incite, instigate
ant foment

quench *vb* 1 *syn* see EXTINGUISH 1
2 *syn* see CRUSH 5
rel end, terminate
3 *syn* see DESTROY 1
4 to bring (as thirst) to an end with or as if with a refreshing drink < after being in the hot sun, he found it difficult to *quench* his thirst >
syn slake, ‖squench
rel appease, content, gratify, satisfy; sate, satiate; allay, alleviate, assuage, lighten, mitigate, relieve; decrease, diminish, lessen, reduce
quenching *n syn* see REPRESSION 1
quenchless *adj* 1 *syn* see INSATIABLE
2 *syn* see INDESTRUCTIBLE
querulent *adj syn* see IRRITABLE
querulential *adj syn* see IRRITABLE
querulous *adj syn* see IRRITABLE
rel blubbering, crying, wailing, weeping, whimpering; bemoaning, deploring, lamenting
query *n* 1 *syn* see INQUIRY 2
2 *syn* see UNCERTAINTY
query *vb syn* see ASK 1
quest *n* 1 *syn* see INQUIRY 1
2 *syn* see PURSUIT 2
quest *vb* 1 *syn* see HOWL 1
2 *syn* see SEEK 1
question *n* 1 *syn* see INQUIRY 2
2 *syn* see PROBLEM 2
3 *syn* see DEMUR 2
question *vb* 1 *syn* see ASK 1
2 to express doubt about < *questioned* his decision to take a new job >
syn challenge, dispute, doubt, mistrust
rel suspect, ‖suspicion; hesitate (over), puzzle (over), wonder (about)
questionable *adj* 1 *syn* see IMPROBABLE 1
ant unquestionable
2 *syn* see MOOT
rel refutable; equivocal, obscure, vague
con dependable, true, trustworthy, trusty; genuine, indubitable, real, undoubted, undubitable, veritable, very
ant authoritative; unquestionable, unquestioned
3 *syn* see UNRELIABLE 1
questioning *n syn* see INQUIRY 2
questioning *adj* 1 *syn* see INCREDULOUS
ant questionless, unquestioning
2 *syn* see INQUISITIVE 1
questionless *adj syn* see AUTHENTIC 2
queue *n syn* see LINE 5
quibble *vb* 1 to find fault with something usually on minor grounds < was a peevish critic, always ready to *quibble* >
syn cavil, chicane, hypercriticize
rel carp, criticize
idiom split hairs
con applaud, commend, compliment, recommend; approve, endorse, sanction
2 *syn* see ARGUE 2
quick *adj* 1 *syn* see FAST 3
rel agile, brisk, nimble; abrupt, impetuous
idiom quick on the trigger
con dilatory, laggard, leisurely, slow, unhasty, unhurried; comatose
ant sluggish
2 able to respond without delay or hesitation or indicative of such ability < very *quick* in perception > < his *quick* eye spotted the trouble >

---

syn synonym(s)   *rel* related word(s)
ant antonym(s)   *con* contrasted word(s)
idiom idiomatic equivalent(s)
‖ use limited; if in doubt, see a dictionary

syn apt, prompt, ready; *compare* INSTAN-
TANEOUS

rel clever, intelligent, quick-witted, smart;
adroit, deft, dexterous; acute, keen, sharp;
able, capable, competent, effective, effectual

con comatose, lethargic, logy, poky, torpid; crass, dense, dull, dumb, stupid

ant slow; sluggish

3 *syn* see WISE 4

quick *adv syn* see FAST 2

quick *n syn* see CENTER 3

quicken *vb* **1** to make alive or lively
<warm spring days that *quicken* the
earth>

syn animate, enliven, liven, vivificate,
vivify

rel activate, energize, vitalize; arouse,
awaken, rouse, stir, wake

con blunt, dull; slow (down)

ant deaden

2 *syn* see PROVOKE 4

rel activate, actuate, motivate; goad, induce, spur

con check, halt, interrupt, stall, stay;
curb, inhibit, restrain

ant arrest

3 *syn* see SPEED 3

con bog (down), detain, embog, hang up,
mire

ant slacken

quickening *adj syn* see INVIGORATING

quick-lunch *n syn* see EATING HOUSE

quickly *adv syn* see FAST 2

quickness *n syn* see SPEED 2

ant slowness

quick-sighted *adj syn* see SHARP 4

quick-tempered *adj syn* see IRASCIBLE

quick-witted *adj* **1** *syn* see SHARP 4

2 *syn* see INTELLIGENT 2

rel apt, prompt, quick, ready

3 *syn* see WISE 4

rel acute, keen; facetious, humorous,
witty

ant slow-witted

quidnunc *n* **1** *syn* see BUSYBODY

2 *syn* see GOSSIP 1

quiescence *n syn* see ABEYANCE

quiescency *n syn* see ABEYANCE

quiescent *adj syn* see LATENT

rel calm, halcyon, hushed, placid, quiet,
still, stilly, untroubled

quiet *n* **1** a period of intensified silence
<the *quiet* before the storm>

syn calm, hush, lull

rel cessation, stop, termination

con din, hubbub, racket, uproar

2 *syn* see SILENCE 1

quiet *adj* **1** *syn* see CALM 1

con harsh, rough; disquieted, disturbed,
perturbed, upset

ant unquiet

2 *syn* see INACTIVE

3 *syn* see STILL 3

con blatant, boisterous, clamorous, strident, vociferous

4 not showy or obtrusive <always
dressed in *quiet* good taste>

syn inobtrusive, restrained, subdued,
tasteful, tasty, unobtrusive

rel homely, plain, simple, unpretentious

con blatant, brazen, flashy, garish, glaring, meretricious, tawdry, tinsel; elaborate

ant gaudy, loud

quiet *vb* **1** *syn* see SILENCE 1

rel abate, decrease, lessen

con excite, provoke, quicken, stimulate;
awaken, rally, stir

2 *syn* see CALM 1

con agitate; unhinge, untune

ant disquiet; excite

‖**quieten** *vb* **1** *syn* see SILENCE 1

2 *syn* see CALM 1

ant arouse; excite

quietive *adj syn* see SEDATIVE

quietness *n syn* see SILENCE 1

quietude *n syn* see SILENCE 1

quietus *n syn* see DEATH 1

‖**quiff** *n syn* see GIRL 1

quilt *n* a bed coverlet made of two layers
of cloth with a stuffing (as of cotton,
wool, or feathers) between <a warm *quilt*
is nice on a winter night>

syn ‖comfortable, comforter, pouf, puff

rel bedcover, bedspread, counterpane;
eiderdown

quinary *adj syn* see QUINTUPLE

quinta *n syn* see ESTATE 3

quintessence *n* **1** *syn* see ESSENCE 2

2 *syn* see APOTHEOSIS 1

quintessential *adj syn* see TYPICAL 1

quintessential *n syn* see ESSENCE 2

quintuple *adj* consisting of five <the
problem is viewed as having *quintuple*
aspects>

syn fivefold, quinary

rel quintuplicate

quip *n syn* see JOKE 1

quip (at) *vb syn* see SCOFF

quipster *n syn* see HUMORIST 2

quit *vb* **1** *syn* see CLEAR 5

2 *syn* see BEHAVE 1

3 *syn* see GO 2

4 *syn* see ABANDON 1

rel relinquish, resign, surrender

5 *syn* see STOP 3

6 to give up (as a habit, activity, or employment) especially with finality <*quit* a
job> <determined to *quit* smoking>

syn drop, leave, resign, terminate

rel retire, secede, withdraw

idiom draw one's time, give notice

con hire on, hire out

quite *adv* **1** *syn* see WELL 3

2 *syn* see ALTOGETHER 2

3 *syn* see ALL 1

4 *syn* see WELL 8

quittance *n syn* see REPARATION

quitter *n syn* see COWARD

quiver *n syn* see FLASH 1

quiver *vb syn* see SHAKE 1

rel beat, palpatate, pulsate, pulse, throb

quivering *adj syn* see TREMULOUS

quivery *adj syn* see TREMULOUS

quiz *n syn* see ECCENTRIC

quiz *vb* **1** *syn* see RIDICULE

2 *syn* see ASK 1

quizzical *adj syn* see INCREDULOUS

rel curious, inquisitive; probing, searching

‖**quod** *vb syn* see IMPRISON

quodlibetic *adj syn* see PEDANTIC

quondam *adj syn* see FORMER 2

quota *n* **1** *syn* see SHARE 1

2 *syn* see RATION

quota *vb syn* see APPORTION 2

quotidian *adj* **1** *syn* see DAILY

2 *syn* see ORDINARY 1

R

rabbity *adj syn* see SHY 1

rabble *n* 1 *syn* see MOB 2
2 the lowest class of people < the *rabble* of the city >
  syn canaille, doggery, dreg(s), hoi polloi, mass(es), mob, other half, polloi, proletariat, raff, ‖ragabash, ragtag, ragtag and bobtail, riffraff, roughscuff, rout, scum, scurf, tag and rag, tagrag and bobtail, trash, unwashed
  rel bourgeoisie, commonalty, many, people, populace, public, rank and file
  idiom the great unwashed, the scum of the earth, the submerged tenth
  con aristocracy, aristoi, elite, Four Hundred, gentility, nobility, upper class, upper crust, upper ten, upper ten thousand

rabble-rouser *n syn* see DEMAGOGUE

rabid *adj* 1 *syn* see FURIOUS 2
  rel crazed, crazy, demented, deranged, insane
2 *syn* see EXTREME 3
  rel enthusiastic, keen, obsessed, zealous

race *n syn* see CREEK 2

race *vb* 1 *syn* see RUSH 1
2 *syn* see COURSE

race *n syn* see FAMILY 1
  rel culture, nation, nationality, people; breed, type, variety

rachis *n syn* see SPINE

rachitic *adj syn* see RICKETY

racial *adj syn* see ETHNIC 2

racialism *n syn* see RACISM

racism *n* racial prejudice or discrimination < an act of overt *racism* >
  syn racialism
  rel discrimination, prejudice; illiberality, unfairness; bias, one-sidedness, partiality
  con broad-mindedness, liberalness, open-mindedness, tolerance; indifference, neutrality

rack *vb syn* see AFFLICT
  rel distress, pain; oppress, persecute

‖**rack back** *vb syn* see REPROVE

racket *n* 1 *syn* see DIN
  ‖2 *syn* see WORK 1

racketry *n syn* see DIN

rackety *adj* 1 *syn* see NOISY
2 *syn* see RICKETY

racking *adj syn* see EXCRUCIATING
  rel barbarous, cruel, ferocious, fierce, inhuman, savage

rack up *vb syn* see GAIN 1

racy *adj* 1 *syn* see PUNGENT
  rel fiery, gingery, mettlesome, spirited
  con banal, inane, jejune
2 *syn* see RISQUÉ

radiant *adj* 1 *syn* see BRIGHT 1

2 *syn* see GLAD 2

radiate *vb* 1 *syn* see SHINE 1
2 *syn* see SPREAD 1
  rel diverge

radical *adj* 1 *syn* see FUNDAMENTAL 1
  rel cardinal, essential, vital; constitutional, inherent, intrinsic
  ant superficial
2 *syn* see EXTREME 3
3 *syn* see LIBERAL 3

radical *n* one who favors rapid and sweeping changes < the *radicals* advocated overthrow of the government >
  syn extremist, revolutionary, revolutionist, ultraist; *compare* REACTIONARY
  rel liberal, progressive, reformer; agitator, insurgent, insurrectionist, rebel; anarchist, nihilist, red, subversive; out-and-outer; secessionist, separatist
  con bitter-ender, diehard, fogy, intransigent, mossback, reactionary, rightist, standpatter
  ant conservative

radius *n syn* see RANGE 2

raff *n syn* see RABBLE 2

raffish *adj syn* see WILD 7

rag *vb* 1 *syn* see SCOLD 1
2 *syn* see BANTER

‖**ragabash** *n syn* see RABBLE 2

ragamuffin *n* a person dressed in ragged clothing < a poor *ragamuffin* found begging >
  syn ragshag, scarecrow, tatterdemalion
  rel hobo, tramp, vagabond, vagrant; bum, loafer, wastrel; orphan, waif
  con buck, coxcomb, dandy, dude, fop

rage *n* 1 *syn* see ANGER
  rel acerbity, acrimony, asperity; frenzy, hysteria, mania; agitation, perturbation, upset
2 *syn* see FASHION 3
  rel caprice, conceit, crotchet, fancy, freak, vagary, whim

rage *vb syn* see ANGER 2

ragged *adj* torn or worn to tatters < never saw such *ragged* clothes >
  syn frayed, frazzled, shreddy, tattered
  rel rent, torn; battered, patched; dilapidated, dingy, faded, seedy, shabby, threadbare, worn-out

raging *adj syn* see WILD 6

rags *n pl* 1 poor or ragged clothing < a beggar in *rags* >
  syn ‖duds, tatters
  rel odds and ends, ribbons, shreds
2 *syn* see CLOTHES

ragshag *n syn* see RAGAMUFFIN

ragtag *n syn* see RABBLE 2

ragtag and bobtail *n syn* see RABBLE 2

raid *n* 1 *syn* see INVASION
  rel assault, onset, onslaught
2 a sudden attack by officers of the law < a *raid* on a gambling joint >
  syn ‖bust

---

syn synonym(s)   *rel* related word(s)
ant antonym(s)   *con* contrasted word(s)
idiom idiomatic equivalent(s)
‖ use limited; if in doubt, see a dictionary

raid *vb* **1** to make a raid on < Indians *raided* the settlers frequently >
syn foray, harass, harry, maraud
rel despoil, devastate, ravage, sack, spoliate, waste; loot, plunder, rifle, rob
2 *syn* see INVADE 1
raider *n syn* see MARAUDER
rail *n syn* see RAILING
rail *vb syn* see SCOLD 1
railing *n* a usually protective barrier consisting essentially of an elongated raised member < a staircase without a *railing* >
syn balustrade, banister, rail
raillery *n syn* see SATIRE
railroad station *n* a building containing accommodations for railroad passengers or freight < an old *railroad station* fallen into disrepair >
syn depot, station, station house
raiment *n syn* see CLOTHES
raiment *vb syn* see CLOTHE
rainbow *n syn* see PIPE DREAM
rainless *adj syn* see FAIR 2
ant rainy
raise *vb* **1** *syn* see LIFT 1
ant lower
2 *syn* see INCITE
3 *syn* see RESURRECT 1
4 *syn* see ERECT 3
5 *syn* see BUILD 1
6 *syn* see BRING UP 1
7 *syn* see GROW 1
8 *syn* see GATHER 6
9 to make larger in amount < *raised* the rent >
syn boost, hike, increase, jack (up), jump, put up, up
rel inflate
idiom send through the roof
con cut back, decrease, drop, lessen, reduce, roll back; minimize
ant lower
raise *n syn* see ADDITION
raised *adj* **1** *syn* see ELEVATED 1
2 *syn* see ERECT
rake *vb syn* see SCOUR 2
rakehell *adj syn* see WILD 7
raking *adj syn* see FAST 3
rakish *adj syn* see WILD 7
rally *vb* **1** *syn* see MOBILIZE 3
2 *syn* see STIR 1
rel fire; refresh, renew, restore
3 *syn* see RECOVER 2
rel brace (up), enliven, invigorate, perk (up), pick up
rally *vb syn* see RIDICULE
rel harass, harry, tantalize, tease, worry
rallying cry *n syn* see BATTLE CRY
ram *vb* **1** *syn* see THRUST 2
2 *syn* see CRAM 1
ramble *vb* **1** *syn* see WANDER 1
2 *syn* see DIGRESS 2
3 *syn* see SPRAWL 2
ramble *n syn* see WALK 1
rambler *n syn* see ROVER
rambunctious *adj syn* see TURBULENT 1
rampage *n syn* see SPREE 1
rel turmoil, uproar
rampant *adj* **1** *syn* see RANK 1
rel excessive, immoderate, inordinate
con moderate, temperate; checked, curbed, restrained
2 *syn* see PREVAILING

rampart *n syn* see BULWARK
rancid *adj syn* see MALODOROUS 1
rel ‖reasty; loathsome, repulsive
ant sweet
rancor *n syn* see ENMITY
rel bitterness, vindictiveness, virulence
rancorous *adj* **1** *syn* see MALICIOUS
2 *syn* see BITTER 3
rancorously *adv syn* see HARD 6
random *adj* lacking a definite plan, purpose, or pattern < a *random* choice >
syn aimless, designless, desultory, haphazard, hit-or-miss, indiscriminate, irregular, objectless, promiscuous, purposeless, slapdash, spot, unaimed, unconsidered, unplanned; *compare* ACCIDENTAL
rel contingent, fluky, fortuitous, incidental, odd
con arranged, organized, planned; methodical, systematic; deliberate, purposeful
ant purposive
random *adv syn* see ABOUT 4
ant orderly
randomly *adv syn* see ABOUT 4
ant orderly
randy *adj syn* see LICENTIOUS 2
range *vb* **1** *syn* see LINE 1
rel assort, classify, sort; bias, dispose, incline, predispose
2 *syn* see WANDER 1
3 to change or differ within limits < discounts *range* from 10% to 40% >
syn extend, go, run, vary
rel differ, fluctuate
range *n* **1** *syn* see HABITAT
2 sphere of action, expression, or influence < a political movement worldwide in its *range* and power >
syn ambit, circle, compass, confine(s), dimension(s), extension, extensity, extent, length, orbit, panorama, purview, radius, reach, realm, scope, stretch, sweep, width
rel area, space, span; domain, field, province, sphere, territory; amplitude, expanse, gamut, spread
3 *syn* see KEN
rel compass
idiom range of comprehension
4 *syn* see ORDER 4
rangy *adj syn* see GANGLING
ant compact
rank *adj* growing or increasing at an immoderate rate < *rank* weeds >
syn rampant
rel exuberant, lavish, lush, luxuriant, profuse
con scanty, sparse, thin
2 *syn* see OVERGROWN
3 *syn* see OBSCENE 2
4 *syn* see EGREGIOUS
rel conspicuous, noticeable, outstanding
5 *syn* see UTTER
6 *syn* see MALODOROUS 1
rel dank, humid; loathsome, repulsive
rank *n* **1** *syn* see LINE 5
2 *syn* see ESTATE 2
3 *syn* see STATUS 1
4 *syn* see STATUS 2
rank *vb* **1** *syn* see CLASS 2
rel arrange, order; assort, sort
2 *syn* see PRECEDE 1
rank and file *n syn* see COMMONALTY
rankle *vb* to produce continual or progressive anger, irritation, or bitterness < this

decision has long *rankled* as an act of injustice >
syn fester
rel annoy, bother, irk, vex; aggravate, exasperate, irritate; harass, obsess, plague, torment

ransack *vb* 1 *syn* see SCOUR 2
2 *syn* see ROB 1

ransom *vb* to liberate by paying a price < *ransomed* the king >
syn buy, redeem
rel recover, regain, retrieve; emancipate, free, liberate; extricate, release

rant *vb* 1 *syn* see ORATE
rel bluster, huff; rage, storm
2 *syn* see SCOLD 1

rant *n syn* see BOMBAST

ran–tan *n syn* see BINGE 1

rantankerous *adj* *syn* see CANTAN-KEROUS

rap *n* 1 *syn* see HIT 1
2 *syn* see REBUKE

rap *vb* 1 *syn* see TAP 1
2 *syn* see CRITICIZE

rap *n* 1 *syn* see CHAT 2
2 *syn* see CONFERENCE 1

rapacious *adj* 1 subsisting on prey < the *rapacious* wolf seized the lamb >
syn predacious, predative, predatorial, predatory, raptorial, vulturine, vulturish, vulturous
2 *syn* see VORACIOUS
rel ferocious, fierce

rapacity *n syn* see CUPIDITY
rel claim, demand, exaction

rape *vb* to have sexual intercourse with a woman without her consent and chiefly by force or deception < *rape* a young girl >
syn defile, deflorate, deflower, force, outrage, ravish, spoil, violate
rel debauch, devirginate, dishonor, ruin; betray, deceive, mislead; entice, lure, seduce, tempt; compromise, shame, wrong

rapid *adj syn* see FAST 3
rel agile, brisk, nimble; hurried, quickened
ant deliberate; leisurely

rapidity *n syn* see SPEED 2

rapidly *adv syn* see FAST 2

rapidness *n syn* see SPEED 2

‖rapper *n syn* see LIE

rapport *n syn* see HARMONY 3

rapprochement *n syn* see RECONCILIA-TION

rapscallion *n syn* see SCAMP

rap session *n syn* see CONFERENCE 2

rapt *adj syn* see INTENT

raptorial *adj syn* see RAPACIOUS 1

rapture *n syn* see ECSTASY

rare *adj* 1 *syn* see THIN 2
2 *syn* see CHOICE
rel excellent, fine, unique
3 *syn* see INFREQUENT
con accustomed, customary, habitual, usual, wonted; abounding, profuse
4 *syn* see EXCEPTIONAL 1

rarefied *adj syn* see THIN 2

rarefy *vb syn* see THIN 2

rarely *adv* 1 *syn* see SELDOM
2 *syn* see EXTRA

raring *adj syn* see EAGER

rascal *n* 1 *syn* see VILLAIN 1
2 *syn* see SCAMP

rash *adj* 1 acting, done, or expressed with undue haste or disregard for consequences < don't do anything *rash* > < that was a very *rash* statement >
syn brash, hasty, hotheaded, ill-advised, incautious, incogitant, inconsiderate, mad-brained, madcap, reckless, thoughtless, unadvised, unconsidered, unwary; compare CARELESS 1
rel abrupt, headlong, impetuous, precipitate, precipitous, sudden; foolhardy, foolish, impulsive, silly; careless, heedless, imprudent, indiscreet, injudicious, unthinking, unwise
con careful, cautious, chary, circumspect, wary; advised, considered, deliberate, designed, premeditated, studied; calm, cool, level-headed
ant calculating
2 *syn* see ADVENTUROUS

rash *n syn* see EPIDEMIC

rasp *vb syn* see SCRAPE 1

raspberry *n* a sound of disapproval, contempt, or derision < the crowd gave the umpire a *raspberry* >
syn bazoo, bird, boo, ‖Bronx cheer, catcall, hiss, hoot, pooh, pooh-pooh, ‖razz

rasping *adj syn* see HARSH 3

raspish *adj syn* see IRRITABLE

raspy *adj syn* see IRRITABLE

rat *n* 1 *syn* see RENEGADE
2 *syn* see SNOT 1

rat *vb* 1 *syn* see DEFECT
2 *syn* see INFORM 3

rate *vb syn* see SCOLD 1

rate *n* 1 *syn* see PRICE 1
2 *syn* see DEGREE 2

rate *vb* 1 *syn* see ESTIMATE 1
2 *syn* see CLASS 2
3 *syn* see EARN 2

rather *adv* 1 *syn* see ENOUGH 2
2 *syn* see INSTEAD
3 *syn* see SOMEWHAT 2
4 *syn* see WELL 8

ratherish *adv syn* see SOMEWHAT 2

ratify *vb* to make something legally valid or operative usually by formal approval or sanctioning < agreed to *ratify* the treaty >
syn confirm
rel accredit, authorize, commission, license; approve, endorse, sanction; authenticate, validate
con disown, reject, repudiate

ratio *n syn* see DEGREE 2

ratiocination *n* 1 *syn* see INFERENCE 1
ant intuition
2 *syn* see INFERENCE 2

ratiocinative *adj syn* see LOGICAL 2

ration *n* an amount allotted or made available especially from a limited supply < saved up their gasoline *ration* for a vacation trip >
syn allotment, allowance, apportionment, measure, meed, part, portion, quantum, quota, share; compare SHARE 1
rel assignment, consignment, distribution, division

---

syn synonym(s)   **rel** related word(s)
ant antonym(s)   **con** contrasted word(s)
idiom idiomatic equivalent(s)
‖ use limited; if in doubt, see a dictionary

ration *vb syn see* APPORTION 2
   rel allocate, allot, assign, mete (out)
rational *adj* agreeable to reason < offered a *rational* explanation>
   syn consequent, intelligent, logical, reasonable, sensible, sound
   rel calm, cool, level-headed, sober, stable; circumspect, judicious, prudent; lucid, normal, sane
   con rash, reckless, wild; groundless, illogical, unreasonable, unreasoning, unsound; crazy, demented, deranged
   ant animal, irrational; absurd
rationale *n syn see* EXPLANATION 2
rationalization *n syn see* EXPLANATION 2
rationalize *vb syn see* EXPLAIN 3
rattle *vb* 1 to make a rapid succession of short sharp noises < the window *rattled* in the wind>
   syn bicker, clack, clatter, clitter, ‖ruttle, shatter
   2 *syn see* CHAT 1
   3 *syn see* EMBARRASS
   rel addle, muddle; disturb, upset; bewilder, distract, perplex
rattlebrain *n syn see* SCATTERBRAIN
rattlebrained *adj syn see* GIDDY 1
rattlehead *n syn see* SCATTERBRAIN
rattletrap *n, usu* **rattletraps** *pl syn see* KNICKKNACK
rattletrap *adj syn see* RICKETY
rattling *adv syn see* VERY 1
ratty *adj syn see* IRASCIBLE
raucous *adj* 1 *syn see* HARSH 3
   rel brusque, gruff
   2 *syn see* TURBULENT 1
raunchy *adj* 1 *syn see* SLOVENLY 1
   2 *syn see* OBSCENE 2
ravage *vb* to lay waste (as by plundering or destroying) < the countryside was *ravaged* by the invading soldiers>
   syn deflower, depredate, desecrate, desolate, despoil, devast, devastate, devour, harry, havoc, pillage, sack, scourge, spoil, spoliate, strip, waste
   rel demolish, destroy, raze; loot, plunder, ransack, rob; ruin, wreck; encroach, invade, trespass; crush, overpower, overrun, overthrow, overwhelm
   idiom lay in ruins, lay waste
   con build, improve, rehabilitate
ravager *n syn see* MARAUDER
rave *vb* 1 *syn see* ORATE
   2 *syn see* ENTHUSE 2
ravel *vb syn see* COMPLICATE
raven *adj syn see* BLACK 1
ravening *adj syn see* VORACIOUS
ravenous *adj* 1 *syn see* VORACIOUS
   2 *syn see* HUNGRY
ravine *n* a small narrow steep-sided valley < followed the *ravine* high up into the hills>
   syn arroyo, chasm, cleft, clough, clove, gap, gorge, gulch
   rel cut, notch; defile, pass; abyss, gulf; crevasse, crevice, fissure; ‖dry wash, gully, gutter, ‖wash; canyon
raving *adj syn see* DELIRIOUS 1
ravish *vb* 1 *syn see* TRANSPORT 2
   2 *syn see* RAPE
ravisher *n syn see* MARAUDER
raw *adj* 1 not cooked < a *raw* egg>

   syn uncooked
   2 *syn see* UNREFINED 3
   3 *syn see* RUDE 1
   4 *syn see* NUDE 2
   5 *syn see* INEXPERIENCED
   rel untaught, untutored; unmatured, unripe
   con drilled, exercised; hardened; adult, grown-up, mature, matured, ripe
   6 *syn see* COARSE 3
   ‖7 *syn see* OBSCENE 2
rawboned *adj syn see* LEAN
rawhider *n syn see* SLAVE DRIVER
rawness *n syn see* INEXPERIENCE
ray *n* 1 one of the lines of light that appear to radiate from a bright or luminous object < the *rays* of the sun>
   syn beam, shaft, shoot
   rel raylet; pencil, streak, stream; moonbeam, sunbeam
   con gleam, glow, incandescence, shine
   2 *syn see* PARTICLE
raze *vb syn see* DESTROY 1
razor-sharp *adj syn see* SHARP 1
‖razz *n syn see* RASPBERRY
razz *vb* 1 *syn see* BANTER
   2 *syn see* RIDICULE
re *prep syn see* APROPOS
reach *vb* 1 *syn see* COME 1
   2 *syn see* GAIN 1
   3 to get into contact with especially intellectually or emotionally < there was no common ground on which she could *reach* him>
   syn approach
   rel affect, influence, sway; get, move, touch
   idiom establish contact with, find a common denominator, get through to, get to, have a meeting of minds, make advances to, make overtures to, make up to, reach (or share) common ground
   4 to communicate with < you can *reach* me at this number>
   syn contact, get
   idiom get in touch (or contact) with, get through to, get to, keep in touch (or contact) with, maintain connections with
   5 *syn see* PASS 9
   6 *syn see* RUN 8
reach *n* 1 *syn see* RANGE 2
   2 *syn see* KEN
react *vb* 1 *syn see* ACT 5
   2 *syn see* RETURN 1
reactionarist *n syn see* REACTIONARY
reactionary *adj syn see* CONSERVATIVE 1
reactionary *n* one who strongly resists change and often favors a prior condition < he is a staunch political *reactionary*>
   syn blimp, Bourbon, diehard, reactionarist, reactionist, royalist, ultraconservative, white; *compare* DIEHARD 1, RADICAL
   rel bitter-ender, conservative, intransigent, rightist, right-winger, standpatter; fogy, mossback
   con extremist, radical, revolutionary, revolutionist, ultraist; liberal, progressive, reformer
reactionist *n syn see* REACTIONARY
reactivate *vb syn see* REVIVE 3
read *vb syn see* SHOW 5
readily *adv syn see* EASILY 1

readiness *n* **1** *syn* see ALACRITY
2 *syn* see ADDRESS 1
3 the power of doing something without
evidence of effort < his *readiness* in repartee >
syn ease, facility
rel eloquence, fluency, volubility
con effort, exertions, pains, trouble

reading *n* *syn* see INTERPRETATION 2
readjust *vb* *syn* see REORGANIZE
ready *adj* **1** in a state of mental or physical
fitness for some experience or action
< *ready* to leave at a moment's notice >
syn prepared, set
rel adjusted, fit, qualified; primed
idiom all ready, all set, champing at the
bit
con unprepared, unqualified
ant unready
2 *syn* see WILLING 1
3 *syn* see QUICK 2
rel adept, expert, masterly, proficient,
skilled, skillful; active, dynamic, live
ready *vb* **1** *syn* see PREPARE 1
2 *syn* see GIRD 3
ready–made *adj* made for general sale or
use rather than prepared according to
individual specifications < *ready-made*
clothing >
syn bought, ‖boughten, ready-to-wear,
store, store-bought, ‖store-boughten
idiom off the rack
con custom-built, made-to-order, tailor=
made; handmade
ant custom-made
ready–to–wear *adj* *syn* see READY-MADE
ready–witted *adj* *syn* see INTELLIGENT 2
real *adj* **1** *syn* see AUTHENTIC 2
ant bogus
2 *syn* see GENUINE 3
3 corresponding to known facts < discovered the *real* reason for his hasty departure >
syn actual, indisputable, true, undeniable,
unfabled, veridical
rel being, existing, subsisting; certain,
inevitable, necessary; sound, valid, well=
grounded
idiom deniable, disputable, doubtful,
questionable; improbable, uncertain, unlikely
ant unreal; apparent; imaginary
realistic *adj* having no illusions and facing
reality squarely < he made a *realistic* appraisal of his chances for advancement >
syn down-to-earth, earthy, hard, hard=
boiled, hardheaded, matter-of-fact, practic,
practical, pragmatic, pragmatical, sober,
unfantastic, unidealistic, unromantic, unsentimental, utilitarian
rel rational, reasonable, sane, sensible,
sound; astute, prudent, shrewd; nonaca-
demic
con dreamy, fantastic, imaginative; idealistic, impractical, irrational, romantic,
visionary; theoretical
ant unrealistic; fanciful
reality *n* **1** *syn* see FACT 1

2 *syn* see ACTUALITY 2
realize *vb* **1** *syn* see GAIN 1
2 *syn* see THINK 1
really *adv* **1** *syn* see VERY 2
2 *syn* see WELL 7
realm *n* *syn* see RANGE 2
ream *n, usu* reams *pl syn* see SCAD
ream *vb* *syn* see CHEAT
‖**ream out** *vb* *syn* see SCOLD 1
reanimation *n* *syn* see REVIVAL
reap *vb* to do the work of collecting ripened crops < storms hampered his *reaping* >
syn garner, gather, harvest, ingather
rel glean
reaping *n* *syn* see HARVEST 1
reappearance *n* *syn* see RECURRENCE
rear *vb* **1** *syn* see BUILD 1
2 *syn* see ERECT 3
3 *syn* see LIFT 1
4 *syn* see BRING UP 1
rel foster, nurse, nurture; breed, propagate
rear *n* **1** *syn* see BACK 1
ant front
2 *syn* see BUTTOCKS
rear *adj* *syn* see POSTERIOR 2
ant front
rear end *n* *syn* see BUTTOCKS
rearmost *adj* *syn* see LAST
rearrange *vb* *syn* see REORGANIZE
rearward *n* *syn* see BACK 1
reason *n* **1** *syn* see EXPLANATION 2
2 *syn* see MOTIVE 1
3 a point or points that support something open to question < he soon gave
sensible *reasons* for the proposed change >
syn argument, ground, proof, wherefore,
why, whyfor
rel explanation, justification, rationalization
4 *syn* see CAUSE 1
5 the power of the mind by which man
attains truth or knowledge < we all must
use *reason* to solve this problem >
syn intellect, understanding
rel inference, ratiocination
6 *syn* see WIT 2
reason *vb* *syn* see THINK 5
reasonable *adj* **1** *syn* see CONSERVATIVE
2
2 *syn* see MODERATE 2
3 *syn* see CHEAP 1
ant extravagant
4 *syn* see RATIONAL
ant unreasonable
reasoned *adj* *syn* see DEDUCTIVE
reasonless *adj* **1** *syn* see INSANE 1
2 *syn* see ILLOGICAL
reassume *vb* *syn* see RESUME 1
reassure *vb* *syn* see DECREASE
rebate *vb* *syn* see DECREASE
rebate *n* *syn* see DEDUCTION 1
rebel *n* one who breaks with or opposes
constituted authority or the established
order < he is a *rebel* among educators >
syn anarch, anarchist, frondeur, insurgent, insurrectionist, malcontent, mutineer,
revolter
rel adversary, antagonist, opponent; assailant, attacker; extremist, radical, revolutionary, revolutionist, ultraist; debunker,
iconoclast
con authoritarian, intransigent, traditionalist; conservative, reactionary, white

---

syn synonym(s)   *rel* related word(s)
ant antonym(s)   *con* contrasted word(s)
idiom idiomatic equivalent(s)
‖ use limited; if in doubt, see a dictionary

rebel *vb syn* see REVOLT 1

rebellious *adj syn* see INSUBORDINATE
rel alienated, disaffected, estranged
con acquiescent, resigned; submissive

rebirth *n* 1 *syn* see CONVERSION 1
2 *syn* see REVIVAL

rebound *vb syn* see RECOVER 3

rebuff *vb syn* see FEND (off)
idiom give the cold shoulder

rebuild *vb syn* see MEND 2

rebuke *vb syn* see REPROVE

rebuke *n* an expression of strong disapproval <his bad behavior earned him a sharp *rebuke* >
syn admonishment, admonition, chiding, rap, reprimand, reproach, reproof, wig
rel dressing down, earful, lecture, lesson, scolding, talking-to, tongue-lashing
idiom a flea in one's ear, slap on the wrist
con applause, compliment, praise

rebut *vb* 1 *syn* see FEND (off)
2 *syn* see DISPROVE 1

recalcitrance *n syn* see DEFIANCE 2

recalcitrant *adj syn* see UNRULY 1
rel obstinate, stubborn; opposing, resisting, withstanding
ant amenable

recall *vb* 1 *syn* see REMEMBER
rel educe, elicit, evoke, extract; arouse, awaken, rouse, stir, waken
2 *syn* see ABJURE
3 *syn* see REVOKE 2
4 *syn* see RESTORE 1

recall *n syn* see MEMORY 2

recant *vb syn* see ABJURE

recapitulation *n syn* see SUMMARY

recede *vb* 1 to move backward <they will return after the floodwaters *recede* >
syn back, fall back, retract, retreat, retrocede, retrograde
rel regress, retrogress; depart, retire, withdraw
ant proceed; advance
2 *syn* see DECREASE

receipts *n pl syn* see REVENUE

receive *vb syn* see TAKE 10

received *adj syn* see ORTHODOX 1

recension *n syn* see REVISION 1

recent *adj* 1 *syn* see NEW 1
2 *syn* see MODERN 1

recently *adv syn* see NEW

receptive *adj* 1 open to ideas, impressions, or suggestions <he has a most *receptive* mind>
syn acceptant, acceptive, influenceable, persuadable, persuasible, responsive, suasible, swayable
rel open, open-minded; accessible, amenable, suggestible
con closed, closed-minded, inhospitable
ant unreceptive
2 *syn* see SYMPATHETIC 2

recess *vb syn* see ADJOURN 2

recession *n syn* see DEPRESSION 3

recherché *adj syn* see CHOICE
rel fresh, new, novel, original; exotic, uncommon, unusual
ant commonplace

recidivate *vb syn* see LAPSE

reciprocal *n syn* see MATE 5

reciprocate *vb* to give back, usually in kind or quantity <they were glad of the chance to *reciprocate* her kindness>

syn recompense, requite, retaliate, return
rel exchange, interchange; compensate, repay; retort, serve out
con accept, acquire, pocket, take

recital *n syn* see DESCRIPTION 2
rel discourse, story; enumeration

recite *vb syn* see RELATE 1
rel count, enumerate, number, tell

reckless *adj* 1 *syn* see ADVENTUROUS
rel desperate, hopeless
2 *syn* see RASH 1
ant calculating
3 *syn* see IRRESPONSIBLE

reckon *vb* 1 *syn* see CALCULATE
rel count, enumerate, number; add, cast, foot, sum, total
2 *syn* see CONSIDER 3
rel conjecture, guess, surmise
3 *syn* see ESTIMATE 3
‖4 *syn* see UNDERSTAND 3

reckon (on) *vb syn* see RELY (on *or* upon)

reckoning *n* 1 *syn* see BILL 1
2 *syn* see COMPUTATION

reclaim *vb syn* see RESTORE 3

recline *vb* 1 *syn* see SLANT 1
2 *syn* see REST 1

reclining *adj syn* see PRONE 4

recluse *adj syn* see SECLUDED

recluse *n* a person who leads a secluded or solitary life <a man who led the life of a *recluse* although living in a busy city>
syn hermit, solitary
rel anchorite, cenobite, eremite

reclusion *n syn* see SECLUSION

reclusive *adj syn* see ANTISOCIAL

recognition *n* 1 a learning process that relates a perception of something new to knowledge already possessed < *recognition* of a genuine diamond>
syn apperception, assimilation, identification
rel cognizance, realization; awareness, consciousness, sensibility
ant irrecognition
2 *syn* see CREDIT 4
ant unrecognition

recognize *vb* 1 to make out as or perceive to be something previously known <said they would *recognize* that face anywhere>
syn know
rel recall, recollect, remember
2 *syn* see IDENTIFY
3 *syn* see ACKNOWLEDGE 2
rel note, notice, observe, remark

recoil *vb* to draw back usually through fear or disgust < *recoiled* from the snake>
syn blanch, blench, flinch, quail, shrink, squinch, start, wince
rel falter, hesitate, waver; balk, shy, stick, stickle; dodge, duck, swerve; quake, shake, shudder, tremble; reel (back)
con advance, approach, near
ant confront; defy

re—collect *vb syn* see COMPOSE 4

recollect *vb syn* see REMEMBER
rel arouse, awaken, rally, rouse, stir, waken

recollection *n* 1 *syn* see MEMORY 2
2 *syn* see MEMORY 1

recommence *vb syn* see RESUME 2

recommend *vb* 1 *syn* see COMMEND 2
ant discommend
2 *syn* see COUNSEL

recommendation *n syn* see CREDENTIALS
rel approval, endorsement; commendation

recompense *vb* **1** *syn* see COMPENSATE 3
rel accord, award, grant, vouchsafe; balance, offset
2 *syn* see RECIPROCATE

recompense *n syn* see REPARATION

reconcile *vb* **1** *syn* see HARMONIZE 3
idiom bury the hatchet, make peace
ant estrange
2 *syn* see ADAPT

reconcilement *n syn* see RECONCILIATION

reconciliate *vb syn* see HARMONIZE 3

reconciliation *n* establishment of harmony < a *reconciliation* between the two countries was effected after ten years >
syn harmonizing, rapprochement, reconcilement
rel appeasement, conciliation, mollification, propitiation, satisfying
ant disagreement

recondite *adj* beyond the reach of the average intelligence < a *recondite* subject >
syn abstruse, acroamatic, deep, esoteric, heavy, hermetic, occult, orphic, profound, secret
rel erudite, learned, scholarly; academic, pedantic; difficult, hard; dark, enigmatic, obscure; anagogic, cabalistic, mystic, mystical; cryptic, runic, sibylline
con easy, facile, simple, straightforward

recondition *vb* **1** *syn* see RESTORE 3
2 *syn* see MEND 2

reconnoiter *vb syn* see SCOUT

reconsider *vb* to consider again with a view to changing or reversing < was asked to *reconsider* his decision >
syn reevaluate, reexamine, rethink, retreat, review, reweigh, think (over)
rel draw off; sleep (on); amend, correct, revise
idiom revise one's thoughts, think better of, view in a new light

reconsideration *n syn* see REVIEW 5

reconstitute *vb syn* see REORGANIZE

reconstruct *vb* **1** *syn* see MEND 2
2 *syn* see REORGANIZE
3 *syn* see RESTORE 3

record *vb syn* see SHOW 5

record *n syn* see DOCUMENT 2

recount *vb syn* see RELATE 1

recountal *n syn* see DESCRIPTION 2

recounting *n syn* see DESCRIPTION 2

recoup *vb syn* see RECOVER 1

recourse *n syn* see RESOURCE 3

recover *vb* **1** to obtain again < *recover* a lost watch >
syn get back, recoup, recruit, regain, repossess, retrieve
rel reclaim, redeem; reacquire, recapture, retake, rewin; reoccupy, resume; rediscover; balance, compensate, offset
con lose, mislay, misplace; forfeit, sacrifice
2 to regain health < *recovering* from a bout of pneumonia >

syn come round, rally
rel convalesce, improve, mend, recuperate; perk (up), revive; heal; refresh, rejuvenate, renew, restore
idiom get back in shape, get better, sit up and take nourishment, take a turn for the better
con decline, fail, weaken, worsen; die, expire, perish
3 to regain a former or normal state < the textile industry was *recovering* quickly from the depression >
syn bounce (back), rebound, snap back
rel rally, revive
con decline, fail
ant worsen
4 *syn* see RESTORE 3

recreancy *n syn* see DEFECTION

recreant *adj syn* see FAITHLESS

recreant *n syn* see RENEGADE

recreate *vb* **1** *syn* see AMUSE
rel refresh, rejuvenate, renew, restore
2 *syn* see PLAY 1

recreation *n* **1** *syn* see ENTERTAINMENT
rel ease, relaxation, repose; frolic, rollick; hilarity, jollity, mirth
2 *syn* see PLAY 1

recrementitious *adj* *syn* see SUPERFLUOUS

recrudesce *vb syn* see RETURN 1
rel refurbish, renew, renovate
con repress, suppress; cease, discontinue, stop

recruit *n syn* see NOVICE

recruit *vb syn* see RECOVER 1
rel refresh, renew, renovate, restore; mend, rebuild, repair

rectify *vb syn* see CORRECT 1
rel rebuild, repair

rectitude *n syn* see GOODNESS
rel conscientiousness, justness, scrupulousness

recumbent *adj syn* see PRONE 4
ant erect, upright

recuperate *vb syn* see IMPROVE 3

recur *vb* **1** *syn* see RETURN 1
rel iterate, reiterate, repeat
2 *syn* see RESORT 2

recurrence *n* a periodic or frequent returning < the *recurrence* of the nightmare upset him >
syn reappearance, reoccurrence, return
rel repetition, reproduction; crebrity, frequency

recurrent *adj syn* see INTERMITTENT

recurring *adj syn* see INTERMITTENT

Red *n syn* see COMMUNIST

red–blooded *adj syn* see VIGOROUS

redden *vb* **1** to make red < blood soon *reddened* the bandage >
syn incarnadine, rubify, rubric, ruby, rud, ruddle, ruddy
2 *syn* see BLUSH

redeem *vb* **1** *syn* see RANSOM
2 *syn* see FREE
3 *syn* see COMPENSATE 1

red–handed *adv* in the act of committing a misdeed < caught *red-handed* >
syn dead to rights, flagrante delicto
rel blatantly, openly

red–hot *adj* **1** *syn* see HOT 1
2 *syn* see IMPASSIONED
3 *syn* see UP-TO-DATE

---

syn synonym(s)   *rel* related word(s)
ant antonym(s)   *con* contrasted word(s)
idiom idiomatic equivalent(s)
‖ use limited; if in doubt, see a dictionary

red–letter adj syn see NOTEWORTHY

red–light district n a district characterized by brothels <sailors frequented the *red-light district*>
syn levee, stew(s), tenderloin
idiom street of fallen women

red–neck n syn see RUSTIC

redolence n syn see FRAGRANCE

redolent adj 1 syn see SWEET 2
2 syn see REMINISCENT

redouble vb syn see INTENSIFY

redoubt n syn see FORT

redoubtable adj 1 syn see FEARFUL 3
2 syn see FAMOUS 2

redound vb syn see CONTRIBUTE 2

redraft n syn see REVISION 1

redraft vb syn see REVISE

redraw vb syn see REVISE

redress vb 1 syn see AVENGE
2 syn see NEUTRALIZE

redress n syn see REPARATION
rel balancing, offsetting; retaliation, vengeance

reduce vb 1 syn see DECREASE
2 to decrease in amount <they decided to *reduce* prices to stimulate sales>
syn clip, cut, cut back, cut down, lower, mark down, pare, shave, slash
rel curtail, decrease, diminish, lessen; deflate, depreciate; scale (down), step down; roll back
con boost, hike, jack (up), jump, put up, raise, up
ant increase
3 syn see CONQUER 1
rel cripple, disable, enfeeble, undermine, weaken; debase, degrade, humble, humiliate
4 syn see DEGRADE 1
ant advance
5 to lose body weight especially by dieting <ate no cake while *reducing*>
syn slenderize, slim (down)
rel bant, diet
idiom lose flesh, take off weight
ant fatten

reduction n 1 syn see DEDUCTION 1
2 syn see DEMOTION

redundancy n syn see VERBIAGE 1
rel flatulence, inflatedness, inflation, tumidity, turgidity

redundant adj syn see WORDY
rel extra, spare, superfluous, supernumerary, surplus; iterating, reiterating, repetitious
ant concise

reduplicate vb syn see COPY

reduplication n syn see REPRODUCTION

reedy adj syn see THIN 1

reek vb syn see SMELL 3

reeking adj syn see MALODOROUS 1

reeky adj syn see MALODOROUS 1

reel vb 1 syn see SPIN 2
2 to move uncertainly or uncontrollably (as in intoxication) <*reeled* down the street>
syn stagger, titubate, totter, wheel
rel careen, lurch, ‖swaver, sway, swing, weave, wobble; falter, ‖stammer, stumble, teeter, topple; bob, waver

reestablish vb syn see RESTORE 1

reevaluate vb syn see RECONSIDER

reexamination n syn see REVIEW 5

reexamine vb syn see RECONSIDER

refashion vb syn see CHANGE 1

refection n syn see MEAL

refer vb 1 syn see ASCRIBE
2 syn see SUBMIT 2
3 to call or direct attention to something <no one *referred* to his recent divorce>
syn advert, allude, bring up, point (out)
rel insert, interpolate, introduce; cite, quote; instance, mention, name, specify; glance, touch
idiom make an allusion to
4 syn see RESORT 2
rel advise, commune, confer, consult

referee n syn see JUDGE 1

referee vb syn see JUDGE 1

reference n syn see CREDENTIALS

refine vb syn see POLISH 2

refined adj 1 syn see GENTEEL 1
ant earthy
2 syn see FINE 1

refinement n syn see CULTURE
rel finish, suavity, urbanity; civility, courtesy, politeness; dignity, elegance, grace
ant vulgarity

reflect vb 1 to reproduce or show as a mirror does <the trees on the shore were *reflected* in the water>
syn glass, image, mirror
rel repeat, reproduce
2 syn see THINK 5
rel study, weigh

reflecting adj syn see THOUGHTFUL 1

reflection n 1 syn see ANIMADVERSION
rel assault, attack, onset, onslaught; depreciation, derogation, disparagement
2 syn see THOUGHT 1

reflective adj syn see THOUGHTFUL 1

reformatory n syn see JAIL

refractory adj syn see OBSTINATE
ant malleable

refrain vb 1 to hold oneself back from doing or indulging in something <*refrained* from speaking out of turn>
syn abstain, forbear, keep, withhold
rel arrest, check, halt, interrupt, stop; curb, inhibit, restrain
2 syn see DENY 3

refresh vb syn see RENEW 1
rel animate, enliven, quicken, vivify; recover, recruit, regain; amuse, divert, recreate
con exhaust, tire
ant addle; jade

refreshed adj made or become fresh <awoke a *refreshed* man>
syn new, regenerated, reinvigorated, renewed, revived
rel recreated, renovated; animated, exhilarated, invigorated, stimulated
con exhausted, fagged, fatigued, jaded, tired, tuckered, wearied, worn-down, worn-out

refuge n 1 the state of being covered or protected <exiles seeking *refuge* in neutral countries>
syn asylum, harborage, sanctuary, shelter; *compare* SHELTER 1
rel protection, shield; immunity
con exposure, liability, openness; vulnerability
2 syn see SHELTER 1
3 syn see RESOURCE 3

refugee *n* one who flees for safety < the villagers fed and housed the *refugees* from the bombed city >
  syn displaced person, DP, émigré, evacuee, fugitive
  rel exile; emigrant, expatriate
  idiom stateless person

refulgent *adj syn* see BRIGHT 1

refurbish *vb syn* see RENEW 1

refusal *n syn* see DENIAL 1

refuse *vb* 1 *syn* see DECLINE 4
  2 *syn* see DENY 2

refuse *n* matter that is regarded as worthless and fit only for throwing away < heaps of *refuse* left by the former tenant >
  syn ‖collateral, debris, dreck, ‖dust, garbage, junk, kelter, litter, ‖muck, ‖mullock, offal, outsweepings, ‖pelf, riffraff, rubbish, ‖sculch, spilth, sweepings, swill, trash, waste
  rel dump, dustheap; rejectamenta, scraps; lumber; offscouring(s)

refute *vb syn* see DISPROVE 1

regain *vb syn* see RECOVER 1
  rel achieve, attain, compass, gain, reach; reclaim, redeem, save; renew, restore

regal *adj syn* see KINGLY
  rel august, imposing, magnificent, stately; glorious, resplendent, splendid, sublime

regale *n syn* see DINNER

regalia *n pl syn* see FINERY 1

regard *n* 1 *syn* see NOTICE 1
  2 *syn* see CONSIDERATION 3
    ant disregard
  3 *syn* see INTEREST 3
  4 a feeling of deferential approval and liking < held in high *regard* by his neighbors >
    syn account, admiration, consideration, esteem, estimation, favor, respect
    rel deference, homage, honor, reverence; appreciation, cherishing, prizing, valuing; approbation, approval, satisfaction
    con deprecation, disapproval; disfavor, disgust, dislike, distaste; contempt, disdain, scorn; detestation, hate, hatred
    ant despite
  5 *syn* see CARE 4

regard *vb* 1 *syn* see ADMIRE 2
    con reject, repudiate, scorn
    ant despise
  2 *syn* see CONSIDER 3
    rel assay, assess, estimate, rate, value

regardful *adj* 1 *syn* see ATTENTIVE 1
  2 *syn* see MINDFUL 2
  3 *syn* see RESPECTFUL

regarding *prep syn* see APROPOS

regardless *adj syn* see NEGLIGENT

regardless of *prep syn* see AGAINST 4

regenerated *adj syn* see REFRESHED

region *n* 1 *syn* see AREA 1
  rel neighborhood, vicinity; division, part, section, sector
  2 *syn* see FIELD

register *n syn* see LIST

register *vb* 1 *syn* see ENROLL 1
  2 *syn* see SHOW 5

regnant *adj* 1 *syn* see DOMINANT 1
  2 *syn* see PREVAILING

regress *vb syn* see REVERT 2

regret *vb* to be very sorry for < *regrets* his mistakes > < *regret* the problems facing minorities >
  syn deplore, repent, rue
  rel bemoan, bewail, lament; grieve, mourn, sorrow; deprecate, disapprove

regret *n* 1 *syn* see SORROW
  rel compunction, contrition, penitence, remorse, repentance; demur, qualm, scruple
  2 **regrets** *pl syn* see APOLOGY 2

regretful *adj syn* see REMORSEFUL

regretless *adj syn* see REMORSELESS

regrettable *adj syn* see DEPLORABLE

regular *adj* 1 *syn* see GENERAL 1
  rel customary, ordinary
  ant irregular
  2 *syn* see ORDERLY 1
  rel fixed, set, settled; constant, equable, even, steady, uniform
  ant irregular; sporadic
  3 *syn* see UTTER

regulate *vb syn* see ADJUST 2
  rel arrange, methodize, order, organize, systematize; moderate, temper

regulation *n syn* see LAW 1

rehabilitate *vb syn* see RESTORE 3

rehearse *vb* 1 *syn* see RELATE 1
  rel iterate, reiterate, repeat
  2 *syn* see EXERCISE 3
  rel run through

reify *vb syn* see MATERIALIZE 2

reign *vb* 1 *syn* see GOVERN 1
  idiom sit on the throne
  2 *syn* see RULE 2

reimburse *vb syn* see COMPENSATE 3
  rel recover; balance, compensate, offset
  con default, dishonor, repudiate; welsh

rein *vb syn* see COMPOSE 4

reinforce *vb syn* see STRENGTHEN 2
  rel augment, enlarge, increase, multiply; bolster, buttress, pillar, prop, sustain
  ant undermine

reinstate *vb* 1 *syn* see RESTORE 5
  2 *syn* see RESTORE 1

reintroduce *vb syn* see RESTORE 1

reinvigorated *adj syn* see REFRESHED

reissue *n syn* see EDITION

reiterate *vb syn* see REPEAT

reject *vb* 1 *syn* see DECLINE 4
  rel debar, eliminate, exclude, shut out
  ant accept; choose, select
  2 *syn* see DISCARD

rejection *n syn* see DENIAL 1

rejoin *vb syn* see ANSWER 1

rejoinder *n syn* see ANSWER 1

rejuvenate *vb* 1 *syn* see RENEW 1
  2 *syn* see RESTORE 3

rekindle *vb syn* see REVIVE 3

relapse *n syn* see LAPSE 2

relapse *vb syn* see LAPSE

relate *vb* 1 to tell orally or in writing the details or circumstances of a situation < *related* the story of his life >
  syn describe, narrate, recite, recount, rehearse, report, state
  rel disclose, divulge, reveal, tell; detail, itemize, particularize; depict, express, render; pronounce
  idiom make public

---

syn synonym(s)   *rel* related word(s)
ant antonym(s)   *con* contrasted word(s)
idiom idiomatic equivalent(s)
‖ use limited; if in doubt, see a dictionary

2 *syn* see JOIN 1

rel ascribe, assign, credit, impute, refer

3 *syn* see BEAR (on *or* upon)

related *adj* connected by or as if by family ties < persons *related* in the first degree > < physics and mathematics are closely *related* >

syn affiliated, agnate, akin, allied, cognate, connate, connatural, consanguine, incident, kindred

rel associated, connected; complementary, convertible, correlative, corresponding, reciprocal; alike, analogous, identical; germane, pertinent, relevant

con different, dissimilar, divergent, unconnected, unlike

ant unrelated

relation *n* *syn* see RELATIVE

relative *n* a person connected with another by blood < all of his *relatives* live out of state >

syn kin, kinsman, kinswoman, relation

rel brother, half brother, half sister, sib, sibling, sister; father, mother, parent; child, daughter, son; grandfather, grandmother, grandparent; grandchild, granddaughter, grandson; aunt, half aunt, half uncle, uncle; half nephew, half niece, nephew, niece; cousin, cross-cousin, half cousin, ortho-cousin; agnate, cognate

relative *adj* 1 *syn* see DEPENDENT 1

2 *syn* see COMPARATIVE

relax *vb* 1 *syn* see LOOSE 5

2 to become less tense or reserved < couldn't *relax* in crowds >

syn ease off, loosen up, unbend, unlax, unwind

rel calm (down), collect (oneself), compose (oneself), cool (off), simmer down

idiom be at ease, breathe easily, feel at home, make oneself at home

con rack (oneself), tense (up)

3 *syn* see REST 2

relaxation *n* *syn* see REST 1

rel amusement, diversion, recreation; alleviation, assuagement, mitigation, relief

ant tension

relaxed *adj* 1 *syn* see LOOSE 1

rel flexuous, sinuous; gentle, lenient, mild, soft

ant stiff

2 *syn* see EASYGOING 3

con ascetic, austere, severe, stern

ant tense

release *vb* 1 *syn* see FREE

rel acquit, exculpate, exonerate; relinquish, resign, surrender, yield

idiom cast loose, set at large

ant detain

2 *syn* see EMIT 2

3 *syn* see TAKE OUT (on)

ant check

relegate *vb* 1 *syn* see BANISH

2 *syn* see COMMIT 1

rel accredit, charge, credit, refer

relegation *n* 1 *syn* see EXILE 1

2 *syn* see DISPOSAL 2

relent *vb* *syn* see ABATE 4

relentless *adj* 1 *syn* see GRIM 3

rel rigorous, strict, stringent; cruel, ferocious, fierce, inhuman

con submissive, yielding

2 *syn* see INFLEXIBLE 2

relevance *n* *syn* see USE 3

relevant *adj* relating to or bearing upon the matter in hand < *relevant* testimony >

syn ad rem, applicable, applicative, applicatory, apposite, apropos, germane, material, pertinent, pointful

rel allied, cognate, related; appropriate, apt, fit, fitting, proper, suitable; important, significant, weighty; admissible, allowable

idiom in point, in question, to the point

con impertinent, inadmissible, inapplicable, inapposite, inappropriate; unallied, unassociated, unconnected, unrelated; alien, extrinsic, foreign

ant irrelevant; extraneous

reliable *adj* 1 having qualities that merit confidence or trust < a *reliable* friend >

syn dependable, secure, tried, tried and true, trustworthy, trusty

rel safe; inerrable, inerrant, infallible, unerring; apposite, cogent, compelling, convincing, meaningful, significant, sound, telling, valid; attested, authenticated, circumstantiated, confirmed, proven, validated, verified; unimpeachable, unquestionable

con doubtful, dubious, problematic, questionable, suspect; independable, undependable, untried, untrustworthy; unattested, unauthenticated, unconfirmed, unvalidated

ant unreliable

2 *syn* see CERTAIN 3

reliance *n* *syn* see TRUST 1

reliant *adj* *syn* see DEPENDENT 1

relic *n* 1 *syn* see REMEMBRANCE 3

2 *syn* see VESTIGE 1

relief *n* 1 *syn* see EASE 3

rel lightening, softening; allayment, appeasement, assuagement, mollification

ant anguish

2 *syn* see HELP 1

relieve *vb* 1 to make less grievous or more tolerable < drugs that *relieve* pain >

syn allay, alleviate, assuage, ease, lighten, mitigate, mollify

rel comfort, console, solace; appease, palliate, relieve, soften; quiet, soothe, subdue; moderate, qualify, temper; decrease, diminish, lessen, reduce; aid, benefit, help

con aggravate, enhance, heighten, sharpen; reinforce

ant intensify

2 *syn* see ROB 1

3 to take the place of for a time < sent to *relieve* the sentry >

syn spell, take over

rel fill in, sub, substitute; replace, supply

4 *syn* see EXEMPT

religion *n* 1 a system of religious belief < tolerant of all *religions* >

syn creed, cult, faith, persuasion

rel belief, doctrine

2 the body of persons who accept a system of religious belief < all the members of my *religion* strive for tolerance >

syn church, communion, connection, creed, cult, denomination, faith, persuasion, sect

religious *adj* *syn* see DEVOUT

rel faithful, staunch, steadfast, true; ethical, moral, noble, righteous, virtuous; honest, honorable, just, upright

con godless, ungodly
ant irreligious

relinquish *vb* to let out of one's possession or control completely <few leaders willingly *relinquish* power>
syn abandon, cede, give up, hand over, lay down, leave, resign, surrender, ‖turn up, waive, yield; *compare* ABDICATE 1
rel lay aside; quit, throw up; abdicate, renounce; desert, forsake; abnegate, forbear, forgo, sacrifice; cast, discard, shed
ant keep

relish *n* 1 *syn* see TASTE 3
2 *syn* see TASTE 4
rel enjoying, liking, loving; bias, prejudice; flair, leaning, penchant, propensity
3 *syn* see ENJOYMENT 1

relish *vb* 1 *syn* see ENJOY 1
2 to eat or drink with pleasure <so hungry that he will *relish* plain food>
syn savor
3 *syn* see ADMIRE 1

relishing *adj syn* see PALATABLE
rel delighting, gratifying, pleasing, regaling, rejoicing, tickling
con banal, flat, inane, insipid, jejune

reluct *vb syn* see DISGUST

reluctant *adj syn* see DISINCLINED
rel calculating, cautious, chary, circumspect, wary

rely (on *or* upon) *vb* to place full confidence <*relied* on the doctor for an accurate diagnosis>
syn bank (on *or* upon), build (on), calculate (on *or* upon), count (on), depend (on *or* upon), ‖lot (on *or* upon), reckon (on), trust (in *or* to)
rel commit, confide, entrust; await, expect, hope, look
idiom put faith in, swear by
con distrust, mistrust

remain *vb syn* see STAY 2
ant depart

remainder *n* a remaining group, part, or trace <he spent the *remainder* of his life in prison>
syn balance, heel, leavings, remains, remanet, remnant, residual, residue, residuum, rest
rel excess, surplus; hangover, leftover

remains *n pl* 1 *syn* see REMAINDER
2 *syn* see CORPSE

remanet *n syn* see REMAINDER

remark *vb* 1 *syn* see SEE 1
2 to make observations and pass on one's judgment <he *remarked* on the lack of modern paintings at the gallery>
syn animadvert, comment, commentate, observe
rel mention, note

remark *n* 1 *syn* see NOTICE 1
2 an expression of opinion or judgment <a *remark* that led to a vehement argument>
syn comment, commentary, note, obiter dictum, observation
rel assertion, reflection, saying, statement, utterance; clarification, elucidation, explanation, explication, exposition, interpreta-

tion; annotation, exegesis, gloss, postil, scholium

remarkable *adj* 1 *syn* see NOTICEABLE
rel exceptional; important, momentous, significant, weighty; peculiar, singular, strange, unique
2 *syn* see EXCEPTIONAL 1

remarkably *adv syn* see VERY 1

remedial *adj syn* see CURATIVE

remedy *n* 1 something used for the treatment of disease <a cold *remedy*>
syn cure, medicament, medicant, medication, medicine, pharmacon, physic
rel biologic, drug, medicinal, pharmaceutical
2 something that corrects or counteracts <no easy *remedy* for discontent>
syn antidote, corrective, counteractant, counteractive, counteragent, countermeasure, counterstep, cure
rel cure-all, elixir, panacea; nostrum

remedy *vb syn* see CURE

remedying *adj syn* see CURATIVE

remember *vb* to bring an image or idea from the past into the mind <*remembers* the old days>
syn bethink, cite, ‖mind, recall, recollect, remind, reminisce, retain, retrospect, revive, revoke
rel look back (on *or* upon), think (of), treasure; relive; educe, elicit, evoke, extract
con disregard, ignore, neglect, overlook; disremember, lose
ant forget

remembrance *n* 1 *syn* see MEMORY 1
2 *syn* see MEMORY 2
3 something that serves to keep a person or thing in mind <wanted to give her a small *remembrance*>
syn keepsake, memento, memorial, relic, remembrancer, reminder, souvenir, token, trophy
rel favor, gift, present

remembrancer *n syn* see REMEMBRANCE 3

remind *vb syn* see REMEMBER
rel hint, imply, intimate, suggest; admonish, advise, warn; jog, prompt
idiom put in mind

reminder *n* 1 *syn* see EXPRESSION 3
2 *syn* see REMEMBRANCE 3
rel memo, memorandum, note, notice; hint, intimation, suggestion; admonition, warning

remindful *adj syn* see REMINISCENT

reminisce *vb syn* see REMEMBER

reminiscence *n* 1 *syn* see MEMORY 1
2 *syn* see MEMORY 2

reminiscent *adj* tending to remind <shoes *reminiscent* of those worn fifty years ago>
syn redolent, remindful
rel evocative, suggestive
idiom bringing to mind

remise *vb syn* see TRANSFER 4

remiss *adj syn* see NEGLIGENT
rel faineant, indolent, lazy, slothful
ant scrupulous

remit *vb* 1 *syn* see EXCUSE 1
2 *syn* see DEFER
3 *syn* see SEND 1

remittable *adj syn* see VENIAL

remnant *n syn* see REMAINDER

remonstrance *n syn* see DEMUR 2

syn synonym(s)   *rel* related word(s)
ant antonym(s)   *con* contrasted word(s)
idiom idiomatic equivalent(s)
‖ use limited; if in doubt, see a dictionary

remonstrate vb syn see OBJECT 1
  rel combat, fight, oppose, resist, withstand

remonstration n syn see DEMUR 2

remorse n syn see PENITENCE

remorseful adj motivated or marked by remorse < a remorseful confession >
  syn apologetic, attritional, compunctious, contrite, penitent, penitential, regretful, repentant, sorry
  rel mournful, rueful, sorrowful
  con impenitent, regretless, unregretful; hard, obdurate
  ant remorseless

remorsefulness n syn see PENITENCE

remorseless adj having no remorse < a remorseless villain >
  syn impenitent, regretless, uncontrite, unregretful, unremorseful, unrepentant, unsorry
  rel compassionless, merciless, pitiless, ruthless, uncompassionate, unmerciful
  con penitent, regretful, sorry
  ant remorseful

remote adj 1 syn see DISTANT 1
  ant close; adjacent
  2 syn see BACK 1
  3 syn see OBSCURE 2
  4 small in degree < a remote possibility >
  syn ||fat, negligible, off, outside, slender, slight, slim, small
  con great, large; important, significant, weighty
  5 syn see INDIFFERENT 2

remotest adj syn see EXTREME 5

remove vb 1 syn see MOVE 4
  2 to take something from a place or position < removed the book from the shelf >
  syn take away, take off, take out, withdraw
  rel move, shift, transfer; extract
  3 to take (as a hat) from one's person < removed her coat when she entered the house >
  syn doff, douse, put off, take off
  rel cast off, throw off
  idiom off with
  con don, put on, replace
  4 to get rid of < remove the causes of poverty >
  syn clear away, eliminate, take out
  rel dispose (of), eradicate, exterminate, extirpate; blot out, efface, erase, expunge, obliterate
  idiom do away with
  5 syn see PURGE 3

removed adj 1 syn see DISTANT 1
  ant adjoining
  2 syn see OBSCURE 2
  3 syn see ALONE 1

remunerate vb 1 syn see PAY 1
  rel accord, award, grant, vouchsafe
  2 syn see COMPENSATE 3

remunerative adj syn see ADVANTAGEOUS 1

renaissance n syn see REVIVAL

renascence n syn see REVIVAL

rencontre n syn see CONTEST 2

rend vb syn see TEAR 1
  rel divide, separate

render vb 1 syn see RETURN 3
  2 syn see REPRESENT 1
  3 syn see TRANSLATE 1

  4 syn see ADMINISTER 1

rendering n 1 syn see INTERPRETATION 2
  2 syn see VERSION 1

rendezvous n 1 syn see ENGAGEMENT 3
  2 syn see RESORT 2

rendezvous vb syn see GATHER 6

rendition n syn see INTERPRETATION 2

renegade n a person who forsakes his faith, party, cause, or allegiance and aligns himself with another < the renegade derided his former beliefs >
  syn apostate, defector, rat, recreant, runagate, tergiversator, turnabout, turncoat
  rel iconoclast, insurgent, rebel; abandoner, deserter, forsaker; heretic, schismatic
  con liege man; disciple, follower
  ant adherent

renege vb syn see BACK DOWN

renew vb 1 to make like new < rested to renew their strength >
  syn modernize, refresh, refurbish, rejuvenate, renovate, restore, update
  rel make over, remodel; mend, rebuild, repair; correct, rectify, reform, revise
  con bankrupt, deplete, drain, exhaust, impoverish; consume
  ant wear out
  2 syn see RESTORE 1
  3 syn see REVIVE 3
  4 syn see REPEAT
  5 syn see RESUME 2

renewed adj syn see REFRESHED

renounce vb 1 syn see ABDICATE 1
  ant arrogate
  2 syn see ABANDON 1
  idiom wash one's hands of
  3 syn see DEFECT

renouncement n syn see RENUNCIATION

renovate vb 1 syn see REVIVE 3
  2 syn see RENEW 1
  rel clean, cleanse

renown n 1 syn see FAME 2
  2 syn see EMINENCE 1

renowned adj syn see FAMOUS 2
  rel acclaimed, extolled, lauded, praised; outstanding, signal

rent vb syn see HIRE 1

rent adj syn see LACERATED

rent n syn see BREACH 3

rental n syn see APARTMENT 1

renunciation n voluntary surrender or putting aside of something desired or desirable < led a life of total renunciation as a monk >
  syn abnegation, denial, renouncement, self-abnegation, self-denial, self-renunciation
  rel abjurement, eschewing, forbearing, forgoing, forswearing, sacrifice, self-sacrifice; rejection, repudiation, surrender, yielding
  con gripping, holding, keeping
  ant retention

reoccupy vb syn see RESUME 2

reoccurrence n syn see RECURRENCE

reopen vb syn see RESUME 2

reorder vb syn see REORGANIZE

reorganization n syn see SHAKE-UP

reorganize vb to arrange in a different way < reorganize a bankrupt company >
  syn readjust, rearrange, reconstitute, reconstruct, reorder, reorient, reorientate, reshuffle, retool

rel reestablish, refound, resettle; rebuild, regenerate, renovate

con disarrange, disorder, disorganize

reorient *vb syn* see REORGANIZE

reorientate *vb syn* see REORGANIZE

‖**rep** *n* 1 *syn* see FAME 2

2 *syn* see REPUTATION 2

repair *vb* 1 *syn* see GO 1

2 *syn* see RESORT 2

repair *vb syn* see MEND 2

repair *n* 1 *syn* see ORDER 9

2 *syn* see ORDER 10

reparation *n* a return for something lost or suffered, usually through the fault of another < war *reparations* >

syn amends, compensation, indemnification, indemnity, quittance, recompense, redress, reprisal, restitution

rel atonement, expiation; remuneration, requital, retribution, reward; adjustment, settlement

repartee *n* 1 *syn* see RETORT 2

2 *syn* see BANTER

rel humor, irony, sarcasm, satire, wit; rejoinder, response, retort

repast *n syn* see MEAL

repay *vb syn* see COMPENSATE 3

rel balance, offset; accord, award

repeal *vb syn* see REVOKE 2

ant establish; enact

repeat *vb* to say or do again < *repeat* a command>

syn ingeminate, iterate, reiterate, renew, reprise, resay

rel recite, recount, rehearse, relate; hash over, recapitulate, rehash, restate, retell; chime, din, echo, harp, ring; duplicate, reproduce; copy, ditto, imitate; recrudesce, recur, return, revert

repeatedly *adv syn* see OFTEN

idiom day after day, day by day, day in and day out

repel *vb* 1 *syn* see FEND (off)

2 *syn* see RESIST

3 *syn* see DISGUST

ant allure; attract

repellent *adj* 1 *syn* see REPUGNANT 1

con alluring, bewitching, captivating, charming; enticing, luring, seductive, tempting

ant attractive; pleasing

2 *syn* see OFFENSIVE

3 *syn* see ANTIPATHETIC 2

repent *vb syn* see REGRET

repentance *n syn* see PENITENCE

con complacency, self-complacency, self-satisfaction

repentant *adj syn* see REMORSEFUL

rephrase *vb syn* see PARAPHRASE

repine *vb syn* see COMPLAIN

replace *vb* 1 *syn* see RETURN 4

2 *syn* see RESTORE 5

3 to put out of a usual or proper place or into the place of another < the old bridge was *replaced* by a new one last year>

syn outplace, supersede, supplant

rel renew, restore; alter, change; recoup, recover, regain, retrieve

4 *syn* see CHANGE 5

replacement *n syn* see SUBSTITUTE

replete *adj* 1 *syn* see ALIVE 5

2 *syn* see FULL 1

replica *n syn* see REPRODUCTION

replicate *vb syn* see COPY

replication *n syn* see REPRODUCTION

reply *vb syn* see ANSWER 1

con accuse, charge, impeach, indict; address, greet, salute

reply *n syn* see ANSWER 1

con argument, dispute; greeting, salute

report *n* 1 common talk or an instance of it that spreads rapidly < spread a false *report* >

syn buzz, cry, gossip, grapevine, hearsay, murmur, on-dit, rumble, rumor, scuttlebutt, talk, tattle, tittle-tattle, whispering, word

rel conversation, speech; chat, chatter, chitchat, prating, small talk; canard, dirt, scandal; advice, intelligence, news, tidings

2 *syn* see REPUTATION 2

3 *syn* see ACCOUNT 7

rel declaration, statement; comment, notice, review; brief, bulletin

report *vb syn* see RELATE 1

rel communicate, impart

repose *vb syn* see REST 1

repose *n syn* see REST 1

rel refreshment, renewal, restoration

con strain, stress; agitation, discomposure, perturbation

repository *n syn* see DEPOT 2

repossess *vb* 1 *syn* see RECOVER 1

2 *syn* see RESUME 1

3 to resume possession of (an item purchased on installment) in default of payments due < *repossessed* the car >

syn take back

rel get back, reclaim, recover, retrieve

reprehend *vb syn* see CRITICIZE

rel admonish, chide, rebuke, reprimand, reproach, reprove; berate, rate, scold, upbraid

reprehensible *adj syn* see BLAMEWORTHY

represent *vb* 1 to present an image or lifelike imitation of (as in art) < the painting *represents* a spring scene>

syn delineate, depict, describe, image, interpret, limn, picture, portray, render

rel express, realize, show; display, exhibit; hint, suggest; draft, outline, sketch; narrate, relate

con color, distort, falsify, garble, misinterpret, pervert, twist, warp

2 to serve as the counterpart or image of < a movie hero who *represents* the ideals of the culture>

syn body (forth), emblematize, embody, epitomize, exemplify, illustrate, mirror, personalize, personate, personify, symbolize, typify; *compare* EMBODY 1

rel denote, mean, signify; impersonate, substitute; copy, imitate, reproduce

con belie, distort, garble, twist, warp

ant misrepresent

representant *n syn* see DELEGATE

representation *n* the act of delineating < an exponent of *representation* in art>

syn delineation, depiction, description, picture, portraiture, portrayal, presentment

---

syn synonym(s)   *rel* related word(s)
ant antonym(s)   *con* contrasted word(s)
idiom idiomatic equivalent(s)
‖ use limited; if in doubt, see a dictionary

rel demonstration, exemplification, illustration

representative *adj syn* see TYPICAL 1
ant atypical

representative *n* 1 *syn* see INSTANCE
2 *syn* see DELEGATE

repress *vb* 1 *syn* see SUPPRESS 2
2 *syn* see COMPOSE 4

repression *n* 1 the action or process of putting down by authority or force < *repression* of unpopular opinions >
syn choking, extinguishment, quashing, quenching, smothering, squashing, squelching, stifling, strangling, suppression, throttling
rel check, control, curb, restraint; crushing, quelling, subdual
con emboldening, encouragement, support
2 an instance of putting down by authority or force < racial *repressions* >
syn clampdown, crackdown, suppression
rel crushing, extinction, smothering; limitation, repression, restriction

reprieve *n syn* see RESPITE 1

reprimand *n syn* see REBUKE

reprimand *vb syn* see REPROVE

reprinting *n syn* see EDITION

reprisal *n* 1 *syn* see REPARATION
2 *syn* see RETALIATION

reprise *vb syn* see REPEAT

reproach *n syn* see REBUKE
rel blame, censure, discredit

reproach *vb syn* see REPROVE

reprobate *vb* 1 *syn* see CRITICIZE
2 *syn* see DECLINE 4

reprobate *adj* 1 *syn* see ABANDONED 2
2 *syn* see WRONG 1

reprobate *n syn* see VILLAIN 1

reproduce *vb* 1 *syn* see PROCREATE 1
2 *syn* see COPY

reproduction *n* one thing which closely or essentially resembles another that has already been made, produced, or written < printed *reproductions* of the great masters >
syn carbon, carbon copy, copy, ditto, duplicate, facsimile, reduplication, replica, replication
ant original

reproof *n syn* see REBUKE

reprove *vb* to criticize adversely, especially in order to warn of or to correct a fault < *reproved* him for talking in class >
syn admonish, call down, chide, lesson, monish, ‖rack back, rebuke, reprimand, reproach, ‖sneap, tick off; *compare* CRITICIZE, LAMBASTE 3, SCOLD 1
rel counsel, warn; blame, censure, criticize, reprehend, reprobate; chasten, correct, discipline, punish
idiom haul over the coals, slap one's wrist, take to task

reptile *n syn* see SYCOPHANT

repudiate *vb* 1 *syn* see DECLINE 4
con acknowledge, admit, avow, confess, own
ant adopt
2 *syn* see DEFECT
3 *syn* see DISCLAIM
rel abandon, desert, forsake; cast, discard
con allow, concede, grant
ant own

repugnance *n syn* see ABOMINATION 2

repugnancy *n syn* see ABOMINATION 2

repugnant *adj* 1 so alien or unlikable as to arouse antagonism and aversion < the idea of moving again became *repugnant* to her >
syn abhorrent, invidious, obnoxious, repellent, revulsive
rel alien, extraneous, extrinsic, foreign; incompatible, incongruous, inconsonant, uncongenial
con acceptable, bearable, tolerable; agreeable, gratifying, pleasant, pleasing, pleasurable
ant congenial
2 *syn* see OFFENSIVE
3 *syn* see ANTIPATHETIC 2

repulse *vb* 1 *syn* see FEND (off)
2 *syn* see DISGUST
ant captivate

repulsion *n syn* see ABOMINATION 2

repulsive *adj syn* see OFFENSIVE
ant alluring

reputable *adj syn* see RESPECTABLE 1

reputation *n* 1 *syn* see FAME 2
rel authority, credit, influence, prestige, weight
2 the estimation in which one is generally held < a good *reputation* >
syn character, fame, name, ‖rep, report, repute

repute *n* 1 *syn* see FAME 2
ant disrepute
2 *syn* see REPUTATION 2

reputed *adj* 1 *syn* see RESPECTABLE 1
2 *syn* see SUPPOSED 1

request *vb syn* see ASK 2
rel appeal, petition, pray, sue

requiescence *n syn* see REST 1

require *vb* 1 *syn* see DEMAND 1
2 *syn* see DEMAND 2
3 *syn* see LACK

required *adj* 1 *syn* see NEEDFUL
2 *syn* see MANDATORY
ant optional

requirement *n* 1 something wanted or needed < production was not sufficient to satisfy *requirements* for cars >
syn demand, need, want
2 *syn* see ESSENTIAL 2

requisite *adj* 1 *syn* see NEEDFUL
2 *syn* see JUST 3

requisite *n syn* see ESSENTIAL 2

requisition *vb syn* see DEMAND 1

requital *n syn* see RETALIATION

requite *vb* 1 *syn* see RECIPROCATE
rel content, satisfy; revenge
2 *syn* see COMPENSATE 3

resay *vb syn* see REPEAT

rescind *vb syn* see REVOKE 2

rescript *n syn* see REVISION 1

rescue *vb* to set free (as from confinement or risk) < *rescue* a drowning child >
syn deliver, save
rel emancipate, free, liberate, manumit, release; conserve, preserve; disembarrass, disentangle, extricate; recover, regain, retrieve; buy, ransom, redeem

research *n syn* see INQUIRY 1

resect *vb syn* see EXCISE

resemblance *n syn* see LIKENESS
rel parallel
ant dissemblance

resemble *vb* to be like or similar to < he *resembles* his father >

syn favor, ‖feature, simulate
idiom be a dead ringer for, bear a resemblance to, be the spit and image of, be the very image of, bring to mind, have all the earmarks of, look like, put one in mind of, remind one of, take after
con differ, vary

resentfully *adv syn* see HARD 6

resentment *n syn* see OFFENSE 2
rel animosity, animus, antagonism, antipathy, rancor; ill will, malice, malignancy, malignity, spite

reservation *n syn* see CONDITION 1
rel circumscription

reserve *vb syn* see KEEP 5
2 to set or have set aside or apart < *reserve* a hotel room >
syn bespeak, book, preengage
rel contract, engage, retain

reserve *n* something stored or kept available for future use or need < keep a *reserve* of canned foods on hand >
syn backlog, hoard, inventory, nest egg, reservoir, stock, stockpile, store
rel fund, supply
idiom something for a rainy day, something in the sock

reserved *adj* 1 inclined to cautious restraint in the expression of knowledge or opinions < too *reserved* to offer a spontaneous criticism >
syn constrained, incommunicable, noncommittal, restrained
rel bashful, diffident, modest, shy; ceremonious, conventional, formal
con demonstrative, expansive, unconstrained, unrestrained; boisterous, loud, ostentatious; extroverted, open, outgoing
ant unreserved
2 *syn* see SILENT 3
ant effusive
3 *syn* see UNSOCIABLE
ant affable
4 *syn* see ANTISOCIAL
5 *syn* see QUALIFIED 2

reservoir *n syn* see RESERVE

reshuffle *vb syn* see REORGANIZE

reside *vb* 1 to have as one's habitation or domicile < he *resides* in Boston >
syn abide, bide, ‖dig, dwell, hang out, live
rel inhabit, occupy, people, tenant; continue, endure
2 *syn* see CONSIST 1

residence *n* 1 *syn* see HABITATION 1
2 *syn* see HABITATION 2

residency *n syn* see HABITATION 2

resident *n syn* see INHABITANT

‖**residenter** *n syn* see INHABITANT

resider *n syn* see INHABITANT

residual *n syn* see REMAINDER

residue *n syn* see REMAINDER

residuum *n syn* see REMAINDER

resign *vb* 1 *syn* see RELINQUISH
2 *syn* see ABDICATE 1
3 *syn* see QUIT 5

resignation *n* 1 *syn* see ACQUIESCENCE
rel humbleness, lowliness, meekness, modesty

---

syn synonym(s)   *rel* related word(s)
ant antonym(s)   *con* contrasted word(s)
idiom idiomatic equivalent(s)
‖ use limited; if in doubt, see a dictionary

2 *syn* see PATIENCE

resigned *adj syn* see PASSIVE 2
ant rebellious

resile *vb syn* see BACK DOWN

resilient *adj* 1 *syn* see ELASTIC 1
2 *syn* see ELASTIC 2
ant flaccid

resist *vb* to stand firm against a person or influence < the criminal *resisted* the police > < we must learn to *resist* temptation >
syn buck, combat, contest, dispute, duel, fight, oppose, repel, traverse, withstand
rel assail, assault, attack; contradict, contravene, gainsay, impugn; baffle, balk, foil, frustrate, thwart; check, counter, hinder, obstruct, stem
con bow, capitulate, surrender
ant submit, yield

resolute *adj* 1 *syn* see DECIDED 2
rel obstinate, pertinacious, stubborn
2 *syn* see FAITHFUL 1

resoluteness *n syn* see DECISION 2

resolution *n* 1 *syn* see ANALYSIS 1
2 *syn* see DECISION 1
3 *syn* see DECISION 2
4 *syn* see COURAGE

resolve *vb* 1 *syn* see ANALYZE
ant blend
2 *syn* see SOLVE 1
3 *syn* see SOLVE 2
rel dispel, disperse, dissipate; clear, disabuse, purge, rid
4 *syn* see DECIDE

resolve *n syn* see DECISION 2

resolved *adj syn* see DECIDED 2

resonant *adj* marked by conspicuously full and rich sounds or tones (as of speech or music) < a deep *resonant* voice rang out >
syn consonant, fat, orotund, plangent, resounding, ringing, rotund, round, sonorant, sonorous, vibrant
rel full, mellow, rich; deep, profound; enhanced, heightened, intensified; earsplitting, loud, powerful, stentorian, strident; beating, pulsating, pulsing, throbbing; booming, clangorous, noisy, reverberant, reverberating, sounding, thundering, thunderous; electrifying, thrilling
con faint, low, murmurous, muted, smothered, soft, weak; flat, toneless, unmusical; cacophonous, discordant, inharmonious, off-key

resort *n* 1 *syn* see RESOURCE 3
2 a place that is habitually frequented < a favorite *resort* of teenagers >
syn hangout, haunt, purlieu, rendezvous, stamping ground, watering hole
rel harbor, haven, refuge, retreat; den, nest
3 a place providing recreation and entertainment especially to vacationers < returned to the same *resort* every year >
syn pleasure dome, spa, watering place
rel hotel, inn, lodge; bath(s), hot spring(s), mineral spring(s), spring(s), thermal spring(s)

resort *vb* 1 *syn* see FREQUENT
ant avoid
2 to betake oneself or to have recourse when in need of help or relief < they were unwilling to *resort* to her parents for aid >
syn apply, go, recur, refer, repair run, turn

rel address, devote, direct, employ, use, utilize

idiom avail oneself of, fall back on (*or* upon)

resound *vb syn* see PRAISE 2

resounding *adj* 1 *syn* see RESONANT
2 *syn* see EMPHATIC

resource *n* 1 resources *pl syn* see MEAN 3
2 resources *pl syn* see WEALTH 2
3 something to which one turns for assistance in difficulty or need in the absence of a usual means or source of supply < has exhausted every *resource* he can think of >
syn dernier ressort, expediency, expedient, makeshift, recourse, refuge, resort, shift, stopgap, string, substitute, surrogate
rel contraption, contrivance, device, lash=up; creation, invention; fashion, manner, method, mode, system, way; means, measure, step; artifice, dodge, stratagem, subterfuge; hope, opportunity, possibility, relief

respect *n syn* see REGARD 4
rel awe, fear, reverence; adoration, veneration, worship
ant scorn

respect *vb syn* see ADMIRE 2
rel revere, reverence, venerate
ant abuse; misuse; scorn

respectable *adj* 1 worthy of esteem or deference < a *respectable* scientist >
syn creditable, estimable, reputable, reputed, well-thought-of
rel honorable, worthy
ant disreputable, unrespectable
2 *syn* see DECOROUS 1
3 *syn* see DECENT 4
4 *syn* see CONSIDERABLE 2
5 acceptable in appearance or standing < wore old but *respectable* clothes >
syn decent, presentable, tolerable; *compare* DECENT 4
rel adequate, satisfactory; acceptable, appropriate, proper, suitable
ant disreputable

respectful *adj* marked by or showing respect or deference < a *respectful* glance >
syn deferential, duteous, dutiful, regardful
rel reverent, reverential, venerating; attentive, civil, courteous, gracious, polite
con abusive, insolent, insulting, offensive; contemptuous, impudent, irreverent, rude
ant disrespectful

respecting *prep syn* see APROPOS

respective *adj syn* see SEVERAL 1

respire *vb syn* see BREATHE 3

respite *n* 1 a temporary suspension of the execution of a capital offender < the murderer won a *respite* >
syn reprieve
2 *syn* see BREAK 4
rel intermission, lull, pause, recess; ease, leisure, rest

resplendent *adj syn* see SPLENDID 2
rel blazing, flaming, glowing

respond *n syn* see ANSWER 1

respond *vb syn* see ANSWER 1
rel act, behave, react

response *n syn* see ANSWER 1

responsible *adj* subject to an authority which may exact redress in case of default < he is *responsible* for the safe delivery of the goods >

syn accountable, amenable, answerable, liable
rel exposed, open, subject
con clear, exempt, immune; irresponsible, unaccountable, unanswerable, unliable
ant irresponsible

responsive *adj* 1 *syn* see RECEPTIVE 1
ant unresponsive
2 *syn* see SENTIENT 3
rel answering, replying, responding
3 *syn* see TENDER
con cold, cool, indifferent

rest *n* 1 freedom from toil or strain < enjoyed his well-deserved *rest* >
syn ease, leisure, relaxation, repose, requiescence
rel deferring, intermission, suspension; quiet, silence, stillness; calm, peace, peacefulness, placidity, restfulness, serenity, tranquillity
con action, work; restlessness, strain
2 *syn* see BASE 1

rest *vb* 1 to dispose oneself at ease in order to relieve or avoid fatigue < she is *resting* in the bedroom after a hard day's work >
syn lie, lie down, recline, repose, stretch (out)
rel doze, nap, nod, sleep, slumber, snooze
2 to refrain from labor or exertion < planned to do nothing but *rest* during his vacation >
syn relax, rest up, unbend, unlax
rel loaf, loll, lounge; ease off, ease up, let down, let up, slacken, slack off
idiom take it easy, take life easy
con labor, toil, work; drudge, grind, slave
3 to allow an interval of rest from exertion < they *rested* for ten minutes before going back to work >
syn breathe, lay off, lie by, spell
idiom lie (*or* rest) on one's oars, stop for breath, take a break (*or* rest), take five (*or* ten), take time out
4 *syn* see BASE
rel depend, hang, hinge; count, rely

rest *n syn* see REMAINDER
rel excess, overplus, superfluity, surplus, surplusage

restart *vb syn* see RESUME 2

restate *vb syn* see PARAPHRASE

restatement *n syn* see VERSION 1

restitute *vb* 1 *syn* see RESTORE 3
2 *syn* see RETURN 4

restitution *n syn* see REPARATION

restive *adj* 1 *syn* see CONTRARY 3
2 *syn* see TENSE 2

restiveness *n syn* see UNREST

restless *adj* lacking rest or giving no rest < the patient was *restless* from pain > < *restless* sleep >
syn uneasy, unpeaceful, unquiet, unrestful, unsettled, untranquil
rel agitated, disturbed, perturbed, troubled; fidgety, jittery, jumpy, nervous, restive; fitful, intermittent, spasmodic
con easy, peaceful, quiet, tranquil
ant restful

restlessness *n syn* see UNREST

restorative *adj* 1 *syn* see CURATIVE
2 *syn* see TONIC 1

restore *vb* 1 to put or bring back (as into existence or use) < *restore* peace in the world >

syn recall, reestablish, reinstate, reintroduce, renew, revive

rel get back, recover, regain, retrieve, win (back)

2 *syn* see RENEW 1

3 to put into a previous good state < made plans to *restore* slum areas >

syn reclaim, recondition, reconstruct, recover, rehabilitate, rejuvenate, restitute

rel redeem, rescue, save; amend, reform, revise; recoup, recruit, regain, retrieve; better, improve; correct, rectify, remedy, right; return

ant deteriorate

4 to help or cause to regain signs of life and vigor < *restore* him to health >

syn resuscitate, revive, revivify

rel cure, heal, remedy; arouse, rally, rouse, stir

5 to put again in possession of something < *restore* the king to his throne >

syn give back, put (back), reinstate, replace, return

6 *syn* see RETURN 4

restrain *vb* 1 to prevent from or control in doing something < *restrained* the child from picking all the flowers >

syn bit, bridle, check, coarct, constrain, crimp, curb, hold back, hold down, hold in, inhibit, keep, pull in, withhold; *compare* HAMPER

rel arrest, interrupt, stop; prevent; forbear, refrain; block, hinder, impede, obstruct; gag, muzzle

idiom keep in line, put (*or* lay) under restraint

con countenance, encourage; incline, induce, move, prompt; persuade; allow, permit

ant impel; incite

2 *syn* see COMPOSE 4

ant abandon

3 *syn* see MODERATE 1

restrained *adj* 1 *syn* see QUIET 4

ant unrestrained

2 *syn* see UNDEMONSTRATIVE

3 *syn* see RESERVED 1

4 *syn* see CONSERVATIVE 2

ant extravagant

restraint *n* *syn* see RESTRICTION 2

restrict *vb* *syn* see LIMIT 2

rel bind, tie; shrink

restricted *adj* *syn* see DEFINITE 1

restriction *n* 1 something that restricts or restrains < they both wanted to be free of the *restriction* of the school >

syn ‖ball and chain, circumscription, cramp, limitation, stint, stricture

rel brake, check, control, curb

2 an act of restricting or the condition of being restricted < undue *restriction* of children >

syn circumscription, confinement, constrainment, constraint, cramp, restraint

rest up *vb* *syn* see REST 2

restyle *vb* *syn* see REVISE

result *n* 1 *syn* see EFFECT 1

rel close, conclusion, end, finish, termination; product, production

con origin, root, source

2 *syn* see ANSWER 2

resume *vb* 1 to assume or take again < *resumed* her place in society >

syn reassume, reoccupy, repossess, retake

rel reclaim, recoup, recover, regain, retrieve

2 to return to or begin again after interruption < *resumed* her work >

syn continue, pick up, recommence, renew, reopen, restart, take up

rel carry on, go on, keep up

con cease, discontinue, end, halt, postpone, quit, stop; check, intermit, interrupt

résumé *n* *syn* see SUMMARY

resurgence *n* *syn* see REVIVAL

resurrect *vb* 1 to restore to life < believed that his body would be literally *resurrected* >

syn raise

idiom raise from the dead

2 *syn* see REVIVE 3

resurrection *n* *syn* see REVIVAL

resuscitate *vb* 1 *syn* see RESTORE 4

2 *syn* see REVIVE 3

resuscitation *n* *syn* see REVIVAL

retail *vb* *syn* see SELL 3

retain *vb* 1 *syn* see HAVE 1

2 *syn* see KEEP 5

con abdicate, resign; abjure, forswear, recant, renounce, retract

3 *syn* see REMEMBER

retake *vb* *syn* see RESUME 1

retaliate *vb* *syn* see RECIPROCATE

rel avenge, revenge

idiom even the score, get back at, get even with, give in kind, give one a dose of his own medicine, give one tit for tat, pay one in his own coin, settle (*or* square) accounts, turn the tables on

retaliation *n* the act of inflicting or the intent to inflict injury in return for injury < they had no opportunity for *retaliation* >

syn avengement, avenging, counterblow, reprisal, requital, retribution, revanche, revenge, vengeance

rel correction, discipline, punishment; indemnification, recompense, repayment; amends, indemnity, redress, reparation, restitution

idiom an eye for an eye, blow for blow, measure for measure, tit for tat

con clemency, grace, lenity, mercy; forgiveness, pardon, remission

retard *vb* *syn* see DELAY 1

rel decrease, lessen, reduce; clog, fetter, hamper; baffle, balk

ant accelerate; advance

retarded *adj* limited in intellectual or emotional development < a *retarded* child >

syn backward, dim-witted, dull, feebleminded, half-witted, imbecile, moronic, quarter-witted, simple, simpleminded, slow, slow-witted; *compare* SIMPLE 3, STUPID 1

rel dim, ‖dough-baked, ‖dunny, opaque; exceptional, underachieving; touched

idiom not all there, soft in the head

con bright, capable, intelligent

retch *vb* to make an effort to vomit < started to *retch* after drinking it >

syn gag, heave, keck

---

syn synonym(s)   *rel* related word(s)
ant antonym(s)   *con* contrasted word(s)
idiom idiomatic equivalent(s)
‖ use limited; if in doubt, see a dictionary

rethink *vb syn* see RECONSIDER

reticent *adj syn* see SILENT 3
con candid, open, plain
ant frank, unreticent

retinue *n syn* see ENTOURAGE

retire *vb* 1 *syn* see RETREAT 2
2 *syn* see GO 2
rel recede, retreat; abandon, relinquish, surrender, yield
ant advance
3 to cause to withdraw from one's position or occupation < all employees are automatically *retired* at age sixty-five >
syn pension (off), superannuate
rel discharge, dismiss; drop, leave, quit, resign, terminate, vacate
4 to go to bed < youngsters should always *retire* before midnight >
syn bed, ||flop, pile (in), roll in, turn in
idiom go beddie-bye, go night-night, hit the hay (*or* sack)
con arise, get out, get up, pile (out), roll out, turn out, uprise
ant rise

retired *adj syn* see OBSCURE 2

retirement *n syn* see SECLUSION

retiring *adj* 1 *syn* see SHY 1
ant assertive
2 *syn* see UNDEMONSTRATIVE
ant forward

retool *vb syn* see REORGANIZE

retort *vb syn* see ANSWER 1

retort *n* 1 *syn* see ANSWER 1
2 a quick, witty, or cutting reply < he made a very clever *retort* >
syn back answer, comeback, repartee, riposte
rel reprisal, retaliation, revenge; crack, gag, jape, jest, joke, quip, sally, wisecrack, witticism

retouch *vb syn* see TOUCH UP

retract *vb* 1 *syn* see RECEDE 1
ant protract
2 *syn* see ABJURE
rel eliminate, exclude, rule out, suspend

retral *adj* 1 *syn* see POSTERIOR 2
2 *syn* see BACKWARD 1

retreat *n syn* see SHELTER 1

retreat *vb* 1 *syn* see RECEDE 1
rel quail, recoil, shrink
ant advance
2 to draw back from action or danger < the army *retreated* in disarray >
syn fall back, give back, retire, withdraw
rel abandon, depart, evacuate, go, leave, pull out, quit, vacate; decamp, escape, flee, fly; back down, back out, bow out, climb down
idiom beat a retreat, drop back, give ground, give way, sound a retreat
con advance, move, proceed, progress
ant attack

re-treat *vb syn* see RECONSIDER

retrench *vb syn* see SHORTEN

retribution *n syn* see RETALIATION
rel affliction, trial, tribulation, visitation

retrieve *vb* 1 *syn* see RECOVER 1
2 *syn* see REVIVE 3

retrocede *vb syn* see RECEDE 1

retrograde *adj syn* see BACKWARD 1

retrograde *vb* 1 *syn* see RECEDE 1
rel return, revert; invert, reverse; backslide, lapse, relapse

2 *syn* see DETERIORATE 1

retrogress *vb syn* see REVERT 2

retrospect *n syn* see REVIEW 5

retrospect *vb syn* see REMEMBER

retrospection *n syn* see REVIEW 5

return *vb* 1 to go or come back (as to a person, place, or condition) < the converted sinner soon *returned* to his old ways >
syn react, recrudesce, recur, revert, turn back
rel advert; revolve, rotate, turn; renew, restore; recover, regain; rebound, reflect, repercuss, reverberate
con abandon, depart, leave, quit
ant forsake
2 *syn* see ANSWER 1
3 to bring back (as a writ or verdict) to an office or tribunal < *return* a verdict of not guilty >
syn render
4 to bring, send, or put back to a former or proper place < *return* the gun to its holster >
syn replace, restitute, restore, take back
ant remove
5 *syn* see RESTORE 5
6 *syn* see YIELD 7
7 *syn* see RECIPROCATE
rel bestow, give

return *n* 1 *syn* see RECURRENCE
2 *syn* see ANSWER 1
3 *syn* see PROFIT
ant outlay

returnless *adj syn* see INEVITABLE

revamp *vb* 1 *syn* see MEND 2
2 *syn* see REVISE

revanche *n syn* see RETALIATION

reveal *vb* 1 to make known what has been or should be concealed < he solemnly promised he would not *reveal* the truth >
syn betray, blab (out), disclose, discover, divulge, give away, let on, ||let out, mouth, spill, tell, unbosom, unclose, uncover, uncurtain, unveil
rel break, communicate, impart; announce, blow (about *or* abroad), broadcast, declare, give out, publish, vent; breathe, whisper; leak; acknowledge, admit, avow, confess, let on; peach, rat, ||split, squeak, squeal (on), ||stool, talk
idiom let slip, let the cat out of the bag, spill the beans
con cover (up), hide, obscure, veil
ant conceal
2 *syn* see OPEN 2

revel *vb* 1 to be festive in a noisy or riotous manner < they *reveled* all night long >
syn carouse, frolic, hell, riot, roister, spree, wassail
idiom blow off steam, cut loose, kick up one's heels, let go, let loose, paint the town red, whoop it up
2 *syn* see WALLOW 3

revel *n* 1 *syn* see MERRYMAKING
2 *syn* see REVELRY 2

revelation *n* disclosure or something disclosed by or as if by divine or preternatural means < a *revelation* closely guarded by members of the sect >
syn apocalypse, oracle, prophecy, vision
ant adumbration

reveling n syn see MERRYMAKING
revelment n 1 syn see MERRYMAKING
2 syn see REVELRY 2
revelry n 1 syn see MERRYMAKING
2 boisterous partying <they were exhausted after the night of *revelry*>
syn high jinks, revel, revelment, skylarking, wassail, whoop-de-do, whoopee, whoopla, whoop-up
revenant n syn see APPARITION
revenge vb syn see AVENGE
rel defend, justify
idiom get one's own back, have one's revenge, take an eye for an eye
revenge n syn see RETALIATION
revengeful adj syn see VINDICTIVE
rel adamant, inexorable, inflexible, obdurate
revenue n amount received or gained usually measured in money <still holds property that yields a good *revenue*>
syn coming(s) in, income, receipts
rel earnings, gains, salary, wages; proceeds, profit, returns, yield
con expenditure, expense(s), outgoings, outlay
reverberant adj syn see HOLLOW 1
revere vb to honor and admire profoundly and respectfully <he is *revered* for his wisdom>
syn adore, reverence, venerate, worship
rel admire, esteem, regard, respect; appreciate, cherish, prize, treasure, value; exalt, magnify; enjoy, love
con contemn, despise, disdain, scorn; scout; insult, mock, scoff
ant flout
revered adj syn see VENERABLE 1
reverence n 1 syn see HONOR 1
rel devotion, fealty, loyalty, piety
2 the emotion inspired by what arouses one's deep respect or veneration <a deep *reverence* for honesty>
syn awe, fear
con contempt, despite, disdain, hatred, scorn; insult, mockery
reverence vb syn see REVERE
idiom hold in reverence
reverend adj syn see VENERABLE 1
reverend n syn see CLERGYMAN
reverential adj syn see VENERABLE 1
reverie n the condition of being lost in thought <spent the day in *reverie* before the fire>
syn brown study, muse, study, trance
rel absorption, abstraction, preoccupation; contemplation, meditation, thought; castle-building, daydreaming, dreaming
reversal n 1 a causing to move or face in an opposite direction or to appear in an inverted position <a *reversal* in policy> <the *reversal* of objects seen through a simple lens>
syn about-face, changeabout, inversion, reverse, reversement, reversion, rights-about, right-about-face, turn, turnabout, turning, volte-face
rel bouleversement, overturning

syn synonym(s)   rel related word(s)
ant antonym(s)   con contrasted word(s)
idiom idiomatic equivalent(s)
‖ use limited; if in doubt, see a dictionary

2 syn see SETBACK
reverse adj syn see OPPOSITE
reverse vb 1 to change to the contrary or opposite side or position <the chairman *reversed* the order in which they would speak>
syn change, inverse, invert, revert, transplace, transpose, turn
rel capsize, overturn, upset; exchange, interchange; shift, transfer
2 syn see REVOKE 2
reverse n 1 syn see OPPOSITE
2 syn see REVERSAL 1
3 syn see SETBACK
reversement n syn see REVERSAL 1
reversion n 1 a return to an ancestral type or condition or an instance of such a return <the law was a shocking *reversion* to earlier times>
syn atavism, throwback
rel backsliding, lapse, relapse
con advance, amendment, bettering, betterment, improvement; reform
2 syn see REVERSAL 1
revert vb 1 syn see RETURN 1
2 to come or go back to a lower or worse condition <*reverted* to savagery>
syn regress, retrogress, throw back
rel backslide, lapse, relapse; decline, degenerate, deteriorate, retrograde
con advance, progress
3 syn see REVERSE 1
review n 1 syn see REVISION 1
2 syn see EXAMINATION
3 syn see CRITICISM
4 syn see JOURNAL
5 a retrospective view of or meditation on past events <an occurrence that in *review* did not surprise him>
syn afterlight, reconsideration, reexamination, retrospect, retrospection, revision
rel reflection, study; second thought
con anticipation, contemplation, foreseeing
review vb syn see RECONSIDER
reviewal n syn see CRITICISM
revile vb syn see SCOLD 1
rel asperse, calumniate, defame, libel, malign, slander, traduce, vilify
con acclaim, eulogize, extol, praise
ant laud
revisal n syn see REVISION 1
revise vb to make a new, amended, improved, or up-to-date version of <the many problems involved in *revising* a dictionary>
syn redraft, redraw, restyle, revamp, rework, rewrite, work over
rel overhaul, reorganize; perfect, polish, upgrade
con discard, disregard
revise n syn see REVISION 1
revision n 1 an act of revising <the *revision* of a manuscript>
syn recension, redraft, rescript, review, revisal, revise
rel amendment, correction, emendation, rectification
2 syn see REVIEW 5
revitalize vb syn see REVIVE 3
revival n a renewal of life, activity, or prominence <a *revival* of weaving>
syn reanimation, rebirth, renaissance, renascence, resurgence, resurrection, resus-

citation, revivification, reviviscence, risorgimento
rel regeneration, rejuvenation, renewal, restoration

revive *vb* 1 *syn* see RESTORE 4
rel gain, improve, recuperate
2 *syn* see RESTORE 1
3 to restore from a depressed, inactive, or unused state < *revived* his hope of escape>
syn reactivate, rekindle, renew, renovate, resurrect, resuscitate, retrieve, revitalize, revivify
rel reanimate, regenerate, reinvigorate, rejuvenate; arouse, galvanize, quicken, stimulate; activate, energize, vitalize
con extinguish, put down, put out, quell, quench, suppress; inhibit
4 *syn* see REMEMBER

revived *adj syn* see REFRESHED

revivification *n syn* see REVIVAL

revivify *vb* 1 *syn* see REVIVE 3
2 *syn* see RESTORE 4

reviviscence *n syn* see REVIVAL

revoke *vb* 1 *syn* see REMEMBER
2 to annul by recalling or taking back < *revoke* a privilege>
syn dismantle, lift, recall, repeal, rescind, reverse
rel abrogate, annul, void; cancel, erase, expunge; invalidate, nullify; countermand, counterorder; abjure, forswear, recant, retract
ant confirm

revolt *vb* 1 to renounce allegiance or subjection < *revolted* against the king>
syn insurrect, mutiny, rebel, rise (against)
rel defy, oppose, resist; break, renounce, turn (against); boycott, strike; overthrow, overturn, riot
idiom kick over the traces, take up arms against
con obey, submit; aid, assist, help, succor, support; bolster, prop (up), sustain, uphold
2 *syn* see DISGUST

revolter *n syn* see REBEL

revolting *adj syn* see OFFENSIVE

revolute *vb syn* see REVOLUTIONIZE

revolution *n* 1 the action or an act of moving around an orbit or circular course < the *revolution* of the earth around the sun>
syn circuit, circulation, circumvolution, gyration, gyre, revolve, rotation, round, turn, wheel, whirl
rel cycle, pirouette, reel, roll, spin, twirl
2 *syn* see SHAKE-UP

revolution *vb syn* see REVOLUTIONIZE

revolutional *adj syn* see EXTREME 3

revolutionary *adj syn* see EXTREME 3

revolutionary *n syn* see RADICAL

revolutionist *n syn* see RADICAL

revolutionist *adj syn* see EXTREME 3

revolutionize *vb* to change fundamentally or completely < he *revolutionized* manufacturing processes>
syn revolute, revolution
rel alter, change, modify; recast, refashion, reform, remodel; redraw, restyle, revamp, revise; metamorphose, transfigure, transform, transmogrify; overthrow, overturn

idiom break with the past, make a clean sweep, make a radical change

revolve *vb* 1 *syn* see PONDER 2
2 *syn* see TURN 1

revolve *n syn* see REVOLUTION 1

revulsion *n syn* see ABOMINATION 2

revulsive *adj syn* see REPUGNANT 1

reward *n* something that is offered or given for some service or attainment < the miner received a *reward* for his hard work>
syn carrot, dividend, guerdon, meed, plum, premium, prize
rel compensation, recompense, remuneration, requital

reweigh *vb syn* see RECONSIDER

reword *vb syn* see PARAPHRASE

rework *vb syn* see REVISE

rewrite *vb syn* see REVISE

rhadamanthine *adj syn* see JUST 3

rhapsodize *vb syn* see ENTHUSE 2
rel acclaim, extol, praise
con blame, condemn, denounce; decry, derogate, detract, minimize

rhapsody *n* 1 *syn* see BOMBAST
2 *syn* see ECSTASY

rhapsody *vb syn* see ENTHUSE 2

rhetoric *n* 1 *syn* see ORATORY
2 *syn* see BOMBAST

rhetorical *adj* emphasizing style often at the expense of thought < the candidate was given to windy *rhetorical* speeches>
syn aureate, bombastic, declamatory, euphuistic, florid, flowery, grandiloquent, highfalutin, high-flown, magniloquent, ‖mouthy, oratorical, orotund, overblown, pompous, purple, sonorous, stilted, swelling, swollen, tumescent, tumid, turgid
rel chichi, orchidaceous, ostentatious, pretentious, showy; gassy, inflated, windy; exaggerated, overdone, overwrought; grand, grandiose, high-sounding, imposing; flamboyant, ornate; embellished; articulate, eloquent, fluent, glib, vocal, voluble
con homely, literal, plain, simple, unpretentious; unadorned, undecorated, unembellished, ungarnished, unornamented
ant unrhetorical

rhino *n syn* see MONEY

rhubarb *n syn* see QUARREL

rhyme *n* 1 *syn* see POETRY 1
2 *syn* see POEM
3 *syn* see RHYTHM

rhyme *vb syn* see AGREE 4

rhymer *n syn* see POETASTER

rhymester *n syn* see POETASTER

rhythm *n* the regular rise and fall in intensity of sounds that is associated chiefly with poetry and music < the *rhythm* of the music made it easy to dance to>
syn beat, cadence, cadency, measure, meter, rhyme, rhythmus, swing
rel lilt; accent

rhythmus *n syn* see RHYTHM

riant *adj syn* see MERRY

‖rib *n syn* see WIFE

rib *vb syn* see BANTER 1

ribald *n syn* see SCAMP

ribbon *n syn* see STRIP 1

rich *adj* 1 having goods, property, and money in abundance < he was a *rich* man, having accumulated his wealth in business>

syn affluent, moneyed, ‖oofy, opulent, wealthy

rel comfortable, easy, independent, prosperous, well-fixed, well-heeled, well-off, well-to-do; fat, flush

idiom flush with money, having money to burn, in the money, rich as Croesus, rolling in money

con destitute, indigent, penurious, poverty-stricken

ant poor

2 *syn* see ORNATE

3 highly seasoned and fatty, oily, or sweet < ate *rich* desserts every day >

syn heavy

rel cloying, oversweet; filling, satiating, sating; fat

con natural, simple, unseasoned

ant plain

4 *syn* see FERTILE

5 *syn* see EXPRESSIVE

richen *vb syn* see ENRICH

riches *n pl syn* see WEALTH 2

rick *n syn* see PILE 1

‖rick *vb syn* see SPRAIN

rickety *adj* likely to give way or break down < a *rickety* old chair >

syn rachitic, rackety, rattletrap, shaky, wobbly; *compare* WEAK 2

rel unsound, unsteady

con firm, rugged, solid, sturdy, substantial, well-made

ant stable

‖rickle *n syn* see PILE 1

ricochet *vb syn* see GLANCE 1

rel bound, rebound, recoil

rid *vb* to set a person or thing free of something that encumbers < *rid* himself of his troubles >

syn clear, lose, shake (off), throw off, unburden

rel free, liberate, release; disembosom, unbosom; eradicate, exterminate, extirpate, remove, uproot; abolish, extinguish

con burden, charge, clog, cumber, encumber, lade, load, lumber, saddle, task, tax, weigh, weight

ant weigh down

riddance *n syn* see DISPOSAL 2

riddle *n syn* see MYSTERY

ride *vb* 1 to travel by automobile < often *rode* out to the countryside >

syn auto, motor

idiom go for a spin

2 *syn* see DRIFT 1

3 *syn* see BAIT 1

rel oppress, persecute; torment, torture

4 *syn* see OVERLAP

ride (out) *vb syn* see SURVIVE 2

ride *n syn* see DRIVE 1

rel excursion, expedition, journey, tour, trip

rider *n syn* see APPENDIX 1

ridge *n* 1 a top or upper part especially when long and narrow < topped the mountain *ridge* >

syn chine, crest, hogback

2 *syn* see WRINKLE

‖ridge runner *n syn* see RUSTIC

ridicule *vb* to make an object of laughter < *ridiculed* him for his inability to perform the feat >

syn deride, lout, mock, quiz, rally, razz, scout, taunt, twit

rel ‖barrack, flout, gibe, jape, jeer, scoff, sneer; burlesque, caricature, mimic, travesty; haze, ride, roast

idiom laugh out of court, make fun (*or* game *or* sport) of, poke fun at

ridiculous *adj* 1 *syn* see LAUGHABLE

rel absurd, foolish, preposterous, silly; antic, bizarre, fantastic, grotesque

2 *syn* see INDECOROUS

riding *n* 1 *syn* see SHIVAREE

2 *syn* see HARBOR 3

rife *adj* 1 *syn* see PREVAILING

2 *syn* see ALIVE 5

riff (through) *vb syn* see BROWSE

riffle *vb syn* see RIPPLE

riffle (through) *vb syn* see BROWSE

riffraff *n* 1 *syn* see RABBLE 2

2 *syn* see REFUSE

rifle *vb syn* see ROB 1

rift *n* 1 *syn* see CRACK 3

2 *syn* see BREACH 3

rel gap, hiatus, interruption, interval

rig *vb syn* see FURNISH 1

rig *n syn* see COSTUME

‖rig *n* 1 *syn* see IMPOSTURE

2 *syn* see PRANK

‖rig *vb syn* see DUPE

rigamajig *n syn* see DOODAD, business, dingus, dofunny, doohickey, gadget, gizmo, thingum, thingumajig, thingumbob

rigging *n syn* see CLOTHES

‖riggish *adj syn* see FAST 7

right *adj* 1 *syn* see UPRIGHT 2

2 *syn* see DECOROUS 1

3 *syn* see JUST 3

4 *syn* see TRUE 3

con specious, unsound; misguided, mistaken

ant unright, wrong

5 *syn* see CORRECT 2

6 *syn* see FIT 1

7 *syn* see AUTHENTIC 2

8 *syn* see SANE 2

9 *syn* see HEALTHY 1

10 *syn* see CONSERVATIVE 1

11 *syn* see DECENT 4

right *n* 1 qualities (as adherence to duty or obedience to lawful authority) that together constitute the ideal of moral propriety or merit moral approval < the *right* is not all on one side >

syn good, straight

rel correctitude, correctness, properness, propriety, rightness

con debt, sin, wickedness; improperness, impropriety, incorrectness, unrightness

ant unright, wrong

2 something to which one has a just claim < the *right* to life, liberty, and the pursuit of happiness >

syn appanage, birthright, perquisite, prerogative, privilege

rel claim, interest, title; freedom, liberty, license

3 *usu* rights *pl syn* see DUE 1

4 *syn* see DIEHARD 1

‖5 *syn* see OBLIGATION 2

---

syn synonym(s)   *rel* related word(s)

ant antonym(s)   *con* contrasted word(s)

idiom idiomatic equivalent(s)

‖ use limited; if in doubt, see a dictionary

‖6 *syn* see EXCUSE 1
right *adv* 1 *syn* see JUST 1
2 *syn* see WELL 4
ant wrong, wrongly
3 *syn* see DIRECTLY 1
4 *syn* see WELL 3
5 *syn* see AWAY 3
6 *syn* see VERY 1
right *vb* 1 *syn* see CORRECT 1
‖2 *syn* see MEND 2
right–about *n syn* see REVERSAL 1
right–about–face *n syn* see REVERSAL 1
right away *adv syn* see AWAY 3
righteous *adj* 1 *syn* see MORAL 1
con corrupt, flagitious, nefarious; bad,
evil, immoral, reprobate, sinful, vicious,
wicked, wrong
ant iniquitous, unrighteous
2 *syn* see GOOD 11
ant unrighteous
righteousness *n syn* see GOODNESS
unrighteousness
rightful *adj* 1 *syn* see JUST 3
rel equitable, fair, impartial
ant unrightful
2 *syn* see TRUE 8
ant unrightful
3 *syn* see FIT 1
right hand *n syn* see RIGHT-HAND MAN
right–handed *adj* having the same direction or course as the movement of the
hands of a watch viewed from in front
< a *right-handed* propeller >
syn clockwise, dextrorotatory, positive
right–hand man *n* a reliable or indispensable person < the boss viewed his efficient
assistant as his *right-hand man* >
syn girl Friday, man Friday, right hand
rightist *n syn* see DIEHARD 1
ant leftist
‖**rightle** *vb syn* see MEND 2
rightly *adv syn* see WELL 1
right–minded *adj syn* see MORAL 1
rightness *n* 1 *syn* see GOODNESS
2 *syn* see ORDER 11
right off *adv syn* see AWAY 3
‖**right smart** *adj syn* see CONSIDERABLE
2
‖**right smart** *adv syn* see VERY 1
right wing *n syn* see DIEHARD 1
right–winger *n syn* see DIEHARD 1
ant left-winger
rigid *adj* 1 *syn* see STIFF 1
rel firm, hard, solid
ant elastic
2 *syn* see INFLEXIBLE 2
3 extremely severe or stern < was regarded as a *rigid* disciplinarian >
syn draconian, ironhanded, rigorist, rigorous, strict, stringent, unpermissive
rel austere, severe, stern; hard-line, inflexible, tough, uncompromising, unyielding;
adamant, adamantine, inexorable, obdurate
con humoring, indulgent, pampering;
loose, relaxed; easy, gentle, mild
ant lax
rigor *n syn* see DIFFICULTY 1
rel austerity, severity, sternness; harshness, roughness; affliction, trial, tribulation, visitation
ant amenity
rigorist *adj syn* see RIGID 3

rigorous *adj* 1 *syn* see RIGID 3
rel inflexible, stiff; ascetic; burdensome,
exacting, onerous, oppressive
con easy, effortless, facile, light, smooth
ant mild
2 *syn* see SEVERE 3
rel drastic
con bland, faint, lenient, smooth
3 *syn* see CORRECT 2
rigorously *adv syn* see HARD 5
rile *vb* 1 *syn* see ROIL 1
2 *syn* see IRRITATE
riley *adj syn* see TURBID
rim *n syn* see BORDER 1
rim *vb syn* see BORDER 1
rima *n syn* see CRACK 3
rimation *n syn* see CRACK 3
rime *n syn* see CRACK 3
rime *vb syn* see CAKE 1
rimple *n syn* see WRINKLE
rimple *vb syn* see CRUMPLE 1
‖**rimption** *n, usu* **rimptions** *pl syn* see
SCAD
‖**rindle** *n syn* see CREEK 2
ring *n* 1 *syn* see LOOP 2
2 *syn* see LOOP 1
3 *syn* see BOXING
4 *syn* see CLIQUE
5 *syn* see COMBINATION 2
ring *vb syn* see SURROUND 1
ring *vb* to sound clearly and resonantly
< the church bells were *ringing* >
syn bell, bong, chime, knell, peal, toll
rel resound, reverberate, sound
‖**ring (up)** *vb syn* see TELEPHONE
ringer *n syn* see IMAGE 1
ringing *adj syn* see RESONANT
‖**ring off** *vb syn* see SHUT UP 2
riot *n* 1 *syn* see DISORDER 2
2 something or someone wildly amusing
< the new comedy is a *riot* >
syn howl, ‖panic, scream, sidesplitter
rel sensation, smash, wow
riot *vb syn* see REVEL 1
riot (away) *vb syn* see WASTE 2
riotous *adj syn* see PROFUSE
rip *vb syn* see TEAR 1
rip (out) *vb syn* see SPUTTER 1
ripe *adj* 1 *syn* see MATURE 1
rel seasonable, timely, well-timed; overdue
con callow, crude, raw, rude; immature,
unmatured, unmellow
ant unripe; green
2 *syn* see CONSUMMATE 1
3 brought by aging to full flavor or the
best state < *ripe* cheese >
syn aged, matured, mellow, ripened
rel ready
ant unripe
‖**ripe** *vb syn* see MATURE
ripen *vb syn* see MATURE
rel better, improve; enhance, heighten,
intensify, season
ripened *adj* 1 *syn* see MATURE 1
ant unripened
2 *syn* see RIPE 3
riposte *n syn* see RETORT 2
ripper *n syn* ‖DILLY, ‖corker, crackerjack,
dandy, ‖dinger, humdinger, jim-dandy,
‖lulu, nifty, peach
ripping *adj syn* see MARVELOUS 2

464   ripple

ripple *vb* to become fretted or lightly ruffled on the surface (as water) <the pond was *rippled* by rain>
syn cockle, dimple, fret, riffle

ripsnorter *n syn* ‖DILLY, ‖corker, crackerjack, ‖daisy, dandy, ‖dinger, ‖doozer, humdinger, jim-dandy, ‖lulu

rise *vb* **1** to assume an upright or standing position <he *rose* from his chair>
syn get up, stand up, uprise, upspring
rel sit up; straighten up
idiom come to one's feet
con lie, lounge, recline, sit; loll, sprawl
2 *syn* see ROLL OUT
ant retire
3 *syn* see ADJOURN 2
ant sit
4 to move or come up from a lower to a higher level <smoke *rose* from the chimneys>
syn arise, ascend, aspire, lift, mount, soar, up, uprear
rel surge, tower; climb, scale; elevate, raise, rear
con descend, drop, lower; dip, plummet, sink
ant fall; decline
5 *syn* see INTENSIFY
6 *syn* see SURFACE
7 *syn* see INCREASE 2
ant abate; fall
8 *syn* see HAPPEN 1
9 *syn* see SPRING 1

rise (against) *vb syn* see REVOLT 1
rise (to) *vb syn* see APPLAUD 2
rise *n* **1** *syn* see ASCENT
ant fall
2 *syn* see ADDITION
3 an increment in amount, number, or volume <crime is on the *rise*>
syn boost, breakthrough, hike, increase, upgrade, wax
con declension, decline, lessening, letup, reduction, slump; decrement, loss
ant drop

rise and shine *vb syn* see ROLL OUT
risible *adj syn* see LAUGHABLE
ant lachrymose, larmoyant
rising *n syn* see ASCENT
ant falling
risk *n syn* see DANGER
rel accident, chance, fortune, luck; exposedness, exposure, liability, liableness, openness
risk *vb* **1** *syn* see ENDANGER
rel beard, brave, dare, defy, face; confront, encounter, meet
idiom go out of one's depth
2 *syn* see VENTURE 1
3 *syn* see GAMBLE 2
riskless *adj syn* see SAFE 2
risky *adj* **1** *syn* see DANGEROUS 1
rel delicate, precarious, sensitive, ticklish, touchy; speculative
idiom on thin ice
2 *syn* see RISQUÉ
risorgimento *n syn* see REVIVAL
risqué *adj* verging on impropriety or indecency <blushed at his *risqué* stories>

syn blue, broad, off-color, purple, racy, risky, salty, sexy, shady, spicy, suggestive, wicked; *compare* OBSCENE 2
rel naughty, warm; coarse, crude, earthy, gross, lewd, obscene, raunchy, raw, ribald, vulgar; dirty, foul; indecent, indecorous, indelicate, inelegant, unrefined
con clean, decent, proper; restrained; euphemistic

‖rissom *n syn* see PARTICLE
rite *n* **1** *syn* see FORM 2
2 forms (as religious rites) appropriate to a particular event <the marriage *rites*>
syn ceremonial, ceremony, formality, liturgy, observance, ritual, service
rel celebration, occasion, solemnity; sacrament, sacramental; form
‖rithe *n syn* see CREEK 2
ritual *n* **1** *syn* see RITE 2
2 *syn* see FORM 2
rival *n* one of two or more striving for what only one can possess <political *rivals* for the nomination>
syn competition, competitor, corrival
rel contender, contestant, entrant; adversary, antagonist, opponent
rival *vb* **1** *syn* see COMPETE 1
2 to strive to equal or surpass <*rivaling* each other for the most work done>
syn compete, emulate, rivalize
rel attempt, strive, struggle, try; contend, fight
3 *syn* see EQUAL 3
4 *syn* see AMOUNT 2
rivalize *vb syn* see RIVAL 2
rivalry *n syn* see CONTEST 1
rive *vb* **1** *syn* see TEAR 1
rel divide, separate; chop, hew
2 *syn* see SHATTER 1
rivel *n syn* see WRINKLE
rivet *vb* **1** *syn* see FASTEN 1
2 *syn* see FASTEN 3
rivulet *n syn* see CREEK 2
road *n* **1** *often* **roads** *pl syn* see HARBOR 3
2 *syn* see WAY 1
3 *syn* see WAY 2
roadblock *n syn* see BAR 2
roadhouse *n syn* see HOTEL
roadman *n syn* see PEDDLER
roadstead *n syn* see HARBOR 3
roadster *n syn* see VAGABOND
roam *vb syn* see WANDER 1
roamer *n syn* see ROVER
roar *vb* to make a very loud and often a continuous or protracted noise <the crowd *roared* their disapproval of the speech>
syn bawl, bellow, bluster, clamor, rout; *compare* BAWL 2
rel rebound, repercuss, reverberate; shout, vociferate, yell; din
con breathe, murmur, mutter, whisper
roaring *adj* **1** *syn* see LOUD 1
2 *syn* see FLOURISHING
roast *vb* **1** *syn* see BURN 3
2 *syn* see LAMBASTE 3
rob *vb* **1** to take possessions unlawfully <*rob* a bank> <he was mugged and *robbed*>
syn ‖knock off, knock over, loot, plunder, ransack, relieve, rifle, stick up; *compare* BURGLARIZE, HOUSEBREAK
rel ‖heist, hold up; jackroll, roll; strongarm; filch, hijack, lift, pilfer, purloin, steal,

syn synonym(s)   *rel* related word(s)
ant antonym(s)   *con* contrasted word(s)
idiom idiomatic equivalent(s)
‖ use limited; if in doubt, see a dictionary

thieve; cheat, defraud, hustle, swindle; despoil, pillage, ravage, sack

2 *syn* see DEPRIVE 2

robber *n* one who commits the crime of robbery <only one *robber* was involved in the holdup>

syn yegg; *compare* THIEF

rel hijacker; sandbagger; crook, swindler; cat burglar, cat man, housebreaker, raffles, second-story man; rifler; holdup man, stickup man; ‖bushranger, highwayman, ‖sticker-up

roborant *adj syn* see TONIC 1

robot *n* 1 a machine that looks like a human being and performs various complex acts (as walking or talking) of a human being <a *robot* that performed household chores>

syn android, automaton

rel golem

2 an efficient, insensitive, often brutalized person <working on an assembly line can often turn a man into a *robot*>

syn automaton, golem, machine

robust *adj* 1 *syn* see FLOURISHING

2 *syn* see STRONG 3

robustious *adj syn* see BOORISH

rock *vb* 1 *syn* see SHAKE 4

rel oscillate, sway, swing, undulate; quake, totter, tremble

2 *syn* see TOSS 2

3 *syn* see HURRY 2

rock *n* 1 *syn* see ERROR 2

2 *syn* see DOLLAR

3 **rocks** *pl syn* see MONEY

rock bottom *n syn* see ESSENCE 2

rock–bottom *adj syn* see BOTTOMMOST

rockbound *adj* 1 *syn* see ROCKY 1

2 *syn* see INFLEXIBLE 2

rocket *vb* 1 *syn* see SKYROCKET

rel arise, ascend, levitate, mount, surge, tower

2 *syn* see HURRY 2

rock pile *n syn* see JAIL

rock–ribbed *adj* 1 *syn* see ROCKY 1

2 *syn* see INFLEXIBLE 2

rocky *adj* 1 abounding in or consisting of rocks <a *rocky* shore>

syn rockbound, rock-ribbed

rel bebouldered, bouldery; stony

2 *syn* see INSENSIBLE 5

rocky *adj* 1 *syn* see UNSTABLE 2

2 *syn* see OBSCENE 2

‖**Rocky Mountain canary** *n syn* see DONKEY 1

rococo *adj* 1 *syn* see OLD-FASHIONED

2 *syn* see ORNATE

rod *n* 1 *syn* see BAR 1

2 *syn* see PUNISHMENT

idiom rod in pickle

rodomont *n syn* see BRAGGART

rodomontade *n* 1 *syn* see BOMBAST

rel boasting, bragging, vaunting; pride, vainglory, vanity

2 *syn* see BRAGGART

rodomontade *vb syn* see BOAST

rodomontade *adj syn* see BOASTFUL

rogue *n* 1 *syn* see VILLAIN 1

rel culprit, delinquent

2 *syn* see SWINDLER

3 *syn* see SCAMP

roguery *n syn* see MISCHIEVOUSNESS

roguish *adj* 1 *syn* see DISHONEST

2 *syn* see PLAYFUL 1

3 *syn* see COY 2

roguishness *n syn* see MISCHIEVOUSNESS

roil *vb* 1 to make turbid <*roiled* the brook with his splashings>

syn mud, muddle, muddy, rile

rel befoul, contaminate, dirty, pollute

con clear, purify, settle

2 *syn* see IRRITATE

roily *adj syn* see TURBID

roister *vb syn* see REVEL 1

role *n* 1 characteristic exterior properties and aspects, style, and atmosphere in which something intangible is discerned <the moral *role* of the legislature>

syn character, clothing

rel appearance, face, guise, seeming, semblance, show; aspect, look

2 *syn* see FUNCTION 1

roll *n* 1 *syn* see LIST

2 *syn* see ROSTER 1

‖3 *syn* see FORTUNE 4

roll *vb* 1 *syn* see PONDER 1

2 *syn* see SWATHE

3 to wrap around on itself or something else <this cloth *rolls* unevenly>

syn furl

4 *syn* see WALLOW 3

5 *syn* see TURN 1

6 *syn* see WANDER 1

7 *syn* see POUR 2

8 *syn* see RUMBLE

9 *syn* see TOSS 2

roll call *n syn* see LIST

rollick *vb* 1 *syn* see GAMBOL

2 *syn* see WALLOW 3

rollick *n syn* see ESCAPADE

rollicking *adj syn* see ANTIC 2

rel cheerful, glad, happy, joyful, joyous, lighthearted

roll in *vb syn* see RETIRE 4

ant roll out

rolling stone *n syn* see ROVER

roll out *vb* to leave one's bed <*rolled* out at dawn>

syn arise, get up, pile (out), rise, rise and shine, turn out, uprise

ant roll in

roll up *vb syn* see ACCUMULATE

roly–poly *adj syn* see ROTUND 2

romance *n syn* see LOVE AFFAIR

romanesque *adj syn* see EXOTIC 2

romantic *adj syn* see EXOTIC 2

2 *syn* see SENTIMENTAL

rel fanciful, fantastic, imaginary, quixotic, visionary; created, invented

ant unromantic; matter-of-fact

Romeo *n syn* see GALLANT 2

romp *n syn* see RUNAWAY

romp *vb syn* see GAMBOL

idiom cut capers, horse around

rondure *n syn* see BALL

roof *n syn* see TOP 1

roof *vb syn* see HARBOR 1

rook *vb syn* see FLEECE 1

rookie *n syn* see NOVICE

room *n* 1 space in a building enclosed or set apart by a partition <the house had seven *rooms*>

syn apartment, chamber

2 **rooms** *pl syn* see APARTMENT 1

3 enough space or range for free movement <no *room* for hope>

syn elbowroom, latitude, leeway, margin, play, scope

rel clearance; license, range, rein, sway; rope

room *vb syn* see HARBOR 2

room and board *n syn* see ACCOMMODATIONS

roomy *adj syn* see SPACIOUS

ant cramped

‖**roose** *vb syn* see COMMEND 2

roost *vb* 1 *syn* see ALIGHT

2 *syn* see HARBOR 2

root *n* 1 *syn* see SOURCE

rel basis, foundation, ground

2 *syn* see BASIS 1

3 *syn* see CENTER 3

4 *syn* see ESSENCE 2

root *vb syn* see ENTRENCH 1

ant uproot

root *vb syn* see APPLAUD 2

rootage *n syn* see SOURCE

rootless *adj syn* see WEAK 2

root out *vb syn* see ANNIHILATE 2

rel demolish, destroy, raze

ant enroot

rootstock *n syn* see SOURCE

roperipe *n syn* see VILLAIN 1

ropes *n pl syn* see INS AND OUTS

ropy *adj syn* see MUSCULAR 1

rose *vb syn* see BLUSH

roseate *adj syn* see HOPEFUL 2

rose-colored *adj syn* see HOPEFUL 2

rose-colored spectacles *n pl syn* see OPTIMISM

roster *n* 1 a list of officers or enlisted men <an army *roster*>

syn muster, muster roll, roll

2 *syn* see LIST

rosy *adj syn* see HOPEFUL 2

rot *vb* 1 *syn* see DECAY

rel corrupt, debase, vitiate

2 *syn* see DETERIORATE 1

3 *syn* see DEBASE 1

rot *n syn* see NONSENSE 2

rotate *vb* 1 *syn* see TURN 1

2 to succeed or cause to succeed each other in turn <the drivers in the car pool *rotated* each week>

syn alternate

rel bandy, exchange, interchange; ensue, follow, succeed; relieve, spell

rotation *n syn* see REVOLUTION 1

rote *n syn* see ROUTINE

rotten *adj* 1 *syn* see BAD 5

rel foul; tainted, touched; sour

2 *syn* see VICIOUS 2

3 *syn* see BAD 8

4 *syn* see BAD 1

rotter *n syn* see CAD

rotund *adj* 1 *syn* see RESONANT

2 rounded or swollen with fat <a wheezing *rotund* man lumbered by>

syn chubby, plump, plumpish, plumpy, podgy, puddy, pudgy, roly-poly, round, roundabout, spuddy, tubby; *compare* FAT 2

rel beefy, chunky, dumpy, heavyset, squat, stocky, stubby, thick, thickset; paunchy, potbellied; buxom, ‖crummy

idiom on the plump side

con angular, gaunt, lank, lanky, lean, rawboned, scrawny, skinny, spare; slender, slight, slim, thin

roturier *n syn* see UPSTART

rouge *vb syn* see BLUSH

rough *adj* 1 not smooth or even <a *rough* undressed block of stone>

syn asperous, cragged, craggy, hairy, harsh, ironbound, jagged, rugged, scabrous, scraggy, uneven, unlevel, unsmooth

rel bumpy, choppy; burred; firm, hard, solid; coarse, gross

con flat, flush, level, plain, plane

ant smooth

2 *syn* see WILD 6

con calm, halcyon, peaceful, placid, serene, tranquil

3 *syn* see TOUGH 8

4 *syn* see TIGHT 3

5 *syn* see INDECOROUS

6 *syn* see RUDE 1

idiom in the rough

7 *syn* see RUDE 3

8 *syn* see HARSH 3

9 *syn* see COARSE 3

rel discourteous, impolite, uncivil, ungracious

10 *syn* see BLUFF

11 *syn* see HARD 6

rough *n syn* see TOUGH

rough (out) *vb syn* see SKETCH

rough (up) *vb syn* see MANHANDLE

rough-and-ready *adj syn* see MAKESHIFT

rough-and-tumble *n syn* see BRAWL 2

rough-and-tumble *adj syn* see MAKESHIFT

roughhewn *adj syn* see RUDE 1

roughhouse *n syn* see HORSEPLAY

roughhouse *vb syn* see MANHANDLE

roughhousing *n syn* see HORSEPLAY

roughly *adv* 1 *syn* see HARD 5

ant smoothly

2 *syn* see NEARLY

roughneck *n syn* see TOUGH

roughness *n syn* see INEQUALITY 1

ant smoothness

roughscuff *n syn* see RABBLE 2

round *adj* 1 having every part of the circumference equally distant from a center within <flowers crowded in stiff *round* beds>

syn circular

rel annular, globular, orbed, orbicular, rounded, spherical, spiral

2 *syn* see CURVED

3 *syn* see ROTUND 2

4 *syn* see OUTSPOKEN

5 *syn* see RESONANT

round *adv* 1 *syn* see ABOUT 1

2 *syn* see NEARLY

3 *syn* see THROUGH 1

4 *syn* see ABOUT 6

round *prep* 1 *syn* see NEAR 2

2 *syn* see ABOUT 4

round *n* 1 *syn* see BALL

2 *syn* see REVOLUTION 1

3 *syn* see TOUR 2

4 *syn* see CYCLE 1

5 *syn* see CURVE

round *vb* 1 *syn* see BALL

2 *syn* see SURROUND 1

---

syn synonym(s)   *rel* related word(s)
ant antonym(s)   *con* contrasted word(s)
idiom idiomatic equivalent(s)
‖ use limited; if in doubt, see a dictionary

3 *syn* see POLISH 2

4 *syn* see CURVE

round about *adv* 1 *syn* see ABOUT 1

2 *syn* see ABOUT 6

3 *syn* see ABOUT 2

roundabout *n* 1 *syn* see DETOUR

2 *syn* see VERBIAGE 1

3 *syn* see TOUR 2

4 *syn* see EXCURSION 1

roundabout *adj* 1 *syn* see INDIRECT 1

2 *syn* see ROTUND 2

rounded *adj* 1 *syn* see CURVED

2 *syn* see CURVACEOUS

rounder *n syn* see WASTREL 1

roundheel *n syn* see DOXY 1

roundly *adv* 1 *syn* see WELL 3

2 *syn* see NEARLY

round off *vb syn* see CLIMAX

round trip *n syn* see TOUR 2

round up *vb syn* see GROUP 1

rouse *vb* 1 *syn* see WAKE 1

  rel animate, enliven, quicken, vivify; excite, provoke, stimulate; foment, incite, instigate

  con calm, compose, lull, quiet, quieten, settle, soothe, still, tranquilize

2 *syn* see INTENSIFY

3 *syn* see PROVOKE 4

4 *syn* see STIR 1

rouser *n syn* see ‖DILLY

rousing *adj* 1 *syn* see EXCITING

2 *syn* see LIVELY 1

‖**roust** *vb syn* see PROVOKE 4

roustabout *n syn* see WORKER

rout *n* 1 *syn* see MOB 2

2 *syn* see RABBLE 2

3 *syn* see MULTITUDE 1

rout *vb syn* see ROAR

rout *vb syn* see RUMMAGE 3

rout *n* 1 *syn* see DEFEAT 1

2 *syn* see RUNAWAY

rout *vb* 1 to put to precipitate flight < the army regrouped and *routed* the enemy>

  syn derout, stampede

  rel chase, dispel, drive, expel

  idiom put to flight

2 *syn* see WHIP 2

route *n syn* see WAY 2

route *vb* 1 *syn* see SEND 1

2 *syn* see GUIDE

routine *n* habitual or mechanical and sometimes monotonous performance of an established procedure < settled into the *routine* of factory work>

  syn grind, groove, pace, rote, rut, treadmill

  rel squirrel cage; ‖drill

  idiom the beaten path, the drab monotony of habit

routine *adj* 1 *syn* see ORDINARY 1

2 *syn* see USUAL 1

rove *vb syn* see WANDER 1

rover *n syn* see PIRATE

rover *n* one who roams habitually < he spent most of his life as a *rover* always on the move>

  syn drifter, meanderer, rambler, roamer, rolling stone, wanderer

  rel gad, gadabout, gadder, runabout; itinerant, peripatetic; floater

  idiom bird of passage

  con homebody

  ant stay-at-home

roving *adj syn* see ITINERANT

row *vb* to propel a boat by means of oars < *rowed* across the lake>

  syn oar, paddle, pull

  rel scull; punt; sail, scud

row *n* 1 *syn* see LINE 5

2 *syn* see SUCCESSION 2

row *n* 1 *syn* see BRAWL 2

2 *syn* see QUARREL

3 *syn* see MOUTH 1

row *vb* ‖1 *syn* see SCOLD 1

2 *syn* see QUARREL

rowdiness *n syn* see HORSEPLAY

rowdy *adj syn* see TURBULENT 1

rowdy *n syn* see TOUGH

rowdydow *n* 1 *syn* see COMMOTION 4

2 *syn* see BRAWL 2

3 *syn* see BINGE 1

rowdydowdy *adj syn* see TURBULENT 1

rowdyish *adj syn* see TURBULENT 1

royal *adj* 1 *syn* see KINGLY

  rel glorious, resplendent, splendid, superb; august, imposing, stately

2 *syn* see EASY 1

3 *syn* see GRAND 1

4 *syn* see EXCELLENT

royalist *n syn* see REACTIONARY

‖**rozzer** *n syn* see POLICEMAN

rub *vb* 1 *syn* see ABRADE 1

2 *syn* see CHAFE 3

  rel aggravate, exasperate, nettle, peeve, provoke, rile; annoy, bother, irk, vex

3 *syn* see POLISH 1

rub *n syn* see OBSTACLE

rubber *n syn* see BUSYBODY

rubberneck *n* 1 *syn* see BUSYBODY

2 *syn* see TOURIST

rubberneck *vb syn* see LOOK 7

rubber stamp *n syn* see COMMONPLACE

rubbish *n* 1 *syn* see REFUSE

2 *syn* see NONSENSE 2

3 *syn* see PAP 2

rubbishing *adj syn* see CHEAP 2

rubbishly *adj syn* see CHEAP 2

rubbishy *adj syn* see CHEAP 2

rube *n syn* see RUSTIC

rubicund *adj syn* see RUDDY

rubify *vb syn* see REDDEN 1

rub out *vb* 1 *syn* see DESTROY 1

2 *syn* see MURDER 1

rubric *n syn* see NAME 1

rubric *adj syn* see NOTEWORTHY

rubric *vb syn* see REDDEN 1

ruby *vb syn* see REDDEN 1

ruck *n* ‖1 *syn* see PILE 1

2 *syn* see GATHERING 2

ruck *n syn* see WRINKLE

ruck (up) *vb syn* see CRUMPLE 1

‖**ruckle** *vb syn* see CRUMPLE 1

rucksack *n syn* see BACKPACK

ruckus *n* 1 *syn* see COMMOTION 3

  rel brawl, broil, melee, scrap

2 *syn* see QUARREL

ruction *n* 1 *syn* see BRAWL 2

2 *syn* see COMMOTION 4

‖**ructious** *adj syn* see BELLIGERENT

rud *vb syn* see REDDEN 1

ruddle *vb syn* see REDDEN 1

ruddy *adj* having a healthy reddish color < has a *ruddy* complexion after being out in the cold>

  syn florid, flush, flushed, full-blooded, glowing, rubicund, sanguine

rel bronzed; blooming; blowsy
con ashen, ashy, livid, pale, pallid, wan, waxy; anemic, bloodless

ruddy *vb syn* see REDDEN 1

rude *adj* 1 lacking in craftsmanship or artistic finish < a *rude* sketch>
syn angular, crude, lumpy, raw, rough, roughhewn, undressed, unfashioned, unfinished, unformed, unhewn, unpolished, unworked, unwrought
rel unlicked; unprocessed; primitive, rudimental, rudimentary
con dressed, fashioned, finished, formed, hewn, polished, worked, wrought
2 *syn* see DISSONANT 1
3 hastily executed and admittedly imperfect or imprecise < *rude* estimates of the cost of building the house>
syn approximate, proximate, rough
rel crude, imperfect, imprecise, inexact
idiom ‖in the ball park
con accurate, correct; faultless, perfect; exact, precise; meticulous, scrupulous
4 *syn* see COARSE 3
5 *syn* see IGNORANT 1
6 lacking in social refinement < gave a *rude* reply to a polite question>
syn discourteous, disgracious, disrespectful, ill, ill-bred, ill-mannered, impertinent, impolite, incivil, incondite, inurbane, mannerless, ‖mismannered, uncalled-for, uncivil, uncourteous, uncouth, ungracious, unhandsome, unmannered, unmannerly, unpolished
rel brusque, crusty, curt, gruff; harsh; intrusive, meddlesome; crabbed, surly; boorish, churlish, clownish, loutish
con courteous, genteel, mannerly, polite, well-mannered; bland, diplomatic, politic, smooth, suave; affable, considerate, gracious
ant civil; urbane
7 *syn* see BARBARIAN 1
8 *syn* see INEXPERIENCED

rudely *adv syn* see NEARLY

rudiment *n* 1 *syn* see ESSENTIAL 1
2 **rudiments** *pl syn* see ALPHABET 2

rudimental *adj syn* see ELEMENTARY 1

rudimentary *adj syn* see ELEMENTARY 1

rue *vb syn* see REGRET

rue *n* 1 *syn* see SORROW
2 *syn* see PENITENCE
3 *syn* see PITY

rueful *adj* 1 *syn* see PITIFUL 1
2 *syn* see WOEFUL 1
3 *syn* see MELANCHOLY 2
rel depressed, oppressed, weighed down; piteous, pitiful; despairing, despondent, hopeless

ruffian *n* 1 *syn* see TOUGH
2 *syn* see THUG 1

ruffle *vb* 1 *syn* see BLOW 1
2 *syn* see ABRADE 1
3 *syn* see ANNOY 1
‖4 *syn* see INTIMIDATE

rugged *adj* 1 *syn* see ROUGH 1
2 *syn* see SEVERE 3
rel arduous, difficult

---

3 *syn* see HARSH 3
4 *syn* see BOORISH
5 *syn* see TOUGH 4
rel brawny, burly, husky, muscular
ant fragile
6 *syn* see HARD 6

ruin *n* 1 *syn* see DETERIORATION 1
2 *syn* see DOWNFALL 2
3 the bringing about of or the results of disaster < met *ruin* at the hands of the enemy>
syn confusion, destruction, devastation, havoc, loss, ruination
rel crumbling, disintegration; break up, dissolution; disrepair; wreck
con rebuilding, reconstruction, re-creation
4 *syn* see INJURY 1

ruin *vb* 1 *syn* see DESTROY 1
rel deface, disfigure; maim, mangle, mutilate; depredate, desecrate, desolate, despoil, devastate, devour, pillage, sack, spoliate, waste
ant restore
2 to subject to forces that are destructive of soundness, worth, or usefulness < in danger of being *ruined* by prosperity>
syn bankrupt, dilapidate, do in, shipwreck, wreck
rel corrupt, debase, degenerate, vitiate
idiom play hob (*or* the devil) with
con rebuild, renew, restore; reclaim, redeem, retrieve, salvage
3 to overthrow the fortunes of < was *ruined* during the great crash>
syn bankrupt, break, bust, fold up, impoverish, pauper, pauperize
rel beggar, clean out, deplete, drain, draw, draw down, exhaust, use up; wipe (out); reduce
idiom go under, lose one's shirt (*or* pants), take to the cleaners
4 *syn* see FRUSTRATE 1

‖**ruinate** *vb syn* see DESTROY 1

ruination *n* 1 *syn* see RUIN 3
2 *syn* see DOWNFALL 2

ruinator *n syn* see VANDAL

ruiner *n syn* see VANDAL

ruinous *adj* 1 *syn* see DESTRUCTIVE
2 *syn* see FATAL 2

rule *n* 1 *syn* see LAW 1
rel order; axiom, fundamental, principle; decorum, etiquette, propriety
2 *syn* see MAXIM
rel fundamental, principle

rule *vb* 1 *syn* see GOVERN 1
rel guide, lead
2 to hold preeminence in (as by ability, strength, or position) < an actor who rightfully *rules* the Shakespearian stage>
syn dominate, domineer, predominate, preponderate, prevail, reign
rel guide, lead; preside
idiom be number one, take first place (*in or* on)
3 *syn* see DECIDE
rel deduce, gather, infer, judge

rule out *vb* 1 *syn* see EXCLUDE
2 *syn* see PREVENT 2

ruling *n syn* see EDICT 1

ruling *adj* 1 *syn* see CENTRAL 1
con peripheral
2 *syn* see PREVAILING

‖**rum** *adj syn* see STRANGE 4

---

syn synonym(s)   *rel* related word(s)
ant antonym(s)   *con* contrasted word(s)
idiom idiomatic equivalent(s)
‖ use limited; if in doubt, see a dictionary

rumble *vb* to make a low heavy rolling sound < thunder *rumbling* in the distance >
syn growl, grumble, roll
rel boom, roar, thunder; peal, resound; blast, burst, clap, crack, crash

rumble *n syn see* REPORT 1

rumble–bumble *n syn see* MISCELLANY 1

rumbustious *adj syn see* TURBULENT 1

rum–dum *adj syn see* INTOXICATED 1

rumdum *n syn see* DRUNKARD

‖**rum–hole** *n syn see* BAR 5

ruminate *vb* 1 *syn see* PONDER 2
rel consider, excogitate, weigh
2 *syn see* CHEW 1

ruminative *adj syn see* THOUGHTFUL 1

rummage *n syn see* CLUTTER 2
rel conglomeration, hash, hotchpotch, miscellany, patchwork, potpourri

rummage *vb* 1 *syn see* DISORDER 1
2 *syn see* SCOUR 2
3 to produce by searching < *rummaged* an old dress out of the attic >
syn dig out, hunt (down *or* out *or* up), rout
rel ferret (out), find; fish, search (out), spy (out); poke

rummery *n syn see* BAR 5

‖**rum–mill** *n syn see* BAR 5

rummy *adj syn see* STRANGE 4

rummy *n syn see* DRUNKARD

rumor *n* 1 *syn see* REPORT 1
2 *syn see* MURMUR 1

rumor *vb syn see* GOSSIP

rumorer *n syn see* GOSSIP 1

rumormonger *n syn see* GOSSIP 1

rump *n syn see* BUTTOCKS

rumple *vb syn see* CRUMPLE 1

‖**rumpot** *n syn see* DRUNKARD

rumpus *n* 1 *syn see* COMMOTION 3
2 *syn see* ARGUMENT 2

rumshop *n syn see* BAR 5

run *vb* 1 to move at a fast springing gait in which both feet are momentarily off the ground in the course of each pace < the boy *ran* down the walk >
syn dash, scamper, scoot, scurry, shin, sprint; *compare* SCUTTLE
rel career, course, race; bustle, hurry, hustle, rush, speed; scorch
con crawl, creep, drag, inch, mosey, poke, saunter, stroll, toddle
2 to hasten away from something that frightens or perturbs < afraid to fight but ashamed to *run* >
syn bolt, flee, fly, make off, scamper, scoot, ‖screw, skedaddle, skip, skirr
idiom ‖dog it, make a break, run for it, show a clean pair of heels, take flight, take French leave, take to one's heels
3 *syn see* HURRY 2
idiom go all out, go like (greased) lightning
4 *syn see* RESORT 2
5 *syn see* FUNCTION 3
6 *syn see* BECOME 1
7 *syn see* LIQUEFY
8 to lie in or take a certain course < the path *runs* along the crest of the hill >
syn extend, go, make, reach, stretch
9 *syn see* RANGE 3
10 *syn see* HUNT 1
11 *syn see* DRIVE 3

12 *syn see* THRUST 2
13 *syn see* SMUGGLE
14 *syn see* OPERATE 3
15 *syn see* CONDUCT 3

run (through *or* over) *vb syn see* BROWSE

run (to *or* into) *vb syn see* AMOUNT 1

run *n* 1 ‖*syn see* CREEK 2
2 an uninterrupted course of occurrence or repetition especially of like things or events < the play had a long *run* >
syn continuance, continuation, duration, persistence
rel continuity, endurance, prolongation
3 *syn see* TENDENCY 1
rel course, set; bearing, direction, line, swing
4 *syn see* TRIP 1
‖5 **runs** *pl but sing or pl in constr syn see* DIARRHEA

runagate *n* 1 *syn see* RENEGADE
2 *syn see* VAGABOND

run along *vb syn see* GO 2

runaround *n* 1 *syn see* DETOUR
2 *syn see* ESCAPE 2

run away *vb syn see* ELOPE

runaway *n* a one-sided or overwhelming victory < the game was a *runaway*, the home team winning by 30 points >
syn cakewalk, romp, rout, walkaway, walkover
rel breather, cinch, duck soup, pushover; setup; shutout; conquest, triumph, victory, win
con photo finish, tossup

run down *vb syn see* DECRY 2

run–down *adj* 1 *syn see* SHABBY 1
2 *syn see* NEGLECTED
rel abandoned, derelict, deserted, desolate, forsaken, lorn

rune *n* 1 *syn see* SPELL
2 *syn see* POEM

rung *n syn see* DEGREE 1

run in *vb* 1 *syn see* ARREST 2
2 *syn see* VISIT 2

run–in *n* 1 *syn see* ENCOUNTER
2 *syn see* QUARREL

runnel *n syn see* CREEK 2

running *n syn see* OVERSIGHT 1

running *adj* 1 *syn see* ACTIVE 1
2 *syn see* EASY 9

running *adv syn see* TOGETHER 2

running mate *n syn see* ASSOCIATE 3

run–of–mine *adj* 1 *syn see* UNREFINED 3
2 *syn see* MEDIUM

run–of–the–mill *adj* 1 *syn see* MEDIUM
rel uncommon, unexceptional
2 *syn see* GENERAL 1

run on *vb syn see* CHAT 1

run out *vb* 1 *syn see* FAIL 2
2 *syn* BANISH

run over *vb syn see* OVERFLOW 2

runt *n syn see* DWARF

runted *adj syn see* STUNTED

run through *vb syn see* GO 4

runtish *adj syn see* STUNTED

runty *adj syn see* STUNTED

run up *vb* 1 *syn see* INCREASE 2
2 *syn see* THROW UP 1

rupture *n* 1 *syn see* BREACH 3
rel division, divorce, parting
2 *syn see* SEPARATION 1

rupture *vb* 1 *syn see* OPEN 3
rel divide, divorce, part, separate, sunder; cleave, rend, rive, split

2 *syn* see SEPARATE 1
rural *adj syn* relating to or characteristic of the country <a peaceful *rural* scene>
  syn agrestic, bucolic, campestral, countrified, country, out-country, outland, pastoral, provincial, rustic
  rel arcadian, idyllic; natural, simple, unsophisticated
  con metropolitan, municipal, oppidan; crammed, crowded, packed, populous; bustling, busy, hustling; artificial, mundane, sophisticated; worldly
  ant urban; citified
ruse *n syn* see TRICK 1
rush *vb* 1 to move or cause to move quickly, impetuously, and often heedlessly <*rushed* around madly trying to get things done>
  syn boil, bolt, charge, chase, dash, fling, lash, race, shoot, ‖swither, tear; *compare* COURSE, HURRY 2, PLUNGE 2, STAMPEDE 2
  rel hasten, hurry, speed; dart, fly, scud; break
  idiom go off half-cocked, not look before one leaps
2 *syn* see HURRY 2
3 *syn* see COURSE
rush *n* 1 *syn* see HASTE 2
2 *syn* see FLOW
rushing *adj syn* see PRECIPITATE 1
rushlight *n syn* see NONENTITY

rustic *adj syn* see RURAL
rustic *n* an inhabitant of a rural or remote area who is usually characterized by an utter lack of sophistication and cultivation <an unbelieving *rustic* gawking at the skyscrapers>
  syn ‖apple knocker, ‖backwoodser, backwoodsman, bucolic, bumpkin, chawbacon, clodhopper, clown, country jake, countryman, greenhorn, hayseed, hick, hillbilly, hillman; ‖hodge, hoosier, jake, jay, joskin, mossback, mountaineer, peasant, provincial, redneck, ‖ridge runner, rube, ‖wayback, woodsy, yap, ‖yob, yokel
  rel rural; exurbanite, suburbanite; agriculturalist, farmer, granger, husbandman
  con burgher, oppidan, townsman; cityite, urbanite; cosmopolitan, cosmopolite
  ant city slicker
rustle *n syn* see HASTE 1
rustler *n syn* see HUSTLER 1
rusty *adj syn* see HARSH 3
‖**rusty** *adj syn* see ILL-TEMPERED
rut *n syn* see ROUTINE
ruth *n* 1 *syn* see PITY
2 *syn* see PENITENCE
ruthful *adj syn* see WOEFUL 1
ruthless *adj syn* see GRIM 3
ruttish *adj syn* see LUSTFUL 2
‖**ruttle** *vb syn* see RATTLE 1
rutty *adj syn* see LUSTFUL 2

S

sable *adj syn* see BLACK 1
  rel dark, dusky, murky; gloomy, somber
sabotage *n* willful effort by indirect means to hinder, prevent, undo, or discredit (as a plan or activity) <*sabotage* of the project by disgruntled officials>
  syn subversion, undermining, wreckage, wrecking
  rel subversiveness, subversivism; damage, impairment, injury
sabotage *vb* to practice sabotage on <*sabotaged* his opponent's campaign with rumors and smears>
  syn subvert, undermine, wreck
  rel frustrate, hamper, hinder; block, obstruct; damage; break up, destroy
  idiom throw a monkey wrench into
  con assist, back, support
saccharine *adj syn* see INGRATIATING
  rel candied, cloying, honeyed, oversweet, sugar-candy, sugar-coated, sugared, sugary, sweet, syrupy
sacerdotal *adj* of, relating to, or belonging to priests or priesthood <*sacerdotal* vestments>
  syn hieratic, priestal, priestish, priestlike, priestly, sacerdotical

  rel churchly, ecclesiastical, religious; clerical, ministerial; apostolic, papal
sacerdotical *adj syn* see SACERDOTAL
sack *n syn* see BAG 1
  rel container; pocket
sack *vb syn* see DISMISS 3
  rel expel, ship; ‖bump, ‖chuck
  idiom give one the sack, send packing
sack *vb syn* see RAVAGE
  rel forage, raid; strip
sacker *n syn* see MARAUDER
sacred *adj* 1 *syn* see HOLY 1
  rel sacramental; angelic, godly, saintly; cherished
  con lay, secular, temporal; earthly; unhallowed
  ant profane
2 dedicated to or hallowed by association with a deity <*sacred* songs>
  syn numinous, spiritual; *compare* HOLY 1
  rel hallowed, sanctified
3 protected (as by law, custom, or human respect) against abuse <a fund *sacred* to charity>
  syn inviolable, inviolate, sacrosanct
  rel defended, guarded, protected, shielded; immune, untouchable
Sacred Writ *n syn* see BIBLE
  idiom Good Book
sacrifice *n syn* see VICTIM 1
  rel burnt offering, oblation; sacrification; hecatomb; sin offering
sacrifice *vb* 1 to offer as a victim in sacrifice <Abraham about to *sacrifice* Isaac>

---

syn synonym(s)   *rel* related word(s)
ant antonym(s)   *con* contrasted word(s)
idiom idiomatic equivalent(s)
‖ use limited; if in doubt, see a dictionary

syn immolate, victimize
rel offer (up); consecrate, dedicate, devote; donate, give, yield
2 *syn* see LOSE 1
idiom kiss good-bye
3 *syn* see FORGO
rel cede, yield
idiom part with

sacrilege *n syn* see PROFANATION
rel irreverence; heresy; crime, impiety, offense, sin

sacrilegious *adj* involving or marked by debasement or defilement of what is sacred < *sacrilegious* despoilers of ancient churches >
syn blasphemous, profane
rel impious, irreverent, ungodly; evil, sinful, wicked; irreligious
con godly, pious, reverent; religious

sacrosanct *adj syn* see SACRED 3
rel esteemed, regarded, respected

sad *adj* 1 affected with or expressing sadness < was *sad* to see him go >
syn heavyhearted, melancholy, mournful, saddened, sorry, unhappy; *compare* DOWNCAST, MELANCHOLY 2
rel blue, dejected, dispirited, down, downbeat, downcast, drear, dumpish, dumpy; grieving, unenjoying; depressed, morose; depressing, dismal, joyless, mirthless, saddening, triste; desolate
con happy, joyful, joyous; blithe, gay, lighthearted; exalted, fired, inspired, uplifted
ant glad
2 causing sadness < felt miserable after listening to that *sad* song >
syn depressing, joyless, melancholic, melancholy, mournful, saddening, triste; *compare* MELANCHOLY 2
rel dismal, gloomy; afflicting, doleful, dreary, lamentable, sorrowful; pathetic, tear-jerking
con bright, gay, lively; exhilarating, heartwarming, stimulating, stirring
ant happy

sadden *vb syn* see DEPRESS 2
idiom make blue, ‖put into a funk
ant gladden

saddened *adj syn* see SAD 1

saddening *adj syn* see SAD 2

saddle *vb syn* see BURDEN
rel hamper, impede, restrict; impose, inflict
idiom hang like a millstone around one's neck

sadness *n* the quality, state, or an instance of being sad < her feelings of *sadness* and longing persisted long after he left >
syn blues, dejection, depression, dinge, (the) dismals, (the) dolefuls, dumps, dysphoria, gloom, heavyheartedness, melancholy, mopes, mournfulness, suds, unhappiness
rel dispiritedness, doldrums, downcastness, downheartedness, downs, ‖funk, listlessness, moodiness; anguish, grief, sorrow, sorrowfulness, woe; desolation, disconsolateness, disconsolation, forlornness, misery, mourning; blue devils, despondency, hopelessness, megrims, melancholia
idiom slough of despond

con happiness, joy, joyfulness, joyousness; cheerfulness, cheeriness, gayness, lightheartedness, liveliness; exhilaration, ups
ant gladness

safe *adj* 1 having been freed from risk, danger, harm, or injury < refugees who found themselves *safe* at last in a neutral country >
syn scatheless, unharmed, unscathed
rel unhurt, uninjured; intact
idiom in (*or* with) a whole skin, out of harm's way, safe and sound
con damaged, harmed, hurt, injured
ant unsafe
2 affording security from threat of harm, injury, risk, or loss < found a *safe* place to hide >
syn riskless, secure
rel guarding, protecting, safeguarding, sheltering, shielding; defended, guarded, protected, sheltered, shielded; unthreatened; impregnable, inviolable, invulnerable, unassailable
idiom safe as a bank vault
con insecure, undefended, unguarded, unprotected, vulnerable; threatened; hazardous, risky
ant dangerous, unsafe
3 not threatening danger < it's *safe* to go there only in the daytime >
syn healthy, uninjurious, wholesome; *compare* HARMLESS
rel innocent, innocuous, inoffensive
con hazardous, perilous, precarious, risky; harmful, injurious, unhealthy
ant dangerous, unsafe
4 *syn* see CAUTIOUS

safeguard *n syn* see DEFENSE 1
rel palladium; buffer, screen

safeguard *vb syn* see DEFEND 1
rel conserve, preserve, save; assure, ensure, insure

safekeeping *n* 1 *syn* see CUSTODY
2 *syn* see PRESERVATION 1

safeness *n syn* see SAFETY

safety *n* the quality, state, or condition of being safe < there's *safety* in numbers >
syn assurance, safeness, security
rel cover, protection, shelter; defense; impregnability, inviolability, invulnerability
con hazard, jeopardy, peril, risk, threat; instability, vulnerability
ant danger

sag *vb* 1 *syn* see SLIP 6
2 *syn* see DROOP 3
rel bend, decline; dangle, flap, flop
idiom ‖have a case of the sags
ant tauten

sag *n* 1 *syn* see DEPRESSION 2
rel settling, sinking
2 *syn* see DECLINE 3

sagacious *adj* 1 *syn* see WISE 1
rel clever, intelligent, smart; far-seeing; judicious, prudent, sapient
idiom wise as an owl
con dumb, stupid, unintelligent; ignorant, unlearned, untaught; unperceptive; unwise
2 *syn* see SHREWD
rel critical, discerning, discriminating
idiom wise in the ways of the world

sagaciousness *n syn* see SAGACITY

rel judgment, wiseness

sagacity *n* intelligent application of knowledge < *sagacity* acquired from years of learning and experience>
  syn insight, sagaciousness, sageness, sapience, wisdom
  rel discernment, penetration, perception, perceptiveness, sensitivity; understanding; judiciousness, prudence; comprehension, grasp

sage *adj* **1** *syn* see WISE 1
  rel philosophic; learned; profound
  2 *syn* see WISE 2
  rel acute, penetrating, probing

sage *n* one distinguished for his breadth of knowledge, experience, wisdom, and sound judgment < was one of the renowned *sages* of constitutional law>
  syn savant, scholar, wise man
  rel expert, master

sageness *n* *syn* see SAGACITY

said *adj* *syn* see SUCH 1

sail *vb* **1** *syn* see FLY 1
  2 *syn* see FLY 4

sailor *n* *syn* see MARINER

sailorman *n* *syn* see MARINER

saintliness *n* *syn* see HOLINESS
  rel righteousness, worthiness

saintly *adj* being of deeply religious and wholly upright character < a *saintly* old couple>
  syn angelic, godly, holy
  rel righteous, upright, upstanding, virtuous, worthy; devout, God-fearing, pious; sainted; seraph, seraphic, seraphlike
  idiom pure in mind and heart

salable *adj* *syn* see MARKETABLE
  ant unsalable

salacious *adj* *syn* see LICENTIOUS 2

salad *n* *syn* see MISCELLANY 1

salary *n* *syn* see WAGE

salient *adj* *syn* see NOTICEABLE
  rel important, pertinent, significant, weighty; impressive, moving; obvious, pronounced; intrusive, obtrusive

saliferous *adj* *syn* see SALTY 1

saline *adj* *syn* see SALTY 1

saliva *n* a liquid secreted into the mouth and helpful to digestion < *saliva* drooled down the baby's chin>
  syn slaver, spit, spittle, water
  rel sputum

salivate *vb* *syn* see DROOL 2

sally *n* **1** *syn* see OUTBURST 1
  2 *syn* see JOKE 1
  3 *syn* see EXCURSION 1

salmagundi *n* *syn* see MISCELLANY 1

salon *n* **1** a spacious elegant apartment or living room (as in a fashionable house) < her *salon* was decorated à la Louis XV>
  syn drawing room, saloon
  rel parlor; suite
  2 a fashionable assemblage of notables held by custom at the home of a prominent person < was famous for her literary *salons*>
  syn saloon

---

syn synonym(s)   *rel* related word(s)
ant antonym(s)   *con* contrasted word(s)
idiom idiomatic equivalent(s)
‖ use limited; if in doubt, see a dictionary

rel at home; reception; levee; evening, soiree

saloon *n* **1** *syn* see SALON 1
  rel gallery; hall
  2 *syn* see SALON 2
  rel gathering, party
  3 *syn* see BAR 5

saloonist *n* *syn* see SALOONKEEPER

saloonkeeper *n* one who owns or manages a bar < the traditional image of the fat cigar-smoking *saloonkeeper*>
  syn barkeeper, boniface, innholder, innkeeper, ‖publican, saloonist, taverner; *compare* BARTENDER
  rel victualler

salt *n* **1** *syn* see LIVING
  2 *syn* see MARINER

salt *adj* *syn* see SALTY 1

saltate *vb* *syn* see JUMP 1

salt away *vb* *syn* see SAVE 4

saltimbanque *n* *syn* see CHARLATAN
  rel impostor, pretender; cheat, fraud

salty *adj* **1** of, relating to, or containing salt < *salty* deposits>
  syn saliferous, saline, salt
  rel brackish, briny, saltish; salted
  ant saltless
  2 *syn* see RISQUÉ
  3 *syn* see CAUSTIC 1

salubrious *adj* *syn* see HEALTHFUL
  rel bracing, invigorating, stimulating
  ant insalubrious

salutary *adj* *syn* see HEALTHFUL
  rel restorative, sanative, sanatory, tonic
  con debilitating, enfeebling, weakening; bad, evil
  ant deleterious; unsalutary

salutation *n* **1** *syn* see GREETING
  2 *syn* see ENCOMIUM

salute *vb* *syn* see ADDRESS 7

salute *n* *syn* see GREETING

salutiferous *adj* *syn* see HEALTHFUL

salvage *vb* to rescue and save from wreckage, destruction, or loss < *salvaged* the torpedoed vessel>
  syn salve
  rel deliver, redeem, rescue, save; reclaim, recover, regain, retrieve; ransom
  con dump, jettison

salvation *n* **1** *syn* see PRESERVATION 1
  2 *syn* see CONSERVATION 1

salve *n* *syn* see OINTMENT
  rel emollient, lubricant; counterirritant; aid, remedy

salve *vb* *syn* see SALVAGE

salvo *n* **1** *syn* see BARRAGE
  rel discharge; spray
  2 *syn* see TESTIMONIAL 3

same *adj* **1** being one rather than another or more < went to the *same* hotel each summer>
  syn exact, identical, selfsame, very
  rel comparable, like, similar
  ant different
  2 agreeing fundamentally or absolutely < all the family have the *same* dark eyes>
  syn duplicate, equal, equivalent, identic, identical, indistinguishable, tantamount; *compare* LIKE
  rel comparable, like, similar; coequal
  ant different
  3 not changing or fluctuating < treated everyone with the *same* courtesy>

syn consistent, constant, invariable, unchanging, unfailing, unvarying

con changeable, fluctuant, inconsistent, inconstant, irregular, variable, varying

sameness *n* 1 *syn* see IDENTITY 1
rel alikeness; uniformity, uniformness, unity

2 *syn* see EQUIVALENCE
rel analogy; resemblance, similarity

sample *n* *syn* see INSTANCE
rel indication, sign; fragment, part, piece, portion, segment; constituent, element; individual, unit

sampling *n* *syn* see INSTANCE

sanative *adj* *syn* see CURATIVE
rel healthful, hygienic, salutary, sanitary

sanatory *adj* *syn* see CURATIVE

sanctified *adj* *syn* see HOLY 1
rel canonized, deified, sainted
ant unsanctified

sanctify *vb* *syn* see BLESS 1

sanctimonious *adj* *syn* see HYPOCRITICAL
rel deceiving, false; snuffling
ant unsanctimonious

sanctimoniousness *n* *syn* see HYPOCRISY
idiom odor of sanctity
ant unsanctimoniousness

sanctimony *n* *syn* see HYPOCRISY

sanction *n* 1 explicit authoritative permission or recognition that gives validity to acts of a subordinate <a colonial governor acting under the *sanction* of the king>
syn endorsement, fiat
rel approval, authorization, consent, permission; approbation, confirmation, encouragement, ratification, recommendation, support
con restraint; debarment; interdict, prohibition; disapprobation, disapproval, objection
ant interdiction

2 *syn* see PERMISSION

sanction *vb* *syn* see APPROVE 2
rel authorize, commission, license
con ban, disallow, forbid, prohibit
ant interdict

sanctioned *adj* *syn* see ORTHODOX 1
ant unsanctioned

sanctity *n* *syn* see HOLINESS
rel godliness; righteousness, uprightness

sanctorium *n* *syn* see SHRINE

sanctuary *n* 1 *syn* see SHRINE

2 *syn* see SHELTER 1
rel bamah; oasis

3 *syn* see REFUGE 1

sanctum *n* *syn* see SHRINE

sand *n* *syn* see FORTITUDE
rel chutzpah, gall
idiom true (or clear) grit

sandwich shop *n* *syn* see EATING HOUSE

sane *adj* 1 *syn* see HEALTHY 1

2 free from mental disorder <a thoroughly *sane* and well-balanced man>
syn all there, compos mentis, lucid, normal, right
rel balanced, oriented; levelheaded, rational, sensible, sober, sound
idiom of sound mind
con abnormal, unbalanced; neurotic, paranoid, psychopathic, psychotic, schizophrenic; balmy, crazy, ‖cuckoo, non compos, non compos mentis, nuts, screwy; deranged, lunatic, mad, wild
ant insane

3 *syn* see WISE 2
rel logical, rational, reasonable; good, right; cogent, compelling, convincing, sound
con imprudent, injudicious, unwise

saneness *n* *syn* see WIT 2
rel clear-mindedness, perception; comprehension, ‖smarts, understanding

sangfroid *n* *syn* see EQUANIMITY
rel self-containment, self-control; aloofness, coolheadedness, indifference, unconcern

sanguinary *adj* 1 *syn* see MURDEROUS

2 *syn* see BLOODY 1
ant unsanguinary

sanguine *adj* 1 *syn* see BLOODY 1

2 *syn* see MURDEROUS

3 *syn* see RUDDY

4 *syn* see CONFIDENT 1
rel expectant; hopeful, undespairing
idiom full of hope
ant hopeless

5 *syn* see OPTIMISTIC
ant unsanguine

sanguineness *n* *syn* see OPTIMISM

sanguineous *adj* 1 *syn* see BLOODY 1

2 *syn* see MURDEROUS

sanguinity *n* *syn* see OPTIMISM

sanity *n* *syn* see WIT 2
rel intelligence; comprehension
idiom sound mind
ant insanity

sans *prep* *syn* see WITHOUT 2

sap *n* *syn* see FOOL 3

sap *vb* *syn* see WEAKEN 1
rel deplete, drain, exhaust, knock out; ruin, wreck; destroy

saphead *n* *syn* see FOOL 3
rel ‖boob, jerk

sapid *adj* *syn* see PALATABLE
idiom fit for a king
con bland, tasteless; repulsive, unpalatable
ant insipid

sapidity *n* *syn* see TASTE 3
ant insipidity

sapience *n* *syn* see SAGACITY

sapient *adj* *syn* see WISE 2
rel erudite, learned, scholarly; thinking; discriminating, sapiential

sapless *adj* *syn* see INSIPID 3

sapor *n* *syn* see TASTE 3

saporous *adj* *syn* see PALATABLE

sappy *adj* *syn* ‖1 *syn* SUCCULENT, juicy

2 *syn* see SENTIMENTAL

3 *syn* see FOOLISH 2

sarcasm *n* a savage bitter form of humor usually intended to hurt or wound <a speech full of personal jabs and *sarcasm*>
syn acerbity, causticity, corrosiveness, sarcasticness
rel humor, irony, raillery, satire, wit; jest, repartee; gibe, lampooning; mockery, ridicule, scorn, sneering; acrimony, invective; rancor, sharpness
con playfulness, waggishness, whimsicality

sarcastic *adj* marked by, expressive of, or given to sarcasm <a critic noted for his

sarcastic comments on actors' performances >

syn acerb, acerbic, archilochian, caustic, corrosive, ‖sarky; *compare* CAUSTIC 1

rel dry; cynical, ironic, sardonic, satiric; jeering, mocking, scornful; biting, cutting, incisive; mordant, scathing, sharp, stinging; pungent, tart, trenchant

con droll, playful, sportive, waggish, whimsical

sarcasticness *n* *syn* see SARCASM

rel bitingness, cuttingness, incisiveness, trenchancy; derision, mocking, taunting

sardonic *adj* characterized by or expressing disdainful, skeptical humor < had a *sardonic* smile that mirrored his fixed expectation of the worst from everyone >

syn cynical, ironic, wry

rel contemptuous, disdainful, scornful; derisive, jeering, mocking, saturnine, sneering; caustic, corrosive, sarcastic, satiric

‖**sarky** *adj* *syn* see SARCASTIC

sash *n* *syn* see BELT 1

sashay *vb* to move about often self-consciously and usually in a conspicuous manner < *sashaying* around, trying to walk like a model >

syn flounce, mince, prance, ‖prink, strut

rel swagger

sass *n* *syn* see BACK TALK

rel impertinence, insolence, sassiness

sassy *adj* 1 *syn* see WISE 5

rel brazen, unabashed; audacious

2 *syn* see DAPPER

Satan *n* 1 *syn* see DEVIL 1

rel deuce; Mephistopheles; devil-god

idiom fallen angel, lord of the underworld, prince of darkness

2 *syn* see DEVIL 2

rel renegade, villain; beast, viper

satanic *adj* 1 of, relating to, or characteristic of Satan < *Satanic* rites >

syn devilish, diabolic, Mephistophelian

rel saturnine

2 *syn* see FIENDISH

rel evil, wicked

satanism *n* the worship of Satan usually marked by the travesty of Christian rites < interpreted *satanism* as an offshoot of the belief in two coequal and coeternal principles of good and evil >

syn diabolism

rel Black Mass

sate *vb* *syn* see SATIATE

rel overfill, overstuff, stuff

idiom have (*or* give) a bellyful of, have (*or* give) an overdose of

sated *adj* *syn* see SATIATED

ant unsated

satellite *n* *syn* see FOLLOWER

rel favorite, minion

satellite *adj* *syn* see CONCOMITANT

satiate *adj* *syn* see SATIATED

idiom stuffed to the gills

con insatiable, unsatiable

ant insatiate, unsatiate

satiate *vb* to satisfy fully or to repletion < tried to titillate rather than *satiate* his readers' interest >

syn cloy, fill, glut, gorge, jade, pall, sate, ‖stall, stodge, surfeit; *compare* SATISFY 3

rel content, fulfill, gratify, indulge, satisfy; overdose, stuff

con coax, court, invite, pique, tantalize, tempt, titillate

satiated *adj* filled to repletion < the mob, *satiated* with violence, finally dispersed >

syn full, glutted, gorged, jaded, sated, satiate, surfeited

rel fulfilled, gratified, indulged, satisfied

con avid, greedy, ravening; craving, hungering, hungry, lusting, thirsting, thirsty

ant unsatiated

satiny *adj* *syn* see SOFT 3

satire *n* humorous ridicule often used to convey rebuke or criticism or to expose folly or vice < a brilliant writer noted for his *satire* >

syn lampoonery, raillery, satiricalness

rel banter, chaffing; causticity, irony; mockery, ridicule; pasquinade, persiflage, squib; parody, spoof, spoofery, takeoff

satiric *adj* of, relating to, characterized by, or based on satire < witty, eloquent, and *satiric* sermons >

syn lampooning, satirizing

rel bantering, chaffing; caustic, ironic; mocking, ridiculing; parodying, spoofing; farcical; Rabelaisian

satiricalness *n* *syn* see SATIRE

satirizing *adj* *syn* see SATIRIC

satisfactorily *adv* *syn* see WELL 4

rel competently, sufficiently

ant unsatisfactorily

satisfactory *adj* 1 *syn* see SUFFICIENT 1

ant unsatisfactory

2 *syn* see VALID

ant unsatisfactory

3 *syn* see DECENT 4

rel fair, goodish, passable

ant unsatisfactory

satisfy *vb* 1 *syn* see CLEAR 5

2 *syn* see SUIT 6

3 to satiate desires or longings < strove to *satisfy* his lust for money and power >

syn appease, content, gratify; *compare* SATIATE

rel gladden, humor, indulge, please; sate, satiate; pacify, placate

con tantalize, tease; excite, pique, provoke, stimulate; arouse

4 *syn* see ASSURE 2

rel induce, inveigle, win (over)

5 measure up to a set of criteria or requirements < courses taken to *satisfy* requirements for graduation >

syn answer, fill, fulfill, meet

rel comply (with), conform (to), serve; do, suffice

idiom fill the bill, make good

satisfying *adj* *syn* see VALID

ant unsatisfying

satisfyingly *adv* *syn* see WELL 5

rel gratifyingly, pleasingly

ant unsatisfyingly

saturate *vb* 1 *syn* see SOAK 1

rel bathe, douche, wash; imbue, infuse, suffuse

2 *syn* see PERMEATE

---

syn synonym(s)   **rel** related word(s)
ant antonym(s)   **con** contrasted word(s)
idiom idiomatic equivalent(s)
‖ use limited; if in doubt, see a dictionary

rel pierce, probe; inoculate, instill

saturate *adj syn* see WET 1

saturated *adj syn* see WET 1

saturnalia *n syn* see ORGY 2

saturnine *adj syn* see SULLEN
rel grave, serious, solemn, somber, staid; moping; dark, funereal; reserved, silent, taciturn, uncommunicative
con cheerful, cheery, happy; cordial, polite
ant genial

satyric *adj* 1 *syn* see LICENTIOUS 2
2 *syn* see LUSTFUL 2

sauce *n* 1 *syn* see BACK TALK
rel pertness, sauciness
‖2 *syn* see LIQUOR 2

saucebox *n syn* see MINX

saucy *adj* 1 flippant and bold in manner or attitude < a *saucy* little flirt >
syn arch, bantam, ‖cocket, malapert, pert
rel flippant, frivolous, light-minded, volatile; bold, brash, combative; impertinent, impudent, insolent; intrusive, meddlesome, obtrusive; smart, smart-alecky, wise
con gentle, meek, mild, quiet, subdued
ant deferential
2 *syn* see INSOLENT 2

sault *n syn* see WATERFALL

saunter *vb* to walk slowly in an idle or leisurely manner < *sauntered* about the streets, stopping in at various shops >
syn amble, bummel, drift, linger, mope, mosey, ‖muck, stroll; *compare* WANDER 1
rel meander, ramble, roam, rove, spatiate, ‖stravage, wander; loiter, tarry
con bustle, chase, hustle, scurry, tear

saunter *n syn* see WALK 1

savage *adj* 1 being undomesticated and often destructive or ferocious through lack of restraints or human control < *savage* dogs >
syn feral, vicious, wild; *compare* WILD 1
rel uncivilized, undomesticated, unsocialized; unbroken, unsubdued, untamed; bestial, brutal, brute; ferocious, fierce
con civilized, domesticated, socialized; broken, subdued, tamed; domestic, tame
2 *syn* see FIERCE 1
rel coldhearted, heartless, implacable, relentless, unrelenting; rapacious, ravenous, voracious; bloodthirsty, bloody, butcherly, murderous, rabid
3 *syn* see BARBARIAN 1
rel primeval, primitive; uncontrolled, unharnessed; harsh, rough, rugged

savant *n syn* see SAGE

save *vb* 1 *syn* see RESCUE
rel unchain, unshackle
idiom snatch from the jaws of death
con desert, leave; condemn, damn
2 *syn* see MAINTAIN 1
3 to keep secure or maintain intact from injury, decay, or loss < regular painting helps *save* the wood >
syn conserve, preserve; *compare* MAINTAIN 1
rel defend, guard, protect, safeguard, shield
con draw (out), withdraw; consume, spend, use up
4 to accumulate and store up (a supply) for future use < *saved* his money for college >

syn lay aside, lay away, lay by, lay in, lay up, put by, salt away, ‖spare; *compare* HOARD
rel accumulate, cache, collect, stockpile, store (up); hoard, husband, manage; keep, reserve, set by; deposit, stow
idiom feather one's nest, keep as a nest egg, save for a rainy day, save to fall back on
con lose, squander, use up, waste
ant consume, spend
5 *syn* see ECONOMIZE

save *prep syn* see EXCEPT

save *conj* 1 *syn* see ONLY
2 *syn* see EXCEPT 1

save-all *adj syn* see STINGY

saving *n* 1 *syn* see PRESERVATION 1
2 *syn* see CONSERVATION 1

saving *prep syn* see EXCEPT

saving *conj syn* see EXCEPT 1

saving *adj syn* see SPARING

savoir faire *n syn* see TACT
rel manners; dignity, elegance, grace; refinement, savoir vivre, taste; aplomb, confidence, self-assurance, self-possession; experience, blaséness, sophistication
con awkwardness, clumsiness, gaucherie, ineptness, maladroitness

savor *n* 1 *syn* see TASTE 3
rel scent, tinge
2 *syn* see QUALITY 1

savor *vb* 1 *syn* see SMACK
2 *syn* see FEEL 2
3 *syn* see RELISH 2

savorless *adj syn* see UNPALATABLE 1
rel bland; thin, watery, weak; unpleasing
con appetizing, pleasing, tempting; piquant, spicy
ant savory

savorous *adj syn* see PALATABLE

savorsome *adj syn* see PALATABLE

savory *adj* 1 *syn* see PALATABLE
rel pleasing, tempting; gustful
con acrid, sharp, strong
ant unsavory
2 *syn* see SWEET 2

‖**savvy** *adj syn* see SHREWD

saw *n syn* see SAYING

‖**sawbones** *n syn* see PHYSICIAN

sawbuck *n syn* see SAWHORSE

saw-edged *adj syn* see SERRATE

sawhorse *n* a rack on which something (as a board) is laid for sawing < *sawhorses* in the carpentry shop >
syn buck, horse, sawbuck, trestle, workhorse

sawtooth *adj syn* see SERRATE

saw-toothed *adj syn* see SERRATE

say *vb* 1 to express in words < learn to *say* what you mean >
syn bring out, chime in, come out (with), declare, deliver, state, tell, throw out, utter; *compare* EXPRESS 2
rel breathe; articulate, enunciate, pronounce; announce, proclaim; animadvert, comment, give, remark; cite, quote, recite, repeat; affirm, assert, aver, avow, protest
idiom out with, put in (*or* into) words, put it
2 *syn* see ARTICULATE 2
rel speak, talk
3 *syn* see SHOW 5

say *n syn* see VOICE 2
　rel authority; decision

say *adv syn* see NEARLY

saying *n* an oft-repeated statement usually involving common experience or observation <the old *saying* that ignorance is bliss>
　syn adage, byword, proverb, saw, word
　rel dictum, maxim; truism

say–so *n syn* see VOICE 2

scabrous *adj syn* see ROUGH 1
　rel scabby, scaly, scurfy; downy; knobby, knotty; bristly, prickly, thorny
　con bald, glabrescent
　ant glabrous, smooth

scad *n, usu* **scads** *pl* a great number or abundance <*scads* of opportunities>
　syn gob(s), heap, jillion, load(s), million, oodles, quantities, ream(s), ‖rimption(s), slather(s), slew, thousand, trillion, wad(s); *compare* MUCH, MULTITUDE 1
　rel great deal, lot
　con few, handful, scattering, sprinkle, sprinkling

scalawag *n syn* see SCAMP

scalding *adj syn* see HOT 1
　ant freezing

scale *vb* 1 *syn* see SKIN 2
　2 to shed scales or fragmentary surface matter <*scaling* skin>
　syn desquamate, exfoliate, flake (off), peel
　rel chip (off), spall (off)

scale *n syn* see DEGREE 2

scale *vb* 1 *syn* see ASCEND 1
　2 *syn* see MEASURE 2

‖**scamble** *vb syn* see SPRAWL 1

scamp *n* a pleasantly mischievous person <what have those little *scamps* done now>
　syn devil, enfant terrible, limb, mischief, pixie, rapscallion, rascal, ribald, rogue, scalawag, skeezicks, slyboots, villain
　rel bird, chap, dog, ‖duck; ‖bleeder; joker, prankster
　con sobersides

scamper *vb* 1 *syn* see RUN 2
　rel hasten (off), hurry (away *or* off), light out, speed (away); dash (off), rush (off), shoot, tear (off), whip (off), whiz (off)
　2 *syn* see RUN 1
　rel scud, scuddle, scuttle

scan *vb syn* see BROWSE
　idiom pass one's eye over

scan *n syn* see EXAMINATION
　rel perusal; observation, reconnaissance

scandal *n syn* see DETRACTION
　rel aspersion; reproach; discredit, disrepute

‖**scandal** *vb syn* see MALIGN

scandalize *vb* 1 *syn* see MALIGN
　2 *syn* see SHOCK 1

scandalizer *n syn* see GOSSIP 1
　rel blabber, blabbermouth, talker

scandalmonger *n syn* see GOSSIP 1
　rel meddler, snoop; backbiter; muckraker

scandalous *adj* 1 *syn* see LIBELOUS
　2 *syn* see OUTRAGEOUS 2

‖**scant** *n syn* see SCARCITY

scant *adj* ‖1 *syn* see STINGY
　2 *syn* see SHORT 3
　3 *syn* see MEAGER 2
　ant ample

scant *vb syn* see SPARE 3

scantiness *n syn* see FAILURE 3
　rel scarceness, scarcity; sparseness, sparsity
　con excess, overage, surplus

scanty *adj* 1 *syn* see MEAGER 2
　rel scarce, wanting
　con ample, enough; profuse
　ant plentiful
　2 *syn* see SHORT 3

scape *vb syn* see ESCAPE 1

‖**scape** *n syn* see ESCAPE 1

scape *n syn* see VISTA

scapegoat *n* one that bears the blame for another or others <was made the *scapegoat* for his boss's errors>
　syn fall guy, goat, patsy, whipping boy
　rel mark, target; victim

scapegrace *n syn* see WASTREL 1

scar *n* a mark left by the healing of injured tissue <still had *scars* from the operation>
　syn cicatrix, scarification
　rel blemish, defect, flaw; blister, pockmark, scab; disfigurement

scar *vb* to mark with a scar <burns that had *scarred* his face>
　syn cicatrize, scarify
　rel cut, score, scratch; blemish, disfigure, flaw, mar; damage, deface

scarce *adj* 1 *syn* see SHORT 3
　rel curtailed, shortened, truncated
　con adequate, sufficient, unwanting
　ant abundant
　2 *syn* see INFREQUENT
　idiom scarce as ice water in hell, scarcer than hen's teeth, seldom met with

scarce *adv syn* see JUST 2

scarcely *adv syn* see JUST 2
　idiom just barely, only just

scarceness *n syn* see SCARCITY

scarcity *n* smallness of supply, quantity, or number in proportion to demand <a serious *scarcity* of grain>
　syn insufficience, insufficiency, paucity, poverty, ‖scant, scarceness; *compare* FAILURE 3
　rel deficiency, shortage, underage; meagerness; rareness, uncommonness; absence, dearth, lack
　con sufficiency; great deal, much; overabundance, overage, oversupply, surplus
　ant abundance

scare *vb syn* see FRIGHTEN
　rel panic, shake up; freeze, paralyze, petrify
　idiom give a scare to, strike terror into the heart of, throw a scare into

scarecrow *n syn* see RAGAMUFFIN

scared *adj syn* see AFRAID 1
　rel startled; panicked, panicky, terror=stricken
　con emboldened, heartened, reassured; aggressive, bold
　ant unafraid, unscared

scarification *n syn* see SCAR

scarify *vb* 1 *syn* see SCAR
　rel deform, disfigure, maim, mar
　2 *syn* see LAMBASTE 3

---

syn synonym(s)　　　*rel* related word(s)
ant antonym(s)　　　*con* contrasted word(s)
idiom idiomatic equivalent(s)
‖ use limited; if in doubt, see a dictionary

scary *adj syn* see AFRAID 1

scathe *vb syn* see LAMBASTE 3
idiom ‖give holy hell, give the business, rip (someone) up one side and down the other

scatheless *n syn* see SAFE 1

scathing *adj syn* see CAUSTIC 1
rel brutal; burning, scorching, searing, sulphurous

scatological *adj syn* see OBSCENE 2

scatter *vb* **1** to cause to separate or break up < the rain *scattered* the crowd >
syn dispel, disperse, dissipate
rel break up, shatter; disband; diverge, divide, part, separate, sever
con assemble, congregate, convene; accumulate, amass, collect, concentrate, crowd
ant gather
2 *syn* see STREW 1
rel dispense, distribute; cast, discard, shed; besprinkle, sprinkle
con accumulate, amass, concentrate
ant collect

scatterbrain *n* a flighty thoughtless person < his wife is a *scatterbrain* >
syn birdbrain, featherbrain, featherhead, flibbertigibbet, harebrain, rattlebrain, rattlehead, shatterbrain
rel fool, goose, silly, simpleton

scatterbrained *adj syn* see GIDDY 1

scattergood *n syn* see SPENDTHRIFT

scattering *n syn* see FEW

scene *n* **1** the total arrangement of the objects that form the scenic environment in which a drama is enacted < spectacle plays that attempt a realistic, three-dimensional *scene* >
syn mise-en-scène, scenery, set, setting, stage set, stage setting
rel hangings, scene cloth; ‖back cloth, backdrop, background; tableau
2 *syn* see VIEW 4
3 the place of an occurrence or action < the *scene* of the crime >
syn locale, mise-en-scène, site
rel locality, location, place, spot
4 a sphere of activity, interest, or controversy < the drug *scene* >
syn arena
rel compass, field, setting, sphere; culture, environment, milieu

scenery *n syn* see SCENE 1
rel decor; furnishings, furniture; properties, props

scent *vb* **1** *syn* see SMELL 1
2 to imbue or fill with an odor < air *scented* with herbs >
syn aromatize, odorize, perfume

scent *n* **1** *syn* see SMELL 1
rel essence, whiff
2 *syn* see FRAGRANCE

scented *adj* **1** *syn* see SWEET 2
2 *syn* see ODOROUS
ant scentless, unscented

scentless *adj syn* see ODORLESS

schedule *n* **1** *syn* see LIST
rel chart, table
2 *syn* see PROGRAM 1

schedule *vb* **1** to place in a schedule < *schedule* a new train >
syn card, sked
rel list, record, slate
2 *syn* see TIME 1

scheme *n* **1** *syn* see PLAN 1
rel presentation, proposal, proposition, suggestion; arrangement, order, ordering; contrivance, device, expedient
2 *syn* see PLOT 2

scheme (out) *vb syn* see PLOT

schism *n* **1** *syn* see BREACH 3
2 *syn* see HERESY
3 a division of a group into two discordant groups < a *schism* within a political party >
syn chasm, cleavage, cleft, split; *compare* BREACH 3
rel divergence, division, separation; breach, break, rupture; estrangement
con unification, unity; reconciliation

schismatic *n syn* see HERETIC
rel protester; skeptic; radical, Young Turk

schismatic *adj syn* see HERETICAL
rel rebellious; unconventional

schismatist *n syn* see HERETIC

‖**schlemiel** *n syn* see FOOL 3

‖**schmo** *n syn* see FOOL 1

‖**schmuck** *n syn* see FOOL 1

‖**schnook** *n syn* see DUNCE

‖**schnorrer** *n syn* see BEGGAR 1

‖**schnozzle** *n syn* see NOSE 1

scholar *n syn* see SAGE
rel pupil, student; bookman; polymath

scholarliness *n syn* see ERUDITION 2
ant unscholarliness

scholarly *adj syn* see LEARNED
rel studious; intellectual, long-hair; educated, taught, trained
con untaught, untrained
ant unscholarly

scholarship *n* **1** *syn* see EDUCATION 2
2 *syn* see ERUDITION 2

scholastic *adj* **1** *syn* see PEDANTIC
rel lettered, literary; scholarly; formal
2 *syn* see LEARNED
rel conversant, versed
con unconversant, unscholarly

school *vb syn* see TEACH
rel inform; guide, lead, show; advance, cultivate; control, direct, manage

schooling *n syn* see EDUCATION 1
rel knowledge; book learning, booklore

schoolmasterish *adj syn* see DIDACTIC

science *n* **1** *syn* see KNOWLEDGE 2
2 *syn* see EDUCATION 2

scilicet *adv syn* see NAMELY

scintillate *vb syn* see FLASH 1

scintillating *adj syn* see CLEVER 5

scintillation *n syn* see FLASH 1

scions *n pl syn* see OFFSPRING

scoff *vb* to show contempt by derision or mockery < heard his tale and *scoffed* at it >
syn fleer, flout, gibe, gird, jeer, jest, quip (at), scout (at), sneer
rel pooh-pooh; deride, mock, rally, ridicule, taunt, twit; contemn, despise, disdain, scorn; boo
con accept, approve, commend; compliment; acclaim, laud, praise

scoff *n syn* see FOOL 1

scold *n syn* see VIRAGO

scold *vb* **1** to reproach angrily and abusively < loudly *scolded* him for staying out late >
syn baste, bawl out, berate, ‖bless out, ‖cample, ‖carpet, ‖chew, ‖chew out, dress

down, jaw, lash, ‖mob, rag, rail, rant, rate, ‖ream out, revile, ‖row, tell off, tongue, tongue-lash, ‖tongue-walk, upbraid, vituperate, wig; *compare* CRITICIZE, LAMBASTE 3, REPROVE

rel blame, censure, criticize, denounce, reprehend, reprobate; admonish, chide, rebuke, reprimand, reproach, reprove; execrate, objurgate; brace, grill, harass, hound; blister, excoriate

idiom jump down one's throat, rake over the coals, read one the riot act, walk into

2 *syn* see GRUMBLE 1

sconce *n syn* see HEAD 1

scoop *n* a news story first obtained and reported by only one source (as a newspaper) < the story was a *scoop* by just a few hours >

syn beat, exclusive

scoop *vb* 1 *syn* see DIP 2

rel gather; lift, pick up

2 *syn* see DIG 2

rel gouge, grub

3 to report a news item in advance of competitors < CBS *scooped* NBC on that story >

syn beat

scoot *vb* 1 *syn* see HURRY 2

2 *syn* see RUN 1

3 *syn* see RUN 2

scope *n* 1 *syn* see ROOM 3

2 *syn* see RANGE 2

3 *syn* see BREADTH 2

scopic *adj syn* see EXTENSIVE 1

scopious *adj syn* see EXTENSIVE 1

scorch *vb* 1 *syn* see LAMBASTE 3

2 *syn* see BURN 3

rel seethe, simmer, stew; ‖plot

scorching *adj syn* see HOT 1

idiom scorching hot, sizzling hot

score *n* 1 *scores pl syn* see MULTITUDE 1

2 a slight cut or line made with or as if with a sharp instrument < cut *scores* on the ham before baking it >

syn scotch, scratch

rel line, mark; nick, notch, serration; cut, slit; cleft, furrow, groove, indentation; gash

3 *syn* see BILL 1

4 an obligation or injury kept in mind for future reckoning < had a *score* to settle with him >

syn account

rel grudge

5 the number of points gained by contestants in a game or contest < a record *score* of 263 for 72 holes >

syn tally

rel account, record; summary, total

idiom the final count

score *vb* 1 *syn* see LAMBASTE 3

rel ream out

idiom tear to pieces

2 *syn* see GAIN 1

3 *syn* see SUCCEED 3

scorn *n syn* see DESPITE 1

rel flouting, gibing, jeering, scoffing; derision, mockery, ridicule, taunt, taunting

---

con consideration, respectfulness

ant respect

scorn *vb syn* see DESPISE

rel flout, gibe, jeer, scoff; mock, ridicule, taunt

idiom hold in utter contempt

con accept, acknowledge, welcome

ant respect

scotch *n syn* see SCORE 2

Scotch *adj syn* see SPARING

scoundrel *n syn* see VILLAIN 1

scour *vb* 1 *syn* see HURRY 2

2 to make a thorough search or examination of < *scoured* the neighborhood for the lost child >

syn beat, comb, finecomb, fine-tooth-comb, forage, grub, rake, ransack, rummage, search

rel rout; look (for); seek; fan, range; rifle; ferret (out), find

idiom beat the bushes, leave no stone unturned, look high and low, look up and down, turn inside out, turn upside down

scour *vb* 1 *syn* see SCRUB 1

2 *syn* see EAT 3

scour *n, usu scours pl syn* see DIARRHEA

scourge *n syn* see PLAGUE 1

scourge *vb* 1 *syn* see WHIP 1

rel hit; knout; frail, whop

idiom whip to ribbons

2 *syn* see RAVAGE

3 *syn* see LAMBASTE 3

scout *vb* to explore in order to obtain information < forward observers *scouted* the terrain before the attack >

syn probe, reconnoiter

rel look (over), survey; observe; check out, examine; ‖case, inspect

idiom run reconnaissance

scout *vb* 1 *syn* see RIDICULE

2 *syn* see DESPISE

rel mock, ridicule

scout (at) *vb syn* see SCOFF

scowl *vb syn* see FROWN 1

idiom look black as thunder, pull a face (*or* scowl)

scrabble *vb* 1 *syn* see SCRIBBLE

2 *syn* see SCRAMBLE 1

scrag *vb* 1 *syn* see HANG 2

2 *syn* see KILL 1

3 *syn* see MURDER 1

scraggy *adj* 1 *syn* see ROUGH 1

2 *syn* see LEAN

rel gangling, spindling, spindly; skeletal; dwarfed, scrubby, stunted, undersize

scram *vb syn* see GET OUT 1

idiom ‖beat it, ‖cheese it, ‖get the hell out

scramble *vb* 1 to move or climb hastily on all fours < *scrambled* across the rocks >

syn clamber, scrabble, ‖spartle, ‖sprauchle

rel scurry, scuttle

2 *syn* see SPRAWL 2

scramble *n syn* see CLUTTER 2

rel conglomeration

scrap *n* 1 *syn* see END 4

rel chip, cutting; scrappage, waste

2 *syn* see PARTICLE

scrap *vb syn* see DISCARD

idiom consign to the scrap heap

scrap *n syn* see BRAWL 2

scrap *vb syn* see QUARREL

scrape *vb* 1 to rub or slide against something that is often harsh, rough, or sharp < chalk *scraping* on the blackboard >

---

syn synonym(s)   *rel* related word(s)
ant antonym(s)   *con* contrasted word(s)
idiom idiomatic equivalent(s)
‖ use limited; if in doubt, see a dictionary

syn grate, rasp, scratch
rel graze, rub, scuff; abrade, chafe, grind
2 *syn* see SCRIMP
3 to make one's way with great difficulty
or succeed by a narrow margin < the
student barely *scraped* through the exam >
syn shave
rel struggle; get along, get by
idiom cut it (*or* the corner) pretty close,
have a close shave

scrape *n syn* see PREDICAMENT
rel trouble; discomfiture, embarrassment

scrapping *n syn* see DISPOSAL 2

scrappy *adj syn* see QUARRELSOME 2
2 *syn* see BELLIGERENT

scratch *vb* 1 *syn* see SCRAPE 1
rel squeak, squeal
2 *syn* see SCRIBBLE

scratch *n* 1 *syn* see SCORE 2
‖2 *syn* see MONEY

scrawl *vb syn* see SCRIBBLE
rel inscribe; doodle

scrawny *adj syn* see LEAN
idiom just (*or* nothing but) skin and
bones
ant brawny

screak *vb syn* see SQUEAL 2

scream *vb* 1 to voice a sudden piercing
loud cry often in shock, terror, or pain
< *screamed* at the sight of the accident
and then fainted >
syn screech, shriek, shrill, squeal; *compare*
SHOUT 1
rel screak, squeak; cry, yell; bellow, roar;
caterwaul, howl, wail, ‖yawl
idiom let out a scream (*or* shriek *or*
screech)
2 *syn* see SQUEAL 2
3 *syn* see YELL 2
rel complain, grumble, protest; blare
idiom raise a howl
4 to produce a vivid, blatant, or startling
effect < clothes and furnishings that
screamed nouveau riche >
syn blare, shout, shriek

scream *n syn* see RIOT 2

screech *vb* 1 *syn* see SCREAM 1
rel penetrate, pierce; vent, voice
2 *syn* see SQUEAL 2

screen *vb* 1 *syn* see DEFEND 1
2 *syn* see SHADE
3 to cut off from view by interposing
something resembling a screen < *screen* a
view with a tall hedge >
syn block out, close, obstruct, shroud,
shut off, shut out
rel conceal, hide; separate, wall off; protect, seclude; embosk
idiom throw up a screen
con bare, disclose, expose, open, reveal
4 *syn* see HIDE
rel defend, guard, protect, safeguard,
shield; camouflage, cloak, cover up, disguise
5 to examine carefully and methodically in
order to separate, select, or eliminate
< the personnel department *screened* sev-
enty candidates for ten jobs >
syn sieve, sift; *compare* SORT 2
rel choose, pick out, select; extract, filter
(out), riddle, sort (out), winnow (out)
6 *syn* see CENSOR

‖**screeve** *vb syn* see EXUDE
‖**screw** *n syn* see SHAFT 3
screw *vb* 1 *syn* see CRUMPLE 1
2 *syn* see EXTORT 1
‖3 *syn* see CHEAT
4 *syn* see SCRIMP
‖5 *syn* see RUN 2
‖**screw** (up) *vb syn* see BOTCH
rel confuse, muddle, snafu; spoil
screwball *n syn* see CRACKPOT
‖**screwing** *n syn* see SHAFT 3
screwy *adj* ‖1 *syn* see INTOXICATED 1
2 *syn* see INSANE 1
idiom having a screw loose
scribble *vb* to write or draw hastily or
roughly < *scribbled* a quick note to her on
his way out >
syn scrabble, scratch, scrawl, squiggle
rel jot (down); scribe, write
scribe *vb syn* see WRITE
scrimmage *n* 1 *syn* see CLASH 2
rel scuffle; fight; free-for-all
2 *syn* see BRAWL 2
scrimp *adj syn* see MEAGER 2
scrimp *vb* to be extremely frugal and parsimonious in an effort to economize
< *scrimped* all year to buy that fur coat >
syn pinch, scrape, screw, skimp, ‖skinch,
spare, stint; *compare* SPARE 3
rel scamp; scratch; save (up)
idiom pinch pennies
‖**scrimption** *n syn* see PITTANCE
scrimpy *adj* 1 *syn* see MEAGER 2
2 *syn* see SHORT 3
3 *syn* see STINGY
scrimy *adj syn* see STINGY
script *n syn* see HANDWRITING
Scripture *n syn* see BIBLE
scrooch (down) *vb syn* see CROUCH
scrooge *n syn* see MISER
scrub *n syn* see INFERIOR
scrub *vb* 1 to clean by abrasive action
< *scrubbed* the pots and pans >
syn scour
rel brush; rub; cleanse, wash; buff, polish
2 *syn* see CANCEL 2
scrubby *adj syn* see SHABBY 1
scruffy *adj syn* see SHABBY 1
scrumptious *adj syn* see DELIGHTFUL
scrunch *vb* 1 *syn* see CHEW 1
2 *syn* see CRUMPLE 1
‖**scrunty** *adj syn* see STUNTED
scruple *n syn* see PARTICLE
scruple *n syn* see QUALM
rel faltering, hesitancy, hesitation, pause;
reconsideration, second thought
scruple *vb syn* see DEMUR
rel question; fret, worry
scrupulous *adj* 1 *syn* see UPRIGHT 2
rel fair-minded; strict; upstanding
con questionable; shifty, slippery; dishonorable, unprincipled; dishonest
ant unscrupulous
2 *syn* see CAREFUL 2
rel critical, fastidious
con careless; undiscriminating, unparticu-
lar
ant remiss
scrutinize *vb* 1 to look at or over critically
and searchingly < the jeweler *scrutinized*
the diamonds to see if they were fakes >
syn canvass, ‖case, check over, check up,
con, examine, inspect, perlustrate, study,
survey, vet, view

rel look over, overlook, peruse, pore (over), scan; consider, contemplate, weigh; penetrate, pierce, probe; analyze, dig (into), dissect; comb
idiom turn a careful (*or* heedful) eye to (*or* on)
2 *syn* see EYE 2

scrutiny *n* 1 *syn* see EXAMINATION
rel look-in, lookover, look-see
2 *syn* see EYE 3

scud *vb syn* see FLY 1

scuddle *vb syn* see SCUTTLE

scuff *vb syn* see SHUFFLE 3

scuffle *vb* 1 *syn* see WRESTLE
rel cuff, scuff
2 *syn* see SHUFFLE 3

scuffle *n syn* see BRAWL 2

∥sculch *n syn* see REFUSE

sculp *vb syn* see SCULPTURE

sculpt *vb syn* see SCULPTURE

sculpture *vb* to form an image or representation from solid material (as wood or stone) < *sculptured* a colossal statue of a horse >
syn carve, chisel, sculp, sculpt
rel cast, form; model, mold, shape

scum *n* 1 *syn* see RABBLE 2
idiom scum of the earth
2 *syn* see SNOT 1

scummy *adj syn* see CONTEMPTIBLE

scurf *n syn* see RABBLE 2

scurrile *adj syn* see ABUSIVE

scurrility *n syn* see ABUSE
rel scurrilousness; maligning, traducing, vilification

scurrilous *adj* 1 *syn* see ABUSIVE
rel coarse, gross; filthy, foul; insulting, offending, offensive, outrageous, outraging
2 *syn* see OBSCENE 2

scurry *vb* 1 *syn* see SCUTTLE
2 *syn* see RUN 1
rel shoot, tear; dart, fly; scuffle, skelter

scurvy *adj syn* see CONTEMPTIBLE
rel base, low, vile

scutter *vb syn* see SCUTTLE
rel hasten, hurry, run, speed

scuttle *vb* to move with or as if with short rapidly alternating steps < armies of fiddler crabs *scuttled* across the road >
syn scuddle, scurry, scutter; *compare* RUN 1
rel scoot; scramble; scud

scuttlebutt *n syn* see REPORT 1

sea *n syn* see OCEAN

sea dog *n syn* see PIRATE

seal *n* an adhesive-backed device bearing a symbolic, pictorial, or official design < the *seal* on a diploma >
syn stamp, sticker

seam *n syn* see JOINT 1
rel bond

seaman *n syn* see MARINER

sear *vb* 1 *syn* see DRY 1
2 to burn or scorch with a sudden application of intense heat < *seared* the steaks in the broiler >
syn sizzle
rel scorch, shrivel, parch; burn (up)

search *vb* 1 *syn* see SCOUR 2
rel run down, scout (around), scrimmage, skirmish
idiom search high and low
2 to subject (a person) to a thorough check for concealed or contraband articles < police *searching* the suspects for weapons >
syn ∥fan, frisk, shake down
rel check, examine; inspect, look over, scan, scrutinize, study

search (for *or* out) *vb syn* see SEEK 1
rel pry (out), scout (out)

search *n syn* see PURSUIT 2

searchingly *adv syn* see HARD 4

sea robber *n syn* see PIRATE

sea rover *n syn* see PIRATE

season *n* a particular period of the year < the Christmas *season* >
syn time
rel period, term

season *vb syn* see HARDEN 2
rel discipline, school, train; fit, prepare; case harden, steel

seasonable *adj syn* see TIMELY 1
rel apropos, pertinent, relevant; appropriate, apt; convenient
con irrelevant; inappropriate, inapt; ill=timed, inconvenient, inopportune
ant unseasonable

seasonably *adv syn* see EARLY 1
ant unseasonably

seasoned *adj syn* see EXPERIENCED
rel acclimated, acclimatized, hardened, toughened; case-hardened, steeled
con inexperienced, unpracticed, unskilled, unversed; unacclimated, unacclimatized, unsteeled, untempered, untried
ant unseasoned

seat *n* 1 *syn* see BUTTOCKS
2 *syn* see CENTER 2
rel fulcrum
3 *syn* see BASE 1

seat *vb* to cause to be seated < an usher *seated* her in the third row >
syn sit
rel establish, place, put

seating *n syn* see BASE 1

sea wolf *n syn* see PIRATE

seclude *vb* to remove or separate (oneself or another) from external influences < in the convent she was *secluded* from secular life >
syn cloister, sequester
rel retire, separate, withdraw; closet, confine, enclose, immure, isolate; screen, shut off

secluded *adj* disposed to, living in, or characterized by seclusion < *secluded* monks > < they enjoyed *secluded* country living >
syn cloistered, hermetic, recluse, secluse, seclusive, sequestered
rel retired, withdrawn; close, hidden, private, screened, shy; alone, isolated, solitary
con communal, public

secluse *adj syn* see SECLUDED

seclusion *n* the act or condition of secluding or of being secluded < the queen went into *seclusion* when her husband died >
syn reclusion, retirement, sequestration; *compare* SOLITUDE

---

syn synonym(s)   *rel* related word(s)
ant antonym(s)   *con* contrasted word(s)
idiom idiomatic equivalent(s)
∥ use limited; if in doubt, see a dictionary

rel detachment, separation, withdrawal; reclusiveness, seclusiveness; privacy, privateness; aloneness, isolation, separateness, solitude

seclusive *adj syn see* SECLUDED

second *n syn see* INSTANT 1
idiom the flash of an eyelid

secondary *adj* 1 *syn see* SUBORDINATE
rel accessory, subservient
con major, prime; first, first-ranking, first-string
ant primary

2 formed from something original, primary, or basic < a *secondary* historical analysis based on original archives>
syn derivate, derivational, derivative, derived
rel borrowed, secondhand; consequent, resultant, subsequent
con basic, principle; first, firsthand, original, uncopied, underived
ant primary

3 *syn see* MINOR 2

secondary *n syn see* INFERIOR
rel second fiddle, second-in-command

second childhood *n syn see* DOTAGE

second–class *adj syn see* INFERIOR 2

second–drawer *adj syn see* INFERIOR 2

second–rate *adj syn see* INFERIOR 2
ant first-rate

secours *n syn see* HELP 1

secrecy *n* the practice or policy of keeping secrets or maintaining concealment < *secrecy* is an inherent feature of intelligence operations>
syn hugger-mugger, hugger-muggery, hush, hush-hush, secretiveness, secretness, silence
rel clandestineness, covertness, furtiveness; concealment, stealth, subterfuge; censorship, suppression
ant openness

secret *adj* 1 existing or done in such a way as to maintain concealment < was involved in *secret* negotiations with the enemy>
syn clandestine, covert, furtive, hole-and-corner, hugger-mugger, hush-hush, mystical, sneak, stealthy, sub-rosa, surreptitious, undercover, ||underneath, under-the-table; *compare* STEALTHY 2, UNDERHAND
rel underhand, underhanded; unacknowledged, unavowed, undeclared; concealed, hidden, screened; classified, confidential, ||eyes-only, restricted, top secret
con acknowledged, avowed, declared; revealed, aboveboard, straightforward, unconcealed; declassified, unclassified, unrestricted; clear, evident, manifest, obvious, patent, plain
ant open, public

2 *syn see* OBSCURE 2

3 *syn see* RECONDITE

secret *n* secrets *pl syn see* GENITALIA

secretaire *n syn see* DESK

secretary *n syn see* DESK

secrete *vb syn see* HIDE
rel deposit; withhold

secretiveness *n syn see* SECRECY

secretly *adv* in a secret manner < negotiated *secretly* with both sides>

syn by stealth, clandestinely, covertly, furtively, hugger-mugger, in camera, privately, stealthily, sub rosa, surreptitiously
rel confidentially; privatim, privily
idiom behind closed doors, on the qt, on the quiet, under the rose, under the table
con forthrightly, plainly, publicly; manifestly, overtly
ant openly

secretness *n syn see* SECRECY

sect *n syn see* RELIGION 2

sectarian *adj* 1 *syn see* HERETICAL
rel splinter
con unified, united
ant nonsectarian

2 *syn see* INSULAR

sectary *n* 1 *syn see* HERETIC
rel beatnik, Bohemian, hippie; maverick; liberal, radical, Young Turk; rebel, revolutionary
con advocate, conformist, follower

2 *syn see* FOLLOWER
rel bigot

sectator *n syn see* FOLLOWER

section *n* 1 *syn see* PART 1
rel district, locality, subdivision, vicinity; area, belt, zone; region, tract; field, sphere, territory

2 *syn see* QUARTER 2

section *vb* to divide into sections < *sectioned* the class on the basis of ability>
syn sectionalize, sectionize; *compare* SEGMENT
rel break up, divide, separate, slice, split; sector, segment

sectionalize *vb syn see* SECTION

sectionize *vb syn see* SECTION

sector *n syn see* QUARTER 2

secular *adj syn see* PROFANE 1
rel nonclerical, nonreligious
con clerical, ecclesiastical, ministerial, priestly, regular; eternal
ant religious

securable *adj syn see* AVAILABLE 1
rel convenient, handy, reachable, ready
idiom at one's disposal
con unavailable, unreachable

secure *adj* 1 *syn see* CONFIDENT 1

2 *syn see* SAFE 2
rel firm, stable, strong
con open, wide-open; assailable, weak; dangerous, precarious
ant insecure

3 *syn see* RELIABLE 1

4 *syn see* FAST 4
rel strong; iron

5 *syn see* STABLE 4

6 *syn see* SURE 1
rel established, settled; balanced
con precarious; unbalanced; unstable, wobbly
ant insecure

secure *vb* 1 *syn see* DEFEND 1

2 *syn see* ENSURE
rel underwrite

3 *syn see* CATCH 1

4 *syn see* FASTEN 2
rel batten (down), clamp, clinch, pinion, rivet, tie down; cement
con unfasten, untie

5 *syn see* GET 1

6 *syn see* EFFECT 1

security *n* 1 *syn see* SAFETY

ant insecurity

2 *syn* see STABILITY

3 *syn* see PLEDGE 1

4 *syn* see GUARANTEE 1

rel assurance; certification; pledge

5 *syn* see DEFENSE 1

sedate *adj syn* see SERIOUS 1
rel calm, placid, serene, tranquil; collected, composed, dispassionate, imperturbable, unruffled; decorous, dignified, proper, seemly
con indecorous, undignified, unseemly; airy, flippant, light
ant flighty

sedative *n* an agent or drug that relieves irritability, nervousness, or excitement < took a *sedative* to help her sleep >
syn calmant, calmative, quietive
rel balm; pacifier, tranquilizer; sleeping pill, sleeping tablet; depressant, ∥downer
con energizer; stimulant; ∥upper

sediment *n* matter which settles to the bottom of a liquid < rocks hidden by *sediment* spoiled the cove for diving >
syn deposit, dreg(s), grounds, lees, precipitate, precipitation, settlings
rel bottoms, dross, recrement, scoria, slag; draff, heeltap

sedition *n* an offense against official ruling authority (as a government or sovereign) to which one owes allegiance < considered the defense industry strike to be overt *sedition* >
syn seditiousness, treason
rel alienation, disaffection, estrangement; action, protest, strike; coup, coup d'etat, putsch; insurrection, mutiny, rebellion, revolt, revolution, uprising; quislingism
con allegiance, fealty, fidelity, loyalty; duty, respect, responsibility

seditious *adj syn* see INSUBORDINATE
rel alienated, disaffected, dissident; faithless, disloyal, perfidious, traitorous, treacherous; lawless, violent
con faithful, loyal, patriotic

seditiousness *n syn* see SEDITION

seduce *vb* **1** *syn* see LURE
rel coax, tease; betray, deceive, delude, mislead; enslave, entrance; overpower, overwhelm
2 to persuade or entice into sexual partnership < lechers who *seduce* silly young girls >
syn debauch, undo
rel deflower; rape, ravish, violate; corrupt, degrade, pervert, ruin

seducement *n* **1** *syn* see SEDUCTION 1
rel undoing
2 *syn* see LURE 2

seduction *n* **1** the act or an instance of seducing or being seduced into a sexual relationship < women who lay themselves open to *seduction* >
syn seducement
rel deflowering; rape, ravishment, violation; corruption, degradation, perversion, ruin
2 *syn* see ATTRACTION 1

rel lorelei, siren song, temptation

seductive *adj syn* see ATTRACTIVE 1
rel desirable, mouth-watering, provocative

seductress *n syn* see SIREN

sedulous *adj syn* see ASSIDUOUS
rel active; busy; hustling, persevering, persistent, unremitting

see *vb* **1** to take cognizance of by physical or mental vision < *saw* that the boat was being driven ashore > < the only one who *saw* the truth >
syn behold, descry, discern, distinguish, espy, mark, mind, note, notice, observe, perceive, remark, twig, view
rel sight; make out; examine, inspect, scan, scrutinize; penetrate, pierce, probe; consider, study; appraise, ponder, weigh
idiom fix one's eyes (*or* mind *or* thoughts) on, occupy oneself with, pay heed (*or* attention) to, take notice of
2 to perceive something by means of the eyes < she *sees* clearly with her new glasses >
syn ∥dekko, look, watch
rel gape, gaze, glare, peek, peep, peer, stare
idiom give the eye, hold in view, keep one's eye on, lay eyes on, turn one's eyes to
3 *syn* see EXPERIENCE 1
4 *syn* see DISCOVER 3
5 *syn* see THINK 1
6 *syn* see APPREHEND 1
rel discern, discriminate, recognize
7 *syn* see FORESEE
idiom see the day when
8 *syn* see LOOK 1
rel look out, watch out
idiom see to it that
9 *syn* see VISIT 2
10 *syn* see DATE
11 *syn* see GUIDE
rel accompany, go (with); attend

seeable *adj syn* see VISUAL 2
ant unseeable

seed *n* **1** *syn* see OFFSPRING
2 a beginning or source from which something (as a conception) may later develop < the growing *seeds* of suspicion in her mind >
syn bud, embryo, germ, nucleus, spark
rel rudiment; core, kernel; conceit, concept, conception, image, impression, notion

seed *vb syn* see PLANT 1

seedy *adj syn* see SHABBY
rel drooping, droopy, flagging, sagging, wilted, wilting; messy, slovenly, unkempt, untidy; neglected, overgrown
idiom gone to seed
con manicured, polished, shined

seeing *n syn* see EYE 2

seeing *conj syn* see BECAUSE
idiom ∥being as how, in that

∥**seeing glass** *n syn* see MIRROR 1

seek *vb* **1** to look for < has gone to *seek* a doctor >
syn cast about, ferret out, hunt, quest, search (for *or* out)
rel bird-dog, delve, dig, fish, mouse, nose, root, smell out, sniff
idiom go in quest (*or* search) of
2 *syn* see TRY 5

---

seeker *n syn* see CANDIDATE
rel bidder; petitioner; solicitant; claimant
seeking *n syn* see PURSUIT 2
seem *vb* to give the impression of being without necessarily being so in fact <things are not always the way they *seem*>
syn appear, look, sound
rel resemble, suggest; hint, imply, insinuate, intimate
idiom have (*or* show) every sign of, have the earmarks of
seeming *n* 1 *syn* see APPEARANCE 2
rel feigning, pretense, sham; facade; illusion
idiom false face (*or* front), outward show
2 *syn* see APPEARANCE 1
rel bearing, demeanor, posture; image, style; effect, impression
seeming *adj syn* see APPARENT 2
seemingly *adv syn* see OSTENSIBLY
seemliness *n* 1 *syn* see ORDER 7
2 *syn* see DECORUM 1
ant unseemliness
seemly *adj syn* see DECOROUS 1
rel compatible, congenial, congruous, consistent, consonant; pleasing
con inappropriate, unfit, unseasonable, unsuitable, untimely; incompatible, uncongenial; displeasing, unpleasing
ant unseemly
seep *vb syn* see EXUDE
rel drip; leak; flow
seer *n syn* see PROPHET
seesaw *vb* to move backward and forward or up and down from a central axis usually in a swaying often unsteady way <planes landing on the *seesawing* flight deck>
syn lurch, pitch, swag, tilt, tilter, yaw; *compare* TEETER, TOSS 2
rel cant, incline, lean, list; rock, roll, sway
seethe *vb* 1 *syn* see BOIL 2
2 *syn* see SOAK 1
3 *syn* see ANGER 2
idiom ‖do a slow burn
con calm (down), simmer (down)
ant cool (down)
4 to be in a state of internal and especially mental agitation, excitement, or turmoil <his brain *seethed* with unanswered questions>
syn boil, bubble, churn, ferment, ‖moil, simmer, smolder, stir
rel abound, swarm, teem; fret, fume, sizzle, steam; bubble over, erupt, overflow
see–through *adj syn* see TRANSPARENT 1
segment *n syn* see PART 1
segment *vb* to separate into segments <tried to *segment* the poem into understandable units>
syn segmentalize, segmentize; *compare* SECTION
rel categorize, compartmentalize; divide, separate; isolate, seclude, set off
segmentalize *vb syn* see SEGMENT
segmentize *vb syn* see SEGMENT
segregate *vb syn* see ISOLATE
rel disconnect; choose, select, single
con mix
ant desegregate
segregation *n* the quality, state, or condition of being socially or racially excluded

or separated <fought against racial *segregation* in the schools>
syn apartheid, separateness, separation, separatism
rel discrimination, jim crowism; ghettoization; isolation, seclusion
ant desegregation
seity *n syn* see INDIVIDUALITY 4
seize *vb* 1 *syn* see APPROPRIATE 1
rel occupy; usurp
2 to take possession or control of usually suddenly and forcibly <the cat *seized* the fish and made off > < *seized* the rope and dragged the boat ashore>
syn catch, clutch, ‖cotch, grab, grapple, nab, ‖nail, snatch, take; *compare* CATCH 1
rel fasten (onto), grasp, latch (onto), snap (at); apprehend, arrest; capture, secure, take over; abduct, carry off, kidnap, spirit (away *or* off)
idiom get into one's clutches, get one's hands (*or* paws) on, lay hold (on *or* of)
con free, loose, release
3 to affect especially as if by laying hold of <was *seized* with a coughing fit>
syn catch, strike, take
rel overtake; afflict
seizure *n syn* see ATTACK 3
rel convulsion; breakdown
seldom *adv* in few instances <she *seldom* writes home anymore>
syn hardly ever, infrequently, little, rarely, unfrequently, unoften
rel occasionally; semioccasionally; irregularly, sporadically; hardly, scarcely
idiom once in a blue moon
con regularly; frequently; usually
ant often
seldom *adj syn* see INFREQUENT
select *adj* 1 singled out from a number or group by fitness or preference <this hotel caters to a *select* clientele>
syn chosen, elect, exclusive, pick, picked, selected
rel culled, screened, weeded (out), winnowed (out); favored, preferred; best, elite
con random; indiscriminate; average, commonplace, mediocre, run-of-the-mill
2 *syn* see CHOICE
rel blue-chip, fine; best; top
3 *syn* see ECLECTIC 1
select *vb syn* see CHOOSE 1
idiom make a choice (*or* selection)
con ignore, pass (over); drop
ant reject
selected *adj syn* see SELECT 1
rel singled (out); appointed, tagged, tapped
selection *n syn* see CHOICE 1
rel choosing, culling, draft, drafting, picking; acumen, discernment, discrimination, insight
ant rejection
selective *adj syn* see ECLECTIC 1
rel particular, scrupulous
self–abandoned *adj syn* see ABANDONED 2
self–abnegating *adj syn* see SELF-SACRIFICING
self–abnegation *n syn* see RENUNCIATION

rel abandonment, relinquishment, resignation

self–absorbed *adj syn see* EGOCENTRIC 2
rel arrogant, cocky, self–important

self–abuse *n syn see* SELF–REPROACH

self–accusation *n* *syn* *see* SELF–RE-
PROACH

self–admiration *n syn see* CONCEIT 2

self–asserting *adj syn see* PRESUMPTU-
OUS
rel aggressive, militant
con meek, modest, unassuming; docile,
passive
ant self–effacing

self–assertive *adj* 1 *syn see* AGGRESSIVE
rel impertinent, intrusive, meddlesome,
obtrusive, officious; audacious, bold; cocksure, sure
2 *syn see* PRESUMPTUOUS

self–assurance *n syn see* CONFIDENCE 2
rel collectedness, coolness, imperturbability; composure, equanimity, sangfroid
con insecurity, uncertainness

self–assured *adj syn see* CONFIDENT 1
rel self–satisfied, smug

self–assuredness *n syn see* CONFIDENCE
2

self–centered *adj* 1 *syn see* SELF–SUFFI-
CIENT
2 *syn see* EGOCENTRIC 2
idiom wrapped up in oneself

self–centeredness *n syn see* SELFISHNESS

self–command *n syn see* WILL 3
rel self–containment, uncommunicative-
ness

self–complacency *n syn see* CONCEIT 2

self–complacent *adj* *syn* *see* COM-
PLACENT

self–composed *adj syn see* CALM 2

self–conceit *n syn see* CONCEIT 2

self–conceited *adj syn see* VAIN 3

self–concern *n syn see* SELFISHNESS

self–concerned *adj syn see* EGOCENTRIC
2

self–confidence *n syn see* CONFIDENCE 2
rel sanguineness, sureness; cockiness,
overconfidence
con diffidence, shyness; self–distrust;
doubt, uneasiness
ant self–doubt

self–confident *adj syn see* CONFIDENT 1

self–conscious *adj* aware of the scrutiny
of others to the point of not appearing
natural or spontaneous < felt *self–conscious*
about wearing platform shoes >
syn affected, conscious, mannered
rel self–aware; anxious, ill at ease, uncomfortable, uneasy; formal, stiff, stilted; arti-
ficial; ||mim, prim; exhibitionist, flaunty,
ostentatious
con unaware, unconcerned; blithe, easy;
natural, spontaneous, unaffected

self–consequence *n syn see* CONCEIT 2

self–contained *adj* *syn* *see* SELF–SUF-
FICIENT

self–contemplation *n* *syn* *see* INTRO-
SPECTION

self–contented *adj syn see* COMPLACENT

self–control *n syn see* WILL 3
rel constraint, reserve, self–containedness;
balance, stability; dignity
idiom presence of mind
ant self–abandonment

self–criticism *n syn see* SELF–REPROACH

self–deceit *n syn see* SELF–DECEPTION

self–deception *n* the act or an instance of
deceiving oneself or of being so deceived
< to presume agreement where none exists
is a dangerous form of *self–deception* >
syn self–deceit, self–delusion
rel misconception, misinterpretation,
misunderstanding; deception, delusion,
illusion
idiom kidding oneself

self–defense *n* an act, instance, or means
of defending oneself, one's property, or a
close relative < sought some measure of
self–defense against society's lawless elements >
syn self–protection
rel self–preservation

self–delusion *n syn see* SELF–DECEPTION

self–denial *n syn see* RENUNCIATION
rel abstaining, abstemiousness, abstinence;
asceticism, selflessness, self–sacrifice, self=
sacrificing; self–forgetful, self–forgetting
ant self–indulgence

self–denying *adj* *syn* *see* SELF–SAC-
RIFICING

self–dependence *n syn see* SELF–RELI-
ANCE

self–destruction *n syn see* SUICIDE

self–discipline *n syn see* WILL 3

selfdom *n syn see* INDIVIDUALITY 4

self–educated *adj syn see* SELF–TAUGHT

self–effacing *adj syn see* SHY 1

self–esteem *n* 1 *syn see* PRIDE 2
rel self–content, self–contentment; self=
satisfaction
con self–distrust, self–doubt; self–contempt
ant self–hate
2 *syn see* CONCEIT 2
rel self–flattery, self–glorification
con self–distrust, self–doubt; self–hate
ant self–contempt

self–evidencing *adj syn see* SELF–EVI-
DENT

self–evident *adj* evident in itself without
need of argument or proof < *self–evident*
truths >
syn prima facie, self–evidencing
rel clear, manifest, obvious, plain; unmistakable, unquestionable
con enigmatic, hidden, mysterious, obscure; doubtable, doubtful, questionable,
uncertain

self–exaltation *n syn see* CONCEIT 2

self–examination *n syn see* INTROSPEC-
TION

self–existent *adj* existing of or by itself
and having no antecedent cause < argues
backward to a first great cause, which is
itself *self–existent* >
syn increate, self–existing, unbegotten,
uncaused, uncreated, unoriginated
rel self–generated, self–originated; self=
produced
con consequent, resultant, sequential
ant derivative

self–existing *adj syn see* SELF–EXISTENT

self–explaining *adj* *syn* *see* SELF–EX-
PLANATORY

---

syn synonym(s)   *rel* related word(s)
ant antonym(s)   *con* contrasted word(s)
idiom idiomatic equivalent(s)
|| use limited; if in doubt, see a dictionary

self-explanatory *adj* capable of being understood without explanation < his actions are *self-explanatory:* he wants to resign >
  syn self-explaining; *compare* CLEAR 5
  rel clear, evident, obvious, manifest, plain, self-evident; comprehensible, understandable
  con equivocal, obscure, uncertain, unclear, vague; complex; incomprehensible, mysterious; inexplicable, unexplainable

self-forgetful *adj syn* see SELFLESS

self-forgetting *adj syn* see SELFLESS

self-giving *adj syn* see SELF-SACRIFICING

self-glorifying *adj syn* see BOASTFUL

self-glory *n syn* see CONCEIT 2
  rel self-aggrandizement; self-glorification

self-governing *adj syn* see DEMOCRATIC

self-government *n syn* see WILL 3

self-gratification *n* the act of pleasing oneself or of satisfying one's desires < human beings driven by unconscious forces toward *self-gratification* >
  syn onanism, self-indulgence
  rel self-abandonment; self-pleasing; self-satisfaction; autotheism, narcissism, self-worship

selfhood *n* 1 *syn* see INDIVIDUALITY 4
  2 see SELFISHNESS

self-importance *n* 1 *syn* see CONCEIT 2
  2 *syn* see EGOTISM 1
  rel arrogance, pomposity

self-important *adj syn* see POMPOUS 1

self-imposed *adj* imposed by oneself or itself < insists on working under *self-imposed* handicaps >
  syn self-inflicted
  rel self-generated, self-produced

self-indulgence *n syn* see SELF-GRATIFICATION
  rel indulgence; excess, intemperance, overindulgence
  ant abstinence

self-indulgent *adj syn* see SYBARITIC

self-inflicted *adj syn* see SELF-IMPOSED
  rel self-determined; accepted; voluntary

self-instructed *adj syn* see SELF-TAUGHT

self-interest *n syn* see SELFISHNESS

self-interested *adj syn* see EGOCENTRIC 2

self-involved *adj syn* see EGOCENTRIC 2

selfish *adj syn* see EGOCENTRIC 2
  idiom ‖looking out for number one
  con self-denying, selfless, self-sacrificing; altruistic, benevolent, charitable, generous, magnanimous
  ant unselfish

selfishness *n* a concern for one's own welfare at the expense of or in disregard of others < his *selfishness* was consummate: he cared for no one but himself >
  syn self-centeredness, self-concern, selfhood, self-interest, self-regard, self-seeking
  rel egoism, egotism, self-absorption; self, selfism, selfness; autotheism, self-worship
  con self-denial, selflessness, self-sacrificing; benevolence, charity, generosity
  ant unselfishness

self-knowledge *n* knowledge or understanding of one's own character, motivations, and capabilities < a poet whose verse reflected deep *self-knowledge* and honesty >

  syn autognosis, self-understanding
  rel self-awareness; introspection, self-examination, self-observation

selfless *adj* having no concern for oneself < *selfless* service to community, state, and nation >
  syn self-forgetful, self-forgetting, unselfish
  rel self-giving, self-sacrificing; self-renouncing; elevated, generous, high-minded, magnanimous
  con self-devoted, self-loving, self-serving
  ant self-centered, selfish

self-love *n syn* see CONCEIT 2
  idiom the sixth insatiable sense
  con self-abuse, self-accusation, self-reproach; self-forgetfulness, selflessness
  ant self-hate

self-mastery *n syn* see WILL 3

self-murder *n syn* see SUICIDE

selfness *n syn* see INDIVIDUALITY 4

self-observation *n syn* see INTROSPECTION

self-opinion *n syn* see CONCEIT 2

self-pleased *adj syn* see COMPLACENT

self-possessed *adj syn* see CALM 2
  rel aloof, reserved; self-contained, self-controlled; self-assured

self-possession *n syn* see EQUANIMITY

self-pride *n syn* see CONCEIT 2

self-proclaimed *adj syn* see SELF-STYLED

self-protection *n syn* see SELF-DEFENSE

self-questioning *n syn* see INTROSPECTION

self-recrimination *n syn* see SELF-REPROACH

self-reflection *n syn* see INTROSPECTION

self-regard *n* 1 *syn* see SELFISHNESS
  2 *syn* see PRIDE 2

self-reliance *n* reliance on one's own resources, efforts, and ability < a strong people characterized by bravery and *self-reliance* >
  syn self-dependence
  rel confidence, self-assurance, self-confidence; self-sufficiency, self-support

self-renouncing *adj syn* see SELF-SACRIFICING

self-renunciation *n syn* see RENUNCIATION

self-reproach *n* an act or instance of reproaching oneself < experienced both guilt and *self-reproach* after the quarrel >
  syn self-abuse, self-accusation, self-criticism, self-recrimination, self-reproof
  rel contrition, regret, remorse; self-castigation, self-condemnation, self-flagellation, self-punishment; self-contempt
  con self-contentment, self-satisfaction; self-applause
  ant self-approbation

self-reproof *n syn* see SELF-REPROACH

self-respect *n syn* see PRIDE 2

self-restraining *adj syn* see ABSTEMIOUS

self-restraint *n syn* see WILL 3
  ant abandon

self-righteous *adj*   *syn*   see HYPOCRITICAL

self-ruling *adj syn* see DEMOCRATIC

self-sacrificing *adj* sacrificing or denying oneself for others < a *self-sacrificing* love >
  syn self-abnegating, self-denying, self-giving, self-renouncing

rel selfless, unselfish; charitable, generous, kindly, philanthropic
con self-centered, selfish, self-seeking

selfsame *adj syn* see SAME 1
rel alike, like
idiom (the) very same
con different, unalike
ant diverse

selfsameness *n syn* see IDENTITY
ant diverseness

self–satisfied *adj syn* see COMPLACENT

self–scrutiny *n syn* see INTROSPECTION

self–searching *n syn* see INTROSPECTION

self–seeking *n syn* see SELFISHNESS

self–seeking *adj syn* see EGOCENTRIC 2

self–serving *adj syn* see EGOCENTRIC 2

self–slaughter *n syn* see SUICIDE

self–starter *n syn* see HUSTLER 1

self–styled *adj* given a specified designation or title by oneself often without justification <a department cluttered with *self-styled* experts>
syn self-proclaimed, soi-disant
rel self-appointed, self-created, self-given; so-called; quasi; would-be

self–sufficient *adj* maintaining or able to maintain oneself without outside aid <organisms are not *self-sufficient*, closed systems>
syn closed, independent, self-centered, self-contained, self-sufficing, self-supported, self-supporting, self-sustained, self-sustaining
rel self-dependent, self-reliant; self-subsistent, self-subsisting; individual, one-man, unit
idiom one's own man, sufficient unto oneself (*or* itself)
con dependent

self–sufficing *adj syn* see SELF-SUFFICIENT

self–supported *adj syn* see SELF-SUFFICIENT

self–supporting *adj syn* see SELF-SUFFICIENT

self–sustained *adj syn* see SELF-SUFFICIENT

self–sustaining *adj syn* see SELF-SUFFICIENT

self–taught *adj* having knowledge or skills acquired by one's own efforts without formal instruction <a *self-taught* painter>
syn autodidactic, self-educated, self-instructed

self–trust *n syn* see CONFIDENCE 2

self–understanding *n syn* see SELF-KNOWLEDGE

self–violence *n syn* see SUICIDE

self–willed *adj syn* see OBSTINATE
con weak, weak-willed, wishy-washy; spineless

sell *vb* **1** *syn* see BETRAY 2
2 to give up (property) to another for money or other valuable consideration <can *sell* you the house now>
syn give, market, vend
ant buy, purchase

3 to deal in or offer (articles) for sale on a regular basis <he *sells* small appliances>
syn market, merchandise, retail
rel barter, deal (in), exchange, trade, traffic; hawk, peddle; vend
ant buy

4 to command a specified price <that coat *sells* for $300>
syn bring, bring in, fetch
rel command, draw; realize, return, yield; gross, net

sell *n syn* see IMPOSTURE

sellable *adj syn* see MARKETABLE

sell off *vb syn* see SELL OUT 1

sell out *vb* **1** to dispose of entirely by selling <*sold out* his share of the business>
syn close out, sell off, ‖sell up
rel dump, move, unload; sacrifice
2 *syn* see DECEIVE
3 *syn* see BETRAY 2

‖sell up *vb syn* see SELL OUT 1

selvage *n syn* see BORDER 1

semblance *n* **1** *syn* see AIR 3
rel aspect, look
2 *syn* see LIKENESS
3 *syn* see APPEARANCE 2
rel air, pose
4 *syn* see MASK 2

semblant *adj syn* see APPARENT 2

seminar *n syn* see CONFERENCE 2

semioccasional *adj syn* see INFREQUENT

sempiternal *adj syn* see INFINITE 1

sempiternity *n syn* see ETERNITY 1

send *vb* **1** to cause to go or be taken from one place, person, or condition to another <*send* a messenger to the bank> <his cold *sent* him to bed>
syn address, consign, dispatch, forward, remit, route, ship, transmit
rel allocate, assign, commit, delegate; advance, launch; expedite, rush
ant receive
2 *syn* see THRILL

senectitude *n syn* see OLD AGE

senescence *n syn* see OLD AGE

senile *adj* exhibiting the weakness and loss of mental faculties often associated with old age <a *senile* professor now unable to lecture coherently>
syn doddering, doddery, ‖doted, doting
rel aging, senescent; aged, ancient, old; enfeebled, feeble, weak; decrepit, doddered, shattered
idiom in one's second childhood

senility *n syn* see DOTAGE
rel decline; senescence

senior *n* **1** *syn* see OLDSTER
2 one older than another <he was her *senior* by eight years>
syn elder
ant junior
3 *syn* see SUPERIOR
con inferior, subordinate, underling

senior citizen *n syn* see OLDSTER

sensation *n* **1** the power to respond or an act of responding to stimuli <the stage of *sensation* precedes that of rational comprehension>
syn feeling, sense, sensibility, sensitivity
rel susceptibility; consciousness; sensitiveness, sensitivity; impression, perception, response
2 *syn* see WONDER 1

---

syn synonym(s)   *rel* related word(s)
ant antonym(s)   *con* contrasted word(s)
idiom idiomatic equivalent(s)
‖ use limited; if in doubt, see a dictionary

rel bomb, bombshell

sensational *adj* **1** *syn* see SENSORY

2 arousing or designed to arouse a quick, intense, and usually superficial emotional response < *sensational* crime reporting >
syn livid, lurid, sensationalistic, sensationist, sultry, tabloid
rel juicy, piquant, pungent; colored, extravagant; coarse, vulgar
con exact, factual; dignified, formal, proper, restrained

3 *syn* see NOTICEABLE
rel impressive, stunning

4 *syn* see MARVELOUS 2
rel boffo, crashing, rousing, slambang, smash, smashing, superfine

sensationalistic *adj* *syn* see SENSATIONAL 2

sensationist *adj* *syn* see SENSATIONAL 2

sensatory *adj* *syn* see SENSORY

sense *n* **1** *syn* see MEANING 1
rel gist, pith, substance; center, core, focus, nucleus

2 *syn* see SUBSTANCE 2

3 *syn* see SENSATION 1
rel awareness, cognizance; discernment, discrimination, penetration; appreciation; recognition

4 *usu* senses *pl* *syn* see WIT 2
rel consciousness

5 *syn* see INTELLIGENCE 1

6 ability to make intelligent choices and to reach intelligent conclusions or decisions < had enough *sense* to study something practical >
syn common sense, good sense, gumption, horse sense, judgment, wisdom
rel discretion, foresight, prudence; appreciation, comprehension, understanding; brains, intelligence, ‖smarts, wit
ant folly

sense *vb* *syn* see FEEL 3
rel anticipate; know, realize

senseless *adj* **1** *syn* see NUMB 1
rel oblivious, unaware; inanimate, wooden

2 *syn* see INSENSATE 1

3 *syn* see INSENSIBLE 2

4 *syn* see SIMPLE 3
rel irrational, surd

5 having no meaning < an ancient custom, now outdated and *senseless* >
syn insignificant, meaningless, pointless, purportless, unmeaning
rel purposeless; trivial, unimportant
idiom without rhyme or reason
con purposeful; important, meaning, meaningful, significant

senselessness *n* *syn* see FOOLISHNESS
rel illogicality, stupidity

sensibility *n* *syn* see SENSATION 1
rel discernment, discrimination, insight, keenness, penetration, responsiveness; affection, emotion, heart
con apathy, indifference, insensibleness, insentience, unfeelingness, unresponsiveness
ant insensibility

sensibilize *vb* *syn* see SENSITIZE

sensible *adj* **1** *syn* see MATERIAL 1
rel concrete, solid
con immaterial, insubstantial; unreal

2 *syn* see PERCEPTIBLE

rel imaginal, perceptual, sensational; weighable; evident, manifest, obvious, patent
con imperceptible; cloudy, unclear
ant insensible

3 *syn* see CONSIDERABLE 2

4 *syn* see SENTIENT 3

5 *syn* see AWARE
rel sensitive, susceptible; noting, observing, perceiving, remarking, seeing; appreciating, comprehending, understanding; intelligent, knowing
con anesthetic, insensate, insensitive
ant insensible

6 *syn* see RATIONAL
rel sensemaking

7 *syn* see WISE 2
rel rational, reasonable; down-to-earth, matter-of-fact
con unreasonable, unsound, unwise; asinine, fatuous
ant absurd, foolish

sensile *adj* *syn* see SENTIENT 3

sensitive *adj* **1** *syn* see SENTIENT 3
rel hypersensitive, supersensitive
con impervious, insensible, unfeeling, unimpressionable, unresponsive; wooden
ant insensitive, unsensitive

2 *syn* see EMOTIONAL 1
rel high-strung, irritable, nervous, tense; insultable, oversensitive, umbrageous; unstable
con impervious, insensate, insensible, unaffected, unemotional
ant insensitive, unsensitive

3 *syn* see ACUTE 3
rel perceiving, seeing; aware, cognizant, conscious; knowing, understanding

4 *syn* see LIABLE 2
rel affected, impressed, influenced; disposed, inclined, predisposed
ant insensitive

5 *syn* see DELICATE 7

6 *syn* see SENSORY

sensitivity *n* *syn* see SENSATION 1

sensitize *vb* to cause to become sensitive or more sensitive < *sensitizing* corporate officers to social and environmental problems >
syn sensibilize
rel animate, excite, quicken, sharpen, stimulate, whet
ant desensitize

sensorial *adj* *syn* see SENSORY

sensory *adj* of or relating to sensation or the senses < *sensory* perception >
syn sensational, sensatory, sensitive, sensorial, sensual
rel sensate; receptive

sensual *adj* **1** *syn* see SENSORY

2 *syn* see CARNAL 2
rel irreligious, unspiritual

3 *syn* see SENSUOUS

4 *syn* see MATERIALISTIC

sensualistic *adj* *syn* see SENSUOUS

sensuous *adj* producing or characterized by gratification of the senses < *sensuous* pleasures >
syn epicurean, luscious, lush, luxurious, sensual, sensualistic, voluptuous; *compare* CARNAL 2, SYBARITIC
rel bacchic, dionysiac, Dionysian, hedonistic, pleasure-loving, pleasure-seeking;

self-indulgent, sybaritic; carnal, fleshly, fleshy
con ascetic, disciplined, restrained

sentence *vb* to decree the fate or punishment of one adjudged guilty, unworthy, or unfit <was *sentenced* to exile>
syn condemn, damn, doom, proscribe
rel adjudge, adjudicate, judge; ordain, rule; blame, denounce; penalize, punish; devote
idiom pass sentence on
con absolve, acquit, exculpate, exonerate, vindicate; discharge, free, liberate, release

sententious *adj syn see* EXPRESSIVE
rel aphoristic, concise, crisp, epigrammatic, piquant, pithy, terse

sentient *adj* 1 *syn see* AWARE
2 *syn see* EMOTIONAL 1
3 capable of receiving and of being readily affected by external stimuli <deeply disturbed in the most *sentient* reaches of his mind>
syn impressible, impressionable, responsive, sensible, sensile, sensitive, susceptible, susceptive
rel sensate; open, receptive, susceptive; reactive
con insensate; closed, unreceptive; unreactive

sentiment *n* 1 *syn see* LEANING 2
2 *syn see* OPINION
rel leaning, predilection, propensity; position, posture
idiom way of thinking
3 *syn see* FEELING 3
rel conception; sensation; emotionalism, sentimentality

sentimental *adj* unduly or affectedly emotional <*sentimental* love stories>
syn bathetic, drippy, gooey, lovey-dovey, maudlin, mawkish, moist, mushy, romantic, sappy, slushy, sobby, sobful, soft‡ boiled, ‖soppy, soupy, sticky, syrupy, tear‡ jerking
rel dreamy, misty-eyed, moonstruck, nostalgic, oversentimental; inane, insipid, jejune, namby-pamby, schoolgirlish, vapid; rosewater, saccharine, soft, sugar-candy, sugary, sweet; loving, tender; affectionate, demonstrative, effusive; gushing, gushy; passionate
con unaffectionate, undemonstrative; dispassionate, emotionless, unemotional, unresponsive; unfeeling, unloving; dry
ant unsentimental

sentinel *n syn see* GUARD 2
sentry *n syn see* GUARD 2
separate *vb* 1 to become or cause to become disunited or disjoined <forces that *separate* families>
syn break up, dichotomize, disjoin, disjoint, dissect, dissever, disunite, divide, divorce, part, rupture, sever, split (up), sunder, uncombine
rel alienate, discontinue, disunify, estrange; dislink, uncouple, unjoin, unlink; disaggregate, disassemble, disgregate, dispel, disperse, dissolve, scatter; detach,

disengage, disrelate, dissociate; halve, quarter
con assemble, associate, blend, mingle, mix; connect, couple, join, link; unify, unite; agglutinate, bind, cement, fuse, weld
ant combine
2 *syn see* KNOW 4
3 *syn see* SORT 2
rel compartment, compartmentalize
4 *syn see* DISCHARGE 7
5 *syn see* ISOLATE

separate *adj* 1 *syn see* SINGLE 2
rel distinctive, peculiar; detached, disconnected, disengaged
2 *syn see* FREE 1
3 *syn see* DISTINCT 1
rel free, independent

separately *adv syn see* APART 1
rel distinctly; solely
con conjointly, jointly
ant together

separateness *n syn see* SEGREGATION
ant togetherness

separation *n* 1 the act, process, or an instance of separating or of being separated <*separation* of church and state> <their *separation* was a sad occasion>
syn detachment, dissolution, disunion, division, divorce, divorcement, partition, rupture, split-up
rel disrelation, dissociation; disunity, parting, shedding; disconnection, disjointedness, disjointure; breakup, disjunction, dissection, sequestration; diffluence, dispersal; dichotomy, diremption, trichotomy
con combination; unification
ant union
2 *syn see* SEGREGATION

separatism *n syn see* SEGREGATION
separatist *n syn see* HERETIC
sepulcher *n syn see* GRAVE
sepulcher *vb* 1 *syn see* ENTOMB 1
2 *syn see* BURY 1

sepulchral *adj* 1 of, relating to, or serving as a sepulcher or a memorial to the dead <*sepulchral* inscriptions>
syn mortuary, tumulary
rel exequial, funebrial, funeral, funerary, funereal
2 *syn see* HOLLOW 1

sepulture *n* 1 *syn see* BURIAL 2
2 *syn see* GRAVE
sepulture *vb* 1 *syn see* ENTOMB 1
2 *syn see* BURY 1

sequel *n* 1 *syn see* SUCCESSION 2
2 *syn see* EFFECT 1
rel end, ending, termination; close, closing, finish, finishing
3 *syn see* EPILOGUE 2
rel continuation, development; aftermath, outcome, result

sequence *n* 1 *syn see* SUCCESSION 2
rel arrangement, disposition, ordering; procession
2 *syn see* ORDER 3
rel classification, grouping; placement
3 *syn see* EFFECT 1
4 *syn see* ORDER 5

sequent *adj syn see* CONSECUTIVE
sequential *adj syn see* CONSECUTIVE
sequester *vb* 1 *syn see* ISOLATE
2 *syn see* SECLUDE

---

syn synonym(s)   *rel* related word(s)
ant antonym(s)   *con* contrasted word(s)
idiom idiomatic equivalent(s)
‖ use limited; if in doubt, see a dictionary

rel hide, secrete
3 *syn* see APPROPRIATE 1
rel attach; impound; dispossess
sequestered *adj syn* see SECLUDED
rel sheltered; closeted
sequestration *n syn* see SECLUSION
rel retreat
sequitur *n syn* see INFERENCE 2
seraglio *n syn* see BROTHEL
sere *adj syn* see DRY 1
serene *adj syn* see CALM 2
rel noiseless, quiet, still; quiescent, resting; undisturbed
con agitated, disquieted, upset
serfage *n syn* see BONDAGE
serfdom *n syn* see BONDAGE
serial *adj syn* see CONSECUTIVE
series *n syn* see SUCCESSION 2
rel continuance, continuation, run; category, group, set; column, tier; gradation,
scale
serious *adj* 1 not light or frivolous (as in
disposition, appearance, or manner) <he
was disturbed by her stern, *serious* look>
syn earnest, grave, no-nonsense, poker-
faced sedate, sober, sobersided, solemn,
somber, staid, weighty
rel businesslike, ‖dern, determined,
steady, steady-going; intent, serious-
minded; contemplative, meditative, pensive, reflective, thoughtful; austere, severe,
stern; humorless, unhumorous; grim
idiom serious as a judge
con flighty, ‖flip, flippant, frivolous, volatile; casual, easy, relaxed
ant light, unserious
2 expressing, involving, or characterized
by seriousness or gravity (as of consequence) <a *serious* economic situation>
syn grave, heavy, severe, weighty
rel important, significant; sobering;
unamusing, unfunny, unhumorous; grim
idiom no joke, no laughing matter
con inconsequential, insignificant, unimportant, unserious
ant trifling, trivial
3 *syn* see HARD 6
4 *syn* see GRAVE 3
rel menacing, threatening
seriously *adv* 1 in a serious manner <at
last settled *seriously* to work>
syn actively, down, earnestly, for real
rel gravely, soberly, solemnly; intently;
vigorously, zealously; determinedly, pur-
posefully, resolutely; fervently, passionately
idiom all joking aside, in all seriousness,
in earnest
con airily, casually, flippantly, lightly,
unconcernedly; carelessly, haphazardly
2 to a serious extent <the cities are
seriously overcrowded>
syn gravely, intensely, severely
rel decidedly, quite, very; dangerously;
critically, deplorably, regrettably
serious–mindedness *n syn* see EARNEST-
NESS
rel thoughtfulness; sober-mindedness
seriousness *n syn* see EARNESTNESS
rel sedateness, sobriety, solemnity, staidness
con gaiety, jollity; lightness
ant flippancy, frivolity

sermon *n* a religious discourse delivered in
public by a clergyman as part of a worship service <preached his first *sermon* on
Sunday>
syn preach, preaching, preachment, sermonizing
rel preachification; sermonary, ser-
monology; sermonette; exhortation, harangue, lecture, tirade
sermonic *adj syn* see DIDACTIC
sermonize *vb* 1 *syn* see PREACH 1
2 *syn* see DISCOURSE 1
3 *syn* see MORALIZE
sermonizer *n syn* see CLERGYMAN
sermonizing *n syn* see SERMON
sermonizing *adj syn* see DIDACTIC
serpent *n syn* see DEVIL 1
serpentine *adj* 1 *syn* see FIENDISH
2 *syn* see WINDING
rel serpentiform, serpentile, serpentlike,
snakelike; crooked, devious
serrate *adj* notched or toothed on the edge
<jagged peaks and *serrate* ridges>
syn denticulate, saw-edged, sawtooth,
saw-toothed, serrated, serried
rel indented, notched, scored, toothed;
serrulate
serrated *adj syn* see SERRATE
serried *adj syn* see SERRATE
serve *vb* 1 *syn* see BENEFIT
2 *syn* see ACT 4
3 to prove adequate or sufficient <will
not *serve* as a true translation>
syn do, suffice, suit
rel service; function, work; fit; satisfy;
make
idiom fill the bill
4 *syn* see MINISTER (to)
5 to put in (a term of imprisonment)
<*served* ten years for armed robbery>
syn do
rel put in, spend; undergo
idiom do a hitch (or stretch), serve (out)
a sentence, serve time, ‖take a vacation
6 *syn* see ADVANCE 1
7 *syn* see TREAT 2
service *n* 1 the performance of military
duty in wartime and especially in a combat zone <saw a year's *service* in Viet-
nam>
syn action, combat
rel active duty, duty; fighting
2 *syn* see FAVOR 4
3 *syn* see RITE 2
4 *syn* see USE 3
serviceability *n syn* see USE 3
rel serviceableness; durability
serviceable *adj* 1 *syn* see HELPFUL 1
ant unserviceable
2 *syn* see PRACTICAL 2
ant unserviceable
serviceman *n* 1 *syn* see SOLDIER
2 servicemen *pl syn* see TROOP 2
servile *adj* 1 *syn* see SUBSERVIENT 2
rel obedient, submissive; passive, unresisting; bootlicking, groveling, toadish
con aggressive
ant authoritative
2 *syn* see BASE 3
servility *n syn* see BONDAGE
servitude *n syn* see BONDAGE
con freedom, independence
set *vb* 1 to position (something) in a specified place <*set* the lamp on the table>

syn establish, fix, lay, place, put, settle, stick
rel bestow, deposit, park; emplace, ensconce, install; affix, anchor, wedge
con displace, replace, supplant; remove, take (away); uproot
2 *syn* see DIRECT 2
idiom set one's sights on
3 *syn* see STATION
4 *syn* see DICTATE
rel designate, direct, instruct, specify, stipulate; establish; make, name
5 to put in order for a meal <she quickly *set* the table for dinner>
syn lay, spread
rel fix, prepare, ready; arrange
ant clear
6 *syn* see GAMBLE 1
7 *syn* see INCITE
∥**8** *syn* see SIT 1
9 *syn* see BELONG 1
10 *syn* see COAGULATE
11 *of a fowl* to incubate eggs by crouching upon them <a chicken house filled with hens *setting* on eggs>
syn brood, ∥clock, cover, sit
rel hatch, incubate; hover
12 *of a celestial body* to pass below the horizon <the sun *set* at seven o'clock>
syn decline, dip, go down, sink
rel descend, drop
con ascend, climb, come up
ant rise
13 *syn* see HARDEN 1
rel crystallize, granulate; fix
set (at) *vb syn* see ESTIMATE 1
set *adj* **1** *syn* see SITUATED
2 *syn* see DECIDED 2
3 *syn* see FIRM 4
rel confirmed, entrenched, established, inveterate, rooted, well-set, well-settled; prescribed, specified
4 *syn* see LITTLE 2
rel diehard, inflexible, obstinate, pigheaded, rigid, unbending, unyielding
5 *syn* see FAST 4
rel fastened; close; sound
6 *syn* see EXPRESS 2
7 *syn* see READY 1
set *n* **1** *syn* see GIFT 2
2 *syn* see BEARING 1
3 *syn* see SCENE 1
4 *syn* see GROUP 3
rel assortment, gaggle; kit, pack
5 a number of people having something (as habit, interest, occupation, or age) in common <the horsey *set* was gathered at the bar>
syn bunch, circle, crowd, group, lot, push; *compare* CLIQUE
rel clan, clique, crew, gang, mob; cénacle; camp, faction; company
set back *vb syn* see DELAY 1
setback *n* a checking of progress <loss of his fellowship was a serious *setback* to his education>
syn backset, check, reversal, reverse; *compare* COMEDOWN

rel delay, retardation, slowdown; hindrance, impediment, obstacle, stumbling block; disappointment; rebuff; defeat; regress, regression
idiom reverse of fortune
con advancement, forwarding, progressing
set down *vb syn* see ALIGHT
set off *vb* **1** *syn* see COMPENSATE 1
2 *syn* see MOBILIZE 1
set on *vb syn* see INCITE
set out *vb* **1** *syn* see DESIGN 3
2 *syn* see HEAD 3
idiom set one's course for
setout *n* **1** *syn* see COSTUME
2 *syn* see BEGINNING
setting *n syn* see SCENE 1
setting–out *n syn* see DEPARTURE 1
settle *vb* **1** *syn* see ENSCONCE 2
2 *syn* see CALM
rel assure, reassure
ant unsettle
3 *syn* see SET 1
rel found, ground, lodge, seat
con dislodge, uproot, unseat
ant unsettle
4 *syn* see DECIDE
rel fix, seal
idiom come to a decision (*or* conclusion), form a judgment, make a decision
5 *syn* see NEGOTIATE 1
rel mediate, reconcile, straighten (out)
idiom bring to terms (*or* agreement)
6 *syn* see CLEAR 5
idiom settle the score, settle up (*or* square) accounts
7 to put in order for final disposal <waiting to *settle* an estate>
syn clean up, wind up
8 *syn* see ALIGHT
rel flop (down), plop (down)
settled *adj* **1** *syn* see FIRM 4
rel decided, determined
con uncertain, undecided
ant unsettled
2 *syn* see INVETERATE 1
3 *syn* see DECIDED 2
rel certain, fixed
con irresolute, undecided, undetermined, unresolved, vacillating, wavering
ant unsettled
settlement *n* **1** *syn* see HABITATION 1
2 *syn* see DECISION 1
rel showdown; quietus
settlings *n pl syn* see SEDIMENT
set to *vb* **1** *syn* see BEGIN 1
2 *syn* see PITCH IN 1
set–to *n* **1** *syn* see BRAWL 2
2 *syn* see QUARREL
3 *syn* see ENCOUNTER
set up *vb* **1** *syn* see ERECT 5
ant tear down
2 *syn* see ELATE
3 *syn* see ERECT 3
con disassemble, take down
4 *syn* see FOUND 2
rel generate, originate; start up; open
5 *syn* see INTRODUCE 3
6 *syn* see TREAT 3
setup *n syn* see SNAP 1
seventh heaven *n syn* see ECSTASY
rel exhilaration; bliss, paradise
con sadness, unhappiness; blues, doldrums, dumps

---

syn synonym(s)   *rel* related word(s)
ant antonym(s)   *con* contrasted word(s)
idiom idiomatic equivalent(s)
∥ use limited; if in doubt, see a dictionary.

sever *vb* **1** *syn* see SEPARATE 1
2 *syn* see KNOW 4
3 *syn* see CUT 5
several *adj* **1** possessed by or attributed to a specific individual < the debaters expressed their *several* opinions >
syn individual, particular, respective, singular
rel independent; personal, special, specific
2 *syn* see DISTINCT 1
3 consisting of an indefinite number more than two and less than many < *several* days passed >
syn divers, some, sundry, various
rel particular, separate, single; few; considerable; many, numerous
idiom not a few
‖**4** *syn* see MANY
‖**several** *pron syn* see SUNDRY
severalize *vb syn* see KNOW 4
severally *adv syn* see APART 1
rel discretely; exclusively
idiom one at a time
severe *adj* **1** given to or characterized by strict discipline and firm restraint < treated all the students with *severe* impartiality >
syn ascetic, astringent, austere, mortified, stern
rel exacting, heavy-handed, onerous, oppressive; disciplined, iron-willed, self-disciplined; inflexible, restrictive, rigid, rigorous, strict, stringent, uncompromising, unyielding
con easy, easygoing, gentle, mild, soft; clement, forbearing, indulgent, lax, lenient, merciful
ant tender, tolerant
2 *syn* see GRIM 2
rel serious, sober, stern
3 of a kind to cause discomfort or hardship < a *severe* winter storm >
syn bitter, brutal, hard, harsh, inclement, intemperate, rigorous, rugged
rel crimpy, unpleasant; forbidding, hostile, inhospitable; bleak, disagreeable, grim; painful, raw, sharp, smart; blistering, extreme, intense, savage; blustering, blustery, stormy, wintry
con balmy, calm, equable, gentle, moderate, soft, temperate
ant mild
4 *syn* see HARD 6
5 *syn* see SERIOUS 2
rel consequential; dear, sore
severely *adv* **1** *syn* see HARD 5
2 *syn* see SERIOUSLY 2
rel markedly
‖**sew** *vb syn* see EXUDE
sew up *vb* ‖**1** *syn* see EXHAUST 4
2 *syn* see MONOPOLIZE
sexy *adj syn* see RISQUÉ
shabby *adj* **1** being ill-kept and showing signs of wear and tear < a *shabby* neighborhood full of depressing tenements >
syn bedraggled, broken-down, decrepit, dilapidated, dingy, disreputable, down-at-heel, faded, mangy, moth-eaten, run-down, scrubby, scruffy, seedy, shoddy, sleazy, slipshod, squalid, tacky, tagrag, tattered, threadbare, tired
rel disfigured, dog-eared; decaying, deteriorated, deteriorating; ramshackle, ratty, rickety; bare, miserable, neglected, poor,

poverty-stricken; sordid; worm-eaten; outworn, worn-out; abandoned, desolate, ruined, ruinous, wrecked
idiom gone to seed
con neat, spick-and-span, tidy, trig, trim, well-kept; brand-new, fresh, new; unused
ant spruce
2 *syn* see CONTEMPTIBLE
3 *syn* see DISREPUTABLE 1
‖**shack** *n syn* see VAGABOND
shack *n syn* see HUT
shackle *n, usu* **shackles** *pl* something that confines the legs or arms so as to prevent free movement < slaves in *shackles* >
syn bond(s), chains, fetter(s), gyve(s), iron(s)
rel anklet, bilbo, leg-iron, trammel; bracelet, handcuff, manacle; straitjacket; collar, garrote
shackle *vb syn* see HAMPER
rel lash, rope, strap; chain, enchain, manacle; handcuff; pinion, secure
con unchain, unfetter, untie
ant unshackle
shade *n* **1** comparative darkness or obscurity due to interception of light rays < trees providing *shade* from the sunlight >
syn adumbration, penumbra, shadow, umbra, umbrage
rel blackness, darkness, dimness, obscuration, obscurity; cover, shelter
con brightness, brilliancy, effulgence, radiance; blaze, glare, glow
2 *syn* see APPARITION
3 *syn* see COLOR 1
rel intensity, saturation
4 *syn* see GRADATION
rel difference, distinction, variation
5 *syn* see HINT 2
shade *vb* to cast into shadow by intercepting light rays < avenues *shaded* by large trees >
syn inumbrate, screen, shadow, umbrage
rel shelter; cover
con roast, scorch, swelter; expose
shaded *adj syn* see SHADY 1
ant unshaded
shadow *n* **1** *syn* see SHADE 1
2 *syn* see APPARITION
3 *syn* see VESTIGE 1
4 *syn* see HINT 2
shadow *vb* **1** *syn* see SHADE
2 *syn* see OBSCURE
3 *syn* see TAIL
shadow (forth) *vb* **1** *syn* see SUGGEST 5
2 *syn* see ADUMBRATE 1
rel forecast, foretell, predict
shadow *adj syn* see SHADY 1
shadowed *adj syn* see SHADY 1
ant unshadowed
shadowy *adj* **1** *syn* see IMAGINARY 1
2 *syn* see GHASTLY 2
3 *syn* see FAINT 1
rel amorphous; foggy
4 *syn* see SHADY 1
ant bright
shady *adj* **1** producing, affording, or abounding in shade < a *shady* day > < cool, *shady* streets >
syn shaded, shadow, shadowed, shadowy, umbrageous, umbrous
rel bosky, screened, sheltered; dusky; dark

con exposed, unshaded, unshadowed; unsheltered; bright, light
ant sunny
2 *syn* see DOUBTFUL 1
3 *syn* see DISREPUTABLE 1
rel subreputable
4 *syn* see RISQUÉ
rel disreputable, shameful

shaft *n* **1** *syn* see RAY 1
2 a scornful, cutting, or pithily critical remark <the target of his latest *shaft* is the president himself>
syn barb, dart
rel cut, jab, thrust; potshot
3 harsh or unfair treatment <he really got the *shaft*: he was fired without notice>
syn ‖screw, ‖screwing
rel short end
idiom ‖a royal screwing, the dirty end of the stick, ‖the royal shaft

shake *vb* **1** to move irregularly to and fro or up and down often in a wavering or oscillating manner <was so frightened that her hands *shook*>
syn ‖didder, dither, quake, quaver, quiver, shiver, shudder, tremble, tremor, twitter
rel palpitate, quail, waver; flicker, flit, flitter, flutter; fluctuate, oscillate; chatter, shimmy, vibrate
idiom shake like an aspen leaf
2 to undergo strong vibration especially as the result of a physical blow or shock <the platform *shook* as the train passed>
syn jar, quake, tremble, tremor, vibrate
rel bounce, jounce; chatter, quiver, shimmy; rock, stagger
3 to cause to move in a quick, jerky manner <rattling and *shaking* the latch>
syn jiggle, joggle
rel bounce, ‖chounce, jounce; jostle; rattle; jerk
4 to cause to move to and fro or up and down violently <an earthquake that *shook* the whole coast>
syn agitate, concuss, convulse, rock
rel jog, jostle, rattle, ‖shog; commove, discompose, disorder, jar, jolt; disquiet, disturb, perturb, upset; churn, roil, ruffle, stir up, whip
5 to get or keep away from (a pursuer) <tried unsuccessfully to *shake* the man tailing him>
syn lose, slip, throw off; *compare* ESCAPE 2
rel avoid, elude; outwit
idiom get rid of, give (someone) the shake (*or* slip), slip from under the eye of
6 *syn* see DISMAY 1
rel disturb, jar, rattle, unsettle, upset; bother, worry; unnerve, unstring

shake (off) *vb syn* see RID

shake *n* **1** *syn* see EARTHQUAKE
2 shakes *pl syn* see JITTERS
3 *syn* see INSTANT 1
4 *syn* see DEAL 2

shake down *vb* **1** *syn* see EXTORT 1
2 *syn* see SEARCH 2

shake up *vb syn* see SPEED 3
shake–up *n* an extensive and often drastic rearrangement <a personnel *shake-up* effected by new management>
syn overturn, reorganization, revolution, turnover
rel liquidation, purge; cleanout, cleanup, clearing out, clear-up; removal, riddance
idiom break with the past, clean sweep

shakiness *n syn* see INSTABILITY
shaking *adj syn* see TREMULOUS
rel unsettled, unstable, unsteady; tottering
con unshakable, unshaken
shaky *adj* **1** *syn* see WEAK 2
rel unsettled; infirm, unsound, unsteady; precarious, tottering, tottery
2 *syn* see DOUBTFUL 1
3 *syn* see TREMULOUS
4 *syn* see RICKETY

shallow *adj* **1** lacking physical depth <buried in a *shallow* grave>
syn shoal, superficial
rel shallowish; surface
idiom as deep as a mud puddle, no deeper than a heavy dew, not deep enough to float a match
con bottomless, unfathomable
ant deep
2 *syn* see SUPERFICIAL 2
rel paltry, petty, trifling, trivial; empty, hollow, idle, vain; bird-witted, feather-brained, flighty
con heavy, profound; discerning, penetrating
ant deep

shallow *n syn* see SHOAL
ant deep

sham *n* **1** *syn* see IMPOSTURE
rel facade, fakery, false front, Potemkin village
2 *syn* see HYPOCRISY
3 *syn* see MOCKERY 2

sham *vb syn* see ASSUME 4
rel ape, copy, imitate, mock; create, invent; lie, mislead

sham *adj* **1** *syn* see FICTITIOUS 2
rel affected, assumed, feigned; pseudo, so-called; make-believe, pretend
2 *syn* see COUNTERFEIT
3 *syn* see ARTIFICIAL 2
rel plaster, synthetic; adulterated; bogus

shamble *vb syn* see SHUFFLE 3
shambles *n pl but usu sing in constr syn* see MESS 3

shame *n syn* see DISGRACE
rel chagrin, embarrassment; guilt, mortification, self-reproach, self-reproof
con pride, self-admiration, self-love, self-respect
ant glory

shamed *adj syn* see ASHAMED
rel crestfallen; shamefaced, shamefast; crushed, disgraced
idiom loaded (*or* bowed down) with shame
ant proud

shameful *adj syn* see DISREPUTABLE 1
shameless *adj* characterized by or exhibiting boldness and a lack of shame <a *shameless* hussy>
syn arrant, barefaced, blatant, brassy, brazen, brazenfaced, impudent, overbold, unabashed, unblushing

---

syn synonym(s)   *rel* related word(s)
ant antonym(s)   *con* contrasted word(s)
idiom idiomatic equivalent(s)
‖ use limited; if in doubt, see a dictionary

rel audacious, bold, cheeky, presumptuous; baldfaced, high-handed; abandoned, dissolute, profligate; immodest, lewd; disgraceful, outrageous
idiom bold as brass, dead (*or* lost) to shame
con bashful, diffident, mousy, shy; chaste, decent, modest, pure

‖**shamus** *n syn* see PRIVATE DETECTIVE
Shangri-la *n syn* see UTOPIA
shanty *n syn* see HUT
shape *vb syn* see MAKE 3
rel devise, plan, work up; tailor
shape *n* 1 *syn* see FORM 1
rel appearance, aspect, look, semblance
2 *syn* see ORDER 9
3 *syn* see ORDER 10
rel state, whack
shapeful *adj syn* see SHAPELY
ant shapeless
shapeless *adj syn* see FORMLESS
rel unshapely; deformed, misshapen
con proportional, proportionate, proportioned, shapeful, symmetrical
ant shapeful, shapely
shapely *adj* having a regular or pleasing shape < a *shapely* girl >
syn clean-limbed, shapeful, statuesque, trim, well-proportioned, well-turned; *compare* CURVACEOUS
rel balanced, clean-cut, proportioned, regular, symmetrical; comely, pleasing; ‖built, full-figured, rounded, ‖stacked; buxom
con dumpy, squat, stumpy; angular, lank, lean; ill-favored, ill-looking
ant shapeless, unshapely
share *n* 1 something belonging to, assumed by, or falling to one (as in division or apportionment) < wanted his *share* of the prize money >
syn allotment, allowance, bite, cut, lot, part, partage, portion, quota, slice; *compare* RATION
rel proportion, quotient, quotum; commission, percentage; divide, ‖divvy; rake-off
idiom piece of the action, slice of the melon
2 *syn* see RATION
3 *syn* see INTEREST 1
share *vb* 1 *syn* see APPORTION 2
rel assign, deal (out), dispense, dole (out), give out, mete (out)
idiom ‖go snucks, share and share alike
con retain, withhold; combine, unite
2 to have, get, or use in common with another or others < she *shared* her husband's fate >
syn partake, participate
rel experience
idiom have a share (*or* part) in, have (*or* take) a hand in
shared *adj syn* see COMMON 1
ant unshared
share out *vb syn* see ADMINISTER 2
sharer *n syn* see PARTICIPANT
sharp *adj* 1 having a fine edge < a *sharp* knife makes a clean cut >
syn honed, keen, razor-sharp, unblunted, whetted
rel acute
idiom sharp as a razor blade

con blunted, dulled; unsharpened
ant blunt, dull
2 *syn* see POINTED 1
3 *syn* see INTELLIGENT 2
4 possessing or indicative of alert competence and clear understanding < people of *sharp* judgment and refined sensibilities >
syn acute, keen, penetrating, penetrative, quick-sighted, quick-witted, sharp-sighted, sharp-witted; *compare* SHREWD
rel alert, bright; clever, cute, ingenious, original, resourceful; fast, quick
idiom sharp as a knife (*or* tack)
con dull-witted; unintelligent; foolish, simple, slow, stupid
ant dull
5 *syn* see ACUTE 3
6 *syn* see WISE 4
rel adroit, nimble; clever, cute; sly, unethical
idiom nobody's fool
7 *syn* see SHORT 5
rel acrimonious, biting, double-edged, incisive, penetrating, piercing, stabbing, stinging; caustic, virulent, vitriolic
8 causing intense mental or physical distress < a *sharp* pain >
syn acute, knifelike, piercing, shooting, stabbing
rel intense, severe, smart; biting, drilling, stinging; penetrating; agonizing, excruciating; paralyzing
9 *syn* see ACRID
rel odorous; strong-scented, strong-smelling; suffocating
10 *syn* see ACUTE 4
11 *syn* see STYLISH
‖**sharp** *vb syn* see SHARPEN
sharp *adv syn* see JUST 1
sharpen *vb* to give a keen edge to < *sharpen* an ax >
syn edge, hone, ‖sharp, whet
rel dress, file, grind, stroke
idiom hone to a razor edge, hone to razor sharpness
ant blunt, dull
sharper *n syn* see SWINDLER
sharp-eyed *adj* having keen vision < the *sharp-eyed* child found all the Easter eggs >
syn eagle-eyed, hawk-eyed, lyncean, lynx-eyed, sharp-sighted
rel alert, attentive, aware, keen, lynxlike, observant, sharp, vigilant, watchful
con myopic, nearsighted, shortsighted; dim-sighted, purblind; blind
sharpie *n syn* see SWINDLER
sharply *adv syn* see HARD 4
rel intensely, penetratingly, piercingly
sharpness *n syn* see EDGE 2
ant bluntness, dullness
sharp practice *n syn* see DECEPTION 1
sharp-sighted *adj* 1 *syn* see SHARP-EYED
2 *syn* see SHARP 4
sharp-witted *adj* 1 *syn* see SHARP 4
2 *syn* see WISE 4
shatter *vb* 1 to break into small pieces by or as if by a blow < *shatter* a windowpane with a rock >
syn burst, fragment, ‖pash, rive, shiver, smash, ‖smatter, splinter, splinterize, splitter; *compare* PULVERIZE 1
rel break, crack, rend, snap, ‖spalt, split; crunch, crush; crash, dash; fragmentalize,

fragmentize, pulverize; demolish, destroy, disintegrate, ruin, ||total, wreck
idiom smash to smithereens (*or* bits)
2 *syn* see DESTROY 1
3 *syn* see RATTLE 1
shatterable *adj syn* see FRAGILE 1
ant shatterproof
shatterbrain *n syn* see SCATTERBRAIN
shattering *adj syn* see DESTRUCTIVE
shattery *adj syn* see FRAGILE 1
idiom as delicate as an eggshell
shave *vb* 1 *syn* see SLIVER
2 *syn* see CUT 6
rel shingle
3 *syn* see REDUCE 2
4 *syn* see BRUSH
idiom cut (*or* shave) it close
5 *syn* see SCRAPE 3
shaveling *n syn* see BOY 1
shear *vb syn* see CUT 6
rel mow; barb, barber; manicure, snip
sheath *n syn* see SKIN 3
sheathe *vb* to cover (a surface) with something that protects <a house *sheathed* with aluminum siding>
syn clad, face, side, skin
rel envelop, surround, wrap; case, cover, encase, jacket; panel
con bare, expose, strip
sheathing *n syn* see SKIN 3
shed *vb* 1 *syn* see DISCARD
rel drop; divest
2 to cast off (a body covering) in a periodic process of growth or renewal <a snake *shedding* its skin>
syn exuviate, molt, slip, slough
rel cast off, discard; doff, take off
sheen *n syn* see LUSTER
rel finish; shininess
sheeny *adj syn* see LUSTROUS 1
sheepheaded *adj syn* see SIMPLE 3
sheer *adj* 1 *syn* see FILMY
rel airy, chiffon, thin; see-through
2 *syn* see UTTER
3 *syn* see PURE 2
rel arrant, bald-faced, complete, outright
4 *syn* see STEEP 1
sheer *vb* 1 *syn* see TURN 6
2 *syn* see SWERVE 1
||**shekels** *n pl syn* see MONEY
shell *n syn* see HULL
shell *vb* 1 *syn* see SHUCK
2 *syn* see BOMBARD
rel pepper; rake
idiom open fire on
shellac *vb syn* see WHIP 2
shellacking *n syn* see DEFEAT 1
rel ||clobbering, whipping
shell out *vb syn* see SPEND 1
shelter *n* 1 something (as a structure or place) that covers or affords protection <a bomb *shelter*>
syn asylum, cover, covert, harbor, harborage, haven, port, refuge, retreat, sanctuary; *compare* REFUGE 1
rel buen retiro, den, hermitage, hide, hideaway, hideout, hidey-hole, retirement, tower

2 dwellings provided for numbers of people or for a community < *shelter* for the aged>
syn housing, quarterage
rel dwellings, lodging; roof
3 *syn* see REFUGE 1
shelter *vb syn* see HARBOR 1
shelve *vb syn* see DEFER
rel dish, drop, give up
idiom put on the shelf
shenanigan *n* 1 *syn* see TRICK 1
rel fast one, game, legerdemain
2 *syn* see PRANK
rel frolic; goings-on, mischievousness; stunt
Sheol *n syn* see HELL
shepherd *vb syn* see GUIDE
Sherlock *n syn* see DETECTIVE
Sherlock Holmes *n syn* see DETECTIVE
shibboleth *n* 1 *syn* see CATCHWORD
rel platitude, truism
2 *syn* see COMMONPLACE
||**shick** *adj syn* see INTOXICATED 1
||**shicker** *adj syn* see INTOXICATED 1
||**shicker** *n syn* see DRUNKARD
shield *n syn* see DEFENSE 1
rel buffer, bumper; screen
shield *vb* 1 *syn* see HARBOR 1
idiom give cover (*or* shelter) to; take (*or* shield) under one's wing
ant expose
2 *syn* see DEFEND 1
shift *vb* ||1 *syn* see APPORTION 2
2 *syn* see CHANGE 5
3 *syn* see MOVE 4
rel alter, change, vary; budge, stir; shuffle; relocate
idiom shift place
4 *syn* see CONSUME 5
5 to carry on one's affairs independently and self-sufficiently often under difficult circumstances <had to *shift* for his own maintenance on very meager pay>
syn do, fare, get along, get by, get on, ||make out, manage, muddle through, stagger (on *or* along)
rel contrive, survive; freelance; progress, succeed
idiom fend for oneself, make do, make it alone, make shift, paddle one's own canoe, stand on one's own two feet
shift *n* 1 *syn* see CONVERSION 2
2 *syn* see RESOURCE 3
rel gambit, maneuver, ploy, strategy
3 *syn* see SPELL 1
4 *syn* see TRANSITION
5 *syn* see TURN 2
shifty *adj* 1 *syn* see EVASIVE 1
rel dodging, elusive; cagey, collusive, conniving, crafty, cunning; furtive, shifty-eyed, sneaky, tricky; insidious, shady; deceitful, dishonest, fraudulent; treacherous
idiom shifty as the sand
2 *syn* see DISHONEST
3 *syn* see UNDERHAND
4 *syn* see MUTABLE 2
shill *n syn* see DECOY 2
shillaber *n syn* see DECOY 2
||**shillelagh** *n syn* see CUDGEL
shilling shocker *n syn* see DIME NOVEL
shilly-shally *adj syn* see VACILLATING 2
shilly-shally *n syn* see HESITATION

shilly–shally *vb syn* see HESITATE

shilly–shallying *adj syn* see VACILLATING 2

   rel halfhearted, lukewarm

shimmer *vb syn* see FLASH 1

shimmer *n syn* see FLASH 1

   rel blinking; spangle; spark, sparking

shin *vb syn* see RUN 1

shindig *n* 1 a large, festive, and often overly lavish party <threw the *shindig* of the year for the debs>

   syn bash, ‖blowout, shindy

   rel fête, gala; ball, dance; party; affair, shebang; ‖shivoo

   2 *syn* see COMMOTION 3

shindy *n* 1 *syn* see SHINDIG 1

   2 *syn* see COMMOTION 3

shine *vb* 1 to emit rays of light <the storm is over and the sun is *shining*>

   syn beam, burn, gleam, radiate

   rel glimmer, glow; incandesce, luminesce; flash, sparkle, twinkle; flare; glare

   2 *syn* see POLISH 1

shine *n* 1 *syn* see DISPLAY 2

   2 *syn* see LUSTER

   rel finish

   3 *usu* shines *pl syn* see PRANK

shiner *n syn* see BLACK EYE 1

shingle *vb syn* see OVERLAP

shining *adj syn* see LUSTROUS 1

shiny *adj syn* see LUSTROUS 1

ship *vb* 1 *syn* see SEND 1

   rel direct; freight; export

   ant receive

   2 *syn* see MOVE 4

shipshape *adj syn* see NEAT 2

shipwreck *vb* 1 to destroy, disable, or seriously damage a ship (as by running aground or causing to founder) <the typhoon *shipwrecked* the entire fishing fleet>

   syn beach, cast away, pile up, strand, wreck

   rel break up; scuttle; founder, capsize; go down, sink

   idiom go aground, go to the bottom (*or* Davy Jones's locker), run on the rocks

   2 *syn* see RUIN 2

shirk *vb* 1 *syn* see SNEAK

   2 *syn* see DODGE 1

   rel bilk, burke; bypass, double, eschew, get around; shuffle off, shun

shirker *n syn* see SLACKER

shirty *adj syn* see ANGRY

shivaree *n* a noisy mock serenade to a newly married couple <*shivarees* and other such disappearing rural customs>

   syn ‖belling, ‖bull band, ‖callithump, charivari, ‖horning, ‖riding, ‖skimmelton

   rel entertainment, reception, welcome

shiver *vb syn* see SHATTER 1

shiver *vb syn* see SHAKE 1

‖shivereens *n pl syn* see SMITHEREENS

shivering *adj syn* see TREMULOUS

shivers *n pl syn* see JITTERS

shivery *adj* 1 *syn* see TREMULOUS

   2 *syn* see COLD 1

shoal *adj syn* see SHALLOW 1

shoal *n* a place where a body of water (as a sea or river) is not deep <dangerous *shoals* in uncharted waters>

   syn shallow

   rel barrier, barrier reef, coral reef, fringing reef, reef, sand reef; bank, bar, sand-

bank, sandbar, tombolo; hook, spit; seamount

   con abyss, deep, depth

shock *n syn* see PILE 1

shock *n* 1 *syn* see IMPACT

   2 *syn* see EARTHQUAKE

   3 *syn* see TRAUMA

   rel prostration, stupefaction

shock *vb* 1 to offend the moral sense of <were *shocked* by pornography>

   syn scandalize

   rel astonish, astound, startle, surprise; jar, jolt, shake up; insult, offend, outrage; appall, horrify; floor, knock out; disgust, nauseate, sicken

   idiom stink in one's nostrils, turn one's stomach

   2 to cause to undergo a physical or psychological shock <his slap *shocked* her out of hysterics>

   syn jolt, startle

   rel shake; jar; electrify

shocked *adj syn* see AGHAST 2

   rel jarred, jolted, shaken up, ‖shook up; offended, outraged; appalled, horrified

shocker *n* 1 *syn* see THRILLER

   2 *syn* see DIME NOVEL

shocking *adj* 1 *syn* see FEARFUL 3

   rel heinous, monstrous

   2 *syn* see OUTRAGEOUS 2

   rel burning, glaring; disgraceful, shameful; unspeakable

shoddy *adj* 1 *syn* see CHEAP 2

   rel makeshift, scambling

   2 *syn* see SHABBY 1

   3 *syn* see DISREPUTABLE 1

shoeless *adj syn* see BAREFOOT 1

   ant shod

shoestring *adj syn* see LITTLE 3

‖shog *vb syn* see PUSH 2

shoo–in *n syn* see SURE THING

‖shool *vb syn* see SHUFFLE

shoot *vb* 1 to cause (a weapon) to drive a projectile forward <*shoot* an arrow at a target>

   syn discharge, fire, loose

   rel trigger; launch, project; expel; blast; poop

   idiom let fly

   2 *syn* see DESTROY 1

   3 *syn* see DISCREDIT 2

   ‖4 *syn* see DISCARD

   5 *syn* see VOMIT

   ‖6 *syn* see PASS 9

   7 *syn* see SHOOT UP 2

   8 *syn* see FLY 1

   9 *syn* see RUSH 1

   rel gallop, highball, hotfoot; spurt

   10 *syn* see PHOTOGRAPH

shoot *n syn* see RAY 1

shooting *adj syn* see SHARP 8

   ant stationary

shooting match *n syn* see AFFAIR 1

shoot up *vb* 1 *syn* see SKYROCKET

   2 to take (a drug) by hypodermic needle <had been *shooting up* heroin for weeks>

   syn ‖mainline, shoot

shop *n syn* see STORE 4

   rel boutique

shoplift *vb* to steal displayed goods from a store <the manager caught them *shoplifting* records>

   syn ‖boost

rel bag, cop, ‖nick, palm, pilfer, pinch, rip off, snitch, swipe

shopworn *adj syn see* TRITE
rel overused, overworked, overworn

shore *n* the land bordering a usually large body of water < watched the ships while walking along the *shore* >
syn bank, beach, coast, strand
rel coastline, shoreline, waterfront, waterside; coastland, seacoast, seashore; foreshore, littoral, shoreface, shoreside; brink, embankment, riverbank, riverside

shore (up) *vb syn see* SUPPORT 4

shore *n syn see* SUPPORT 3

short *adj* 1 having little length in space or time < a *short* visit >
syn brief
rel abbreviate, abbreviated, abridged, curtailed, decreased, diminished, lessened, shortened; curtate, decurtate
con extensive, lengthy; drawn-out, overlong; extended, prolonged, protracted
ant long
2 having small physical stature < he was the *shortest* boy present >
syn ‖low, low-set, low-statured
rel chunky, dumpy, squat, squatty, stubby, thick, thickset
con gangling, gangly, lanky, rangy; elevated, high, lofty, spiring, towering
ant tall
3 not coming up to a measure or need < fuel was very *short* that year >
syn deficient, failing, inadequate, insufficient, scant, scanty, scarce, scrimpy, shy, skimpy, slender, unsufficient, wanting; *compare* MEAGER 2
rel lacking, needing; exiguous, meager, sparse
con abounding, overflowing, teeming; abundant, ample, copious, plenteous, plentiful
ant long
4 *syn see* BLUFF
ant expansive
5 lacking in graciousness or consideration < his manner was *short* and abrupt >
syn inconsiderate, sharp, thoughtless, unceremonious, ungracious
rel bluff, blunt, brusque, crusty, curt; short-spoken; gruff, irascible
con considerate, gracious, kindly; bland, smooth; ceremonious
6 readily breaking or crumbling < a rich *short* pastry >
syn brittle, crisp, crumbly, ‖crump, crunchy, friable
rel delicate, fragile
con soggy, tough
7 *syn see* CONCISE
rel compact; pointed
idiom to the point
con extended, protracted, spun-out
ant lengthy, long-drawn-out

short *adv* 1 without hesitation or delay < stopped *short* >
syn abruptly, asudden, forthwith, sudden, suddenly

con hesitantly; gradually, slowly
2 *syn see* UNAWARES

short *n syn see* SUBSTANCE 2

short *vb syn see* SPARE 3

shortage *n syn see* FAILURE 3
rel curtailment, pinch, tightness; shortfall
ant overage

short and sweet *adj syn see* CONCISE

shortcoming *n syn see* IMPERFECTION
idiom weak point
con forte, long suit

shortcut *n* a route shorter or more direct than the one ordinarily taken < they took a *shortcut* down the back roads >
syn cutoff
rel bypass
ant detour

shorten *vb* to reduce in extent (as of length or duration) < decided to *shorten* their visit > < *shorten* a skirt for summer wear >
syn abbreviate, abridge, curtail, cut, cut back, retrench, slash
rel decrease, diminish, elide, excerpt, lessen, reduce; compress, condense, contract, shrink; bobtail, clip, dock; minimize
idiom cut short
con draw out, protract
ant elongate; lengthen; extend, prolong

shorthanded *adj* short of the necessary number of people < the office was critically *shorthanded* >
syn underhanded, undermanned, understaffed
rel short, wanting
con overmanned, overstaffed

short-lived *adj syn see* TRANSIENT
rel short-haul, short-run, short-term
con long-run, long-term
ant agelong; long-lived

shortly *adv* 1 *syn see* BRIEFLY
2 *syn see* PRESENTLY 1
rel pronto, quickly

short-range *adj syn see* TACTICAL 1
ant long-range

shortsighted *adj syn see* MYOPIC
ant farsighted, longsighted

short-spoken *adj syn see* BLUFF
ant windy

shot *n* 1 *syn see* FLING 1
2 *syn see* OPPORTUNITY
3 *syn see* DRAM

‖**shot** *adj syn see* INTOXICATED 1

shotgun *vb syn see* FORCE 2

should *vb syn see* WANT 3

shoulder *vb syn see* PUSH 2

shout *vb* 1 to utter a sudden loud cry (as to express joy or triumph or to attract attention) < the mob *shouted* for a speech >
syn cry, whoop, yell; *compare* CALL 1, SCREAM 1
rel exclaim; howl, scream, shriek; bawl, bellow, clamor, roar, vociferate
con murmur, whisper
2 *syn see* SCREAM 4
3 *syn see* CALL 1
rel bark; bray
4 *syn see* TREAT 3

shove *vb* 1 *syn see* PUSH 1
rel cram, jam; dig, jab, poke, prod
idiom push and shove
2 *syn see* PUSH 2

---

syn synonym(s)   *rel* related word(s)
ant antonym(s)   *con* contrasted word(s)
idiom idiomatic equivalent(s)
‖ use limited; if in doubt, see a dictionary

3 *syn* see PUSH 6

shove (off) *vb syn* see GO 2
ant pull in

shovel *vb* 1 *syn* see DIG 1

2 *syn* see DIG 2

shovel *vb syn* see SHUFFLE

show *vb* 1 to set out or place on view for customers <we're *showing* lots of long dresses this fall>
syn display, offer
rel afford, supply; exhibit; present, proffer, submit; deal (in), sell

2 to reveal outwardly or make apparent <asked a question or two to *show* his intelligence>
syn demonstrate, evidence, evince, exhibit, illustrate, manifest, mark, ostend, proclaim; *compare* LOOK 4
rel disclose, discover, divulge, lay out, reveal, unveil; present, project
con camouflage, conceal, dissemble, hide, obscure
ant disguise

3 *syn* see STAGE

4 to present in such a way as to invite notice, attention, and admiration <she loved to *show* her jewels to everyone>
syn brandish, display, disport, exhibit, expose, flash, flaunt, parade, show off, trot out
rel air, lay out, set out, spread; blazon, flourish, sport, vaunt
con belittle, deprecate, depreciate, minimize

5 to give an exact and usually automatic reading or indication of <the speedometer *shows* 70 MPH>
syn indicate, mark, read, record, register, say
rel point (to); ring up

6 *syn* see LOOK 4
rel lay out, reveal, unveil

7 *syn* see GUIDE

8 *syn* see ESTABLISH 6
rel present; plead; allege

9 *syn* see APPEAR 1
rel come, show up; materialize

10 *syn* see COME 1
idiom ‖make the scene, put in an appearance, show one's face

11 *syn* see TURN UP 3

show *n syn* see APPEARANCE 2
rel likeness; effect, impression
idiom outward show

2 *syn* see MASK 2

3 *syn* see DISPLAY 2

4 *syn* see OPPORTUNITY

5 *syn* see EXHIBITION 1

6 *syn* see EXHIBITION 2

7 *syn* see MOVIE

8 *syn* see SHOWING 1

shower *n syn* see BARRAGE
rel shatter, spatter, spray

shower *vb syn* see BATHE 1

showing *n* 1 performance in a test of skill, power, or effectiveness <he made a good *showing* in the race>
syn out, show
rel record

2 *syn* see APPEARANCE 2

show–me *adj syn* see INCREDULOUS

show off *vb syn* see SHOW 4
rel boast, brag, swagger

showpiece *n* a prime or outstanding example used or suitable for exhibition <a Fabergé Easter egg was the *showpiece* of the collection>
syn chef d'oeuvre, masterpiece, pièce de résistance
rel gem, jewel; prize
con claptrap, rubbish, trash, trivia, truck

showroom *n syn* see STORE 4

show up *vb syn* see EXPOSE 4
rel discredit; invalidate

2 *syn* see TURN UP 3

3 *syn* see COME 1

showy *adj* given to or marked by excessive outward display <*showy* decorations>
syn chichi, flamboyant, orchidaceous, ostentatious, peacockish, peacocky, pretentious, splashy, swank
rel sporty; flashy, garish, gaudy, jazzy, meretricious, tawdry; gorgeous, resplendent; luxurious, opulent, ornate, sumptuous; overdone, overwrought; sensational
con muted, quiet, restrained, subdued; elegant, graceful, restrained; appropriate, seemly
ant unshowy

shred *n syn* see PARTICLE

shred *vb syn* see SLIVER

shreddy *adj syn* see RAGGED

shrew *n syn* see VIRAGO
rel she-devil; spitfire

shrewd *adj* marked by clever discerning awareness and hardheaded acumen <the captain was a *shrewd* judge of character>
syn argute, astucious, astute, cagey, heady, perspicacious, sagacious, ‖savvy; *compare* SHARP 4, WISE 2, 4
rel canny, crafty, foxy, ingenious, ‖pawky, slick, ‖sly, tidy; clever, intelligent, knowing, quick-witted, smart; polite, smooth; judicious, prudent, sensible, wise; penetrating, piercing, probing; acute, keen, sharp; farsighted, foresighted
con green, naive, simple, soft; foolable, gullible, slow

shrewdness *n syn* see WIT 3
rel canniness, foxiness

shriek *vb* 1 *syn* see SCREAM 1
rel squawk, ‖yarm

2 *syn* see SQUEAL 2

3 *syn* see SCREAM 4

shrill *vb syn* see SCREAM 1

shrill *adj syn* see ACUTE 4

shrine *n* a structure or place considered sacred by a religious group <pilgrims going to the *shrine* at Lourdes hoping to be healed>
syn holy place, sanctorium, sanctuary, sanctum
rel reliquary; enshrinement

shrink *vb* 1 *syn* see CONTRACT 3
rel shrivel (up), wither
con amplify, expand
ant swell

2 *syn* see FAIL 3
idiom shrink (*or* dwindle) down to nothing

3 *syn* see RECOIL
rel cower, cringe, crouch, huddle, slink; draw (back), recede, retire, retreat, withdraw; boggle, demur, scruple

shrinking *adj syn* see UNDEMONSTRATIVE

shrivel *vb syn* see WITHER
　rel parch; fossilize
shroud *vb* 1 *syn* see ENFOLD 1
　2 *syn* see SCREEN 3
shrouded *adj syn* see ULTERIOR
shuck *n syn* see HULL
shuck *vb* to strip, break off, or remove the
　enclosing case or cover of < *shuck* corn >
　syn hull, husk, shell; *compare* SKIN 2
　rel decorticate, peel; skin, strip
shuck (off) *vb syn* see DISCARD
shudder *vb syn* see SHAKE 1
　rel gyrate, shimmy
shuffle *vb* 1 *syn* see DISORDER 1
　2 *syn* see EQUIVOCATE 2
　3 to walk awkwardly in a sliding, drag-
　ging way without lifting the feet < an old
　drunk *shuffling* along in filthy bedroom
　slippers >
　syn scuff, scuffle, shamble, ‖shool, shovel
　rel drag, pad, scrape, slipper, slip-slop,
　slur; draggle, straggle, trail (along)
　4 *syn* see STUMBLE 6
shuffle *n syn* see CLUTTER 2
shuffling *adj syn* see EVASIVE 1
shun *vb syn* see ESCAPE 2
　rel decline, refuse, reject; snub; despise,
　disdain, scorn
　idiom have nothing to do with, keep
　away from, stand aloof from, steer clear
　of, turn away from, turn one's back upon
　con accept, adopt, welcome
shunning *n syn* see ESCAPE 2
shunt *vb* 1 to push or turn off to one side
　< *shunt* a railroad car onto a siding >
　syn sidetrack, switch; *compare* TURN 6
　rel change, move, shift, transfer; avert,
　deflect, divert, head off
　idiom push aside (*or* to the side)
　2 *syn* see SHUTTLE
shush *vb* 1 *syn* see SILENCE
　2 *syn* see SUPPRESS 2
shut *vb syn* see CLOSE 1
　rel lock, seal; batten (down)
　ant open
‖**shut–eye** *n syn* see SLEEP 1
shut in *vb syn* see ENCLOSE 1
　ant shut out
shut-in *adj syn* see UNSOCIABLE
shut–mouthed *adj syn* see SILENT 3
　ant openmouthed
shut off *vb syn* see SCREEN 3
shut out *vb syn* see SCREEN 3
shuttle *vb* to travel back and forth fre-
　quently < *shuttled* between New York and
　Washington every week >
　syn shunt
　rel shuttlecock; alternate
shut up *vb* 1 *syn* see SILENCE
　2 to cease speaking < told the boy to sit
　down and *shut up* >
　syn dry up, dumb (up), ‖dummy (up),
　pipe down, ‖ring off
　rel hush, quiet (down), shush, soft-pedal
　idiom button (*or* seal) one's lips, keep
　quiet
shy *adj* 1 disinclined to obtrude oneself
　< *shy* in the presence of strangers >

　syn backward, bashful, coy, demure,
　diffident, modest, rabbity, retiring, self=
　effacing, timid, unassertive, unassured
　rel backhanded, hesitant; reluctant; con-
　scious, self-conscious, self-distrustful,
　shamefaced, sheepish; introversive, intro-
　vert, introverted, inturned; circumspect,
　reserved; cautious, chary, suspicious, wary;
　apprehensive, fearful, nervous, skittish,
　timorous
　con brash, forward; aggressive, audacious,
　intrusive, obtruding, pushing, pushy;
　blunt, crass
　ant bold, obtrusive
　2 *syn* see DISINCLINED
　3 *syn* see SHORT 3
　con excess, over, surplus
shy *vb* 1 *syn* see DEMUR
　rel blench, quail, recoil, shrink
　2 *syn* see ESCAPE 2
shy *n syn* see POTSHOT
Shylock *n syn* see LOAN SHARK
shyster *n syn* see PETTIFOGGER
‖**sib** *adj syn* see SYMPATHETIC 2
sibilate *vb syn* see HISS
sibylline *adj* 1 *syn* see PROPHETIC
　2 *syn* see OBSCURE 3
sic *vb syn* see URGE
　rel agitate, catalyze, inspirit, instigate;
　abet, aid, countenance, favor
sick *adj* 1 affected with illness or disease
　< was *sick* with pneumonia >
　syn down, ill; *compare* UNWELL
　rel diseased, disordered, fevered; ailing,
　‖cronk, ‖crook, funny, indisposed, unwell;
　debilitated, sickly, unhealthy; rocky, tot-
　tering, wobbly; confined, laid up; lousy,
　mean, rotten
　idiom ‖on the sick list, sick as a dog
　con healthy, strong
　ant well
　2 *syn* see MORBID
　3 *syn* see FED UP
　idiom ‖up to here with
　4 *syn* see FAULTY
　5 *syn* see SICKLY 2
sick (up) *vb syn* see VOMIT
sicken *vb* 1 *syn* see UPSET 5
　2 *syn* see DISGUST
sicken (with *or* of) *vb syn* see CONTRACT
　1
sickening *adj syn* see OFFENSIVE
‖**sicker** *vb syn* see EXUDE
sickliness *n syn* see INFIRMITY 1
sickly *adj* 1 *syn* see UNWELL
　rel ‖cranky, down
　con hale, hearty; healthy, well
　ant robust
　2 accompanying, indicating, or suggesting
　sickness < a *sickly* complexion >
　syn peaked, ‖peaking, peaky, sick
　rel ‖pimping, puny, sickish, weak; dis-
　eased; unhealthy
　con healthy, hearty
　3 *syn* see UNWHOLESOME 1
　4 *syn* see MORBID
sickness *n* 1 the condition of being ill
　< finally recovered from her *sickness* >
　syn affliction, diseasedness, disorder,
　illness, indisposition, infirmity, unhealth;
　compare DISEASE 1, INFIRMITY 1
　rel indisposedness, unhealthfulness, un-
　healthiness, unwellness; affection, ailment,
　ill

---

syn synonym(s)　　*rel* related word(s)
ant antonym(s)　　*con* contrasted word(s)
idiom idiomatic equivalent(s)
‖ use limited; if in doubt, see a dictionary

idiom ill health
con haleness, healthiness, heartiness
ant health
2 *syn* see DISEASE 1

side *n* **1** a place, space, or direction with respect to a center or a line of division <lived on the north *side* of the street> <the morning *side* of the hill> <turned to one *side*>
syn hand
rel direction, flank, sector
2 *syn* see PHASE
3 *syn* see VIEWPOINT 2
4 the attitude, position, or action of one person or group as opposed to another <could understand her *side* as well as his in the quarrel>
syn part; *compare* POSITION 1
rel attitude, disposition; posture, stance, stand; position, standpoint, viewpoint
side *vb syn* see SHEATHE
side (with) *vb syn* see SUPPORT 2
side action *n syn* see SIDE EFFECT
sideboards *n pl syn* see SIDE-WHISKERS
sideburns *n pl syn* see SIDE-WHISKERS
side effect *n* a secondary and usually adverse effect (as of a drug) <drowsiness is a common *side effect* of antihistimines>
syn side action, side reaction
rel effect; reaction, response
side-glance *n* a look or glance directed to one side <she shot an impatient *side-glance* at him>
syn side-look
rel glance; stare
sideling *adv syn* see SIDEWAYS 1
sideling *adj syn* see STEEP 1
||**sidelings** *adv syn* see SIDEWAYS 1
sidelong *adv syn* see SIDEWAYS 1
side-look *n syn* see SIDE-GLANCE
side reaction *n syn* see SIDE EFFECT
sidereal *adj syn* see STELLAR 1
sidesplitter *n syn* see RIOT 2
sidestep *vb* **1** *syn* see EQUIVOCATE 2
2 *syn* see SKIRT 3
3 *syn* see DODGE 1
sideswipe *n syn* see POTSHOT
sidetrack *vb syn* see SHUNT 1
sideward *adv syn* see SIDEWAYS 1
sideways *adv* **1** to, toward, or at one side <slipped *sideways* on the ice>
syn crabwise, laterally, sideling, ||sidelings, sidelong, sideward, sidewise; *compare* ASIDE 1
rel obliquely; indirectly
con straight; directly
2 *syn* see ASIDE 1
side-whiskers *n pl* the usually shaped growth of whiskers on both sides of a man's face <grew *side-whiskers* and a moustache in order to look older>
syn burnsides, dundrearies, muttonchops, sideboards, sideburns
sidewise *adv* **1** *syn* see SIDEWAYS 1
2 *syn* see ASIDE 1
sidle *vb* to move sideways or obliquely especially in an unobtrusive or furtive manner <a suspicious-looking man *sidled* up to her>
syn edge, ||slive
rel ease, slip
siege *n* a sometimes prolonged period of disorder or stress (as of body or mind) <endured a three-week *siege* of flu>

syn bout, go; *compare* ATTACK 3
rel attack, onslaught, seizure, spell
siesta *n syn* see NAP
siesta *vb syn* see NAP
sieve *n syn* see GOSSIP 1
sieve *vb syn* see SCREEN 5
sift *vb* **1** *syn* see SCREEN 5
2 *syn* see SORT 2
3 *syn* see EXPLORE
sigh *vb* **1** to take in and let out a deep audible breath (as in weariness, grief, or relief) <flopped down in the chair and *sighed* deeply>
syn ||sock, sough, suspire
rel breathe, respire; exhale; gasp, pant, wheeze; groan, moan; sob
idiom heave a sigh
2 to make a sound like sighing <the wind *sighed* in the branches>
syn sough
rel blow; murmur, whisper; moan; whine; whistle; howl, roar
3 *syn* see LONG
sighful *adj syn* see MELANCHOLY 2
sight *n* **1** *syn* see EYESORE
||**2** *syn* see MUCH
3 *syn* see EYE 2
4 *syn* see LOOK 1
5 *syn* see VIEW 4
6 *syn* see VIEW 5
sightless *adj syn* see BLIND 1
ant sighted
sightseer *n syn* see TOURIST
sign *n* **1** a motion, action, gesture, or word by which a command, thought, or wish is expressed <put a finger to her lips as a *sign* to keep quiet>
syn high sign, signal
rel gesticulation; gesture, motion; hint, indication, suggestion, warning
2 *syn* see CHARACTER 1
3 *syn* see EXPRESSION 3
rel symbolization; attestation, evidence, proof
4 *syn* see INDICATION 3
rel earmark, exponent, indicator; exhibit, show
sign *vb* **1** to affix a signature to <he refused to *sign* a confession>
syn autograph, ink, signature, subscribe
idiom put one's John Hancock on, put one's John Henry down (*or* on)
2 *syn* see SIGNAL
sign (over) *vb syn* see TRANSFER 4
signal *n syn* see SIGN 1
rel alarm, alert, tocsin; movement
signal *vb* to notify by or as if by a signal <*signaled* his wife to keep quiet>
syn flag, gesture, motion, sign, signalize
idiom give the high sign (to)
signal *adj syn* see NOTICEABLE
rel characteristic, distinctive, individual, peculiar, significative; eminent, famous, illustrious, renowned
signalize *vb* **1** *syn* see CHARACTERIZE 2
2 *syn* see SIGNAL
signature *vb syn* see SIGN 1
significance *n* **1** *syn* see MEANING 1
2 *syn* see IMPORTANCE
rel authority, credit, influence, merit, prestige; excellence, perfection, virtue
con indifference; triviality, unimportance, worthlessness; irrelevance

ant insignificance

significancy *n syn* see MEANING 1

significant *adj* 1 *syn* see EXPRESSIVE
rel cogent, compelling, convincing, sound, telling, valid; forceful, powerful; important, momentous, weighty
con meaningless, unexpressive; unimportant
ant insignificant

2 *syn* see IMPORTANT 1
con inconsequential, meaningless, unimportant
ant insignificant

significant *n syn* see INDICATION 3

significantly *adv syn* see WELL 8
ant insignificantly

signification *n* 1 *syn* see MEANING 1
rel implying, signifying; construction, implication; essence, gist, substance
‖2 *syn* see IMPORTANCE

significative *adj syn* see INDICATIVE

signify *vb* 1 *syn* see MEAN 2
rel bear, carry, convey; bespeak, purport
2 *syn* see MATTER

sign on *vb syn* see ENTER 3

sign up *vb syn* see ENTER 3

silence *n* 1 absence of sound or noise < the heavy *silence* of the night >
syn noiselessness, quiet, quietness, quietude, soundlessness, still, stillness
rel calm, hush, lull
con din, uproar
ant noise

2 *syn* see SECRECY

3 *syn* see DEATH 1

silence *vb* to compel or reduce to silence < *silenced* the courtroom chatter by pounding his gavel >
syn choke (off), hush, quiet, ‖quieten, shush, shut up, still
rel dampen, deaden, dumb, lull, muffle, mute; quash, quell, squash, squelch, suppress; gag, muzzle

silent *adj* 1 *syn* see DUMB 1

2 characterized by absence of speech < was *silent* as he faced the altar >
syn dumb, mum, ‖mumchance, mute, speechless, wordless; *compare* DUMB 1
rel inarticulate, muted, tongue-tied, voiceless
con speaking, talking

3 showing marked restraint in speaking < a stern, *silent* man >
syn close, close-lipped, closemouthed, close-tongued, dumb, inconversable, reserved, reticent, shut-mouthed, silentious, speechless, taciturn, tight-lipped, tight-mouthed, uncommunicative, wordless
rel checked, curbed, inhibited, restrained; unconversational, unsociable; inarticulate, incoherent; mute, voiceless; mum, secretive
con articulate, fluent, glib, vocal, voluble; babblative, garrulous, loquacious, windy; blabbering, blabbery, chattering
ant talkative

4 *syn* see STILL 3
idiom silent as a post (*or* stone), silent as the grave (*or* tomb)

ant noisy

5 *syn* see UNSPOKEN 1

silentious *adj syn* see SILENT 3

silhouette *n syn* see OUTLINE
rel ‖shade, shadow

silken *adj* 1 *syn* see SOFT 3

2 *syn* see INGRATIATING

silky *adj* 1 *syn* see SOFT 3

2 *syn* see INGRATIATING

silliness *n syn* see FOOLISHNESS
rel illogicality
con logic, logicality, logicalness, sanity, sensibleness; wisdom

silly *adj* 1 *syn* see SIMPLE 3
rel empty, empty-headed, vacuous; irrational, unreasonable; ignorant, unintelligent, unwise
ant sensible

2 *syn* see GIDDY 1
rel ‖balmy, crazy, ‖dippy, irrational, off, ‖wacked-out
idiom silly as a goose
con level-headed, practical, rational, serious
ant sensible

3 *syn* see FOOLISH 2
rel funny, senseless

silvern *adj syn* see SILVERY

silver-tongued *adj syn* see GLIB

silvery *adj* relating to, containing, or resembling silver < repeated polishings gave the wood a *silvery* sheen >
syn argent, argentate, argenteous, argentine, silvern
rel silver; brilliant, glittering, shimmering, shining

similar *adj syn* see LIKE
rel complementary, correlative; reciprocal
idiom much of a muchness, much the same
con antithetical, antonymous, contradictory, contrary, opposite
ant dissimilar

similarity *n syn* see LIKENESS
rel approximation; collation, correlation; association, interrelation; parallel; closeness; coincidence, synonymity
con unlikeness, variance
ant dissimilarity

similarly *adv syn* see ALSO 1
idiom by the same token

simile *n* 1 *syn* see ANALOGY 2

2 *syn* see LIKENESS

similitude *n* 1 *syn* see LIKENESS
rel copy, image, replica
ant dissimilitude

2 *syn* see ANALOGY 2

simmer *vb* 1 *syn* see BOIL 2

2 *syn* see SEETHE 4

simmer down *vb syn* see COMPOSE 4
rel quiet (down), subside
idiom ‖cool it, take it easy
con boil, seethe; explode, fulminate
ant boil over

Simon Legree *n syn* see SLAVE DRIVER

simon-pure *adj syn* see AUTHENTIC 2

simp *n syn* see DUNCE

simper *vb syn* see SMIRK

simple *adj* 1 *syn* see NATURAL 5
rel childish, childlike; amateur, green, unexperienced; trusting; ‖square

2 *syn* see PLAIN 1
ant elaborate

---

syn synonym(s)   *rel* related word(s)
ant antonym(s)   *con* contrasted word(s)
idiom idiomatic equivalent(s)
‖ use limited; if in doubt, see a dictionary

3 actually or apparently deficient in intelligence < a poor *simple* woman easily duped >
syn asinine, brainless, ‖buffle-headed, fatuous, foolish, insensate, mindless, nit-witted, senseless, sheepheaded, silly, soft, spoony, unintelligent, unwitty, weak-headed, weak-minded, witless; *compare* RETARDED, STUPID 1
rel amateur, green, inexperienced, inexpert; credulous, gullible; childish, childlike, naive; ignorant, illiterate, uneducated, unschooled, untaught; crass, dense, dopey, dull, dumb, slow, stupid; doting, feeble-minded, idiotic, retarded, simpleminded
con able, competent; alert, clever, keen; bright, intelligent, understanding
ant wise
4 *syn* see RETARDED
5 *syn* see PURE 2
rel inelaborate, stark; bald, bare, mere; fundamental, uncompounded
6 *syn* see EASY 1
rel incomplex, incomplicate
idiom simple as ABC
ant complex, complicated
simple *n syn* see FOOL 3
simplehearted *adj syn* see NATURAL 5
simpleminded *adj syn* see RETARDED
simplest *adj syn* see ELEMENTARY 1
simpleton *n* 1 *syn* see FOOL 4
2 *syn* see DUNCE
rel bungler, ‖clot
simplify *vb* to make simple or simpler < *simplify* a manufacturing process >
syn boil down, streamline
rel clarify, clean up, disentangle, disinvolve, straighten (out), unscramble; abridge, cut down, reduce, shorten; oversimplify
ant complicate
simply *adv syn* see JUST 3
simulacrum *n* 1 *syn* see IMAGE 1
2 *syn* see IMITATION
3 *syn* see APPEARANCE 2
simulate *vb* 1 *syn* see ASSUME 4
rel ape, copy, imitate, mimic; play-act, pose
idiom ‖make out like (*or* as if)
2 *syn* see RESEMBLE
simulated *adj* 1 *syn* see FICTITIOUS 2
ant genuine
2 *syn* see ARTIFICIAL 2
ant genuine
simultaneous *adj syn* see CONTEMPORARY 1
rel agreeing, concurring, coinciding
simultaneously *adv syn* see TOGETHER 1
idiom in one breath
sin *n* 1 *syn* see EVIL 3
2 *syn* see EVIL 2
3 *syn* see IMPERFECTION
sin *vb syn* see TRESPASS 1
since *prep syn* see AFTER 2
ant before
since *conj syn* see BECAUSE
sincere *adj* 1 genuine in feeling or expression < had a *sincere* dislike for politics >
syn heartfelt, hearty, unfeigned, wholehearted, whole-souled; *compare* GENUINE 3
rel candid, frank, frankhearted, open, plain; faithful, honest, truthful; aboveboard, forthright, pretensionless, straight-

forward, unpretentious; dear, devout, heartful; meant, unaffected
con affected, artificial, feigned, put-on, unmeant
ant insincere
2 *syn* see GENUINE 3
rel authentic, bona fide; serious; actual
idiom honest to God
ant insincere
sincereness *n syn* see GOOD FAITH
sincerity *n syn* see GOOD FAITH
rel heart; goodwill; singleness, straightforwardness
con cunning, deceit, guile; ill will
ant insincerity
sine qua non *n syn* see ESSENTIAL 2
sinew *n* 1 *syn* see POWER 4
2 *usu* sinews *pl syn* see MAINSTAY
sinewy *adj syn* see MUSCULAR 1
rel strong, sturdy, tenacious, tough
ant flabby
2 *syn* see MUSCULAR 2
sinful *adj* 1 *syn* see WRONG 1
rel base, low, vile; disgraceful, shameful; culpable, damnable
2 *syn* see BLAMEWORTHY
ant sinless
sing *vb* 1 to utter words in musical tones and with musical inflections and modulations < children often can *sing* before they converse >
syn chant, tune, vocalize
rel descant; carol, serenade, troll; croon, hum, lull, lullaby; cantillate, hymn, intone; singsong; roar
2 *syn* see TALK 6
‖3 *syn* see INFORM 3
single *adj* 1 being without a spouse < enjoying life as a *single* girl >
syn sole, spouseless, unmarried, unwed
rel free, unattached, unfettered; celibate; maiden, virgin
idiom footloose and fancy-free
con attached; united; wed
ant married
2 one as distinguished from two or more or all others < a *single* instance of dishonesty has been cited >
syn lone, one, only, particular, separate, sole, solitary, unique
rel individual, singular; especial, special, specific; distinguished, singled-out; distinct
con several; manifold, many, numerous
ant multiple
3 *syn* see FRANK
4 *syn* see SOLE 4
single (out) *vb syn* see CHOOSE 1
rel screen, winnow (out); accept, admit, receive
single-eyed *adj syn* see FRANK
single-hearted *adj syn* see FRANK
single-minded *adj* 1 *syn* see FRANK
2 *syn* see INFLEXIBLE 2
rel diehard; bigoted
singleness *n* 1 *syn* see UNIQUENESS
2 *syn* see UNITY 1
ant multifariousness
singly *adv syn* see APART 1
ant together
singular *adj* 1 *syn* see SEVERAL 1
rel discrete; certain, definite; exclusive
2 *syn* see EXCEPTIONAL 1
ant usual

3 *syn* see ONLY 2
idiom first and last, one and only, one only
4 *syn* see STRANGE 4
idiom passing strange
singularity *n* 1 *syn* see INDIVIDUALITY 4
2 *syn* see INDIVIDUALITY 3
3 *syn* see UNITY 1
ant multiplicity
singularize *vb syn* see CHARACTERIZE 2
singularness *n syn* see UNITY 1
ant multifariousness
sinister *adj* seriously threatening disaster < a *sinister* plot >
syn baleful, malefic, maleficent, malign; *compare* OMINOUS
rel fateful, ill-omened, inauspicious, ominous, portentous, unpropitious; apocalyptic, dire, doomful, ill-boding, threatening; lowering, menacing; evil, malicious
con harmless, innocent, innocuous
sink *vb* 1 to become submerged < the overloaded raft *sank* below the surface >
syn founder, go down, go under, submerge, submerse
rel capsize, overturn, tip (over); dive, plunge; scuttle; shipwreck, wreck
idiom go to Davy Jones's locker, go to the bottom, sink like a rock
con come up, rise
ant float
2 *syn* see SET 12
3 *syn* see DETERIORATE 1
ant rise
4 *syn* see STOOP 2
5 *syn* see LOWER 3
6 *syn* see THRUST 2
7 *syn* see HUMBLE
ant uplift
sink *n* 1 a place marked by a staggering amount of corruption and filth < that area of the city was a *sink* of vice and crime >
syn Augean stable, cesspit, cesspool, den, pandemonium, Sodom, sty
rel hellhole; fleshpot
idiom Alsatian den, den of iniquity, sink of corruption
2 *syn* see DEPRESSION 2
sinkage *n syn* see DEPRESSION 2
sinkhole *n syn* see DEPRESSION 2
sinuous *adj syn* see WINDING
rel twisted; snake-shaped
idiom twisting and turning
sip *vb syn* see DRINK 1
siphon *vb* 1 *syn* see CONDUCT 4
2 *syn* see DRAIN 1
sire *n syn* see FATHER 2
sire *vb* 1 *syn* see FATHER 1
2 *syn* see GENERATE 1
siren *n* an enticingly attractive woman who lures men into dangerous or compromising situations < a slinky *siren* of the silent screen era >
syn femme fatale, Lorelei, seductress, temptress
rel charmer, vamp
siren *adj syn* see ATTRACTIVE 1

rel sirenic
siren song *n syn* see LURE 2
sissified *adj syn* see EFFEMINATE
sissy *n syn* see WEAKLING
sissy *adj syn* see EFFEMINATE
sissy–pants (*or* **sissy-britches**) *n pl but sing or pl in constr syn* see WEAKLING
sit *vb* 1 to rest on the buttocks or haunches < she was *sitting* in a chair >
syn ‖set
rel perch, rest; ‖plop (down), seat, sit down; squat
con arise, get up, rise, stand, stand up
2 *syn* see CONVENE 1
3 *syn* see POSE 3
4 *syn* see SET 11
5 *syn* see SEAT
rel ensconce, install, settle
sit down *vb syn* see ALIGHT
site *n* 1 *syn* see PLACE 1
2 *syn* see SCENE 3
3 a place where an archaeological excavation is made < a burial *site* >
syn dig
4 *syn* see HABITAT
sited *adj syn* see SITUATED
‖**sitfast** *adj syn* see IMMOVABLE 1
sitting duck *n syn* see TARGET 1
rel sitter
situate *adj syn* see SITUATED
situated *adj* having a site, situation, or location < a town *situated* on a hill >
syn located, placed, positioned, set, sited, situate
situation *n* 1 *syn* see PLACE 1
2 *syn* see PREGNANCY
3 *syn* see JOB 2
4 *syn* see STATUS
5 *syn* see STATE 1
rel bargain
sizable *adj* 1 *syn* see CONSIDERABLE 2
2 *syn* see BIG 1
rel man-sized; giant-sized
sizableness *n syn* see SIZE 2
size *n* 1 the amount of measurable space or area occupied by or comprising a thing < the *size* of the card is 3″x 5″ >
syn admeasurement, dimension(s), dimensionality, extent, magnitude, measure, proportion
rel area; body, bulk, mass, volume; height; extension, length; amplitude, breadth, expanse, spread, stretch, width; measurement
2 considerable amount, proportion, volume, character, or importance < left an estate of some *size* >
syn amplitude, bigness, greatness, largeness, magnitude, sizableness
rel dimension, extent
con littleness, smallness; minuteness, tininess
sizz *vb syn* see HISS
sizzle *vb* 1 *syn* see SEAR 2
2 *syn* see HISS
sizzling *adj syn* see HOT 1
‖**skag** *n syn* see CIGARETTE
skate *n syn* see MAN 3
sked *n syn* see PROGRAM 1
sked *vb syn* see SCHEDULE 1
skedaddle *vb* 1 *syn* see RUN 2
rel ‖split; cut out
2 *syn* see GET OUT 1

---

syn synonym(s)   *rel* related word(s)
ant antonym(s)   *con* contrasted word(s)
idiom idiomatic equivalent(s)
‖ use limited; if in doubt, see a dictionary

idiom lift them up and set them down,
‖take off like a bat out of hell
‖**skeet** *vb syn* see HURRY 2
skeezicks *n syn* see SCAMP
skein *n syn* see MAZE 1
skeletal *adj syn* see EMACIATED
skeleton *vb syn* see SKETCH
skeletonize *vb syn* see SKETCH
‖**sken** *vb syn* see SQUINT
skeptic *n* a doubting or incredulous person
< men of long experience are often *skeptics* >
  syn doubter, doubting Thomas, head-shaker, Pyrrhonian, Pyrrhonist, unbeliever, zetetic
  rel questioner; agnostic; pessimist; scoffer; cynic, misanthrope; disbeliever
  con accepter; apostle, disciple, follower; devotee, diehard
  ant believer
skeptical *adj syn* see INCREDULOUS
  rel freethinking; dissenting; suspicious; cynical
  idiom ‖from Missouri
  ant believing
skeptically *adv syn* see ASKANCE 2
  idiom with a grain of salt, with a note of skepticism, with a skeptical eye
  con trustingly
  ant gullibly
skepticism *n syn* see UNCERTAINTY
  rel qualm, qualmishness
  idiom question in one's mind, shadow of doubt
  con belief, trust
  ant gullibility
sketch *n syn* see COMPENDIUM 1
sketch *vb* to present succinctly < let's *sketch* our plan of action >
  syn adumbrate, block (out), chalk (out), characterize, draft, outline, rough (out), skeleton, skeletonize
  rel depict; diagram, diagrammatize; blueprint, delineate; line; draw, plot, trace; design, develop; detail, lay out, map (out)
sketchy *adj syn* see SUPERFICIAL 2
skew *vb* 1 *syn* see SLANT 3
  2 *syn* see SWERVE 1
  rel skid, slide, slip
skewer *vb syn* see IMPALE
skid *vb* 1 *syn* see SLIDE 3
  rel sheer, skew, slue, veer
  idiom go into a skid
  2 *syn* see PLUMMET
skiddoo *vb syn* see GET OUT 1
  idiom go (*or* take) off like a shot
skid road *n syn* see SKID ROW
skid row *n* a city street or district notorious for cheap bars, flophouses, and homeless derelicts < boozy old men wandering the *skid row* >
  syn bowery, skid road
skill *n* 1 *syn* see ABILITY 2
  2 *syn* see ART 1
  3 *syn* see ADDRESS 1
  rel ease, skillfulness
skilled *adj* 1 *syn* see PROFICIENT
  con skill-less, unproficient
  ant unskilled, unskillful
  2 *syn* see EXPERIENCED
  rel prepared, primed, trained
  con unfit, unqualified, untrained
  ant unskilled

skillet *n syn* see FRYING PAN
skillful *adj* 1 *syn* see PROFICIENT
  rel learned, versant, well-versed
  ant unskillful
  2 accomplished or done with proficiency or skill < his answer was a very *skillful* evasion >
  syn adroit, clever, good, pretty, ‖skilly, wicked, workmanlike, workmanly; *compare* CLEVER 4, PROFICIENT
  rel expert, masterful
  con clumsy; unskilled
  ant inept, unskillful
‖**skilly** *adj syn* see SKILLFUL 2
skim *vb* 1 *syn* see BRUSH
  2 *syn* see GLANCE 1
  3 *syn* see FLY 1
skim (through) *vb syn* see BROWSE
  con examine, inspect, scrutinize
skimble-skamble *n syn* see GIBBERISH 1
‖**skimmelton** *n syn* see SHIVAREE
skimp *adj syn* see MEAGER 2
skimp *vb* 1 *syn* see SCRIMP
  2 *syn* see SPARE 3
skimpy *adj* 1 *syn* see MEAGER 2
  2 *syn* see SHORT 3
skin *n* 1 *syn* see HIDE
  2 *syn* see HULL
  3 a usually thin casing forming the outside surface of a structure or thing < aircraft *skins* made of aluminum alloys >
  syn sheath, sheathing
  rel facing, siding; case, casing, cover, jacket; shell
  4 *syn* see MISER
  5 *syn* see SWINDLER
  ‖6 *syn* see DOLLAR
skin *vb* 1 *syn* see SHEATHE
  2 to remove the surface, skin, or thin outer covering of < *skin* a Bermuda onion >
  syn decorticate, excorticate, peel, scale, strip; *compare* SHUCK
  rel cut off, pull off; pare, shave (off), trim; hull, husk, shuck; bark, rind; excoriate, flay, gall
  3 *syn* see OVERCHARGE 1
  4 *syn* see CRITICIZE
  5 *syn* see HURRY 2
‖**skinch** *vb* 1 *syn* see SCRIMP
  2 *syn* see SPARE 3
skinflint *n syn* see MISER
‖**skinhead** *n syn* see BALDHEAD
skinny *adj syn* see LEAN
  rel twiggy, weedy; emaciated; skeletal
  idiom mere skin and bones, skinny as a rail
  ant fleshy
skip *vb* 1 to move or proceed with a light bounding step < children *skipping* home from school >
  syn hop, lope, skitter, spring, trip
  rel caper, cavort, curvet, frisk, gambol; bounce, hippety-hop; jump; leap; bound
  con hobble, shamble, shuffle; hitch, limp, stagger, totter
  2 *syn* see GLANCE 1
  3 *syn* see RUN 2
  idiom ‖split the scene
skip *n syn* see OMISSION
skirmish *n* 1 *syn* see CLASH 2
  rel assault, attack; ambush
  con pitched battle

2 *syn* see ENCOUNTER
skirr *vb* **1** *syn* see RUN 2
  2 *syn* see FLY 1
skirt *n* *syn* see BORDER 1
  rel skirting
skirt *vb* **1** *syn* see BORDER 1
  2 to make a detour or circuit (as around a congested area) < *skirted* the city to avoid traffic >
    syn bypass, circumnavigate, circumvent, detour
    idiom go around
  3 to avoid (as a topic or question) because of difficulty, complexity, controversy, or danger < *skirted* all touchy issues >
    syn burke, bypass, circumvent, ‖polly-fox, sidestep; *compare* EQUIVOCATE 2, ESCAPE 2
    rel avoid, dodge, duck, evade, hedge; elude, escape; ignore, skip
    idiom get around
    con confront, face, meet, take on
‖**skite** *n* *syn* see PRANK
skitter *vb* *syn* see SKIP 1
skittery *adj* *syn* see EXCITABLE
skittish *adj* **1** *syn* see GIDDY 1
  rel irresponsible, undependable, unreliable
  2 *syn* see EXCITABLE
  rel restive; nervous
skive *vb* *syn* see CUT 6
skiver *vb* *syn* see IMPALE
skookum *adj* *syn* see EXCELLENT
skookum–house *n* *syn* see JAIL
skulk *vb* *syn* see SNEAK
skunk *n* *syn* see SNOT 1
skunk *vb* *syn* see WHIP 2
sky *n* the expanse of space surrounding the earth < blue *sky* crisscrossed with jet trails >
    syn empyrean, firmament, heaven(s), welkin
    rel azure; celestial sphere
    idiom the wild blue yonder
sky-high *adv* *syn* see APART 3
sky-high *adj* *syn* see EXCESSIVE 1
skylarking *n* **1** *syn* see HORSEPLAY
    idiom ‖making whoopee
  2 *syn* see REVELRY 2
sky pilot *n* *syn* see CLERGYMAN
  rel chaplain; padre
skyrocket *vb* to rise abruptly and rapidly (as to an unprecedented level or amount < when the election was over taxes and prices *skyrocketed* >
    syn rocket, shoot up, soar
    rel climb, rise; upsoar, upspring
    con slide; drop
    ant crash, plummet
skyscraping *adj* *syn* see LOFTY 6
slab *n* *syn* see BAR 1
  rel chunk, lump
‖**slab** *n* *syn* see SLIME
slabber *vb* *syn* see DROOL 2
slack *adj* *syn* see NEGLECTFUL
  rel dilatory, lackadaisical, lethargic, sluggish; faineant, indolent, lazy, slothful; inert, stagnant
  con assiduous, busy, diligent, industrious, sedulous

  2 *syn* see LOOSE 1
  rel feeble, infirm, soft, unsteady, weak; inactive, inert, passive, supine; laggard, leisurely, slow
  con tensed, tightened; constant, equable, even, steady, uniform; firm, hard
  ant taut, tight
  3 *syn* see SLOW 3
slack *vb* *syn* see LOOSE 5
  idiom ‖cut some slack, make slack
  ant tighten
slack *n* *syn* see SLOWDOWN 1
slacken *vb* **1** *syn* see DELAY 1
  idiom keep back
  ant quicken
  2 *syn* see ABATE 4
  3 *syn* see LOOSE 5
  ant tighten
slackening *n* *syn* see SLOWDOWN 1
slacker *n* one who shirks work, responsibility, or an obligation < didn't want any *slackers* in his office >
    syn goldbrick, shirker, slinker, ‖spiv
    rel idler, loafer; slugabed, sluggard
slack–spined *adj* *syn* see WEAK 4
slake *vb* *syn* see QUENCH 4
slam *n* **1** *syn* see BLOW 1
  2 *syn* see BANG 2
  3 *syn* see ANIMADVERSION
  rel fling, swipe; crack, potshot; rap, slap; dig, jab
slam *vb* **1** to strike with extreme force or violence < *slammed* the ball out of the park > < the car *slammed* into the fence >
    syn belt, blast, clobber, slug, smash, wallop; *compare* STRIKE 2
    rel bang, bat, hit, knock, slap, swat, thwack; cudgel, hammer, mace; batter, beat, pound
  2 *syn* see LAMBASTE 3
‖**slam** *adv* *syn* see WELL 3
slammer *n* *syn* see JAIL
slander *n* *syn* see DETRACTION
  rel black wash, muckraking, mud-slinging, roorback, scandal-mongering
slander *vb* *syn* see MALIGN
  rel assail, attack; damage, hurt, injure; blackwash, muckrake; belie, strumpet
  idiom dish the dirt, run a smear campaign, sling the mud
  ant panegyrize
slanderous *adj* *syn* see LIBELOUS
  rel blackwashing, muckraking, scandalmongering
  ant panegyrical
slang *n* *syn* see DIALECT 2
  rel slanginess, slanguage
slangism *n* *syn* see BARBARISM
slant *adv* *syn* see ASIDE 1
slant *vb* **1** to set or be set at an angle < *slanted* the ladder against the wall >
    syn cant, heel, incline, lean, list, recline, slope, tilt, tip
    rel bank, decline, descend; bend, deviate, diverge, splay, swerve, veer
  2 to direct (written or spoken material) to the interests of a particular audience or group < a magazine *slanted* to farm families >
    syn aim, angle
    rel direct, orient, point, train; concentrate, focus; spoon-feed; bias, skew, warp
  3 to orient (material) from objective presentation so as to favor a particular bias

---

syn synonym(s)   *rel* related word(s)
ant antonym(s)   *con* contrasted word(s)
idiom idiomatic equivalent(s)
‖ use limited; if in doubt, see a dictionary

< accused the media of *slanting* the news against the president >
syn angle, bias, skew; *compare* PREJUDICE 2
rel influence, prejudice; color, distort, twist, warp
ant objectify, objectivize

slant *n* **1** *syn* see SLOPE
2 *syn* see VIEWPOINT 2
rel predilection, predisposition, prejudice

slanted *adj syn* see DIAGONAL

slanting *adj syn* see DIAGONAL

slantingly *adv syn* see ASIDE 1

slantingways *adv* **1** *syn* see ASIDE 1
2 *syn* see DIAGONALLY

slantly *adv syn* see ASIDE 1

slantways *adv* **1** *syn* see ASIDE 1
2 *syn* see DIAGONALLY

slantwise *adv* **1** *syn* see ASIDE 1
2 *syn* see DIAGONALLY

slap *n* **1** *syn* see CUFF
2 *syn* see AFFRONT
3 *syn* see FLING 1

slap *vb* **1** to strike quickly and sharply with the hand < *slapped* the hysterical girl >
syn blip, box, buffet, cuff, smack, spank, ‖wherret; *compare* STRIKE 2
rel ‖biff, ding, hit, sock, swat, whack; ‖wap, wham; bash
2 *syn* see LAMBASTE 3

‖**slap** *adv syn* see WELL 3

slap around *vb syn* see MANHANDLE

slapdash *adj* **1** *syn* see RANDOM
2 *syn* see SLIPSHOD 3

‖**slap-up** *adj syn* see EXCELLENT

slash *vb* **1** *syn* see CUT 1
2 *syn* see HACK
3 *syn* see LAMBASTE 3
idiom ‖light into
4 *syn* see REDUCE 2
5 *syn* see SHORTEN

slate *n syn* see TICKET 3

‖**slate** *vb syn* see LAMBASTE 3

slather *n, often* **slathers** *pl syn* see SCAD

slattern *n* **1** an untidy slovenly woman < two blowsy *slatterns* gossiping at the bar >
syn dowd, dowdy, drab, draggle-tail, ‖malkin, slut, ‖streel, traipse
rel frump; slob, ‖slommack, sloven; crone, gammer, hag, witch
2 *syn* see WANTON
rel prostitute, whore

slattern *adj syn* see SLATTERNLY

slatternly *adj* being habitually untidy and very dirty especially in dress or appearance < a filthy, *slatternly* old woman >
syn blowsy, dowdy, draggletailed, frowsy, slattern, sordid; *compare* SLOVENLY 1
rel careless, disordered, neglected, poky; bedraggled, disheveled, draggled, draggly, messy, mussy, slipshod, sloppy, slovenly, unkempt, untidy; dirty, filthy, foul, grimy, squalid
con clean, fresh, neat, tidy, trim; smart; immaculate, spotless
ant bandbox

slaughter *n syn* see MASSACRE
rel slaughtery; annihilation, destruction

slaughter *vb* **1** to kill (animals) for food < *slaughtered* a beef for the winter >
syn butcher, slay
rel stick

2 to kill (a person) in an especially bloody or barbarous manner < Jack the Ripper *slaughtered* his victims with a knife >
syn butcher, slay
rel kill, murder, ‖total, ‖waste; maim, mangle, mutilate, torture
3 to kill (people) in large numbers < millions *slaughtered* in death camps >
syn annihilate, decimate, exterminate, massacre, wipe (out)

‖**slaunchways** *adv* **1** *syn* see DIAGONALLY
2 *syn* see ASIDE 1

slave *n* **1** a person held in servitude or bondage < plantations worked by *slaves* >
syn bondman, bondslave, bondsman, chattel, mancipium
rel help, menial, retainer, servant; helot, serf, thrall, vassal
con freedman, freedwoman; ‖deditician
ant freeman
2 one who works at a hard, monotonous, usually menial task < *slaves* working all night on a senator's speech >
syn dray horse, drudge, galley slave, peon, slavey, toiler, workhorse
rel ‖coolie

slave *vb syn* see DRUDGE
idiom work like a slave

slave driver *n* a person in authority who exacts extreme effort from his subordinates < the chief proofreader was a real *slave driver* >
syn rawhider, Simon Legree, taskmaster
rel martinet
idiom a hard taskmaster

slaver *vb* **1** *syn* see DROOL 2
2 *syn* see FAWN

slaver *n syn* see SALIVA

slavery *n* **1** *syn* see WORK 2
2 *syn* see BONDAGE
idiom involuntary servitude, the yoke (*or* chains) of slavery

slavey *n* **1** *syn* see SLAVE 2
2 *syn* see HACK 2

slavish *adj* **1** *syn* see HARD 6
2 *syn* see SUBSERVIENT 2
rel spineless, subdued, tame; miserable, wretched
ant independent
3 copying obsequiously something superior < the painting was a *slavish* copy of an old master >
syn apish, emulative, imitative
rel uninspired; unoriginal
con fresh, new, novel, original; fanciful, imaginative, ingenious, inspired; extravagant, high-flown

slay *vb* **1** *syn* see KILL 1
2 *syn* see MURDER 1
3 *syn* see SLAUGHTER 2
4 *syn* see SLAUGHTER 1

slayer *n syn* see MURDERER

sleazy *adj* **1** *syn* see LIMP 1
rel slight, tenuous, thin; gossamery
2 *syn* see CHEAP 2
3 *syn* see SHABBY 1

sleek *vb syn* see POLISH 2

sleek *adj* having a very smooth or lustrous surface or texture < the car's *sleek* new paint job >
syn glassy, glossy, polished, ‖sleekit, sleeky, smarmy

rel smooth; glistening, lustrous

||**sleekit** *adj syn* see SLEEK

sleeky *adj syn* see SLEEK

sleep *n* **1** the natural suspension of consciousness during which the powers of the body are restored < needed eight hours of *sleep* to function efficiently >
syn ||doss, ||shut-eye, slumber; *compare* DOZE, NAP
rel repose, rest; slumberland
idiom land of Nod, the arms of Morpheus
con wakefulness
2 *syn* see LETHARGY 1
3 *syn* see DEATH 1

sleep *vb* to rest in a state of sleep < *slept* for over eight hours >
syn ||doss, slumber; *compare* DOZE, NAP
rel relax, repose, rest; oversleep, sleep in
idiom be in the land of Nod, be sunk in sleep, pound one's ear, rest in the arms of Morpheus, sleep like a top (*or* log)
con arouse, awaken, wake (up)

sleeplessness *n syn* see INSOMNIA

sleepy *adj* **1** having an inclination for or affected by sleep < was *sleepy* after the long day >
syn dozy, drowsy, nodding, ||peepy, ||sloomy, slumberous, slumbery, snoozy, somnolent, soporific
rel heavy, heavy-eyed, lethargic, sluggish, torpid; dazed, dopey, listless, oscitant, yawning; asleep, sleeping, slumbering; nepenthean, poppied; comatose, ||out
con awake, conscious, restless, sleepless, unsleeping; alert, wide-awake
ant wakeful
2 *syn* see INACTIVE
3 *syn* see SOPORIFIC 1

||**sleer** *vb syn* see SNEER 1

sleight *n* **1** *syn* see ADDRESS 1
2 *syn* see TRICK 1

||**sleighty** *adj syn* see CLEVER 4

slender *adj* **1** *syn* see THIN 1
rel slenderish, slimmish; lithe, svelte, trim
idiom slender as a reed
2 *syn* see SHORT 3
3 *syn* see REMOTE 4

slenderize *vb syn* see REDUCE 5

sleuth *n syn* see DETECTIVE

slew *n syn* see SCAD

slewed *adj syn* see INTOXICATED 1

slice *n syn* see SHARE 1
rel segment
idiom a slice of the pie (*or* melon)

slice *vb* **1** *syn* see CUT 1
2 *syn* see CUT 5

slick *vb* **1** *syn* see POLISH 2
2 *syn* see DRESS UP 1
3 *syn* see SLIDE 1

slick *adj* **1** having a glassy surface that often offers insecure footing < a floor *slick* with wax >
syn greasy, lubricious, ||sliddery, ||slipper, slippery, slithery
rel oily; ||slape, smooth; soapy
idiom slick as a greased pig
con coarse, gritty, rough, uneven

2 *syn* see FULSOME
rel glossy; slippery
3 *syn* see WISE 4

slicker *n syn* see SWINDLER

||**slidder** *vb* **1** *syn* see SLIDE 3
2 *syn* see SLITHER 2

||**sliddery** *adj syn* see SLICK 1

slide *vb* **1** to go or progress with a smooth continuous motion < goldfish *slid* across the pool >
syn glide, glissade, slick, slip, slither
rel flow, stream
2 *syn* see SLIP 6
3 to fall or nearly fall because of loss of balance or footing < stumbled and *slid* on the ice >
syn skid, ||slidder, slip, ||slur
idiom take a slide (*or* a skid)
4 to shift or be shifted out of place or away from one's grasp < the packages *slid* from her arms >
syn slip
rel shift; move; fall, spill, tumble
5 *syn* see CREEP 1
6 to take a natural course < preferred to let the matter *slide* for a while >
syn coast, drift
rel glide
idiom run its course
7 *syn* see STEAL 3
8 *syn* see SNEAK

slide *n syn* see DECLINE 3

slight *adj* **1** *syn* see THIN 1
rel slightish, ||slighty; smallish; pint-sized
2 *syn* see DELICATE 5
rel gossamery, sleazy
3 *syn* see REMOTE 4

slight *vb syn* see NEGLECT
rel skip; contemn, despise; flout, scoff

slightest *adj syn* see FIRST 4
rel ||fat, negligible

slighting *adj syn* see DEROGATORY

slim *adj* **1** *syn* see THIN 1
rel lissome, lithe, lithesome, svelte
ant chubby
2 *syn* see CLEVER 4
3 *syn* see REMOTE 4

slim (down) *vb syn* see REDUCE 5

slime *n* a viscous and usually dirty or offensive substance < a layer of *slime* formed in the bottom of the pool >
syn muck, ||slab, slum
rel ooze, ||sleech, sludge; scum

sling *vb* **1** *syn* see THROW 1
rel catapult; sock
2 *syn* see STRIDE 1

sling *vb syn* see HANG 1

slink *vb syn* see SNEAK

slink *n syn* see SNEAK

slinker *n syn* see SLACKER

slip *vb* **1** *syn* see SLIDE 1
2 *syn* see SNEAK
3 *syn* see STEAL 3
4 *syn* see SLIDE 4
5 *syn* see SLIDE 3
6 to decline gradually from a standard or accustomed level < sales in some lines *slipped* >
syn drop (off), fall (off *or* away), sag, slide, slump
rel erode, soften; decline, go down, sink; dip; drop; nose-dive, plummet, topple; crash

---

con better, gain, improve, rally, rebound;
ascend, climb, rise; skyrocket, soar
7 *syn* see SHAKE 5
8 *syn* see SHED 2
slip (on) *vb syn* see DON 1
   ant slip (off)
slip *n* 1 *syn* see WHARF
   2 *syn* see ESCAPE 1
   3 *syn* see ERROR 2
   4 *syn* see DECLINE 3
‖**slipper** *adj syn* see SLICK 1
slippery *adj* 1 *syn* see SLICK 1
   2 *syn* see MUTABLE 2
slippy *adj syn* see SLICK 1
slipshod *adj* 1 *syn* see SHABBY 1
   2 *syn* see SLOVENLY 1
   3 marked by indifference to exactness,
   precision, and accuracy <a *slipshod* piece
   of research>
     syn botchy, careless, messy, slapdash,
   sloppy, slovenly, unthorough, untidy
     rel neglected, negligent; haphazard, slap-
   happy, unmeticulous; botched-up, fouled=
   up, messed-up, ‖screwed-up; faulty, imperfect, inaccurate, inexact
     con fastidious, meticulous, neat; accurate,
   exact, precise; methodical, orderly, systematic; thorough
slipslop *n syn* see NONSENSE 2
slipup *n syn* see ERROR 2
slit *vb syn* see CUT 1
slither *vb* 1 *syn* see SLIDE 1
   rel ‖sluther
   2 to walk or move in a sinuous way <a
   slinky blonde *slithered* over from the
   bar>
     syn ‖slidder, snake, undulate
     rel creep, glide, sidle, steal; lurk, prowl,
   slink, sneak
slithery *adj syn* see SLICK 1
‖**slive** *vb syn* see SIDLE
sliver *vb* to cut into very thin slices < *sliv-*
   ered cheese>
     syn shave, shred
     rel carve, haggle, slice
     con chop, dice, mince; comminute, pow-
   der, pulverize; crush, mash
slobber *vb syn* see DROOL 2
slobbering *adj syn* see EFFUSIVE
slobbery *adj* 1 *syn* see EFFUSIVE
   2 *syn* see SLOVENLY 1
slog *vb* 1 *syn* see STRIKE 2
   2 *syn* see PLOD 1
   3 *syn* see DRUDGE
slogan *n syn* see CATCHWORD
   rel expression, idiom, locution
slogging *n syn* see WORK 2
‖**slommacky** *adj syn* see SLOVENLY 1
sloom *n syn* see DOZE
sloom *vb syn* see DOZE
‖**sloomy** *adj syn* see SLEEPY 1
slop *n syn* see PAP 2
slop *vb* 1 *syn* see SPILL 1
   2 *syn* see SPLASH
   3 *syn* see GULP
   4 *syn* see PLOD 1
slope *vb syn* see SLANT 1
slope *n* a natural or artificial inclined surface <the steep *slope* of the hill>
     syn grade, gradient, inclination, incline,
   lean, leaning, slant, tilt
     rel acclivity, ascent, rise; declivity, de-
   scent; deflection, deviation, obliqueness,

obliquity; pitch, swag, sway, tip; bend,
skew
   con champaign, flat, flatland, mesa,
plain(s), plateau, tableland
   ant level
sloped *adj syn* see INCLINED 3
slopeways *adv syn* see ASIDE 1
sloping *adj syn* see INCLINED 3
slopped *adj syn* see INTOXICATED 1
sloppy *adj* 1 *syn* see SLIPSHOD 3
   rel amateurish; mediocre; awkward,
clumsy; poor
   ant exact, precise
   2 *syn* see SLOVENLY 1
   3 *syn* see EFFUSIVE
   rel soft; oversentimental
   4 *syn* see INTOXICATED 1
slosh *n syn* see BLOW 1
slosh *vb* 1 *of a liquid* to move with a gentle
lapping motion or sound <heard water
sloshing in the bottom of the boat>
   syn bubble, burble, gurgle, lap, swash,
wash
   rel babble, ripple; dash, plash, splash,
tumble; bespatter, spatter; churn, whirl;
gush, rush; roar
   2 *syn* see SPLASH
   3 *syn* see GULP
‖4 *syn* see STRIKE 2
sloth *n* 1 disinclination to action or labor
<a bland *sloth*-provoking summer day>
   syn idleness, indolence, laze, laziness,
slothfulness, slouch, sluggishness
   rel ergophobia, faineancy, idling, lazing,
loafing; apathy, heaviness, languidness,
languor, lassitude, lethargy, listlessness,
torpidity; shiftlessness
   con assiduity, assiduousness, busyness,
diligence, sedulity, sedulousness
   ant industriousness, industry
   2 sluggishness and apathy in the practice
of virtue <the deadly sin of *sloth*>
   syn acedia
   rel heedlessness, inattention, inattentive-
ness
   con assiduity
slothful *adj syn* see LAZY
   con assiduous, busy, diligent, sedulous
   ant industrious
slothfulness *n syn* see SLOTH 1
slouch *n* 1 *syn* see OAF 2
   2 *syn* see SLUGGARD
   3 *syn* see SLOTH 1
slouch *vb* to assume, have, or move with
an awkwardly drooping posture, carriage,
or gait <three drunks *slouched* across the
room>
   syn droop, loll, ‖lollop, lop, slump, trollop
   rel loaf, lounge, saunter, shamble, shuffle;
bend, lean, stoop; sag, wilt
   con erect, straighten (up); sit up, stand
up
slough *n* 1 *syn* see SWAMP
   2 *syn* see INLET
‖**slough** *n syn* see HULL
slough *vb* 1 *syn* see SHED 2
   2 *syn* see DISCARD
   idiom ‖get shut (*or* shed) of
slough over *vb syn* see NEGLECT
sloven *adj syn* see SLOVENLY 1
slovenly *adj* 1 negligent of or marked by
lack of neatness and order especially in
appearance or dress < *slovenly* attire>

syn careless, disheveled, ill-kempt, messy, mussy, raunchy, slipshod, slobbery, ‖slommacky, sloppy, sloven, uncombed, unfastidious, unkempt, unneat, untidy; *compare* SLATTERNLY

rel down-at-heel, shabby, sleazy, sluttish, slutty; blowsy, dowdy, frowsy, frumpish

con fastidious, neat, tidy, trim; combed, groomed, well-groomed; immaculate

ant neat

2 *syn* see SLIPSHOD 3

slow *adj* 1 *syn* see RETARDED

rel limited; ‖dunch

2 moving, flowing, or proceeding at less than the usual, desirable, or required speed <a *slow* advance toward mutual understanding>

syn deliberate, dilatory, laggard, leisurely, unhasty, unhurried

rel measured, slowish, steady; unhasting, unhurrying; slow-footed, slow-going, slow-paced; plodding, poky, rusty; dragging, flagging, halting, lagging, straggling; dawdling, delaying, postponing, procrastinating; leaden, sluggish; crawling, snaillike, snail-paced, ultra-slow

idiom as slow as a swamp turtle, as slow as molasses in January

con blitz, lightning, quick, rapid, swift; fast-going, fast-moving, fast-paced, rapid-paced

ant fast

3 marked by reduced economic activity (as in sales or patronage) <trading was *slow* on the commodity exchange today>

syn down, off, slack, sluggish

rel moderate; reduced; low; inactive, stagnant

con active; up; heavy

slow (up *or* down) *vb syn* see DELAY 1

rel moderate, qualify, temper; abate, decrease, lessen, reduce

ant speed

slow coach *n syn* see LAGGARD

slowdown *n* 1 a slowing or gradual decrease in activity <a *slowdown* in car sales this quarter>

syn slack, slackening, slow-up

rel decline, downtrend, downturn; drop, drop-off, falloff; inactivity, stagnation; freeze

con increase, rise, upswing, upturn; acceleration, quickening

ant speedup

2 a deliberate slowing down by workers in the rate and quantity of production <air traffic snarled by a controllers' *slowdown*>

syn ‖ca' canny

rel action; protest; slow-up; sit-down; strike, walkout; stoppage

ant speedup

slowgoing *adj syn* see LAZY

slowpoke *n syn* see LAGGARD

slow–up *n syn* see SLOWDOWN 1

slow–witted *adj syn* see RETARDED

ant quick-witted

‖slubberdegullion *n syn* see VILLAIN 1

---

syn synonym(s)　　*rel* related word(s)
ant antonym(s)　　*con* contrasted word(s)
idiom idiomatic equivalent(s)
‖ use limited; if in doubt, see a dictionary

slue *vb syn* see SWERVE 1

slug *n syn* see SLUGGARD

rel slacker, sloven

slug *n syn* see DRAM

slug *vb syn* see SLAM 1

slugabed *n syn* see SLUGGARD

sluggard *n* an habitually lazy, shiftless, and inactive person <a *sluggard* who wanted to sleep all day>

syn bum, dolittle, do-nothing, faineant, idler, lazybones, loafer, slouch, slug, slugabed

rel lie-abed, sleepyhead; dawdler, laggard, slow coach, slowpoke; goldbrick, shirker

idiom ‖his idleship, ‖Weary Willie

con go-getter, hustler, live wire

ant dynamo

sluggish *adj* 1 *syn* see LETHARGIC

rel dragging, draggy, leaden, lumpish; costive, stiff; apathetic, stupefied

con go-getting, hustling, vigorous; expeditious

ant brisk

2 *syn* see SLOW 3

sluggishness *n syn* see SLOTH 1

sluice *vb syn* see POUR 2

rel flush, wash; douse, drench, soak

slum *n* a densely populated usually urban area marked by run-down housing, poverty, and social disorganization <a *slum* full of vagrants, junkies, pimps, and pushers>

syn stew

rel slumdom, slumland; tobacco road; tenderloin; skid row; ghetto; hive, kennel, rookery, warren

idiom desolation row, the wrong side of the tracks

slum *n syn* see SLIME

slumber *vb* 1 *syn* see DOZE

2 *syn* see SLEEP

slumber *n* 1 *syn* see SLEEP 1

2 *syn* see DOZE

3 *syn* see LETHARGY 1

slumberous *adj* 1 *syn* see SLEEPY 1

2 *syn* see SOPORIFIC 1

3 *syn* see LETHARGIC

slumbery *adj syn* see SLEEPY 1

slump *vb* 1 *syn* see FALL 2

rel droop, flag, sag

idiom come down like a rock (*or* a ton of bricks)

2 *syn* see SLOUCH

rel cave in, collapse

3 *syn* see SLIP 6

slump *n* 1 *syn* see DECLINE 3

2 *syn* see DEPRESSION 3

slup *vb syn* see SLURP

‖slur *vb syn* see SLIDE 3

slur *vb syn* see MALIGN

slur (over) *vb syn* see NEGLECT

slur *n* 1 *syn* see ANIMADVERSION

2 *syn* see STIGMA

slurp *vb* to eat or drink noisily <*slurping* soup with a large spoon>

syn slup

rel guzzle, lap (up), slosh, swill; suck; wolf (down); smack

con nibble, pick (at); sip

slushy *adj syn* see SENTIMENTAL

slut *n* 1 *syn* see SLATTERN 1

2 *syn* see WANTON

3 *syn* see MINX

sly *adj* **1** *syn* see CLEVER 4
rel smart; cagey; masterful

2 attaining or seeking to attain one's ends by devious means <a *sly* way of upping sales>
syn artful, astute, crafty, cunning, deep, ||downy, foxy, guileful, insidious, subdolous, subtle, tricky, vulpine, wily; *compare* UNDERHAND
rel disingenuous, unfrank; calculating, designing, Machiavellian, scheming; cagey, devious, shady, shifty, ||slanter, slick, slippery, smooth; clandestine, covert, furtive, stealthy; underhand, underhanded, unscrupulous; predatory; crooked, dishonest
idiom crazy like a fox, cunning as a fox (*or* serpent), sly as a fox
con candid, forthright, frank, honest, open, sincere, straightforward

sly *vb syn* see SNEAK

slyboots *n pl but sing in constr syn* see SCAMP

slyness *n syn* see CUNNING 2

smack *n* **1** *syn* see TASTE 3
2 *syn* see HINT 2

smack *vb* to have a trace, vestige, or suggestion of something <that plan *smacks* of radicalism>
syn savor, smell
rel resemble, suggest; reek, stink

smack *vb* **1** *syn* see KISS 1
idiom ||plant a juicy kiss on
2 *syn* see SLAP 1

smack *n* **1** *syn* see CUFF
2 *syn* see BLOW 1

||**smack–dab** *adv syn* see JUST 1

||**smacker** *n syn* see DOLLAR

||**smackeroo** *n syn* see DOLLAR

small *adj* **1** being the opposite of large <a *small* white house>
syn bantam, little, monkey, petite, smallish; *compare* TINY
rel cramped, limited, narrow, two-by-four; puny, undersized; paltry, petty, piddling, trivial
con big, great; considerable, sizable; enormous, huge, immense, vast
ant large

2 *syn* see MINOR 2
3 *syn* see LITTLE 2
4 *syn* see LITTLE 3
5 *syn* see PETTY 2
6 *syn* see REMOTE 4

small beer *n syn* see TRIVIA

small–beer *adj syn* see LITTLE 3

small change *n syn* see TRIVIA

smallest *adj syn* see FIRST 4

small–fry *adj syn* see MINOR 2

smallish *adj syn* see SMALL 1
ant largish

small–minded *adj syn* see ILLIBERAL
ant large-minded

small potato *n, usu* small potatoes *pl but sing or pl in constr syn* see TRIVIA

small talk *n* light or casual conversation <had to make *small talk* at the cocktail party>
syn bavardage, by-talk, chitchat, chitterchatter, trifling
rel badinage, banter, repartee; babble, babbling, bibble-babble, chatter, prattle, prattling, prittle-prattle

small–time *adj syn* see MINOR 2

ant big-time

small–town *adj syn* see INSULAR

||**smarm** *vb syn* see SMEAR 1

smarmy *adj* **1** *syn* see SLEEK
2 *syn* see FULSOME

smart *vb syn* see HURT 4

smart *vb* to cause or produce a sharp stinging and usually localized pain <gave him a slap that was hard enough to *smart*>
syn bite, burn, ||stang, sting; *compare* HURT 4
rel prick; tingle; hurt

smart *adj* **1** *syn* see INTELLIGENT 2
ant stupid
2 *syn* see WISE 4
idiom knowing the score, on the ball
ant dull, dumb
3 *syn* see CLEVER 5
rel pert, saucy
4 *syn* see WISE 5
5 *syn* see STYLISH
rel dapper, ||dinky, spruce
ant dowdy
||**6** *syn* see CONSIDERABLE 2

smart aleck *n* an obnoxiously conceited and self-assertive person with pretensions to smartness or cleverness <was heckled by a *smart aleck* in the back row>
syn know-it-all, smarty, smarty-pants, wiseacre, wisecracker, wise guy, wisehead, wisenheimer
rel blowhard, boaster, braggadocio, braggart, gasbag, windbag; exhibitionist, grandstander, show-off
idiom hot-air artist

smart–alecky *adj syn* see WISE 5

smarten (up) *vb syn* see DRESS UP 1

smart set *n* ultrafashionable often international society <the *smart set* that suns in Cannes and skis in St. Moritz>
syn beautiful people, jet set, ton
rel aristocracy, aristoi, blue bloods, bon ton, elite, Four Hundred, society, upper crust, who's who

smarty *n syn* see SMART ALECK

smarty–pants *n pl but sing in constr syn* see SMART ALECK

smash *vb* **1** *syn* see SHATTER 1
2 *syn* see SLAM 1
3 *syn* see DESTROY 1

smash *n* **1** *syn* see BLOW 1
2 *syn* see BANG 2
3 *syn* see IMPACT
4 *syn* see CRASH 3
5 *syn* see COLLAPSE 2
6 a striking success <the new musical was a box-office *smash*>
syn bang, bell ringer, hit, succès fou, tenstrike, wow
rel sensation; knockout
idiom howling (*or* roaring) success, smash hit
con disaster, dud, failure
ant flop

||**smash** *n syn* see MONEY

||**smashed** *adj syn* see INTOXICATED 1

smashup *n* **1** *syn* see COLLAPSE 2
2 *syn* see CRASH 3

smatch *n* **1** *syn* see HINT 2
2 *syn* see FEW

smatter *vb* ||**1** *syn* see SHATTER 1
2 *syn* see CHAT 1

smatter *n syn* see FEW
smatterer *n syn* see AMATEUR 2
smattering *n syn* see FEW
smaze *n syn* see HAZE 1
smear *vb* **1** to overspread with something unctuous, viscous, or adhesive < *smeared* the crack with wet concrete >
  syn bedaub, besmear, dab, daub, plaster, ||smarm, smudge
  rel rub; coat, cover, overlay, overspread, spread; smirch, soil
  2 *syn* see TAINT 1
  3 *syn* see MALIGN
  idiom use smear tactics (on *or* against)
  4 *syn* see WHIP 2
  rel foil, frustrate; repulse
  idiom mop up the floor (*or* earth) with
smell *vb* **1** to perceive by means of the olfactory organs < *smelled* a dead skunk >
  syn nose, scent, sniff, ||snift, snuff
  rel detect, perceive, sense; whiff; ||snaffle, snuffle
  idiom get a whiff of
  2 *syn* see SMACK
  3 to have or emit an offensive odor < the canal *smells* today >
  syn funk, reek, stench, stink
  idiom offend the nostrils, smell (*or* stink) to high heaven
smell *n* **1** a quality that makes a thing perceptible to the olfactory sense < the *smell* of a ham cooking >
  syn aroma, odor, scent
  rel bouquet, fragrance, incense, perfume, redolence, spice; flavor, savor, stench, stink
  2 *syn* see HINT 2
smeller *n syn* see NOSE 1
||**smellful** *adj syn* see MALODOROUS 1
  ant odorless, smell-less
smellfungus *n syn* see CRITIC
smell-less *adj syn* see ODORLESS
  ant ||smellful, smelly
smelly *adj syn* see MALODOROUS 1
  con odorless, scentless, smell-less; fragrant, fresh, sweet
smidgen *n syn* see PARTICLE
smile *vb* to express amusement, satisfaction, or pleasure by brightening one's eyes and curving the corners of one's mouth upward < *smiled* as she greeted him >
  syn beam, grin
  rel simper, smirk
  idiom break into a smile, crack a smile
  con grimace; glare, glower, lower, scowl
  ant frown
smirch *vb syn* see SOIL 2
  rel discolor; smear
smirk *vb* to smile in an affected manner < *smirking* children imitating their teacher >
  syn simper, ||smirkle; *compare* SNEER 1
  rel grin, smile; fleer, leer, sneer
||**smirkle** *vb syn* see SMIRK
smitch *n syn* see PARTICLE
smite *vb* **1** *syn* see STRIKE 2
  rel bat, belt, clobber; dash

idiom smite a blow
  2 *syn* see AFFLICT
smithereens *n pl* very small particles or fragments < a house blown to *smithereens* by a bomb >
  syn ||shivereens, smithers
  rel fragments, particles, pieces
smithers *n pl syn* see SMITHEREENS
smitten *adj syn* see ENAMORED 1
  idiom bitten by the love bug
smoke *n syn* see CIGARETTE
smoke *vb syn* see HURRY 2
smolder *vb syn* see SEETHE 4
  rel burst, erupt, explode; fulminate
smooch *vb syn* see SOIL 2
smooch *vb syn* see KISS 1
  idiom ||plant a smooch on
||**smoodge** *vb syn* see KISS 1
smooth *adj* **1** *syn* see LEVEL
  rel glossy, sleek, slick; rippleless, unbroken, unwrinkled
  con harsh, rugged, scabrous, uneven
  ant rough
  2 *syn* see HAIRLESS
  3 *syn* see EASY 9
  4 *syn* see EASY 1
  rel smooth-running
  idiom smooth and easy
  ant labored
  5 *syn* see SUAVE
  rel courteous, courtly, polite; smooth-faced, smooth-tongued
  con bluff, blunt, brusque, crusty, curt, gruff, harsh
  6 *syn* see GENTLE 1
  rel agreeable, soothing
smooth *vb* **1** *syn* see EVEN 1
  con corrugate; roughen; wrinkle
  ant unsmooth
  2 *syn* see POLISH 2
smooth *adv syn* see EVENLY 3
smoothen *vb syn* see EVEN 1
smoothly *adv* **1** *syn* see EVENLY 3
  con unevenly, ununiformly
  ant roughly
  2 *syn* see EASILY 1
  ant unsmoothly
smooth–spoken *adj syn* see VOCAL 3
  ant rough-spoken
smorgasbord *n syn* see MISCELLANY 1
smother *vb* **1** *syn* see SUFFOCATE
  2 *syn* see COMPOSE 4
  rel hush up, muffle; cork; quash, quell, squelch; quench
  3 *syn* see WHIP 2
smothering *adj syn* see STIFLING 1
smothering *n syn* see REPRESSION 1
smothery *adj syn* see STIFLING 1
||**smouch** *vb syn* see KISS 1
smouch *vb syn* see STEAL 1
smudge *vb* **1** *syn* see SOIL 2
  rel smear; blotch, splotch
  2 *syn* see SMEAR 1
  3 *syn* see TAINT 1
||**smudgy** *adj syn* see STIFLING 1
smug *adj syn* see COMPLACENT
  idiom pleased with oneself
smug *vb syn* see DRESS UP 1
smuggle *vb* to import or export secretly and in violation of the law < *smuggling* weapons into the country >
  syn bootleg, contraband, run
  idiom run contraband

smut *vb* **1** *syn* see STAIN 1
2 *syn* see TAINT 1

smutch *vb* **1** *syn* see SOIL 2
2 *syn* see TAINT 1

smutty *adj syn* see OBSCENE 2

snack *n* food served or taken informally and usually in small amounts and typically under other circumstances than a regular meal <a milk-and-cookie *snack* after school >
  syn ‖bait, ‖bever, bite, ‖chack, morsel, mug-up, ‖piece, tapa
  rel collation, refreshment, tea
  idiom bite to eat

snack bar (*or* counter) *n syn* see EATING HOUSE

‖**snaffle** *vb syn* see STEAL 1

‖**snafu** *vb syn* see CONFUSE 5

snag *n syn* see OBSTACLE
  rel brake, clog, curb, drag; hold-up
  idiom ‖snags and sawyers

snake *n syn* see SNOT 1

snake *vb* ‖**1** *syn* see STEAL 1
2 *syn* see CREEP 1
3 *syn* see SLITHER 2
‖**4** *syn* see SNEAK

snaky *adj syn* see WINDING

snap *vb* **1** to speak in a curt, biting tone < *snapped* at his subordinates for inefficiency >
  syn bark, snarl
  rel growl, grumble, grunt, snort; roar, yell
  idiom bite one's head off, snap off one's head (*or* nose)
2 *syn* see JERK
  rel clutch, grab, grasp, seize, snaffle, snatch

snap *n* **1** something easily managed or accomplished <that exam was a *snap* >
  syn breeze, child's play, cinch, duck soup, kid stuff, picnic, pie, ‖pipe, pushover, setup, ‖snip, soft touch
  rel sinecure
  idiom a simple twist of the wrist, simplicity itself, soft snap
  con difficulty, headache, problem, trouble; bother, inconvenience, pain
  ant chore
2 *syn* see PARTICLE
3 *syn* see MAN 3
4 *syn* see VIGOR 2

snap back *vb syn* see RECOVER 3

‖**snapper** *vb syn* see STUMBLE 3

snapping *adv syn* see VERY 1

snappish *adj syn* see IRRITABLE
  rel curt, short, ungracious; crabbed, morose, surly

snappy *adj* **1** *syn* see IRRITABLE
2 *syn* see FAST 3
3 *syn* see PUNGENT
  rel animated, lively, vivacious; prompt, quick, ready
4 *syn* see STYLISH

snare *n syn* see LURE 2
  rel chicane, chicanery, deception; ensnarement, entrapment

snare *vb syn* see CATCH 3
  rel seduce, tempt; involve; embrangle, enmesh, ensnarl, trammel

‖**snark** *vb syn* see SNORE

snarl *n* **1** *syn* see CONFUSION 3

  rel entanglement, tangle; complexity, complication, intricacy, intricateness; labyrinth, maze; mishmash, swarm; jam
  idiom tangled skein, wheels within wheels
2 *syn* see MAZE 1

snarl *vb* **1** *syn* see ENTANGLE 1
2 *syn* see COMPLICATE

snarl *vb syn* see SNAP 1

snarl up *vb syn* see CONFUSE 5

snatch *vb* **1** *syn* see SEIZE 2
  rel jerk, wrench, yank; nip (up), whip (up)
‖**2** *syn* see KIDNAP

sneak *vb* to move or go stealthily and furtively < *sneaked* into the garage and stole the car >
  syn creep, glide, gumshoe, lurk, ‖meech, pussyfoot, shirk, skulk, slide, slink, slip, sly, ‖snake, ‖snook, steal; *compare* STEAL 3
  rel crawl, slither, worm, prowl
  idiom go on (little) cat's feet, move under cover
  con barge, strut, swagger; clump, stamp, stump; stride; march, parade

sneak *n* a person who behaves in a stealthy, furtive, or shifty manner < found out that he was a liar, a cheat, and a *sneak* >
  syn slink, sneaker, sneaksby, weasel
  rel blackguard, knave, scoundrel; cur, heel, louse, reptile, skunk, snake; toad
  idiom Jerry Sneak

sneak *adj syn* see SECRET 1

sneaker *n syn* see SNEAK

sneaking *adj syn* see UNDERHAND
  ant forthright

sneaksby *n syn* see SNEAK

sneaky *adj syn* see UNDERHAND

‖**sneap** *vb syn* see REPROVE

sneer *vb* **1** to smile with attendant facial contortions expressing scorn or contempt < *sneered* haughtily at the beggar >
  syn fleer, leer, ‖sleer; *compare* SMIRK
  rel grin, smile
  idiom curl one's lip, make a scornful (*or* mocking) face
2 *syn* see SCOFF
  rel belittle, detract, disparage, underrate
  idiom cock a snook at, give the Bronx cheer to, give the raspberry, sneeze at, thumb one's nose at

‖**sneezer** *n syn* see NOSE 1

snicker *vb syn* see LAUGH
  idiom have a case of the snickers

snide *adj syn* see COUNTERFEIT
2 *syn* see CROOKED 2

sniff *vb syn* see SMELL 1

‖**snift** *vb syn* see SMELL 1
  rel ‖snifter

snifter *n syn* see DRAM

‖**sniggle** *vb syn* see LAUGH

snip *n* **1** *syn* see MINX
‖**2** *syn* see SNAP 1

snippety *adj syn* see BLUFF
  rel impolite, insolent, rude

snippy *adj syn* see BLUFF

snip–snap *n syn* see BANTER

snit *n* a state of agitation or excited irritation especially over a trivial matter < was in a *snit* because his secretary was one minute late >
  syn fume, stew, sweat, swivet, tizzy

rel huff, pique; conniption, fit, frenzy, seizure, taking; dither, flap, panic, ‖swither

snitch *vb* 1 *syn* see INFORM 3
2 *syn* see STEAL 1

snitch *n* ‖1 *syn* see NOSE 1
2 *syn* see INFORMER

snob *n* one inclined to rebuff or ignore people or things that he regards as inferior (as in culture or social status) < appeals to real lovers of music rather than musical *snobs* >
syn high-hat, snoot, snot
rel name-dropper, snobling; bootlicker, hanger-on, lickspittle, sycophant, toady

snob *vb* *syn* see CUT 7

snobbish *adj* of, relating to, or characteristic of a snob < a *snobbish* group of jet-set sophisticates >
syn ‖dicty, high-hat, potty, snobby, snooty
rel aloof, remote; high-flown, pretentious, snotty, supercilious; haughty, hoity-toity, pompous, ritzy; condescending, patronizing; insecure, uncertain, unconfident, unselfconfident, unsure
con certain, confident, secure, self-confident

snobby *adj* *syn* see SNOBBISH
rel snubbing, snubby

‖**snook** *vb* 1 *syn* see SNOOP
2 *syn* see SNEAK

snoop *vb* to look, inquire, or search impertinently or intrusively < he knew he had no right to *snoop* into her private life >
syn busybody, mouse, nose, ‖piroot, poke, pry, ‖snook
rel peek, peep, peer, stare; interfere, intrude, meddle, mess
idiom stick (*or* poke) one's nose into

snoop *n* *syn* see BUSYBODY

snoopy *adj* *syn* see CURIOUS 2

snoot *n* 1 *syn* see NOSE 1
2 *syn* see SNOB

snooty *adj* *syn* see SNOBBISH

snooze *vb* *syn* see NAP

snooze *n* *syn* see NAP

‖**snoozle** *vb* *syn* see DOZE

snoozy *adj* *syn* see SLEEPY 1

snore *vb* to breathe during sleep with a rough hoarse noise due to vibration of the soft palate < driven to distraction by her sister's *snoring* >
syn ‖snark
rel wheeze; snuffle; snort, ‖snotter
idiom ‖drive pigs to market, ‖saw logs (*or* wood)

snort *n* *syn* see DRAM

snorter *n* *syn* see DRAM

snot *n* 1 an utterly contemptible person < a despicable *snot* whom everyone shunned >
syn ‖bugger, cur, dog, louse, ‖prick, puke, rat, scum, skunk, snake, sod, stinkard, stinkaroo, stinker, toad, wretch; *compare* VILLAIN 1
rel ‖creep, ‖crumb, lowlife; knave, rogue, scoundrel, ‖skite; pig, reptile
2 *syn* see SNOB

snout *n* *syn* see NOSE 1

snowball *vb* *syn* see INCREASE 2

snub *vb* *syn* see CUT 7
rel high-hat, ‖ritz, swank; put down
idiom look coldly upon, turn a cold shoulder (on *or* upon)

‖**snudge** *vb* *syn* see SNUGGLE

‖**snuff** *n* *syn* see OFFENSE 2

snuff *vb* *syn* see SMELL 1

‖**snuff** (out) *vb* *syn* see DIE 1

snug *adj* 1 *syn* see NEAT 2
2 *syn* see COMFORTABLE 2
idiom snug as a bug in a rug
‖3 *syn* see PROSPEROUS 3

snug *vb* *syn* see SNUGGLE

snuggle *vb* to assume or be in a warm comfortable position usually near another person or thing < a baby *snuggling* close to his mother >
syn burrow, ‖croodle, cuddle, nestle, nuzzle, ‖snudge, snug, ‖snuzzle
rel curl up; huddle; spoon
idiom snuggle up like a bug in a rug
con flinch, recoil, shrink

‖**snuzzle** *vb* *syn* see SNUGGLE

‖**sny** *vb* *syn* see TEEM

so *adv* 1 *syn* see ALSO 1
2 *syn* see THUS 1
3 *syn* see VERY 1
4 *syn* see THEREFORE

so *conj* with the purpose that < repeated it aloud *so* there'd be no mistake >
syn so as, so that
idiom in order that, to the end that, with the intent that

soak *vb* 1 to permeate or be permeated with or as if with water < *soak* a sponge with water > < rain *soaked* her to the skin >
syn drench, ‖drouk, impregnate, insteep, saturate, seethe, sodden, ‖sog, sop, souse, steep, waterlog; *compare* WET
rel dip, immerse, submerge; draw, infuse; infiltrate, penetrate, permeate, pervade; water-soak; drown
2 *syn* see WET
3 *syn* see ENGAGE 4
4 *syn* see OVERCHARGE 1
5 *syn* see DRINK 3
idiom ‖soak it up like a sponge

soak *n* 1 *syn* see DRUNKARD
2 *syn* see BINGE 1

soaked *adj* *syn* see WET 1

soaker *n* *syn* see DRUNKARD

soaking *adj* *syn* see WET 1
idiom soaking wet

so-and-so *adj* *syn* see DAMNED 2

soapbox *vb* *syn* see ORATE

soapy *adj* *syn* see FULSOME

soar *vb* 1 *syn* see RISE 4
rel climb; shoot
2 *syn* see SKYROCKET
ant plummet

soaring *adj* *syn* see LOFTY 6
idiom high as the sky

so as *conj* *syn* see SO

sob *vb* *syn* see CRY 2

sobby *adj* *syn* see SENTIMENTAL

sober *adj* 1 *syn* see ABSTEMIOUS
rel controlled, restrained; self-possessed
con indulgent, overindulgent; uncontrolled, unrestrained; immoderate, intemperate; excessive; profligate

2 *syn* see SERIOUS 1
rel decorous, proper; calm, placid, serene, tranquil
con flippant, light, light-minded; unstable, volatile
ant gay

3 having or exhibiting self-control and avoiding extremes of behavior < his bearing was *sober*, his comments judicious >
syn moderate, temperate, unimpassioned; *compare* ABSTEMIOUS
rel rational, reasonable; calm, collected, composed, cool, imperturbable; constrained, disciplined, inhibited, reserved, restrained, self-controlled, self-disciplined; abstaining, forbearing, refraining; abnegating, eschewing, forgoing
con irrational, unreasonable; emotional, hotheaded, impassioned, overemotional, passionate; intemperate, uncontained, uncontrolled; excited; drunk, intoxicated; abandoned
ant unsober

4 *syn* see SUBDUED 2

5 *syn* see REALISTIC
rel sober-eyed, sober-minded

sobersided *adj syn* see SERIOUS 1

sobful *adj syn* see SENTIMENTAL

sobriety *n syn* see TEMPERANCE 2
rel gravity, sedateness, seriousness, soberness
con excitement; drunkenness, intoxication; abandonment
ant insobriety

sobriquet *n syn* see NICKNAME

so-called *adj* 1 *syn* see NOMINAL
2 *syn* see ALLEGED

sociable *adj* 1 *syn* see SOCIAL 2
ant nonsocial
2 *syn* see GRACIOUS 1
rel companionable, convivial; gregarious; close, familiar, intimate; good-natured
ant unsociable
3 *syn* see SOCIAL 1
ant unsociable, unsocial

social *adj* 1 conducive to, marked by, or passed in pleasant companionship with one's friends or associates < a relaxed, *social* evening >
syn companionable, convivial, sociable
rel amusing, entertaining, pleasant, pleasurable; cordial, friendly, genial, gracious, hospitable
con unfriendly, unhospitable, unsociable; eremitic, solitary
ant unsociable, unsocial
2 inclined by nature to association or community life with others of the same species < man is a *social* animal >
syn gregarious, sociable
rel social-minded; intersocial
con eremitic, solitary, unsociable; antisocial, asocial, unsocial; remote, withdrawn
ant nonsocial

social evil *n, used with the* syn *see* PROSTITUTION

socialize *vb* to participate actively in a social group < *socializes* with his colleagues >
syn mingle
rel associate, mix

society *n* 1 *syn* see COMPANY 1
2 *syn* see ASSOCIATION 2

3 an organized aggregate of persons who are responsible for a prevailing social order < rules made in the interests of *society* rather than for the chosen few >
syn community, people, public
rel masses, populace
idiom people in general, society at large, the general public
4 *syn* see ARISTOCRACY
idiom high society (or life)

sock *vb syn* see STRIKE 2

sock *n* 1 *syn* see BLOW 1
2 *syn* see CUFF

‖**sock** *vb syn* see SIGH 1

sod *n syn* see SNOT 1

sodality *n syn* see ASSOCIATION 2

sodden *adj syn* see WET 1

sodden *vb syn* see SOAK 1

Sodom *n syn* see SINK 1
rel Babylon

so far *adv syn* see HITHERTO 1
idiom up till now

soft *adj* 1 *syn* see GENTLE 1
rel moderate, temperate
2 *syn* see SUBDUED 2
ant loud
3 smooth or delicate in texture, grain, or fiber < the dog's fur was *soft* >
syn cottony, satiny, silken, silky, velvety
rel smooth; sleek
con coarse, rough
ant harsh
4 *syn* see COMFORTABLE 2
ant rough
5 *syn* see SIMPLE 3
idiom ‖soft in the head
6 giving way easily to physical touch or pressure < a *soft* cheese >
syn mushy, pappy, pulpous, pulpy, quaggy, spongy, squashy, squelchy, squishy, squushy, yielding
rel softish; compressible, malleable, pliable, pliant, workable; doughy, formless; flabby, fleshy
idiom soft as butter
con firm, solid; resistant, rigid, tough, unyielding; nail-hard, rock-hard
ant hard

soft (on) *adj syn* see ENAMORED 1

soft-boiled *adj syn* see SENTIMENTAL
ant hard-boiled

soften *vb syn* see DEPRECIATE 1

softened *adj syn* see SUBDUED 2

softhead *n syn* see FOOL 4

softhearted *adj syn* see TENDER
ant hardhearted

soft-pedal *vb* to reduce the emphasis, importance, or effect of something (as an issue) < tried to *soft-pedal* military spending >
syn de-emphasize, play (down)
rel tone (down), tune (down); cushion, dampen, muffle, subdue; hush (up), silence, suppress; conceal, disguise
con emphasize, play (up); focus (on), spotlight

soft-shell *adj syn* see MODERATE 4

soft soap *n syn* see FLATTERY
rel ‖snow job

soft-soap *vb syn* see COAX

soft spot *n* 1 *syn* see APPETITE 3
2 a vulnerable point < the major *soft spot* in the West's armor >

idiom one and only
4 belonging, granted, or attributed to the one person or group < *sole* rights of publication >
syn exclusive, single, unshared
con multiple; shared

solecism *n* 1 *syn* see ANACHRONISM 2
2 *syn* see BARBARISM
3 *syn* see FAUX PAS
solely *adv syn* see ONLY 1
solemn *adj* 1 *syn* see CEREMONIAL
rel full, plenary; august, grand, impressive, magnificent, majestic, overwhelming; ostentatious
2 *syn* see SERIOUS 1
idiom as solemn as an owl, grave as an undertaker
solemnize *vb syn* see KEEP 2
rel dignify, honor, solemnify, venerate
solicit *vb* 1 to seek (as advertising, orders, or votes) especially on a large scale < *solicited* contributions all over the district >
syn canvass, drum, drum up
rel ask, request; beg, beseech, implore; claim, demand, exact
2 *syn* see ASK 2
rel apply, go, refer, resort, turn
3 *syn* see DEMAND 1
solicitous *adj syn* see EAGER
solicitude *n* 1 *syn* see CARE 2
rel attention, heed, watchfulness; presentiment; compunction, qualm, scruple
con carelessness, heedlessness, indifference, neglect, negligence
ant unmindfulness
2 *syn* see CONSIDERATION 3
solid *adj* 1 *syn* see FIRM 2
rel compacted, concentrated, consolidated
con spongy; disintegrated; fluid, liquid
2 *syn* see STABLE 4
3 *syn* see VALID
rel firm, hard
ant insubstantial
4 *syn* see UNANIMOUS
solid *adv syn* see HARD 9
solidarism *n syn* see SOLIDARITY
solidarity *n* a feeling of unity (as in interests, standards, and responsibilities) that binds members of a group together < *solidarity* among union members is essential in negotiations >
syn cohesion, solidarism, togetherness
rel cohesiveness; oneness, singleness, undividedness; integrity, solidity, union, unity; esprit, esprit de corps; firmness, fixity
con separation; discord, dissension, schism; confusion, disorder, disorganization
ant division
solidify *vb syn* see HARDEN 1
rel compress, contract
idiom make (or become) hard as a rock
con soften; disintegrate, dissolve
ant liquefy
solidly *adv* 1 *syn* see HARD 9
2 *syn* see HARD 7
solitariness *n syn* see SOLITUDE
solitary *adj* 1 *syn* see ANTISOCIAL
ant gregarious
2 *syn* see UNSOCIABLE
3 *syn* see DERELICT 1
4 *syn* see LONE 1

---

syn Achilles' heel
rel vulnerability, vulnerableness, weakness; chink, loophole
idiom heel of Achilles, weak link (or point), weak link in the chain
con impregnability, invulnerability; invincibility
soft touch *n* 1 someone who can be easily talked into giving help (as a loan) < recognized him as a *soft touch* when she was broke >
syn easy mark
rel softy; dupe, fool, pushover; sucker; mark, sitting duck, target
con cynic, doubting Thomas, hard case, skeptic
2 *syn* see SNAP 1
∥**sog** *vb syn* see SOAK 1
∥**sog** *vb syn* see DOZE
soggy *adj syn* see HUMID
soi–disant *adj syn* see SELF-STYLED
soil *vb* 1 *syn* see CONTAMINATE 1
ant purify
2 to make or become unclean < a shirt *soiled* with grease and grime >
syn begrime, besoil, dirty, foul, grime, muck, ∥mucky, muddy, murk, smirch, smooch, smudge, smutch, tarnish; *compare* STAIN 1
rel ∥becoom, ∥benasty, ∥nasty; bedaub, daub, smear; drabble, draggle; mess, spoil
con brighten, cleanse, freshen, renew; purify
ant clean
3 *syn* see TAINT 1
soil *n* 1 *syn* see EARTH 2
2 *syn* see COUNTRY
soily *adj syn* see DIRTY 1
soiree *n syn* see EVENING 3
sojourn *n* a temporary but sometimes extended stay < a summer *sojourn* in Nice >
syn stopover, tarriance, visit
rel stay, stop; layover
sojourn *vb syn* see VISIT 3
rel linger; abide
Sol *n syn* see SUN 1
solace *vb syn* see COMFORT
idiom offer (or give) solace to, wipe one's tears away
soldier *n* a person engaged in military service < *soldiers* fighting and dying in futile wars >
syn fighter, fighting man, GI, man-at-arms, serviceman, swad, ∥swaddy, ∥sweat, warrior
rel dogface, doughboy, ∥doughfoot, infantryman; trooper; guerrilla, partisan; condottiere, free companion, free lance, mercenary, soldier of fortune
soldierly *adj syn* see BRAVE 1
rel martial; aggressive, combative, militant, pugnacious, warlike
con unsoldierly
sole *n syn* see BOTTOM 1
sole *adj* 1 *syn* see SINGLE 1
2 *syn* see SINGLE 2
3 *syn* see ONLY 2

---

syn synonym(s)   *rel* related word(s)
ant antonym(s)   *con* contrasted word(s)
idiom idiomatic equivalent(s)
∥ use limited; if in doubt, see a dictionary

rel companionless, unaccompanied, unattended
ant accompanied
5 *syn* see SINGLE 2
6 *syn* see ONLY 2
solitary *n syn* see RECLUSE
solitude *n* the state of one who is alone < a very social person who could not bear *solitude* >
syn aloneness, isolation, loneness, solitariness; *compare* SECLUSION
rel detachment, separateness; retirement, withdrawal; confinement, quarantine; loneliness, lonesomeness
con companionship, company
solo *adj syn* see ONLY 2
so long *interj syn* see GOOD-BYE
solution *n syn* see ANSWER 2
solve *vb* **1** to find an answer or solution for (a problem or difficulty) < mass transit partially *solved* the traffic problem >
syn fix, resolve, work, work out
rel decide, determine, settle
idiom hit upon a solution
2 to find an explanation or solution for something obscure, mysterious, or incomprehensible < the mystery of the missing cookies was never *solved* >
syn break, ‖cipher, clear up, decipher, dissolve, ‖dope out, figure out, puzzle out, resolve, unfold, unravel, unriddle
rel enlighten, illuminate; construe, elucidate, explain, interpret
idiom get to the bottom of, have it, put two and two together
somatic *adj syn* see BODILY
somber *adj* **1** *syn* see DARK 1
2 *syn* see GLOOMY 3
3 *syn* see SERIOUS 1
idiom as somber as an undertaker
some *adj* **1** *syn* see CERTAIN 2
2 *syn* see SEVERAL 3
some *adv* **1** *syn* see NEARLY
2 *syn* see SOMEWHAT 2
somebody *pron* one or some individual of no certain or known identity < *somebody* should be home >
syn someone
rel anybody, one
con none
ant nobody, no one
somebody *n* **1** *syn* see NOTABLE 1
ant nobody
2 *syn* see CELEBRITY 2
someday *adv syn* see YET 2
‖somegate *adv syn* see SOMEHOW
somehow *adv* in some way not yet known or specified < this thing must be done *somehow* >
syn ‖somegate, someway, somewise
rel anyhow, anyway, anywise
idiom by hook or by crook, in one way or another, in some such way, somehow or other (*or* another)
con nohow, noway, nowise
someone *pron syn* see SOMEBODY
someplace *adv syn* see SOMEWHERE 1
ant no place
something *adv syn* see SOMEWHAT 2
something *n syn* see ENTITY 1
sometime *adv syn* see YET 2
idiom one of these days
sometime *adj syn* see FORMER 2

sometimes *adv* at intervals < illustrated by beautiful and *sometimes* outstanding photographs >
syn at times, ‖betimes, ever and again, ever and anon, here and there, now and again, now and then, once and again, ‖otherwhile; *compare* OCCASIONALLY
rel intermittently, periodically, recurrently; frequently; consistently, constantly
idiom every now and then (*or* again), every once in a while, every so often, from time to time
con continually, continuously, unceasingly, uninterruptedly; endlessly, ever, interminably
someway *adv syn* see SOMEHOW
somewhat *adv* **1** *syn* see WELL 8
2 to some extent or in some degree < felt *somewhat* better but not fine >
syn fairly, kind of, moderately, more or less, pretty, rather, ratherish, some, something, sort of
rel adequately, bearably, tolerably; insignificantly, slightly
idiom rather more than less
somewhen *adv syn* see YET 2
somewhere *adv* **1** to, at, or in some unknown or unspecified location < lived on a farm *somewhere* in the Midwest >
syn someplace, ‖somewheres
rel somewhither; elsewhere, otherwhere
idiom someplace or other
con anyplace, anywhere, ‖anywheres; no place, ‖nowheres
ant nowhere
2 *syn* see NEARLY
‖somewheres *adv syn* see SOMEWHERE 1
ant ‖nowheres
somewise *adv syn* see SOMEHOW
somnifacient *adj syn* see SOPORIFIC 1
somniferous *adj syn* see SOPORIFIC 1
somnific *adj syn* see SOPORIFIC 1
somnolent *adj* **1** *syn* see SOPORIFIC 1
2 *syn* see SLEEPY 1
rel inactive, passive, supine
somnorific *adj syn* see SOPORIFIC 1
so much as *adv syn* see EVEN 4
son *n syn* see BOY 1
rel sonny; junior
sonance *n syn* see SOUND 1
sonant *adj syn* see VOCAL 1
song *n* **1** *syn* see POETRY 1
2 music or a piece of music intended for vocal expression < played and sang a *song* >
syn aria, descant, ditty, hymn, lay, lied; *compare* MELODY
rel lyric; piece
3 *syn* see CALL 1
song and dance *n syn* see SPIEL
songful *adj syn* see MELODIOUS 2
sonorant *adj syn* see RESONANT
sonorous *adj* **1** *syn* see RESONANT
2 *syn* see RHETORICAL
3 *syn* see NOISY
‖sonsy *adj* **1** *syn* see LUCKY
2 *syn* see GRACIOUS 1
3 *syn* see EASYGOING 3
soon *adv* **1** *syn* see PRESENTLY 1
rel forthwith, instantly, pronto, quickly
idiom in the near future
2 *syn* see FAST 2
3 *syn* see EARLY 1

‖**soon** *adj syn* see EARLY 2

sooner *adv syn* see BEFORE 3

sooner or later *adv syn* see YET 2

soothe *vb syn* see CALM
 rel comfort, console; hush, subdue
 con annoy, irritate, vex
 ant excite

‖**soother** *n syn* see CALM

soothsay *vb syn* see FORETELL

soothsayer *n syn* see PROPHET

sop *n* 1 *syn* see WEAKLING
 2 a conciliatory or propitiatory gift or advance <provided the $400 raise as a *sop*> <the new office was a *sop* to his wounded feelings>
 syn sugarplum
 rel douceur, gratuity; ‖baksheesh, ‖boodle, bribe, ‖palm oil
 idiom sop in the pan, sop to Cerberus

sop *vb* 1 *syn* see WET
 2 *syn* see SOAK 1
 3 *syn* see BRIBE

sophic *adj syn* see WISE 1

sophism *n syn* see FALLACY 2
 rel illogicality, irrationality; invalidity, unsoundness; claptrap

sophistic *adj syn* see ILLOGICAL

sophisticate *adj syn* see SOPHISTICATED 2

sophisticate *vb syn* see ADULTERATE

sophisticated *adj* 1 *syn* see COMPLEX 2
 ant unsophisticated
 2 being experienced in the ways of the world <a *sophisticated*, well-traveled man>
 syn blasé, disenchanted, disentranced, disillusioned, knowing, mondaine, sophisticate, worldly, worldly-wise, world-wise; *compare* COSMOPOLITAN 1
 rel adult, mature; experienced, practiced, schooled, seasoned; salty, uncelestial; couth, well-bred; smooth, suave, svelte, urbane; bored, jaded, world-weary; brittle; cynical, skeptical
 con artless, gee-whiz, ingenuous, natural; green, inexperienced, unseasoned, virginal; unworldly
 ant naive, unsophisticated

sophistry *n syn* see FALLACY 2
 rel ambiguity, tergiversation

soporiferous *adj syn* see SOPORIFIC 1

soporific *adj* 1 tending to induce sleep <a *soporific* drug> <*soporific* prose>
 syn hypnotic, narcotic, opiate, sleepy, slumberous, somnifacient, somniferous, somnific, somnolent, somnorific, soporiferous, soporifical
 rel calming, quietening, sedative, tranquilizing; anesthetic, deadening, numbing
 con arousing, waking; invigorating, stimulating
 2 *syn* see SLEEPY 1

soporifical *adj syn* see SOPORIFIC 1

sopping *adj syn* see WET 1

soppy *adj* 1 *syn* see WET 1
 ‖2 *syn* see SENTIMENTAL

sorcerer *n syn* see MAGICIAN 1

sorceress *n syn* see WITCH 1

sorcerous *adj syn* see MAGIC

sorcery *n syn* see MAGIC 1

sordid *adj* 1 *syn* see DIRTY 1
 2 *syn* see SLATTERNLY
 3 *syn* see BASE 3
 rel foul, nasty, seamy, sodden

sore *adj syn* see PAINFUL 1

sorehead *n syn* see GROUCH

sorely *adv syn* see HARD 6

sorrow *n* distress of mind <felt great *sorrow* at the loss of her friend>
 syn affliction, anguish, care, ‖dole, grief, heartache, heartbreak, regret, rue, woe
 rel mournfulness, sadness, sorrowfulness, unhappiness; grieving, lamentation, mourning, sorrowing; dejection, depression, melancholy; agony, distress, dolor, misery, suffering, wretchedness
 con cheerfulness, gaiety, gladness, happiness, joyfulness; ecstasy
 ant joy

sorrow *vb syn* see GRIEVE 2
 rel groan, moan, sob
 idiom break one's heart over, eat one's heart out
 ant rejoice

sorrowful *adj* 1 *syn* see WOEFUL 1
 rel sorrow-laden, sorrow-stricken, sorrow-struck
 idiom full of (*or* filled with) sorrow
 con sorrowless
 ant joyful
 2 *syn* see MELANCHOLY 2
 ant gay

sorry *adj* 1 *syn* see SAD 1
 rel bad, regretful, remorseful; miserable, wretched
 ant glad
 2 *syn* see REMORSEFUL
 3 *syn* see CONTEMPTIBLE
 rel inadequate, paltry, poor, trifling; cheesy, scruffy, shoddy; disgraceful

sort *n* 1 *syn* see TYPE
 2 *syn* see GROUP 3

sort *vb* 1 *syn* see ASSORT
 2 to analyze and assort (as individuals or things) to obtain those desired or required <he knew he must *sort* out facts from fancy>
 syn comb, separate, sift, winnow; *compare* SCREEN 5
 rel riddle, screen; choose, cull, pick, select
 con consolidate, join, lump, merge; aggregate, amalgamate, blend, fuse, mix; unify

sort of *adv syn* see SOMEWHAT 2

SOS *n syn* see ALARM 1

soshed *adj syn* see INTOXICATED 1

so–so *adv syn* see ENOUGH 2

so–so *adj syn* see MEDIUM

sot *n syn* see DRUNKARD

‖**sot** *adj syn* see OBSTINATE

so that *conj syn* see SO

sotto voce *adv* in an inaudible or barely audible voice <made a snide remark to her *sotto voce*>
 syn faintly, mutedly, weakly
 rel low, quietly, softly; muffledly; mutteringly; aside, privately
 idiom below one's breath, between one's teeth, in an aside, in an undertone, in a whisper, out of earshot, under one's breath
 con aloud, out, out loud

---

syn synonym(s)   *rel* related word(s)
ant antonym(s)   *con* contrasted word(s)
idiom idiomatic equivalent(s)
‖ use limited; if in doubt, see a dictionary

sough *vb* **1** *syn* see SIGH 2
2 *syn* see SIGH 1

soul *n* **1** an animating essence or principle held to be inseparably associated with life or living beings < philosophers who teach that life is a manifestation of *soul* >
syn anima, animus, élan vital, pneuma, psyche, spirit, vital force
rel life, vitality
idiom breath of life
2 the immortal part of man believed to have permanent individual existence < into God's hands I commit my *soul* >
syn spirit
rel life; noumenon
idiom one's immortal soul
con flesh
ant body
3 *syn* see HEART 1
rel character, personality, psyche; conscience; spirit
idiom heart of hearts, heart's core, one's inmost soul (*or* mind), one's secret (*or* inner) self, (the) secret recesses of the heart
4 *syn* see ESSENCE 2
5 *syn* see HUMAN

soul–searching *n* *syn* see INTROSPECTION

soul–sick *adj* *syn* see DOWNCAST

sound *adj* **1** *syn* see HEALTHY 1
rel intact, unimpaired; perfect
idiom sound as a bell (*or* whistle), sound of mind and body
con impaired; unfit
ant unsound
2 *syn* see WHOLE 1
3 *syn* see STABLE 4
ant unsound
4 *syn* see VALID
rel errorless, faultless, flawless, impeccable; accurate, correct, exact, precise; rational, reasonable; well-founded, well-grounded
con questionable, shaky; invalid
ant unsound
5 *syn* see ORTHODOX 1
6 *syn* see RATIONAL
rel right-minded, sober, sober-minded, sound-minded
ant unsound

sound *n* **1** a sensation or effect resulting from stimulation of the auditory receptors < the *sound* of thunder >
syn noise, sonance
rel vibration; resonance; sonancy; reverberation
con quiet, soundlessness
ant silence
2 *syn* see EARSHOT

sound *vb* **1** *syn* see SEEM
2 *syn* see DECLARE 1

sound *vb* to measure the depth of (as a body of water) typically with a weighted line < *sounding* the distance to the bottom >
syn fathom, plumb, plumb-line
idiom ‖cast (*or* sling) the lead, make a sounding, take soundings

sound (out) *vb* *syn* see PROBE 2

soundless *adj* *syn* see BOTTOMLESS 2
ant soundable

soundless *adj* *syn* see STILL 3

soundlessness *n* *syn* see SILENCE 1

soundness *n* **1** *syn* see HEALTH
ant unsoundness
2 *syn* see STABILITY
3 *syn* see WIT 2
rel level-headedness, sensibleness
idiom sound mind, soundness of mind
ant unsoundness

sound off *vb* *syn* see SPEAK UP

soup *n* *syn* see PREDICAMENT

soupçon *n* *syn* see HINT 2

soupy *adj* *syn* see SENTIMENTAL

sour *adj* **1** causing or characterized by the one of the basic taste sensations produced chiefly by acids < *sour* pickles >
syn acerb, acerbic, acetose, acid, acidulous, dry, tart
rel keen, sharp, tangy; ‖blinky, sourish; fermented, soured, turned; acrid, bitter, vinegary
ant sweet
2 *syn* see BAD 8

source *n* the point at which something begins its course or existence < the *source* of his wisdom was long practical experience >
syn derivation, fount, fountain, fountainhead, inception, mother, origin, provenance, provenience, root, rootage, rootstock, spring, well, wellhead, wellspring, whence
rel birthplace; beginning, commencement, dawn, dawning, onset, opening, start, starting; authorship, origination, rise, rising; antecedent, cause, determinant; parent, paternity
con end, ending, terminus
ant termination; outcome

sourpuss *n* *syn* see GROUCH
rel killjoy

souse *vb* **1** *syn* see DIP 1
2 *syn* see WET
3 *syn* see SOAK 1

souse *n* *syn* see BINGE 1

soused *adj* *syn* see WET 1

souvenir *n* *syn* see REMEMBRANCE 3
idiom token of remembrance

sovereign *adj* **1** *syn* see FREE 1
rel self-determined, self-governed
2 *syn* see DOMINANT 1
rel commanding, directing, guiding; highest, loftiest
3 *syn* see EXCELLENT
4 *syn* see KINGLY

sovereignty *n* *syn* see SUPREMACY

sow *vb* **1** *syn* see PLANT 1
2 *syn* see STREW 1
rel fling, toss; drill

‖sowf *vb* *syn* see HUM

sozzled *adj* *syn* see INTOXICATED 1

spa *n* **1** a locality featuring mineral springs or water cures < hoped a week at a *spa* would help his arthritis >
syn baths, ‖hydro, springs, watering place, wells
rel waters
idiom health spa
2 *syn* see RESORT 3

space *n* **1** *syn* see WHILE 1
rel lapse; interval, term; duration
2 *syn* see EXPANSE
rel room, roomage; spaciousness

spaced–out *adj* *syn* see DRUGGED

spacious *adj* larger in extent or capacity than the average <a mansion with *spacious* rooms and gardens>
syn ample, capacious, commodious, roomy, wide
rel big, generous, great, large, spacy; enormous, immense, vast; expansive, extended, extensive; boundless, spaceless
con circumscribed, confined, cramped, limited, narrow, restricted; small, tiny
ant strait

spade *vb* 1 *syn* see DIG 2
2 *syn* see DIG 1

span *n* *syn* see TERM 2
rel interval; space

spang *adv* *syn* see JUST 1

spangle *vb* 1 to adorn with small brilliant objects <a tutu *spangled* with sequins>
syn bespangle, glitter
rel adorn, decorate, ornament, trim
2 *syn* see FLASH 1

spang-new *adj* *syn* see BRAND-NEW

spaniel *n* *syn* see SYCOPHANT

spank *vb* *syn* see SLAP 1

spank *n* *syn* see CUFF
idiom a sound spank

spanking *adv* *syn* see VERY 1

spanking-new *adj* *syn* see BRAND-NEW

span-new *adj* *syn* see BRAND-NEW

spare *vb* 1 *syn* see EXEMPT
2 *syn* see SAVE 4
3 to refrain from the free use or consumption of <don't *spare* the syrup on my pancakes>
syn scant, short, skimp, ‖skinch, stint; *compare* SCRIMP
rel pinch
4 *syn* see SCRIMP

spare *adj* 1 *syn* see SUPERFLUOUS
idiom enough and to spare, more than enough
2 *syn* see LEAN
ant corpulent
3 *syn* see MEAGER 2
ant profuse

sparing *adj* careful in the use of money, goods, or resources <was *sparing* in his expenditures>
syn canny, chary, economical, frugal, provident, saving, Scotch, stewardly, thrifty, unwasteful, wary; *compare* STINGY
rel parsimonious, ‖scant, tight, tightfisted, ungiving
con exuberant, liberal, prodigal, profuse
ant lavish, unsparing

spark *n* *syn* see SEED 2

spark *n* *syn* see SUITOR 2

spark *vb* *syn* see ADDRESS 8

sparker *n* *syn* see SUITOR 2

sparkish *adj* *syn* see DAPPER

sparkle *vb* *syn* see FLASH 1

sparkle *n* *syn* see FLASH 1

sparse *adj* *syn* see MEAGER 2
rel dispersed, scattered; infrequent, occasional, sporadic; rare, scarce, uncommon
con close, compact, thick

‖spartle *vb* *syn* see SCRAMBLE 1

spasmodic *adj* *syn* see FITFUL

rel spurtive
con continual, continuous, uninterrupted

spat *n* 1 *syn* see QUARREL
‖2 *syn* see CUFF

spat *vb* *syn* see QUARREL

spate *n* 1 *syn* see FLOOD 2
rel progression, series, succession; rain, river, spurt
2 *syn* see FLOW

spatter *vb* 1 *syn* see SPLASH
rel sparge
2 *syn* see SPOT 1
3 *syn* see MALIGN
4 *syn* see SPUTTER 2

spatter *n* *syn* see FEW

spattering *n* *syn* see FEW

spawn *vb* *syn* see GENERATE 1

spawning *adj* *syn* see FERTILE

speak *vb* 1 to articulate words in order to express thoughts <always *speak* clearly>
syn talk, utter, verbalize, vocalize, voice
rel drawl, gasp, mouth, mumble, murmur, mutter, shout, splutter, spout, whisper; descant, dilate (on *or* upon), expatiate, perorate; converse, discourse; allege, assert, aver, convey, declare, tell
idiom break silence, give voice (*or* tongue *or* utterance) to, let fall, make public (*or* known), open one's mouth (*or* lips), put in (*or* into) words, say one's say, speak one's piece
con gabble, gibber, jabber; maunder, mumble, mutter; mispronounce, misspeak
2 *syn* see TALK 2
3 to have oral command of (a language) <he *speaks* fluent German>
syn converse (in), parley, talk, use
idiom be at ease in
con falter, hesitate, stumble

speaker *n* *syn* see SPOKESMAN

speaking *n* *syn* see SPEECH 1

speak out *vb* *syn* see SPEAK UP

speak up *vb* to speak strongly, boldly, or vigorously <we'll never know how you feel if you don't *speak up*>
syn sound off, speak out
idiom come out with it, have one's say, let one's voice be heard, make oneself heard, speak one's mind, stand up and be counted

spear *vb* *syn* see IMPALE
rel stick; bore, drill, penetrate, pierce; gouge, ream

special *adj* 1 of or relating to one thing or class <*special* soap for infants>
syn especial, individual, particular, specific
rel characteristic, distinctive, peculiar; exceptional, occasional, rare, uncommon; unique
con common, familiar, ordinary; customary, habitual, usual
2 *syn* see EXPRESS 2
rel defined, determinate; designated, earmarked

special *adv* *syn* see ESPECIALLY 1

specialize *vb* *syn* see ITEMIZE 1

specially *adv* 1 *syn* see ESPECIALLY 1
2 *syn* see EXPRESSLY 2

species *n* *syn* see TYPE

specific *adj* 1 *syn* see SPECIAL 1
rel limited, reserved, restricted, specialized

---

syn synonym(s)   *rel* related word(s)
ant antonym(s)   *con* contrasted word(s)
idiom idiomatic equivalent(s)
‖ use limited; if in doubt, see a dictionary

con general, generic
ant nonspecific, unspecific
2 *syn* see EXPLICIT
con ambiguous, cloudy, indefinite, uncertain, unexplicit, unspecified, vague
ant nonspecific, unspecific
3 *syn* see EXPRESS 2
ant nonspecific, unspecific
specifically *adv* **1** *syn* see EXPRESSLY 2
2 *syn* see ESPECIALLY 1
3 *syn* see EXPRESSLY 1
specificate *vb syn* see SPECIFY 3
specificize *vb syn* see SPECIFY 3
specify *vb* **1** *syn* see MENTION
2 *syn* see ITEMIZE 1
3 to make something (as a condition or requirement) specific < his will *specified* how the money would be divided >
syn detail, particularize, specificate, specificize, stipulate; *compare* ITEMIZE 1
rel determine, establish, fix, settle; condition, limit, set; pin (down); enumerate, list; precise
specimen *n syn* see INSTANCE
rel sort, species, type, variety
specious *adj syn* see FALSE 1
rel apparent, seeming; colorable, plausible; beguiling; illogical, spurious; empty, hollow, idle, nugatory, vain
ant valid
speciousness *n syn* see FALLACY 2
rel speciosity
ant validity
speck *n* **1** *syn* see POINT 11
rel pinpoint; tick
2 *syn* see PARTICLE
speck *vb syn* see SPECKLE 1
speckle *vb* **1** to produce on or mark with small spots, speckles, or blemishes < a *speckled* egg >
syn bespeckle, dot, freckle, pepper, speck, sprinkle, stipple; *compare* SPOT 1
rel dapple, flake, fleck
2 *syn* see SPOT 2
spectacle *n syn* see EXHIBITION 1
spectacled *adj syn* see BESPECTACLED
spectacular *adj syn* see MARVELOUS 1
rel eye-popping, sensational, striking, thrilling; dramatic, histrionic, stagy, theatrical
ant unspectacular
spectator *n* one who sees or looks upon something < sports *spectators* >
syn beholder, by-sitter, bystander, eyewitness, looker-on, observer, onlooker, stander-by, viewer, watcher, witness
rel gazer; perceiver; seer
specter *n syn* see APPARITION
spectral *adj syn* see GHASTLY 2
rel phantom, phantomlike, shadowlike; disembodied, unearthly; spooky
spectrum *n syn* see APPARITION
speculate *vb syn* see THINK 5
rel excogitate, review, study, weigh
idiom ‖beat one's brains, turn over in one's mind, ‖use the gray matter
speculation *n* **1** *syn* see THOUGHT 1
rel excogitation, review, studying, weighing
2 *syn* see THEORY 2
speculative *adj* **1** *syn* see THEORETICAL 1
2 *syn* see THOUGHTFUL 1
rel musing, ruminating; curious, inquiring, questioning

ant unspeculative
speech *n* **1** communication, expression, or interchange of thoughts in spoken words < considered *speech* as a means of reproducing for one's listeners the images in one's mind >
syn discourse, speaking, talk, utterance, verbalization; *compare* VOCALIZATION
rel articulation, uttering, vocalization, vocalizing, voice, voicing; expressing, expression; language
idiom oral communication, vocal expression
2 a usually formal discourse delivered to an audience < a televised *speech* to the nation >
syn address, allocution, lecture, talk
rel debate, parlance, parley; declamation, harangue, oration, speechification
3 *syn* see LANGUAGE 1
speechcraft *n syn* see ORATORY
speechless *adj* **1** *syn* see DUMB 1
rel aphonic
2 *syn* see SILENT 2
3 *syn* see SILENT 3
speed *n* **1** *syn* see HASTE 1
rel alacrity, legerity; headway
con dilatoriness, tardiness
2 rate of movement, performance, or occurrence < ran through the exercise at a high *speed* >
syn ‖bat, celerity, gait, pace, quickness, rapidity, rapidness, swiftness, velocity; *compare* TEMPO
rel fastness, fleetness; clip, hickory
speed *vb* **1** *syn* see HURRY 2
idiom make haste
ant slow (up *or* down)
2 *syn* see COURSE
3 to cause to move fast or faster < *sped* our craft forward >
syn accelerate, hasten, hurry, quicken, shake up, step up, swiften
rel advance, aid, ease, encourage, expedite, facilitate, forward, further, help (along), smooth; cheer (on), drive (on), goad (on), spur (on); burn (up)
idiom ‖get the lead out
con hamper, restrain, retard; check, stay; delay, postpone, put off
ant slow (up *or* down)
speedily *adv syn* see FAST 2
idiom against the clock, hell-bent for leather, like a bat out of hell, like all forty, ‖like all get-out, on the double, to beat the band
con deliberately, languidly, leisurely; lazily, lethargically, sluggishly; crawlingly, creepingly
ant slow, slowly
speediness *n syn* see HASTE 1
ant slowness
speedy *adj syn* see FAST 3
rel agile, brisk, nimble; prompt, ready
idiom fast as greased lightning, speedy as an arrow
ant dilatory; slow
speerings *n pl syn* see NEWS
‖**spelder** *vb syn* see SPRAWL 1
spell *n* a spoken word or set of words believed to have magic power < cause death by muttering *spells* over her >
syn charm, conjuration, ‖devil-devil, incantation, rune

rel bewitching, enchanting, hexing

spell *vb syn see* BEWITCH 1

spell *vb syn see* MEAN 2

spell *vb* **1** *syn see* RELIEVE 3
2 *syn see* REST 3

spell *n* **1** a limited period or amount of activity < each *spell* of work was followed by a brief rest >
syn bout, go, shift, stint, time, tour, trick, turn
rel streak; ||patch, period; stretch; relay
2 *syn see* WHILE 1
3 *syn see* ATTACK 3

spellbind *vb syn see* ENTHRALL 2

spell out *vb syn see* EXPLAIN 1

spend *vb* **1** to distribute or consume in payment or expenditure < *spent* fifty dollars for that dress >
syn disburse, expend, fork (out), give, lay out, outlay, pay, shell out
rel blow, drop, hand out; contribute; consume, dissipate, lavish, squander, throw away, waste
ant save
2 *syn see* GO 4
3 to cause or permit to elapse < *spent* the summer at the beach >
syn pass, while (away)

spender *n syn see* SPENDTHRIFT
ant saver

spending money *n syn see* POCKET MONEY

spendthrift *n* one who dissipates his resources foolishly and wastefully < a *spendthrift* who lost his estate through gambling >
syn high roller, prodigal, profligate, scattergood, spender, squanderer, unthrift, waster, wastethrift, wastrel
con hoarder, miser, saver

spent *adj syn see* EFFETE 2

spew *vb* **1** *syn see* VOMIT
2 *syn see* ERUPT 1
rel flood, gush

sphere *n* **1** *syn see* BALL
2 *syn see* FIELD
rel circle, jurisdiction, realm

sphere *vb syn see* BALL

spice *n* **1** *syn see* HINT 2
2 *syn see* FRAGRANCE

spick-and-span *adj* **1** *syn see* BRAND-NEW
2 *syn see* NEAT 2

spicy *adj* **1** *syn see* SWEET 2
2 *syn see* PUNGENT
rel fiery, gingery, high-spirited, spirited, zestful
3 *syn see* RISQUÉ
rel sophisticated; piquant

spider *n syn see* FRYING PAN

spiel *n* voluble, glib, or extravagant talk often intended to impress, persuade, or deceive < gave her a long sales *spiel* >
syn ||line, pitch, song and dance
rel demagoguery; dramatics, pyrotechnics, sensationalism

||spieler *n syn see* SWINDLER

spiff *vb syn see* DRESS UP 1

---

spiffy *adj syn see* DAPPER

||spiflicated *adj syn see* INTOXICATED 1

spigot *n syn see* FAUCET

spike *vb syn see* IMPALE

spill *vb* **1** to cause or allow (something) to fall, flow, or run out and be lost or wasted < accidentally dropped the cup and *spilled* his tea >
syn slop, squab
rel dribble, drip, drop; spatter, splash, spray
2 *syn see* OVERFLOW 2
3 *syn see* REVEAL 1

spilth *n syn see* REFUSE

spin *vb* **1** to turn or cause to turn rapidly < pinwheels *spinning* in the wind >
syn gyrate, gyre, ||pirl, pirouette, ||purl, twirl, whirl, whirligig; *compare* TURN 1
rel revolve, rotate, wheel; swirl; oscillate, pendulate, vibrate
idiom spin like a top
2 to feel as if revolving < her head was *spinning* with figures >
syn reel, swim, turn, whirl
rel dizzy, giddy; fluster, mix up, muddle
idiom be in a whirl

spin (out) *vb syn see* EXTEND 3

spin *n syn see* DRIVE 1

spinal column *n syn see* SPINE

spindling *adj syn see* GANGLING

spindly *adj syn see* GANGLING

spine *n* the articulated column of bones that is the central and axial feature of a vertebrate skeleton < fractured his *spine* >
syn back, backbone, rachis, spinal column, vertebrae, vertebral column
rel spinal cord

spineless *adj syn see* WEAK 4
rel weak-kneed, weak-willed
idiom as spineless as an amoeba
con self-willed, strong-willed

spin-off *n syn see* OUTGROWTH 2

spinster *n* a woman who is past the common age for marrying or who seems unlikely ever to marry < a gentle *spinster,* happy in her solitary life >
syn maiden lady, old maid, spinstress, ||tabby

spinstress *n syn see* SPINSTER

spiny *adj syn see* THORNY

spiral *vb syn see* WIND 2

spiring *adj syn see* LOFTY 6

spirit *n* **1** *syn see* SOUL 1
2 *syn see* APPARITION
3 *syn see* SOUL 2
4 *syn see* TEMPER 1
5 a lively or brisk quality in a person or his actions < a man of great *spirit* and courage >
syn animation, brio, dash, élan, esprit, gimp, life, oomph, verve, vim, zing; *compare* VIGOR 2
rel ardor, briskness, enthusiasm, liveliness; drive, get-up-and-go, ginger, go, pep, snap, starch, vigor, vitality, zip; character, force, substance
6 *syn see* COURAGE
rel ardor, fervor, passion, zeal; energy, force, might, power, strength
7 *often* spirits *pl syn see* LIQUOR

spirit (away) *vb syn see* KIDNAP

spirit (up) *vb syn see* ELATE

spirited *adj* **1** *syn see* LIVELY 1

rel sharp; fiery, gingery, peppery
idiom full of life (*or* go)
ant spiritless
2 having or manifesting a high degree of vitality, spirit, and daring <the lawyer gave a *spirited* defense of his client>
syn beany, fiery, gingery, high-hearted, high-spirited, mettlesome, peppery, spunky
rel game, gritty, resolute; audacious, bold, brave, courageous, dauntless, fearless, intrepid, nervy, plucky, valiant; avid, eager, hot, keen; ardent, enthusiastic, fervent, hot, passionate, peppy, zealous
con unenthusiastic; flabby, languid, limp; boneless, spineless
ant spiritless
spiritless *adj* **1** *syn* see DEAD 1
2 *syn* see DOWNCAST
idiom down in the dumps
3 *syn* see LANGUID
rel tame; broken, subdued, submissive
ant spirited
spiritual *adj* **1** *syn* see IMMATERIAL 1
rel supernatural, supramundane
ant physical
2 *syn* see SACRED 2
3 *syn* see ECCLESIASTICAL
4 appealing to, coming from, or related to the higher emotions or to the aesthetic senses <man's *spiritual* and intellectual life as opposed to his animal instincts>
syn numinous
rel cerebral, intellectual, mental; elevated, high, high-minded, lofty; saintly
con low, lower; base
ant animal
spirituous *adj* containing a considerable amount of alcohol <*spirituous* liquors>
syn alcoholic, ardent, hard, strong
rel spiked; inebriating, intoxicating, intoxicative; heady
con nonalcoholic, nonintoxicating, soft
‖**spiry** *adj syn* see LIVELY 1
‖**spit** *vb syn* see IMPALE
spit *n* **1** *syn* see SALIVA
2 *syn* see IMAGE 1
rel counterpart; look-alike; twin
spit *vb* **1** *syn* see SPUTTER 1
2 *syn* see SPUTTER 2
spite *n syn* see MALICE
rel rancor; revenge, revengefulness, vengeance, vengefulness, vindictiveness
con sympathy; affection, love, tenderness
spiteful *adj syn* see MALICIOUS
rel antagonistic, hostile; revengeful, vengeful, vindictive
con charitable; sympathetic; affectionate, loving
ant spiteless
spitefulness *n syn* see MALICE
spitish *adj syn* see MALICIOUS
spitting image *n syn* see IMAGE 1
rel mirror image
spittle *n syn* see SALIVA
spit up *vb syn* see VOMIT
‖**spiv** *n* **1** *syn* see PARASITE
2 *syn* see SLACKER
splash *vb* to dash a liquid or semiliquid substance upon or against <*splashed* water onto her face>
syn douse, plash, slop, slosh, spatter, splatter, splosh, splurge, spurtle, swash
rel dash, throw; spray; sprinkle; ‖sprent, squirt; drench, drown, soak, sop, wet

splashy *adj syn* see SHOWY
splathering *adj syn* see CLUMSY 1
splatter *vb syn* see SPLASH
splay *adj syn* see CLUMSY 1
spleen *n syn* see MALICE
rel revenge, revengefulness, vindictiveness; wrath
splendid *adj* **1** *syn* see GRAND 2
rel baroque, flamboyant
2 extraordinarily or transcendently impressive <a *splendid* new city>
syn glorious, gorgeous, magnificent, proud, resplendent, splendiferous, splendorous, sublime, superb
rel eminent, illustrious; grand, impressive, lavish, luxurious, royal, sumptuous; divine, exquisite, lovely; incomparable, matchless, peerless, superlative, supreme, unparalleled, unsurpassed; surpassing, transcendent
con common, ordinary, run-of-the-mill
ant unimpressive
splendiferous *adj syn* see SPLENDID 2
rel dazzling, marvelous; smashing, walloping; rattling, ripping, screaming, terrific
splendorous *adj syn* see SPLENDID 2
splice *vb syn* see MARRY 2
splinter *vb syn* see SHATTER 1
splinterize *vb syn* see SHATTER 1
split *vb* **1** *syn* see CUT 5
rel crack, rive
2 *syn* see TEAR 1
‖**3** *syn* see BETRAY 2
split (up) *vb syn* see SEPARATE 1
split *n* **1** *syn* see CRACK 3
2 *syn* see SCHISM 3
3 *syn* see BREACH 3
rel alienating, estranging
split second *n syn* see INSTANT 1
splitter *vb syn* see SHATTER 1
split–up *n syn* see SEPARATION 1
‖**splodge** *vb syn* see SPLOTCH
splosh *vb syn* see SPLASH
splotch *vb* to mark or spot with irregular patches especially of contrasting color <a pallid face *splotched* with red>
syn blotch, mottle, ‖splodge
rel blot, stain; dapple, fleck, marble, motley, variegate; bespot, spot; harlequin
‖**splunge** *vb syn* see PLUNGE 2
splurge *n syn* see SPREE 1
rel extravagance; splash
splurge *vb syn* see SPLASH
splurt *vb syn* see SQUIRT
splutter *vb* **1** *syn* see SPUTTER 2
2 *syn* see SPUTTER 1
spoil *n* something taken from another by force or craft <gold, jewels, and paintings are often *spoils* of war>
syn boodle, booty, loot, plunder, plunderage, prize, ‖spreaghery, ‖spulzie, swag
rel acquisition, grab, haul, take; pickings, stealings; pillage, spoliation
spoil *vb* **1** *syn* see RAVAGE
2 *syn* see INJURE 1
rel ‖snafu; ruin, wreck; demolish, destroy
3 *syn* see RAPE
4 *syn* see BABY
rel accommodate, favor, oblige
idiom spoil (one) rotten, spoil to death
5 *syn* see DECAY
spoiled *adj* **1** *syn* see DAMAGED
ant unspoiled

2 *syn* see BAD 5
  rel off, tainted; putrefying, rotting
  ant unspoiled
spoiler *n syn* see MARAUDER
spoken *adj* 1 *syn* see ORAL 2
  ant written
  2 *syn* see VOCAL 1
  ant unspoken
spokesman *n* one who speaks as a representative of another <selected as *spokesman* for the party's views>
  syn mouth, mouthpiece, speaker, spokesperson, spokeswoman
  rel delegate, deputy, representative; champion, protagonist; prophet
spokesperson *n syn* see SPOKESMAN
spokeswoman *n syn* see SPOKESMAN
spoliate *vb syn* see RAVAGE
  rel raid; maraud; gut, ravish, sweep
spoliator *n syn* see MARAUDER
sponge *n* 1 *syn* see DRUNKARD
  2 *syn* see PARASITE
sponger *n syn* see PARASITE
spongy *adj syn* see SOFT 6
  idiom as soft as a sponge
sponsor *n* one that accepts responsibility for another person or thing <the major *sponsor* of this project is the government>
  syn angel, backer, backer-up, guarantor, patron, surety
  rel advocate, champion, mainstay, supporter, upholder; preferrer, promoter; benefactor, Maecenas
sponsorship *n syn* see BACKING
spontaneity *n syn* see UNCONSTRAINT
  rel extemporaneousness, offhandedness, unpremeditatedness
spontaneous *adj* acting or activated without apparent thought or deliberation <a *spontaneous* burst of applause>
  syn automatic, impulsive, instinctive, involuntary, unmeditated, unpremeditated, unprompted, will-less
  rel unconstrained, unforced; unreasoned, unstudied; extemporaneous, extempore, impromptu, improvised, offhand; natural, simple, unsophisticated
  con deliberate, intended, intentional, planned, predetermined, preplanned, studied, thought-out, voluntary, willed, willful; forced, prompted; conventional, formal, stylized
  ant premeditated
spontoon *n syn* see CUDGEL
spoof *vb syn* see DUPE
spoof *n syn* see IMPOSTURE
spook *n* ‖1 *syn* see APPARITION
  ‖2 *syn* see ECCENTRIC
  3 *syn* see SPY
‖**spook** *vb* 1 *syn* see FRIGHTEN
  2 *syn* see GHOSTWRITE
spooky *adj* 1 *syn* see WEIRD 1
  rel spookish; ominous
  2 *syn* see NERVOUS
‖**spoon** *n syn* see DUNCE
spoony *adj syn* see SIMPLE 3
spoony (over *or* on) *adj syn* see ENAMORED 1

---

syn synonym(s)   *rel* related word(s)
ant antonym(s)   *con* contrasted word(s)
idiom idiomatic equivalent(s)
‖ use limited; if in doubt, see a dictionary

spoor *n syn* see FOOTPRINT
sporadic *adj* 1 *syn* see FITFUL
  ant regular
  2 *syn* see INFREQUENT
  rel separate, single
  ant frequent
sporadically *adv syn* see OCCASIONALLY
  ant regularly
sport *vb syn* see PLAY 1
sport *n* 1 *syn* see PLAY 1
  2 **sports** *pl syn* see ATHLETICS
  3 *syn* see FUN 1
  rel jollification; antics, high jinks, horseplay
  4 *syn* see LAUGHINGSTOCK
  5 *syn* see CHANGE 2
sporting girl *n syn* see PROSTITUTE
sporting house *n syn* see BROTHEL
sportive *adj syn* see PLAYFUL 1
sportiveness *n syn* see MISCHIEVOUSNESS
sportsmanlike *adj syn* see FAIR 5
  ant unsporting, unsportsmanlike
sportsmanly *adj syn* see FAIR 5
  ant unsporting, unsportsmanlike
sporty *adj syn* see WILD 7
spot *n* 1 *syn* see STIGMA
  2 *syn* see DRAM
  3 *syn* see PARTICLE
  4 *syn* see PLACE 1
  rel scene; section, sector
  5 *syn* see JOB 2
  idiom job slot
  6 *syn* see PREDICAMENT
spot *vb* 1 to mark or stain (something) with spots <a white dress *spotted* with red mud>
  syn bespatter, bespot, spatter; *compare* SPECKLE 1
  rel blot, blotch, mottle; fleck, marble, streak, stripe; dot, pepper, speck, speckle, sprinkle, stipple; splash; dirty, soil, stain
  2 to form or appear as spots on <a bleak landscape *spotted* with cottages>
  syn dot, pimple, speckle, sprinkle, stud
  rel intersperse
  3 *syn* see IDENTIFY
  rel ascertain; see
  4 *syn* see FIND 1
spot *adj syn* see RANDOM
spotless *adj* 1 *syn* see CLEAN 1
  rel hygienic, sanitary
  2 *syn* see CHASTE
  ant spotted
spotty *adj* 1 lacking uniformity <*spotty* illumination>
  syn irregular, patchy, uneven
  rel unequal; flickering, fluctuating
  con equal, even, regular, uniform
  2 *syn* see FITFUL
spousal *n syn* see WEDDING
spousal *adj syn* see MATRIMONIAL
spouse *n* a marriage partner <consulted with her *spouse* before buying the dress>
  syn consort, mate
spouseless *adj syn* see SINGLE 1
  con espoused
‖**spout** *vb syn* see PAWN
spout *n syn* see WATERFALL
spraddle *vb syn* see SPRAWL 1
sprain *vb* to injure (a joint) by a sudden twisting motion that stretches and lacerates the ligaments <*sprained* her ankle>
  syn ‖rick, turn, twist, wrench

rel pull, strain, stretch; tear; dislocate, throw; break, fracture

sprangle *vb syn* see SPRAWL 2

sprat *n syn* see TWERP

||**sprauchle** *vb syn* see SCRAMBLE 1

sprawl *vb* 1 to lie or sit with arms and legs stretched out carelessly and awkwardly < the dog lay *sprawled* out on the sofa > *syn* drape, ||scamble, ||spelder, spraddle, spread-eagle
rel loll, lounge; slouch, slump
2 to grow, develop, or spread irregularly and without apparent design or plan < the city *sprawls* down the whole coast > *syn* ramble, scramble, sprangle, spread= eagle, straddle, straggle
rel extend, stretch; spread

spread *vb* 1 to extend or cause to extend over a considerable area or space < they *spread* the news far and wide > < clouds *spread* over the sky > *syn* circulate, diffuse, disperse, dissemi= nate, distribute, propagate, radiate, strew; *compare* STREW 1
rel deal, dispense; broadcast, communi= cate, pass (on), transmit; dissipate, scatter, sow; peddle, push, retail
idiom spread abroad (*or* far and wide)
con hold (in); contain; compress
2 *syn* see OPEN 4
con fold; close
3 *syn* see SET 5

spread *n* 1 *syn* see EXPANSION 2
rel diffusion; profusion; stretch, sweep
2 *syn* see EXPANSE
3 *syn* see DINNER
4 *syn* see BEDSPREAD

spread–eagle *vb* 1 *syn* see SPRAWL 1
2 *syn* see SPRAWL 2

||**spreaghery** *n syn* see SPOIL

spree *n* 1 an unrestrained indulgence in or outburst of an activity < a shopping *spree* >
syn binge, fling, orgy, rampage, splurge
2 *syn* see BINGE 1

spree *vb syn* see REVEL 1

sprightful *adj syn* see LIVELY 1

sprightly *adj* 1 *syn* see LIVELY 1
rel perky; breezy
2 *syn* see ANTIC 2
rel sportive; coltish, frisky
3 *syn* see AGILE
4 *syn* see CLEVER 5
rel pungent, sharp; keen-witted, quick= witted

spring *vb* 1 to have something as a source < the primitive cultures from which civili= zation *springs* >
syn arise, birth, come (from), derive (from), emanate, flow, head, issue, origi= nate, proceed, rise, stem, upspring; *com= pare* BEGIN 2
rel appear, emerge, come out, loom; ar= rive, come; begin, commence, hatch, start
2 *syn* see SKIP 1
3 *syn* see JUMP 1
4 *syn* see START 1
||5 *syn* see FREE

spring *n* 1 *usu* **springs** *pl syn* see SPA 1
2 *syn* see SOURCE
3 *syn* see YOUTH 1
ant autumn
4 *syn* see MOTIVE 1

rel excitant, impetus, incitement, stimu= lant, stimulus
5 the season between winter and summer < planting flowers in the *spring* >
syn budtime, springtide, springtime
rel ||blackberry winter
idiom prime of the year
con autumn, fall

spring *adj syn* see VERNAL

springe *n syn* see PITFALL

springlike *adj syn* see VERNAL

springtide *n* 1 *syn* see SPRING 5
2 *syn* see YOUTH 1
ant autumn

springtime *n* 1 *syn* see SPRING 5
2 *syn* see YOUTH 1
ant autumn

springy *adj syn* see ELASTIC 1
rel rebounding, recoiling
ant rigid; springless

sprinkle *vb* 1 to scatter (something) in small drops or particles < *sprinkle* choco= late shot on whipped cream >
syn besprinkle, dust, powder, ||strinkle; *compare* STREW 1
rel shake; scatter; pepper; sparge
2 *syn* see SPECKLE 1
3 *syn* see SPOT 2
4 *syn* see BAPTIZE
5 to rain lightly < it's only *sprinkling*, so we can still take our walk >
syn drizzle, ||mizzle
rel mist; shower; spit
con pour, stream

sprinkling *n* 1 *syn* see HINT 2
2 *syn* see DUSTING
3 *syn* see FEW

sprint *vb syn* see RUN 1

sprit *vb syn* see SQUIRT

sprite *n syn* see FAIRY

||**spritz** *vb syn* see SQUIRT

spruce *adj syn* see DAPPER
ant slouchy

spruce (up) *vb syn* see DRESS UP 1

sprucy *adj syn* see DAPPER

spry *adj syn* see AGILE
rel prompt, quick, ready; energetic, vigor= ous; healthy, robust, sound
ant doddering

spuddy *adj syn* see ROTUND 2

||**spulzie** *n syn* see SPOIL

spume *n syn* see FOAM

spunk *n* 1 *syn* see FORTITUDE
rel bulldoggedness, doggedness
idiom clear (*or* true) grit
ant funk
2 *syn* see COURAGE

spunkless *adj syn* see COWARDLY
ant spunky

spunky *adj* 1 *syn* see BRAVE 1
idiom full of spunk
ant spunkless; funky
2 *syn* see SPIRITED 2
ant funky

spur *n syn* see STIMULUS
rel excitant; activation, actuation
ant checkrein; curb

spur *vb syn* see URGE
rel rowel; arouse, awaken, rally, rouse, stir; instigate; countenance, favor
ant curb

spurious *adj* 1 *syn* see ILLEGITIMATE 1
2 *syn* see ARTIFICIAL 2

3 of doubtful authenticity < claimed they had bought a *spurious* painting >
syn apocryphal, bastard, unauthentic, ungenuine; *compare* ARTIFICIAL 2, COUNTERFEIT
rel bogus, counterfeit, fake, phony, pseudo, sham; false, unreal
idiom not what (*or* all) it's cracked up to be
con actual, real, true; bona fide, genuine, veritable
ant authentic
4 *syn see* ARTIFICIAL 3
rel make-believe, pretend, pretended, pseudo
5 *syn see* COUNTERFEIT
spuriousness *n syn see* FALLACY 2
spurn *vb syn see* DECLINE 4
rel conspue, contemn, despise, disdain, scorn, scout; flout, scoff, sneer
con crave, desire, want
ant embrace
spur-of-the-moment *adj syn see* EXTEMPORANEOUS
spurt *vb syn see* SQUIRT
spurtle *vb syn see* SPLASH
sputter *vb* 1 to utter (words or ejaculations) hastily, explosively, and sometimes indistinctly < pompously *sputtering* his objections >
syn rip (out), spit, splutter
rel ejaculate, eject, throw (out); gibber, jabber; bluster, heckle, hector, rage, rant, rave, storm
2 to make a series of sudden short crackling or popping sounds < bacon *sputtering* in the pan >
syn spatter, spit, splutter
rel crackle, pop; hiss
spy (on *or* upon) *vb* to make furtive, stealthy, or secret observations of < had private detectives *spying* on his wife >
syn ‖stag
rel stake out; watch
spy *n* one who keeps secret watch to obtain information < was convicted on evidence produced by a *spy* >
syn agent, spook, undercover man; *compare* INFORMER
rel detective, investigator, sleuth; scout; beagle
idiom inside man, secret agent
spying *n syn see* ESPIONAGE
squab *adj syn see* STOCKY
‖**squab** *vb syn see* PRESS 1
squab *vb syn see* SPILL 1
squabble *n syn see* QUARREL
squabble *vb* 1 *syn see* QUARREL
rel clash, encounter
idiom have a squabble over
2 *syn see* ARGUE 2
idiom get into (*or* have) a hassle, have a verbal wrestling match
squalid *adj syn see* DIRTY 1
rel disheveled, slipshod, sloppy, slovenly, unkempt; frowzy, slatternly; dingy, shoddy, sleazy
2 *syn see* SHABBY 1

3 *syn see* BASE 3
squall *vb* 1 to make a raucous noise < angry street urchins fighting and *squalling* at each other >
syn caw, ‖quawk, squark, squawk, yawp (*or* yaup)
rel bellow, howl, roar, shout, yell; bark, yap, yip; croak
2 *syn see* BAWL 2
rel squeal; screech, shriek; yelp
squall *n syn see* QUARREL
squander *vb syn see* WASTE 2
idiom make ducks and drakes of, play ducks and drakes with
squander *n syn see* EXTRAVAGANCE 2
squanderer *n syn see* SPENDTHRIFT
square *n* 1 *syn see* COMMON 2
2 *syn see* FOGY
square *adj* 1 having four equal sides and four right angles < a large *square* Georgian mansion >
syn foursquare, quadrate, quadratic, quadratical
rel boxlike, boxy, squarish
2 *syn see* EVEN 5
3 *syn see* FAIR 4
4 *syn see* CONVENTIONAL 1
square *vb* 1 *syn see* ADAPT
2 *syn see* CLEAR 5
3 *syn see* BRIBE
4 *syn see* AGREE 4
rel balance; coincide
square *adv syn see* JUST 1
squarehead *n syn see* DUNCE
squarely *adv* 1 *syn see* EVENLY 1
2 *syn see* JUST 1
squark *vb syn see* SQUALL 1
squash *vb* 1 *syn see* PRESS 1
2 *syn see* CRUSH 2
3 *syn see* CRUSH 5
4 *syn see* PRESS 7
squash *n* 1 *syn see* SQUELCH
2 *syn see* CROWD 1
squashing *n syn see* REPRESSION 1
squashy *adj syn see* SOFT 6
ant firm
squat *vb* to sit on one's haunches < they were *squatting* around the fire >
syn hunker (down), ‖quat, ‖swat; *compare* CROUCH
rel crouch; hunch; stoop
squat *adj syn see* STOCKY
rel squattish, squatty
con long, tall; twiggy
ant lanky
‖**squaw** *n syn see* WIFE
squawk *vb* 1 *syn see* SQUALL 1
2 *syn see* GRIPE
rel yap, yip
squawker *n syn see* INFORMER
squawky *adj syn see* HARSH 3
con liquid, mellow, smooth
squdgy *adj syn see* STOCKY
squeak *vb* 1 to utter or make a short shrill cry or noise < mice *squeaking* in the barn >
syn ‖queak; *compare* SQUEAL 2
rel creak, grate, screak, screech, squeal; pipe; scream
2 *syn see* TALK 6
3 *syn see* INFORM 3
squeak *n syn see* OPPORTUNITY
‖**squeaker** *n syn see* INFORMER

---

syn synonym(s)   *rel* related word(s)
ant antonym(s)   *con* contrasted word(s)
idiom idiomatic equivalent(s)
‖ use limited; if in doubt, see a dictionary

squeal *vb* **1** *syn* see SCREAM 1
  idiom squeal like a stuck pig
  2 to make a harsh piercing sometimes rasping noise <tires *squealing* on wet pavement>
  syn screak, scream, screech, shriek; *compare* SQUEAK 1
  rel creak, grate, rasp
  3 *syn* see INFORM 3
  4 *syn* see TALK 6
  5 *syn* see YELL 2
  rel bitch, beef, complain, gripe, squawk
  idiom raise a howl, scream bloody murder
squealer *n syn* see INFORMER
squeam *n syn* see QUALM
squeamish *adj* **1** inclined to become nauseated <felt *squeamish* after the heavy meal on the ship>
  syn ‖pensy, qualmish, qualmy, queasy, queer, ‖wambly; *compare* NAUSEATED
  rel unsettled, upset; dizzy, shaky, vertiginous
  2 *syn* see NAUSEATED
  idiom sick at (*or* to) one's stomach
  3 *syn* see NICE 1
squeamishness *n syn* see NAUSEA
squeamy *adj syn* see NICE 1
squeeze *vb* **1** *syn* see PRESS 1
  rel contract, ‖scruze
  2 *syn* see EMBRACE 1
  3 *syn* see EXTORT 1
  4 *syn* see EKE OUT 2
  5 *syn* see PRESS 8
  6 *syn* see PRESS 7
squeezy *adj syn* see CRAMPED
squelch *n* a sound of or as if of semiliquid matter under suction <the *squelch* of his feet in the mud>
  syn squash, squidge, squish
squelch *vb syn* see SUPPRESS 2
squelching *n syn* see REPRESSION 1
squelchy *adj syn* see SOFT 6
‖**squench** *vb* **1** *syn* see EXTINGUISH 1
  2 *syn* see QUENCH 4
squidge *n syn* see SQUELCH
squiffed *adj syn* see INTOXICATED 1
squiggle *vb* **1** *syn* see WRIGGLE
  2 *syn* see SCRIBBLE
squinch *vb* **1** *syn* see RECOIL
  2 *syn* see SQUINT
squinny *vb syn* see SQUINT
squinny *adj syn* see THIN 1
squint *vb* to look or peer with the eyes partly closed <*squinted* in the bright sunlight>
  syn ‖sken, squinch, squinny
  idiom look asquint, screw up one's eyes
  ant goggle
squirm *vb* **1** *syn* see WRIGGLE
  2 *syn* see WRITHE 1
squirrel *vb syn* see HOARD
squirt *vb* to come forth in a sudden rapid usually narrow stream <water *squirting* from the hose>
  syn jet, splurt, sprit, ‖spritz, spurt, ‖squitter
  rel pour, stream, surge; spatter; spray
  con dribble, drip, trickle
squirt *n* ‖**1** squirts *pl syn* see DIARRHEA
  2 *syn* see TWERP
squish *n* **1** *syn* see PRESS 1
  2 *syn* see SQUELCH

squishy *adj syn* see SOFT 6
‖**squit** *n syn* see TWERP
‖**squitter** *vb syn* see SQUIRT
squush *vb syn* see PRESS 1
squushy *adj syn* see SOFT 6
stab *n* **1** *syn* see PRICK 1
  2 *syn* see POKE 1
  3 *syn* see FLING 1
stab *vb syn* see THRUST 2
  rel dagger, dirk, poniard, prong
stabbing *adj syn* see SHARP 8
stabile *adj syn* see STEADY 2
stabilify *vb syn* see STABILIZE
stabilitate *vb syn* see STABILIZE
stability *n* the ability to withstand force or stress without alteration of position and without material change <the structural *stability* of the bridge>
  syn firmness, security, soundness, stableness, steadiness, strength
  rel dependability, durability, reliability; solidity, solidness, sturdiness; cohesion, toughness
  con insecurity, undependability, unreliability, unsoundness, unsteadiness; weakness
  ant instability, unstability
stabilize *vb* to make or keep stable, steadfast, or firm <a policy that *stabilized* the economy>
  syn ballast, poise, stabilify, stabilitate, steady
  rel balance, counterbalance, counterpoise, equalize, equipoise; prop, support, sustain; fix, secure, set, settle
  ant unstabilize
stable *adj* **1** *syn* see SURE 1
  rel balanced, poised; fixed, set, solid, sound, steadfast
  con wobbling, wobbly
  ant instable, unstable
  2 *syn* see STEADY 2
  3 *syn* see LASTING
  rel constant, steady; safe, secure, sound; staunch, steadfast, resolute
  4 marked by solidity, firmness, and stability especially in design or construction <a *stable* foundation for the building>
  syn firm, secure, solid, sound; *compare* FAST 4, SURE 1
  rel strong, sturdy; unassailable, unshakable
  idiom as firm as (the rock of) Gibraltar, solid as a rock
  con insecure, shaky, unsound, weak, wobbling, wobbly
  ant instable, unstable
stableness *n syn* see STABILITY
  ant unstableness
stack *n syn* see PILE 1
stack *vb syn* see HEAP 1
‖**stacked** *adj syn* see CURVACEOUS
stade *n syn* see STADIUM
stadium *n* a large usually unroofed structure with tiered seats enclosing a field used especially for sports <a football *stadium*>
  syn bowl, coliseum, stade
  rel arena, garden, gymnasium
‖**stag** *vb syn* see SPY (on *or* upon)
stage *n* **1** *used with the syn* see DRAMA
  2 *syn* see DEGREE 1
  rel level; phase; period

stage *vb* to present on the stage < *staged* a
play >
   syn mount, produce, put on, show
   rel bring out, open; give, present; do,
   execute, perform, play
stage set *n syn* see SCENE 1
stage setting *n syn* see SCENE 1
stagger *vb* 1 *syn* see REEL 2
   2 *syn* see LURCH 2
   idiom pitch and plunge
   3 *syn* see TEETER
   rel ‖stiver, ‖stoit, ‖stoiter, ‖stot
   4 *syn* see HESITATE
   5 to affect with great wonder or bewilderment < a plot so bizarre as to *stagger* the
   imagination >
   syn boggle, dumbfound, nonplus
   rel perplex, puzzle, stump; amaze, astonish, astound, flabbergast; bowl (over),
   floor, knock over; devastate, overpower,
   overwhelm, shatter; paralyze
   idiom take (one) aback
stagger (on *or* along) *vb syn* see SHIFT 5
‖**stagger** *n syn* see FLING 1
staggering *adj syn* see MARVELOUS 1
stagnant *adj syn* see STATIC
stagnate *vb* 1 *syn* see VEGETATE
   2 *syn* see STULTIFY
stagnation *n syn* see DEPRESSION 3
staid *adj syn* see SERIOUS 1
   rel decorous, formal; collected, composed,
   cool; priggish, smug; starchy, stuffy
   con breezy, devil-may-care, easy, frivolous; debonair, jaunty; playful, sportive;
   hoydenish, rakish; fresh, irreverent; uncontrolled, unrestrained
   ant unstaid
stain *vb* 1 to soil often permanently with
foreign matter < a shirt *stained* with
grease >
   syn bestain, blot, discolor, smut; *compare*
   SOIL 2
   rel tinge; bedaub, daub, smear; besmirch,
   smirch, smudge, smutch
   2 *syn* see TAINT 1
   3 *syn* see DEBASE 1
stain *n* 1 *syn* see STIGMA
   rel blemish, defect, flaw
   idiom blot on the escutcheon
   2 *syn* see COLOR 6
stainless *adj syn* see CHASTE
   con tainted, tarnished
   ant stained
stake *n* 1 *syn* see BET
   2 *syn* see INTEREST 1
stake *vb* 1 *syn* see GAMBLE 1
   rel stake down
   2 *syn* see CAPITALIZE
stale *adj* 1 *syn* see MALODOROUS 1
   2 *syn* see TRITE
   rel dusty, fusty; dead
   ant fresh
‖**stale** *n syn* see LURE 2
stalemate *n syn* see DRAW 4
stalk *vb* 1 to pursue (game) stealthily or
under cover < *stalk* deer >
   syn still-hunt
   rel follow, track; drive, chase, pursue;
   walk up; flush (out); ambush

---

   2 *syn* see STRIDE 1
stalky *adj syn* see THIN 1
stall *vb* ‖1 *syn* see SATIATE
   2 *syn* see ARREST 1
   rel brake, slow (down); hold off, put off,
   stand off; suspend; shut down
   idiom pull the checkstring
   con spur
stalwart *adj* 1 *syn* see STRONG 2
   rel athletic, brawny, husky, muscular,
   sinewy
   2 *syn* see BRAVE 1
stamina *n syn* see TOLERANCE 1
stammer *vb* 1 to make involuntary stops
and repetitions in uttering syllables and
words < the frightened child *stammered*
and fell silent >
   syn ‖hammer, ‖stut, stutter
   rel falter, hesitate; stumble; splutter, sputter; gibber, jabber
   ‖2 *syn* see TEETER
stamp *vb* 1 *syn* see TRAMPLE 2
   rel clomp, clump, stump
   2 *syn* see IMPRESS 3
   rel etch, imprint, infix, inscribe, print
   idiom impress on the mind
stamp *n* 1 *syn* see IMPRESSION 1
   2 *syn* see TYPE
   3 *syn* see SEAL
stampede *vb* 1 *syn* see ROUT 1
   2 to take to sudden headlong flight in
panic < cattle *stampeding* across the
plain >
   syn pell-mell; *compare* RUSH 1
   rel bolt, charge, chase, crash, dash, fling,
   hurry, rush, shoot, tear
   idiom run like a pack of scalded dogs
stamping ground *n* 1 *syn* see HABITAT
   2 *syn* see RESORT 2
stance *n* 1 *syn* see POSTURE 1
   2 *syn* see POSITION 1
stanch *vb syn* see STEM
stand *vb* 1 *syn* see BEAR 10
   idiom ‖hack it, take lying down
   2 *syn* see TREAT 3
stand (on *or* upon) *vb syn* see DEPEND (on
or upon) 1
   idiom be contingent on
stand *n syn* see POSITION 1
standard *n* 1 *syn* see FLAG
   2 *syn* see MODEL 2
   3 a means of determining what a thing
should be < each generation has its own
standards of morality >
   syn benchmark, criterion, gauge, measure,
   touchstone, yardstick
   rel average, mean, median, norm, par;
   axiom, belief, fundamental, principle; law,
   rule; exemplar, model, pattern
   idiom rule of thumb
   4 a fixed, customary, or official measure
(as of quantity, quality, or price) < governmental *standards* of weights and
measures >
   syn assize
   rel ‖dick
stander-by *n syn* see SPECTATOR
stand-in *n syn* see SUBSTITUTE
   rel second; assistant
standing *n* 1 *syn* see TERM 5
   2 *syn* see STATUS 1
   3 *syn* see STATUS 2
standoff *adj syn* see UNSOCIABLE

standoff *n syn* see DRAW 4

standoffish *adj* 1 *syn* see UNSOCIABLE
2 *syn* see ANTISOCIAL

stand out *vb* 1 *syn* see BULGE
2 *syn* see LOOM 3

standout *adj syn* see SUPERB 3

stand over *vb syn* see DEFER

standpat *n syn* see DIEHARD 1

standpatter *n syn* see DIEHARD 1

standpoint *n syn* see VIEWPOINT 2

standstill *n* cessation of movement < the
car came to a *standstill* in the mud >
syn stay, stillstand, stop
rel arrest, check; pause; cessation, halt
con start; movement
ant start-up

stand up *vb syn* see RISE 1

stand-up *adj syn* see ERECT
con lowered; flat, horizontal

∥**stang** *vb syn* see SMART

staple *n syn* see LOOP 2

staple *n syn* see BODY 3

star *n syn* see CHIEF 2

starch *n syn* see VIGOR 2

star-crossed *adj syn* see UNLUCKY

stare *vb* 1 *syn* see LOOK 7
idiom ∥take a gander at
2 *syn* see GAZE 1
idiom fix (*or* rivet) one's eyes on

stare down *vb* to overcome (someone) by
or as if by staring < the teacher could not
stare the boy *down* >
syn look down, outstare
rel glare; master, quell, subdue, suppress;
overcome, overwhelm

stark *adj* 1 *syn* see UTTER
2 *syn* see NUDE 2
3 *syn* see EMPTY 1

stark-naked *adj syn* see NUDE 2
idiom bare (*or* naked) as a newborn babe,
∥naked as a jaybird, naked as the day one
was born

∥**starny** *adj syn* see STELLAR 1

starry *adj syn* see STELLAR 1

start *vb* 1 to move suddenly and violently
from a state of stillness or rest < *started*
from his bed at the sound of shots >
syn bolt, jump, spring, startle
rel dart; bounce; bound, leap; draw
(back), flinch, recoil
idiom jump out of one's skin, start aside
ant stay
2 *syn* see RECOIL
3 *syn* see BEGIN 2
rel proceed, spring
ant end
4 *syn* see FOUND 2
5 *syn* see BEGIN 1
ant stop

start *n* 1 *syn* see BEGINNING
ant finish
2 *syn* see ADVANTAGE 3

startle *vb* 1 *syn* see START 1
2 *syn* see SHOCK 2
3 *syn* see FRIGHTEN
rel astonish, surprise
idiom make one jump out of one's skin,
∥scare the pants off

startlish *adj syn* see EXCITABLE

starved *adj syn* see HUNGRY
rel underfed, undernourished; weakened;
half-famished, half-starved
con fed, nourished; overfed

ant well-fed

starving *adj syn* see HUNGRY
rel craving, famishing, hungering; dying,
perishing
idiom crazy for food

stash *vb* 1 *syn* see HOARD
2 *syn* see HIDE
rel hoard, squirrel

stasis *n syn* see BALANCE 1

state *n* 1 the way in which one manifests
existence or the circumstances under
which one exists or by which one is given
distinctive character < remained in a
weakened *state* for weeks >
syn condition, mode, posture, situation,
status
rel circumstances; attitude, position,
stand
idiom state of being
2 *syn* see STATUS 1
3 *syn* see STATUS 2

state *vb* 1 *syn* see RELATE 1
rel elucidate, explain, expound, interpret;
set forth
2 *syn* see ENUNCIATE 1
3 *syn* see SAY 1
4 *syn* see EXPRESS 2
ant imply

stated *adj syn* see FIRM 4

stately *adj* 1 *syn* see CEREMONIAL
rel dignified, grand, noble; imperial,
kingly, princely, regal, royal
2 *syn* see COURTLY
3 *syn* see GRAND 1
con lowly, poor; shabby; cheap

statement *n* 1 *syn* see EXPRESSION 1
rel outgoing; articulation, presentation,
presentment, verbalization, vocalization
2 *syn* see WORD 1
rel description, narrative, recital
3 *syn* see BILL 1

static *adj* characterized by relatively little
or no movement, progression, or change
(as in conditions) < a *static* economy >
syn immobile, stagnant, stationary, unmoving; *compare* STEADY 2
rel constant, stabile, stable, unchanging,
unfluctuating; fixed, immovable, rigid,
sticky; inactive, inert; stalled, stopped,
stuck
idiom at a standstill, standing still
con active, changing, mobile, moving,
progressing; erratic, fluctuating, inconstant, unstable
ant dynamic

station *n* 1 *syn* see PLACE 1
2 *syn* see RAILROAD STATION
3 *syn* see STATUS 1

station *vb* to appoint or assign to an office
or duty < *stationed* guards around the
camp >
syn post, set
rel appoint, assign; place, position

stationary *adj syn* see STATIC
rel motionless, stock-still
ant moving

station house *n syn* see RAILROAD STA-
TION

statuesque *adj syn* see SHAPELY

stature *n* 1 *syn* see QUALITY 2
rel prestige, standing, status; ability, capacity; competence, qualification
2 *syn* see STATUS 2

status *n* **1** rating or positioning in relation to others (as in a social order, community, class, or profession) < his *status* as a slave >
syn capacity, character, footing, place, position, quality, rank, situation, standing, state, station
rel rating
2 social or professional importance or distinction < a lawyer of international *status* >
syn cachet, consequence, dignity, position, prestige, rank, standing, state, stature
rel caliber, merit, worth; distinction, renown; eminence, prominence
con inconsequence, insignificance, unimportance
3 *syn* see STATE 1
rel status quo
idiom state of affairs

statute *n* *syn* see LAW 1

staunch *adj* **1** *syn* see SURE 1
2 *syn* see FAITHFUL 1
rel firm, strong
idiom as staunch as an oak, tried and true
con mercurial; shaky, unsteady

stave *vb* *syn* see HURRY 2

stave off *vb* **1** *syn* see FEND (off)
rel beat off, drive (off), fight (off); block, parry
2 *syn* see PREVENT 2

staving *adv* *syn* see VERY 1
ant barely

stay *vb* **1** *syn* see ARREST 1
rel postpone, prorogue, put off
2 to continue to be in one place for a noticeable time < *stayed* late at the office >
syn abide, bide, linger, remain, stick around, tarry, wait
rel dally, delay, dillydally, lag, procrastinate; hang around, loiter; outstay, stay out
ant go
3 *syn* see VISIT 3
rel bide, dwell, live
4 *syn* see DEFER

stay *n* *syn* see STANDSTILL

stay *n* *syn* see SUPPORT 3

stay *vb* *syn* see BASE

stead *vb* *syn* see HELP 1

steadfast *adj* **1** *syn* see IMMOVABLE 1
2 *syn* see INFLEXIBLE 2
ant unsteadfast, vacillating
3 *syn* see SURE 2
ant capricious
4 *syn* see FAITHFUL 1
rel unfaltering, unflinching, unquestioning, unwavering

steadfastly *adv* *syn* see HARD 7
rel staunchly, strongly

steadiness *n* *syn* see STABILITY
ant unsteadiness

steady *adj* **1** *syn* see SURE 2
rel unswerving; eternal, never-ending

2 being neither markedly varying nor variable in course or extent < a *steady* rain > < *steady* prices >
syn constant, equable, even, stabile, stable, unchanging, unfluctuating, uniform, unvarying; *compare* STATIC
rel steady-going; certain, changeless, fixed, set, sure, unchangeable; unflickering, unwavering; durable, reliable
con inconstant, uneven, unstable; changeable; changing, fluctuating, uncertain, undependable, undulating, unsure, varying, wavering
ant unsteady
3 *syn* see FAITHFUL 1

steady *vb* *syn* see STABILIZE

steady *n* **1** *syn* see BOYFRIEND 2
2 *syn* see GIRL FRIEND 2

steal *vb* **1** to take another's possession illegally and without his knowledge < *stole* a car >
syn abstract, annex, appropriate, cabbage, ||clout, ||cly, collar, ||coon, ||cop, ||crook, filch, ||heist, hook, lift, nab, ||nail, ||nick, nim, nip, pilfer, pillage, pinch, pocket, ||prig, purloin, smouch, ||snaffle, ||snake, snitch, swipe, thieve, vulture
rel mooch; fleece, frisk; grab, grasp, seize, snatch, take; hijack, shanghai; poach, rustle; burglarize, rob; loot, plunder, rifle
idiom make off (or away) with, run away (or off) with
2 *syn* see SNEAK
3 to move or go quietly so as not to disturb < *stole* out of the sickroom on tiptoe >
syn creep, glide, mouse, slide, slip; *compare* SNEAK
rel tiptoe
con clump, stamp, stomp, stump

steal *n* **1** *syn* see THEFT
2 *syn* see BARGAIN 1

stealage *n* *syn* see THEFT

stealer *n* *syn* see THIEF

stealing *n* *syn* see THEFT

stealthily *adv* *syn* see SECRETLY
ant openly

stealthy *adj* **1** *syn* see SECRET 1
rel crafty, cunning, sly, wily; skulking, slinking, sneaking; catlike
con direct, straight, straightforward
ant open
2 being so quiet, slow, and deliberate in movement as to escape observation < the *stealthy* movements of the cat burglar >
syn catlike, catty, feline, furtive; *compare* SECRET 1
rel noiseless, pantherine, pantherish, quiet, silent; shifty, skulking, sly, sneak, sneaking, sneaky

steam *n* *syn* see POWER 4

steamroller *vb* *syn* see WHIP 2

steam up *vb* *syn* see ANGER 1

steel *vb* **1** *syn* see GIRD 3
rel rally; nerve; buck up; reinforce
idiom grit one's teeth, set one's jaw, take the bit in one's teeth
ant unsteel
2 *syn* see ENCOURAGE 1

steep *adj* **1** having an incline approaching the perpendicular < a *steep* trail up the mountain >

---

syn synonym(s)   *rel* related word(s)
ant antonym(s)   *con* contrasted word(s)
idiom idiomatic equivalent(s)
|| use limited; if in doubt, see a dictionary

syn abrupt, arduous, precipitate, precipitous, sheer, sideling, steepdown, steep-to, steep-up, ‖stickle
rel elevated, lifted, raised; steepish; high, lofty; prerupt; perpendicular, straight-up; breakneck
con easy, gentle, gradual, moderate; shelfy, shelving, shelvy
2 *syn* see EXCESSIVE 1

steep *vb* 1 *syn* see SOAK 1
2 *syn* see INFUSE 1

steepdown *adj syn* see STEEP 1

steep–to *adj syn* see STEEP 1

steep–up *adj syn* see STEEP 1

steer *vb syn* see GUIDE
idiom steer one's course

steer *n syn* see TIP

stellar *adj* 1 of, relating to, or suggestive of a star or group of stars < *stellar* light >
syn astral, sidereal, ‖starny, starry, stellular
rel gleaming, luminous, lustrous, shining, starlike, twinkling; star-spangled
con starless
2 *syn* see CHIEF 2

stellify *vb syn* see EXALT 1

stellular *adj syn* STELLAR 1, astral, sidereal, ‖starny, starry

stem *vb syn* see SPRING 1

stem *vb* to hinder or prevent by or as if by damming < *stem* the flow of blood >
syn stanch, stop
rel arrest, check, control

stemma *n syn* see GENEALOGY

stench *n syn* see SMELL 3

stenchful *adj syn* see MALODOROUS 1

stenchy *adj syn* see MALODOROUS 1

stentorian *adj syn* see LOUD 1
rel orotund; clamorous, vociferous; gravelly, rough; clarion-voiced, loudmouthed, loud-voiced, trumpet-tongued

stentorious *adj syn* see LOUD 1
rel orotund; clamorous, vociferous; gravelly, rough; clarion-voiced, loudmouthed, loud-voiced, trumpet-tongued

stentorophonic *adj syn* see LOUD 1

step *n* 1 *syn* see FOOTPRINT
2 *syn* see DEGREE 1
3 *syn* see MEASURE 7
rel act, action; motion

step *vb* 1 *syn* see WALK 1
2 *syn* see DANCE 1

step–by–step *adj syn* see GRADUAL

step in *vb* 1 *syn* see VISIT 2
2 *syn* see INTERPOSE 1

step up *vb syn* see SPEED 3
ant step down

stereotyped *adj syn* see TRITE
idiom worn thin

stereotypical *adj syn* see TRITE
ant original

sterile *adj* 1 lacking the power to produce offspring or produce fruit < a hybrid that is completely *sterile* >
syn barren, effete, impotent, infecund, infertile, unfruitful
rel childless; fallow, fruitless, unproductive; unprolific; arid, bare, dry; dead, desolate
con potent, productive, rich; bearing, fruiting, fruitive, producing, turning out, yielding; fecund, fruitful, prolific, teeming
ant fertile

2 *syn* see UNORIGINAL
rel flat, insipid, jejune, vapid; stale; effete, worn-out; impotent
con fertile, fruitful, potent, producing, productive, prolific
ant fecund

sterilize *vb* to make incapable of producing offspring < *sterilizing* animals in medical experiments >
syn alter, castrate, change, desexualize, fix, geld, mutilate, neuter, unsex
rel emasculate; caponize, poulardize; spay

sterling *adj syn* see HONORABLE 1
rel pure, true

stern *adj syn* see SEVERE 1
rel grim, implacable, unrelenting; inexorable, inflexible
ant lenient, soft

‖**stern** *n syn* see BUTTOCKS

stew *n* 1 *syn* see BROTHEL
2 *usu* stews *pl syn* see RED-LIGHT DISTRICT
3 *syn* see SLUM
4 *syn* see MISCELLANY 1
5 *syn* see SNIT
rel boil
6 *syn* see COMMOTION 2

stew *vb* 1 *syn* see BOIL 2
2 *syn* see WORRY 3
idiom be in a stew

stewardly *adj syn* see SPARING

‖**stewed** *adj syn* see INTOXICATED 1

stick *n* 1 *syn* see BAR 1
2 *syn* see DECOY 2
3 sticks *pl, used with the syn* see FRONTIER 2
idiom the middle of nowhere

stick *adv syn* see ALL 1

stick *vb* 1 *syn* see THRUST 2
2 to become or cause to become closely and firmly attached < papers all *stuck* together >
syn adhere, cleave, cling, cohere
rel affix, attach, fasten, fix; glue; cement; fuse, weld; braze, solder
idiom stick close, stick like a wet shirt, stick like the paper on the wall, stick like wax, stick to like a barnacle (*or* leech)
con loosen; detach, disengage
ant unstick
3 *syn* see SET 1
4 *syn* see NONPLUS 1
5 *syn* see FLEECE 1
6 *syn* see OVERCHARGE 1
‖7 *syn* see BEAR 10
8 *syn* see DEMUR

stickage *n syn* see ADHERENCE 1

stick around *vb syn* see STAY 2

stick–at–nothing *adj syn* see UNSCRUPULOUS

sticker *n syn* see SEAL

sticking *n syn* see ADHERENCE 1

stick–in–the–mud *n syn* see FOGY

‖**stickle** *adj syn* see STEEP 1

stickle *vb syn* see DEMUR
rel hold out, stall; contend, kick, object, protest

stick out *vb syn* see BULGE
rel outstretch, outthrust, pretend, push
2 *syn* see STRIKE 1
3 *syn* see BEAR 10

stick up *vb syn* see ROB 1

sticky *adj* 1 having the quality of sticking by or as if by adhesion < *sticky* syrup >

syn adhesive, ‖claggy, ‖clarty, cloggy, gluey, gooey, gummy, stodgy

rel tacky; viscid, viscous

2 *syn* see HUMID

3 *syn* see HARD 6

4 *syn* see SENTIMENTAL

‖**stickybeak** *n syn* see BUSYBODY

sticky–fingered *adj syn* see LARCENOUS

stiff *adj* **1** incapable of or highly resistant to bending or flexing <a *stiff* cardboard packing box>

syn immalleable, impliable, incompliant, inelastic, inflexible, rigid, unbending, unflexible, unyielding; *compare* INFLEXIBLE 2

rel stiffish; hard, resistant; hardened, petrified; stark

idiom stiff as a board (*or* poker)

con soft, softened; yielding; bendable, pliable, pliant; limber, supple, willowy

ant flexible, flexile

2 *syn* see INTOXICATED 1

3 *syn* see OBSTINATE

4 characterized by a lack of ease, grace, or spontaneity especially in style <a play whose dialogue and characters were *stiff* and perfunctory>

syn buckram, cardboard, muscle-bound, stilted, wooden

rel rigid, set, studied; machine-made, mechanical, stereotyped, stock; arid, dry, dull

con expressive, graphic, vivid; easy, fluent, graceful, smooth

5 *syn* see EXCESSIVE 1

stiff *n* **1** *syn* see CORPSE

2 *syn* see DRUNKARD

3 *syn* see MISER

stiff–necked *adj syn* see OBSTINATE

stifle *vb* **1** *syn* see SUFFOCATE

2 *syn* see MUFFLE 2

3 *syn* see SUPPRESS 3

4 *syn* see STULTIFY

stifling *adj* **1** producing or seeming to produce suffocation <*stifling* heat>

syn smothering, smothery, ‖smudgy, suffocating, suffocative; *compare* HUMID, STUFFY 1

rel oppressive, overpowering; unbearable, unendurable

2 *syn* see STUFFY 1

stifling *n syn* see REPRESSION 1

stigma *n* a mark of shame or discredit <the *stigma* of personal cowardice>

syn bar sinister, black eye, blot, blur, brand, odium, onus, slur, spot, stain

rel besmirchment, disfigurement, smudge, smutch, taint, tainting; disgrace, dishonor, shame

con credit, distinction, glory, honor; bay(s), crown, laurel(s)

still *adj* **1** *syn* see MOTIONLESS

2 *syn* see CALM 1

rel peaceful, unperturbed

con roiled, roily, turbid

3 devoid of or making no stir, sound, or noise <the streets were *still* at 3:00 A.M.>

syn hush, hushful, noiseless, quiet, silent, soundless, stilly, whist

rel calm, hushed, peaceful, placid, serene, tranquil; deathlike, deathly

idiom deathly still, still as death

ant noisy

still *vb* **1** *syn* see CALM

ant agitate

2 *syn* see SILENCE

still *adv* **1** *syn* see HOWEVER

2 *syn* see YET 1

idiom still (*or* even) more

3 *syn* see ALSO 2

still *n syn* see SILENCE 1

still and all *adv syn* see HOWEVER

still–hunt *vb syn* see STALK 1

stillness *n syn* see SILENCE 1

stillstand *n syn* see STANDSTILL

stilly *adj* **1** *syn* see STILL 3

con agitated, disturbed, noisy

ant noiseful

2 *syn* see CALM 1

stilted *adj* **1** *syn* see RHETORICAL

2 *syn* see STIFF 4

3 *syn* see GENTEEL 3

rel conventional, formal; decorous; prim

stimulant *n syn* see STIMULUS

stimulate *vb* **1** *syn* see PROVOKE 4

rel enliven, vivify; activate, dynamize, energize, vitalize

idiom build a fire under, get one started (*or* moving)

con unnerve; deaden

2 *syn* see ELATE

stimulating *adj* **1** *syn* see EXCITING

rel enlivening, lively; provocative, seminal, suggestive; incitory, stimulative, stimulatory

2 *syn* see INVIGORATING

stimulative *adj syn* see INVIGORATING

stimulus *n* something that rouses the mind or spirits or incites to activity <the war proved a *stimulus* to the economy> <sought a *stimulus* to take her mind off her own troubles>

syn catalyst, goad, impetus, impulse, incentive, incitation, incitement, instigation, motivation, propellant, provocative, push, spur, stimulant; *compare* MOTIVE 1

rel boost, encouragement, inducement, invitation, urging; cause, motive; excitement, piquing, provocation, stimulation

sting *vb syn* see SMART

stingy *adj* being unwilling or showing unwillingness to share with others <too *stingy* to tip the waiter>

syn cheeseparing, ‖chinchy, close, close-fisted, costive, hardfisted, hardhanded, ironfisted, mean, mingy, miserly, ‖narrow, narrow-fisted, narrowhearted, niggard, niggardly, parsimonious, penny-pinching, penny-wise, penurious, pinching, pinch-penny, save-all, ‖scant, scrimpy, scrimy, tight, tightfisted, ungenerous, ungiving; *compare* SPARING

rel economical, frugal, Scotch, sparing, thrifty; scaly, screwy

idiom as close as a vise, as close (*or* tight) as paper on a wall, as tightfisted as a kulak, near (*or* close *or* tight) as the bark on a tree

con bountiful, giving, liberal, munificent, open-handed, philanthropic, unsparing, unstinting; prodigal

---

syn synonym(s)   *rel* related word(s)
ant antonym(s)   *con* contrasted word(s)
idiom idiomatic equivalent(s)
‖ use limited; if in doubt, see a dictionary

ant generous

stink *vb syn* see SMELL 3

stinkard *n syn* see SNOT 1

stinkaroo *n syn* see SNOT 1

stinker *n syn* see SNOT 1

stinking *adj* 1 *syn* see MALODOROUS 1
   idiom stinking to high heaven
   ‖2 *syn* see INTOXICATED 1

‖**stinko** *adj syn* see INTOXICATED 1

stinky *adj syn* see MALODOROUS 1

stint *vb* 1 *syn* see SCRIMP
   2 *syn* see SPARE 3

stint *n* 1 *syn* see RESTRICTION 1
   2 *syn* see TASK 1
   rel amount, quantity; allotment, apportionment; participation, share
   3 *syn* see SPELL 1

stipend *n syn* see WAGE
   rel award, consideration, payment

stipple *vb syn* see SPECKLE 1

stipulate *vb syn* see SPECIFY 3
   rel designate; state; provide

stipulated *adj syn* see FIRM 3
   rel designated, pinned down
   con implied, unstated, unwritten

stipulation *n syn* see CONDITION 1
   rel specification; circumscription, limit

stir *vb* 1 to cause to shift from quiescence or torpor into activity <a teacher who *stirred* the minds of his most sluggish students>
   syn arouse, awaken, bestir, challenge, kindle, rally, rouse, wake, waken, whet; *compare* PROVOKE 4
   rel excite, galvanize, inspire, provoke, quicken, stimulate; agitate, foment, incite, instigate; activate, energize, vitalize; actuate, drive, move, impel; ‖roust, rout
   idiom make (*or* have) an impact on, set astir, set on fire
   2 *syn* see WAKE 1
   3 *syn* see SEETHE 4

stir (up) *vb syn* see INCITE
   idiom add fuel to the flame, apply the torch, feed the fire, pour oil on the fire, stir the embers

stir *n* 1 signs of excited activity, hurry, or commotion <noticed a *stir* within the crowd>
   syn ado, bustle, flurry, furore, fuss, pother, whirl, whirlpool, whirlwind; *compare* COMMOTION 4
   rel agitation, disquiet, stir-up; commotion, disturbance; din, hubbub, pandemonium, stirabout, tumult
   con calm, peace, placidity; inaction, inactivity
   ant tranquillity
   2 *syn* see MOTION 1

‖**stir** *n syn* see JAIL

‖**stirra** *n syn* see MAN 3

stirring *n syn* see MOTION 1

stirring *adj syn* see EXCITING
   rel heart-stirring, soul-stirring

stitch *n syn* see PAIN 1

stivy *adj syn* see STUFFY 1

stock *n* 1 *syn* see FAMILY 1
   2 *syn* see ESTIMATION 1
   3 *syn* see TRUST 1
   4 *syn* see SUPPLY
   5 *syn* see RESERVE

stock *vb* to equip, furnish, supply, or have material requisites (as for sale) <a bar that *stocks* all the best brands of liquor>

syn carry, keep
   rel have; furnish, supply
   idiom have (*or* keep) in stock, keep on hand

stockade *n syn* see JAIL

stockpile *n* 1 *syn* see PILE 1
   2 *syn* see RESERVE

stockpile *vb syn* see ACCUMULATE

stock–still *adj syn* see MOTIONLESS

stocky *adj* being compact and broad in build and often short in stature <a *stocky* but quick and hard-hitting catcher>
   syn ‖chuffy, ‖chumpy, chunky, dumpy, heavyset, squab, squat, squdgy, stubby, ‖stuggy, stumpy, thick, thick-bodied, thickset
   rel plump, stout; bunty, low-set, short; lumpish, lumpy, pudgy; corpulent, fat
   con lean, skinny, thin, wiry

stodge *vb* 1 *syn* see SATIATE
   2 *syn* see PLOD 1

stodgy *adj* 1 *syn* see STICKY 1
   2 *syn* see DULL 9
   rel unexciting; pedantic; heavy, ponderous, weighty
   3 *syn* see TACKY 2

stoic *adj syn* see IMPASSIVE 1
   rel aloof, detached, indifferent, unconcerned; self-controlled, Spartan; indomitable, unassailable; long-suffering, patient, resigned

stoicism *n syn* see APATHY 1
   rel backbone, fortitude, grit, guts, pluck, sand

‖**stoit** *vb syn* see LURCH 2

‖**stoiter** *vb syn* see LURCH 2

stolid *adj syn* see IMPASSIVE 1
   rel blunt, dull, obtuse; dense, dull, dumb, slow, stupid; inactive, inert, passive, supine
   ant sensitive

stolidity *n syn* see APATHY 1
   rel dullness, dumbness, slowness, stupidity; inactiveness, inactivity, inertia, passivity
   con aptness, quickness, readiness; animation, enlivening, quickening; ardor, enthusiasm, fervor, passion, zeal; fire
   ant sensitivity

stomach *n* 1 *syn* see ABDOMEN
   2 *syn* see APPETITE 1

stomach *vb syn* see BEAR 10

stomachache *n* abdominal pain <she has a terrible *stomachache*>
   syn bellyache, colic, collywobbles, gripe(s)
   rel distress, misery

‖**stomachy** *adj syn* see IRASCIBLE

stomp *vb syn* see TRAMPLE 2

stone–blind *adj syn* see BLIND 1

stone–broke *adj syn* see POOR 1

stoned *adj* 1 *syn* see INTOXICATED 1
   2 *syn* see DRUGGED

stone–still *adj syn* see MOTIONLESS

stony *adj* 1 *syn* see UNFEELING 2
   ant soft
   2 *syn* see POOR 1

stonyhearted *adj syn* see UNFEELING 2
   rel flinty, hard, stonelike
   idiom as cold as marble
   ant softhearted

stooge *n* 1 one who plays a subordinate or compliant role to a principal <an executive who was only a *stooge* with no real power>

syn Charlie McCarthy, dummy, yes-man
2 *syn* see TOOL 2

stool *n syn* see INFORMER

‖**stool** *vb syn* see INFORM 3

stoolie *n syn* see INFORMER

stool pigeon *n syn* see INFORMER

stoop *vb* 1 to descend from one's level (as of rank or dignity) usually to do something < a king who would not *stoop* to consider the common people >
  syn condescend, deign
  rel relax, thaw, unbend; accord, concede; accommodate, favor, oblige
  idiom be so good as to, come (or get) down from one's high horse, lower oneself
2 to drop in status or dignity by indulgence in pettiness or unworthy behavior < a man who would not *stoop* to tell a lie >
  syn descend, sink
  idiom act beneath oneself, debase (or demean) oneself, lower oneself
3 *syn* see DUCK 2

stop *vb* 1 *syn* see STEM
2 *syn* see FILL 1
  rel disrupt, hinder, interrupt; cut off, turn off
  ant unstop
3 to suspend or cause to suspend activity < the conversation *stopped* >
  syn cease, desist, ‖deval, discontinue, give over, halt, knock off, leave off, quit, surcease; *compare* ARREST 1
  rel ‖can, refrain (from); arrest, check, cut off, interrupt; stay, suspend; ‖cheese, lay off; break off, break up, end, terminate
  con continue, go on, keep (on), keep up, persist
  ant start
4 to come to a standstill < the car *stopped* at the intersection >
  syn bring up, draw up, fetch up, halt, haul up, pull up
  con start; move; pull out
  ant go

stop (in *or* by) *vb syn* see VISIT 2

stop (over) *vb syn* see VISIT 3
  idiom make a stopover

stop *n* 1 *syn* see END 2
  ant start
2 *syn* see BAR 2
3 *syn* see STANDSTILL

stopcock *n syn* see FAUCET

stopgap *adj syn* see MAKESHIFT

stopgap *n syn* see RESOURCE 3

stopover *n syn* see SOJOURN

stopper *vb syn* see FILL 1
  ant unstopper

store *vb syn* see STOW

store (up) *vb syn* see ACCUMULATE
  rel deposit; cache

store *n* 1 *syn* see RESERVE
2 *syn* see SUPPLY
3 *syn* see DEPOT 2
4 a business establishment where goods are shown for sale < a food *store* >
  syn market, outlet, shop, showroom
  rel discounter, discount house, discount store, emporium

store *adj syn* see READY-MADE

store–bought *adj syn* see READY-MADE

‖**store–boughten** *adj syn* see READY-MADE

storehouse *n syn* see DEPOT 2

storm *n* 1 *syn* see COMMOTION 4
2 *syn* see BARRAGE

storm *vb syn* see ATTACK 1

storm and stress *n syn* see UNREST

stormful *adj syn* see WILD 6
  rel threatening; dusty, murky; foul; howling, riproaring, roaring
  ant calm

stormily *adv syn* see HARD 2

stormy *adj syn* see WILD 6
  rel threatening; dusty, murky; foul; howling, riproaring, roaring
  ant calm

story *n* 1 *syn* see ACCOUNT 7
2 a recital of real or imaginary happenings that is less elaborate than a novel < told the *story* of his escape > < a simple *story* of heartwarming devotion >
  syn anecdote, narration, narrative, tale, yarn; *compare* ACCOUNT 7
  rel conte; description; fable; folktale, legend, märchen; Canterbury tale, cock-and-bull story, fabrication, fairy tale, fiction
3 *syn* see LIE

storyteller *n syn* see LIAR

‖**stot** *vb syn* see LURCH 2

stout *adj* 1 *syn* see BRAVE 1
  idiom bold as a lion
  con irresolute; fainthearted
2 *syn* see STRONG 2
  rel resolute, steadfast; hard; indomitable, invincible
  idiom as strong (or stalwart) as an English oak
3 *syn* see FAT 2
  rel thick-bodied; ‖plenitudinous
  ant spare

stouthearted *adj syn* see BRAVE 1

stow *vb* to put (articles) into a storage space < *stowed* his gear belowdecks >
  syn bestow, pack, store, warehouse
  ant unstow

straddle *vb* 1 *syn* see BESTRIDE 2
2 *syn* see SPRAWL 2

straggle *vb* 1 *syn* see WANDER 1
2 *syn* see SPRAWL 2

straggler *n syn* see LAGGARD

straight *adv* 1 *syn* see AWAY 3
2 *syn* see DIRECTLY 1

straight *adj* 1 *syn* see DIRECT 2
  idiom as straight as an arrow
  ant circuitous
2 *syn* see STRAIGHTFORWARD 2
3 free from admixture or extraneous matter < a shot of *straight* liquor >
  syn neat, plain, pure, unadulterated, undiluted, unmixed
  rel unmodified; concentrated; strong
  con adulterated, blended, mixed; watered-down; weak
4 *syn* see CONVENTIONAL 1

straight *n syn* see RIGHT 1

straightaway *adv syn* see AWAY 3

straightforward *adj* 1 *syn* see DIRECT 2
2 free from all that is dishonest or secretive < a *straightforward* answer >
  syn aboveboard, forthright, plain dealing, straight; *compare* FRANK

---

rel pretenseless; honest, honorable, just, upright, upstanding; candid, frank, open, plain, unequivocal; direct, outspoken

con equivocal, evasive, shuffling; indirect; prevaricative; dishonest, untruthful

ant devious

3 *syn* see FRANK

rel barefaced, straight-from-the-shoulder

4 *syn* see CLEAR 5

straightly *adv syn* see DIRECTLY 1

straight off *adv syn* see AWAY 3

straight-out *adj syn* see UTTER

straight-up *adj* **1** *syn* see ERECT

2 *syn* see VERTICAL

straightway *adv syn* see AWAY 3

strain *n* **1** *syn* see HINT 2

2 *syn* see MELODY

3 *syn* see MOOD 1

strain *vb* **1** *syn* see TRY 2

rel stretch

idiom put a strain on

2 to injure (as a body part) by overuse or misuse < *strained* a muscle while lifting weights >

syn pull

3 *syn* see LABOR 1

4 *syn* see EXUDE

5 *syn* see DEMUR

strain *n syn* see STRESS 1

strained *adj syn* see FORCED

rel taut, tense, tight

con unforced, unlabored; unconstrained

ant unstrained

strait *n syn* see JUNCTURE 2

rel bind, squeeze; difficulty, hardship, rigor, vicissitude; bewilderment, mystification, perplexity

straitlaced *adj syn* see PRIM 1

rel hidebound, intolerant, narrow, narrow-minded; rigorous, strict

idiom prim and proper

con easygoing, relaxed; broadminded, liberal, liberal-minded; libertine

strake *vb syn* see STREAK

‖**stramash** *n syn* see CRASH 3

strand *n syn* see SHORE

strand *vb syn* see SHIPWRECK 1

stranded *adj syn* see AGROUND

idiom high and dry, run aground

strange *adj* **1** *syn* see EXOTIC 2

2 *syn* see UNFAMILIAR 1

rel unknown; alien

3 *syn* see MARVELOUS 1

4 deviating from what is ordinary, usual, or to be expected < a *strange* unpredictable man >

syn bizarre, curious, eccentric, erratic, idiosyncratic, odd, oddball, outlandish, peculiar, quaint, queer, ‖rum, rummy, singular, uncouth, unusual, weird; *compare* EXCEPTIONAL 1, MYSTERIOUS

rel aberrant, abnormal, atypical, off, off=the-wall; fishy, funny; far-out, freaky, ‖kinky, kooky, offbeat, outré, ‖scatty; crazy, nutty; fantastic, grotesque

idiom as strange as they come

con common, ordinary, unexceptional, usual; expected, predictable

ant familiar

stranger *n* a nonresident or an unknown person in a community < he felt he had become a *stranger* in a foreign land >

syn alien, auslander, foreigner, inconnu, outcomer, outlander, outsider

rel out-of-stater, outstater; transient; visitor; immigrant; wanderer

idiom stranger within the gates

con inhabitant, resident; aboriginal, aborigine, autochthon, indigene, native

strangle *vb* **1** *syn* see CHOKE 1

2 *syn* see SUPPRESS 2

strangling *n syn* see REPRESSION 1

strapped *adj syn* see POOR 1

stratagem *n syn* see TRICK 1

rel conspiracy, intrigue, machination, plot

strategy *n syn* see PLAN 1

stratospheric *adj syn* see EXCESSIVE 1

straw *adj syn* see BLOND 1

rel strawish, strawy

straw *vb syn* see STREW 1

stray *vb* **1** *syn* see WANDER 1

2 *syn* see ERR

idiom stray from the straight and narrow

3 *syn* see DIGRESS 2

idiom get off the track, get sidetracked

stray *adj syn* see ERRATIC 1

rel random, sporadic

streak *n syn* see HINT 2

streak *vb* to make irregular lines or stripes of contrasting colors on or in < hair *streaked* with gray >

syn strake, striate, stripe

rel dapple, fleck, spot; marble, variegate, vein

stream *n* **1** *syn* see CREEK 2

2 *syn* see FLOW

stream *vb syn* see POUR 2

streamer *n syn* see FLAG

streamline *vb syn* see SIMPLIFY

‖**streel** *n syn* see SLATTERN 1

street *n syn* see WAY 1

rel ruelle, streetlet; drive

street arab *n syn* see VAGABOND

street girl *n syn* see PROSTITUTE

streetwalker *n syn* see PROSTITUTE

streetwalking *n syn* see PROSTITUTION

strength *n* **1** *syn* see POWER 4

rel brawn; sturdiness, toughness; healthiness, soundness

con feebleness

ant weakness

2 *syn* see STABILITY

3 *syn* see SUBSTANCE 2

strengthen *vb* **1** *syn* see ENCOURAGE 1

2 to make strong or stronger < exercise is needed to *strengthen* the body >

syn energize, fortify, invigorate, reinforce

rel brace, support, undergird; anneal, ruggedize, sinew, tone (up), toughen; cheer, embolden, encourage, enhearten, ensteel, hearten, inspirit, nerve, steel

con cripple, debilitate, disable, enfeeble, tear down, undermine; deject, discourage, dishearten, dispirit; emasculate, enervate, unman, unnerve

ant weaken

3 *syn* see GIRD 3

idiom gather one's resources, recruit one's strength

‖**strengthy** *adj syn* see STRONG 1

strenuous *adj* **1** *syn* see VIGOROUS

2 *syn* see HARD 6

rel breathless, energy-consuming; mean, wicked; Herculean

idiom a long hard pull, an uphill climb, tough going

con comfortable, cushy, light, unburdensome

ant effortless

stress *n* the action or effect of force exerted within or upon a thing < the bridge trusses slowly yielded to *stress* and buckled under the weight of the deck >
syn pressure, strain, tension
rel pinch; burden, weight
2 *syn* see EMPHASIS
rel import, importance

stress *vb* 1 *syn* see TRY 2
2 *syn* see EMPHASIZE

stretch *vb* 1 *syn* see RUN 8
rel range, roll
2 *syn* see EXTEND 3
con abbreviate, shorten; condense, curtail, cut, trim
3 *syn* see EMBROIDER

stretch (out) *vb* *syn* see REST 1

stretch *n* 1 *syn* see RANGE 2
2 *syn* see DISTANCE 1
3 *syn* see EXPANSE
rel area, region, tract
4 *syn* see WHILE 1

stretch *adj* *syn* see ELASTIC 1

stretchy *adj* *syn* see ELASTIC 1

strew *vb* 1 to spread (something) loosely or at intervals usually over a substantial area < *strew* seed for birds >
syn bestrew, broadcast, disject, disseminate, scatter, sow, straw; *compare* SPREAD 1, SPRINKLE 1
rel dust, pepper; dissipate; cover
2 *syn* see SPREAD 1

striate *vb* *syn* see STREAK

strict *adj* 1 *syn* see RIGID 3
rel exacting, oppressive, unsparing; dour, forbidding, grim, hard-boiled, harsh, tough
idiom not to be trifled (*or* messed) with
con easy, easygoing; lax, loose; permissive
ant lenient
2 *syn* see TRUE 3

stricture *n* 1 *syn* see RESTRICTION 1
2 *syn* see ANIMADVERSION

‖**striddle** *vb* 1 *syn* see BESTRIDE 2
2 *syn* see STRIDE 1

stride *vb* 1 to move or walk with long often purposeful steps < *strode* to the door and slammed it >
syn march, sling, stalk, ‖striddle
rel clump, stamp, stomp, tramp, tromp
2 *syn* see BESTRIDE

strident *adj* 1 *syn* see HARSH 3
rel loud, stentorian, stertorous
2 *syn* see VOCIFEROUS

stridulent *adj* *syn* see HARSH 3

stridulous *adj* *syn* see HARSH 3

strife *n* 1 *syn* see DISCORD
rel argument, controversy, dispute; altercation, quarrel, squabble, wrangle; brawl, broil, fracas; affray, combat, fight, fray
ant accord
2 *syn* see CONTEST 1

strike *vb* 1 to engage in a temporary work stoppage to effect compliance with demands made on an employer < they *struck* for higher wages >
syn stick out, walk out

2 to deliver (a blow) in a strong, vigorous manner < angrily *struck* the boy >
syn ‖biff, catch, clout, ‖devel, ding, hit, ‖nail, pop, slog, ‖slosh, smite, sock, swat, whack; *compare* SLAM 1, SLAP 1
rel beat, pummel, ‖slat, ‖swap, ‖wap, whop; cudgel, hammer, mace; ‖plug, poke, ‖puck, punch; bang, bash, crash, ‖pandy, slam; ‖stoush, thrash
idiom hang one on, let one fly
3 *syn* see GIVE 10
4 *syn* see AFFLICT
5 *syn* see SEIZE 3
6 *syn* see ATTACK 1
7 *syn* see OCCUR 2
8 *syn* see AFFECT
9 *syn* see DON 2

strike *n* *syn* see DISCOVERY

strike out *vb* *syn* see HEAD 3

striker *n* *syn* see HELPER

striking *adj* *syn* see NOTICEABLE
rel showy; forceful, powerful; cogent, compelling, telling

strikingly *adv* *syn* see VERY 1

string *n* 1 *syn* see LINE 5
2 *syn* see RESOURCE 3
3 *syn* see SUCCESSION 2
4 **strings** *pl syn* see POWER 1

string (up) *vb* *syn* see HANG 2

string along *vb* *syn* see TRIFLE 1
idiom keep (someone) dangling

stringent *adj* 1 *syn* see RIGID 3
rel binding, confining, drawing
2 *syn* see GRIM 2

strings *n pl syn* see CONDITION 1

stringy *adj* *syn* see MUSCULAR 1

‖**strinkle** *vb* *syn* see SPRINKLE 1

strip *vb* 1 to remove the clothing of < guards *stripped* and searched the prisoners >
syn denude, disrobe, unclothe, undress
rel doff, peel, take off; bare, denudate, expose, uncover; disfrock, unfrock
idiom strip to the buff
con clothe, dress, robe; cover
2 to take something (as honors, privileges, functions, or trappings) away from < an exiled king now *stripped* of his power >
syn bankrupt, bare, denudate, denude, deprive, dismantle, disrobe, divest; *compare* DEPRIVE 2
rel bereave; deplenish, disfurnish, ‖displenish, dispossess; despoil, rob
con clothe, endow, furnish, grant, vest; install
ant invest
3 *syn* see RAVAGE
4 *syn* see SKIN 2

strip *n* *syn* see STRIPTEASE

strip *n* 1 a relatively long and narrow piece or section < tear old linen into *strips* for bandages >
syn band, bandeau, banding, fillet, ribbon, stripe
rel piece; section; segment; shred
2 *syn* see BAR 1

stripe *vb* *syn* see WHIP 1

stripe *n* 1 *syn* see STRIP 1
2 *syn* see TYPE

stripe *vb* *syn* see STREAK

stripling *n* *syn* see BOY 1

stripped *adj* 1 *syn* see NUDE 2

---

con attired; covered
ant clothed, dressed
2 *syn* see OPEN 2
con covered, unexposed; protected

stripper *n syn* see STRIPTEASER

stripping *n syn* see STRIPTEASE

striptease *n* entertainment in which a female performer removes her clothing piece by piece in view of an audience < a nightclub featuring *striptease* >
syn strip, stripping
idiom exotic dancing

stripteaser *n* one who performs a striptease < worked part-time as a model and *stripteaser* >
syn ecdysiast, peeler, stripper, stripteuse, teaser
idiom exotic dancer, ‖pantie peeler, ‖strip-and-shake artist, strip artist

stripteuse *n syn* see STRIPTEASER

strive *vb* 1 *syn* see LABOR 1
2 *syn* see TRY 5
rel labor, toil, travail, work; drive, strain

striving *n* 1 *syn* see CONTEST 1
rel contending; combat, fight
2 *syn* see ATTEMPT
rel labor, toil, travail, work

stroll *vb syn* see SAUNTER

stroll *n syn* see WALK 1

strong *adj* 1 having great physical strength < had the *strong* hands and arms of a wrestler >
syn mighty, powerful, ‖strengthy, wieldy; compare MUSCULAR 2
rel firm, robust, stark, strapping, sturdy, two-handed; able-bodied, tough; brawny, muscular, sinewy; lusty, vigorous
idiom strong as a bull (*or* ox)
con feeble, frail; puny, weak-bodied; forceless, impotent, powerless, strengthless
ant weak
2 having or manifesting great force or power (as in acting or resisting) < a *strong* constitution >
syn stalwart, stout, sturdy, tenacious, tough
rel hardy, robust, rugged, strapping; firm, solid, staunch; durable, enduring; forceful, potent, powerful; lusty, vigorous
con frail; forceless, impotent, powerless, strengthless; depleted, failing
ant weak
3 being rich in a characteristic ingredient < *strong* coffee >
syn concentrated, full-bodied, lusty, potent, robust
rel strong-flavored, strong-tasting; straight, undiluted, unmixed; rich; heroic, large, potent
con diluted, mixed, watered-down
ant weak
4 *syn* see SPIRITUOUS
5 *syn* see SURE 1
rel solid, substantial, unmoving, unyielding
6 *syn* see MALODOROUS 1

strong arm *n* 1 *syn* see POWER 4
2 *syn* see THUG 1

strong–arm *vb syn* see INTIMIDATE

stronghold *n syn* see FORT

strongly *adv syn* see HARD 1
ant weakly

strong man *n syn* see TYRANT

strong suit *n syn* see FORTE

structure *n* 1 *syn* see BUILDING
rel construction, erection, pile
2 *syn* see EDIFICE
3 something made up of more or less interdependent elements and having a definite organizational pattern < the complex bureaucratic *structure* of modern government >
syn framework
rel anatomy, skeleton; build, construction, frame; arrangement, composition, form, format, makeup, morphology; complex, network, system

struggle *vb syn* see TRY 5
rel compete, vie
idiom make a valiant attempt (*or* try)
ant give up

struggle *n syn* see ATTEMPT

strum *vb syn* see HUM

strumpet *n syn* see WANTON

‖**strunt** *vb syn* see STRUT 2

‖**strunt** *n syn* see LIQUOR 2

strut *vb* 1 *syn* see SASHAY
2 to walk with an air of pomposity or affected dignity < a pompous general *strutting* off the parade ground >
syn ‖strunt, swagger
rel flaunt, parade
con cower, cringe; slink

stubborn *adj* 1 *syn* see OBSTINATE
rel contumacious, insubordinate, rebellious; cantankerous, ornery; ‖stunkard, ‖stunt
idiom set in one's ways, stubborn as a mule
con adaptable, pliable, pliant; amenable, tractable
ant docile
2 *syn* see INFLEXIBLE 2

stubbornness *n syn* see DEFIANCE 2
rel cantankerousness, orneriness

stubby *adj syn* see STOCKY

stube *n syn* see ALEHOUSE

stuck–up *adj syn* see VAIN 3
idiom too big for one's breeches, wise in one's own conceit

stud *vb syn* see SPOT 2

studied *adj syn* see DELIBERATE 1
rel thoughtful; intentional, voluntary, willful, willing
con natural, offhand
ant unstudied

studio *n* the working place of an artist (as a painter) < moved to a larger *studio* >
syn atelier, bottega
rel shop, workroom, workshop

studious *adj syn* see DELIBERATE 1
ant impromptu

study *n* 1 *syn* see REVERIE
2 *syn* see ATTENTION 1
rel contemplation, weighing; abstraction, meditation, musing, pondering, rumination
3 *syn* see EXERCISE 4

study *vb* 1 *syn* see CONSIDER 1
idiom give careful study to
2 *syn* see SCRUTINIZE 1

stuff *n* 1 *syn* see PERSONAL EFFECTS
2 *syn* see MONEY
3 *syn* see THING 4
4 *syn* see ESSENCE 2

stuff *vb syn* see CRAM 1
rel overfill, overstuff

idiom fill to overflowing, fill to the brim

stuffed *adj syn* see FULL 1

stuffed shirt *n* a smug usually pompous person with an inflexibly conservative or reactionary outlook <a *stuffed shirt* with a starched mind>
syn Blimp, Colonel Blimp, fuddy-duddy
rel diehard; prig, prude, smug
con freethinker, latitudinarian, liberal, libertarian, libertine; avant garde

stuffing *n syn* see ENTRAILS
rel ‖tar

stuffy *adj* 1 marked by a heavy oppressive quality of air <a *stuffy* room that needed airing>
syn airless, breathless, close, stifling, stivy, suffocating, sultry; *compare* HUMID, STIFLING 1
rel heavy, oppressive, thick; stagnant; shut-up, unventilated
con airy, breezy; open, ventilated; bracing, invigorating, refreshing, stimulating
2 *syn* see PRIM 1
rel dull, humdrum, stodgy; hidebound, illiberal, narrow, narrow-minded
3 *syn* see POMPOUS 1

‖**stuggy** *adj syn* see STOCKY

stultify *vb* to deprive of vitality and render futile especially by enfeebling or repressive influences <artistic creativity *stultified* by the intrusion of propaganda>
syn constipate, stagnate, stifle, trammel
rel discourage, inhibit, restrain; check, stunt; enfeeble, impair, weaken; deaden, dull; repress, smother, suffocate, suppress; invalidate, nullify
con encourage, foster, nourish; pique, provoke, stimulate

stultiloquence *n syn* see CHATTER

stumble *vb* 1 *syn* see WALLOW 2
rel falter, waver; trip; fall
2 *syn* see DEMUR
3 to move so clumsily and awkwardly as to lose one's balance or trip and fall <*stumbled* across the darkened room and fell>
syn blunder, bumble, lurch, ‖snapper; *compare* WALLOW 2
rel reel, stagger, totter; trip; pitch, topple
4 *syn* see LUMBER
5 *syn* see TEETER
rel careen, swing
6 to act, proceed, or execute in a hesitant and clumsily faltering manner <*stumbled* through his Latin translation>
syn limp, muddle, shuffle
rel falter, hesitate, wobble; blunder, bumble; botch, bungle, ‖muck
ant breeze
7 *syn* see HAPPEN 2
idiom come (*or* run) up against, fall upon, stub one's toe upon (*or* on)
8 *syn* see PUZZLE

stumblebum *n* a clumsy inept or blundering person <a staff consisting of third-raters and *stumblebums*>
syn blunderbuss, blunderer, bungler
rel incompetent

---

syn synonym(s)   *rel* related word(s)
ant antonym(s)   *con* contrasted word(s)
idiom idiomatic equivalent(s)
‖ use limited; if in doubt, see a dictionary

con crackerjack, ‖dab, ‖darb, expert, top-notcher, whiz; natural; professional

stumbling block *n syn* see OBSTACLE

stump *vb* 1 *syn* see NONPLUS 1
2 *syn* see LUMBER

stump *n syn* see DEFIANCE 1

stumpy *adj syn* see STOCKY

‖**stumpy** *n syn* see MONEY

stun *vb syn* see DAZE 2
rel nonplus; amaze, astound, flabbergast; knock out
idiom strike dumb (*or* dead)

stunner *n* 1 *syn* see WONDER 1
2 *syn* see BEAUTY

stunning *adj* 1 *syn* see EXCELLENT
2 *syn* see BEAUTIFUL

‖**stunpoll** *n syn* see DUNCE

‖**stunt** *adj syn* see STUNTED

stunt *vb* to hinder the normal growth and development of <the inhospitable climate had *stunted* all vegetation>
syn dwarf, suppress
rel check, curb, hold back; impair

stunt *n syn* see TRICK 3

stunted *adj* having had one's growth and development hindered or arrested <the children were *stunted* from malnutrition>
syn runted, runtish, runty, ‖scrunty, ‖stunt
rel undersized; dwarf
con able-bodied, robust well-set, well-set-up; giant, oversize; healthy, strong, sturdy, vigorous

‖**stupe** *n syn* see DUNCE

stupefy *vb* 1 *syn* see DULL 5
2 *syn* see DAZE 2
rel addle, faze, rattle; nonplus

stupendous *adj* 1 *syn* see MARVELOUS 1
2 *syn* see MONSTROUS 1

stupid *adj* 1 lacking in or exhibiting a lack of power to absorb ideas or impressions <a willing boy but too *stupid* to succeed in school>
syn beefheaded, beef-witted, beetleheaded, blear-eyed, blear-witted, blockheaded, blockish, chuckleheaded, dense, doltish, dull, dumb, duncical, fatheaded, goosey, hammerheaded, numskulled, pinhead, pinheaded, thick, thickheaded, thick-witted; *compare* RETARDED, SIMPLE 3
rel asinine, fatuous, foolish, simple; brute, brutish, dummel, lumbering, oafish, slow, slow-witted, sluggish; ‖half-assed; crass; backward, half-witted, retarded; idiotic, imbecilic
idiom ‖dead above (*or* between) the ears, ‖dead from the neck up, having a block for a head, having cotton between the ears, ‖muscle-bound between the ears
con acute, alert, bright, clever, keen, knowing, quick, quick-witted, sharp, smart; sage, wise; brilliant; able, competent
ant intelligent
2 *syn* see LETHARGIC

stupid *n syn* see DUNCE

stupor *n syn* see LETHARGY 1
rel sopor; anesthesia, insensibility

sturdy *adj syn* see STRONG 2
rel sound, substantial
ant decrepit

Sturm und Drang *n syn* see UNREST

‖**stut** *vb syn* see STAMMER 1

stutter *vb syn* see STAMMER 1

sty *n* **1** an extremely unkempt or filthy place < the basement was a rat-infested *sty* >
syn dump, pigpen, pigsty
2 *syn* see SINK 1

stygian *adj syn* see INFERNAL 2

style *n* **1** *syn* see VEIN 1
2 *syn* see NAME 1
3 *syn* see FASHION 3
4 an individual's characteristic attitudes and taste as expressed or indicated in his way of life < she liked the man's sophisticated *style* >
syn manner, way
rel behavior; bearing, carriage; characteristic, trait; idiosyncrasy, peculiarity

style *vb syn* see NAME 1

stylish *adj* being in accordance with or conforming to current fashion < she was a *stylish* dresser >
syn a la mode, chic, ‖classy, dashing, exclusive, fashionable, in, modish, posh, sharp, smart, snappy, swank, swish, tonish, tony, ‖trendy, trig, ultrafashionable, with-it; *compare* DAPPER
rel new, new-day, newfangled, new-fashioned; modern, modernistic, up-to-date; chichi, doggish, doggy, natty, rakish, sassy, swagger; ostentatious, pretentious, ritzy, showy, swell; sleek, slick
idiom in fashion, in the mode
con styleless; old-fashioned, outmoded, out-of-date; drab, tasteless
ant dowdy, unstylish

suasible *adj syn* see RECEPTIVE 1

suave *adj* being conspicuously and ingratiatingly tactful and well-mannered < a man of *suave*, well-bred equanimity >
syn bland, civilized, smooth, urbane; *compare* TACTFUL
rel affable, cordial, genial, gracious, sociable; courteous, courtly, polite; diplomatic, politic; cultivated, cultured, distingué, polished, refined, well-bred; sophisticated, worldly; ingratiating, soft, soft-spoken; fulsome, slick, unctuous
con clumsy, unpolished, unskilled; tactless, undiplomatic, untactful
ant bluff

sub *adj syn* see SUBORDINATE

sub *n syn* see SUBSTITUTE

subaltern *n syn* see INFERIOR

subaquatic *adj syn* see SUBMARINE

subaqueous *adj syn* see SUBMARINE

subaverage *adj syn* see LOW 9

subconscious *n* mental activities that occur just below the threshold of consciousness < a motive probably rooted in his *subconscious* >
syn underconsciousness, undersense
rel subconsciousness; subliminal self
idiom subconscious (*or* submerged) mind
con consciousness; awareness

subdolous *adj syn* see SLY 2

subdue *vb syn* see CONQUER 1
rel extinguish, put down, quash, quell, quench, squelch, suppress

subdued *adj* **1** *syn* see QUIET 4
2 reduced or lacking in force, intensity, or vividness < *subdued* colors > < she answered his questions in a timid *subdued* voice >

syn low-key, low-keyed, sober, soft, softened, toned down
rel moderated, tempered; controlled, restrained; mellow; neutral; quiet
con enlivened, intensified; bright, intense, strong; brilliant, vivid; saturated; blaring, glaring, harsh, screaming
3 *syn* see TAME
ant unsubdued

subduer *n syn* see VICTOR 1

subfusc *adj syn* see DULL 8

subitaneous *adj syn* see PRECIPITATE 1

subjacent *adj syn* see INFERIOR 1
ant superjacent

subject *n* **1** *syn* see CITIZEN 2
2 the basic idea or the principal object of attention in a discourse or artistic composition < the Puritans as soldiers of Christ was the *subject* of her paper >
syn argument, head, matter, motif, motive, point, subject matter, text, theme, topic
rel material, substance; problem, question; leitmotiv; core, meat
con elaboration, enlargement, enlarging, expatiation; development, explication

subject *adj* **1** *syn* see SUBORDINATE
rel servile, slavish, subservient
ant dominant, sovereign
2 *syn* see LIABLE 2
rel apt, likely

subject *vb syn* see EXPOSE 1

subjective *adj* peculiar to a particular individual as modified by individual bias and limitations < *subjective* judgments >
syn unobjective
rel biased, prejudiced; abstract, nonobjective, nonrepresentational, nonrepresentative
ant objective

subject matter *n syn* see SUBJECT 2

subjoin *vb syn* see ADD 1
rel combine, conjoin, unite
con part, separate, sever

subjugate *vb* **1** *syn* see CONQUER 1
rel compel, coerce, force
2 *syn* see ENSLAVE
ant liberate

subjugator *n syn* see VICTOR 1

sublease *vb syn* see SUBLET

sublet *vb* to turn over to another one's right of occupancy of (rented or leased housing) < *sublet* her apartment to a friend >
syn sublease, underlease, underlet

sublime *vb syn* see EXALT 1

sublime *adj* **1** *syn* see GRAND 3
2 *syn* see SPLENDID 2
rel abstract, ideal, transcendent, transcendental; divine, holy, sacred, spiritual; august, majestic, noble, stately

sublimity *n syn* see APEX 2

sublunary *adj syn* see EARTHLY 1

submarine *adj* being, acting, growing, or used under water < a *submarine* camera >
syn subaquatic, subaqueous, underwater

submerge *vb* **1** *syn* see DIP 1
rel drench, impregnate, saturate, soak
2 *syn* see DELUGE 1
3 *syn* see SINK 1

submerse *vb* **1** *syn* see DIP 1
2 *syn* see SINK 1

submission *n syn* see SURRENDER

rel bowing, submitting; acquiescence, compliance, resignation; cringing, servility; prostration

ant resistance

submissive *adj* 1 *syn* see TAME

rel complying, conformable, obeying; bowing down, unerect; menial, servile, slavish, subservient

ant rebellious

2 *syn* see PASSIVE 2

submit *vb* 1 *syn* see YIELD 2

ant resist, withstand

2 to offer or commit (something) for consideration, study, or decision < *submitted* his report directly to the general >

syn hand in, refer

rel bring, deliver, present; offer, proffer, tender; send in; provide

3 *syn* see SUGGEST 4

4 *syn* see FALL 3

ant hold out, resist

subnormal *adj* *syn* see LOW 9

rel subpar

subordinate *adj* placed in or occupying a lower class, rank, or status < making the executive *subordinate* to the legislative branch >

syn collateral, dependent, secondary, sub, subject, tributary, under

rel adjuvant, auxiliary, contributory, subsidiary; satellite; inferior, subaltern, subalternate; accessory, parergal, supplementary

con chief, first, leading, main; dominant, master, superior

subordinate *n* *syn* see INFERIOR

sub rosa *adv* *syn* see SECRETLY

ant aboveboard

sub–rosa *adj* *syn* see SECRET 1

ant aboveboard

subscribe *vb* 1 *syn* see SIGN 1

2 *syn* see CONTRIBUTE 1

3 *syn* see ASSENT

rel approve, endorse, favor, sanction

subsequent *adj* 1 being, occurring, or carried out at a time after something else < *subsequent* events disproved his predictions >

syn after, ensuing, later, posterior, postliminary, subsequential

rel following, next, succeeding; consequential, resultant, resulting

con exordial, introductory, prefatory, preliminary, preludial; anterior, precedent, preceding, prior

ant antecedent

2 *syn* see CONSECUTIVE

ant antecedent

subsequential *adj* 1 *syn* see SUBSEQUENT 1

2 *syn* see CONSECUTIVE

ant antecedent

subsequently *adv* *syn* see AFTER

ant antecedently, priorly

subsequent to *prep* *syn* see AFTER 2

subservient *adj* 1 *syn* see AUXILIARY

2 showing extreme compliance or abject obedience < a *subservient* minor bureaucrat >

syn menial, obeisant, obsequious, servile, slavish

rel acquiescent, compliant, resigned, submissive; cowering, cringing, fawning, truckling; abject, ignoble, mean

idiom as obedient as a dog

con aggressive; arrogant, haughty; rebellious; independent, irrepressible, uncontainable

ant domineering, overbearing

subside *vb* *syn* see ABATE 4

idiom dwindle down

subsidiary *adj* *syn* see AUXILIARY

rel back-up; minor, tributary

subsidize *vb* *syn* see ENDOW 2

rel back; promote; help

subsidy *n* *syn* see APPROPRIATION

rel subsidization; gift, reward

subsist *vb* *syn* see BE

subsistence *n* *syn* see LIVING

substance *n* 1 *syn* see TENOR 1

rel import, meaning

idiom the general drift

2 the inner significance or central meaning of something written or said < just give me the *substance* of his speech >

syn amount, body, burden, core, crux, gist, kernel, matter, meat, nub, nubbin, pith, purport, sense, short, strength, sum and substance, sum total, thrust, upshot; *compare* BODY 3, ESSENCE 2, MEANING 1, TENOR 1

rel center, focus, heart, nucleus; point; import, meaningfulness

3 *syn* see BODY 3

rel drift, tenor

4 *syn* see ESSENCE 2

5 *syn* see THING 4

6 *syn* see WEALTH 2

substantial *adj* 1 *syn* see MATERIAL 1

con airy, ethereal

ant unsubstantial

2 *syn* see IMPORTANT 1

rel key, principal; strong; serious

3 *syn* see PROSPEROUS 3

rel solid, solvent

substantiate *vb* 1 *syn* see EMBODY 1

rel substantialize, substantify

2 *syn* see CONFIRM 2

rel demonstrate, prove, test, try

substitutable *adj* *syn* see INTERCHANGEABLE

substitute *n* 1 a person who takes the place of or acts instead of another < found a *substitute* for the sick teacher >

syn alternate, fill-in, locum tenens, pinch hitter, replacement, stand-in, sub, succedaneum, surrogate

rel relay, relief; deputy, procurator, proxy; supply; double, understudy

2 *syn* see RESOURCE 3

substitute *vb* *syn* see EXCHANGE 2

substitute *adj* 1 serving or fitted for use as a substitute < a *substitute* driver was needed for the long trip >

syn alternate, alternative, surrogate

rel additional; another; other, second; back-up, reserve; supplemental, supplementary, suppletory

2 *syn* see ARTIFICIAL 2

substract *vb* *syn* see DEDUCT 1

substral *adj* *syn* see ELEMENTAL 1

---

syn synonym(s) *rel* related word(s)
ant antonym(s) *con* contrasted word(s)
idiom idiomatic equivalent(s)
|| use limited; if in doubt, see a dictionary

substratum *n* 1 *syn* see BASIS 1
  rel core, meat, stuff, substance
  2 *syn* see BASE 1
substruction *n syn* see BASE 1
substructure *n syn* see BASE 1
  ant superstructure
subsume *vb syn* see INCLUDE
subterfuge *n syn* see DECEPTION 1
subterrane *n syn* see CAVE
subterranean *adj* being, lying, functioning,
  or operating under the surface of the earth
  < *subterranean* hot springs that emerge as
  geysers >
  syn subterrestrial, underearth, underfoot,
  underground
  con aboveground, surface, surficial
subterranean *n syn* see CAVE
subterrestrial *adj* *syn* see SUBTER-
RANEAN
subtile *adj syn* see THIN 2
subtle *adj* 1 *syn* see THIN 2
  2 *syn* see FINE 1
  ant unsubtle
  3 *syn* see LOGICAL 2
  rel dexterous, skillful
  con blunt; dense
  4 *syn* see SLY 2
  ant unsubtle
subtract *vb syn* see DEDUCT 1
  ant add
subtraction *n syn* see DEDUCTION 1
  ant addition
suburbs *n pl syn* see ENVIRONS 2
  rel fringes; suburbia
subvention *n syn* see APPROPRIATION
subversion *n syn* see SABOTAGE
  rel demolishing, destroying, destruction
subvert *vb syn* see SABOTAGE
  rel overthrow, overturn, upset; demolish,
  destroy, ruin; corrupt, debase, deprave,
  pervert
  con sustain, uphold
succedaneum *n syn* see SUBSTITUTE
succedent *adj syn* see CONSECUTIVE
succeed *vb* 1 *syn* see FOLLOW 1
  ant precede
  2 to result favorably according to plans
  and desires < that advertising campaign
  really *succeeded* >
  syn click, come off, go, go over, pan out,
  prove out
  rel catch on; prevail
  idiom go over big, go over with a bang,
  hit the mark, make a hit, turn out well
  ant fail, flop
  3 to attain or be attaining a desired end
  < how to *succeed* in big business >
  syn arrive, flourish, go, make out, prosper, score, thrive
  rel ∥dow; get ahead; boom; achieve, attain, gain, reach; accomplish, effect, fulfill;
  conquer, prevail, triumph, win (out)
  idiom do all right by oneself, do well,
  gain one's end, get places, get somewhere,
  get to the top of the ladder, make a success, make it (big), make one's mark,
  ∥make the big time, make the grade
  con dwindle, languish; fall down, flounder, founder; lose (out); bust
  ant fail
succeeding *adj syn* see CONSECUTIVE
succès fou *n syn* see SMASH 6
success *n* a succeeding fully or in accordance with one's desires < attributed his

business *success* to hard work and attention to detail >
  syn arrival, ∥do, flying colors, go, prosperity, successfulness
  rel accomplishment, achievement, attainment; triumph, victory
  ant failure; nonsuccess, unsuccessfulness
successful *adj* resulting in or having
  gained success < a *successful* business
  venture >
  syn prosperous, thriving; *compare* FLOUR-
  ISHING
  rel extraordinary, notable, noteworthy,
  outstanding, smash, smashing
  idiom crowned (*or* blessed *or* flushed)
  with success, ∥out front
  con failing, thriveless, unprosperous; defeated, disappointed, failed, frustrated;
  bankrupt, broken, destroyed, ruined
  ant successless, unsuccessful
successfully *adv syn* see WELL 5
  ant unsuccessfully
successfulness *n syn* see SUCCESS
  ant nonsuccess, unsuccessfulness
succession *n* 1 *syn* see ORDER 5
  2 a number of things that follow each
  other in some order < another *succession*
  of price hikes >
  syn alternation, chain, consecution,
  course, order, progression, row, sequel,
  sequence, series, string, suite, train; *compare* CYCLE 1
  rel successiveness; round, round robin
successional *adj syn* see CONSECUTIVE
successive *adj syn* see CONSECUTIVE
  rel alternating, rotating
successively *adv syn* see TOGETHER 2
succinct *adj syn* see CONCISE
  rel blunt, brusque
  idiom right to the point
  ant discursive
succinctly *adv syn* see BRIEFLY
  ant discursively
succor *n syn* see HELP 1
  rel ministration, ministry; maintenance,
  nourishment, sustenance
succubus *n syn* see DEVIL 2
succulent *adj* full of juice < a *succulent*
  roast >
  syn juicy, ∥sappy
succumb *vb* 1 *syn* see YIELD 2
  rel abandon, relinquish, resign
  2 *syn* see FALL 3
  idiom hand over one's sword, meet one's
  Waterloo, show (*or* wave) the white flag,
  strike (*or* haul down) one's colors
  3 *syn* see COLLAPSE 2
  idiom bite the dust, ∥take the count
  4 *syn* see DIE 1
  idiom yield one's breath
such *adj* 1 being previously characterized
  or specified < authorized to seize illegally
  parked cars and impound *such* vehicles >
  syn aforementioned, aforesaid, said
  2 being of so extreme a degree or quality
  < *such* nonsense as I had never heard
  before >
  syn that
  3 *syn* see LIKE
such *pron* 1 *syn* see SUCH A ONE
  2 *syn* see SUCHLIKE
  idiom the like
such a one *pron* someone or something
  that has been, is being, or will be stated,

implied, or exemplified < the area is full of caverns; *such a one* may be found here >
syn such
suchlike *adj syn* see LIKE
suchlike *pron* a person or thing of the same or similar kind < airplanes, missiles, rockets, and *suchlike* >
syn such
‖**suck** *n syn* see SYCOPHANT
sucker *n* **1** *syn* see PARASITE
2 *syn* see FOOL 3
idiom easy pickings
sucker *vb syn* see CHEAT
suck in *vb syn* see DECEIVE
‖**suck-in** *n syn* see DECEPTION 1
suckle *vb syn* see NURSE 1
sudden *adj syn* see PRECIPITATE 1
rel accelerated, quickened, speeded; expeditious, fast, fleet, rapid, swift
sudden *adv* **1** *syn* see UNAWARES
2 *syn* see SHORT 1
suddenly *adv* **1** *syn* see SHORT 1
2 *syn* see UNAWARES
idiom of (*or* on) a sudden, on the sudden
suds *n pl but sing or pl in constr* **1** *syn* see SADNESS
2 *syn* see FOAM
sue *vb syn* see ADDRESS 8
idiom make (*or* pay) suit to, press one's suit
sue (for *or* to) *vb syn* see PETITION
suffer *vb* **1** *syn* see BEAR 10
rel accept, admit, receive
idiom grin and abide
2 *syn* see EXPERIENCE 1
3 *syn* see LET 2
rel countenance; accept, admit, receive; acquiesce, bow, submit, yield
‖**4** *syn* see HURT 4
sufferable *adj syn* see BEARABLE
ant insufferable
sufferance *n syn* see PERMISSION
suffering *n syn* see DISTRESS
rel adversity, misfortune
suffice *vb syn* see SERVE 3
sufficiency *n syn* see ENOUGH
ant insufficiency
sufficient *adj* **1** being what is requisite or needed especially without superfluity < there is *sufficient* bread left for breakfast >
syn adequate, comfortable, competent, decent, enough, satisfactory, sufficing; *compare* DECENT 4
rel ample, plenteous, plentiful, plenty; commensurable, commensurate, due, proportionate; acceptable, agreeable, pleasing
con inadequate, unsufficing; deficient; failing, lacking, missing, wanting
ant insufficient
2 *syn* see DECENT 4
idiom fair to middling
sufficient *n syn* see ENOUGH
sufficiently *adv syn* see ENOUGH 1
ant insufficiently
sufficing *adj syn* see SUFFICIENT 1

syn synonym(s)   *rel* related word(s)
ant antonym(s)   *con* contrasted word(s)
idiom idiomatic equivalent(s)
‖ use limited; if in doubt, see a dictionary

suffocate *vb* to stop the respiration of (as by asphyxiation) < the child was *suffocated* in an old refrigerator >
syn asphyxiate, choke, ‖quackle, smother, stifle; *compare* CHOKE 1
rel stive; strangle
suffocating *adj* **1** *syn* see STIFLING 1
2 *syn* see STUFFY 1
suffocative *adj syn* see STIFLING 1
suffrage *n* the right, privilege, or power of expressing one's choice or wish (as in an election or in the determination of policy) < universal *suffrage* >
syn ballot, franchise, vote
rel voice
suffuse *vb syn* see INFUSE 1
rel interject, interpose, introduce
‖**sugar** *n syn* see MONEY
sugar (over) *vb syn* see SUGARCOAT 1
sugarcoat *vb* **1** to make (something difficult or unpleasant) superficially easy or attractive < *sugarcoated* the reproach with a smile >
syn candy, honey, sugar (over), sweeten
rel edulcorate
2 *syn* see PALLIATE
sugarplum *n syn* see SOP 2
suggest *vb* **1** to convey an idea indirectly < designing attractive books with jackets that truly *suggest* their contents >
syn connote, hint, imply, insinuate, intimate; *compare* POINT 2
rel advert, allude, refer; denote
idiom bring to mind
con demonstrate, display, exhibit, manifest, set out, show
ant express
2 *syn* see POINT 2
rel promise
idiom be the sign of, point in the direction of
3 *syn* see PROPOSE 1
4 to offer (as an idea or theory) for consideration < this, I *suggest*, is what really happened >
syn submit, theorize
rel conjecture; imagine
5 to represent another thing indirectly, figuratively, and sometimes obscurely by evoking a thought, image, or conception of it < the meaning of a poem is often *suggested* in its title >
syn adumbrate, shadow (forth); *compare* ADUMBRATE 1
rel outline, sketch; betoken, symbolize; typify
con display, flaunt, parade
ant manifest
suggestion *n* **1** *syn* see PROPOSAL
2 *syn* see HINT 1
rel implication, innuendo
3 *syn* see ASSOCIATION 4
rel allusion; reminder
con demonstration, display, exhibition, manifestation, show
ant expression
4 *syn* see HINT 2
suggestive *adj* **1** *syn* see EVOCATIVE
rel significative
2 *syn* see RISQUÉ
rel erotic, sexy
suicide *n* the act or an instance of taking one's own life voluntarily and intention-

ally <committed *suicide* by shooting herself>
syn felo-de-se, hara-kiri, self-destruction, self-murder, self-slaughter, self-violence

suit *n* 1 a legal proceeding instituted for the sake of demanding justice or enforcing a right <filed a *suit* to recover her property>
syn action, case, cause, lawsuit
2 *syn* see PRAYER
rel asking, request, requesting, solicitation, soliciting

suit *vb* 1 *syn* see AGREE 4
idiom be in accord with, check out to the letter
2 *syn* see SERVE 3
3 *syn* see ADAPT
4 to be suitable for or to <the right word is the one that *suits* the occasion>
syn agree (with), become, befit, fit, go (together *or* with); *compare* SUIT 6
rel harmonize (with); benefit; please, satisfy
idiom answer a need (*or* the purpose), hit the spot
con clash, conflict, disaccord, disagree
5 *syn* see FLATTER
6 to meet the needs or desires of <this arrangement *suits* me fine>
syn please, satisfy; *compare* SUIT 4
con discontent, displease, dissatisfy; disappoint, fail, let down

suitability *n* *syn* see ORDER 11
ant unsuitability
suitable *adj* 1 *syn* see GOOD 2
ant unsuitable
2 *syn* see JUST 3
rel reasonable; advisable, expedient, politic
ant unsuitable
3 *syn* see FIT 1
rel nice, presentable, seemly
ant unbecoming, unsuitable
4 *syn* see ELIGIBLE
ant unsuitable
suitableness *n* *syn* see ORDER 11
ant unsuitableness
suitably *adv* *syn* see WELL 4
ant unsuitably
suite *n* 1 *syn* see ENTOURAGE
2 *syn* see GROUP 3
3 *syn* see APARTMENT 1
4 *syn* see SUCCESSION 2
suited *adj* *syn* see ASSORTED 2
ant unsuited
suitor *n* 1 *syn* see SUPPLIANT
2 one who courts a woman or seeks to marry her <a *suitor* for the king's daughter>
syn spark, sparker, swain, wooer
rel beau, boyfriend; cavalier, gallant; lover, man, paramour
sulk *vb* to be sullen or morose in mood usually because of a grievance <*sulked* all day when he didn't call>
syn ‖dort, grump, ‖mump, pet, pout, ‖sull
rel frown, glower, lower, scowl; brood, gloom, mope, take on
idiom be in a sulk, have the sulks, ‖take the dods
sulk *n*, *often* **sulks** *pl* the state, condition, or mood of one sulking <sat in a *sulk* all day after being reprimanded>

syn ‖dods, ‖dorts, grumps, mulligrubs, mumps, pouts, sullens
rel sourness, sulkiness, surliness; glumness, grouchiness
idiom a case of the sulks
sulky *adj* *syn* see SULLEN
rel cranky, testy, touchy; cantankerous, irritable, querulous
idiom having the sulks
‖**sull** *vb* *syn* see SULK
sullen *adj* showing a forbidding or disagreeable mood <stalked out in *sullen* silence>
syn ‖chuff, ‖chuffy, crabbed, crabby, ‖dorty, dour, gloomy, glum, morose, mumpish, saturnine, sulky, surly, ugly
rel moody; tenebrific, tenebrose, tenebrous; frowning, glowering, lowering, scowling; cross, fretful, grumpy, ill-humored, peevish, petulant, pouting, pouty, sour, sourpussed; black, hostile, malevolent, malicious, malign, mean, ‖runty; cynical, pessimistic
con easy, gay, high-spirited, insouciant, lighthearted, smiling
sullens *n pl* *syn* see SULK
sully *vb* *syn* see TAINT 1
rel disgrace, shame
sulphurous *adj* *syn* see INFERNAL 1
sultry *adj* 1 *syn* see HUMID
rel smothering, smothery, ‖smudgy, stifling, suffocating
2 *syn* see STUFFY 1
3 *syn* see HOT 1
idiom hot as Hades, ‖hot as old Billy Hell
4 *syn* see SENSATIONAL 2
sum *n* 1 *syn* see WHOLE 1
2 *syn* see WHOLE 2
rel body, bulk, mass; structure
3 *syn* see SUMMARY
sum *vb* 1 *syn* see ADD 2
2 *syn* see EPITOMIZE 1
sum (to *or* into) *vb* *syn* see AMOUNT 1
sum and substance *n* 1 *syn* see SUBSTANCE 2
2 *syn* see MEANING 1
summarize *vb* *syn* see EPITOMIZE 1
rel recapitulate, résumé, retrograde
summary *adj* 1 *syn* see CONCISE
rel compact, compacted
ant circumstantial
2 done or executed on the spot and without formality <a *summary* trial and speedy execution>
syn drumhead
summary *n* a short restatement of the main points <a *summary* of the news>
syn epitome, recapitulation, résumé, sum, summation, summing-up, sum-up
rel outline; run-through; roundup; inventory
con amplification, elaboration, enlargement, expansion
summate *vb* 1 *syn* see ADD 2
2 *syn* see EPITOMIZE 1
summation *n* *syn* see SUMMARY
summative *adj* *syn* see CUMULATIVE
summer *n* the season between spring and autumn <liked to swim during the *summer*>
syn summertide, summertime
rel midsummer

summerhouse *n* a covered structure in a garden or park designed to provide a shady resting place < watched the sea from the *summerhouse* >
  syn alcove, belvedere, garden house, gazebo, pagoda
summertide *n syn* see SUMMER
summertime *n syn* see SUMMER
summing–up *n syn* see SUMMARY
summit *n* 1 *syn* see TOP 1
  2 *syn* see APEX 2
summon *vb* 1 *syn* see CONVOKE
  2 to demand or request the presence or service of < were *summoned* to the principal's office >
  syn call, call in, convene, summons; *compare* CONVOKE
  rel bid, command, enjoin, order; cite, subpoena
  idiom bid come
summons *vb syn* see SUMMON 2
‖**sump** *n syn* see SWAMP
sumptuous *adj* 1 *syn* see LUXURIOUS 3
  rel gorgeous, resplendent, splendid, superb; lavish, rich
  2 *syn* see GRAND 2
  rel awe-inspiring, grandiose, imposing
sum total *n* 1 *syn* see WHOLE 1
  2 *syn* see SUBSTANCE 2
sum up *vb syn* see EPITOMIZE 1
sum–up *n syn* see SUMMARY
sun *n* 1 the heavenly body about which the earth rotates < up in time to see the *sun* rise >
  syn daystar, phoebus, Sol
  rel celestial body, luminary, orb, star
  idiom old Sol
  2 the radiation of the sun < enjoying the warm spring *sun* >
  syn sunlight, sunshine
  rel daylight; radiance, radiation
sun *vb* to expose to sunshine < *sunned* himself too long and got badly burned >
  syn bask, insolate
  rel sunbathe; sunburn, sun-cure, sun-dry, tan
sunbeamy *adj syn* see CHEERFUL 1
Sunday best *n syn* see FINERY
  idiom Sunday-go-to-meeting clothes
sunder *vb* 1 *syn* see SEPARATE 1
  rel cleave, rend, rive
  2 *syn* see CUT 5
‖**sundowner** *n syn* see VAGABOND
sundries *n pl* miscellaneous small articles, details, or items < supplied such *sundries* as needles, pins, and thread >
  syn etceteras, oddments, odds and ends, this and that(s)
  rel notions
sundry *adj* 1 *syn* MANY, legion, multifarious, multitudinal, multitudinous, numerous, populous, ‖several, various, voluminous
  idiom all and sundry
  2 *syn* see SEVERAL 3
  idiom all sorts of
sundry *pron, pl in constr* an indeterminate number of more than one or two < *sundry* were interviewed; a few were selected >

  syn divers, many, ‖several, various
  idiom all and sundry, quite a few
sunk *adj syn* see DOWNCAST
sunlight *n syn* see SUN 2
sunny *adj* 1 *syn* see FAIR 2
  rel bright, brilliant
  idiom bright and sunny
  2 *syn* see CHEERFUL 1
sunrise *n syn* see DAWN 1
sunset *n syn* see EVENING 2
sunshine *n syn* see SUN 2
sunshine *adj syn* see FAIR 2
sunshining *adj syn* see FAIR 2
sunshiny *adj syn* see FAIR 2
sunup *n syn* see DAWN 1
sup (off *or* up) *vb syn* see DRINK 1
super *adj syn* see MARVELOUS 2
  idiom out of this world
super *adv* 1 *syn* see VERY 1
  2 *syn* see EVER 6
superabundant *adj* abounding to a great, abnormal, or excessive degree < *superabundant* harvests had brought down prices >
  syn overabounding, overabundant, overflowing
  rel abounding, abundant, cornucopian, plenteous, plentiful; excess, excessive, overmuch, surplus; crawling, teeming; overspilling; epidemic, rampant
superadd *vb syn* see ADD 1
superannuate *vb* 1 *syn* see OUTDATE
  2 *syn* see RETIRE 2
superb *adj* 1 *syn* see GRAND 3
  rel noble; majestic
  2 *syn* see SPLENDID 2
  rel imposing, stately; opulent
  3 consummately impressive and supremely excellent of its kind < the writer's style is brilliant and his command of words and imagery, *superb* >
  syn magnificent, outstanding, standout, superexcellent, superlative; *compare* SUPREME
  rel gorgeous, glorious, marvelous, resplendent; crashing, rousing, sensational, slambang, super, superfine, wonderful; best, optimal, optimum, prime; sublime
  idiom very best
  con inferior, mediocre, poor, substandard; atrocious, awful, dreadful, shocking; deplorable, dismal, lamentable, pitiful, woeful; abominable, execrable, outrageous, shameful
  ant wretched
superbity *n syn* see PRIDE 3
supercilious *adj syn* see PROUD 1
  rel sniffish, sniffy, snifty, snippy, snuffy; sneering
superciliousness *n syn* see PRIDE 3
supererogant *adj syn* see SUPEREROGATORY
supererogative *adj syn* see SUPEREROGATORY
supererogatory *adj* given or done without compulsion, need, or warrant < people who offer *supererogatory* advice >
  syn gratuitous, supererogant, supererogative, unasked, uncalled-for, wanton
  rel nonessential, superfluous, supernumerary, unnecessary, unneeded
  con essential, indispensable, vital; compulsory, obligatory; called-for, needful, required, requisite, sought, wanted

---

syn synonym(s)   *rel* related word(s)
ant antonym(s)   *con* contrasted word(s)
idiom idiomatic equivalent(s)
‖ use limited; if in doubt, see a dictionary

superexcellent *adj syn* see SUPERB 3
rel incomparable, matchless, unparalleled, unsurpassed

superficial *adj 1 syn* see SHALLOW 1
2 lacking in depth, solidity, and comprehensiveness <wrote only a *superficial* report on the situation>
syn cursory, depthless, shallow, sketchy, uncritical
rel bird's-eye, general; one-dimensional, skin-deep; smattery
con comprehensive, full, inclusive; deep, detailed, in-depth, thorough; critical
ant exhaustive

superficies *n syn* see TOP 2
superfluent *adj syn* see SUPERFLUOUS
superfluity *n 1 syn* see EXCESS 1
rel overflowing, swarming, teeming
2 *syn* see LUXURY

superfluous *adj* exceeding what is needed or indispensable <omitted all *superfluous* information>
syn de trop, excess, extra, recrementitious, spare, superfluent, supernumerary, surplus
rel unnecessary, unneeded, unwanted; needless, useless; dispensable, nonessential; gratuitous, supererogatory, unasked, uncalled-for
con critical, crucial, imperative; essential, fundamental, vital; consequential, important, momentous, notable, noteworthy; defective, inadequate
ant deficient

superhuman *adj 1 syn* see SUPERNATURAL 1
2 *syn* see SUPERNATURAL 2

superhuman *n syn* see SUPERMAN
superincumbent *adj 1 syn* see SUPERIOR 1
2 *syn* see ONEROUS

superintend *vb syn* see SUPERVISE
superintendence *n syn* see OVERSIGHT 1
rel direction, presidence
superintendency *n syn* see OVERSIGHT 1
rel direction, presidence

superior *adj 1* being or regarded as being above the level of another <the new assistant received a *superior* rating for his work>
syn greater, higher, over, overlying, superincumbent, superjacent
rel major, primary, senior
con lesser, lower, nether, under
ant inferior
2 *syn* see SUPERNATURAL 1
3 *syn* see BETTER 2
ant inferior
4 being of higher quality, accomplishment, or merit <a class of *superior* students>
syn exceptional, premium; *compare* MARVELOUS 2
rel noteworthy, remarkable, unusual
con commonplace, ordinary, unexceptional, unremarkable
ant average
5 *syn* see CHOICE
6 *syn* see EXCELLENT
ant inferior
7 *syn* see PROUD 1

superior *n* one standing above another in a hierarchy of rank <was always respectful to his *superiors* in the department>
syn better, brass hat, elder, higher-up, senior
rel heavyweight
ant inferior

superiority *n syn* see BETTER 2
rel ascendancy, dominance, supremacy
ant inferiority

superjacent *adj syn* see SUPERIOR 1
ant subjacent

superlative *adj syn* see SUPERB 3
rel accomplished, consummate, finished

superman *n* a person of extraordinary power or achievement <a space program run by scientific *supermen*>
syn demigod, superhuman
idiom Triton among the minnows
con also-ran, loser, underdog
ant subhuman

supermundane *adj syn* see SUPERNATURAL 1

supernatural *adj 1* of, relating to, or proceeding from an order of existence beyond the visible observable universe <many then believed in a *supernatural* force that directs history>
syn metaphysical, miraculous, numinous, preternatural, superhuman, superior, supermundane, suprahuman, supramundane, supranatural, unearthly
rel paranormal, rare, unusual; spiritual; celestial, heavenly; divine
2 being much more than is natural or normal <had a *supernatural* ability to win money>
syn superhuman, supernormal, superordinary, supranormal, uncanny, unnatural
rel extraordinary, outstanding, phenomenal, remarkable; paranormal
3 *syn* see EXCESSIVE 1

supernormal *adj syn* see SUPERNATURAL 2
ant subnormal

supernumerary *adj syn* see SUPERFLUOUS

superordinary *adj syn* see SUPERNATURAL 2
ant ordinary

superpatriot *n syn* see PATRIOTEER
superscribe *vb syn* see ADDRESS 6
supersede *vb syn* see REPLACE 3
rel reject, repudiate; abandon, desert, forsake; discard

superseded *adj syn* see OBSOLETE
supersensible *adj syn* see PSYCHIC 1
supersensory *adj syn* see PSYCHIC 1
supertemporal *adj syn* see INFINITE 1
supervene *vb syn* see FOLLOW 1
supervenient *adj syn* see ADVENTITIOUS
supervise *vb* to have or exercise the charge, direction, and oversight of <*supervised* the construction of the new stadium>
syn boss, chaperon, overlook, oversee, quarterback, superintend, survey
rel guide, steer; administer, conduct, direct; manage, run; control; monitor, proctor

supervision *n syn* see OVERSIGHT 1
supper club *n syn* see NIGHTCLUB
supplant *vb 1* to supersede (another) by or as if by force, trickery, or treachery <a wife who found herself *supplanted* by another woman>

syn cut out, displace, usurp

rel crowd (out), force (out); bounce, cast (out), eject, expel, oust

idiom give the bum's rush, give the old heave-ho, step into the shoes of

2 *syn* see REPLACE 3

supple *adj* **1** *syn* see ELASTIC 1

    ant stiff

    2 *syn* see PLASTIC

    3 showing freedom and ease of bodily movement (as in bending or twisting) < the light *supple* spring of a cat >

    syn limber, lissome, lithe, lithesome

    rel agile, graceful, willowy, wiry, withy

    con awkward, clumsy, gawky, maladroit, unhandy; ungraceful; arthritic, creaky, decrepit

    ant stiff

supplement *n* **1** *syn* see COMPLEMENT 1

    2 *syn* see APPENDIX 1

suppliant *n* one who asks (as for a favor or gift) humbly < a room full of *suppliants* waiting to see the king >

    syn asker, beggar, petitioner, prayer, suitor, supplicant, supplicator

    rel solicitant, solicitor

supplicant *n* *syn* see SUPPLIANT

supplicate *vb* *syn* see BEG

    idiom ask on bended knee, ‖come down on one's marrowbones

supplication *n* *syn* see PRAYER

supplicator *n* *syn* see SUPPLIANT

supply *vb* *syn* see GIVE 3

    rel fulfill, outfit, provision

supply *n* an accumulation of something that is a source from which things may be drawn < an unending *supply* of new talent >

    syn armamentarium, fund, inventory, stock, store

    rel accumulation; reserve, reservoir, stockpile, surplus; hoard

supply *adj* *syn* see TEMPORARY

support *vb* **1** *syn* see BEAR 10

    2 to favor actively in the face of opposition < *support* an unpopular economic policy >

    syn advocate, back, backstop, champion, side (with), uphold

    rel applaud, approve, endorse, favor, plunk (for), pull (for); root; adopt, embrace, espouse; defend, maintain, sustain

    idiom align oneself with, be on (someone's) side, take (someone's) side

    con battle, combat, counter, fight, oppose; withstand

    ant buck

    3 to supply what is needed for sustenance < *support* his family >

    syn maintain, provide (for)

    idiom boil the pot, bring home the bacon, make a living for, take care of

    4 to hold up in position by serving as a foundation or base for < pillars *supporting* an arch >

    syn bear up, bolster, brace, buttress, carry, prop, shore (up), sustain, upbear, uphold

    rel stand

    5 to keep from yielding, sinking, or losing courage or stability < her friends *supported* her during the crisis >

    syn bolster, buoy (up), prop, sustain, underprop, uphold; *compare* ENCOURAGE 1

    rel encourage; fortify, stiffen, strengthen

support *n* **1** *syn* see HELP 1

    2 *syn* see HELP 2

    3 a supporting means, agency, medium, or device < girders as structural *supports* > < strong economic *support* for the government >

    syn brace, buttress, column, prop, shore, stay, underpinner, underpinning, underpropping

    rel base, foundation; sustentation

    4 *syn* see LIVING

supportable *adj* *syn* see BEARABLE

    ant insupportable, unsupportable

supporter *n* **1** *syn* see FOLLOWER

    2 *syn* see EXPONENT

    ant antagonist

supposable *adj* *syn* see THINKABLE 2

    ant insupposable

supposal *n* *syn* see THEORY 1

suppose *vb* **1** *syn* see UNDERSTAND 3

    rel presuppose

    2 *syn* see CONJECTURE

suppose *n* *syn* see THEORY 2

supposed *adj* accepted or advanced as true or real on the basis of less than conclusive evidence < the *supposed* efficiency of the new machine >

    syn conjectural, hypothetical, putative, reputed, suppositional, suppositious, supposititious, suppositive, suppository; *compare* ALLEGED

    rel assumed, postulated, postulatory, presumed, presupposed; provisional, tentative; academic, speculative, theoretical; alleged

    con sure; known, proved, proven; ascertained, demonstrated, observed, recognized

    ant certain

    2 *syn* see ALLEGED

    ant proved, proven

supposition *n* **1** *syn* see ASSUMPTION 2

    2 *syn* see THEORY 2

suppositional *adj* *syn* see SUPPOSED 1

suppositious *adj* **1** *syn* see FICTITIOUS 1

    2 *syn* see SUPPOSED 1

    rel doubtful, dubious, questionable; pretended, simulated

supposititious *adj* **1** *syn* see ILLEGITIMATE 1

    2 *syn* see FICTITIOUS 1

    3 *syn* see SUPPOSED 1

supposititiousness *n* *syn* see ILLEGITIMACY 1

suppositive *adj* *syn* see SUPPOSED 1

suppository *adj* *syn* see SUPPOSED 1

suppress *vb* **1** *syn* see CRUSH 5

    idiom ride roughshod over

    2 to hold back more or less forcefully someone or something that seeks an outlet < management tried to *suppress* the workers' discontent > < there was no way to *suppress* her short of murder >

    syn muffle, ‖quelch, repress, shush, squelch, strangle; *compare* CRUSH 5

---

syn synonym(s)   *rel* related word(s)
ant antonym(s)   *con* contrasted word(s)
idiom idiomatic equivalent(s)
‖ use limited; if in doubt, see a dictionary

rel curb, restrain; arrest, check, interrupt; put down, slap down; quash, quell, squash; cut off, spike; abolish, annihilate, extinguish

idiom bring to naught, crack (*or* clamp) down on, put the kibosh on

3 to keep from public knowledge < *suppress* all news from the front >

syn burke, hush (up), stifle

rel repress; censor; silence

idiom put the lid on

con disclose, divulge, leak, ‖let out, reveal; broadcast, circulate, diffuse, publish, spread

4 *syn* see COMPOSE 4

rel drown; swallow

5 *syn* see STUNT

suppression *n* **1** *syn* see REPRESSION 1

2 *syn* see REPRESSION 2

supra *adv* *syn* see ABOVE 2

ant infra

suprahuman *adj* *syn* see SUPERNATURAL 1

supramundane *adj* *syn* see SUPERNATURAL 1

supranatural *adj* *syn* see SUPERNATURAL 1

supranormal *adj* *syn* see SUPERNATURAL 1

supremacy *n* the position of being first (as in rank, power, or influence) < Britain once enjoyed *supremacy* on the seas >

syn ascendancy, ascendant, dominance, domination, dominion, masterdom, preeminence, preponderance, preponderancy, preponderation, prepotence, prepotency, sovereignty

rel authority, control, driver's seat, power, sway; mastership, mastery, principality, superiority; transcendence

supreme *adj* developed to the utmost and not exceeded by any other in degree, quality, or intensity < dying for one's principles is an example of *supreme* sacrifice >

syn incomparable, preeminent, surpassing, towering, transcendent, ultimate, unequalable, unmatchable, unsurpassable; *compare* ALONE 3, EXCELLENT, MARVELOUS 2, MAXIMUM, SUPERB 3

rel crowning, master, sovereign; unequaled, unmatched, unparalleled, unrivaled, unsurpassed; final, last; absolute, perfect

surcease *vb* *syn* see STOP 3

sure *adj* **1** firmly settled or established < trying to find a *sure* footing on the rugged slope >

syn fast, firm, secure, stable, staunch, strong; *compare* FAST 4, STABLE 4

2 free from doubt, hesitation, or fear < upheld a *sure* faith >

syn abiding, enduring, firm, fixed, never-failing, steadfast, steady, unfaltering, unqualified, unquestioning, unshakable, unshaken, unwavering, wholehearted

rel assured, changeless, constant, unchangeable, unchanging, uncompromising, unfailing, unvarying; certain, fixed, set

con insecure, uncertain, unreliable; feeble, infirm, shaky, unsound; doubtful, dubious, hesitant

ant unsure

3 *syn* see INFALLIBLE 1

4 *syn* see INFALLIBLE 2

5 marked by unwavering assurance especially as to the rightness of one's views or actions < was *sure* he knew the answer >

syn certain, cocksure, confident, positive

rel assured, self-assured, self-possessed, self-satisfied; arrogant, cocky, pert; decided, decisive

con doubtful, hesitant, uncertain

ant unsure

6 *syn* see POSITIVE 3

rel convincing, telling; absolute, definite; genuine, real, valid

sure–enough *adj* **1** *syn* see ACTUAL 2

2 *syn* see AUTHENTIC 2

surefire *adj* *syn* see INFALLIBLE 2

sureness *n* *syn* see CERTAINTY

ant unsureness

sure thing *n* one that is bound to be successful < was deemed a *sure thing* in the race >

syn shoo-in

rel certainty; winner

surety *n* **1** *syn* see CERTAINTY

2 *syn* see GUARANTEE 1

3 *syn* see SPONSOR

surface *n* *syn* see TOP 2

rel exterior, outside; cover, covering

con body, mass; inside, interior; lining

surface *vb* to come to the surface (as of water) < a submarine *surfaced* outside the harbor >

syn rise

rel come up

con go down, go under; submerge; dive

surfeit *n* *syn* see EXCESS 1

surfeit *vb* *syn* see SATIATE

rel overfill, overindulge

idiom have all one can take (*or* stand)

ant whet

surfeited *adj* *syn* see SATIATED

ant unsatisfied

surge *vb* *syn* see POUR 2

surly *adj* *syn* see SULLEN

rel discourteous, ill-mannered, rude, ungracious; bearish, boorish, churlish; fractious, irritable, snappish, waspish

idiom as surly as a bear

con affable, cordial, genial, gracious

ant amiable

surmise *vb* *syn* see CONJECTURE

rel consider, regard; hypothesize, theorize

idiom risk assuming, venture a guess

surmount *vb* **1** *syn* see OVERCOME 1

rel best, better, outdo, outstrip, outtop, outtower, surpass

idiom rise superior to

2 *syn* see CLEAR 8

3 to stand or lie at the top of < a cross *surmounts* the cupola >

syn cap, crest, crown, top

rel finish; terminate

4 *syn* see TOP

surpass *vb* **1** to be or become greater than or superior to < *surpassed* all his fellows in scholarship >

syn ‖bang, beat, best, better, cap, cob, ding, exceed, excel, outdo, outgo, outmatch, outshine, outstrip, pass, top, transcend, trump

rel distance, outdistance, outpace, outperform, outpoint, outrange, outrival, outrun, outvie; eclipse, outrank, outtop, outtower, outweigh, overshadow, overtop, rank

idiom have it all over, put to shame
2 *syn* see EXCEED 1

surpassing *adj syn* see SUPREME

surpassingly *adv syn* see VERY 1

surplus *n* **1** *syn* see EXCESS 1
ant deficiency
2 *syn* see EXCESS 2
ant shortage

surplus *adj syn* see SUPERFLUOUS

surplusage *n* **1** *syn* see EXCESS 2
ant shortage, underage
2 *syn* see EXCESS 1
ant shortage

surprise *vb* **1** to attack unawares <hijack-ers *surprised* the truck driver and took his cargo>
syn ambush, lay (for), waylay
rel bushwhack, dry-gulch; capture, catch; grab, grasp, seize, take
2 to impress forcibly through unexpected-ness, startlingness, or unusualness <was *surprised* by his violent jealousy>
syn amaze, astonish, astound, dumb-found, flabbergast
rel startle; bewilder, confound, discomfit, disconcert, dismay, nonplus, ||swan; faze, rattle, rock; bowl (over), floor, stagger; stun, stupefy
idiom leave open-mouthed (*or* aghast), take aback (*or* by surprise)

surprising *adj syn* see MARVELOUS 1
rel unexpected, unforeseen, unlooked-for; eye-opening, eye-popping

surrender *vb* **1** *syn* see RELINQUISH
rel commit, consign, entrust
2 *syn* see FALL 3
rel give in, give up
idiom haul down one's colors, strike the (*or* one's) flag

surrender *n* the yielding of one's person, forces, or possessions to another <the victors demanded unconditional *surren-der*>
syn capitulation, dedition, submission
rel appeasement, Munich; relenting, suc-cumbing, yielding; white flag

surreptitious *adj syn* see SECRET 1
rel skulking, slinking, slinky, sneaking, sneaky
con obvious, open, overt
ant brazen

surreptitiously *adv syn* see SECRETLY
con openly, overtly, plainly
ant brazenly

surrogate *n* **1** *syn* see SUBSTITUTE
2 *syn* see RESOURCE 3

surrogate *adj syn* see SUBSTITUTE 1

surround *vb* **1** to close in or as if in a ring about something <a crowd *surrounded* the accident victim>
syn begird, beset, circle, compass, encir-cle, encompass, environ, gird, girdle, hem, loop, ring, round
rel embosom, enclave, enclose, envelop; circumscribe, circumvent, confine, limit
2 *syn* see BORDER 1

surroundings *n pl syn* see ENVIRONMENT

surveillance *n* **1** *syn* see EYE 3

idiom peeled eye
2 *syn* see LOOKOUT 3
rel surveyance
idiom watchful (*or* weather) eye

survey *vb* **1** *syn* see ESTIMATE 1
rel measure, size, size up
2 *syn* see SUPERVISE
3 to view from or as if from a high place or position <*surveyed* the view from his penthouse window>
syn overlook, oversee
4 *syn* see SCRUTINIZE 1

survey *n* **1** *syn* see EXAMINATION
2 *syn* see COMPENDIUM 1

||**survigrous** *adj syn* see VIGOROUS

survive *vb* **1** *syn* see OUTLIVE
2 to continue to exist or function in spite of a usually adverse condition or develop-ment <a company that managed to *sur-vive* the recession>
syn come through, pull through, ride (out)
rel carry on, carry through, continue, endure, last, persist; live down, outlast, outlive; recover, revive
idiom come out of it, live to fight again, make it through, ride out (*or* weather) the storm
con collapse, crash, fold, fold up, go down, go under; founder, sink; close (down), close up; bankrupt, bust
ant perish

susceptible *adj* **1** *syn* see LIABLE 2
rel disposed, inclined, predisposed
ant immune, unsusceptible
2 *syn* see EASY 3
rel nonresistant, soft; movable, persuad-able
ant unsusceptible
3 *syn* see SENTIENT 3
rel affected, impressed, influenced, swayed, touched; aroused, roused, stirred
ant unsusceptible

susceptive *adj syn* see SENTIENT 3

suscitate *vb syn* see PROVOKE 4

suspect *adj syn* see DOUBTFUL 1
idiom ||a bit thin (*or* thick), open to suspi-cion

suspect *vb* **1** *syn* see DISTRUST
idiom have doubts about
2 *syn* see UNDERSTAND 3
idiom be inclined to think

suspend *vb* **1** *syn* see EXCLUDE
2 *syn* see DEFER
rel arrest, check, interrupt; cease, discon-tinue, stop
idiom lay on the table, put on the shelf
3 *syn* see HANG 1

suspended *adj* hung or seeming as if hung from a support <bunches of grapes *sus-pended* from the vines>
syn hanging, pendent, pendulant, pendu-lous, pensile
rel dangling, swinging

suspenders *n pl* a pair of supporting bands worn across the shoulders to sup-port trousers, skirt, or belt <*suspenders* are out of style>
syn braces, ||gallows, ||galluses

suspense *n syn* see SUSPENSION 2

suspension *n* **1** *syn* see ABEYANCE
2 a temporary withholding of action or cessation of activity <asked for *suspension*

of judgment until all the evidence was in >
syn moratorium, suspense
rel cessation, concluding, conclusion, end, ending, finish, period, termination
con resumption; continuance
suspicion *n* 1 *syn* see UNCERTAINTY
rel apprehension, foreboding, misgiving, presentiment; distrust
2 *syn* see HINT 2
‖**suspicion** *vb syn* see DISTRUST
suspicious *adj* 1 *syn* see DOUBTFUL 1
rel questionable; queer
2 given or prone to suspicion < was *suspicious* of everyone's motives >
syn distrustful, jealous, mistrustful
rel careful, cautious; leery, wary, watchful; skeptical, unbelieving
con trustful, trusting, unsuspecting; naive; dupable, easy, exploitable, gullible
ant unsuspicious
suspiciously *adv syn* see ASKANCE 2
rel distrustingly, mistrustingly
ant unsuspiciously
suspire *vb* 1 *syn* see SIGH 1
idiom draw a long breath
2 *syn* see LONG
sustain *vb* 1 *syn* see MAINTAIN 1
rel nourish, support; prolong
2 *syn* see SUPPORT 4
rel lug, pack, tote
3 *syn* see SUPPORT 5
rel befriend, favor
idiom stand by
con abandon, forsake; ignore
4 *syn* see BEAR 10
5 *syn* see EXPERIENCE 1
rel bear, endure
sustainable *adj syn* see BEARABLE
ant unsustainable
sustenance *n* 1 *syn* see FOOD 2
idiom bodily sustenance
2 *syn* see LIVING
sustentation *n syn* see PRESERVATION 1
susurration *n syn* see MURMUR 1
‖**swack** *n syn* see CUFF
‖**swacked** *adj syn* see INTOXICATED 1
swad *n syn* see SOLDIER
swaddle *vb syn* see SWATHE
rel ‖sweel
ant unswaddle
‖**swaddy** *n syn* see SOLDIER
swag *vb* 1 *syn* see SEESAW
2 *syn* see DROOP 3
swag *n* 1 *syn* see SPOIL
2 *syn* see MONEY
swagger *vb* 1 *syn* see LORD
rel swash, swashbuckle
2 *syn* see STRUT 2
rel bluster, brandish, flourish
con blench, quail; shrink, wince; truckle
‖**swagger** *n syn* see VAGABOND
‖**swagman** *n syn* see VAGABOND
swain *n* 1 *syn* see BOYFRIEND 1
2 *syn* see SUITOR 2
swainish *adj syn* see BOORISH
swallow *vb* 1 to receive through the esophagus into the stomach < *swallowed* the pills easily with a sip of water >
syn down, take
rel drop, gulp, ‖quilt, toss; ingest, ingurgitate
2 *syn* see DRINK 1

3 *syn* see BELIEVE 1
idiom swallow (something) hook, line, and sinker
4 *syn* see BEAR 10
5 *syn* see ACCEPT 2
6 *syn* see MUMBLE
swamp *n* wet spongy land saturated and sometimes partially covered with water < hunted alligators in the Florida *swamps* >
syn baygall, bog, fen, marsh, marshland, mire, morass, ‖moss, muskeg, ‖purgatory, ‖puxy, quag, quagmire, slough, ‖sump, swampland, ‖swang, ‖vlei
rel bottoms, ‖holm; ‖glade; ‖heel; quake ooze; shaking prairie, trembling prairie
swamp *vb* 1 *syn* see DELUGE 1
2 *syn* see DELUGE 3
swampland *n syn* see SWAMP
‖**swang** *n syn* see SWAMP
swank *vb syn* see LORD
swank *adj* 1 *syn* see SHOWY
2 *syn* see STYLISH
swap *vb* 1 *syn* see EXCHANGE 2
2 *syn* see TRADE 1
idiom ‖swap horses, swap out of
‖**swap** *n syn* see BLOW 1
‖**swapping** *adj syn* see HUGE
‖**swarf** *vb syn* see FAINT
swarm *vb syn* see TEEM
idiom gather (*or* swarm) like bees
swarming *adj syn* see ALIVE 5
swart *adj syn* see DARK 3
swarth *adj syn* see DARK 3
swarthy *adj syn* see DARK 3
swash *vb* 1 *syn* see SLOSH 1
2 *syn* see SPLASH
swashy *adj syn* see INSIPID 3
swat *vb* ‖1 *syn* see SQUAT
2 *syn* see STRIKE 2
rel blip, box, buffet, cuff, smack; belt, clobber, slug, smash, wallop
swat *n syn* see HIT 1
swathe *vb* to cover or bind completely with clothing or material < legs *swathed* in bandages > < the baby was *swathed* in a warm shawl >
syn drape, enswathe, envelop, enwrap, roll, swaddle, wrap (up); *compare* ENFOLD 1
rel enfold; encase; cover
con bare, denude, expose, strip, uncover, unswaddle, unwrap
ant unswathe
sway *vb* 1 *syn* see SWING 2
2 *syn* see LURCH 2
3 *syn* see GOVERN 1
4 *syn* see AFFECT
rel bias, dispose, incline, predispose; conduct, control, direct, manage; govern, rule
sway *n syn* see POWER 1
rel range, reach, scope, sweep; amplitude, expanse, spread, stretch
swayable *adj syn* see RECEPTIVE 1
swear *vb* 1 *syn* see VOW
idiom swear on a stack of Bibles, swear to God, swear up and down
2 *syn* see TESTIFY 2
3 to use profane, blasphemous, or obscene language < *swore* when the horse threw him >
syn bedamn, curse, cuss, damn, execrate, imprecate

rel blaspheme; rail, rant; abuse, revile, vilify, vituperate

idiom ‖chew the dirty rag, curse and swear, fall a-cursing, ‖let out religion, make the air blue, rip (*or* rap) out an oath, swear like a sailor (*or* trooper), use language

swear *n syn* see SWEARWORD

swearing *n syn* see BLASPHEMY 1

swearword *n* a profane, blasphemous, or obscene word < let loose with a string of *swearwords* >

syn curse, cuss, cussword, expletive, oath, swear

rel four-letter word, obscenity, scurrility

idiom blue word, one-horse oath, raw one, ripe (*or* juicy) word, sailor's blessing, six-cornered oath, strong word

sweat *vb* 1 *syn* see EXUDE

2 *syn* see FLEECE 1

sweat *n* 1 *syn* see WORK 2

2 *syn* see SNIT

‖3 *syn* see SOLDIER

sweatful *adj syn* see SWEATY

sweating *adj syn* see SWEATY

sweat out *vb syn* see BEAR 10

sweaty *adj* producing, accompanied by, or characterized by sweat < he still held the racket tight in *sweaty* hands >

syn asweat, perspiring, perspiry, ‖puggy, sweatful, sweating

rel clammy; sticky; wet

idiom bathed in sweat, covered with sweat, drenched (*or* in) sweat, in a muck of a sweat, wet with sweat (*or* perspiration)

sweep *vb syn* see FLY 4

sweep *n syn* see RANGE 2

sweeping *n* sweepings *pl syn* see REFUSE

sweeping *adj* 1 *syn* see ALL-AROUND 2

rel all-embracing, all-encompassing

2 *syn* see INDISCRIMINATE 1

rel all-out, out-and-out, whole-hog; across-the-board, blanket

sweet *adj* 1 distinctly pleasing or charming < a *sweet* smile >

syn dulcet, engaging, winning, winsome

rel agreeable, pleasant, pleasing; beautiful, fair, lovely; delectable, delicious, delightful, luscious; angelic, heavenly

con disagreeable, unpleasant; displeasing, obnoxious, repulsive

ant bitter

2 having a pleasant smell < the *sweet* odor of flowers and incense >

syn ambrosial, aromal, aromatic, balmy, fragrant, perfumed, perfumy, redolent, savory, scented, spicy; *compare* ODOROUS

rel clean, fresh; sweetish

con funky, fusty, musty, noisome, putrid, rancid, rotten, stale, stinking, strong, whiffy; fetid, foul, olid, rank, smelly

ant malodorous

3 *syn* see MELODIOUS 1

sweet *n syn* see SWEETHEART 1

sweeten *vb* 1 *syn* see PACIFY

2 *syn* see SUGARCOAT 1

sweetheart *n* 1 one who is dearly beloved — often used as a term of endearment

< was her childhood *sweetheart* > < *sweetheart*, you know I'll wait >

syn beloved, darling, dear, flame, heartthrob, honey, honeybunch, love, loveling, sweet, sweetling, turtledove

rel ‖cutie pie, deary, pigsney; pet, puggy

2 *syn* see GIRL FRIEND 2

rel doll baby, lovey-dovey, ‖tootsie

3 *syn* see BOYFRIEND 2

rel paramour; ‖dreamboat

sweetheart *vb syn* see ADDRESS 8

sweetie *n syn* see GIRL FRIEND 2

rel sweetie pie

sweetling *n syn* see SWEETHEART 1

sweetness and light *n syn* see AMENITY 1

sweet–talk *vb syn* see COAX

swell *vb* 1 *syn* see EXPAND 3

rel balloon, belly, bloat, blow up, bosom; pouch, pout; overblow

con compress, condense, constrict, contract

ant shrink

2 *syn* see LORD

rel puff

idiom act the grand seigneur, swell it

swell *n syn* see EXPERT

swell *adj syn* see MARVELOUS 2

swelled head *n syn* see CONCEIT 2

swellheadedness *n syn* see CONCEIT 2

swelling *adj syn* see RHETORICAL

‖**swelt** *vb* 1 *syn* see DIE 1

2 *syn* see FAINT

swelter *vb syn* see BURN 3

sweltering *adj syn* see HOT 1

idiom ‖hot as the hinges of hell

ant frigid

sweltry *adj syn* see HOT 1

swerve *vb* 1 to turn or be turned away abruptly from a straight line or course < *swerved* the car to avoid collision >

syn dip, sheer, skew, slue, train off, veer

2 to be deflected from a fixed or right course of action or conduct < never *swerved* from the concept of duty, honor, country >

syn depart, deviate, digress, diverge

rel shift; waver; err, stray, wander

idiom deviate from the straight and narrow, get off the proper course (*or* path)

swift *adj syn* see FAST 3

rel headlong, precipitate, sudden; double-quick; supersonic

ant sluggish

swift *adv syn* see FAST 2

ant sluggishly

swiften *vb syn* see SPEED 3

swiftly *adv syn* see FAST 2

con slowly

ant sluggishly

swiftness *n* 1 *syn* see SPEED 3

ant sluggishness

2 *syn* see HASTE 1

ant slowness

swig *n syn* see DRINK 3

swig *vb syn* see DRINK 3

swill *vb* 1 *syn* see DRINK 3

2 *syn* see CONSUME 5

swill *n* 1 *syn* see REFUSE

2 *syn* see DRINK 3

swillbowl *n syn* see DRUNKARD

swiller *n syn* see DRUNKARD

swim *vb syn* see SPIN 2

---

syn synonym(s)   *rel* related word(s)
ant antonym(s)   *con* contrasted word(s)
idiom idiomatic equivalent(s)
‖ use limited; if in doubt, see a dictionary

idiom have one's head swim
swimming *adj syn* see DIZZY 2
rel fluctuating, swaying, wavering
swimmingly *adv syn* see WELL 5
swimmy *adj syn* see DIZZY 2
swindle *vb syn* see CHEAT
rel rogue; victimize
idiom sell one a bill of goods, take for a
ride, take for a sucker
swindle *n syn* see IMPOSTURE
swindler *n* one who defrauds usually of
money and especially by imposture or by
gaining the victim's confidence < lost their
savings to *swindlers* in a get-rich-quick
scheme >
syn bunco steerer, cheat, cheater, chiaus,
come-on, confidence man, con man, defrauder, diddler, double-dealer, flimflammer, ‖grifter, gyp, gypper, ‖mace, mountebank, Peter Funk, rogue, sharper, sharpie,
skin, slicker, ‖spieler, trickster
rel bilk, bilker, blackleg, charlatan, chis-
eler, crook, deceiver, dodger, fraud,
gouger, harpy, highbinder, hoaxer, operator, rook, shark, sharp, sharpster, tricker;
scoundrel
swing *vb 1 syn* see HANDLE 2
2 to move rhythmically to and fro, up and
down, or back and forth < the clock's
pendulum *swung* slowly >
syn oscillate, pendulate, sway
rel undulate, wave; rock, roll; revolve,
rotate, switch, wheel; jiggle, wag, waggle,
wiggle, wigwag
3 *syn* see TURN 6
4 *syn* see LURCH 2
swing *n 1 syn* see RHYTHM
2 *syn* see HANG
‖**swingeing** *adj syn* see EXCELLENT
swinish *adj syn* see BRUTISH
swipe *n syn* see HIT 1
swipe *vb syn* see STEAL 1
swirl *vb* to move swiftly in circles, eddies,
or undulations < water *swirled* into the
storm drains >
syn eddy, gurge, purl, swoosh, whirl,
whirlpool, whorl
rel boil, roil; gush, surge
swish *vb syn* see HISS
swish *adj syn* see STYLISH
switch *vb 1 syn* see WAG
2 *syn* see EXCHANGE 2
3 *syn* see SHUNT 1
‖**swither** *vb syn* see RUSH 1
swivet *n syn* see SNIT
swizzle *vb syn* see DRINK 3
swollen *adj syn* see RHETORICAL
swoon *vb syn* see FAINT
rel die away, drown
swoon *n syn* see FAINT
swoosh *vb syn* see SWIRL
sworn *adj syn* see INVETERATE 1
sybarite *n syn* see HEDONIST
sybaritic *adj* marked by or given to luxury
or voluptuous living < the *sybaritic* grandeur of a sultan's harem > < a man of
sybaritic and self-indulgent habits >
syn hedonistic, onanistic, self-indulgent,
sybaritical, sybaritish; *compare* SENSUOUS
rel apolaustic, pleasure-loving; epicurean,
luxurious; carnal, sensual, voluptuous
sybaritical *adj syn* see SYBARITIC
sybaritish *adj syn* see SYBARITIC

sycophancy *n syn* see DETRACTION
sycophant *n* a base or servilely attentive
flatterer and self-seeker < *sycophants* who
slavishly curried favor with the king >
syn apple-polisher, bootlick, bootlicker,
‖brownnose, ‖brownnoser, ‖clawback,
creature, ‖easy rider, footlicker, groveler,
lickspit, lickspittle, minion, reptile, spaniel,
‖suck, toad, toadeater, toadier, toady,
truckler, yes-man; *compare* PARASITE
rel flunky, gopher, lackey, slave, stooge;
flatterer, self-seeker; snob, tuft-hunter
sycophant *adj syn* see FAWNING
sycophantic *adj syn* see FAWNING
sycophantical *adj syn* see FAWNING
sycophantish *adj syn* see FAWNING
syllable *n syn* see PARTICLE
syllabus *n syn* see COMPENDIUM 1
sylloge *n syn* see COMPENDIUM 1
symbol *n 1* something that stands for
something else by reason of relationship,
association, convention, or accidental
resemblance < the lion is often used as a
symbol of courage >
syn attribute, emblem; *compare* INDICA-
TION 3
rel indication, token, type; badge, mark,
note, sign, stamp; character, design, device, figure, motif, pattern; representation
2 *syn* see CHARACTER 1
symbolism *n syn* see ALLEGORY 1
symbolization *n syn* see ALLEGORY 1
symbolize *vb syn* see REPRESENT 2
symmetrical *adj syn* see PROPORTIONAL
symmetry *n* beauty of form or arrangement arising from balanced proportions
< the superb *symmetry* of the design >
syn balance, harmony, proportion
rel arrangement, order; agreement, conformity; equality, evenness, regularity;
rhythm; finish
con asymmetry, dissymmetry; disproportion, imbalance, irregularity, unbalance
sympathetic *adj 1 syn* see CONSONANT 1
ant unsympathetic
2 favorably inclined < found his hearers
sympathetic to his proposal >
syn friendly, receptive, ‖sib, well-disposed
rel agreeable, congenial, favorable; amenable, open, open-minded, receptive, responsive
con ill-disposed, unfriendly, unreceptive;
cool, indifferent, lukewarm; neutral
ant unsympathetic
3 *syn* see TENDER
rel benign, benignant, kind, kindly; appreciating, comprehending, understanding
ant unsympathetic
sympathize (with) *vb syn* see COMPAS-
SIONATE
rel appreciate, comprehend, understand
sympathy *n 1 syn* see ATTRACTION 2
ant antipathy
2 a feeling for or a capacity for sharing in
the interests of another < he was in *sympathy* with her desire to succeed >
syn compassion, empathy, fellow feeling
rel responsiveness, sensitivity; feelings,
heart; tenderness, warmheartedness,
warmth; benignancy, benignness, kindliness, kindness
con disinterest, unconcern
3 *syn* see PITY

symphonic *adj syn* see HARMONIOUS 1
symphonious *adj syn* see HARMONIOUS 1
symphonize *vb syn* see HARMONIZE 4
symphony *n syn* see ORCHESTRA
  rel concert band, symphony band; symphony orchestra
symptom *n syn* see INDICATION 3
synchronal *adj syn* see CONTEMPORARY 1
synchronic *adj syn* see CONTEMPORARY 1
synchronous *adj syn* see CONTEMPORARY 1
syncope *n syn* see FAINT
syndicate *n* a combination of interlocked companies or enterprises <a large newspaper *syndicate*>
  syn cartel, chain, combine, conglomerate, group, pool, trust
  rel association, organization; partnership, union
syndrome *n syn* see DISEASE 1
synergetic *adj syn* see COOPERATIVE
  ant counteractive
synergic *adj syn* see COOPERATIVE
  ant counteractive
synopsis *n syn* see ABRIDGMENT
synopsize *vb syn* see EPITOMIZE 1
  idiom hit the high spots, put it in a nutshell
synthesize *vb syn* see HARMONIZE 4

synthetic *adj* formed or developed by human art, skill, or effort and not by natural processes <*synthetic* plastics>
  syn artificial, factitious, man-made; *compare* ARTIFICIAL 2
  rel manufactured; constructed, fabricated, made
  con natural
syrupy *adj syn* see SENTIMENTAL
system *n* 1 an organized integrated whole made up of diverse but interrelated and interdependent parts <the capitalist *system*>
  syn complex; *compare* WHOLE 2
  rel aggregation, array; mesh, network; arrangement, disposition, scheme, setup; order, pattern
  con disorganization; chaos
  2 *syn* see WHOLE 2
  3 *syn* see ORDER 8
  rel proceeding, procedure, process
  4 *syn* see METHOD 1
systematic *adj syn* see ORDERLY 1
  rel arranged, ordered, organized, systematized; analytical, logical
  con disorganized; chaotic
  ant unsystematic
systematize *vb syn* see ORDER 1
  rel contrive, frame
  con confuse, disorder, jumble

T

tab *n* 1 *syn* see EYE 3
  2 *syn* see BILL 1
  3 *syn* see CHECK 2
  4 *syn* see PRICE 1
tabby *n* 1 *syn* see GOSSIP 1
  ‖**2** *syn* see SPINSTER
tabernacle *n syn* see HOUSE OF WORSHIP
table *n* 1 a piece of furniture on which food is customarily served <a feast on the *table*>
  syn board, dining table, dinner table, mahogany, ‖table-board
  rel bar, buffet, counter, sideboard
  2 a condensed ordered enumeration of items usually arranged in columns <a *table* of weights and measures>
  syn chart, tabulation
  rel list; diagram
  3 *syn* see PLATEAU
‖**table–board** *n syn* see TABLE 1
tableland *n syn* see PLATEAU
tabloid *adj syn* see SENSATIONAL 2
taboo *n* a restraint imposed by social usage or as a protective measure <a society rife with antiquated moral *taboos*>
  syn ban, forbiddance, interdiction, prohibition, proscription
  rel inhibition, limitation, reservation,

restraint, restriction; regulation, sanction; don't
  con acceptance, toleration; approval, authorization, permission, permit, permittance
taboo *vb syn* see FORBID
tabulation *n syn* see TABLE 2
tacit *adj* 1 expressed or conveyed without words, speech, or forthright reference <they made a *tacit* agreement to work together>
  syn implicit, implied, inarticulate, inferred, undeclared, understood, unexpressed, unsaid, unspoken, unuttered, wordless
  rel alluded (to), hinted (at), intimated, suggested; assumed
  con expressed, spoken, verbal; categorical, explicit, express, unequivocal
  2 *syn* see UNSPOKEN 1
taciturn *adj syn* see SILENT 3
  rel laconic, unexpressive; brooding, dour
  con chatty, communicative, loquacious, talkative; convivial, uninhibited, unreserved, unrestrained
  ant garrulous
tack *n syn* see TURN 2
  rel alteration; digression, tangent; swerve, zigzag
tackle *n syn* see EQUIPMENT
tackle *vb syn* see ATTACK 2
  rel take on, undertake; plunge into, set about
  idiom get on the job, put one's shoulder to the wheel, start the ball rolling

---

syn synonym(s)   *rel* related word(s)
ant antonym(s)   *con* contrasted word(s)
idiom idiomatic equivalent(s)
‖ use limited; if in doubt, see a dictionary

con avoid, delay, hesitate, put off
tackling *n syn* see EQUIPMENT
tacky *adj* 1 *syn* see SHABBY 1
 rel dowdy, outmoded, unstylish; messy, sloppy, slovenly, unkempt, untidy; blowsy, frowzy, frumpish
 idiom gone to seed
 2 marked by a lack of style or good taste <an old *tacky* scarf spoiled her outfit>
 syn dowdy, frumpish, frumpy, outmoded, out-of-date, stodgy, unstylish
 rel unbecoming; crude, inelegant, tasteless; incorrect, unsuitable; cheap, gaudy
 con ‖mod, modern, modish, smart, stylish, tasteful; elegant
tact *n* skill and grace in dealing with others <handled the embarrassing situation with great *tact*>
 syn address, delicatesse, diplomacy, poise, savoir faire, tactfulness; *compare* ADDRESS 1
 rel control, head, presence, repose; amenity, courtesy, gallantry; policy, politicness, smoothness, suavity, urbanity; adroitness, deftness, skill; acumen, finesse, perception, sensitivity
 con abruptness, bluntness, coarseness, discourtesy, rudeness
 ant tactlessness
tactful *adj* marked by or exhibiting tact <his *tactful* skill in handling negotiations>
 syn delicate, diplomatic, politic, tactical; *compare* SUAVE
 rel polished, suave, urbane; adroit, deft, skilled, skillful; perceptive, sensitive
 con clumsy, unpolished, unskilled; discourteous, impolite, rude; undiplomatic
 ant blunt, tactless, untactful
tactfulness *n syn* see TACT
 rel civility, civilness, politeness; polish
 ant tactlessness
tactic *adj syn* see TACTILE 2
tactical *adj* 1 made or carried out with only a limited or immediate end in view <had time only for *tactical* decisions and not strategic planning>
 syn short-range
 con long-range
 ant strategic
 2 *syn* see EXPEDIENT
 3 *syn* see TACTFUL
tactile *adj* 1 *syn* see TANGIBLE 1
 2 of or relating to the sense of touch <*tactile* responses>
 syn tactic, tactual
tactility *n syn* see TOUCH 3
taction *n syn* see TOUCH 2
tactless *adj* marked by a lack of tact <his *tactless* remark hurt her>
 syn brash, impolitic, maladroit, undiplomatic, unpolitic, untactful
 rel impolite, inconsiderate, indelicate, rude; bungling, inept
 con diplomatic, polite, tactical
 ant tactful
tactual *adj syn* see TACTILE 2
tad *n syn* see BOY 1
tag *n* 1 *syn* see COMMONPLACE
 2 *syn* see TICKET 1
tag *vb syn* see TAIL
tag and rag *n syn* see RABBLE 2
tag end *n syn* see TAIL END 2

tagrag *adj syn* see SHABBY 1
tagrag and bobtail *n syn* see RABBLE 2
tail *n syn* see BUTTOCKS
tail *vb* to follow (someone) for purposes of surveillance <detectives *tailing* the suspects>
 syn bedog, dog, shadow, tag, trail; *compare* EYE 2, FOLLOW 2
 rel hound, pursue
tail end *n* 1 *syn* see BUTTOCKS
 2 the hindmost end of something <watched the *tail end* of the parade march off>
 syn tag end
tailor *vb syn* see ADAPT
 rel style; dovetail; shape up
tailor–made *adj syn* see CUSTOM-MADE
tailor–make *vb syn* see ADAPT
taint *vb* 1 to touch or affect with something bad or undesirable <his good reputation was *tainted* by the scandal>
 syn besmear, besmirch, blur, cloud, defile, dirty, discolor, smear, smudge, smut, smutch, soil, stain, sully, tar, tarnish; *compare* CONTAMINATE 1
 rel discredit; brand, stigmatize; blacken; damage, harm, hurt
 idiom cast a slur upon; give a bad name to, give a black mark to
 con brighten, cleanse, clear
 2 *syn* see DECAY
 rel befoul, contaminate, foul
 3 *syn* see CONTAMINATE 1
taintless *adj syn* see CLEAN 1
 ant tainted
take *vb* 1 *syn* see CATCH 1
 2 *syn* see SEIZE 2
 idiom make off with
 con drop, dump, give up, relinquish, surrender
 3 *syn* see APPROPRIATE 1
 con relinquish, yield
 4 to lay hold of (as with the hands or an instrument) <*took* the ax by the handle>
 syn clasp, grasp, grip
 rel hold; handle
 idiom take hold of
 con drop, release
 5 *syn* see SEIZE 3
 rel contract, get; harrow, reach, torment
 6 *syn* see CATCH 7
 7 *syn* see ATTRACT 1
 8 *syn* see SWALLOW 1
 9 *syn* see EAT 1
 10 to bring into and accept in a particular capacity or relationship <*took* his son as a member of the firm>
 syn admit, receive, take in
 rel bring; accept; have, include
 11 *syn* see BUY 1
 12 *syn* see CHOOSE 1
 13 *syn* see DEMAND 2
 14 to obtain from another source by means of derivation <*takes* his name from his father's>
 syn derive, draw
 rel get, obtain; borrow
 15 *syn* see BEAR 10
 rel withstand; undergo; ‖hack
 idiom take it lying down, take it on the chin
 16 *syn* see CONTRACT 1
 idiom take sick with

17 *syn* see APPREHEND 1
18 *syn* see UNDERSTAND 3
19 *syn* see DEDUCT 1
20 *syn* see TREAT 2
21 *syn* see CHEAT
    rel bamboozle, hoodwink
    idiom take for a ride
22 *syn* see ACT 5

take (from) *vb syn* see DECRY 2

take (to) *vb syn* see HABITUATE 2
    rel enjoy, fancy, favor, like
    idiom get used to

take away *vb* 1 *syn* see REMOVE 2
    rel separate
2 *syn* see DEDUCT 1
3 *syn* see DECRY 2

take back *vb* 1 *syn* see RETURN 4
2 *syn* see REPOSSESS 3
3 *syn* see ABJURE

take down *vb syn* see DISMOUNT

take in *vb* 1 *syn* see TAKE 10
2 *syn* see INCLUDE
3 *syn* see APPREHEND 1
    rel perceive; ‖savvy; absorb, assimilate,
    digest
4 *syn* see DECEIVE
    rel flimflam, take; trick

take off *vb* 1 *syn* see REMOVE 2
2 *syn* see REMOVE 3
3 *syn* see DEDUCT 1
4 *syn* see KILL 1
5 *syn* see MIMIC
    idiom do a takeoff on
6 *syn* see GET OUT 1
7 *syn* see HEAD 3
    idiom hit the road (*or* trail)
8 *syn* see GO 2

takeoff *n syn* see CARICATURE 2

take on *vb* 1 *syn* see DON 2
2 *syn* see ADD 1
3 to proceed to deal with < *took* on a new
    job with more responsibilities >
    syn take up, undertake
    rel begin, commence, enter (upon); at-
    tempt, endeavor, try; launch, venture
    idiom set about, take upon oneself
    con abandon, drop, forsake
    ant give up
4 *syn* see ENGAGE 5
5 *syn* see EMPLOY 2
6 *syn* see ADOPT
    ant give up

take out *vb* 1 *syn* see REMOVE 2
2 *syn* see REMOVE 4
3 *syn* see DEDUCT 1
4 *syn* see DATE

take out (on) *vb* to find release for (as
    emotions) < *took* out his anger on the
    dog >
    syn loose, release, unleash, vent
    idiom give vent to, let loose (*or* fly)
    con control, govern, restrain; bottle (up),
    check, keep down, quell, smother; repress,
    suppress

take over *vb syn* see RELIEVE 3

take up *vb* 1 *syn* see LIFT 1
2 *syn* see BEGIN 1
3 *syn* see TAKE ON 3

---

    rel assume; tackle
    idiom address oneself to
4 *syn* see ADOPT
    rel support; affiliate
5 *syn* see RESUME 2

taking *adj syn* see INFECTIOUS 3

tale *n* 1 *syn* see STORY 2
    rel myth, saga
2 *syn* see DETRACTION
3 *syn* see LIE
    rel fiction; yarn
4 *syn* see WHOLE 1

tale *vb syn* see COUNT 1

talebearer *n* 1 *syn* see INFORMER
2 *syn* see GOSSIP 1

talent *n syn* see GIFT 2
    rel art, craft, skill; endowment; expertise,
    forte

talisman *n syn* see CHARM 2
    idiom good-luck piece, lucky piece (*or*
    charm)

talk *vb* 1 *syn* see SPEAK 3
2 *syn* see SPEAK 1
3 *syn* see CONVERSE
4 *syn* see CHAT 1
    rel palaver, spout off
    idiom talk one's arm (*or* ear *or* leg) off,
    flap (*or* wag) the (*or* one's) tongue
5 *syn* see GOSSIP
6 to reveal secret or confidential informa-
    tion usually concerning illegal acts < at
    last the suspect *talked* to the police >
    syn sing, squeak, squeal; *compare* IN-
    FORM 3
    rel inform (on); divulge, reveal; confess
    idiom spill one's guts, spill the beans, tell
    all
7 to give a talk < he *talks* to community
    groups on ecology >
    syn address, lecture, prelect, speak
    rel declaim, harangue, hold forth, per-
    orate, speechify; spout

talk (into) *vb syn* see INDUCE 1

talk *n* 1 *syn* see SPEECH 1
2 *syn* see CONVERSATION 2
3 *syn* see CHAT 2
4 a formal or prearranged discussion,
    exchange, or negotiation usually of a po-
    litical nature < summit *talks* on nuclear
    arms >
    syn conference, meeting, parley, powwow
    rel dialogue, discussion, exchange; negoti-
    ation; deliberation
5 *syn* see REPORT 1
6 *syn* see SPEECH 2
    rel spiel; conference, discussion

talkative *adj* given to talk or talking < a
    talkative, sociable man >
    syn babblative, chatty, gabby, garrulous,
    loose-lipped, loose-tongued, loquacious,
    mouthy, multiloquent, multiloquious,
    talky, tonguey; *compare* GLIB
    rel articulate, eloquent, fluent; vocal,
    voluble; buzzy, gossipy
    con closemouthed, laconic, reserved, reti-
    cent, uncommunicative; speechless
    ant silent

talkee-talkee *n syn* see CHATTER

talky *adj syn* see TALKATIVE

tall *adj syn* see HIGH 1
    rel high-reaching, sky-high, skyscraping
    idiom higher than a cat's back
    con abbreviated, truncated; low

---

syn synonym(s)   *rel* related word(s)
ant antonym(s)   *con* contrasted word(s)
idiom idiomatic equivalent(s)
‖ use limited; if in doubt, see a dictionary

ant short

tally *n syn* see SCORE 5

tally *vb* **1** *syn* see INVENTORY

2 *syn* see COUNT 1

3 *syn* see AGREE 4

rel equal, match; balance, complement

con conflict (with), differ (from), disagree (with)

tame *adj* docilely tractable <a *tame* lion>

syn domestic, domesticated, domitae naturae, subdued, submissive

rel broken (in), ‖busted, housebroken, trained; amenable, biddable, docile, obedient, tractable; pliable, pliant; meek, mild

idiom gentle as a lamb

con fierce, savage, tameless; undomesticated, untrained; unbridled, unbroken

ant untamed, wild

tame *vb syn* see DOMESTICATE

tamp *vb syn* see CRAM 1

rel fill up (or in), plug up; concentrate

tamper (with) *vb* **1** *syn* see BRIBE

2 *syn* see MEDDLE

rel interpose, intervene; doctor, manipulate

tang *n syn* see TASTE 3

rel bite, nip, piquancy, twang; aroma, pungency; spiciness, tanginess

tangible *adj* **1** capable of being perceived especially by the sense of touch <primitives who find *tangible* expression of divinity in idols>

syn palpable, tactile, touchable; *compare* PERCEPTIBLE

rel corporeal, physical; embodied, material, real, substantial

con ethereal, spiritual, unreal

ant intangible

2 *syn* see MATERIAL 1

3 *syn* see PERCEPTIBLE

rel distinct, evident, manifest, obvious, patent, plain

con clouded, cloudy, imperceptible, indistinct, unclear

ant intangible

tangle *vb* **1** *syn* see INVOLVE 1

idiom make a party to

ant untangle

2 *syn* see CATCH 3

ant untangle

3 *syn* see ENTANGLE 1

rel foul up, mix up

4 *syn* see COMPLICATE

ant untangle

tangle *n syn* see MAZE 1

tanked *adj syn* see INTOXICATED 1

tank town *n syn* see BURG

tank up *vb syn* see DRINK 3

tantalize *vb syn* see WORRY 1

rel badger, bait; frustrate

tantamount *adj syn* see SAME 2

rel alike, like, uniform; selfsame, very

idiom as much as to say

tap *n* **1** *syn* see FAUCET

2 *syn* see BAR 5

tap *vb syn* see DRAIN 1

tap *vb* **1** to strike or hit audibly and usually lightly <*tapped* her pencil on the desk>

syn bob, knock, rap, tunk

rel bang, beat, hammer, hit, pound, smite, strike, thud, thump

2 *syn* see DESIGNATE 2

tapa *n syn* see SNACK

taper *vb syn* see DECREASE

taper off *vb syn* see DECREASE

taproom *n syn* see BAR 5

tapster *n syn* see BARTENDER

tar *n syn* see MARINER

tar *vb syn* see TAINT 1

taradiddle *n syn* see LIE

tardy *adj* not arriving, occurring, or done at the set, due, or expected time <be *tardy* for school>

syn behindhand, belated, late, lated, overdue, unpunctual

rel delayed, detained; dilatory, laggard, slow; delinquent

con beforehand, early; convenient, opportune, seasonable, timely; precise, punctilious

ant prompt, punctual

target *n* **1** an object of ridicule, attack, or abuse <made him the chief *target* of political satire>

syn butt, mark, sitting duck

rel victim; fall guy, scapegoat, whipping boy

2 *syn* see AMBITION 2

3 *syn* see USE 4

tariff *n* **1** *syn* see TAX 1

2 *syn* see PRICE 1

‖tarnation *adj syn* see UTTER

tarnish *vb* **1** *syn* see DULL 1

2 *syn* see SOIL 2

rel contaminate, defile, pollute, stain, taint

con clean, cleanse; shine (up)

ant polish

3 *syn* see INJURE 1

4 *syn* see TAINT 1

rel defame, disgrace, embarrass; slander

tarpaulin *n syn* see MARINER

tarriance *n syn* see SOJOURN

tarry *vb* **1** *syn* see DELAY 2

rel falter, flag

2 *syn* see STAY 2

rel dawdle; sojourn

3 *syn* see VISIT 3

tart *adj syn* see SOUR 1

rel piquant, pungent

ant flat

tart *n syn* see DOXY 1

Tartarean *adj syn* see INFERNAL 1

Tartuffe *n syn* see HYPOCRITE

Tartuffery *n syn* see HYPOCRISY

Tartuffism *n syn* see HYPOCRISY

task *n* **1** a piece of work assigned or to be done <laboratory *tasks* assigned to chemistry students>

syn assignment, chare, chore, devoir, duty, job, stint

rel enterprise, project, undertaking; errand, labor, toil, work; charge, function, mission, office, province; business, calling, employment, occupation, vocation

2 a necessary undertaking that is usually difficult, dull, disagreeable, or problematic <deciphering his handwriting is a real *task*>

syn chore, effort, job, taskwork

rel burden, onus, strain, tax; bother, headache, nuisance, pain, trouble

idiom a hard (or long) row to hoe

con child's play, cinch, duck soup, picnic, ‖pipe, sinecure, snap

3 *syn* see LOAD 3

task *vb syn* see BURDEN

taskmaster *n syn* see SLAVE DRIVER

taskwork *n syn* see TASK 2

taste *vb syn* see FEEL 2
idiom be exposed to, run up against

taste *n* 1 *syn* see HINT 2
rel bit, sample, sampling
2 *syn* see APPETITE 1
3 the property of a substance which
makes it perceptible to the gustatory sense
< children often dislike the *taste* of ol-
ives >
syn flavor, relish, sapidity, sapor, savor,
smack, tang
4 a liking for or enjoyment of something
because of the pleasure it gives < had a
taste for fast cars >
syn gusto, heart, palate, relish, zest
rel appreciation, comprehension, understanding; partiality, predilection, prepossession; disposition, inclination, predisposition
con dislike, disrelish; allergy, aversion,
repugnance, repulsion
ant antipathy; distaste
5 *syn* see APPETITE 3
ant distaste
6 the power or practice of discerning and
enjoying whatever constitutes excellence
(as in the fine arts) < a room whose decoration reflected her exquisite *taste* >
syn tastefulness
rel correctness; finesse, polish, refinement;
elegance, grace
con gracelessness, inelegance, unrefine-
ment; incorrectness, vulgarity
ant tastelessness

tasteful *adj* 1 *syn* see PALATABLE
rel rich
ant savorless, tasteless
2 *syn* see QUIET 4
ant tasteless

tastefulness *n syn* see TASTE 6
ant tastelessness

tasteless *adj* 1 *syn* see UNPALATABLE 1
rel bland, dull, stale, vapid; unflavored;
uninteresting
con flavorful, pleasing
ant tasteful, tasty
2 *syn* see BARBARIC 1
rel inelegant, unpolished, unrefined
idiom in bad taste
ant tasteful, tasty

tasty *adj* 1 *syn* see PALATABLE
idiom fit for a king
con unsavory; bland, flavorless, unpalatable
ant savorless, tasteless
2 *syn* see QUIET 4
ant tasteless

||**tats** *n pl syn* see DICE

||**tatter** *vb syn* see HURRY 2

tatterdemalion *n syn* see RAGAMUFFIN

tattered *adj* 1 *syn* see RAGGED
2 *syn* see SHABBY 1

tatters *n pl syn* see RAGS 1

tattle *vb syn* see GOSSIP

idiom tell tales out of school

tattle *n syn* see REPORT 1

tattler *n syn* see INFORMER

tattletale *n syn* see INFORMER

tatty *adj syn* see CHEAP 2

taunt *vb syn* see RIDICULE
rel banter, chaff; provoke; upbraid; disdain, scorn; affront, insult, offend, outrage

taut *adj syn* see TIGHT 3
rel firm, trim; stretched
con flabby; relaxed
ant slack

tautology *adj syn* see VERBIAGE 1
rel reiteration, repetition, repetitiousness;
padding

tavern *n* 1 *syn* see BAR 5
2 *syn* see HOTEL

tavern car *n syn* see PARLOR CAR

taverner *n syn* see SALOONKEEPER

tawdry *adj syn* see GAUDY
rel common, sleazy; flaring, screaming

tax *vb* 1 *syn* see BURDEN
rel overtax
idiom press hard upon, tax the strength
of, weigh heavy on (*or* upon)
2 *syn* see ACCUSE

tax *n* 1 a charge usually of money imposed
by authority upon persons or property for
public purposes < federal, state, and local
taxes bear heavily on the thrifty >
syn assessment, ||cess, duty, impost, levy,
tariff
rel tithe, tribute; boodle, boondoggle,
giveaway, pork barrel
2 *syn* see LOAD 3
rel difficulty, strain; demand, imposition

taxi *n syn* see TAXICAB

taxicab *n* an automobile that carries passengers for a fare < took a *taxicab* from
the airport to his hotel >
syn cab, hack, taxi
rel ||crawler, nighthawk

taxing *adj syn* see ONEROUS
rel wearing; tedious, troublesome

TB *n syn* see TUBERCULOSIS

||**tea** *n syn* see MARIJUANA

teach *vb* to cause to acquire knowledge or
skill < *teach* a child to read >
syn discipline, educate, instruct, school,
train
rel communicate, impart; implant, inculcate, instill; edify, enlighten, indoctrinate;
fit, ground, prepare, rear; drill, exercise,
practice; coach, tutor; lesson
idiom give instruction

teaching *n syn* see EDUCATION 1

teachy *adj syn* see DIDACTIC

tear *vb* 1 to separate (one part of a substance or object from another) forcibly
< *tore* a chunk from the loaf on the ta-
ble >
syn cleave, rend, rip, rive, split
rel cut, gash, incise, slash, slit; devil, pull
(apart), rift, sever, sunder; ribbon, shred;
break, crack, rupture; damage, impair,
injure
2 *syn* see EXTRACT 1
3 *syn* see RUSH 1
4 *syn* see COURSE

tear *n syn* see BINGE 1

tear down *vb* 1 *syn* see DESTROY 1
ant build up
2 *syn* see MALIGN

---

ant build up

teardrops *n pl syn* see TEARS

tearful *adj* flowing with or accompanied by tears < *tearful* entreaties >
syn lachrymose, teary, weeping, weepy
rel lamenting, mournful; sniveling; bawling, blubbering, crying, sobbing
con dry-eyed
ant tearless

tearing *adj syn* see EXCRUCIATING

tear–jerking *adj syn* see SENTIMENTAL

tears *n pl* a profuse secretion of saline fluid that overflows the eyelids and dampens the face < a blow that brought *tears* to his eyes >
syn teardrops, water

teary *adj syn* see TEARFUL
ant tearless

tease *vb syn* see WORRY 1
rel disturb, importune
idiom give a bad time

teaser *n syn* see STRIPTEASER

tease up *vb syn* see TOUCH UP

‖**tec** *n syn* see DETECTIVE

teched *adj syn* see INSANE 1

technique *n syn* see METHOD 1

tedious *adj* 1 *syn* see IRKSOME
2 *syn* see ARID 2
rel dragging, mortal, slow, tiresome

tedium *n* a state of dissatisfaction and weariness < incessant routine without variety breeds *tedium* >
syn boredom, doldrums, ennui, yawn
rel irksomeness, tediousness, tiresomeness, wearisomeness; dullness, monotony
con enlivenment, interest, invigoration, refreshment

teem *vb* to be abundantly stocked or provided < rivers *teeming* with fish >
syn abound, crawl, flow, pullulate, ‖sny, swarm
rel bristle, bustle; cram, crowd, jam, pack; overbrim, overflow, overrun
con lack, want

teem *vb syn* see POUR 3

teeming *adj syn* see ALIVE 5
rel multitudinous, populous, pregnant; bristling
con rare, sparse, uncommon; empty, lacking, void, wanting

teensy *adj syn* see TINY

teensy–weensy *adj syn* see TINY

teenty *adj syn* see TINY

teeny *adj syn* see TINY

teeny–weeny *adj syn* see TINY

tee off *vb syn* see BEGIN 1

teeter *vb* to progress (as by walking) unsteadily < *teetered* along on 4-inch heels >
syn falter, lurch, stagger, ‖stammer, stumble, topple, totter, wobble; *compare* LURCH 2, SEESAW
rel sway, weave

teethy *adj syn* see TOOTHY 1

teetotal *adj syn* see DRY 3

tehee *vb syn* see LAUGH

telephone *vb* to communicate with (a person) by telephone < *telephoned* him yesterday >
syn ‖buzz, call, phone, ‖ring (up)
idiom ‖get (one) on the horn, give (one) a buzz (or ring)

telestic *adj syn* see MYSTICAL 1

tell *vb* 1 *syn* see COUNT 1

2 *syn* see SAY 1
rel communicate, convey, impart
3 *syn* see REVEAL 1
rel recite, recount, rehearse, relate; acquaint, apprise, inform
4 *syn* see INFORM 2
5 *syn* see COMMAND
6 *syn* see WEIGH 3

telling *adj syn* see VALID
rel power-packed; influential, weighty; significant, striking

tell off *vb syn* see SCOLD 1
rel call down; denounce
idiom give (one) a piece of one's mind, tell (one) a thing or two, tell (one) where to get off

telltale *n* 1 *syn* see GOSSIP 1
2 *syn* see HINT 1

tellurian *adj syn* see EARTHLY 1

telluric *adj syn* see EARTHLY 1

temblor (*or* **tremblor**) *n syn* see EARTHQUAKE

temerarious *adj syn* see ADVENTUROUS
rel heedless, imprudent, incautious, injudicious

temerity *n* conspicuous or flagrant boldness (as in speech, behavior, or action) < had the *temerity* to order an attack when hopelessly outnumbered >
syn assurance, audacity, brashness, hardihood, hardiness, nerve
rel daring, foolhardiness, heedlessness, rashness, recklessness, venturesomeness; impetuosity, precipitateness; impertinence, intrusiveness
con deliberation, judgment, judiciousness, prudence; heed, heedfulness
ant caution

temper *vb syn* see MODERATE 1
rel dilute, season; ease, pacify, soften; adjust, modify; curb, tune down
idiom take the edge off

temper *n* 1 a general or prevailing quality or characteristic (as of moral or social attitudes and behavior) < riots reflected the *temper* of the times >
syn mood, spirit, timbre, tone
rel atmosphere, aura, climate; orientation, outlook; disposition, drift, leaning, tendency, trend; character, nature, peculiarity
2 *syn* see DISPOSITION 3
rel condition, posture, state; attribute, property, quality; style, type, way
idiom turn of mind
3 *syn* see MOOD 1
idiom frame (*or* state) of mind
4 an outbreak or display of anger < a childish fit of *temper* >
syn passion
rel anger, fury, ire, rage; conniption, fit, outburst, tantrum

temperament *n syn* see DISPOSITION 3
rel mentality, mind; kind, type, way
idiom inner nature

temperamental *adj* 1 *syn* see MOODY
2 *syn* see INCONSTANT 1
ant steady

temperance *n* 1 an avoidance of extremes (as in action, thought, or feeling) < a man who knew no *temperance* in his opinions >
syn measure, moderateness, moderation
rel reasonableness; constraint, restraint

idiom happy medium
con extremeness, radicalness; excess, excessiveness; immoderateness, immoderation, unconstraint, unreasonableness, unrestraint
ant intemperance, intemperateness
2 strict habitual and usually complete self‑denial in the gratification of appetites or passions <an ascetic who practiced complete *temperance*>
syn abstinence, continence, sobriety
rel abnegation, eschewal, forbearance, forgoing, refrainment, sacrifice, self-denial, self-deprivation; control, restraint, self‑control, self-discipline; asceticism, austerity, mortification
con intemperance, intemperancy, intemperateness, prodigality
ant excess

temperate *adj* **1** *syn* see MODERATE 2
rel constant, equable, even, steady; checked, curbed, regulated, restrained
ant intemperate
2 *syn* see ABSTEMIOUS
rel indulgent; self-indulgent
con intemperate; dissipated, prodigal, profligate
ant excessive
3 *syn* see CONSERVATIVE 2
4 *syn* see SOBER 3

temperish *adj* *syn* see IRASCIBLE

tempersome *adj* *syn* see ILL-TEMPERED

tempestuous *adj* *syn* see WILD 6
rel tumultuous, unbridled, unrestrained, violent
ant calm, quiet

temple *n* *syn* see HOUSE OF WORSHIP

tempo *n* rate of performance or delivery <increased sales and production *tempo*>
syn pace, time; *compare* SPEED 2
rel speed; momentum

temporal *adj* **1** *syn* see MATERIALISTIC
ant nontemporal
2 *syn* see PROFANE 1
rel material, physical; nonsacred, nonspiritual, unhallowed, unsanctified, unspiritual
con celestial, heavenly
ant spiritual

temporary *adj* lasting, continuing, or serving for a limited time <was *temporary* president of the company for nine months>
syn acting, ad interim, interim, pro tem, pro tempore, supply; *compare* TRANSIENT
rel alternate, substitute; interimistic, provisional, provisory; jackleg, make-do, makeshift, stopgap
ant permanent

tempt *vb* *syn* see LURE
rel provoke, rouse; court, invite, solicit, vamp, woo
idiom whet the appetite
con discourage; dissuade; repel, repulse, revolt

temptation *n* *syn* see LURE 2

tempting *adj* *syn* see ENTICING
rel appetizing, mouth-watering; provoking, rousing, tantalizing

con repellent, repulsive
ant untempting

temptress *n* *syn* see SIREN

ten *n* *syn* see BREAK 4

tenable *adj* **1** capable of being defended against attack <the platoon's position was no longer *tenable*>
syn defendable, defensible
rel impregnable, secure
con insecure, vulnerable; defenseless, helpless, unprotected; dangerous, precarious, risky
ant untenable
2 *syn* see JUSTIFIABLE
rel believable, credible, maintainable, plausible
con indefensible, inexcusable, unbelievable, unjustifiable
ant untenable

tenacious *adj* **1** *syn* see STRONG 2
rel bulldogged, bulldoggish, bulldoggy, dogged, obstinate, pertinacious, stubborn; resolute, steadfast, true; persevering, persisting
2 *syn* see VISCOUS
rel cohesive; tacky; sticky
3 *syn* see FAST 4
con lax, slack

tenant *vb* *syn* see INHABIT

tenantable *adj* *syn* see LIVABLE 1
idiom fit to live in
con uninhabitable

tend *vb* **1** *syn* see TILL
2 to supervise or take charge of <employed a girl to *tend* the children each day>
syn attend, care (for), mind, watch
rel cherish, cultivate, foster, minister, nurse, nurture, serve; defend, guard, protect, safeguard, shield; supervise
idiom look after, see after, see to, take care of, take under one's wing
con disregard, ignore, neglect

tend *vb* **1** to have or exhibit an inclination or tendency <he *tends* to praise people too highly>
syn incline, lean, look; *compare* INCLINE 3
idiom be disposed
2 *syn* see CONTRIBUTE 2

tendency *n* **1** a movement or course having a particular direction and character <a growing *tendency* to underestimate the potential strength of that nation>
syn current, drift, run, tenor, trend
rel curve, inclination, leaning, propensity; turn; shift; custom, habit, usage, way
2 *syn* see LEANING 2

tendentious *adj* *syn* see BIASED 2

tender *adj* showing or expressing affectionate interest in another <his mother was very *tender* with her wayward son>
syn compassionate, kindhearted, responsive, softhearted, sympathetic, warm, warmhearted
rel gentle, lenient, mild, soft, yielding; considerate, solicitous, thoughtful; affectionate, fond, loving; benevolent, charitable, humane, mild; commiserative; forgiving, merciful, tolerant
con callous, hard, harsh; inhumane, uncharitable, unfeeling
ant rough, severe

---

syn synonym(s)   *rel* related word(s)
ant antonym(s)   *con* contrasted word(s)
idiom idiomatic equivalent(s)
‖ use limited; if in doubt, see a dictionary

tender *vb syn* see OFFER 1
  rel propose, purpose, submit, suggest
tenderfoot *n syn* see NOVICE
tenderloin *n syn* see RED-LIGHT DISTRICT
tenebrific *adj syn* see GLOOMY 3
tenebrous *adj* **1** *syn* see DARK 1
  2 *syn* see OBSCURE 3
tenement *n syn* see APARTMENT 1
tenet *n syn* see DOCTRINE
  rel belief, conviction, persuasion, view
tenor *n* **1** the course of thought that is
  retained through something spoken or
  written <the *tenor* of the book is first
  expressed in the introduction>
  syn drift, purport, substance; *compare*
  BODY 3, MEANING 1, SUBSTANCE 2
  rel intent; inclination, trend; mood, tone;
  core, gist, meat, stuff
  2 *syn* see TENDENCY 1
tense *adj* **1** *syn* see TIGHT 3
  rel strained, stretched
  ant relaxed
  2 feeling or showing nervous tension <the
  soldiers were *tense* as they waited for the
  order to advance>
  syn edgy, nervy, restive, uneasy, uptight
  rel queasy; jittery, rusty, unquiet; anxious, concerned, overanxious
  con easy; calm, cool, ‖loose, placid, unconcerned; firm, nerveless, unshaken
  ant relaxed
tension *n* **1** *syn* see STRESS 1
  rel tautness, tenseness, tightness
  idiom stress and strain
  ant relaxation
  2 emotional strain <was suffering from
  nervous *tension*>
  syn unease, uptightness
  rel strain, stress; anxiety, nerves, nervousness, uneasiness; agitation, discomfort,
  disquiet, misease
ten-strike *n syn* see SMASH 6
tent *vb syn* see CAMP
tentative *adj* **1** *syn* see CONDITIONAL 1
  rel acting, ad interim, makeshift, temporary; probationary; experimental, test, trial
  con conclusive, decisive, definitive
  ant final
  2 *syn* see VACILLATING 2
  rel disinclined, reluctant
tenue *n syn* see BEHAVIOR
tenuous *adj* **1** *syn* see THIN 2
  2 *syn* see THIN 1
  rel aerial, airy, ethereal, fine
  con abundant
  ant dense
  3 having little substance or strength and
  usually not firmly based <only a *tenuous*
  link in the chain of evidence>
  syn feeble, insubstantial, unsubstantial;
  compare IMPLAUSIBLE
  rel flimsy, weak; insignificant
  con significant, sound, strong
  ant substantial
tenure *n syn* see HOLD
tepid *adj* **1** moderately warm <a *tepid*
  bath>
  syn lukewarm, milk-warm, warmish
  rel mild, temperate, warm
  con cold, cool, freezing, frozen; heated,
  hot, steaming

  2 lacking in animation, force, passion,
  conviction, or commitment <gave only a
  tepid endorsement to the candidate>
  syn halfhearted, lukewarm, unenthusiastic; *compare* ARID 2
  rel indifferent; colorless, dull, lifeless,
  unlively; feeble, marrowless, pithless, sapless, spiritless; dim, faint, forceless, weak
  con animated, forceful; fiery, impassioned,
  passionate, spirited
tergiversate *vb* **1** *syn* see DEFECT
  idiom fall away from
  2 *syn* see EQUIVOCATE 2
  idiom beg the question
tergiversation *n* **1** *syn* see DEFECTION
  rel about-face, reversal, reverse; denial,
  disavowal, forswearing, renunciation, repudiation
  2 *syn* see AMBIGUITY
tergiversator *n syn* see RENEGADE
tergiverse *vb* **1** *syn* see DEFECT
  2 *syn* see EQUIVOCATE 2
term *n* **1** *syn* see LIMIT 1
  rel terminus
  2 a limited, definite, or measurable extent
  of time during which something exists,
  lasts, or is in progress <the office has a
  term of four years>
  syn duration, span, time
  rel phase; go, period, spell, stretch; hitch,
  tour, turn; standing
  3 *syn* see WORD 2
  4 terms *pl syn* see CONDITION 1
  rel detail, item, particular, point; limit
  5 terms *pl* mutual social relationship or
  relative position <fight on equal
  terms> <the two were on *terms* of great
  intimacy>
  syn footing, standing
  rel coequality, equipollence, status; equality, equivalence, par, parity; balance
term *vb syn* see NAME 1
termagant *n syn* see VIRAGO
termagant *adj syn* see TURBULENT 1
terminable *adj* liable to be terminated or
  subject to termination <marriage is a
  terminable institution>
  syn determinable, endable
  rel finite, limited; limitable
terminal *adj syn* see LAST
  con beginning, starting
  ant initial
terminate *vb* **1** *syn* see CLOSE 3
  rel abolish, extinguish; discontinue, wind
  down
  idiom put the lid on
  ant initiate
  2 *syn* see ADJOURN 2
  3 *syn* see DISMISS 3
  4 *syn* see QUIT 6
terminated *adj syn* see COMPLETE 4
terminating *adj syn* see LAST
  ant initial
termination *n syn* see END 2
  rel issue, outcome, ‖pay-off, result
  con source; beginning, start
  ant initiation
terminology *n* the specialized or technical
  terms and expressions peculiar to a field,
  subject, or trade <the *terminology* of the
  plastics industry>
  syn cant, dictionary, jargon, language,
  lexicon, palaver, vocabulary; *compare*
  DIALECT 2

rel shoptalk; gibberish, gobbledygook

terminus *n syn* see END 2

terra firma *n syn* see EARTH 2

terrain *n* **1** the physical configuration and features of a tract of land < made an analysis of the *terrain* via aerial photos >
syn topography
rel contour, form, profile, shape
2 an area devoted to a specified activity < the whole country had become breeding and racing *terrain* >
syn territory, turf
3 *syn* see FIELD

terrene *adj* **1** *syn* see EARTHLY 1
2 *syn* see EARTHY 1

terrestrial *adj* **1** *syn* see EARTHLY 1
rel earthbound, prosaic; profane, secular, unspiritual
ant empyreal
2 *syn* see EARTHY 1

terrible *adj* **1** *syn* see FEARFUL 3
2 *syn* see HARD 6
3 *syn* see INTENSE 1
4 *syn* see GHASTLY 1

terribly *adv syn* see VERY 1

terrific *adj* **1** *syn* see FEARFUL 3
rel terrorizing; agitating, disquieting, upsetting
2 *syn* see MARVELOUS 2
rel magnificent, superb; rattling, screaming

terrified *adj syn* see AFRAID 1
rel horrified, shocked; terrorized; frozen, paralyzed
con unfearful, unfearing, unfrightened
ant unafraid

terrify *vb syn* see FRIGHTEN
rel freeze, paralyze, petrify, stun, stupefy
idiom put the fear of God into, strike fear into the heart of

terrifying *adj syn* see GHASTLY 1
ant unterrifying

territory *n* **1** *syn* see AREA 1
2 *syn* see FIELD
3 *syn* see TERRAIN 2

terror *n syn* see FEAR 1
rel awe, fearfulness

terroristic *adj* characterized by or practicing terror as a means of coercion < used torture and other *terroristic* tactics to extract confessions >
syn gestapo
rel coercive, strong-arm; brutal, cruel, merciless; immoral, improper, unsanctioned

terrorize *vb* **1** *syn* see FRIGHTEN
idiom scare to death
2 *syn* see INTIMIDATE
idiom use gestapo tactics on

terse *adj syn* see CONCISE
rel close, compact; lean, precise; clear-cut, crisp, incisive; taut
con circuitous; pleonastic, redundant, repetitious

tersely *adv syn* see BRIEFLY
rel closely, compactly; crisply, incisively, precisely; abruptly, curtly
idiom in as few words as possible

ant prolixly

test *n syn* see EXPERIMENT
rel inspection, scrutiny; confirmation, corroboration, substantiation, verification

test *vb* **1** *syn* see TRY 1
rel assay, essay; confirm, substantiate, verify
idiom bring to test
2 *syn* see PROVE 1

test (out) *vb syn* see EXPERIMENT

test *adj syn* see EXPERIMENTAL 2
rel proving, testing, trying; probational, speculative

testament *n syn* see TESTIMONY

testify *vb* **1** to serve as evidence of < present conditions *testify* to the accuracy of his predictions >
syn attest, point (to)
rel affirm; demonstrate, show; prove
con discredit, disprove, invalidate; confute, refute
2 to make a solemn declaration under oath for the purpose of establishing a fact (as in court) < *testified* against the defendant >
syn depone, depose, ‖mount, swear
idiom give evidence
3 *syn* see INDICATE 2

testimonial *n* **1** *syn* see TESTIMONY
rel indication, manifestation, show, sign, symbol, token
2 *syn* see CREDENTIALS
3 an expression of great approval and high esteem < a dinner was planned as a *testimonial* in his honor >
syn appreciation, salvo, tribute
rel salute; triumph; jubilee; commemoration, memorialization, remembrance
4 *syn* see MONUMENT 2

testimony *n* something that serves as tangible verification < the results are remarkable *testimony* to the accuracy of his predictions >
syn attestation, confirmation, evidence, proof, testament, testimonial, witness; *compare* INDICATION 3
rel demonstration, illustration; affirmation, corroboration, documentation, substantiation, verification

testy *adj syn* see IRASCIBLE
rel annoyed, exasperated, grouchy, irritable

tetchy *adj syn* see IRASCIBLE
rel ill-humored; cantankerous

tête-à-tête *n* a private conversation between two people < had a *tête-à-tête* with her in a quiet corner >
syn vis-à-vis
rel causerie, chat, coze; conversation, talk; argument, discussion

tetrad *n syn* see QUARTET

‖**tew** *vb syn* see WORRY 3

text *n syn* see SUBJECT 2
rel consideration, issue; fundamentals; idea

texture *n* **1** *syn* see ESSENCE 1
2 a basic often highly complex underlying scheme, structure, or pattern < war destroys the very *texture* of a society >
syn fabric, fiber, web
rel framework, structure; composition, constitution, makeup; pattern, scheme

thalassic *adj syn* see MARINE 1

---

thankful *adj syn* see GRATEFUL 1
  con unappreciative, ungrateful
  ant thankless, unthankful
thankless *adj* 1 not inclined to give thanks
  <a *thankless* guest>
  syn unappreciative, ungrateful, unthankful
  rel self-centered; careless, heedless,
  thoughtless; unappreciative, ungrateful,
  unmindful
  con appreciative, grateful, mindful; careful, heedful, thoughtful
  ant thankful
  2 not likely to obtain thanks <a *thankless*
  job>
  syn unappreciated, ungrateful, unthankful
  rel disagreeable, distasteful, unpleasant;
  miserable, wretched
  con thankworthy
thanks *n pl syn* see GRACE 1
thanksgiving *n syn* see GRACE 1
thankworthy *adj syn* see WORTHY 1
thank-you-ma'am *n syn* see BUMP 3
that *adj* 1 being the other <we argued it
  this way and we argued it *that* way>
  syn another
  ant this
  2 *syn* see SUCH 2
thaumaturgic *adj syn* see MAGIC
thaumaturgy *n syn* see MAGIC 1
thaw *vb syn* see LIQUEFY
theater *n syn* see DRAMA
theatral *adj syn* see DRAMATIC 1
theatric *adj syn* see DRAMATIC 1
theatrical *adj* 1 *syn* see DRAMATIC 1
  2 having qualities resembling a stage play
  or an actor's performance <he slowly
  made an exaggerated *theatrical* bow>
  syn dramatic
  rel histrionic, melodramatic, staged; affected, artificial, exaggerated, mannered,
  unnatural
theft *n* the unlawful taking and carrying
  away of property without the consent of
  its owner <was found guilty of auto
  theft>
  syn larceny, lift, pinch, purloining, steal,
  stealage, stealing, thievery, thieving,
  ‖touch
  rel filching, pilferage, pilfering, swiping;
  robbery, robbing, ‖stouth, ‖stouthrief;
  ‖score
theme *n* 1 *syn* see SUBJECT 2
  2 *syn* see ESSAY 2
then *adv* 1 at another time <science as it
  was taught then>
  syn again, anon, when; *compare* BEFORE
  2
  rel before, formerly
  2 *syn* see AGAIN 4
  3 *syn* see THEREFORE
thence *adv* 1 *syn* see AWAY 1
  2 *syn* see THEREFROM
thenceforth *adv* from that time forward
  <the island which was *thenceforth* to be
  their home>
  syn thenceforward, thereafter; *compare*
  HENCEFORTH
  idiom from then on
thenceforward *adv syn* see THENCE-
  FORTH
theorem *n syn* see PRINCIPLE 1
theoretical *adj* 1 concerned principally
  with abstractions and theories <*theoretical* versus applied physics>

  syn academic, closet, speculative
  rel conjectural, hypothetical, notional,
  suppositional, unproved; analytical, prob-
  lematical
  con practical; factual; proved
  ant applied
  2 *syn* see ABSTRACT 1
  rel idealized, ivory-tower
  ant concrete
theorize *vb syn* see SUGGEST 4
theory *n* 1 a belief, policy, or procedure
  proposed or followed as the basis of action <an educational system that was
  based on the *theory* that men learn best
  by experience>
  syn hypothesis, supposal; *compare* AS-
  SUMPTION 2
  rel base, basis, grounds, position, premise, understanding
  ant practice
  2 something taken for granted especially
  on trivial or inadequate grounds <her
  theory that the house was haunted>
  syn conjecture, perhaps, speculation,
  suppose, supposition
  rel guess, guesswork, surmise; feeling,
  hunch, impression, presentiment, suspicion
  con assurance, certainty, knowledge
there *adv* to or into that place <they seldom go *there* anymore>
  syn thither, thitherward, yon
  rel yonder
  ant here
thereafter *adv syn* see THENCEFORTH
thereby *adv* in consequence of that <lied
  to the jury, *thereby* negating his tes-
  timony>
  syn therethrough; *compare* THEREFROM
therefore *adv* for this or that reason <I
  think, *therefore* I am>
  syn accordingly, consequently, ergo,
  hence, so, then, thereupon, thus
  rel thence, therefrom
therefrom *adv* from that thing, fact, or
  circumstance <public opinion and a policy deriving *therefrom*>
  syn thence, thereof; *compare* THEREBY
thereof *adv syn* see THEREFROM
thereon *adv* on or upon that <knew both
  the text and commentary *thereon*>
  syn thereupon
  rel therein, thereof, thereto
therethrough *adv syn* see THEREBY
theretofore *adv* up to that time <*theretofore* obscure communities>
  syn thereuntil
  rel ‖afore, before, previously
  idiom before then
thereuntil *adv syn* see THERETOFORE
  idiom until then
thereupon *adv* 1 *syn* see THEREON
  2 *syn* see THEREFORE
thesis *n* 1 a position assumed or a point
  made especially in controversy <his *thesis*
  about the assassination was arguable>
  syn contention, contestation
  rel point, position; argument; belief, opinion, sentiment(s), view(s)
  2 *syn* see ASSUMPTION 2
  3 *syn* see DISCOURSE 2
  rel exposition; argument, argumentation
thespian *adj syn* see DRAMATIC 1
thespian *n syn* see ACTOR 1

thew *n syn* see MUSCLE 1

thick *adj* 1 *syn* see STOCKY
rel broad, wide; bulky, burly, husky; blubber, blubbery, massive, obese
con slender, slight, slim; lanky, spare; skeletal
2 *syn* see CLOSE 4
rel concentrated, crammed; localized
con dispersed, scattered
ant diffuse
3 *syn* see STUPID 1
4 *syn* see FAMILIAR 1
idiom hand in glove, thick as thieves
5 *syn* see IMPLAUSIBLE
idiom a little too thick

thick–bodied *adj syn* see STOCKY

thickhead *n syn* see DUNCE
rel ‖clot

thickheaded *adj syn* see STUPID 1

thickset *adj syn* see STOCKY
rel fleshy, portly

thickskull *n syn* see DUNCE
rel lout

thick–witted *adj syn* see STUPID 1

thief *n* one who steals <a *thief* took her money>
syn filcher, larcener, larcenist, nimmer, pilferer, prig, purloiner, stealer; compare ROBBER
rel burglar, cat burglar, cat man, housebreaker; hijacker, robber; ‖booster, ‖dip, lifter, shoplifter; nip, pickpocket

thieve *vb syn* see STEAL 1

thievery *n syn* see THEFT

thieving *adj syn* see LARCENOUS

thieving *n syn* see THEFT

thievish *adj syn* see LARCENOUS

thin *adj* 1 not thick, heavy, or broad (as in configuration or physique) <a *thin* body>
syn attenuate, reedy, slender, slight, slim, squinny, stalky, tenuous, twiggy; compare LEAN
rel lank, lanky, lathy, lean, macilent, spare; cadaverous, gaunt, pinched, skeletal, wasted; meager, puny, small, twiglike
con broad, wide; compact, dense, solid; heavy, massive; corpulent, fat, obese
ant thick
2 characterized by wide separation of component particles <*thin* air at high altitudes>
syn attenuate, attenuated, rare, rarefied, subtile, subtle, tenuous
rel diffuse, diluted, dispersed; fine, refined
con heavy, thick
ant dense
3 *syn* see DILUTE
4 *syn* see ACUTE 4
rel high-pitched
con low, low-pitched; guttural; deep
5 *syn* see IMPLAUSIBLE
rel vapid; transparent; questionable; untenable
idiom a bit thin
con believable, convincing, sound, substantial

thin *vb* 1 to make thin or thinner <a once powerful frame *thinned* by privation>
syn attenuate, extenuate, wiredraw
rel diminish, reduce; weaken
con broaden, enlarge; strengthen
ant thicken
2 to make or become less dense <the air *thinned* at high altitudes>
syn attenuate, rarefy
ant densify
3 *syn* see DILUTE

thing *n* 1 *syn* see AFFAIR 1
2 *syn* see OCCURRENCE
3 *syn* see ACTION 1
rel exploit, feat, stunt
4 whatever is apprehended as having actual, distinct, and demonstrable existence <there is a place for each *thing* in the lab>
syn article, object
rel entity, item
5 that which can be known as having existence in space or time <virtue is not a *thing*, but an attribute of a *thing*>
syn being, entity, individual, material, matter, object, stuff, substance
rel item, particular
con attribute, characteristic, property, quality
6 *syn* see ENTITY 1
ant nonentity, nonexistence
7 **things** *pl syn* see POSSESSION 2
8 **things** *pl syn* see PERSONAL EFFECTS
9 **things** *pl syn* see CLOTHES
10 *syn* see POINT 1
11 *syn* see FASHION 3
12 *syn* see FETISH 2

thingum *n syn* see DOODAD

thingumajig *n syn* see DOODAD

thingumbob *n syn* see DOODAD

thingummy *n syn* see DOODAD

think *vb* 1 to form an idea of something in the mind <try to *think* exactly how the accident happened>
syn conceive, envisage, envision, fancy, feature, image, imagine, project, realize, see, vision, visualize
rel consider, contemplate, study, weigh; appreciate, comprehend, understand; cerebrate, ideate; conjecture, guess, surmise
2 *syn* see UNDERSTAND 3
3 *syn* see CONJECTURE
4 *syn* see FEEL 3
rel estimate; regard
5 to use one's powers of conception, judgment, or inference <the power to *think* sets humans apart from other animals>
syn cerebrate, cogitate, deliberate, reason, reflect, speculate
rel consider, contemplate; brood, meditate, mull, muse, ponder, ruminate; intellectualize, logicalize, logicize, rationalize; conclude, deduce, infer, judge
idiom put on one's thinking cap, set one's brain to work, use one's head, use the old bean

think (out *or* over) *vb syn* see CONSIDER 1

think (over) *vb syn* see RECONSIDER

thinkable *adj* 1 capable of being thought about <concepts that are easy enough to be *thinkable*>
syn cogitable
rel imaginable, presumable, supposable; comprehendible, comprehensible
con unimaginable; incomprehensible, uncomprehensible

---

syn synonym(s)   *rel* related word(s)
ant antonym(s)   *con* contrasted word(s)
idiom idiomatic equivalent(s)

‖ use limited; if in doubt, see a dictionary

ant unthinkable

2 capable of being made actual < nationalism at this time would be scarcely *thinkable* >
syn conceivable, imaginable, supposable
rel likely, possible; convincing, plausible; feasible, practicable, practical
con inconceivable, unimaginable; impossible, unlikely; implausible; impractical, unfeasible
ant unthinkable

thinking *adj syn* see THOUGHTFUL 1
ant unthinking

third degree *n syn* see CROSS-EXAMINATION

third estate *n syn* see COMMONALTY

thirst *vb syn* see LONG
rel covet; desire, wish

thirsting *adj syn* see THIRSTY 1

thirsty *adj* 1 experiencing a desire for drink < the long hot walk had made him *thirsty* >
syn athirst, dry, thirsting
rel juiceless, parched, sapless
2 *syn* see DRY 1
3 *syn* see EAGER
idiom hungry for, itching for, wild for
ant sated, satiated

this and that *n, often* this and thats *pl*
syn see SUNDRIES

thither *adv syn* see THERE
ant hither

thitherward *adv syn* see THERE
ant hitherward

thorny *adj* bristling with perplexities, points of controversy, or other conflicting elements < the *thorny* question of states' rights >
syn nettlesome, prickly, spiny
rel troublesome, vexatious; difficult; tricky

thorough *adj* 1 *syn* see EXHAUSTIVE
rel absolute
2 *syn* see CIRCUMSTANTIAL

thoroughbred *adj syn* see PUREBRED
con mixed, mongrel

thoroughfare *n syn* see WAY 1

thoroughgoing *adj* 1 *syn* see EXHAUSTIVE
2 *syn* see UTTER

thoroughly *adv* 1 *syn* see WELL 3
2 in a detailed and complete manner < *thoroughly* investigated the accusations >
syn completely, detailedly, exhaustively, in and out, inside out, up and down
idiom item by item, to the last detail
con casually, offhandedly, sketchily, superficially
ant cursorily
3 *syn* see VERY 1
4 *syn* see HARD 3

though *adv syn* see HOWEVER

though *conj* in spite of the fact that < *though* they know the war is lost, they continue to fight >
syn albeit, although, howbeit, much as, when, whereas, while

thought *n* 1 the act or process of thinking < sat immersed in deep *thought* >
syn brainwork, cerebration, cogitation, deliberation, reflection, speculation
rel contemplation; meditation, musing, pondering, rumination

2 *syn* see IDEA

thoughtful *adj* 1 characterized by or exhibiting the power to think < the doctor had a shrewd rather than a *thoughtful* face >
syn cogitative, contemplative, meditative, pensive, ‖pensy, pondering, reflecting, reflective, ruminative, speculative, thinking
rel analytical, calculating, logical, rational; earnest, grave, melancholy, serious, sober, studious; brainy, intellectual; deep, inseeing, introspective
con irrational; dull, slow, stupid, unthinking; empty-headed, shallow, vacuous
ant thoughtless
2 *syn* see MINDFUL 2
3 mindful of others < the thank-you note was a *thoughtful* gesture >
syn attentive, considerate
rel anxious, careful, concerned, heedful, mindful, solicitous; chivalrous, civil, courteous, gallant, gracious, polite, well-bred
con careless, heedless, inattentive, negligent, remiss, unconcerned, unmindful, unthinking; inconsiderate; discourteous, impolite
ant thoughtless, unthoughtful

thoughtfully *adv syn* see WELL 2
rel courteously, politely, solicitously
con discourteously, impolitely; inconsiderately, heedlessly, unkindly
ant thoughtlessly, unthoughtfully

thoughtless *adj* 1 *syn* see RASH 1
2 *syn* see CARELESS 1
con mindful
ant thoughtful
3 *syn* see SHORT 5
rel discourteous, impolite, rude; selfish
ant thoughtful

thought–out *adj syn* see DELIBERATE 1
rel investigated; analyzed
idiom thought over (*or* through)

thousand *n syn* see SCAD

thrall *n syn* see BONDAGE

thralldom *n syn* see BONDAGE

thrash *vb* 1 *syn* see BEAT 1
2 *syn* see WHIP 2
3 *syn* see WHIP 1
rel strike; paddywhack, ‖pail

thrashing *n syn* see DEFEAT 1

thrash out *vb syn* see DISCUSS 1

threadbare *adj* 1 *syn* see SHABBY 1
rel damaged, impaired, injured; frayed, ragged; shopworn, timeworn, worn
idiom the worse for wear, worn to rags (*or* threads)
2 *syn* see TRITE
rel common, familiar; imitative, uncreative; set, stock; banal, corny
con fresh, new; different, novel, original, unconventional, unusual; memorable

threaten *vb* to announce or forecast impending danger or evil < bullies *threatening* the child with a beating >
syn menace
rel browbeat, bulldoze, cow, intimidate; augur, forebode, portend, presage; caution, forewarn, warn
idiom make (*or* utter) threats against

threatening *adj* 1 *syn* see IMMINENT 2
rel impending; forthcoming, upcoming; close, near
2 *syn* see OMINOUS

threesome *n syn* see TRIAD
threshold *n syn* see VERGE 2
thrift *n syn* see ECONOMY
   rel austerity, economizing; saving; parsimony
   ant waste
thriftiness *n syn* see ECONOMY
   ant thriftlessness
thriftless *adj syn* see IMPROVIDENT
   ant thrifty
thrifty *adj* 1 *syn* see FLOURISHING
   rel blooming, burgeoning; growing
   2 *syn* see SPARING
   rel foresighted, prudent; conserving, preserving
   con extravagant, improvident
   ant wasteful
thrill *vb* to fill with emotions that stir or excite or to be so excited <an audience *thrilled* by the brilliant spectacle>
   syn electrify, enthuse, send
   rel animate, excite, galvanize, move, quicken, stimulate; arouse, inspire, rally, rouse, stir
   idiom thrill to pieces (*or* to bits)
   con bore, ennui, weary
thrill *n* sudden emotional stimulation, excitement, or enjoyment <they both got a *thrill* out of small-boat racing>
   syn bang, boot, kick, wallop
   rel excitement, lift, stimulation, titillation
thriller *n* a work of fiction or drama designed to hold the interest by use of a high degree of intrigue, adventure, or suspense <wrote cheap detective *thrillers*>
   syn chiller, shocker, thriller-diller
   rel gothic, mystery; dime novel, penny dreadful, shilling shocker
thriller–diller *n syn* see THRILLER
thrive *vb* 1 *syn* see BOOM
   rel come on, develop, grow; increase; prosper
   con stagnate; fail; bust
   2 *syn* see SUCCEED 3
   rel advance, progress
   idiom make a go, turn out well
thriving *adj* 1 *syn* see FLOURISHING
   rel blooming, growing; advancing, progressing
   idiom going strong
   con shriveling; dying
   2 *syn* see SUCCESSFUL
thriving *n syn* see PROSPERITY 2
throb *vb syn* see PULSATE
   rel thump; resonate
throe *n* 1 *syn* see ATTACK 3
   rel convulsion
   2 *syn* see PAIN 1
   rel stab
throne *n syn* see TOILET
throng *n syn* see CROWD 1
   rel assemblage, assembly, collection, congregation, gathering; bunch, flock, group, pack
thronged *adj syn* see ALIVE 5
   rel crawling
throttle *vb syn* see CHOKE 1

throttling *n syn* see REPRESSION 1
through *prep* 1 *syn* see VIA 1
   2 *syn* see VIA 2
   3 *syn* see OVER 6
   4 *syn* see ABOUT 4
   idiom clear through
through *adv* 1 from beginning to end <the region has a mild climate the whole year *through*>
   syn around, over, round, throughout
   2 *syn* see OVER 5
through *adj* 1 *syn* see DIRECT 2
   con obstructed; interrupted
   2 *syn* see COMPLETE 4
   3 having no further value, strength, or resources <when he lost his voice, his singing career was *through*>
   syn done for, finished, washed-up
   rel ended; over
   4 being at the very end of a course, concern, or relationship <was *through* with his wife>
   syn done, washed-up
   rel finished
through–and–through *adv*   *syn*   see DOWN 2
throughout *adv* 1 *syn* see EVERYWHERE 1
   2 *syn* see THROUGH 1
throughout *prep* 1 *syn* see ABOUT 4
   2 *syn* see DURING
throw *vb* 1 to cause to move swiftly through space by a propulsive movement or a propelling force <*throw* a ball to first base>
   syn ‖bung, cast, fire, fling, heave, hurl, launch, pitch, sling, toss
   rel ding, drive, impel, precipitate, shoot; project, propel, push, shove, thrust; flick, flip; ‖chuck, shy, tumble; lift, lob
   2 to dislodge from one's seat especially in horseback riding <was *thrown* while taking a hurdle>
   syn buck (off), pitch, unhorse, unseat
   rel ding (off), fling (off)
   3 *syn* see OVERCOME 1
   4 *syn* see DON 1
   5 *syn* see EXERT
   6 *syn* see ADDRESS 3
throw away *vb* 1 *syn* see DISCARD
   ant salvage
   2 *syn* see WASTE 2
   con lay away, lay by, lay up
throw back *vb syn* see REVERT 2
throwback *n syn* see REVERSION 1
throw down *vb syn* see FELL 1
   rel cast down
throw in *vb syn* see INTRODUCE 6
   rel contribute
throwing away *n syn* see DISPOSAL 2
   ant salvaging
throw off *vb* 1 *syn* see RID
   2 *syn* see SHAKE 5
   3 *syn* see EMIT 2
   rel disgorge, eject, exhaust, expel
   4 *syn* see CONFUSE 2
throw out *vb* 1 *syn* see EJECT 1
   2 *syn* see DISCARD
   3 *syn* see SAY 1
   4 *syn* see CONFUSE 2
throw over *vb syn* see ABANDON 1
throw up *vb* 1 to construct or erect hastily and often carelessly <makeshift buildings *thrown up* almost overnight>

---

syn synonym(s)   *rel* related word(s)
ant antonym(s)   *con* contrasted word(s)
idiom idiomatic equivalent(s)
‖ use limited; if in doubt, see a dictionary

syn jerry-build, run up
rel roughcast, roughhew
idiom slap together, throw together
2 *syn* see VOMIT

thrum *vb syn* see HUM
rel birr, purr

thrust *vb* 1 *syn* see PUSH 1
rel crowd, jam; bump, elbow, jostle, nudge, prod, shoulder
2 to cause (as a pointed instrument) to penetrate forcibly < *thrust* the dagger through her heart >
syn dig, drive, plunge, ram, run, sink, stab, stick
rel jab, shove; impale; pierce; embed; put

thrust *n syn* see SUBSTANCE 2

thud *vb* to make a dull sound by or as if by striking a surface with something thick and heavy < heard footsteps *thudding* down the hall >
syn clonk, clunk, thump
rel tunk; hit, smite, strike; beat, pound

thug *n* 1 a person inclined or hired to treat another roughly, brutally, or murderously < was beaten and robbed by *thugs* >
syn ‖gorilla, ‖hood, hoodlum, hooligan, ruffian, strong arm; *compare* TOUGH
rel bully, ‖larrikan, plug-ugly, roughneck, rowdy, tough; punk; cutthroat, gangster, gunman, mobster; goon, hatchet man
2 *syn* see TOUGH

thumb *vb syn* see HITCHHIKE
idiom thumb a ride

thumb (through) *vb syn* see BROWSE

thump *vb syn* see THUD
rel hammer, knock

thunder *n* the sound that follows a flash of lightning and is caused by sudden expansion of the air in the path of the electrical discharge < he was more afraid of *thunder* than of lightning >
syn thunderclap, thundercrack, thundering
rel fulmination

thunderbolt *n* a single discharge of lightning with the accompanying thunder < he was startled by the *thunderbolt* >
syn bolt, thunderstroke

thunderclap *n syn* see THUNDER

thundercrack *n syn* see THUNDER

thundering *n syn* see THUNDER

thunderstroke *n syn* see THUNDERBOLT

thunderstruck *adj syn* see AGHAST 2
rel bewildered, staggered; breathless, stunned
idiom struck dumb

thus *adv* 1 in this or that manner < summoned his counselors and spoke *thus* to them >
syn so, thus and so, thus and thus, thusly
2 *syn* see THEREFORE

thus and so *adv syn* see THUS 1

thus and thus *adv syn* see THUS 1

thus far *adv syn* see HITHERTO 1

thusly *adv syn* see THUS 1

thwack *n syn* see BLOW 1

thwart *adj syn* see TRANSVERSE

thwart *vb syn* see FRUSTRATE 1
rel curb, restrain, scotch; cross; foul up, gum up, queer; stymie
con aid, assist, help, support; abet, encourage

‖**tick** *n syn* see INSTANT 1

ticket *n* 1 a slip giving information (as of ownership, identity, or price) < the price of the iron is on the *ticket* >
syn label, tag
rel card; slip; sticker
2 a card of admission < theater *tickets* >
syn carte d'entrée
rel pass
3 a list of candidates for appointment, nomination, or election < vote the party *ticket* >
syn slate
rel choice; lineup; list
4 *syn* see BALLOT 1
5 *syn* see PASSPORT

ticklish *adj* 1 *syn* see UNSTABLE 2
2 *syn* see DELICATE 7
rel critical
3 *syn* see INCONSTANT 1

tick off 1 *syn* see ENUMERATE 2
2 *syn* see REPROVE

tidbit (*or* titbit) *n syn* see DELICACY

‖**tiddly** *adj syn* see INTOXICATED 1

tide *n syn* see FLOW

tidings *n pl syn* see NEWS

tidy *adj syn* see NEAT 2
rel sleek, spruce
ant untidy

tie *n* 1 *syn* see BOND 3
rel fastener, fastening; attachment
2 *syn* see DRAW 4

tie *vb* 1 to make fast and secure < *tie* a bundle with strong cord >
syn bind, tie up
rel attach, fasten; connect, join, link; anchor, moor, rivet, secure; lash, truss (up); band, cinch, gird, rope
con loose, loosen; disconnect
ant untie
2 *syn* see MARRY 2
3 *syn* see HAMPER
idiom tie hand and foot, tie one's hands
ant untie
4 *syn* see EQUAL 3

tier *n* 1 *syn* see LINE 5
rel layer
2 *syn* see CLASS 1

tie up *vb* 1 *syn* see TIE 1
2 *syn* see HAMPER

tie–up *n syn* see ASSOCIATION 1
rel linkup

tiff *n syn* see QUARREL

tiff *vb syn* see QUARREL

tiffany *adj syn* see FILMY

tight *adj* 1 *syn* see FAST 4
rel clasped; solid, steadfast
con lax, limp; shaky
ant loose
2 *syn* see CLOSE 4
ant loose
3 fitting, drawn, or stretched so that there is no slackness or looseness < a *tight* drumhead >
syn close, taut, tense
rel skintight; constricted, contracted, drawn, tightened; inflexible, rigid, stiff
con loosened, slack, unconstricted
ant loose
4 difficult to cope with, get through, or circumvent < a very *tight* diplomatic situation >
syn arduous, rough, tricksy, trying
rel difficult; exacting; tense; critical; punishing; distressing, disturbing, upsetting

5 *syn* see STINGY
6 *syn* see INTOXICATED 1
 idiom tight as a tick
tight *adv syn* see HARD 7
tightfisted *adj syn* see STINGY
 rel grudging, mean, shabby
tight–laced *adj syn* see PRIM 1
tight–lipped *adj syn* see SILENT 3
 idiom with one's lips sealed
tightly *adv syn* see HARD 7
tight–mouthed *adj syn* see SILENT 3
tightwad *n syn* see MISER
till *prep syn* see UNTIL
till *conj* up to the time when < be sure to
wait *till* I come>
 syn until
till *vb* to prepare (soil) for the raising of
crops < *till* the soil>
 syn cultivate, dress, ‖labor, tend, work
 rel harrow, hoe, mulch, plow, turn; plant,
sow
tillable *adj syn* see ARABLE
 ant untillable
tilt *vb* **1** *syn* see SLANT 1
 2 *syn* see SEESAW
tilt *n syn* see SLOPE
tilted *adj syn* see INCLINED 3
tilter *vb syn* see SEESAW
tilting *adj syn* see INCLINED 3
timber *n* **1** *syn* see FOREST
 2 a large squared or dressed piece of
wood < roof *timbers* >
 syn balk, beam
 rel girder, rafter
timberland *n syn* see FOREST
timbre *n syn* see TEMPER 1
time *n* **1** *syn* see WHILE 1
 rel season
 2 *syn* see OCCASION 5
 3 *syn* see OPPORTUNITY
 idiom the proper moment
 4 *syn* see PERIOD 2
 5 *syn* see TERM 2
 6 *syn* see SEASON
 7 *syn* see TEMPO
 8 *syn* see SPELL 1
 ‖**9** *syn* see BINGE 1
time *vb* **1** to arrange or set the time of
< *timed* his visits to coincide with her
vacations>
 syn book, schedule
 rel plan, program, set up
 2 to ascertain or record the time, duration, or rate of < *timed* the car at 100
mph>
 syn clock
 idiom hold the clock on
time and again *adv syn* see OFTEN
timeless *adj* **1** *syn* see CONTINUAL
 2 *syn* see ETERNAL 4
timely *adv syn* see EARLY 1
timely *adj* **1** done or occurring at a
suitable time < await a more *timely* mo-
ment>
 syn auspicious, favorable, opportune,
propitious, prosperous, seasonable, timeous, well-timed
 rel appropriate, fit, fitting, meet, proper,
suitable; likely, promising

 con improper, inappropriate, unfitting;
inauspicious, inopportune, unfavorable,
unpropitious, unsuitable; ill-timed
 ant untimely
 2 *syn* see PUNCTUAL 2
timeous *adj syn* see TIMELY 1
timetable *n syn* see PROGRAM 1
 rel table; plan
timeworn *adj* **1** *syn* see ANCIENT 1
 2 *syn* see TRITE
timid *adj* **1** *syn* see SHY 1
 rel humble; shrinking
 ant bold
 2 marked by or exhibiting a lack of boldness, courage, or determination < was too
timid to ski>
 syn timorous, ‖timorsome, undaring
 rel gentle, mild, milk-toast, milky; cautious, chary, wary; jumpy, nervous, skittish; afraid, apprehensive, fainthearted,
fearful; chicken, chickenhearted, hen-
hearted, mouselike, mousy, pigeonhearted;
cowardly, yellow; funky, panicky
 con audacious, brave, courageous, daring,
doughty, fearless, intrepid, lionhearted,
unafraid, valiant, valorous
 ant bold
 3 *syn* see VACILLATING 2
timorous *adj syn* see TIMID 2
 rel quailing, recoiling, shrinking; quivering, shivering, shuddering, trembling
 ant assured
‖**timorsome** *adj syn* see TIMID 2
tincture *n* **1** *syn* see COLOR 6
 2 *syn* see HINT 2
 rel smattering
tincture *vb syn* see TINT
 rel pigment; stain
ting *vb syn* see TINKLE 1
tinge *vb syn* see TINT
 rel streak
tinge *n* **1** *syn* see COLOR 1
 rel coloration, coloring, tincture; stain
 2 *syn* see HINT 2
tingle *vb* **1** *syn* see TINKLE 1
 rel chime
 2 *syn* see JINGLE
tinker *vb syn* see FIDDLE 2
 idiom play around
tinkle *vb* **1** to make a repeated light high-
pitched ringing sound < wind-bells *tin-
kling* in the breeze>
 syn plink, ting, tingle
 rel clink, jangle, jingle
 2 *syn* see JINGLE
 3 *syn* see CHAT 1
tinsel *adj syn* see GAUDY
tint *n syn* see COLOR 1
 rel tincture, touch; coloration, pigmenta-
tion; dye, stain, wash
tint *vb* to color with a slight shade or stain
< white blossoms *tinted* with pale pink>
 syn complexion, tincture, tinge
 rel color, dye; shade, touch (up); stain,
wash
tintamarre *n syn* see DIN
tiny *adj* exceptionally or remarkably small
< the first *tiny* buds of spring flowers>
 syn ‖bitsy, diminutive, dwarf, dwarfish,
itsy-bitsy, itty-bitty, lilliputian, midget,
miniature, minikin, minute, peewee, pint-
size, pocket, pocket-size, pygmy, teensy,
teensy-weensy, teenty, teeny, teeny-weeny,
wee, weensy, weeny; *compare* SMALL 1

---

syn synonym(s) *rel* related word(s)
ant antonym(s) *con* contrasted word(s)
idiom idiomatic equivalent(s)
‖ use limited; if in doubt, see a dictionary

rel minuscular, minuscule; infinitesimal, microscopic, minim

con colossal, enormous, gigantic, immense, mammoth, vast

ant huge

tip *n syn* see POINT 9

tip *vb syn* see SLANT 1

tip *vb syn* see TIPTOE

rel creep, mince, pussyfoot, steal

tip (over) *vb syn* see OVERTURN 1

idiom turn upside down

tip *n syn* see GRATUITY

tip *n* a piece of advice or confidential information given by one thought to have access to special or inside sources < gave him a *tip* on which horse would win >

syn point, pointer, steer, tip-off

rel advice; information; clue, cue, hint; forecast, prediction

idiom a bit of inside advice, a bug in the ear, a word to the wise

tip-off *n syn* see TIP

tipped *adj syn* see INCLINED 3

tipple *vb syn* see DRINK 3

idiom drown one's cares (*or* sorrows)

tipple *n syn* see LIQUOR 2

tippler *n syn* see DRUNKARD

tipster *n syn* see INFORMER

tipsy *adj syn* see INTOXICATED 1

rel dazed, unsteady

tiptoe *vb* to walk or proceed quietly on or as if on the ends of the toes < *tiptoed* through the dark house >

syn tip, toe

rel creep, gumshoe, pussyfoot, steal

con clomp, clump, stamp, stomp, stump

tirade *n* a violent, often protracted, and usually denunciatory speech or writing < lashed out with a vicious *tirade* of angry protest >

syn diatribe, harangue, jeremiad, philippic

rel rant, rodomontade, screed; abuse, invective, revilement, vituperation; censure, condemnation, denunciation; berating, tongue-lashing; lecture, sermon

tire *vb* 1 to deplete the strength and energy of < the plane trip *tired* him >

syn drain, fatigue, jade, wear, wear down, weary; *compare* EXHAUST 4

rel debilitate, enervate, enfeeble, sap, weaken; exhaust, wear out

con brace (up), invigorate, strengthen; animate, energize, enliven, pep (up), quicken, stimulate, vitalize

2 *syn* see BORE

rel jade, wear; irk; disgust, nauseate, sicken

idiom make one tired, put one to sleep

tired *adj* 1 being depleted of strength and energy < was too *tired* to go on >

syn fatigued, jaded, wearied, weary, worn, worn down

rel overtaxed, overworked; drained, run-down; ‖beat, ‖bushed, dog-tired, exhausted, fagged, frazzled, overworn, ‖pooped, ‖tuckered up, tuckered, worn-out; collapsing, consumed, knocked out, prostrate, spent

idiom worn to a frazzle

con active, energetic, lively, strong, tireless

ant rested; fresh, untired

2 *syn* see SHABBY 1

3 *syn* see FED UP

rel annoyed, bothered, displeased, irked

idiom having a bellyful of, having about enough of

4 *syn* see TRITE

tiredness *n syn* see FATIGUE

rel collapse, prostration

tireless *adj syn* see INDEFATIGABLE

rel active, enthusiastic

con inactive, listless, tired, unenergetic, unenthusiastic, weak

tiresome *adj syn* see IRKSOME

rel dull; jading; burdensome, onerous, oppressive; difficult, hard

tiring *adj syn* see IRKSOME

Titan *adj syn* see HUGE

titanic *adj syn* see HUGE

title *n* 1 *syn* see CLAIM 1

rel argument, ground, justification, proof, reason; desert, due, merit

2 *syn* see NAME 1

title *vb syn* see NAME 1

titter *vb syn* see LAUGH

rel twitter

idiom laugh behind (*or* in) one's hand, laugh in one's beard

tittle *n syn* see PARTICLE

rel fleck, flyspeck, speck; crumb, grain, scrap, snippet

tittle-tattle *n* 1 *syn* see CHATTER

2 *syn* see REPORT 1

titubate *vb syn* see REEL 2

titular *adj syn* see NOMINAL

tizzy *n syn* see SNIT

to *prep* 1 in the direction of and as far as < was driving *to* the city >

syn into

rel toward

ant from

2 *syn* see AGAINST 2

rel on, over, upon

3 *syn* see BEFORE 1

4 *syn* see UNTIL

5 for the particular purpose of < a market study tailored *to* your needs >

syn for

idiom in contemplation (*or* consideration) of, with an eye to, with a view to

6 in complement to < played Romeo *to* her Juliet >

syn opposite

toad *n syn* see SNOT 1

toad *n syn* see SYCOPHANT

toadeater *n syn* see SYCOPHANT

toadier *n syn* see SYCOPHANT

toady *n syn* see SYCOPHANT

toady *vb syn* see FAWN

rel follow, tag, tail, trail

toadying *adj syn* see FAWNING

toadyish *adj syn* see FAWNING

to-and-fro *n* 1 *syn* see HESITATION

2 *syn* see QUARREL

toast *n syn* see DRINK 2

to-be *n syn* see FUTURE

tocsin *n syn* see ALARM 1

rel sign, signal

today *adv* at the present time < youth *today* do not know what poverty is >

syn now, nowadays, presently

idiom in this day and age, these days

con then, yesteryear

today *n syn* see PRESENT

todayish *adj syn* see PRESENT

to–do *n* **1** *syn* see COMMOTION 4
  2 *syn* see COMMOTION 3
toe *vb syn* see TIPTOE
tog (out *or* up) *vb syn* see DRESS UP 1
together *adv* **1** at one and the same time
  <events that occurred *together*>
  syn at once, coincidentally, coincidently,
  coinstantaneously, concurrently, simultaneously
  idiom all at once, all together
  ant separately
  2 in succession usually without intermission <was moody for days *together*>
  syn consecutively, continually, continuously, hand running, night and day, running, successively, unintermittedly, uninterruptedly
  idiom on end
  3 in or by combined action or effort
  <students and faculty protested *together*>
  syn conjointly, jointly, mutually
  rel collectively, concertedly, unanimously
  idiom in one breath, in the same breath,
  with one accord, with one voice
  ant separately
togetherness *n* **1** *syn* see ASSOCIATION 1
  2 *syn* see SOLIDARITY
‖**toggle** *vb syn* see DRESS UP 1
togs *n pl syn* see CLOTHES
toil *n syn* see WORK 2
  idiom sweat of one's brow, toil and trouble
toil *vb* **1** *syn* see LABOR 1
  2 *syn* see DRUDGE
  3 *syn* see PLOD 1
toil *n, usu* **toils** *pl syn* see WEB 2
toiler *n syn* see SLAVE 2
toilet *n* a fixture for defecation and urina-
  tion
  syn ‖can, convenience, ‖donicker, head,
  john, johnny, latrine, lavatory, ‖loo, ‖pot,
  ‖potty, privy, ‖throne, water closet
  rel hopper
toilful *adj syn* see HARD 6
toilsome *adj syn* see HARD 6
toilsomely *adv syn* see HARD 8
token *n* **1** *syn* see INDICATION 3
  rel harbinger, omen, portent; characteristic, earmark; indicator, smack
  2 *syn* see REMEMBRANCE 3
  3 *syn* see EXPRESSION 3
  4 *syn* see PLEDGE 1
‖**tokus** *n syn* see BUTTOCKS
tolerable *adj* **1** *syn* see BEARABLE
  ant intolerable
  2 *syn* see RESPECTABLE 5
  3 *syn* see DECENT 4
  rel fair, goodish, OK, tidy
  idiom better than nothing, good enough
  ant intolerable
tolerably *adv syn* see ENOUGH 2
tolerance *n* **1** the capacity to bear something unpleasant, painful, or difficult
  <had always had a high *tolerance* to
  pain>
  syn endurance, stamina, toleration

rel fortitude, grit, guts; strength, vigor;
long-suffering, patience, sufferance; steadfastness, steadiness; opposition, resistance
  ant intolerance
  2 *syn* see FORBEARANCE 2
  rel liberality, liberalness, open-mindedness, permissiveness
  con narrow-mindedness; prejudice; dogmatism; bigotry
  ant intolerance
tolerant *adj* **1** *syn* see LIBERAL 3
  rel open-minded; permissive
  con narrow, narrow-minded; prejudiced;
  dogmatic; bigoted
  ant intolerant
  2 *syn* see FORBEARING
  rel benevolent, humane; condoning, excusing, forgiving, sympathetic, understanding
  con severe, stern; uncompromising, unforgiving, unsympathetic
  ant intolerant
tolerate *vb* **1** *syn* see ACCEPT 2
  rel condone, countenance; allow, consent
  (to), permit; have, hear (to)
  2 *syn* see BEAR 10
  rel sustain
toleration *n* **1** *syn* see FORBEARANCE 2
  2 *syn* see TOLERANCE 1
toll *n syn* see EXPENSE 2
toll *vb syn* see LURE
toll *vb syn* see RING
‖**tomato** *n syn* see PROSTITUTE
tomb *n syn* see GRAVE
  rel box, coffin, ‖trough
tomb *vb* **1** *syn* see BURY 1
  ant untomb
  2 *syn* see ENTOMB 1
  ant disentomb, untomb
tomboy *n* a girl exhibiting boyish behavior
  <a *tomboy* who still rode, fished, and
  fought with her brothers>
  syn gamine, hoyden
  rel romp
tombstone *n* an inscribed memorial stone
  set at a place of interment <read the
  epitaph on the *tombstone* of her ances-
  tor>
  syn footstone, grave marker, gravestone,
  headstone, ledger, monument
  rel memorial; cenotaph
tome *n syn* see BOOK 1
tomfool *n syn* see FOOL 1
tomfool *adj syn* see FOOLISH 2
tomfoolery *n* **1** *syn* see NONSENSE 2
  2 *syn* see PRANK
tommyrot *n syn* see NONSENSE 2
Tom o' Bedlam *n syn* see LUNATIC 1
Tom Thumb *n syn* see DWARF
ton *n* **1** *syn* see FASHION 3
  2 *syn* see SMART SET
tone *n* **1** *syn* see INFLECTION
  2 *syn* see VEIN 1
  3 *syn* see COLOR 1
  rel blend
  4 the state of a living body or any of its
  organs or parts in which the functions are
  healthy and performed with due vigor
  <diet and exercise contributed to his
  good muscle *tone*>
  syn tonicity, tonus
  rel health, healthiness; elasticity, resiliency; strength, vigor

---

syn synonym(s)   *rel* related word(s)
ant antonym(s)   *con* contrasted word(s)
idiom idiomatic equivalent(s)
‖ use limited; if in doubt, see a dictionary

5 *syn* see TEMPER 1
  rel current, movement
  idiom (the) state of things
  6 *syn* see MOOD 1
toned down *adj syn* see SUBDUED 2
tongue *n syn* see LANGUAGE 1
tongue *vb syn* see SCOLD 1
tongue–lash *vb syn* see SCOLD 1
  idiom give one the rough side of one's
  tongue
tongue–tied *adj syn* see INARTICULATE 3
  con loose-lipped, loose-tongued
∥**tongue–walk** *vb syn* see SCOLD 1
  idiom give one the rough side of one's
  tongue
tonguey *adj syn* see TALKATIVE
tonic *adj* 1 increasing or restoring physical
  or mental tone < the *tonic* effect of a
  syn astringent, restorative, roborant
  rel invigorating, refreshing, renewing,
  strengthening; bracing, sharp
  con debilitating, enfeebling, weakening;
  enervating; exhausting, grueling, sapping
  2 *syn* see INVIGORATING
tonicity *n syn* see TONE 4
tonish *adj syn* see STYLISH
tonus *n syn* see TONE 4
tony *adj syn* see STYLISH
too *adv* 1 *syn* see ALSO 2
  2 *syn* see EVER 6
  rel exorbitantly, immoderately, unconscio-
  nably, unmeasurably
  3 *syn* see VERY 1
∥**toodle–oo** *interj syn* see GOOD-BYE
tool *n* 1 *syn* see IMPLEMENT
  rel machine, mechanism
  2 one used or manipulated by another to
  accomplish his purposes < had no intention of being used as a *tool* by either faction >
  syn cat's-paw, pawn, puppet, stooge
  rel agent, hireling, vehicle; chump, sucker
tool *vb syn* see DRIVE 5
toot *vb syn* see DECLARE 1
toot *n syn* see BINGE 1
toothful *n syn* see DRAM
toothsome *adj syn* see PALATABLE
  rel agreeable, pleasant, pleasing
toothy *adj* 1 having or showing prominent
  teeth < a wide *toothy* grin >
  syn teethy
  2 *syn* see PALATABLE
too–too *adj syn* see GENTEEL 3
  rel chichi
∥**tootsie** *n syn* see DOXY 1
top *n* 1 the highest point < hiked to the *top*
  of the mountain >
  syn apex, crest, crown, fastigium, peak,
  roof, summit, vertex
  rel acme, climax, culmination, height,
  pinnacle; cusp, head, point, tip
  con base, foot, sole; nadir
  ant bottom
  2 the outer or upper part < the *top* of the
  table >
  syn face, superficies, surface
  3 *syn* see BEST
  ant bottom
top *vb* 1 to remove or cut back the top of
  < *top* a tree >
  syn crop, detruncate, pollard, truncate
  rel clip, dock, prune, trim; curtail,
  shorten

  2 *syn* see SURPASS 1
  3 *syn* see SURMOUNT 3
top *adj* 1 of, relating to, or being at the top
  < the *top* floor of the house >
  syn apical, highest, loftiest, topmost,
  uppermost
  con bottommost, lowest
  ant bottom
  2 *syn* see EXCELLENT
  3 *syn* see MAXIMUM
top–drawer *adj syn* see EXALTED 1
tope *vb syn* see DRINK 3
toper *n syn* see DRUNKARD
Tophet *n syn* see HELL
topic *n syn* see SUBJECT 2
  rel proposition; issue
topless *adj syn* see LOFTY 6
toploftical *adj syn* see PROUD 1
toplofty *adj syn* see PROUD 1
  rel inflated, puffed; egotistic
  con crestfallen
topmost *adj* 1 *syn* see TOP 1
  ant bottommost
  2 *syn* see MAXIMUM
top–notch *adj syn* see EXCELLENT
top off *vb syn* see CLIMAX
topography *n syn* see TERRAIN 1
topple *vb* 1 *syn* see FALL 2
  2 *syn* see TEETER
  3 *syn* see OVERTURN 1
  4 *syn* see OVERTHROW 1
top–ranking *adj syn* see EXALTED 1
topsy–turviness *n syn* see CONFUSION 3
topsy–turvy *adj* 1 *syn* see UPSIDE-DOWN
  1
  2 *syn* see UPSIDE-DOWN 2
  rel cockeyed, disarranged, disjointed,
  disordered, unhinged
torch *n syn* see INCENDIARY
toreador *n syn* see BULLFIGHTER
torero *n syn* see BULLFIGHTER
torment *vb* 1 *syn* see AFFLICT
  rel distress, trouble; hurt, pain, punish
  2 *syn* see MOLEST
tormented *adj syn* see DISTRAUGHT
tormenting *adj syn* see EXCRUCIATING
torn *adj syn* see LACERATED
tornado *n* a violent destructive whirling
  wind accompanied by a funnel-shaped
  cloud extending downward from a cumu-
  lonimbus cloud < the *tornado* caused
  extensive destruction >
  syn cyclone, twister; *compare* HURRI-
  CANE, WHIRLWIND 1
torpedo *n syn* see ASSASSIN
torpid *adj syn* see LETHARGIC
  rel dull, leaden, sodden; motionless,
  static; numb
  con lively; frisky, sprightly, vigorous; fast
  ant active
torpidity *n syn* see LETHARGY 1
  rel listlessness, passivity, stagnation
torpidness *n syn* see LETHARGY 1
  ant activeness
torpor *n syn* see LETHARGY 1
  rel stolidity; passivity
  ant activity; animation
torrent *n syn* see FLOOD 2
  rel flux, rush
torrid *adj* 1 *syn* see HOT 1
  idiom burning hot, hot enough to roast
  an ox
  ant arctic

2 *syn* see IMPASSIONED
rel sultry
ant frigid
tort *n syn* see EVIL 3
tortuous *adj syn* see WINDING
rel involute, vermiculate; cranky; involved
torture *vb* **1** *syn* see AFFLICT
rel oppress, persecute, wrong; hurt,
wound; maim, mangle, mutilate
idiom put on the rack, put to torture
2 *syn* see DEFORM
torturing *adj syn* see EXCRUCIATING
torturous *adj syn* see EXCRUCIATING
tory *n syn* see DIEHARD 1
rel loyalist, traditionalist
tory *adj syn* see CONSERVATIVE 1
tosh *n syn* see NONSENSE 2
toss *vb* **1** *syn* see THROW 1
2 to rise and fall often rhythmically or
with alternate motions <a small boat
tossing in heavy seas>
syn heave, pitch, rock, roll; *compare* SEE-
SAW
rel bob; sway
3 *syn* see DRINK 1
4 *syn* see WRITHE 1
idiom toss and turn
toss (around) *vb syn* see DISCUSS 1
rel bandy (about)
tosspot *n syn* see DRUNKARD
tot *n syn* see DRAM
tot *vb syn* see ADD 2
total *adj* **1** *syn* see WHOLE 4
rel overall; comprehensive, full, inclusive,
plenary; teetotal
ant partial
2 *syn* see UTTER
3 *syn* see TOTALITARIAN 1
rel authoritative; absolute, arbitrary, despotic; omnipotent
4 *syn* see TOTALITARIAN 2
rel monopolistic
5 concentrating and employing all resources on a single objective <a *total*
offensive>
syn all-out, full-blown, full-out, full-scale,
totalitarian, unlimited
rel out-and-out, unreserved, unrestricted
con hampered, impeded, trammeled; restrained, restricted; stinted
ant limited
total *n* **1** *syn* see WHOLE 1
2 *syn* see BODY 5
total *vb* **1** *syn* see ADD 2
2 *syn* see AMOUNT 1
rel comprise, consist (of); stack up; equal,
result (in), yield
idiom mount up to, pile up to
3 to make a total wreck of < *totaled* his
car when he hit the wall>
syn demolish, wreck; *compare* DESTROY 1
rel crack up, smash
totalistic *adj syn* see TOTALITARIAN 1
con democratic; individualistic
totalitarian *adj* **1** of or relating to central-
ized control by one autocratic leader or
party considered to be infallible <Nazi
Germany was a *totalitarian* state>

syn authoritarian, total, totalistic; *compare* ABSOLUTE 4, DICTATORIAL
con democratic, popular; constitutional
2 having or exercising dictatorial powers
often tending toward monopoly <anti-
trust legislation reversing the trend toward
the *totalitarian* collectivism of big busi-
ness>
syn total
3 *syn* see TOTAL 5
totalitarianism *n syn* see TYRANNY
totality *n* **1** *syn* see WHOLE 1
2 *syn* see ENTIRETY 1
3 *syn* see WHOLE 2
rel configuration, form
totalize *vb syn* see ADD 2
totally *adv syn* see ALL 1
tote *vb syn* see CARRY 1
rel cart, haul; shoulder
‖**tote** *n syn* see WHOLE 1
tote *vb syn* see ADD 2
totter *vb* **1** *syn* see TEETER
rel shimmy
2 *syn* see REEL 2
rel blunder, stumble, trip; dodder, ‖dot-
ter; flounder
touch *vb* **1** to probe with a sensitive part of
the body (as a finger) so as to get or produce a sensation often in the course of
examining or exploring < *touch* an iron to
test its temperature>
syn feel, finger, handle, palpate, paw
rel brush, graze; caress, fondle, rub,
stroke, toy (with); palm, thumb; examine,
inspect, probe, scrutinize; investigate
2 *syn* see ADJOIN
3 *syn* see EQUAL 3
4 *syn* see AFFECT
rel arouse, stir; excite, quicken, stimulate
idiom touch a chord
5 *syn* see AMOUNT 2
rel come (to), verge (on)
touch *n* **1** *syn* see CONTACT 1
rel junction; communication
2 an act of touching or feeling <woke her
with a light *touch* on her hand>
syn palpation, taction
rel brush, pat, stroke; contact
3 tactile sensitivity <a blanket soft to the
touch>
syn feel, tactility
rel feeling
4 a specified sensation conveyed through
the tactile receptors <the velvety *touch* of
a fabric>
syn feel, feeling
5 *syn* see HINT 1
6 distinctive manner or method <this
house needs a woman's *touch*>
syn hand
rel manner, style, way
‖**7** *syn* see THEFT
touchable *adj syn* see TANGIBLE 1
ant untouchable
touch down *vb syn* see ALIGHT
touching *prep* **1** *syn* see AGAINST 2
idiom up against
2 *syn* see APROPOS
touching *adj* **1** *syn* see ADJACENT 3
rel meeting; impinging; overlapping
2 *syn* see MOVING 2
rel compassionate, responsive, sympathetic, tender; piteous, pitiable, pitiful, tear=
jerking

---

syn synonym(s)   *rel* related word(s)
ant antonym(s)   *con* contrasted word(s)
idiom idiomatic equivalent(s)
‖ use limited; if in doubt, see a dictionary

touch—me—not—ish *adj syn* see UNSOCIABLE

touchstone *n syn* see STANDARD 3
  rel check, test, trial; barometer, scale; demonstration, proof

touch up *vb* to improve or perfect by small additional strokes or alterations < *touch up* a picture>
  syn brush up, retouch, tease up
  rel improve, perfect, polish; do (up), fix (up)
  idiom put finishing touches on

touchy *adj* 1 *syn* see IRASCIBLE
  rel hypersensitive, oversensitive, sensitive, thin-skinned; temperamental, volatile; miffy
  ant imperturbable
  2 *syn* see DELICATE 7
  rel dicey, risky, unpredictable; harmful, hazardous, unsafe

tough *adj* 1 *syn* see STRONG 2
  rel flinty, hard, unyielding; resistant, unbreakable, withstanding
  idiom tough as leather (*or* nails)
  con breakable; brittle; yielding
  ant fragile
  2 *syn* see VISCOUS
  3 advocating a persistently firm course of action < a *tough* foreign policy>
  syn hard-line, inflexible, uncompromising, unyielding
  rel stiff, taut; fixed, confirmed, hard-shell, narrow, rigid; arbitrary, immutable, unalterable; hard-boiled, hardened, obdurate, harsh, procrustean, rigorous, severe, strict; drastic
  con liberal, relaxed; compromising, flexible, laissez-faire, yielding
  ant soft
  4 having or exhibiting great physical endurance (as to strain, hardship, or labor) < the rigorous climate created a *tough* people>
  syn hardy, rugged
  rel conditioned, hard-bitten, hardened, seasoned, steeled; fit, healthy, lusty, robust, vigorous; stalwart, strong, sturdy
  con delicate, fragile, frail, tender; half-hardy, puny; weakened
  ant weak
  5 *syn* see OBSTINATE
  rel hardfisted, hardhanded, hardheaded, tough-minded
  6 *syn* see HARD 6
  ant soft
  7 *syn* see ONEROUS
  ant soft
  8 frequented by rowdy or criminal elements < lived in a *tough* neighborhood>
  syn bad, rough
  rel disorderly, rowdy; dangerous, unsafe; ghetto, inner-city, underprivileged
  con orderly, quiet, safe

tough (out) *vb syn* see ACCEPT 2

tough *n* a rough or unruly person often taking part in bullying or violent behavior < attacked by a gang of *toughs*>
  syn ‖b'hoy, bullyboy, mucker, mug, plugugly, punk, rough, roughneck, rowdy, ruffian, thug, toughie, yahoo; *compare* BULLY 1, THUG 1
  rel goon, hood, hoodlum, hooligan

toughen *vb syn* see HARDEN 2

  rel develop, strengthen
  ant weaken

toughie *n syn* see TOUGH
  rel ‖heavy

tour *n* 1 *syn* see SPELL
  2 a journey in which one eventually returns to the starting point < made a quick *tour* of all the bars>
  syn circuit, round, roundabout, round trip; *compare* TRIP 1
  rel turn; circle tour

tour de force *n* 1 *syn* see FEAT 2
  2 *syn* see MASTERPIECE 1

tourist *n* one who makes a tour for pleasure or culture < *tourists* going through the castle>
  syn rubberneck, sightseer, ‖tripper
  rel day-tripper, excursionist; traveler; visitor

tout *n syn* see LOOKOUT 3

tout *vb* to overly publicize < was *touted* as the world's most modern shopping center>
  syn ballyhoo, herald, trumpet
  rel proclaim, publicize; plug, promote; acclaim, laud, praise
  idiom praise to the skies

tow *vb syn* see PULL 2
  rel propel; push
  idiom take in tow

toward *adj syn* see GOOD 1
  ant untoward

toward *prep* 1 *syn* see APROPOS
  2 *syn* see AGAINST 1

tower (above *or* over) *vb syn* see OVERLOOK 2

towering *adj* 1 *syn* see LOFTY 6
  rel altitudinous, high, tall; stratospheric
  2 *syn* see SUPREME
  3 *syn* see MONSTROUS 1
  4 reaching a high point of greatness, intensity, or violence < a *towering* rage>
  syn monumental, overwhelming
  rel ‖crashing; overpowering; mind-blowing
  con minor, petty, piddling, puny, trivial
  5 *syn* see EXCESSIVE 1

towery *adj syn* see LOFTY 6

to wit *adv syn* see NAMELY

towner *n syn* see TOWNSMAN

townish *adj* of, relating to, or characteristic of a town or of urban life < enjoyed a fast-paced, competitive, *townish* life-style>
  syn towny
  rel city, metropolitan, urban
  con bucolic, rural; isolated, lonely, solitary

townman *n syn* see TOWNSMAN

townsman *n* a town dweller < population composed mostly of *townsmen* and a few countrymen>
  syn burgher, cit, citizen, towner, townman, towny

towny *n syn* see TOWNSMAN

towny *adj syn* see TOWNISH

tow–row *n syn* see COMMOTION 4

toxic *adj syn* see POISONOUS
  ant nontoxic

toxicant *adj syn* see POISONOUS

toy *n* 1 *syn* see KNICKKNACK
  2 something for a child to play with < games, dolls, and other *toys*>
  syn ‖die, ‖play-pretty, plaything, ‖pretty

toy *vb syn* see TRIFLE 1
  rel disport, frolic, play, sport; fiddle (with); tease; caress, cosset, cuddle, dandle, pet
  idiom fool (*or* mess) around with

trace *n* 1 *syn* see TRACK 1
  rel evidence, proof
2 *syn* see VESTIGE 1
  rel mark, token
3 *syn* see HINT 2

trace *vb syn* see TRACK 1

track *n* 1 detectable evidence that something has passed < the *track* of a sleigh in the snow >
  syn trace, tread
  rel impress, imprint, mark, print; sign, vestige
2 *syn* see TRAIL
  rel footpath, footway, walk
  idiom beaten path
3 *syn* see WAY 1
  rel roadway, trackway
4 *syn* see FOOTPRINT
  rel scent, slot

track *vb* 1 to follow the tracks or traces of < *track* a wounded deer >
  syn trace, trail
  rel follow; dog, shadow, tail; chase, pursue; find, hunt (down), smell (out)
  idiom be hot on the trail of
2 *syn* see TRAVEL 2

tract *n* 1 *syn* see AREA 1
  rel amplitude, spread, stretch; part, portion, section, sector
2 *syn* see LOT 3
3 *syn* see FOOTPRINT

tractable *adj syn* see OBEDIENT
  rel flexible, pliable, pliant; manageable; subdued
  con headstrong, unmanageable, willful; obstinate, refractory, stubborn
  ant intractable, unruly

tractate *n syn* see DISCOURSE 2

trade *n* 1 a pursuit followed as an occupation or means of livelihood and requiring technical knowledge and skill < the *trade* of a carpenter >
  syn art, calling, craft, handicraft, métier, profession, vocation
  rel employment, occupation, pursuit, work
  con avocation, hobby
2 *syn* see BUSINESS 4
  rel market
3 *syn* see PATRONAGE 2

trade *vb* 1 to give one thing in return for another with an expectation of gain < *traded* furs for tobacco and rum >
  syn bargain, barter, exchange, swap, traffic, truck; *compare* EXCHANGE 2
  rel market, merchandise, sell; deal; argue, chaffer, dicker, haggle, wrangle
  idiom make (*or* strike) a bargain, make a deal
2 *syn* see EXCHANGE 2

trademark *n syn* see MARK 7

trader *n syn* see MERCHANT

tradesman *n syn* see MERCHANT

---

syn synonym(s)   *rel* related word(s)
ant antonym(s)   *con* contrasted word(s)
idiom idiomatic equivalent(s)
‖ use limited; if in doubt, see a dictionary

tradition *n* 1 an inherited or established way of thinking, feeling, or doing < America's Puritan *tradition* is still very much alive >
  syn heritage
  rel culture; convention, custom, ethic, form; birthright, inheritance, legacy
2 *syn* see LORE 2

traditional *adj* 1 of or relating to tradition < a *traditional* interpretation of the Bible >
  syn conventional, tralatitious; *compare* CONVENTIONAL 1
  rel ancestral, immemorial, old; customary, habitual, usual; acknowledged, established, establishmentarian, fixed; common, popular
  con new; unconventional, unusual; individualistic, original, personal
2 *syn* see ORAL 2

traditionalist *n syn* see PURIST

traditionalistic *adj syn* see CONSERVATIVE 1

traduce *vb syn* see MALIGN
  rel mock; disgrace; betray; violate

traducing *adj syn* see LIBELOUS

traffic *n* 1 *syn* see BUSINESS 4
2 *syn* see COMMERCE 2
  rel relations, relationship; closeness, connection, familiarity; intimacy
3 *syn* see PATRONAGE 2
4 the number or volume of vehicles or pedestrians moving along a route < freeway *traffic* is heavy during the rush hour >
  syn travel

traffic *vb* 1 *syn* see TRADE 1
2 to engage in illegal or disreputable business or activity < *trafficked* in drugs >
  syn truck
  rel deal (in), push, shove; black-market; bootleg, moonshine; fence
  idiom handle (*or* deal in) under the counter

trafficable *adj syn* see MARKETABLE

trafficker *n syn* see MERCHANT

tragedy *n* 1 *syn* see DISASTER
  rel blow, shock
2 *syn* see MISFORTUNE
  rel unluckiness; curse, lot; woe(s)
  con prosperity, success
  ant triumph

trail *vb* 1 *syn* see DRAG 3
2 *syn* see DELAY 2
  rel plod, trudge; falter, flag; halt
3 *syn* see TRACK 1
  rel nose (out), sniff (out)
  idiom follow a scent
4 *syn* see TAIL
5 *syn* see FOLLOW 2

trail *n* a rough course or way formed by or as if by repeated chance footsteps < an old Indian *trail* >
  syn path, pathway, track, ‖trod
  rel footpath, footwalk, footway

train *vb syn* see LURE

train *n* 1 *syn* see ENTOURAGE
2 *syn* see SUCCESSION 2
  rel course, run; line, thread; gradation, scale, tier

train *vb* 1 *syn* see TEACH
  rel cultivate, develop, shape; accustom, habituate; harden, season

2 *syn* see DIRECT 2

training *n syn* see EDUCATION 1

train off *vb syn* see SWERVE 1

traipse *vb* 1 *syn* see WANDER 1

  2 *syn* see WALK 1

  3 *syn* see DRAG 3

traipse *n syn* see SLATTERN 1

trait *n* 1 *syn* see QUALITY 1

  2 *syn* see CHARACTERISTIC 1

  rel denominator; attribute, quality

traitorous *adj syn* see FAITHLESS

  rel apostate, renegade; mutinous, rebellious, seditious; alienated, disaffected, estranged; unpatriotic

  con faithful; patriotic

traject *vb syn* see CONDUCT 4

tralatitious *adj syn* see TRADITIONAL 1

  idiom handed down from time immemorial

tralucent *adj syn* see TRANSLUCENT 3

trammel *vb* 1 *syn* see ENTANGLE 3

  2 *syn* see HAMPER

  rel circumscribe, confine, limit; bind, enchain, handcuff, manacle

  3 *syn* see STULTIFY

tramp *vb* 1 to walk, tread, or step especially heavily < heard hobnailed boots *tramping* across the square >

  syn trample, tromp; *compare* PLOD 1

  rel march; thud; footslog, stodge, trudge; stamp, stomp

  2 *syn* see HIKE 2

  3 *syn* see TRAMPLE 2

tramp *n* 1 *syn* see VAGABOND

  2 *syn* see WANTON

  3 a journey on foot or a walking trip < took a long *tramp* through the woods >

  syn hike, walkabout

  rel ramble, saunter, stroll, walk; traipse

tramper *n syn* see VAGABOND

trample *vb* 1 *syn* see TRAMP 1

  2 to tread on forcibly and repeatedly so as to crush or injure < was *trampled* to death by his horse >

  syn stamp, stomp, tramp, tromp

  rel ‖stoach, ‖stramp, ‖stunt; pound; tread (on); override

trance *vb syn* see TRANSPORT 2

trance *n syn* see REVERIE

tranquil *adj syn* see CALM 2

  rel irenic, pacific, peaceful; quiet, still; stable, steady

  con stirred up, troubled

  ant agitated

tranquilize *vb syn* see CALM

  rel hush; sedate; subdue

  idiom pour oil on troubled waters

  ant agitate

transaction *n syn* see CONTRACT

transcend *vb syn* see SURPASS 1

  idiom go beyond, rise above

transcendent *adj* 1 *syn* see SUPREME

  rel accomplished, consummate, finished; entire, intact, perfect, whole

  2 *syn* see ABSTRACT 1

  rel absolute, ultimate; boundless, eternal, infinite

transcendental *adj* 1 *syn* see OTHERWORLDLY 1

  2 *syn* see ABSTRACT 1

  rel supernatural, supranatural, ultimate

transfer *vb* 1 *syn* see MOVE 4

  rel carry, convey; relocate

2 *syn* see GIVE 3

  rel convey, transmit

  3 *syn* see TRANSFORM

  4 to shift the title of (property) from one owner to another < to preserve the farm intact he *transfers* it to a single heir >

  syn abalienate, alien, alienate, assign, cede, convey, deed, make over, remise, sign (over)

transfigure *vb syn* see TRANSFORM

transfix *vb syn* see IMPALE

transform *vb* to make over to a radically different form, composition, state, or disposition < the interaction of social forces *transforms* custom and produces a new tradition >

  syn change, commute, convert, metamorphize, metamorphose, mutate, transfer, transfigure, translate, transmogrify, transmute, transpose, transubstantiate; *compare* CHANGE 1

  rel alter; denature

transformation *n syn* see CONVERSION 2

transfuse *vb syn* see PERMEATE

transgress *vb* 1 *syn* see VIOLATE 1

  2 *syn* see TRESPASS 1

transgression *n syn* see BREACH 1

  rel erring, error, lapse, slip; overstepping; misbehavior, misstepping

transient *adj* lasting or staying only a short time < features of a *transient* culture now extinct >

  syn ephemeral, evanescent, fleeting, fugacious, fugitive, impermanent, momentaneous, momentary, passing, short-lived, transitory, volatile; *compare* TEMPORARY

  rel deciduous, flitting, unstable; temporal, temporary; insubstantial

  idiom as transient as the clouds, here today and gone tomorrow

  con lasting, perdurable, permanent, substantial; durable, stable

  ant perpetual

transit *n* 1 *syn* see PASSAGE 1

  2 *syn* see TRANSITION

  3 *syn* see TRANSPORTATION 1

  4 public conveyance of passengers or goods as a commercial enterprise < mass *transit* >

  syn transport, transportation

transition *n* passage from one state or condition to another < the *transition* from boyhood to manhood >

  syn alteration, passage, shift, transit

  rel change, conversion, metamorphosis, transformation; development, evolution; growth, progress

transitional *adj* involving or characterized by passage from one stage, condition, or state to another < a *transitional* phase of social development >

  syn transitive, transitory

  rel developing, evolving; altering, changing, shifting

  idiom being in a state of flux

transitive *adj syn* see TRANSITIONAL

transitory *adj* 1 *syn* see TRANSIENT

  rel changeable; nonpermanent, unenduring; brief, short-term

  2 *syn* see TRANSITIONAL

translate *vb* 1 to make a version of in another language < *translated* many secret documents from French to English >

syn put, render, transpose, turn
rel transliterate; transcribe; interpret; metaphrase, paraphrase
2 *syn* see TRANSFORM
translate (into) *vb syn* see PARAPHRASE
translation *n syn* see VERSION 1
translucent *adj* 1 *syn* see TRANSPARENT 1
2 *syn* see CLEAR 4
rel apparent, obvious, unmistakable
3 admitting and diffusing light so that objects beyond cannot be clearly distinguished < *translucent* amber>
syn clear, tralucent, translucid, transparent; *compare* TRANSPARENT 1
rel lucent, lucid
translucid *adj syn* see TRANSLUCENT 3
transmarine *adj syn* see OVERSEAS
transmigrate *vb syn* see MIGRATE
transmigratory *adj syn* see MIGRATORY
transmit *vb* 1 *syn* see SEND 1
rel convey, transport
2 *syn* see COMMUNICATE 1
3 *syn* see HAND DOWN
rel instill; transfuse, translate
4 *syn* see CONDUCT 4
transmogrify *vb syn* see TRANSFORM
transmundane *adj syn* see OTHER-WORLDLY 1
transmute *vb syn* see TRANSFORM
transparent *adj* 1 admitting light without appreciable diffusion or distortion so that objects beyond are entirely visible <a sheet of *transparent* plastic>
syn clear, limpid, pellucid, see-through, translucent; *compare* TRANSLUCENT 3
rel crystal, crystalline, glassy; diaphanous
idiom clear as glass (*or* crystal)
con dark, smoky; cloudy, foggy hazy, misty, nubilous
ant opaque
2 *syn* see FILMY
3 *syn* see TRANSLUCENT 3
4 *syn* see CLEAR 4
rel distinguishable, recognizable; articulate, distinct, plain; unambiguous, unequivocal
con muddy, turbid
transpicuous *adj syn* see CLEAR 4
transpierce *vb syn* see IMPALE
transpire *vb* 1 *syn* see GET OUT 2
2 *syn* see HAPPEN 1
rel eventuate, result
transplace *vb syn* see REVERSE 1
rel remove; rearrange
transport *vb* 1 *syn* see CARRY 1
2 to carry away by strong and usually pleasant emotion < *transported* with ecstasy>
syn enrapture, enravish, entrance, ravish, trance
rel excite, move, provoke, quicken, stimulate; agitate, inflame, stir (up); elevate, uplift; carry away, delight, imparadise; ‖send, slay, thrill, ‖wow
3 *syn* see BANISH
transport *n* 1 *syn* see TRANSPORTATION 1

2 *syn* see ECSTASY
rel ardor, enthusiasm, fervor, passion; happiness
3 *syn* see VEHICLE 3
4 *syn* see TRANSIT 4
transportable *adj syn* see PORTABLE
transportation *n* 1 an act, process, or instance of transporting or being transported <arranged for the *transportation* of his luggage>
syn carriage, carrying, conveyance, transit, transport, transporting
rel hauling, moving
2 *syn* see VEHICLE 3
3 *syn* see TRANSIT 4
transporting *n syn* see TRANSPORTATION 1
transpose *vb* 1 *syn* see TRANSFORM
2 *syn* see TRANSLATE 1
3 *syn* see REVERSE 1
transubstantiate *vb syn* see TRANSFORM
transude *vb syn* see EXUDE
transversal *adj syn* see TRANSVERSE
rel bent; intersecting
transverse *vb syn* see TRAVERSE 4
transverse *adj* extended or lying in a direction across something else <the *transverse* arches of the cathedral ceiling>
syn crossing, crosswise, thwart, transversal, traverse
rel diagonal, oblique; across, crossed
con perpendicular
ant longitudinal
transversely *adv syn* see OVER 1
transversely *adv syn* see OVER 1
trap *n* 1 *syn* see LURE 2
rel artifice, feint, gambit, maneuver, ploy, ruse, stratagem, wile; birdlime, net; ambuscade, ambush; conspiracy, intrigue, machination, plot
‖ 2 *syn* see POLICEMAN
‖ 3 *syn* see MOUTH 1
trap *vb syn* see CATCH 3
rel mousetrap, snag
trapfall *n syn* see PITFALL
traps *n pl syn* see PERSONAL EFFECTS
trash *n* 1 *syn* see REFUSE
rel leavings
2 *syn* see NONSENSE 2
3 *syn* see RABBLE 2
‖**trash** *vb syn* see VANDALIZE
trash *vb syn* see PLOD 1
trashy *adj syn* see CHEAP 2
rel third-rate
trauma *n* intense mental, emotional, or physical disturbance resulting from stress <a broken home may produce persistent *trauma* in children>
syn shock, traumatism
rel blow, stress; traumatization; derangement, disturbance, upset; collapse
traumatism *n syn* see TRAUMA
travail *n* 1 *syn* see WORK 2
rel task; struggle
idiom toil and trouble
con relaxation, rest
2 *syn* see LABOR 2
rel contractions, pains
idiom birth throe
travel *vb* 1 *syn* see GO 1
rel move (on); voyage; roam, trek; explore

2 to journey over (as by conveyance) <certain roads can be *traveled* only on horseback>
syn cover, do, pass (over), track, traverse
rel cross
travel *n* 1 *syn* see PASSAGE 1
2 *often* **travels** *pl syn* see JOURNEY
3 *syn* see TRAFFIC 4
travelable *adj syn* see PASSABLE
‖**traveler** *n syn* see VAGABOND
traverse *n syn* see OBSTACLE
traverse *vb* 1 *syn* see RESIST
2 *syn* see DENY 4
rel oppose; dismiss; squash, squelch
3 *syn* see TRAVEL 2
4 to extend or lie across (something) <a highway *traversing* the entire state>
syn cross, transverse
rel crisscross, intersect, quarter
idiom cut across
5 to pass over, along, or to and fro especially on foot <deep in thought he *traversed* the terrace again and again>
syn perambulate, walk
rel peregrinate; track, tread; pace
traverse *adj syn* see TRANSVERSE
travesty *n* 1 *syn* see CARICATURE 2
rel mimicry; distortion, exaggeration; ridicule
2 *syn* see MOCKERY 2
travesty *vb syn* see MIMIC
treacherous *adj* 1 *syn* see FAITHLESS
rel undependable, unreliable, untrustworthy; betraying, deceptive, double=crossing, falsehearted, misleading, Punic
ant dependable; trustworthy
2 *syn* see DANGEROUS 1
rel deceptive, ticklish, tricky; precarious
treacherousness *n syn* see TREACHERY
ant dependability; trustworthiness
treachery *n* betrayal of a trust or confidence <corruption in public office is little short of *treachery*>
syn disloyalty, faithlessness, perfidiousness, perfidy, treacherousness, treason; *compare* INFIDELITY
rel falseheartedness, falseness; double cross, double-dealing; sellout
idiom dirty pool, dirty work at the crossroads
con incorruptibility, reliability; probity, rectitude, uprightness; constancy, fidelity, loyalty, staunchness
ant dependability; trustworthiness
tread *vb* 1 *syn* see DANCE 1
2 *syn* see WALK 1
rel march, stride; tromp
tread *n syn* see TRACK 1
treadmill *n syn* see ROUTINE
treason *n* 1 *syn* see TREACHERY
rel deceit, deceitfulness; duplicity; Machiavellianism
idiom breach of trust (*or* faith)
con allegiance, loyalty
ant staunchness
2 *syn* see SEDITION
rel disloyalty, treacherousness, treachery; high treason; misprision
ant allegiance
treasure *n syn* see FIND 1
rel catch, plum, prize; pearl
treasure *vb syn* see APPRECIATE 1
rel conserve, guard, preserve, save; idolize, revere, reverence, venerate, worship

idiom hold dear
treasure–house *n* 1 *syn* see TREASURY 1
2 *syn* see BONANZA
treasure trove *n* 1 *syn* see FIND 1
2 *syn* see BONANZA
treasury *n* 1 a place (as a room or building) where valuables are kept <priceless gold candlesticks kept in the *treasury* of the cathedral>
syn treasure-house
rel archive(s), gallery, museum; depository, repository, storehouse
idiom treasure room
2 the place of deposit, retention, and disbursement of collected funds <the union *treasury* held emergency strike funds>
syn chest, coffer, exchequer, war chest
rel depositary, depository
3 *syn* see BONANZA
treat *vb* 1 *syn* see CONFER 2
rel consider, study, weigh; deliberate, reason, think
2 to have to do with or behave toward (a person or thing) in a specified manner <*treat* all employees fairly and impartially>
syn deal (with), handle, play, serve, take, use
rel conduct, do with, manage, ‖wield; regard, respect; account, consider, hold; appraise, estimate, evaluate, rate, value
idiom act with regard to, conduct oneself toward, do by
3 to pay for another's entertainment <*treated* her to a few drinks>
syn blow, set up, ‖shout, stand
rel stake
idiom go treat, pick up the tab for, stand treat
4 to give medical treatment to <was *treated* by an eye specialist>
syn doctor
rel attend, care (for), minister (to), nurse
treat *n syn* see DELICACY
treatise *n syn* see DISCOURSE 2
rel writing; book; argument, discussion, exposition
treaty *n* a formal, usually written, arrangement made by negotiation between two or more political authorities <the two nations finally signed an arms-limitation *treaty*>
syn agreement, concord, convention, pact; *compare* CONTRACT
rel arrangement, entente, understanding, bargain, contract; charter, compact, concordat, covenant; alliance, cartel, league; accord, reconciliation, settlement
treble *adj syn* see ACUTE 4
ant bass
tree *vb syn* see CORNER
trek *n syn* see JOURNEY
tremble *vb* 1 *syn* see SHAKE 1
rel shrink, wince
idiom tremble like a leaf
2 *syn* see SHAKE 2
trembling *adj syn* see TREMULOUS
ant steady
tremendous *adj* 1 *syn* see FEARFUL 3
2 *syn* see MONSTROUS 1
3 *syn* see HUGE
rel amazing, astounding, flabbergasting; terrific

idiom great big
ant minute

tremendousness *n syn* see ENORMITY 2
rel bigness, largeness

tremor *n syn* see EARTHQUAKE

tremor *vb* **1** *syn* see SHAKE 1
2 *syn* see SHAKE 2

tremorous *adj syn* see TREMULOUS

tremulant *adj syn* see TREMULOUS

tremulous *adj* characterized by or affected with trembling or tremors < her *tremulous* hands could scarcely hold the book >
syn aquake, aquiver, ashake, ashiver, quaking, quaky, quivering, quivery, shaking, shaky, shivering, shivery, trembling, tremorous, tremulant
rel aguish; aspen; palpitating; vibrating
idiom having the shakes
con firm, settled, stable, steady, unmoving

trench *n* a long narrow furrow in the ground < dig a *trench* for a sewer pipe >
syn cut, ditch
rel gully; drill, furrow; fosse; trough; drain, sink

trench *vb syn* see BORDER 3

trenchant *adj* **1** *syn* see INCISIVE
rel piercing, probing, razor-sharp; sarcastic, sardonic, satiric; acrid; piquant, poignant, pungent
2 *syn* see CAUSTIC 1
rel scalding, scorching

trend *n* **1** *syn* see TENDENCY 1
rel movement; flow; direction, orientation; swing, wind; progression
2 *syn* see FASHION 3

‖**trendy** *adj syn* see STYLISH
rel ultramodern
con dated, outmoded

trepidation *n syn* see FEAR 1
ant unapprehensiveness

trepidity *n syn* see FEAR 1
ant intrepidity, intrepidness

trespass *n syn* see BREACH 1
rel encroachment, entrenchment, invasion; intrusion, obtrusion

trespass *vb* **1** to commit an offense < exhibited scrupulous fairness even to those who *trespassed* against him >
syn offend, sin, transgress
rel deviate, err, lapse
idiom do wrong by
2 to make inroads on the property, territory, or rights of another < warned the hunters not to *trespass* on his land >
syn encroach, entrench, infringe, invade
rel enter, penetrate, pierce, probe; interlope, intermeddle, intrude; transgress
idiom crash the gate

trestle *n syn* see SAWHORSE

triad *n* a union or group of three often closely related individuals or things < a *triad* of deities >
syn threesome, trine, trinity, trio, triple, triumvirate, triune, troika; *compare* TRIUMVIRATE 1

trial *n* **1** the state or fact of being tested (as by suffering) < the Vietnam war period was a time of great national *trial* >

syn affliction, calvary, cross, crucible, ordeal, tribulation, visitation
rel agony, distress, misery, suffering; anguish, grief, heartbreak, sorrow, woe; adversity, misfortune; difficulty, hardship, rigor, vicissitude
idiom crown of thorns, fiery ordeal, trial and tribulation
2 a source of vexation or annoyance < living in a crowded hotel is a real *trial* >
syn care, trouble, worry
rel complication, difficulty; annoyance, distress, misfortune; ordeal
3 *syn* see EXPERIMENT
4 *syn* see ATTEMPT

trial *adj syn* see EXPERIMENTAL 2

trial and error *n syn* see EXPERIMENT

trial balloon *n syn* see FEELER
rel trial

trial run *n syn* see EXPERIMENT

tribe *n syn* see FAMILY 1

tribulation *n syn* see TRIAL 1
rel oppression, persecution, wronging

tribunal *n syn* see COURT 2

tributary *adj syn* see SUBORDINATE
rel conquered, subdued, subjugated, vanquished; accessory, minor; satellite

tribute *n* **1** *syn* see TESTIMONIAL 3
rel recognition; monument
2 *syn* see ENCOMIUM

trice *n syn* see INSTANT 1

trick *n* **1** an indirect, ingenious, and often cunning means to gain an end < used every *trick* in the bag to cover up the scandal >
syn artifice, chouse, device, feint, gambit, gimmick, jig, maneuver, play, ploy, ‖prat, ruse, shenanigan, sleight, stratagem, whizzer, wile; *compare* PRANK
rel contrivance, craft, expediency; blind, bluff, diversion, dodge, dodgery, red herring; curve, deception, sham, stall; fraud, ‖rort, scheme, shift, skin game
2 *syn* see PRANK
rel boutade; escapade; practical joke
3 an ingenious or dexterous act or procedure designed to puzzle or amuse < a juggler's *trick* >
syn feat, stunt
rel accomplishment
4 **tricks** *pl syn* see PERSONAL EFFECTS
5 *syn* see HANG
6 *syn* see HABIT 1
7 *syn* see SPELL

trick *adj* somewhat defective and inclined to function abnormally on occasion < a *trick* lock that doesn't always catch >
syn tricky, undependable
rel catchy, touchy; unreliable, untrustworthy; insecure, shaky, unstable; defective, dysfunctioning, malfunctioning

trick *vb syn* see DUPE
rel outtrick, outtrump, outwit; have
idiom take (someone) for a ride

trick (off, out, *or* up) *vb syn* see DRESS UP 1

trickery *n syn* see DECEPTION 1
rel double-cross; underhandedness
idiom underhand dealing

trickle *vb syn* see DRIP
ant gush

trickster *n* **1** *syn* see SWINDLER
idiom gyp artist

---

syn synonym(s)   *rel* related word(s)
ant antonym(s)   *con* contrasted word(s)
idiom idiomatic equivalent(s)
‖ use limited; if in doubt, see a dictionary

2 *syn* see MAGICIAN 2

tricksy *adj syn* see TIGHT 4

tricky *adj* 1 *syn* see SLY 2
  rel deceptive, delusive; delusory, misleading; deceitful, dishonest
  2 *syn* see UNSTABLE 2
  rel catchy, difficult, trappy; quirky
  3 *syn* see DELICATE 7
  4 *syn* see TRICK

tried *adj syn* see RELIABLE 1
  rel constant, faithful, staunch, steadfast; demonstrated, proved, tested; approved, certified
  ant untried

tried and true *adj syn* see RELIABLE 1

trifle *n* 1 *syn* see KNICKKNACK
  rel rope yarn
  2 *syn* see HINT 2

trifle *vb* 1 to behave amorously without serious intent <was interested only in *trifling* with her, not marrying her>
  syn coquet, dally, flirt, fool, lead on, string along, toy, wanton
  rel play (with); mess around, ‖muck, mucker; philander; mash
  2 *syn* see FIDDLE 1

trifle (away) *vb syn* see WASTE 2
  rel misuse; burn (up), use up
  con retain, save

trifling *n syn* see SMALL TALK

trifling *adj syn* see PETTY 2
  rel banal, inane, insipid, jejune, vapid; empty, frivolous, hollow, idle, nugatory, otiose, vain; insignificant, unimportant

trig *adj* 1 *syn* see NEAT 2
  2 *syn* see STYLISH
  ‖3 *syn* see FULL 1

triggerman *n syn* see ASSASSIN

trill *vb syn* see DRIP

trillion *n syn* see SCAD

trim *vb* 1 *syn* see ADORN
  2 *syn* see WHIP 2
  rel ‖skin
  3 *syn* see CUT 6

trim *adj* 1 *syn* see NEAT 2
  rel clean, clean-cut, fit, spruce; shapely, streamlined, symmetrical
  con disordered, shapeless, straggly
  ant frowsy
  2 *syn* see SHAPELY

trim *n syn* see ORDER 10
  rel commission; whack

trine *n syn* see TRIAD

trinity *n syn* see TRIAD

trinket *n syn* see KNICKKNACK
  rel plaything; frippery, showpiece, tinsel; trinketry, trinkums

trio *n syn* see TRIAD

trip *vb syn* see SKIP 1

trip *n* 1 a single passage of a vehicle between two points or to a point and return <a regular bus *trip* to and from the city>
  syn run; *compare* DRIVE 1, JOURNEY, TOUR 2
  rel drive; progress
  2 *syn* see JOURNEY
  rel run
  3 *syn* see ERROR 2

tripes *n pl syn* see ENTRAILS

triple *n syn* see TRIAD

tripped out *adj syn* see DRUGGED

‖**tripper** *n syn* see TOURIST

triste *adj syn* see SAD 2

trite *adj* used or occurring so often as to have lost interest, freshness, or force <unrequited love has become a *trite* theme>
  syn bathetic, chain, cliché, clichéd, commonplace, corny, hack, hackneyed, musty, old hat, shopworn, stale, stereotyped, stereotypical, threadbare, timeworn, tired, twice-told, warmed-over, well-worn, worn-out
  rel common, ordinary; banal, dull, flat, jejune, mildewed, vapid; bedridden, drained, exhausted, used-up; bromidic, platitudinous, prosaic, ready-made, set, stock
  con first, new, seminal; novel, unique; creative, imaginative; uncopied; memorable; distinctive
  ant fresh, original

triturate *vb syn* see PULVERIZE 1

triumph *n* 1 *syn* see VICTORY 1
  rel ascendancy, gain; surmounting, vanquishing, vanquishment
  ant defeat
  2 *syn* see EXULTATION
  rel joy; festivity, merriment, reveling

triumph *vb* 1 *syn* see EXULT
  rel gloat
  2 *syn* see WIN 1
  rel prosper, succeed; conquer, surmount
  idiom get the best (*or* better) of
  con lose
  ant fail
  3 *syn* see CONQUER 2

triumphal *adj syn* see EXULTANT

triumphant *adj syn* see EXULTANT
  rel rejoicing, triumphing

triumvirate *n* 1 an administrative or ruling body of three <a monarchy replaced by a *triumvirate* of generals>
  syn troika; *compare* TRIAD
  rel junta
  2 *syn* see TRIAD

triune *n syn* see TRIAD

trivia *n pl but sometimes sing in constr* unimportant matters <they became bored with the *trivia* of everyday life>
  syn minutia(e), small beer, small change, small potato(es), triviality

trivial *adj* 1 *syn* see LITTLE 3
  rel slight; negligible
  idiom no great shakes
  con considerable
  ant momentous, weighty
  2 *syn* see PETTY 2
  rel captious, fribbling, frivolous; shallow, superficial

triviality *n syn* see TRIVIA
  rel shallowness, superficiality, unimportance
  con basic(s), essential(s), fundamental(s)

‖**trod** *n syn* see TRAIL

troika *n* 1 *syn* see TRIUMVIRATE 1
  2 *syn* see TRIAD

trollop *n syn* see WANTON
  idiom (a) fast number

trollop *vb syn* see SLOUCH

tromp *vb* 1 *syn* see TRAMP 1
  2 *syn* see HIKE 2
  rel slog, trudge
  3 *syn* see TRAMPLE 2
  4 *syn* see BEAT 1

troop *n* 1 *syn* see COMPANY 4
  rel assemblage, assembly, collection, gathering; army, host, legion, multitude
  2 **troops** *pl* members of a nation's military units < Marines, GI's, and Seabees were among the *troops* sent to war >
  syn armed forces, forces, military, servicemen
  rel combatants; soldiers, troopers
  idiom fighting men
troop *vb syn* see WALK 1
trophy *n syn* see REMEMBRANCE 3
tropic *adj syn* see TROPICAL
  rel baking, broiling, scorching, sweltering
  con arctic
tropical *adj* of, relating to, or occurring in the tropics < *tropical* fruits >
  syn tropic
  rel equatorial, semitropical, subtropical; warm; hot, sultry, torrid
  con temperate
tropical cyclone *n syn* see HURRICANE
tropical storm *n syn* see HURRICANE
trot *n* 1 *syn* see HAG 2
  2 *syn* see PONY
troth *n syn* see ENGAGEMENT 2
trot out *vb syn* see SHOW 4
troubadour *n syn* see BARD 1
  rel balladist; rhymer, rhymester
trouble *vb* 1 to cause to be uneasy or upset < sorrows that *trouble* the strongest of men >
  syn ail, cark, distress, upset, worry
  rel agitate, concern, discompose, disquiet, disturb, perturb, rowel, ||worrit; annoy, bother, fret, irk, vex; ||destroy, haunt
  2 *syn* see TRY 2
  rel upset, worry; discompose, disconcert, disturb; harry, irritate; afflict, torment
  3 *syn* see INCONVENIENCE
  rel annoy, pester, plague, worry; impose (on *or* upon), intrude
trouble *n* 1 *syn* see TRIAL 2
  2 *syn* see EFFORT 1
  rel ado, bustle, flurry, fuss, pother; bother, inconvenience; difficulty, hardship, rigor; strain, stress
  3 a condition of annoyance, disturbance, or distress < got him into *trouble* by repeating gossip >
  syn Dutch, hot water
  rel bind, difficulty, predicament
troubled *adj syn* see DISTRAUGHT
troublemaker *n* a person who consciously or unconsciously causes trouble < a *troublemaker* who set father against daughter >
  syn bad actor, mischief-maker
  rel agitator, inciter, inflamer, instigator
troublesome *adj* giving trouble or anxiety < a *troublesome* infection >
  syn mean, pesky, troublous, ugly, vexatious, wicked
  rel annoying, bothersome, vexing; alarming, disquieting, disturbing, upsetting; infestive; painful
  con untroublesome
  ant innocuous

syn synonym(s)   *rel* related word(s)
ant antonym(s)   *con* contrasted word(s)
idiom idiomatic equivalent(s)
|| use limited; if in doubt, see a dictionary

troublesomeness *n syn* see INCONVENIENCE
  rel difficulty; irritation, vexation
troublous *adj syn* see TROUBLESOME
  rel troubling
trounce *vb syn* see WHIP 2
  idiom walk all over
trouncing *n syn* see DEFEAT 1
troupe *n syn* see COMPANY 4
trouper *n syn* see ACTOR 1
  rel entertainer; artiste
trove *n syn* see ACCUMULATION
truce *n* a suspension of or an agreement for suspending hostilities < the high command ordered a *truce* for the holidays >
  syn armistice, cease-fire
  rel break, ||breather, letup, lull, pause, respite; de-escalation, ||wind-down; accord, reconciliation; peace
truck *vb* 1 *syn* see TRADE 1
  rel handle; peddle, retail
  2 *syn* see TRAFFIC 2
  idiom have truck with
truck *n syn* see COMMERCE 2
truckle *vb syn* see FAWN
  rel knuckle down, knuckle under, succumb; follow, tag, tail, trail
  idiom kiss (*or* lick) one's boots, lick the feet of, make a doormat of oneself
truckler *n syn* see SYCOPHANT
truckling *adj syn* see FAWNING
truculent *adj* 1 *syn* see FIERCE 1
  rel browbeating, bullying, cowing, intimidating; frightening, terrifying, terrorizing
  2 *syn* see ABUSIVE
  rel caustic, mordacious, mordant, scathing, sharp, trenchant; harsh, rough, severe; vitriolic
  3 *syn* see BELLIGERENT
trudge *vb syn* see PLOD 1
true *adj* 1 *syn* see FAITHFUL 1
  rel sincere, unfeigned, whole-hearted, whole-souled
  ant false, fickle
  2 *syn* see UPRIGHT 2
  rel creditable, estimable, worthy; high=principled, right-minded, truehearted
  3 conformable to fact or to a standard, rule, or model < gave a *true* account of the accident >
  syn faithful, just, right, strict, undistorted, veracious, veridical
  rel careful, conscientious, meticulous, punctilious, scrupulous; finicky, fussy, overnice; accurate, precise; absolute, mathematical
  idiom true to the letter
  con imprecise, inaccurate, incorrect, inexact; erroneous, false
  ant untrue
  4 *syn* see GENUINE 3
  con deceitful
  5 *syn* see AUTHENTIC 2
  rel genuine, kosher; sincere, unfaked, unfeigned
  con artificial, fake, faked, feigned; insincere
  ant false
  6 *syn* see REAL 3
  rel natural, normal, regular, typical
  ant false
  7 being such as it should be < meanings presented in their *true* relationship >

syn appropriate, desired, fitting, proper
rel acceptable; applicable, befitting, likely, suitable
con inappropriate, unfitting
8 being such by right < the *true* heir >
syn legitimate, rightful
rel lawful, legal, proper
con illegitimate, spurious, supposititious
ant false
9 that can be relied on < polls can provide a *true* projection of public sentiment >
syn authoritative, dependable, trustable, trustworthy
rel meaningful, significant; expressive, indicative, suggestive
con independable, undependable, untrustworthy; doubtful, questionable
truelove *n* **1** *syn* see GIRL FRIEND 2
2 *syn* see BOYFRIEND 2
idiom one and only
true–tongued *adj* *syn* see TRUTHFUL
truism *n* **1** *syn* see VERACITY 2
2 *syn* see MAXIM
3 *syn* see COMMONPLACE
trull *n* *syn* see WANTON
truly *adv* **1** *syn* see VERY 2
rel absolutely, positively
2 *syn* see EVEN 3
rel confidently, really
3 *syn* see WELL 7
rel probably; surely
trump *n* *syn* see TRUMP CARD
trump *vb* *syn* see SURPASS 1
trump card *n* something decisive or telling often held in reserve < kept a political *trump card* up his sleeve till election eve >
syn clincher, trump
rel ace; coup, coup de grace, coup de main
idiom ace in the hole
trumpery *n* *syn* see NONSENSE 2
trumpery *adj* *syn* see CHEAP 2
trumpet *vb* *syn* see TOUT
truncate *vb* *syn* see TOP 1
rel abbreviate, abridge; cut off, lop; shear
truncheon *n* *syn* see CUDGEL
trust *n* **1** complete assurance and certitude regarding the character, ability, strength, or truth of someone or something < they continue to have *trust* in his judgment >
syn confidence, dependence, faith, hope, reliance, stock
rel assurance, certainty, certitude, conviction; belief, credence, credit; positiveness, sureness; entrustment; overconfidence, oversureness
con doubt, dubiety, dubiosity, skepticism, suspicion, uncertainty
ant mistrust
2 *syn* see SYNDICATE
3 *syn* see CUSTODY
trust *vb* *syn* see ENTRUST 1
rel commit, consign, hand over
trust (in *or* to) *vb* *syn* see RELY (on *or* upon)
rel assume, imagine, presume
idiom have no reservations
trustable *adj* *syn* see TRUE 9
ant trustless
trustless *adj* *syn* see UNRELIABLE 1
rel unworthy; unfaithful; suspect, suspicious; dishonest; deceitful; treacherous

ant trustable, trustworthy
trustworthy *adj* **1** *syn* see RELIABLE 1
rel veracious, truthful; honest, scrupulous, upright
con deceitful; dishonest
ant untrustworthy
2 *syn* see TRUE 9
rel accurate, exact; valid; realistic
con inaccurate, inexact; invalid; unrealistic; suspect
ant untrustworthy
3 *syn* see AUTHENTIC 1
trusty *adj* **1** *syn* see RELIABLE 1
rel predictable, stable; firm, sound; responsible; ‖straight
con capricious
ant untrusty
2 *syn* see AUTHENTIC 1
ant untrusty
truth *n* **1** *syn* see VERACITY 1
rel precision, rightness, trueness; authenticity, genuineness, veritableness; candor
idiom unvarnished truth (*or* truthfulness)
con equivocation, evasion, hedging; deception, deceptiveness, falseness
ant falsity, untruth
2 *syn* see VERACITY 2
rel reality
idiom (the) gospel truth, (the) truth of the matter
ant lie, untruth
truthful *adj* observant of or telling the truth < a *truthful* witness >
syn true-tongued, truth-speaking, truth-telling, veracious, veridical
rel candid, frank, honest, sincere; accurate, factual; real, realistic
con false, insincere, truthless, uncandid; inaccurate; unrealistic
ant untruthful
truthfulness *n* *syn* see VERACITY 1
ant untruthfulness
truthlessness *n* *syn* see MENDACITY
truth–speaking *adj* *syn* see TRUTHFUL
truth–telling *adj* *syn* see TRUTHFUL
try *vb* **1** to subject to testing < *try* the door to be sure it's locked >
syn check, examine, prove, test
rel inspect, scrutinize; appraise, judge, weigh
idiom make trial of, put to proof, put to the test
2 to subject to stress < the fine print *tried* her eyes >
syn distress, harass, irk, pain, strain, stress, trouble
rel annoy, bother, vex
3 *syn* see AFFLICT
4 *syn* see PROVE 1
5 to make an effort to do or accomplish something < the baby is *trying* to walk >
syn assay, attempt, endeavor, essay, offer, seek, strive, struggle, undertake
rel aim, aspire, hope, strike
idiom do one's best (*or* utmost) to, have a go at
try (out) *vb* *syn* see EXPERIMENT
rel examine, inspect, scrutinize; demonstrate, prove
idiom cut and try, put to trial, try for size
try *n* **1** *syn* see ATTEMPT
2 *syn* see FLING 1

rel dab, jab

trying *adj* 1 *syn* see TIGHT 4
rel annoying, bothersome, irksome, irritating, troublesome, vexing; strenuous; sticky, tricky
2 *syn* see ONEROUS

try on *vb syn* see EXPERIMENT

tryst *n syn* see ENGAGEMENT 3

‖**tub** *n syn* see FATTY
tub *vb syn* see BATHE 1

tubby *adj syn* see ROTUND 2
idiom plump as a dumpling (*or* partridge)

tuberculosis *n* a communicable bacterial disease typically marked by wasting, fever, and formation of cheesy tubercles often in the lungs < Victorian heroines fading away with *tuberculosis* >
syn consumption, phthisis, TB, white plague

tuck (in) *vb syn* see BED
rel snug (down *or* up), snuggle

‖**tuck** *n syn* see FOOD 1

tuck *n syn* see ENERGY 2

‖**tucked up** *adj syn* see CRAMPED

tucker *vb syn* see EXHAUST 3
rel gruel; wilt; drop
idiom take the tuck out of

tug *vb* 1 *syn* see CONTEND 1
2 *syn* see LABOR 1
3 *syn* see PULL 2

tug–of–war *n syn* see CONTEST 1

tuition *n syn* see EDUCATION 1

tumble *vb* 1 *syn* see FALL 2
rel trip; come (down), descend
2 *syn* see PLUMMET
rel depreciate; sag, slump
idiom take a downward spiral, take a nosedive
3 *syn* see HAPPEN 2
4 *syn* see DISCOVER 3
5 *syn* see OVERTHROW 2
6 *syn* see FELL 1
7 *syn* see CONFUSE 5
8 *syn* see DISORDER 1

tumble (to) *vb syn* see APPREHEND 1

tumble *n syn* see CLUTTER 2

tumescent *adj* 1 *syn* see INFLATED
rel bloated; bulging
2 *syn* see RHETORICAL

tumid *adj* 1 *syn* see INFLATED
rel dilated, distended, expanded, swollen
2 *syn* see RHETORICAL

tummy *n syn* see ABDOMEN

tumulary *adj syn* see SEPULCHRAL 1

tumult *n* 1 *syn* see COMMOTION 1
rel disturbance, turmoil, uproar
2 *syn* see COMMOTION 4
rel babel, din, hullabaloo, pandemonium, racket
con calm, hush, lull, quietude
3 *syn* see COMMOTION 2
rel seething; disorder, unsettlement; ferment, maelstrom, paroxysm
4 *syn* see DIN
rel noise; ‖corroborate
idiom ‖all hell broken loose

tumultuous *adj syn* see TURBULENT 1

tumultuously *adv syn* see HARD 2

tun *n syn* see CASK
rel vat

tune *n* 1 *syn* see MELODY
rel carol; composition, number, piece
2 *syn* see HARMONY 1
3 *syn* see HARMONY 2
4 *syn* see ORDER 4

tune *vb* 1 *syn* see SING 1
2 *syn* see HARMONIZE 3
rel fix, regulate
3 to adjust with respect to resonance < *tune* a TV set to a local station >
syn dial

tune (up) *vb syn* see ADJUST 2

tuned *adj syn* see MELODIOUS 2

tuneful *adj* 1 *syn* see MELODIOUS 2
2 *syn* see MELODIOUS 1
ant tuneless

tunk *vb syn* see TAP 1

turbid *adj* clouded with or as if with roiled sediment < a *turbid* stream >
syn muddy, riley, roily
rel dark, dense, obscure; mucky, thick; clouded, cloudy, murky, opaque, smoky; dull
con translucent; lucid, pellucid, transparent; crystal, crystalline; clean, pure, undefiled
ant clear, limpid

turbulence *n syn* see COMMOTION 2
rel babel, din, pandemonium, uproar; unruliness; fracas, fight
con calmness, composure, placidity, quiet

turbulent *adj* 1 given to insubordination and disorder < a *turbulent* and irresponsible group >
syn boisterous, disorderly, rambunctious, raucous, rowdy, rowdydowdy, rowdyish, rumbustious, termagant, tumultuous, unruly; *compare* UNRULY 1
rel mutinous; fast, roisterous, uncontrollable, uninhibited, wild; clamorous, loud-mouthed; brawling, quarrelsome, rough, roughhouse; hell-for-leather, rip-roaring, tempestuous
con calm, placid, quiet, tranquil; controlled, orderly, peaceful, restrained
2 *syn* see WILD 6
rel agitated, convulsed, moiling, stirred up; boiling, roily, ruffled, swirling; howling, riotous, roaring; tempest-tossed

turbulently *adv syn* see HARD 2
rel blusteringly

turf *n syn* see TERRAIN 2
rel area, region, sphere

turgid *adj* 1 *syn* see INFLATED
rel swelling, turgescent
2 *syn* see RHETORICAL

turmoil *n* 1 *syn* see COMMOTION 2
rel jitteriness, nervousness, restlessness, unease, uneasiness; disorder, disruption; moil; riot, strife, uproar
2 *syn* see UNREST
rel distress; anxiety, anxiousness
ant tranquillity
3 *syn* see COMMOTION 4

turn *vb* 1 to move or cause to move in a curved or circular path on or as if on an axis < *turned* the wheel sharply to avoid a collision >
syn circle, circumduct, gyrate, gyre, revolve, roll, rotate; *compare* SPIN 1

---

syn synonym(s)   *rel* related word(s)
ant antonym(s)   *con* contrasted word(s)
idiom idiomatic equivalent(s)
‖ use limited; if in doubt, see a dictionary

rel orbit; pirouette, spin, twirl, whirl; twist, weave, wind; circulate, eddy, swirl; oscillate, sway, swing, vibrate

2 *syn* see SPRAIN

3 *syn* see REVERSE 1

4 *syn* see PLOW

5 *syn* see UPSET 5

rel discompose, undo; unbalance

6 to change or cause to change course or direction < *turned* his car down a side road >

syn avert, deflect, divert, pivot, sheer, swing, veer, volte-face, wheel, whip, whirl; *compare* SHUNT 1

rel depart, detract, deviate, digress, diverge; move, shift; switch, swivel, twist, zigzag; call off, double (back), reverse; shunt, sidetrack; bend, curve, sway; detour, rechannel, turn away

7 *syn* see DIRECT 2

con call off, detract (from), distract, divert (from), draw (away)

8 *syn* see ADDRESS 3

rel employ, use; plunge (into), undertake

idiom turn one's hand (*or* energies) to

con avoid, dodge, shy (away)

9 *syn* see CURDLE

10 *syn* see DECAY

11 *syn* see CHANGE 1

12 *syn* see TRANSLATE 1

13 *syn* see DULL 3

14 *syn* see SPIN 2

15 *syn* see DEFECT

16 *syn* see RESORT 2

17 *syn* see BECOME 1

rel change (into), pass (into)

turn (on *or* upon) *vb syn* see DEPEND (on *or* upon) 1

turn *n* **1** *syn* see REVOLUTION 1

2 an often sudden change in course or trend < his health took a *turn* for the better >

syn bend, deflection, deviation, double, shift, tack, yaw

rel course, drift, trend

3 *syn* see REVERSAL 1

4 a point at which a change of course takes place < hidden by a *turn* in the road >

syn angle, bend, bow, flection, flexure, turning

rel curve, twist; corner

5 *syn* see WALK 1

6 *syn* see DRIVE 1

7 *syn* see SPELL 1

8 *syn* see CHANGE 1

9 *syn* see GIFT 2

rel bias, disposition, predisposition

10 an unusual, unexpected, or special interpretation or construction < gave a new *turn* to the old joke >

syn twist

rel construction, interpretation; device, gimmick, trick

11 *syn* see ATTACK 3

turnabout *n* **1** *syn* see REVERSAL 1

2 *syn* see RENEGADE

rel backslider, coward, quitter, turnback

turn back *vb syn* see RETURN 1

turncoat *n* *syn* see RENEGADE

rel deserter, straggler; betrayer, quisler, quisling, traitor; spy

turn down *vb syn* see DECLINE 4

turned on *adj syn* see DRUGGED

turn in *vb syn* see RETIRE 4

ant turn out

turning *n* **1** *syn* see TURN 4

2 *syn* see DEVIATION 1

rel detour

3 *syn* see REVERSAL 1

turning point *n* *syn* see JUNCTURE 2

rel climax, culmination, peak

idiom moment of truth

turnip *n* *syn* see DUNCE

turn off *vb* **1** *syn* see DISMISS 3

2 *syn* see HANG 2

turn out *vb* **1** *syn* see FURNISH 1

rel deck, dress (out)

2 *syn* see BEAR 9

3 *syn* see ROLL OUT

turnout *n* **1** *syn* see COSTUME

2 *syn* see OUTPUT

turn over *vb* **1** *syn* see OVERTURN 1

2 *syn* see PLOW

3 *syn* see PONDER 2

idiom turn over in one's mind

4 *syn* see GIVE 3

rel assign, confer, consign, convey, delegate, relegate; give up, relinquish, ‖turn up

idiom come across with, put into the hands of

con get back, reclaim, recover, regain, retrieve, take back

5 *syn* see COMMIT 1

turnover *n* *syn* see SHAKE-UP

turn up *vb* **1** *syn* see FIND 1

rel see; uncover, unearth; track (down)

idiom come across

‖**2** *syn* see RELINQUISH

3 to arrive when or where expected < *turned* up for dinner promptly at seven o'clock >

syn show, show up

rel appear, arrive, come, materialize; blow in, pop (in), punch in, roll (in), weigh in

idiom make one's appearance, put in an appearance

4 *syn* see COME 1

turtledove *n* *syn* see SWEETHEART 1

tussle *vb syn* see WRESTLE

rel scrap, skirmish, spar; hassle

idiom get into a tussle

tutelage *n* *syn* see EDUCATION 1

twaddle *n* *syn* see NONSENSE 2

rel gabble; wish-wash

twaddle *vb* **1** *syn* see BABBLE 2

2 *syn* see CHAT 1

twang *n* *syn* see HINT 2

‖**twat** *n* *syn* see BUTTOCKS

tweedle *vb syn* see CHIRP

tween *prep syn* see BETWEEN 2

tweet *vb syn* see CHIRP

twerp *n* a usually young or insignificant upstart who meddles beyond his competence or concern < ignored the protests of that insolent *twerp* >

syn pup, puppy, sprat, squirt, ‖squit

rel upstart; ‖squib; fool, jerk, ‖twit; brat

idiom small-time big shot

twice–told *adj syn* see TRITE

twiddle *vb syn* see FIDDLE 1

rel finger, manipulate, palpate; monkey (with), toy (with)

idiom twiddle around with

twiddle *vb syn* see CHAT 1

twig *vb* **1** *syn* see SEE 1

2 *syn* see APPREHEND 1

||**twig** *n syn* see FASHION 3

twiggy *adj syn* see THIN 1

twilight *n* 1 *syn* see EVENING 1
rel afterglow, afterlight
2 *syn* see EVENING 1
rel decline; end

twin *adj* made up of two very closely matched or identical aspects, elements, individuals, or parts < the *twin* threats of inflation and recession >
syn double, dual, paired
rel bifold, binary, twofold; identical, matched, matching; like, similar
con independent, separate; dissimilar, unlike

twin *n syn* see MATE 5

twine *vb syn* see WIND 2
rel interweave; undulate; enmesh, entangle, tangle

twinge *n syn* see PAIN 1

twinkle *vb* 1 *syn* see BLINK 2
rel illuminate, light, light up; shine
2 *syn* see FLASH 1
3 *syn* see WINK

twinkle *n* 1 *syn* see INSTANT 1
2 *syn* see FLASH 1

twinkling *n syn* see INSTANT 1
idiom the twinkling of an eye

twirl *vb syn* see SPIN 1

twist *vb* 1 *syn* see SPRAIN
2 *syn* see MISREPRESENT
3 *syn* see WIND 2
ant untwist

twist *n syn* see TURN 10

twister *n syn* see TORNADO

twisting *adj syn* see CROOKED 1

twit *vb syn* see RIDICULE
rel jive, josh; twitter; chide, reproach, reprove; blame, censure, reprehend

twitch *vb syn* see JERK
rel clutch, grasp, pluck, snatch; nip, pinch

twitter *vb* 1 *syn* see CHIRP
2 *syn* see CHAT 1
3 *syn* see SHAKE 1

twittery *adj syn* see NERVOUS
rel flustered; twittering
idiom all atwitter, all fluttery, all of a twitter

twitty *adj syn* see IRRITABLE

twixt *prep syn* see BETWEEN 2

twofold *adj* 1 having two parts, elements, or aspects < the problem is *twofold*: to find gasoline and to be able to pay for it >
syn bifold, binary, double, double-barreled, dual, dualistic, duple, duplex
rel dyadic; paired, twin
con distinct, separate
2 being twice as large, as great, or as many < a *twofold* increase in enrollment >
syn double, double-barreled
idiom twice over

two-handed *adj* 1 designed for or requiring the use of both hands < a *two-handed* sword >
syn bimanual

2 having or being efficient with two hands < *two-handed* tennis players are rare >
syn ambidextrous, bimanual

twosome *n syn* see COUPLE

two-time *vb syn* see DECEIVE

two-wheeler *n syn* see BICYCLE

tycoon *n syn* see MAGNATE

tyke *n syn* see DOG 1

type *n* a number of individuals thought of as a group because of a common quality or qualities < political radicals of whatever *type* >
syn breed, cast, character, class, cut, description, feather, ilk, kidney, kind, lot, mold, nature, order, persuasion, sort, species, stamp, stripe, variety, way
rel blazon, brand, form; sample, specimen; category, group, rubric

typhoon *n syn* see HURRICANE

typic *adj syn* see GENERAL 1
rel average, ordinary

typical *adj* 1 constituting or having the nature of a type < a *typical* instance of guilt by association >
syn archetypal, classic, classical, exemplary, ideal, model, paradigmatic, prototypal, prototypical, quintessential, representative
rel characteristic; emblematic, symbolic; absolute, consummate, perfect
con uncharacteristic; unusual
ant atypical, untypical
2 *syn* see GENERAL 1
rel old hat, unexceptional; collective, quintessential, representative; characteristic, specific
idiom being the rule and not the exception
con distinctive; exceptional, extraordinary, unusual; abnormal
ant atypical, untypical

typification *n syn* see ALLEGORY 1

typify *vb* 1 *syn* see REPRESENT 2
2 *syn* see EPITOMIZE 2
rel model

tyrannical *adj syn* see ABSOLUTE 4
rel brutal, harsh, oppressive; roughshod

tyrannize *vb* to exercise arbitrary power over often with unjust and oppressive severity < a country *tyrannized* by a dictator and his secret police >
syn despotize
rel dictate, dominate, domineer, overlord; crush, oppress, trample; shackle; terrorize

tyrannous *adj syn* see ABSOLUTE 4
rel lordly; fascistic, totalitarian

tyranny *n* absolute government in which unlimited power is vested in a single usually severe and oppressive ruler < the *tyranny* of Hitler >
syn autocracy, despotism, dictatorship, totalitarianism
rel monocracy; absolutism, authoritarianism, fascism; domination, oppression, totality; terrorism
idiom iron heel (*or* boot)
con democracy; freedom; anarchy

tyrant *n* a ruler who exercises absolute power oppressively and brutally < Hitler and Stalin as twentieth-century *tyrants* >
syn despot, dictator, duce, oppressor, strong man
rel autocrat, totalitarian

---

syn synonym(s)   *rel* related word(s)
ant antonym(s)   *con* contrasted word(s)
idiom idiomatic equivalent(s)
|| use limited; if in doubt, see a dictionary

idiom man on horseback
tyro *n* **1** *syn* see AMATEUR 2

2 *syn* see NOVICE

U

uberrima fides *n syn* see GOOD FAITH
ubiquitous *adj* *syn* see OMNIPRESENT
ugly *adj* **1** *syn* see GRAVE 3
2 unpleasing to the sight < an *ugly* decaying neighborhood >
syn hideous, ill-favored, ill-looking, unbeautiful, uncomely, unsightly
rel homely, plain; bizarre, grotesque; repelling, repugnant, repulsive; unattractive, uninviting, unpleasing, unprepossessing
idiom homely as a mud (*or* hedge) fence, not much to look at, short on looks
con comely, fair, good-looking, handsome, lovely, pretty; attractive, prepossessing
ant beautiful
3 *syn* see BASE 3
4 *syn* see TROUBLESOME
5 *syn* see SULLEN
ukase *n syn* see EDICT 1
ulterior *adj* lying behind what is manifest or avowed < an *ulterior* motive >
syn buried, concealed, covert, guarded, hidden, obscured, privy, shrouded
rel ambiguous, cryptic, dark, enigmatic, equivocal, obscure
idiom hidden under the rug, kept behind a screen, under cover, under wraps
con clear, open, overt, plain, straightforward; explicit, expressed
ultimate *adj* **1** *syn* see LAST
2 *syn* see SUPREME
3 being so fundamental as to stand at the extreme limit of the actually or conceivably knowable < *ultimate* realities >
syn absolute, categorical
rel empyreal, empyrean, sublime, transcendental; exalted, grand, lofty
ultimate *n syn* see APOTHEOSIS 1
ultimate *vb syn* see CLOSE 3
ultimately *adv syn* see YET 2
ultra *adj* **1** *syn* see EXTREME 3
2 *syn* see OUTLANDISH 3
ultraconservative *n* *syn* see REACTIONARY
ultrafashionable *adj syn* see STYLISH
ultraist *n syn* see RADICAL
ultraist *adj syn* see EXTREME 3
ultramarine *adj syn* see OVERSEAS
ululate *vb syn* see HOWL 1
rel bewail, lament
umbra *n* **1** *syn* see APPARITION
2 *syn* see SHADE 1
umbrage *n* **1** *syn* see SHADE 1
2 *syn* see FOLIAGE
3 *syn* see OFFENSE 2
rel annoyance, irking, vexation; exasperation, irritation, nettling, provoking; fury, ire, rage, wrath
umbrage *vb* **1** *syn* see SHADE
2 *syn* see ANGER 1

umbrageous *adj syn* see SHADY 1
umbrous *adj syn* see SHADY 1
umpire *n syn* see JUDGE 1
umpire *vb syn* see JUDGE 1
unabashed *adj syn* see SHAMELESS
ant abashed
unabbreviated *adj syn* see UNABRIDGED
ant abbreviated
unabridged *adj* not shortened by omission of parts (as words) < published an *unabridged* edition of Shakespeare's plays >
syn complete, unabbreviated, uncondensed, uncut, undocked, whole-length
rel entire, intact, whole
con condensed, cropped, curtailed, cut, incompleted, shortened, trimmed
ant abridged
unacceptable *adj* *syn* see OBJECTIONABLE
ant acceptable
unaccompanied *adj syn* see ALONE 1
ant accompanied, companioned
unaccomplished *adj syn* see AMATEURISH
ant accomplished, skilled
unaccountable *adj* **1** *syn* see INEXPLICABLE
ant accountable
2 *syn* see MYSTERIOUS
unaccustomed *adj syn* see UNFAMILIAR 1
ant accustomed, familiar
unacquaintance *n syn* see IGNORANCE 2
ant acquaintance
unacquainted *adj syn* see IGNORANT 2
ant acquainted
unacquaintedness *n syn* see IGNORANCE 2
ant acquaintance
unacquired *adj syn* see INNATE 1
ant acquired
unadorned *adj syn* see PLAIN 1
ant adorned
unadulterated *adj* **1** *syn* see PURE 2
2 *syn* see STRAIGHT 3
ant adulterated
unadvisable *adj syn* see INADVISABLE
ant advisable
unadvised *adj syn* see RASH 1
ant advised, thought-out
unaffable *adj syn* see UNDEMONSTRATIVE
ant affable
unaffected *adj syn* see NATURAL 5
ant affected, artificial
unafraid *adj syn* see BRAVE 1
rel composed, cool, imperturbable; assured, confident, sure
con apprehensive, fearful
ant afraid
unaimed *adj syn* see RANDOM
unalert *adj syn* see INCAUTIOUS 1
ant alert

unalike *adj syn* see DIFFERENT 1
    ant alike
unalloyed *adj syn* see PURE 2
unalluring *adj syn* see PLAIN 5
    ant alluring, attractive
unalterable *adj syn* see INFLEXIBLE 3
    ant alterable
unambiguous *adj* 1 *syn* see CLEAR 4
    ant ambiguous, obscure
    2 *syn* see EXPLICIT
    ant ambiguous
    3 *syn* see CLEAR 5
unanimated *adj syn* see DEAD 1
unanimous *adj* being of one mind <they
    were *unanimous* in their determination to
    win>
    syn consentaneous, consentient, solid
    rel agreed, agreeing, concordant, concur-
    rent, harmonious
    idiom of one accord, of one (*or* the same)
    mind, with one voice
    con differing, disagreed, disagreeing, dis-
    cordant, inharmonious
unanticipatedly *adv syn* see UNAWARES
unapparent *adj syn* see IMPERCEPTIBLE
    ant apparent, detectable
unappeasable *adj* 1 *syn* see INSATIABLE
    ant appeasable
    2 *syn* see GRIM 3
    ant appeasable, placable
unappetizing *adj syn* see UNPALATABLE
    1
    ant appetizing
unappreciable *adj syn* see IMPERCEPTI-
    BLE
    ant appreciable
unappreciated *adj syn* see THANKLESS 2
    ant appreciated
unappreciative *adj syn* see THANKLESS 1
    ant appreciative
unapproachable *adj* 1 *syn* see INACCESSI-
    BLE
    ant approachable, attainable
    2 *syn* see UNSOCIABLE
    ant accessible, approachable
unapt *adj* 1 *syn* see IMPROPER 1
    2 *syn* see UNSKILLFUL 1
    ant apt
unarm *vb syn* see DISARM 2
unartful *adj syn* see NATURAL 5
    ant artful
unarticulate *adj syn* see DUMB 1
    ant articulate
unartificial *adj syn* see NATURAL 5
    ant affected, artificial
unasked *adj* 1 not asked or invited <an-
    noyed by his *unasked* advice>
    syn unbidden, uninvited, unrequested,
    unsought
    rel arrogant, impudent, overbearing, pre-
    sumptuous; spontaneous, voluntary; unac-
    ceptable, unwanted, unwelcome
    con desired, invited, sought, wanted;
    acceptable, welcome
    ant asked
    2 *syn* see SUPEREROGATORY
unassailable *adj syn* see INVINCIBLE 1
    rel stalwart, stout, strong, sturdy, tena-
    cious, tough

    ant assailable
unassertive *adj syn* see SHY 1
    ant aggressive, assertive
unassorted *adj syn* see MISCELLANEOUS
unassuming *adj syn* see HUMBLE 1
    ant assuming, presumptuous
unassured *adj* 1 *syn* see UNSAFE
    2 *syn* see SHY 1
    ant assured
    3 *syn* see INSECURE 1
unattainable *adj* 1 *syn* see INACCESSIBLE
    ant attainable
    2 *syn* see IMPOSSIBLE 1
unattractive *adj syn* see PLAIN 5
    ant alluring, attractive
unauthentic *adj syn* see SPURIOUS 3
    ant authentic, genuine
unavailable *adj syn* see FUTILE
unavailing *adj syn* see FUTILE
unavoidable *adj syn* see INEVITABLE
    ant avoidable
unavoidably *adv syn* see WILLY-NILLY
unaware *adv syn* see UNAWARES
unaware *adj syn* see IGNORANT 2
    ant aware, conscious
unawaredly *adv syn* see UNAWARES
unawareness *n syn* see IGNORANCE 2
    ant awareness, consciousness
unawares *adv* without warning <caught
    unawares by company>
    syn aback, short, sudden, suddenly, unan-
    ticipatedly, unaware, unawaredly, unex-
    pectedly
    rel unprepared, unready
    idiom like a bolt from the blue, off base,
    out of a clear sky, out of the blue
unbalance *vb syn* see MADDEN 1
unbalance *n syn* see INSANITY 1
    rel disorientation, instability
unbalanced *adj* 1 *syn* see LOPSIDED
    ant balanced
    2 *syn* see INSANE 1
unbearable *adj syn* see INSUFFERABLE
    ant bearable, supportable
unbearing *adj syn* see BARREN 2
unbeatable *adj syn* see INVINCIBLE 1
    ant beatable, defeatable
unbeauteous *adj syn* see PLAIN 5
    ant beauteous
unbeautified *adj syn* see PLAIN 1
    ant beautified, embellished
unbeautiful *adj* 1 *syn* see PLAIN 5
    ant beautiful
    2 *syn* see UGLY 2
    ant beautiful
unbecoming *adj* 1 *syn* see INDECOROUS
    rel awkward, clumsy, gauche, inept, mal-
    adroit
    ant becoming, seemly
    2 *syn* see IMPROPER 1
unbecomingness *n syn* see IMPROPRIETY
    1
    ant becomingness, seemliness
unbefitting *adj syn* see IMPROPER 1
    ant apropos, befitting
unbegotten *adj syn* see SELF-EXISTENT
unbelief *n* the attitude or state of mind of
    one who does not believe <after so much
    deception, so many lies, she could offer
    nothing but *unbelief* to his words>
    syn disbelief, incredulity, unbelievingness,
    unfaith

---

syn synonym(s)   *rel* related word(s)
ant antonym(s)   *con* contrasted word(s)
idiom idiomatic equivalent(s)
‖ use limited; if in doubt, see a dictionary

rel doubt, dubiety, dubiosity, skepticism, uncertainty; distrust, mistrust, suspicion; apprehension, misgiving, qualm
con assurance, certitude, security, trust; dependence, reliance, stock, store
ant belief

unbelievable *adj* 1 *syn* see INCREDIBLE 1
ant believable, credible
2 *syn* see IMPLAUSIBLE
ant believable, credible

unbelieve *vb syn* see DISBELIEVE
ant believe, credit

unbeliever *n syn* see SKEPTIC
ant believer

unbelieving *adj syn* see INCREDULOUS
ant believing

unbelievingness *n syn* see UNBELIEF

unbend *vb* 1 *syn* see RELAX 2
2 *syn* see REST 2

unbendable *adj syn* see INFLEXIBLE 2
ant bendable

unbending *adj* 1 *syn* see STIFF 1
ant bendable
2 *syn* see INFLEXIBLE 2
3 *syn* see UNSOCIABLE

unbiased *adj syn* see FAIR 4
rel aloof, uninterested
ant biased

unbidden *adj syn* see UNASKED

unbind *vb* 1 *syn* see LOOSE 3
ant bind
2 *syn* see FREE
ant bind

unblamable *adj syn* see GOOD 11
ant blamable, blameworthy

unblemished *adj* 1 *syn* see WHOLE 1
ant blemished, flawed
2 *syn* see CHASTE

unblenched *adj syn* see BRAVE 1

unblenching *adj syn* see BRAVE 1

unblock *vb syn* see OPEN 1
ant block

unblunted *adj syn* see SHARP 1
ant blunt, blunted

unblurred *adj syn* see CLEAR 4
ant blurred

unblushing *adj syn* see SHAMELESS

unbodied *adj syn* see IMMATERIAL 1
ant bodied, incarnate

unbookish *adj syn* see UNSCHOLARLY
ant bookish

unbosom *vb syn* see REVEAL 1

unbounded *adj syn* see LIMITLESS
ant bounded, limited

unbrace *vb syn* see WEAKEN 1
ant brace, reinforce

unbroken *adj syn* see WHOLE 1
ant broken

unbrookable *adj syn* see INSUFFERABLE

unbuild *vb syn* see DESTROY 1
ant build

unburden *vb syn* see RID
rel discharge, disencumber, unload
con encumber, lade, load, saddle, tax, weight
ant burden

unbury *vb syn* see EXHUME
ant bury

uncalled-for *adj* 1 *syn* see UNNECESSARY
ant required
2 *syn* see SUPEREROGATORY
3 *syn* see BASELESS

rel absurd, foolish, preposterous, silly; impertinent, intrusive, officious
ant well-founded
4 *syn* see RUDE 6

uncandid *adj syn* see DISINGENUOUS
ant candid

uncanny *adj* 1 *syn* see WEIRD 1
2 *syn* see SUPERNATURAL 2

uncared-for *adj syn* see NEGLECTED
ant cared-for

uncareful *adj syn* see IRRESPONSIBLE
ant careful

uncaring *adj syn* see CARELESS 1
ant careful

uncaused *adj syn* see SELF-EXISTENT

unceasing *adj syn* see CONTINUAL

uncelebrated *adj syn* see OBSCURE 5
ant celebrated, noted

uncelestial *adj syn* see EARTHLY 1
ant celestial

unceremonious *adj* 1 *syn* see INFORMAL 1
ant ceremonious
2 *syn* see SHORT 5

uncertain *adj* 1 not stable, consistent, or predictable <was in very *uncertain* health>
syn capricious, chancy, erratic, fluctuant, iffy, incalculable, unpredictable, whimsical; *compare* INCONSTANT 1
rel questionable, undependable, unsettled; fickle, inconstant, insecure, unstable, unsure; changeable, mutable, protean, variable; unexpectable, unforeseeable
idiom in a state of uncertainty, in suspense
2 *syn* see INCONSTANT 1
3 *syn* see MUTABLE 2
4 *syn* see DOUBTFUL 1
ant certain
5 *syn* see MOOT
ant certain
6 *syn* see OBSCURE 3
7 *syn* see VACILLATING 2
idiom at a loss
ant certain, set

uncertainty *n* a feeling of unsureness about someone or something <troubled by a growing *uncertainty* about the future>
syn concern, doubt, doubtfulness, dubiety, dubiosity, dubitancy, incertitude, mistrust, query, skepticism, suspicion, uncertitude, wonder
rel anxiety, bother, disquiet, trouble, worry; agitation, distress, perturbation, uneasiness; disfaith, distrust; hesitation, reserve, salt
con assurance, certitude, confidence, conviction; complacency, content, satisfaction
ant certainty

uncertitude *n syn* see UNCERTAINTY
ant certitude

unchain *vb syn* see FREE
ant chain

unchangeable *adj syn* see INFLEXIBLE 3
ant changeable

unchanging *adj* 1 *syn* see STEADY 2
2 *syn* see SAME 3
ant changeable, changing

uncharnel *vb syn* see EXHUME

unchaste *adj* 1 *syn* see IMPURE 1
ant chaste

2 *syn* see FAST 7
ant chaste

unchristian *adj syn* see OUTRAGEOUS 1
ant ‖Christian

uncivil *adj* 1 *syn* see BARBARIAN 1
2 *syn* see RUDE 6
rel coarse, crass, crude
con polished, smooth, urbane
ant civil

uncivilized *adj* 1 *syn* see BARBARIAN 1
ant civilized
2 *syn* see BOORISH
ant civilized
3 *syn* see OUTRAGEOUS 1

unclad *adj syn* see NUDE 2

unclean *adj* 1 *syn* see IMPURE 1
ant clean, pure
2 *syn* see DIRTY 1
ant clean, cleanly
3 *syn* see IMPURE 3
ant clean; purified

uncleanly *adj* 1 *syn* see IMPURE 1
ant cleanly
2 *syn* see DIRTY 1
ant clean, cleanly

unclear *adj* 1 *syn* see OBSCURE 3
ant clear
2 *syn* see FAINT 2
ant clear, distinct
3 *syn* see DOUBTFUL 1
ant clear

uncloak *vb syn* see EXPOSE 4
ant cloak

unclose *vb* 1 *syn* see OPEN 1
ant close
2 *syn* see REVEAL 1

unclosed *adj syn* see OPEN 1
ant closed

unclothe *vb* 1 *syn* see STRIP 1
ant clothe, dress
2 *syn* see OPEN 2

unclothed *adj syn* see NUDE 2
ant clothed, dressed

unclouded *adj syn* see FAIR 2
ant clouded, cloudy

uncluttered *adj syn* see NEAT 2
ant cluttered

uncolored *adj syn* see FAIR 4
ant colored, partial

uncombed *adj syn* see SLOVENLY 1

uncombine *vb syn* see SEPARATE 1
ant combine

un‑come‑at‑able *adj syn* see INACCESSI-
BLE
ant come-at-able

uncomely *adj* 1 *syn* see IMPROPER 1
2 *syn* see PLAIN 5
ant comely
3 *syn* see UGLY 2
ant comely

uncomfortable *adj* causing or likely to
cause discomfort <kept an *uncomfortable*
chair for uninvited callers>
syn comfortless, discomforting, harsh,
uncomforting, uncomfy
rel distressing, easeless, uneasy
con comforting, easy, soothing
ant comfortable

uncomforting *adj syn* see UNCOMFORT-
ABLE
ant comforting

uncomfy *adj syn* see UNCOMFORTABLE
ant comfy

uncommon *adj* 1 *syn* see INFREQUENT
con commonplace, everyday, ordinary
ant common
2 *syn* see EXCEPTIONAL 1
ant common, commonplace

‖uncommon *adv syn* see EXTRA

uncommonly *adv* 1 *syn* see OCCASION-
ALLY
ant commonly
2 *syn* see EXTRA

uncommunicative *adj* 1 *syn* see SILENT 3
ant communicative
2 *syn* see UNSOCIABLE

uncompanionable *adj syn* see UNSOCIA-
BLE
ant companionable

uncompassionate *adj syn* see UNFEEL-
ING 2
ant compassionate

uncompensated *adj syn* see UNPAID 1
ant compensated

uncomplainingness *n syn* see PATIENCE
ant complainingness, discontent

uncomplete *adj syn* see DEFICIENT 1
ant complete

uncompliant *adj syn* see INFLEXIBLE 2
ant compliant

uncomplimentary *adj syn* see DEROGA-
TORY
ant complimentary

uncomprehensible *adj syn* see INCOM-
PREHENSIBLE 1
ant comprehensible, graspable

uncompromising *adj* 1 *syn* see INFLEXI-
BLE 2
2 *syn* see TOUGH 3

unconcealed *adj syn* see FRANK

unconceivable *adj syn* see IMPLAUSIBLE
ant conceivable

unconcern *n syn* see APATHY 2
ant concern

unconcerned *adj syn* see INDIFFERENT 2
rel collected, composed, cool, nonchalant
con anxious, careful, solicitous, worried
ant concerned

uncondensed *adj syn* see UNABRIDGED
ant condensed

unconfident *adj syn* see INSECURE 1
ant confident

unconfined *adj syn* see FREE 2
ant confined

uncongenial *adj* 1 *syn* see ANTIPATHETIC
2
rel displeasing, unattractive, unlikable,
unpleasing
ant congenial
2 *syn* see INHARMONIOUS 2

unconnected *adj syn* see INCOHERENT 2
ant connected, ordered

unconquerable *adj* 1 *syn* see INVINCIBLE
1
rel insuperable, unsurmountable; proof,
resistant, secure, tight
idiom more than a match for
con beatable, vincible; expungable, preg-
nable, vulnerable; insecure, open, unprotected
ant conquerable

---

syn synonym(s)   *rel* related word(s)
ant antonym(s)   *con* contrasted word(s)
idiom idiomatic equivalent(s)
‖ use limited; if in doubt, see a dictionary

2 *syn* see INSUPERABLE
ant conquerable
unconscionable *adj* **1** *syn* see UNSCRUPU-
LOUS
ant conscientious, conscionable
2 *syn* see EXCESSIVE 1
3 *syn* see UNREASONABLE 2
4 *syn* see OUTRAGEOUS 1
unconscious *adj syn* see INSENSIBLE 2
ant conscious
unconsequential *adj syn* see PETTY 2
ant consequential
unconsidered *adj* **1** *syn* see PETTY 2
2 *syn* see RANDOM
ant considered, planned
3 *syn* see RASH 1
ant considered
unconsolable *adj syn* see INCONSOLABLE
ant consolable
unconspicuous *adj syn* see INCONSPICU-
OUS
ant conspicuous
unconstrained *adj* **1** *syn* see EASYGOING
3
2 *syn* see DEMONSTRATIVE
ant constrained
unconstraint *n* freedom from constraint or
pressure < had always been due to the
unconstraint of a happy affectionate family >
syn abandon, ease, naturalness, spontaneity, unrestraint; *compare* ABANDON 2
rel impulsiveness, instinctiveness; ingenuousness, naiveté, simplicity, unsophistication
con pressure, strain, stress, tension; formality, rigidity; sophistication
ant constraint
uncontainable *adj syn* see IRREPRESSI-
BLE
uncontent *adj syn* see DISCONTENTED
ant content, contented
uncontented *adj syn* see DISCONTENTED
ant content, contented
uncontestable *adj syn* see POSITIVE 3
ant contestable
uncontinuous *adj syn* see INCOHERENT 2
uncontrite *adj syn* see REMORSELESS
ant contrite
uncontrollable *adj* **1** *syn* see UNRULY 1
ant controllable
2 *syn* see IRREPRESSIBLE
ant controllable
uncontrovertible *adj syn* see POSITIVE 3
ant controvertible, disputable
unconversant *adj* *syn* see INEXPERI-
ENCED
ant conversant, versed
unconvincing *adj syn* see IMPLAUSIBLE
ant convincing
uncooked *adj syn* see RAW 1
ant cooked
‖**uncorporal** *adj syn* see IMMATERIAL 1
uncorrectable *adj syn* see HOPELESS 2
ant correctable
uncostly *adj syn* see CHEAP 1
ant costly
uncountable *adj* **1** *syn* see INNUMERA-
BLE
ant countable
2 *syn* see INCALCULABLE 1
uncounted *adj syn* see INNUMERABLE
uncouple *vb syn* see DETACH

ant couple
uncourteous *adj syn* see RUDE 6
ant courteous
uncouth *adj* **1** *syn* see STRANGE 4
2 *syn* see DERELICT 1
3 *syn* see COARSE 3
ant couth
4 *syn* see RUDE 6
uncover *vb* **1** *syn* see REVEAL 1
2 *syn* see EXPOSE 1
3 *syn* see OPEN 2
ant cover
uncovered *adj syn* see OPEN 2
uncreate *vb syn* see ANNIHILATE 2
uncreated *adj syn* see SELF-EXISTENT
ant created
uncreative *adj syn* see UNORIGINAL
ant creative
uncritical *adj syn* see SUPERFICIAL 2
rel imprecise, inaccurate, inexact; careless,
casual, offhand, perfunctory, slipshod
con accurate, exact, precise; careful; discerning, discriminating, penetrating
ant critical
uncrown *vb syn* see DEPOSE 1
ant coronate, crown
unction *n syn* see OINTMENT
unctious *adj syn* see FULSOME
unctuous *adj* **1** *syn* see FATTY 2
2 *syn* see FULSOME
uncultivated *adj* **1** *syn* see COARSE 3
ant cultivated
2 *syn* see BARBARIAN 1
ant cultivated
3 *syn* see WILD 1
ant cultivated
uncultured *adj* **1** *syn* see BOORISH
ant cultured
2 *syn* see COARSE 3
uncurable *adj syn* see HOPELESS 2
ant curable
uncurbed *adj syn* see AUDACIOUS 4
ant curbed
uncurious *adj syn* see INDIFFERENT 2
ant curious
uncurtain *vb syn* see REVEAL 1
uncustomary *adj syn* see EXCEPTIONAL 1
ant customary
uncut *adj syn* see UNABRIDGED
ant cut
undamaged *adj syn* see WHOLE 1
ant damaged
undaring *adj syn* see TIMID 2
ant daring
undarkened *adj syn* see FAIR 3
undauntable *adj syn* see BRAVE 1
undaunted *adj syn* see BRAVE 1
ant daunted
undear *adj syn* see CHEAP 1
ant dear
undeceive *vb syn* see DISABUSE
ant deceive
undecided *adj* **1** *syn* see PENDING
ant decided
2 *syn* see DOUBTFUL 1
undecipherable *adj syn* see ILLEGIBLE
ant decipherable
undecisive *adj syn* see VACILLATING 2
ant decisive
undeclared *adj syn* see TACIT
undecorated *adj syn* see PLAIN 1
ant decorated
undecorous *adj syn* see INDECOROUS

ant decorous

undefeatable *adj syn* see INVINCIBLE 1
  ant defeatable

undefiled *adj syn* see CHASTE

undefined *adj syn* see FAINT 2
  ant defined

undeflowered *adj syn* see VIRGIN 1
  ant deflowered

undelude *vb syn* see DISABUSE
  ant delude

undemonstrated *adj syn* see UNTRIED 1
  ant demonstrated

undemonstrative *adj* not socially outgoing < a shy *undemonstrative* person yet capable of deep feeling >
  syn aseptic, restrained, retiring, shrinking, unaffable, unexpansive, withdrawn; *compare* UNSOCIABLE
  rel chill, cold, frigid, glacial, icy; emotionless, indifferent, unemotional, uninterested; aloof, distant, reserved, standoffish
  con free and easy, hail-fellow-well-met, outgiving, outgoing, palsy-walsy; sociable
  ant demonstrative

undeniable *adj* 1 *syn* see POSITIVE 3
  ant deniable
  2 *syn* see REAL 3

undenominational *adj syn* see NONSECTARIAN
  ant denominational

undependable *adj* 1 *syn* see UNRELIABLE 1
  ant dependable
  2 *syn* see UNSAFE
  ant dependable
  3 *syn* see TRICK
  ant dependable

under *adv syn* see BELOW 1
  ant above, over

under *prep syn* see BELOW 1
  ant over

under *adj* 1 *syn* see INFERIOR 1
  2 *syn* see SUBORDINATE

underage *n syn* see FAILURE 3
  ant overage

underconsciousness *n syn* see SUBCONSCIOUS

undercover *adj syn* see SECRET 1

undercover man *n syn* see SPY

undercroft *n syn* see CRYPT

underdeveloped *adj syn* see BACKWARD 6

underdog *n syn* see VICTIM 1
  ant overdog, top dog

underearth *adj syn* see SUBTERRANEAN

underfoot *adj* 1 *syn* see SUBTERRANEAN
  2 *syn* see DOWNTRODDEN

undergo *vb syn* see EXPERIENCE 1
  rel abide, bear, endure, tolerate; bow, defer, submit, yield

underground *adj* *syn* see SUBTERRANEAN

underhand *adj* characterized by sly unobtrusive craft or deceit < ready to use the most *underhand* methods to gain his ends >
  syn devious, duplicitous, guileful, indirect, shifty, sneaking, sneaky, underhanded; *compare* SECRET 1, SLY 2

rel deceitful, dishonest; crooked, oblique; crafty, cunning, insidious, sly, tricky, wily; furtive, hangdog
  con candid, frank, open, plain; forthright, straight-forward
  ant aboveboard

underhanded *adj* 1 *syn* see UNDERHAND
  ant aboveboard
  2 *syn* see SHORTHANDED

underivative *adj syn* see PRIMARY 5
  ant derivative

underived *adj syn* see PRIMARY 5
  ant derived

underlease *vb syn* see SUBLET

underlet *vb syn* see SUBLET

underline *vb syn* see EMPHASIZE

underline *n syn* see CAPTION

underling *n syn* see INFERIOR

underly *adj syn* see UNWELL

underlying *adj* 1 *syn* see FUNDAMENTAL 1
  rel cardinal, essential, vital; critical, crucial; indispensable, necessary, needful
  2 *syn* see ELEMENTAL 1

undermanned *adj* *syn* see SHORTHANDED
  ant overmanned

undermine *vb* 1 *syn* see WEAKEN 1
  rel ruin, wreck; foil, frustrate, thwart
  idiom bore from within
  ant reinforce
  2 *syn* see SABOTAGE

undermining *n syn* see SABOTAGE

undermost *adj syn* see BOTTOMMOST
  ant uppermost

underneath *prep syn* see BELOW 1

underneath *adv syn* see BELOW 1

‖**underneath** *adj syn* see SECRET 1

underneath *n syn* see BOTTOM 1

underpinner *n syn* see SUPPORT 3

underpinning *n* 1 *syn* see BASIS 1
  2 *syn* see BASE 1
  3 *syn* see SUPPORT 3

underprivileged *adj* deficient in basic economic and social resources < the role of the school in bettering the lot of *underprivileged* children >
  syn depressed, deprived, disadvantaged
  rel handicapped; hapless, ill-fated, ill-starred, unfortunate, unlucky; impoverished, needy, poor
  idiom badly off, in adverse circumstances, out of luck
  con advantaged, fortunate, privileged; coddled, indulged, spoiled

underprize *vb syn* see DEPRECIATE 1
  ant overprize

underprop *vb syn* see SUPPORT 5

underpropping *n syn* see SUPPORT 3

underrate *vb syn* see DEPRECIATE 1
  ant overrate

underscore *vb syn* see EMPHASIZE

undersense *n syn* see SUBCONSCIOUS

undersexed *adj syn* see FRIGID 3
  ant oversexed

underside *n syn* see BOTTOM 1

understaffed *adj syn* see SHORTHANDED
  ant overstaffed

understand *vb* 1 *syn* see APPREHEND 1
  idiom get the drift
  ant misunderstand
  2 *syn* see KNOW 1
  idiom get the hang of

---

syn synonym(s)   *rel* related word(s)
ant antonym(s)   *con* contrasted word(s)
idiom idiomatic equivalent(s)
‖ use limited; if in doubt, see a dictionary

3 to view as plausible or likely < I *understand* he is expected home soon >
syn ASSUME, believe, ||conceit, conceive, expect, gather, imagine, ||reckon, suppose, suspect, take, think, ||wit; *compare* CONJECTURE
  rel conclude, deduce, infer; conjecture, guess, presume, surmise; fancy; consider
  con know; challenge, doubt, question
understandable *adj* of a kind to be readily understood < her style was smooth and easy, her language *understandable* >
syn apprehensible, comprehendible, comprehensible, fathomable, graspable, intelligible, knowable, lucid, luminous; *compare* CLEAR 4, 5
  rel clear-cut, unambiguous, unblurred; plain, simple, straightforward; exoteric, lay, popular
  con mysterious, obscure, strange, vague; cryptic, esoteric, hidden
understanding *n* **1** *syn* see REASON 5
  rel discernment, discrimination, insight, penetration; awareness, intuition; apprehension, comprehension, grasp
2 *syn* see AGREEMENT 2
3 *syn* see MEANING 1
understood *adj syn* see TACIT 1
understrapper *n syn* see INFERIOR
understructure *n syn* see BASE 1
  ant superstructure
undersurface *n syn* see BOTTOM 1
undertake *vb* **1** *syn* see TRY 5
  rel begin, commence, start
  idiom put (*or* set) one's hand to
2 *syn* see TAKE ON 3
3 *syn* see PROMISE 1
  rel certify, warrant
  idiom stand back of (*or* behind)
undertaker *n* **1** *syn* see ENTREPRENEUR 1
2 *syn* see MORTICIAN
undertaking *n* **1** *syn* see ATTEMPT
2 *syn* see PROJECT 2
under-the-table *adj syn* see SECRET 1
  ant aboveboard
undertone *n* **1** *syn* see MURMUR 1
2 *syn* see ASSOCIATION 4
undervalue *vb syn* see DEPRECIATE 1
  ant overvalue
underwater *adj syn* see SUBMARINE
underwit *n syn* see FOOL 4
underworld *n syn* see HELL
undescribable *adj syn* see UNUTTERABLE
  ant describable
undesignated *adj syn* see ANONYMOUS
undesigned *adj syn* see UNINTENTIONAL
  ant designed
undesigning *adj syn* see GENUINE 3
  ant designing
undesirable *adj syn* see OBJECTIONABLE
  ant desirable
undesired *adj syn* see UNWELCOME 1
  ant desired
undestroyable *adj syn* see INDESTRUCTIBLE
  ant destroyable, destructible
undeterminable *adj syn* see INDEFINITE 1
  ant determinable
undetermined *adj* **1** *syn* see PENDING
  ant determined

2 *syn* see FAINT 2
undeveloped *adj* **1** *syn* see BACKWARD 6
  ant developed
2 *syn* see PRIMITIVE 3
  ant advanced
undeviatingly *adv syn* see DIRECTLY 1
undevised *adj syn* see UNINTENTIONAL
  ant devised
undexterous *adj syn* see UNSKILLFUL 1
  ant dexterous
undifferenced *adj syn* see LIKE
undifferentiated *adj syn* see LIKE
  ant differentiated
undiluted *adj* **1** *syn* see STRAIGHT 3
  ant diluted
2 *syn* see PURE 2
undiplomatic *adj syn* see TACTLESS
  ant diplomatic
undiscernible *adj syn* see IMPERCEPTIBLE
  ant discernible
undisciplinable *adj syn* see UNRULY 1
undisciplined *adj syn* see UNRULY 1
  ant disciplined
undiscriminated *adj syn* see INDISCRIMINATE 1
  ant discriminate, discriminated
undiscriminating *adj syn* see INDISCRIMINATE 1
undisguised *adj syn* see FRANK
undisputable *adj syn* see POSITIVE 3
  ant controvertible, disputable
undissembled *adj* **1** *syn* see GENUINE 3
  ant dissembled, feigned
2 *syn* see FRANK
undissembling *adj syn* see FRANK
  ant dissembling
undistinct *adj syn* see FAINT 2
  ant clear, distinct
undistinctive *adj syn* see FAIR 4
undistinguishing *adj syn* see INDISCRIMINATE 1
undistorted *adj syn* see TRUE 3
  ant distorted
undistracted *adj syn* see WHOLE 5
undivided *adj syn* see WHOLE 5
  ant divided
undo *vb* **1** *syn* see LOOSE 3
2 *syn* see OPEN 1
  rel loose, untie
3 *syn* see ABOLISH 1
4 *syn* see DESTROY 1
5 *syn* see OUTWIT
  idiom bring down (*or* low), bring to naught
6 *syn* see SEDUCE 2
undocked *adj syn* see UNABRIDGED
  ant docked
undoing *n syn* see DOWNFALL 2
undomesticated *adj syn* see WILD 1
  ant domesticated
undoubtable *adj syn* see POSITIVE 3
  ant doubtable, questionable
undoubted *adj syn* see AUTHENTIC 2
  ant doubtful, questionable
undoubtedly *adv syn* see WELL 7
undoubtful *adj syn* see CONFIDENT 1
  ant doubtful
undress *vb* **1** *syn* see STRIP 1
  ant dress
2 *syn* see EXPOSE 4
  ant dress up
undressed *adj* **1** *syn* see NUDE 2

ant dressed
2 *syn* see RUDE 1
ant dressed, finished
undubitable *adj syn* see AUTHENTIC 2
ant dubitable
undue *adj* 1 *syn* see IMPROPER 1
2 *syn* see EXCESSIVE 1
3 *syn* see UNREASONABLE 2
undulate *vb syn* see SLITHER 2
unduly *adv syn* see EVER 6
ant duly
unduteous *adj syn* see IMPIOUS 2
ant duteous
undutiful *adj syn* see IMPIOUS 2
ant dutiful
undying *adj syn* see IMMORTAL 1
rel continuing, persistent; interminable, unceasing; inextinguishable, unquenchable
ant mortal
uneager *adj syn* see DISINCLINED
ant eager
unearth *vb syn* see DISCOVER 3
rel exhibit, expose, show; disclose, reveal; delve, dig
unearthing *n syn* see DISCOVERY
unearthly *adj* 1 *syn* see SUPERNATURAL 1
2 *syn* see WEIRD 1
3 *syn* see FOOLISH 2
unease *n* 1 *syn* see CARE 2
2 *syn* see TENSION 2
3 *syn* see EMBARRASSMENT
ant ease, easiness
uneasiness *n* 1 *syn* see CARE 2
2 *syn* see EMBARRASSMENT
ant ease, easiness
uneasy *adj* 1 *syn* see TENSE 2
rel anxious, careful, concerned, solicitous, worried; agitated, disquieted, disturbed, perturbed
idiom on pins and needles
ant easy
2 *syn* see RESTLESS
3 *syn* see DOUBTFUL 1
uneatable *adj syn* see INEDIBLE
ant eatable
uneducated *adj syn* see IGNORANT 1
ant educated, lettered
unelaborate *adj syn* see PLAIN 1
ant elaborate
unembellished *adj syn* see PLAIN 1
ant embellished
unembodied *adj syn* see IMMATERIAL 1
unembroidered *adj syn* see PLAIN 1
unemotional *adj* 1 *syn* see COLD 2
rel dispassionate; unfeeling; impassive
con affective, feeling; affectionate, demonstrative
ant emotional
2 *syn* see UNFEELING 2
unemphatic *adj syn* see INCONSPICUOUS
unemployed *adj* lacking a gainful occupation <the problems of *unemployed* workers>
syn jobless, workless
rel free, unengaged, unoccupied; underemployed; fired, laid off
idiom at liberty, let go, on layoff, out of work

ant employed
unending *adj* 1 *syn* see EVERLASTING 1
2 *syn* see CONTINUAL
unendurable *adj syn* see INSUFFERABLE
ant endurable
unenlarged *adj syn* see ILLIBERAL
unenlightened *adj syn* see BACKWARD 5
ant enlightened
unennobled *adj syn* see IGNOBLE 1
ant ennobled, noble
unentangle *vb syn* see EXTRICATE 2
ant entangle
unenthusiastic *adj syn* see TEPID 2
ant enthusiastic
unequal *adj* 1 *syn* see DIFFERENT 1
2 *syn* see LOPSIDED
unequalable *adj syn* see SUPREME
unequaled *adj syn* see ALONE 3
ant equaled
unequipped *adj syn* see UNFIT 2
unequitable *adj syn* see INEQUITABLE
ant equitable
unequivocal *adj* 1 *syn* see CLEAR 5
ant equivocal
2 *syn* see POSITIVE 1
ant equivocal
3 *syn* see POSITIVE 3
unequivocally *adv syn* see EASILY 2
uneradicable *adj syn* see INDELIBLE
ant eradicable
unerasable *adj syn* see INDELIBLE
ant erasable
unerring *adj syn* see INFALLIBLE 1
unescapable *adj syn* see INEVITABLE
ant escapable
unessential *adj* 1 *syn* see UNNECESSARY
ant essential
2 *syn* see DISPENSABLE
ant essential
unethical *adj syn* see CORRUPT 2
ant ethical
unevadable *adj syn* see INEVITABLE
ant evadable
uneven *adj* 1 *syn* see ROUGH 1
ant even
2 *syn* see LOPSIDED
ant even
3 *syn* see SPOTTY 1
rel differing, disparate, unequal; discrepant, inconsistent
con consistent, equal, regular
unevenness *n* 1 *syn* see DISPARITY
2 *syn* see INEQUALITY 1
uneventful *adj syn* see COMMON 6
ant eventful
unevolved *adj syn* see PRIMITIVE 3
ant advanced, evolved
unexaminable *adj syn* see MYSTERIOUS
unexampled *adj syn* see ONLY 2
unexceptionable *adj syn* see DECENT 4
ant exceptionable
unexceptional *adj* 1 *syn* see DECENT 4
2 *syn* see COMMON 6
ant exceptional
unexcessive *adj syn* see CONSERVATIVE 2
ant excessive
unexpansive *adj syn* see UNDEMONSTRATIVE
ant expansive
unexpectedly *adv syn* see UNAWARES
unexpedient *adj syn* see INADVISABLE
ant expedient
unexperienced *adj syn* see INEXPERIENCED

---

syn synonym(s)   *rel* related word(s)
ant antonym(s)   *con* contrasted word(s)
idiom idiomatic equivalent(s)
‖ use limited; if in doubt, see a dictionary

ant experienced

unexpert *adj syn* see INEFFICIENT 2
ant expert

unexplainable *adj syn* see INEXPLICABLE
ant explainable, explicable

unexplicit *adj syn* see OBSCURE 3
ant explicit

unexpressed *adj* 1 *syn* see UNSPOKEN 1
ant expressed
2 *syn* see TACIT 1
ant expressed

unexpressible *adj syn* see UNUTTERABLE
ant expressible

unexpressive *adj syn* see EXPRESSION-
LESS
ant expressive

unextreme *adj syn* see CONSERVATIVE 2

unfabled *adj syn* see REAL 3
ant fabled

unfacile *adj syn* see UNSKILLFUL 1

unfailing *adj* 1 *syn* see SAME 3
2 *syn* see INFALLIBLE 2
ant fallible

unfair *adj syn* see INEQUITABLE
ant fair

unfairness *n syn* see INJUSTICE 1
ant fairness

unfaith *n syn* see UNBELIEF
ant faith

unfaithful *adj syn* see FAITHLESS
ant faithful

unfaithfulness *n syn* see INFIDELITY
ant faithfulness

unfaltering *adj syn* see SURE 2

unfamed *adj syn* see OBSCURE 5
ant famed

unfamiliar *adj* 1 not well known <trying
to find her way about the *unfamiliar*
room in the dark>
syn new, strange, unaccustomed
rel exotic, foreign; curious, peculiar, remarkable; unknown
con accustomed, commonplace, customary, ordinary, usual, wonted
ant familiar
2 *syn* see IGNORANT 2
ant familiar

unfamiliarity *n syn* see IGNORANCE 2

unfantastic *adj syn* see REALISTIC
ant fantastic

unfashioned *adj syn* see RUDE 1

unfasten *vb syn* see LOOSE 3
ant fasten

unfastidious *adj syn* see SLOVENLY 1
ant fastidious

unfathered *adj syn* see ILLEGITIMATE 1

unfathomable *adj* 1 *syn* see BOTTOMLESS
2
ant fathomable
2 *syn* see INCOMPREHENSIBLE 1
ant fathomable

unfathomed *adj syn* see HUGE

unfavorable *adj* 1 *syn* see ADVERSE 2
ant favorable
2 *syn* see EVIL 5

unfavorably *adv syn* see AMISS 2

unfearful *adj syn* see BRAVE 1
ant fearful

unfearing *adj syn* see BRAVE 1
ant fearing

unfeasible *adj syn* see IMPOSSIBLE 1
ant feasible, practicable

unfeeling *adj* 1 *syn* see INSENSATE 1

ant feeling
2 lacking in normal human sympathy
<an *unfeeling* response to a plea for
help>
syn callous, cold-blooded, coldhearted,
compassionless, hard-boiled, hardened,
hardhearted, heartless, ironhearted, marblehearted, obdurate, stony, stonyhearted,
uncompassionate, unemotional, unsympathetic; *compare* PITILESS
rel brutal, cruel, indurated, merciless,
roughhearted, ruthless, tough; exacting,
severe; unamiable, uncordial, unkind;
cantankerous, churlish, crotchety, curmud-
geonly, surly
idiom hard of heart
con considerate, gentle, thoughtful; kind,
merciful; compassionate, sympathetic,
warmhearted
ant feeling
3 *syn* see NUMB 1

unfeigned *adj* 1 *syn* see SINCERE 1
ant feigned
2 *syn* see GENUINE 3
ant dissembled, feigned

unfertile *adj syn* see BARREN 2
ant fertile

unfinished *adj* 1 *syn* see RUDE 1
ant dressed, finished
2 *syn* see AMATEURISH
ant finished

unfit *adj* 1 not adapted or appropriate to a
particular end <land *unfit* for farming>
syn ill-adapted, ill-suited, inappropriate,
inapt, unfitted, unmeet, unsuitable, unsuited
rel discordant, inharmonious; improper,
infelicitous, unbecoming; incompatible,
incongruous, uncongenial
idiom out of drawing, out of one's element, out of place
con adapted, appropriate, apt, suitable,
suited; congruous, harmonious
ant fit
2 lacking essential qualifications <politi-
cians *unfit* to govern>
syn disqualified, incapable, incompetent,
ineligible, unequipped, unfitted, unqualified
rel awkward, blundering, bungling; butterfingered, heavyhanded, maladjusted,
maladroit, unhandy; inefficient, inexpert,
unproficient, unskillful
con capable, competent, qualified; adroit,
dexterous, handy; expert, skilled

unfitted *adj* 1 *syn* see UNFIT 1
2 *syn* see UNFIT 2
ant fitted

unfitting *adj syn* see IMPROPER 1
ant fitting

unfix *vb* 1 *syn* see LOOSE 3
ant fix
2 *syn* see DETACH

unfixedness *n syn* see INSTABILITY

unflagging *adj syn* see INDEFATIGABLE
rel constant, steady
ant flagging

unflappable *adj syn* see COOL 2
rel easy, relaxed

unflawed *adj syn* see PERFECT 2
ant flawed

unfledged *adj syn* see YOUNG 1
ant fledged

unfleshed *adj syn* see INEXPERIENCED

unfleshly *adj syn* see IMMATERIAL 1
  ant fleshly

unflexible *adj syn* see STIFF 1
  ant flexible

unflinching *adj syn* see GRIM 3

unfluctuating *adj syn* see STEADY 2
  ant fluctuant, fluctuating

unfold *vb* **1** *syn* see OPEN 4
  ant fold
  2 *syn* see SOLVE 2
  3 to disclose by degrees to the sight or understanding <shyly she *unfolded* her hopes for the future>
  syn develop, elaborate, evolve
  rel demonstrate, evidence, evince, manifest, show; disclose, display, exhibit, expose, reveal

unfolding *n syn* see DEVELOPMENT

unforbearing *adj syn* see INTOLERANT 1
  ant forbearing

unforced *adj syn* see VOLUNTARY
  ant forced

unforgivable *adj syn* see INEXCUSABLE
  ant forgivable

unformed *adj* **1** *syn* see FORMLESS
  rel unfinished
  ant formed
  2 *syn* see RUDE 1

unfortunate *adj* **1** *syn* see UNLUCKY
  rel infelicitous; deplorable, miserable, sad, wretched; malefic
  con auspicious, favorable, propitious
  ant fortunate
  2 *syn* see INFELICITOUS
  3 *syn* see DEPLORABLE

unfounded *adj syn* see BASELESS
  rel deceptive, misleading; dishonest, mendacious, untruthful
  ant well-founded

unframe *vb syn* see DESTROY 1

unfrank *adj syn* see DISINGENUOUS
  ant frank

unfrequent *adj syn* see INFREQUENT
  ant frequent

unfrequently *adv syn* see SELDOM
  ant frequently

unfriendly *adj syn* see HOSTILE 1
  ant friendly

unfruitful *adj syn* see STERILE 1
  con fecund, fertile
  ant fruitful, prolific

unfunctional *adj syn* see IMPRACTICABLE 2
  ant functional

unfussy *adj syn* see EASYGOING 3
  ant fussy

ungainly *adj syn* see CLUMSY 1
  rel blundering, lubberly, maladroit
  con graceful, supple, willowy; gainly

ungarnished *adj syn* see PLAIN 1
  ant garnished

ungenerous *adj* **1** *syn* see PETTY 2
  ant generous
  2 *syn* see STINGY
  ant generous

ungenial *adj syn* see ANTIPATHETIC 2
  ant genial

---

syn synonym(s)   *rel* related word(s)
ant antonym(s)   *con* contrasted word(s)
idiom idiomatic equivalent(s)
|| use limited; if in doubt, see a dictionary

---

ungenuine *adj syn* see SPURIOUS 3
  ant genuine

ungetatable *adj syn* see INACCESSIBLE
  ant getatable

ungifted *adj syn* see AMATEURISH
  ant gifted

ungiving *adj syn* see STINGY

ungodly *adj* **1** *syn* see IMPIOUS 1
  ant godly
  2 *syn* see INDECOROUS
  3 *syn* see OUTRAGEOUS 1

ungovernable *adj syn* see UNRULY 1
  ant governable

ungoverned *adj syn* see AUDACIOUS 4

ungracious *adj* **1** *syn* see RUDE 6
  ant gracious
  2 *syn* see SHORT 5
  ant gracious

ungraded *adj syn* see UNREFINED 3

ungraspable *adj syn* see INCOMPREHENSIBLE 1
  ant comprehensible, graspable

ungrateful *adj* **1** *syn* see THANKLESS 1
  ant grateful
  2 *syn* see THANKLESS 2
  3 *syn* see OFFENSIVE

ungratified *adj syn* see DISCONTENTED
  ant gratified

ungrounded *adj syn* see BASELESS

unguarded *adj syn* see INCAUTIOUS 1
  ant guarded

unguent *n syn* see OINTMENT

unguessed *adj syn* see MYSTERIOUS

unguilty *adj syn* see INNOCENT 2
  ant guilty

unhallowed *adj* **1** *syn* see IMPIOUS 1
  2 *syn* see FIENDISH

unhampered *adj syn* see AUDACIOUS 4
  ant hampered

unhandsome *adj* **1** *syn* see PLAIN 5
  ant handsome
  2 *syn* see RUDE 6

unhandy *adj* **1** *syn* see UNWIELDY
  2 *syn* see UNSKILLFUL 1
  ant handy
  3 *syn* see AWKWARD 2
  ant handy

unhappiness *n* **1** *syn* see MISERY 1
  ant happiness
  2 *syn* see SADNESS
  ant happiness

unhappy *adj* **1** *syn* see UNLUCKY
  ant happy
  2 *syn* see INFELICITOUS
  ant happy
  3 *syn* see AWKWARD 2
  ant happy
  4 *syn* see SAD 1
  ant happy
  5 *syn* see BAD 8
  6 *syn* see GLOOMY 3

unharmed *adj syn* see SAFE 1

unharmonious *adj* **1** *syn* see DISSONANT 1
  ant harmonious
  2 *syn* see INHARMONIOUS 2
  ant harmonious

unhasty *adj syn* see SLOW 2
  ant hasty

unhealth *n syn* see SICKNESS 1
  ant health

unhealthful *adj syn* see UNWHOLESOME 1
  ant healthful

unhealthiness *n syn* see INFIRMITY 1

ant healthiness

unhealthy *adj* **1** *syn see* UNWHOLESOME 1
ant healthy
2 *syn see* DANGEROUS 1
3 *syn see* VICIOUS 2

unheard–of *adj syn see* OBSCURE 5

unheavy *adj syn see* LIGHT 1
ant heavy

unheeding *adj* **1** *syn see* INATTENTIVE
ant heedful, heeding
2 *syn see* CARELESS 1
ant heedful, heeding

unhewn *adj syn see* RUDE 1

unhinge *vb* **1** *syn see* UPSET 5
2 *syn see* MADDEN 1
3 *syn see* DISCOMPOSE 1

unholy *adj* **1** *syn see* IMPIOUS 1
ant holy
2 *syn see* BLAMEWORTHY
3 *syn see* OUTRAGEOUS 1

unhonest *adj syn see* DISHONEST
ant honest

unhorse *vb* **1** *syn see* THROW 2
2 *syn see* OVERTHROW 2

unhurried *adj syn see* SLOW 2
ant hurried

unhurt *adj syn see* WHOLE 1

unicity *n syn see* UNIQUENESS

unidealistic *adj syn see* REALISTIC
ant idealistic

unification *n* a bringing together or being brought together into an integrated whole < *unification* of mass transit facilities is increasingly needed >
syn coadunation, coalition, combination consolidation, melding, mergence, merger, merging, union; *compare* ALLIANCE 2
rel affiliation, connection, interlocking, joining, linkage; coupling, hookup
con dissociation, disunion, division, parting, partition, separation
ant disunification

uniform *adj* **1** *syn see* LIKE
ant various
2 *syn see* STEADY 2
rel compatible, consistent, consonant; ordered, orderly, regular
ant multiform

uniformly *adv syn see* EVENLY 3
ant variably

unify *vb* **1** to gather or combine parts or elements into a close mass or a coherent whole < minorities that are *unified* by persecution >
syn compact, concentrate, consolidate, integrate; *compare* UNITE 1
rel articulate, concatenate; order, organize, systematize; bind, tie
idiom make one
con divide, part, scatter; disorder, disorganize; disunite, divide, separate
ant break up, disunify
2 *syn see* HARMONIZE 4
ant disunify

unifying *adj syn see* INTEGRATIVE
ant disunifying

unilluminated *adj syn see* DARK 1
ant illuminated

unimaginable *adj* **1** *syn see* INCONCEIVABLE 1
ant imaginable
2 *syn see* EXCEPTIONAL 1

3 *syn see* INCREDIBLE 1

unimpaired *adj syn see* WHOLE 1
ant impaired

unimpassioned *adj* **1** *syn see* MATTER=OF-FACT 3
ant impassioned
2 *syn see* SOBER 3
rel impassive, phlegmatic, stoic, stolid; calm, placid, tranquil
con ardent, fervent, fervid, heated, keen
ant impassioned, passionate

unimpeachable *adj syn see* DECENT 4

unimportant *adj syn see* LITTLE 3
ant important

unimpressible *adj syn see* INSUSCEPTIBLE
ant impressible

unimpressionable *adj syn see* INSUSCEPTIBLE
ant impressionable

unindifferent *adj syn see* BIASED 2
ant indifferent

unindulgent *adj syn see* INTOLERANT 1
ant indulgent

uninflammable *adj syn see* NONCOMBUSTIBLE
ant flammable, inflammable

uninformed *adj syn see* IGNORANT 2
ant informed

uninhibited *adj syn see* AUDACIOUS 4
ant inhibited

uninhibitedness *n syn see* ABANDON 2

uninitiate *n syn see* AMATEUR 2

uninjured *adj syn see* WHOLE 1
ant injured

uninjurious *adj syn see* SAFE 3

uninspired *adj* **1** *syn see* UNORIGINAL
ant inspired
2 *syn see* PONDEROUS 2
ant inspired

uninstructed *adj* **1** *syn see* IGNORANT 2
2 *syn see* IGNORANT 1

unintelligent *adj syn see* SIMPLE 3
ant intelligent

unintelligible *adj* **1** *syn see* INCOMPREHENSIBLE 1
ant intelligible
2 *syn see* OBSCURE 3
ant intelligible

unintended *adj syn see* UNINTENTIONAL
ant intended

unintentional *adj* not the result of intent or design < her slight of the newcomer was quite *unintentional* >
syn inadvertent, undesigned, undevised, unintended, unplanned, unpremeditated, unpurposed, unthought; *compare* ACCIDENTAL, EXTEMPORANEOUS
rel causeless, chance, haphazard, purposeless, random; unanticipated, unexpected, unforeseen, unlooked-for; unthinking, unwitting
con deliberate, designed, devised, intended, planned, premeditated, purposed
ant intentional

uninterested *adj syn see* INDIFFERENT 2
ant interested

uninteresting *adj syn see* ARID 2
ant interesting

unintermitted *adj syn see* CONTINUAL
ant intermitted, intermittent

unintermittedly *adv syn see* TOGETHER 2

unintermittent *adj syn see* CONTINUAL
ant intermitted, intermittent

uninterrupted *adj* 1 *syn* see CONTINUAL
ant interrupted
2 *syn* see DIRECT 2
uninterruptedly *adv* *syn* see TOGETHER
2
ant interruptedly
uninventive *adj* *syn* see UNORIGINAL
ant inventive
uninvited *adj* *syn* see UNASKED
ant invited
union *n* 1 *syn* see UNIFICATION
ant disunion
2 *syn* see ASSOCIATION 2
3 *syn* see JOINT 1
4 *syn* see ALLIANCE 2
unique *adj* 1 *syn* see ONLY 2
2 *syn* see SINGLE 2
3 *syn* see ALONE 3
4 *syn* see EXCEPTIONAL 1
uniqueness *n* the quality or state of standing alone and without a peer < the time
she rode in an old-time sleigh — never
would she forget the *uniqueness* of that
experience >
syn oneness, singleness, unicity, uniquity
rel curiousness, oddity, peculiarity,
quaintness, singularity, strangeness; import, mark, moment, note, significance;
memorability, notability, remarkableness,
unusualness
con commonness, commonplaceness,
ordinariness, routineness; monotony,
sameness, tediousness
uniquity *n* *syn* see UNIQUENESS
unite *vb* 1 *syn* see JOIN 1
rel amalgamate, blend, merge, mix
ant alienate; disunite, divide
2 to join forces especially in order to act
more effectively < citizen groups *uniting*
to further the fight against crime >
syn band, coadjute, combine, concur,
conjoin, cooperate, league; *compare* UNIFY
1
rel affiliate, ally, associate, confederate;
coalesce, commingle, fuse, mingle, weld
idiom draw together, hook up with, join
forces (with), make common cause (with),
throw in with
con break up, disband, separate, split
(up)
ant disunite, part
unity *n* 1 the condition of being or consisting of one < *unity* — the idea conveyed
by whatever we visualize as one thing >
syn individuality, oneness, singleness,
singularity, singularness
rel identity, selfsameness, soleness,
uniqueness, uniquity
ant multiplicity
2 *syn* see HARMONY 3
rel agreement, identity, oneness, union;
solidarity; conformance, congruity
ant disunity
universal *adj* 1 *syn* see OMNIPRESENT
2 present or significant throughout the
world < *universal* aspirations for a better
world >
syn catholic, cosmic, cosmopolitan, ecumenical, global, planetary, worldwide

rel all-embracing, all-inclusive; broad,
extensive, sweeping; all, entire, total,
whole
con narrow, petty, provincial
ant parochial
3 *syn* see GENERAL 2
ant particular
universe *n* the totality of physical entities
< theories of the expanding *universe* >
syn cosmos (*or* kosmos), creation, macrocosm, macrocosmos, megacosm, nature,
world
univocal *adj* *syn* see CLEAR 5
ant ambiguous
unjust *adj* *syn* see INEQUITABLE
ant just
unjustifiable *adj* 1 *syn* see UNREASON-
ABLE 2
ant justifiable
2 *syn* see INEXCUSABLE
ant justifiable
unjustness *n* *syn* see INJUSTICE 1
ant justice, justness
unkempt *adj* *syn* see SLOVENLY 1
ant kempt
unknow *vb* *syn* see FORGET 1
unknowable *adj* 1 *syn* see INCOMPRE-
HENSIBLE 1
ant knowable
2 *syn* see INCONCEIVABLE 1
ant knowable
3 *syn* see MYSTERIOUS
unknowing *adj* *syn* see IGNORANT 2
ant knowing
unknowingness *n* *syn* see IGNORANCE 2
ant knowingness
unknown *adj* *syn* see OBSCURE 5
ant well-known
unlade *vb* *syn* see UNLOAD
ant lade, load
unlawful *adj* contrary to or prohibited by
law < the spread of *unlawful* wiretap-
ping >
syn criminal, illegal, illegitimate, illicit,
lawless, wrongful
rel flagitious, iniquitous, nefarious; black-
market, bootleg, under-the-counter; exceptionable, improper, intolerable, objectionable
idiom against the law
con condign, due, rightful; allowable,
justifiable, permissible
ant lawful
unlawfulness *n* *syn* see ILLEGALITY
ant lawfulness
unlax *vb* 1 *syn* see RELAX 2
2 *syn* see REST 2
unlearned *adj* *syn* see UNSCHOLARLY
ant erudite, learned
unleash *vb* *syn* see TAKE OUT (on)
unless *conj* *syn* see EXCEPT 1
unlettered *adj* *syn* see IGNORANT 1
ant educated, lettered
unlevel *adj* *syn* see ROUGH 1
ant level
unlike *adj* *syn* see DIFFERENT 1
ant like
unlikely *adj* *syn* see IMPROBABLE 1
ant likely
unlikeness *n* *syn* see DISSIMILARITY
rel incompatibility, incongruousness,
inconsistence
ant likeness

syn synonym(s)   *rel* related word(s)
ant antonym(s)   *con* contrasted word(s)
idiom idiomatic equivalent(s)
‖ use limited; if in doubt, see a dictionary

unlimited *adj* 1 *syn* see LIMITLESS
   ant limited, measured
   2 *syn* see TOTAL 5
   ant limited
unload *vb* to remove cargo or the cargo of
   < *unload* cattle from a truck >
   syn disburden, discharge, off-load, unlade,
   unship, unstow
   rel disencumber, dump, jettison, lighten;
   stevedore; debark, disembark, land
   idiom break bulk
   ant lade, load
unloose *vb syn* see LOOSE 3
unloosen *vb syn* see LOOSE 3
unloyal *adj syn* see FAITHLESS
   ant loyal
‖**unluck** *n syn* see MISFORTUNE
   ant luck
unlucky *adj* 1 *syn* see OMINOUS
   2 involving or suffering misfortune that
   results from chance < in spite of careful
   planning the expedition was *unlucky* from
   the start >
   syn hapless, ill-fated, ill-starred, luckless,
   misfortunate, star-crossed, unfortunate,
   unhappy, untoward
   rel calamitous, cataclysmic, catastrophic,
   dire, disastrous, tragical
   idiom down on one's luck, out of luck
   con fortunate, happy, providential; prosperous, successful; coming, made
   ant lucky
unmake *vb* 1 *syn* see DESTROY 1
   2 *syn* see DEPOSE 1
   ant make
unman *vb syn* see UNNERVE
   rel deplete, drain, exhaust, impoverish;
   abase, degrade; disqualify, paralyze, prostrate, unfit
   idiom knock the bottom (*or* stuffing) out
   of
   con brace, fortify
   ant man
unmanageable *adj syn* see UNRULY 1
   ant manageable
unmanly *adj* 1 *syn* see COWARDLY
   ant manly
   2 *syn* see EFFEMINATE
   ant manly
unmannered *adj* 1 *syn* see RUDE 6
   2 *syn* see FRANK
unmannerly *adj syn* see RUDE 6
   ant mannerly
unmarred *adj syn* see WHOLE 1
   ant marred
unmarried *adj syn* see SINGLE 1
   ant married, wed
unmarry *vb syn* see DIVORCE 2
unmask *vb syn* see EXPOSE 4
unmatchable *adj syn* see SUPREME
unmatched *adj* 1 *syn* see ALONE 3
   2 *syn* see ODD 1
   ant matched
unmaterial *adj syn* see IMMATERIAL 1
   ant material
unmeaning *adj syn* see SENSELESS 5
   ant meaningful
unmeasurable *adj* 1 *syn* see INCALCULA-
   BLE 1
   ant measurable
   2 *syn* see EXCESSIVE 1
unmeasured *adj* 1 *syn* see INCALCULA-
   BLE 1

   ant measurable
   2 *syn* see LIMITLESS
   ant limited, measured
unmeditated *adj syn* see SPONTANEOUS
   ant meditated
unmeet *adj syn* see UNFIT 1
   ant meet
unmeetness *n syn* see IMPROPRIETY 1
unmellowed *adj syn* see YOUNG 1
   con developed, matured, ripened
   ant mellow, mellowed
unmerciful *adj syn* see PITILESS
   ant merciful
unmindful *adj syn* see FORGETFUL
   con anxious, careful, concerned
   ant mindful; solicitous
unmindfulness *n syn* see APATHY 2
   ant mindfulness
unmistakable *adj syn* see CLEAR 5
   ant mistakable
unmitigated *adj* 1 *syn* see PURE 2
   2 *syn* see UTTER
unmixable *adj syn* see INCONSONANT 1
unmixed *adj* 1 *syn* see STRAIGHT 3
   ant blended, mixed
   2 *syn* see PURE 2
unmodern *adj syn* see OLD-FASHIONED
   ant modern
unmodifiable *adj syn* see INFLEXIBLE 3
   ant modifiable
unmovable *adj* 1 *syn* see IMMOVABLE 1
   ant mobile, movable
   2 *syn* see INFLEXIBLE 3
unmoving *adj syn* see STATIC
   ant mobile
unmusical *adj syn* see DISSONANT 1
   ant musical
unnamed *adj syn* see ANONYMOUS
unnatural *adj* 1 *syn* see IRREGULAR 1
   2 *syn* see SUPERNATURAL 2
   ant natural
unneat *adj syn* see SLOVENLY 1
   ant neat
unnecessary *adj* not needed or unavoidable < *unnecessary* loss of life >
   syn inessential, needless, uncalled-for,
   unessential, unneeded, unneedful, unrequired
   rel excess, redundant, superfluous, surplus; lavish, prodigal, profuse; gratuitous,
   supererogatory
   con essential, needed, required, vital;
   inevitable, unescapable
   ant necessary; unavoidable
unneeded *adj syn* see UNNECESSARY
   ant needed; unavoidable
unneedful *adj syn* see UNNECESSARY
   ant needful; unavoidable
unnerve *vb* to deprive of strength, spirit,
   and vigor < a man so *unnerved* as to be
   bereft of sense and judgment >
   syn castrate, emasculate, enervate, unman, unstring
   rel enfeeble, sap, undermine, weaken;
   bewilder, confound, distract; agitate, perturb, upset
   con brace (up), inspirit, invigorate, reinforce, strengthen; encourage, hearten, steel
   ant nerve
unneutral *adj syn* see BIASED 2
   ant neutral
unnoted *adj syn* see OBSCURE 5
   rel unconsidered, unobserved, unre-
   marked

ant noted

unnoteworthy *adj syn* see COMMON 6
ant noteworthy

unnoticeable *adj syn* see INCONSPICUOUS
ant noticeable

unnoticing *adj syn* see INATTENTIVE
ant noticing

unnumberable *adj syn* see INNUMERA-
BLE

unnumbered *adj syn* see INNUMERABLE
ant numbered

unobjectionable *adj syn* see DECENT 4
ant objectionable

unobjective *adj syn* see SUBJECTIVE
ant objective

unobservable *adj syn* see IMPERCEPTIBLE

unobservant *adj syn* see INATTENTIVE
ant observant, observing

unobserving *adj syn* see INATTENTIVE
ant observant, observing

unobstructed *adj syn* see OPEN 1
con clogged, plugged
ant obstructed

unobtainable *adj syn* see INACCESSIBLE

unobtrusive *adj syn* see QUIET 4
ant obtrusive

unoffending *adj syn* see HARMLESS
ant offending

unoffensive *adj syn* see HARMLESS
ant offensive

unofficial *adj syn* see INFORMAL 1

unoften *adv syn* see SELDOM
ant often

unordinary *adj syn* see EXCEPTIONAL 1
ant ordinary

unorganized *adj syn* see INCOHERENT 2
ant organized

unoriginal *adj* lacking or manifesting a
lack of capacity for originality < a good
man but with a mind stolid and *unoriginal* >
syn noncreative, sterile, uncreative, uninspired, uninventive, unoriginative; *compare*
ARID 2
rel arid, barren, dry; dull, prosaic, staid,
stodgy, stuffy, unfired
con creative, inspired, inventive, originative; alert, aware, keen; constructive, productive
ant original

unoriginated *adj syn* see SELF-EXISTENT

unoriginative *adj syn* see UNORIGINAL
ant originative

unornamented *adj syn* see PLAIN 1

unorthodox *adj syn* see HERETICAL
ant orthodox

unorthodoxy *n syn* see HERESY
ant orthodoxy

unostentatious *adj syn* see PLAIN 1
ant ostentatious

unpaid *adj* 1 serving without pay < a charity manned by *unpaid* assistants >
syn uncompensated, unrecompensed,
unremunerated
rel freewill, gratuitous, voluntary, volun-
teer
con compensated, recompensed, remunerated

ant paid

2 not cleared by payment < an *unpaid*
bill >
syn due, mature, outstanding, overdue,
owing, payable, unsettled
idiom in arrears
con cleared, discharged, liquidated, settled
ant paid

unpaired *adj syn* see ODD 1
ant paired

unpalatable *adj* 1 lacking appeal to the
sense of taste < threw together a greasy
unpalatable meal >
syn distasteful, flat, flavorless, ill-flavored,
insipid, savorless, tasteless, unappetizing,
unsavory
rel loathsome, nauseous, sickening; thin,
washy, watery, weak
con appetizing, delectable, delicious, flavorsome, sapid, savory, tasty
ant palatable

2 *syn* see BITTER 2

unparagoned *adj syn* see ALONE 3
ant paragoned

unparalleled *adj syn* see ALONE 3
ant paralleled

unpardonable *adj syn* see INEXCUSABLE
ant pardonable

unparented *adj syn* see ORPHAN

unpassioned *adj syn* see NEUTRAL
ant impassioned, passionate

unpatient *adj syn* see IMPATIENT 1
ant patient

unpeace *n syn* see DISCORD
ant peace

unpeaceful *adj syn* see RESTLESS
ant peaceful

unpedantic *adj syn* see LIVELY 1
ant pedantic

unperceivable *adj syn* see IMPERCEPTI-
BLE

unperceiving *adj* 1 *syn* see IMPERCEP-
TIVE
ant perceiving, perceptive, percipient
2 *syn* see INATTENTIVE

unperceptive *adj syn* see IMPERCEPTIVE
ant perceiving, perceptive, percipient

unperishable *adj syn* see INDESTRUCTI-
BLE
ant perishable

unpermissive *adj syn* see RIGID 3
ant permissive

unphysical *adj syn* see IMMATERIAL 1
ant physical

unpierceable *adj syn* see IMPASSABLE 1
ant pierceable

unpitying *adj syn* see PITILESS
ant pitying

unplanned *adj* 1 *syn* see RANDOM
ant planned
2 *syn* see UNINTENTIONAL
ant planned

unpleasant *adj syn* see BAD 8

unpliable *adj syn* see OBSTINATE
ant pliable, pliant

unpliant *adj syn* see OBSTINATE
ant pliable, pliant

unpolished *adj* 1 *syn* see RUDE 1
idiom in the rough
ant polished
2 *syn* see RUDE 6
3 *syn* see BOORISH

---

syn synonym(s)   *rel* related word(s)
ant antonym(s)   *con* contrasted word(s)
idiom idiomatic equivalent(s)
‖ use limited; if in doubt, see a dictionary

ant polished
unpolitic *adj syn see* TACTLESS
   ant politic
unpractical *adj syn see* IMPRACTICAL 1
   ant practical
unpracticed *adj* 1 *syn see* UNTRIED 1
   2 *syn see* INEXPERIENCED
   ant practiced
unpredictable *adj syn see* UNCERTAIN 1
   ant predictable
unprejudiced *adj syn see* FAIR 4
   ant prejudiced
unpremeditated *adj* 1 *syn see* SPONTANE-
   OUS
   2 *syn see* UNINTENTIONAL
   ant premeditated
unprepossessed *adj syn see* FAIR 4
   ant prepossessed
unprescribed *adj syn see* VOLUNTARY
   ant prescribed
unpretentious *adj syn see* PLAIN 1
   ant pretentious
unpretty *adj syn see* PLAIN 5
   ant pretty
unprevailing *adj syn see* FUTILE
unprincipled *adj* 1 *syn see* UNSCRUPU-
   LOUS
   ant principled
   2 *syn see* ABANDONED 2
   rel corrupt, crooked, unscrupulous; dishonest, unconscientious, unethical
   3 *syn see* CORRUPT 2
   ant principled
unproductive *adj* 1 *syn see* BARREN 2
   rel impotent, infecund, unprolific
   ant productive
   2 *syn see* FUTILE
   ant productive
unprofane *adj syn see* HOLY 1
   ant profane
unproficient *adj syn see* UNSKILLFUL 1
   ant proficient, skilled
unprogressive *adj* 1 *syn see* BACKWARD
   6
   ant progressive
   2 *syn see* BACKWARD 5
   ant progressive
unprompted *adj syn see* SPONTANEOUS
unpropitious *adj syn see* OMINOUS
   rel adverse, antagonistic, counter
   con cheering, encouraging, reassuring
   ant propitious
unproportionate *adj syn see* LOPSIDED
   ant proportionate
unprosperous *adj syn see* POOR 1
   ant prosperous
unprosperousness *n syn see* POVERTY 1
   ant prosperousness
unprotected *adj syn see* HELPLESS 1
   rel undefended, unguarded, unsheltered,
   unshielded; insecure, unsafe
   ant protected
unproved *adj syn see* UNTRIED 1
   ant proved
unpunctual *adj syn see* TARDY
   ant punctual
unpurposed *adj* 1 *syn see* UNINTEN-
   TIONAL
   2 *syn see* FECKLESS 1
unqualified *adj syn see* UNFIT 2
   rel unskilled; unsuitable
   ant qualified
   2 *syn see* SURE 2

rel unconditional, unlimited, unreserved;
clear, explicit, express; entire, perfect,
utter
   ant qualified
   3 *syn see* UTTER
   4 *syn see* PURE 2
unquenchable *adj syn see* INSATIABLE
   ant quenchable
unquestionable *adj* 1 *syn see* AUTHENTIC
   2
   ant doubtable, questionable
   2 *syn see* POSITIVE 3
   rel dependable, reliable; established, well=
   founded, well-grounded
   ant doubtable, questionable
   3 *syn see* DOWNRIGHT 2
unquestionably *adv syn see* EASILY 2
   ant questionably
unquestioning *adj syn see* SURE 2
   ant questioning
unquiet *adj syn see* RESTLESS
   ant quiet
unravel *vb syn see* SOLVE 2
   rel disentangle, extricate, untangle
unreachable *adj syn see* INACCESSIBLE
   ant reachable
unreadable *adj syn see* ILLEGIBLE
   ant legible, readable
unreal *adj syn see* FICTITIOUS 1
   ant real
unrealistic *adj syn see* IMPRACTICAL 1
   ant realistic
unrealizable *adj syn see* IMPOSSIBLE 1
   ant realizable
unreasonable *adj* 1 *syn see* ILLOGICAL
   rel incongruous, loose, self-contradictory
   ant reasonable
   2 exceeding the bounds of reason or right
   < the constitutional guarantees against
   unreasonable searches and seizures >
   syn unconscionable, undue, unjustifiable,
   unwarrantable, unwarranted
   rel arbitrary, peremptory; excessive, immoderate, inordinate, overmuch; improper,
   unlawful, unrightful, wrongful
   con lawful, licit; proper, right, tolerable
   ant reasonable
unreasoned *adj syn see* ILLOGICAL
   ant reasoned
unrecking *adj syn see* CARELESS 1
unreckonable *adj syn see* INCALCULA-
   BLE 1
unrecompensed *adj syn see* UNPAID 1
   ant recompensed
unrecoverable *adj syn see* HOPELESS 2
unrefined *adj* 1 *syn see* BOORISH
   ant refined
   2 *syn see* COARSE 3
   ant refined
   3 not freed from unwanted material
   < shipped the *unrefined* ore >
   syn crude, impure, native, raw, run-of=
   mine, ungraded, unsorted
   rel rough, roughcast, roughhewn; coarse,
   natural, undressed, unprocessed
   idiom in the rough
   con dressed, processed
   ant refined
unreflective *adj syn see* CARELESS 1
unregretful *adj syn see* REMORSELESS
   ant regretful
unregular *adj syn see* IRREGULAR 1
   ant regular

unrehearsed adj syn see EXTEMPORANE-
OUS
 ant rehearsed
unrelenting adj syn see GRIM 3
 ant relenting
unreliable adj 1 not to be counted on < it
is certain that much of the testimony was
unreliable >
 syn dubious, fly-by-night, questionable,
 trustless, undependable, unsure, untrustworthy, untrusty
 rel fickle, inconstant, unstable, vacillating;
 faithless, false, untrue; falsehearted, perfidious; shifty, slick, slippery, tricky; inaccurate, inexact, unfaithful
 idiom not to be depended (*or* relied) on
 con dependable, trustworthy, trusty; constant; faithful, true
 ant reliable
 2 *syn* see UNSAFE
 ant reliable
unreligious adj syn see IRRELIGIOUS
 ant religious
unremarkable adj syn see ORDINARY 1
unremitting adj syn see CONTINUAL
unremittingly adv syn see HARD 3
unremorseful adj syn see REMORSELESS
 ant remorseful
unremunerated adj syn see UNPAID 1
 ant remunerated
unrenowned adj syn see OBSCURE 5
 ant renowned
unrepealable adj syn see IRREVOCABLE
 ant repealable
unrepeatable adj syn see ONLY 2
unrepentant adj syn see REMORSELESS
 ant repentant
unrepresentative adj syn see ABNORMAL
1
unrequested adj syn see UNASKED
unrequired adj 1 syn see UNNECESSARY
 ant required
 2 *syn* see DISPENSABLE
 ant required
unreserved adj 1 syn see FRANK 1
 ant reserved
 2 *syn* see DEMONSTRATIVE
 ant reserved
 3 *syn* see EASYGOING 3
unresistant adj syn see PASSIVE 2
 ant resistant, resisting
unresisting adj syn see PASSIVE 2
 ant resistant, resisting
unresolved adj syn see VACILLATING 2
 ant resolved
unrespectable adj syn see DISREPUTABLE
1
 ant respectable
unresponsive adj 1 syn see INSUSCEPTI-
BLE
 ant responsive
 2 *syn* see FRIGID 3
unresponsiveness n syn see APATHY 1
 ant responsiveness
unrest n a disturbed uneasy state < that
popular *unrest* that, unchecked, can lead
to insurrection and anarchy >
 syn ailment, disquiet, disquietude, ferment, inquietude, restiveness, restlessness,

storm and stress, Sturm und Drang, turmoil
 rel agitation, commotion, confusion, convulsion, tumult, turbulence, upheaval;
anarchy, chaos, disorder
 con calm, easiness, peace, quiet
unrestful adj 1 syn see RESTLESS
 ant restful
 2 *syn* see NERVOUS
unrestrainable adj syn see IRREPRESS-
IBLE
 ant restrainable
unrestrained adj 1 syn see EXCESSIVE 2
 2 *syn* see FREE 2
 ant restrained
 3 *syn* see AUDACIOUS 4
 rel candid, frank, open; forthright, plainspoken, straightforward; bluff, blunt,
brusque
 ant restrained
 4 *syn* see DEMONSTRATIVE
 ant restrained
unrestraint n 1 syn see UNCONSTRAINT
 ant restraint
 2 *syn* see ABANDON 2
unrestricted adj syn see OPEN 4
unriddle vb syn see SOLVE 2
unrighteous adj syn see INEQUITABLE
 ant righteous
unripe adj syn see YOUNG 1
unrivaled adj syn see ALONE 3
unromantic adj syn see REALISTIC
 ant romantic
unruffled adj syn see COOL 2
 ant discomposed, ruffled
unruly adj 1 resistant to discipline or control < a stubborn *unruly* boy >
 syn fractious, indocile, indomitable, intractable, recalcitrant, uncontrollable,
undisciplinable, undisciplined, ungovernable, unmanageable, untoward, wild; *compare* OBSTINATE, TURBULENT 1
 rel contumacious, incorrigible, insubordinate, rebellious; contrary, froward, perverse, wayward; boisterous, obstreperous,
rampageous; disorderly, raffish, rambunctious, rowdy, turbulent
 idiom out of hand
 con controlled, easy, mild, restrained;
disciplined, governable, manageable; amenable, biddable, obedient; correct, proper
 ant docile, tractable
 2 *syn* see TURBULENT 1
 rel hard, ruffianly, tough
 3 *syn* see DISOBEDIENT
unsacred adj syn see PROFANE 1
 ant sacred
unsafe adj not to be depended on or
trusted < an *unsafe* investment >
 syn unassured, undependable, unreliable,
untrustworthy
 rel insecure, shaky, tottery, unsound,
unstable; chancy, hazardous, risky; dangerous, jeopardous, perilous; erratic, uncertain
 con dependable, trustworthy; secure,
sound, stable, substantial
 ant safe
unsaid adj syn see TACIT 1
unsalutary adj syn see UNWHOLESOME 1
 ant salutary
unsandaled adj syn see BAREFOOT 1
 ant sandaled

---

syn synonym(s)   *rel* related word(s)
ant antonym(s)   *con* contrasted word(s)
idiom idiomatic equivalent(s)
‖ use limited; if in doubt, see a dictionary

unsane *adj syn* see INSANE 1
ant sane

unsatiate *adj syn* see INSATIABLE
ant satiate, satiated

unsatisfactory *adj syn* see BAD 1
ant satisfactory

unsatisfiable *adj syn* see INSATIABLE
ant satisfiable

unsavory *adj syn* see UNPALATABLE 1
ant savory

unsay *vb syn* see ABJURE

unscathed *adj syn* see SAFE 1

unscholarly *adj* not devoted to scholarly pursuits < *unscholarly* concerns>
syn inerudite, unbookish, unlearned, unstudious
rel unenlightened, uninformed, uninitiated; callow, green, unripe; inexperienced, naive
con bookish, erudite, learned; enlightened, informed; experienced
ant scholarly

unschooled *adj* 1 *syn* see IGNORANT 1
2 *syn* see NATURAL 5

unscramble *vb syn* see EXTRICATE 2

unscrupulous *adj* 1 lacking in moral scruples < *unscrupulous* conduct of political leaders>
syn conscienceless, stick-at-nothing, unconscionable, unprincipled
rel crafty, deceitful, scheming; improper, unseemly, wrongful; corrupt, crooked, dishonest; questionable, shady, sinister, underhand
con conscientious, dutiful, proper, upright; dependable, reliable, responsible
ant scrupulous
2 *syn* see CORRUPT 2
con meticulous, particular, punctilious, strict
ant scrupulous

unseasonable *adj* 1 involving or occurring at an inappropriate or unexpected time < his wife's sudden return proved most *unseasonable* >
syn ill-seasoned, ill-timed, inopportune, malapropos, mistimed, untimely
rel deplorable, inappropriate, inconvenient, unsuitable; inauspicious, infelicitous, undesirable, unfavorable, unfortunate
con apropos, opportune, timely, well-timed
ant seasonable
2 *syn* see IMPROPER 1

unseasoned *adj syn* see INEXPERIENCED
ant seasoned

unseat *vb syn* see THROW 2

unsectarian *adj syn* see NONSECTARIAN
ant sectarian

unseemliness *n syn* see IMPROPRIETY 1
ant propriety, seemliness

unseemly *adj* 1 *syn* see INDECOROUS
rel coarse, crude, inelegant, unrefined; raffish, rowdy, ruffianly
con prim, restrained, starchy, stiff, stilted; elegant, gracious, polished, refined
ant seemly
2 *syn* see IMPROPER 1
ant seemly

unselfish *adj syn* see SELFLESS
ant selfish

unsentimental *adj syn* see REALISTIC
ant sentimental

unserviceable *adj syn* see IMPRACTICABLE 2
ant serviceable

unsettle *vb* 1 *syn* see DISORDER 1
rel agitate, disquiet, perturb; discommode, incommode, trouble
con calm, ease, quiet, stabilize, steady
ant settle
2 *syn* see UPSET 5
ant settle
3 *syn* see DISCOMPOSE 1

unsettled *adj* 1 *syn* see RESTLESS
2 *syn* see CHANGEABLE 1
ant settled
3 *syn* see DOUBTFUL 1
ant settled
4 *syn* see PENDING
ant settled
5 *syn* see BACK 1
6 *syn* see UNPAID 2
ant settled

unsettledness *n syn* see INSTABILITY

unsex *vb syn* see STERILIZE

unshackle *vb syn* see FREE
ant shackle

unshakable *adj syn* see SURE 2
ant shakable

unshaken *adj syn* see SURE 2
ant shaken

unshaped *adj syn* see FORMLESS
ant shaped

unshared *adj syn* see SOLE 4
ant shared

unship *vb syn* see UNLOAD

unshod *adj syn* see BAREFOOT 1
ant shod

unshroud *vb syn* see EXPOSE 4
ant shroud

unshut *vb syn* see OPEN 1
ant shut

unsightly *adj syn* see UGLY 2
rel ill-shaped, unshapely; unesthetic; drab, dull, lackluster
ant sightly

unsimilar *adj syn* see DIFFERENT 1
ant similar

unskilled *adj* 1 *syn* see AMATEURISH
ant skilled
2 *syn* see INEFFICIENT 2
ant skilled

unskillful *adj* 1 lacking in skill or proficiency < an ardent but *unskillful* home mechanic>
syn inadept, inapt, inept, inexpert, unapt, undexterous, unfacile, unhandy, unproficient
rel incapable, incompetent; unfitted, unqualfied, unready
con adept, apt, dexterous, expert, handy, proficient
ant skillful
2 *syn* see INEFFICIENT 2

unsleeping *adj syn* see WATCHFUL
ant sleeping

unsmooth *adj syn* see ROUGH 1
ant smooth

unsober *adj syn* see INTOXICATED 1
ant sober

unsociable *adj* disinclined to active social intercourse < tried to hide his basically shy *unsociable* nature under a professional heartiness of manner>
syn aloof, cool, distant, inosciable, offish, reserved, shut-in, solitary, standoff, standoffish, touch-me-not-ish, unapproachable,

unbending, uncommunicative, uncompanionable, withdrawn; *compare* INDIFFERENT 2, UNDEMONSTRATIVE
rel self-contained, self-sufficient; exclusive, inaccessible, remote; prickly, sensitive; brooding, secretive; diffident, shy, timid
con cordial, genial, hearty, outgoing; companionable, friendly, gregarious
ant sociable, social
unsoiled *adj syn* see CLEAN 1
ant soiled, sullied
unsoluble *adj syn* see INSOLUBLE
ant soluble, solvable
unsolvable *adj syn* see INSOLUBLE
ant soluble, solvable
unsophisticated *adj syn* see NATURAL 5
rel authentic, bona fide, genuine; callow, crude, green, uncouth
con finished, polished, smooth, suave
ant sophisticated
unsorry *adj syn* see REMORSELESS
ant sorry
unsorted *adj* 1 *syn* see MISCELLANEOUS
2 *syn* see UNREFINED 3
ant sorted
unsought *adj* 1 *syn* see UNASKED
2 *syn* see UNWELCOME 1
unsound *adj* 1 *syn* see INSANE 1
ant sound
2 *syn* see WEAK 1
rel damaged, faulty, flawed, imperfect
con solid, strong, substantial
ant sound
3 *syn* see FALSE 1
ant sound
4 *syn* see DANGEROUS 1
unsparing *adj syn* see LIBERAL 1
ant close, sparing
unspeakable *adj syn* see UNUTTERABLE
rel loathsome, offensive, repulsive, revolting; abominable, detestable, hateful, odious; distasteful, obnoxious, repellent, repugnant; atrocious, disgusting, outrageous
unspoiled *adj syn* see VIRGIN 1
unspoken *adj* 1 not put into words <met regularly by a sort of *unspoken* agreement>
syn silent, tacit, unexpressed, unuttered, unvoiced, wordless
rel implicit, implied, understood; hinted, intimated, suggested; mute, unsaid, unstated
con mentioned, said, stated, told, voiced
ant spoken
2 *syn* see TACIT 1
ant spoken
unstability *n syn* see INSTABILITY
ant stability
unstable *adj* 1 *syn* see MOVABLE
ant stable
2 difficult to manage because of lack of physical steadiness <the canoe is an inherently *unstable* craft>
syn rocky, ticklish, tricky
rel insecure, uncertain, unsteady
con secure, steady
ant stable
3 *syn* see WEAK 2

ant stable
4 *syn* see INCONSTANT 1
rel buoyant, effervescent, elastic, resilient; freakish
ant stable
5 *syn* see CHANGEABLE 1
ant stable
6 *syn* see MUTABLE 2
ant stable
7 *syn* see DOUBTFUL 1
unstableness *n syn* see INSTABILITY
ant stability, stableness
unsteadfast *adj syn* see MOVABLE
ant steadfast
unsteadfastness *n syn* see INSTABILITY
ant steadfastness
unsteadiness *n syn* see INSTABILITY
ant steadiness
unsteady *adj* 1 *syn* see MOVABLE
2 *syn* see CHANGEABLE 1
ant steady
3 *syn* see MUTABLE 2
ant steady
unsteel *vb syn* see DISARM 2
unstop *vb syn* see OPEN 1
ant stop
unstow *vb syn* see UNLOAD
unstrengthen *vb syn* see WEAKEN 1
ant strengthen
unstring *vb syn* see UNNERVE
unstudied *adj* 1 *syn* see NATURAL 5
ant studied
2 *syn* see EXTEMPORANEOUS
unstudious *adj syn* see UNSCHOLARLY
ant studious
unstylish *adj syn* see TACKY 2
ant stylish
unsubstantial *adj* 1 *syn* see TENUOUS 3
ant substantial
2 *syn* see IMPLAUSIBLE
3 *syn* see IMMATERIAL 1
ant substantial
4 *syn* see WEAK 1
rel insecure, shaky, undependable
ant substantial
unsuccess *n syn* see FAILURE 2
ant success, successfulness
unsuccessfulness *n syn* see FAILURE 2
ant success, successfulness
unsufferable *adj syn* see INSUFFERABLE
ant sufferable
unsufficient *adj syn* see SHORT 3
ant sufficient
unsuitable *adj* 1 *syn* see UNFIT 1
rel undesirable, unhappy
ant suitable
2 *syn* see IMPROPER 1
ant suitable
unsuited *adj syn* see UNFIT 1
rel inadmissible, objectionable, unacceptable; disappointing, inadequate
ant suited
unsullied *adj* 1 *syn* see CHASTE
ant sullied
2 *syn* see CLEAN 1
ant soiled, sullied
unsupportable *adj* *syn* see INSUFFERABLE
ant bearable, supportable
unsure *adj* 1 *syn* see INSECURE 1
ant sure
2 *syn* see WEAK 2
3 *syn* see DOUBTFUL 1

---

syn synonym(s)   *rel* related word(s)
ant antonym(s)   *con* contrasted word(s)
idiom idiomatic equivalent(s)
‖ use limited; if in doubt, see a dictionary

ant sure
4 *syn* see UNRELIABLE 1

unsurmountable *adj* *syn* see INSUPER-
ABLE
  ant surmountable

unsurpassable *adj* *syn* see SUPREME
  ant surpassable

unsusceptible *adj* *syn* see INSUSCEPTIBLE
  ant susceptible

unsuspecting *adj* *syn* see CREDULOUS
  ant suspecting, suspicious

unsuspicious *adj* *syn* see CREDULOUS
  ant suspecting, suspicious

unswayable *adj* *syn* see INFLEXIBLE 2
  ant suasible

unswerving *adj* *syn* see WHOLE 5
  rel constant, steadfast, steady, unremitting; firm, unfaltering, unwavering

unsymmetrical *adj* *syn* see LOPSIDED
  ant symmetrical

unsympathetic *adj* **1** *syn* see ANTIPA-
THETIC 2
  rel dislikable, unlikable; displeasing, unpleasant, unpleasing
  con appealing, congenial, likable; pleasant, pleasing
  ant sympathetic
2 *syn* see UNFEELING 2
  rel cold, cool, frigid; disinterested, halfhearted, indifferent, lukewarm
  ant sympathetic

untactful *adj* *syn* see TACTLESS
  ant tactful

untangle *vb* *syn* see EXTRICATE 2
  ant entangle, tangle

untapped *adj* *syn* see VIRGIN 2

untaught *adj* *syn* see IGNORANT 1

untellable *adj* *syn* see UNUTTERABLE
  ant expressible

untempered *adj* *syn* see EXCESSIVE 2
  ant temperate, tempered

untenable *adj* *syn* see INEXCUSABLE

untended *adj* *syn* see NEGLECTED

untested *adj* *syn* see UNTRIED 1
  ant tested, tried

unthankful *adj* **1** *syn* see THANKLESS 2
2 *syn* see THANKLESS 1
  ant thankful

unthinkable *adj* **1** *syn* see EXCEPTIONAL
1
2 *syn* see INCREDIBLE 1
  ant thinkable

unthinking *adj* *syn* see CARELESS 1

unthorough *adj* *syn* see SLIPSHOD 3
  ant thorough

unthought *adj* *syn* see UNINTENTIONAL
  ant aforethought

unthrift *n* **1** *syn* see EXTRAVAGANCE 2
  ant thrift
2 *syn* see SPENDTHRIFT

unthrift *adj* *syn* see IMPROVIDENT

unthrifty *adj* *syn* see IMPROVIDENT
  ant thrifty

untidy *adj* **1** *syn* see SLOVENLY 1
  ant tidy
2 *syn* see SLIPSHOD 3

untie *vb* *syn* see EXTRICATE 2

untighten *vb* *syn* see LOOSE 5
  ant tighten

until *prep* up to a stipulated time < we
never met him *until* last night >
  syn before, in advance of, prior to, till,
to, up till, up to; *compare* BEFORE 1

until *conj* *syn* see TILL

untimely *adj* **1** *syn* see EARLY 2
  ant timely
2 *syn* see UNSEASONABLE 1
  con opportune, pat, seasonable, well=
timed
  ant timely
3 *syn* see IMPROPER 1
  ant timely

untiring *adj* *syn* see INDEFATIGABLE
  con casual, disinterested, intermittent

untold *adj* **1** *syn* see HUGE
2 *syn* see INNUMERABLE

untouchable *n* *syn* see OUTCAST
  rel déclassé, outcaste, outsider

untouched *adj* **1** *syn* see WHOLE 1
2 *syn* see VIRGIN 2

untoward *adj* **1** *syn* see UNRULY 1
2 *syn* see UNLUCKY
3 *syn* see INDECOROUS

untowardness *n* *syn* see IMPROPRIETY

untrammeled *adj* *syn* see AUDACIOUS 4

untranquil *adj* *syn* see RESTLESS

untried *adj* **1** not subjected to test or proof
(as by experience or use) < the fledgling's
untried wings >
  syn undemonstrated, unpracticed, unproved, untested
  rel inexperienced, unseasoned; callow,
green, immature; fresh, half-baked, unripe
  con practiced, proven, tested; accomplished, finished, skilled; initiated
  ant tested, tried
2 *syn* see INEXPERIENCED

untroubled *adj* *syn* see CALM 1
  ant troubled

untroublesome *adj* *syn* see EASY 1

untrue *adj* **1** *syn* see FAITHLESS
  ant true
2 *syn* see FALSE 1
  rel imprecise, inexact, unprecise; for-
sworn, perjured
  con exact, precise
  ant true

untruism *n* *syn* see LIE
  ant truism

untrustworthy *adj* **1** *syn* see UNRELI-
ABLE 1
  ant trustworthy
2 *syn* see UNSAFE
  ant trustworthy

untrusty *adj* *syn* see UNRELIABLE 1
  ant trusty

untruth *n* **1** *syn* see FALLACY 1
  ant truth
2 *syn* see LIE
  ant truth

untruthful *adj* *syn* see DISHONEST
  rel deceptive, delusive, delusory, misleading; false, wrong; inaccurate, incorrect
  ant truthful

untruthfulness *n* *syn* see MENDACITY
  ant truthfulness

untune *vb* *syn* see DISCOMPOSE

untutored *adj* **1** *syn* see IGNORANT 1
2 *syn* see NATURAL 5

untwine *vb* *syn* see EXTRICATE 2

untypical *adj* *syn* see ABNORMAL 1
  ant typical

ununderstandable *adj* *syn* see INCON-
CEIVABLE 1
  ant understandable

unusable *adj* *syn* see IMPRACTICABLE 2

ant usable

unused *adj syn* see VACANT 4

unusual *adj* 1 *syn* see EXCEPTIONAL 1
idiom the exception rather than the rule
ant usual
2 *syn* see STRANGE 4
ant usual

unusually *adv syn* see EXTRA

unutterable *adj* being beyond human
power to tell or describe < *unutterable*
spiritual bliss >
syn incommunicable, indefinable, indescribable, ineffable, inenarrable, inexpressible, undescribable, unexpressible, unspeakable, untellable
rel inconceivable, incredible, unbelievable,
unimaginable; awesome, awful, marvelous,
prodigious, wonderful, wondrous
idiom beyond expression
con commonplace, humdrum, ordinary;
monotonous, samely, unvarying

unuttered *adj* 1 *syn* see UNSPOKEN 1
ant uttered
2 *syn* see TACIT 1
ant uttered

unvarnished *adj syn* see FRANK

unvarying *adj* 1 *syn* see STEADY 2
ant varying
2 *syn* see SAME 3
ant variable, varying

unveil *vb* 1 *syn* see OPEN 2
ant veil
2 *syn* see REVEAL 1
ant veil

unveracity *n syn* see MENDACITY
ant veracity

unversed *adj syn* see INEXPERIENCED
ant versed

unvigilant *adj syn* see INCAUTIOUS 1
ant vigilant

unvital *adj syn* see PETTY 2
ant vital

unvocal *adj syn* see INARTICULATE 3
ant vocal

unvoiced *adj syn* see UNSPOKEN 1
ant voiced

unwanted *adj* 1 *syn* see UNWELCOME 1
ant wanted
2 *syn* see OBJECTIONABLE
ant wanted

unwarrantable *adj syn* see UNREASON-
ABLE 2
ant warrantable

unwarranted *adj* 1 *syn* see BASELESS
2 *syn* see UNREASONABLE 2

unwary *adj* 1 *syn* see INCAUTIOUS 1
ant wary
2 *syn* see CREDULOUS
3 *syn* see RASH 1
ant wary

unwashed *adj syn* see IGNOBLE 1

unwashed *n syn* see RABBLE 2

unwasteful *adj syn* see SPARING
ant wasteful

unwatchful *adj* 1 *syn* see INATTENTIVE
ant watchful
2 *syn* see INCAUTIOUS 1
ant watchful

unwatered *adj syn* see DRY 1

ant watered

unwavering *adj syn* see SURE 2
ant wavering

unweariable *adj syn* see INDEFATIGABLE
ant weariable

unwearying *adj syn* see INDEFATIGABLE
rel constant, steady; interminable, unceasing

unwed *adj syn* see SINGLE 1
ant married, wed

unwelcome *adj* 1 not of a kind to be welcome <an *unwelcome* interruption that
scattered his train of thought >
syn undesired, unsought, unwanted, unwished
rel distasteful, obnoxious, repellent; unasked; undesirable, unpleasant, unpleasing
con desired, sought, wanted; agreeable,
desirable, pleasant, pleasing
ant welcome
2 *syn* see OBJECTIONABLE
ant welcome

unwell *adj* somewhat disordered in health
<had felt *unwell* from the moment she
got up >
syn ailing, ‖donsie, indisposed, low, mean,
off-color, offish, poorly, sickly, underly;
compare SICK 1
rel rocky, shaky, wobbly; feeble, frail,
infirm, weakly; ill, sick; qualmish, queasy,
squeamish
idiom out of sorts, under the weather
ant well

unwholesome *adj* 1 likely to be detrimental to physical, mental, or moral health
<an *unwholesome* crime-ridden neighbor-
hood >
syn insalubrious, insalutary, noisome,
noxious, sickly, unhealthful, unhealthy,
unsalutary
rel baneful, deleterious, detrimental, pernicious; harmful, hurtful, injurious, mischievous
con healthful, hygienic, salubrious, salutary
ant wholesome
2 *syn* see OFFENSIVE
ant wholesome

unwieldy *adj* clumsy and difficult to handle usually because of excessive weight
and awkward form <a massive *unwieldy*
sledgehammer >
syn cumbersome, cumbrous, ponderous,
unhandy; *compare* HEAVY 1
rel awkward, inconvenient; uncontrollable, unmanageable; bulky, clumsy, lumbering, massive; burdensome, encumbering,
onerous
con compact, neat, trig, trim; adaptable,
convenient, handy; easy, facile, light
ant wieldy

unwilling *adj syn* see DISINCLINED
ant willing

unwind *vb syn* see RELAX 2

unwise *adj* not marked by or according
with good sense or sound judgment <his
decision to quit school was most *unwise* >
syn ill-advised, ill-judged, impolitic, imprudent, indiscreet, injudicious
rel senseless, thoughtless, witless; impractical, unsound; fatuous, inane, inept; inappropriate, undesirable, unfortunate; fool-

---

syn synonym(s)   *rel* related word(s)
ant antonym(s)   *con* contrasted word(s)
idiom idiomatic equivalent(s)
‖ use limited; if in doubt, see a dictionary

ish, misguided, unintelligent; childish,
immature, naive
idiom penny-wise and pound-foolish
con discreet, judicious, prudent; sane,
sensible, sound; appropriate, apt, desirable
ant wise

unwished *adj syn see* UNWELCOME 1

unwishful *adj syn see* DISINCLINED
ant wishful

unwitting *adj* 1 *syn see* FORGETFUL
ant witting
2 *syn see* IGNORANT 2
ant witting

unwitty *adj syn see* SIMPLE 3
ant ‖witty

unwonted *adj* 1 *syn see* EXCEPTIONAL 1
ant wonted

unworkable *adj* 1 *syn see* IMPOSSIBLE 1
2 *syn see* IMPRACTICABLE 2
ant workable

unworked *adj syn see* RUDE 1
ant worked, wrought

unworkmanlike *adj syn see* INEFFICIENT
2
ant workmanlike, workmanly

unworldly *adj* 1 *syn see* DREAMY 1
2 *syn see* NATURAL 5
ant worldly

unworthy *adj syn see* WORTHLESS 1
ant worthy

unwritten *adj syn see* ORAL 2
ant written

unwrought *adj syn see* RUDE 1
ant worked, wrought

unyielding *adj* 1 *syn see* STIFF 1
ant yielding
2 *syn see* OBSTINATE
rel firm, fixed, rigid
ant yielding
3 *syn see* GRIM 3
4 *syn see* TOUGH 3
ant yielding
5 *syn see* INFLEXIBLE 2

up *adj* 1 *syn see* BAD 1
2 *syn see* FAMILIAR 3
3 *syn see* UP-TO-DATE

up *vb* 1 *syn see* RISE 4
2 *syn see* RAISE 9

up-and-coming *adj syn see* ENTERPRIS-
ING 2
rel alert, eager, keen, ready

up and down *adv syn see* THOROUGHLY
2

up-and-down *adj syn see* DOWNRIGHT 2

upbear *vb syn see* SUPPORT 4

upbeat *adj syn see* OPTIMISTIC

upbraid *vb syn see* SCOLD 1

upchuck *vb syn see* VOMIT

upclimb *vb syn see* ASCEND 1

upcoming *adj syn see* FORTHCOMING
rel foreseen, prospective
idiom in prospect, on the horizon

up-country *n syn see* FRONTIER 2

update *vb syn see* RENEW 1

upend *vb syn see* WHIP 2

upgo *vb syn see* ASCEND 1

upgrade *vb syn see* ADVANCE 2
ant downgrade

upgrade *n syn see* RISE 3

upgrading *n syn see* ADVANCEMENT 1
ant downgrading

upgrowth *n syn see* DEVELOPMENT

upheaval *n syn see* COMMOTION 1

rel cataclysm, catastrophe, disaster; alteration, change; churning, heaving, stirring

upheaved *adj syn see* ELEVATED 1
ant downthrown

uphill *adj syn see* HARD 6

uphold *vb* 1 *syn see* SUPPORT 5
rel defend, justify, maintain, vindicate;
aid, assist, help
ant contravene; subvert
2 *syn see* SUPPORT 2
3 *syn see* SUPPORT 4
4 *syn see* LIFT 1

upholstered *adj* 1 *syn see* LUXURIOUS 3
2 *syn see* FAT 2

upland *n syn see* PLATEAU

uplay *vb syn see* ACCUMULATE

uplift *vb* 1 *syn see* LIFT 1
2 *syn see* ILLUMINATE 2
ant degrade

uplifted *adj syn see* ELEVATED 1

upon *prep* 1 *syn see* OVER 3
2 *syn see* OVER 4

upper class *n syn see* ARISTOCRACY

upper crust *n syn see* ARISTOCRACY
rel (the) Four Hundred

upper hand *n syn see* BETTER 2

uppermost *adj syn see* TOP 1
ant lowermost

‖upper story *n syn see* MIND 1

‖upperworks *n pl syn see* MIND 1

uppish *adj syn see* PRESUMPTUOUS

uppity *adj syn see* PRESUMPTUOUS

upraise *vb* 1 *syn see* LIFT 1
2 *syn see* COMFORT
ant depress

upraised *adj syn see* ELEVATED 1

uprear *vb* 1 *syn see* LIFT 1
2 *syn see* BUILD 1
3 *syn see* EXALT 1
con bust, demote, downgrade
ant degrade
4 *syn see* RISE 4

upright *adj* 1 *syn see* ERECT
2 having or manifesting a strict regard for
what is morally right <an *upright* man
ready to give even the devil his due>
syn conscientious, honest, honorable, just,
right, scrupulous, true
rel ethical, moral, principled, righteous,
virtuous; equitable, fair, impartial; elevated, high-minded, noble; blameless,
exemplary, good, pure
con crooked, devious, oblique; depraved;
base, low, vile; ignoble, mean
ant corrupt

uprightness *n syn see* GOODNESS
rel nobility, reputability, worthiness;
honesty, integrity
ant corruption

uprise *vb* 1 *syn see* RISE 1
2 *syn see* ROLL OUT

uprisen *adj syn see* ELEVATED 1

uproar *n* 1 *syn see* DIN
rel chaos, confusion, disorder; brawl,
broil, fracas, melee; commotion, confusion,
turbulence, turmoil
con calm, peace, quiet
2 *syn see* COMMOTION 4
3 *syn see* COMMOTION 3

uproarious *adj syn see* NOISY

uproot *vb* 1 *syn see* ANNIHILATE 2
rel demolish, destroy; overthrow, overturn, subvert; displace, replace, supersede,
supplant; move, shift, transplant

ant establish; inseminate

upset *vb* **1** *syn* see OVERTURN 1
rel invert, reverse; bend, curve, turn
2 *syn* see DISCOMPOSE 1
rel bewilder, confound, distract; unman, unnerve
idiom rock the boat
3 *syn* see TROUBLE 1
4 *syn* see DISORDER 1
5 to disturb the normal functioning especially of body or mind < her stomach was badly *upset* by too many sweets >
syn derange, disorder, sicken, turn, unhinge, unsettle
rel afflict, indispose, lay up; ail, suffer; debilitate, incapacitate, invalid

upshot *n* **1** *syn* see EFFECT 1
rel ending, termination; climax, culmination; completion, conclusion, finish
2 *syn* see SUBSTANCE 2

upside–down *adj* **1** having the upper and lower parts reversed in position < *upside=down* letters >
syn inverted, topsy-turvy
rel reversed
2 confused utterly even to the point of inversion of the normal or reasonable < *upside-down* logic that confused cause with effect >
syn arsy-varsy, downside-up, topsy-turvy
rel inverted, reversed; chaotic, confused, helter-skelter, jumbled, mixed-up; fouled-up, haywire, ‖snafu
con orderly, well-ordered; logical, reasonable, sensible, sound; legitimate, plausible

upspring *vb* **1** *syn* see SPRING 1
2 *syn* see RISE 1

upstanding *adj* *syn* see ERECT

upstart *n* a usually crude and pushing person who has recently reached a position of prominence, power, or wealth < declared the new executive an *upstart* lacking all breeding and culture >
syn arriviste, nouveau riche, parvenu, roturier
rel bounder, cad, outsider; guttersnipe, mucker, slob, vulgarian; boor, lout, roughneck, rowdy; comer; social climber

upsurge *vb* *syn* see INCREASE 2

uptight *adj* *syn* see TENSE 2

uptightness *n* *syn* see TENSION 2

up till *prep* *syn* see UNTIL

up to *prep* *syn* see UNTIL

up–to–date *adj* completely modern (as in style or outlook) < using *up-to-date* methods of study >
syn abreast, au courant, contemporary, down-to-date, red-hot, up, up-to-the-minute
rel convenient, opportune, timely; expedient, fitting, suitable; advanced, modern, stylish; a la mode, dashing, modish
idiom abreast of the times
con dusty, rusty, stale, timeworn; antiquated, outmoded, superannuated
ant out-of-date; archaic

up–to–the–minute *adj* *syn* see UP-TO=DATE

---

upturn *n* *syn* see COMMOTION 1

uranian *adj* *syn* see HOMOSEXUAL

uranian *n* *syn* see HOMOSEXUAL

uranist *n* *syn* see HOMOSEXUAL

urban *adj* of, relating to, or characteristic of a city < *urban* disorders >
syn burghal, city, municipal
rel inner city; metropolitan; civic, popular, public; oppidan, town, village
ant rural

urbane *adj* **1** *syn* see COSMOPOLITAN 1
2 *syn* see SUAVE
rel balanced, poised
ant bucolic, clownish
3 *syn* see GENTEEL 1
rel affable, civil, courteous, gracious, obliging
ant rude

urchin *n* a pert or roguish youngster < *urchins* pilfering apples on their way from school >
syn gamin, imp, monkey
rel brat, bratling, cub, dickens, pup, whelp, whippersnapper; guttersnipe, mudlark, ragamuffin, street arab; hobbledehoy

urge *vb* to press or impel to action, effort, or speed < his conscience *urged* him to tell the truth >
syn egg (on), exhort, goad, prick, prod, prompt, propel, sic, spur
rel hurry, hustle, push, rush, shove; blandish, cajole, coax, encourage, incite, needle, solicit, wheedle; constrain, drive, high-pressure, press, pressure; provoke, set (on), tar (on)
idiom bring pressure to bear on, twist one's arm
con brake, check, constrain, curb, hold back, inhibit, restrain

urge *n* *syn* see DESIRE 1
rel goad, incentive, motive, spring, spur

urgent *adj* *syn* see PRESSING
rel driving, impelling; demanding

usable *adj* *syn* see OPEN 5
ant unusable

usage *n* **1** *syn* see HABIT 1
rel choice, preference; procedure, proceeding, process; guidance, guiding, lead
2 *syn* see FORM 3
rel ceremony, formality

usance *n* *syn* see USE 1

use *n* **1** the act or practice of using something or the state of being used < all tools must be kept ready for instant *use* >
syn appliance, application, employment, operation, play, usance; *compare* EXERCISE 1
con desuetude, disuse
ant nonuse
2 *syn* see EXERCISE 1
3 the quality of being appropriate or valuable to some end < even the scraps had some *use* >
syn account, advantage, applicability, appropriateness, avail, fitness, relevance, service, serviceability, usefulness, utility
rel adaptability, availability, benefit, efficacy; profit, value, worth
con inadequacy, inapplicability, inappropriateness, insufficiency, unfitness, unserviceability, uselessness, worthlessness
4 a particular service or end < industrial *uses* of atomic energy >

---

syn synonym(s)   *rel* related word(s)
ant antonym(s)   *con* contrasted word(s)
idiom idiomatic equivalent(s)
‖ use limited; if in doubt, see a dictionary

syn duty, function, goal, mark, object, objective, purpose, target
5 *syn* see HABIT 1
rel ceremony, formality
6 *syn* see NEED 3

use *vb syn* see ACCUSTOM
2 to put into action or service < it is necessary to *use* resources wisely >
syn apply, bestow, employ, exercise, exploit, handle, utilize
rel manipulate, operate, ply, wield; control, govern, manage, regulate
idiom avail oneself of, bring into play, fall back (on *or* upon), make use of, press into service, put into action, put to use
con dissipate, exhaust, use up; waste
3 *syn* see OPERATE 3
4 *syn* see SPEAK 3
5 *syn* see EXPLOIT 2
idiom make the most of, make use of
6 *syn* see TREAT 2

used up *adj syn* see EFFETE 2
useful *adj* **1** *syn* see PRACTICAL 2
2 *syn* see GOOD 1
ant useless
3 *syn* see GOOD 2
ant useless

usefulness *n syn* see USE 3
ant uselessness

useless *adj* **1** *syn* see FUTILE
ant useful
2 *syn* see IMPRACTICABLE 2
ant useful
3 *syn* see FECKLESS 1

use up *vb* **1** *syn* see CONSUME 1
2 *syn* see GO 4
3 *syn* see DEPLETE

usher *vb syn* see PRECEDE 3

usher in *vb syn* see INTRODUCE 3

usual *adj* **1** familiar through frequent or regular repetition < the sort that would perform her *usual* chores while waiting for the end of the world >
syn accepted, accustomed, chronic, customary, habitual, routine, wonted
rel natural, normal, regular, typical; common, familiar, ordinary; current, prevailing, prevalent, rife
idiom that make up one's daily round
con exceptional, rare, unaccustomed; remarkable, strange, unexpected
ant unusual
2 *syn* see GENERAL 1
3 *syn* see ORDINARY 1

usually *adv* **1** by or in accord with habit or custom < establishments of a kind *usually* restricted to back streets >
syn as usual, consistently, customarily, habitually, wontedly
2 more often than not < he is *usually* late for work >
syn as a rule, by ordinary, commonly, frequently, generally, ordinarily

rel now and again (*or* now and then), occasionally, once and again, sometimes
idiom for the most part, in the main
con infrequently, seldom, uncommonly
ant rarely

usurer *n syn* see LOAN SHARK

usurp *vb* **1** *syn* see ARROGATE 1
ant abdicate
2 *syn* see SUPPLANT 1

utensil *n syn* see IMPLEMENT

utile *adj syn* see PRACTICAL 2
ant inutile

utilitarian *adj syn* see REALISTIC

utility *n syn* see USE 3
ant inutility

utilize *vb syn* see USE 2
rel advance, forward, further, promote

utmost *adj* **1** *syn* see EXTREME 5
2 *syn* see MAXIMUM
3 *syn* see EXTREME 1

utopia *n* an often imaginary place or situation of perfection and delight < able to make an enduring *utopia* of the humblest house >
syn arcadia, Cockaigne, fairyland, heaven, lubberland, paradise, promised land, Shangri-la, wonderland, Zion
rel dreamland, dreamworld, never-never

utopian *adj* **1** *syn* see IDEALISTIC
rel abstract, ideal, transcendental
2 *syn* see AMBITIOUS 2
rel impossible, impracticable, unfeasible; arcadian, edenic, millennial, otherworldly

utopian *n syn* see DREAMER

utter *adj* being such without qualification — used especially to intensify the noun modified < acted like an *utter* idiot >
syn absolute, all-fired, arrant, black, blamed, blank, blankety-blank, blasted, bleeding, blessed, blighted, blinding, ‖blinking, blithering, ‖blooming, blue, complete, confounded, ‖consarned, consummate, crashing, dad-blamed, dad-blasted, dad-burned, damned, dang, darn (*or* durn), dashed, deuced, doggone, double-distilled, double-dyed, downright, flatout, goldarn, gross, hell-fired, infernal, out-and-out, outright, perfect, positive, ‖proper, pure, ‖puredee (*or* pure-D), rank, regular, sheer, stark, straight-out, ‖tarnation, thoroughgoing, total, unmitigated, unqualified; *compare* PURE 2

utter *vb* **1** *syn* see SPEAK 1
idiom give utterance to
2 *syn* see SAY 1

utterance *n* **1** *syn* see WORD 1
2 *syn* see VOCALIZATION
3 *syn* see EXPRESSION 1
4 *syn* see SPEECH 1

uttering *n syn* see VOCALIZATION

utterly *adv* **1** *syn* see WELL 3
2 *syn* see ALL 1

uttermost *adj* **1** *syn* see EXTREME 5
2 *syn* see EXTREME 1

V

vacancy *n syn* see VACUITY 2
rel desertedness
ant occupancy

vacant *adj* **1** *syn* see EMPTY 1
rel tenantless, unfilled, unoccupied, untaken
con inhabited, tenanted
ant occupied
2 *syn* see VACUOUS 2
3 *syn* see EXPRESSIONLESS
rel empty-headed, inane, thoughtless, witless
4 not being put to normal or appropriate use < *vacant* land >
syn idle, unused
rel bare, empty; unfilled, unoccupied
con filled; used
ant occupied

vacate *vb* **1** *syn* see ANNUL 4
rel repeal, rescind, retract, reverse, revoke
idiom declare null and void
2 to make something (as an office, post, or dwelling) vacant or empty < *vacate* a house>
syn clear, empty, void
rel abandon, give up, part (with *or* from), relinquish; leave, quit

vacation *n* a period spent away from one's usual activity or work often in travel or recreation < took a two-week *vacation* to Florida>
syn holiday, leave
rel break, breathing space (*or* breathing spell), intermission, recess; time off; respite, rest; furlough

vacillant *adj syn* see VACILLATING 2

vacillate *vb syn* see HESITATE
rel swag, sway, ‖swither; alternate, seesaw, teeter, teeter-totter, wag, waggle, wigwag, wobble; dally, dawdle, fiddle-faddle
idiom blow hot and cold, hem and haw, swing from one thing to another
con decide, resolve, settle

vacillating *adj* **1** *syn* see WEAK 2
rel unfixed; unsettled, unsteady; changeable, fickle, inconstant; eccentric, erratic, mercurial, volatile
con constant, steady, unchanging; strong
2 given to or manifesting hesitation or vacillation < a *vacillating* witness>
syn double-minded, faltering, halting, hesitant, hesitating, indecisive, irresolute, pendulous, shilly-shally, shilly-shallying, tentative, timid, uncertain, undecisive, unresolved, vacillant, vacillatory, wavering, weak-kneed, whiffling, wiggle-waggle, wobbly

---

syn synonym(s)   *rel* related word(s)
ant antonym(s)   *con* contrasted word(s)
idiom idiomatic equivalent(s)
‖ use limited; if in doubt, see a dictionary

rel doubtful, doubting, unsure; fluctuating, oscillating, shifting; dallying, dawdling, demurring, dillydallying, stalling
con certain, decisive, resolute, resolved, sure; definite, positive

vacillation *n syn* see HESITATION
rel dallying, demurral, dillydallying, stalling

vacillatory *adj syn* see VACILLATING 2
rel alternating, seesawing, varying; indecisive, irresolute, uncertain

vacuity *n* **1** *syn* see HOLE 3
2 the condition, fact, or quality of being vacuous < the utter *vacuity* of his expression >
syn blankness, emptiness, vacancy, vacuousness, voidness
rel bareness, barrenness, bleakness, desolateness, hollowness; dullness, inaneness, inanity, stupidity
3 *syn* see NOTHINGNESS

vacuous *adj* **1** *syn* see EMPTY 1
2 characterized by a lack of substance, thought, or intellectual content < a *vacuous* mind >
syn empty-headed, vacant; *compare* STUPID 1
rel shallow, superficial; blank, empty; dull, foolish, inane, silly

vacuousness *n syn* see VACUITY 2
vade mecum *n syn* see HANDBOOK
vag *n syn* see VAGABOND
vagabond *adj syn* see ITINERANT
rel vagabondish
vagabond *n* a person who wanders at will or as a habit < a park full of *vagabonds* sleeping on benches>
syn arab, ‖bindle stiff, bum, canter, clochard, derelict, drifter, floater, ‖gangrel, hobo, piker, roadster, runagate, ‖shack, street arab, ‖sundowner, ‖swagger, ‖swagman, tramp, tramper, ‖traveler, vag, vagrant, Weary Willie
rel roamer, rover, wanderer; boomer, migrant, runabout, straggler, stray, transient; bohemian, gypsy, picaro, picaroon; ‖casual; stiff; beggar, rogue
idiom knight of the road

vagabond *vb syn* see WANDER 1
vagabondage *n syn* see VAGRANCY
vagabondia *n syn* see VAGRANCY
vagabondism *n syn* see VAGRANCY
vagabondize *vb syn* see WANDER 1
vagarious *adj syn* see ARBITRARY 1
rel unreasonable; kinky
vagary *n syn* see CAPRICE
rel daydream, dream, fantasy; kink, quirk
idiom passing fancy
vagrancy *n* the act or state of wandering from place to place usually with no means of support < dropped out of society and lived a life of *vagrancy* >
syn hoboism, vagabondage, vagabondia, vagabondism

rel itineracy, itinerancy, nomadism; rambling, roaming, roving, wandering

vagrant *n syn* see VAGABOND

vagrant *adj syn* see ITINERANT
rel aimless, errant, erratic; straying; sauntering, strolling

vague *adj* **1** *syn* see OBSCURE 3
rel indeterminate, indistinct, unplain; cloudy, dim, hazy, nebulous; muddy
con clear, distinct
ant express
2 *syn* see FAINT 2
rel nebulous, unsubstantial; indefinite, unplain; uncertain, unrecognizable; dreamlike, dreamy
3 *syn* see HAZY
rel bleared, bleary, blurry

vain *adj* **1** devoid of worth or significance
< the *vain* pursuits of a luxurious life >
syn empty, hollow, idle, nugatory, otiose
rel profitless, unprofitable, useless, valueless, void, worthless; ineffective, ineffectual, inefficacious; bootless, fruitless; abortive, futile
con useful, valuable, worthy; effective, effectual, efficacious
2 *syn* see FUTILE
rel paltry, petty, puny, trifling, trivial; delusive, delusory, misleading
3 having or exhibiting undue or excessive pride especially in one's appearance or achievements < was *vain* about his clothes >
syn conceited, ||conceity, narcissistic, self-conceited, stuck-up, vainglorious; *compare* PROUD 1
rel arrogant, egocentric, egoistic, haughty, ||pensy, proud, self-important, swollen-headed; boastful, self-exalting; coxcombical, dandyish, foppish
idiom stuck on oneself
con humble, meek, modest; bashful, diffident, retiring, shy

vainglorious *adj syn* see VAIN 3
rel boastful, bragging, vaunting; disdainful, insolent, supercilious

vainglory *n syn* see CONCEIT 2
rel arrogance, haughtiness; boastfulness, bombast; exhibition, flaunting, parading
con lowliness, meekness; bashfulness, diffidence, self-effacement, shyness; modesty
ant humility

vainness *n syn* see CONCEIT 2

vale *n syn* see VALLEY

valedictory *adj syn* see PARTING

valiance *n syn* see HEROISM
con feebleness, ineffectiveness; fear

valiancy *n syn* see HEROISM
con feebleness, ineffectiveness; fear

valiant *adj syn* see BRAVE 1
ant pusillanimous

valid *adj* having the power to impress others as right and well-founded < a *valid* conclusion >
syn cogent, convincing, satisfactory, satisfying, solid, sound, telling
rel persuasive, potent, strong; attested, confirmed, corroborated, demonstrated, determined, established, substantiated, validated, verified; lawful, legal, licit; effective, effectual; conclusive, decisive, definitive, determinative; acceptable

con groundless, shaky, unconvincing, unfounded, unsound; fallacious, false, misleading, sophistical; counterfeit, fictitious
ant invalid

validate *vb syn* see CONFIRM 2
rel approve, endorse, legalize, ratify, rubber-stamp, sanction
con abolish, abrogate, annul, cancel, repeal; void
ant invalidate

validity *n syn* see POINT 3
rel efficacy, gravity, soundness; persuasiveness, potency
con inconsistency; unsoundness; fallacy, falsity
ant invalidity, invalidness

validness *n syn* see POINT 3
ant invalidity, invalidness

valley *n* an elongate depression of the earth's surface commonly situated between ranges of hills or mountains < small farms dotted the floor of the *valley* >
syn ||combe, dale, glen, vale
rel dell, dingle, hollow; ||rincon; canyon

valor *n syn* see HEROISM
rel mettle, resolution, spirit, tenacity; indomitableness, invincibility, unconquerableness; backbone, fortitude, guts, sand
con cowardliness, fear
ant pusillanimity, pusillanimousness

valorous *adj syn* see BRAVE 1
ant pusillanimous

valorousness *n syn* see HEROISM
rel chivalrousness, chivalry; manliness
con cowardliness
ant pusillanimity, pusillanimousness

valuable *adj syn* see PRECIOUS 1
rel dear, expensive; appreciated, prized, treasured, valued; admired, esteemed, respected
idiom of great value
con cheap, inexpensive, trashy; unmarketable, unsalable; unworthy
ant valueless, worthless

valuate *vb syn* see ESTIMATE 1

valuation *n* **1** *syn* see ESTIMATE 1
rel judgment, opinion, rating
2 *syn* see WORTH 1
rel charge, cost, price

value *n* **1** *syn* see WORTH 1
rel appraisal, assessment; charge, cost, expense, price
2 *syn* see QUALITY 2

value *vb* **1** *syn* see ESTIMATE 1
rel compute, figure, gauge, reckon
idiom place a value (*or* price) on
2 *syn* see APPRECIATE 1
rel care (for); revere, reverence, venerate
idiom set much by

valueless *adj syn* see WORTHLESS 1
ant valuable

valve *n syn* see FAUCET
rel shutoff

||**vamoose** *vb syn* see GET OUT 1

vamp *vb syn* see MEND 2
rel brush up, fix up, touch up; furbish, refurbish

vamp (up) *vb syn* see CONTRIVE 2

vamp *n syn* see FLIRT
rel charmer, enchantress, enticer, femme fatale, gold digger, inveigler, seductress, siren, temptress

vandal *n* one who willfully destroys or mars something valuable < *vandals* had knocked off the head of the statue>
  syn defacer, despoiler, destroyer, ruinator, ruiner, wrecker
  rel hoodlum, hooligan, lout, ruffian; devastator, ravager, spoiler, spoliator; looter, pillager, plunderer; iconoclast

vandalize *vb* to destroy or deface (as public or private property) willfully or maliciously < youths *vandalized* the shop>
  syn ‖trash, wreck
  rel ‖rip off; destroy, tear up

vanish *vb* to pass from view or out of existence < the moon *vanished* behind a cloud>
  syn clear, disappear, evanesce, evanish, evaporate, fade
  rel dematerialize, dissolve, melt (away); die
  idiom do the vanishing act, vanish from sight, vanish into thin air, vanish like a dream
  con arise, break out (*or* through), come (forth *or* out), emerge, issue, loom (up), materialize, show (up)
  ant appear

vanished *adj syn* see EXTINCT 2
  rel expired, passed away; annihilated, no more, perished

vanity *n syn* see CONCEIT 2
  rel autotheism, self-worship

vanquish *vb syn* see CONQUER 1
  rel surmount; overturn, subvert; humble, trample

vanquisher *n syn* see VICTOR 1
  rel champ, champion
  con loser

vanquishment *n syn* see DEFEAT 1
  rel mastery, subdual, subjugation

vantage *n syn* see ADVANTAGE 3
  ant disadvantage

vapid *adj syn* see INSIPID 3
  rel flavorless, milk-toast, tasteless, weak; dull, unimaginative, uninteresting
  idiom neither hot nor cold, neither one thing nor the other
  con brisk, lively, tangy, zesty; crisp, forceful, incisive, trenchant; expressive, meaningful, pregnant, significant, telling

vaporous *adj* 1 *syn* see HAZY
  2 *syn* see AIRY 3
  rel unsubstantial, wispy; illusory, unreal

vapory *adj* 1 *syn* see HAZY
  2 *syn* see AIRY 3
  rel gaseous

variable *adj* 1 *syn* see CHANGEABLE 1
  rel fitful, spasmodic; irregular, unequable, unequal, ununiform
  con unchanging, unvarying; immobile, stable, unmoving; equable, equal, uniform
  ant constant, invariable
  2 *syn* see MUTABLE 2
  3 *syn* see INCONSTANT 1

variance *n* 1 the quality, state, or fact of being variable < a daily *variance* of 1°F.>
  syn difference, variation
  rel change, deviation, fluctuation

  ant invariance
  2 *syn* see DISCORD
  rel division, separation, severing, sundering

variation *n* 1 *syn* see CHANGE 1
  rel difference, dissimilarity; deflection, discrepancy
  con stability, unchangeableness
  2 *syn* see VARIANCE 1
  rel shift; divergence; discrepancy, disparity
  con uniformity

varicolored *adj syn* see VARIEGATED
  ant solid

varied *adj syn* see MISCELLANEOUS

variegated *adj* having a pattern involving different colors or shades of color < *variegated* leaves>
  syn dappled, discolor, motley, multicolor, multicolored, multihued, parti-color, particolored, polychromatic, polychrome, varicolored, versicolor, versicolored
  rel checked, checkered; piebald, pied, skewbald; freaked, streaked; flecked, stippled; marbled; mottle, mottled, spattered, speckled, spotted; calico; pinto
  ant solid

variety *n* 1 the quality or state of being composed of different parts, elements, or individuals < the *variety* of the city's cultural life>
  syn diverseness, diversity, multeity, multifariousness, multiformity, multiplicity, variousness
  rel diversification, heterogeneity, variation
  2 a collection of different things, forms, or qualities especially of a particular class < had a great *variety* of jobs in his lifetime>
  syn assortment
  rel conglomeration, medley, miscellany
  3 *syn* see TYPE
  rel classification; grade, rank

various *adj* 1 *syn* see MANY
  rel assorted, heterogeneous, miscellaneous, omnifarious, omnigenous
  2 *syn* see DIFFERENT 1
  rel changing, variant, varied, varying; distinct, separate; distinctive, individual, peculiar
  ant uniform
  3 *syn* see SEVERAL 3
  ant many, numerous
  4 *syn* see DISTINCT 1
  5 *syn* see CERTAIN 2

various *pron, pl in constr syn* see SUNDRY

variously *adv syn* see OTHERWISE 1

variousness *n syn* see VARIETY 1

varnish *vb syn* see PALLIATE

vary *vb* 1 *syn* see CHANGE 1
  rel modulate, qualify
  2 *syn* see DIFFER 1
  3 *syn* see DIFFER 2
  rel depart, deviate, digress, diverge; divide, part, separate
  ant agree
  4 *syn* see RANGE 3

vast *adj syn* see HUGE
  rel big, large; ample, capacious, spacious; broad, expansive, far-flung, wide, widespread; astronomical, cosmic
  con confined, limited, narrow, restricted

vastness *n syn* see ENORMITY 2

---

syn synonym(s)   *rel* related word(s)
ant antonym(s)   *con* contrasted word(s)
idiom idiomatic equivalent(s)
‖ use limited; if in doubt, see a dictionary

vatic *adj syn see* PROPHETIC

vaticinal *adj syn see* PROPHETIC

vaticinate *vb syn see* FORETELL

vault *n syn see* CRYPT

vault *vb* **1** *syn see* JUMP 1
  rel upleap, upspring; overjump, overleap; clear; rise, soar; ascend, mount; surmount
  2 *syn see* CLEAR 8

vaulting *adj syn see* AMBITIOUS 1
  rel enthusiastic; opportunistic

vaunt *vb syn see* BOAST
  rel brandish, display, exhibit, expose, flaunt, parade, show off
  idiom puff oneself

vaunter *n syn see* BRAGGART

vaunting *adj syn see* BOASTFUL

vector *n* an agent capable of transmitting a pathogen from one organism to another <fleas are *vectors* of bubonic plague>
  syn carrier, vehicle

veer *vb* **1** *syn see* TURN 6
  2 *syn see* SWERVE 1
  rel depart, deviate, digress, diverge; angle off, bear off; twist; pivot, turn, wheel

vegetate *vb* to lead a passive existence without exertion of body or mind <he never really lived his life—he merely *vegetated*>
  syn stagnate
  rel idle; languish; hibernate
  idiom idle life away, live the life of a clam, pass the time

vehement *adj syn see* INTENSE 1
  rel emphatic, pronounced; energetic, hearty, lively, zealous; forceful, potent, powerful; ardent, fervent, fervid, heated, impassioned, passionate, perfervid; delirious, frantic, furious, rabid, wild

vehicle *n* **1** *syn see* VECTOR
  rel agent
  2 *syn see* MEAN 2
  rel implement, tool
  3 a means of transporting goods or passengers <his *vehicle* was an old battered coupe>
  syn conveyance, transport, transportation

veil *n syn see* MASK 2

veil *vb syn see* ENFOLD 1
  rel mantle, overspread, spread (over); blanket, curtain; camouflage, cloak, cover (up), disguise, mask; conceal, hide, screen, secrete
  con exhibit, lay (open), open up, reveal, uncover, unmask; bare, expose, show
  ant unveil

vein *n* **1** a distinctive method of expression <wrote his speech in the proper *vein* for a very sophisticated audience>
  syn fashion, manner, mode, style, tone
  rel way; line; mood, tenor
  2 *syn see* HINT 2
  3 *syn see* MOOD 1
  rel complexion, disposition, fettle, temperament; character, nature, spirit

velitation *n syn see* ENCOUNTER

velleity *n syn see* WILL 1
  rel volition; wish

vellicate *vb syn see* JERK
  rel nip, pinch; fidget, jig, jiggle

velocipede *n syn see* BICYCLE

velocity *n syn see* SPEED 2
  rel headway, impetus, momentum; dispatch, expedition, haste, hurry

velutinous *adj syn see* VELVETY

velvetlike *adj syn see* VELVETY
  idiom soft as velvet

velvety *adj* **1** having the extreme softness associated with the surface or appearance of velvet <wore a *velvety* red flower in her hair>
  syn velutinous, velvetlike
  rel plush, plushy, smooth, soft; glossy, sleek, slick; satiny, silken, silky
  2 *syn see* SOFT 3

venal *adj* **1** open to corrupt influence and especially bribery <a *venal* legislator>
  syn bribable, buyable, corruptible, purchasable; *compare* CORRUPT 2, CROOKED 2
  rel corrupt, flagitious, infamous, iniquitous, nefarious, vicious; hack, hireling, mercenary, paid; ignoble, sordid; unethical, unprincipled, unscrupulous
  2 *syn see* CORRUPT 2

vend *vb* **1** *syn see* SELL 2
  2 *syn see* PEDDLE 2
  3 *syn see* DECLARE 1

vendee *n syn see* PURCHASER

vendetta *n* a prolonged mutual enmity marked by bitter hostility and conflict <a long-standing *vendetta* between two rival gangs>
  syn feud
  rel dispute, quarrel; rhubarb, row, wrangle; conflict, fight, set-to; blood feud, blood vengeance

vendible *adj syn see* MARKETABLE
  ant unvendible

vendible *n, usu* **vendibles** *pl syn see* MERCHANDISE

vendor *n syn see* PEDDLER

veneer *n syn see* MASK 2

veneer *vb syn see* PALLIATE

venerable *adj* **1** deserving to be venerated usually by reason of prolonged testing (as of character) <a *venerable* judge with an impressive knowledge of the law>
  syn patriarchal, revered, reverend, reverential; *compare* HONORABLE 1
  rel dignified, imposing, stately; admirable, estimable; honored, reverenced; worshipful; sacred
  ant unvenerable
  2 *syn see* ANCIENT 1
  rel elderly; patriarchal, reverenced, reverend, venerated
  con contemporary, current; fresh, inexperienced, new, untried, unused

venerate *vb syn see* REVERE
  rel honor; idolize
  idiom put on a pedestal

venery *n syn see* HUNTING

venge *vb syn see* AVENGE
  idiom even (up) the score, repay in kind, settle accounts (*or* an account)

vengeance *n syn see* RETALIATION
  rel return; repayment; revengefulness, vengefulness

vengeful *adj syn see* VINDICTIVE
  rel antagonistic, hostile, inimical, rancorous
  con charitable, forgiving, kind; benevolent, benign, inoffensive

venial *adj* of a kind that can be remitted and that does not warrant punishment or penalty <the *venial* indiscretions of youth>

syn excusable, forgivable, pardonable, remittable

rel allowable, unobjectionable; insignificant, minor, trifling, trivial; harmless, tolerable

con criminal, damning, deadly, mortal; grievous, outrageous, serious; inexcusable, unforgivable, unpardonable, unremittable

ant heinous

venom *n syn* see POISON

rel ill will, malignity, rancor, venomousness, virulence, vitriol

con antidote, remedy

venomous *adj syn* see POISONOUS

rel malevolent, malign, malignant; baleful, malefic, maleficent; viperish, viperlike, viperous

vent *vb* 1 *syn* see EMIT 2

rel cast out, discharge, exhaust

2 *syn* see EXPRESS 2

rel utter, voice; assert, declare

idiom come out with, give vent to

con check, curb, inhibit, restrain; repress, suppress

3 *syn* see TAKE OUT (on)

vent *n* 1 *syn* see APERTURE

2 *syn* see EXPRESSION 1

rel articulation, verbalization, vocalization

venter *n syn* see ABDOMEN

ventilate *vb* 1 *syn* see BROACH

2 *syn* see EXPRESS 2

rel go into, take up; debate, deliberate, discourse (about), discuss, ||rap (about), talk over (*or* of *or* about), thresh out; advertise, broadcast, publish

idiom chew the fat (*or* the rag)

ventilation *n syn* see CONFERENCE 1

venture *vb* 1 to expose to risk or loss < *ventured* their capital in foreign trade>

syn adventure, chance, hazard, risk, wager; *compare* GAMBLE 2

rel endanger, imperil, jeopard, jeopardize, jeopardy, peril; expose, lay (open)

idiom take chances (*or* risks) on (*or* with)

2 *syn* see GAMBLE 2

rel bet, operate, play (for), speculate, stake; jeopard, jeopardize, jeopardy

idiom luck it

3 *syn* see FACE 3

venture *n syn* see ADVENTURE

rel attempt, undertaking; crack, fling; dare, gamble, risk, speculation

idiom leap in the dark

venturesome *adj syn* see ADVENTUROUS

rel stalwart, stout, sturdy; brave; overbold

con timid, timorous; afraid, apprehensive, fearful

venturous *adj syn* see ADVENTUROUS

rel aggressive, enterprising, hustling

veracious *adj* 1 *syn* see TRUTHFUL

rel direct; undeceitful, undeceptive

con equivocal; deceitful, dishonest, insincere; false, untruthful

ant unveracious

2 *syn* see TRUE 3

rel unquestionable, valid

con illusory, invalid, wrong

ant unveracious

veraciousness *n syn* see VERACITY 1

rel artlessness, openness; trustworthiness

con falseness, insincerity

veracity *n* 1 the quality or state of keeping close to fact and avoiding distortion or misrepresentation <questions the *veracity* of that witness>

syn truth, truthfulness, veraciousness, veridicality, verity

rel accuracy, correctness, exactness, factualness; frankness, honesty

con inaccuracy, incorrectness; deception, dishonesty, untruth, untruthfulness

ant unveracity

2 something that is true <can make lies sound like *veracities*>

syn gospel, truism, truth, verity

rel verisimilitude; actuality; fact

con lie, untruth

ant unveracity

verbal *adj* 1 *syn* see ORAL 2

2 *syn* see VERBATIM

verbalism *n* 1 *syn* see WORDING

rel styling

2 *syn* see VERBOSITY

verbality *n syn* see VERBIAGE 1

rel verbalism, verboseness, verbosity, wordiness

verbalization *n syn* see SPEECH 1

verbalize *vb syn* see SPEAK 1

rel air, express, give, say, state, vent, ventilate, word

idiom couch in terms, find words to express

verbatim *adv* in the same words <repeated their earlier conversation *verbatim*>

syn direct, directly, literally, literatim, word for word

rel accurately, exactly, precisely

idiom to the letter

con basically, essentially, in essence; carelessly, imprecisely, inaccurately, inexactly

verbatim *adj* using the same words <court stenographers took down the *verbatim* testimony>

syn literal, verbal, word-for-word

rel close, faithful, strict; exact, precise

idiom following the letter, true to the letter

con careless, imprecise, inaccurate, inexact

verbiage *n* 1 a stylistic fault involving excessive wordiness that obscures or unduly complicates expression <the florid *verbiage* of the dissertation>

syn circumambages, circumbendibus, circumlocution, periphrase, periphrasis, pleonasm, redundancy, roundabout, tautology, verbality; *compare* VERBOSITY

rel nimiety; repetition; expansiveness, floridity, floridness; longiloquence, longwindedness

idiom purple prose

con breviloquence, brevity, briefness, terseness

ant concision

2 *syn* see WORDING

verbose *adj syn* see WORDY

rel flowery, grandiloquent, magniloquent; circumlocutory, periphrastic, pleonastic, tautologous

con precise; close, compact, lean, tight

---

syn synonym(s)   *rel* related word(s)
ant antonym(s)   *con* contrasted word(s)
idiom idiomatic equivalent(s)
|| use limited; if in doubt, see a dictionary

ant concise; laconic

verboseness *n syn* see VERBOSITY
  ant conciseness

verbosity *n* the quality or state or an
instance of being wordy <his two-hour
lecture was the epitome of *verbosity*>
<flowery *verbosities* weakened his
speech>
  syn prolixity, prolixness, verbalism, verboseness, windiness, wordiness; *compare*
VERBIAGE 1
  rel bombast, grandiloquence; long-wind-
edness; redundancy
  con conciseness, preciseness, succinctness,
terseness; leanness, tightness

verboten *adj syn* see FORBIDDEN
  rel disallowed, disapproved; unauthorized,
unlicensed, unsanctioned; outlawed, taboo
  con allowed, permitted; authorized, licensed; approved, endorsed, sanctioned

verdure *n syn* see FOLIAGE

verge *n* 1 *syn* see BORDER 1
  2 a time interval or set of circumstances
marking the imminent beginning of a new
state, condition, or action <on the *verge*
of war>
  syn brink, edge, point, threshold
  rel border line

verge *vb* 1 *syn* see BORDER 1
  rel approach; incline, lean, tend (to *or*
toward); touch (on *or* upon)
  2 *syn* see ADJOIN
  3 *syn* see BORDER 3

veridical *adj* 1 *syn* see TRUTHFUL
  2 *syn* see REAL 3
  3 *syn* see TRUE 3
  rel uncolored, undistorted, unvarnished;
actual, real
  con invalid; illusory, unreal

veridicality *n syn* see VERACITY 1
  rel genuineness

verificatory *adj syn* see CORROBORATIVE

verify *vb syn* see CONFIRM 2
  rel demonstrate, prove, test, try; document, establish, settle

verily *adv syn* see EVEN 3

verisimilitude *n* the quality of a representation that causes it to appear true <his
characters are too stilted for *verisimilitude*>
  syn color, plausibility, verisimility
  rel authenticity, genuineness, veritableness; likeness, resemblance, similarity

verisimility *n syn* see VERISIMILITUDE

veritable *adj syn* see AUTHENTIC 2
  rel undenied, unrefuted; actual, factual
  con doubtful, questionable; imaginary,
unreal, untrue; artificial, factitious; counterfeit, false, spurious

veritably *adv syn* see VERY 2

verity *n* 1 *syn* see VERACITY 2
  ant falsity
  2 *syn* see VERACITY 1

vernacular *adj* of or relating to everyday
speech < *vernacular* Welsh differs greatly
from literary Welsh>
  syn colloquial, vulgar, vulgate

vernacular *n* 1 *syn* see LANGUAGE 1
  rel mother tongue
  idiom native tongue
  2 *syn* see DIALECT 2
  3 a commonly spoken as opposed to a
prestige variety of a language <literary
Chinese and the various *vernaculars*>

  syn colloquial, patois, vulgate; *compare*
DIALECT 2
  rel dialect, lingo, slang

vernacularism *n syn* see BARBARISM

vernacularity *n syn* see BARBARISM

vernal *adj* of, relating to, or resembling the
spring of the year < *vernal* sunshine>
  syn spring, springlike

versant *adj syn* see FAMILIAR 3
  ant unversed

versatile *adj* having a wide range of skills,
aptitudes, or interests <a *versatile* artist,
who is at home in any medium>
  syn adaptable, all-around, ambidextrous,
many-sided, mobile, myriad-minded
  rel elastic, flexible, plastic, pliable; adroit,
dexterous, facile; able, skilled, skillful;
accomplished, conversant; gifted, talented;
well-rounded
  con inadequate, limited

verse *n* 1 *syn* see POETRY 1
  2 *syn* see POEM
  rel jingle; ballad, lay; sonnet; lyric; ode;
epic

versed *adj* 1 *syn* see EXPERIENCED
  rel competent
  con incompetent
  ant unversed
  2 *syn* see FAMILIAR 3
  ant unversed

verseman *n syn* see POETASTER

versemonger *n syn* see POETASTER

verser *n syn* see POETASTER

versesmith *n syn* see POETASTER

versicolor *adj syn* see VARIEGATED

versicolored *adj syn* see VARIEGATED

versificator *n syn* see POETASTER

versifier *n syn* see POETASTER

version *n* 1 a restating often in simpler
language of something previously stated
or written <a simple *version* of Beowulf
for the use of children>
  syn paraphrase, rendering, restatement,
translation
  rel rendition; clarification, interpretation;
condensation, simplification; rewording;
restipulation
  2 *syn* see ACCOUNT 7
  rel tale
  3 *syn* see INTERPRETATION 2

versus *prep* 1 in conflict with <the case of
John Doe *versus* Richard Roe>
  syn against
  rel con, contra
  idiom at cross-purposes with (*or* to), at
odds with, at outs with, at variance with,
on the outs with
  2 in contrast with <the age-old argument
about free trade *versus* protection>
  syn over against, vis-à-vis
  idiom as opposed to

vertebrae *n syn* see SPINE

vertebral column *n syn* see SPINE

vertex *n syn* see TOP 1
  rel cap; tip-top; apogee, zenith
  idiom upper extremity

vertical *adj* situated at right angles to the
plane of the horizon or extending from
that plane at such an angle < *vertical*
walls>
  syn perpendicular, plumb, straight-up
  rel erect, upright; steep, up-and-down
  con flat, plane

ant horizontal

verticalism *n syn* see VERTICALITY

verticality *n* the quality or state of being vertical <the soaring *verticality* of the spires>
syn perpendicularity, plumbness, verticalism, verticalness
rel erectness, uprightness
con flatness, lowness
ant horizontality

verticalness *n syn* see VERTICALITY

vertiginous *adj syn* see DIZZY 2

verve *n syn* see SPIRIT 5
rel liveliness, vivacity; bounce, buoyancy, elasticity, resiliency; spring; fire, gusto, zest

very *adj* 1 *syn* see AUTHENTIC 2
rel hundred-percent, perfect; correct, exact, right
con fake, fraudulent, mock, sham
2 *syn* see PRECISE 4
rel especial, express, special
3 *syn* see PERFECT 3
4 being as stated without addition or superfluity <the *very* thought of it makes me ill>
syn bare, mere
5 *syn* see SAME 1
idiom (the) very same

very *adv* 1 to a high or exceptional degree <a *very* successful meeting>
syn ‖awful, awfully, ‖big, ‖crazy, damned, ‖dreadful, dreadfully, eminently, exceedingly, exceptionally, extremely, greatly, highly, hugely, insatiably, ‖larruping, ‖main, mightily, mighty, ‖monstrous, mortacious, mortally, most, much, notably, parlous, pesky, ‖pure, rattling, remarkably, right, ‖right smart, snapping, so, spanking, staving, strikingly, super, surpassingly, terribly, thoroughly, too, vitally, whacking, whopping
rel passing, quite, somewhat; perfectly, seriously, significantly, tellingly
idiom nothing if not
con inconsiderably, little, scarcely, slightly
2 in actual fact <told the *very* same story>
syn actually, de facto, genuinely, really, truly, veritably
rel exactly, precisely; almost, nearly, practically, well-nigh
idiom in point of fact, in truth
con apparently, ostensibly, outwardly, seemingly

vest *vb* 1 *syn* see INVEST 2
2 *syn* see BELONG 2

vestibule *n* an entrance chamber between the outer door and the interior of a building <the *vestibule* of a theater>
syn foyer, lobby
rel entrance hall, entry, entryway; portal, portico; antechamber, anteroom; narthex

vestige *n* 1 something (as a mark or visible sign) left by a material thing formerly present but now lost or unknown <digging for the *vestiges* of past civilizations>

syn memento, relic, shadow, trace
rel remainder, remains; rag, remnant, scrap, tag
2 *syn* see FOOTPRINT
rel path; trail

vet *vb syn* see SCRUTINIZE 1
idiom go over with a fine-tooth comb

vet *adj syn* see EXPERIENCED

vet *n syn* see VETERAN

veteran *n* one having knowledge or ability gained through long experience <was a political campaign *veteran* of long standing>
syn longtimer, old hand, old-timer, vet
rel expert, master, past master
con amateur, freshman, youngster
ant novice

veteran *adj syn* see EXPERIENCED
rel wise; sophisticated, worldly
idiom dry behind the ears, not born yesterday, wise in the ways of the world
con inexperienced, unpracticed, unversed; unqualified, unskilled, untrained

veto *vb* to refuse to admit or approve <the President *vetoed* the bill>
syn kill, negative, ‖nix, non-placet
rel decline, deny, disallow, forbid, prohibit, refuse, reject; defeat
idiom put one's veto on
con admit, approve, assent (to); pass

vex *vb syn* see ANNOY 1
rel ‖chaw, embarrass; plague; anger, infuriate
con appease, mollify, pacify, propitiate, smooth (over); please, regale
ant soothe

vexation *n syn* see ANNOYANCE 1
rel aggravation, irritation

vexatious *adj syn* see TROUBLESOME

vexing *n syn* see ANNOYANCE 1

via *prep* 1 over a route that passes through <shipped to New York *via* the Panama Canal>
syn by, by way of, through
rel along; over
2 using as a means of approach or action <reached the voters *via* mass-media advertising>
syn by, by dint of, by means of, by virtue of, by way of, per, through, with
idiom through the medium of

viable *adj syn* see POSSIBLE 1

viands *n pl syn* see FOOD 1
rel fare

vibrant *adj syn* see RESONANT

vibrate *vb syn* see SHAKE 1

vice *n* 1 degrading or immoral habits and practices <an exposé of *vice* and crime in the city>
syn corruption, depravity, immorality, wickedness
rel decay, rot, squalor; evil, ill, sin, wrong; indecency, unchastity; debasement, debauchery, licentiousness, perversion
con morality; respectability; uprightness
ant virtue
2 *syn* see FAULT 2
rel shortcoming
idiom weak point
3 *syn* see BLEMISH

vice versa *adv syn* see AGAIN 5

vicinage *n syn* see LOCALITY 1

vicinity *n* 1 *syn* see LOCALITY 1

---

syn synonym(s)   *rel* related word(s)
ant antonym(s)   *con* contrasted word(s)
idiom idiomatic equivalent(s)
‖ use limited; if in doubt, see a dictionary

2 *syn* see ORDER 4

vicious *adj* 1 *syn* see WRONG 1

2 highly offensive or reprehensible in character, nature, or conduct < *vicious* parents who were a bad influence on their children>

syn corrupt, degenerate, depraved, flagitious, infamous, miscreant, nefarious, perverse, putrid, rotten, unhealthy, villainous

rel bad, faulty, poor, unsound; opprobrious, reprehensible; contaminated, obnoxious, septic

con good, moral, righteous, right-minded

ant virtuous

3 *syn* see SAVAGE 1

rel brutish; bloodthirsty

4 *syn* see MALICIOUS

5 *syn* see INTENSE 1

rel severe

vicissitude *n* 1 *syn* see CHANGE 2

rel alternation; reversal; transposition; progression; diversity, variety

2 *syn* see DIFFICULTY 1

rel chop and change, ups and downs; adversity, mischance, misfortune; affliction, trial, tribulation

victim *n* 1 a living being sacrificed (as in a religious rite) <offered up human *victims* to appease their bloodthirsty gods>

syn offering, sacrifice

2 one subjected to oppression, loss, or suffering < *victims* of social injustice>

syn bottom dog, casualty, prey, underdog

rel quarry

3 *syn* see FOOL 3

idiom easy mark, easy pickings

victimize *vb* 1 *syn* see SACRIFICE 1

2 *syn* see DUPE

victor *n* 1 one that defeats an enemy <the Allies were the *victors* of World War II>

syn conqueror, defeater, master, subduer, subjugator, vanquisher

rel winner

con conquered, defeated, subjugated; loser

ant vanquished

2 a successful contender <emerged as *victor* in the swimming meet>

syn winner

rel champ, champion; first, top

idiom conquering hero

ant loser

Victorian *adj* *syn* see PRIM 1

rel old-fashioned, old-maidish; hidebound; starchy

con easy going; trendy, with-it

victory *n* 1 the overcoming of an opponent <won a knockout *victory* in the first round>

syn conquest, triumph, win

rel command, control, dominion, mastery, subjugation; superiority, supremacy; walkaway, walkover

idiom a feather in one's cap

con loss; bust, failure, fizzle, flop, ||floperoo, washout; comedown, cropper

ant defeat

2 *syn* see BETTER 2

victuals *n pl* *syn* see FOOD 1

videlicet *adv* *syn* see NAMELY

vie *vb* 1 *syn* see COMPETE 1

rel challenge; match; outvie

2 *syn* see OPPOSE 1

view *n* 1 *syn* see LOOK 1

rel examination, inspection, scan, scrutiny

2 *syn* see EXAMINATION

3 *syn* see EYE 4

4 what is revealed to the vision or can be seen <the *view* from the window>

syn outlook, scene, sight

rel panorama, picture, prospect, vista

5 extent or range of vision <there were still no ships in *view*>

syn sight

rel look; apprehension, scan

6 something (as an aim, end, or motive) to or by which the mind is directed <kept this *view* in mind while negotiating>

syn object

rel intent, intention, purpose; aim, ambition, goal, objective; design, plan, project; consideration, notion; expectation

7 *syn* see OPINION

rel concept, conception; deduction, inference

view *vb* 1 *syn* see SCRUTINIZE 1

2 *syn* see EYE 1

rel observe

3 *syn* see SEE 1

4 *syn* see CONSIDER 3

viewable *adj* *syn* see VISUAL 2

viewer *n* *syn* see SPECTATOR

viewpoint *n* 1 *syn* see EYE 4

2 the position or attitude that determines how something is seen, presented, or evaluated <from this *viewpoint* the picture looks askew> <consider totalitarianism from the German *viewpoint*>

syn angle, direction, outlook, side, slant, standpoint; *compare* EYE 4

rel estimation; attitude, position, posture, stand; long view, perspective

idiom frame of reference, point of view, vantage point

viewy *adj* *syn* see IMPRACTICAL 1

vigil *n* *syn* see LOOKOUT 3

vigilance *n* *syn* see LOOKOUT 3

vigilant *adj* *syn* see WATCHFUL

rel agog, anxious, avid, eager, keen; acute, sharp, sharp-eyed; attentive

idiom on one's guard, with a weather eye open

con lax, neglectful, negligent, remiss, slack; forgetful, oblivious, unmindful

vigor *n* 1 *syn* see POWER 4

2 a quality of physical or mental force or forcefulness <the *vigor* of youth>

syn bang, drive, getup, get-up-and-go, go, pep, punch, push, snap, starch, vitality; *compare* ENERGY 2, ENTERPRISE 4, SPIRIT 5

rel bounce, energy, force, might, muscularity, power, strength; healthiness, soundness; lustiness, manliness, virility

con slowness, sluggishness

ant weakness

3 *syn* see ENERGY 2

rel dash, drive, dynamism, fire, punch, starch, steam, vim, zing, zip; ability, capability, capacity

con ineffectiveness; impotence; incompetence, uselessness, worthlessness

vigorous *adj* having or manifesting great vitality and force <seemed as *vigorous* as a youth half his age>

syn dynamic, energetic, lusty, red=
blooded, strenuous, ‖survigrous, vital
rel brisk, dashing, lively, slashing; exuberant, mettlesome, proud, spirited; driving,
hard-driving, hard-hitting, robust, rough=
and-ready, zealous; bouncing, hardy,
healthy, hearty, masterful, potent, powerful, strong, tough; rude, stout, sturdy;
athletic, husky, muscular, sinewy
con languorous, unenergetic; decrepit,
feeble, infirm, weak; impotent
ant lethargic

vigorously *adv syn* see HARD 1
rel alertly, eagerly; boldly, firmly, pur-
posefully, resolutely, unfalteringly, zealously; lustily, robustly
con aimlessly, languorously; falteringly,
indecisively; impotently

vile *adj* 1 *syn* see BASE 3
rel corrupted, debased, debauched, depraved, perverted; coarse, gross, obscene,
vulgar; disgusting, foul, nasty; abhorrent,
contemptible, loathsome, offensive, repulsive, revolting
2 *syn* see OFFENSIVE

vilify *vb syn* see MALIGN
rel abuse, mistreat, misuse, outrage; assail, attack, berate; denounce
con commend, compliment; acclaim, exalt; celebrate, glorify, honor; adore, worship
ant eulogize

vilifying *adj syn* see LIBELOUS

villa *n syn* see MANSION

villain *n* 1 a low, mean, reprehensible person utterly lacking in principle < was an
insufferable bully, a tyrant, and a *villain*
in general >
syn blackguard, heel, knave, lowlife, miscreant, rascal, reprobate, rogue, roperipe,
scoundrel, ‖slubberdegullion; *compare*
SNOT 1, DEVIL 2
rel meanie; evildoer, offender, sinner;
criminal, malefactor
2 *syn* see SCAMP

villainize *vb syn* see MALIGN
ant eulogize

villainous *adj syn* see VICIOUS 2
rel contrary, detestable, objectionable,
offensive; debased, perverted; atrocious,
heinous, outrageous; abandoned, dissolute,
profligate

villenage *n syn* see BONDAGE

vim *n syn* see SPIRIT 5
rel pepper; kick, push

vinculum *n syn* see BOND 3

vindicable *adj syn* see JUSTIFIABLE
rel inoffensive, unobjectionable, venial
con indefensible, unjustifiable; inexcusable, unforgivable; heinous, mortal

vindicate *vb* 1 *syn* see AVENGE
2 *syn* see MAINTAIN 2
rel advocate, plead (for), second, support,
uphold; rationalize; bear out, prove
3 *syn* see EXCULPATE
rel confute, disprove, refute; defend,
guard, protect, shield
con accuse, attack, calumniate

ant convict

vindictive *adj* showing or motivated by a
desire for vengeance < *vindictive* hatred
for his brother >
syn revengeful, vengeful, wreakful
rel grim, implacable, merciless, relentless,
unrelenting; malicious, malign, malignant,
spiteful
con charitable, forgiving, merciful, relenting
ant unvindictive

vinegarish *adj syn* see CANTANKEROUS

vinegary *adj syn* see CANTANKEROUS

vintage *adj* 1 being of old, recognized, and
enduring interest, importance, or quality
< a *vintage* comedy from the silent movie
era >
syn classic, classical
2 *syn* see OLD-FASHIONED

violate *vb* 1 to fail to keep < people who
thoughtlessly *violate* the law >
syn breach, break, contravene, infract,
infringe, offend, transgress
rel disregard, trample (on *or* upon); err,
sin; overpass, trespass
con abide by, carry out, fulfill, submit
(to); heed, keep, mind
ant observe; obey
2 *syn* see RAPE

violation *n* 1 *syn* see BREACH 1
rel break; encroachment; illegality, misdemeanor, offense, wrong
ant observance
2 *syn* see PROFANATION
rel defacement, defacing

violence *n syn* see FORCE 4
rel frenzy, fury, savagery; assault, attack,
clash, foul play, onslaught, rampage,
struggle, tumult, uproar
con passiveness, passivity; peace, peacefulness
ant nonviolence

violent *adj syn* see INTENSE 1
rel forceful, forcible, mighty, potent, powerful, strong; extreme, immoderate, inordinate; acute, cutting, piercing, splitting
con calm, moderate, peaceful
ant nonviolent

violently *adv syn* see HARD 2
rel combatively; destructively, ruinously
idiom like fury, with a vengeance

VIP *n syn* see NOTABLE 1

virago *n* a woman of extremely pugnacious
temperament < an overbearing *virago* who
screamed at her children and squabbled
with her neighbors >
syn amazon, fishwife, harpy, ogress,
scold, shrew, termagant, vixen, Xanthippe
rel cat; dragon; fury

virgin *adj* 1 never having had sexual relations < *virgin* girls were sacrificed >
syn intact, maiden, undeflowered, virginal
rel innocent, untouched; single, spouseless, unmarried, unwed; abstinent, celibate
2 not marred or altered from a natural or
original state < a *virgin* forest >
syn unspoiled, untapped, untouched,
virginal
rel primeval, pristine; fresh, new; unmarred, unsullied

virginal *adj* 1 *syn* see VIRGIN 1
2 *syn* see VIRGIN 2

virginity *n* the quality or state of being a
virgin < lost her *virginity* >

syn ‖cherry, maidenhead, maidenhood
rel chasteness, chastity, purity

virile *adj* 1 *syn* see POTENT 3
2 characterized by the energy and drive considered typical of a man or of men <developed a strong *virile* prose style>
syn male, manlike, manly, masculine
rel manful, mannish; decisive, forceful; energetic, potent, robust; ultramasculine
con effeminate, womanish; emasculated, weak, weakened; impotent

virtual *adj* 1 *syn* see IMPLICIT 3
rel basic, essential, fundamental
ant actual

virtuality *n* *syn* see ESSENCE 2

virtually *adv* not absolutely or actually, yet so nearly so that the difference is negligible <that request is *virtually* an order>
syn in essence, morally, practically; *compare* ALMOST 2
rel basically, essentially, fundamentally; absolutely, actually
idiom for all practical purposes, in effect, in substance, to all intents and purposes

virtue *n* 1 *syn* see GOODNESS
rel fealty, fidelity, loyalty, piety; virtuousness
con dishonesty; disloyalty, infidelity; evil; immorality; depravity
ant vice
2 *syn* see EXCELLENCE
rel attribute, characteristic, feature, property; effectiveness, effectualness, efficacy; force, might, power, strength
3 *syn* see QUALITY 1
4 *syn* see QUALITY 2
5 *syn* see POWER 4

virtuosic *adj* *syn* see CONSUMMATE 1

virtuoso *n* 1 *syn* see EXPERT
2 *syn* see MUSICIAN

virtuous *adj* 1 *syn* see EFFECTIVE
ant virtueless
2 *syn* see MORAL 1
rel spotless, unsullied, untainted, untarnished; worthy
con dishonest; unjust; unworthy; impure, tainted; immodest, immoral, indecent; vicious, wicked
ant unvirtuous, virtueless
3 *syn* see GOOD 11
rel faultless, sinless
idiom innocent as a lamb, in the clear, without reproach
con bad, impure, unrighteous
ant unvirtuous, virtueless; vicious

virulent *adj* 1 *syn* see POISONOUS
rel malign, malignant
2 *syn* see BITTER 3
rel biting, cutting, scathing, sharp, stabbing; hateful, spiteful, unfriendly

virus *n* *syn* see POISON
rel corruption, taint

visage *n* 1 *syn* see FACE 1
2 *syn* see LOOK 2

vis-à-vis *n* 1 *syn* see OPPOSITE NUMBER
2 *syn* see TÊTE-À-TÊTE

vis-à-vis *prep* 1 *syn* see AGAINST 1
rel opposite
2 *syn* see VERSUS 2

viscera *n pl* *syn* see ENTRAILS

visceral *adj* 1 *syn* see INNER 2

2 *syn* see INSTINCTIVE 1

viscerous *adj* *syn* see INNER 2

viscid *adj* *syn* see VISCOUS
rel jellylike, slabby

viscose *adj* *syn* see VISCOUS
rel smeary

viscous *adj* having a glutinous adhesive consistency or quality <a *viscous* scum covered the surface of the platter>
syn tenacious, tough, viscid, viscose
rel ‖slab, slimy, thick; glutinous, gummy, ropy, sticky; semifluid; stiff

visibility *n* the quality or state of being visible <very poor *visibility* due to fog>
syn visuality

visible *adj* *syn* see VISUAL 2
rel seen

vision *n* 1 *syn* see REVELATION
rel apparition, phenomenon, presence
2 *syn* see FANCY 4
rel muse
idiom phantom of the mind
3 *syn* see EYE 2

vision *vb* *syn* see THINK 1

visional *adj* *syn* see VISUAL 1

visionary *adj* 1 *syn* see DREAMY 1
rel abstracted, introspective, musing; impractical
idiom out of this world, up in the clouds
2 *syn* see IDEALISTIC
rel exalted, grandiose, lofty, noble, pretentious
ant pragmatic, pragmatical
3 *syn* see AMBITIOUS 2
rel radical

visionary *n* *syn* see DREAMER
ant pragmatist

visionless *adj* *syn* see BLIND 1

visit *vb* 1 *syn* see INFLICT 2
rel afflict, bother, pain, trouble; avenge, punish
idiom bring down upon
2 to make a social call upon <*visited* friends briefly in the evening>
syn call, come by, come over, drop (in *or* by), look in, look up, pop (in), run in, see, step in, stop (in *or* by)
3 to reside with temporarily as a guest <*visited* with friends in the country for a few weeks>
syn sojourn, stay, stop (over), tarry
rel frequent; reside
4 *syn* see CONVERSE

visit *n* 1 a coming to stay with another temporarily and usually briefly <pay a *visit* to friends>
syn call, visitation
2 *syn* see SOJOURN

visitant *n* *syn* see VISITOR 1

visitation *n* 1 *syn* see VISIT 1
2 *syn* see TRIAL 1
rel mischance; calamity, catastrophe, disaster

visitor *n* 1 one who visits another <there are *visitors* in the living room>
syn caller, guest, visitant; *compare* COMPANY 2
rel invitee
2 **visitors** *pl* *syn* see COMPANY 2

visor *n* 1 a projecting front brim on a cap or hat for shading the eyes <the *visor* kept out the sun>
syn bill, peak

rel eyeshade
2 *syn* see MASK 1
vista *n* an extensive or distant view < a
long flat tree-lined *vista* >
syn lookout, outlook, perspective, prospect, scape
rel panorama, scene, sight, view; range,
scope, survey
idiom long view
visual *adj* 1 of or relating to or used in
vision < the *visual* sense >
syn ocular, optic, optical, visional
2 capable of being seen < *visual* objects >
syn ocular, seeable, viewable, visible
rel discernible, perceivable, perceptible
visuality *n syn* see VISIBILITY
visualize *vb* 1 *syn* see THINK 1
rel picture, view; objectify; call up, conjure (up)
idiom bring (or call) to mind, conjure up
a mental image (*or* picture) of, see in the
mind's eye
2 *syn* see FORESEE
vital *adj* 1 *syn* see LIVING 1
rel breathing
2 *syn* see VIGOROUS
3 *syn* see ESSENTIAL 2
rel indispensable, needed, needful, required, requisite; integral, prerequisite
vital force *n syn* see SOUL 1
vitality *n syn* see VIGOR 2
rel animation, life, liveliness, pulse; endurance, energy, spirit, vim
vitalize *vb* to arouse to activity, animation, or life < atomic energy is a force
that can *vitalize* or destroy human civilization >
syn actify, activate, activize, energize
rel animate, enliven, invigorate, quicken,
vivify; dynamize, excite, galvanize, provoke, stimulate; pep up, strengthen
idiom put life into
con eviscerate, weaken
ant atrophy; devitalize
vitalizing *adj syn* see INVIGORATING
ant devitalizing
vitally *adv syn* see VERY 1
vitiate *adj syn* see DEBASED
ant purified
vitiate *vb* 1 *syn* see INJURE 1
rel twist, warp
2 *syn* see DEBASE 1
rel defile, soil, sully, taint; prostitute;
contaminate
idiom drive to the dogs
ant purify
3 *syn* see ABOLISH 1
vitiated *adj syn* see DEBASED
rel contaminated, defiled, polluted,
tainted; impaired, injured, spoiled
ant purified
vitriolic *adj syn* see BITTER 3
vituperate *vb syn* see SCOLD 1
rel condemn, lambaste; asperse, calumniate, malign, traduce; bark (at), growl (at),
yell (at); abuse, curse
idiom rip into
con applaud, commend, compliment;
eulogize, extol, praise

ant acclaim
vituperation *n syn* see ABUSE
rel blame, censure, revilement, scolding,
tongue-lashing
con eulogy, extolment
ant acclaim, praise
vituperative *adj syn* see ABUSIVE
rel censorious, critical; severe; railing,
scolding
vituperatory *adj syn* see ABUSIVE
rel censorious, critical; severe; railing,
scolding
vituperous *adj syn* see ABUSIVE
rel censorious, critical; severe; railing,
scolding
vivacious *adj* 1 *syn* see LIVELY 1
rel breezy, vibrant, zesty; frolicsome,
playful, sportive
idiom gay as a lark
ant languid
2 *syn* see EXUBERANT 1
viva voce *adj syn* see VOCAL 1
vivid *adj* 1 *syn* see COLORFUL
2 *syn* see GRAPHIC 1
rel acute, intense, keen, sharp; dramatic,
dramaturgic, theatrical; eloquent, expressive, meaningful, rich; animated, lively,
spirited, vigorous
vivificate *vb syn* see QUICKEN 1
rel revive
vivify *vb syn* see QUICKEN 1
rel refresh, renew, restore; excite, galvanize
idiom give life to, imbue with life, put
new life into
vivres *n pl syn* see FOOD 1
vixen *n syn* see VIRAGO
vizard *n syn* see MASK 1
‖**vlei** *n syn* see SWAMP
vocable *n syn* see WORD 2
rel verbalism
vocabulary *n* 1 the sum or set of words
employed by a language, group, individual, or work or in relation to a subject
< Latin contributes heavily to the *vocabu-
lary* of English >
syn lexicon, word-hoard, word-stock
idiom stock of words
2 *syn* see TERMINOLOGY
rel phraseology
vocal *adj* 1 uttered by the voice or having
to do with such utterance < the infant's
primitive *vocal* sounds from which language develops >
syn articulate, oral, sonant, spoken, viva
voce, voiced
rel intonated; expressed, uttered
con unexpressed, unuttered, unvoiced
ant nonvocal
2 *syn* see VOCALIC
ant consonantal
3 being able to express oneself clearly or
easily < he was hardly *vocal*: he could
scarcely express the simplest concepts >
syn articulate, eloquent, fluent, smooth-
spoken
rel expressing, voicing; expressive; outspoken, stentorian, venting
con faltering, halting, hesitant, stumbling
4 *syn* see OUTSPOKEN
vocalic *adj* marked by, consisting of, or
functioning as a vowel or vowels < *vocalic*
and consonantal sounds >

---

syn synonym(s)   *rel* related word(s)
ant antonym(s)   *con* contrasted word(s)
idiom idiomatic equivalent(s)
‖ use limited; if in doubt, see a dictionary

syn vocal, vowel, vowely
rel vowellike
vocalism *n syn* see VOCALIZATION
vocalization *n* the exercise of the vocal
organs in song or speech < his *vocalization*
of a previously unstated thought >
  syn articulation, utterance, uttering, vocalism; *compare* SPEECH 1
  rel mouth, mouthing; sounding, voice,
voicing; diction, enunciation, verbalization;
speaking, speech
vocalize *vb* 1 *syn* see SPEAK 1
  rel emit, let out; express; enunciate, pronounce; communicate, convey, impart
  idiom execute vocally
2 *syn* see SING 1
vocation *n* 1 *syn* see TRADE 1
2 *syn* see MISSION
vocative *adj syn* see GLIB
  rel chatty, garrulous, loquacious, talkative, windy; slick, smooth
vociferant *adj syn* see VOCIFEROUS
vociferate *vb syn* see CALL 1
vociferous *adj* so loud, noisy, and insistent
as to compel attention < the crowd made
vociferous protests against the speaker's
statement >
  syn blatant, boisterous, clamorous, ‖din-
some, loudmouthed, multivocal, obstreperous, openmouthed, strident, vociferant
  rel distracting; loud, noisy, shrill
  con close-lipped, reserved, silent, uncommunicative; noiseless, quiet, still
vogue *n syn* see FASHION 2
  rel bon ton, fashionableness, stylishness
voice *n* 1 *syn* see EXPRESSION 1
  rel speech
2 the right to express a wish, choice, or
opinion or to influence a situation < even
the youngest had a *voice* in planning the
party >
  syn say, say-so
voice *vb syn* see SPEAK 1
  rel sound; articulate, enunciate, pronounce; formulate, phrase, present, put;
recount, tell
voiced *adj syn* see VOCAL 1
voiceless *adj syn* see DUMB 1
void *adj* 1 *syn* see EMPTY 1
  ant full
2 *syn* see DEVOID
  rel scant, short, shy; bare, bereft, denuded, deprived
3 *syn* see NULL
  rel negated
void *n syn* see HOLE 3
void *vb* 1 *syn* see VACATE 2
  rel evacuate; deplete, drain, eliminate;
eject, remove, throw out
2 *syn* see DISCHARGE 5
void *vb syn* see ANNUL 4
  idiom declare (*or* make) null and void
voidness *n syn* see VACUITY 2
  ant fullness
volage *adj syn* see GIDDY 1
volant *adj syn* see AGILE
volatile *adj* 1 *syn* see ELASTIC 1
  rel capricious, fickle, inconstant, mercurial, unstable; flighty, flippant, frivolous,
light-minded; changeable, protean, variable
2 *syn* see EXCITABLE
  rel explosive

3 *syn* see INCONSTANT 1
4 *syn* see TRANSIENT
volatility *n syn* see LIGHTNESS
  rel animation, sprightliness; inconstancy,
instability, mercurialness; changeability,
variability
volition *n syn* see WILL 2
  rel choice, election, option, selection;
desire, preference
  con coercion, compulsion, duress, force
volley *n syn* see BARRAGE
volte-face *n syn* see REVERSAL 1
volte-face *vb syn* see TURN 6
  rel about-face, face (about), right-about-
face
voluble *adj syn* see GLIB
volume *n* 1 *syn* see BOOK 1
2 *syn* see BULK 1
  rel amount, content, quantity
3 *syn* see BODY 4
voluminous *adj syn* see MANY
voluntary *adj* consisting of or proceeding
from an exercise of free will < the law
requires that a confession be *voluntary* >
  syn deliberate, intentional, unforced, unprescribed, willful, willing, witting
  rel chosen, elected, opted, volitional;
autonomous, free, independent
  con coerced, compelled, forced; unintentional, unplanned, unwilling, unwitting
  ant involuntary
voluptuous *adj syn* see SENSUOUS
  rel indulgent, self-gratifying; abandoned,
dissipated, dissolute, excessive, wanton
  con self-contained, self-denying
  ant ascetic
vomit *vb* to discharge the contents of the
stomach through the mouth < the churning seas made several passengers *vomit* >
  syn barf, bring up, ‖cack, ‖cascade, ‖cast,
‖cat, disgorge, ‖heave, shoot, sick (up),
spew, spit up, throw up, upchuck
  rel gag, regurgitate, retch; keck; eject,
expel
  idiom ‖blow one's lunch, holler New
York, lose one's cookies
voodoo *n* 1 *syn* see MAGICIAN 1
2 *syn* see JINX
voodoo *vb syn* see BEWITCH 1
voodooist *n syn* see MAGICIAN 1
voracious *adj* excessively greedy (as in
appetite, reactions, or behavior) < the
wolverine is an extremely *voracious* eater >
  syn edacious, gluttonous, rapacious, ravening, ravenous
  rel acquisitive, covetous, grasping, greedy;
devouring, gorging, satiating, sating, surfeiting; avid, insatiable
vortex *n syn* see EDDY
  rel spiral, spout
votary *n* 1 *syn* see ADDICT
  rel disciple; freak
2 *syn* see AMATEUR 1
  rel hound
vote *n* 1 *syn* see BALLOT 1
2 *syn* see SUFFRAGE
vote (in) *vb syn* see ELECT 2
  rel choose, decide
  idiom cast one's vote for
vouch *vb syn* see CERTIFY 1
  rel support, uphold; confirm, corroborate,
prove, substantiate, verify; assure, guarantee

vouchsafe *vb syn* see GRANT 1
rel condescend, deign, stoop; accommodate, favor, oblige

vow *vb* to promise solemnly < *vowed* never to leave each other >
syn covenant, pledge, plight, swear; *compare* PROMISE 1
rel assert, declare, ‖swan; promise
idiom give (*or* make) a solemn promise, give one's word of honor

vowel *adj syn* see VOCALIC

vowely *adj syn* see VOCALIC

voyage *n* a journey by water < took the new ship on a long *voyage* >
syn cruise
rel journey, tour, trip

voyeur *n syn* see PEEPING TOM

vulgar *adj* 1 *syn* see VERNACULAR
rel conversational, spoken; idiomatic
2 *syn* see PUBLIC 4
3 *syn* see COARSE 3
4 *syn* see OBSCENE 2
rel base, low, vile; loathsome, offensive,

repulsive, revolting; indecorous, indelicate, uncouth
con decent, delicate, refined; high-minded, lofty, noble
5 *syn* see BARBARIC 1
rel inelegant, ungraceful; improper, incorrect, unseemly; uncouth, unpolished, unrefined
idiom in very poor taste
con elegant, graceful; correct, proper, seemly

vulgarism *n syn* see BARBARISM

vulgate *adj syn* see VERNACULAR

vulgate *n syn* see VERNACULAR 3

vulnerability *n syn* see EXPOSURE
rel vincibility

vulnerableness *n syn* see EXPOSURE
rel weakness

vulnerary *adj syn* see CURATIVE

vulpine *adj syn* see SLY 1

vulture *vb syn* see STEAL 1

vulturine *adj syn* see RAPACIOUS 1

vulturish *adj syn* see RAPACIOUS 1

vulturous *adj syn* see RAPACIOUS 1

W

‖**wack** *n syn* see ECCENTRIC

wacky *adj* 1 *syn* see FOOLISH 2
2 *syn* see INSANE 1

wad *n* 1 *syn* see LUMP 1
2 *often* **wads** *pl syn* see SCAD
3 *syn* see FORTUNE 4

wade (in *or* into) *vb syn* see PITCH IN 1

‖**waffle** *vb syn* see BABBLE 2

wag *vb* to move to and fro < the dog *wagged* his tail briskly >
syn beat, lash, switch, waggle, wave, woggle
rel shake, twitch, wiggle; oscillate; wigwag

wag *n* 1 a person full of sportive humor < a gay young *wag*, always full of fun >
syn card, comedian, humorist, joker, zany
rel clown, cutup, madcap, prankster, show-off; jester, kidder, quipster, wisecracker, wit
idiom life of the party
2 *syn* see ZANY 2
3 *syn* see HUMORIST 2

wage *n, often* **wages** *pl* the price paid a person for his labor or services < high *wages* are often seen as a factor in inflation >
syn emolument, fee, hire, pay, pay envelope, salary, stipend
rel compensation, recompense, remuneration, reward; earnings, income, receipts, return(s), take

wager *n syn* see BET

wager *vb* 1 *syn* see VENTURE 1
2 *syn* see GAMBLE 1

idiom lay a wager

waggery *n* 1 *syn* see MISCHIEVOUSNESS
2 *syn* see JOKE 1

waggish *adj syn* see PLAYFUL 1
rel facetious, humorous, jocose, jocular, witty; comic, comical, droll, funny, laughable, ludicrous; arch, pert, saucy
con earnest, grave, sedate, serious, sober, staid

waggishness *n syn* see MISCHIEVOUSNESS

waggle *vb syn* see WAG
rel sway, waddle, wobble

wail *vb* 1 *syn* see CRY 2
idiom make an outcry
2 *syn* see HOWL 1
3 *syn* see BAWL 2
4 *syn* see COMPLAIN

wailful *adj syn* see MELANCHOLY 2

waistband *n syn* see BELT 1

wait *vb syn* see STAY 2
rel anticipate, foresee; await, expect
idiom bide one's time, cool one's heels, look forward to, mark time
con depart, go, leave

wait (on) *vb syn* see MINISTER (to)

waive *vb* 1 *syn* see RELINQUISH
rel allow, concede, grant
con claim, demand, exact, require; assert, defend, maintain
2 *syn* see DEFER

wake *vb* 1 to stop sleeping < she usually *woke* before dawn >
syn awake, awaken, rouse, stir, waken
rel arise, get up, roll out
con catnap, doze, drowse, nap, nod, snooze; sleep, slumber
2 *syn* see STIR 1
rel freshen, renew
con calm, ease, mollify, relax

waken *vb* 1 *syn* see STIR 1
rel freshen, renew

---

syn synonym(s)   *rel* related word(s)
ant antonym(s)   *con* contrasted word(s)
idiom idiomatic equivalent(s)
‖ use limited; if in doubt, see a dictionary

con calm, ease, mollify, relax
2 *syn* see WAKE 1

wale *n syn* see WHEAL

walk *vb* 1 to advance on foot step by step
< often *walked* to work on pleasant
mornings >
syn ambulate, foot (it), hoof, pace, step,
traipse, tread, troop
rel circumambulate, perambulate, promenade, ramble, stroll; hike, tramp; lumber,
plod, slog, stride, stump, trudge; leg, race,
run
idiom beat one's feet, heel and toe it, ride
shanks' mare
con drive, ride
2 *syn* see TRAVERSE 5

walk *n* 1 a usually brief journey on foot
for pleasure or exercise < always took a
walk before breakfast >
syn constitutional, ramble, saunter, stroll,
turn
rel hike, march, tramp; deambulation,
parade, promenade; airing, stretch
2 *syn* see FIELD

walkabout *n syn* see TRAMP 3

walkaway *n syn* see RUNAWAY

walk out *vb syn* see STRIKE 1

walkover *n syn* see RUNAWAY

wall *n syn* see BAR 2

wall *vb syn* see ENCLOSE 1

wallop *n* 1 *syn* see BLOW 1
2 *syn* see IMPACT
3 *syn* see THRILL

wallop *vb* 1 *syn* see BEAT 1
2 *syn* see WHIP 2
3 *syn* see SLAM 1

walloping *adj syn* see HUGE

wallow *vb* 1 to roll or move in an indolent
and ungainly yet comfortable fashion
< hogs *wallowing* in a cool mudhole >
syn welter
rel flounder, roll, tumble; cuddle, nestle,
snuggle
2 to move or progress unsteadily and
clumsily as if beset by obstacles < *wal-
lowed* through the mire for miles trying to
get help >
syn blunder, flounder, lurch, stumble;
compare STUMBLE 3
rel reel, stagger, sway, totter, wamble,
welter
idiom make heavy weather (of)
3 to become deeply or excessively involved
in or with something subjectively felt as
pleasant < *wallowing* in luxury >
syn bask, indulge, luxuriate, revel, roll,
rollick, welter
rel baby, humor, pamper, spoil; appreciate, delight (in), enjoy, relish
con abstain, refrain; avoid, eschew, shun

waltz *vb syn* see BREEZE

‖**wambly** *adj syn* see SQUEAMISH 1

‖**wampum** *n syn* see MONEY

wan *adj* 1 *syn* see PALE 1
rel cadaverous, haggard, worn; blanched,
bleached, washed-out; anemic, bloodless
2 *syn* see WEAK 4

wander *vb* 1 to move about from place to
place more or less aimlessly and without
obvious plan < *wandering* through the
forest >
syn bat, circumambulate, drift, gad, gallivant, maunder, meander, mooch, ‖project,
ramble, range, roam, roll, rove, straggle,

stray, traipse, vagabond, vagabondize;
compare SAUNTER
rel amble, saunter, stroll; divagate, diverge; trail; boom, bum, tramp
2 *syn* see DIGRESS 2
3 *syn* see ERR

wanderer *n syn* see ROVER

wandering *adj* 1 *syn* see ITINERANT
2 *syn* see ERRATIC 1
3 *syn* see DELIRIOUS 1

wane *vb* 1 *syn* see ABATE 4
ant wax
2 *syn* see FAIL 3
ant wax

wangle *vb syn* see ENGINEER
rel outflank, outgeneral, outmaneuver,
overreach

waning *n syn* see FAILURE 4
ant waxing

‖**wanky** *adj syn* see WEAK 1

want *vb* 1 *syn* see LACK
idiom be found wanting, fall short, feel
the want of
2 *syn* see DESIRE 1
rel choose, prefer
idiom could do with, have a mind (*or* an
eye) to
3 to have as a duty or responsibility
< you *want* to behave yourself >
syn must, ought, should
rel become, befit, behoove; need (to)
idiom be wise to, had better (*or* best)

want *n* 1 *syn* see ABSENCE
rel exigency, necessity, need
con sufficiency
2 *syn* see POVERTY 1
rel exiguousness, meagerness, scantiness,
skimpiness; inadequacy, insufficiency
con riches
3 *syn* see REQUIREMENT 1

wanting *adj* 1 *syn* see ABSENT 1
2 *syn* see SHORT 3
3 *syn* see DEFICIENT 1

wanting *prep syn* see WITHOUT 2

wanton *adj* 1 *syn* see FAST 7
rel lax, slack; wayward
idiom of easy virtue, of loose morals
con austere, puritanical, restrained, self=
restrained
ant chaste
2 *syn* see SUPEREROGATORY
rel malevolent, malicious, spiteful; contrary, perverse; wayward

wanton *n* a woman who engages in lewd
unseemly conduct < giddy *wantons* flaunting themselves in bars >
syn baggage, ‖bim, ‖bimbo, cyprian,
hussy, jade, jezebel, ‖pig, slattern, slut,
strumpet, tramp, trollop, trull, wench;
compare DOXY, HARLOT 1, PROSTITUTE
idiom loose woman

wanton *vb syn* see TRIFLE 1

wantwit *n syn* see DUNCE

war *vb syn* see CONTEND 1
rel attempt, endeavor, essay, strive, struggle; challenge, engage, take on
idiom draw the sword against, lift one's
hand against, take up the cudgels

warble *n syn* see MELODY

war chest *n syn* see TREASURY 2

war club *n syn* see CUDGEL

war cry *n syn* see BATTLE CRY

ward *n* 1 *syn* see GUARD 2

2 *syn* see DEFENSE 1

3 *syn* see CUSTODY

ward *vb* 1 to cause to miss an objective by or as if by turning aside < *warded* the stroke of his enemy's sword with his shield >

syn deflect, fend, parry

rel block, check, halt, stay, stymie; avert, divert, turn

idiom keep at arm's length, turn aside

2 *syn* see PREVENT 2

rel balk, foil, frustrate, thwart; check, interrupt

ant conduce (to)

ward (off) *vb syn* see FEND (off)

ant bring on

warden *n syn* see CUSTODIAN

ware *adj syn* see AWARE

warehouse *vb syn* see STOW

rel accommodate; guard, protect, shelter

wares *n pl syn* see MERCHANDISE

warfare *n syn* see CONTEST 1

warhorse *n syn* see COURSER

warlike *adj* 1 *syn* see BELLIGERENT

ant peaceable

2 *syn* see MARTIAL

rel battling, contending, fighting, warring

ant unwarlike

warlock *n syn* see MAGICIAN 1

warm *adj* 1 *syn* see ENTHUSIASTIC

2 *syn* see TENDER

rel ardent, fervent, passionate; affable, cordial, gracious; heartfelt, hearty, sincere, wholehearted

ant cool; austere

warmed–over *adj syn* see TRITE

warmhearted *adj syn* see TENDER

rel benign, benignant, kind, kindly, outgoing

con austere, cold, cool, frigid, frosty, severe, stern

ant coldhearted

warming *n syn* see DEFEAT 1

warmish *adj syn* see TEPID 1

warn *vb* 1 to let one know of approaching danger or risk < police and the weather service join to *warn* travelers of hazardous road conditions >

syn caution, forewarn

rel advise, alert, apprise, inform, notify, tip; counsel, direct, guide

idiom address a warning to, give warning, put a flea in one's ear, put one on guard

2 *syn* see INFORM 2

3 *syn* see COMMAND

warning *n* something and especially a statement that warns or is intended to warn < gave them *warning* that disobedience would lead to punishment >

syn admonition, caution, caveat, commonition, forewarning, monition

rel advice, counsel, guidance, recommendation; hint, suggestion, tip

idiom flea (*or* word) in the ear, word to the wise

warning *adj syn* see MONITORY

warp *vb* 1 *syn* see DEBASE 1

rel contort, crook, distort, twist

con disentangle, rectify, straighten, unkink

2 *syn* see DEFORM

rel bend, crook, kink, twist

3 *syn* see MISREPRESENT

war paint *n* 1 *syn* see FINERY

2 *syn* see MAKEUP 3

warped *adj syn* see BIASED 2

ant unwarped

warrant *n* 1 *syn* see PLEDGE 1

2 *syn* see BASIS 3

3 *syn* see WORD 8

warrant *vb* 1 *syn* see MAINTAIN 2

rel state; assure, ensure, insure

2 to give assurance of the worth of something especially in respect to quality, quantity, or condition < *warranted* the merchandise to be exactly as described in the catalog >

syn certify, guarantee, guaranty

rel assure, insure, secure; back, sponsor, stipulate; affirm, claim, state

idiom stand behind

3 *syn* see JUSTIFY 4

rel endorse; call (for), need, require

warrantable *adj syn* see JUSTIFIABLE

ant unwarrantable

warranty *n syn* see GUARANTEE 1

warrior *n syn* see SOLDIER

wary *adj* 1 *syn* see CAUTIOUS

rel distrustful, doubting, leery, suspicious; vigilant, watchful

idiom on one's guard

con careless, heedless, thoughtless; devil=may-care, reckless, venturesome

ant foolhardy; unwary

2 *syn* see SPARING

wash *vb* 1 *syn* see BATHE 1

2 *syn* see BATHE 2

3 *syn* see DRIFT 1

4 *syn* see SLOSH 1

washed–out *adj syn* see EFFETE 2

washed–up *adj* 1 *syn* see THROUGH 3

2 *syn* see THROUGH 4

wash out *vb* 1 *syn* see FAIL 4

2 *syn* see DISCARD

wash up *vb syn* see GO 4

washy *adj syn* see DILUTE

waspish *adj* 1 *syn* see IRRITABLE

rel contrary, impatient, perverse; malicious, sharp, spiteful; crabbed, cross=grained

2 *syn* see CANTANKEROUS

waspy *adj* 1 *syn* see IRRITABLE

rel contrary, impatient, perverse; malicious, sharp, spiteful; crabbed, cross=grained

2 *syn* see CANTANKEROUS

wassail *n* 1 *syn* see BINGE 1

2 *syn* see REVELRY 2

wassail *vb syn* see REVEL 1

waste *n* 1 an area of the earth unsuitable for cultivation or general habitation < the scattered dwellers of southern Africa's dry *wastes* >

syn badland, barren, desert, wasteland, wild, wilderness, wild land, wildness

rel brush, brushland, bush; jungle

2 *syn* see EXTRAVAGANCE 2

3 *syn* see REFUSE

rel rubble, rummage

waste *vb* 1 *syn* see RAVAGE

idiom reduce to a shambles

---

syn synonym(s)   *rel* related word(s)

ant antonym(s)   *con* contrasted word(s)

idiom idiomatic equivalent(s)

‖ use limited; if in doubt, see a dictionary

ant conserve

2 to spend or expend freely and usually foolishly or futilely < *wasted* his inheritance on women and gambling > < *waste* one's time on trifles >

syn blow, blunder (away), cast away, consume, dissipate, dribble (away), drivel, fool (away), fritter, frivol away, muddle (away), ‖piss away, potter (away), prodigalize, riot (away), squander, throw away, trifle (away)

rel disburse, expend, spend; dispense, distribute; deplete, drain, exhaust, impoverish; dispel, disperse, scatter; misspend

idiom let slip through one's fingers, pour down the drain, throw good money after bad

ant save; conserve

waste (away) *vb syn* see FAIL 3

wasted *adj syn* see EMACIATED
rel meager; shriveled, withered, wizened
con healthy, robust; stalwart, stout, strong, sturdy

wastefulness *n syn* see EXTRAVAGANCE 2
ant frugality

wasteland *n syn* see WASTE 1

waster *n* **1** *syn* see SPENDTHRIFT
rel dissipater, fritterer; idler, loafer, lounger
2 *syn* see WASTREL 1

wastethrift *n syn* see SPENDTHRIFT

wastrel *n* **1** a worthless, self-indulgent, and reprehensible person < loafers and other *wastrels* lounging on the corner >
syn ‖bad lot, good-for-nothing, ne'er-do-well, no-good, profligate, rounder, scapegrace, waster
rel lecher, libertine, rake, rip, roué; blackguard, black sheep, knave, rascal, rogue, scoundrel; rapscallion, scalawag, scamp
idiom sad case
2 *syn* see SPENDTHRIFT
rel dissipater, fritterer; idler, loafer, lounger

watch *vb* **1** *syn* see SEE 2
rel examine, follow, inspect, scan, scrutinize
idiom keep an eye on, keep tabs on
2 *syn* see EYE 2
3 *syn* see TEND 2
idiom keep watch over
4 *syn* see LOOK 1

watch *n* **1** *syn* see LOOKOUT 3
2 *syn* see GUARD 2
3 *syn* see EYE 3

watch and ward *n syn* see LOOKOUT 3

watchdog *n syn* see CUSTODIAN

watcher *n syn* see SPECTATOR

watchfire *n syn* see BEACON 1

watchful *adj* paying close attention usually with a view to anticipating approaching danger or opportunity < adopted a policy of *watchful* waiting >
syn alert, open-eyed, unsleeping, vigilant, wakeful, wide-awake
rel cautious, chary, circumspect, wary; prompt, quick, ready
idiom keeping one's eyes peeled (*or* open), on the watch (*or* lookout)
con careless, heedless, thoughtless; inadvertent; absentminded, abstracted, faraway
ant unwatchful

watchman *n syn* see GUARD 2

watch out *vb syn* see BEWARE

watchword *n* **1** *syn* see PASSWORD 1
2 *syn* see PASSWORD 3
3 *syn* see CATCHWORD

water *n* **1** *syn* see TEARS
2 *syn* see SALIVA

water *vb syn* see DROOL 1

water closet *n syn* see TOILET

watercourse *n syn* see CHANNEL 1

watered–down *adj syn* see DILUTE

waterfall *n* a precipitous descent of water or the site of this < heard the roar of the *waterfall* >
syn cascade, cataract, chute, fall(s), ‖force, sault, spout
rel rapid(s), riffle, shoot; eddy, surge, vortex, whirlpool

watering hole *n* **1** *syn* see RESORT 2
2 *syn* see BAR 5
3 *syn* see NIGHTCLUB

watering place *n* **1** *syn* see SPA 1
2 *syn* see RESORT 3
3 *syn* see BAR 5
4 *syn* see NIGHTCLUB

waterish *adj* **1** *syn* see DILUTE
2 *syn* see PALE 2
3 *syn* see INSIPID 3

waterless *adj syn* see DRY 1
ant watered

waterlog *vb syn* see SOAK 1

watery *adj* **1** *syn* see DILUTE
2 *syn* see PALE 2
3 *syn* see INSIPID 3

wave *vb syn* see WAG

waver *vb syn* see HESITATE
rel palter, shift, trim; seesaw, teeter
idiom back and fill, hem and haw

wavering *n syn* see HESITATION

wavering *adj* **1** *syn* see VACILLATING 2
ant unwavering
2 *syn* see WEAK 2

wax *vb* **1** *syn* see INCREASE 2
ant wane
2 *syn* see BECOME 1

wax *n syn* see RISE 3
ant wane

waxen *adj syn* see PALE 1

waxy *adj syn* see ANGRY

way *n* **1** a public and unobstructed passage leading from one place to another < tracing the remains of an old lumberman's *way* >
syn artery, avenue, boulevard, ‖drag, highway, path, road, street, thoroughfare, track
rel course, line, passage, route; alley, byway, lane, ride, row
2 that along which one passes in going from one place to another < his *way* led through wooded hills >
syn course, line, passage, path, road, route
3 *syn* see DOOR 2
4 *syn* see METHOD 1
rel custom, habit, habitude, practice, usage, use, wont
5 *syn* see STYLE 4
6 *syn* see HABIT 1
7 *syn* see DISTANCE 3
8 *syn* see TYPE

‖wayback *n syn* see RUSTIC

wayfaring *adj syn* see ITINERANT

waylay *vb syn* see SURPRISE 1
   rel lurk, prowl, skulk, slink
   idiom lay wait for, lie in wait for
ways *n pl but sing in constr syn* see DISTANCE 2
wayward *adj* 1 *syn* see CONTRARY 3
   rel capricious, fickle, inconstant, unstable, variable
   con complaisant, good-natured
   2 *syn* see ARBITRARY 1
weak *adj* 1 lacking physical, mental, or moral strength <a *weak* spirit in a *weak* body>
   syn decrepit, feeble, flimsy, fragile, frail, infirm, insubstantial, puny, unsound, unsubstantial, ‖wanky, weakly
   rel debilitated, enfeebled, sickly, spindly, weakened; forceless, impotent, impuissant, powerless
   con stalwart, stout, sturdy, tenacious, tough; dynamic, energetic, forceful, vigorous
   ant strong
   2 deficient in stability <a love too *weak* to bear the trials of daily life>
   syn dickey, fluctuant, insecure, rootless, shaky, unstable, unsure, vacillating, wavering, wobbly; *compare* RICKETY
   rel hesitant, irresolute, trimming, uncertain; insubstantial, undependable, unreliable
   con certain, secure, solid, stable, sure; dependable, reliable, substantial
   ant strong
   3 *syn* see IMPLAUSIBLE
   4 not equal to the requirements and demands of a situation <a *weak* executive>
   syn boneless, emasculate, forceless, impotent, inadequate, ineffective, ineffectual, invertebrate, slack-spined, spineless, wan
   rel unfit, unqualified, unsuitable; bungling, incompetent, inept
   con able, competent, effective, efficient; adequate, fit, qualified, satisfactory, sufficient, suitable; manly, masculine, virile
   ant strong
   5 *syn* see DILUTE
   ant strong
weaken *vb* 1 to lose or cause to lose strength, vigor, or energy <his hesitation *weakened* the force of his argument>
   syn attenuate, blunt, cripple, debilitate, disable, enfeeble, sap, unbrace, undermine, unstrengthen; *compare* PARALYZE 1
   rel emasculate, enervate, incapacitate, unman, unnerve; damage, impair, injure; lessen, minimize, reduce; dilute, thin
   con better, improve; activate, energize, invigorate, vitalize
   ant strengthen
   2 *syn* see FAIL 1
   3 *syn* see FAIL 3
   4 *syn* see DILUTE
weak-headed *adj syn* see SIMPLE 3
weak-kneed *adj syn* see VACILLATING 2
weakling *n* a person lacking in stamina and character <his speech deplored the characterless *weaklings* in critical positions>

syn baby, doormat, invertebrate, jellyfish, milksop, Milquetoast, ‖molly, mollycoddle, namby-pamby, pantywaist, sissy, sissy-pants (*or* sissy-britches), sop
   rel butt, mark, pushover, sucker; drip, mama's boy, misfit, mother's boy, sad sack, weak sister
   idiom shrinking violet
weakly *adv syn* see SOTTO VOCE
   ant strongly
weakly *adj syn* see WEAK 1
weak-minded *adj syn* see SIMPLE 3
weakness *n syn* see APPETITE 3
weal *n syn* see WHEAL
weald *n syn* see FOREST
wealth *n* 1 *syn* see MEAN 3
   2 one's worldly possessions <at that point his *wealth* consisted of the clothes he stood in and a solitary quarter>
   syn fortune, property, resources, riches, substance, worth
   rel assets, estate, goods, holdings, possessions
wealthy *adj syn* see RICH 1
   con impoverished, penniless, poor
   ant indigent
wean *vb syn* see ESTRANGE
   ant addict
wear *vb* 1 *syn* see ABRADE 1
   2 *syn* see TIRE 1
wear (away) *vb syn* see EAT 3
wear down *vb syn* see TIRE 1
wearied *adj syn* see TIRED 1
   ant refreshed; unwearied, unweary
weariful *adj syn* see ARID 2
weariless *adj syn* see INDEFATIGABLE
weariness *n syn* see FATIGUE
   2 *syn* see ARID 2
wear out *vb* 1 *syn* see EXHAUST 4
   ‖**2** *syn* see WHIP 1
weary *vb* 1 *syn* see TIRE 1
   rel debilitate, enfeeble, weaken; depress, oppress, weigh
   con animate, energize, vitalize; enliven, quicken, vivify
   ant refresh
   2 *syn* see BORE
weary *adj* 1 *syn* see TIRED 1
   ant refreshed, unwearied, unweary
   2 *syn* see FED UP
Weary Willie *n syn* see VAGABOND
weasel *n syn* see SNEAK
weasel *vb syn* see EQUIVOCATE 2
weathery *adj syn* see CHANGEABLE 1
weave *vb syn* see LURCH 2
web *n* 1 *syn* see TEXTURE 2
   2 something by which one is ensnared, held fast, or inextricably involved <diplomacy caught in its own *web* of double-dealing>
   syn cobweb, entanglement, mesh(es), toil(s); *compare* ENTANGLEMENT 1
   rel complexity, complication; labyrinth, maze, morass, skein, snarl, tangle; embroilment, enmeshment, ensnarement, entrapment, involvement
   idiom a tangled web
   3 *syn* see MAZE 1
wed *vb* 1 *syn* see MARRY 1
   2 *syn* see MARRY 2
   3 *syn* see JOIN 1
wedded *adj syn* see MATRIMONIAL
   con unwed, unwedded

---

syn synonym(s)   *rel* related word(s)
ant antonym(s)   *con* contrasted word(s)
idiom idiomatic equivalent(s)
‖ use limited; if in doubt, see a dictionary

wedding n the marriage ceremony usually with its accompanying festivities <one of the most elaborate *weddings* of the social season>
syn bridal, espousal(s), marriage, nuptial(s), spousal

wedlock n *syn* see MARRIAGE 1

wee adj *syn* see TINY

weed n *syn* see MARIJUANA

weensy adj *syn* see TINY

weeny adj *syn* see TINY

weep vb 1 *syn* see DEPLORE 1
2 *syn* see EXUDE
3 *syn* see CRY 2
4 *syn* see DRIP

weeping adj *syn* see TEARFUL

weepy adj *syn* see TEARFUL

weigh vb 1 *syn* see CONSIDER 1
rel appraise, evaluate, rate
2 *syn* see BURDEN
3 to carry intellectual weight <this evidence *weighed* heavily against him>
syn count, militate, tell
rel import, matter, register, signify
idiom amount to some shucks, be something, carry weight, cut (some) ice
4 *syn* see MATTER

weigh down vb *syn* see DEPRESS 2
ant raise (one's spirits)

weight n 1 *syn* see LOAD 2
2 *syn* see IMPORTANCE
3 *syn* see INFLUENCE 1
rel effectiveness, efficacy; forcefulness, forcibleness, potency, powerfulness
4 *syn* see LOAD 3

weight vb 1 *syn* see ADULTERATE
rel burden, cumber, encumber; contaminate, corrupt, foul up, spoil
2 *syn* see BURDEN

weightiness n *syn* see IMPORTANCE

weightless adj *syn* see LIGHT 1
ant weighty

weighty adj 1 *syn* see IMPORTANT 1
2 *syn* see SERIOUS 1
3 *syn* see SERIOUS 2
4 *syn* see HEAVY 1
ant weightless
5 *syn* see FAT 2
6 *syn* see ONEROUS

weird n 1 *syn* see FATE
2 *syn* see PREDICTION

weird adj 1 fearfully and mysteriously strange or fantastic <shuddered at the *weird* unearthly glow that swept across the sky>
syn eerie, spooky, uncanny, unearthly
rel creepy, haunting, unnatural; preternatural, supernatural; supernal; curious, odd, peculiar, queer, strange; inscrutable, mysterious; awe-inspiring, awful, dreadful, fearful, horrific
con common, commonplace, everyday, quotidian; natural, normal, ordinary
2 *syn* see STRANGE 4

welcome adj *syn* see PLEASANT 1
rel congenial, cordial, genial, sympathetic; contenting, satisfying
ant unwelcome

welfare n a state of thriving and progress <parents who seek their children's *welfare*>
syn advantage, benefit, good, interest, prosperity, well-being

rel fortune, luck, success; contentment, felicity, happiness, satisfaction
ant illfare

welkin n *syn* see SKY

well n 1 wells pl *syn* see SPA 1
2 *syn* see SOURCE

well adv 1 in a good, proper, or acceptable manner <the children behaved very *well* at the party>
syn aright, befittingly, correctly, decently, decorously, fitly, fittingly, justly, nicely, properly, rightly
rel bearably, passably, tolerably, unobjectionably; considerately, pleasantly, thoughtfully, white; appropriately
con badly, improperly, objectionably, obnoxiously, outrageously
ant ill
2 in a pleasant, cooperative, or thoughtful manner <he speaks *well* of your new proposal>
syn considerately, generously, heedfully, kindly, thoughtfully
rel concernedly, interestedly; approvingly
con contemptuously, disdainfully, scornfully
3 to a full extent or degree <you are *well* aware of the problems we face>
syn à fond, altogether, clear, ‖cleverly, completely, entirely, fully, perfectly, ‖plumb, quite, right, roundly, ‖slam, ‖slap, thoroughly, utterly, wholly
rel certainly, obviously, surely, undoubtedly, unquestionably; sublimely
idiom all the way
con barely, hardly, scarcely
4 in an adequate or appropriate manner <any large box will answer our need very *well*>
syn acceptably, adequately, amply, appropriately, becomingly, fittingly, properly, right, satisfactorily, suitably
5 in a desirable or pleasing manner <everything went *well* on the trip>
syn favorably, fortunately, happily, prosperously, satisfyingly, successfully, swimmingly
rel comfortably, easily, smoothly
con amiss, wrong
ant badly
6 *syn* see EASILY 1
7 in all likelihood <the fighting may *well* continue for years>
syn doubtlessly, easily, indeed, really, truly, undoubtedly
rel conceivably, perhaps, possibly; likely, probably
8 to a considerable extent or degree <they landed *well* beyond the wharf>
syn considerably, far, quite, rather, significantly, somewhat
idiom by a long way, by a wide margin

well adj 1 *syn* see PROSPEROUS 3
2 *syn* see HEALTHY 1
ant ill, unwell
3 *syn* see LUCKY

well—behaved adj *syn* see GOOD 13

well—being n 1 *syn* see PROSPERITY 2
ant ill-being
2 *syn* see WELFARE
ant ill-being

well—bred adj *syn* see GENTEEL 1
ant ill-bred

well–conditioned *adj syn* see HEALTHY 1
well–developed *adj syn* see CURVACEOUS
well–disposed *adj syn* see SYMPATHETIC 2
    ant ill-disposed
well–favored *adj syn* see BEAUTIFUL
    ant ill-favored
well–fixed *adj syn* see PROSPEROUS 3
    ant badly off
well–founded *adj* having a firm foundation in fact or logic <offered *well-founded* arguments to support his position>
    syn cogent, good, just, justified, well-grounded
    rel sound, substantial, telling, valid; rational, reasonable, reasoned; fundamental, meaty, pithy
    con unjustified; insubstantial, invalid, unsound; irrational, unreasonable
well–groomed *adj* 1 *syn* see NEAT 2
    2 *syn* see DAPPER
well–grounded *adj syn* see WELL-FOUNDED
wellhead *n syn* see SOURCE
well–heeled *adj syn* see PROSPEROUS 3
    ant badly off
well–hung *adj syn* see GLIB
well–known *adj* much talked about <a *well-known* hospital>
    syn famous, leading, noted, notorious, popular, prominent; *compare* FAMOUS 2
    rel conspicuous, important, outstanding
    idiom on everyone's tongue
    con inconspicuous, obscure, unheard-of, unimportant, unnoted, unpopular
    ant unknown
well–liked *adj syn* see FAVORITE 2
well–liking *adj syn* see HEALTHY 1
well–mannered *adj syn* see CIVIL 2
    ant ill-mannered
well–nigh *adv* 1 *syn* see NEARLY
    2 *syn* see ALMOST 2
well–off *adj syn* see PROSPEROUS 3
    ant badly off
well over *vb syn* see OVERFLOW 2
well–paying *adj syn* see ADVANTAGEOUS 1
well–proportioned *adj syn* see SHAPELY
wellspring *n syn* see SOURCE
well–thought–of *adj syn* see RESPECTABLE 1
well–timed *adj syn* see TIMELY 1
    con premature, untimely; behindhand, late, tardy
    ant ill-timed
well–to–do *adj syn* see PROSPEROUS 3
    ant badly off
well–turned *adj syn* see SHAPELY
well–worn *adj syn* see TRITE
welsh *vb syn* see BACK DOWN
welt *n* 1 *syn* see WHEAL
    ‖2 *syn* see BLOW 1
weltanschauung *n syn* see IDEOLOGY
welter *vb* 1 *syn* see WALLOW 1
    rel strive, struggle; toss, tumble, writhe; grovel
    2 *syn* see WALLOW 3
welter *vb syn* see WITHER

---

syn synonym(s)   *rel* related word(s)
ant antonym(s)   *con* contrasted word(s)
idiom idiomatic equivalent(s)
‖ use limited; if in doubt, see a dictionary

---

wench *n* 1 *syn* see GIRL 1
    2 *syn* see WANTON
wend *vb syn* see GO 1
western *n* a motion picture or radio or television play with its scene laid in the western U.S. and having cowboys as its main characters <young boys delighting in Saturday morning *westerns*>
    syn horse opera, oater
    rel shoot-'em-up
wet *vb* to make wet by or as if by saturating with water <they were *wet* thoroughly by the pouring rain>
    syn deluge, douse, drench, drown, soak, sop, souse; *compare* SOAK 1
    rel damp, dampen, moisten; humidify, humify; fill, impregnate, saturate; irrigate; lave, rinse, wash
    ant desiccate, dry
wet *adj* 1 containing or impregnated with liquid <change *wet* clothing for dry>
    syn drenched, dripping, madid, saturate, saturated, soaked, soaking, sodden, sopping, soppy, soused, wringing-wet
    rel soggy, water-logged; damp, dank, moist, wettish
    idiom dripping (*or* soaking *or* sopping) wet
    con bone-dry, dehydrated, desiccated, parched, sere, waterless
    ant dry
    2 *syn* see INTOXICATED 1
‖**wet** *n syn* see DRAM
wettish *adj syn* see DAMP
whack *vb syn* see STRIKE 2
whack *n* 1 *syn* see BLOW 1
    2 *syn* see FLING 1
whacking *adj syn* see HUGE
whacking *adv syn* see VERY 1
whale *n syn* see GIANT
whale *vb syn* see WHIP 1
whaling *adj syn* see HUGE
wham *n syn* see BANG 2
whammy *n syn* see JINX
whangdoodle *n syn* see NONSENSE 2
wharf *n* a structure used by boats and ships for taking on or landing cargo and passengers <brought the boat alongside the *wharf* and moored her>
    syn berth, dock, jetty, levee, pier, quay, slip
what–do–you–call–it *n* a thing or person that the speaker cannot (as from not knowing or from forgetting) name <hand me one of those little *what-do-you-call-its*> <went to *what-do-you-call-her's* house last week>
    syn what-is-it, whatsis, what's its name, what-you-call-it, what-you-may-call-it, whatyoumayjigger; *compare* DOODAD, GADGET 1
what–is–it *n syn* see WHAT-DO-YOU-CALL-IT
whatnot *n syn* see KNICKKNACK
whatsis *n syn* see WHAT-DO-YOU-CALL-IT
what's its name *n syn* see WHAT-DO-YOU-CALL-IT
what–you–call–it *n syn* see WHAT-DO-YOU-CALL-IT
what–you–may–call–it *n syn* see WHAT-DO-YOU-CALL-IT
whatyoumayjigger *n syn* see WHAT-DO-YOU-CALL-IT

wheal *n* a ridge raised on the skin by or as if by a stroke of a lash <the convict's back was covered with *wheals* and old scars>
syn wale, weal, welt, whelk, ||whelp
rel strake, streak, stripe

wheedle *vb syn* see COAX

wheel *n* **1** *syn* see CYCLE 1
2 *syn* see REVOLUTION 1
3 *syn* see LEAGUE 4

wheel *vb* **1** *syn* see REEL 2
2 *syn* see DRIVE 5
3 *syn* see TURN 6

wheeze *vb syn* see HISS

wheeze *n syn* see PRANK

whelk *n syn* see WHEAL

whelm *vb* **1** *syn* see DELUGE 1
2 *syn* see DELUGE 3
3 *syn* see OVERWHELM 4

||**whelp** *n syn* see WHEAL

when *adv syn* see THEN 1

when *conj syn* see THOUGH

whence *n syn* see SOURCE

where *adv* **1** *syn* see WHEREVER
2 *syn* see WHITHER 1

where *n syn* see PLACE 1

whereabouts *adv syn* see WHITHER 1
con hereabouts, thereabouts

whereas *conj* **1** *syn* see BECAUSE
2 *syn* see THOUGH

||**whereaway** *adv syn* see WHITHER 1

wherefore *n syn* see REASON 3

whereto *adv syn* see WHITHER 2

whereunto *adv syn* see WHITHER 2

wherever *adv* at, in, or to any or every place in or to which <he goes *wherever* he is needed>
syn everywhere, where
con here, there

||**wherret** *vb syn* see SLAP 1

||**wherret** *vb syn* see WORRY 1

whet *vb* **1** *syn* see SHARPEN
2 *syn* see STIR 1

whet *n* ||**1** *syn* see WHILE 1
2 *syn* see APPETIZER

whether or no *adv syn* see WILLY-NILLY

whetted *adj syn* see SHARP 1

whicker *vb syn* see NEIGH

whiff *n syn* see HINT 2

whiffet *n syn* see NONENTITY

whiffle *vb syn* see HESITATE

whiffling *adj syn* see VACILLATING 2

whiffy *adj syn* see MALODOROUS 1

whigmaleerie *n* **1** *syn* see CAPRICE
2 *syn* see KNICKKNACK

while *n* **1** a somewhat indefinite period of time <sat down to rest for a *while*>
syn bit, space, spell, stretch, time, ||whet
2 *syn* see OCCASION 5
3 *syn* see EFFORT 1

while *conj syn* see THOUGH

while *vb* to pass time and especially leisure time without boredom or in pleasant ways <*whiled* odd hours away in dreaming>
syn beguile, fleet, wile
rel amuse, divert, entertain; brighten, enliven, lighten

while (away) *vb syn* see SPEND 3

whilom *adj syn* see FORMER 2

whim *n syn* see CAPRICE
rel idea; disposition, inclination, thought; dream, fantasy, vision

whimper *vb* to cry feebly and often plaintively or peevishly <a baby *whimpering* in its sleep>
syn pule, whine; *compare* CRY 2

whimsical *adj* **1** *syn* see ARBITRARY 1
2 *syn* see UNCERTAIN 1

whimsied *adj syn* see ARBITRARY 1

whimsy *n syn* see CAPRICE
rel idea; disposition, inclination, thought; dream, fantasy, vision

whim–whams *n pl syn* see JITTERS

whine *vb* **1** *syn* see WHIMPER
2 *syn* see COMPLAIN

||**whinner** *vb syn* see NEIGH

whinny *vb syn* see NEIGH

whiny *adj syn* see IRRITABLE

whip *vb* **1** to strike repeatedly with or as if with a lash or rod <*whip* a dog for stealing from the table>
syn flagellate, flog, hide, ||larrup, lash, lather, scourge, stripe, thrash, ||wear out, whale, ||yerk
rel beat, belabor, drub, wallop; bastinado, birch, bludgeon, cane, cudgel, quirt, switch
2 to defeat utterly <*whipped* their traditional rival by a score of 40 to 7>
syn beat, blast, ||bowl (down *or* out), ||clean up (on), ||clobber, ||cream, curry, drub, dust, lambaste, ||larrup, lick, mop (up), overrun, overwhelm, rout, shellac, skunk, smear, smother, steamroller, thrash, trim, trounce, upend, wallop, whomp; *compare* CONQUER 1, DEFEAT 2
rel conquer, defeat, overcome, subdue, vanquish
idiom cook one's goose, deal a crushing defeat, settle one's hash, snow one under
3 to agitate with an instrument so as to stiffen and increase the bulk of by incorporation of air <*whip* cream for a shortcake>
syn beat, whisk
4 *syn* see TURN 6

whip (up) *vb syn* see INCITE
ant calm (down)

whip hand *n syn* see BETTER 2

whippersnapper *n syn* see NONENTITY

whipping boy *n syn* see SCAPEGOAT

whippy *adj syn* see ELASTIC 1

whipster *n syn* see NONENTITY

whirl *vb* **1** *syn* see SPIN 1
2 *syn* see SWIRL
3 *syn* see TURN 6
4 *syn* see HURRY 2
5 *syn* see SPIN 2

whirl *n* **1** *syn* see REVOLUTION 1
2 *syn* see EDDY
3 *syn* see COMMOTION 4
4 *syn* see STIR 1
5 *syn* see FLING 1

whirlblast *n syn* see WHIRLWIND 1

whirligig *vb syn* see SPIN 1

whirlpool *n* **1** *syn* see EDDY
2 *syn* see STIR 1

whirlpool *vb syn* see SWIRL

||**whirlpuff** *n syn* see WHIRLWIND 1

whirlwind *n* **1** a rotating windstorm of limited extent that is often accompanied by a column of dust or vapor <*whirlwinds* moved across the plowed land>
syn whirlblast, ||whirlpuff, whirly; *compare* HURRICANE, TORNADO

rel dust devil, rainspout, sand column, sand spout, waterspout
2 *syn* see STIR 1

whirly *n syn* see WHIRLWIND 1

whish *vb* 1 *syn* see HISS
2 *syn* see HURRY 2

whisk *vb* 1 *syn* see HURRY 2
2 *syn* see WHIP 3

whisker *n syn* see HAIR

whiskered *adj* 1 *syn* see BEARDED
2 *syn* see HAIRY 1

whiskers *n pl syn* see BEARD

whisper *vb* 1 *syn* see HISS
2 *syn* see CONFIDE 1

whisper *n* 1 *syn* see MURMUR 1
2 *syn* see HINT 2

whispering *n syn* see REPORT 1

whist *adj syn* see STILL 3

whistle–stop *n syn* see BURG

whit *n syn* see PARTICLE

white *adj syn* see FAVORABLE 5
ant black

white *n syn* see REACTIONARY
ant red

white *vb* 1 *syn* see WHITEN 1
2 *syn* see PALLIATE

whited sepulcher *n syn* see HYPOCRITE

white–haired *adj syn* see FAVORITE 1

white–headed *adj syn* see FAVORITE 1

white–hot *adj* 1 *syn* see HOT 1
2 *syn* see IMPASSIONED

white lightning *n syn* see MOONSHINE 2

white–livered *adj syn* see COWARDLY

whiten *vb* 1 to free from color and make white or whiter < *whiten* linen in the sun >
syn blanch, bleach, blench, decolor, decolorize, white
rel dim, dull, fade, lighten, pale; etiolate; frost, grizzle, silver
con color, darken
ant blacken
2 *syn* see PALLIATE

white plague *n syn* see TUBERCULOSIS

whitewash *vb syn* see PALLIATE

whither *adv* 1 to what place < *whither* did they go? >
syn where, whereabouts, ‖whereaway
2 to what point, conclusion, or end < *whither* is our nation drifting? >
syn whereto, whereunto

whiz *vb* 1 *syn* see HISS
2 *syn* see HURRY 2

whiz *n syn* see EXPERT
ant dub, dud, duffer

whiz–bang *adj syn* see EXCELLENT

whizzer *n syn* see TRICK 1

whole *adj* 1 free from damage, defect, or flaw < feared the eggs were broken but found them *whole* >
syn entire, flawless, good, intact, perfect, sound, unblemished, unbroken, undamaged, unhurt, unimpaired, uninjured, unmarred, untouched
rel complete, plenary; healthy, well
con broken, damaged, defective, impaired, injured, marred
2 *syn* see HEALTHY 1

---

3 lacking nothing that properly belongs to it < the effect of the *whole* mural >
syn choate, complete, entire, full, integral, perfect
rel orbicular, rounded, well-rounded
ant partial
4 including every constituent element or individual < the *whole* community rose to his defense >
syn all, complete, entire, gross, outright, total
ant partial
5 not scattered or dispersed < gave the matter his *whole* attention >
syn concentrated, exclusive, fixed, undistracted, undivided, unswerving

whole *n* 1 the total supply or amount < the *whole* of our creative literature >
syn aggregate, all, be-all and end-all, entirety, gross, sum, sum total, tale, total, totality, ‖tote
rel amount, supply; result, resultant, summation; bulk, mass, quantity, quantum
con detail, division, fraction, fragment, portion, section, segment, share
ant part
2 an organized array of parts or elements forming or functioning as a unit < stars, planets, galaxies — all but parts of one stupendous *whole*, the universe >
syn entity, integral, integrate, sum, system, totality; *compare* SYSTEM 1
rel being, organism, organization; coherence, cohesion, linkage; unity
con accumulation, aggregation, heap, pile, mass; section, segment; selection
ant part; agglomeration

wholehearted *adj* 1 *syn* see SURE 2
2 *syn* see SINCERE 1
rel ardent, fervent, impassioned, passionate; earnest, serious; authentic, bona fide, genuine

whole–hog *adj syn* see EXHAUSTIVE

whole–length *adj syn* see UNABRIDGED

wholeness *n* 1 *syn* see HEALTH
rel integrity; heartiness, robustness, vigor
2 *syn* see ENTIRETY 1
3 *syn* see INTEGRITY 2

whole number *n syn* see NUMBER

wholesale *adj syn* see INDISCRIMINATE 1

wholesome *adj* 1 *syn* see HEALTHFUL
ant noxious; unwholesome
2 *syn* see CURATIVE
3 *syn* see HEALTHY 1
4 *syn* see SAFE 3
ant noxious

whole–souled *adj syn* see SINCERE 1
rel ardent, fervent, impassioned; earnest, intense, serious

wholly *adv* 1 *syn* see WELL 3
2 *syn* see ALL 1

whomp *vb syn* see WHIP 2

whoop *vb syn* see SHOUT 1

whoop *n syn* see PARTICLE

whoop–de–do *n syn* see REVELRY 2

whoopee *n* 1 *syn* see REVELRY 2
2 *syn* see MERRYMAKING

whoopla *n* 1 *syn* see COMMOTION 4
2 *syn* see REVELRY 2

whoop–up *n syn* see REVELRY 2

whoosh *vb syn* see HISS

whop *vb syn* see BEAT 1

whop n syn see BLOW 1

whopping adj syn see HUGE

whopping adv syn see VERY 1

whore n 1 syn see HARLOT 1
  2 syn see PROSTITUTE

whoredom n syn see PROSTITUTION

whorehouse n syn see BROTHEL

whoreson n syn see BASTARD 1

whorish adj syn see FAST 7

whorl vb syn see SWIRL

who's who n syn see ARISTOCRACY

why n 1 syn see REASON 3
  2 syn see MYSTERY

whyfor n syn see REASON 3

wicked adj 1 syn see WRONG 1
  ant upright
  2 syn see PLAYFUL 1
  3 syn see RISQUÉ
  4 syn see MALICIOUS
  5 syn see DANGEROUS 1
  6 syn see TROUBLESOME
  7 syn see OUTRAGEOUS 1
  8 syn see SKILLFUL 2
  9 syn see ABLE

wickedness n 1 syn see EVIL 2
  2 syn see VICE 1

wide adj 1 syn see SPACIOUS
  2 syn see EXTENSIVE 2
  3 syn see LIBERAL 3

wide–awake adj syn see WATCHFUL
  rel alive, awake, aware, conscious, sensible

widen vb syn see BROADEN

wideness n syn see BREADTH 2

widespread adj syn see PREVAILING

widget n syn see GADGET 1

width n syn see RANGE 2

wield vb 1 syn see HANDLE 2
  rel conduct, control
  2 syn see EXERT

wieldy adj syn see STRONG 1

wiener n syn see FRANKFURTER

wienerwurst n syn see FRANKFURTER

wienie n syn see FRANKFURTER

wife n the female partner in a marriage
  < wives unwilling to share responsibility>
  syn ‖ball and chain, lady, ‖little woman,
  ‖missus, Mrs., ‖old lady, ‖old woman,
  ‖rib, ‖squaw, woman
  rel consort, helpmate, helpmeet, mate,
  other half, spouse; bride, dowager, matron; concubine
  idiom better half
  con maid, maiden; widow

wig n syn see REBUKE

wig vb syn see SCOLD 1

wiggle vb syn see WRIGGLE

wiggle–waggle adj syn see VACILLATING
  2

wiggle–waggle vb syn see HESITATE

wiggy adj syn see POMPOUS 1

wight n syn see HUMAN

wild adj 1 living and growing in a state of
  nature and without human intervention
  < lived on wild plants and game animals>
  syn agrarian, agrestal, native, natural,
  uncultivated, undomesticated; compare
  SAVAGE 1
  rel escaped, feral; unsubdued, untamed
  ant cultivated, domesticated
  2 syn see SAVAGE 1
  ant tame, tamed

  3 syn see IRRESPONSIBLE
  rel adventurous, audacious, daring, dashing; brash, cocksure, rash
  4 syn see FURIOUS 2
  rel bewildered, distracted, perplexed;
  agitated, perturbed, upset; addled, confused, muddled; crazy, demented, deranged, mad
  con easy, relaxed
  5 syn see UNRULY 1
  6 marked by turmoil and fury especially
  of natural elements <a wild night of
  howling winds and driving snow>
  syn blustering, blustery, ‖coarse, dirty,
  furious, raging, rough, stormful, stormy,
  tempestuous, turbulent
  rel blatant, boisterous, clamorous, ungovernable, unruly; brutal, harsh, severe
  con calm, peaceful, placid, quiet, stormless; halcyon, irenic, serene
  7 given to unrestrained self-indulgence
  and pursuit of pleasure <her son got in
  with a wild bunch and took to drink>
  syn devil-may-care, fast, gay, raffish,
  rakehell, rakish, sporty
  rel boisterous, roisterous, rollicking,
  swaggering; careless, heedless, irresponsible, thoughtless; lewd, loose, unchaste,
  wanton
  con moderate, restrained, sober, sparing,
  temperate; bridled, controlled, curbed;
  self-controlled
  8 syn see EXTRAVAGANT 1
  9 syn see BARBARIAN 1
  ant cultivated, cultured
  10 syn see BARBARIC 1

wild n syn see WASTE 1

wilderness n syn see WASTE 1
  rel backcountry, backland(s), hinterland
  idiom back of beyond

wild land n syn see WASTE 1

wildly adv syn see HARD 2

wildness n syn see WASTE 1

wile n syn see TRICK 1
  rel chicane, chicanery, trickery; cunning,
  deceit, dissimulation, guile
  con candor, frankness, openness, plain
  dealing, straightforwardness, unconstraint;
  artlessness, naturalness, sincerity

wile vb 1 syn see ATTRACT 1
  2 syn see WHILE

wiliness n syn see CUNNING 2

will vb to be inclined <you may decide
  whichever way you will>
  syn choose, elect, like, please, wish
  rel crave, desire, want
  idiom have a mind to, see (or think) fit

will n 1 a desire to act in a particular way
  or have a particular thing <I've no will
  to be sociable tonight>
  syn fancy, inclination, liking, mind, pleasure, velleity
  rel appetite, desire, passion, urge; hankering, longing, pining, yearning
  idiom heart's desire
  con aversion, dislike, distaste, repugnance,
  repulsion, revulsion
  2 the aspect of mind involved in choosing
  or deciding <problems arise when one's
  will and judgment come in conflict>
  syn volition
  rel design, intent, purpose, wishes; character, disposition, temper

3 power of controlling one's actions, impulses, or emotions < a self-indulgent man of feeble character and little *will* >
syn discipline, self-command, self-control, self-discipline, self-government, self-mastery, self-restraint, willpower
rel aplomb, assurance, confidence, poise, self-possession; control, discretion, restraint
con gratification, indulgence, self-indulgence

will *vb* to give to another by will < *will* family treasures to a relative >
syn bequeath, devise, leave, legate

willful *adj* **1** *syn* see OBSTINATE
rel contumacious, factious
idiom having the bit in one's teeth, not yielding an inch
con amenable, docile, obedient, tractable
ant biddable
2 *syn* see VOLUNTARY
rel intentional, purposive; decided, determined, resolved; dogged, obstinate, pertinacious, stubborn
con accidental, chance, involuntary, unintentional, unplanned

willies *n pl syn* see JITTERS

willing *adj* **1** prepared in mind or by disposition < *willing* to help >
syn disposed, fair, inclined, minded, predisposed, prone, ready
rel agreeable, compliant, favorable; forward, game, prompt
idiom in the mood
con averse, disinclined, indisposed, loath, reluctant, unminded
ant unwilling
2 *syn* see VOLUNTARY
rel disposed, inclined, predisposed; open, prone

will-less *adj syn* see SPONTANEOUS

willpower *n syn* see WILL 3

willy-nilly *adv* surely and without regard to plans or inclination < it seems that we must drift *willy-nilly* toward disaster >
syn helplessly, inescapably, inevitably, perforce, unavoidably, whether or no
idiom as a matter of course, come what may, of necessity, without let or choice

‖**willy-willy** *n syn* see HURRICANE

wilt *vb* **1** *syn* see WITHER
2 *syn* see COLLAPSE 2
3 *syn* see DROOP 3

wily *adj syn* see SLY 2
rel sagacious, shrewd; clever, knowing
con aboveboard, forthright, straightforward; guileless, open, trusting

win *vb* **1** to gain the victory < the home team *won* by a wide margin >
syn beat, overcome, prevail, triumph; *compare* CONQUER 1
idiom bear off the palm (*or* prize), bring home the bacon, carry the day, come out first (*or* ahead), finish in front
ant lose
2 *syn* see GAIN 1
3 *syn* see EARN 1
rel produce, yield

4 *syn* see GET 1
ant lose

win (over) *vb* **1** *syn* see DISARM 2
2 *syn* see INDUCE 1

win *n syn* see VICTORY 1

wince *vb syn* see RECOIL
rel dodge, duck, jib, sheer, swerve, turn; cower, cringe

wind *n* **1** *syn* see NOTHING 1
2 *syn* see HINT 1

wind *vb syn* see BLOW 1

wind *vb* **1** *syn* see DEFORM
2 to follow a circular, spiral, or writhing course < the vine *wound* its way up the pillar >
syn coil, corkscrew, curl, entwine, spiral, twine, twist, wreathe; *compare* CURVE
rel bend, curve, meander, weave; circle, encircle, enlace, gird, girdle, surround; enclose, envelop

windbaggery *n syn* see NONSENSE 2

windiness *n syn* see VERBOSITY

winding *adj* curving repeatedly first one way then another < a *winding* country road >
syn anfractuous, convoluted, flexuous, meandering, meandrous, serpentine, sinuous, snaky, tortuous; *compare* CROOKED 1
rel bending, curving, twisting; crooked, devious; circuitous, indirect, roundabout
con direct, straight

window dressing *n syn* see MASK 2

windrow *n syn* see PILE 1

wind up *vb* **1** *syn* see CLOSE 3
2 *syn* see SETTLE 7

windup *n syn* see FINALE

windy *adj* **1** marked by more wind than usual < a *windy* March day >
syn airy, blowy, breezy, gusty
rel brisk, fresh; drafty
con breathless, motionless, still
ant windless
2 *syn* see INFLATED
3 *syn* see WORDY

wing *n syn* see ANNEX
rel expansion, prolongation; bulge, projection, protrusion, protuberance

wing *vb syn* see FLY 4

wink *vb* to close and open the eyelids quickly < *winking* involuntarily as the light struck his eyes >
syn bat, blink, nictate, nictitate, twinkle
rel squinch, squinny, squint; flutter

wink (at) *vb syn* see CONNIVE 1

wink *n* **1** *syn* see INSTANT 1
2 *syn* see HINT 2

winker *n syn* see EYE 1

winner *n syn* see VICTOR 2
ant loser

winning *adj syn* see SWEET 1

winnow *vb* **1** *syn* see BLOW 1
2 *syn* see SORT 2

winsome *adj syn* see SWEET 1
rel adorable, lovable, lovesome

wipe (out) *vb* **1** *syn* see ERASE
2 *syn* see ANNIHILATE 2
3 *syn* see SLAUGHTER 3

wipe *n* **1** *syn* see HIT 1
‖**2** *syn* see HANDKERCHIEF

‖**wiped out** *adj syn* see DRUGGED

‖**wiper** *n syn* see HANDKERCHIEF

wire *n syn* see PICKPOCKET

wiredraw *vb syn* see THIN 1

---

syn synonym(s)   *rel* related word(s)
ant antonym(s)   *con* contrasted word(s)
idiom idiomatic equivalent(s)
‖ use limited; if in doubt, see a dictionary

wiry *adj syn* see MUSCULAR 1
wisdom *n* 1 *syn* see KNOWLEDGE 2
2 *syn* see SAGACITY
3 *syn* see SENSE 6
   rel judiciousness, sageness, saneness, sapience; perspicacity, sagacity, shrewdness
   ant folly
wise *n syn* see METHOD 1
wise *adj* 1 having or exhibiting a capacity for discernment and the intelligent application of knowledge <to be *wise* is to use knowledge well>
   syn discerning, gnostic, insighted, insightful, knowing, knowledgeable, perceptive, sagacious, sage, sophic, wisehearted
   rel aware, grasping, intuitive, sensing; acute, keen, perspicacious; cogitative, contemplative, reflective, thoughtful; astute, sharp, shrewd
   con dull, obtuse, slow, slow-witted; insensitive, unaware, unknowing
   ant unwise
2 exercising or involving sound judgment <*wise* management of scarce resources>
   syn judgmatic, judicious, prudent, sage, sane, sapient, sensible; *compare* SHREWD
   rel canny, discreet, foresighted, provident; astute, perspicacious, sagacious, shrewd; alert, bright, intelligent, keen, smart
   con careless, heedless, injudicious; improvident, imprudent, indiscreet, short-sighted
   ant foolish, unwise
3 *syn* see EXPEDIENT
4 shrewdly aware and subtly resourceful <a *wise* operator with his eye always on the main chance>
   syn canny, hep, knowing, nimble-witted, quick, quick-witted, sharp, sharp-witted, slick, smart; *compare* INTELLIGENT 2, SHREWD
   rel cagey, foresighted, shrewd; artful, crafty, cunning, slippery, smooth, tricky, wily; steel-trap
   idiom in the groove, not born yesterday, on the beam
   con narrow, prim, puritanical, straitlaced; conservative, plodding, ‖square
5 presumptuously confident and self-assured <a bunch of *wise* kids tearing up the neighborhood>
   syn ‖biggety, bold, bold-faced, cheeky, forward, fresh, impudent, nervy, pert, procacious, sassy, smart, smart-alecky
   rel arrogant, brash, cocky, insolent; flip, flippant, impertinent, lippy, sassy
   con demure, mannerly, modest, proper; dull, priggish, stuffy
wise (up) *vb syn* see INFORM 2
wiseacre *n syn* see SMART ALECK
wisecrack *n syn* see JOKE 1
wisecracker *n syn* see SMART ALECK
wise guy *n syn* see SMART ALECK
wisehead *n syn* see SMART ALECK
wisehearted *adj syn* see WISE 1
wise man *n syn* see SAGE
wisenheimer *n syn* see SMART ALECK
wish *vb* 1 *syn* see DESIRE 1
   rel expect, hope; fancy
2 *syn* see WILL
3 *syn* see IMPOSE 4
wishy-washy *adj* 1 *syn* see INSIPID 3

   rel enervated, languid, listless, spiritless; flavorless, savorless
   idiom neither flesh, fowl, nor good red herring, neither one thing nor the other
2 *syn* see CHARACTERLESS
wistful *adj syn* see PENSIVE 2
‖**wit** *vb syn* see UNDERSTAND 3
wit *n* 1 *syn* see MIND 1
   rel perspicacity, sagacity; apprehension, awareness, comprehension
2 *often* **wits** *pl* mental soundness and health <frightened nearly out of her *wits*>
   syn lucidity, ‖marbles, mind, reason, saneness, sanity, sense(s), soundness
   rel balance, rationality
   con aberration; craziness, derangement, insanity, lunacy, madness, mania
   ant witlessness
3 acuteness of perception or judgment <had the *wit* to know that he was out of his depth in such a discussion>
   syn acumen, astucity, astuteness, clearsightedness, discernment, discrimination, keenness, penetration, percipience, perspicacity, shrewdness; *compare* PRUDENCE 1
   rel awareness, comprehension, grasp, insight, perception, understanding; prudence, sagaciousness, sagacity, sageness, sapience, wisdom; clairvoyance, divination, ESP, sensing
   con aridity, dullness, prosaicness, unimaginativeness; fatuity, foolishness, inanity, silliness, stupidity
4 *syn* see INTELLIGENCE 1
5 a talent for banter or persiflage <a jolly man, noted for his kindly *wit*>
   syn esprit, humor
   rel alertness, keenness, quick-wittedness; brilliance, cleverness, intelligence, smartness
6 *syn* see HUMOR 5
7 *syn* see HUMORIST 2
witch *n* 1 a woman who practices the black arts <ancient laws against *witches*>
   syn bruja, enchantress, hag, hex, lamia, sorceress, witchwoman; *compare* MAGICIAN 1
2 *syn* see HAG 2
witch *vb syn* SEE BEWITCH 1
witchcraft *n* 1 *syn* see MAGIC 1
2 *syn* see CHARM 3
witchery *n* 1 *syn* see MAGIC 1
2 *syn* see CHARM 3
witching *n syn* see MAGIC 1
witchwoman *n syn* see WITCH 1
witchy *adj syn* see MAGIC
with *prep* 1 *syn* see OVER 3
2 *syn* see FOR 2
3 *syn* see VIA 2
withal *adv* 1 *syn* see ALSO 2
2 *syn* see HOWEVER
withdraw *vb* 1 *syn* see REMOVE 2
   ant deposit
2 *syn* see ABJURE
3 *syn* see GO 3
   rel quail, recoil, retreat, shrink; recede
   idiom give ground, give way
   con advance, progress; arrive, come
4 *syn* see RETREAT 2
   ant advance
withdrawal *n syn* see DEPARTURE 1

ant approach

withdrawn *adj* **1** *syn* see UNDEMONSTRA-
TIVE
ant outgiving
2 *syn* see INDIFFERENT 2
3 *syn* see UNSOCIABLE
ant outgoing

wither *vb* to lose substance and freshness
by or as if by loss of natural moisture
< projects that *wither* and die from lack
of popular interest >
syn dry up, mummify, mummy, shrivel,
welter, wilt, wizen
rel cave in, collapse, deflate, fold; constrict, contract, shrink; decline, wane
con freshen, revive, revivify; develop,
grow, increase, wax
ant flourish

withhold *vb* **1** *syn* see RESTRAIN 1
2 *syn* see KEEP 5
con award, concede, grant, vouchsafe
ant accord
3 *syn* see DENY 2
4 *syn* see REFRAIN 1

within *adv* *syn* see INDOORS
ant without

within *n* *syn* see INTERIOR
ant without

withindoors *adv* *syn* see INDOORS
ant withoutdoors

withinside *adv* *syn* see INDOORS
ant withoutside

with-it *adj* *syn* see STYLISH

without *prep* **1** *syn* see BEYOND 1
2 not having < living *without* decent housing or adequate food >
syn awanting, lacking, minus, sans, wanting

without *adv* *syn* see OUTDOORS
ant within

without *n* *syn* see OUTDOORS

‖**without** *conj* *syn* see EXCEPT 1

withoutdoors *adv* *syn* see OUTDOORS
ant indoors, withindoors

with respect to *prep* *syn* see APROPOS

withstand *vb* *syn* see RESIST
rel bear, endure, stand, suffer, tolerate
con capitulate, submit, yield

witless *adj* **1** *syn* see SIMPLE 3
2 *syn* see INSANE 1

witlessness *n* *syn* see FOOLISHNESS

witness *n* **1** *syn* see TESTIMONY
2 *syn* see SPECTATOR

witness *vb* **1** *syn* see CERTIFY 1
rel affirm; endorse, subscribe
2 *syn* see INDICATE 2

witticism *n* *syn* see JOKE 1

wittiness *n* *syn* see HUMOR 4

witting *adj* **1** *syn* see AWARE
ant unwitting
2 *syn* see VOLUNTARY
ant unwitting

witty *adj* provoking or intended to provoke
mirth < a whimsical *witty* discussion on
the foreignness of honesty to politics >
syn facetious, humorous, jocose, jocular
rel amusing, diverting, entertaining; scintillating, sparkling; penetrating, piercing,
probing; funny, ridiculous, risible

con foolish, senseless, silly; brash, cheeky,
fresh; earnest, serious, sober, solemn
ant unwitty

wiz *n* *syn* see EXPERT
ant dub, dud, duffer

wizard *n* **1** *syn* see MAGICIAN 1
2 *syn* see EXPERT
ant dub, dud, duffer

wizardly *adj* *syn* see MAGIC

wizardry *n* *syn* see MAGIC 1

wizen *vb* *syn* see WITHER
rel decrease, diminish, dwindle, reduce

wobble *vb* **1** *syn* see LURCH 2
2 *syn* see TEETER
3 *syn* see SHAKE

wobbly *adj* **1** *syn* see RICKETY
2 *syn* see WEAK 2
3 *syn* see VACILLATING 2

woe *n* **1** *syn* see SORROW
rel bemoaning, bewailing, deploring, lamentation
con bliss, felicity, happiness
2 *syn* see MISERY 1
3 *usu* **woes** *pl* *syn* see DISASTER

woebegone *adj* **1** *syn* see DOWNCAST
rel lugubrious, melancholy
con alert, concerned, interested, spirited;
lively, vigorous; avid, eager, keen
2 *syn* see GLOOMY 3
rel dilapidated, outworn, shabby, worn
con bright, crisp, fresh, gay

woeful *adj* **1** full of or expressive of woe
< a *woeful* countenance >
syn afflicted, doleful, dolent, dolorous,
miserable, rueful, ruthful, sorrowful,
wretched
rel harrowed, racked, tortured, wrung;
crushed, overcome, stricken; disconsolate,
heartsick, inconsolable; dejected, depressed, dispirited, downcast, downhearted, low-spirited
idiom cut to the heart, cut up, in the
dumps (or depths or doldrums), on the
rack
con content, satisfied; easy, peaceful,
quiet; cheerful, gay, lighthearted
ant joyful
2 *syn* see MELANCHOLY 2
3 *syn* see DEPLORABLE
rel dismal, grave, sad; unprecedented

woggle *vb* *syn* see WAG

wolf *n* a man forward, direct, and zealous
in amorous pursuit of women < known
far and wide as a lecherous old *wolf* >
syn Casanova, chaser, Don Juan, ladies'
man, lady-killer, masher, philander, philanderer, womanizer
rel amorist; lecher, libertine, Lothario,
profligate, rip, roué, rounder
idiom man on the make, skirt chaser

wolf *vb* **1** *syn* see GULP
2 *syn* see PHILANDER

wolfish *adj* *syn* see FIERCE 1

woman *n* **1** *syn* see WIFE
2 *syn* see MISTRESS

womanize *vb* *syn* see PHILANDER

womanizer *n* *syn* see WOLF

wonder *n* **1** something that causes fascinated astonishment or admiration < the
seven *wonders* of the ancient world >
syn marvel, miracle, phenomenon, portent, prodigy, sensation, stunner
rel curiosity, cynosure, gazingstock, spectacle

---

syn synonym(s)　　*rel* related word(s)
ant antonym(s)　　*con* contrasted word(s)
idiom idiomatic equivalent(s)
‖ use limited; if in doubt, see a dictionary

idiom one for the book(s), something to shout (*or* write home) about

2 the complex emotion aroused by the strange and incomprehensible and especially the awe-inspiring <stood gazing in wide-eyed *wonder* at the scene unveiled before her>
syn admiration, amaze, amazement, marveling, wonderment
rel awe, fear, reverence; bewilderment, perplexity, puzzlement; astonishment, marvel, shock
con disinterest, incuriosity, indifference, unconcern; dispassion, impassivity; casualness, offhandedness; boredom, ennui

3 *syn* see UNCERTAINTY
rel assailability, vulnerability
con unconcern

wonderful *adj* **1** *syn* see MARVELOUS 1
2 *syn* see MARVELOUS 2
ant lousy

wonderland *n syn* see UTOPIA
wonderment *n syn* see WONDER 2
wondrous *adj syn* see MARVELOUS 1
wont *n syn* see HABIT 1
wont *vb syn* see ACCUSTOM
wonted *adj syn* see USUAL 1
ant unwonted
wontedly *adv syn* see USUALLY 1
ant unwontedly
woo *vb syn* see ADDRESS 8
idiom bill and coo, pitch woo
wood *n, often* **woods** *pl but sing or pl in constr syn* see FOREST
wooden *adj* **1** *syn* see STIFF 4
rel awkward, clumsy; heavy, ponderous, weighty
con limber, supple; plastic, pliable, pliant
2 *syn* see AWKWARD 2
woodenhead *n syn* see DUNCE
woodland *n syn* see FOREST
woods colt *n syn* see BASTARD 1
woodsy *n syn* see RUSTIC
wooer *n syn* see SUITOR 2
woolly *adj syn* see HAIRY 1
word *vb* to convey (as an impression, a thought, or a need) in words <seemed scarcely to know how to *word* her appeal>
syn couch, express, formulate, phrase, put; *compare* EXPRESS 2
rel convey, offer, submit; say, state, tell
word *n* **1** something that is said <didn't tell a *word* about his plans>
syn statement, utterance
rel announcement, declaration, pronouncement
2 a pronounceable sound or combination of sounds that expresses and symbolizes an idea <be sure you learn the meaning of each *word*>
syn term, vocable
rel expression, idiom, locution, phrase
3 *syn* see COMMAND 1
4 *syn* see NEWS
5 *syn* see REPORT 1
6 *syn* see MESSAGE 1
7 *syn* see SAYING
8 a statement whose weight or worth depends on the truthfulness or authority of its maker <had the doctor's *word* that no operation would be needed>
syn assurance, guarantee, pledge, warrant; *compare* PROMISE

rel commitment, engagement, undertaking; oath, vow; promise
9 *syn* see PROMISE
10 *usu* **words** *pl syn* see QUARREL
11 *syn* see PASSWORD 3
12 *syn* see PASSWORD 1
wordage *n syn* see WORDING
word for word *adv syn* see VERBATIM
word–for–word *adj syn* see VERBATIM
word–hoard *n syn* see VOCABULARY 1
wordiness *n syn* see VERBOSITY
con crispness, pithiness, trenchancy
ant laconicism, laconism
wording *n* manner or style of verbal expression <take care with the *wording* of a formal invitation>
syn diction, parlance, phrase, phraseology, phrasing, verbalism, verbiage, wordage
rel language, mode, style
wordless *adj* **1** *syn* see TACIT 1
2 *syn* see SILENT 2
3 *syn* see SILENT 3
4 *syn* see UNSPOKEN 1
ant wordy
word–of–mouth *adj syn* see ORAL 2
word–stock *n syn* see VOCABULARY 1
wordy *adj* using or marked by the use of more words than are needed to express an idea <tired of dull *wordy* editorials>
syn diffuse, long-winded, palaverous, prolix, redundant, verbose, windy
rel flatulent, inflated, tumid, turgid; garrulous, glib, loquacious, talkative, voluble; bombastic, highfalutin, rhetorical
con compendious, concise, pithy, succinct, summary, terse; lean, taut
ant laconic
work *n* **1** the activity that affords one his livelihood <laborers hurrying to *work* at dawn>
syn business, calling, employment, job, line, occupation, pursuit, ‖racket; *compare* JOB 2
rel art, craft, handicraft, métier, profession, trade, vocation, walk
2 strenuous activity that involves difficulty and effort and usually affords no pleasure <had done much hard *work* during his life>
syn bullwork, donkeywork, drudge, drudgery, grind, labor, moil, plugging, slavery, slogging, sweat, toil, travail
rel effort, exertion, pains, trouble; chore, duty, job; elucubration; striving; spadework
ant play
3 works *pl syn* see FACTORY
work *vb* **1** *syn* see OPERATE 3
2 *syn* see TILL
3 *syn* see SOLVE 1
4 *syn* see LABOR 1
5 *syn* see FUNCTION 3
6 *syn* see ACT 5
work (for) *vb syn* see BENEFIT
workable *adj syn* see POSSIBLE 1
rel applicable, exploitable, usable
ant unworkable
workaday *adj* **1** *syn* see PROSAIC 3
2 *syn* see ORDINARY 1
workday *adj syn* see PROSAIC 3
worker *n* one who earns a living by labor and especially by manual labor <weary *workers* straggling home each night>

syn hand, laborer, ‖mozo, operative, roustabout, workhand, workingman, workman

rel artisan, craftsman, handicraftsman, mechanic; employee

ant idler

workhand *n syn* see WORKER

workhorse *n* 1 *syn* see SLAVE 2

2 *syn* see SAWHORSE

work in *vb syn* see INSINUATE 3

working *adj* 1 *syn* see ACTIVE 1

2 *syn* see BUSY 1

workingman *n syn* see WORKER

workless *adj syn* see UNEMPLOYED

workman *n syn* see WORKER

workmanlike *adj syn* see SKILLFUL 2

ant unworkmanlike

workmanly *adj syn* see SKILLFUL 2

work off *vb syn* see FOIST 2

work out *vb syn* see SOLVE 1

work over *vb syn* see REVISE

work–shy *adj syn* see LAZY

work up *vb syn* see GENERATE 3

world *n* 1 *syn* see EARTH 1

2 *syn* see UNIVERSE

worldly *adj* 1 *syn* see EARTHLY 1

ant otherworldly

2 *syn* see MATERIALISTIC

ant otherworldly, unworldly

3 *syn* see SOPHISTICATED 2

ant unworldly

worldly–wise *adj syn* see SOPHISTICATED 2

rel callous, hard-boiled, hardened

con naive, unsophisticated, unworldly

worldwide *adj syn* see UNIVERSAL 2

con parochial

world–wise *adj syn* see SOPHISTICATED 2

world–without–end *adj syn* see EVER-LASTING 1

world–without–end *n syn* see ETERNITY 2

worm *n syn* see WRETCH 1

worm *vb* 1 *syn* see INSINUATE 3

2 *syn* see WRIGGLE

wormling *n syn* see WRETCH 1

worn *adj* 1 *syn* see TIRED 1

2 *syn* see HAGGARD

worn down *adj syn* see TIRED 1

worn–out *adj* 1 *syn* see EFFETE 2

2 *syn* see TRITE

worried *adj syn* see DISTRAUGHT

ant unworried

worry *vb* 1 to disturb one or destroy one's peace of mind by repeated or persistent tormenting attacks < vain regrets that *worry* his spirit >

syn annoy, bedevil, beleaguer, dun, gnaw, hagride, harass, harry, needle, pester, plague, tantalize, tease, ‖wherret

rel beset, bother, fret, pelt, trouble, vex; goad, test, try; afflict, torment, torture; aggrieve, oppress, persecute, wrong

idiom give one gyp

con comfort, console, solace; alleviate, assuage, ease, relieve

2 *syn* see TROUBLE 1

3 to experience concern, disquietude, or anxiety < *worrying* over her children's health >

syn cark, fret, fuss, pother, stew, ‖tew

rel carry on, take on; despair, give up; bother, concern (oneself); agitate, disquiet, disturb, trouble

idiom be upset, bite one's nails

con accept, submit; abide, bear, endure, stand, support; disregard, ignore, overlook, pass over

worry *n* 1 *syn* see CARE 2

rel presentiment; doubt, mistrust, uncertainty; anguish, heartache, woe

con composure, equanimity, sangfroid; assurance, certainty, certitude, confidence, security

2 *syn* see TRIAL 2

worrywart *n syn* see PESSIMIST

worsen *vb syn* see DETERIORATE 1

rel blast, blight, debase, degrade, humble, lower; corrupt, foul, taint

idiom get worse, grow worse

ant better

worship *n syn* see ADORATION

worship *vb* 1 *syn* see REVERE

con contemn, despise, disdain, flout, scorn; curse, execrate, vilify

2 *syn* see ADORE 3

ant abominate; scorn

3 *syn* see LOVE 2

worst *vb syn* see DEFEAT 2

worth *n* 1 equivalence in good qualities (as utility, importance, or desirability) express or implied < impossible to estimate the *worth* of such a man to the community >

syn account, valuation, value

rel class, excellence, merit, perfection, quality, virtue; rate; use, usefulness, utility; consequence, importance, mark, moment, note, significance, weight

con baseness, meanness, paltriness, poorness

ant worthlessness

2 *syn* see QUALITY 2

3 *syn* see WEALTH 2

worthless *adj* 1 lacking all excellence or value < gave me a *worthless* check >

syn draffy, drossy, good-for-nothing, inutile, ‖no-account, no-good, nothing, unworthy, valueless

rel inferior, mediocre, poor, second-rate; defective, flawed, imperfect; bootless, ineffectual, unavailing, useless; contemptible, dusty, mean, sad, sorry

idiom dear at any price, of no earthly value (*or* worth)

con esteemed, precious; useful, valuable, worthwhile; invaluable, priceless

ant worthful

2 *syn* see FECKLESS 1

rel incapable, incompetent, unqualified

worthwhile *adj syn* see ADVANTAGEOUS 1

worthy *adj* 1 having worth or merit < a *worthy* custom handed down from our ancestors >

syn admirable, commendable, deserving, estimable, laudable, meritable, meritorious, praisable, praiseworthy, thankworthy

rel invaluable, precious, priceless; desirable, pleasing, satisfying; divine

con good-for-nothing, ‖no-account, no-good, valueless; contemptible, sad, sorry

---

syn synonym(s)   *rel* related word(s)
ant antonym(s)   *con* contrasted word(s)
idiom idiomatic equivalent(s)
‖ use limited; if in doubt, see a dictionary

ant worthless
2 *syn* see HONORABLE 1
ant unworthy
wound *vb syn* see INJURE 3
wow *n syn* see SMASH 6
‖**wowser** *n syn* see PRUDE
wrack *vb syn* see DESTROY 1
wrackful *adj syn* see DESTRUCTIVE
wraith *n syn* see APPARITION
wrangle *vb* **1** *syn* see QUARREL
2 *syn* see ARGUE 2
wrangle *n syn* see QUARREL
wrap *vb syn* see ENFOLD 1
rel camouflage, cloak, mask
ant unwrap
wrap (up) *vb* **1** *syn* see BUNDLE UP
2 *syn* see SWATHE
wrapped *adj syn* see INTENT
wrapped up *adj syn* see INTENT
wrap up *vb syn* see CLOSE 3
wrath *n syn* see ANGER
rel acerbity, acrimony, asperity; offense,
resentment
wrathful *adj syn* see ANGRY
wrathy *adj syn* see ANGRY
‖**wraxle** *vb syn* see WRESTLE
wreak *vb syn* see INFLICT 2
wreakful *adj syn* see VINDICTIVE
wreath *n* a circlet of intertwined leaves or
flowers worn upon the head as an ornament or as a mark of honor or esteem
<received the laurel *wreath* of victory
from the emperor's own hand>
syn anadem, chaplet, coronal, coronet,
crown, garland
rel bay(s), laurel
wreathe *vb syn* see WIND 2
wreck *n* **1** *syn* see CRASH 3
2 *syn* see COLLAPSE 2
3 *syn* see JALOPY
wreck *vb* **1** *syn* see VANDALIZE
2 *syn* see DESTROY 1
rel despoil, loot, plunder, ravage; cripple,
disable
3 *syn* see TOTAL 3
4 *syn* see SABOTAGE
5 *syn* see SHIPWRECK 1
6 *syn* see RUIN 2
7 *syn* see INFLICT 2
wreckage *n* **1** *syn* see SABOTAGE
2 *syn* see DRIFTWOOD
wrecker *n syn* see VANDAL
wreckful *adj syn* see DESTRUCTIVE
wrecking *n syn* see SABOTAGE
wrench *vb* to shift the position of or
move by or as if by vigorous twisting
<suddenly *wrenched* her around to face
him>
syn wrest, wring, wry
rel bend, twist; coerce, compel, constrain,
force; drag, rend, tear; contort, distort
2 *syn* see SPRAIN
3 *syn* see MISREPRESENT
4 *syn* see EXTORT 1
wrest *vb* **1** *syn* see WRENCH 1
rel arrogate, confiscate, usurp; elicit,
extort, extract
2 *syn* see EXTORT 1
3 *syn* see MISREPRESENT
wrestle *vb* to struggle with an opponent at
close quarters <determined to solve the
problem if he had to *wrestle* with it all
night>

syn grapple, scuffle, tussle, ‖wraxle
rel contend, fight, struggle; endeavor,
essay; labor, moil, toil, travail, work; exert, strain, stretch, strive
wretch *n* **1** a worthless and often vicious
or contemptible person <a treacherous
drink-sodden *wretch*>
syn ‖blighter, lowlife, mucker, no-good,
worm, wormling
rel good-for-naught, good-for-nothing,
ne'er-do-well; blackguard, caitiff, devil,
knave, rapscallion, rascal, rogue, rotter,
scalawag, scoundrel, villain
idiom sad case
2 *syn* see SNOT 1
wretched *adj* **1** *syn* see WOEFUL 1
rel melancholy; abject, mean, sordid;
piteous, pitiable, pitiful; despairing, despondent, forlorn, hopeless
con animated, gay, lively; content, contented, satisfied; gratified, pleased
2 *syn* see BASE
wretchedness *n syn* see MISERY 1
wriggle *vb* to move or advance with worm-
like motions <the attackers *wriggled*
stealthily through the underbrush>
syn squiggle, squirm, wiggle, worm,
writhe
rel flow, glide, ooze, slide, slip
wring *vb* **1** *syn* see EXTORT 1
2 *syn* see WRENCH 1
rel press, squeeze
3 *syn* see AFFLICT
wringing-wet *adj syn* see WET 1
wrinkle *n* a small linear prominence or
depression on a surface <a benign old
face netted with *wrinkles*>
syn corrugation, crease, crinkle, fold,
furrow, plica, ridge, rimple, rivel, ruck
rel crow's foot; pleat, pucker
wrinkle *vb syn* see CRUMPLE 1
write *vb* to form characters or words on a
surface (as of paper) usually with pen or
pencil <learned to *write* at an early age>
syn engross, indite, inscribe, scribe
rel dot (down), jot, note; chalk, pen,
pencil; scratch, scrawl, scribble; draft,
draw, make out; write down, write up
idiom push one's pen, put in writing, take
down
write down *vb syn* see DEPRECIATE 1
ant write up
write off *vb* **1** *syn* see DEPRECIATE 1
2 *syn* see DECRY 2
write-up *n syn* see PUFF 3
writhe *vb* **1** to twist and turn in physical
or mental distress <*writhing* in anguish
with a throbbing tooth-ache>
syn agonize, squirm, toss
rel blench, flinch, recoil, shrink, wince;
contort, distort; bend, twist; thrash, tumble
2 *syn* see WRIGGLE
writing *n syn* see PRINT 2
writing desk *n syn* see DESK
wrong *n* **1** *syn* see INJUSTICE 2
2 *syn* see EVIL 2
3 *syn* see EVIL 3
4 *syn* see INJUSTICE 1
wrong *adj* **1** rejecting or deviating from the
dictates of moral or divine law <had a
wrong outlook on life> < *wrong* principles
of conduct>

syn bad, evil, immoral, iniquitous, reprobate, sinful, vicious, wicked

rel blamable, blameworthy, censurable, reprehensible; corrupt, debauched, depraved; abandoned, dissolute, infamous, villainous; blasphemous, unholy, unrighteous; accursed, unblessed

con ethical, high-principled, moral, righteous, upright; chaste, innocent, pure, virtuous

ant right

2 *syn* see FALSE 1

idiom at fault, barking up the wrong tree, in error, on the wrong track

con exact, precise

ant right

3 *syn* see BAD 1

rel improper, inappropriate, inapt, infelicitous, unfit, unfitting, unhappy, unsuitable

con appropriate, fit, fitting, proper, suitable

4 *syn* see MISTAKEN

ant right

5 *syn* see INSANE 1

wrong *adv syn* see AMISS 2

ant right

wrong *vb* to inflict injury on another without justification < these men who have *wronged* the public trust deserve no consideration >

syn aggrieve, oppress, outrage, persecute

rel abuse, ill-treat, maltreat, mistreat; harm, hurt, injure; offend

idiom do wrong to (*or* by)

con guard, protect, safeguard; care (for), cherish; honor, love, respect

wrongdoing *n* **1** *syn* see EVIL 3

2 *syn* see MISCONDUCT

wrongful *adj syn* see UNLAWFUL

ant rightful

wrongheaded *adj* **1** *syn* see OBSTINATE

2 *syn* see CONTRARY 3

wrongly *adv syn* see AMISS 1

ant rightly

wroth *adj syn* see ANGRY

wrothful *adj syn* see ANGRY

wrothy *adj syn* see ANGRY

wry *vb syn* see WRENCH 1

wry *adj syn* see SARDONIC

X

x *n syn* see ERROR 1

x (out) *vb syn* see ERASE

Xanthippe *n syn* see VIRAGO

Xmas *n syn* see CHRISTMAS

Y

yahoo *n syn* see TOUGH

yak *n syn* see CHATTER

yak *vb syn* see CHAT 1

‖**yak** *n syn* see JOKE 1

yakety-yak *n syn* see CHATTER

yakety-yak *vb syn* see CHAT 1

yak–yak *n syn* see CHATTER

yak–yak *vb syn* see CHAT

yammer *vb* **1** *syn* see GRIPE

2 *syn* see CHAT 1

yank *vb* **1** *syn* see JERK

rel tug; clutch, grab, snatch

2 *syn* see EXTRACT 1

yap *n* **1** *syn* see RUSTIC

‖**2** *syn* see MOUTH 1

yard *n syn* see COURT 1

yardstick *n syn* see STANDARD 3

yare *adj syn* see AGILE

yarn *n* **1** *syn* see STORY 2

2 *syn* see CHAT 2

yarn *vb syn* see CONVERSE

yatter *n syn* see CHATTER

yatter *vb syn* see CHAT 1

yaw *n syn* see TURN 2

yaw *vb syn* see SEESAW

yaw *vb syn* see YAWN

yawn *vb* to breathe deeply with jaws widespread usually in reaction to fatigue or boredom < *yawned* again and again in the stuffy room >

syn gape, yaw

rel doze, drowse, nap, snooze

yawn *n syn* see TEDIUM

yawning *adj syn* see CAVERNOUS 1

yawp (*or* yaup) *vb* **1** *syn* see SQUALL 1

2 *syn* see GRIPE

yea *adv* **1** *syn* see ALSO 2

2 *syn* see YES 1

3 *syn* see EVEN 3

yearbook *n* a book issued yearly to chronicle a particular part of the preceding year's activities < sports editor of his school *yearbook* >

syn annual, annuary

yearn *vb syn* see LONG

rel covet, desire, wish; pant

ant dread

years *n pl syn* see OLD AGE

yeast *n syn* see FOAM

yeasty *adj syn* see GIDDY 1

yegg *n syn* see ROBBER

yell *vb* **1** *syn* see SHOUT 1

---

syn synonym(s)   *rel* related word(s)
ant antonym(s)   *con* contrasted word(s)
idiom idiomatic equivalent(s)
‖ use limited; if in doubt, see a dictionary

2 to complain vigorously or vociferously <let the opposition *yell;* we got the vote>
syn howl, scream, squeal, yip, yowl
rel cry, lament, squall, wail, weep; bemoan, bewail, deplore
idiom beat one's breast, make an outcry, tear one's hair, yell to high heaven
con acclaim, applaud, cheer, hail
3 *syn* see CALL 1

yellow *adj syn* see COWARDLY
yellowback *n syn* see DIME NOVEL
yellowbelly *n syn* see COWARD
rel fink, rat, stinker
yellow dog *n syn* see CAD
yen *vb syn* see LONG
‖**yep** *adv syn* see YES 1
ant ‖nope
‖**yerk** *vb syn* see WHIP 1
yes *adv* 1 —used as a function word to express assent, agreement, understanding, or acceptance < *yes,* I can do that>
syn agreed, all right, aye, OK (*or* okay), ‖okeydoke, yea, ‖yep
rel assuredly, certainly, gladly, willingly; undoubtedly, unquestionably
idiom beyond a doubt, beyond any shade (*or* shadow) of doubt, with all my heart, without the least doubt
2 *syn* see EXACTLY 3
yes *vb syn* see ASSENT
yes-man *n* 1 *syn* see STOOGE 1
2 *syn* see SYCOPHANT
yesterday *n syn* see PAST
ant tomorrow
yesteryear *n syn* see PAST
yet *adv* 1 beyond this — used as an intensive to stress the comparative degree <in spite of her protest he went *yet* faster>
syn even, still
2 at some future time <just wait, we'll get there *yet*>
syn eventually, finally, someday, sometime, somewhen, sooner or later, ultimately
idiom after a while, in due course, in the course of time
3 *syn* see ALSO 2
4 *syn* see HITHERTO 1
5 *syn* see HOWEVER
yet *conj syn* see ONLY
yield *vb* 1 *syn* see RELINQUISH
con appropriate, arrogate, confiscate
2 to give way before a force that one cannot longer resist < *yielded* to temptation>
syn bow, buckle (under), capitulate, cave, defer, knuckle, knuckle under, submit, succumb
rel accord, award, concede, grant; cede, surrender, waive; break, fail
idiom give ground, give place, give way
con bear up, hold out, resist
ant withstand
3 *syn* see BEAR 9

4 *syn* see GIVE 7
rel discharge, eject, emit, vent
5 to produce as return or revenue <an investment that *yields* 10 percent>
syn bring in, pay, return
rel afford, furnish, provide, supply; hold out, offer, proffer, tender
idiom afford (*or* give *or* provide) a return of, put at one's disposal
6 *syn* see GIVE 12
yield *n syn* see OUTPUT
yielding *adj* 1 *syn* see SOFT 6
ant unyielding
2 *syn* see PASSIVE 2
yip *vb syn* see YELL 2
‖**yob** *n syn* see RUSTIC
yoke *n* 1 *syn* see BONDAGE
2 *syn* see BOND 3
yoke *vb* 1 *syn* see HITCH 2
2 *syn* see JOIN 1
yokel *n syn* see RUSTIC
yon *adv* 1 *syn* see BEYOND 1
2 *syn* see THERE
yonder *adv syn* see BEYOND 1
yore *n syn* see PAST
young *adj* 1 being in an early stage of life, growth, or development < *young* shoots of new grass>
syn callow, green, immature, infant, juvenile, unfledged, unripe, youthful
rel fresh, new; crude, raw, unfinished, unformed
con full-grown, grown-up, mature, ripe; aged, elderly, superannuated
ant old; adult
2 *syn* see INEXPERIENCED
youngling *n syn* see CHILD 1
young man *n syn* see BOYFRIEND 1
young one *n syn* see CHILD 1
youngster *n syn* see CHILD 1
youth *n* 1 the period of life in which one passes from childhood to maturity <the thought of regaining one's *youth*>
syn adolescence, greenness, juvenility, prime, puberty, pubescence, spring, springtide, springtime, youthfulness, youthhood
rel callowness, immaturity, inexperience, unripeness; dewiness
idiom awkward age, flower (*or* springtime *or* May) of life, salad days
ant age
2 *syn* see CHILD 1
youthful *adj syn* see YOUNG 1
rel beardless, boyish, puerile; maiden, virgin, virginal
con adult, matured
ant aged, elderly
youthfulness *n syn* see YOUTH 1
youthhood *n syn* see YOUTH
yowl *vb* 1 *syn* see YELL 2
2 *syn* see BAWL 2
yule *n syn* see CHRISTMAS
yuletide *n syn* see CHRISTMAS
yummy *adj syn* see DELIGHTFUL

Z

zakuska *n syn* see APPETIZER

zany *n* 1 *syn* see CLOWN 3
rel comic, farceur, funnyman
2 one who makes an exhibition of himself for the amusement of others <tired of having her parties spoiled by drunken *zanies*>
syn clown, cutup, farceur, joker, jokester, wag
rel practical joker, pranker, prankster, trickster; exhibitionist, show-off
3 *syn* see WAG 1
4 *syn* see FOOL 4

zeal *n syn* see PASSION 6
rel energy, gusto, spirit, zest; fierceness, intensity, vehemence; avidity, keenness, readiness, urgency; earnestness, seriousness, sincerity
con coolness, halfheartedness, indifference, lukewarmness; carelessness, heedlessness, insouciance, negligence, unmindfulness; disinterest, lackadaisy, unconcern
ant apathy

zealot *n syn* see ENTHUSIAST
rel adherent, disciple, follower, partisan, sectary

zealous *adj syn* see ENTHUSIASTIC
rel afire, ardent, fervent, fervid, fired; avid, eager; dedicated, fanatic, frenetic, rabid, wild-eyed; infatuated, obsessed, possessed
con cool, halfhearted, indifferent, lukewarm; careless, heedless, insouciant, negligent, unmindful; disinterested, lackadaisical, uninterested
ant apathetic

zemi *n syn* see CHARM 2

zenith *n syn* see APEX 2
ant nadir

zero *n* 1 a numerical symbol 0 denoting the absence of all magnitude or quantity <wrote a row of *zeros* after the decimal point>
syn aught (*or* ought), cipher, goose egg, naught (*or* nought), nothing, zilch
rel blank, nil, void
2 *syn* see NONENTITY

zero (in) *vb syn* see DIRECT 2

zero hour *n syn* see JUNCTURE 2

zest *n syn* see TASTE 4
rel ardor, eagerness, enthusiasm, fervor, passion, zeal; delectation, delight, enjoyment, pleasure, satisfaction; bliss, ecstasy, elation

zesty *adj syn* see PUNGENT

zetetic *n syn* see SKEPTIC

zilch *n* 1 *syn* see ZERO 1
2 *syn* see NONENTITY

zing *n* 1 *syn* see EAGERNESS
2 *syn* see SPIRIT 5

Zion *n* 1 *syn* see HEAVEN 2
2 *syn* see UTOPIA

zip *vb* 1 *syn* see BREEZE
2 *syn* see HURRY 2

zippy *adj syn* see AGILE
rel alert, keen, ready; dynamic, forceful, intense

zoetic *adj syn* see LIVING 1

Zoilus *n syn* see CRITIC

zombie *n* 1 *syn* see DUNCE
2 *syn* see ECCENTRIC

zone *n syn* see AREA 1
rel section, sector, segment

zonked *adj* 1 *syn* see INTOXICATED 1
2 *syn* see DRUGGED
